THE SUPREME COURT AND INDIVIDUAL RIGHTS

Fifth Edition

David G. Savage

CQ PRESS

A Division of SAGE
Washington, D.C.

CQ Press
2300 N Street, NW, Suite 800
Washington, DC 20037

Phone: 202-729-1900; toll-free, 1-866-4CQ-PRESS (1-866-427-7737)

Web: www.cqpress.com

Cover design: Cynthia Richardson, RICHdesign Studio
Cover photos: (*top*) Landov, (*bottom left*) AP Images, (*bottom center*) AP Images, (*bottom right*) CORBIS
Composition: C&M Digitals (P) Ltd.

♾ The paper used in this publication exceeds the requirements of the American National Standard for Information Sciences—Permanence of Paper for Printed Library Materials, ANSI Z39.48-1992.

Printed and bound in the United States of America

13   12   11   10   09   1   2   3   4   5

LIBRARY OF CONGRESS CATALOGING-IN-PUBLICATION DATA

Savage, David G.,
  The supreme court and individual rights / David G. Savage. — 5th ed.
      p. cm.
  Includes bibliographical references and index.
  ISBN 978-0-87289-424-2 (pbk. : alk. paper) 1. Civil rights—United States—Cases.
2. United States. Supreme Court. I. Title.

  KF4748.W53 2009
  342.7308′5—dc22

                              2009019747

THE SUPREME COURT AND INDIVIDUAL RIGHTS

★ TABLE OF CONTENTS

★ PREFACE

It is hard to imagine Dick Heller, Patrick Kennedy, and Lakhdar Boumediene having much in common, or for that matter, being in the same room together. They all, however, brought individual rights claims before the Supreme Court in spring 2008. Heller, a security guard in Washington, D.C., wanted to keep his handgun at home, but the District of Columbia's gun control laws, the strictest in the nation, prohibited him from doing so: They made handguns illegal, even if kept only in the home. Heller argued that the handgun ordinance violated his Second Amendment right "to keep and bear arms." Kennedy had been sentenced to die for the rape of his stepdaughter in Louisiana; at the time, he was the only person on death row in the United States for a crime other than murder. He contended that his punishment was "cruel and unusual" and therefore a violation of the Eighth Amendment. Boumediene had been arrested in Bosnia, where he held citizenship, and turned over to U.S. authorities who then held him as a prisoner at the U.S. naval base at Guantánamo Bay, Cuba. The U.S. military claimed that Boumediene had links to the al-Qaida network, which he denied. He contended that he was being wrongly held and sought to plead his innocence before a judge. He pointed to the Constitution's protection for the "the privilege of the Writ of Habeas Corpus."

All three men won their cases in late June 2008. In *District of Columbia v. Heller,* the Supreme Court struck down the D.C. handgun ordinance as unconstitutional, ruling that the Second Amendment had always been intended to protect an individual's right to possess a firearm for self-defense. In *Kennedy v. Louisiana,* the Court held that the ultimate punishment—execution—must be reserved for crimes that result in another person's death. In *Boumediene v. Bush,* the Court disagreed with Congress and President George W. Bush and ruled that the prisoners held at Guantánamo Bay were entitled to hearings before a judge.

The rulings were much debated, by the public, in the press, and among the justices. Only Justice Anthony M. Kennedy was in the majority in all three decisions. No one questioned, however, the Supreme Court's extraordinary authority to protect the rights of individuals and to strike down laws—whether passed by a city, a state, or Congress—if they conflicted with the Constitution.

In the Guantánamo case, Justice Kennedy declared that an individual's "freedom from unlawful restraint" by the government had been a fundamental principle at the nation's founding. The "protection for the habeas corpus privilege was one of the few safeguards of liberty specified in a Constitution that, at the outset, had no Bill of Rights," he wrote. If lawmakers and the chief executive could revoke this right for some prisoners, it would "lead to a regime in which [Congress and the president], not this Court, say 'what the law is,'" wrote Kennedy, citing Chief Justice John Marshall's landmark opinion in *Marbury v. Madison.*

To people unfamiliar with U.S.-style democracy—and perhaps to many who know it well—the notion of placing so much power in the hands of nine unelected justices must seem remarkable. It is a paradox, but it is not an accident. Americans place great faith in the rule of law and in a constitution that defines the powers of government and the rights of individuals. If the U.S. Constitution is to stand as the highest law—the law that governs the lawmakers—some person or persons must decide what it means when a dispute arises between the government and an individual. The black-robed justices who sit atop the federal court system are those persons.

The Supreme Court and Individual Rights tells the long and still-unfolding story of the Court's role as the protector of rights that many hold dear. They include the right to speak freely and to publish or broadcast views without interference by the government; religious freedom, including the right to be free of government-imposed religion; and the right to vote in elections that are free and fair. The government must enforce the law and punish those who break it, but the Constitution also protects the rights of those who are charged with a crime. Official searches and seizures are limited; forced self-incrimination is prohibited. Trials must be fair, and punishments may not be extreme and excessive. Because of Dick Heller's case, the Second Amendment right to

"bear arms" has been awakened from hibernation. Other old rights continue to evolve. The rights to equality and liberty were invoked to strike down racial segregation laws in the 1950s and gender discrimination and abortion laws in the 1970s. More recently, they have been used to protect gays and lesbians from discrimination.

If there is a surprise in the chapters that follow, it is that these robust rights are of recent vintage. Though the Bill of Rights was ratified in 1791, its impact on American life and law was minimal until the middle part of the twentieth century. Only then did the Supreme Court enforce these as truly national rights, binding not just on the federal government, but on state agencies, local police, public schools, and municipal authorities. This transformation is recounted here, as are the famous cases of recent history—from *Brown v. Board of Education* (1954) to *Roe v. Wade* (1973) to *Bush v. Gore* (2000)—as are the hundreds of lesser-known cases and litigants who, like Heller, Kennedy, and Boumediene, have shaped the Constitution as we know it today.

The Court and the Individual

The most stirring words in the United States' founding documents speak of freedom and equality. The Declaration of Independence in 1776 set forth what its authors saw as the "self-evident truth" that "all men are created equal" and that they possess "unalienable rights," including "Life, Liberty and the Pursuit of Happiness." The purpose of government, it states, is "to secure these rights." Eleven years later, "We the People of the United States," in order to "secure the Blessings of Liberty to ourselves and our Posterity," adopted the Constitution as a plan of government. Yet, for most of U.S. history, constitutional law and the decisions of the Supreme Court had little to do with individual liberties and equal rights.

To those who came of age after World War II, this may come as startling news. The Court's role as the protector of individual rights emerged rather late in its history. In its first century, the Court's great debates concerned the powers of the new federal government versus the residual authority of the states. At the time, it was generally believed that freedom and liberty could be protected best by limiting the powers of government. Especially feared was the potential for an all-powerful central authority. Critics of the new Constitution—the so-called Anti-Federalists—were so concerned that they pressed to have it amended to add protections for individual rights. They succeeded in winning approval of ten amendments, the first of which begins with the phrase, "Congress shall make no law . . . abridging the freedom of speech or of the press" or to prohibit "the free exercise

of religion." Contrary to what is often assumed today, however, these ten amendments—the Bill of Rights—did not give individuals a right to freedom of speech or the right to the free exercise of his or her religion. It simply protected them from federal laws that would restrict speech or religion. The Anti-Federalists put their trust in the states, and the states retained their sovereign powers, including the authority to restrict speech and religion.

In the decades prior to the Civil War, southern states moved to suppress speech that criticized slavery.[1] In 1859 the Virginia postmaster banned the sale or distribution of the *New York Tribune*, a newspaper with abolitionist leanings. Twenty years earlier, the state had prosecuted citizens for circulating an antislavery petition to Congress.[2] Neither the newspaper's publisher nor the censored Virginians looked to the U.S. Constitution or Supreme Court for relief. The justices had ruled that the first ten amendments limited Congress only; they did not apply to the states nor give citizens true rights as individuals.

The Constitution as it is known today emerged later and in two stages. In the Gettysburg Address, President Abraham Lincoln had foreseen the Civil War leading to a "new birth of freedom" in the nation, and in 1866 the northern Republicans who controlled Congress sought to put his vision into the Constitution: "All persons born or naturalized in the United States . . . are citizens of the United States," they said in the Fourteenth Amendment. "No State shall make or enforce any law which shall abridge the privileges or immunities of citizens of the United States, nor shall any State deprive any person of life, liberty, or property, without due process of law, nor deny to any person within its jurisdictions the equal protection of the laws." By the middle of the twentieth century, these few sentences had become the most important in the Constitution. For the first time, the rights of individual Americans were to be protected by the national government and its federal courts, made off-limits to suppression by the states. The Equal Protection Clause marks the first time that the Constitution incorporated the Declaration of Independence's self-evident truth that all were equal before the law. "The Reconstruction Amendment transformed the original Bill of Rights" from one that protected states' rights to one that "vested citizens with rights against states," wrote Akhil Reed Amar.[3] "The central role of the Bill of Rights today owes at least as much to the Reconstruction (in 1866) as to the Creation (in 1787 and 1791)."[4]

Yet, in the decades after their enactment, the Reconstruction-era amendments had surprisingly little effect. After the Civil War, the Supreme Court stood in the way of this new vision of individual rights being protected by federal authorities. Instead, the Court weakened the new rights adopted by the Reconstruction Congress and restored the sovereign authority of the states. Rep. John Bingham, R-Ohio, the sponsor of the Fourteenth Amendment, had stood on the House floor and asserted that the "privileges or immunities" of a U.S. citizen were the individual rights set out in the Bill of Rights, but the Supreme Court ignored his view and treated the Fourteenth Amendment as having made a minor alteration in the balance between federal authority and states' rights. By the end of the nineteenth century, the Court had rendered the Reconstruction amendments all but meaningless. They were rarely invoked, except to strike down worker protection laws. Segregation of the races was seen as an unassailable fact of life, a matter of tradition and custom in the South. Constitutional change during the first half of the twentieth century came slowly, and the shift was hardly noticed at first. In the 1920s, the Court breathed life into the First Amendment as a protection for the right to freedom of speech against local and state

prosecutions. In *Stromberg v. California* (1931), the justices for the first time voided a state conviction on the ground that it violated the free speech rights of a citizen.[5] In that case a nineteen-year-old California girl had been prosecuted for carrying a Soviet flag at a summer camp. In time, the Court came to believe it had a duty to protect the basic rights described in the Bill of Rights against violations by the state, and it did so by ruling that a state's violations of an individual's freedom of speech, the press, religion, or any of the fair trial provisions violated the right to liberty set out in the Fourteenth Amendment.

In 1954 the Court struck down state segregation laws as violations of the equal protection component of the Fourteenth Amendment. Excluding black children from the better white schools in the South was "inherently unequal," said Chief Justice Earl Warren, "and cannot stand." The unanimous ruling in *Brown v. Board of Education* touched off a civil rights revolution that transformed race relations nationwide and led to an ever-widening attack on discrimination against women, minorities, the disabled, and gays and lesbians. By the latter decades of the twentieth century, the Court's role as the enforcer of the Constitution and the protector of individual rights was so well established that many have assumed that it was always so.

IN THE BEGINNING: FEW RIGHTS AND NARROW PROTECTION, 1789–1865

The Supreme Court deals with cases that arise under the Constitution and the laws of the United States. Only half a dozen sentences in the original Constitution deal directly with matters of individual rights. The Constitution forbids suspension of the privilege of the writ of habeas corpus except in time of public emergency,[6] and it prohibits the passage of bills of attainder or ex post facto laws.[7] For almost all crimes, the Constitution requires jury trials in the state where the crime was committed.[8] It defines the crime of treason, sets the standard of evidence, and limits the penalty for that crime.[9] It also provides for extradition of fugitives[10] and forbids religious tests for federal officeholders.[11]

The Demand for Guarantees

Not surprisingly, many persons active in the formulation of the new government—with all-too-fresh memories of governmental oppression—found the lack of more comprehensive guarantees of individual rights a serious deficiency. Historian Charles Warren describes the situation:

> Men on all sides contended that, while the first object of a Constitution was to establish a government, its second object, equally important, must be to protect the people against the government. That was something which all history and all human experience had taught.
>
> The first thing that most of the colonies had done, on separating from Great Britain, had been to assure to the people a Bill of Rights, safeguarding against state legislative despotism those human rights which they regarded as fundamental. Having protected themselves by specific restrictions on the power of their state legislatures, the people of this country were in no mood to set up and accept a new national government, without similar checks and restraints. As soon as the proposed Constitution was published, the demand for a national Bill of Rights was heard on all sides.[12]

Thus, a number of the states that ratified the Constitution did so only with the assurance that a top priority of the First Congress would be the approval of a bill of rights to be added to the Constitution.

The Bill of Rights

In June 1789 during the First Congress, Rep. James Madison of Virginia introduced a dozen proposed constitutional amendments as a bill of rights generally modeled after existing state bills of rights.[13] Congress approved the amendments in September 1791. Ten of them took effect in December after ratification by the requisite number of states.[14] These amendments, now known as the Bill of Rights, were conceived to protect the individual against the government. As Chief Justice Earl Warren noted, its provisions do not guarantee novel rights, but do "summarize in a striking and effective manner the personal and public liberties which Americans [of that time] regarded as their due and as being properly beyond the reach of any government."[15] Warren continued, "The men of our First Congress . . . knew . . . that whatever form it may assume, government is potentially as dangerous a thing as it is a necessary one. They knew that power must be lodged somewhere to prevent anarchy within and conquest from without, but that this power could be abused to the detriment of their liberties."[16] As Zechariah Chafee Jr. points out, the guarantees perform an affirmative as well as a negative function: "They fix a certain point to halt the government abruptly with a 'thus far and no farther'; but long before that point is reached they urge upon every official of the three branches of the state a constant regard for certain declared fundamental policies of American life."[17]

The First Amendment protects freedom of thought and belief. It forbids Congress to restrict freedom of religion, speech, the press, peaceable assembly, and petition. The Second Amendment ensures the right of the states to maintain militia and the right of the people to keep and bear arms. The Third Amendment restricts the government's power to quarter soldiers in people's homes. Neither the Second nor the Third Amendment has been the subject of many cases before the federal courts.[18] The Fourth Amendment protects the individual's right to be secure in his or her person, house, papers, and effects against unreasonable searches or seizures. This security is ensured by requiring that searches and arrests be authorized by warrants issued only if there is probable cause for the action and when the person to be arrested or the place to be searched and the objects sought are precisely described.

The Fifth Amendment requires indictment of all persons charged in civilian proceedings with capital or otherwise serious crimes. It forbids trying a person twice for the same offense or compelling a person to incriminate himself. It states that no one should be deprived of life, liberty, or property without due process of law, and it protects private property against being taken for public use without just compensation. The Sixth Amendment sets out certain requirements for criminal trials, guaranteeing a speedy and public jury trial for all persons accused of a crime, with an impartial jury selected from the area of the crime. The defendant is further guaranteed the right to be notified of the charge or charges against him, to confront witnesses testifying against him, to compel witnesses to come to testify in his favor, and to have the aid of an attorney in his defense.

The Seventh Amendment provides for a jury trial in all common law suits involving more than $20. The Eighth Amendment forbids excessive bail, excessive fines, and cruel and unusual punishment. The Ninth and Tenth Amendments do not guarantee specific rights. The Ninth declares that the mention in the Constitution of certain rights should not be interpreted as denying or disparaging other rights retained by the people. The Tenth reserves to the states, or to the people, all powers not delegated by the Constitution to the national government or prohibited by the Constitution to the states.

The Judicial Role

James Madison, father of the first ten amendments, expected the federal courts to play a major role in implementing their guarantees. "Independent tribunals of justice will consider themselves in a peculiar manner the guardians of those rights; they [the courts] will be an impenetrable bulwark against every assumption of power in the Legislative or Executive; they will naturally be led to resist every encroachment upon rights expressly stipulated for in the Constitution by the declaration of rights," he told his fellow members of Congress.[19] The Supreme Court, however, had little occasion to make good on Madison's assumptions in its first 130 years. The Alien and Sedition Acts of 1798—which were severe infringements of the rights and liberties of the individual, particularly those protected by the First Amendment—were never challenged before the high court; they expired early in 1801. It is worth noting that most of the early members of the Court, in their roles as circuit judges, presided over trials of persons charged with sedition and displayed no disinclination to enforce that law.[20] Slavery, despite the prolonged national debate it engendered, was never dealt with by the Court as a matter of individual rights. The few pronouncements by the Court on the issue demonstrate clearly that the justices saw it as a matter of property rights, not human rights. *(See box, The Court and the Issue of Slavery, pp. 6–7.)*

In the early 1830s the Court ruled in a benchmark case that the Bill of Rights provided no protection against state action, only against federal authority. The case, *Barron v. Baltimore* (1833), arose when the owner of a wharf in Baltimore, Maryland, challenged city action that seriously impaired the value of his property by creating shoals and shallows around it. Barron argued that this was a "taking" of his property without just compensation in violation of the Fifth Amendment.[21] When Barron's case came before the Supreme Court, Chief Justice John Marshall found the question it posed to be "of great importance, but not of much difficulty." Marshall described Barron's argument: the Fifth Amendment "being in favor of the liberty of the citizen ought to be so construed as to restrain the legislative power of a State, as well as that of the United States."[22] That argument could not, however, prevail, continued the chief justice. The Bill of Rights was adopted to secure individual rights against the "apprehended encroachments of the general government—not against those of the local governments."[23] The Court could find no indication that Congress intended the Bill of Rights to safeguard the individual against state action, and it would not undertake such an extension of those provisions on its own. Marshall concluded: "Had Congress engaged in the extraordinary occupation of improving the constitutions of the several States by affording the people additional protection from the exercise of power by their own governments in matters which concerned themselves alone, they would have declared this purpose in plain and intelligible language."[24] *Barron v. Baltimore* stands to this day, unreversed in its precise finding—that the First Congress, in approving the Bill of Rights, did not intend these amendments to protect the individual against state action but only against action by federal authorities.

THE CIVIL WAR AMENDMENTS

After the Civil War, Congress added three new amendments to the Constitution. The language of these additions appeared, at least on the surface, to overturn the restrictions *Barron v. Baltimore* placed on the guarantees of the Bill of Rights. The Thirteenth Amendment, adopted in 1865, abolished slavery and involuntary servitude, except for persons sentenced to such service as punishment for crime. It authorizes Congress to pass laws to enforce this guarantee. The Fifteenth Amendment, adopted in 1870, forbids state or federal authorities to deny or abridge the right of U.S. citizens to vote because of race, color, or previous condition of servitude. It, too, authorizes Congress to pass legislation enforcing its prohibition.

The Fourteenth Amendment, the most complex and most litigated of the three, was adopted in 1868. It declares that all persons born or naturalized in the United States are citizens. This is the Constitution's only definition of citizenship. In addition, the amendment forbids states to abridge any privilege or immunity of U.S. citizens; to deprive any person of life, liberty, or property without due process of law; or to deny to any person the equal protection of the law. These guarantees are supported by a grant of power to Congress to enforce them through legislation. They became the foundation of the modern revolution in civil rights and criminal procedure, although for decades after their addition to the Constitution they seemed almost useless as protection for individual rights, in large part because of the decisions of the late-nineteenth-century Court.

The Intent of Congress

The Privileges and Immunities, Due Process, and Equal Protection Clauses were intended by their author, Rep. John A. Bingham, R-Ohio, to extend the guarantees of the Bill of Rights against state action. Bingham thought that the privileges and immunities section of the Fourteenth Amendment would be the chief vehicle for this extension. In 1871 Bingham explained this view in response to a query from a fellow member of the House. He stated that "the privileges and immunities of citizens of the United States . . . are chiefly defined in the first eight amendments to the Constitution. . . . These eight articles . . . were never limitations upon the power of the States, until made so by the Fourteenth Amendment."[25]

During Senate consideration of the amendment, the chief Senate spokesman in behalf of the proposal had stated that "the great object of the first section of this amendment is . . . to restrain the power of the States and compel them at all times to respect these great fundamental guarantees."[26] During the process of ratification, however, the other sections of the amendment—concerning apportionment of representatives among the states, the holding of federal posts by persons who had forsaken such offices to support the rebellious states, and the validity of the public debt—were given far more attention than section 1.

Frustration of the Promise

Almost a century would pass before the hopes explicit in the adoption of the Thirteenth, Fourteenth, and Fifteenth Amendments were fulfilled. Partly in response to waning public enthusiasm for Reconstruction, partly out of concern for healing the wounds of war, partly because the nation had not developed its sensitivity to issues of individual rights, the Supreme Court in the postwar decades severely curtailed the use of the Civil War amendments to protect individual citizens. The restrictive interpretation of these amendments came in two lines of rulings. In the first, the Court defined narrowly the Privileges and Immunities, Due Process, and Equal Protection Clauses of the Fourteenth Amendment and the similar substantive phrases of the Thirteenth and Fifteenth Amendments. In the second, the Court rigidly confined the enforcement power these three amendments granted Congress.

The Court first indicated its limited view of the effect of these amendments early in the 1870s. In the *Slaughterhouse Cases* (1873), the Court ruled that the privileges and immunities of U.S. citizenship were a brief list and did not include, for example, the right to vote.[27] The Thirteenth Amendment did no more than abolish the institution of slavery, the Court ruled in *United States v. Reese* (1876). Also, according to the decision in *United States v. Cruikshank* (1876), the Fifteenth Amendment did not grant to anyone a federal right to vote, only the right to exercise the state-granted franchise free of racial discrimination.[28] A decade later the Court held in *Hurtado v. California* (1884) that the due process guarantee did not extend the specific protections of the Bill of Rights against state action,[29] and in the well-known *Plessy v. Ferguson* (1896) decision, the Court found no denial of equal protection in the requirement of segregated public facilities for blacks and whites.[30]

THE COURT AND THE ISSUE OF SLAVERY: A QUESTION OF LEGALITY, NOT MORALITY

The issue of slavery came to the Supreme Court in its first decades only as a question of international or commercial law or of states' rights and federal power. Not until after the Civil War did the status of the nation's blacks become a question of individual rights rather than property rights. As the United States celebrated the bicentennial of the Constitution in 1987, Justice Thurgood Marshall reminded everyone that "when the Founding Fathers used the phrase 'We the People' in 1797, they did not have in mind the majority of America's citizens."[1] At the time of the nation's founding, the phrase was not meant to include blacks or women.

The framers, Marshall noted, "could not have imagined, nor would they have accepted, that the document they were drafting would one day be construed by a Supreme Court to which had been appointed a woman and a descendant of an African slave." Marshall pointed out that "the record of the Framers' debates on the slave question is especially clear: the Southern states acceded to the demands of the New England states for giving Congress broad power to regulate commerce, in exchange for the right to continue the slave trade."[2] Slavery continued to influence constitutional history up to the pre–Civil War. As Carl B. Swisher explained,

> Concern for the preservation of slavery furnished the driving power back of theories of state rights and of limitation upon the power of the federal government which for many decades hampered the expansion of federal power. Concern for the protection of slavery entered into the interpretation of the commerce clause ... of clauses having to do with the rights of citizenship, and of other important constitutional provisions. The clash of interest between slavery and non-slavery groups brought on the crisis of a civil war which threatened the complete destruction of the American constitutional system.[3]

Historian Charles Warren also viewed the slavery issue as underlying the early debate over the scope of the commerce power:

> [T]hroughout the long years when the question of the extent of the federal power over commerce was being tested in numerous cases in the court, that question was, in the minds of Southerners, simply

coincident with the question of the extent of the Federal power over slavery.[4]

The Court gave firm support to federal power over the subject of fugitive slaves. At the same time, it left as much as possible to the states the question of the status of slaves who had spent time in both slave and free areas. The Court's divergence from this position—in *Scott v. Sandford* (1857)—added fuel to the conflagration that ignited the Civil War.

INTERNATIONAL LAW

In 1825 in the Court's first decision on slavery, the justices held that the slave trade, even though illegal in the United States by that time, was not illegal under international law. The case involved slaves who had arrived in the United States after being removed from *The Antelope*, a vessel captured by an American warship. Chief Justice John Marshall made clear in his opinion that the legality of the situation alone, not its morality, was before the Court:

> In examining claims of this momentous importance; claims in which the sacred rights of liberty and of property come in conflict with each other ... this Court must not yield to feelings which might seduce it from the path of duty, but must obey the mandates of the law.... Whatever might be the answer of a moralist to this question, a jurist must search for its legal solution in those principles of action which are sanctioned by the usages, the national acts, and the general assent of that portion of the world of which he considers himself as a part.[5]

COMMERCIAL LAW

Four years later the Court ruled that a slave who had died in an abortive rescue attempt after a steamboat fire was a passenger, not freight, for purposes of his owners' damage suit against the vessels involved. "A slave has volition, and has feelings which cannot be entirely disregarded," wrote Chief Justice Marshall. "He cannot be stowed away as a common package.... The carrier has not, and cannot have, the same absolute control over him that he has over inanimate matter. In the nature of things, and in his character, he resembles a passenger, and not a package of goods."[6] In 1841 the

The Court refused to acknowledge that the enforcement clauses of these amendments significantly enlarged federal power to protect individual rights. Rather, the enforcement power granted to Congress to implement these provisions remained constrained by state prerogatives. Congress enacted a number of statutes to enforce the Thirteenth, Fourteenth, and Fifteenth Amendments, but by the end of the century, most of their provisions had either been declared invalid by the Court, repealed directly, or rendered obsolete by subsequent legislation.[31] Charles Warren, writing in the 1920s, describes the effect of the Civil War amendments upon the nation's black citizens, as a result of these Supreme Court decisions:

Court was faced with a case challenging Mississippi's ban on the importation of slaves, but the justices found a way to decide the case without ruling directly on the importation ban.[7]

FUGITIVE SLAVE LAWS

As tensions between slave and free states built, and the operations of the underground railway accelerated, an increasing number of cases challenged the federal fugitive slave law, enacted in 1793 to govern the return of fugitive slaves from one state to another. In 1842 the Court affirmed the exclusive power of Congress to regulate these disputes. The justices struck down a Pennsylvania law providing that before a fugitive was returned to his alleged owner or the owner's representative, a hearing should be held before a magistrate to determine the validity of the claim to the supposed fugitive slave.[8] Six years later, the Court reaffirmed the validity of the federal fugitive slave law and specifically disclaimed any power to resolve the moral dilemma it posed:

> [S]ome notice should be taken of the argument, urging on us a disregard of the Constitution and the act of Congress in respect to this subject, on account of the supposed inexpediency and invalidity of all laws recognizing slavery or any right of property in man. But that is a political question, settled by each state for itself; and the federal power over it is limited and regulated by the people of the states in the Constitution itself, as one of its sacred compromises, and which we possess no authority as a judicial body to modify or overrule.[9]

On the eve of the Civil War, the Court resolved the most famous of the fugitive slave cases, *Ableman v. Booth* (1859). Sherman Booth, an abolitionist editor, was prosecuted under the federal fugitive slave law for helping a fugitive slave to escape. The state courts of Wisconsin, Booth's residence, repeatedly issued writs of habeas corpus ordering federal authorities to release Booth from custody on the grounds that the federal fugitive slave law was unconstitutional. The Court in March 1859 resoundingly defended the freedom of federal courts from such state interference and upheld Booth's conviction.[10]

SLAVE OR FREE?

The Court in 1850 was asked to decide what effect residence in a free state or territory had on the status of a slave. This first case on the matter was resolved with restraint and without incident. The individuals involved were slaves in Kentucky who worked for a time in the free state of Ohio but returned to Kentucky to live. The Court ruled that their status depended on the state where they were residing; no constitutional provision controlled state action on this matter, it held.[11]

The Court reached a similar conclusion seven years later in the landmark *Scott v. Sandford*, but it did not stop there. Dred Scott, the alleged slave, brought the case on his own behalf. By holding that Scott's status was determined by the law of the state in which he resided—the slave state of Missouri—the Court also ruled that as a slave he could not bring the suit, and thus it had no jurisdiction over the matter at all. The Court then held that slaves were not citizens and that Congress lacked the power to exclude slavery from the territories.[12] Thus slavery became an issue to be resolved only on the battlefield. The Supreme Court did not speak again on the subject.

---

1. *Thurgood Marshall, speech at the annual seminar of the San Francisco Patent and Trademark Law Association, May 6, 1987.*

2. Ibid.

3. Carl B. Swisher, *American Constitutional Development,* 2d ed. (Cambridge, Mass.: Houghton Mifflin, 1954), 230.

4. Charles Warren, *The Supreme Court in United States History,* 2 vols. (Boston: Little, Brown, 1926), 1:627.

5. *The Antelope,* 10 Wheat. (23 U.S.) 66 at 114, 121 (1825).

6. *Boyce v. Anderson,* 2 Pet. (2 U.S.) 150 at 154–155 (1829).

7. *Groves v. Slaughter,* 15 Pet. (40 U.S.) 449 (1841).

8. *Prigg v. Pennsylvania,* 16 Pet. (41 U.S.) 539 (1842).

9. *Jones v. Van Zandt,* 5 How. (46 U.S.) 215 at 231 (1848).

10. *Ableman v. Booth,* 21 How. (62 U.S.) 506 (1859).

11. *Strader v. Graham,* 10 How. (51 U.S.) 82 (1851).

12. *Dred Scott v. Sandford,* 19 How. (60 U.S.) 393 (1857).

The first section of the 14th Amendment is a prohibitory measure, and the prohibitions operate against the states only, and not against acts of private persons; the fifth section only gives Congress power, by general legislation, to enforce these prohibitions, and Congress may, within bounds, provide the modes of redress against individuals when a State has violated the prohibitions; and though Congress cannot act directly against the states, Congress may regulate the method of appeal to United States courts by any persons whose right under the Amendment has been affected by action of the states. As to the 15th Amendment, though theoretically it is capable of being enforced to a

Lithograph commemorating the celebration in Baltimore of the enactment of the Fifteenth Amendment. Featured are likenesses of prominent supporters of the amendment. *Top, left to right:* President Ulysses S. Grant, Vice President Schuyler Colfax, President Abraham Lincoln, abolitionist martyr John Brown, and Baltimore jurist Hugh Lennox Bond. *Bottom, left to right:* abolitionist Frederick Douglass and Mississippi senator Hiram R. Revels.

certain extent by direct congressional action, Congress has, in fact, taken few steps toward such enforcement; and only a few acts of a state or of a state officer have been found by the courts to violate it. Meanwhile, the southern states, by constitutional and statutory provisions, which have been in general upheld by the court, have found methods of limiting the negro right to vote.[32]

Early in the twentieth century, one student of these Court rulings declared that the enforcement acts were struck down because "they were in fact out of joint with

the times. They did not square with public consciousness, either North or South. They belonged ... to a more arbitrary period. They fitted a condition of war, not of peace, and suggested autocracy, rather than a democracy!"[33] The Court's narrow view of these amendments eventually, however, gave way to a more expansive one, with these amendments providing the basis for the modern revolution in civil and criminal rights. Congress made possible this shift in federal judicial concern by expanding the class of persons who could ask a federal court to issue a writ of habeas corpus ordering their release from custody. This new law allowed persons detained by state officials to win their release if they could show that their detention was in violation of their constitutional rights. In 1875 Congress enlarged the jurisdiction of the federal courts and expanded the categories of cases they could hear, giving them the right to hear all cases arising under the Constitution or federal laws. Several years later Congress further expanded Supreme Court jurisdiction, authorizing the Court to hear appeals in criminal cases.

Property, Not People

In one of the most ironic chapters in Supreme Court history, these new powers and guarantees were for half a century wielded much more effectively to protect property than to protect people. Developing the doctrine of substantive due process, the Court found the Fourteenth Amendment a useful tool for striking down a wide range of "progressive" state laws ranging from those setting minimum wages and maximum hours for working men and women to consumer-oriented measures concerning weights and measures of items produced for sale. Only a few isolated cases kept alive the hope that the Court would eventually exercise its authority to protect the individual against the government.

In 1886 the Court held that the Equal Protection Clause ensured Chinese aliens the right to run laundries in San Francisco free of the discriminatory application of licensing requirements by city officials.[34] That same year the Court held that the Fourth and Fifth Amendments provided absolute protection from federal seizure of an individual's private papers.[35] Twenty-eight years later, in 1914, the Court provided for enforcement of this protection through an exclusionary rule—declaring that persons from whom federal agents take evidence illegally have the right to demand that the evidence be excluded from use in federal court.[36] In 1915 the Court invoked the Fourteenth Amendment to strike down state laws restricting the right of aliens to work.[37] The Court also held that year that the Fifteenth Amendment was violated by Oklahoma's use of a grandfather clause that effectively required all blacks—and only blacks—to take a literacy test before being considered qualified to vote.[38] World War I brought the most restrictive set of federal laws concerning speech and the press since 1798. Challenged as violating the First Amendment, these laws were upheld by the Court, but the cases posing these questions to the Court were the first steps in the still-continuing process of shaping the standards by which to judge the government's actions restricting individual freedom.

Broadening Protection

Despite some advances in the protection of individual rights, the Bill of Rights continued to be viewed as applicable only to federal action. Because state authorities exert far more influence on the everyday lives of individual citizens than do their federal counterparts, this state of affairs left most citizens inadequately protected against arbitrary, coercive, and unfair state government action. The Supreme Court's ruling in *Gitlow v. New York* (1925) marked the beginning of the expansion of federal protection for individual rights. Benjamin Gitlow, a socialist, was indicted for violating New York's criminal anarchy law by publishing and distributing documents considered to be subversive. The material at issue was a "Left Wing Manifesto" calling for "class revolution" and the organization of a "proletariat state" to suppress the "bourgeoisie." He went before the Supreme Court to argue that New York's law was unconstitutional because it denied him the rights of free speech and free press, guaranteed by the First Amendment.[39]

The Court upheld the law, but in so doing the majority stated that it now assumed "that freedom of speech and of the press—which are protected by the First Amendment from abridgment by Congress—are among the fundamental personal rights and 'liberties' protected by the due process clause of the Fourteenth Amendment from impairment by the states."[40] Thus the Court began reading into the due process guarantee many of the specific rights and liberties set out in the Bill of Rights. This process, variously described as the "incorporation," or absorption, of the Bill of Rights into the Fourteenth Amendment, continued for a half a century. By the mid-1970s, the Court had at last extended the Bill of Rights to the point that Representative Bingham had intended a century earlier when Congress approved section 1 of the Fourteenth Amendment.

INCORPORATION: APPLICATION OF THE BILL OF RIGHTS TO THE STATES

When constitutional law experts refer to "incorporation," they are probably not discussing the legal steps for turning a business into a corporation. Rather, they are likely referring to the awkward process by which the Supreme Court extended the Bill of Rights to state and local governments and thereby gave individuals true rights against the government. Most public employees and most government authority rests with state and local agencies. This includes police, prosecutors, and public school officials and personnel. Yet, the Bill of Rights begins with the words "Congress shall make no law respecting the establishment of religion, or prohibiting the free exercise thereof; or abridging the freedom of speech, of the press." Other provisions forbid "unreasonable searches and seizures" or the taking of "private property" for public use. Early in the nineteenth century, however, the Court determined that these first ten amendments to the Constitution limited only the federal government.[1]

After the Civil War, the Reconstruction Congress sought to extend these "great fundamental guarantees" involving freedom of speech and religion to all citizens. The Fourteenth Amendment, ratified in 1868, declares, "No state shall make or enforce any law which shall abridge the privileges or immunities of citizens of the United States." Just five years after the ratification of the Fourteenth Amendment, the Court drained the privileges or immunities clause of most of its meaning in the *Slaughterhouse Cases* (1873). The Court ruled that these "privileges" were distinctly national rights, such as the right to be protected "when on the high seas." By contrast, the "entire domain of civil rights" such as free speech and private property remained the province of the states, the Court said.

In the twentieth century, the Court used a different phrase in the Fourteenth Amendment to accomplish the same goal of extending the protections of the Bill of Rights. The amendment reads, "No state shall ... deprive any person of life, liberty, or property, without due process of law," and the Court held that punishing a person for his speech or his religion, or prosecuting him

without a lawyer, deprived him of "liberty ... without due process of law." The fundamental rights set out in the Bill of Rights were said to be "incorporated" in or embodied by the notion of "due process of law." In 1925 the Court seemed to adopt this theory in a casual statement in *Gitlow v. New York*. Benjamin Gitlow, a communist, had been convicted of violating a state sedition law for publishing a radical newspaper. "For present purposes we may and do assume that the freedom of speech and of the press—which are protected by the First Amendment from abridgment by Congress—are among the fundamental personal rights and liberties protected by the due process clause of the Fourteenth Amendment from impairment by the States."[2] Gitlow lost his appeal, but constitutional law was forever changed. From the late 1940s to the mid-1960s, debate raged in the Court: Which rights were so fundamental that they should be incorporated into "due process of law"? Justice Hugo L. Black argued for total incorporation. Others favored a step-by-step approach. In time, nearly all the rights mentioned in the Bill of Rights were applied to the states, with a few exceptions. The Third Amendment's guarantees against having soldiers "quartered in any house" has little significance today. The Fifth Amendment states that persons can be held to answer for a serious crime only on "indictment of a Grand Jury," but that provision has not been extended to states. The Seventh Amendment asserts that the "right to trial by jury shall be preserved" in civil suits, but those who file a state civil suit are not guaranteed a jury trial. In 2008 the Second Amendment's right to "keep and bear arms" was interpreted for the first time as giving individuals the right to have a gun at home. The case leading to this decision involved a Washington, D.C., law, but because the District of Columbia is not a state, the Court did not address whether the right protected by the Second Amendment extends to the states.

---

1. *Barron v. Baltimore*, 32 U.S. 243 (1833).

2. *Gitlow v. New York*, 268 U.S. 652 at 666 (1925).

The first rights absorbed into the Due Process Clause and thus protected against state action were those set out in the First Amendment. In 1931 the Court for the first time struck down some state laws as infringing on the freedom to speak and freedom of the press.[41] In 1934 it assumed that freedom of religion was likewise protected against state infringement,[42] and in 1937 the Court held the right of peaceable assembly to be so protected.[43] The Court also began in the 1930s to enforce the equal protection guarantee against racial discrimination

by state officials and to use the Due Process Clause to require fundamental fairness in state dealings with criminal suspects. With these legal doctrines and precedents in place, the groundwork for revolution was laid.

A Double Standard

As the federal courts, led by the Supreme Court, began to assume the role intended for them by Madison and the drafters of the Fourteenth Amendment, the Court indicated that it would apply a stricter standard to laws

"FOOTNOTE FOUR"

In *United States v. Carolene Products Co.* (1938), the Supreme Court foreshadowed a shift in its concern from economic rights to individual rights. Justice Harlan Fiske Stone, writing for the majority, penned what is now known simply as Footnote Four, which set out the Court's new path concerning its application of the Fourteenth Amendment:

4. There may be narrower scope for operation of the presumption of constitutionality when legislation appears on its face to be within a specific prohibition of the Constitution, such as those of the first ten Amendments, which are deemed equally specific when held to be embraced within the Fourteenth. See *Stromberg v. California,* 283 U.S. 359, 369, 370, 51 S.Ct. 532, 535, 536, 75 L.Ed. 1117, 73 A.L.R. 1484; *Lovell v. Griffin,* 303 U.S. 444, 58 S.Ct. 666, 82 L.Ed. 949, decided March 28, 1938.

It is unnecessary to consider now whether legislation which restricts those political processes which can ordinarily be expected to bring about repeal of undesirable legislation, is to be subjected to more exacting judicial scrutiny under the general prohibitions of the Fourteenth Amendment than are most other types of legislation. On restrictions upon the right to vote, see *Nixon v. Herndon,* 273 U.S. 536, 47 S.Ct. 446, 71 L.Ed. 984; *Nixon v. Condon,* 286 U.S. 73, 52 S.Ct 484, 88 A.L.R. 458; on restraints upon the dissemination of information, see *Near v. Minnesota,* 283 U.S. 697, 713–714, 718–720, 722, 51 S.Ct. 625, 630, 632, 633, 75 L.Ed. 1357; *Grosjean v. American Press Co.,* 297 U.S. 233, 56 S.Ct. 444, 80 L.Ed. 660; *Lovell v. Griffin,* supra; on interferences with political organizations, see *Stromberg v. California,* supra, 283 U.S. 359, 369, 51 S.Ct. 532, 535, 75 L.Ed. 1117, 73 A.L.R. 1484; *Fiske v. Kansas,* 274 U.S. 380, 47 S.Ct. 655, 71 L.Ed. 1108; *Whitney v. California,* 274 U.S. 357, 373–378, 47 S.Ct. 641, 647, 649, 71 L.Ed. 1095; *Herndon v. Lowry,* 301 U.S. 242, 57 S.Ct. 732, 81 L.Ed. 1066; and see Holmes, J. in *Gitlow v. New York,* 268 U.S. 652, 673, 45 S.Ct. 625, 69 L.Ed. 1138; as to prohibition of peaceable assembly, see *De Jonge v. Oregon,* 299 U.S. 353, 365, 57 S.Ct. 255, 260, 81 L.Ed. 278.

Nor need we enquire whether similar considerations enter into the review of statutes directed at particular religious, *Pierce v. Society of Sisters,* 268 U.S. 510, 45 S.Ct. 571, 69 L.Ed. 1070, 39 A.L.R. 468, or national, *Meyer v. Nebraska,* 262 U.S. 390, 43 S.Ct. 625, 67 L.Ed. 1042, 29 A.L.R. 1446; *Bartels v. Iowa,* 262 U.S. 404, 43 S.Ct. 628, 67 L.Ed. 1047; *Farrington v. Tokushige,* 273 U.S. 284, 47 S.Ct. 406, 71 L.Ed. 646, or racial minorities, *Nixon v. Herndon,* supra; *Nixon v. Condon,* supra: whether prejudice against discrete and insular minorities may be a special condition which tends seriously to curtail the operation of these political processes ordinarily to be relied upon to protect minorities, and which may call for a correspondingly more searching judicial inquiry. Compare *McCulloch v. Maryland,* 4 Wheat. 316, 428, 4 L.Ed. 579; *South Carolina State Highway Department v. Barnwell Bros.,* 303 U.S. 177, 58 S.Ct. 510, 82 L.Ed. 734, decided February 14, 1938, note 2, and cases cited.[1]

---

1. *United States v. Carolene Products Co.,* 304 U.S. 144 (1938).

---

challenged as infringing on individual rights than it used for those attacked as abridging economic rights. In *United States v. Carolene Products Co.* (1938), the Court upheld a federal law barring interstate shipment of certain types of skimmed milk.[44] This ruling reflected the Court's shift away from disapproval of all such interstate regulation as interfering too much with states' rights and the free flow of commerce.

Writing for the majority, Justice Harlan Fiske Stone stated that the Court would now uphold economic regulation against a constitutional challenge so long as the regulation had a rational basis.[45] In a footnote—the famous "Footnote Four"—Stone asserted that "[t]here may be narrower scope for operation of the presumption of constitutionality when legislation appears on its face to be within a specific prohibition of the Constitution, such as those of the first ten Amendments."[46] *(See box, "Footnote Four.")* This meant, Justice Robert H. Jackson observed several years later, that the "presumption of validity which attaches in general to legislative acts is frankly reversed in the case of interferences with free speech and free assembly."[47] He explained the reasoning behind this double standard:

Ordinarily, legislation whose basis in economic wisdom is uncertain can be redressed by the processes of the ballot box or the pressures of opinion. But when the channels of opinion or of peaceful persuasion are corrupted or clogged, these political correctives can no longer be relied on, and the democratic system is threatened at its most vital point. In that event the Court, by intervening, restores the processes of democratic government; it does not disrupt them.[48]

FREEDOM FOR IDEAS

The First Amendment protects against the government suppressing the unrestricted exchange of ideas. The guarantees of freedom for speech, press, and religion have been "first" in several ways—the first listed in the Bill of Rights and the first of those amendments to be fully applied against state action. Furthermore, many argue, this amendment is in fact first in importance among the Constitution's guarantees of individual rights. Such a "preferred position" is linked to the function of these freedoms in maintaining an environment that fosters responsive democratic government. In 1937 Chief Justice Charles Evans Hughes explained:

> The greater the importance of safeguarding the community from incitement to the overthrow of our institutions by force and violence, the more imperative is the need to preserve inviolate the constitutional rights of free speech, free press and free assembly in order to maintain the opportunity for free political discussion, to the end that government may be responsive to the will of the people and that changes, if desired, may be obtained by peaceful means. Therein lies the security of the Republic, the very foundation of constitutional government.[49]

A Charter for Government

Eight years later, in 1945, Justice Wiley B. Rutledge brought together the Court's acknowledgment of its new role with respect to the rights of the individual, the view of the First Amendment freedoms as "preferred," and the stricter test for laws challenged as violating those freedoms:

> The case confronts us again with the duty our system places on this Court to say where the individual's freedom ends and the State's power begins. Choice on that border, now as always delicate, is perhaps more so where the usual presumption supporting legislation is balanced by the preferred place given in our scheme to the great, the indispensable democratic freedoms secured by the First Amendment. . . . That priority gives these liberties a sanctity and a sanction not permitting dubious intrusions. And it is the character of the right, not of the limitation, which determines what standard governs the choice. . . .

For these reasons any attempt to restrict those liberties must be justified by clear public interest, threatened not doubtfully or remotely, but by clear and present danger. The rational connection between the remedy provided and the evil to be curbed, which in other contexts might support legislation against attack on due process grounds, will not suffice. These rights rest on firmer foundation.[50]

"The First Amendment," added Justice Rutledge later in his opinion, "is a charter for government, not for an institution of learning."[51] Concurring, Justice Rober H. Jackson wrote,

> [I]t cannot be the duty, because it is not the right, of the state to protect the public against false doctrine. The very purpose of the First Amendment is to foreclose public authority from assuming a guardianship of the public mind through regulating the press, speech and religion. In this field every person must be his own watchman for truth, because the forefathers did not trust any government to separate the true from the false for us. . . .
>
> This liberty was not protected because the forefathers expected its use would always be agreeable to those in authority or that its exercise would always be wise, temperate, or useful to society.
>
> As I read their intentions, this liberty was protected because they knew of no other way by which free men could conduct representative democracy.[52]

In 1979 Justice William J. Brennan Jr. discussed the way in which the First Amendment operates to "foster the values of democratic self-government":

> The First Amendment bars the State from imposing upon its citizens an authoritative vision of truth. It forbids the State from interfering with the communicative processes through which its citizens exercise and prepare to exercise their rights of self-government. And the Amendment shields those who would censure the State or expose its abuses.[53]

No Absolute Right

Neither the intrinsic importance of free expression nor its "societal function" enshrines in the First Amendment an absolute ban on all official restrictions on speech, the press, assembly, or religion. The collective good—the nation's security or the public's safety—warrants some restriction on the individual's freedom to speak, to publish, to gather in groups, and to exercise his or her religious beliefs. The task of the Court has been to balance the community's interest against the individual's rights, to determine when order and safety demand that limits be set to individual freedom. Wartime, the cold war, and the civil rights era put the Court in the position of reconciling these competing concerns. The Court's course has been uneven: the justices have sometimes discarded "tests" for determining permissible government constraints almost as soon as they have developed them.

The often mentioned clear and present danger test, although little used by the modern Court, nevertheless stands as a symbol of the basic position still held by the Court on free speech questions: only for very good reason may the government suppress speech, and the Court will evaluate the reasons. Freedom of the press has come more and more frequently before the Court since 1960. The Court has steadfastly rejected all restraints upon publication, most dramatically exhibited in the *Pentagon Papers Case* (1971).[54] Although the Court has rejected efforts by the news media to expand the protection of the First Amendment into special privileges for the press, it has extended protection to the media from libel suits brought by public officials or public figures.

Freedom of religion, a guarantee reflecting the original purpose for many of the nation's earliest settlers setting sail for the New World, has been at issue in some of the Court's most controversial modern rulings. Although it has generally upheld laws enacted to enhance the public welfare against challenges that they incidentally curtail the freedom to exercise one's religious beliefs, the Court has applied the standard of strict scrutiny to laws challenged as violating the First Amendment's ban on the establishment of religion. Such scrutiny has resulted in decisions rejecting state efforts to require devotional exercises in public schools or to use public funds to aid parochial schools. The Court has, however, upheld school funding laws that allow some tax money to flow to religious schools, so long as the schools are not singled out for special treatment.

POLITICAL RIGHTS

For the first 130 years of U.S. history, the privilege of political participation was strictly limited. Until well into the twentieth century, the right to vote was the prerogative of the adult white man, and often only those adult white men who could pay a poll tax, pass a literacy test, or meet other qualifications. The Constitution barely mentions the right to vote, and there is no mention at all of the right to have that vote counted equally with others or of the protected freedom of political association. During the twentieth century, however, these rights won judicial recognition and protection. By 1975 the right to vote belonged to all citizens eighteen years of age and older, regardless of sex or race.

Since 1962, when the Supreme Court abandoned its traditional aloofness from the issue of electoral districting, the right to have one's vote counted as equal to those of other city or state residents has become firmly established. As it has implemented that right, the Court has redistributed the balance of political power in every state of the Union. Unrestricted political association—the freedom to associate with others who share one's political views—has been recognized as an individual and institutional right. Although the Court during the peak of the cold war upheld state and federal programs and statutes curtailing the exercise of the freedom to associate, the modern Court determined this freedom to be a core value the First Amendment was intended to protect.

The Suffrage

Congress, not the Supreme Court, has led in expansion of the suffrage. Three constitutional amendments were required to lower the barriers of race, sex, and age. Indeed, it was the Court's narrow view of the privileges, immunities, and rights protected by the Civil War amendments that necessitated adoption of the Nineteenth Amendment to enfranchise women[55] and that rendered the Fifteenth Amendment a hollow promise for most of a century.[56]

After the Civil War, despite the clear language of the Fourteenth and Fifteenth Amendments, the Supreme Court continued to defer to state power to set

Despite such obstacles as an 1875 Supreme Court ruling that the right to vote was not guaranteed by the Fourteenth Amendment, women's suffrage groups in the nineteenth and early twentieth centuries persevered. Under the auspices of the National American Woman Suffrage Association, many women, like these on Pennsylvania Avenue in Washington, D.C., in 1913, took to the streets to protest sex discrimination. In 1920 their efforts paid off when the Nineteenth Amendment, giving women the right to vote, was added to the Constitution.

voter qualifications, steadily upholding a variety of devices used to exclude blacks from voting. In the twentieth century, the Court slowly asserted itself and began to strike down the most blatant of these mechanisms—the grandfather clause in 1915 and the white primary in 1927 and again in 1944.[57] It was left to Congress, however, to take the lead, as it did in the 1960s, abolishing poll tax requirements through a constitutional amendment, suspending literacy tests, and imposing federal control over the electoral machinery of states with high minority populations and low voter registration or participation. The Court's role, although secondary, was crucial. A century earlier, the Court had undercut similar efforts by Congress

to guarantee the right to vote against racial discrimination, by adopting a constricted view of the power of Congress to enforce the constitutional amendments adopted in the wake of the Civil War.

In the 1950s and 1960s, the Court gave full backing to the exercise of unprecedented federal power to guarantee civil rights to the nation's blacks. The most aggressive and effective of the major civil rights statutes was the Voting Rights Act of 1965, which superimposed federal power and machinery upon the electoral processes of states that had long denied blacks the right to vote. In 1966 the Court upheld the law against every point of a multifaceted constitutional challenge by the affected states.[58] Within five years of enactment, more than 1 million blacks had been newly registered to vote.

Redistricting Revolution

The Supreme Court's unexpected plunge into legislative redistricting and the apportionment of legislative power stands in stark contrast to its early reluctance to enforce the clear ban of the Fifteenth Amendment. After decades of declaring such issues "political" and unsuitable for judicial resolution, the Court in the early 1960s reconsidered its stance. In *Baker v. Carr* (1962), the Court announced its reversal, holding that constitutionally based challenges to the malapportionment of state legislative bodies were "federal questions" that federal courts might properly consider.[59] Although the Court in its ruling went no further than that declaration, *Baker v. Carr* set off a judicial revolution.

The following year, 1963, the justices declared that the Fourteenth Amendment's guarantee of equal protection—when applied to voting rights—meant "one person, one vote."[60] Prior to this decision, a rural district with 50,000 residents could have as much clout in the state legislature as a city with 1 million persons. Though each person had the same one vote, it was clear in such states that each rural vote carried more weight than a dozen city votes. The "one person, one vote" rule called for the state to value each vote equally in the legislature. The application of this rule to federal and state electoral divisions transformed the political base of every legislative body of any significance in the nation.

Beliefs and Association

Out of the unlikely context of the antisubversive and anti–civil rights laws, the protected freedom of political association won judicial affirmation in the 1950s and 1960s. In addition to its constitutional basis in the First Amendment, the right of association has a clear practical basis: no point of view can win recognition in an increasingly complex American society without organized backing. War had slowed the progress of this right toward acknowledged constitutional status, as during World War II and the subsequent cold war Congress and state legislatures sought to protect the

nation against subversion with laws and programs that declared a belief in communism or a similar political system and affiliation with such a system to be criminal and tantamount to treason.

As it had during the Civil War and World War I, the Court reflected a sensitivity to the national mood in its decisions upholding the validity of these antisubversive devices. The Court backed the power of Congress to enact laws that effectively made it illegal for anyone aware of the Communist Party's aims to participate in the party's activities. The Court seemed to sanction the use of guilt by association as a basis for depriving or denying persons jobs. Yet within a few years of these rulings, the Court began to circumscribe the methods by which such laws could be enforced. Enforcement became so difficult that in many instances it was altogether abandoned.

In one line of rulings beginning in 1957, the Court set strict standards of proof for government efforts to prosecute persons who were members of the U.S. Communist Party. Simple association could not properly serve as the basis for denying people a job, firing them, depriving them of a U.S. passport, or refusing them admission to the bar.[61] Almost simultaneously, in another series of decisions, the Court began to give full recognition to the right of association. These rulings, most of which dealt with civil rights activists, soon influenced the Court's view of legislation penalizing membership in "subversive" organizations.[62] By 1967 the right of association had gained clear constitutional status. As Justice Byron R. White wrote,

> The right of association is not mentioned in the Constitution. It is a judicial construct appended to the First Amendment rights to speak freely, to assemble, and to petition for redress of grievances. While the right of association has deep roots in history and is supported by the inescapable necessity for group action in a republic as large and complex as ours, it has only recently blossomed as the controlling factor in constitutional litigation; its contours as yet lack delineation.[63]

In the past quarter century, the Court has further defined these contours in applying the right of association to curtail the exercise of state power over radical student groups, national political party delegations, independent candidates, and party-switching voters. The Court held that this freedom also shields some government workers from being fired or denied promotions because they belong to the "wrong" political party. It has steadfastly refused, however, to allow private clubs to invoke this right to protect discriminatory practices.

EQUALITY BEFORE THE LAW

The Fourteenth Amendment's promise of equal protection of the laws was intended, said one of its key advocates, Sen. Jacob M. Howard, R-Mich., to give "to the humblest, the poorest, the most despised of the race, the same rights and the same protection before the law as it gives to the most powerful, the most wealthy, or the most haughty."[64] Not until well past the middle of the next century, however, was the protection of this guarantee actually extended to the nation's black citizens, to aliens, to women, and to the poor. Even then, however, the extension was less than complete.

At first, the Supreme Court seemed in accord with the intent of this portion of the Fourteenth Amendment. The Equal Protection Clause, wrote Justice Samuel F. Miller in 1873, was clearly meant to guarantee equal treatment of blacks. He expressed doubt "whether any action of a State not directed by way of discrimination against the negroes as a class . . . will ever be held to come within the purview of this provision."[65] Seven years later, the Court used the Equal Protection Clause to strike down a state law excluding blacks from jury duty. The equal protection guarantee, declared the Court, meant that "the law in the States shall be the same for the black as for the white; that all persons, whether colored or white, shall stand equal before the laws of the States."[66]

This declaration soon eroded into superficiality. In the *Civil Rights Cases* (1883), the Court held that the Fourteenth Amendment applied only to state, not individual, action; that individual discrimination did not violate the Thirteenth Amendment; and that Congress could act only to remedy discrimination by a state, not to prevent it before it occurred.[67] In *Plessy v. Ferguson* (1896), the Court upheld as reasonable Louisiana's

requirement of "equal but separate" accommodations for black and white passengers on railway trains.[68] This ruling, wrote one commentator, left the Fourteenth Amendment's guarantees "virtually nonexistent except as a bulwark of the rights of corporations."[69] *Plessy* was the logical outcome of a conservative view of the power of the law. In the majority opinion, written by Justice Henry B. Brown, the Court declared,

> If the two races are to meet upon terms of social equality, it must be the result of natural affinities, a mutual appreciation of each other's merits and a voluntary consent of individuals. . . . Legislation is powerless to eradicate racial instincts or to abolish distinctions based upon physical differences, and the attempt to do so can only result in accentuating the difficulties of the present situation. If the civil and political rights of both races be equal one cannot be inferior to the other civilly or politically. If one race be inferior to the other socially, the Constitution of the United States cannot put them upon the same plane.[70]

Business interests, generally more able than individuals to present their views to the Court in the late nineteenth and early twentieth century, did not hesitate to use the Equal Protection Clause as a basis from which to challenge state taxes, police regulations, and labor laws. They too met with no more than a modicum of success. The Court adopted rationality as the test for such challenges and would uphold all such laws so long as they had a reasonable basis. Nevertheless, businessmen persisted; economic cases accounted for the vast majority of equal protection questions before the Court until 1960.[71]

The Modern View

In 1938, the seventieth anniversary of the Fourteenth Amendment's adoption, the amendment began to take on new strength in its intended role as protector of individual rights. In the first of a line of rulings that would erode the declaration of *Plessy v. Ferguson* into uselessness, the Supreme Court in 1938 held that a state that did not maintain a "black" law school was in violation of the equal protection promise when it refused to admit a black resident to its "white" state law school solely because of his race.[72] Six years later, even as the Court upheld the war power of the federal government to remove Japanese Americans from their homes on the West Coast, the justices signaled their waning tolerance for laws using racial classifications. In *Korematsu v. United States,* the majority stated that "all legal restrictions which curtail the civil rights of a single racial group are immediately suspect" as violations of the Fourteenth Amendment's guarantee of equal protection. Such laws were subject to "the most rigid scrutiny," declared the Court. "Pressing public necessity may sometimes justify the existence of such restrictions; racial antagonism never can."[73]

Led by the National Association for the Advancement of Colored People (NAACP) and its legal defense fund, civil rights groups quickly accepted this clear judicial invitation to challenge the segregation that pervaded American life. In several subsequent cases decided in the late 1940s, the justices indicated their increasing skepticism that separate facilities could ever be truly equal. In *Brown v. Board of Education* (1954), the Court finally abandoned the separate but equal doctrine and declared state segregation of public schools unconstitutional.[74] Eighty-six years after adoption of the Fourteenth Amendment, the Court at last set the United States on the road to fulfilling its promise of equal protection.

Although the Court mandated a change in the nation's direction, progress was slow. In the 1960s, the frustration of the nation's blacks erupted in demonstrations, boycotts, sit-ins, and other types of protest. The reaction was often violent. This recurrence of protest and reaction sparked legislative action, leading Congress to pass the most comprehensive civil rights measure since Reconstruction. The Civil Rights Act of 1964 translated the guarantee of equal protection into a statutory requirement of equal opportunity in employment and equal access to public facilities for blacks and whites. Historian Irving Brant wrote that the 1964 act brought to fruition "all that a once-aroused nation had attempted" in adopting the Fourteenth Amendment.[75] The act was immediately challenged as unconstitutional and was just as quickly upheld by a unanimous Supreme Court.[76] In 1968 Congress approved the Fair Housing Act. The Court

reinforced its provisions with a broadened interpretation of the Civil Rights Act of 1866, which guaranteed similar rights of equal treatment to blacks and whites seeking to sell, buy, or rent housing.[77]

The Expanding Guarantee

In the last quarter of the twentieth century, the Supreme Court wrestled with a range of "second generation" questions raised by the national effort to ensure equal treatment for blacks and whites, including the problem of defining proper remedies for past discrimination. White plaintiffs charged that employers engaged in "reverse discrimination," that is, they penalized members of the majority group in order to compensate minority group members for past unfairness. Mindful of history, however, the Court generally condoned "affirmative action" to make up for past discrimination. In the closing years of the twentieth century, the Court began to question the continuing appropriateness of programs that favored racial minorities. Ruling in favor of a white highway contractor who challenged a decision awarding a contract to a Hispanic firm instead of his own, the Court asserted that policies based on race must undergo the strictest judicial scrutiny to ensure that no individual's right to equal protection of the laws is infringed.[78] Despite such scrutiny, the Court in 2003 upheld well-designed affirmative action policies at colleges and universities, ruling that officials may consider a student's race as one factor in the admissions process.[79]

The protection of the Fourteenth Amendment's guarantee of equality before the law was broadened as the Court brought aliens and women within its scope. In 1971 the Court formally declared alienage, like race, to be in all circumstances a suspect classification upon which to base laws. Absent a compelling state justification, such laws would be held invalid.[80] Women as a class fared less well. The Court has not yet declared gender a suspect classification in all circumstances, but in 1971 the Court for the first time nullified a state law because it violated the equal protection guarantee by treating men and women differently without a sufficient justification.[81] Since then, the Court has struck down a variety of federal regulations and state laws for this same reason. It generally employs the rule that classification by gender must serve important governmental objectives, and be substantially related to achieving those objectives, in order to be upheld.

FUNDAMENTAL FAIRNESS

The Constitution twice promises the individual that government will not deprive her of life, liberty, or property without due process of law. None of these guarantees—in the Fifth and Fourteenth Amendments—protects absolutely against loss of life, liberty, or property. They simply assure the individual that this deprivation will occur only after the government has adhered to certain standard, approved procedures. What is due process for the person faced with a sentence of death or life in prison or loss of property? The Supreme Court has spent more than a century debating this issue. The first time it considered the matter, it noted that the phrase "due process" probably meant no more to those who wrote it into the Bill of Rights than simply "by the law of the land," that is, by accepted legal procedures.[82] From that matter-of-fact origin, however, the guarantee of due process has expanded into the basic constitutional assurance to the individual that the government will deal fairly with him, even when it suspects or charges him with serious crimes.

The close relationship between procedure and substance, particularly in the nation's judicial system, was noted by Justice Wiley B. Rutledge in 1947. "At times," he wrote, "the way in which courts perform their function becomes as important as what they do in the result. In some respects matters of procedure constitute the very essence of ordered liberty under the Constitution."[83] Despite the many landmark due process decisions that dot the history of the Supreme Court in the twentieth century, the definition of due process remains incomplete. Justice Felix Frankfurter explained why:

> Due process of law . . . conveys neither formal nor fixed nor narrow requirements. It is the compendious expression for all those rights which the courts must enforce because they are basic to our free society. But basic rights do not become petrified as of any one time, even though, as a

matter of human experience, some may not too rhetorically be called eternal verities. It is of the very nature of a free society to advance in its standards of what is deemed reasonable and right. Representing as it does a living principle, due process is not confined within a permanent catalogue of what may at a given time be deemed the limits or the essentials of fundamental rights.[84]

Frankfurter wrote this in 1949. In the following two decades, the Court expanded the meaning of due process to include virtually all the specific guarantees of the Bill of Rights.

The Long Debate

The original due process guarantee is contained in the Fifth Amendment, but *Barron v. Baltimore* made plain that its reach was limited to federal action. The Fourteenth Amendment, added in 1868, included a similar guarantee, specifically directed against state action, but in one of history's odd turnabouts, this provision was used at first by the Court as a means of dismantling state economic regulation. At the same time, the justices refused to read into the Due Process Clause any requirement that states use the indictment process for persons charged with capital crimes, that they provide twelve-person juries to try people charged with serious crimes, or that they observe the privilege against compelled self-incrimination.[85]

For a century after 1868, the Court and legal scholars argued over whether the Fourteenth Amendment's due process guarantee incorporated the Bill of Rights, making each guarantee applicable against state action. As the debate continued from decision to decision, it tended to obscure the growing consensus among the justices that due process meant more than "by the law of the land," that it indeed represented a promise of fundamental fairness. Justice Frankfurter described it as "representing a profound attitude of fairness between man and man, and more particularly between the individual and the government."[86] Eventually, this consensus rendered the incorporation debate moot.

A fundamentally conservative Court in the 1920s began the enlargement of due process. Inherent in the concept of due process, that Court declared, were the guarantees that one's trial would be free from mob domination, that the judge would be impartial, that the jury would be representative of the community, and that one should have the effective aid of an attorney.[87] The Court first recognized these guarantees as being essential in cases where the crimes were serious and the defendant young, ignorant, or a member of a minority group. In the 1930s, the Court began to apply constitutional standards to the evidence used by state prosecutors. Decades before formally extending the Fifth Amendment privilege against compelled self-incrimination to state defendants, the Court held that confessions extracted by torture could not fairly be used against persons so forced to incriminate themselves.[88] In the 1940s, the Court simply assumed that the ban on cruel and unusual punishment applied to the states as well as the federal government.[89] It held that the Fourth Amendment guarantee of personal security against unreasonable search and seizure applied against state action, but it declined to require state judges to exclude evidence seized in violation of that guarantee.[90]

The Due Process Revolution

The decade of the 1960s saw the most rapid expansion of the meaning of due process. Led by Chief Justice Earl Warren, the Supreme Court firmly applied the guarantees of the Fourth, Fifth, Sixth, and Eighth Amendments against state action. Right by right, the Court read into the Constitution greater protection for criminal defendants. In 1960 the Court forbade federal agents to use evidence seized illegally by state agents. In 1961 it required the exclusion of illegally obtained evidence from state trials.[91] Since 1938 all federal defendants had been guaranteed the aid of an attorney. In 1963 the Supreme Court finally closed the gap between the right of state and federal defendants in that regard; the Court declared that all persons charged with serious crimes in state court were assured the aid of an attorney, who would be appointed by the court and paid by the state if necessary.[92]

Rejecting "the notion that the Fourteenth Amendment applies to the states only a 'watered-down subjective version of the Bill of Rights,'" the Court in 1964 held that state suspects, like federal suspects, are protected against being forced to incriminate themselves.[93] In 1965 the Court held that this privilege also barred adverse comment, by judge or prosecutor, on a defendant's failure to testify in his own defense.[94] Also that year, the Court held that due process required states to provide a defendant with the opportunity to confront and cross-examine persons who testified against her.[95] In 1967 the Court held that states were obliged to provide a speedy trial to criminal defendants.[96] In 1968 it added the requirements of a jury trial for all persons charged by the state with serious crimes.[97] Then, on the last day of Chief Justice Warren's tenure, the Court in 1969 applied the ban on double jeopardy to state criminal proceedings.[98]

By the early 1970s, the Court had grown so confident of its role as protector of individual rights that within a seven-month period, it overturned all state laws that imposed the death penalty or prohibited abortion. Neither ruling gained the type of public acceptance that the *Brown* decision had, and the Court four years later reinstated capital punishment.[99] The Court was widely criticized for pursuing a liberal, "activist" agenda. Although the *Roe v. Wade* (1973) abortion ruling survived, it remained under constant attack. Chastened, the Court retreated from its role as the champion of new rights and liberties.

In the late 1980s, the justices dealt a defeat to the emerging gay rights movement. By a 5-4 vote in *Bowers v. Hardwick* (1986), the Court upheld Georgia's prosecution of two gay men for having sex at home and ruled the right of privacy recognized in *Roe* did not extend to homosexuals.[100] In the 1990s, the Court refused to recognize a "right to die" in the Constitution. A small but growing movement asserted that persons who were terminally ill were entitled to the option of obtaining lethal medication from a physician, despite state laws against assisted suicide. The Court unanimously rejected the claim that the Fourteenth Amendment's protection for liberty and equality protected individuals who wanted to end their lives this way. This "asserted right has no place in our Nation's traditions," said Chief Justice William H. Rehnquist in *Washington v. Glucksberg* (1997), "and therefore, this change, if it is to be established in law, must be done through legislation."[101]

Still, even if the Court were no longer in the vanguard of change, it recognized shifts in public sentiment on matters of freedom and equality. In *Lawrence v. Texas* (2003), the Court struck down a Texas law that criminalized sex between gays and lesbians, calling this state "intrusion into the personal and private life" of homosexuals a violation of the Fourteenth Amendment's right to "liberty."[102] The opinion overruled *Bowers v. Hardwick* and highlighted, as had the *Brown* and *Roe* decisions for earlier generations, that notions of equality and liberty are not frozen forever in law, but evolve as the nation changes. "As the Constitution endures," wrote Justice Anthony M. Kennedy, "persons in every generation can invoke its principles in their own search for greater freedom."

At the same time, however, some members of the Court found old rights in the Constitution—some for the first time. In 2008 Justice Antonin Scalia argued that the right to have a gun for self-defense was a "pre-existing right" held by Americans before the Constitution. This right was incorporated into the Constitution, but then lay barren through much of the nation's legal history. Reviving the Second Amendment as a personal right, not just a protection for state militias, Scalia said residents have a right to a have a handgun at home to protect themselves and their families. "Undoubtedly some think that the Second Amendment is outmoded in a society where our standing army is the pride of our nation, where well-trained police forces provide personal security, and where gun violence is a serious problem," Scalia wrote. "That is perhaps debatable, but what is not debatable is that it is not the role of this Court to pronounce the Second Amendment extinct."[103]

NOTES

1. See Michael Kent Curtis, *Free Speech: The People's Darling Privilege* (Durham, N.C.: Duke University Press, 2000).

2. See Akhil Reed Amar, *The Bill of Rights: Creation and Reconstruction* (New Haven, Conn.: Yale University Press, 1998), 160–161.

3. Amar, *Bill of Rights,* 215.

4. Ibid., 291.

5. *Stromberg v. California,* 283 U.S. 359 (1931).

6. Article I, section 9, clause 2.

7. Article I, section 9, clause 3.

8. Article III, section 2, clause 3.

9. Article III, section 3.

10. Article IV, section 2, clause 2.

11. Article VI, section 3.

12. Charles Warren, *Congress, the Constitution and the Supreme Court* (Boston: Little, Brown, 1925), 79–80.

13. As a delegate to the Constitutional Convention in 1787, Madison had not felt that a bill of rights was a necessary safeguard against the power of the national government. The importance of a national bill of rights to secure support for the new plan of government, however, became clear to Madison (and other framers) during the ratification fights at several state conventions. Madison was elected to the new Congress and viewed it as his duty as floor leader in the House of Representatives to propose the twelve amendments, despite his personal views about their necessity.

14. Irving Brant, *The Bill of Rights* (Indianapolis: Bobbs-Merrill, 1965), 42–67; Julius Goebel Jr., *History of the Supreme Court of the United States,* vol. 1, *Antecedents and Beginnings to 1801* (New York: Macmillan, 1971), 413–456.

15. Henry M. Christman, ed., *The Public Papers of Chief Justice Earl Warren* (New York: Simon and Schuster, 1959), 70.

16. Ibid.

17. Zechariah Chafee Jr., *Free Speech in the United States* (Cambridge, Mass.: Harvard University Press, 1941; reprint, New York: Atheneum, 1969), 6–7.

18. Brant, *Bill of Rights,* 486; see also Goebel, *Antecedents and Beginnings,* 633–651.

19. Brant, *Bill of Rights,* 49–50.

20. Ibid., 314; see also Goebel, *Antecedents and Beginnings,* 633–651.

21. *Barron v. Baltimore,* 7 Pet. (32 U.S.) 243 (1833).

22. Id. at 247.

23. Id. at 250.

24. Id.

25. Brant, *Bill of Rights,* 333; see also Carl B. Swisher, *American Constitutional Development,* 2d ed. (Cambridge, Mass.: Houghton Mifflin, 1954), 331.

26. Brant, *Bill of Rights,* 336.

27. *Slaughterhouse Cases,* 16 Wall. (83 U.S.) 36 (1873); *Minor v. Happersett,* 21 Wall. (88 U.S.) 162 (1875).

28. *United States v. Reese,* 92 U.S. 214 (1876); *United States v. Cruikshank,* 92 U.S. 542 (1876).

29. *Hurtado v. California,* 110 U.S. 516 (1884).

30. *Plessy v. Ferguson,* 163 U.S. 537 (1896).

31. Charles Warren, *The Supreme Court in United States History,* 2 vols. (Boston: Little, Brown, 1926), 2:618.

32. Ibid., 617.

33. William W. Davis, "The Federal Enforcement Acts," in *Studies in Southern History and Politics,* cited by Warren, *Supreme Court in United States History,* 2:618.

34. *Yick Wo v. Hopkins,* 118 U.S. 356 (1886).

35. *Boyd v. United States,* 116 U.S. 616 (1886).

36. *Weeks v. United States,* 232 U.S. 383 (1914).

37. *Truax v. Raich,* 239 U.S. 33 (1915).

38. *Guinn v. United States,* 238 U.S. 347 (1915).

39. *Gitlow v. New York,* 268 U.S. 652 (1925).

40. Id. at 666.

41. *Stromberg v. California,* 283 U.S. 359 (1931); *Near v. Minnesota,* 283 U.S. 697 (1931).

42. *Hamilton v. Board of Regents,* 293 U.S. 245 (1934).

43. *DeJonge v. Oregon,* 299 U.S. 353 (1937).

44. *United States v. Carolene Products Co.,* 304 U.S. 144 (1938).

45. Id. at 152.

46. Id.

47. Robert H. Jackson, *The Struggle for Judicial Supremacy* (New York: Random House, Vintage Books, 1941), 284–285.

48. Ibid.

49. *DeJonge v. Oregon,* 299 U.S. 353 at 365 (1937).

50. *Thomas v. Collins,* 323 U.S. 516 at 529–530 (1945).

51. Id. at 537.

52. Id. at 545–546.

53. *Herbert v. Lando,* 441 U.S. 153 (1979).

54. *New York Times Co. v. United States,* 403 U.S. 713, *United States v. Washington Post,* 403 U.S. 713 (1971).

55. *Minor v. Happersett,* 21 Wall. (88 U.S.) 162 (1875).

56. *United States v. Reese,* 92 U.S. 214 (1876); *United States v. Cruikshank,* 92 U.S. 542 (1876).

57. *Guinn v. United States,* 238 U.S. 347 (1915); *Nixon v. Herndon,* 273 U.S. 536 (1927); *Smith v. Allwright,* 321 U.S. 649 (1944).

58. *South Carolina v. Katzenbach,* 383 U.S. 301 (1966).

59. *Baker v. Carr,* 369 U.S. 186 (1962).

60. *Gray v. Sanders,* 372 U.S. 368 (1963).

61. *Yates v. United States,* 354 U.S. 298 (1957); *Scales v. United States,* 367 U.S. 203 (1961); *Noto v. United States,* 367 U.S. 290 (1961); *Elfbrandt v. Russell,* 384 U.S. 11 (1966); *Aptheker v. Secretary of State,* 378 U.S. 500 (1964); *Schware v. Board of Bar Examiners,* 353 U.S. 232 (1957); *Keyishian v. Board of Regents,* 385 U.S. 589 (1967); *United States v. Robel,* 389 U.S. 258 (1967).

62. *National Association for the Advancement of Colored People v. Alabama,* 357 U.S. 449 (1958); *National Association for the Advancement of Colored People v. Button,* 371 U.S. 415 (1963).

63. *United States v. Robel,* 389 U.S. 258 at 282–283 (1967).

64. Brant, *Bill of Rights,* 337.

65. *Slaughterhouse Cases,* 16 Wall. (83 U.S.) 36 at 81 (1873).

66. *Strauder v. West Virginia,* 100 U.S. 303 at 307 (1880).

67. *Civil Rights Cases,* 100 U.S. 3 (1883).

68. *Plessy v. Ferguson,* 163 U.S. 537 (1896).

69. Brant, *Bill of Rights,* 367.

70. *Plessy v. Ferguson,* 163 U.S. 537 at 551–552 (1896).

71. Robert J. Harris, *The Quest for Equality* (Baton Rouge: Louisiana State University Press, 1960), 59; cited by C. Herman Pritchett, *The American Constitution,* 2d ed. (New York: McGraw-Hill, 1968), 682.

72. *Missouri ex rel. Gaines v. Canada,* 305 U.S. 337 (1938).

73. *Korematsu v. United States,* 323 U.S. 214 at 216 (1944).

74. *Brown v. Board of Education,* 347 U.S. 483 (1954).

75. Brant, *Bill of Rights,* 377.

76. *Heart of Atlanta Motel v. United States,* 379 U.S. 241 (1964).

77. *Jones v. Alfred H. Mayer Co.,* 392 U.S. 409 (1968).

78. *Adarand Constructors Inc. v. Peña,* 515 U.S. 200 (1995).

79. *Gratz v. Bollinger,* 539 U.S. 244 (2003); *Grutter v. Bollinger,* 539 U.S. 306 (2003).

80. *Graham v. Richardson,* 403 U.S. 365 (1971).

81. *Reed v. Reed,* 404 U.S. 71 (1971).

82. *Murray's Lessee v. Hoboken Land & Improvement Co.,* 18 How. (59 U.S.) 272 (1856).

83. *United States v. United Mine Workers,* 330 U.S. 258 at 342 (1947).

84. *Wolf v. Colorado,* 338 U.S. 25 at 27 (1949).

85. *Hurtado v. California,* 110 U.S. 516 (1884); *Maxwell v. Dow,* 176 U.S. 581 (1900); *Twining v. New Jersey,* 211 U.S. 78 (1908).

86. *Joint Anti-Fascist Refugee Committee v. McGrath,* 341 U.S. 123 at 162 (1951).

87. *Moore v. Dempsey,* 261 U.S. 86 (1923); *Tumey v. Ohio,* 273 U.S. 510 (1927); *Norris v. Alabama,* 294 U.S. 587 (1935); *Powell v. Alabama,* 287 U.S. 45 (1932).

88. *Brown v. Mississippi,* 297 U.S. 278 (1936).

89. *Louisiana ex rel. Francis v. Resweber,* 329 U.S. 459 (1947).

90. *Wolf v. Colorado,* 338 U.S. 25 (1949).

91. *Elkins v. United States,* 364 U.S. 206 (1960); *Mapp v. Ohio,* 367 U.S. 643 (1961).

92. *Gideon v. Wainwright,* 372 U.S. 335 (1963).

93. *Malloy v. Hogan,* 378 U.S. 1 at 10–11 (1964).

94. *Griffin v. California,* 380 U.S. 609 (1965).

95. *Pointer v. Texas,* 380 U.S. 400 (1965).

96. *Klopfer v. North Carolina,* 386 U.S. 213 (1967).

97. *Duncan v. Louisiana,* 391 U.S. 145 (1968).

98. *Benton v. Maryland,* 395 U.S. 784 (1969).

99. *Furman v. Georgia,* 408 U.S. 238 (1972); *Roe v. Wade,* 410 U.S. 113 (1973); *Gregg v. Georgia,* 428 U.S. 153 (1976).

100. *Bowers v. Hardwick,* 478 U.S. 186 (1986).

101. *Washington v. Glucksberg,* 521 U.S. 702 (1997).

102. *Lawrence v. Texas,* 539 U.S. 558 (2003).

103. *District of Columbia v. Heller,* 554 U.S __ (2008).

chapter 2

Freedom for Ideas: The First Amendment and the Right to Believe, to Speak, to Assemble, to Petition, and to Publish

O F ALL THE LIBERTIES GUARANTEED by the Bill of Rights, the freedoms of the First Amendment are the most widely cherished. Won through revolution, the freedoms of speech, press, religion, peaceable assembly, and petition are values fundamental to the American ideals of individual freedom and representative self-government. The guarantee of freedom for the individual's expression of ideas and opinions reflects a belief in the worth of each person. So, too, does the decision to entrust the government of society to the will of its members.

The "First Amendment protects two kinds of interests on free speech," wrote Professor Zechariah Chafee Jr. "There is an individual interest, the need of many men to express their opinions on matters vital to them if life is to be worth living, and a social interest in the attainment of truth, so that the country may not only adopt the wisest course of action but carry it out in the wisest way."[1] The two interests are inextricably bound together. Professor Thomas I. Emerson observed that freedom of individual expression is essential to preserve a stable community in the face of ever-changing political, economic, and social circumstances and to maintain "the precarious balance between healthy cleavage and necessary consensus."[2] Suppression of free expression, on the other hand, endangers the development and liberty of the individual and the stability of representative government. In the words of constitutional historian Thomas M. Cooley,

> Repression of full and free discussion is dangerous in any government resting upon the will of the people. The people cannot fail to believe that they are deprived of rights, and will be certain to become discontented, when their discussion of public measures is sought to be circumscribed by the judgment of others upon their temperance or fairness. They must be left at liberty to speak with the freedom which the magnitude of the supposed wrongs appears in their minds to demand; and if they exceed all the proper bounds of moderation, the consolation must be, that the evil likely to spring from the violent discussion will probably be less, and its correction by public sentiment more speedy, than if the terrors of the law were brought to bear to prevent the discussion.[3]

Justice Louis D. Brandeis also explained this relationship:

> Those who won our independence believed that the final end of the State was to make men free to develop their faculties; and that in its government the deliberative forces should prevail over the arbitrary. They valued liberty both as an end and as a means.... They believed that freedom to think as you will and to speak as you think are means indispensable to the discovery and spread of political

truth; that without free speech and assembly discussion would be futile; that with them, discussion affords ordinarily adequate protection against the dissemination of noxious doctrine; that the greatest menace to freedom is an inert people; that public discussion is a political duty; and that this should be a fundamental principle of the American government. They recognized the risks to which all human institutions are subject. But they knew that order cannot be secured merely through fear of punishment for its infraction; that it is hazardous to discourage thought, hope and imagination; that fear breeds repression; that repression breeds hate; that hate menaces stable government; that the path of safety lies in the opportunity to discuss freely supposed grievances and proposed remedies; and that the fitting remedy for evil counsels is good ones. Believing in the power of reason as applied through public discussion, they eschewed silence coerced by law—the argument of force in its worst form. Recognizing the occasional tyrannies of governing majorities, they amended the Constitution so that free speech and assembly should be guaranteed.[4]

Freedom of individual expression, including the right to speak one's mind without fear of repression, has been crucial to the success of representative government in the United States.

THE FIRST AMENDMENT

The First Amendment states, "Congress shall make no law respecting an establishment of religion, or prohibiting the free exercise thereof; or abridging the freedom of speech, or of the press; or the right of the people peaceably to assemble, and to petition the Government for a redress of grievances." Given the fundamental character of these rights, it seems somewhat ironic that they were not enumerated in the main body of the Constitution. In that document the framers sought to prevent federal infringement of certain crucial personal rights by specifically prohibiting Congress to enact ex post facto laws and bills of attainder or to require religious oaths from government officers. The framers also limited suspension of the writ of habeas corpus.

The Constitution's authors were apparently convinced, however, that the limited powers given the central government and their division among three separate and coequal branches of government were sufficient guarantees against abuse of the freedoms of belief and expression. Many of the framers also thought

any enumeration of individual rights was bound to be incomplete and would imply that those freedoms not listed were not protected. Participants in the state ratifying conventions were, however, unsatisfied with these explanations. Some of the colonies agreed to ratify the Constitution only on the condition that these and other critical rights—such as indictment and trial by jury—be added. The First Congress thus approved twelve amendments and submitted them to the states in the fall of 1789. Two of these—dealing with apportionment of U.S. representatives and compensation of members of Congress—were not ratified at the time. The other ten—comprising the Bill of Rights—were made part of the Constitution late in 1791.

No Absolute Rights

For nearly 130 years, the Supreme Court had very little occasion to review or interpret the First Amendment. Seven years after its ratification, however, Congress, fearing war with France, curtailed speech and the press by passing the Alien and Sedition Acts of 1798. This measure proved so unpopular that it precipitated the fall of the Federalist Party, which sponsored it, and was allowed to expire before constitutional challenges to it reached the Supreme Court. In the late 1800s, the Court reviewed a pair of federal territorial laws outlawing polygamy, which were challenged as abridging the free exercise of religion. The Court held polygamy a crime that could not be justified as a religious practice. The laws against it therefore did not violate the First Amendment.[5] Not until World War I, when Congress enacted new sedition and espionage acts, was the Supreme Court forced to consider whether the First Amendment's prohibition against federal interference with speech, the press, religion, and assembly was absolute or whether certain emergencies might limit its protection. In a series of nine cases testing the constitutionality of these two wartime laws, the Supreme Court made clear that the guarantees of free speech and press were not absolute. The justices, however, disagreed on the point at which government might curb exercise of these freedoms.

Rights and the States

The First Amendment explicitly prohibits only Congress from abridging the First Amendment's guaranteed freedoms. The Supreme Court was called upon to consider whether the amendment also prohibited state as well as federal abridgment of its guarantees. In *Barron v. Baltimore* (1833), the Court ruled that the Bill of Rights restricted the federal government only, not the states.[6] In 1868 the Fourteenth Amendment was added to the Constitution, forbidding the states to deprive anyone of "liberty" without due process of law. By 1890 the Court had defined liberty to include economic and property rights, but not personal liberties, which remained outside the Court's view of the Fourteenth Amendment. As historians Alpheus T. Mason and William M. Beaney observed, "This illogical position could not long endure."[7]

Application of First Amendment strictures to state action is traced to the minority opinion in *Gilbert v. Minnesota* (1920). Justice Brandeis, dissenting, said he could not believe "that the liberty guaranteed by the Fourteenth Amendment includes only liberty to acquire and enjoy property."[8] Nonetheless, as late as 1922 a majority of the Court still declared, "[T]he Constitution of the United States imposes upon the States no obligation to confer upon those within their jurisdiction ... the right of free speech."[9] The following year, however, the Court began to include personal

freedoms in the definition of liberty protected by the Fourteenth Amendment. Liberty, the majority wrote in *Meyer v. Nebraska* (1923),

> denotes not merely freedom from bodily restraint but also the right of the individual to contract, to engage in any of the common occupations of life, to acquire useful knowledge, to marry, establish a home and bring up children, to worship God according to the dictates of his own conscience, and generally to enjoy those privileges long recognized at common law as essential to the orderly pursuit of happiness by free men.[10]

Two years later, and with little explanation, the Court decided that the First Amendment guarantees of free speech and free press were applicable to the states. This view is expressed, almost as an aside, in *Gitlow v. New York* (1925):

> For present purposes we may and do assume that freedom of speech and of the press—which are protected by the First Amendment from abridgment by Congress—are among the fundamental personal rights and "liberties" protected by the due process clause of the Fourteenth Amendment from impairment by the States.[11]

That same year, the Court moved toward including religious liberty within this protection when it struck down an Oregon law requiring all children to attend public schools. In *Pierce v. Society of Sisters* (1925), the Court said that the right of parents to rear their children included the right to send them to private and parochial schools.[12] It would be fifteen more years before the Court explicitly applied the First Amendment ban on governmental interference with the free exercise of religion to the states. In *Cantwell v. Connecticut* (1940), the Court declared that the Fourteenth Amendment "has rendered the legislatures of the states as incompetent as Congress to enact" such restrictions. The states were specifically barred from passing any laws respecting establishment of religion by the Court's ruling in *Everson v. Board of Education* (1947).[13]

In *Near v. Minnesota* (1931), the Supreme Court, for the first time, struck down a state law as an unconstitutional prior restraint on the press. Six years later, the Court held that the freedom of assembly was guaranteed against state infringement by the First and Fourteenth Amendments. In *DeJonge v. Oregon* (1937), the Court held the right of peaceful assembly to be as fundamental as the rights of free speech and press and therefore equally entitled to protection from restriction by the states. The right of assembly, the Court wrote, "is one that cannot be denied without violating those fundamental principles of liberty and justice which lie at the base of all civil and political institutions, principles which the Fourteenth Amendment embodies in the general terms of its due process clause."[14]

GOVERNMENT RESTRAINTS

Government has restrained the exercise of First Amendment free speech and free press rights in two ways: first, suppression of the utterance before it is spoken or published, and second, punishment of the person who made the offending utterance. Prohibition of prior restraints—censorship, severe taxation, and licensing systems, for example—is particularly vital to ensure freedom of the press. The English legal commentator Sir William Blackstone thought that liberty of the press lay entirely in allowing "no previous restraints upon publications and not in freedom from censure for criminal matter when published."[15] The First Amendment has been interpreted by the Supreme Court to limit subsequent punishment as well as prior restraint. As Cooley wrote,

> [t]he mere exemption from previous restraints cannot be all that is secured by the constitutional provisions, inasmuch as of words to be uttered orally there can be no previous censorship, and the liberty of the press might be rendered a mockery and a delusion, and the phrase itself a byword, if, while every man was at liberty to publish what he pleased, the public authorities might nevertheless punish him for harmless publications.... The evils to be prevented were not the censorship of the press merely, but any action of the government by means of which it might prevent such free and general discussion of public matters as seems absolutely essential to prepare the people for an intelligent exercise of their rights as citizens.[16]

Although the First Amendment is stated absolutely—"Congress shall make no law ... "—few contend that the amendment is an absolute ban on governmental restriction of the amendment's guarantees. Most justices and constitutional scholars distinguish between pure expression and expression that is in itself conduct or that incites conduct. The first, with a few exceptions, is absolutely protected against governmental infringement; the second is not. The Court's explanation of this distinction in *Cantwell v. Connecticut* (1940), although it was speaking specifically of the freedom of religion, may be applied to all First Amendment freedoms: "[T]he Amendment embraces two concepts—freedom to believe and freedom to act. The first is absolute but, in the nature of things, the second cannot be. Conduct remains subject to regulation for the protection of society."[17]

Unprotected Speech

Some forms of expression that fall outside protection of the First Amendment are fairly obvious. Few would apply First Amendment protection to a person who counsels murder or, as Justice Oliver Wendell Holmes Jr. said, to a "man in falsely shouting fire in a theatre and causing a panic."[18] Few would argue that publishers are free to print deliberately false and defamatory material about public or private individuals. The outer bounds of First Amendment protection are not fixed. The Supreme Court initially held commercial speech—speech proposing a financial transaction—to be outside the amendment's reach. In a line of rulings beginning in 1975, the Court reversed that position. The Court has held that the First Amendment protects commercial advertising, but it has emphasized that the protection is less than that accorded political and other noncommercial speech.

The Court once ruled that libelous statements were unprotected. It has since held false and defamatory statements about public officials and figures protected unless actual malice is proved. Obscenity is still outside the scope of First Amendment protection, but even there the standards for determining what is obscene and what is not have undergone significant change in recent decades, bringing additional material under protection.

STUDENT RIGHTS AND FREEDOM FOR IDEAS

The Supreme Court's support for students' rights has waxed and waned. During World War II, as the United States and its European allies fought the spread of Nazism, the Court ruled that students in U.S. schools could not be forced to salute the flag. "Freedom to differ is not limited to things that do not matter much," wrote Justice Robert H. Jackson in *West Virginia State Board of Education v. Barnette* (1943). "That would be mere shadow freedom. The test of its substance is the right to differ as to things that touch the heart of the existing order."[1] *(See "Flag Salute Cases II," pp. 136–138.)*

The Court issued its strongest endorsement for free speech rights during the nation's divisive war in Vietnam. In December 1965, school officials in Des Moines, Iowa, suspended Mary Beth Tinker and her brother for defying a school policy and wearing black armbands to protest the war. Justice Abe Fortas described their actions as a "silent, passive expression of opinion" that did not "materially disrupt" the school or invade the rights of others. In such circumstances, school officials cannot punish students for expressing their views, the Court ruled in *Tinker v. Des Moines School District* (1969). Fortas noted that students do not "shed their constitutional rights to freedom of speech and expression at the school house gate."[2] He continued,

> In our system, state-operated schools may not be enclaves of totalitarianism. School officials do not possess absolute authority over their students. Students in school as well as out of school are "persons" under our Constitution [and] they are possessed of fundamental rights which the State must respect.[3]

It is noteworthy that Justice Fortas, the author of the opinion, was a close adviser and longtime friend of President Lyndon B. Johnson, the chief target of Vietnam War protesters. Since *Tinker,* however, the Court has generally sided with school officials, rejecting student claims of First Amendment violations. In the last two decades, the justices declared that school authorities have broad authority to limit what students say in school assemblies, to search their lockers and purses, and to censor school newspapers. Students are "children who have been committed to the temporary custody of the state as school master," Justice Antonin Scalia wrote in *Vernonia School District v. Acton* (1995), upholding an Oregon school's policy of drug testing all its student athletes.[4]

In 1986 the Supreme Court decided that free speech is not entirely free at school assemblies. Matthew Fraser had been asked to give a nominating speech for a fellow student at Bethel High School in Pierce County,

Washington. His brief statement began by describing the candidate as "a man who is firm—he's firm in his pants, firm in his shirt, his character is firm, but most of all, his belief in you, the students of Bethel, is firm." School officials were not amused. They said that Fraser had overstepped the bounds of decency, so they suspended him for three days. He sued and won in the lower federal courts. The Supreme Court reversed the decision, upholding the school district, 7-2. "Even the most heated political discourse in a democratic society requires consideration for the personal sensibilities of other participants and audiences," wrote Chief Justice Warren E. Burger.[5] Moreover,

> the constitutional rights of students in public school are not automatically coextensive with the rights of adults in other settings.... Surely it is a highly appropriate function of public school education to prohibit the use of vulgar and offensive terms in public discourse.[6]

Although the Court did not overturn *Tinker,* it determined that the school has more authority over what is said at an official school event than over an emblem worn on a sleeve. "The First Amendment does not prevent the school officials from determining that ... a high school assembly or classroom is no place for a sexually explicit monologue directed towards an unsuspecting audience of teenage students," Burger declared.[7] In dissent, Justice Thurgood Marshall argued that there was no evidence that Fraser's humorous speech had disrupted the school, and therefore, it should have been protected as free speech. "'Frankly, my dear, I don't give a damn.' When I was a high school student [in the 1930s], the use of those words in a public forum shocked the nation," said Justice John Paul Stevens in a separate dissent. "Today, Clark Gable's four-letter expletive is less offensive than it was then." He argued that the 600 students who attended the assembly would be a better judge of whether Fraser's sexual metaphor was offensive, certainly better "than a group of judges who are at least two generations and 3,000 miles away from the scene of the crime," Stevens wrote.[8] He thought that the student should have been given a hearing before a student government board before he was found guilty of violating the school speech policy and suspended.

Just as school officials may limit what students say in a school assembly, they may also control what appears in a school-sponsored newspaper. Students at Hazelwood East High School near St. Louis wrote and edited *Spectrum,* the school newspaper, as part of a journalism class. In May 1983, the principal deleted two pages of the six-page paper that contained stories on teen pregnancies, the impact of divorce, and references to unnamed students at the school. Principal Robert Reynolds said the material was not appropriate for younger students, and he worried that the content would invade the privacy of some persons. Three students sued and won a ruling from the U.S. Court of Appeals in St. Louis on the ground that the school had violated the free press rights of students by censoring the paper.

The Court disagreed, 6-3. "School officials retained ultimate control over what constituted 'responsible journalism' in a school-sponsored newspaper," wrote Justice Byron R. White in *Hazelwood School District v. Kuhlmeier* (1988).[9] He characterized the school newspaper as part of the curriculum, and therefore, subject to regulation by school authorities. Moreover, most of the money to fund the paper came from the school, and the journalism instructor was charged with editing the paper. In this instance, the principal stepped in because the teacher had left to take a new job. "We conclude that Principal Reynolds act[ed] reasonably in requiring the deletion" of the two articles, White said.[10]

In dissent, Justices William J. Brennan Jr., Marshall, and Harry A. Blackmun contended that school officials had broken a promise to "not restrict free expression or diverse viewpoints" in the school paper. "In my view, the principal broke more than just a promise. He violated the First Amendment's prohibitions against censorship of any expression that neither disrupts classwork nor invades the rights of others," Brennan wrote.[11]

The speech rights of high school students were limited further in 2007 when the Court ruled that a student could be suspended for "unfurling a pro-drug banner at a school event." Joseph Frederick, a senior, skipped school on January 24, 2002, the day that the Olympic Torch was to pass by his school in Juneau, Alaska, en route to the winter games in Salt Lake City. Frederick arrived outside the school with a fourteen-foot banner that read, "BONG HiTS 4 JESUS." The words were "just nonsense meant to attract television cameras," he said. Instead, they attracted the attention of school principal Deborah Morse. She took Frederick's banner and suspended him for ten days. Frederick sued her for violating his free speech rights. By a 6–3 vote, the Court shielded the principal from the suit.[12] "At a school-sanctioned and school-supervised event, a high school principal [may forbid] speech that can reasonably be regarded as encouraging illegal drug use," said Chief Justice John G. Roberts Jr.

The justices were sharply divided, however. Justice Clarence Thomas joined Roberts, but said he would overrule *Tinker* entirely, if given a chance.

"As originally understood, the Constitution does not afford students a right to free speech in public schools," Thomas wrote. Justices Samuel A. Alito Jr. and Anthony M. Kennedy agreed with Roberts, because the Alaska case was said to involve illegal drugs, but they also said that they would oppose "any restriction on speech that can be plausibly interpreted as commenting on any political or social issue." Justices Stevens, David H. Souter, and Ruth Bader Ginsburg dissented, arguing that school officials should have ignored "this nonsense banner."

When religion at school is the issue, the Court has drawn a sharp distinction between school-sponsored religious messages and a student's prayer or religious expression. "There is a crucial difference between government speech endorsing religion, which the Establishment Clause forbids, and private speech endorsing religion, which the Free Speech and Free Exercise Clause protect," Justice Sandra Day O'Connor noted in upholding a federal "equal access" law that allows students to meet on campus to pray or read the Bible.[13] The Court has thus barred schools from sponsoring prayers and Bible readings, posting the Ten Commandments in classrooms, teaching creationism, or selecting a student to deliver a prayer before high school athletic games.[14] It has also ruled, however, that students may pray on their own or with friends at school and that church-sponsored groups may not be prohibited from using school facilities simply because of their religious nature.[15]

1. *West Virginia State Board of Education v. Barnette,* 319 U.S. 642 (1943).

2. *Tinker v. Des Moines School District,* 393 U.S. 503 at 506 (1969).

3. Id. at 511.

4. *Vernonia School District v. Acton,* 515 U.S. 646 at 654 (1995).

5. *Bethel School District v. Fraser,* 478 U.S. 675 at 681 (1986).

6. Id. at 682–683.

7. Id. at 685.

8. Id. at 691–692.

9. *Hazelwood School District v. Kuhlmeier,* 484 U.S. 260 at 269 (1988).

10. Id. at 274.

11. Id. at 278.

12. *Morse v. Frederick,* 551 U.S. ___ (2007).

13. *Westside Community Board of Education v. Mergens,* 496 U.S. 226 at 250 (1990).

14. On creationism, see *Edwards v. Aguillard,* 482 U.S. 578 (1987); on student-led prayers, *Santa Fe Independent School District v. Doe,* 530 U.S. 290 (2000).

15. *Good News Club v. Milford Central School,* 533 U.S. 98 (2001).

Speech and Conduct

Commercial speech, libel, and obscene material are examples of pure expression. What has proved difficult for the Court to determine with consistency is the precise point at which expression becomes conduct that breaches the bounds of First Amendment protection and becomes subject to government restraint and regulation. Assume, for example, that a man is making an intemperate speech on a controversial issue on a public street corner. Does the First Amendment protect him against punishment for any consequences his speech might have? If not, must the government wait to stop the speech until his listeners take action either against the speaker or the object of his speech? May it stop him at the point that it thinks his words will lead to a breach of the peace, or can the government, knowing from past experience that the speaker is a rabble-rouser, prevent him from speaking at all? Finding answers to these questions is made more difficult by the emotional response generated by many forms of expression. As Justice Robert H. Jackson once observed, the "freedom to differ is not limited to things that do not matter much."[19]

The voicing of a popular opinion held by a majority rarely raises a First Amendment challenge. It is the unpopular opinion and minority position on matters of crucial concern that are most likely to draw hostility and hatred from the majority upon whose goodwill the rights of the minority depend. If the unpopular opinion is perceived as a threat to a way of life or a form of government, it may prompt the majority to petition the government to repress the expression. Such suppression is just what the First Amendment was designed to curb, explained Justice Holmes in a dissenting opinion:

> Persecution for the expression of opinions seems to me perfectly logical.... But when men have realized that time has upset many fighting faiths, they may come to believe even more than they believe the very foundations of their own conduct that the ultimate good desired is better reached by free trade in ideas— that the best test of truth is the power of the thought to get itself accepted in the competition of the market, and that truth is the only ground upon which their wishes safely can be carried out. That at any rate is the theory of our Constitution.[20]

THE TASK OF BALANCING

The Supreme Court's job has been to balance the scales so that personal rights are restricted only so much as needed to preserve an organized and orderly society. This has not been an easy task, for some justices give more weight to certain factors in the equation than do others. If, for instance, a judge believes the preservation of First Amendment rights to be worth more than the tranquility of the established society, the judge may require the society to show that the expression places it in some grave and immediate jeopardy. If, on the other hand, the judge gives the need for an orderly society the same or greater weight than the need for free expression, even a small degree of disruption may be enough for him to justify governmental restraint of the threatening idea.

The Absolute Position

Very few justices have believed that the First Amendment is absolute, that the government may under no circumstances restrict the exercise of free speech, press, religion, or assembly. Justice Hugo L. Black was one who held the view that there are limits. "[T]he Amendment provides in simple words that Congress shall make no law ... abridging freedom of speech or of the press," he wrote in one case. "I read 'no law abridging' to mean no law abridging."[21] Black elaborated on this in a 1961 dissent:

> I believe that the First Amendment's unequivocal command that there shall be no abridgment of the rights of free speech and assembly shows that the men who drafted our Bill of Rights did all the "balancing" that was to be done in this field.... [T]he very object of adopting the First Amendment, as well as the other provisions of the Bill of Rights, was to put the freedoms protected there completely out of the area of any congressional control that may be attempted through the exercise of precisely those powers that are now being used to "balance" the Bill of Rights out of existence.[22]

Black's view of the First Amendment meant that he would extend its protection to obscenities and libel, but even Black placed certain kinds of expression outside the reach of the First Amendment. In 1949 he wrote an opinion holding that a particular instance of picketing was so intertwined with illegal labor practices that it lost any First Amendment protection it might otherwise have, and in two cases in the mid-1960s, Black contended that civil rights demonstrations were not protected if they occurred in inappropriate places. *(See details of Brown v. Louisiana and Adderly v. Florida, p. 66.)*

Preferred Position

If First Amendment rights generally have not been viewed as absolute, most justices still accord them what came to be called a "preferred position" when weighed against competing rights and interests. This position arises from the judicial belief that preservation of these rights is so essential to the maintenance of democratic values as to warrant special judicial consideration. Justice Benjamin N. Cardozo first voiced this view from the bench in *Palko v. Connecticut* (1937). He suggested that because the freedom of "thought and speech ... is the matrix, the indispensable condition, of nearly every other form of freedom," First Amendment rights are on a "different plane of social and moral values" than the other rights and freedoms guaranteed by the Bill of Rights.[23]

Cardozo's statement was followed in 1938 by a broad hint that the Court might apply stricter standards to test the validity of laws restricting First Amendment rights than it did to cases involving property and economic rights. Traditionally the Court had deferred to legislative judgment in enacting statutes levying taxes and regulating business. So long as there was a reasonable basis for the regulation, the Court would presume it constitutional. In the famous "Footnote Four" of *United States v. Carolene Products Co.* (1938), however, Justice Harlan Fiske Stone wrote, "There may be a narrower scope for operation of the presumption of constitutionality when legislation appears on its face to be within a specific prohibition of the Constitution, such as those of the first ten Amendments."[24] *(See box, "Footnote Four," p. 11.)*

The following year all but one member of the Court endorsed the premise implicit in that footnote:

"Mere legislative preferences or beliefs respecting matters of public convenience may ... be insufficient to justify such [regulation] as diminishes the exercise of rights [of freedom of speech and press] so vital to the maintenance of democratic institutions," the majority wrote. Furthermore, it was the duty of the courts "to weigh the circumstances and to appraise the substantiality of the reasons advanced" to support regulation of First Amendment rights rather than to defer to legislative judgment.[25]

This special treatment of the First Amendment was called the "preferred position" by Stone when as chief justice he first used the expression in a dissent in *Jones v. Opelika* (1942). Its first recognition by a majority came in the decision that overturned *Jones*. In *Murdock v. Pennsylvania* (1943), the majority flatly stated that "[f]reedom of press, freedom of speech, freedom of religion are in a preferred position."[26] The fullest elaboration of this attitude came in *Thomas v. Collins* (1945). Justice Wiley B. Rutledge wrote that it was the Court's duty

> to say where the individual's freedom ends and the State's power begins. Choice on that border, now as always delicate, is perhaps more so where the usual presumption supporting legislation is balanced by the preferred place given in our scheme to the great, the indispensable democratic freedoms secured by the First Amendment.... That priority gives these liberties a sanctity and a sanction not permitting dubious intrusions....
>
> ... [A]ny attempt to restrict those liberties must be justified by clear public interest, threatened not doubtfully or remotely, but by clear and present danger. The rational connection between the remedy provided and the evil to be curbed, which in other contexts might support legislation against attack on due process grounds, will not suffice. These rights rest on firmer foundation. Accordingly, whatever occasion would restrain orderly discussion and persuasion, at appropriate time and place, must have clear support in public danger, actual or impending. Only the gravest abuses, endangering paramount interests, give occasion for permissible limitation.[27]

Use of the phrase "preferred position" faded, but the concept did not. The Court considers statutes that limit First Amendment rights highly suspect, requiring close judicial attention and compelling justification for their existence. Chief Justice Warren E. Burger stated that consensus in 1978:

> Deference to a legislative finding cannot limit judicial inquiry when First Amendment rights are at stake.... A legislature appropriately inquires into and may declare the reasons impelling legislative action but the judicial function commands analysis of whether the specific conduct charged falls within the reach of the statute and if so whether the legislation is consonant with the Constitution. Were it otherwise, the scope of freedom of speech and of the press would be subject to legislative definition and the function of the First Amendment as a check on legislative power would be nullified.[28]

A few justices opposed the preferred position concept. Chief among these was Felix Frankfurter, a vigorous advocate of judicial restraint. In 1949 he characterized the preferred position approach to the First Amendment as "a mischievous phrase, if it carries the thought, which it may subtly imply, that any law touching communication is infected with presumptive invalidity."[29] When he balanced First Amendment rights against competing interests, Frankfurter placed great weight on legislative judgment. Two years later he wrote,

> Free speech cases are not an exception to the principle that we are not legislators, that direct policy making is not our province. How best to reconcile competing interests is the business of legislatures, and the balance they strike is a judgment not to be displaced by ours, but to be respected unless outside the pale of fair judgment.[30]

THE SEARCH FOR A STANDARD

The Supreme Court has never held the freedoms of speech, press, religion, and assembly to be absolute. Although it has written specific rules for determining whether speech is obscene or libelous, the Court has been unable to settle on a general standard for determining at what point a form of expression becomes sufficiently threatening to society to justify its being regulated or otherwise restrained by government.

Clear and Present Danger

The first time the Supreme Court ruled directly on the extent to which government might limit speech, Justice Oliver Wendell Holmes Jr. proposed the "clear and present danger" test as the standard for such regulation. *Schenck v. United States* (1919) was the first of several cases challenging convictions under the World War I espionage and sedition acts that made it a federal crime to obstruct the U.S. war effort. Writing for a unanimous Court, Holmes stated,

> The question in every case is whether the words are used in such circumstances and are of such a nature as to create a clear and present danger that they will bring about the substantive evils that Congress has a right to prevent. It is a question of proximity and degree.[31]

In the eyes of the justices, the fact that the country was engaged in a war made Schenck's efforts to obstruct recruitment a clear and present danger punishable under federal law. *(See "Schenck v. United States," pp. 35–36.)*

Eight months after the *Schenck* decision, a majority of the Court moved away from the clear and present danger standard and toward what became known as the "bad tendency" test. This test held that government may punish any speech that tends to interfere with the successful prosecution of a war effort, no matter how remote in time or unlikely the effect of the interference might be. The majority applied the bad tendency test in several cases.[32] In 1937, however, it renewed reliance on the clear and present danger doctrine, in a case concerning a black communist who went to Georgia to solicit members for the Communist Party and to encourage black Georgians to demand equal rights with whites. The man was convicted under a state law after a trial court found that his speeches and documents had a dangerous tendency to incite insurrection. A majority of the Court overturned the conviction on the ground that the speech and documents did not threaten "a clear and present danger of forcible obstruction of a particular state function."[33] *(See "Herndon v. Lowry," pp. 47–48.)*

Until 1937 the Court had considered free speech questions primarily in the context of seditious speech—that is, utterances that threatened the viability of the established governing and economic system. After 1937 the Court began to review more cases weighing the constitutional guarantee of free speech against state limitations designed to preserve public peace. In these cases it frequently employed the clear and present danger test. Thus in 1940 the Court held that a state could not constitutionally punish a person for peacefully picketing an employer with whom he had a labor dispute.[34] In another 1940 case, the Court overturned the conviction of a Jehovah's Witness for breach of the peace. His verbal attack on other religions highly incensed two passersby who had consented to listen to it. In the absence of a definitive statute making such conduct a clear and present danger to a substantial interest of the state, the Court said the situation had threatened no "clear and present menace to public peace and order."[35] *(See "Disturbing the Peace," pp. 50–52.)*

It became apparent that the justices could seldom reach a consensus on whether a danger was "clear and present." In 1949 a majority of the Court held that the clear and present danger to public order was not threatened by a speaker whose speech in a private hall sparked a near riot by several hundred protesters gathered outside the hall. In 1951, however, the Court upheld the conviction of a speaker whose utterances caused one listener to threaten to stop the speaker from continuing his remarks. Here the Court majority held that a clear and present danger of greater disorder warranted restraint of the speaker.[36]

The widely held fear that the American system of government was in danger of subversion by communists led to enactment of a federal law outlawing membership in the Communist Party and the advocacy of the violent overthrow of the established government. *(See "Freedom of Political Association," pp. 217–247.)* Whether this act was an unconstitutional infringement on free speech came before the Supreme Court in *Dennis v. United States* (1951). A majority of the Court upheld the federal law, using a substantially revised version of the clear and present danger test. The justices read the traditional rule as being applicable only when the probability of success of the intended

dangerous effect was imminent. Chief Justice Fred M. Vinson, however, found this an inadequate protection from subversive activity that included advocacy of the future overthrow of the government by force. The clear and present danger test must be reinterpreted, he wrote in his dissent: "In each case [courts] must ask whether the gravity of the 'evil' discounted by its improbability, justified such invasion of free speech as is necessary to avoid the danger."[37] With this restatement, the original meaning of the clear and present danger test appeared to be lost. The doctrine was little used after *Yates v. United States* (1957).[38]

The Balancing Doctrine

The clear and present danger test was replaced for a time by the so-called balancing doctrine, in which the Court weighed the value of preserving free speech against the value of preserving whatever governmental interest that speech might adversely affect. This standard first appeared in a 1950 decision sustaining a federal law that denied the protection of the National Labor Relations Act to any union whose officers failed to swear that they were not communists and did not believe in the violent overthrow of the government. The majority found that the law's primary purpose was to prevent a union official from using his power to force a strike to advance the communist cause. In the Court's view, this law limited speech only incidentally. It found application of the clear and present danger test inappropriate and turned instead to the balancing test:

> When particular conduct is regulated in the interest of public order, and the regulation results in an indirect, conditional, partial abridgment of speech, the duty of the courts is to determine which of these two conflicting interests demands the greater protection under the particular circumstances presented.[39]

Throughout the cold war period—roughly the late 1940s to the late 1980s—the Court employed the balancing test to determine the validity of numerous state and federal laws restricting the speech and actions of individuals associated with the Communist Party and other allegedly subversive organizations.[40] When the Court was asked to weigh the interest of a state in obtaining the membership lists of a state branch of the National Association for the Advancement of Colored People (NAACP) against the members' right to privacy in association, it balanced the scales in favor of the right of association. The Court did not apply the balancing test to other 1960s civil rights cases involving picketing and demonstrations. In 1967 the Court specifically rejected the use of that test in a national security case.[41]

The Court disposed of some of the cold war cases by using the "incitement test," which distinguished between advocacy of unlawful conduct (such as the violent overthrow of the government) as abstract doctrine, and advocacy that actually incited action. The first was protected by the First Amendment; the second was not.[42]

Alternative Approaches

Recognizing the inadequacy of earlier substantive tests, the Court now relies on several standards that focus on the challenged statute rather than on the conduct or speech it regulates. The three standards most frequently employed are "statutory vagueness," "facial overbreadth," and the "least restrictive means" test. They are based on the premise that laws imposing restrictions that are too broad, or vague, might inhibit

some persons from exercising their constitutionally protected freedoms. An overly broad statute restricts forms of expression that are protected as well as those that are not. Under the least restrictive means test, government may restrain expression only as much as necessary to achieve its purpose: "[E]ven though the governmental purpose be legitimate and substantial, that purpose cannot be pursued by means that broadly stifle fundamental personal liberties when the end can more narrowly be achieved."[43]

Statutes deficient in any of these respects may be challenged by persons whose speech may in fact be properly punished by the state under the law. In 2003, for example, the Court struck down a Virginia law that made all cross burnings a crime, even as it said some cross burnings may be banned. Because burning a cross on the property of an African American family sends a message of terror and intimidation, states may make such acts a crime, said Justice Sandra Day O'Connor. Burning a cross at a Ku Klux Klan rally on private property, however, may be a symbol of group solidarity. Such "symbolic expressions" are generally protected by the First Amendment, she said. The Court thus struck down the Virginia law because it was overbroad but also maintained that states may prosecute persons who burn a cross with an "intent to intimidate" others.[44]

Freedom of Speech

Speech is the basic vehicle for communicating ideas, thoughts, and beliefs. The right to speak freely is necessary to the free flow of ideas that is considered so crucial to the success of representative government in the United States. This belief spurred the people of the new nation to add to the Constitution a prohibition on government action "abridging" the freedom of speech. Although the First Amendment states its protection absolutely, few contend that the right it protects is without limit. The forms of speech that merit no First Amendment protection include libel and obscenity. The speech-related cases before the Supreme Court repeatedly come down to two questions: What is protected speech? When may such speech be curbed?

The Court approaches speech that stands alone in a manner different from speech that is accompanied by a course of conduct, such as picketing. Verbal expression of thought and opinion, whether spoken calmly in the privacy of one's home or delivered passionately in a soapbox harangue, is the purest form of speech. Constitutional historian C. Herman Pritchett has observed that the "distinctive qualities of pure speech are that it relies for effect only on the power of the ideas or emotions that are communicated by speech and that usually the audience is a voluntary one which chooses to listen to the speaker's message."[1]

Because pure speech does not interfere with or inconvenience others, it is subject to the least amount of government control. The Court, however, recognizes the right of government to curb pure speech that threatens the national security or public safety. It also acknowledges that government has a right to regulate pure speech that interferes with others. The broadest official restrictions on pure speech have come during times of war, when the Court has upheld federal and state controls on seditious and subversive speech. It has sustained punishment of nonseditious speech that stimulates a violent and hostile reaction by those who hear it. Because the Court considers the varying circumstances attending each free speech case, it has been unable to develop and apply consistently a standard for determining when the threat to national security or public safety warrants a restriction on or punishment of the speech.

Certain forms of pure speech and expression fall outside the protection of the First Amendment because they are not essential to the communication of ideas and have little social value. "Fighting words"—public insults calculated to elicit a violent response—fall into this category, as does obscenity. Here again, however, the Court has had great difficulty settling on a standard by which to define the obscene. Initially the Court placed speech that advertised products and services outside the protection of the First Amendment. Since 1975, however, it has recognized that advertisements convey ideas and information of substantial value to the public and so has brought commercial speech under First Amendment coverage.

Expression that makes a symbolic statement has been considered pure speech by the Court. The justices have upheld the right of students to wear armbands and to fly the flag upside down in symbolic protest of the Vietnam War. Although such symbolism may make itself felt on an involuntary audience, it relies for effect, like pure speech, primarily on evocation of an idea or emotion. The Court has also held, however, that symbolic speech, like pure speech, may be so intertwined with conduct that the state may regulate both. When speech is combined with conduct—usually parading, demonstrating, or picketing—the Court is more open to allowing government regulation. Pritchett wrote that such "speech plus" involves

> physical movement of the participants, who rely less upon the persuasive influence of speech to achieve their purposes and more upon the public impact of assembling, marching and patrolling. Their purpose is to bring a point of view—by signs, slogans, singing or their mere presence—to the attention of the widest possible public, including those uninterested or even hostile.[2]

The Court has upheld the right of persons to engage in speech plus conduct, but at the same time it has accorded government the right to regulate the conduct aspect to ensure public safety and order. Such regulation must be precisely drawn and applied in a nondiscriminatory fashion. The government also must have a legitimate and substantial interest to justify the regulation, and the regulation must restrict the speech aspect as little as possible. One area of speech plus conduct—picketing—has been held by the Court to have almost no First Amendment protection. Although the Court at first ruled that the information conveyed to the public by labor picketing merited some degree of First Amendment protection, later decisions have virtually reversed this holding. Peaceful labor picketing is, however, protected under federal labor law.

The Court has also established that government has limited power to prevent public property from being used for public speech and assembly. It has, however, made an exception of property, such as a jail yard, that is dedicated to specific uses making it an inappropriate public forum. Because the First Amendment bars only government action abridging speech, it generally does not affect speech on private property. Here, too, there are exceptions. The First Amendment applies to privately owned company towns that provide all services to its residents that a municipally owned town would. The owners of private property dedicated to specific public purposes—for example, a shopping mall—may restrict speech on their property that is not directly related to its public use.

SEDITIOUS SPEECH AND NATIONAL SECURITY

Just seven years after ratification of the First Amendment, the Federalist-dominated Congress passed the Sedition Act of 1798. This act set stiff penalties for false, scandalous, or malicious writings about the president, either chamber of Congress, or the government if published with intent to defame any of them, excite hatred against them, stir up sedition, or aid foreign countries hostile to the United States. The Republicans charged that it abridged the freedoms of speech and press, but no challenge got to the Supreme Court

before the act expired. Although only twenty-five people were arrested and ten convicted under the act, it was extremely unpopular and is credited with bringing about the demise of the Federalist Party. Upon taking office in 1801, Democratic-Republican Thomas Jefferson pardoned all those convicted under it, and several years later Congress refunded their fines with interest. Although martial law imposed in some areas during the Civil War substantially curtailed freedoms of speech and press, the constitutionality of these actions was never presented to the Court. In 1917, after the United States had entered World War I, Congress again passed legislation restricting free speech and free press.

Espionage and Sedition

The Espionage Act of 1917 made it a crime to make false statements with the intent to interfere with the operation of the armed forces or to cause insubordination, disloyalty, or mutiny in the armed forces or to obstruct recruiting and enlistment efforts. The Sedition Act of 1918, passed the year World War I ended, expanded the grounds for prosecuting persons for disloyal speech. The law made it a crime to say or do anything to obstruct the sale of government war bonds; to utter, print, write, or publish anything intended to cause contempt and scorn for the government of the United States, the Constitution, the flag, or the uniform of the armed forces; or to say or write anything urging interference with defense production. The act also made it a crime to advocate, teach, defend, or suggest engaging in any conduct proscribed by the law.

Nearly two thousand persons were prosecuted under the act, and nine hundred were convicted, including Eugene V. Debs, the Socialist Party candidate for president.[3] Challenges to these two laws reached the Supreme Court in 1919 and 1920, presenting the Court with its first opportunity to grapple with the First Amendment and its protection for speech. World War I was deeply unpopular in some quarters, and the men and women who were appealing their convictions argued that they had simply voiced strong views opposing the war. Moreover, the First Amendment's provision that "Congress shall make no law … abridging the freedom of speech" appeared as though it were written to nullify measures such as the Sedition Act of 1918.

TREASON

Article III, section 3, of the Constitution defines treason against the United States as consisting "only in levying War against them, or in adhering to their Enemies, giving them Aid and Comfort. No Person shall be convicted of Treason unless on the Testimony of two Witnesses to the same overt Act, or on Confession in open Court." The Supreme Court has reviewed only three charges of treason, all arising from incidents during World War II. Two of these decisions left interpretation of part of the law in some doubt; the third added little to the discussion.

Cramer v. United States (1945) concerned a German-born laborer, Anthony Cramer, who became a U.S. citizen in 1936. Six years later, Cramer befriended two Germans who had landed in the United States to sabotage the American war effort. He met twice with them in public places and held some money in safekeeping for one of them. Cramer was charged with giving aid and comfort to the enemy, but the Supreme Court held, 5-4, that Cramer's traitorous intent had not been proved and that eating and drinking with the enemy did not establish guilt.[1]

Haupt v. United States (1947) grew out of the same incident. Hans Max Haupt, the father of one of the saboteurs, was convicted of giving aid and comfort to the enemy after he sheltered his son, helped him try to find employment, and bought him an automobile. Sustaining the conviction, the Court ruled, 8-1, that sheltering the enemy was an overt act that gave aid and comfort, and there was no further need to prove that Haupt had traitorous intent when he took in his son.[2]

In *Kawakita v. United States* (1952), the Court held that charges of treason could be brought against an American citizen who had committed a treasonous act against the United States in a foreign country.[3]

---

1. *Cramer v. United States*, 325 U.S. 1 (1945).

2. *Haupt v. United States*, 330 U.S. 631 (1947).

3. *Kawakita v. United States*, 343 U.S. 717 (1952).

The Court, nonetheless, repeatedly rejected the First Amendment challenges concerning these laws and upheld the prosecutions, often unanimously. The justices stated that the freedom of speech was not an absolute right and therefore could be swept aside in wartime emergencies. At such times, criticizing the government represented a danger that could not and need not be tolerated. The Court thus deferred to Congress's judgment that certain disloyal words and acts would interfere with the war effort and needed to be suppressed. The post–World War I cases are remembered best, not for their decisions, but for the dissents written by Justices Oliver Wendell Holmes Jr. and Louis D. Brandeis. After upholding the first three of the sedition prosecutions, Holmes had a change of heart and penned several eloquent essays on the freedom of speech and the "free trade in ideas." His words outshined and outlived the majority opinions that held for the government.

Schenck v. United States

The first of the six major seditious speech cases was *Schenck v. United States* (1919). It is best known for Justice Holmes's offhand comment that the freedom of speech does not "protect a man in falsely shouting fire in a theatre" and his invocation of the "clear and present danger" standard. Charles Schenck, the secretary of the Socialist Party, and others were convicted of conspiring to foment insubordination in the armed forces and to obstruct recruiting and enlistment. Schenck printed and distributed fifteen thousand leaflets opposing the recently passed Selective Service Law; many were mailed to draftees.

Justice Holmes, who wrote the unanimous opinion affirming Schenck's conviction, described the leaflet's message: "In impassioned language it intimated that conscription was despotism in its worst form and a monstrous wrong against humanity in the interest of Wall Street's chosen few." The leaflet urged its readers to oppose the draft. Again in Holmes's words, the pamphlet

> described the arguments on the other side [in favor of the draft] as coming from cunning politicians and a mercenary capitalist press, and even silent consent to the conscription law as helping to support an infamous conspiracy. It denied the power to send our citizens away to foreign shores to shoot up the people of other lands, and added that words

could not express the condemnation such cold-blooded ruthlessness deserves … winding up, "You must do your share to maintain, support and uphold the rights of the people of this country."[4]

Schenck had not denied at trial that the intended effect of this circular was to persuade people to resist conscription, but he also argued that such expression was protected by the First Amendment. The Court rejected this contention.

> We admit that in many places and in ordinary times the defendants in saying all that was said in the circular would have been within their constitutional rights. But the character of every act depends upon the circumstances in which it is done…. The most stringent protection of free speech would not protect a man in falsely shouting fire in a theatre and causing panic. It does not even protect a man from an injunction against uttering words that may have all the effect of force…. The question in every case is whether the words used are used in such circumstances and are of such a nature as to create a clear and present danger that they will bring about the substantive evils that Congress has a right to prevent. It is a question of proximity and degree. When a nation is at war many things that might be said in time of peace are such a hindrance to its effort that their utterance will not be endured as long as men fight and that no Court could regard them as protected by any constitutional right.[5]

It made no difference that Schenck and his compatriots had not succeeded in obstructing recruitment. "The statute … punishes conspiracies to obstruct as well as actual obstruction," Holmes concluded. "If the act (speaking or circulating a paper), its tendency and the intent with which it is done are the same, we perceive no ground for saying that success alone warrants making the act a crime."[6]

Frohwerk v. United States

The next two cases, decided a week after *Schenck,* also unanimously affirmed convictions under the espionage and sedition laws, but in both cases the evidence showing intent to create a clear and present danger was less convincing than in *Schenck.* Jacob Frohwerk had placed in a German-language newspaper twelve articles that the government considered attempts to cause disloyalty and insubordination among the armed forces. Justice Holmes, who wrote the opinion in *Frohwerk v. United States* (1919), indicated that the defendant might well have been acquitted had more evidence been presented. There was little in the language of the articles, Holmes said, to distinguish them from the language Schenck had used in his leaflets, but from the trial record the Court was unable to determine whether the circumstances surrounding the publishing and distribution of the articles were such that no clear and present danger was raised:

> It may be that all this might be said or written even in time of war in circumstances that would not make it a crime. We do not lose our right to condemn either measures or men because the Country is at war. It does not appear that there was any special effort to reach men who were subject to the draft…. But we must take the case on the record as it is, and on that record it is impossible to say that it might not have been found that the circulation of the paper was in quarters where a little breath would be enough to kindle a flame and that the fact was known and relied upon by those who sent the paper out.[7]

Debs v. United States

In the other case, the Court upheld the conviction of Socialist Party leader Eugene V. Debs for violating the espionage act by a speech he gave in Canton, Ohio. The government alleged the speech was intended to interfere with recruiting and to incite insubordination in the armed forces. Debs's speech was primarily about socialism. He discussed its growing popularity and predicted its eventual success. He also spoke, however, in support of several people serving sentences for violations of the espionage and sedition acts, saying of one that if she was guilty, then so was he. He stated, "You need to know that you are fit for something better than slavery and cannon fodder" and "You have your lives to lose; you certainly ought to have the right to declare war if you consider a war necessary." On this evidence, a trial jury convicted Debs.

The Supreme Court affirmed the conviction in *Debs v. United States* (1919). Based on these statements,

Socialist leader Eugene V. Debs was convicted for inciting insubordination, disloyalty, and mutiny in the armed forces and for obstructing military recruitment after he told listeners, "You need to know that you are fit for something better than slavery and cannon fodder." The Supreme Court upheld his conviction in *Debs v. United States* (1919). Here, Debs is released from the federal penitentiary in Atlanta, Georgia, in 1921.

In *Abrams v. United States* (1919) the Court upheld the conviction on espionage charges of Russian emigrés Samuel Lipman, Hyman Lychowsky, Mollie Steimer, and Jacob Abrams. They had thrown leaflets from the windows and roofs of New York City buildings calling for weapons workers to strike.

wrote Justice Holmes, a jury could reasonably conclude that Debs was opposed "not only [to] war in general but this war, and that the opposition was so expressed that its natural and intended effect would be to obstruct recruiting."[8] The Court then considered whether Debs actually intended his speech to have this effect and decided that he did. Here Holmes looked at evidence showing that just before speaking, Debs endorsed the view that U.S. involvement in World War I was unjustifiable and should be opposed by all means.[9]

Abrams v. United States

Eight months after *Debs,* the Court issued its first divided decision in a seditious speech case. *Abrams v. United States* (1919) concerned the convictions of five

Russian-born immigrants for writing, publishing, and distributing in New York City two allegedly seditious pamphlets criticizing the U.S. government for sending troops into Russia in 1918. One of the pamphlets described President Woodrow Wilson as a coward and a hypocrite, implying that the real reason for sending troops to Russia was not to protect supplies for use in the war against Germany but to aid those fighting the takeover of Russia by communist revolutionaries. The pamphlet also described capitalism as the "one enemy of the workers." The second pamphlet, printed in Yiddish, warned workers in munitions factories that their products would be used to kill Russians as well as Germans. It also called for a general strike. The five immigrants distributed some of these pamphlets by tossing them from a window; others were circulated secretly around the city. The five were each sentenced to twenty years in prison.

A seven-justice majority upheld the convictions. Justice John H. Clarke, writing for the majority, quickly dismissed the direct free speech issue by citing *Schenck* and *Frohwerk* as precedents. The only question the Court need answer, Clarke said, was whether there was sufficient evidence presented to the jury to sustain its guilty verdict. Clarke quoted sections of the two pamphlets—the evidence in the case—and from these excerpts concluded that

> the plain purpose of their propaganda was to excite, at the supreme crisis of war, disaffection, sedition, riots, and, as they hoped, revolution, in this country for the purpose of embarrassing and if possible defeating the military plans of the [U.S.] Government in Europe.... Thus it is clear not only that some evidence but that much persuasive evidence was before the jury tending to prove that the defendants were guilty as charged.[10]

This reasoning strayed too far from the clear and present danger test to win the concurrence of Justices Holmes and Brandeis. Holmes agreed with the majority that the five defendants had advocated a general strike and curtailment of war materials production, but he questioned whether their intent to hinder the war effort had been proved. Holmes further contended that the espionage and sedition acts required conviction of a speaker only if it was proved that he intended his speech to have the criminal effect proscribed by the law and that the speech must produce or be intended to produce a "clear and imminent danger that it will bring about forthwith certain substantive evils that the United States constitutionally may seek to prevent." Holmes continued:

> But as against dangers peculiar to war ... the principle of the right to free speech is always the same. It is only the present danger of immediate evil or an intent to bring it about that warrants Congress in setting a limit to the expression of opinion where private rights are not concerned. Congress certainly cannot forbid all effort to change the mind of the country. Now nobody can suppose that the surreptitious publishing of a silly leaflet by an unknown man, without more, would present any immediate danger that its opinions would hinder the success of the government arms or have any appreciable tendency to do so.[11]

Then, warming to his task, the seventy-eight-year-old Holmes memorably set forth his "theory of our Constitution" and its protection for the "free trade in ideas." Having written terse opinions that had sent Schenck, Frohwerk, and Debs to jail, Holmes "in the course of a few short months ... underwent a spectacular conversion experience," observed Rodney Smolla.[12] According to Smolla, Holmes's dissent is "a haunting, poetic masterpiece, and to this day one of the sacred icons in the free speech tradition." Wrote Holmes in *Abrams,*

> But when men have realized that time has upset many fighting faiths, they may come to believe even more than they believe the very foundations of their own conduct that the ultimate good desired is better reached by free trade in ideas—that the best test of truth is the power of the thought to get itself accepted in the competition of the market, and the truth is the only ground upon which their wishes safely can be carried out. That at any rate is the theory of our Constitution. It is an experiment, as all life is an experiment. Every year if not every day we have to wager our salvation upon some prophecy based upon imperfect knowledge. While that experiment is part of our system I think that we should be eternally vigilant against attempts to check the expression of opinions that we loathe and believe to be fraught with death, unless they so imminently threaten immediate interference with the lawful and pressing purposes of the law that an immediate check is required to save the country. I wholly disagree with the argument of the Government that the First Amendment left the common law as to seditious libel in force. History seems to be against the notion. I had conceived that the United States through many years has shown its repentance for the Sedition Act of 1798, by repaying fines that it imposed. Only the emergency that makes it immediately dangerous to leave the correction of evil counsels to time warrants making any exception to the sweeping command, "Congress shall make no law ... abridging the freedom of speech."[13]

While not speaking for the Court, Holmes thus reshaped his clear and present danger standard to refer only to a national emergency or an "immediate evil," not harmless rantings in "a silly leaflet by an unknown man."

Schaefer v. United States

In the next case, the Court majority moved even farther away from Holmes's clear and present danger test.

Schaefer v. United States (1920) arose after five officers of a German-language newspaper in Philadelphia were convicted of publishing false news items with the intent to promote Germany's success in the war and hamper U.S. recruiting efforts. The articles, generally unfavorable to the U.S. war effort, were reprinted from other publications, but the paper's officers had either added to or omitted parts of the original texts. One article was found objectionable by the trial court solely because one word had been mistranslated so that "bread lines" read "bread riots."

Six of the justices voted to reverse the convictions of two of the men but sustained the convictions of the other three. Speaking through Justice Joseph McKenna, the majority said it had no doubt that the statements were deliberately falsified, "the purpose being to represent that the war was not demanded by the people but was the result of the machinations of executive power." [14] The majority further contended that it was not unreasonable for a jury to conclude that the additions and omissions were made with the intent that the reprinted articles would have the effect alleged. To readers, McKenna wrote, the articles' "derisive contempt may have been truly descriptive of American feebleness and inability to combat Germany's prowess, and thereby [may have served] to chill and check the ardency of patriotism." [15] Furthermore, the majority held that there was no need to show that the articles presented an immediate danger but only that they tended to have a bad effect. Were the articles, McKenna asked,

the mere expression of peevish discontent, aimless, vapid and innocuous? We cannot so conclude. We must take them at their word, as the jury did, and ascribe to them a more active and sinister purpose. They were the publications of a newspaper, deliberately prepared, systematic, always of the same trend, more specific in some instances, it may be, than in others. Their effect or the persons affected could not be shown, nor was it necessary. The tendency of the articles and their efficacy were enough for offense ... and to have required more would have made the law useless. It was passed in precaution. The incidence of its violation might not be immediately seen, evil appearing only in disaster, the result of disloyalty engendered and the spirit of mutiny. [16]

Holmes and Brandeis would have acquitted all five defendants on the ground that the articles did not raise a clear and present danger to the government's war efforts. Of one of the reprints, Brandeis wrote,

It is not apparent on a reading of this article ... how it could rationally be held to tend even remotely or indirectly to obstruct recruiting. But ... the test to be applied ... is not the remote or possible effect. There must be the clear and present danger. Certainly men judging in calmness and with this test presented to them could not reasonably have said that this coarse and heavy humor immediately threatened the success of recruiting. [17]

Brandeis not only chided the majority for failing to apply the test in its review of the case, but criticized the lower courts for failing to offer the test to the jury as the standard to be used. Instead, the jury had been instructed to convict if they found that any of the articles would diminish "our will to win" the war. Brandeis concluded with a strong warning against restricting free speech too readily:

To hold that such harmless additions to or omissions from news items and such impotent expressions of editorial opinion, as were shown here, can afford the basis even of a prosecution will doubtless discourage criticism of the policies of the Government. To hold that such publications can be suppressed as false reports, subjects to new perils the constitutional liberty of the press....

... Nor will this grave danger end with the passing of the war. The constitutional right of free speech has been declared to be the same in peace and in war. In peace, too, men may differ widely as to what loyalty to our country demands; and an intolerant majority, swayed by passion or by fear, may be prone in the future, as it has often been in the past, to stamp as disloyal opinions with which it disagrees. Convictions such as these, besides abridging freedom of speech, threaten freedom of thought and of belief. [18]

Justice Clarke also dissented, but not on free speech grounds.

Pierce v. United States

The final major case in this series centered on a pamphlet entitled "The Price We Pay," written by an eminent Episcopal clergyman and published by the Socialist Party. A federal district judge in Baltimore acquitted several persons accused of violating the espionage act by distributing the pamphlet in that city. The judge found that the booklet was an attempt to recruit persons to the Socialist Party and its philosophy, not an attempt to persuade them to interfere with the war effort. An Albany, New York, judge and jury, however, found the latter to be true. Consequently, several persons who distributed the pamphlet in Albany were convicted of conspiring to attempt to cause insubordination in the armed forces. They appealed to the Supreme Court on the ground that the government failed to show intent to cause insubordination or to prove that distribution of the pamphlet created a clear and present danger that insubordination would result.

Seven justices upheld the convictions in *Pierce v. United States* (1920). A jury could conclude that several of the statements were false, the majority reasoned, and that the distributors knew them to be false or distributed them without any regard for whether the statements were false. Among those statements the Court majority thought a jury might consider false were the following:

> Into your homes the recruiting officers are coming. They will take your sons of military age and impress them into the army.... And still the recruiting officers will come; seizing age after age, mounting up to the elder ones and taking the younger ones as they grow to soldier size.

> The Attorney General of the United States is so busy sending to prison men who do not stand up when the Star Spangled Banner is played, that he has no time to protect the food supply from gamblers.

> Our entry into [the war] was determined by the certainty that if the allies do not win, J. P. Morgan's loans to the allies will be repudiated, and those American investors who bit on his promises would be hooked.

A jury would also be warranted in concluding that such statements, when circulated, would have a tendency to cause insubordination and that that was the intent of the distributors. Even if a jury did not agree on the probable effect of the pamphlet, said Justice Mahlon Pitney,

> at least the jury fairly might believe that, under the circumstances existing, it would have a tendency to cause insubordination, disloyalty and refusal of duty in the military and naval forces.... Evidently it was intended, as the jury found, to interfere with the conscription and recruitment services; to cause men eligible for the service to evade the draft; to bring home to them, and especially to their parents, sisters, wives, and sweethearts, a sense of impending personal loss, calculated to discourage the young men from entering the service.[19]

Holmes and Brandeis dissented in an opinion written by Brandeis. They disagreed that the statements cited by the majority were false. The first, regarding recruiting, was eventually proved true. The second, concerning the attorney general, was false if taken literally but was clearly meant to suggest that the attorney general could spend his time in better ways than prosecuting people for allegedly seditious statements. The third, regarding the reason for U.S. entry into the war, was an expression of opinion rather than fact. To buttress this last statement, Brandeis noted that some members of Congress found the loans instrumental in the government's decision to enter the war. Brandeis then said,

> To hold that a jury may make punishable statements of conclusions or of opinion, like those here involved, by declaring them to be statements of facts and to be false would practically deny members of small political parties freedom of criticism and of discussion in times when feelings run high and the questions involved are deemed fundamental.[20]

Furthermore, Brandeis continued, even if the statements were false, the government offered no proof showing that the men who distributed the pamphlet knew they were false. Nor was there any proof that the pamphlet intended to dampen military morale. The defendants did not even distribute the pamphlet to military men, Brandeis observed. Finally, he said, there was no indication that distribution of "The Price We Pay" raised a clear and present danger of causing insubordination. Brandeis again concluded his dissent with a warning that the Court majority had placed the guarantee of free speech in a precarious position:

> The fundamental right of free men to strive for better conditions through new legislation and new institutions will not be preserved, if efforts to secure it by argument to fellow citizens may be construed as criminal incitement to disobey the existing law—merely, because the argument presented seems to those exercising judicial power to be unfair in its portrayal of existing evils, mistaken in its assumptions, unsound in reasoning or intemperate in language.[21]

Hartzel v. United States

Distance in time from actual combat brought calmer voices to the debate on seditious speech. The 1918 sedition law was repealed in 1921, and many of those convicted of violating it, including Debs, were ultimately pardoned or had their sentences reduced. The Espionage Act was still in force when the United States entered World War II in 1941. The Supreme Court reviewed only one conviction under it. The case concerned a man who printed and sent out several articles urging in hostile and intemperate language that the white race stop fighting each other and band together to confront the yellow races. The question in *Hartzel v. United States* (1944) was not whether what Hartzel said fell within the reach of the federal law, but whether there was enough evidence to sustain his conviction, the same question prominent in the World War I cases of *Pierce, Schaefer,* and *Abrams*. A five-justice majority concluded that the government had not proved beyond a reasonable doubt that Hartzel had intended his statements to incite insubordination in the armed forces.[22]

State Sedition Laws

From time to time in U.S. history, states have perceived their internal security to be threatened by radical political forces and, like the federal government, they have sought to minimize those threats by restricting the exercise of free speech, free press, and free assembly. The first round of such state laws was enacted after President William McKinley was assassinated in 1901 by a professed anarchist. The model for these criminal anarchy laws—and for the federal Smith Act of 1940—was New York's 1902 law that defined criminal anarchy as "the doctrine that organized government should be overthrown by force or violence, or by assassination of the executive head or any of the executive officials of government, or by any unlawful means." The law made it a felony for anyone to advocate criminal anarchy by speech or by printing and distributing any material promoting or teaching it.

Following the Russian Revolution of 1917 and World War I, which ended the next year, thirty-three states enacted peacetime sedition or criminal syndicalism statutes. Similar to but broader than the criminal anarchy laws, these statutes made it unlawful to advocate, teach, or aid the commission of a crime, sabotage, or other unlawful act of violence in order to bring about political change or a change in industrial ownership. These laws also made it unlawful to organize or knowingly become a member of an organization that advocated criminal syndicalism. The Supreme Court initially sustained the constitutionality and application of these laws, but by the late 1930s it began to reverse convictions in lower courts, holding either that the law in dispute was too vague or broad or that it had been applied to persons whose advocacy of overthrow of the government presented no immediate threat.

During the cold war years, states focused exclusively on preventing communist infiltration of government. Many required public employees to swear that they did not advocate forceful overthrow of the government. Persons refusing to take such oaths were liable to dismissal; those who lied were subject to prosecution for perjury. At first the Court sustained convictions under these laws, but as the threat of infiltration receded, the justices began to find several of the loyalty oath statutes unconstitutionally vague. In some instances, the Court found their application violated due process requirements. (*See "Federal Loyalty Programs," pp. 233–236.*)

THE RIGHT AND FREEDOM OF ASSOCIATION: AN IMPLICIT FIRST AMENDMENT GUARANTEE

The right of an individual to associate with others—for instance, with people who share similar beliefs and aspirations—is not explicitly granted by the Constitution or the Bill of Rights, but the Supreme Court has found this right to be implicit within the First Amendment freedoms of speech and assembly and in the concept of liberty protected by the Fourteenth Amendment. The right of association, however, did not gain recognition by the Court until the late 1950s, and its boundaries remain unclear.

At the height of the cold war, the Court was unwilling to say that communists had a right to associate freely; in a similar vein, members of a drug gang or a terrorist cell can be prosecuted for associating with like-minded persons. In 1927 a majority of the justices upheld the conviction of a woman for violating California's criminal syndicalism law by associating with people in an organization that advocated overthrow of the government by unlawful means.[1] In 1928 the Court upheld the conviction of a Ku Klux Klan officer who disobeyed a New York statute that required certain organizations to file membership lists with the state. The Court ruled that the statute was a proper exercise of the state's police power.[2]

A distaste for implying guilt by association underpinned the Court's decision in *DeJonge v. Oregon* (1937), reversing Dirk DeJonge's conviction for conducting a public meeting under the auspices of the Communist Party. The Court distinguished between the party's illegal intent to overthrow the U.S. government and the protected right of a party member to speak and assemble for lawful purposes.[3] *(See details of DeJonge v. Oregon, p. 47.)* The right of association was sorely tested during the cold war years, when Americans thought that communist subversion threatened U.S. national security. Laws intended to protect the nation against communist activities were repeatedly challenged on the basis that political associations were constitutionally protected. The Court, however, upheld these laws, and leaders of the Communist Party in the United States received prison sentences for organizing a political group whose goal was to overthrow the government. *(See further discussion, pp. 220–244.)*

THE NAACP CASES

The civil rights movement late in the 1950s won judicial recognition of a constitutionally protected right of association by addressing the issue of membership in the National Association for the Advancement of Colored People (NAACP). Several southern states, incensed by the association's influential role in the civil rights movement, tried to prevent the NAACP from continuing its activities within their borders. The NAACP challenged these measures. Not only did the Supreme Court strike them down, but in so doing it found in the First and Fourteenth Amendments an implicit right of association on an equal plane with the explicitly guaranteed freedoms of speech, press, assembly, and religion.

The first case arose in Alabama. Like many other states, Alabama required all out-of-state corporations to register before doing business there. Although local branches of the NAACP had operated in Alabama since 1915, it had never registered, nor had the state indicated that it should do so. In 1956 the state attorney general, charging the NAACP with failure to register, won a temporary restraining order prohibiting the organization from operating in Alabama. The attorney general also requested, and the state court ordered, that the NAACP turn over certain records, including lists of all its members in the

state. The NAACP eventually produced all the records requested, except for the membership lists. The state court held the organization in contempt and fined it $100,000. The Supreme Court unanimously reversed the contempt conviction in *NAACP v. Alabama ex rel. Patterson* (1958). Justice John Marshall Harlan wrote the Court opinion:

> Effective advocacy of both public and private points of view, particularly controversial ones, is undeniably enhanced by group association, as this Court has more than once recognized by remarking upon the close nexus between the freedoms of speech and assembly.... It is beyond debate that freedom to engage in association for the advancement of beliefs and ideas is an inseparable aspect of the "liberty" assured by the Due Process Clause of the Fourteenth Amendment.[4]

Furthermore, Justice Harlan said, the right of association also entails the right to privacy in that association: "It is hardly a novel perception that compelled disclosure of affiliation with groups engaged in advocacy may constitute [an] effective ...restraint on freedom of association."[5] Turning to the NAACP in specific, he observed that the association had offered unrebutted evidence that previous public disclosures of its membership had resulted in economic reprisal, loss of employment, and physical violence to members. The Court held that Alabama had not presented a sufficient reason to justify an infringement of this protected right. The reversal of the contempt citation was not the end of this particular story, however. The Court sent the case back to the state court for a decision on whether the NAACP had violated Alabama law by failing to register. The state court forbade the NAACP to operate in Alabama.[6] The Supreme Court reversed that decision in 1964.[7]

TEACHERS' ASSOCIATIONS

In 1960 the Court struck down an even more subtle attempt to discourage membership in the NAACP. An Arkansas law required teachers in state-supported schools to file affidavits listing all the organizations they had belonged to or contributed to within the past five years. It was widely understood that this law was aimed at exposing teachers who belonged to the NAACP. The case of *Shelton v. Tucker* (1960) came to the Court after teachers whose contracts were not renewed, because they had refused to comply with the statute, charged that the law violated their rights to personal, academic, and associational liberties. For the majority, Justice Potter Stewart stated that there was no question that a state might, in an appropriate investigation of the fitness and competence of its teachers, consider their associational ties. In this case, however, the law's "comprehensive interference with associational freedom goes far beyond what might be justified in the exercise of the State's legitimate inquiry into the fitness and competency of its teachers."[8]

WOMEN, BOY SCOUTS, GAYS, AND PRIVATE CLUBS

During the 1980s, the Court rejected claims of freedom of association brought by large, business-oriented clubs that sought to preserve their policies of excluding women. They had come under challenge due to state and local antidiscrimination laws that had opened doors to blacks and women. The

Jaycees, a national organization of young men who seek to rise in the business world, contended that the freedom of association permitted it to maintain its male-only policy. The Court disagreed unanimously in 1984, ruling that the state's "compelling interest in eradicating discrimination against its female citizens" in the business world outweighed the Jaycees' right to freedom of association.[9] Justice William J. Brennan Jr. had described the Jaycees as "large and basically unselective groups." Young men could join freely, and the chapters in Minneapolis and St. Paul had more than 400 members. Clubs that are small and selective might have a stronger claim, he noted.

Lawyers for Rotary International and New York City's highly exclusive private clubs seized on these issues to defend their men's only policies, but the Court rejected their claims as well. It upheld a California law that prohibited race or gender discrimination in business-oriented clubs, dealing a defeat to Rotary's many, small local chapters.[10] In addition, it upheld a New York City ordinance that barred such discrimination by private clubs with more than 400 members and regular meal service.[11]

In cases involving dance clubs limited to teenagers only, the Court made clear that there is no right of "social association." Dallas had licensed teens-only dance clubs that closed their doors to anyone younger than fourteen or older than eighteen. This age restriction was successfully challenged in the Texas courts on the ground that it violated the freedom to associate of those who were excluded. Disagreeing, Chief Justice William H. Rehnquist said, "[T]he Constitution does not recognize a generalized right of social association."[12]

The Court continued, however, to hold that the First Amendment included a right of "expressive association." Surely, an avowedly racist group such as the Ku Klux Klan could not be required to include African Americans in its membership, nor could a civil rights march be required to include a contingent from the Ku Klux Klan. In Boston, the annual St. Patrick's Day parade had been organized since 1947 by the South Boston Allied War Veterans Council. A predominantly Irish group, the vets said the parade was intended to celebrate "traditional religious and social values." A local group of Irish gays and lesbians wanted to join the march to portray a somewhat different picture of the Boston Irish. The war vets refused their request to join the parade. The gay and lesbian group sued, and Massachusetts judges ruled that their exclusion from the public parade violated the state's antidiscrimination law. The Court took up the veterans' appeal and ruled unanimously that the parade's organizers had the freedom not to associate with the gays and lesbians.

"Parades are a form of expression, not just motion, and the inherent expressiveness of marching to make a point" brings them under the protection of the First Amendment, Justice David H. Souter said. The organizers may not be compelled "to alter the expressive content of their parade" since the "fundamental rule of protection under the First Amendment [is] that a speaker has the autonomy to choose the content of his own message."[13]

Five years later, the Court extended the "freedom of expressive association" to uphold the Boy Scouts' decision to dismiss an openly gay scoutmaster. The New Jersey courts had ruled illegal the dismissal of James Dale, a gay scoutmaster, under the terms of the state's antidiscrimination law. In a 5-4 vote, the Court reversed the state's decision. "The forced inclusion of an unwanted person in a group infringes the group's freedom of expressive

association if the presence of that person affects in a significant way the group's ability to advocate public or private viewpoints," said Chief Justice Rehnquist. The Boy Scouts of America had repeatedly and "sincerely" voiced the view that "avowed homosexuals were not to be Scout leaders," he said, and Dale had stepped forward as "a gay rights activist" in his college days.[14] As such, Dale's mere presence as a scoutmaster conflicts with the group's message, Rehnquist asserted. The dissenters—Justices John Paul Stevens, Souter, Ruth Bader Ginsburg, and Stephen J. Breyer—questioned whether the exclusion of gays was an integral part of the Boy Scouts' mission and message.

In 2006 the Court unanimously rejected a freedom of association claim from several law schools and law professors who objected to having military recruiters on campus. The law schools had adopted policies prohibiting recruiters for employers who discriminated against gays and lesbians. The Defense Department forbids openly gay persons from serving in the military through the "Don't Ask, Don't Tell" policy. Congress had also passed the Solomon Amendment, thereby threatening to cut off federal funds to colleges or universities that did not give military recruiters equal access to the campus and students.

In *Rumsfeld v. Forum for Academic and Institutional Rights,* the Court upheld the funding restriction and rejected the First Amendment challenge. "The Solomon Amendment neither limits what law schools may say nor requires them to say anything," wrote Chief Justice John G. Roberts Jr. He also said that a military recruiter who visits campus is not analogous to the scoutmaster in *Dale.* "Recruiters are, by definition, outsiders who come onto campus for the limited purpose of trying to hire students—not to become members of the school's expressive association. This distinction is critical," he wrote. "Students and faculty are free to associate to voice their disapproval of the military's message.... A military recruiter's mere presence on campus does not violate a law school's right to associate, regardless of how repugnant the law school considers the recruiter's message."[15]

1. *Whitney v. California, 274 U.S. 357 (1927).*

2. *Bryant v. Zimmerman, 278 U.S. 63 (1928).*

3. *DeJonge v. Oregon, 299 U.S. 353 (1937).*

4. *NAACP v. Alabama ex rel. Patterson,* 357 U.S. 449 at 460–461 (1958).

5. Id. at 461.

6. *NAACP v. Alabama ex rel. Patterson,* 360 U.S. 240 (1959); *NAACP v. Gallion,* 368 U.S. 16 (1961).

7. *NAACP v. Alabama ex rel. Flowers,* 377 U.S. 288 (1964); see also *Louisiana ex rel. Gremillion v. NAACP,* 366 U.S. 293 (1961); *Bates v. City of Little Rock,* 361 U.S. 516 (1960).

8. *Shelton v. Tucker,* 464 U.S. 479 at 490 (1960).

9. *Roberts v. United States Jaycees,* 468 U.S. 609 (1984).

10. *Board of Directors of Rotary International v. Rotary Club of Duarte,* 481 U.S. 537 (1987).

11. *New York State Club Association v. City of New York,* 487 U.S. 1 (1988).

12. *Dallas v. Stanglin,* 490 U.S. 19 at 25 (1988).

13. *Hurley v. Irish-American Gay, Lesbian and Bisexual Group of Boston,* 515 U.S. 557 at 568, 573 (1995).

14. *Boy Scouts of America v. Dale,* 530 U.S. 640 at 648, 652 (2000).

15. *Rumsfeld v. Forum for Academic and Institutional Rights,* 547 U.S. 47 (2006).

By the late 1960s, the fear that communists would destroy the established order was replaced by concern that the public peace was in jeopardy from civil rights activists, antiwar protesters, and members of the so-called New Left. Once again, several states turned to their criminal anarchy and syndicalism laws to restrain what they perceived as disturbing speech from dissident elements of the society. In the Court's first review of this latest application of a criminal syndicalism law, however, the justices cast doubt on the validity of all such laws. The First Amendment protected the advocacy of forceful overthrow of the government, the Court said, unless that advocacy actually incited someone to undertake such action.

Gitlow v. New York

The first of the state sedition laws to be tested before the Court was New York's criminal anarchy law. Benjamin Gitlow, a member of the left wing of the Socialist Party, was convicted under the law for printing and distributing some sixteen thousand copies of the "Left Wing Manifesto." This tract repudiated the moderate stance of the main body of the Socialist Party and called for the overthrow of the democratic state by "*class action of the proletariat in any form* having as its objective the conquest of the power of the state." It also urged the proletariat to "organize its own state *for the coercion and suppression of the bourgeoisie.*" Gitlow appealed his conviction to the Supreme Court on the ground that the statute unconstitutionally restricted his rights of free speech and free press by condemning certain classes of speech without considering whether they presented a clear and present danger of bringing about the evil that the state had the right to prevent.

Gitlow won one of his arguments. The First Amendment explicitly prohibited only Congress, and not the states, from restricting free speech. Gitlow argued, however, that the First Amendment rights of free speech and free press were implicit in the concept of liberty guaranteed by the Fourteenth Amendment. The Court agreed, almost casually, with this contention, but a majority of the Court nonetheless sustained the conviction in *Gitlow v. New York* (1925). *(See mention of this case, pp. 218–219.)* The majority opinion, written by Justice Edward T. Sanford, first held that Gitlow's manifesto fell within the speech

proscribed by the law. It was neither abstract doctrine nor the "mere prediction that industrial disturbances and revolutionary mass strikes will result spontaneously in an inevitable process of evolution in the economic system."[23] Rather, the manifesto urged mass strikes for the purpose of fomenting industrial disturbance and revolutionary action to overthrow the organized government.

The Court next held that the state was within its police power when it punished "those who abuse this freedom [of expression] by utterances inimical to the public welfare, tending to corrupt public morals, incite to crime, or disturb the public peace."[24] The state need not show that such utterances created a clear and present danger of inciting overthrow of the government but only that they tended to have that effect. Sanford explained:

> That utterances inciting to the overthrow of organized government by unlawful means present a sufficient danger of substantive evil to bring their punishment within the range of legislative discretion is clear. Such utterances, by their very nature, involve danger to the public peace and to the security of the State. They threaten breaches of the peace and ultimate revolution. And the immediate danger is none the less real and substantial, because the effect of a given utterance cannot be accurately foreseen. The State cannot reasonably be required to measure the danger from every such utterance in the nice balance of a jeweler's scale. A single revolutionary spark may kindle a fire that, smouldering for a time, may burst into a sweeping and destructive conflagration. It cannot be said that the state is acting arbitrarily or unreasonably when in the exercise of its judgment as to the measures necessary to protect the public peace and safety, it seeks to extinguish the spark without waiting until it has enkindled the flame or blazed into the conflagration. It cannot reasonably be required to defer the adoption of measures for its own peace and safety until the revolutionary utterances lead to actual disturbances of the public peace or imminent and immediate danger of its own destruction; but it may, in the exercise of its judgment, suppress the threatened danger in its incipiency.[25]

Having upheld the authority of the state to determine that a certain class of speech presented a danger, the majority then refused to consider whether the First Amendment protected specific utterances falling

Benjamin Gitlow and William Z. Foster, Communist Workers' Party candidates for president and vice president in 1928, at Madison Square Garden. Three years earlier the Supreme Court had upheld Gitlow's conviction for publishing an article calling for workers to overthrow capitalism and the government by force.

within that class. The majority's reasoning was different from the Court's traditional approach to convictions under federal sedition laws, which condemned certain kinds of actions. Under those laws, speech was unprotected only if the government could prove that the circumstances in which it was uttered made it the equivalent of the proscribed action.

Justices Holmes and Brandeis dissented, arguing that the clear and present danger test should be applied to state as well as to federal statutes restricting the right of free speech. In Gitlow's case, wrote Holmes,

> there was no present danger of an attempt to overthrow the government by force on the part of the admittedly small minority who shared [Gitlow's]

views. It is said that this manifesto was more than a theory, that it was an incitement. Every idea is an incitement. It offers itself for belief and if believed it is acted on unless some other belief outweighs it or some failure of energy stifles the movement at its birth. The only difference between the expression of an opinion and an incitement in the narrower sense is the speaker's enthusiasm for the result. Eloquence may set fire to reason. But whatever may be thought of the redundant discourse before us it had no chance of starting a present conflagration. If in the long run the beliefs expressed in proletarian dictatorship are destined to be accepted by the dominant forces of the community, the only meaning of free speech is that they should be given their chance and have their way.[26]

Whitney v. California

California's criminal syndicalism statute was the second state sedition law tested in the Supreme Court. Anita Whitney, a niece of former Supreme Court justice Stephen J. Field, participated in a convention establishing the California branch of the Communist Labor Party. At the convention, Whitney advocated adoption of a resolution dedicating the party to seek political change through the ballot, but this proposition was rejected in favor of a resolution urging revolutionary class struggle as the means to overthrow capitalism. Despite her defeat, Whitney continued to participate in the convention and the party. Whitney testified that she had no intention of helping to create an unlawful organization, but she was convicted of violating the California law prohibiting organization and participation in groups advocating criminal syndicalism.

The Supreme Court unanimously sustained her conviction. After holding that the state law was not unconstitutionally vague, Justice Sanford said the majority saw little to distinguish Whitney's actions from Gitlow's manifesto. In fact, Whitney's actions in assembling with others to form a group advocating forceful overthrow of the government posed an even greater danger to the state. Wrote Sanford,

> The essence of the offense denounced by the Act is the combining with others in an association for the accomplishment of the desired ends through the advocacy and use of criminal and unlawful methods. It partakes of the nature of a criminal conspiracy.... That such united and joint action involves even greater danger to the public peace and security than the isolated utterances and acts of individuals is clear. We cannot hold that, as here applied, the Act is an unreasonable or arbitrary exercise of the police power of the State, unwarrantedly infringing any right of free speech, assembly or association, or that those persons are protected from punishment by the due process clause who abuse such rights by joining and furthering an organization thus menacing the peace and welfare of the state.[27]

Although Justices Holmes and Brandeis concurred with the majority, their separate opinion, written by Brandeis, sounded more like a dissent. Under the California statute, Brandeis wrote,

> [t]he mere act of assisting in forming a society for teaching syndicalism, of becoming a member of it, or of assembly with others for that purpose is given the dynamic quality of crime. There is guilt although the society may not contemplate immediate promulgation of the doctrine. Thus the accused is to be punished, not for contempt, incitement or conspiracy, but for a step in preparation, which, if it threatens the public order at all, does so only remotely. The novelty in the prohibition introduced is that the statute aims, not at the practice of criminal syndicalism, nor even directly at the preaching of it, but at association with those who propose to preach it.[28]

Brandeis did not deny that the freedom of assembly, like the freedoms of speech and press, could be restricted by the state, but he again insisted that the restriction be permitted only if the assembly presented a clear and present danger of resulting in the intended evil. The danger must be imminent and serious, he wrote; fear of danger is not enough to restrict the First Amendment freedoms:

> To justify suppression of free speech there must be reasonable ground to fear that serious evil will result if free speech is practiced. There must be reasonable ground to believe that the danger apprehended is imminent. There must be reasonable ground to believe that the evil to be prevented is a serious one. Every denunciation of existing law tends in some measure to increase the probability that there will be violation of it. Condonation of a breach enhances the probability. Expressions of approval add to the probability. Propagation of the criminal state of mind by teaching syndicalism increases it. Advocacy of law-breaking heightens it still further. But even advocacy of violation, however reprehensible morally, is not a justification for denying free speech where the advocacy falls short of incitement and there is nothing to indicate that the advocacy would be immediately acted on. The wide difference between advocacy and incitement, between preparation and attempt, between assembling and conspiracy, must be borne in mind. In order to support a finding of clear and present danger it must be shown either that immediate serious violence was to be expected or was advocated, or that the past conduct furnished reason to believe that such advocacy was then contemplated....

... The fact that speech is likely to result in some violence or in destruction of property is not enough to justify its suppression. There must be the probability of serious injury to the State. Among free men, the deterrents ordinarily to be applied to prevent crime are education and punishment for violations of the law, not abridgement of the rights of free speech and assembly.[29]

Although Brandeis and Holmes believed that under these standards the California law improperly restricted Whitney's rights of free speech and assembly, they felt compelled to concur in Whitney's conviction for technical reasons. A few months later, California's governor pardoned Whitney for reasons that echoed Brandeis's opinion.

Fiske v. Kansas

The same day that it decided *Whitney,* the Supreme Court for the first time reversed a conviction for violating a state criminal syndicalism act. In *Fiske v. Kansas* (1927), the Court held that the First Amendment guarantee of free speech had been violated by the conviction of Fiske, an organizer for International Workers of the World (IWW). The only evidence introduced at trial to show the unlawful nature of the organization was the IWW preamble, which read in part, "Between these two classes a struggle must go on until the workers of the world organize as a class, take possession of the earth and the machinery of production, and abolish the wage system." The trial jury apparently assumed that this class struggle would involve the violent overthrow of the government, which would make the IWW and participation in it unlawful under the Kansas statute.

The Supreme Court reversed, seeing no evidence that the IWW actually advocated violence or other criminal acts to bring about political and industrial change.[30] *Fiske* was a turning point. The Court heard three more major cases testing the constitutionality of state criminal syndicalism laws as applied in particular circumstances. In all three, the Court reversed convictions for violating these laws.

DeJonge v. Oregon

Two of these cases came to the Court ten years after *Fiske. DeJonge v. Oregon* (1937) arose after Dirk DeJonge

was convicted for conducting a public meeting under Communist Party auspices. DeJonge maintained he was innocent because he had not advocated or taught any criminal doctrine at the meeting but merely discussed issues of public concern. The state courts, however, interpreted the statute to make criminal any participation in any meeting sponsored by an organization that advocated at any time the forceful overthrow of the established government. The Court unanimously reversed DeJonge's conviction, holding that the state's interpretation of the statute was unnecessarily restrictive of the rights of free speech and assembly. In one of the Court's first expositions on the right of assembly, Chief Justice Charles Evans Hughes wrote that

peaceable assembly for lawful discussion cannot be made a crime. The holding of meetings for peaceable political action cannot be proscribed. Those who assist in the conduct of such meetings cannot be branded as criminals on that score. The question, if the rights of free speech and peaceable assembly are to be preserved, is not as to the auspices under which the meeting is held but as to its purpose; not as to the relations of the speakers, but whether their utterances transcend the bounds of the freedom of speech which the Constitution protects. If the persons assembling have committed crimes elsewhere, if they have formed or are engaged in a conspiracy against the public peace and order, they may be prosecuted for their conspiracy or other violation of valid laws. But it is a different matter when the State, instead of prosecuting them for such offense, seizes upon mere participation in a peaceable assembly and a lawful public discussion as the basis for a criminal charge.[31]

Herndon v. Lowry

In *Herndon v. Lowry* (1937), a majority of the Court abandoned the "bad tendency" test adopted in *Gitlow* in favor of something more like the clear and present danger standard. Herndon, a black organizer, was sent to Atlanta to recruit members for the Communist Party. He held three meetings and signed up a few members. He had with him membership blanks, literature on the party, and a booklet entitled "The Communist Position on the Negro Question." This booklet called for self-determination for blacks living in the southern "black belt," and its authors envisioned a black-dominated government separate from the rest of the United States. To achieve this goal, the tract advocated strikes, boycotts, and a revolutionary power struggle against the white ruling class.

Herndon was arrested and convicted of violating a Georgia law that made it unlawful for anyone to attempt to persuade anyone else to participate in an insurrection against the organized government. Herndon appealed his conviction on the grounds that he had said or done nothing to create any immediate danger of an insurrection. A five-justice majority agreed, holding the state statute too vague and too broad. The state needed to show more than that Herndon's words and actions might tend to incite others to insurrection at some future time. Justice Owen J. Roberts wrote,

> The power of a state to abridge freedom of speech and of assembly is the exception rather than the rule and penalizing even of utterances of a defined character must find its justification in a reasonable apprehension of danger to organized government. The judgment of the legislature is not unfettered. The limitation upon individual liberty must have appropriate relation to the safety of the state.[32]

The majority did not accept the state court's view that Herndon was guilty if he intended an insurrection to occur "at any time within which he might reasonably expect his influence to continue to be directly operative in causing such action by those whom he sought to induce." This view left a jury without any precise standard for measuring guilt, Roberts said, and could conceivably allow a jury to convict a person simply because it disagreed with his opinion:

> The statute, as construed and applied, amounts merely to a dragnet which may enmesh anyone who agitates for a change of government if a jury can be persuaded that he ought to have foreseen his words would have some effect in the future conduct of others. No reasonably ascertainable standard of guilt is prescribed. So vague and indeterminate are the boundaries thus set to the freedom of speech and assembly that the law necessarily violates the guarantee of liberty embodied in the Fourteenth amendment.[33]

The four dissenters would have used the bad tendency test to uphold the conviction. They said Herndon's

possession of the booklets on black self-determination showed that he intended to distribute them. He had not denied that intention, they noted. They also said it was apparent that by endorsing the self-determination plan, Herndon was advocating insurrection. "Proposing these measures was nothing short of advising a resort to force and violence, for all know that such measures could not be effected otherwise," they wrote.[34]

Brandenburg v. Ohio

State criminal syndicalism laws reemerged in the late 1960s as states sought ways to restrain civil rights and antiwar activists. The Court, however, in a per curiam opinion called into question the continuing validity of most criminal syndicalism laws. In the case of *Brandenburg v. Ohio* (1969), the Court extended the *Herndon* decision by setting out what has been called the "incitement" test. This standard distinguishes between advocacy of the use of force as an abstract doctrine, which is protected by the First Amendment, and actual incitement to use force, which is not protected.

Clarence Brandenburg, the leader of a Ku Klux Klan group, invited a newsman and photographer to film a Klan rally. Parts of the film were subsequently broadcast locally and nationally. They showed Brandenburg declaring that "if our President, our Congress, our Supreme Court, continues to suppress the white Caucasian race, it's possible that there might have to be some revengance [*sic*] taken." As a result of the speech shown on the film, Brandenburg was convicted of violating Ohio's criminal syndicalism act. The Supreme Court reversed the conviction in an unsigned opinion. It observed that the *Brandenburg* case was similar to *Whitney*. Both had assembled with others in a group that advocated unlawful means to change the political order. Although the Court sustained Whitney's conviction in 1927,

> later decisions have fashioned the principle that the constitutional guarantees of free speech and free press do not permit a State to forbid or proscribe advocacy of the use of force or of law violation except where such advocacy is directed to inciting or producing imminent lawless action and is likely to incite or produce such action…. Measured by this test, Ohio's Criminal Syndicalism Act cannot be sustained.[35]

The Court also overturned *Whitney*.

The Ku Klux Klan marches in Washington, D.C., in 1926. In *Brandenburg v. Ohio* (1969), which concerned the Klan, the Supreme Court held that it is unconstitutional to punish a person who advocates violence as a means of accomplishing political reform.

PUBLIC SPEECH AND PUBLIC SAFETY

Speech that threatens the community peace and order is far more prevalent than speech that jeopardizes the national security. The Supreme Court's role in community peace cases has been much the same as its role in national security cases—to find the balance among the right of an individual to make a public speech, the right of listeners to assemble to hear that speech, and the obligation of the state to maintain public order, safety, and tranquility. If the incident involves only verbal or symbolic expression, the balance tips in favor of the right to speak. Government may place no restraint on or punish such speech unless it threatens or actually harms public safety, the Court has held. Because the Court examines the individual circumstances of each case, the point at which speech becomes an incitement or a threat to the welfare of the community varies considerably. The Court thus far has been unable to devise a general standard for determining the point at which First Amendment protection must give way to government restriction.

Government cannot place any prior restraints on speech, but it can legally regulate the time, place, and manner of speech that is likely to interfere with other rightful uses of public property—especially speech that is combined with potentially disruptive conduct, such as parading or demonstrating. These regulations must be precisely drawn to restrict speech only as much as is necessary, and they must be applied and enforced in a nondiscriminatory manner.

Permits and Prior Restraint

Until the Supreme Court applied the First Amendment to the states, it conceded to municipalities absolute authority to regulate and even to prohibit speech on public property. In 1897 the Court sustained the validity of a Boston ordinance prohibiting public speeches on Boston Common without a permit from the mayor. The Supreme Court endorsed the holding of the Massachusetts Supreme Court, which, in an opinion written by Oliver Wendell Holmes Jr., declared that a legislature as representative of the public … may and does exercise control over the use which the public may make of such places…. For the legislature absolutely or constitutionally to forbid public speaking in a highway or public park is no more an infringement of the rights of a member of the public than for the owner of a private house to forbid it in his house.[36]

Some forty years passed before the Court was obliged to rule again on this question. By that time, it had decided that the First Amendment acted as a bar against state infringement of free speech. In line with that view, cases claiming that government was abridging free speech were getting special scrutiny.

Hague v. C.I.O. (1939) arose from Jersey City, New Jersey, mayor Frank Hague's opposition to attempts to organize workers in the city into closed-shop unions. To discourage these efforts, Hague harassed members of the Committee for Industrial Organization (C.I.O.), searching them when they entered the city, arresting them for distributing union literature, and forcibly throwing some of them out of the city. He also refused to grant any member of the union the permit required by city ordinance before a public speech could be made on public property. The C.I.O. brought suit to stop Hague from enforcing this statute. The Supreme Court granted the injunction against continued enforcement of the ordinance. Writing for two members of the majority, Justice Roberts said that the right to speak and assemble in public was a privilege and immunity of national citizenship that states and cities could not abridge:

Wherever the title of streets and parks may rest, they have immemorially been held in trust for the use of the public and, time out of mind, have been used for purposes of assembly, communicating thoughts between citizens, and discussing public questions. Such use of the streets and public places has, from ancient times, been a part of the privileges, immunities, rights and liberties of citizens. The privilege of a citizen of the United States to use the streets and parks for communication of views on national questions may be regulated in the interest of all; it is not absolute, but relative, and must be exercised in subordination to the general comfort and convenience, and in consonance with peace and good order; but it must not, in the guise of regulation, be abridged or denied.[37]

In a concurring opinion, Justices Harlan Fiske Stone and Stanley F. Reed viewed the rights of free speech and assembly as included not in the Privileges and Immunities Clause of the Fourteenth Amendment but in that amendment's prohibition against state deprivation of personal liberty without due process of law. Under the due process guarantee, these rights were secured to all persons in the United States and not just to citizens. This broader view was eventually accepted by a majority of the Court.

In *Hague,* Roberts indicated that states and cities might regulate certain aspects of public speaking. In 1941 the Court elaborated on this, holding that the time, manner, and place of public speeches or other forms of expression could be regulated so long as the regulation was precisely and narrowly drawn and applied neutrally to all speakers and demonstrators.[38] *(See details of Cox v. New Hampshire, p. 63.)*

Disturbing the Peace

Having established in *Hague* the right of individuals to communicate ideas in public places, the Court was quickly faced with the question whether the First Amendment protected speech that sparked a breach of the peace.

Speech to Passersby. The first case raising this issue concerned a Jehovah's Witness named Jesse Cantwell. Seeking converts to his faith in New Haven, Connecticut, in 1938, Cantwell stopped two men on a sidewalk and asked if he could play a record for them. They agreed, and he played "Enemies," which attacked organized religion in general and Catholicism in particular. The two men, both Catholics, were offended and told Cantwell to go away. There was no violence or other disturbance. Nonetheless, Cantwell was convicted of inciting others to a breach of the peace. The Supreme Court reversed the conviction in *Cantwell v. Connecticut* (1940), finding the breach-of-the-peace ordinance too vague as applied to Cantwell:

The offense known as breach of the peace embraces a great variety of conduct destroying or menacing public order and tranquility. It includes not only violent acts but acts and words likely to produce violence in others. No one would have the hardihood to suggest that the principle of freedom of speech sanctions incitement to riot or that religious liberty connotes the privilege to exhort others to physical attack upon those belonging to another sect. When clear and present danger of riot, disorder, interference with traffic upon the public streets, or other immediate threat to public safety, peace or order, appears, the power of the State to prevent or punish is obvious. Equally obvious is it that a State may not unduly suppress free communication of views, religious or other, under the guise of conserving desirable conditions. Here we have a situation analogous to a conviction under a statute sweeping in a great variety of conduct under a general and indefinite characterization, and leaving to the executive and judicial branches too wide a discretion in its application.[39]

Looking at the facts of the situation, the Court said it found "no assault or threatening of bodily harm, no truculent bearing, no intentional discourtesy, no personal abuse." Absent a statute narrowly drawn to define and punish the conduct Cantwell engaged in, his conduct, the Court said, "raised no such clear and present menace to public peace and order as to render him liable" under the general breach-of-the-peace statute.[40]

Near Riot. The next breach-of-the-peace case required the Court to decide to what extent the First Amendment protected speech that provoked a near riot. Arthur Terminiello was a defrocked Catholic priest who in 1946 spoke at a private meeting in Chicago sponsored by the Christian Veterans of America. In his speech Terminiello virulently attacked Jews, blacks, and the Roosevelt administration but did not urge his five hundred listeners to take any specific action. While he spoke, some one thousand protesters gathered outside the hall, shouting, throwing rocks through windows, and trying to break into the meeting. The police restrained the mob, though with difficulty. As a result of the disturbance, Terminiello was arrested for and convicted of disorderly conduct under an ordinance that made it illegal for anyone to aid in a "breach of the peace or a diversion tending to a breach of the peace."

The Supreme Court reversed Terminiello's conviction in a 5 to 4 vote but without reaching the constitutional issues involved. Instead, the majority held that the trial judge had improperly instructed the jury when he defined a breach of the peace as speech that "stirs the public to anger, invites dispute, brings about a condition of unrest, or creates a disturbance." Some parts of this instruction, the majority felt, would punish speech protected by the First Amendment, and since it was not apparent under which part the jury had convicted Terminiello, the conviction must fall. Justice William O. Douglas explained the majority position in *Terminiello v. Chicago* (1949):

> [A] function of free speech under our system of government is to invite dispute. It may indeed best serve its high purpose when it induces a condition of unrest, creates dissatisfaction with conditions as they are, or even stirs people to anger. Speech is often provocative and challenging. It may strike at prejudices and preconceptions and have profound unsettling effects as it presses for acceptance of an idea. That is why freedom of speech, though not absolute,... is nevertheless protected against censorship or punishment, unless shown likely to produce a clear and present danger of a serious substantive evil that rises far above public inconvenience, annoyance or unrest.... There is no room under our Constitution for a more restrictive view. For the alternative would lead to standardization of ideas either by legislatures, courts, or dominant political or community groups.[41]

Chief Justice Fred M. Vinson dissented, contending that Terminiello's speech consisted of "fighting words" that are outside the protection of the First Amendment. *(See box, Fighting Words and Hate Crimes, pp. 54–55.)* In a separate dissent joined by Justices Felix Frankfurter and Harold H. Burton, Justice Robert H. Jackson maintained that Terminiello's speech created a clear and present danger that a riot would ensue and that the authorities were entitled to act to preserve the public peace "at least so long as danger to public order is not invoked in bad faith, as a cover for censorship or suppression." The choice [for the courts], Jackson wrote,

> is not between order and liberty. It is between liberty with order and anarchy without either. There is danger that, if the court does not temper its doctrinaire logic with a little practical wisdom, it will convert the constitutional Bill of Rights into a suicide pact.[42]

Street Meeting. Two years later, the Supreme Court drew closer to Jackson's position when it affirmed the breach-of-the-peace conviction of a student whose street corner speech seemed much less threatening to public order than Terminiello's. The different conclusions in these two cases illustrate the difficulty the Court has had in settling on a general standard by which to determine when speech oversteps the bounds of First Amendment protection. *(See "The Search for a Standard," pp. 30–32.)* Irving Feiner spoke at an open-air gathering in Syracuse, New York, inviting listeners to attend a meeting that evening of the Progressive Party. In the course of his speech, Feiner made insulting remarks about President Harry S. Truman, the American Legion, and the mayor of Syracuse. He also urged blacks to fight for equal rights. Someone complained to the police, who sent two officers to investigate. The crowd was restless, and some passersby were jostled and forced into the street. Finally one listener told the officers that if they did not stop Feiner, he would. The police then asked Feiner to stop speaking. When he refused they arrested him for breach of the peace.

The six justices voting to sustain the conviction in *Feiner v. New York* (1951) found that the police had acted not to suppress speech but to preserve public order. Chief Justice Vinson wrote,

> We are well aware that the ordinary murmurings and objections of a hostile audience cannot be allowed to silence a speaker, and are also mindful of the possible danger of giving overzealous police officials complete discretion to break up otherwise lawful public meetings.... But we are not faced here with such a situation. It is one thing to say that the police cannot be used as an instrument for the oppression of unpopular views, and another to say that, when as here the speaker passes the bounds of argument or persuasion and undertakes incitement to riot, they are powerless to prevent a breach of the peace.[43]

In dissent, Justice Hugo L. Black said that the majority's decision in effect made the police censors of public speech. Instead, the duty of the police should be to protect the speaker in the exercise of his First Amendment rights, even if that necessitates the arrest of those who would interfere, he said. Justices Douglas and Sherman Minton also dissented.

Prior Restraint

In contrast with its difficulty in defining the point at which speech loses its First Amendment protection, the Court has steadfastly rejected state efforts to place prior restraints on speech. In 1931 the Court held that an injunction against continued publication of a newspaper was an unconstitutional prior restraint of the press.[44] In 1940 it held that a statute permitting city officials to determine what was a religious cause and what was not amounted to an unconstitutional restraint on the free exercise of religion.[45] Not until 1945, however, did the Court overturn a state statute as an improper prior restraint on speech.

Union Organizer. The case of *Thomas v. Collins* (1945) arose after Thomas, a union organizer, refused to apply for the organizer's permit required by Texas law. The state issued an injunction to stop Thomas from soliciting for union members. He made a speech advocating union membership anyway and was convicted of contempt. He appealed to the Supreme Court, which voted 5-4 to overturn his conviction. Elaborating on the reasoning behind the Court's earlier permit decisions, Justice Wiley B. Rutledge said it was clear that the injunction against soliciting restrained Thomas's right to speak and the rights of the workers to assemble to hear him. The statute prohibiting solicitation without a permit was so imprecise that it in essence forbade "any language which conveys, or reasonably could be found to convey, the meaning of invitation." Rutledge continued, "How one might 'laud unionism,' as the State and the State Supreme Court concede Thomas was free to do, yet in these circumstances not imply an invitation, is hard to conceive."[46]

The law operated to require Thomas to obtain a permit in order to make a public speech. This was incompatible with the First Amendment, Rutledge said:

> If the exercise of the rights of free speech and assembly cannot be made a crime, we do not think this can be accomplished by the device of requiring previous registration as a condition for exercising them and making such a condition the foundation for restraining in advance their exercise.[47]

The dissenters would have affirmed Thomas's conviction. Justice Roberts contended that the contempt conviction was based not on Thomas's speech but on his explicit solicitation of workers to join the union in violation of the order not to solicit without a permit. The dissenters thought the registration requirement was well within the powers of the state to regulate business transactions.

Street Speaker. In *Kunz v. New York* (1951), which was decided on the same day as *Feiner,* a solid majority of the Court struck down as an unconstitutional prior restraint a New York City ordinance that barred worship services on public streets without a permit. Carl J. Kunz, an ordained Baptist minister, had been granted a permit for one year, but his application for renewal was rejected because his vituperative denunciations of Catholics and Jews had created public disturbances. When Kunz spoke without the permit, he was convicted and fined ten dollars. He appealed his conviction to the Supreme Court, which overturned it by an 8-1 vote. Writing for the majority, Chief Justice Vinson rejected as too arbitrary the New York court's rationale that the permit had been revoked "for good reasons":

> We have here … an ordinance which gives an administrative official discretionary power to control in advance the right of citizens to speak on religious matters on the streets of New York. As such, the ordinance is clearly invalid as a prior restraint on the exercise of First Amendment rights.[48]

In lone dissent, Justice Jackson contended that Kunz's speeches were filled with "fighting words," the kind of verbal abuses and insults that were likely to incite violent response and that city officials were entitled to restrain. "The question … is not whether New York could, if it tried, silence Kunz, but whether it must place its streets at his service to hurl insults at the passer-by," Jackson said.[49]

Congress in 1917 had made it a crime to threaten the life of the president. An eighteen-year-old named Watts who said he was facing induction into the army joined a discussion at a rally near the Washington Monument on August 27, 1966. "I've got to report for my physical this Monday. I am not going. If they ever make me carry a rifle, the first man I want to get in my sights is LBJ. They are not going to make me kill my black brothers." An army intelligence investigator reported Watts's statement, and he was convicted of threatening the president. In *Watts v. United States* (1969), the Court ruled that although the government can punish speech that carries a "true threat," the First Amendment protects "political hyperbole." In a short, unsigned opinion, the Court said Watt's statements could not be seen as true threats to shoot the president, but were more aptly described as a "kind of very crude offensive method of stating a political opposition to the President."[50]

The *Watts* decision, like *Brandenburg v. Ohio,* demonstrated that the Court finally had adopted the clear and present danger standard, put forth by Justice Holmes in *Schenck* in 1919 and advocated throughout the late 1920s, as well as Justices Brandeis's standard in *Whitney* that speech could be punished only where "immediate serious violence was to be expected." Although neither *Brandenburg* nor *Watts* set forth an eloquent essay on free speech, both adopted the view that only "imminent lawless action" or a "true threat" of violence could void the speaker's First Amendment free speech shield.

Symbolic Speech

Symbolic speech, the expression of ideas and beliefs through symbols rather than words, has generally been held protected by the First Amendment. The Supreme Court first dealt with the issue in 1931, when it found California's "red flag" law unconstitutional. The statute had made it a crime to raise a red flag as a symbol of opposition to organized government or as "an invitation … to anarchistic action, or as an aid to propaganda that is of a seditious character." A state jury convicted Yetta Stromberg of raising a reproduction of the Soviet flag every morning at a children's summer camp, but it did not say which part of the law she violated. The Supreme Court held that the first clause of the statute was an unconstitutional restriction of free speech, because the flying of any banner symbolizing advocacy of a change in government through peaceful means could be penalized. Because it was possible that the jury had believed Stromberg guilty of violating

FIGHTING WORDS AND HATE CRIMES

"Fighting words"—words so insulting that they provoke violence from the person to whom they are addressed—are generally unprotected by the First Amendment guarantee of free speech. Laws criminalizing "hate speech"—which targets persons because of their race, religion, or sexual orientation—have, however, run afoul of the First Amendment.

The Supreme Court first addressed the issue of fighting words in *Chaplinsky v. New Hampshire* (1942). Chaplinsky, a Jehovah's Witness, provoked a public disturbance when he publicly assailed another religion as "a racket," and called a police officer "a God damned racketeer" and "a damned Fascist." He was convicted of violating a state statute making it a crime to call another person "offensive and derisive names" in public. The Supreme Court sustained the conviction, upholding the statute against a challenge that it violated the guarantee of free speech. "[R]esort to epithets or to personal abuse is not in any proper sense communication of information or opinion safeguarded by the Constitution," the unanimous Court declared:

> Allowing the broadest scope to the language and purpose of the ... Amendment, it is well understood that the right of free speech is not absolute at all times and under all circumstances. There are certain well-defined and narrowly limited classes of speech, the prevention and punishment of which has never been thought to raise any Constitutional problem. These include the lewd and obscene, the profane, the libelous, and the insulting or "fighting" words—those which by their very utterance inflict injury or tend to incite an immediate breach of the peace. It has been well observed that such utterances are no essential part of any exposition of ideas, and are of such slight social value as a step to truth that any benefit that may be derived from them is clearly outweighed by the social interest in order and morality.[1]

The Court, however, was willing to uphold the statute only because the state court had narrowly construed its language to apply to fighting

words and no other speech. The Supreme Court has continued to insist that statutes penalizing fighting words be narrowly drawn and strictly interpreted. In 1972 the Court affirmed the reversal of a Georgia man's conviction for calling a police officer a "son of a bitch" and threatening the officer with physical abuse. The justices concluded that the state court's interpretation of the statute was too broad, making it applicable to protected speech as well as to fighting words.[2]

In 1971 the Court ruled that a state may not punish as a crime the public display of an offensive word, in this case used as an expression of legitimate protest and not resulting in a breach of the peace. In protest of the Vietnam War, Paul Cohen wore into a Los Angeles courthouse a jacket inscribed with the slogan "Fuck the Draft." He was arrested and convicted under a state breach-of-the-peace law making "offensive conduct" a crime. Writing for the majority in *Cohen v. California* (1971), Justice John Marshall Harlan described the offending slogan not as conduct but as speech expressing a political viewpoint. Such expression is entitled to First Amendment protection, Harlan said, unless it provokes or intends to provoke a breach of the peace. The state cannot properly prohibit public display of the offending expletive, Harlan continued. For if a state had the power to outlaw public use of one word, he wrote, it could outlaw the use of other words and such action would run "a substantial risk of suppressing ideas in the process. Indeed, governments might soon seize upon the censorship of particular words as a convenient guise for banning the expression of unpopular views."[3] The Court later held that the Federal Communications Commission could regulate the times at which radio and television may broadcast offensive words.[4] *(See "Content and Context," pp. 121–124.)*

During the 1980 s verbal and physical attacks on victims who were chosen because of their race, religion, ethnic origin, or sexual orientation spurred enactment of numerous laws forbidding "hate speech" and "hate

only this clause of the law, its unconstitutionality rendered her conviction a denial of due process. Chief Justice Charles Evans Hughes wrote,

> The maintenance of the opportunity for free political discussion to the end that government may be responsive to the will of the people and that changes may be obtained by lawful means, an opportunity essential to the security of the Republic, is a fundamental principle of our constitutional system. A statute which upon its face, and as authoritatively construed, is so vague and indefinite as to permit the punishment of the fair use of this opportunity is repugnant to the guaranty of liberty contained in the Fourteenth Amendment.[51]

crimes." In the early 1990 s, two of these laws were challenged before the Supreme Court as violations of free speech rights. The first case, decided in 1992, arose after three white teenagers in St. Paul, Minnesota, put up and burned a makeshift cross in the yard of a black family. The crudely made cross recalled the use of this symbol by the Ku Klux Klan. The youths were charged under an ordinance prohibiting the display of a symbol that one knows "arouses anger, alarm or resentment in others on the basis of race, color, creed, religion or gender." The justices struck down the ordinance, saying it unconstitutionally singled out specific types of "hate speech" for criminal punishment. Although the judgment was unanimous, the justices split sharply in their rationale. A five-person majority in an opinion penned by Justice Antonin Scalia said, "content-based regulations are presumptively invalid." Government may not ban speech "based on hostility—or favoritism—toward the underlying message expressed."[5]

Scalia said that if a municipality wants to outlaw a particular kind of speech that would be considered "fighting words," it must outlaw all fighting words, not just race-, religion-, or gender-based epithets. Government, he continued, cannot treat various conducts differently within a category of prohibited speech. "Thus, the government may proscribe libel; but it may not make the further content discrimination of proscribing only libel critical of the government," he said.

Dissenting justices, led by Byron R. White, called the majority's method "a simplistic, all-or-nothing-at-all approach" to the First Amendment, but they joined the judgment of the Court, finding the ordinance too sweeping: "Although the ordinance reaches conduct that is unprotected [by the First Amendment], it also makes criminal expressive conduct that causes only hurt feelings, offense, or resentment, and is protected by the First Amendment."

The second ruling, in 1993, upheld a law that required enhanced penalties for crimes committed because of prejudice. That case began when a group of black youths beat a white teenager in Kenosha, Wisconsin. The assailants, angry after having watched a movie about the abuse of blacks, spotted the white youth as he was walking along a street. "There goes a white boy," yelled one of them. "Go get him." The white teenager was beaten into unconsciousness. The young man who led the attack was charged under Wisconsin's hate crime law, which allows judges to add up to five years to the sentence of a defendant who "intentionally selects" his victim on the basis of race, religion, ethnic origin, disability, or sexual orientation. After the leader was convicted of aggravated battery, the judge imposed the maximum two-year sentence for the offense and an additional two years under the hate crime law.

The Supreme Court unanimously upheld the sentence. Chief Justice Willam H. Rehnquist wrote that judges traditionally have been permitted to consider "a wide variety of factors" in sentencing a defendant, including the motive for the crime. Courts cannot consider a defendant's abstract beliefs, he said, but they can take racial bias or other prejudice into account when that is part of the motive for the offense. Wisconsin lawmakers passed the measure, he said, because "bias-inspired conduct ... is thought to inflict greater individual and societal harm.... The State's desire to redress these perceived harms provides an adequate explanation for its penalty-enhancement provisions over and above mere disagreement with offenders' belief or biases."[6]

---

1. *Chaplinsky v. New Hampshire,* 315 U.S. 568 at 571, 572 (1942).

2. *Gooding v. Wilson,* 405 U.S. 518 (1972); see also *Lewis v. City of New Orleans,* 415 U.S. 130 (1974).

3. *Cohen v. California,* 403 U.S. 15 at 26 (1971).

4. *Federal Communications Commission v. Pacifica Foundation,* 438 U.S. 726 (1978).

5. *R. A. V. v. City of St. Paul,* 505 U.S. 377 (1992).

6. *Wisconsin v. Mitchell,* 508 U.S. 476 (1993).

Saluting the Flag

The fullest exposition of symbolism as a form of communication protected by the First Amendment came in the Court's decision in the second wartime "flag salute" case. The Court ruled that states could not compel schoolchildren to pledge allegiance to the American flag. For the majority in *West Virginia State Board of Education v. Barnette* (1943), Justice Jackson wrote,

> There is no doubt that, in connection with the pledges, the flag salute is a form of utterance. Symbolism is a primitive but effective way of communicating ideas. The use of an emblem or flag to symbolize some system, idea, institution, or

personality, is a shortcut from mind to mind. Causes and nations, political parties, lodges and ecclesiastical groups seek to knit the loyalty of their followings to a flag or banner, a color or design. The State announces rank, function, and authority through crowns and maces, uniforms and black robes, the church speaks through the Cross, the Crucifix, the altar and shrine, and clerical raiment. Symbols of State often convey political ideas just as religious symbols come to convey theological ones. Associated with many of these symbols are appropriate gestures of acceptance or respect: a salute, a bowed or bared head, a bended knee. A person gets from a symbol the meaning he puts into it, and what is one man's comfort and inspiration is another's jest and scorn.[52]

The First Amendment, Jackson said, no more permitted a state to compel allegiance to a symbol of the organized government than it permitted the state to punish someone who used a symbol to express peaceful opposition to organized government. *(See details of West Virginia State Board of Education v. Barnette, pp. 136–138.)*

Sit-Ins

Another form of symbolic speech reviewed by the Supreme Court were the sit-ins of the early 1960s. To protest racial discrimination in public accommodations, black students and others requested service at "whites only" lunch counters and remained there quietly until ejected or arrested. At least one justice believed that these sit-ins were a form of expression guaranteed constitutional protection under some circumstances. In a concurring opinion in *Garner v. Louisiana* (1961), Justice John Marshall Harlan wrote that a sit-in was

> as much a part of the "free trade in ideas"… as is verbal expression, more commonly thought of as "speech." It, like speech, appeals to good sense and to "the power of reason as applied through public discussion"… just as much, if not more than, a public oration delivered from a soapbox at a street corner. This Court has never limited the right to speak … to mere verbal expression.[53]

The Court avoided answering the question whether the First and Fourteenth Amendments protected the protesters from conviction for trespassing on private property.[54] Two decades later the Court held that civil rights demonstrators who boycotted the shops of white merchants could not be assessed damages for economic losses. Such a sustained, nonviolent boycott the Court held in *NAACP v. Claiborne Hardware Co.* (1982) was protected by the First Amendment. Violence, however, was not protected, and those who practiced it could be held liable for damages inflicted.[55]

Antiwar Protests

The unpopularity of the Vietnam War generated several symbolic speech cases. In *United States v. O'Brien* (1968), the Supreme Court refused to view draft card burning, an expression of protest against the war and the draft, as symbolic speech protected by the First Amendment. "We cannot accept the view that an apparently limitless variety of conduct can be labeled 'speech' whenever the person engaging in the conduct intends thereby to express an idea," the majority said. Even if that view were adopted, the majority continued, the First Amendment would not protect draft card burning:

> This Court has held that when "speech" and "non-speech" elements are combined in the same course of conduct, a sufficiently important governmental interest in regulating the nonspeech element can justify incidental limitations on First Amendment freedoms.[56]

Here, the majority said, Congress had a substantial interest in maintaining the draft registration system as part of its duty to raise and maintain armies. (Almost thirty years later in quite a different context the Court cited this idea of a substantial public interest that permits some restriction on freedom of expression when it upheld a state law that forbade nude dancing.)[57] In another case during the Vietnam War, *Tinker v. Des Moines School District* (1969), the Court ruled that school officials improperly suspended students for wearing black armbands in symbolic protest of the war. The officials said they based the suspensions on their fear that the armbands might

LOUD SOUNDS AND FREE SPEECH

Does a city impermissibly interfere with freedom of speech by regulating the use of loudspeakers and other amplification devices? Over the years the Court's position has changed several times. The Court first considered the question in *Saia v. New York* (1948). A Lockport, New York, ordinance prohibited the use of sound equipment without permission from the chief of police. Samuel Saia, a Jehovah's Witness, obtained a permit to amplify religious lectures in a public park. Because some people complained about the noise, Saia's permit was not renewed. He spoke with the loudspeaker anyway and was arrested and convicted of violating the ordinance. He countered that the ordinance violated his right to free speech. The Court, 5-4, struck down the ordinance because it set no standards for granting or denying permits. Justice William O. Douglas explained:

> The present ordinance would be a dangerous weapon if it were allowed to get a hold on our public life.... Any abuses which loudspeakers create can be controlled by narrowly drawn statutes. When a city allows an official to ban them in his uncontrolled discretion, it sanctions a device for suppression of free communication of ideas.[1]

In dissent, Justice Felix Frankfurter insisted that a city has a right to regulate the use of sound amplification to protect the privacy of other users of the park. "Surely there is not a constitutional right to force unwilling people to listen," he said.[2] In a separate dissent, Justice Robert H. Jackson drew a distinction between speech and amplification of speech. Regulating amplification, even prohibiting it altogether, in no way interfered with the freedom of speech itself, he said.

Just a year later, however, the four dissenters in *Saia* and Chief Justice Fred M. Vinson joined to sustain a Trenton, New Jersey, ordinance prohibiting the use on all public streets of any sound equipment that emitted "loud and raucous noise." This language might have been interpreted as barring all use of sound equipment in city streets, but a three-justice plurality in *Kovacs v. Cooper* (1949), for whom Justice Stanley F. Reed spoke, distinguished between "loud and raucous noise" and other sounds that might come from amplifying systems. Reed agreed that "[a]bsolute prohibition within municipal limits of all sound amplification, even though reasonably regulated in place, time and volume, is undesirable and probably unconstitutional as an unreasonable interference with normal activities." Regulation of noise was, however, permissible. The ordinance in no way restricts "communication of ideas or discussion of issues by the human voice, by newspapers, by pamphlets."[3]

Justice Hugo L. Black, in dissent, disagreed with Reed's interpretation of the ordinance, contending that it prohibited all sound amplification. This repudiation of *Saia,* he wrote, was "a dangerous and unjustifiable breach in the constitutional barriers designed to insure freedom of expression."[4]

In 1952 the Court majority held that individuals do not have an absolute right to privacy in public places. A private transit company in the District of Columbia piped music, occasionally interspersed with commercials, into its streetcars. Despite a challenge from passengers that the practice violated their right to privacy, the programming was approved by the local public utilities commission. The Court held that courts had no authority to interfere with such a decision by the commission so long as it was arrived at through proper procedures. Justice Douglas dissented, calling the programming "a form of coercion to make people listen."[5]

The Court issued its definitive answer in *Ward v. Rock Against Racism* (1989), in which the justices, 6-3, upheld New York City's regulation requiring all performers at its band shell in Central Park to use the sound amplification system and sound technician provided by the city. "Music, as a form of expression and communication, is protected under the First Amendment," Justice Anthony M. Kennedy wrote, and the city's regulation did not violate that protection. The regulation was justified by the city's substantial interest in protecting its citizens from unwelcome noise, it was reasonable, and it was narrowly tailored to accomplish its purpose.

The lower court had invalidated the regulation, holding that it was not the least restrictive means of attaining the city's objective. The Supreme Court held that that was an unnecessary additional criterion. "A regulation of the time, place or manner of protected speech must be narrowly tailored to serve the government's legitimate content-neutral interests, but ... it need not be the least restrictive or least intrusive means of doing so."[6]

---

1. *Saia v. New York,* 334 U.S. 558 at 562 (1948).

2. Id. at 563.

3. *Kovacs v. Cooper,* 336 U.S. 77 at 8 –82, 89 (1949).

4. Id. at 101 –102.

5. *Public Utilities Commission of the District of Columbia v. Pollak,* 343 U.S. 451 at 468 (1952).

6. *Ward v. Rock Against Racism,* 491 U.S. 781 (1989).

A RIGHT TO BE SILENT

The First Amendment guarantees individuals the right to speak freely. The Supreme Court also has held that this guarantee includes a right to remain silent. In other words, the state may not coerce or compel a person to state a position or belief he or she does not voluntarily endorse. Among the most dramatic examples of this right are the two 1940 cases arising from the refusal of children of Jehovah's Witnesses to salute the American flag in school. In their view, pledging allegiance to the flag violated their religious belief that they should not worship graven images.

The first time the Court considered this matter, it held that the flag salute requirement did not violate religious freedom. Three years later, the Court reversed itself to rule that compulsory flag salutes indeed abridged the freedom guaranteed by the First Amendment for speech and religious belief.[1] *(See details of cases, pp. 133–138.)* More recently, the Court held that

First Amendment freedom includes the right to refuse to carry a state-required ideological message on your car license plates. George Maynard was convicted of a misdemeanor for obscuring the motto on his New Hampshire license plate, which read "Live Free or Die." A member of the Jehovah Witnesses, he protested the motto on religious and moral grounds. Affirming a lower court's reversal of Maynard's conviction, the Supreme Court stated, "[T]he right of freedom of thought protected by the First Amendment against state action includes both the right to speak freely and the right to refrain from speaking at all."[2]

---

1. *Minersville School District v. Gobitis,* 310 U.S. 586 (1940), overruled by *West Virginia State Board of Education v. Barnette,* 319 U.S. 624 (1943).

2. *Wooley v. Maynard,* 430 U.S. 705 at 714 (1977).

On March 31, 1966, David O'Brien and three other antiwar protesters demonstrated their opposition to U.S. military action in Vietnam by burning their draft cards on the steps of the South Boston courthouse. Their convictions for violating the Selective Service Act were affirmed in *United States v. O'Brien.*

create a disturbance among the students. The majority wrote that

> undifferentiated fear or apprehension of disturbance is not enough to overcome the right to freedom of expression.... In order for the State in the person of school officials to justify prohibition of a particular expression of opinion, it must be able to show that its action was caused by something more than a mere desire to avoid the discomfort and unpleasantness that always accompany an unpopular viewpoint.[58]

In yet another form of protest against the Vietnam War, an actor wore an army uniform while he and others performed a protest play on a sidewalk outside an army induction center in Houston. The play depicted U.S. soldiers killing Vietnamese women and children. The actor was arrested and convicted of violating a federal law that made it a crime to wear an official military uniform in a theatrical production unfavorable to the armed forces. The Court unanimously overturned that conviction in *Schacht v. United States* (1970), concluding that the wearing of the uniform was part of the actor's speech. "An actor, like everyone else in our country enjoys a constitutional right to freedom of speech, including the right openly to criticize the Government during a dramatic performance," the Court said.[59]

Protest and the Flag

The Supreme Court in five modern cases—one in 1969, two in 1974, one in 1989, and one in 1990—reversed the convictions of persons who used the American flag to symbolize opposition to government policy and the course of public events. *Street v. New York* (1969) concerned a man who protested the shooting of civil rights activist James Meredith by publicly burning a flag while declaring, "If they did that to Meredith, we don't need an American flag." He was convicted under a New York law that made it illegal to mutilate a flag or to cast contempt upon it either by words or conduct. Overturning the conviction, the Supreme Court said the statute as applied to Street was too broad because it permitted the punishment of his words, which were protected by the First and Fourteenth Amendments.[60]

In *Smith v. Goguen* (1974), the Court overturned the conviction of a man who wore a small flag on the seat of his pants. The Massachusetts statute that made contemptuous treatment of the flag a crime was unconstitutionally vague, the Court said, because it "fails to draw reasonably clear lines between the kinds of non-ceremonial treatment [of the flag] that are criminal and those that are not."[61] In *Spence v. Washington* (1974), the Supreme Court directly confronted the question whether using the flag for protest was expression protected by the First Amendment. The case arose when a student flew a flag, on which he had superimposed a peace symbol, upside down from his apartment window. The student was protesting the U.S. invasion of Cambodia and the shooting deaths of four student demonstrators by members of the Ohio National Guard at Kent State University. He was arrested and convicted for violating a Washington statute prohibiting defacement of the flag. In a per curiam opinion, the Court majority overturned the conviction, holding that the student's conduct was a form of symbolic speech protected under the First Amendment:

> [T]here can be little doubt that appellant communicated through the use of symbols.... [This communication] was a pointed expression of anguish by appellant about the then-current domestic and foreign affairs of his government. An intent to convey a particularized message was present, and in the surrounding circumstances the likelihood was great that the message would be understood by those who viewed it.[62]

Because the communication was protected by the First Amendment, the majority continued, the state could punish the communication only if it clashed with some substantial interest of the state. There was, however, no evidence that the flag caused a breach of the peace, and the possibility that some passersby might be offended by the message was not sufficient to warrant restraint of speech.

Flag Burning. In 1989 the Court set off a storm of protest when it struck down laws that made it a crime to burn an American flag. Congress in 1967 had made it a federal offense, punishable by one year in prison, to

THE PLEDGE OF ALLEGIANCE: "ONE NATION, UNDER GOD"

Does the daily recital of the Pledge of Allegiance in the public schools, along with its reference to "one nation, under God," violate the Constitution's ban on "laws respecting an establishment of religion"? The Supreme Court began to decide the issue in 2004 in *Elk Grove Unified School District v. Newdow,* but a 5-3 majority ultimately dismissed the case on the ground that the divorced father who had brought the suit did not have standing to sue as a parent or on behalf of his daughter.[1]

The Pledge of Allegiance was written in 1892 as part of the four hundredth anniversary of Christopher Columbus's voyage to America. It ended with the words, "One Nation, indivisible, with Liberty and Justice for all." In 1954, at the height of the cold war, Congress amended the pledge to add the phrase "under God." Several decades later, Michael Newdow—a doctor, lawyer, and atheist—sued the California school district where his nine-year-old daughter attended school, claiming that the teacher-led recitation of the Pledge of Allegiance amounted to religious indoctrination. His daughter was free not to say the pledge, if she preferred: In 1943 the Court had ruled that students cannot be compelled to salute the flag, and therefore it was generally assumed that children had a free speech right not to say the pledge.[2] Newdow's claim went further. He alleged that the daily recitation of the pledge in a public school violated the First Amendment's ban on an establishment of religion.

To the surprise of many, Newdow won his case in the U.S. Ninth Circuit Court of Appeals, which held that he had a right to challenge what was said in his daughter's school and that the reference to God "conveys an impermissible message of endorsement" of a religious belief by the government.[3] The ruling set off a national uproar, and the Supreme Court agreed to hear the school district's appeal challenging both conclusions.

Justice Antonin Scalia withdrew from the case because he had criticized the Ninth Circuit's ruling in a speech he had given. His absence created the prospect of a 4-4 split, which would have had the effect of affirming the circuit court ruling declaring the pledge unconstitutional. On June 14, 2004—Flag Day—the Court announced that it was dismissing Newdow's appeal and vacating the Ninth Circuit's ruling. Justices John Paul Stevens, Anthony M. Kennedy, David H. Souter, Ruth Bader Ginsburg, and Stephen G. Breyer agreed that because Newdow's ex-wife had "sole legal custody" of their daughter, Newdow did not have the legal standing to sue the school system.

The three dissenters argued that they would have given Newdow standing, but would have rejected his claim that the pledge was unconstitutional. "Reciting the Pledge, or listening to others recite it, is a patriotic exercise, not a religious one; participants promise fidelity to our flag and our Nation, not to any particular God, faith or church," wrote Chief Justice William H. Rehnquist and Justice Sandra Day O'Connor.[4] In a separate dissent, Justice Clarence Thomas said he would have gone much further and ruled that the First Amendment's ban on "an establishment of religion" does not restrict states, cities, or school boards that seek to promote an official religion. The First Amendment says, "Congress shall make no law respecting an establishment of religion," he noted. "Quite simply, the Establishment Clause is best understood as a federalism provision—it protects state establishments from federal interference but does not protect any individual right," Thomas wrote.[5]

---

1. *Elk Grove Unified School District v. Newdow*, 542 U.S. 1 (2004).

2. *West Virginia State Board of Education v. Barnette*, 319 U.S. 624 (1943).

3. *Elk Grove Unified School District v. Newdow*, 328 F.3d 466 (9th Cir. 2003).

4. *Elk Grove Unified School District v. Newdow*, 542 U.S. 1 at 6 (2004).

5. Id. at 50.

"knowingly cast contempt upon any flag of the United States by publicly mutilating, defacing, defiling, burning or trampling" upon it. Texas and forty-seven other states had laws against flag desecration. In 1984 Gregory Johnson went to the Republican National Convention in Dallas to protest the policies of the Reagan administration. Standing outside the city hall, he doused a flag with kerosene and set it on fire. He was arrested, charged with violating the Texas law against flag desecration, convicted, fined $2,000, and sentenced to a year in prison. The Texas Court of Criminal Appeals voided his conviction on free speech grounds. When the state appealed, the Court agreed to hear the case to decide whether the First Amendment protects the right to burn a flag.

In a 5-4 decision, the Court upheld the appeals court decision. "If there is a bedrock principle underlying the First Amendment, it is that the government may

Gregory Johnson, who has a record of flag burning, holds the American flag while another protester sets it alight. In 1989 the Supreme Court ruled that the conviction of Johnson for burning a flag during a demonstration in Dallas violated his First Amendment rights.

not prohibit the expression of an idea simply because society finds the idea itself offensive or disagreeable," said Justice William J. Brennan Jr. "We have not recognized an exception to this principle even where our flag has been involved."[63] Lawyers for the state had argued that the flag is a symbol of national unity and thereby deserves special protection. The Court agreed that the flag is a special symbol, but it then went on to say that the freedom it symbolizes includes the right to disagree in a very public way. Wrote Brennan, "We never before have held that the Government may ensure that a symbol be used to express only one view of that symbol."[64] Further, he stated,

We are fortified in today's conclusion by our conviction that forbidding criminal punishment for conduct such as Johnson's will not endanger the special role played by our flag or the feelings it inspires. To paraphrase Justice Holmes, we submit that nobody can suppose that this gesture of an unknown man will change our Nation's attitude towards its flag. We are tempted to say, in fact, that the flag's deservedly cherished place in our community will be strengthened, not weakened, by our holding today. Our decision is a reaffirmation of the principles of freedom and inclusiveness that the flag best reflects, and of the conviction that our toleration of Johnson's is a sign and source of our strength.... The way to preserve the flag's special role is not to punish those who feel differently about these matters. It is to persuade them that they are wrong. We can imagine no more appropriate response to burning a flag than waving one's own, no better way to counter a flag-burner's message than by saluting the flag that burns.... We do not consecrate the flag by punishing its desecration, for in doing so we dilute the freedom that this cherished emblem represents.[65]

Justices Thurgood Marshall, Harry A. Blackmun, Antonin Scalia, and Anthony M. Kennedy joined Brennan. In a concurring opinion, Kennedy described the outcome as "painful" but required by the Constitution. "The hard fact is that sometimes we must make decisions we do not like. We make them because they are right, right in the sense that the law and the Constitution, as we see them, compel the result.... It is poignant but fundamental that the flag protects those who hold it in contempt," Kennedy wrote.[66]

Chief Justice William H. Rehnquist dissented:

The flag symbolizes the Nation in peace as well as in war.... It does not represent the views of any particular political party, and it does not represent any particular political philosophy. The flag is not simply another "idea" or "point of view" competing for recognition in the marketplace of ideas. Millions and millions of Americans regard it with an almost mystical reverence regardless of what sort of social, political, or philosophical beliefs they may have. I cannot agree that the First Amendment invalidates the Act of Congress, and the laws of 48 of the 50 states, which make criminal the public burning of a flag.[67]

Justices Byron R. White, John Paul Stevens, and Sandra Day O'Connor joined him in dissent.

Within weeks Congress attempted to reverse the Court by passing the Flag Protection Act, which would have subjected to arrest anyone who "knowingly mutilates, defaces, physically defiles, burns, maintains on the floor or ground, or tramples upon any flag." The same five-justice majority in *Texas v. Johnson* struck down the 1989 law in June 1990. Brennan, again writing for the majority, said, "Although Congress cast the Flag Protection Act in somewhat broader terms than the Texas statute at issue in Johnson, the act still suffers from the same fundamental flaw: it suppresses expression out of concern for its likely communicative impact."[68]

Protest of the Persian Gulf War in 1990 led to a Court ruling limiting the authority of cities to prohibit residents from displaying signs on their own lawns. The unanimous 1994 decision struck down an ordinance enacted by Ladue, Missouri, to minimize "visual clutter" by prohibiting most signs on residential property. A community activist who put up signs in her yard and window opposing the war challenged the ordinance as a violation of her free speech rights. In a broadly worded decision, Justice John Paul Stevens said the ordinance "almost completely foreclosed a venerable means of communication that is both unique and important."[69]

Cross Burning

The Court ruled in 2003 that cross burning in certain instances is protected, but the government may prosecute those who burn a cross to "intimidate" or terrorize others. In August 1998, a Ku Klux Klan member, Barry Black, led a small Klan rally in a farm field near a rural highway in southwestern Virginia. Several speakers ranted at "the blacks and the Mexicans," and one said he would "love to take a .30/.30" and randomly shoot them. At the rally's end, the group sang "Amazing Grace" and watched as a thirty-foot cross was burned. In 1952 Virginia had adopted an anti-Klan law that made it a crime to burn a cross in any "public place." Black was arrested, convicted, and fined $2,500.

In *Virginia v. Black* (2003), the Court struck down the Virginia law that made all cross burnings a crime because the First Amendment protects even hateful expressions.[70] "The burning of a cross is symbolic expression," said Justice O'Connor. "Sometimes the cross burning is a statement of ideology, a symbol of a group solidarity. It is ritual used at Klan gatherings, and it is used to represent the Klan itself. Thus, burning a cross at a political rally would almost certainly be protected expression," she said. This portion of her opinion overturned Black's conviction. The vote was 7-2. "It is true that a cross burning, even at a political rally, arouses a sense of anger or hatred among the vast majority of citizens who see a burning cross. But this sense of anger or hatred is not sufficient to ban all cross burnings," O'Connor said.

Justices Clarence Thomas and Scalia dissented. Thomas, the only black justice, accused his colleagues of minimizing the threat posed by the Klan. It is "a terrorist organization, which, in its endeavor to intimidate, or even eliminate those it dislikes, uses the most brutal of methods," he said. "In our culture, cross burning has almost invariably meant lawlessness and understandably instills in its victims well-grounded fear of physical violence." Virginia's law against cross burning "prohibits only conduct, not expression," he added. "And, just as one cannot burn down someone's house to make a political point and then seek refuge in the First Amendment, those who hate cannot terrorize and intimidate to make their point," he said.

Cross burnings originated in the fourteenth century as a means for Scottish clans to signal each other from distant hillsides. The first Ku Klux Klan was formed shortly after the Civil War and carried out "a veritable reign of terror" throughout the South, but the group did not then burn crosses, the Court noted. The mythology of the Klan and cross burnings appeared in a 1905 book that celebrated the legendary white knights. *The Clansmen: An Historical Romance of the Ku Klux Klan,* by Thomas Dixon, depicted cross burnings to celebrate acts of violence. In 1915 filmmaker D. W. Griffith turned Dixon's book into a movie, *The Birth of a Nation*. Posters advertising the film showed a hooded Klansman atop a horse with a burning cross in his right hand. Within months, a new Ku Klux Klan emerged with the burning of a giant cross at Stone Mountain, Georgia, near Atlanta. With an assist from Hollywood, the Klan had found a new symbol for itself.

In the second part of the split decision, the Court held that states may make it a crime to burn a cross in a yard or on a street if it is done to threaten persons, because, O'Connor said, "burning a cross is a particularly virulent form of intimidation." Authorities in Virginia Beach had brought charges against two white men who burned a small cross in the yard of an African American neighbor. That conviction can be upheld, the Court said. "In light of cross burning's long and pernicious history as a signal of impending violence,… the First Amendment permits Virginia to outlaw cross burnings done with intent to intimidate," O'Connor said.

THE FREEDOM OF ASSEMBLY

The Supreme Court initially considered the right to peaceable assembly a privilege and immunity of national citizenship guaranteed by the Fourteenth Amendment. In *United States v. Cruikshank* (1876), the Court stated,

> The right of the people peaceably to assemble for the purpose of petitioning Congress for a redress of grievances, or for any thing else connected with the powers or the duties of the national government, is an attribute of national citizenship, and, as such, under the protection of, and guaranteed by, the United States. The very idea of a government, republican in form, implies a right on the part of its citizens to meet peaceably for consultation in respect to public affairs and to petition for a redress of grievances.[71]

It would be more than sixty years before the Court again addressed the issue of the right of assembly. In *DeJonge v. Oregon* (1937), a majority of the Court had recognized, first, that the right of assembly was on an equal status with the rights of free speech and free press, and, second, that it was applicable to the states through the Due Process Clause of the Fourteenth Amendment. The meaning of this First Amendment protection was simple, the Court said, "peaceable assembly for lawful discussion cannot be made a crime."[72] *(See DeJonge v. Oregon, p. 47.)* Two years later, in *Hague v. C.I.O.* (1939), a plurality of three justices again held that the right of peaceable assembly was protected by the Privileges and Immunities Clause of the Fourteenth Amendment. Two

other justices found this right included in the "liberty" guaranteed by the Fourteenth Amendment's Due Process Clause. It is this latter view that has prevailed.[73] *(See details of Hague v. C.I.O., p. 50.)*

Parades and Demonstrations

The right to parade or demonstrate peacefully to make known one's views or to support or oppose an issue of public policy is based on the twin guarantees of the rights of free speech and free assembly. Because parading and demonstrating involve conduct that might interfere with the ability of other members of the public to use the same public places, however, they have always been considered subject to greater regulation than exercises of pure speech and assembly. To preserve the freedoms of speech and assembly, the Supreme Court has insisted that parade and demonstration regulations be precisely worded and applied in nondiscriminatory fashion. To preserve the public welfare, the Court has held that not all public places are appropriate sites for public protests.

Time, Place, and Manner

The primary precedent on parades and demonstrations is *Cox v. New Hampshire* (1941). Cox was one of sixty-eight Jehovah's Witnesses convicted of parading without a permit. He challenged the statute as an improper infringement on his rights of free speech and assembly, but the Supreme Court rejected his argument in a unanimous decision. As construed and applied, the ordinance did not allow denial of permits, the Court said, because the views of the paraders might be unpopular; the ordinance was intended only to ensure that paraders would not unduly interfere with others using the streets. Chief Justice Charles Evans Hughes explained:

> If a municipality has authority to control the use of its public streets for parades and processions, as it undoubtedly has, it cannot be denied authority to give consideration, without unfair discrimination, to time, place and manner in relation to the other proper uses of the streets.[74]

Half a century later, the Court again spoke to this point, declaring in a 1992 ruling that parade

THE RIGHT OF PETITION

The First Amendment right "to petition the Government for a redress of grievances" has its origins in the Magna Carta, the medieval English charter of political and civil liberties. One of the earliest exercises of the right in the United States occurred in the 1830s, when Congress received scores of petitions seeking the abolition of slavery in the District of Columbia. The right of petition was later invoked by the unemployed petitioners of Jacob S. Coxey's Ohio army of 1894, the bonus marchers in 1932, and participants in the Poor People's Campaign of 1968. Petitioners are not restricted to seeking redress of grievances only from Congress. They may petition administrative agencies and the courts.

Application of the First Amendment to the states through the Due Process Clause of the Fourteenth Amendment has also ensured citizens the right to make their views known to state governments. In addition, petition of government is not limited solely to seeking a redress of grievances; petitioners may seek benefits. Individuals, citizen groups, and corporations all lobby government to persuade it to adopt policies that will benefit their particular interests. The major decision defining lobbyists' right to petition came in 1954, when the Court upheld the authority of Congress to require certain lobbyists to register.[1]

In 1980 the Court ruled that the right of petition is not infringed by military regulations requiring the approval of the base commander before military personnel may send a petition to members of Congress.[2] This right, however, does not protect those who exercise it from being sued for libel for what they include in their petition, the Court decided in 1985.[3] Also that year, the Court held that the ten-dollar limit on what a veteran can pay an attorney for representation in pursuing claims with the Veterans Administration did not abridge the veteran's right effectively to petition the government for redress.[4]

---

1. *United States v. Harriss,* 347 U.S. 612 (1954).

2. *Brown v. Glines,* 444 U.S. 348 (1980).

3. *McDonald v. Smith,* 472 U.S. 479 (1985).

4. *Walters v. National Association of Radiation Survivors,* 473 U.S. 305 (1985).

---

regulations must be neutral and not give unbridled discretion to a local official. A Forsyth County, Georgia, ordinance required organizers of a parade to pay up to $1,000 for police protection. The Court ruled 5-4 that this ordinance violated the First Amendment because it allowed a county administrator to set an excessive fee. The ordinance lacked definite standards to guide the administrator, the Court said, noting that the administrator could decide not to assess the fee and was not required to provide an explanation for the action taken.[75] Three years later, the Court held unanimously that parade organizers cannot be required by state law to include participants with whom they disagree. Boston veterans wanted to exclude marchers whose main purpose was to proclaim their homosexual identity. When a parade is privately organized, the Court said, it is a form of private expression protected by the First Amendment's guarantee of free speech.[76]

Civil Rights Protests

Cases arising out of the civil rights movement of the late 1950s and 1960s gave the Court the opportunity to explore more fully the extent of First Amendment protection for peaceable demonstrations and protests. In a series of cases involving nonviolent demonstrations in southern states, the Supreme Court ruled that peaceful protests conducted according to valid regulations on public property designated for general use were protected by the First Amendment. Peaceful protests on public property reserved for specific purposes, however, might not be protected.

Breach of Peace. The first case in this series arose in Columbia, South Carolina, where in early 1961 some 180 black high school and college students marched to the state capitol grounds to protest discrimination. Between two hundred and three hundred people gathered to watch the peaceful demonstration. Although there was no threat of violence or other disturbance, the police grew concerned that trouble might flare up and therefore ordered the demonstrators to disperse within fifteen minutes. The students refused, were arrested, and subsequently convicted of breach of the peace. The Supreme Court overturned the convictions in *Edwards v. South Carolina* (1963).[77] The Court

A group of demonstrators march in Washington, D.C., in August 1963 to demand equal rights. The civil rights movement led to the Court exploring more fully First Amendment protections concerning free speech and peaceable protest.

accepted the state courts' finding that the students' conduct constituted a breach of the peace under state law, but the justices held that the state law was unconstitutionally broad because it penalized the exercise of free speech, assembly, and petition for redress of grievances "in their most pristine and classic form." Justice Potter Stewart wrote for the Court:

These petitioners were convicted of an offense so generalized as to be, in the words of the South Carolina Supreme Court, "not susceptible of exact definition." And they were convicted upon evidence which showed no more than that the opinions which they were peaceably expressing were sufficiently opposed to the views of the majority of the community to attract a crowd and necessitate police protection.[78]

Recalling that the majority in *Terminiello v. Chicago* (1949) had held provocative and unsettling speech to be constitutionally protected, Stewart declared that "the Fourteenth Amendment does not permit a State to make criminal the peaceful expression of unpopular views."[79] In lone dissent, Justice Tom C. Clark would have upheld the convictions because the police were trying to preserve the peace and did not intend to suppress speech.

Similar circumstances attended the arrest and conviction of the Reverend B. Elton Cox for breach of the peace in Baton Rouge, Louisiana. In 1961 Cox led some two thousand black college students in a two-and-one-half block march from the state capitol to a courthouse, where twenty-three other students were in jail for their attempts to integrate whites-only lunch counters. Prior to the march, police officials asked Cox to abandon the demonstration, but he refused. The march was orderly. Once at the courthouse, Cox and the students complied with police instructions to stay on the sidewalk. Between one hundred and three hundred white onlookers watched the students wave picket signs and sing patriotic and religious songs. Cox then spoke to explain the reasons for the demonstration. At its conclusion, he urged the marchers to seek service at the lunch counters.

At this point, the sheriff ordered the demonstrators to disperse. Soon afterwards the police fired a tear gas canister into the crowd and the demonstrators left the area. Cox was arrested and convicted of disturbing the peace. The Supreme Court, 7-2, set aside his conviction in *Cox v. Louisiana* (1965). As in *Edwards*, the majority found Louisiana's breach-of-the-peace statute unconstitutionally broad in scope because it penalized persons who were lawfully exercising their rights of free speech, assembly, and petition.[80]

Courthouse Picketing. In a second charge arising from Cox's protest that day in 1961, the Court, 5-4, overturned his conviction for violating a Louisiana statute prohibiting picketing or parading "in or near" a courthouse.[81] The Court sustained the validity of the statute, as justified by the state interest protecting the administration of justice from outside influence. The statute was precisely drawn so that it did not restrict the rights of free speech and assembly but instead regulated conduct that, though entwined with speech and assembly, was not constitutionally protected. The Court also held, however, that the term *near* was so vague that it was not unreasonable for Cox to rely on the interpretation of the police as to how close they might come to the courthouse. By specifically confining the demonstration to a particular segment of the sidewalk, the police had in effect given permission for the demonstration to take place at that particular place. Thus the statute had been applied improperly to convict Cox.

Library Protest. The following year the Court overturned the breach-of-the-peace convictions of five black men who staged a peaceful and orderly protest against racial segregation by refusing to leave a library reserved for white use. The Court held this demonstration to be constitutionally protected in the case of *Brown v. Louisiana* (1966). The First Amendment freedoms

> embrace appropriate types of action which certainly include the right in a peaceable and orderly manner to protest by silent and reproachful presence, in a place where the protestant has every right to be, the unconstitutional segregation of public facilities.[82]

In dissent Justice Hugo L. Black maintained that the First Amendment did not "guarantee to any person the right to use someone else's property, even that owned by the government and dedicated to other purposes, as a stage to express dissident ideas."[83]

Jailhouse Demonstration. Justice Black's views won the adherence of a majority in a later case. *Adderly v. Florida* (1966) arose after blacks demonstrated at a county jail to protest the arrests of several students who had tried to integrate a segregated theater. The demonstrators were convicted of criminal trespass. Writing the opinion for the five-justice majority, Black acknowledged that the jail, like the capitol grounds in *Edwards*, was public property, but there the similarities ended. "Traditionally, state capitol grounds are open to the public. Jails, built for security purposes, are not," he said. Black continued:

> The State, no less than a private owner of property, has power to preserve the property under its control for the use to which it is lawfully dedicated. For this reason there is no merit to the [demonstrators'] argument that they had a constitutional right to stay on the property over the jail custodian's objections, because this "area chosen for the peaceful civil rights demonstration was not only 'reasonable' but also particularly appropriate...." Such an argument has as its major unarticulated premise the assumption that people who want to propagandize protests or views have a constitutional right to do so whenever and however and wherever they please. That concept of constitutional law was vigorously and forthrightly rejected in [previous cases].... We reject it again.[84]

For the four dissenters, Justice William O. Douglas said the Court was effectively negating *Edwards* and *Cox*. Douglas wrote:

> The jailhouse, like an executive mansion, a legislative chamber, a courthouse, or the statehouse itself ... is one of the seats of government, whether it be the Tower of London, the Bastille, or a small county jail. And when it houses political prisoners or those who many think are unjustly held, it is an obvious center for protest.... Conventional methods of petitioning may be, and often have been, shut off to large groups of our citizens.... Those who do not control television and radio, those who cannot afford to advertise in newspapers or circulate elaborate pamphlets may have only a more limited type of access to public officials. Their methods should not be condemned as tactics of obstruction and harassment as long as the assembly and petition are peaceable, as these were.[85]

Residential Area. In 1969 the Court upheld the right of peaceful demonstrators to parade in a residential neighborhood on the public sidewalks near Chicago mayor Richard Daley's home. The demonstrators advocated desegregation of Chicago public schools. White residents grew threatening, so to ward off potential violence police asked the marchers to disperse. They refused and were arrested. Five were convicted of disorderly conduct. In a unanimous decision in *Gregory v. City of Chicago* (1969), the Supreme Court overturned the convictions. Because there was no evidence that the marchers' conduct had been disorderly, the Court said the convictions violated due process. The Court also said that the "march, if peaceful and orderly, falls well within the sphere of conduct protected by the First Amendment."[86] Almost twenty years later, however, the Court in *Frisby v. Schultz* (1988) upheld a Brookfield, Wisconsin, ordinance forbidding picketing of an individual residence. The Court found the ordinance narrowly tailored enough to preserve residential privacy while leaving open alternative methods of expression. "The First Amendment permits the government to prohibit offensive speech as intrusive when the 'captive' audience cannot avoid the objectionable speech," wrote Justice Sandra Day O'Connor for the Court.[87]

Boycotts and Sleep-Ins. In *NAACP v. Claiborne Hardware Co.* (1982), the Court unanimously ruled that a nonviolent boycott in 1966 by civil rights demonstrators, intended to curtail business at the shops of white merchants in Port Gibson, Mississippi, was speech and conduct protected by the First Amendment. Damages for economic losses suffered as a result of the boycott could not be assessed against those who merely participated in it. Violence, on the other hand, the Court explained, was not protected activity, and a state court could assess damages against those responsible for such violence; the liability, however, must reflect the individual's participation in violence and cannot be lodged against someone simply because he or she was part of the boycotting group.[88]

In 1983 the Court struck down as unconstitutional a federal law barring demonstrations on the sidewalks adjacent to the Supreme Court building on Capitol Hill in Washington, D.C.[89] The following year, the Court took up *Clark v. Community for Creative Non-Violence* (1984). CCNV, protesting the Reagan administration's treatment of the nation's poor and homeless, challenged the administration's ban on camping in certain national parks. When applied to Lafayette Park, which sits across from the White House and is the site of a variety of periodic and ongoing demonstrations, CCNV argued, the ban violated the First Amendment freedom of expression. The Court, 7-2, upheld the ban—which defined camping as sleeping overnight—as a reasonable restriction on the time, place, and manner in which First Amendment rights could be exercised.[90]

Abortion Protests

During the 1980s and 1990s, the front line in the abortion battle was often the sidewalk in front of a medical clinic. Sidewalk protests made for a daily clash between the free speech rights of the abortion foes and the rights of patients who sought to end their pregnancies. The confrontations were often loud, angry, and sometimes violent. In three rulings, the Court held that patients and clinic workers can be shielded from "abusive face-to-face encounters" with abortion protesters, so long as the protesters remain otherwise free to deliver their message.

In 1994 the Court upheld a Florida judge's order that established a "36-foot buffer zone" in the driveway leading to an abortion clinic in Melbourne. As many as four hundred protesters gathered there daily to sing and chant. When cars approached, they blocked them and confronted the patients. Under the judge's order, police were told to arrest any protester who stood in the driveway. In upholding this order, Chief Justice William H. Rehnquist described it as a "time, place and manner regulation" of speech, not a regulation of the content of the speech itself. The buffer zone simply allows patients and the clinic staff to enter and exit the facility and "burdens no more speech than necessary," he said for the 6-3 majority in *Madsen v. Women's Health Center* (1994).[91] The decision also upheld part of the order that prohibited loud singing, chanting, or the use of bullhorns outside the clinic during the hours patients were undergoing surgery, but struck down another part of the order that imposed a three-hundred-foot "no approach" zone that followed patients and staff outside the clinic. In dissent, Justices Scalia, Kennedy, and Thomas said the judge's entire order should have been struck down as a free speech violation.

In 1997 the Court by the same 6-3 margin handed down a similar ruling in a Buffalo, New York, case. Upheld was a judge's order that kept protesters fifteen feet from the entrance to an abortion facility, but struck down was part of the order that prevented protesters from approaching within fifteen feet of patients on the sidewalks leading to the clinic.[92] The most significant ruling concerning a law (rather than one judge's injunction) came in 2000, when the Court held that patients had "a right to be let alone" as they approached a medical facility. The 6-3 decision upheld a model Colorado law that made it illegal to confront a person face-to-face within 100 feet of any health care facility. Protesters and sidewalk "counselors" were told that they could not come within eight feet of any person, without their consent so as to "engage in oral protest, education or counseling" or pass out a leaflet.

In upholding this restriction on free speech, Justice Stevens said states were entitled to protect "the unwilling listener's right to be let alone," a phrase first used by Justice Louis Brandeis in a wiretap case.[93] *(See "Electronic Eavesdropping," pp. 309–312.)* Patients, their families, and friends may be shielded, at least somewhat, from "aggressive counselors who sometimes used strong and abusive language in face-to-face encounters," Stevens wrote in *Hill v. Colorado* (2000).[94] Because the protesters need stay only eight feet away, however, they remain free to voice their message, he added. Justice Scalia read his dissent from the bench and condemned the ruling as "one of the many aggressively pro-abortion novelties announced by the Court in recent years.... 'Uninhibited, robust and wide open debate' is replaced by the power of the state to protect an unheard of 'right to be let alone' on the public streets," he said.[95] Justices Kennedy and Thomas joined in dissent.

Labor Picketing

The question of how much protection the First Amendment affords labor picketing has troubled the Supreme Court. Picketing conveys a message to the public about the issues in labor disputes and is therefore a form of expression, but unlike other sorts of parades and demonstrations, picketing also uses economic pressure and coercion to bring about better working conditions and, as conduct, can be regulated by government.

Permissible Pickets

Initially, courts considered all labor picketing illegal. As labor unions grew in power and acceptability, however, that view began to change. In a 1921 decision the Supreme Court permitted a union to post one picket at each entrance and exit of a factory for the purpose of explaining a union grievance against the employer. Although the First Amendment issue of free speech was not directly raised in this case, the Court acknowledged that "[w]e are a social people and the accosting by one of another in an inoffensive way and an offer by one to communicate and discuss information with a view to influence the other's action are not regarded as aggression or a violation of the other's rights."[96]

In a 1930s decision, the Court moved closer to the First Amendment question. In *Senn v. Tile Layers Union* (1937), it upheld a Wisconsin statute permitting peaceful picketing against a challenge that such picketing constituted a "taking" of the employer's property without due process of law guaranteed by the Fourteenth Amendment. "Clearly, the means which the state

authorizes—picketing and publicity—are not prohibited by the Fourteenth Amendment. Members of a union might make known the facts of a labor dispute, for freedom of speech is guaranteed by the Federal Constitution," Justice Brandeis wrote for a slim majority.[97]

Full Protection

In 1940 a substantial majority of the Court drew industrial picketing under the protective wing of the First Amendment. In *Thornhill v. Alabama* (1940), Byron Thornhill appealed his conviction under an Alabama law that forbade picketing. He argued that the statute violated his rights of free speech, assembly, and petition for redress of grievances. Speaking through Justice Frank Murphy, eight justices held the statute invalid. "In the circumstances of our times the dissemination of information concerning the facts of a labor dispute must be regarded as within that area of free discussion that is guaranteed by the Constitution," Murphy wrote.[98] The picketing did not lose its First Amendment protection just because it might result in some degree of economic coercion, Murphy explained:

> It may be that effective exercise of the means of advancing public knowledge may persuade some of those reached to refrain from entering into advantageous relations with the business establishment which is the scene of the dispute. Every expression of opinion ... has the potentiality of inducing action in the interests of one rather than another group in society. But the group in power at any moment may not impose penal sanctions on peaceful and truthful discussion of matters of public interest merely on a showing that others may thereby be persuaded to take action inconsistent with its interests.[99]

The following year, the Court in *AFL v. Swing* (1941) relied on *Thornhill* to rule that a state policy limiting picketing to cases where union members had a dispute with their employer was an unconstitutional infringement of the First Amendment guarantee of free speech. The Court said the state could not forbid organizational picketing by unions hoping to persuade nonunion workers to join.[100]

The Court has struggled with the question of how much protection the First Amendment affords labor picketing. While recognizing picketing as a form of expression, the Court has stopped short of granting it unlimited First Amendment protection.

Prior Restraint of Violence

In a case decided the same day as *AFL v. Swing*, the Court indicated that the First Amendment did not foreclose prior restraint of picketing in the interest of public safety. By a 6-3 vote, the majority upheld an injunction forbidding a union of milk wagon drivers to engage in picketing because their past picketing had resulted in violence. Justice Felix Frankfurter wrote the opinion for the majority in *Milk Wagon Drivers Union v. Meadowmoor Dairies Inc.* (1941). "Peaceful picketing is the workingman's means of communication," said Frankfurter, but the First Amendment does not protect "utterance in a context of violence" that becomes "part of an instrument of force." Under the circumstances of the case, he continued, "it could justifiably be concluded that the momentum of fear generated by past violence would survive even though future picketing might be wholly peaceful."[101]

Third-Party Picketing

Also in the early 1940s, the Court delivered two conflicting decisions on the permissibility of picketing of persons not directly involved in a labor dispute. In *Bakery and Pastry Drivers v. Wohl* (1940), the Court lifted an injunction against a union of bakery truck drivers that had picketed bakeries and groceries using nonunion drivers in order to induce the nonunion drivers to give some of their work to union drivers. The Court majority observed that the mobility and "middle-man" status of the nonunion drivers separated them from the public. Therefore picketing those who did business with them was "the only way to make views, admittedly accurate and peaceful, known."[102] In *Carpenters and Joiners Union v. Ritter's Cafe* (1942), the Court sustained an injunction against a carpenters' union, forbidding it to picket a cafe owned by a man whose nearby house was being built by a nonunion contractor. The five-justice majority noted that the union's real complaint was with the contractor and thus concluded,

> As a means of communication of the facts of a labor dispute, peaceful picketing may be a phase of the constitutional right of free utterance. But recognition of peaceful picketing as an exercise of free speech does not imply that the state must be without power to confine the sphere of communication to that directly related to the dispute.[103]

PUBLIC SPEECH ON PRIVATE PROPERTY: THE FIRST AMENDMENT RESTRICTED

The First Amendment prohibits only government action abridging the freedom of speech. Most First Amendment cases thus involve situations in which speech occurs or is abridged in a public forum or on public property. Some private property is dedicated to public use, however, and there the question arises whether the property owner becomes subject to the First Amendment prohibition. If that is so, then a private owner may no more restrict exercise of First Amendment freedoms on his property than may a government.

THE COMPANY TOWN

The Court first confronted this issue in *Marsh v. Alabama* (1946). Chickasaw, Alabama, a suburb of Mobile, was wholly owned by a private corporation. A Jehovah's Witness, Grace Marsh, passed out handbills on a Chickasaw street in violation of a regulation forbidding such distribution. She challenged her subsequent arrest and conviction, claiming that her First Amendment rights had been infringed. A majority of the Supreme Court agreed. Save for its private ownership, wrote Justice Hugo L. Black, Chickasaw had all the characteristics of any other American town, and its residents had the same interest as residents of municipally owned towns in keeping channels of communication open. "There is no more reason for depriving these people of the liberties guaranteed by the First and Fourteenth Amendments than there is for curtailing these freedoms with respect to any other citizens," Black said.[1]

PICKETING AND PRIVATE MALLS I

In 1968 the Court relied on *Marsh v. Alabama* when it forbade the owner of a private shopping mall to prohibit union picketing of a store in the mall. A nonunion supermarket in a privately owned mall near Altoona, Pennsylvania, was picketed by members of a food employees union who wished to point out that the supermarket did not employ union workers or abide by union pay and working condition requirements. The owners of the store and the shopping center won an injunction against picketing in the mall and its private parking lots.

By a 6-3 vote, the Supreme Court declared the injunction invalid in *Amalgamated Food Employees Union Local 590 v. Logan Valley Plaza* (1968). Noting the similarities between the shopping center and the business district in the company town involved in *Marsh*, Justice Thurgood Marshall observed that the general public had unrestricted access to the mall and that it served as the functional equivalent of a town business district. These circumstances, the majority said, rendered the mall public for purposes of the First Amendment, and consequently its owners could not invoke state trespass laws to prohibit picketing that advanced the communication of ideas. Marshall noted the narrowness of the ruling:

> All we decide here is that because the shopping center serves as the community business block "and is freely accessible and open to the people in the area and those passing through"…the State may not delegate the power, through the use of its trespass laws, wholly to exclude those members of the public wishing to exercise their First Amendment rights on the premises in a manner and for a purpose generally consonant with the use to which the property is actually put.[2]

Justice Black dissented, contending that the majority erred in its reliance on *Marsh* as a precedent. *Marsh* held that the First Amendment applied when the private property had taken on *all* of the aspects of a town, he said, adding,

> I can find nothing in Marsh which indicates that if one of these features is present, e.g., a business district, this is sufficient for the Court to confiscate a part of an owner's private property and give its use to people who want to picket on it.[3]

HANDBILL PROTESTS IN SHOPPING CENTERS

Within four years a majority of the Court qualified the ruling in *Logan Valley Plaza*, holding that owners of a private shopping mall could prohibit the

---

The conclusion of the two holdings seemed to be that a third party to a labor dispute could be picketed only if the union had no other means to make its views effectively known. In both these cases the majority recognized that industrial picketing, in Justice William O. Douglas's words,

is more than free speech, since it involves patrol of a particular locality and since the very presence of a picket line may induce action of one kind or another, quite irrespective of the nature of the ideas which are being disseminated. Hence those aspects of picketing make it the subject of restrictive regulation.[104]

distribution of leaflets unrelated to business conducted in the mall. The circumstances in *Lloyd Corporation, Ltd. v. Tanner* (1972) were similar to those in *Marsh* with one major difference. The Lloyd Center was not a company town but a privately owned and operated shopping mall that prohibited the circulation of handbills. Inside the mall, several people attempted to distribute handbills inviting the general public to attend a meeting to protest the Vietnam War. When asked to desist, they did, but then brought suit charging they had been denied their right to free speech. By a 5-4 vote, the Supreme Court rejected the charge. Writing for the majority, Justice Lewis F. Powell Jr. held that although the shopping mall served the public, it still maintained its private character:

> The invitation is to come to the Center to do business with the tenants. There is no open-ended invitation to the public to use the Center for any and all purposes, however incompatible with the interests of both the stores and the shoppers whom they serve. This Court has never held that a trespasser or an uninvited guest may exercise general rights of free speech on property privately owned and used nondiscriminatorily for private purposes only.[4]

Writing for the dissenters, Justice Marshall saw nothing to distinguish this case from the Court's holdings in *Marsh* and *Logan Valley Plaza*.

PICKETING AND PRIVATE MALLS II

In 1976 the Court moved a step closer to divesting speech on private property used for specific public purposes of any First Amendment protection, but a majority of the Court still refused to overturn the *Logan Valley Plaza* decision, leaving the issue unsettled. *Hudgens v. National Labor Relations Board* (1976) arose after striking employees of a shoe company warehouse decided also to picket the company's retail stores. One of these was situated in a shopping mall whose owners threatened to have the pickets arrested for trespassing if they did not desist. The picketers withdrew but challenged the owners' threat as an unfair labor practice under the National Labor Relations Act.

Before answering that question, the Supreme Court majority felt it necessary to determine whether the picketing was entitled to any First Amendment protection. A majority concluded it was not. Three of the members of the majority held that the *Lloyd* decision had in effect overruled the *Logan Valley Plaza* decision and that, consequently, uninvited speech on private property was not protected. The three other justices comprising the majority did not believe that the *Logan Valley Plaza* decision had been overruled, but they distinguished between the pickets in that case, who conveyed information about the operation of a store actually located in the mall, and the pickets in *Hudgens*, who tried to convey information about a warehouse located away from the mall.

Justices Marshall and William J. Brennan Jr. dissented. Marshall insisted that when an owner of a private shopping mall invited the public onto his property to conduct business he gave up a degree of privacy to the interests of the public. One public interest was "communicating with one another on subjects relating to businesses that occupy" the shopping center. "As far as these groups are concerned," said Marshall, "the shopping center owner has assumed the traditional role of the state in its control of historical First Amendment forums."[5] Just four years later, however, the Court seemed to move again on this question, holding unanimously that a state could require the owner of a shopping mall to permit students to collect signatures on a petition to Congress within his mall.[6]

---

1. *Marsh v. Alabama, 326 U.S. 501 at 508–509 (1946);* see also *Tucker v. Texas, 326 U.S. 517 (1946).*

2. *Amalgamated Food Employees Union Local 590 v. Logan Valley Plaza, 391 U.S. 308 at 319–320 (1968).*

3. *Id.* at 332.

4. *Lloyd Corporation, Ltd. v. Tanner, 407 U.S. 551 at 564–565, 568 (1972).*

5. *Hudgens v. National Labor Relations Board, 424 U.S. 507 at 543 (1976).*

6. *Prune Yard Shopping Center v. Robins, 447 U.S. 74 (1980).*

Illegal Conduct

The Court moved another step away from *Thornhill* in the late 1940s. Picketing as "conduct" may in some circumstances be so intertwined with illegal labor practices that states may prohibit it, held a unanimous Court in *Giboney v. Empire Storage & Ice Co.* (1949).

A Missouri court issued an injunction against a union of ice drivers that had picketed an ice company in order to persuade the company to refuse to sell ice to nonunion drivers. Other unions had observed the picket line, and the company's sales fell by 85 percent. If the company had entered into the proposed union agreement, however, it would have violated Missouri's restraint of trade law. The union contended that because its picketing publicized the facts about the labor dispute, the picketing was entitled to First Amendment protection. The Supreme Court rejected this thesis. In an opinion written by Justice Black, the Court found that the picketing was an integral part of conduct that violated a valid state law and was therefore not protected by the First Amendment. Wrote Black, "It has never been deemed an abridgment of freedom of speech or press to make a course of conduct illegal merely because the conduct was in part initiated, evidenced or carried out by means of language."[105]

State Regulation

In a series of cases beginning with *Giboney* and ending with three decisions in 1950, the Court effectively reversed *Thornhill,* making clear that the expressive aspects of picketing did not protect it from state regulation and prohibition. If the purpose of the picketing could be construed as contrary to state statute or policy, the Court would hold a state-imposed injunction valid. The first of the 1950 cases blended the aspects of industrial picketing and civil rights demonstrations. In *Hughes v. Superior Court of California* (1950), the Court upheld an injunction forbidding picketing by blacks trying to force a grocer to hire a certain percentage of black employees. Although no state law prohibited racial hiring quotas, the California judge who issued the injunction held the picketing inimical to the state's policy of supporting nondiscrimination.[106] In two other cases decided the same day, the Court upheld injunctions against picketing aimed at forcing an employer to pressure his employees to choose the picketing union as their bargaining representative and against picketing to compel a family business with no employees to operate by union standards.[107]

In *Local Plumbers Union # 10 v. Graham* (1953), the Court again held that the speech aspects of picketing did not protect it from regulation. The union claimed that its picketing simply announced to the public that the picketed employer hired nonunion workers, but the Supreme Court found that the major

purpose of the picketing was to force the employer to replace his nonunion employees with union workers, action that would violate the state's "right-to-work" law.[108] Three years later, the Court upheld an injunction against unions engaged in picketing of a nonunion gravel pit. Such picketing violated a state law making it an unfair labor practice to force an employer "to interfere with any of his employees in the enjoyment of their legal rights." Writing for the majority in *International Brotherhood of Teamsters, Local 695 v. Vogt* (1957), Justice Frankfurter reviewed the cases decided by the Court since the *Thornhill* finding that picketing was protected by the First Amendment. *Thornhill* was still valid, he said, because "[s]tate courts, no more than state legislatures, can enact blanket prohibitions against picketing." He added, however, that the cases decided since then had

> established a broad field in which a state, in enforcing some public policy, whether of its criminal or its civil law, and whether announced by its legislature or its courts, could constitutionally enjoin peaceful picketing aimed at preventing effectuation of that policy.[109]

For the three dissenters, Justice Douglas said that the majority had completely abandoned *Thornhill.* Douglas urged the Court to return to the proposition that the First Amendment protects from state restriction all picketing that is not violent or a part of illegal conduct:

> [W]here, as here, there is no rioting, no mass picketing, no violence, no disorder, no fisticuffs, no coercion—indeed nothing but speech, the principles announced in Thornhill ... should give the advocacy of one side of a dispute First Amendment protection.[110]

In 1968 the Court held that the First Amendment forbade a state to delegate to the owner of a shopping mall the power to restrict labor picketing of a store in the mall. The continuing validity of this decision has since been called into question, and the decision in *Vogt* stands as the Court's position on labor picketing's relation to the First Amendment.[111] *(See box, Public Speech on Private Property, pp. 70–71.)*

Soliciting and Canvassing

Door-to-door noncommercial solicitation of a neighborhood by persons seeking financial and moral support for their religious, political, or civic cause squarely sets the freedoms of speech, press, and religion against the right of privacy in one's home. Must the right to disseminate ideas give way to privacy, or does privacy yield to the uninvited dissemination of ideas? Professor Zechariah Chafee Jr. argued that privacy may be the value more worthy of preservation:

> Of all the methods of spreading unpopular ideas … [solicitation] seems the least entitled to extensive [First Amendment] protection. The possibilities of persuasion are slight compared with the certainties of annoyance. Great as is the value of exposing citizens to novel views, home is one place where a man ought to be able to shut himself up in his own ideas if he desires.[112]

The Supreme Court, however, has generally held in solicitation cases that freedom of ideas takes precedence over privacy. To protect their citizens from annoyance, governments may regulate the time and manner of solicitation, and to protect the public from fraud or crime, governments may require solicitors to identify themselves, but such regulations must be narrowly drawn and precisely defined to avoid infringing First Amendment rights.

One of the first solicitation ordinances to fall under Supreme Court scrutiny was a Connecticut statute that prohibited solicitation of money or services without the approval of the secretary of the local public welfare office. The secretary had the discretion to determine if the solicitation was in behalf of a bona fide religion or charitable cause. The Supreme Court struck down the statute in *Cantwell v. Connecticut* (1940):

> Without doubt a State may protect its citizens from fraudulent solicitation by requiring a stranger in the community, before permitting him publicly to solicit funds for any purpose, to establish his identity and his authority to act for the cause which he purports to represent. The State is likewise free to regulate the time and manner of solicitation generally, in the interest of public safety, peace, comfort or convenience. But to condition the solicitation of

aid for the perpetuation of religious views or systems upon a license, the grant of which rests in the exercise of a determination by state authority as to what is a religious cause, is to lay a forbidden burden upon the exercise of liberty protected by the Constitution.[113]

Although continuing to uphold the authority of a town to require solicitors to meet identification requirements, the Court in 1976 ruled a New Jersey town ordinance too vague to meet First Amendment standards, and in 1980 it held invalid an Illinois village's ordinance denying the right to solicit funds door-to-door to any group that spent more than a certain percentage on administrative costs. That, the Court said, was an undue infringement upon free speech.[114] This point was subsequently reaffirmed when the Court struck down Maryland and North Carolina laws regulating the professional solicitation of funds.[115]

Membership Solicitations

A Texas law required all labor union organizers to register with the state before soliciting union members there. To test the statute, union organizer R. J. Thomas announced that he would solicit members without registering. A Texas court issued an order restraining Thomas from addressing an organizing rally without the proper credentials, but he defied the order and was subsequently convicted of contempt. Thomas challenged the registration requirement as violating his right of free speech. The Supreme Court agreed. In *Thomas v. Collins* (1945), the Court held that the First Amendment clearly protected a speech made to solicit persons for membership in a lawful organization:

> That there was restriction upon Thomas' right to speak and the right of the workers to hear what he had to say, there can be no doubt. The threat of the restraining order, backed by the power of contempt, and of arrest for crime, hung over every word…. We think a requirement that one must register before he undertakes to make a public speech to enlist support for a lawful movement is quite incompatible with the requirements of the First Amendment.[116]

MONEY AND POLITICAL SPEECH

When legislators limit the amount anyone can contribute to a candidate or a political campaign or the amount a candidate may spend, they restrict free speech. After avoiding the issue for years, the Supreme Court in *Buckley v. Valeo* (1976) struck down limits that Congress had imposed on campaign spending.[1] Similar limits on campaign contributions, however, were upheld. The contribution and spending provisions in question were part of the Federal Election Campaign Act of 1974. The justices concluded that restricting how much a candidate spends to campaign is a much greater limit on political speech than restricting how much a wealthy person can contribute to the campaign.

"A restriction on the amount of money a person or group can spend on political communication during a campaign necessarily reduces the quantity of expression," declared the Court, "by restricting the number of issues discussed, the depth of their exploration and the size of the audience reached.... [V]irtually every means of communicating ideas in today's mass society requires the expenditure of money."[2] Although acknowledging that contribution limits also curtail free speech, the Court nonetheless found them justified by the government's interest in preventing corruption.

This two-part rule has survived, despite much criticism, including from within the Court. Justices Antonin Scalia, Anthony M. Kennedy, and Clarence Thomas have said they would overrule one part of the *Buckley* decision and give donors a free speech right to give as much as they wish to candidates or political parties. Justice John Paul Stevens would overrule the other half of the *Buckley* decision and permit lawmakers to put limits on spending by candidates. "Money is property; it is not speech.... These property rights are not entitled to the same protection as the right to say what one pleases," Stevens wrote in a 2000 concurring opinion.[3] Shortly after joining the court, Chief Justice John G. Roberts Jr. and Justice Samuel A. Alito Jr. said they mostly agreed with Scalia, Kennedy, and Thomas that campaign money is entitled to full free speech protection under the First Amendment.

Federal limits on funding election campaigns have been on the books for more than a century. President Theodore Roosevelt called on Congress to forbid corporations and national banks from funding candidates and their campaigns, and the Tillman Act of 1907 did just that. The Taft-Hartley Act of 1947 put similar limits on labor unions. The Watergate scandal that brought down President Richard Nixon also put a spotlight on the role of big cash contributions from wealthy supporters and led directly to the 1974 law that was challenged in the *Buckley* case.

Regulating campaign funding has proven to be as tricky and as frustrating as seeking to devise a simple and fair tax code. Candidates and interest groups have regularly found ways to evade the fund-raising limits, and lawmakers and regulators have responded with a series of new rules to stop them. In 2002, for example, Congress passed the Bipartisan Campaign Reform Act of 2002 (BCRA)—also known as the McCain-Feingold Act—to plug loopholes that had allowed corporations, unions, and the wealthy to funnel huge amounts of money into campaigns. The BCRA sought to ban the "soft money" contributions that were channeled through

Doorbells

The Court in *Martin v. Struthers* (1943) struck down a Struthers, Ohio, ordinance that prohibited distributors of handbills or other advertisements from knocking on doors or ringing bells to ensure that residents would receive the flyer. Ignoring this ordinance, a Jehovah's Witness distributed a flyer, which advertised a religious meeting, in a neighborhood where many of the residents were night workers and consequently slept in the daytime. He was arrested and defended himself with the claim that the ordinance was unconstitutional. The Court agreed by a 5-4 vote. "While door to door distributors of literature may be either a nuisance or a blind for criminal activities, they may also be useful members of society engaged in dissemination of ideas," wrote Justice Black. He enumerated causes that depended on door-to-door solicitation for their success, observing that this form of dissemination of ideas "is essential to the poorly financed causes of little people." The First Amendment prohibited the community from substituting its judgment for that of an individual in determining whether the individual may receive information. In dissent Justice Reed maintained that the ordinance did not violate any First Amendment right but simply respected a homeowner's privacy:

political parties and curtail "electioneering communication," or broadcast ads funded by corporations or unions that targeted specific candidates close to an election. In 2003 the Court upheld the law as constitutional under the rules set in the *Buckley* decision. Writing for the 5-4 majority, Justices John Paul Stevens and Sandra Day O'Connor noted that the law was "designed to purge national politics of what was conceived to be the pernicious influence of 'big money' campaign contributions." The law will "protect the integrity of the political process" and have "only a marginal impact on the ability of contributors, candidates, officeholders and parties to engage in effective political speech.... Congress has a fully legitimate interest in maintaining the integrity of federal office holders and preventing corruption of the federal electoral process," the Court held.[4]

Having upheld the BCRA in principle, the Court backtracked in 2007 and removed some political ads from its restrictions. In *Federal Election Commission v. Wisconsin Right to Life,* the Court explained that "issue advocacy" differs from urging voters to elect or defeat a candidate. It also deserves more protection under the First Amendment, the Court said in a 5-4 decision.[5] The antiabortion group from Wisconsin had sought to broadcast radio ads in 2004 that faulted Sen. Russ Feingold, D-Wis., for not supporting President George W. Bush's judicial nominees. These ads appeared to run afoul of the BCRA because Feingold, a co-sponsor of the law, was then running for reelection. Moreover, corporate donations helped pay for the group's ads. Speaking for the Court, Chief Justice Roberts described the ads as "pure political speech" and said that ads of this sort deserve an exemption from the law. "The First Amendment requires us to err on the side of protecting speech rather than suppressing it," he said. Scalia, Kennedy, Thomas, and Alito agreed.

Efforts by liberal reformers to eliminate big money from state politics also were dealt a defeat by the Roberts Court. Vermont's lawmakers had sought to restore small-town democracy to state politics by strictly limiting how much candidates could raise and spend. For example, candidates for the state senate were told they could spend no more than $4,000 on their campaigns. Contributions to senate candidates were limited to $400. These limits posed a direct challenge to *Buckley v. Valeo* because they restricted spending as well as contributions. In *Randall v. Sorrell* (2006), the Court in a 6-3 decision struck down the entire Vermont law as unconstitutional under the First Amendment.[6] Breyer said the limits were so low that they would make it impossible for challengers to run an effective campaign for state office. Stevens, David H. Souter, and Ruth Bader Ginsburg dissented.

1. *Buckley v. Valeo,* 424 U.S. 1 (1976); see also *United States v. CIO,* 335 U.S. 106 (1948); *United States v. United Auto Workers,* 352 U.S. 567 (1957); *Pipefitters v. United States,* 407 U.S. 385 (1972).

2. *Buckley v. Valeo,* 424 U.S. 1 at 19 (1976).

3. *Nixon v. Shrink Missouri Government PAC,* 528 U.S. 377 at 398–399 (2000).

4. *McConnell v. Federal Election Commission,* 540 U.S. 93 (2003).

5. *Federal Election Commission v. Wisconsin Right to Life,* 551 U.S. ___ (2007).

6. *Randall v. Sorrell,* 548 U.S. 230 (2006).

No ideas are being suppressed. No censorship is involved. The freedom to teach or preach by word or book is unabridged, save only the right to call a householder to the door of his house to receive the summoner's message.[117]

In 2002 the Court went a step further and ruled that cities may not require religious solicitors, political activists, or other advocates to register and obtain a permit before they go door-to-door. In an 8-1 decision, the justices struck down an ordinance adopted by the tiny Village of Stratton, Ohio, whose residents were irritated by the activities of Jehovah's Witnesses. Had the ordinance been limited to "commercial" soliciting, it could be upheld, said Justice John Paul Stevens, but a registration requirement that applies to all solicitors goes too far and violates the freedom of speech. In a rare solo dissent, Chief Justice Rehnquist faulted the Court for depriving the village residents "of the degree of accountability and safety" that comes with registering door-to-door solicitors.[118]

Airport Solicitations

In 1992 the Court, divided 6-3, said airports may prohibit individuals and groups from soliciting money in their terminals. The case was brought by the Krishnas, a religious group that disseminates religious literature and solicits funds in public places. The group challenged regulations by the Port Authority of New York and New Jersey, which operated three major airports in the New York City area. Airports, the Court ruled, are not traditional forums for public speech, so a solicitations ban need only be reasonable to be upheld. Solicitation may disrupt business by slowing the path of those who are approached for money or who change their paths to avoid being solicited, the justices said. In a separate decision involving the same parties, the Court ruled that the airport authority's ban on the mere distribution of literature in the terminals was invalid.[119]

Religious Speech

The First Amendment gives public officials, particularly in schools, a somewhat contradictory message. It says they must protect the freedom of speech, but at the same time they may not take any action "respecting an establishment of religion." Following the school prayer decisions of the 1960s, many educators came to believe that the Constitution required the public school to be a "religion-free zone," as some put it. In a series of rulings in the 1990s, however, the Court stressed that officials may not exclude or discriminate against "religious speech," even in public schools that must abide by the ban on promoting religion. "There is a crucial difference between government speech endorsing religion, which the Establishment Clause forbids, and private speech endorsing religion, which the Free Speech and Free Exercise Clauses protect," wrote Justice Sandra Day O'Connor in a 1990 decision.[120] In 1984 Congress had passed the Equal Access Act, requiring schools to allow student-led religious clubs to have the same rights as other student groups. The Court's 1990 unanimous ruling upheld the rights of a group of students to organize a Christian club to meet on campus so they could pray and read the Bible together. "We think that secondary school students are mature enough and are likely to understand that a school does not endorse or support student speech that it merely permits on a nondiscriminatory basis," O'Connor said.[121]

Also in the early 1990s, a small evangelical Christian church on Long Island challenged a New York state law prohibiting the use of public schools for religious purposes. The school board of Center Moriches had rejected the church's request to use a school building in the evening to show films on raising families and children that presented "a Christian perspective." In a unanimous decision in 1993, the Court said the state ban violated the church group's freedom of speech and held that public school systems must open their facilities for use by religious groups on the same basis as other organizations. Justice Byron R. White concluded that it "discriminates on the basis of viewpoint to permit school property to be used for the presentation of all views about family issues and child-rearing except those dealing with the subject matter from a religious viewpoint."[122]

Two years later, in 1995, a divided Court extended that decision to colleges and universities in a case holding that a state university that subsidizes newspapers and magazines written by students cannot refuse funding for a student publication with an evangelical Christian perspective.[123] The University of Virginia used student fees to pay the printing costs of campus publications, but it refused Robert Rosenberger's request to pay for *Wide Awake,* a newspaper with a religious perspective. In a 5-4 vote the Court ruled that the university's policy violates the Free Speech Clause. Justice Anthony M. Kennedy wrote that because it "selects for disfavored treatment those student journalistic efforts with religious editorial viewpoints … [i]t is axiomatic that the government may not regulate speech based on its substantive content or the message it conveys."[124] The four dissenters, led by Justice David H. Souter, said the problem was not regulating speech but funding it. "The Court today, for the first time, approves direct funding of core religious activities by an arm of the state," Souter wrote.[125] In 2000 the Court again chided a public school system for refusing to allow religious activists to use their school facilities. In this case, it was a minister and his wife who wanted to offer a Bible study program to elementary school children at the end of the regular school day. Citing *Lamb's Chapel* and *Rosenberger,* Justice Thomas, speaking for a 6-3 majority, said officials cannot "discriminate … because of a religious viewpoint."[126]

In a decision handed down on the same day as *Rosenberger,* the Court had held that state officials may not exclude citizens from displaying religious symbols on public land where other symbols and messages may be displayed. Officials at the state capitol in Columbus, Ohio, tried to prevent the Ku Klux Klan from erecting a large wooden cross on the capitol grounds during the Christmas season. The officials refused the Klan's request, claiming that such a display would violate the Establishment Clause. In a 7-2 decision, the Court disagreed, stating that the exclusion violated the guarantee of freedom of speech. "Private religious speech, far from being a First Amendment orphan, is as fully protected under the Free Speech Clause as secular private expression," said Justice Antonin Scalia.[127] Justice Clarence Thomas concurred in the ruling, but questioned the premise that the Klan's use of the cross was religious. "The Klan simply has appropriated one of the most sacred of religious symbols as a symbol of hate," he said.[128]

Justices Stevens and Ruth Bader Ginsburg dissented, arguing that adorning a state building with religious symbols would be seen by many as an endorsement of religion. The Court majority, however, was more concerned about discrimination against private religious expressions than an inference of government promotion of religion.

Commercial Speech

The Supreme Court had originally held that commercial speech—advertising or any speech that proposes a commercial transaction—was unprotected by the First Amendment and therefore subject to regulation and even prohibition by the states. In a series of decisions in the 1970s, the Court changed its view. Finding that commercial speech provides information to which the consuming public has a right, the Court struck down state and local prohibitions of certain advertisements. The Court, however, continued to emphasize that commercial advertising remained subject to regulation to prevent false, deceptive, and misleading information. The result has been a hodgepodge of rulings and inconsistently applied standards for assessing advertising, leading Alex Kozinski, a federal appeals court judge in California, to observe, "The commercial speech doctrine is the stepchild of First Amendment jurisprudence. Liberals don't much like commercial speech because it's commercial; conservatives mistrust

it because it's speech. Yet, in a free market economy, the ability to give and receive information about commercial matters may be as important, sometimes more important," than noncommercial expression.[129]

Unprotected Speech

Commercial speech was first discussed by the Court in *Schneider v. Irvington* (1939). The majority ruled that the First Amendment prohibits a city from requiring a person soliciting for religious causes to first obtain permission from city officials. The Court cautioned, however, that it was not ruling on whether such a condition would be unconstitutional if applied to commercial solicitation and canvassing.[130] *Schneider* was followed by the Court's unanimous opinion in *Valentine v. Chrestensen* (1942), which became the early precedent on commercial speech. Here the Court held that the First Amendment did not protect commercial handbills even if one side of a handbill contained a statement protesting the ordinance banning the circulation of commercial handbills:

> This Court has unequivocally held that the streets are proper places for the exercise of the freedom of communicating information and disseminating opinion and that, though the states and municipalities may appropriately regulate the privilege in the public interest, they may not unduly burden or proscribe its employment in these public thoroughfares. We are equally clear that the Constitution imposes no such restraint on government as respects purely commercial advertising. Whether, and to what extent, one may promote or pursue a gainful occupation in the streets, to what extent such activity shall be adjudged a derogation of the public right of the user, are matters for legislative judgment.[131]

In a 1951 case, salesmen of nationally known magazines claimed that freedom of the press was infringed by ordinances prohibiting door-to-door solicitation for subscriptions without prior consent of the homeowners. The Court rejected the claim. "We agree that the fact that periodicals are sold does not put them beyond the protection of the First Amendment. The selling, however, brings into the transaction a commercial feature," the Court wrote.[132]

PUBLIC EMPLOYEES AND THE FIRST AMENDMENT

Public employees have the same First Amendment rights as other citizens to speak freely, but they may be punished for speaking out about problems in the workplace. This two-part standard has been refined over more than four decades.

Until the mid-twentieth century, however, the "unchallenged dogma" was that public employees, like private sector workers, had no right to object to conditions set by their employer. As Justice Oliver Wendell Holmes Jr. had observed when he sat on the Massachusetts high court, a policeman "may have a constitutional right to talk politics, but he has no constitutional right to be a policeman."[1] In the 1950s, the Court and the public came to question the loyalty oaths that were imposed on teachers and college professors.

The First Amendment rights of public employees won recognition in the late 1960s in the case of an Illinois high school teacher who had been fired after sending a letter to a local newspaper. In the letter, Marvin Pickering criticized the superintendent for mishandling a bond drive and for spending too much money on school sports programs. The superintendent said that his actions were detrimental to the school system and dismissed him. In *Pickering v. Board of Education of Township High School District* (1968), the justices rejected the premise that "teachers may be constitutionally compelled to relinquish the First Amendment rights they would otherwise enjoy as citizens to comment on matters of public interest in connections with the operation of the public schools in which they work."

Justice Thurgood Marshall said a balance was called for between the speech rights of the employees and the employers' need to maintain an efficient and effective workforce. Pickering's letter did not contain blatant false statements, he said, and it was not likely to disrupt the workforce. In such a case, the Court concluded, a public employee deserves the right to speak publicly as a citizen on a matter of public concern.[2]

The Court, however, has rejected First Amendment claims from public employees fired over workplace disputes. In *Connick v. Myers* (1983), the Court upheld New Orleans district attorney Harry Connick's decision to fire prosecutor Sheila Myers after she objected to a transfer and sent a questionnaire throughout the office asking about low morale. The office dispute was not a matter of public concern, the Court ruled.[3] In 2006 the Court went a step further and ruled that the First Amendment does not protect disgruntled public employees disciplined by a supervisor, even when they seek to reveal internal matters that could be of great public concern. Richard Ceballos, a deputy district attorney in Los Angeles County, had come to believe that a police officer may have lied to obtain a search warrant. He took his suspicions to other prosecutors and to his superiors. When they disagreed with his view, he aided a defense lawyer and testified in court for the defendant. Afterward, Ceballos said he was transferred to another office and given lesser duties. He sued, claiming that he was retaliated against for having spoken out on a matter of public concern. In *Garcetti v. Ceballos* (2006), the Court in a 5-4 decision ruled that internal

Communication of Information

The selling of magazines was enough to allow states to bar door-to-door solicitation, but the commercial aspect of a paid political advertisement in a newspaper was not enough to deprive paid political advertisement of all First Amendment protection. In the landmark libel case *New York Times Co. v. Sullivan* (1964), the Court held that an advertisement seeking support for the civil rights movement

> was not a commercial advertisement in the sense in which the word was used in Chrestensen. It communicated information, expressed opinion, recited grievances, protested claimed abuses, and sought financial support on behalf of a movement whose

existence and objectives are matters of the highest public interest.... That the *Times* was paid for publishing this advertisement is as immaterial in this connection as is the fact that newspapers and books are sold. Any other conclusion would discourage newspapers from carrying "editorial advertisements" of this type.[133]

More than a decade later, the Court used this same reasoning when it held that Virginia had violated the First Amendment when it punished a local newspaper editor for printing an advertisement concerning the availability of legal abortions in New York. The advertisement did more than propose a commercial transaction, the Court said in *Bigelow v. Virginia* (1975). It whistleblowers cannot depend on the First Amendment for protection."We hold that when public employees make statements pursuant to their official duties, the employees are not speaking as citizens for First Amendment purposes, and the Constitution does not insulate their communications from employer discipline," wrote Justice Anthony M. Kennedy.[4]

At times, the Court has tipped the balance in favor of the free speech rights of employees when they have made troubling comments that do not affect the work of an agency. In *Rankin v. McPherson* (1987), the justices prevented the firing of a police desk officer in Texas who in 1981 on the day President Ronald Reagan was shot and wounded, commented, "If they go for him again, I hope they get him." Outraged by this comment, a supervisor fired the officer. Justice Harry A. Blackmun explained that as long as a public employee is not in a confidential, policymaking, or public-contact role, the danger to the agency's successful function from that employee's private speech is minimal. At some point, he wrote, "such concerns are so removed from the effective functioning of the public employer that they cannot prevail over the free speech rights of the public employee. This is such a case." The vote was 5-4. The dissenters—Chief Justice William H. Rehnquist and Justices Byron R. White, Sandra Day O'Connor, and Antonin Scalia—maintained that "no law enforcement agency is required by the First Amendment to permit one of its employees to 'ride with the cops and cheer for the robbers.'"[5]

The justices also upheld the rights of public employees to speak and write on non-work-related topics on their own time. In the closely watched *United States v. National Treasury Employees Union* (1995), the Court struck down a federal law barring most executive branch workers from earning outside income by giving speeches and writing articles. The ban had the commendable intent of preventing influence buying and the appearance of impropriety among government workers, but it had the unconstitutional consequence of restricting the free speech rights of government workers. The justices ruled 6-3 that the ban was unconstitutional because it applied when neither the subject of a freelance piece nor the person paying for it had any link to the worker's official duties. The Court cited examples of a mail handler who gave lectures on the Quaker religion and a government microbiologist who wrote dance reviews. Justice John Paul Stevens emphasized that a ban on payment is effectively a ban on free speech: "Publishers compensate authors because compensation provides a significant incentive toward more expression."[6]

1. *McAuliffe v. Mayor of New Bedford,* 155 Mass. 216, 220, 29 N.E. 517 (1892), cited in *Connick v. Myers,* 461 U.S. 138 at 143 (1983).

2. *Pickering v. Board of Education of Township High School District,* 205, 395 U.S. 563 (1968).

3. *Connick v. Myers,* 461 U.S. 138 (1983).

4. *Garcetti v. Ceballos,* 547 U.S. 410 (2006).

5. *Rankin v. McPherson,* 483 U.S. 378 (1987).

6. *United States v. National Treasury Employees Union,* 513 U.S. 454 (1995).

conveyed information not only to women who might be interested in seeking an abortion but to people interested in the general issue of whether abortions should be legalized.[134]

The Consumer's Right

In *Virginia State Board of Pharmacy v. Virginia Citizens Consumer Council Inc.* (1976), the Court majority abandoned its distinction between advertising that publicly conveyed important information and thereby merited some First Amendment protection and advertising that did not. Agreeing with a lower court that Virginia could not constitutionally forbid pharmacists from advertising the prices of prescription drugs, the Court wrote,

Advertising, however tasteless and excessive it sometimes may seem, is nonetheless dissemination of information as to who is producing and selling what product, for what reason, and at what price. So long as we preserve a predominantly free enterprise economy, the allocation of our resources in large measure will be made through numerous private economic decisions. It is a matter of public interest that those decisions, in the aggregate, be intelligent and well informed. To this end, the free flow of commercial information is indispensable.... And if it is indispensable to the proper allocation of resources in a free enterprise system, it is also indispensable to the formation of intelligent opinions as to how that system ought to be regulated or altered. Therefore, even if

FEDERAL MONEY AND FREE SPEECH

"Free speech" is speech free of government control, but when the government funds the speech, it can exercise at least some control of it without violating the First Amendment. That was the message of several Supreme Court decisions on matters ranging from abortion to "indecent" art and Internet pornography. When Congress sought to restrict the courtroom speech of subsidized lawyers, however, the justices, all of whom are lawyers, took a different approach.

In 1976 in the Hyde Amendment, named for Henry Hyde, Congress had legislated that federal money was not to be used to pay for abortions, and the Reagan administration had gone a step further in 1988 by telling doctors and nurses at federally supported clinics that they could not advise patients about abortion. This "gag rule" was challenged as a violation of the free speech rights of doctors and their patients. In a 5-4 decision in *Rust v. Sullivan* (1991), the Court upheld the abortion speech restriction. "This is not a case of the Government suppressing a dangerous idea, but of a prohibition on a project grantee or its employees from engaging in activities outside of its scope," Chief Justice William H. Rehnquist said. He added, "The government may validly choose to fund childbirth over abortion.... When Congress established a National Endowment for Democracy to encourage other countries to adopt democratic principles, it was not constitutionally required to fund a program to encourage competing lines of political philosophy such as Communism and Fascism."[1]

The Court also rejected a free speech challenge to the congressional requirement that the National Endowment for the Arts (NEA) take into account "general standards of decency" before awarding arts grants. While most of the NEA's money goes to support conventional projects, such as symphonies, theaters, and established artists, on occasion its small grants provoke a public outcry. In the 1990s, a furor arose over a grant that funded an exhibit that included starkly homoerotic photographs taken by the late Robert Mapplethorpe and a second one that helped pay for *Piss Christ*, a photograph of a cross in urine taken by Andres Serrano. Some outraged members of Congress pressed to abolish the arts endowment entirely, but lawmakers settled ultimately on a compromise that instructed the NEA to consider standards of decency in deciding what projects to fund. Several performance artists sued after their bids for grants were rejected by the NEA.

The lead plaintiff, Karen Finley, was known for appearing on stage covered in chocolate and feathers. In an 8-1 decision in *National Endowment for the Arts v. Finley* (1998), the Court rejected the free speech challenge, but it did so after concluding that the congressional requirement was mostly advice, not a hard-and-fast rule. Quoting *Rust v. Sullivan*, Justice Sandra Day O'Connor said, "Congress may selectively fund a program to encourage certain activities it believes to be in the public interest," without taking on the duty to fund other, less desirable

---

the First Amendment were thought to be primarily an instrument to enlighten public decision-making in a democracy, we could not say that the free flow of information does not serve that goal.[135]

In other words, the ability to obtain drug price information assists consumers in making a multitude of economic decisions, small and large. In subsequent cases the Court used this reasoning to rule that a state could not prohibit advertisement of contraceptives, advertisement of prices for routine legal services, or the posting of "For Sale" and "Sold" signs in private yards.[136] Using traditional First Amendment tests, the Court found that the right of the public to the commercial information outweighed any interest the government had in suppressing that information.

Since the 1970s, the Court has recognized a corporate right of free speech, first acknowledged in the political arena, and often entwined with commercial speech. *(See box, Money and Political Speech, p. 74–75.)* Lawyers' advertising has been the backdrop for several rulings. The Court in 1977 held that lawyers could not be stopped from advertising the price of "routine legal services." The Court has also held that the First Amendment was not violated by a state bar's disciplinary action against an attorney who solicited clients in person, for pecuniary gain, under circumstances that posed dangers of fraud, undue influence, and intimidation—all of which was conduct the Court thought the state had a right to prevent.[137] The Court has since ruled that states may regulate advertising by attorneys only to ensure that it is not deceptive or misleading.[138] Modifying the

activities.[2] O'Connor had dissented in the 1991 abortion counseling case. Justice David H. Souter, who supplied the crucial fifth vote in 1991, cast the lone dissent in the arts endowment case, arguing that the "decency" rule seeks to exclude "art that disrespects the ideology, opinions or convictions" of the majority.[3]

Federally subsidized lawyers fared better when they challenged a congressional requirement that they not go to court seeking to strike down welfare reform laws. The Legal Services Corporation, which gets much of its funding from Congress, helps provide lawyers to represent low-income individuals with legal problems, including losses of government benefits. By law, these attorneys handle only civil disputes, not criminal cases. In a further limit, Congress forbids these lawyers from making broad challenges in court to changes in welfare rules. In *Legal Services Corp. v. Velasquez* (2001), the Court, 5-4, struck down this restriction on free speech grounds. Handcuffing lawyers "distorts the legal system," said Justice Anthony M. Kennedy.[4] "We must be vigilant when Congress imposes rules and conditions which in effect insulate its own laws from legitimate judicial challenge."[5] Justices John Paul Stevens, Souter, Ruth Bader Ginsberg, and Stephen G. Breyer joined Kennedy's opinion.

Congress also funds public libraries, and as a condition of receiving the money, lawmakers decided in 2000 that libraries must install software filters on their computers to screen out sexually explicit material to prohibit its access by minors. The American Library Association challenged this requirement on the ground that it forced its members to violate the free speech rights of library patrons. A three-judge panel struck down the law after concluding that the clumsy software filters blocked out too much useful non-pornographic material. In *United States v. American Library Association* (2003), the Court overruled the lower court and upheld the law in a 6-3 decision. "When the Government appropriates public funds to establish a program it is entitled to define the limits of that program," Chief Justice Rehnquist said, citing *Rust v. Sullivan*.[6] "Especially because public libraries have traditionally excluded pornographic material from their other collections, Congress could reasonably impose a parallel limitation on its Internet assistance programs." Concurring, Justices Kennedy and Breyer noted that adult patrons may ask to have the filter disconnected on the computer they intend to use.

---

1. *Rust v. Sullivan*, 500 U.S. 173 at 194 (1991).

2. *National Endowment for the Arts v. Finley*, 524 U.S. 569 at 588 (1998).

3. Id. at 606.

4. *Legal Services Corp. v. Velasquez*, 531 U.S. 533 at 544 (2001).

5. Id. at 548.

6. *United States v. American Library Association*, 539 U.S. (2003).

Court's stance slightly in 1995, a 5-4 majority upheld a Florida regulation prohibiting lawyers from soliciting accident victims by mail for thirty days after an accident.[139] In two other cases, the Court said states may not prohibit lawyers from truthfully advertising themselves as certified public accountants or bar accountants from personally soliciting new clients.[140]

A Question of Government Interests

The prevailing standard for assessing government regulation of commercial speech can be traced to a 1980 case in which the Court reviewed a New York regulation that banned promotional advertising by an electrical utility. According to the Court, whether commercial speech will be protected turns on the nature of the expression as well as the governmental interest served by the regulation. The Court concluded that a state cannot ban all promotional advertising by a utility, even in light of the state's legitimate interest in energy conservation.[141] Justice Lewis F. Powell Jr. wrote in that case involving Central Hudson Gas & Electric Corp.,

In commercial speech cases ... a four-part analysis has developed. At the outset, we must determine whether the expression is protected by the First Amendment. For commercial speech to come within that provision, it at least must concern lawful activity and not be misleading. Next, we ask whether the asserted governmental interest is substantial. If both inquiries yield positive answers, we must determine whether the regulation directly advances the governmental interest asserted, and whether it is not more extensive than is necessary to serve that interest.[142]

The Court in 1980 also held that a state cannot forbid a utility from distributing statements of its views on controversial matters of public policy as inserts in customer bills. Six years later, it also said that the state cannot force a utility to send out inserts carrying messages with which the company does not agree.[143]

Advertising Beer, Cigarettes, and Gambling

In the 1990s, protection for commercial speech grew stronger, as the Court threw out a series of limits on the advertising of legal products that may be harmful. There is no general "vice exception" to the First Amendment, said Justice Stevens in a 1996 decision striking down Rhode Island's ban on the advertising of beer prices.[144] At one time, the Court had believed that the government could strictly regulate the advertising of undesirable products. For instance, in 1986 the justices on a 5-4 vote upheld a Puerto Rican law prohibiting the advertising of gambling on the island. The territory's authorities hoped to draw tourists to the casinos, not native Puerto Ricans.[145] In 1999 the Court would reverse course on such advertising and unanimously strike down a federal law prohibiting radio and television stations from broadcasting ads for casino gambling.[146] The justices ruled that authorities are not entitled to shield the public from accurate information about a lawful product.

A post–Prohibition era federal law had made it illegal for brewers to advertise the alcohol content of their beer, thereby giving rise to a mystery that was the perennial topic of barroom debates. In *Rubin v. Coors Brewing Co.* (1995), the Court struck down the ban, declaring it paternalistic for the government to deny customers the right to know and brewers the right to disclose the alcohol content of their beer. It was an unnecessary and outdated restriction on the freedom of speech.[147] The most far-reaching opinion concerning advertising was the unanimous decision delivered in *44 Liquormart v. Rhode Island* (1996). It resulted in the striking down of laws against advertising beer and liquor prices in ten states. As in *Rubin v. Coors,* the justices said they could not see who benefited from shielding consumers from accurate information. A

Rhode Island retailer challenged a state law after he was fined $400 for having included in a newspaper ad the word "WOW" next to pictures of rum and vodka. This implied he was offering bargain prices, the state board said. "There is no question that Rhode Island's price advertising ban constitutes a blanket prohibition against truthful, non-misleading speech about a lawful product," Justice Stevens wrote.[148] While advertising can be regulated to protect consumers from fraudulent sales pitches, there is no common sense reason for preventing consumers from knowing in advance the retail prices they will pay.

In *FDA v. Brown & Williamson* (2000), the justices on a 5-4 vote had halted the Clinton administration's attempt to regulate tobacco as a dangerous drug.[149] In that decision, the Court said Food and Drug Administration authorities had exceeded their power under the Pure Food and Drug Act when they reclassified cigarettes as drugs. Another tobacco-related case the following year involved Massachusetts and several other states that separately had moved to restrict outdoor ads for tobacco products. Massachusetts attorney general Scott Harshbarger said he wanted to "stop Big Tobacco from recruiting new customers among the children of Massachusetts." He thus imposed a ban on outdoor ads for cigarettes, cigars, and smokeless tobacco within a thousand feet of a school, park, or playground. The big tobacco firms sued, and by the same 5-4 vote as in the *FDA* case, the Court struck down the state's regulations as violating the First Amendment and the federal law governing warning labels on cigarette packs.

In dense cities such as Boston, "these regulations would constitute a nearly complete ban on the communication of truthful information" about tobacco products, said Justice O'Connor, since nearly all the city's land is near a school, park, or playground. "So long as the sale and use of tobacco is lawful for adults, the tobacco industry has a protected interest in communicating information about its products and adult consumers have an interest in receiving that information," she said.[150] The Court's three regular smokers— Chief Justice Rehnquist and Justices Scalia and Thomas—joined her, as did Justice Kennedy.

Freedom of the Press

Much of the significance of free speech would be lost if speech could not be transcribed and circulated freely. Not only is it difficult for individuals to disseminate their views on public matters without help from "the press"—including, in modern times, the broadcast media, cable television, and the Internet—but it is also impossible for individuals otherwise to procure for themselves the reliable information they need to make informed judgments on the conduct of government and other matters of public concern. Indeed, in the Internet Age, where the volume and speed of information dissemination can be overwhelming at times, the press provides people with important cues concerning where to find reputable news and analysis. Thomas Jefferson spelled out the importance of the press's information function in 1787, when he criticized omission of a free press guarantee from the Constitution. Writing from France, where he had been during the Constitutional Convention, Jefferson proffered,

> The people are the only censors of their governors; and even their errors will tend to keep these to the true principles of their institution. To punish these errors too severely would be to suppress the only safeguard of the public liberty. The way to prevent these irregular interpositions of the people is to give them full information of their affairs thru the channel of the public papers, & to contrive that those papers should penetrate the whole mass of the people. The basis of our government being the opinion of the people, the very first object should be to keep that right; and were it left to me to decide whether we should have a government without newspapers or newspapers without a government, I should not hesitate for a moment to prefer the latter.[1]

Nearly two hundred years later, Justice Lewis F. Powell Jr. stated the same case for a free press in the context of modern communications:

> An informed public depends on accurate and effective reporting by the news media. No individual can obtain for himself the information needed for the intelligent discharge of his political responsibilities. For most citizens the prospect of personal familiarity with newsworthy events is hopelessly unrealistic. In seeking out the news the press therefore acts as an agent of the public at large. It is the means by which the people receive that free flow of information and ideas essential to intelligent self-government. By enabling the public to assert meaningful control over the political process, the press performs a crucial function in effecting the societal purpose of the First Amendment.[2]

The "societal purpose" of the First Amendment can be achieved only if publishers are free to determine for themselves what they will print. Although the First Amendment is usually thought of in terms of individual freedoms, the societal value of a free press is what the Supreme Court has stressed in its decisions. At the least, the guarantee of freedom of the press means freedom from prior restraint or censorship by the government before publication. At the most, the guarantee also means that governments may not punish the press for what it publishes. As is true of many other constitutional guarantees, however, only a few justices have advocated this absolute view of free press. Most justices have viewed freedom of the press as subject to certain restrictions. With the rise of methods of "publication" unforeseen by the framers—for instance, via radio, television, and the Internet—the Court's search for the proper balance between a free press and governmental interests has become more complicated.

The Supreme Court has struck down a number of laws as prior restraints on the press. This list includes statutes that forbade continued publication of malicious criticisms of government officials, prohibited circulation of noncommercial handbills, or placed a discriminatory tax on newspapers. In 1971 the Supreme Court rejected a request by the Nixon administration to stop publication of the Pentagon Papers, articles revealing the content of classified government documents about U.S.

involvement in Vietnam.[3] The Court said the government had failed to show sufficient justification for restraining continued publication of the documents, but in that case and in others the Court has strongly implied that prior restraints might be permissible under certain, extreme circumstances. The Court also has upheld the right of government to regulate certain aspects of publishing, including labor and business practices and the manner and place of distribution of circulars and handbills. These regulations may operate from time to time as prior restraints on the press.

The Court has not guarded the press quite so rigorously against punishment after publication as against prior restraint of publication. During World War I, it upheld the convictions of several people for publication of articles the Court found in violation of the Espionage Act of 1917 and the Sedition Act of 1918. (See "Espionage and Sedition," pp. 34–41.) Libel, the printed defamation of an individual, was long thought by the Court to be outside the protection of the First Amendment, but in the 1960s the Court began to reverse this posture, extending to publishers considerable protection against libel suits brought by public officials and public figures. The Court has held that the First Amendment affords the press less protection from libel suits brought by private individuals and little if any when the case does not involve a matter of public concern. A corollary issue is whether the First Amendment protects the press against claims that published articles or broadcast reports have impermissibly interfered with individual privacy. In the few cases it has decided involving this issue, the Court has ruled against the privacy claims unless the claimants could prove that the publisher acted with actual malice or displayed reckless disregard for the truth of the report. The Court still considers "obscene" publications to be outside the protection of the First Amendment and subject to prior restraint as well as subsequent punishment. Child pornography, for instance, is considered obscene and outside the bounds of First Amendment protection. The justices, however, have had great difficulty in defining what else is obscene, and the standard, which has been changed many times, continues to evolve as societal mores change.

In the mid-twentieth century, freedom of the press collided upon occasion with the right to impartial and fair administration of justice. Comprehensive reporting of the workings of the justice system is crucial to its fair administration, but news reports—especially of sensational crimes—may injure a defendant's rights to a fair trial by prejudicing the community against him. Gag rules are one response of trial judges to this situation. With such orders, the trial court judge restricts the information the press may report about the trial in question. In 1976 the Court reviewed such a gag order and found it an unconstitutional prior restraint,[4] but the Court has upheld several contempt citations against reporters who defied court-ordered gag rules. To protect a defendant's right to a fair trial, some judges have excluded the press and the public from pretrial hearings. In 1979 the Supreme Court upheld such an exclusion order, but in 1980 the Court read the First Amendment to guarantee both the press and the public the right to attend trials.[5]

Does the role of the press in a representative government entitle reporters to special access to sources? The Supreme Court has ruled against journalists' arguments that the First Amendment gives them special privileges. Gag rules are just one aspect of this access question. Another aspect—access to prisons to view conditions and interview inmates—has been answered negatively by a majority of the Court. Confidentiality is a more troubling area. Can reporters be required to divulge their anonymous sources to court officials and other law enforcement officers investigating alleged criminal activity? Reporters contend that their relationships with news sources should be privileged as are the relationships between doctor and patient, lawyer and client, and husband and wife. The Court has, however, so far rejected this argument, holding that a reporter has no more constitutional right to withhold information that might help resolve a crime than does an ordinary citizen.[6] In another ruling disappointing to the press, the Court held that the First Amendment does not require police to use subpoenas instead of search warrants when it seeks evidence of a crime from newspaper offices and files.[7] Congress responded to that ruling by passing a law in 1980 imposing the subpoena requirement.

PRIOR RESTRAINT: CENSORSHIP

Professor Thomas I. Emerson had this to say about the effect of censorship on the press:

> A system of prior restraint is in many ways more inhibiting than a system of subsequent punishment: It is likely to bring under government scrutiny a far wider range of expression; it shuts off communication before it takes place; suppression by a stroke of the pen is more likely to be applied than suppression through a criminal process; the procedures do not require attention to the safeguards of the criminal process; the system allows less opportunity for public appraisal and criticism; the dynamics of the system drive toward excesses, as the history of all censorship shows.[8]

It was a history of excesses that impelled the framers to add the free press guarantee to the First Amendment. Prior restraint of the press had been widely practiced—and sharply attacked—in England. Church officials and state authorities there had imposed a licensing system on the press from the development of the printing press in the fifteenth century until 1695, when the licensing laws were repealed. Indirect censorship through heavy taxation also was common. Several of the colonies also attempted to censor the press, but these efforts were unpopular and short-lived. Consequently, when the guarantee of freedom of the press was written, it was widely assumed to mean freedom from prior restraint. In fact, few prior restraints have been imposed on the press throughout U.S. history.

Public Nuisance

It was not until *Near v. Minnesota* (1931) that the Supreme Court reviewed a case of prior restraint of the press. The case concerned a state law that prohibited, as a public nuisance, publication of malicious, scandalous, and defamatory newspapers, magazines, and other publications; the truth of the defamatory allegations could be an acceptable defense only if the allegations were made with good motive and for justifiable ends. In 1927 the county attorney for Hennepin County sought an injunction under this statute. The attorney wanted to halt publication of a weekly periodical

The only known photograph of *Saturday Press* editor Jay Near appeared April 19, 1936, in the *Minneapolis Tribune*. Near's successful appeal to the Supreme Court in 1931 marked the first time the Court enforced the First Amendment's guarantee of freedom of the press to strike a state law that imposed a prior restraint on a newspaper.

charging that county officials were derelict in their duties regarding a Jewish gangster who ran gambling, bootlegging, and racketeering operations in Minneapolis. The articles charged that the police chief was in collusion with the gangster, that a member of the grand jury investigating the rackets was sympathetic to the gangster, and that the county attorney seeking the injunction had failed to take adequate measures to stop the vice operations. The publication, the county argued, was clearly a scandal sheet, and its managers seemed prejudiced against Jews.

A state court issued a temporary injunction forbidding continued publication of the newspaper. At the ensuing trial it was concluded that the paper had, indeed, violated the state statute, and a permanent injunction forbidding further publication was issued. At every opportunity, J. M. Near, the manager of the

THE PRESS AS BUSINESS

When the Court in 1936 struck down certain state taxes on the press as an unconstitutional prior restraint, Justice George Sutherland made clear that the First Amendment does not immunize newspapers from payment of ordinary business taxes.[1] The First Amendment also does not exempt the press from compliance with general laws regulating business and labor relations. "The publisher of a newspaper has no special immunity from the application of general laws," the Court said in 1937, ruling that the National Labor Relations Act applied to the press.[2] It also held that the press must abide by federal minimum wage and maximum hour standards.[3] The Court in addition has ruled that the press is subject to antitrust laws. In *Associated Press v. United States* (1945), Justice Hugo L. Black said that antitrust laws were vital to preservation of a free press:

> The First Amendment, far from providing an argument against application of the Sherman Act, here provides powerful reasons to the contrary. That Amendment rests on the assumption that the widest possible dissemination of information from diverse and antagonistic sources is essential to the welfare of the public, that a free press is a condition of a free society. Surely a command that the government itself shall not impede the free flow of ideas does not afford nongovernment combinations a refuge if they impose restraints upon that constitutionally guaranteed freedom. Freedom to publish means freedom for all and not for some. Freedom to publish is guaranteed ... but freedom to combine to keep others from publishing is not.[4]

1. *Grosjean v. American Press Company,* 297 U.S. 233 (1936).

2. *Associated Press v. National Labor Relations Board,* 301 U.S. 103 at 132 (1937).

3. *Oklahoma Press Publishing Co. v. Walling,* 327 U.S. 186 (1946).

4. *Associated Press v. United States,* 326 U.S. 1 at 20 (1945). See also *Lorain Journal Co. v. United States,* 342 U.S. 143 (1951); *United States v. Radio Corporation of America,* 358 U.S. 334 (1959); *Citizen Publishing Company v. United States,* 394 U.S. 131 (1969); *United States v. Greater Buffalo Press Inc.,* 402 U.S. 549 (1971).

paper, raised the argument that the law as applied to his paper violated his rights under the First and Fourteenth Amendments. When the state supreme court affirmed the order for the permanent injunction, Near appealed to the Supreme Court. By a 5-4 vote the Supreme Court lifted the injunction, holding that the Minnesota statute was an unconstitutional prior restraint on the press in violation of the First and Fourteenth Amendments. Admittedly, the statute did not operate exactly like the old English licensing laws that required editors to submit all articles to government censors for approval prior to publication, wrote Chief Justice Charles Evans Hughes for the majority, but "if we cut through mere details of procedure," he continued,

> the operation and effect of the statute in substance is that public authorities may bring the owner or publisher of a newspaper or periodical before a judge upon a charge of conducting a business of publishing scandalous and defamatory matter—in particular that the matter consists of charges against public officers of official dereliction—and unless the owner or publisher is able and disposed to bring competent evidence to satisfy the judge that the charges are true and are published with good motives and for justifiable ends, his newspaper or periodical is suppressed and further publication is made punishable as a contempt. This is of the essence of censorship.[9]

Acknowledging that freedom of the press from prior restraint was not absolute, Hughes suggested four exceptional situations in which government censorship might be permissible: publication of crucial war information, such as the number and location of troops; obscene publications; publications inciting "acts of violence" against the community or violent overthrow of the government; and publications that invade "private rights." The nature of these exceptions, none of which applied in the pending case, placed "in a strong light the general conception that liberty of the press ... has meant, principally although not exclusively, immunity from prior restraints or censorship," Hughes wrote.[10] The passage of time had not lessened the necessity for that immunity, he continued:

> While reckless assaults upon public men, and efforts to bring obloquy upon those who are endeavoring

faithfully to discharge official duties, exert a baleful influence and deserve the severest condemnation in public opinion, it cannot be said that this abuse is greater, and it is believed to be less, than that which characterized the period in which our institutions took shape. Meanwhile, the administration of government has become more complex, the opportunities for malfeasance and corruption have multiplied, crime has grown to most serious proportions, and the danger of its protection by unfaithful officials and of the impairment of the fundamental security of life and property by criminal alliances and neglect, emphasizes the primary need of a vigilant and courageous press, especially in great cities. The fact that the liberty of the press may be abused by miscreant purveyors of scandal does not make any the less necessary the immunity of the press from previous restraint in dealing with official misconduct. Subsequent punishment for such abuses as may exist is the appropriate remedy, consistent with constitutional privilege.[11]

Hughes said the Minnesota statute could not be justified on the grounds that a publisher might avoid its penalties by showing that the defamatory material was true and printed with good motives and for justifiable ends. This would place the legislature in the position of deciding what were good motives and justifiable ends and thus "be but a step to a complete system of censorship."[12] In addition, the statute could not be justified because it was intended to prevent scandals that might disturb the public peace and even provoke assaults and the commission of other crimes. "Charges of reprehensible conduct, and in particular of official malfeasance, unquestionably create a public scandal," Hughes wrote, "but the theory of the constitutional guaranty is that even a more serious public evil would be caused by authority to prevent publication."[13]

The four dissenters, in an opinion written by Justice Pierce Butler, contended that the Minnesota law did not "operate as a *previous* restraint ... within the proper meaning of that phrase." The restraint occurred only after publication of articles adjudged to constitute a public nuisance and served only to prohibit further illegal publications of the same kind. "There is nothing in the statute purporting to prohibit publications that have not been adjudged to constitute a nuisance,"

Butler said.[14] Furthermore, the dissenters thought the threat of subsequent punishment inadequate to protect against this sort of evil. Libel laws are ineffective against false and malicious assaults printed by "insolvent publishers who may have purpose and sufficient capacity to contrive to put into effect a scheme ... for oppression, blackmail or extortion."[15]

Sixty years later, the Court invoked *Near* when it struck down a New York law that denied criminals the right to proceeds from any book or article written about their crimes; the law instead required that such profits be directed to a victims' fund. In the case of *Simon & Schuster Inc. v. Members of New York State Crime Victims Board* (1991), the Court held that this "Son-of-Sam" law was too broad in its sweep and thereby violated the First Amendment. Justice Sandra Day O'Connor explained in her opinion that the so-called Son-of-Sam laws are named for a 1970s serial killer in New York, David Berkowitz, who was known popularly as Son of Sam and whose story was worth a substantial amount of money to publishers. Justice Anthony M. Kennedy summarized the Court's view in his concurring opinion: "Here a law is directed to speech alone where the speech in question is not obscene, not defamatory, not words tantamount to an act otherwise criminal, not an impairment of some other constitutional right, not an incitement to lawless action, and not calculated or likely to bring about imminent harm the State has the substantive power to prevent. No further inquiry is necessary to reject the State's argument that the statute should be upheld."[16]

Restrictive Taxation

The Supreme Court prohibited the use of a more traditional kind of prior restraint in *Grosjean v. American Press Co.* (1936). The Louisiana legislature, under the direction of Governor Huey Long, placed a state tax of 2 percent on the gross receipts of newspapers that sold advertisements and had circulation in excess of twenty thousand per week. The tax was promoted as a tax on the privilege of doing business, but it had been calculated to affect only nine big city newspapers opposed to the Long regime. The papers immediately sought an injunction in federal district court to stop enforcement of the law on the grounds that the tax violated freedom of the press, and

Vending Rights

The First Amendment protects the right of newspaper publishers to sell their papers on sidewalk racks, even though the sidewalks are public property, the Court held in *Lakewood v. Plain Dealer Publishing Co.* (1988).[1] By the narrowest of margins, 4-3, the Court struck down an ordinance enacted by the town of Lakewood, Ohio, which gave the mayor almost total discretion to grant or deny vending rack permits to the *Cleveland Plain Dealer.*

Lakewood and other cities may regulate or license newspaper racks, said Justice William J. Brennan Jr. in the opinion announcing the decision, but they must do so by using neutral criteria to ensure that the decision to grant a license is not based on the content or the point-of-view of the newspaper seeking a license. Lakewood's procedure left so much discretion to the mayor that it raised a "real and substantial threat of … censorship," Brennan asserted. "It is not difficult to visualize a newspaper … feeling significant pressure to endorse the incumbent mayor, … or to refrain from criticizing him, in order to receive a favorable and speedy disposition" of its application for a permit to sell papers in sidewalk boxes.

Justices Byron R. White, John Paul Stevens, and Sandra Day O'Connor dissented. Neither Chief Justice William H. Rehnquist nor Justice Anthony M. Kennedy participated.

In 1993 the Court struck down a Cincinnati ordinance prohibiting news racks on public property from being used to distribute commercial handbills; the ordinance, however, permitted newspapers to be sold from sidewalk vending machines. Writing for a six-justice majority, Justice Stevens said the city had failed to show a "reasonable fit" between the ordinance and its interest in "the safety and attractive appearance of its streets and sidewalks."[2] The dissenting justices, Rehnquist, White, and Clarence Thomas, argued that the city's selective ban on commercial news racks was permitted by the lower degree of constitutional protection for commercial speech. *(See "Commercial Speech," pp. 77–82.)*

---

1. *Lakewood v. Plain Dealer Publishing Co.,* 486 U.S. 750 (1988).

2. *City of Cincinnati v. Discovery Network,* 507 U.S. 410 (1993).

because smaller newspapers were exempt, denied them equal protection. The federal district court issued the injunction, and a unanimous Supreme Court affirmed that decision solely on First Amendment grounds.

The tax "operates as a restraint in a double sense," wrote Justice George Sutherland. "First, its effect is to curtail the amount of revenue realized from advertising, and, second, its direct tendency is to restrict circulation."[17] Sutherland then reviewed the history of restrictive taxation of the press. The British Parliament had frequently imposed "taxes on knowledge" to suppress criticism of the government. Despite strong opposition, these stamp taxes persisted until 1855. Massachusetts in 1785 and 1786 imposed a stamp tax and an advertising tax on newspapers and magazines, but hostility to the taxes was so strong that they were quickly repealed. Given this background, Sutherland said, the framers of the First Amendment must have meant to prohibit the imposition of such taxes. He continued:

> The predominant purpose of the grant of immunity here invoked was to preserve an untrammeled press as a vital source of public information. The newspapers, magazines and other journals of the country, it is safe to say, have shed and continue to shed, more light on the public and business affairs of the nation than any other instrumentality of publicity; and since informed public opinion is the most potent of all restraints upon misgovernment, the suppression or abridgement of the publicity afforded by a free press cannot be regarded otherwise than with grave concern. The tax here involved is bad … because, in the light of its history and of its present setting, it is seen to be a deliberate and calculated device in the guise of a tax to limit the circulation of information to which the public is entitled in virtue of the constitutional guaranties: A free press stands as one of the great interpreters between the government and the people. To allow it to be fettered is to fetter ourselves.[18]

Handbills

The Supreme Court has always considered handbills, leaflets, circulars, and other types of flyers containing an individual or group opinion on public issues to be a

THE COMMAND TO PUBLISH

Freedom of the press means that government may not stop the press from printing nor command it to print. The Supreme Court has found only one exception to the rule that government may not dictate the form or content of what the press prints: gender-based advertisements for help.

THE "HELP-WANTED" CASE

In the early 1970s, the Court upheld a government order to a newspaper forbidding it to organize help-wanted advertisements under columns labeled "Jobs—Male Interest" and "Jobs—Female Interest" in violation of an ordinance that prohibited discrimination by sex in employment. The Court reached that decision in *Pittsburgh Press Co. v. Pittsburgh Commission on Human Relations* (1973) by a 5-4 vote. The majority explained that the ads were commercial speech unprotected by the First Amendment and that the column heads added by the newspaper were indistinguishable from that speech. *(See "Commercial Speech," pp. 77–82.)* Even if commercial speech merited First Amendment protection, the majority said, illegal commercial speech did not:

> The advertisements, as embroidered by their placement, signaled that the advertisers were likely to show an illegal sex preference in their hiring decisions. Any First Amendment interest which might be served by advertising an ordinary commercial proposal and which might arguably outweigh the governmental interest supporting the regulation is altogether absent when the commercial activity itself is illegal and the restriction on advertising is incidental to a valid limitation on economic activity.[1]

THE RIGHT OF REPLY

In a later decision, the Court emphasized the narrowness of the *Pittsburgh Press* ruling when it struck down a Florida statute that required newspapers to grant political candidates equal space to reply to the paper's criticism of their public records. Writing for a unanimous Court in *Miami Herald Publishing Co. v. Tornillo* (1974), Chief Justice Warren E. Burger carefully reviewed the arguments in favor of the law, while acknowledging that the diminishing number of newspapers and the concentration of media ownership meant that frequently only one view of an issue was published:

> Chains of newspapers, national newspapers, national wire and news services, and one-newspaper towns are the dominant features of a press that has become noncompetitive and enormously powerful and influential in its capacity to manipulate popular opinion and change the course of events.[2]

Nonetheless, a governmental command to print specific information collides with the freedom of the press guaranteed by the First Amendment, he said, and under the decisions of the Court

> any such compulsion to publish that which "'reason' tells them should not be published" is unconstitutional. A responsible press is an undoubtedly desirable goal, but press responsibility is not mandated by the Constitution and like many other virtues it cannot be legislated.[3]

In conclusion, Burger wrote,

> A newspaper is more than a passive receptacle or conduit for news, comment and advertising. The choice of material to go into a newspaper, and the decisions made as to limitations on the size and content of the paper, and treatment of public issues and public officials—whether fair or unfair—constitute the exercise of editorial control and judgment. It has yet to be demonstrated how governmental regulation of this crucial process can be exercised consistent with First Amendment guarantees of a free press as they have evolved to this time.[4]

---

1. *Pittsburgh Press Co. v. Pittsburgh Commission on Human Relations,* 413 U.S. 376 at 389 (1973).

2. *Miami Herald Publishing Co. v. Tornillo,* 418 U.S. 241 at 249 (1974).

3. Id. at 256.

4. Id. at 258.

---

part of the press entitled to First Amendment protection. Chief Justice Hughes voiced this principle in 1938:

> The liberty of the press is not confined to newspapers and periodicals. It necessarily embraces pamphlets and leaflets. These indeed have been historic weapons in the defense of liberty, as the pamphlets of Thomas Paine and others in our own history abundantly attest. The press in its historic connotation comprehends every sort of publication which affords a vehicle of information and opinion.[19]

The Court has consequently been unsympathetic to efforts of municipalities to restrict distribution of handbills on public property. The arguments that some restriction is necessary to protect the public from fraud or to keep the streets clean have not been considered sufficient to justify the resulting infringement on the

Obscenity: An Elusive Definition and a Changing Standard

The Supreme Court has never considered obscenity to be protected by the First Amendment. Obscenity is one category of expression that is unprotected because it is "no essential part of any exposition of ideas, and of ... slight social value as a step to truth."[1] To place obscenity outside the protection of the First Amendment, however, does not end the matter. It only shifts the focus of judicial effort to the problem of defining what is obscene. The problem has proved frustrating.

The only criterion the Court has consistently agreed upon is that to be obscene, material must deal with sex. Blasphemous or sacrilegious expression is not considered obscene, nor, generally, are scatological profanities. Violence has been found obscene only when linked with sex. As Justice John Marshall Harlan explained when the Court ruled that the phrase "Fuck the Draft" on a jacket worn in a courtroom was not obscene, "Whatever else may be necessary to give rise to the States' broader power to prohibit obscene expression, such expression must be, in some significant way, erotic."[2]

Most state laws restricting the dissemination of obscene materials date back to the Victorian era. The earliest standard for obscenity, stated by a British court in *Regina v. Hicklin* (1868), was "whether the tendency of the matter charged as obscenity is to deprave and corrupt those whose minds are open to such immoral influences and into whose hands a publication of this sort may fall."[3] As Thomas I. Emerson observed, the *Hicklin* test "brought within the ban of the obscenity statutes any publication containing isolated passages that the courts felt would tend to exert an immoral influence on susceptible persons."[4] By the 1930s that standard was being rejected as too rigid. In 1934 appeals court judge Augustus Hand proposed a new standard:

> While any construction of the statute that will fit all cases is difficult, we believe that the proper test of whether a given book is obscene is in its dominant effect. In applying this test, relevancy of the objectionable parts to the theme, the established reputation of the work in the estimation of approved critics, if the book is modern, and the verdict of the past, if it is ancient, are persuasive pieces of evidence; for works of art are not likely to sustain a high position with no better warrant for their existence than their obscene content.[5]

THE *ROTH* STANDARD

The Supreme Court did not express any opinion on a definition of obscenity until the 1950s, when, in one ruling, it considered a federal and a state obscenity law. *Roth v. United States* (1957) concerned a federal statute making it a crime to mail materials that were "obscene, lewd, lascivious or filthy." *Alberts v. California* (1957) concerned a state law making it illegal to publish, sell, distribute, or advertise any "obscene or indecent" material. The majority relied heavily on Judge Hand's test in establishing what became known as the "*Roth* standard." Obscene matter, declared the Court, has no First Amendment protection. Justice William J. Brennan Jr. wrote:

All ideas having even the slightest redeeming social importance—unorthodox ideas, controversial ideas, even ideas hateful to the prevailing climate of opinion—have the full protection of the guaranties, unless excludable because they encroach upon the limited area of more important interests. But implicit in the history of the First Amendment is the rejection of obscenity as utterly without redeeming social importance.[6]

Brennan then proposed a definition of obscenity:

> [S]ex and obscenity are not synonymous. Obscene material is material which deals with sex in a manner appealing to prurient interest. The portrayal of sex, e.g., in art, literature, and scientific works is not itself sufficient reason to deny material the constitutional protection of freedom of speech and press.... It is therefore vital that the standards for judging obscenity safeguard the protection of freedom of speech and press for material which does not treat sex in a manner appealing to prurient interest.[7]

The standard for making this determination, Brennan said, was "whether to the average person, applying contemporary standards, the dominant theme of the material taken as a whole appeals to the prurient interest."[8] Finding that the trial courts in *Roth* and *Albert* had applied this standard to hold the material in question obscene, the majority upheld convictions under both the federal and state laws.

After *Roth* the Court grew increasingly fragmented on what makes material obscene. In *Manual Enterprises v. Day* (1962), Justice Harlan held that to be obscene, material must not only appeal to prurient interest but also be patently offensive. That is, he wrote, obscene materials are those "so offensive on their face as to affront current community standards of decency."[9] Because the case involved a federal obscenity statute, Harlan thought the community and the standards of decency should be national in scope. Two years later, in *Jacobellis v. Ohio* (1964), Justice Brennan added the requirement that the materials in question must be found "utterly without redeeming social importance."[10] Justice Stewart added in a concurrence in *Jacobellis* that while obscenity is hard to define, "I know it when I see it."[11]

The height of confusion over a definition of obscenity was reached one day in 1966, when the Court, deciding three cases, issued fourteen separate opinions. In one case the Court ruled that the book *Fanny Hill* was not obscene. The threefold test to be applied was that the dominant theme of the book must appeal to prurient interest, that the book must be found patently offensive when judged by contemporary community standards, and that it must be found utterly without redeeming social value. Because the trial court had found that the book might have "some minimal literary value," it was not obscene.[12] In a second case the Court came up with the "pandering" test: material that might not be obscene on its own merits might become so if it was placed "against a background of commercial exploitation of erotica solely for the sake of their prurient appeal."[13]

The Court then retreated, indicating in a per curiam opinion in *Redrup v. New York* (1967) that it would sustain obscenity convictions only to protect juveniles or unwilling adults from exposure to obscene materials or in cases of pandering.[14]

THE *MILLER* STANDARD

In the early 1970s, for the first time since the 1957 *Roth* decision, a slim majority of the Court endorsed a standard for determining what was obscene. This new standard gave governments at all levels much more latitude to ban obscene materials than did the *Roth* test. Writing for the five-justice majority in *Miller v. California* (1973), Chief Justice Warren E. Burger held that states could regulate

> works which depict or describe sexual conduct. That conduct must be specifically defined by the applicable state law, as written or authoritatively construed. A state offense must also be limited to works which, taken as a whole, appeal to the prurient interest in sex, which portray sexual conduct in a patently offensive way, and which, taken as a whole, do not have serious literary, artistic, political or scientific value.[15]

Under this standard, Burger said, the majority intended to exclude only hard-core materials from First Amendment protection. As a guideline, he suggested that such materials were those that included "patently offensive representations or descriptions of ultimate sexual acts, normal or perverted, actual or simulated" and "patently offensive representations or descriptions of masturbation, excretory functions, and lewd exhibition of the genitals."[16]

The majority specifically rejected the *Jacobellis* test that to be obscene, materials must be "utterly without redeeming social value." It also rejected the idea that the community standard must be national in scope. "It is neither realistic nor constitutionally sound to read the First Amendment as requiring that the people of Maine or Mississippi accept public depiction of conduct found tolerable in Las Vegas or New York City," Burger wrote.[17]

The majority stressed that First Amendment values would be adequately protected by this standard. Burger noted that appellate courts had the authority to "conduct an independent review of constitutional claims when necessary."[18] The Court did just that when it overturned a Georgia jury's finding that the movie *Carnal Knowledge* was obscene. Holding that local juries did not have "unbridled discretion" to determine what is patently offensive, the Court in *Jenkins v. Georgia* (1974) found nothing in the movie that fit its *Miller* standards for what might constitute hard-core obscenity.[19] The Court subsequently upheld state laws prohibiting the promotion of sexual performances by children but struck down a state law banning material just because it incited lust. That covered material that did no more than "arouse 'good, old-fashioned, healthy' interest in sex."[20]

In 1982 the Court held that the First Amendment limited the power of public school officials to take books off the library shelves because some parents found the contents objectionable.[21] Four years later the Court held that the First Amendment was not abridged when school officials suspended a student for a lewd speech at a school assembly. "It is a highly appropriate function of public school education to prohibit the use of vulgar and offensive terms in public discourse," the Court declared.[22]

In *Pope v. Illinois* (1987), the Court revisited the *Miller* test for "literary, artistic, political, or scientific value." The justices declared that local community standards should not be used in deciding whether an allegedly obscene book or film has any such value. Instead, an objective, national standard should be used, with the overriding question being whether a reasonable person would find value in the material, taken as a whole.[23]

In recent decades, prosecutions for obscenity have all but disappeared, even as hard-core material has become abundant on the Internet. The Court, perhaps welcoming the respite, has chosen not to revisit the issue.

---

1. *Chaplinsky v. New Hampshire,* 315 U.S. 568 at 572 (1942).

2. *Cohen v. California,* 403 U.S. 15 at 20 (1971).

3. *Regina v. Hicklin,* L.R. 3 Q.B. 360 at 371 (1868), quoted in Thomas I. Emerson, *The System of Freedom of Expression* (New York: Random House, Vintage Books, 1970), 469.

4. Emerson, *System,* 469.

5. *United States v. One Book Entitled "Ulysses,"* 72 F. 2d. 705 at 708 (2d Cir. 1934).

6. *Roth v. United States, Alberts v. California,* 354 U.S. 476 at 484 (1957).

7. Id. at 487–488.

8. Id. at 489.

9. *Manual Enterprises v. Day,* 370 U.S. 478 at 482 (1962).

10. *Jacobellis v. Ohio,* 378 U.S. 184 at 191 (1964).

11. Id. at 197.

12. *A Book Named "John Cleland's Memoirs of a Woman of Pleasure" [Fanny Hill] v. Attorney General of Massachusetts,* 383 U.S. 413 at 419 (1966).

13. *Ginzburg v. United States,* 383 U.S. 463 at 466 (1966); the third case was *Mishkin v. New York,* 383 U.S. 502 (1966).

14. *Redrup v. New York,* 386 U.S. 767 (1967).

15. *Miller v. California,* 413 U.S. 15 at 24 (1973).

16. Id. at 25.

17. Id. at 32.

18. Id. at 25.

19. *Jenkins v. Georgia,* 418 U.S. 153 (1974).

20. *New York v. Ferber,* 458 U.S. 747 (1982); *Brockett v. Spokane Arcades, Eikenberry v. JR Distributors,* 472 U.S. 491 (1985).

21. *Board of Education, Island Trees Union Free School District #26 v. Pico,* 457 U.S. 853 (1982).

22. *Bethel School District No. 403 v. Fraser,* 478 U.S. 675 (1986).

23. *Pope v. Illinois,* 481 U.S. 497 (1987).

PRIOR RESTRAINT OF OBSCENITY

In *Near v. Minnesota* (1931), the Supreme Court indicated that obscenity was one form of expression that might be subject to prior restraint. Twenty-six years later, a majority of five justices upheld, against a challenge of unconstitutional prior restraint, a New York statute that allowed public officials to seek injunctions against the sale of obscene publications.

Contrary to the discussion in *Near*, the majority indicated that the First Amendment might protect even obscene publications from licensing or censorship before publication. The challenged statute, however, was not such a prior restraint. Instead, the majority said, it "studiously withholds restraint upon matters not already published and not yet found to be offensive." As such it was a valid means "for the seizure and destruction of the instruments of ascertained wrongdoing."[1]

In another 5–4 decision, the Court upheld a Chicago ordinance that prohibited public showings of movies found to be obscene. In *Times Film Corp. v. City of Chicago* (1961), the majority held that the doctrine of prior restraint was not absolute and that the censorship procedure was a valid means for controlling the dissemination of obscene movies. In dissent, Chief Justice Earl Warren said the majority decision "gives formal sanction to censorship in its purest and most far-reaching form."[2]

In 1965 the Court limited the impact of this decision by prescribing strict rules authorities must follow when censoring films. The burden of proving the film obscene falls on the censor, who must license it quickly or seek a restraining order in court. Furthermore, the process must "assure a prompt final judicial decision." The Court has been consistent in enforcing these procedural safeguards.[3]

---

1. *Kingsley Books v. Brown*, 354 U.S. 436 at 445, 444 (1957).

2. *Times Film Corp. v. City of Chicago*, 365 U.S. 43 at 55 (1961).

3. *Freedman v. Maryland*, 380 U.S. 51 at 59 (1965); see also *Southeastern Promotions, Ltd. v. Conrad*, 420 U.S. 546 (1975); *Roaden v. Kentucky*, 413 U.S. 496 (1973).

---

freedoms of speech and press. The Court has only limited distribution of noncommercial handbills when distribution has occurred on private property dedicated to specific public purposes. *(See box, Public Speech on Private Property, pp. 70–71.)*

The Lovell Case

The first test of a city ordinance controlling distribution of handbills came in *Lovell v. Griffin* (1938). Alma Lovell, a Jehovah's Witness, distributed religious tracts in Griffin, Georgia, in violation of an ordinance that prohibited circulation of literature without written permission. The Court struck down the ordinance as a prior restraint on the press. Wrote Chief Justice Hughes,

> The ordinance prohibits the distribution of literature of any kind at any time, at any place, and in any manner without a permit from the City Manager.... Whatever the motive which induced its adoption, its character is such that it strikes at the very foundation of the freedom of the press by subjecting it to license and censorship.[20]

The Handbill Cases

In cases considered together in the 1930s, the Court struck down four ordinances seeking to regulate handbill circulation. The first of these cases, *Schneider v. Irvington* (1939), again involved a Jehovah's Witness, who was convicted of canvassing and distributing religious tracts without the required permit. The Court held that, as in *Lovell*, the ordinance left too much to official discretion. In the other three cases, the Court held unconstitutional ordinances that prohibited all distribution of handbills on public streets.[21] In *Schneider*, Justice Owen J. Roberts attempted to explain how a city might properly regulate circulation of handbills:

> Municipal authorities, as trustees for the public, have the duty to keep their communities' streets open and available for movement of people and property, the primary purpose to which the streets are dedicated. So long as legislation to this end does not abridge the constitutional liberty of one rightfully upon the street to impart information through speech or the distribution of literature, it may lawfully regulate the conduct of those using the streets. For example,

a person could not exercise this liberty by taking his stand in the middle of a crowded street, contrary to traffic regulations, and maintain his position to the stoppage of all traffic; a group of distributors could not insist upon a constitutional right to form a cordon across the street and to allow no pedestrian to pass who did not accept a tendered leaflet; nor does the guarantee of freedom of speech or of the press deprive a municipality of power to enact regulations against throwing literature broadcast in the streets. Prohibition of such conduct would not abridge the constitutional liberty since such activity bears no necessary relationship to the freedom to speak, write, print or distribute information or opinion.[22]

The desire to prevent litter was not a sufficient reason to limit circulation of handbills, the Court held. Cities could prevent litter by other methods. Responding to the argument that cities should be permitted to prohibit the dissemination of handbills in public streets so long as other public places were available for distribution, Roberts wrote that "one is not to have the exercise of his liberty of expression in appropriate places abridged on the plea that it may be exercised in some other place."[23]

Anonymous Handbills

Twenty-one years after *Schneider,* the Supreme Court struck down a Los Angeles ordinance that required all handbills to include the name and address of the person preparing, sponsoring, or distributing them. "There can be no doubt that such an identification requirement would tend to restrict freedom to distribute information and thereby freedom of expression," wrote Justice Hugo L. Black in *Talley v. California* (1960).[24] Throughout history, he observed, persecuted groups and sects have had to resort to anonymous criticism of oppressive practices to avoid further persecutions. Three justices dissented, maintaining that the Court should weigh the state's interest in preventing fraud against the individual's claimed rights.

In another decision on the side of pamphleteers, *McIntyre v. Ohio Elections Commission* (1995), the Court invalidated an Ohio prohibition on anonymous campaign literature. The Court said that part of an individual's freedom of speech is the freedom to remain anonymous. The vote was 7-2, and Justice John Paul Stevens, writing for the majority, praised the U.S. tradition of pamphleteering: "Under our Constitution, anonymous pamphleteering is not a pernicious, fraudulent practice, but an honorable tradition of advocacy and of dissent. Anonymity is a shield from the tyranny of the majority."[25]

Injunctions

In *Organization for a Better Austin v. Keefe* (1971), the Supreme Court ruled that a temporary injunction against the publication of certain handbills was an unconstitutional abridgment of the freedoms of speech and press. An organization that sought to maintain the racial composition of its neighborhood grew upset with the tactics real estate agent Jerome Keefe used to induce whites to sell their homes to blacks. After Keefe denied the allegations and refused to cooperate with the association, it began to circulate handbills in Keefe's neighborhood describing what it considered to be his unsavory real estate activities. Keefe then sought and was granted the injunction. The Supreme Court held that "the injunction, so far as it imposes prior restraint on speech and publication, constitutes an impermissible restraint on First Amendment rights." The aim of the organization in circulating the handbills—namely, to coerce Keefe into cooperation with it—was "not fundamentally different from the function of a newspaper," the majority said. In addition, the injunction could not be justified as protecting Keefe's privacy. Keefe was "not attempting to stop the flow of information into his own household, but to the public."[26]

Election-Day Editorials

The basic need to protect free discussion of government lay at the heart of the Court's 1966 decision to strike down an Alabama statute that made it a crime to solicit votes on election day. A newspaper editor who printed an editorial on election day urging his readers to vote a certain way on a ballot proposition was convicted under this law. A statute setting criminal penalties "for publishing editorials such as the one here silences the press at a time when it can be most effective," wrote Justice Black for the majority in *Mills v. Alabama* (1966). "It is difficult to conceive of a more obvious and flagrant abridgment of the constitutionally guaranteed freedom of the press."[27]

The Pentagon Papers

Publication in June 1971 of articles based upon a classified history of U.S. involvement in Vietnam precipitated an unprecedented confrontation between the U.S. government and the press. The forty-seven-volume, seven-thousand-page history, which soon became known as the Pentagon Papers, covered the Truman, Eisenhower, Kennedy, and Johnson administrations. It indicated that the U.S. government was more involved in the Vietnamese civil war at almost every stage than U.S. officials had ever publicly admitted. Copies of the Pentagon Papers were made available to the press by Daniel Ellsberg, an analyst who had helped prepare the history and then had become an antiwar activist. The *New York Times* was the first newspaper to publish articles based on the papers; the first installment appeared in its June 13, 1971, edition. The following day, after the second installment appeared, the Justice Department asked the *Times* to return the documents and to halt publication of the series. The articles, they said, would cause "irreparable injury to the defense interests of the U.S." The *Times* refused to comply.

On June 15, U.S. district court judge Murray I. Gurfein granted the temporary restraining order requested by the Justice Department against the *Times*. He put the order in effect until he could hold hearings on the government's request for a permanent injunction. After the hearings, Gurfein ruled June 19 that the government was not entitled to a permanent injunction against publication by the *Times* of further articles. Judge Irving R. Kaufman of the U.S. Court of Appeals, however, immediately granted a restraining order against the *Times*, at the Justice Department's request, to permit the government to appeal Judge Gurfein's decision. The appeals court on June 23 returned the case to the lower court for further (closed) hearings, and it extended until June 25 a restraining order against the *Times*. The *Times* on June 24 petitioned the Supreme Court to review the order by the court of appeals.

The government also sought to restrain the *Washington Post,* which had published its first Pentagon Papers article on June 18, from further publications. The *Post* case arrived at the Supreme Court through an involved succession of hearings and temporary restraining orders similar to those in the *Times* case. The district court and the court of appeals in Washington, however, refused the Justice Department's request for a permanent injunction against the *Post*. The government appealed on June 24.

The Court heard arguments in the *Pentagon Papers Case* (1971) on June 26 and announced its decision four days later. By a 6-3 vote, the Court on June 30 ruled that the government had failed to meet "the heavy burden of showing justification" for restraining further publications of the Pentagon Papers.[28] Each of the nine justices wrote a separate opinion. Taken together, these opinions covered the wide range of sentiment that exists when a First Amendment right must be weighed against national security claims. In separate concurring opinions, Justices Black and William O. Douglas maintained that freedom of the press was absolute and could not be abridged by the government under any circumstances. "[E]very moment's continuance of the injunctions against these newspapers amounts to a flagrant, indefensible, and continuing violation of the First Amendment," Black asserted in the last opinion he wrote before his retirement. "Both the history and language of the First Amendment support the view that the press must be left free to publish news, whatever the source, without censorship, injunctions or prior restraints."[29] Douglas wrote, "The First Amendment provides that 'Congress shall make no law … abridging the freedom of speech or of the press.' That leaves, in my view, no room for governmental restraint on the press."[30]

Justice William J. Brennan Jr. thought the government might properly restrain the press in certain clear emergencies, but the circumstances of this case did not present such an emergency, according to him, so there should have been no injunctive restraint. The government sought the injunction on the grounds that the publication "could," "might," or "may" damage national security, Brennan said, "But the First Amendment

Daniel Ellsberg, a former Defense Department analyst, speaks in 1971 before a House panel investigating the significance of the Pentagon Papers, classified documents that he leaked to the press detailing U.S. military involvement in Vietnam. In the *Pentagon Papers Case* (1971) the Court ruled that the government could not restrain the *New York Times* and the *Washington Post* from publishing the documents.

tolerates absolutely no prior judicial restraints of the press predicated upon surmise or conjecture that untoward consequences may result."[31] Justices Potter Stewart and Byron R. White both also thought that prior restraints might be permissible under certain conditions and that disclosure of some of the information in the Pentagon Papers might be harmful to national interests. "But I cannot say that disclosure of any of [the papers] will surely result in direct, immediate, and irreparable damage to our Nation or its people," concluded Stewart. "That being so, there can under the First Amendment be but one judicial resolution of the issues before us."[32] White said he concurred with the majority "only because of the concededly extraordinary protection against prior restraints enjoyed by the press under our constitutional system."

The government's position, White said, is that the necessity to preserve national security is so great that the president is entitled

> to an injunction against publication of a newspaper story whenever he can convince a court that the information to be revealed threatens "grave and irreparable" injury to the public interest; and the injunction should issue whether or not … publication would be lawful … and regardless of the circumstances by which the newspaper came into possession of the information.

> At least in the absence of legislation by Congress … I am quite unable to agree that the inherent powers of the Executive and the courts reach so far as to authorize remedies having such a sweeping potential for inhibiting publications by the press.[33]

The critical factor for Justice Thurgood Marshall was that Congress had twice refused to give the president authority to prohibit publications disclosing matters of national security or to make such disclosures criminal. It would be a violation of the doctrine of separation of powers, Marshall said,

> for this Court to use its power of contempt to prevent behavior that Congress has specifically declined to prohibit.... The Constitution provides that Congress shall make laws, the President execute laws, and courts interpret law.... It did not provide for government by injunction in which the courts and the Executive can "make law" without regard to the action of Congress.[34]

Chief Justice Warren E. Burger and Justices John Marshall Harlan and Harry A. Blackmun dissented. All three lamented the haste with which the cases had been decided. Holding that the press did not enjoy absolute protection from prior restraint, Burger said that the exception that might permit restraint "may be lurking in these cases and would have been flushed had they been properly considered in the trial courts, free from unwarranted deadlines and frenetic pressures."[35] Burger also thought the newspapers had been derelict in their duty to report the discovery of stolen property or secret government documents. That duty "rests on taxi drivers, Justices and the *New York Times*," he said.[36]

Justice Harlan listed a number of questions that he said should and would have been considered if the cases had been deliberated more fully. On the merits of the cases, the judiciary should not "redetermine for itself the probable impact of disclosure on the national security."[37] Therefore, Harlan would have sent the cases back to the lower courts for further proceedings, during which time he would have permitted the temporary restraining orders to remain in effect. Harlan said he could "not believe that the doctrine prohibiting prior restraints reaches to the point of preventing courts from maintaining the *status quo* long enough to act responsibly in matters of such national importance."[38]

Justice Blackmun wrote in his dissent,

> The First Amendment, after all, is only one part of the entire Constitution. Article II ... vests in the Executive Branch primary power over the conduct of foreign affairs.... Each provision of the Constitution is important and I cannot subscribe to a doctrine of unlimited absolutism for the First Amendment at the cost of downgrading other provisions.... What is needed here is a weighing, upon properly developed standards, of the broad right of the press to print and of the very narrow right of the government to prevent.[39]

The three dissenters and Stewart and White from the majority indicated that they believed the newspapers might be subject to criminal penalties for publishing classified government documents, but the question never arose. The government's prosecution of Ellsberg for espionage, theft, and conspiracy for leaking the papers was dismissed because of government misconduct. (Four members of a secret White House investigative team burglarized the office of Ellsberg's psychiatrist in an effort to find Ellsberg's records, presumably to use against him in the *Pentagon Papers Case*.) The government brought no further prosecutions.

SUBSEQUENT PUNISHMENT: LIBEL

Libel occurs when something printed or broadcast defames the character or reputation of an individual. The effort to punish publishers for printing defamatory statements can be traced back to England, where state and church authorities suppressed criticism of their policies, calling it sedition. It is not certain whether the First Amendment guarantee of a free press was intended to prohibit Congress from enacting similar seditious libel laws. Whatever the case, the Federalist-dominated Congress enacted a libel law in 1789, but it proved extremely unpopular and was allowed to expire. Although the validity of the law was never tested, later justices assumed it was unconstitutional.[40]

In any event, Congress has never again enacted a law making general criticism of government officials and their conduct unlawful. It is now well accepted that criticism of government policies and officials is protected by the First Amendment, although specific types of criticism may be punishable. The Sedition Act of 1918, for example, set penalties for interfering with the war effort, and the Smith Act of 1940 punished those

FREEDOM TO CIRCULATE

"Liberty of circulating is as essential to that freedom [of the press] as liberty of publishing; indeed, without the circulation, the publication would be of little value," the Supreme Court said as early as 1878.[1] In that case and others, however, the Court nonetheless upheld the right of Congress to prohibit the use of the mails to circulate materials considered injurious to public morals.

Circulation through the mails of publications espousing unpopular political opinions and doctrines also has been restricted. During the World Wars I and II, the government permitted the postmaster general to withdraw second-class mailing privileges from publications that violated the espionage laws. In 1921 the Court upheld this delegation of authority when it sustained the postmaster general's withdrawal of second-class mail rates from the Socialist *Milwaukee Leader* without directly addressing the First Amendment questions implied in the case.[2]

The Court, however, appeared more willing to protect publications that clearly posed no threat to national security. In 1946 it ruled that the postmaster general had exceeded his authority when he withdrew second-class mail privileges from *Esquire* because he determined the magazine's contents fell outside the matter eligible for the special mailing rates. The Court said that Congress had authorized the postmaster general to decide only whether publications contained "information of a public character, literature or art" and not "whether the contents meet some standard of the public good or welfare."[3] The Court also extended some protection to dissident publications in 1965, when it struck down a 1962 federal statute permitting the postmaster general to deliver "Communist political propaganda" only at the recipient's specific request.[4]

Because obscenity has no First Amendment protection, the Court has consistently sustained federal statutes restricting its dissemination. In 1957 the Court upheld a law prohibiting the mailing of obscene materials, and in 1970 it sustained a federal statute allowing individuals to request the post office not to deliver obscene materials to them.[5] In other cases the Supreme Court has upheld the right of Congress to bar the importation of obscene matter and to prohibit the transport of such matter by common carrier through interstate commerce.[6] In 1983 the Court unanimously struck down a federal law barring the mailing of unsolicited ads for contraceptives.[7]

---

1. *Ex parte Jackson*, 96 U.S. 727 at 733 (1878); see also *In re Rapier*, 143 U.S. 110 (1892).

2. *United States ex rel. Milwaukee Social Democratic Publishing Co. v. Burleson*, 255 U.S. 407 (1921).

3. *Hannegan v. Esquire*, 327 U.S. 146 at 158–159 (1946).

4. *Lamont v. Postmaster General*, 381 U.S. 301 (1965).

5. *Roth v. United States*, 354 U.S. 476 (1957); *Rowan v. Post Office Department*, 397 U.S. 728 (1970).

6. *United States v. Thirty-seven Photographs*, 402 U.S. 363 (1971); *United States v. 12 200-Ft. Reels of Super 8mm. Film*, 413 U.S. 123 (1973); *United States v. Orito*, 413 U.S. 139 (1973).

7. *Bolger v. Youngs Drug Products Corp.*, 463 U.S. 60 (1983).

---

who conspired to advocate overthrow of the government. Both types of conduct are considered outside the protection of the First Amendment.

Civil Libel

When someone is libeled, the question arises as to the proper balance between the need for open discussion of public issues and personalities and the need of individuals for protection against false, irresponsible, and malicious publications. Certain public figures—judges, legislators, and executive officials—enjoy absolute immunity from libel suits. Certain professionals, such as doctors and lawyers, enjoy a more limited or qualified immunity, but publishers historically have been liable to damage suits. Libelous publications include those charging that an individual is guilty of a criminal offense, carries a dread disease (such as leprosy or AIDS, acquired immune deficiency syndrome), is incompetent in his or her profession, or if a public official, is guilty of misconduct.

In the United States, truth is a defense to libel—but truth can be expensive to prove—and when the truth involves a matter of judgment, as in a political opinion, it may be impossible to prove. Placing this burden of proof on publishers can lead to self-censorship, a hesitancy to print information about public

GROUP LIBEL

From time to time states have sought to quell racial and religious intolerance and unrest by enacting libel laws that make it illegal for anyone to defame groups of people. Such laws clearly restrain the freedom of the press to discuss public issues concerning particular groups, but the Supreme Court sustained them in the only case it has heard on the validity of group libel laws. The justices held that the First Amendment offered no protection for such statements.

Beauharnais v. Illinois (1952) concerned a man who headed an organization called the White Circle League. He distributed on Chicago streets leaflets making clearly racist statements about blacks and calling on the mayor and city council to protect white residents and neighborhoods against harassment by blacks. Beauharnais was convicted of violating an Illinois group libel statute that made it illegal to publish anything defamatory or derogatory about "a class of citizens of any race, color, creed or religion." He appealed his conviction, but the Supreme Court sustained it, 5–4.

For the majority, Justice Felix Frankfurter observed that it would be libelous to accuse an individual falsely of being a rapist or robber, and, he said, "if an utterance directed at an individual may be the object of criminal sanctions, we cannot deny to a State power to punish the same utterance directed at a defined group" unless the state had acted arbitrarily when it passed its group libel law.[1] Frankfurter mentioned the First Amendment only at the end of his opinion, holding it irrelevant to this case on the basis of the Court's earlier *dicta* that the First Amendment afforded no protection for libel.

In a separate dissenting opinion, Justice William O. Douglas wrote,

> Today a white man stands convicted for protesting in unseemly language against our decisions invalidating restrictive covenants. Tomorrow a negro will be hailed before a court for denouncing lynch law in heated terms.... Intemperate speech is a distinctive characteristic of man. Hot-heads blow off and release destructive energy in the process.... So it has been from the beginning; and so it will be throughout time. The Framers of the Constitution knew human nature as well as we do.[2]

The viability of the *Beauharnais* decision as a precedent has been called into question by the Court's later decisions that both civil and criminal libels are within the scope of the First Amendment protections, but the Court has not reconsidered the 1952 decision.[3]

---

1. *Beauharnais v. Illinois,* 343 U.S. 250 at 258 (1952).

2. Id. at 286–287.

3. See *New York Times Co. v. Sullivan,* 376 U.S. 254 (1964); *Garrison v. Louisiana,* 379 U.S. 64 (1964); *Ashton v. Kentucky,* 384 U.S. 195 (1966).

officials and others influential in public life. Such self-censorship impairs the societal function of the press in a democratic system. Cognizant of this restrictive impact, several states early in the twentieth century began to enact laws protecting publishers from libel suits except where the publisher prints the charges in actual malice. The seminal decision came from the Kansas Supreme Court in the 1908 case of *Coleman v. MacLennan,* in which a political candidate sued a newspaper publisher for libel:

> [W]here an article is published and circulated among voters for the ... purpose of giving what the defendant believes to be truthful information concerning a candidate for public office, and for the purpose of enabling such voters to cast their ballots more intelligently, and the whole thing is done in good faith, and without malice, the article is privileged, although the principal matters contained in the article may be untrue in fact and derogatory to the character of the plaintiff, and in such a case the burden is on the plaintiff to show actual malice in the publication of the article.[41]

To protect the communication of information relevant to public affairs, the U.S. Supreme Court—fifty years later—adopted this "actual malice" rule for libel suits brought against publishers by public officials and other personalities in the public eye. Now libel cases involving anyone of public note immediately pull the First Amendment into play. In the mid 1980s, however, the Court reminded the country that the First Amendment provides no shield against damage awards in a libel case that involves only private parties and no "matter of public concern." "We have long recognized that not all speech is of equal First Amendment importance," wrote Justice Powell for the Court in *Dun & Bradstreet Inc. v. Greenmoss Builders Inc.* (1985). "It is speech on 'matters of public concern' that is 'at the heart of the First Amendment's protection.'"[42]

New York Times Co. v. Sullivan

The Supreme Court revised the rules for libel in *New York Times Co. v. Sullivan* (1964). L. B. Sullivan was an elected commissioner of the city of Montgomery, Alabama, responsible for the police department. He sued the *New York Times* and four black clergymen—Ralph D. Abernathy, Fred L. Shuttlesworth, S. S. Seay Sr., and J. E. Lowery—for libel as a result of an advertisement the clergymen had placed in the newspaper on March 29, 1960. The advertisement, entitled "Heed Their Rising Voices," called attention to the fledgling struggle for civil rights in the South and appealed for funds to support the black student movement, the "struggle for the right-to-vote," and the legal defense of civil rights leader Dr. Martin Luther King Jr., who had been indicted for perjury in Montgomery. The advertisement recounted the violence with which the civil rights movement had been met. Sullivan's libel suit was based on the following two paragraphs:

> In Montgomery, Alabama, after students sang "My Country, 'Tis of Thee" on the State Capitol steps, their leaders were expelled from school, and truckloads of police armed with shotguns and tear-gas ringed the Alabama State College Campus. When the entire student body protested to state authorities by refusing to re-register, their dining hall was padlocked in an attempt to starve them into submission….
>
> Again and again the Southern violators have answered Dr. King's peaceful protests with intimidation and violence. They have bombed his home almost killing his wife and child. They have assaulted his person. They have arrested him seven times—for "speeding," "loitering" and similar "offenses." And now they have charged him with "perjury"—a felony under which they could imprison him for ten years.[43]

The advertisement did not refer to Sullivan personally, but Sullivan contended that the references to police included him. He also contended that because arrests are usually made by police, the "they" in "They have arrested" referred to him, and that the "they" who made the arrests were equated with the "they" who bombed King's home and assaulted him.

The two paragraphs contained errors. The students sang the national anthem, not "My Country, 'Tis of Thee." Several students were expelled from the school for demanding service at an all-white lunch counter, but not for leading the demonstration at the capitol. Police were deployed near the campus, but they did not "ring" it. Students protested the expulsions by boycotting classes for a day, not by refusing to re-register. The campus dining room was never padlocked; the only students denied access to it were those who did not have meal tickets. King had been arrested four times, not seven times.

The suit was tried under Alabama libel law, and Sullivan was awarded damages of $500,000. Other plaintiffs brought suits against the *Times* seeking damages totaling $5.6 million. The *Times* appealed the decision to the Supreme Court, which unanimously reversed it. Writing for six justices, Justice Brennan dismissed the Court's earlier *dicta* viewing all libel as outside the protection of the First Amendment. "None of … [those] cases sustained the use of libel laws to impose sanctions upon expression critical of the official conduct of public officials," he said. "[L]ibel can claim no talismanic immunity from constitutional limitations. It must be measured by standards that satisfy the First Amendment."[44] At the outset Brennan distinguished the civil rights advertisement from the kind of commercial speech the Court still held unprotected. The ad, he explained, primarily communicated information about a public issue of great concern. *(See "Commercial Speech," pp. 77–82.)* Reviewing the role of a free press in a democratic society, Brennan stated,

> we consider this case against the background of a profound national commitment to the principle that debate on public issues should be uninhibited, robust, and wide-open, and that it may well include

THE NEW YORK TIMES, TUESDAY, MARCH 29, 1960

"The growing movement of peaceful mass demonstrations by Negroes is something new in the South, something understandable.... Let Congress heed their rising voices, for they will be heard."

—New York Times editorial
Saturday, March 19, 1960

Heed Their Rising Voices

As the whole world knows by now, thousands of Southern Negro students are engaged in widespread non-violent demonstrations in positive affirmation of the right to live in human dignity as guaranteed by the U. S. Constitution and the Bill of Rights. In their efforts to uphold these guarantees, they are being met by an unprecedented wave of terror by those who would deny and negate that document which the whole world looks upon as setting the pattern for modern freedom...

In Orangeburg, South Carolina, when 400 students peacefully sought to buy doughnuts and coffee at lunch counters in the business district, they were forcibly ejected, tear-gassed, soaked to the skin in freezing weather with fire hoses, arrested en masse and herded into an open barbed-wire stockade to stand for hours in the bitter cold.

In Montgomery, Alabama, after students sang "My Country, 'Tis of Thee" on the State Capitol steps, their leaders were expelled from school, and truckloads of police armed with shotguns and tear-gas ringed the Alabama State College Campus. When the entire student body protested to state authorities by refusing to re-register, their dining hall was padlocked in an attempt to starve them into submission.

In Tallahassee, Atlanta, Nashville, Savannah, Greensboro, Memphis, Richmond, Charlotte, and a host of other cities in the South, young American teenagers, in face of the entire weight of official state apparatus and police power, have boldly stepped forth as protagonists of democracy. Their courage and amazing restraint have inspired millions and given a new dignity to the cause of freedom.

Small wonder that the Southern violators of the Constitution fear this new, non-violent brand of freedom fighter... even as they fear the upswelling right-to-vote movement. Small wonder that they are determined to destroy the one man who, more than any other, symbolizes the new spirit now sweeping the South—the Rev. Dr. Martin Luther King, Jr., world-famous leader of the Montgomery Bus Protest. For it is his doctrine of non-violence which has inspired and guided the students in their widening wave of sit-ins; and it is this same Dr. King who founded and is president of the Southern Christian Leadership Conference—the organization which is spearheading the surging right-to-vote movement. Under Dr. King's direction the Leadership Conference conducts Student Workshops and Seminars in the philosophy and techniques of non-violent resistance.

Again and again the Southern violators have answered Dr. King's peaceful protests with intimidation and violence. They have bombed his home almost killing his wife and child. They have assaulted his person. They have arrested him seven times—for "speeding," "loitering" and similar "offenses." And now they have charged him with "perjury"—a *felony* under which they could imprison him for *ten years*. Obviously, their real purpose is to remove him physically as the leader to whom the students and millions of others—look for guidance and support, and thereby to intimidate *all* leaders who may rise in the South. Their strategy is to behead this affirmative movement, and thus to demoralize Negro Americans and weaken their will to struggle. The defense of Martin Luther King, spiritual leader of the student sit-in movement, clearly, therefore, is an integral part of the total struggle for freedom in the South.

Decent-minded Americans cannot help but applaud the creative daring of the students and the quiet heroism of Dr. King. But this is one of those moments in the stormy history of Freedom when men and women of good will must do more than applaud the rising-to-glory of others. The America whose good name hangs in the balance before a watchful world, the America whose heritage of Liberty these Southern Upholders of the Constitution are defending, is *our* America as well as theirs...

We must heed their rising voices—yes—but we must add our own.

We must extend ourselves above and beyond moral support and render the material help so urgently needed by those who are taking the risks, facing jail, and *even death* in a glorious re-affirmation of our Constitution and its Bill of Rights.

We urge you to join hands with our fellow Americans in the South by supporting, with your dollars, this combined appeal for all three needs—the defense of Martin Luther King—the support of the embattled students—and the struggle for the right-to-vote.

Your Help Is Urgently Needed ... NOW!!

Stella Adler
Raymond Pace Alexander
Harry Van Arsdale
Harry Belafonte
Julie Belafonte
Dr. Algernon Black
Marc Blitzstein
William Branch
Marlon Brando
Mrs. Ralph Bunche
Diahann Carroll

Dr. Alan Knight Chalmers
Richard Coe
Nat King Cole
Cheryl Crawford
Dorothy Dandridge
Ossie Davis
Sammy Davis, Jr.
Ruby Dee
Dr. Philip Elliott
Dr. Harry Emerson Fosdick

Anthony Franciosa
Lorraine Hansbury
Rev. Donald Harrington
Nat Hentoff
James Hicks
Mary Hinkson
Van Heflin
Langston Hughes
Morris Iushewitz
Mahalia Jackson
Mordecai Johnson

John Killens
Eartha Kitt
Rabbi Edward Klein
Hope Lange
John Lewis
Viveca Lindfors
Carl Murphy
Don Murray
John Murray
A. J. Muste
Frederick O'Neal

L. Joseph Overton
Clarence Pickett
Shad Polier
Sidney Poitier
A. Philip Randolph
John Raitt
Elmer Rice
Jackie Robinson
Mrs. Eleanor Roosevelt
Bayard Rustin
Robert Ryan

Maureen Stapleton
Frank Silvera
Hope Stevens
George Tabor
Rev. Gardner C. Taylor
Norman Thomas
Kenneth Tynan
Charles White
Shelley Winters
Max Youngstein

We in the south who are struggling daily for dignity and freedom warmly endorse this appeal

Rev. Ralph D. Abernathy
(Montgomery, Ala.)

Rev. Fred L. Shuttlesworth
(Birmingham, Ala.)

Rev. Kelley Miller Smith
(Nashville, Tenn.)

Rev. W. A. Dennis
(Chattanooga, Tenn.)

Rev. C. K. Steele
(Tallahassee, Fla.)

Rev. Matthew D. McCollom
(Orangeburg, S.C.)

Rev. William Holmes Borders
(Atlanta, Ga.)

Rev. Douglas Moore
(Durham, N.C.)

Rev. Wyatt Tee Walker
(Petersburg, Va.)

Rev. Walter L. Hamilton
(Norfolk, Va.)

I. S. Levy
(Columbia, S.C.)

Rev. Martin Luther King, Sr.
(Atlanta, Ga.)

Rev. Henry C. Bunton
(Memphis, Tenn.)

Rev. S.S. Seay, Sr.
(Montgomery, Ala.)

Rev. Samuel W. Williams
(Atlanta, Ga.)

Rev. A. L. Davis
(New Orleans, La.)

Mrs. Katie E. Whickham
(New Orleans, La.)

Rev. W. H. Hall
(Hattiesburg, Miss.)

Rev. J. E. Lowery
(Mobile, Ala.)

Rev. T. J. Jemison
(Baton Rouge, La.)

COMMITTEE TO DEFEND MARTIN LUTHER KING AND THE STRUGGLE FOR FREEDOM IN THE SOUTH

312 West 125th Street, New York 27, N.Y. UNiversity 6-1700

Chairmen: A. Philip Randolph, Dr. Gardner C. Taylor; *Chairmen of Cultural Division:* Harry Belafonte, Sidney Poitier; *Treasurer:* Nat King Cole; *Executive Director:* Bayard Rustin; *Chairmen of Church Division:* Father George B. Ford, Rev. Harry Emerson Fosdick, Rev. Thomas Kilgore, Jr., Rabbi Edward E. Klein; *Chairman of Labor Division:* Morris Iushewitz

Please mail this coupon TODAY!

Committee To Defend Martin Luther King
and
The Struggle For Freedom In The South
312 West 125th Street, New York 27, N.Y.
UNiversity 6-1700

I am enclosing my contribution of $_____
for the work of the Committee.

Name _____

Address _____

City _____ Zone ____ State ____

☐ I want to help   ☐ Please send further information

Please make checks payable to:
Committee to Defend Martin Luther King

The purpose of this ad was to publicize and raise money for the cause of civil rights. Commissioner L. B. Sullivan of Montgomery, Alabama, claimed the ad libeled him. In deciding against Sullivan, the Supreme Court established a new standard for libel suits.

vehement, caustic, and sometimes unpleasantly sharp attacks on government and public officials.... The present advertisement, as an expression of grievance and protest on one of the major public issues of our time, would seem clearly to qualify for the constitutional protection. The question is whether it forfeits that protection by the falsity of some of its factual statements and by its alleged defamation of ... [Sullivan].[45]

The courts, said Brennan, have recognized that "erroneous statement is inevitable in free debate, and that it must be protected if the freedoms of expression are to have the 'breathing space' that they 'need ... to survive.'"[46] This was true of speech about public officials as well as public issues, Brennan noted,

> A rule compelling the critic of official conduct to guarantee the truth of all his factual assertions—and to do so on pain of libel judgments virtually unlimited in amount—leads to a comparable "self-censorship."... Under such a rule, would-be critics of official conduct may be deterred from voicing their criticism, even though it is believed to be true and even though it is in fact true, because of doubt whether it can be proved in court or fear of the expense of having to do so.... The rule thus dampens the vigor and limits the variety of public debate. It is inconsistent with the First and Fourteenth Amendments.[47]

Drawing heavily on *Coleman v. MacLennan*, Brennan then set out the standard for determining whether defamatory statements about public officials were protected by the First Amendment:

> The constitutional guarantees require, we think, a federal rule that prohibits a public official from recovering damages for a defamatory falsehood relating to his official conduct unless he proves that the statement was made with "actual malice"—that is, with knowledge that it was false or with reckless disregard of whether it was false or not.[48]

This oft-relied-upon standard became known as the *New York Times* rule or actual malice rule. In applying that rule to the circumstances of the *Sullivan* case, the Court discovered no evidence that the individual clergymen knew their statements to be false or were reckless in that regard. Although the *Times* had information in its news files that would have corrected some of the

errors contained in the advertisement, the Court did not find that the *Times* personnel had acted with any actual malice. The evidence against the *Times*, said Brennan, "supports at most a finding of negligence in failing to discover the misstatements, and is constitutionally insufficient to show the recklessness that is required for a finding of actual malice."[49]

Concurring, Justice Black, joined by Justice Douglas, contended that the First and Fourteenth Amendments prevented a state from ever awarding libel damages to public officials for false statements made about their public conduct. The newspaper and the individual clergymen "had an absolute, unconditional constitutional right to publish in the *Times* advertisement their criticisms of the Montgomery agencies and officials," he wrote.[50] In another concurring opinion, Justice Arthur J. Goldberg, also joined by Douglas, held that the First Amendment provided an absolute right to criticize the public conduct of public officials. He also questioned how much protection the actual malice rule would afford publishers. Can "freedom of speech which all agree is constitutionally protected ... be effectively safeguarded by a rule allowing the imposition of liability upon a jury's evaluation of the speaker's state of mind?" he asked.[51]

In a series of subsequent decisions, the Court elaborated on its *New York Times* rule. In *Garrison v. Louisiana* (1964) the Court determined that the actual malice rule limited state power to impose criminal as well as civil sanctions against persons criticizing the official conduct of public officials. In 1968 the Court ruled that to prove reckless disregard for the truth or falsity of the allegedly libelous statement there must be "sufficient evidence to permit the conclusion that the defendant in fact entertained serious doubts as to the truth of his publications."[52] In *Herbert v. Lando* (1979), the Court by a 6-3 vote rejected a television producer's claim that the First Amendment protected him from having to answer questions about the editorial process of a certain story. The Court held that the *New York Times* actual malice standard required inquiry into the editorial process—the prepublication thoughts, conclusions, and conversations of editors and reporters—by persons who charge they have been libeled by the product of that process. The Court said that nothing in the First Amendment restricted a person alleging libel from obtaining the evidence necessary to prove actual malice under the *New York Times* rule. To the contrary, *New York Times Co. v. Sullivan*

> and its progeny made it essential to proving liability that plaintiffs [alleging libel] focus on the conduct and state of mind of the defendant [publishers]. To be liable, the alleged defamer of public officials or of public figures must know or have reason to suspect that his publication is false. In other cases [brought by private individuals] proof of some kind of fault, negligence perhaps, is essential to recovery. Inevitably, unless liability is to be completely foreclosed, the thoughts and editorial processes of the alleged defamer would be open to examination.[53]

Since *Herbert v. Lando,* the Court has been seriously divided in determining against what category of person the *New York Times* rule operates. All the justices have agreed that public officials and public figures must show actual malice to win damages. After a brief period when the Court seemed to apply the actual malice standard to suits brought by private individuals involving matters of public concern, it now allows states to set less stringent standards of proof for private citizens alleging libel.

Public Officials

Two years after *New York Times Co. v. Sullivan,* the Court further defined the category of "public official." In *Rosenblatt v. Baer* (1966), a former supervisor of a county ski resort sued a newspaper columnist for an allegedly libelous statement about his management of the recreation area. Without being instructed to use the *New York Times* rule, the jury found in favor of the supervisor. The Supreme Court reversed, but the justices in the majority disagreed in their reasoning. Justice Brennan, who wrote the formal Court opinion in which only two other justices concurred, put in context the issue of freedom of the press:

> There is, first, a strong interest in debate on public issues, and second, a strong interest in debate about

those persons who are in a position significantly to influence the resolution of those issues. Criticism of government is at the very center of the constitutionally protected area of free discussion. Criticism of those responsible for government operations must be free, lest criticism of government itself be penalized.

He then defined "public officials":

> It is clear, therefore, that the "public official" designation applies at the very least to those among the hierarchy of government employees who have, or appear to the public to have, substantial responsibility for or control over the conduct of governmental affairs.... Where a position in government has such apparent importance that the public has an independent interest in the qualifications and performance of the person who holds it, beyond the general public interest in the qualifications and performance of all government employees, both elements we identified in *New York Times* are present and the *New York Times* malice standards apply.[54]

Although this has come to be the accepted definition of "public official," a majority of the Court did not initially endorse it. Justice Tom C. Clark concurred in the judgment without an opinion. Justice Douglas concurred, but thought the question should turn on whether the alleged libel involved a public issue rather than a public official. Justice Stewart also agreed with the judgment but cautioned that the actual malice rule should be applied only "where a State's law of defamation has been unconstitutionally converted into a law of seditious libel."[55] Justice Harlan concurred with the judgment but disagreed with part of Brennan's opinion. Justice Black concurred, maintaining that the First and Fourteenth Amendments forbade all libel judgments against newspaper comment on public issues. Justice Abe Fortas dissented for technical reasons. The Court was considerably more unified in 1971 when it ruled that candidates for public office were public officials and that the *New York Times* rule protected publishers from libel charges resulting from their decision to print information on the criminal records of these persons.[56]

Performance, Publicity, and the Press

In August 1972, an Ohio television station filmed, without the performer's consent, the entire fifteen-second act of Hugo Zacchini, a "human cannonball" whose "act" consisted of being shot from a cannon into a net two hundred feet away. After the station showed the film clip on its nightly news program as an item of interest, Zacchini sued, charging that the television station had appropriated his right to control publicity concerning his performance.

The Ohio Supreme Court ruled in favor of the television station. Unless Zacchini showed that the station intentionally meant to harm him or to use the film for some private purpose, its airing of Zacchini's act was protected by the First and Fourteenth Amendments, the court held. By a 5-4 vote, the Supreme Court overturned that ruling in *Zacchini v. Scripps-Howard Broadcasting Co.* (1977).[1]

"Wherever the line in particular situations is to be drawn between media reports that are protected and those that are not, we are quite sure that the First and Fourteenth Amendments do not immunize the media when they broadcast a performer's entire act without his consent," wrote Justice Byron R. White for the majority. "The Constitution no more prevents a State from requiring ... [the station] to compensate petitioner for broadcasting his act on television than it would privilege ... [the station] to film and broadcast a copyrighted dramatic work without liability to the copyright owner." Three of the dissenters held that the broadcast was privileged under the First and Fourteenth Amendments. The film was a simple report on a newsworthy event and shown as part of an ordinary daily news report. The broadcast was therefore no more than a "routine example of the press fulfilling the informing function so vital to our system."[2]

---

1. *Zacchini v. Scripps-Howard Broadcasting Co.,* 433 U.S. 562 (1977).

2. Id. at 574–575, 580.

Public Figures

The wide diversity of views on the applicability of the actual malice rule was again evident a year after *Rosenblatt* in two decisions in which the Court applied the *New York Times* rule to persons who were not public officials but were nonetheless in the public eye. The first of these cases, *Curtis Publishing Co. v. Butts* (1967), concerned a libel action brought by former University of Georgia athletic director Wallace Butts against the *Saturday Evening Post,* which was owned by the Curtis Publishing Company. The *Post* had printed a story in which it alleged that Butts had "fixed" a football game by revealing his team's offensive and defensive plays to the opposing coach, Paul Bryant of the University of Alabama. At the trial, which was completed before the Supreme Court issued its malice rule in *New York Times Co. v. Sullivan,* Butts admitted talking to Bryant but said he had revealed nothing of value to him. Butts was supported by expert witnesses, and there was substantial evidence that the *Post* investigation of the allegation had been gravely inadequate. The jury found in Butts's favor; the final award was $480,000. After the *New York Times* rule was issued, the publishing company asked for another trial, which the state courts denied.[57]

The second case, *Associated Press v. Walker* (1967), concerned an allegedly libelous eyewitness news report that former general Edwin A. Walker had led rioters against federal marshals at the University of Mississippi. The marshals were trying to maintain order during turmoil over the enrollment of a black student, James Meredith. Walker, who had commanded federal troops guarding black students who tried to enter a Little Rock, Arkansas, high school in 1958, was awarded $500,000 in compensatory damages. The Supreme Court combined the cases. It unanimously reversed the award in *Walker,* but by a 5-4 vote upheld the award of damages to Butts.[58] All of the justices agreed that Butts and Walker were both public figures, but four of the justices would not have applied the actual malice rule to their cases. Three of the remaining five justices would have applied the actual malice rule, and the other two maintained that freedom of the press absolutely protects publishers from libel suits.

Justice Harlan, joined by Justices Clark, Stewart, and Fortas, were four members of the majority. (Chief Justice Earl Warren, the fifth member of the majority, agreed with Harlan's result but not with his reasoning.) "Butts may have attained that status by position alone and Walker by his purposeful activity amounting to a thrusting of his personality into the 'vortex' of an important public controversy," Harlan said. Both men "commanded sufficient public interest and had sufficient access to the means of counter-argument to be able to 'expose through discussion the falsehood and fallacies' of the defamatory statements."[59] Those four justices, however, would apply a rule less strict than actual malice in libel cases brought by such public figures. Harlan wrote,

> a "public figure" who is not a public official may also recover damages for a defamatory falsehood whose substance makes substantial danger to reputation apparent, on a showing of highly unreasonable conduct constituting an extreme departure from the standards of investigation and reporting ordinarily adhered to by reasonable publishers.[60]

Using this standard, Harlan found that the *Post* had failed to exercise elementary journalistic precautions to determine if the allegation against Butts was true. The libel award to Butts must be sustained, but the award to Walker must be overturned, Harlan said, because nothing in the evidence suggests a "departure from accepted publishing standards."[61]

The remaining five justices agreed with Chief Justice Warren that public figures must prove actual malice under the *New York Times* rule to win libel damages. Applying that rule, it was evident that Walker had not proved actual malice, Warren said. In Butts's case, however, the conduct of the *Post* showed the "degree of reckless disregard for the truth" that constituted actual malice under the rule.

Narrowing the Definition

In the late 1970s, the Court sharply narrowed the public figure category. In decisions in *Wolston v. Reader's Digest Association Inc.* (1979) and *Hutchinson v. Proxmire* (1979), the justices held that two men who had been involuntarily thrust into the public eye were not public figures and could recover libel damages without proving actual malice in the publications charged. Ilya Wolston was convicted of contempt in 1958 for refusing to appear and testify before a grand jury investigating Soviet espionage attempts. Ronald Hutchinson, a scientist, found himself in the public eye after his research—paid for in part with federal funds—was the target of a "Golden Fleece" award from Sen. William Proxmire, D-Wis., who described the research as a waste of tax dollars. Neither Wolston nor Hutchinson, held the Court, was a public figure as a result of this publicity.

The vote in *Wolston* was 8-1. Only Justice Brennan dissented. Justice William H. Rehnquist explained that the majority felt that "[a] private individual is not automatically transformed into a public figure just by becoming involved in or associated with a matter that attracts public attention." "A libel defendant must show more than mere newsworthiness [on the part of the person charging libel] to justify application of the demanding burden of *New York Times*," wrote Rehnquist.[62] Moving away from definition and toward procedural safeguards, the Court in 1984 ruled that federal appeal courts reviewing libel awards won by public figures must take a new look at the evidence to see if it proved actual malice. Two years later, the Court held that judges should summarily dismiss libel charges brought by a public figure unless they find clear and convincing evidence of actual malice in the challenged article.[63]

Private Individuals

In *Rosenbloom v. Metromedia Inc.* (1971), the Court considered for the first time whether private individuals must prove actual malice to win damages for libel. George Rosenbloom, a distributor of nudist magazines, was arrested in a police crackdown on pornography. A local radio station reported that Rosenbloom had been arrested for possession of obscene literature. After he was acquitted of criminal obscenity charges,

Rosenbloom sued the radio station for libel. A jury awarded him $750,000, but an appeals court reversed on the grounds that the jury should have been required to apply the *New York Times* actual malice standard to the case. In the 5-3 decision affirming the appeals court, the Supreme Court splintered into several groups. Chief Justice Burger and Justices Brennan and Blackmun agreed that the actual malice rule should be applied to all discussion of public issues, even discussion including defamatory statements about private individuals. The First Amendment protects discussion of public issues, Brennan said, and an issue does not become less public

> merely because a private individual is involved.… The public's primary interest is in the event; the public focus is on the conduct of the participant and the content, effect, and significance of the conduct, not the participant's prior anonymity or notoriety.[64]

Justice Black concurred, maintaining that the guarantee of a free press protected publishers against all libel suits. Justice White also concurred, holding that the *New York Times* rule protected newspapers that praised public officials—in this case the police who undertook the pornography investigation—and criticized their adversaries. In dissent, Justices Marshall, Stewart, and Harlan said they would not apply the actual malice rule to libel cases involving private individuals. Justice Douglas did not participate.

Gertz v. Robert Welch Inc.

Three years after *Rosenbloom,* the Court shifted gears and adopted the *Rosenbloom* dissenters' position that the actual malice rule did not apply in libel cases brought by private individuals. Five justices endorsed this view in *Gertz v. Robert Welch Inc.* (1974). Attorney Elmer Gertz sued a Chicago policeman on behalf of the family of a youth killed by the officer. *American Opinion,* the journal of the John Birch Society, printed an article characterizing Gertz as a "Leninist" with a criminal record who was part of a communist conspiracy to discredit local police. Charging that the allegations were false, Gertz sued the journal for

damages. The jury awarded him $50,000, but the trial court overruled the jury. Citing *Rosenbloom,* the court said that the First Amendment protected publishers from libel suits in connection with discussions of public interest even if they defamed private individuals unless the individual could prove actual malice on the part of the publisher.

The Supreme Court reversed, 5-4. The majority included the two newest members of the Court, Powell and Rehnquist, who had succeeded Justices Black and Harlan late in 1971. Voting with them were *Rosenbloom* dissenters Marshall and Stewart and, with reservations, Justice Blackmun. The *New York Times* rule is not appropriate in libel cases involving private individuals, wrote Justice Powell for the majority. Private citizens lack the access of public officials and public figures to "channels of effective communication" to combat allegations about their conduct, he observed. Furthermore, private individuals, unlike public officials and figures, have not voluntarily subjected themselves to public scrutiny. A private person, Powell wrote,

> has relinquished no part of his interest in the protection of his own good name, and consequently he has a more compelling call on the courts for redress of injury inflicted by defamatory falsehood. Thus, private individuals are not only more vulnerable to injury than public officials and public figures; they are also more deserving of recovery.[65]

Therefore, Powell continued, "[S]o long as they do not impose liability without fault, the States may define for themselves the appropriate standard of liability for a publisher or broadcaster of defamatory falsehood injurious to a private individual."[66] To avoid self-censorship, Powell cautioned, the liability of publications to private person libel suits must be limited. Therefore, private individuals who proved, for example, only that a publisher had been negligent when printing false defamatory statements could recover damages only for the actual injury to his reputation. Punitive or presumed damages could be awarded only on a showing that actual malice, as defined by the *New York Times* rule, was intended, Powell held. Turning to the case at hand, Powell maintained that Gertz was a private

THE PRESS AND PERSONAL PRIVACY

Freedom of the press might be justifiably curtailed, wrote Chief Justice Charles Evan Hughes in *Near v. Minnesota* (1931), to prevent the invasion of "private rights." *(See details of Near, pp. 85–87.)* The Court, however, has blocked the press from being sued for publishing newsworthy stories, even if the reports invaded the personal privacy of an unwitting subject. *Time Inc. v. Hill* (1967) brought to the Court a claim of privacy by a family held hostage in their Pennsylvania home in 1952 by three escaped convicts. The convicts treated the family politely and released them unharmed. A 1953 book, *The Desperate Hours,* recounted a story similar to the Hill family's experience, but the convicts in the story, unlike those in the actual event, were violent toward their captives. The novel was made into a play and later a film. In an article on the play, *Life* sent actors to the former Hill house, where they were photographed acting scenes from the play. The article characterized the play as a reenactment of the Hill incident.

Hill sued the magazine under a New York right of privacy statute that made it a misdemeanor for anyone to use without consent another's name for commercial purposes. The jury found in favor of Hill, and the state appeals courts affirmed their verdict. The Supreme Court reversed the ruling, 6-3.[1] The Hill family was newsworthy, albeit involuntarily, wrote Justice William J. Brennan Jr. for the majority. The New York law permitted newsworthy persons to recover if they could show that the article was fictionalized. Stated Brennan, the actual malice standard set out in *New York*

Times Co. v. Sullivan (1964) must be applied to this case even though private individuals were involved.[2] Brennan wrote,

> The guarantees for speech and press are not the preserve of political expression or comment upon public affairs, essential as those are to healthy government. One need only pick up any newspaper or magazine to comprehend the vast range of published matter which exposes persons to public view, both private citizens and public officials. Exposure of the self to others in varying degrees is a concomitant of life in a civilized community. The risk of this exposure is an essential incident of a society which places a primary value on freedom of speech and of press.... We have no doubt that the subject of the *Life* article ... is a matter of public interest.... Erroneous statement is no less inevitable in such a case than in the case of comment upon public affairs, and in both, if innocent or merely negligent, "...it must be protected if the freedoms of expression are to have the 'breathing space' that they need ... 'to survive'...."
>
> ... We create a grave risk of serious impairment of the indispensable service of a free press in a free society if we saddle the press with the impossible burden of verifying to a certainty the facts associated in news articles with a person's name, picture or portrait, particularly ... [in] nondefamatory matter.[3]

Because the jury had not been instructed that it could award damages to the Hills only if it found the article had been published with actual malice, the majority sent the case back to the lower courts.

individual despite his active participation in community and professional affairs:

> Absent clear evidence of general fame or notoriety in the community, and pervasive involvement in the affairs of society, an individual should not be deemed a public personality for all aspects of his life. It is preferable to reduce the public-figure question to a more meaningful context by looking to the nature and extent of an individual's participation in the particular controversy giving rise to the defamation.[67]

The majority sent the case back for a new trial. The jury should not have been allowed to award damages without a finding of fault on the part of *American Opinion.* The majority also said that the trial court had

erred in holding that the actual malice standard should be applied. The dissenting justices, Chief Justice Burger and Justice Brennan, joined by Justice Douglas, maintained that discussions of public interest, including those touching private persons, should be protected by the actual malice rule. Justice White also dissented, claiming that the majority opinion made it almost impossible for private individuals to defend their reputations successfully.

Time Inc. v. Firestone

The Court reaffirmed the principles of *Gertz* in *Time Inc. v. Firestone* (1976). The cause of the libel suit occurred nearly a decade earlier. On December 22, 1967, *Time* carried an item in its "Milestones" section announcing the

In 2001 the Court threw out a suit against a radio commentator who broadcast an illegally intercepted cellphone conversation between Gloria Bartnicki and another official of a Pennsylvania teachers' union, which was locked in negotiations with the local school board. "We're gonna have to go to their homes … to blow off their front porches," one union leader was heard to say. Federal wiretap law prohibits intercepting or disclosing a private phone call, but as the Court noted, the defendant in this suit, radio commentator Frederick Vopper, did not tape the call, but received the taped conversation from a local antitax activist. In a 6-3 decision in *Bartnicki v. Vopper* (2001), the Court ruled that the First Amendment generally forbids "imposing sanctions on the publication of truthful information of public concern. In this case, privacy concerns give way when balanced against the interest in publishing matters of public importance."[4]

In *Cox Broadcasting Corporation v. Cohn* (1975), the Court had struck down a Georgia law making it illegal to broadcast the name of rape victims. The father of a girl who had died as a result of an assault and rape sued a television station for reporting his daughter's name in two of their news reports. The reporter testified that he had obtained the name of the victim at an open court hearing at which five of the suspects pleaded guilty. The Court said that the First Amendment does not allow states to "impose sanctions for the publication of truthful information contained in official court records open to public inspection." The majority held,

If there are privacy interests to be protected in judicial proceedings, the States must respond by means which avoid public documentation or other exposure of private information. Their political institutions must weigh the interests in privacy with the interests of the public to know and of the press to publish.[5]

In 1979 a unanimous Court struck down a state law that forbade newspapers, but not other forms of the press, from reporting the names of juveniles involved in criminal proceedings.[6] A decade later, in *The Florida Star v. B.J.F.,* the Court held that the First Amendment protected a newspaper from being sued for damages for publishing the name of a rape victim when state law barred such disclosure. The paper had obtained the name from a publicly released police report. "We do not hold that a state may never punish publication of the name of a victim of a sexual offense," Justice Thurgood Marshall wrote for the Court. "We hold only that where a newspaper publishes truthful information which it has lawfully obtained, punishment may lawfully be imposed, if at all, only when narrowly tailored to a state interest of the highest order."[7]

---

1. *Time Inc. v. Hill*, 385 U.S. 374 (1967).
2. *The New York Times Co. v. Sullivan*, 376 U.S. 254 (1964).
3. *Time Inc. v. Hill*, 385 U.S. 374 at 388, 389 passim (1967).
4. *Bartnicki v. Vopper*, 532 U.S. 514 at 534 (2001).
5. *Cox Broadcasting Corp. v. Cohn*, 420 U.S. 469 at 495, 496 (1975).
6. *Smith v. Daily Mail Publishing Co.*, 443 U.S. 97 (1979).
7. *The Florida Star v. B.J.F.*, 491 U.S. 524 (1989).

divorce of Russell A. Firestone Jr., heir to the tire fortune, from his third wife, Mary Alice Sullivan. In that item the magazine wrote, "The 17-month intermittent trial produced enough testimony of extra-marital adventures on both sides, said the judge, 'to make Dr. Freud's hair curl.'" This report, as *Time* was soon to discover, was less than accurate. Although Firestone's suit for divorce had charged his wife with adultery and extreme cruelty, the judge in granting him the divorce did not specify that those charges were the grounds upon which the divorce was granted. When *Time* refused to retract the item, the former Mrs. Firestone sued the magazine for libel. She won a $100,000 damage judgment. *Time* appealed, claiming that Mrs. Firestone was a public figure and therefore must prove actual malice to win the suit. The

magazine also argued that reports of court proceedings are of sufficient public interest that they cannot be the basis for libel judgments—even if erroneous or false and defamatory—unless it is proved that they were published maliciously.

The Supreme Court, in a mixed victory for Mrs. Firestone, rejected both of the arguments by *Time* and sent the case back to Florida courts to determine whether *Time* had been negligent or was otherwise at fault. Writing for the majority, Justice Rehnquist stated that Mrs. Firestone was not a public figure despite her involvement in the sensational divorce case. She "did not assume any role of especial prominence in the affairs of society … and she did not thrust herself to the forefront of any particular public controversy in order to

CONFIDENTIAL PROCEEDINGS

A state may not fine a newspaper for printing a true report of confidential proceedings of a state commission considering disciplinary action against a sitting state judge. This was the Supreme Court's unanimous holding in *Landmark Communications Inc. v. Virginia* (1978).[1] After the Norfolk *Virginian-Pilot* printed an accurate report of an inquiry by the state judicial review commission into the conduct of a sitting judge named in the article, the newspaper was indicted, tried, convicted, and fined $500 for violating state law by breaching the confidentiality of the commission's proceedings.

The state justified the law as necessary to protect public confidence in the judicial process, to protect the reputation of judges, and to protect persons who bring complaints to the commission. The Court held that those interests justified the law protecting the confidentiality of proceedings before the commission, but they did not justify imposing criminal penalties on news media, uninvolved in the commission's proceedings, that breached that confidentiality.

---

1. *Landmark Communications Inc. v. Virginia*, 435 U.S. 829 (1978).

---

influence the resolution of the issues involved in it."[68] *Gertz* established that the actual malice rule did not apply to cases brought by private individuals. Rehnquist also noted that in *Gertz* the justices rejected use of the actual malice rule for reports of court proceedings. The public interest in such reports, he added, was sufficiently protected under a 1975 decision forbidding the states to allow the media to be sued for reporting true information available to the public in official court records. *(See box, The Press and Personal Privacy, pp. 106–107.)* Justice White dissented, saying that the libel award to Mrs. Firestone should be upheld. Justice Brennan also dissented, arguing that the First Amendment protected *Time* for reporting of public judicial proceedings unless actual malice was proved. The third dissenter, Justice Marshall, thought Mrs. Firestone was a public figure and that the *New York Times* actual malice rule should therefore apply to protect *Time*.

In 1979 the Court again upheld *Gertz*, ruling that private individuals who were placed in the public eye involuntarily were not "public figures" and did not have to prove actual malice under the *New York Times* rule in order to bring a successful libel suit. Seven years later, however, the Court seemed to rebalance this equation somewhat, holding that private persons who sue for libel must prove the falsity of the challenged report as well as fault of the media before they can recover damages.[69]

Parodies versus Opinions

Satirists and cartoonists who delight in inflicting pain on their chosen targets won a shield from lawsuits in a late 1980s case that pitted one of the nation's foremost Baptist ministers against one of its most outrageous pornographers. Larry Flynt's *Hustler* regularly lampooned public figures and often did so in salacious parodies. The Rev. Jerry Falwell, founder of the Moral Majority, a Christian advocacy group, was targeted in the November 1983 issue, where he was featured in a parody of a Campari ad headlined "Jerry Falwell talks about his first time." In this supposed interview, the Baptist leader talks about an incestuous sexual encounter in an outhouse, with references to flies and a goat. The comments attributed to him may have been outrageous and hurtful, but they clearly were not his words. Falwell sued *Hustler,* contending the mock interview defamed him and caused him emotional distress. A jury in Virginia agreed with the latter claim and awarded him $200,000 in damages, a verdict that was upheld by a federal appeals court, because Hustler had shown "actual malice" and a "reckless disregard for the truth."

The Court unanimously ruled for the pornographer over the preacher in *Hustler Magazine v. Falwell* (1988), holding that cartoonists, satirists, and other commentators are protected from lawsuits when they lampoon public figures, so long as they are not using false statements of "actual facts" to defame their target.[70] Neither the writer's "bad motive" nor the "outrageousness" of the parody is enough to knock down the shield of the First Amendment, said Chief Justice Rehnquist. "Were we to hold otherwise, there can be little doubt that political cartoonists and satirists would be subjected to damages awards without any showing that their work falsely defamed its subject," he said.[71] "The art of the cartoonist is often not reasoned or evenhanded, but slashing and one sided."[72] Throughout U.S. history, famous figures have been mocked in cartoons, he noted, citing portrayals of George Washington sitting on an ass as well as "Lincoln's tall, gangling posture, Teddy Roosevelt's glasses and teeth, and Franklin D. Roosevelt's jutting jaw and cigarette holder."[73] These caricatures and others like them may irritate or even emotionally injure their subjects, but "from the viewpoint of history, it is clear that our political discourse would have been considerably poorer without them," the chief justice said.[74]

Two years later, Rehnquist and the Court made clear that opinion writers, critics, and commentators do not have a First Amendment license to malign others with false statements of fact dressed up as opinions. The case arose when Michael Milkovich, a high school wrestling coach from Ohio, sued a sports columnist for writing that his actions had taught students a bad lesson: "If you get into a jam, lie your way out." In 1974 his team at Maple Heights High was involved in a fight with another team in which several persons were injured; the state athletic association put the team on suspension. After a court hearing, the team's suspension was lifted. A day later, Theodore Diadiun wrote a sports page column for the *Lorain Journal* entitled "Maple Beat the Law with the 'Big Lie.'" A second headline read, "Diadiun Says Maple Told a Lie." The columnist did not report what the coach said under oath during the court hearing, but implied that his testimony was false. "Anyone who attended the meet … knows in his heart that Milkovich and [school superintendent Don] Scott lied at the hearing after each having given his solemn oath to tell the truth. But they got away with it," the columnist wrote.

Milkovich and Scott sued the newspaper for defaming them by saying, in essence, that they had committed perjury by lying under oath. Eventually, the Ohio Supreme Court threw out their lawsuits, holding that the column was "constitutionally protected opinion." In 1990 the Court took up the wrestling coach's appeal and revived his lawsuit, determining that there is no "wholesale defamation exemption for anything that might be labeled opinion."[75] Sometimes, "expressions of opinion … imply an assertion of objective fact," said Chief Justice Rehnquist, and if these assertions of fact are maliciously false and damaging to a person's reputation, they can form the basis of a defamation suit, he said in *Milkovich v. Lorain Journal* (1990).[76] "The statement, 'In my opinion Jones is a liar,' can cause as much damage to reputation as the statement, 'Jones is a liar,'" he said.[77] Rehnquist went on to say that the plaintiff must prove the statement was both factual and false and that it was printed with a reckless disregard for the truth. For example, "the statement, 'In my opinion, Mayor Jones shows his abysmal ignorance by accepting the teachings of Marx and Lenin,' would not be actionable," he said, because it is pure opinion and a "rhetorical hyperbole."[78] In the wrestling coach's case, "We think the connotation that [Milkovich] committed perjury is sufficiently factual to be susceptible as being proved true or false," Rehnquist stated, and therefore, can go to trial.[79] In dissent, Justices Brennan and Marshall said the lawsuit should have been thrown out because the column "offered conjecture and not solid information."[80]

Questionable Quotes, Sensitive Sources

Two high-profile cases involving the methods used by reporters came to the Court in *Masson v. New Yorker* (1991) and *Cohen v. Cowles Media Co.* (1991). The first case arose from the writings of *New Yorker* reporter Janet Malcolm about Jeffrey Masson, a psychoanalyst who was fired from his job as projects director of the Sigmund Freud Archives after disputing some of Freud's theories. Masson challenged some of the direct quotations attributed to him in the stories, saying they were fabricated. Many of the quotes made him sound boastful, and, in one of the more damning quotes, Malcolm wrote that Masson said he was considered an "intellectual gigolo," a phrase he said he never used.

Masson sued for libel.[81] By 7-2 the Court ruled that fabricated quotes may be libelous if they are published with knowledge of falsity or convey a meaning different from what the speaker actually said. Justice Anthony M. Kennedy, writing for the majority, said that a jury should decide whether Malcolm acted with knowledge of falsity or reckless disregard for the truth of the passages in question. In general, quotation marks signify a verbatim reproduction, Kennedy noted. He then explained that the common law of libel does not concern itself with slight inaccuracies; it concentrates instead on issues of truth.

Cohen v. Cowles Media Co. (1991) arose from a Minnesota gubernatorial race. A political consultant offered reporters negative information about a candidate in return for a promise of confidentiality. After two newspapers printed the source's name, the consultant was fired. He then sued the newspapers, alleging breach of contract and fraudulent misrepresentation. The Supreme Court ruled 5-4 that the First Amendment does not shield the news media from lawsuits if they break promises of confidentiality to sources. A state doctrine of promissory estoppel, which protects people who rely to their detriment on promises from others, applied to all citizens' daily transactions, Justice White wrote for the majority.[82] In deciding that the First Amendment does not bar action for a broken contract, White said any resulting constraint on truthful reporting "is no more than the incidental, and constitutionally insignificant, consequence of applying to the press a generally applicable law that requires those who make certain kinds of promises to keep them."[83]

A FREE PRESS VERSUS THE RIGHT TO A FAIR TRIAL

At times the First Amendment guarantee of freedom of the press collides with the Sixth Amendment guarantee of trial by an impartial jury. As Justice Clark wrote in 1966,

> A responsible press has always been regarded as the handmaiden of effective judicial administration, especially in the criminal field…. The press does not simply publish information about trials, but guards against the miscarriage of justice by subjecting the police, prosecutors, and judicial processes to extensive public scrutiny and criticism.[84]

In this way the public may assure itself that justice is attained, to the benefit both of society and of the individual defendant.

The conflict between the freedom of the press and the right to a fair trial arises from the Constitution's promise that a defendant shall be judged by an impartial jury solely on evidence produced in court and that both judge and jury shall be free from outside influence. In cases concerning prominent people or sensational crimes, pretrial publicity can so saturate a community that the pool of unbiased potential jurors is significantly diminished. News accounts and editorials may influence jurors and judges while a case is pending. The question then is what, if any, restrictions on the free press are constitutionally permissible to ensure a fair trial.

Contempt of Court

The Supreme Court has had little tolerance for efforts by judges to restrict criticism of their official conduct. From time to time a judge has held in contempt publishers, editors, and writers who have criticized his handling of a case while it was still pending. The now-discarded argument in support of such punishment was that public criticism of a judge might influence or coerce him to rule in a way that will maintain the goodwill of the publisher and the community at large at the expense of the parties in the case.

Federal Courts

The potential for judicial abuse of the contempt power prompted Congress in 1831 to enact a law forbidding the use of contempt citations to punish misbehavior other than that which occurred in court "or so near thereto as to obstruct the administration of justice." In 1918 the Supreme Court allowed the use of the contempt power to curtail a newspaper's criticisms of a judge's conduct in a pending case.[85] In 1941, however, the Court overturned that decision, holding that the phrase "so near thereto" meant only physical proximity. Thus, federal law as presently construed gives published criticisms of federal judicial conduct absolute protection from summary contempt proceedings.[86]

State Courts

In 1907 the Court sustained a contempt citation against a newspaper publisher for publishing articles and a cartoon critical of a state court's actions on pending cases. If the court determines that a critical publication tends to interfere with the fair administration of justice, wrote Justice Oliver Wendell Holmes Jr., then the publisher may be punished. "When a case is finished, the courts are subject to the same criticism as other people, but the propriety and necessity of preventing interference with the court of justice by premature statement, argument or intimidation hardly can be denied," he said.[87] With the application to the states as well as the federal government of the First Amendment guarantees of free speech and press, the Court has not since 1925 sustained a contempt citation issued by a judge against a newspaper critical of his actions on a pending case.

The leading decision in this area is *Bridges v. California* (1941), in which the Court overturned, 5-4, contempt rulings against a labor leader and an anti-union Los Angeles newspaper. While a motion for a new trial was pending in a dispute between two competing longshoremen's unions, Bridges, the president of one of the unions, sent a telegram to the U.S. secretary of labor describing as outrageous the judge's initial decision favoring the competing union. Bridges threatened to strike the entire Pacific coast if the original decision were allowed to stand. The telegram was reprinted in several California newspapers. A companion case to *Bridges— Times-Mirror Co. v. Superior Court of California—* involved a *Los Angeles Times* editorial that urged a trial judge to give severe sentences to two union members found guilty of beating up nonunion truck drivers.

Writing for the five-justice majority overturning the contempt citation against the newspaper, Justice Black said that punishment for contempt improperly restricted freedom of the press. If the contempt citations were allowed to stand, Black said,

anyone who might wish to give public expression to his views on a pending case involving no matter what problem of public interest, just at the time his audience would be most receptive, would be as effectively discouraged as if a deliberate statutory scheme of censorship had been adopted.[88]

Such a restriction would be permissible only if the criticism raised a clear and present danger that a substantive evil would result, Black continued. The only dangers cited by the court in this case were that the articles might result in disrespect for the court and unfair administration of justice. Black dismissed the first of these rationales:

> The assumption that respect for the judiciary can be won by shielding judges from published criticism wrongly appraises the character of American public opinion. For it is a prized American privilege to speak one's mind, although not always with perfect good taste, on all public institutions. And an enforced silence, however limited, solely in the name of preserving the dignity of the bench, would probably engender resentment, suspicion, and contempt much more than it would enhance respect.[89]

The Court also did not find any evidence that the articles in question created a clear and present danger of interfering with the fair administration of justice. The judge in the *Los Angeles Times* case was likely to know that a lenient sentence for the two union members would result in criticism from the paper. "To regard it [the editorial], therefore, as in itself of substantial influence upon the course of justice would be to impute to judges a lack of firmness, wisdom, or honor, which we cannot accept as a major premise," Black wrote.[90] Likewise, the judge in the *Bridges* case was likely to realize that his decision might result in a labor strike. "If he was not intimidated by the facts themselves," Black said, "we do not believe that the most explicit statement of them could have sidetracked the course of justice."[91]

Speaking for the dissenters, Justice Felix Frankfurter said the judges were within their rights to punish comments that had a "reasonable tendency" to interfere with the impartial dispensation of justice. Wrote Frankfurter,

Freedom of expression can hardly carry implications that nullify the guarantees of impartial trials. And since courts are the ultimate resorts for vindicating the Bill of Rights, a state may surely authorize appropriate historic means [the contempt power] to assure that the process for such vindication be not wrenched from its rational tracks into the more primitive melee of passion and pressure. The need is great that courts be criticized, but just as great that they be allowed to do their duty.[92]

In *Pennekamp v. Florida* (1946), the Court reaffirmed its opinion that editorial comment on judicial handling of a pending case did not present a clear and present danger of interfering with the fair administration of justice and was therefore not punishable. "In the borderline instances where it is difficult to say upon which side the alleged offense falls, we think the specific freedom of public comment should weigh heavily against a possible tendency to influence pending cases," the Court said.[93] The following year, the Court in *Craig v. Harney* (1947) overturned a contempt citation for articles that gave an unfair and inaccurate account of a trial. The majority found that neither the articles nor a critical editorial constituted "an imminent and serious threat to the ability of the court to give fair consideration" to the pending case.[94]

Although the Court almost totally abandoned use of the clear and present danger test in other contexts during the 1950s, it reaffirmed the use of that test in contempt cases in 1962. *(See "The Search for a Standard," pp. 30–32.)* In *Wood v. Georgia* (1962), the Court reversed the contempt citation of a county sheriff who denounced a county judge's order to a grand jury to investigate rumors of purchased votes and other corrupting practices as a "political attempt to intimidate" black voters. The lower court held that the sheriff's criticism, publicized in several news accounts, created a clear and present danger of influencing the grand jury. The Supreme Court disagreed, observing that the lower courts had made no attempt to show how the criticism created "a substantive evil actually designed to impede the course of justice."[95]

Pretrial Publicity

A serious and frequent threat to the fair administration of justice is posed by publications that cast defendants

in such a bad light that their rights to fair treatment are jeopardized. In those instances, the Court has held that trial courts should take regulatory actions to protect the right to a fair trial with the least possible restriction on a free press. Defense attorneys frequently claim that news reports are so inflammatory and pervasive as to deny their clients due process. The Supreme Court rejected such a claim in *Stroble v. California* (1951), noting that the publicity had receded six weeks before the trial, that the defendant had not requested a change of venue, and that his publicized confession was voluntary and placed in evidence in open trial.[96]

In 1959 the Court overturned a federal conviction because jurors had been exposed through news accounts to information that was not admitted in evidence at the trial.[97] Two years later, in *Irvin v. Dowd* (1961), the Supreme Court for the first time reversed a state conviction on grounds that pretrial publicity had denied the defendant due process. Leslie Irvin had been arrested and indicted for one of six murders committed in and around Evansville, Indiana. Shortly after his arrest, the police sent out press releases saying that he had confessed to all six crimes. The media covered the crimes and the confession extensively. It also reported on previous crimes in which Irvin had been implicated.

Irvin's attorney won a change of venue to a neighboring rural county, but that area was just as saturated by the same news reports. A request for a second change of venue was denied. The pervasiveness of the news reports was evident during jury selection. Of the 420 potential jurors asked about Irvin's guilt, 370 said that they had some opinion. Eight of the 12 jurors selected said they thought he was guilty even before the trial began. Given these circumstances, a unanimous Court found that the jury did not meet the constitutional standard of impartiality, but Justice Clark, who wrote the opinion, cautioned that it was not necessary for jurors to

be totally ignorant of the facts and issues involved. In these days of swift, widespread and diverse methods of communication, an important case can be expected to arouse the interest of the public in the vicinity, and scarcely any of those best qualified to serve as jurors will not have formed some impression or opinion as to the merits of the case. This is particularly true in criminal cases. To hold that the mere existence of any preconceived notion as to the guilt or innocence of an accused, without more, is sufficient to rebut the presumption of a prospective juror's impartiality would be to establish impossible standards.[98]

The following year a narrow majority of the Court held that pretrial publicity had not denied Teamsters Union president David D. Beck a fair trial on charges of grand larceny. According to the Court majority, the adverse publicity, stemming largely from a U.S. Senate investigation, had been diluted by time and by the presence of other labor leaders also under investigation, and the grand jury as well as the petit jury had been carefully questioned to avoid selection of those unduly influenced by media reports.[99] In *Rideau v. Louisiana* (1963), however, the Court held that a murder defendant whose filmed confession was broadcast and seen by three jurors had been denied due process when his effort to win a change of venue was rejected. Clark dissented. There was no evidence, he argued, that the telecast confession had indelibly marked the minds of the jurors.[100]

Conduct of Trial

The very presence of working news reporters in and near a courtroom during the course of a trial may also jeopardize its fairness. The Court had little trouble holding in *Estes v. Texas* (1965) that the presence of television cameras, radio microphones, and newspaper photographers at the pretrial hearing and trial of financier Billie Sol Estes denied Estes his right to a fair trial. "[V]ideotapes of these hearings clearly illustrate that the picture presented was not one of that judicial serenity and calm to which petitioner was entitled," the Court said.[101] The following year the Court in *Sheppard v. Maxwell* (1966) laid out some ground rules to ensure fair trials with minimal restriction on the operation of a free press.

Sheppard v. Maxwell

The 1954 beating death of a pregnant woman in her suburban Cleveland home and the subsequent arrest, trial, and conviction of her husband, Dr. Sam Sheppard,

for her murder excited some of the most intense and sensational press coverage the country had witnessed up to that time. Pretrial publicity as much as proclaimed Sheppard's guilt. Reporters had access to witnesses during the trial itself and frequently published information damaging to Sheppard that could have come only from the prosecuting attorneys. Some of this information was never introduced as evidence. Reporters in the courtroom were seated only a few feet from the jury and from Sheppard and his counsel, who were constantly besieged by reporters and photographers as they entered and left the courtroom.

"The fact is that bedlam reigned at the courthouse during the trial and newsmen took over practically the entire courtroom," said the Supreme Court, overturning Sheppard's conviction by an 8-1 vote. "The carnival atmosphere at trial could easily have been avoided since the courtroom and courthouse premises are subject to control of the court," the majority wrote. "[T]he presence of the press at judicial proceedings must be limited when it is apparent that the accused might otherwise be prejudiced or disadvantaged."[102] Change of venue and postponement of the trial until publicity dies down would be proper if pretrial publicity threatens the fair administration of justice, the Court said. Once the trial has begun, the judge may limit the number of reporters permitted in the courtroom and place strict controls on their conduct while there. Witnesses and jurors should be isolated from the press, and the jury may be sequestered to prevent it from being influenced by trial coverage. The majority also indicated that the judge should have acted to prevent officials from releasing certain information to the press:

> [T]he trial court might well have proscribed extrajudicial statements by any lawyer, party, witness or court official which divulged prejudicial matters, such as the refusal of Sheppard to submit to an interrogation or take any lie detector tests; any statement made by Sheppard to officials; the identity of prospective witnesses or their probable testimony; any belief in guilt or innocence; or like statements concerning the merits of the case....

Being advised of the great public interest in the case, the mass coverage of the press, and the

Dr. Sam Sheppard in September 1966 with his son and second wife. The Court decided that negative pretrial publicity had influenced the outcome of Sheppard's trial and overturned his conviction.

potential prejudicial impact of publicity, the court could also have requested the appropriate city and county officials to promulgate a regulation with respect to dissemination of information about the case by their employees. In addition, reporters who wrote or broadcast prejudicial stories could have been warned as to the impropriety of publishing material not introduced in the proceedings.... In this manner, Sheppard's right to a trial free from outside interference would have been given added protection without corresponding curtailment of the news media.[103]

Gag Rules

So-called gag rules bar the press by judicial order from publishing articles containing certain types of information about pending court cases. Refusal to comply with

the order may result in being held in contempt of court. After *Sheppard,* which said a gag rule was needed to ensure the defendant in that case of a fair trial, trial judges began to use such orders. Gag rules are clearly a prior restraint on publication, and their constitutionality has been challenged repeatedly by the press. In the Court's first full-scale review of a gag rule, all nine justices held the challenged order an unconstitutional prior restraint on the press.[104] Only three justices, however, said that all gag rules were unconstitutional. Four felt they might be permissible under some circumstances. The remaining two justices indicated their inclination to agree that all gag rules were unconstitutional.

In the small town of Sutherland, Nebraska, in October 1975, six members of a family were murdered. Police arrested Erwin Charles Simants, who was charged with the crimes. Because of the nature of the

INMATES AND FREE SPEECH

Prison rules limiting inmate communications with persons outside the walls must be measured against the First Amendment, held a unanimous Supreme Court in *Procunier v. Martinez* (1974). The justices thus invalidated California regulations allowing prison mailroom officials wide discretion to censor letters to or from inmates. The traditional "hands-off" policy of the federal courts toward prison regulations is rooted in a realistic appreciation of the fact that "the problems of prisons ... are complex and intractable, and ... not readily susceptible of resolution by decree," Justice Lewis F. Powell Jr. explained.[1] He continued, however, "[w]hen a prison regulation or practice offends a fundamental constitutional guarantee, federal courts will discharge their duty to protect constitutional rights.... This is such a case."[2]

The Court recognized that censorship of inmate mail jeopardized the First Amendment rights of those free persons who wished to communicate with prisoners, but it also acknowledged that the government had a legitimate interest in maintaining order in penal institutions, an interest that might justify the imposition of certain restraints on inmate correspondence. To determine whether a censorship regulation constituted an impermissible restraint on First Amendment liberties, the Court set out a two-part test: the regulation must further a substantial government interest—not simply the suppression of criticism or other expression—and the restraint on speech "must be no greater than is necessary or essential to the protection of the particular governmental interest involved."[3] The Court also held that the inmate and author must be informed of the censorship of a particular letter.

Also in 1974, the Court held that states were under no First Amendment obligation to permit prisoners to have face-to-face interviews with news reporters. An inmate's First Amendment rights might legitimately be constrained by security, rehabilitative, and discipline considerations, the Court said in *Procunier v. Hillery* (1974). Referring to *Martinez*, the Court pointed to the mail as one alternative means inmates had of communicating with persons outside the prison.[4]

The Court in *Turner v. Safley* (1987) announced a standard against which such prison regulations could be measured. If the regulation was reasonably related to legitimate penological interests, said the Court, it would be upheld. The justices then used the *Turner* standard to strike down a state prison rule forbidding most inmate marriages but upheld, 5-4, a regulation barring most correspondence between inmates.[5]

---

1. *Procunier v. Martinez*, 416 U.S. 396 at 404–405 (1974).

2. Id. at 405–406.

3. Id. at 413.

4. *Procunier v. Hillery*, 417 U.S. 817 (1974).

5. *Turner v. Safley*, 482 U.S. 78 (1987).

---

crimes and the location—a rural area with a relatively small number of potential jurors—the judge issued a gag order on the day of the preliminary hearing. Although that hearing took place in open court, the press was forbidden to report any of the testimony given or the evidence presented. The order remained in effect until the jury was chosen.

Writing the Court's opinion in *Nebraska Press Association v. Stuart* (1976), Chief Justice Burger said that the judge could have used less drastic means than the gag order to ensure that excessive publicity did not make it impossible to assemble an unbiased jury and conduct a fair trial. "[P]rior restraints on speech and publication are the most serious and the least tolerable infringement on First Amendment rights," Burger wrote. "A prior restraint ... has an immediate and irreversible sanction. If it can be said that a threat of criminal or civil sanctions after publication 'chills' speech, prior restraint 'freezes' it at least for the time."[105] (See "*Prior Restraint: Censorship,*" pp. 85–96.) Furthermore, said Burger, the right to report evidence given in an open courtroom is a settled principle. "[O]nce a public hearing had been held, what transpired there could not be subject to prior restraint."[106]

The chief justice refused, however, to rule out the possibility that the circumstances of some other case might justify imposition of a gag rule. "This Court has frequently denied that First Amendment rights are absolute and has consistently rejected the proposition that a prior restraint can never be employed."[107] "The right to a fair trial by a jury of one's peers is unquestionably one of the most precious and sacred safeguards enshrined in the Bill of Rights," wrote Justice Brennan in a concurring opinion joined by Justices Marshall and Stewart. Brennan, however, added, "I would hold … that resort to prior restraints on the freedom of the press is a constitutionally impermissible method for enforcing that right." Judges have less drastic means of ensuring fair trials than by prohibiting press "discussion of public affairs."[108] Eight years later, in 1984, however, the Court upheld a state court order restraining the publication of information about a religious organization obtained through pretrial discovery that took place under court order.[109]

Lawyers' extrajudicial statements to the press also became an issue for the Court. By a 5-4 vote, the Court ruled in *Gentile v. State Bar of Nevada* (1991) that the free speech rights of lawyers may be curtailed if their comments present "substantial likelihood of material prejudice" during a trial. The opinion by Chief Justice Rehnquist rejected a higher "clear and present danger standard."[110]

ACCESS AND CONFIDENTIALITY

In a practical sense, the public delegates to the press the job of gathering, sifting, and reporting the news that shapes its political, economic, and social views of the world. As surrogate for the public, the press attends and reports on events that the vast majority of the public does not or cannot attend. The news gathering process has been the subject of several Supreme Court cases as the justices have considered whether the First Amendment guarantees the press special access to or special protection for its news sources. The Court generally has refused to adopt such an expansive view of the First Amendment freedom, although the one exception to that view came when the press linked arms with the general public to argue for access to criminal trials.

The Court in *Gannett Co. Inc. v. DePasquale* (1979) rejected the newspaper chain's claim that it had a constitutional right, under the First and the Sixth Amendments, to attend a pretrial hearing on suppression of evidence in a murder case. By a vote of 5-4, Court held that the judge in the case had properly

granted the request of the defendants to exclude the press and public from the hearing. Upholding the judge's action were Chief Justice Burger, Justices Stewart, Powell, Rehnquist, and John Paul Stevens. Dissenting were Justices Blackmun, Brennan, White, and Marshall. The majority based its decision wholly on the Sixth Amendment, reading it literally and finding that it guaranteed the right to a *public* trial only to the person *charged* with crime, not to the public or the press. In this case, the defendants had requested that the pretrial hearing be closed; the judge had granted that request. Justice Stewart pointed out that closing such a hearing was "often one of the most effective methods that a trial judge can employ to attempt to insure that the fairness of a trial will not be jeopardized by the dissemination of such [prejudicial] information throughout the community before the trial itself has even begun."[111]

Within a year the Court had effectively reversed itself. By 7-1, the Court in *Richmond Newspapers Inc. v. Commonwealth of Virginia* (1980) recognized that the press and the public had a First Amendment right of access to trials and pretrial hearings. Justice Rehnquist dissented; Powell did not participate. In some situations, wrote Chief Justice Burger for the Court, it might be necessary—to ensure a fair trial—to limit access to a trial, but the reasons must be clearly set out and support the finding that closure is essential to preserving some overriding interest.[112] This trend continued to a surprising climax the following year in *Chandler v. Florida* (1981). Nothing in the Constitution—either in the Due Process Clause or the guarantee of a fair trial—precluded a state from permitting television cameras in a courtroom to broadcast trial proceedings, the Court ruled.[113]

When the press asks for special access to institutions and persons not generally available to the public, it almost always gets a judicial cold shoulder. Twice the Supreme Court has confronted such a request, and each time it has rejected the press's arguments. In the companion cases *Saxbe v. Washington Post Co.* (1974) and *Pell v. Procunier* (1974), the Court weighed the right of reporters to gather news within the prison system against society's interest in secure prisons. In both the Court sustained, 5-4, prison regulations that bar interviews by reporters with inmates they request by name to see.[114] The regulations prohibiting face-to-face interviews were apparently written to curtail the so-called "big wheel" phenomenon, in which the influence of certain inmates is so enhanced by publicity that disruption and disciplinary problems result.

Justice Stewart, writing for the majority, held that prison officials were justified in adopting the ban on interviews to minimize disruptive behavior. The ban did not mean that reporters had no access to the prisons, he stressed; reporters could communicate with specific inmates through the mail. Furthermore, the California and federal prison systems permitted reporters to visit prisons and to talk with inmates they met in the course of supervised tours or with inmates selected by prison officials. Nothing in the First or Fourteenth Amendments requires "government to afford the press special access to information not shared by members of the public generally," wrote Stewart.[115] In a dissenting opinion joined by two other justices, Justice Powell saw the ban on interviews as "impermissibly restrain[ing] the ability of the press to perform its constitutionally established function of informing the people on the conduct of their government."[116] Elaborating on this point, Powell said the government had no legitimate interest in withholding the information reporters might gather in personal interviews:

> Quite to the contrary, federal prisons are public institutions. The administration of these institutions, the effectiveness of their rehabilitative programs, the conditions of confinement they maintain, and the experiences of the individuals incarcerated therein are all matters of legitimate societal interest and concern. Respondents [the reporters] do not assert a right to force disclosure of confidential information or to invade in any way the decision-making process of governmental officials. Neither do they seek to question any inmate who does not wish to be interviewed. They only seek to be free of an exceptionless prohibition against a method of newsgathering that is essential to effective reporting in the prison context.[117]

In 1978 the Court, 4-3, reaffirmed its holding that reporters have no right to greater access to institutions and persons than the general public has. A federal judge six years earlier had found conditions in an Alameda County, California, jail to be so shocking as to constitute cruel and unusual punishment. As a result, television station KQED sought access to the prison to interview inmates and film conditions there. The county sheriff agreed to begin monthly scheduled tours of the prison open to the press and general public, but he prohibited the use of cameras or sound equipment as well as interviews with inmates. KQED then won an order from a federal judge directing the sheriff to grant the press wider access, to allow interviews and the use of sound and camera equipment. The sheriff appealed in *Houchins v. KQED Inc.* (1978).

Neither the First Amendment nor the Fourteenth Amendment mandates "a right of access to government information or sources of information within the government's control," wrote Chief Justice Burger, announcing the decision in an opinion only two other justices joined. The First Amendment does not guarantee access to information but only the freedom to communicate information once acquired. "[U]ntil the political branches decree otherwise, as they are free to do, the media has no special right of access to the Alameda County Jail different from or greater than that accorded the public generally," Burger wrote.[118] The fourth member of the majority, Justice Stewart, agreed only that the order was too broad. The three dissenters—Justices Brennan, Stevens, and Powell—argued that "information-gathering is entitled to some measure of constitutional protection ... not for the private benefit of those who might qualify as representatives of the 'press' but to insure that the citizens are fully informed regarding matters of public interest."[119]

Protecting Confidentiality

Does the First Amendment allow reporters to withhold information from the government to protect a news source? Members of the press contend that the threat of exposure will discourage those news sources who, for a variety of reasons, agree to provide information to reporters only if they are assured confidentiality. Not only will the individual reporter's effectiveness be damaged by forced disclosure, they contend, but the public will also suffer, losing information that it is entitled to have. For these reasons, they argue that the First Amendment protects the confidentiality of news sources, even if the sources reveal to the reporter information about crimes. Several states have laws shielding reporters from demands of grand juries, courts, and other investigating bodies for confidential or unpublished information they have collected, but the Supreme Court has refused to recognize a constitutional privilege of journalists to refuse to answer legitimate inquiries from law enforcement officers.

Grand Jury Investigations

In 1972 the Court jointly decided three cases in which reporters challenged grand jury subpoenas for confidential information:

- *Branzburg v. Hayes:* Paul M. Branzburg, an investigative reporter for the Louisville *Courier-Journal* who wrote several articles based on personal observations of drug users, whom he had promised not to identify. He was then subpoenaed by a grand jury to testify on what he had observed.

- *In re Pappas:* Paul Pappas, a television newsman who was allowed to visit a Black Panthers headquarters during a period of civil unrest on the condition that he not report what he saw. He later was subpoenaed to testify about that visit.

- *United States v. Caldwell:* Earl Caldwell, a black reporter for the *New York Times* who gained the confidence of Black Panthers in the San Francisco area and wrote several articles about them. He was then called to testify before a grand jury about alleged criminal activity among the Panthers.

State courts in *Branzburg* and *Pappas* ruled that the reporters must provide the information sought to the grand juries. The two reporters appealed. In *Caldwell*, a federal court of appeals, reversing a lower court, held that freedom of the press protected Caldwell not only from testifying but even from appearing before the grand jury. The Justice Department appealed this ruling to the Supreme Court. By a 5-4 vote, the Supreme Court sustained the state courts in *Branzburg* and *Pappas* and reversed the appeals court in *Caldwell*. "Until now the only testimonial privilege for unofficial witnesses that is rooted in the Federal Constitution is the Fifth Amendment privilege against self-incrimination," wrote Justice White for the majority. "We are asked to create another by interpreting the First Amendment to grant newsmen a testimonial privilege that other citizens do not enjoy. This we decline to do."[120] The majority held that there were no infringements of First Amendment rights in these cases:

> We do not question the significance of free speech, press or assembly to the country's welfare. Nor is it suggested that news gathering does not qualify for First Amendment protection; without some protection for seeking out the news, freedom of the press could be eviscerated. But this case involves no intrusions upon speech or assembly, no prior restraint or restriction on what the press may publish and no express or implied command that the press publish what it prefers to withhold. No exaction or tax for the privilege of publishing, and no penalty, civil or criminal, related to the content of published material is at issue here. The use of confidential sources by the press is not forbidden or restricted; reporters remain free to seek news from any source by means within the law. No attempt is made to require the press to publish its sources of information or indiscriminately to disclose them on request.[121]

White observed that the First Amendment did not protect the press from obeying other valid laws, such as labor and antitrust regulations. The authority of grand juries to subpoena witnesses was vital to their task. "Fair and effective law enforcement aimed at providing security for the person and property of the individual is a fundamental function of government," he wrote, "and the grand jury plays an important constitutionally mandated role in this process."[122] On the record, said the Court, it found that the public interest in law enforcement and in ensuring effective grand jury proceedings outweighed the uncertain burden on newsgathering that might result from insisting that reporters, like other citizens, respond to relevant questions put to them in the course of a valid grand jury investigation or criminal trial. The majority thought that potential exposure would affect few of a reporter's confidential news sources. "Only where news sources themselves are implicated in crime or possess information relevant to the grand jury's task need they or the reporter be concerned about grand jury subpoenas," White wrote. In addition, the Court could not "seriously entertain the notion that the First Amendment protects a newsman's agreement to conceal the criminal conduct of his source ... on the theory that it is better to write about crime than to do something about it," he said.[123]

The majority's "crabbed view of the First Amendment reflects a disturbing insensitivity to the critical role of an independent press in our society," wrote Justice Stewart in a dissent that Justices Marshall and Brennan joined. The majority decision "invites state and federal authorities to undermine the historic independence of the press by attempting to annex the journalistic profession as an investigative arm of government."[124] Stewart contended that a reporter had a constitutional right to maintain a confidential relationship with news sources. The right to publish must include the right to gather news, he said, and that right in turn must include a right to confidentiality. A reporter's immunity to grand jury probes is not a personal right but the right of the public to maintain an access to information of public concern, Stewart said.[125] Stewart did not believe the immunity was absolute. Weighed against other constitutional rights, First Amendment rights must be given a preferred position, he said, and government must show a compelling reason for restricting them. He suggested that a reporter be required to appear before a grand jury only if the government can

(1) show that there is probable cause to believe that the newsman has information which is clearly relevant to a specific probable violation of law; (2) demonstrate that the information sought cannot be obtained by alternative means less destructive of First Amendment rights; and (3) demonstrate a compelling and overriding interest in the information.[126]

Justice Douglas also dissented, holding that the First Amendment immunized reporters from grand jury investigations unless they were implicated in a crime.

Newsroom Searches

The Supreme Court sanctioned a different threat to confidentiality when it ruled in *Zurcher v. The Stanford Daily* (1978) that the First Amendment does not protect newspaper offices from warranted police searches for information or evidence. The lineup of the justices was almost identical to that in the three 1972 "newsman's privilege" cases. Justice Brennan did not participate; Justice Stevens dissented. (Stevens succeeded Justice Douglas, who had dissented in the earlier cases.) By a 5-3 vote, the Court rejected the argument of the nation's press that police should use subpoenas, not search warrants, to obtain information or evidence from news files, at least so long as the reporter or newspaper was not suspected of any involvement in criminal activity.

A subpoena is a less intrusive means for obtaining evidence than is a search by police armed with a warrant. The subpoena requires a person to search his own home, office, or files for certain specified items. The search warrant authorizes police, unannounced, to enter a home or office by force if necessary to search for the particular material the warrant describes. Furthermore, a person faced with a search warrant has no opportunity to contest the search before it takes place, whereas a person subpoenaed to produce information can move to quash the subpoena.

Zurcher v. The Stanford Daily arose from a 1971 police search of the offices of the *Stanford Daily,* the campus newspaper of Stanford University. The search occurred after conflict between police and demonstrators at Stanford University Hospital resulted in injury to nine police officers. Police obtained a warrant to search the files, wastebaskets, desks, and photo labs at the newspaper's offices. The object of the fruitless search was evidence of the identity of the demonstrators responsible for the police injuries. The Supreme Court majority declared that the men who wrote the Fourth Amendment were well aware of the conflict between the government and the press, and if they had felt that special procedures were needed when the government wanted information in the possession of the press, they would have said so. The First Amendment guarantee of a free press that can gather, analyze, and publish news without governmental interference is sufficiently protected by the Fourth Amendment requirement that searches be reasonable and that warrants be issued by neutral magistrates, wrote Justice White for the majority. He continued:

> Properly administered, the preconditions for a warrant—probable cause, specificity with respect to the place to be searched and the things to be seized, and overall reasonableness—should afford sufficient protection against the harms that are assertedly threatened by warrants for searching newspaper offices.[127]

Magistrates could ensure that the search not interfere with publication—and that the warrant be specific enough to prevent officers from rummaging in newspaper files or intruding into editorial decisions. White also said the majority was no more persuaded than it had been in 1972 "that confidential sources will disappear and that the press will suppress news because of fears of warranted searches."[128]

In dissent, Justice Stewart, joined by Justice Marshall, found it

> self-evident that police searches of newspaper offices burden the freedom of the press.... [I]t cannot be denied that confidential information may be exposed to the eyes of police officers who execute a search warrant by rummaging through the files, cabinets, desks and wastebaskets of a newsroom. Since the indisputable effect of such searches will thus be to prevent a newsman from being able to promise confidentiality to his potential sources, it seems obvious to me that a journalist's access to information, and thus the public's, will thereby be impaired.... The end result, wholly inimical to the First Amendment, will be a diminishing flow of potentially important information to the public.[129]

Justice Stevens also disagreed with the majority, arguing that documentary evidence in the possession of an innocent third party should be sought by subpoena rather than search warrant.

The Freedom to Broadcast

The modern expansion of the "press" to include radio and television broadcasters generated a new set of First Amendment issues. Because the number of broadcast frequencies is limited, the government has found it necessary to allocate access to them through a licensing system. With regard to print media, such a system would be considered prior restraint in violation of free speech and free press, but as the Supreme Court noted in 1969, "[w]ithout government control the … [broadcast media] would be of little use because of the cacophony of competing voices, none of which could be clearly and predictably heard."[130] The Court has thus sustained the right of the Federal Communications Commission (FCC) to determine who receives broadcast licenses, but it has also emphasized that such determinations must be made on neutral principles that do not favor one broadcaster over another because of the particular views espoused. As early as 1943 the Court wrote that "Congress did not authorize the Commission to choose among applicants upon the basis of their political, economic or social views or upon any other capricious basis."[131]

The Fairness Doctrine

The unique nature of the broadcast media does not place it altogether outside the protection of the First Amendment, but the freedom guaranteed to those who wish to broadcast is of a different variety, subject to different requirements. For almost forty years, the FCC required broadcasters to give individuals whose views or records were attacked on the air an opportunity to respond. The commission, to protect what it viewed as the public's right to hear a fair presentation of both sides of a dispute, also required broadcasters who editorialized to offer persons with opposing views the right of reply. This policy was known as the fairness doctrine. In *Red Lion Broadcasting Co. v. Federal Communications Commission* (1969), broadcasters challenged the fairness doctrine as a violation of their First Amendment rights to determine the content of broadcasts without governmental interference. The Supreme Court unanimously rejected this argument. "Where there are substantially more individuals who want to broadcast than there are frequencies to allocate, it is idle to posit an unabridgeable First Amendment right to broadcast comparable to the right of every individual to speak, write, or publish," wrote Justice White for the majority.[132]

The First Amendment right of viewers and listeners to diverse viewpoints on matters of political, economic, and social concern is paramount to the rights of broadcasters, White argued. Conversely, the Supreme Court has ruled that radio and television stations are not required by the First Amendment's guarantee to sell time to all individuals and groups who wish to expound their views on public issues across the airwaves. The Court, after voting 7-2, announced this decision in *Columbia Broadcasting System v. Democratic National Committee* (1973). Six of the justices, led by Chief Justice Burger, held that while the fairness doctrine did require broadcasters to provide a right of reply to opposing views, Congress had firmly rejected the idea that all persons wishing to air their views should have access to broadcast facilities.

The fairness doctrine makes the broadcaster responsible for adequate coverage of public issues in a manner that fairly reflects different viewpoints, the six agreed, but since every viewpoint cannot be aired, Congress and the FCC have appropriately left it to the broadcaster to exercise journalistic discretion in selecting those that present a fair picture of the issue. Five of the six justices saw the basic question as "not whether there is to be discussion of controversial issues of public importance in the broadcast media, but rather who shall determine what issues are to be discussed by whom, and when."[133] Providing a right of access to the airwaves would work chiefly to benefit persons who could afford to buy the time, and these persons could not be held accountable for fairness, they said.

In another side of this issue, the justices in *FCC v. League of Women Voters of California* (1984) struck down a federal law barring editorials on public radio and television programs that received federal grants. This curtailed precisely the sort of speech the framers meant to protect, wrote Brennan.[134] President Ronald Reagan opposed the fairness doctrine, and he appointed

to the FCC commissioners who agreed with him. After the Court declined to review a lower court ruling that the FCC could abandon this doctrine without congressional approval, the FCC voted 4-0 in August 1987 to discard it.[135]

Political Gadflies Excluded

Ralph Forbes, an Arkansas man who ran often and unsuccessfully for public office, sued when he was excluded in 1992 from a televised debate between the two leading candidates for a congressional seat. In *Arkansas Educational Television Commission v. Forbes* (1998), the Court ruled that perennial candidates and political gadflies do not have a First Amendment right to appear in debates on public television. State-owned channels must abide by the free speech principles of the First Amendment, but a public broadcaster may nonetheless "exercise substantial editorial discretion in the selection and presentation of its programming," the Court said.[136] Such discretion includes the right to exclude from a candidate's debate a "perennial candidate" who will appear on the ballot but has little public support, the 6-3 majority held. The decision to exclude Forbes was "a reasonable, viewpoint neutral exercise of journalistic discretion consistent with the First Amendment," said Justice Anthony M. Kennedy.[137]

Content and Context

In 1978 the Court upheld against a First Amendment challenge the FCC's power to limit the hours during which radio stations may broadcast material that although possibly offensive to many listeners is not obscene. Around two o'clock one afternoon, a New York radio station owned by the Pacifica Foundation aired a recorded monologue by humorist George Carlin. Entitled "Filthy Words," the sketch satirized society's attitude toward certain words, in particular seven that are usually barred from use on the air. In the monologue, Carlin lists the seven "dirty words"—*shit, piss, fuck, cunt, cocksucker, motherfucker,* and *tits*—and then uses them in various forms throughout the recording. After receiving a parent's complaint that his young son had heard the monologue, the FCC issued an order to the station restricting the hours during which such an "offensive" program could be broadcast. Pacifica challenged the order, arguing that the FCC was regulating the content of a program in violation of the guarantee of free speech.

"No such absolute rule [forbidding government regulation of content] is mandated by the Constitution," said Justice John Paul Stevens for the majority of five. "[B]oth the content and the context of speech are critical elements of First Amendment analysis." While "some uses of even the most offensive words are unquestionably protected" by the First Amendment, "the constitutional protection accorded to such patently offensive language [as used in the monologue] need not be the same in every context.... Words that are commonplace in one setting are shocking in another," he said.[138] The context of the broadcast justified the FCC's regulation, the majority concluded. Because the broadcast media has established a "uniquely pervasive presence," offensive material that is broadcast reaches people in the privacy of their homes "where the individual's right to be let alone plainly outweighs the First Amendment rights of an intruder." Furthermore, the broadcast was "uniquely accessible to children," and the Court has held that speech otherwise protected might be regulated to protect their welfare.[139] Four justices dissented.

The Supreme Court upheld in 1978 the authority of the FCC to decree an end to common ownership of a community's single newspaper and its only radio or television station. The commission has broad power "to regulate broadcasting in the 'public interest,'" wrote Justice Marshall for the unanimous Court. The FCC issued its order to encourage diversity of ownership that could possibly result in diversity of viewpoints aired within a community. This was a valid public interest and a rational means of reaching that goal, Marshall said in *Federal Communications Commission v. National Citizens Committee for Broadcasting* (1978).[140]

Cable Television

The rapid growth of cable television during the 1980s changed the way most Americans received television signals in their homes, and it forced the Supreme Court to rethink the legal rules for this medium. Federal regulation

first of radio and then of broadcast television was based on the notion that the spectrum of frequencies was limited. The government licensed broadcasters to use this frequency, and therefore it had some authority to regulate what was carried over the air. The Court had upheld the fairness doctrine because broadcasters were making use of this scarce public commodity, but in the early 1990s the Court ruled cable television to be fundamentally different from over-the-air broadcasting and therefore deserving of the full free press protections of a newspaper or magazine. "Cable television does not suffer from the inherent limitations that characterized the broadcast medium. Indeed, given the rapid advances in fiber optics and digital compression technology, soon there may be no practical limitation on the number of speakers who use the cable medium," wrote Justice Kennedy in *Turner Broadcasting v. FCC* (1994).[141] "Cable programmers and cable operators engage in and transmit speech, and they are entitled to the protection of the speech and press provisions of the First Amendment."[142] Kennedy said this meant that the government may not regulate "the content of speech" carried by cable operators, except for truly obscene material, which is not protected by the First Amendment.

Two years later, in *Denver Area Telecommunications Consortium v. FCC* (1996), the Court struck down parts of a federal law that sought to protect children and their parents from "indecent" performances on "leased access" cable channels. "The First Amendment embodies an overarching commitment to protect speech from Government regulation through close judicial scrutiny," said Justice Stephen G. Breyer.[143] Parents could obtain "lockboxes" or screening devices to block offensive channels, he noted, and Congress could have even required cable operators to make these lockboxes available to all customers. Blocking the channels by law, however, goes too far, he said.

In *United States v. Playboy Entertainment Group* (2000), the Court invalidated a federal law that required cable operators to block channels "dedicated to sexually-oriented programming" before 10:00 P.M. if their signals could "bleed" into another channel. Parents had complained of coming home to find their children watching fuzzy images from pay-per-view channels to which they had not subscribed. The complaints prompted Congress to pass a law requiring cable operators to block these channels to all their customers during the daytime and evening hours. The Playboy Entertainment Group challenged the law because it prevented its channels from being shown before 10:00 P.M. In a 5-4 decision, the Court struck down the law because it was a "content-based regulation" of speech.

"This case involves speech alone; and even where speech is indecent and enters the home, the objective of shielding children does not suffice to support a blanket ban if the protection can be accomplished by a less restrictive alternative," Kennedy said.[144] Cable subscribers, on request, may fully block the adult-oriented channels, he noted. "Simply put, targeted blocking is less restrictive than banning, and the Government cannot ban speech if targeted blocking is feasible."[145] Justices John Paul Stevens, David H. Souter, Clarence Thomas, and Ruth Bader Ginsburg joined Kennedy's opinion.

The cable industry, however, lost the battle that it had fought the hardest to win. In 1992 Congress repealed rules limiting how much cable companies may charge their subscribers, but it added the requirement that cable systems carry the signals of all over-the-air broadcasters in their area. Otherwise, cable companies could drive those broadcasters (and fellow competitors for advertisements) out of business. The cable industry challenged this requirement as an infringement on its free speech and free press rights, arguing that as a newspaper cannot be required to publish all columnists and feature stories, a cable company similarly cannot be required to carry unpopular local channels. The Court disagreed, and in *Turner Broadcasting v. FCC* (1997) upheld the law in a 5-4 decision. This is a "content-neutral regulation of speech," said Justice Kennedy, because it is not targeted at a particular type of speech or message. It was well justified, he said, because the growing power of the cable television industry threatens "the economic viability of free local broadcast television."[146] Kennedy was joined by Chief Justice William H. Rehnquist and Justices Stevens, Souter, and Breyer.

The Internet and the "New Marketplace of Ideas"

The new medium of the 1990s was the Internet, the worldwide network that allows computer users around the globe to post and obtain all varieties of information. In 1996 Congress passed the Communication Decency Act to protect minors from the free flow of pornography on the Internet by making it a crime to transmit any "obscene or indecent" messages that could be received by someone under age eighteen. Art galleries, librarians, sex advice columnists, the sponsors of Web sites devoted to gays and lesbians, and others challenged the law. Opponents said they had no simple or certain way to prevent young computer users from tapping into their sites, because the material was freely available to all. Moreover, the word "indecent" was vague.

In *Reno v. ACLU* (1997), the Court's first—and unanimous—decision concerning the Internet, the justices had this to say about this popular medium: "From the publishers' point of view, it constitutes a vast platform from which to address and hear from a world wide audience of millions of readers, viewers, researchers and buyers.... It is no exaggeration to conclude that the content on the Internet is as diverse as human thought."[147] In striking down the law as too broad in its reach and vague in its meaning, Justice Stevens wrote, "Could a speaker confidently assume that a serious discussion about birth control practices, homosexuality,... or the consequences of prison rape would not violate the CDA?"[148]

Of more significance for the future, the Court described the "vast democratic forums of the Internet" as deserving full First Amendment protection.[149] Unlike broadcast television, the Internet does not operate over scarce airwaves, and unlike radio, it does not "invade" the home or the auto with an unwanted, offensive message. Computer users usually must take steps on their own to reach the offensive material, Stevens noted. There is "no basis for qualifying the level of First Amendment scrutiny that should be applied to this medium," he said.[150] Citing "the dramatic expansion of this new marketplace of ideas,... in the absence of evidence to the contrary, we presume that governmental regulation of the content of speech is more likely to interfere with the free exchange of ideas than to encourage it."[151]

Despite the unanimous defeat for the anti-indecency law, the issue of pornography and the Internet was sure to return to the Court. Reacting to the initial decision, Congress passed a narrower measure called the Child Online Protection Act of 1998, which applied only to "commercial" Web sites and defined the banned material as that which is "harmful to minors." The American Civil Liberties Union renewed its challenge in the lower court on First Amendment grounds. In 2002 the Court struck down the Child Pornography Protection Act of 1996, which made it a crime to own or sell a "computer-generated image" of what "is, or appears to be,… a minor engaging in sexually explicit conduct." Child pornography is illegal in all circumstances—and it is not protected by the First Amendment—but Congress in 1996 had decided also to ban "virtual child pornography" because of concerns that digital imaging could produce lifelike creations.

The Court's 6-3 decision in *Ashcroft v. Free Speech Coalition* (2002) held that this criminal sanction, complete with a fifteen-year prison term, cannot stand as a punishment for a fictional creation. "These images do not involve, let alone harm, any children in the production process," said Justice Kennedy.[152] "The statute proscribes the visual depiction of an idea—that of teenagers engaging in sexual activity—that is a fact of modern society and has been a theme in art and literature throughout the ages."[153] The Court also invalidated a second part of the law that could have punished a filmmaker for using an actor who "appears to be" a minor engaging in sex, even if the actor were over age eighteen. Justice Sandra Day O'Connor agreed with the majority that this section was unconstitutional, but she said she would have upheld the ban on "virtual child pornography." Chief Justice Rehnquist and Justice Scalia dissented in full.

A year later, in *United States v. American Library Association* (2003), the Court upheld a federal law requiring public librarians to install software filters on their computers to screen out sexually explicit material that would be harmful to minors. In the Children's Internet Protection Act of 1998, Congress said libraries must comply with the law if they want to receive federal funds. Because libraries do not have a right to receive federal money, and because library patrons do not have a right to receive subsidized pornography, the Court upheld the law and said it does not violate the First Amendment.[154] *(See also box, Federal Money and Free Speech, pp. 80–81.)*

Freedom of Religion

It is unthinkable to most Americans that Congress or the president could or would dictate what religious beliefs individuals must hold or what church, if any, they must attend. The freedom to believe as one chooses, or not to believe at all, is as basic to the concept of U.S. democracy as the rights of free speech and press. The First Amendment reads in part, "Congress shall make no law respecting an establishment of religion, or prohibiting the free exercise thereof." These two commands protect what the authors of the Constitution referred to as the "freedom of conscience." One clause asserts that the government may not control, influence, or promote religion. The other states that the government may not forbid individuals from freely practicing their religion. Faith and conscience exist separately from the secular authority of government. The freedom to believe and to worship may be the most absolute of rights in the law.

The First Amendment's guarantees of free exercise of religion and separation of church and state were the direct products of colonial experience. Many of the colonies were established by settlers fleeing religious persecution, primarily in Anglican-dominated England. Some of the colonialists were themselves intolerant, persecuting those whose religious beliefs and practices were different from their own. Several colonies forbade Catholics and non-Christians to hold certain offices and jobs. For a time, there was a state religion in some of the colonies. Others colonies, however—notably Delaware, Pennsylvania, and Rhode Island—tolerated religious diversity.[1] By the time of the American Revolution, belief in religious toleration was well established, and when the First Amendment was written in 1789, it was religious freedom that led the list of individual rights Congress was forbidden to abridge. As Justice Joseph Story wrote in his commentaries on the Constitution,

It was under a solemn consciousness of the dangers from ecclesiastical ambition, the bigotry of spiritual pride, and the intolerance of sects, thus exemplified in our domestic as well as in foreign annals, that it

was deemed advisable to exclude from the national government all power to act upon the subject.[2]

The Supreme Court has struggled mightily, particularly in the second half of the twentieth century, to give precise meaning to the First Amendment's limits on the government. What, after all, is meant by an "establishment of religion"? Is it simply a ban on the official proclamation of a "national religion" as Chief Justice William H. Rehnquist suggested in *Wallace v. Jaffree* (1985), or does it speak more broadly, erecting "a wall of separation between church and state," as President Thomas Jefferson wrote in a letter to the Danbury Baptist Congregation in 1802?[3]

These questions took on a new urgency after World War II. Until then, the key word in the First Amendment was *Congress.* Because the federal legislature rarely passed laws that dealt with churches and the faithful, the ban on laws "respecting an establishment of religion" had little practical significance. By the middle decades of the twentieth century, however, the Supreme Court, led by Justice Hugo L. Black, had become convinced that the framers of the Reconstruction-era Fourteenth Amendment—with its mandate that "No State shall … deprive any person of life, liberty, or property"—extended to all Americans and to all levels of government protections for the "fundamental rights" set forth in the first ten amendments. That meant that the ban on an "establishment of religion" applied to states, cities, and local school boards.

In the late 1940s, the Court took up a New Jersey case that challenged the common practice of using taxpayer money to pay the cost of busing children to parochial schools (as well as public schools). Speaking for a unanimous court in *Everson v. Board of Education* (1947), Justice Black adopted Jefferson's "separation of church and state" as constitutional law:

The "establishment of religion" clause of the First Amendment means at least this: Neither a state nor the Federal Government can set up a church. Neither can pass laws which aid one religion, aid all religions or prefer one religion over another. Neither can force nor influence a person to go to or to remain away from church against his will or force him to profess a belief or disbelief in any religion. No person can be punished for entertaining or professing any religious beliefs or disbeliefs, for church attendance or non-attendance. No tax in any amount, large or small, can be levied to support any religious activities or institutions, whatever they may be called, or whatever form they may adopt to teach or practice religion. Neither a state nor the Federal Government can, openly or secretly, participate in the affairs of any religious organizations or groups and *vice versa*. In the words of Jefferson, the clause against establishment of religion by law was intended to erect "a wall of separation between Church and State."[4]

Since *Everson,* a debate has raged among constitutional scholars and religious activists as to whether the Constitution's framers indeed intended to erect a wall of separation between church and state. Advocates of strict separation rely largely on the words of Jefferson and James Madison, who led the fight in Virginia to forbid tax assessments to support churches or the clergy. The two argued that religious liberty flourished when churches relied on voluntary support. "To compel a man to furnish contributions of money for the propagation of opinions which he disbelieves, is sinful and tyrannical," Jefferson said.[5]

Critics of this view of Madison, Jefferson, and the other framers, however, argue that these men did not intend to remove the influence of religion from government and public life. Chief Justice Rehnquist was a leading critic in this camp and had referred to Jefferson's "wall of separation" as a "misleading metaphor" that does not capture the true meaning of the First Amendment.[6] Moreover, Rehnquist and several of his colleagues, including Justices Clarence Thomas and Anthony M. Kennedy, had condemned legal decisions enforcing strict separation as reflecting "hostility" toward religion. In one opinion, Thomas charged that the rulings limiting government aid to parochial schools stemmed from an anti-Catholic "bigotry."[7] Rehnquist

and Thomas were leading spokesmen for the view that the First Amendment requires only that the government be neutral toward religion; it cannot favor or disfavor religion. Under this theory, tax money can be sent to religious schools so long as it arrives there via an education aid program that supports schooling in general, without regard to whether the institutions are religious in nature. By 2002 their view had won a narrow majority at the Supreme Court in some school funding cases.[8]

The doctrine of strict separation between church and state reached its peak during the 1960s and 1970s, when the Court struck down state-sponsored prayer and Bible readings in public schools. Also invalidated were a series of state laws that subsidized parochial schools. The justices then believed, as Justice Black had written, that "No tax in any amount, large or small, can be levied to support any religious activities or institutions."[9] More recently, only Justices David H. Souter, John Paul Stevens, and Ruth Bader Ginsburg have continued to espouse the separationist view, often in dissent. Souter has authored dissents that carry a tone of dismay and despair, maintaining that constitutional history and Court precedent make clear that tax money cannot flow to parochial schools. "Together with James Madison, we have consistently understood the Establishment Clause to impose a substantive prohibition against public aid to religion, and hence to the religious mission of sectarian schools," he wrote in *Mitchell v. Helms* (2000).[10]

In the religion-and-school cases during the Rehnquist Court, three trends were simultaneously on display. First, public school sponsorship of prayers and religious invocations were strictly forbidden. In this area, the Court refused to budge from its 1960s strict separation decisions.[11] This came as something of a surprise, since President Ronald Reagan had called for restoring prayer in the public schools and appointed to the Court three new justices and the chief justice in the 1980s. Nonetheless, the Court in *Lee v. Weisman* (1992) ruled that public schools may not invite a priest, cleric, or rabbi to deliver an invocation at a graduation ceremony.[12] Justices Sandra Day O'Connor and Kennedy, two Reagan appointees, joined their more liberal, separationist advocates in declaring that such an activity amounts to government sponsorship of a religious practice. Eight years later, in *Santa Fe Independent School District v. Doe* (2000), they joined with their more liberal colleagues again to rule that a public school cannot select a student to deliver a prayer at a football game.[13] This too crosses the line, they said.

Second, however, the Court has made clear that private prayer or religious activity is permitted on a public school campus. Students have a free speech right to pray on their own, to read the Bible at school, or to talk about their faith. In a series of rulings, the justices upheld the principle of "equal access" to public school facilities for religious students and Christian groups. Third, the conservative wing of the Court, led by Chief Justice Rehnquist, shifted the law in favor of allowing tax money to flow to religious schools. In 1997 the Court ruled that federal funds can be used to pay public school tutors to reach remedial reading classes in parochial schools.[14] In 2001 the Court held that federal aid may be used to purchase computers for parochial schools as well as public schools.[15] In 2002 the Court, in a 5-4, decision upheld Ohio's use of state vouchers or tuition grants to pay for children in Cleveland to attend religious schools.[16] On this frontier, the wall of separation erected during the 1960s was thoroughly breached.

Unlike the Establishment Clause, the First Amendment's protection for the "free exercise of religion" has led to minimal conflicts in the Court. The few cases have grown out of clashes between state or local governments and a minority religion: the Mormons, Jehovah's Witnesses, the Amish, and Hare Krishnas, for example. Many of the Court's landmark free speech decisions of the 1940s arose when local and state authorities tried to prevent Jehovah's Witnesses from going door to door to solicit contributions. In the midst of World War II, the Court ruled that the children of Jehovah's Witnesses cannot be compelled to salute the flag at school.[17] In the 1960s and 1970s, the Court continued to rule in general in favor of religious freedom in clashes with government authorities. Here too, however, the Court has since reversed direction. In an opinion authored by Justice Antonin Scalia, the Court ruled that religious adherents are not entitled to an exemption from "neutral, generally applicable laws."[18] This 5-4 decision, handed down in *Employment Division, Department of Human Resources of Oregon v. Smith* (1990), dropped the earlier "strict scrutiny" standard in religious freedom cases and touched off sharp criticism from across the religious and ideological spectrum, ranging from the American Civil Liberties Union to the Christian Coalition. They contended that the Court's watered-down standard would not protect religious liberty, and they went on to win passage of a law to overturn the decision. The Court, unfazed, struck down the new law as unconstitutional in *City of Boerne v. Flores* (1997).[19]

THE FREE EXERCISE OF RELIGION

Freedom of religion is inextricably bound with the other freedoms guaranteed by the First Amendment. Without the freedoms of speech and press, the expression and circulation of religious beliefs and doctrines would be impossible. Without the freedoms of assembly and association, the right to participate with others in public and private religious worship would be curtailed. Before and after the Court held in 1940 that the Fourteenth Amendment protected the free exercise of religion from restriction by the states, it resolved several other cases challenging state infringements on religious liberty by relying on the freedoms of speech and press.[20] The Court held in *Lovell v. Griffin* (1938) that a municipal prohibition against distribution of handbills without a permit was an unconstitutional prior restraint on freedom of the press. At issue in this particular case was the right of a Jehovah's Witness to pass out religious circulars. In *Kunz v. New York* (1951), the Court held that arbitrary denial of a public speech permit to a Baptist minister was a violation of the rights of free speech and assembly as well as of religious liberty.[21] *(See "The Lovell Case," p. 92, and details of the Kunz case, p. 53.)*

As a result of the close relationship among these rights, the Supreme Court uses many of the same tests developed in the context of restrictions on free speech and press to determine if government has impermissibly restricted free exercise of religion. In general, the

RELIGION: AN EVOLVING DEFINITION

As the nation's tolerance for religious diversity has broadened, so has the Supreme Court's definition of beliefs it considers religious and therefore entitled to First Amendment protection. The Court originally considered religion only in the traditional Judeo-Christian sense, which demanded belief in a divine being. "The term 'religion' has reference to one's views of his relations to his Creator, and the obligations they impose of reverence for his being and character, and of obedience to his will," the Court said in *Davis v. Beason* (1890).[1] This view also prevailed in 1931, when Chief Justice Charles Evans Hughes wrote that "[t]he essence of religion is belief in a relation to God involving duties superior to those arising from any human relation."[2] This definition guided Congress in 1948, when it tried to define the belief one must hold to qualify for exemption from military service as a conscientious objector. *(See box, Religion and War, p. 137.)*

In the 1940s, the Court began to move toward a more expansive interpretation of "religion," accepting beliefs that were neither orthodox nor theistically based. In 1943 Justice Felix Frankfurter quoted with approval the words of federal judge Augustus Hand in a case earlier that year:

> It is unnecessary to attempt a definition of religion; the content of the term is found in the history of the human race and is incapable of compression into a few words. Religious belief arises from a sense of the inadequacy of reason as a means of relating the individual to his fellow men and to his universe.... [I]t may justly be regarded as a response of the individual to an inward mentor, call it conscience or God, that is for many persons at the present time the equivalent of what has always been thought a religious impulse.[3]

The following year, 1944, Justice William O. Douglas, speaking for the Court majority, said that the free exercise of religion "embraces the right to maintain theories of life and of death and of the hereafter which are rank heresy to followers of the orthodox faiths."[4] In 1953 Douglas wrote that "it is no business of courts to say that which is religious practice or activity for one group is not religion under the protection of the First Amendment."[5] As one commentator noted, these decisions made clear that "the classification of a belief as religion does not depend upon the tenets of its creed."[6] The breadth of the Court's modern definition of religion was perhaps most clearly stated in *Torcaso v. Watkins* (1961):

> neither a State nor the federal government can constitutionally force a person "to profess a belief or disbelief in any religion." Neither can constitutionally pass laws nor impose requirements which aid all religions as against non-believers, and neither can aid those religions based on a belief in the existence of God as against those religions founded on different beliefs.[7]

In 1965 the Court reaffirmed *Torcaso*, viewing as religious any sincere and meaningful belief that occupies a place in the possessor's life parallel to the place God holds in the faith of an orthodox believer. The Court expanded this definition in 1970 to include moral and ethical beliefs held with the strength of traditional religious convictions.[8]

---

1. *Davis v. Beason,* 133 U.S. 333 at 342 (1890).
2. *United States v. Macintosh,* 283 U.S. 605 at 633–634 (1911).
3. *United States v. Kauten,* 133 P. 2d 703 at 708 (1943), quoted by Justice Felix Frankfurter, dissenting in *West Virginia State Board of Education v. Barnette,* 319 U.S. 624 at 658–659 (1943).
4. *United States v. Ballard,* 322 U.S. 78 at 86 (1944).
5. *Fowler v. Rhode Island,* 345 U.S. 67 at 70 (1953).
6. John Sexton, "Note: Toward a Constitutional Definition of Religion," *Harvard Law Review* 91, no. 5 (March 1978): 1056.
7. *Torcaso v. Watkins,* 367 U.S. 488 at 495 (1961).
8. *United States v. Seeger,* 380 U.S. 163 at 166 (1965); *Welsh v. United States,* 398 U.S. 333 (1970).

Court has ruled that states and the federal government may restrict the free exercise of religion if the exercise involves fraud or other criminal activity and there is no other means of protecting the public. Government also may restrict religious practices that threaten public peace and order but only if the restriction is nondiscriminatory, narrowly drawn, and precisely applied. In some circumstances, the Court has upheld the right of government to compel an individual to take action contrary to his or her religious belief. As the rule was stated late in the 1970s, such a compulsory law will stand against a First Amendment challenge if its primary purpose and effect are to advance a valid secular goal and if the means chosen are calculated to have the least possible restrictive effect on free exercise of religion.

Religion and Crime

In its first direct pronouncement on the First Amendment's protection for the free exercise of religion, the Supreme Court held in the late 1870s that polygamy was a crime, not a religious practice. *Reynolds v. United States* (1879) brought before the Court a Mormon's challenge to the constitutionality of the federal law that barred plural marriages in Utah Territory. Observing that bigamy and polygamy were considered punishable offenses in every state, the Court found "it … impossible to believe that the constitutional guaranty of religious freedom was intended to prohibit legislation in respect to this most important feature of social life."[22] Eleven years later, the Court elaborated on this reasoning when it upheld an Idaho territorial statute denying the vote to bigamists, polygamists, and those who advocated plural marriages. In *Davis v. Beason* (1890), the Court for the first time distinguished between protected belief and unprotected conduct:

> It was never intended or supposed that the [First] Amendment could be evoked as a protection against legislation for the punishment of acts inimical to the peace, good order and morals of society. With man's relations to his Maker and the obligations he may think they impose, and the manner in which an expression shall be made by him of his belief on those subjects, no interference can be permitted provided always the laws of society designed to secure its peace and prosperity, and the morals of its people, are not interfered with. However free the exercise of religion may be, it must be subordinate to the criminal laws of the country, passed with reference to actions regarded by general consent as properly the subjects of punitive legislation.[23]

Justice Stephen J. Field, who wrote the Court's opinion, concluded succinctly: "Crime is not the less odious because sanctioned by what any particular sect may designate as religion."[24]

Fraud

States and municipalities, wishing to protect their citizens from fraud, occasionally have restricted religious groups' freedom to solicit funds to sustain the religion.

In *Cantwell v. Connecticut* (1940), the Court laid out the type of restriction that might be permitted:

> Nothing we have said is intended even remotely to imply that, under the cloak of religion, persons may, with impunity, commit fraud upon the public.… Even the exercise of religion may be at some slight inconvenience in order that a State may protect its citizens from injury. Without doubt a State may protect its citizens from fraudulent solicitation by requiring a stranger in the community … to establish his identity and his authority to act for the cause which he purports to represent. The State is likewise free to regulate the time and manner of solicitation generally, in the interest of public safety, peace, comfort or convenience.[25]

In *Martin v. City of Struthers* (1943), the Court held that the possibility that some persons might use house-to-house solicitations as opportunities to commit crimes did not warrant an ordinance prohibiting all solicitors from ringing doorbells to summon the occupants of the house. The Court said that the municipality must find a way of preventing crime that was less restrictive of those persons soliciting for sincere causes.[26] *(See details of Martin v. City of Struthers, pp. 74–75.)*

Only once has the Supreme Court dealt with the issue of whether a movement designated as religious by its founders was actually fraudulent. Guy Ballard, the leader of the "I Am" movement in the mid-1940s, at one point had approximately 3 million followers. He and two relatives claimed that their spiritual teachings had been dictated by God, that Jesus had personally appeared to them, and that they could cure both curable and incurable diseases. They were indicted by the federal government for mail fraud. The sole question before the Supreme Court in *United States v. Ballard* (1944) was whether the trial jury had been properly instructed that it need not determine whether the Ballards' beliefs were true but only whether the Ballards believed them to be true. A majority of the Court found the instruction proper. Religious freedom, wrote Justice William O. Douglas,

> embraces the right to maintain theories of life and of death and of the hereafter which are rank heresy to followers of the orthodox faiths. Heresy trials are

foreign to our Constitution. Men may believe what they cannot prove. They may not be put to the proof of their religious doctrines or beliefs.... The religious views espoused by respondents might seem incredible, if not preposterous, to most people. But if those doctrines are subject to trial before a jury charged with finding their truth or falsity, then the same can be done with the religious beliefs of any sect.[27]

Chief Justice Harlan Fiske Stone dissented, arguing that a jury could properly be instructed to determine whether the representations were true or false. Stone said he saw no reason why the government could not submit evidence, for instance, showing that Ballard had never cured anyone of a disease. Justice Robert H. Jackson also dissented, on the ground that the case should have been dismissed altogether. *(See box, Religion: An Evolving Definition, p. 128.)*

Laws that make employment of children under a certain age a crime have been upheld against claims that they impinge on religious liberty. In the 1940s, the Court sustained a Massachusetts statute that prohibited girls younger than eighteen from selling newspapers on the streets. The law had been applied to forbid a nine-year-old Jehovah's Witness from distributing religious literature. The state's interest in protecting children from the harmful effects of child labor "is not nullified merely because the parent grounds his claim to control the child's course of conduct on religion or conscience," the Court wrote in *Prince v. Massachusetts* (1944).[28]

Drugs and Sacrifice

A state must prove that it has a "compelling interest" in enforcing a law that infringes on religious practices, the Court ruled in 1963.[29] In 1990 it significantly narrowed that standard and its generous view of the Free Exercise Clause.[30] The latter case, *Employment Division, Department of Human Resources of Oregon v. Smith* (1990), involved two men who were fired from their jobs with a private drug rehabilitation program because they took peyote at a Native American church ceremony. Peyote, a cactus that contains the hallucinogen mescaline, is a traditional element of Native American religious ceremonies. Oregon law subjected anyone who used the drug to criminal penalties, making no exception, as some laws do, for its sacramental use. The workers were denied state unemployment compensation on the grounds that they had been discharged for criminal behavior.

The Supreme Court not only upheld the denial of benefits, but it also declared that states may outlaw all use of peyote without violating the guarantee of free exercise of religion. A five-justice majority, led by Justice Antonin Scalia, said no constitutional violation occurs when a criminal law that applies generally to all people has the incidental effect of infringing on religious exercise for some. Scalia was joined by Chief Justice William H. Rehnquist and Justices Byron R. White, John Paul Stevens, and Anthony M. Kennedy. Justices Harry A. Blackmun, William J. Brennan Jr., Thurgood Marshall, and Sandra Day O'Connor dissented. (O'Connor sought to keep the stricter constitutional standard but joined the majority to uphold the denial of benefits, saying the state of Oregon had convincingly argued that its interest in drug control was compelling and outweighed the law's burden on religious practice.)

In 1993, after extensive lobbying by religious and civil liberty groups, Congress passed the Religious Freedom Restoration Act, which was intended to reverse the *Smith* ruling by making it more difficult for states to enforce laws that incidentally affected some people's freedom to exercise their religion. The law states that government may burden a person's exercise of religion only if it demonstrates that the regulation furthers a compelling governmental interest and is the least restrictive means of furthering that interest.[31]

The Court, however, was determined to have the last word. In 1997 the justices took up a constitutional challenge to the Religious Freedom Restoration Act and struck it down as having exceeded Congress's power. *(See details of City of Boerne v. Flores, p. 127.)* In a bold assertion of its power to determine the meaning of the Constitution, the Court said its decision in the Oregon case spelled out the meaning of the "free exercise of religion," and Congress was not free to change it by passing a new law. Justice Kennedy spoke for the 6-3

Santeria priest Rigoberto Zamora (*left*) and Pedro Flores prepare a goat for a ritual sacrifice. Zamora and other members of his church celebrated the Supreme Court's decision striking down city attempts to prohibit animal sacrifice in religious worship.

majority; dissenting were Justices O'Connor, David H. Souter, and Stephen G. Breyer. Scalia's opinion in *Smith* thus remained the law. Nonetheless, three years after the peyote ruling, the Court made clear that it would invalidate laws that were targeted at particular religious practices. In 1993 the justices unanimously struck down a south Florida city's ban on ritual animal sacrifices, ruling that it interfered with the free exercise of an Afro-Cuban religion. The justices said the city of Hialeah had improperly targeted followers of the Santeria religion. Although the ban against animal killings ostensibly sought to protect public health or prevent cruelty to animals, it was not generally applied, the justices noted. Rather, the ban targeted ritual sacrifice—and as such infringed only on the Santerians' exercise—but not, for instance, other killings, such as by hunters.[32]

Religion and Social Order

At times, society's need for order and tranquility may be strong enough to warrant restriction of religious liberty, but the Supreme Court has made it clear that such restrictions must be narrowly drawn and uniformly applied. The conflict between public order and religious liberty was first raised in *Cantwell v.*

Connecticut (1940). Jesse Cantwell, a Jehovah's Witness, played a recording that attacked the Catholic Church. Two Catholic passersby heard it. When they indicated their displeasure with the message, he stopped the record and moved on. The next day, he was arrested for breach of the peace. The Supreme Court overturned the conviction, finding the statute defining breach of the peace too broad, "sweeping in a great variety of conduct under a general and indefinite characterization." This vagueness left too much discretion to officials charged with applying it. Cantwell had not started a riot or caused anyone else to take action that amounted to a breach of the peace, the majority said. He therefore raised no "clear and present menace to public peace and order as to render him liable to conviction of the common law offense in question."[33] *(See details of Cantwell v. Connecticut, pp. 50–51.)*

Permits

In *Cantwell,* the Court struck down a statute that forbade solicitation for religious causes without a permit because the law allowed a state official discretion to withhold permits if he did not think the cause was a religious one. "[T]o condition the solicitation of aid for the perpetuation of religious views or systems upon a license, the grant of which rests in the exercise of a determination by state authority as to what is a religious cause, is to lay a forbidden burden upon the exercise of [religious] liberty," the Court wrote.[34] Permit systems requiring speakers, demonstrators, and paraders to seek a license before undertaking their activity were valid only if narrowly drawn and precisely applied.

In *Cox v. New Hampshire* (1941), the Court upheld the conviction of a group of Jehovah's Witnesses who paraded without obtaining the required permit. The Court said the statute was not enacted or applied with intent to restrict religious freedom. Rather, it was intended simply to determine the time, manner, and place of parades so as to minimize public disruption and disorder. Such a precisely drawn and applied statute did not unconstitutionally impinge on religious liberty.[35] *(See details of Cox v. New Hampshire, p. 63.)* In *Kunz v. New York* (1951), the Court reversed the conviction of a Baptist minister who continued to give highly inflammatory public street sermons even though his permit to speak on the streets had not been renewed because earlier speeches had caused disorder. The Court ruled that "an ordinance which gives an administrative official discretionary power to control in advance the right of citizens to speak on religious matters on the streets … is clearly invalid as a prior restraint on the exercise of First Amendment rights."[36] (See details of Kunz v. New York, p. 53.)

In another 1951 case, the Supreme Court ruled that a city could not deny a permit for a public meeting to a group of whose religious views it disapproved. Jehovah's Witnesses had applied for a permit to hold a religious meeting in Havre de Grace, Maryland. The permit was denied after officials questioned the adherents about their religious beliefs. The Jehovah's Witnesses held their meeting despite the permit denial and were arrested for disorderly conduct. The Supreme Court reversed their convictions in Niemotko v. Maryland (1951). Denial of a permit to one religious group when permits had been granted to other religious meetings amounted to a denial of equal protection, the Court said.[37] Two years later, the Court reversed the conviction of a Jehovah's Witness who spoke at an open-air meeting in violation of a Pawtucket, Rhode Island, ordinance prohibiting religious addresses in public parks. During the trial, the state admitted that it had allowed ministers of other churches to deliver sermons at church services held in public parks. The Court ruled that such unequal treatment constituted an improper establishment of religion. "To call the words which one minister speaks to his congregation a sermon, immune from regulation, and the words of another minister an address, subject to regulation, is merely an indirect way of preferring one religion over another," the Court stated in Fowler v. Rhode Island (1953).[38]

License Fees

The validity of license fees imposed on peddlers was challenged by Jehovah's Witnesses who contested the application of the fees to Witnesses who sold religious literature from door to door. A five-justice majority initially sustained the license fees in Jones v. Opelika (1942), ruling that the solicitations were more commercial than religious:

> When proponents of religious or social theories use the ordinary commercial methods of sales of articles to raise propaganda funds, it is a natural and proper exercise of the power of the state to charge reasonable fees for the privilege of canvassing. Careful as we may and should be to protect the freedoms safeguarded by the Bill of Rights, it is difficult to see in such enactments a shadow of prohibition of the exercise of religion or of abridgement of the freedom of speech or the press. It is prohibition and unjustifiable abridgement which is interdicted, not taxation.[39]

In 1943 Justice James F. Byrnes, who had voted with the majority, resigned and was replaced by Wiley B. Rutledge, a liberal. The Court decided to address the license fee issue again. The new case concerned a Jeannette, Pennsylvania, ordinance that placed a tax of $1.50 a day on the privilege of door-to-door solicitation. It also required all persons taking orders for or delivering goods door-to-door to obtain a license from the city. Without obtaining such a license, Jehovah's Witnesses went from house to house in the town soliciting new members. They requested "contributions" of specific amounts from persons showing an interest in their books and pamphlets but on occasion gave the literature free of charge to residents who were unable to pay. Arrested and convicted of violating the ordinance, the Witnesses claimed it unconstitutionally restricted their religious liberty.

"A state may not impose a charge for the enjoyment of a right granted by the federal constitution," the five-justice majority said in Murdock v. Pennsylvania (1943), overruling the Court's decision the year before in Jones v. Opelika. The majority held that because Jehovah's Witnesses believe that each Witness is a minister ordained by God to preach the gospel, the license fee constituted a tax on the free exercise of religion. Soliciting new adherents by personal visitation and the sale of religious tracts was an evangelical activity that "occupies the same high estate under the First Amendment as do worship in the churches and preaching from the pulpits," wrote Justice William O. Douglas for the

Court.[40] Unlike the majority in *Opelika,* this majority did not hold that the commercial aspects of religious solicitation deprived it of its First Amendment protection:

> [T]he mere fact that the religious literature is "sold" by itinerant preachers rather than "donated" does not transform evangelism into a commercial enterprise. If it did, then the passing of the collection plate in church would make the church service a commercial project. The constitutional rights of those spreading their religious beliefs through the spoken and printed word are not to be gauged by standards governing retailers or wholesalers of books…. It is plain that a religious organization needs funds to remain a going concern. But an itinerant evangelist, however misguided or intolerant he may be, does not become a mere book agent by selling the Bible or religious tracts to help defray his expenses or to sustain him. Freedom of speech, freedom of the press, freedom of religion are available to all, not merely to those who can pay their own way.[41]

Almost forty years later, the Court addressed a First Amendment challenge by the Hare Krishna sect to a Minnesota law governing conduct at a state fair. The rule required all persons seeking to sell literature or solicit funds at the fair to do so from a fixed booth. In *Heffron v. International Society for Krishna Consciousness* (1981), the Court held that this rule was reasonable in light of the state's interest in maintaining order in a public place and that it was not an abridgement of the sect's freedom to exercise its religion. A few months later, similar considerations of evenhandedness guided the Court in *Widmar v. Vincent* (1981). A state university must grant the same access to university buildings to an organized student group that wishes to hold religious meetings as it does to any organized group that wishes to meet for any other reason, the Court said.[42]

Religion and Patriotism

Under what circumstances may government compel a person to set aside or subordinate his or her religious beliefs in order to fulfill some officially imposed duty? The Supreme Court usually has upheld statutes aimed clearly at maintaining or improving the public health and welfare even if those laws indirectly infringe on religious liberty. In the early twentieth century, a state law requiring compulsory vaccination against smallpox was sustained against a challenge brought by Seventh-Day Adventists opposed to it on religious grounds. The Court ruled in *Jacobson v. Massachusetts* (1905) that the legislature had acted reasonably to require vaccination in order to suppress a disease that threatened the entire population.[43] The Court, however, has remained silent on whether the state can force a person to accept medical treatment, including blood transfusions, if such treatment would violate religious beliefs. Although a number of well-publicized cases have arisen in lower courts, the Supreme Court so far has chosen not to adjudicate the issue.

In several instances, the Court has determined that the government's interest in imposing a duty upon individual citizens is not great enough to warrant the intrusion on their free exercise of religion. Two of the Court's early decisions on this issue illustrate the shifting weights accorded government interests and religious liberty in different situations. In *Pierce v. Society of Sisters* (1925), the Court ruled that Oregon could not constitutionally compel all schoolchildren to attend public schools. Such compulsion violated the liberty of parents to direct the upbringing of their children, a liberty that includes the right to send children to parochial schools. In 1934, however, the Court held that a college student's conscientious objection to war did not excuse him from attending mandatory classes in military science and tactics at the University of California.[44]

Flag Salute Cases I

By far the most dramatic cases to pose the question of government compulsion versus religious liberty involved schoolchildren and the American flag. Could government demand that children be forced to salute the flag against their religious beliefs? These cases arose as Europe and then the United States entered World War II. Lillian and William Gobitas, aged twelve and ten, were expelled from a Minersville, Pennsylvania, school in 1936 for refusing to participate in daily flag salute ceremonies. The children were Jehovah's

JEHOVAH'S WITNESSES: DEFINERS OF FREEDOM

The broad interpretation of the First Amendment guarantee of the free exercise of religion has evolved almost solely in connection with one of the most persecuted religious sects in U.S. history. "Probably no sect since the early days of the Mormon Church has been as much a thorn in the communal side and as much a victim of communal hate and persecution as Jehovah's Witnesses," wrote commentator Leo Pfeffer.[1] Jehovah's Witnesses were originally followers of Charles T. Russell, a Presbyterian who grew disillusioned with existing religious organizations and began to fashion a new religion in the late 1860s and early 1870s. His followers, known as Russellites, adopted the name Jehovah's Witnesses after Joseph F. Rutherford succeeded Russell in 1931 as leader of the group. In 1884 the sect established the Watchtower Bible and Tract Society to print and disseminate religious literature to be distributed by the Witnesses. In 1931 the Witnesses described their mission:

> As Jehovah's Witnesses our sole and only purpose is to be entirely obedient to his commandments; to make known that he is the only true and almighty God; that his Word is true and that his name is entitled to all honor and glory; that Christ is God's King, whom he has placed upon his throne of authority; that his kingdom is now come, and in obedience to the Lord's commandments we must now declare this good news as a testimony or witness to the nations and to inform the rulers and the people of and concerning Satan's cruel and oppressive organization, and particularly with reference to Christendom, which is the most wicked part of that visible organization, which great act will be quickly followed by Christ the King's bringing to the obedient peoples of the earth peace and prosperity, liberty and health, happiness and everlasting life; that God's kingdom is the hope of the world and there is no other, and that this message must be delivered by those who are identified as Jehovah's Witnesses.[2]

To carry this message across the country, the Witnesses organized Watchtower Campaigns in the 1930s and 1940s. Each house in a town would be visited by a Witness. If the occupants were willing, the Witness would give them literature, usually for a monetary contribution, and play a record. The gist of the message was that organized religions, the Roman Catholic church in particular, were "rackets." A typical publication, entitled *Enemies,* claimed that

> the greatest racket ever invented and practiced is that of religion. The most cruel and seductive public enemy is that which employs religion to carry on the racket, and by which means the people are deceived and the name of Almighty God is reproached. There are numerous systems of religion, but the most subtle, fraudulent and injurious to humankind is that which is generally labeled the "Christian religion," because it has the appearance of a worshipful devotion to the Supreme Being, and thereby easily misleads many honest and sincere persons.[3]

A chapter entitled "Song of the Harlot" states in part, "Referring now to the foregoing scriptural definition of harlot: what religious system exactly fits the prophecies recorded in God's Word? There is but one

Witnesses who had been taught not to worship any graven image. Their parents appealed to the local school board to make an exception for their children. When the school board refused, the parents placed the children in a private school and then sued to recover the additional school costs and to stop the school board from requiring the salute as a condition for attendance in the public schools. A federal district court in Philadelphia and then the court of appeals upheld the parents' position. The school board appealed to the Supreme Court.

On three earlier occasions, the Supreme Court in brief, unsigned opinions had dismissed challenges to flag salute requirements, saying that they posed no substantial federal question. In each of those cases the result of the dismissal was to sustain the requirement.[45] A dismissal of the *Gobitis* case would have left the lower court decisions in place, striking down the requirement. The Supreme Court granted review, and *Minersville School District v. Gobitis* was argued in spring 1940. The Gobitas children were represented by attorneys for the American Civil Liberties Union. The American Bar Association filed a "friend of the court" brief in their behalf. The Supreme Court voted 8-1 to reverse the lower courts and sustain the flag salute requirement. Religious liberty must give way to political authority, wrote Justice Felix Frankfurter for the majority, at least so long as that authority was not answer, and that is, the Roman Catholic Church."[4] Thus Jehovah's Witnesses were not popular in many communities. On more than one occasion members of the sect met with violence from those affronted by their views. Several communities enacted laws to curb the activities of the Witnesses, and it was these laws that the Witnesses challenged in court. According to constitutional historian Robert F. Cushman, since 1938 members of the sect have brought some thirty major cases testing the principles of religious freedom to the Supreme Court. In most of those cases, the Court has ruled in their favor.[5]

The first case brought by the Witnesses was *Lovell v. Griffin* (1938), in which the Court held that religious handbills were entitled to protection of freedom of the press. In another important case, *Cantwell v. Connecticut* (1940), the Court held, first, that the Fourteenth Amendment prohibited abridgment by the states of the free exercise of religion; second, that public officials did not have the authority to determine that some causes were religious and others were not; and third, that a breach-of-the-peace law as applied to a Jehovah's Witness whose message angered two passersby was overbroad and vague and therefore unconstitutional.[6] In other significant decisions the Court upheld the right of Witnesses to solicit from door to door and to ring homeowners' doorbells, to refuse to salute the flag, and to be exempt from peddler's fees on sales of their literature.[7]

In 2002 the Court reaffirmed that the Jehovah's Witnesses have rights under the First Amendment to go door to door to solicit donations and without obtaining a city permit in advance. The village of Stratton, Ohio, had adopted the permitting ordinance to protect its residents against "the flim flam con artists who prey on small town populations," the mayor said, but the true target appeared to be Jehovah's Witnesses, who had been chased out of town on several occasions. "The rhetoric used in the World War II–era opinions that repeatedly saved petitioners' coreligionists from prosecutions reflected the Court's evaluation of the First Amendment freedoms … [which] motivated a united democratic people to fight to defend those very freedoms from totalitarian attack. It motivates our decision today," wrote Justice John Paul Stevens for the 8-1 majority.[8]

---

1. Leo Pfeffer, *Church, State and Freedom*, rev. ed. (Boston: Beacon Press, 1967), 650. Pfeffer and Justice Robert H. Jackson's dissenting opinion in *Douglas v. City of Jeannette*, 319 U.S. 157 (1943), are the main sources of the information here.

2. Quoted by Pfeffer, *Church, State and Freedom*, 651.

3. *Douglas v. City of Jeannette*, 319 U.S. 157 at 171 (1943).

4. Id.

5. Robert F. Cushman, *Cases in Civil Liberties*, 2d ed. (Englewood Cliffs, N.J.: Prentice-Hall, 1976), 305.

6. *Lovell v. Griffin*, 303 U.S. 444 (1938); *Cantwell v. Connecticut*, 310 U.S. 296 (1940).

7. *Martin v. City of Struthers*, 319 U.S. 141 (1943); *West Virginia State Board of Education v. Barnette*, 319 U.S. 624 (1943), overruling *Minersville School District v. Gobitis*, 310 U.S. 586 (1940); *Murdock v. Pennsylvania*, 319 U.S. 105 (1943), overruling *Jones v. Opelika*, 316 U.S. 584 (1942).

8. *Watchtower Bible & Tract Society of New York v. Village of Stratton*, 536 U.S. 150 (2002).

---

used directly to promote or restrict religion. "Certainly the affirmative pursuit of one's convictions about the ultimate mystery of the universe and man's relation to it is placed beyond the reach of the law," he wrote. On the other hand, he said, the "mere possession of religious convictions which contradict the relevant concerns of a political society does not relieve the citizen from the discharge of political responsibilities."[46]

Was the flag salute a relevant political concern? Frankfurter sidestepped the question, writing that national unity was the basis for national security and that the Court should defer to the local determination that a compulsory flag salute was an effective means of creating that unity:

> The influences which help toward a common feeling for the common country are manifold. Some may seem harsh and others no doubt are foolish. Surely, however, the end is legitimate. And the effective means for its attainment are still so uncertain and so unauthenticated by science as to preclude us from putting the widely prevalent belief in flag-saluting beyond the pale of legislative power. It mocks reason and denies our whole history to find in the allowance of a requirement to salute our flag on fitting occasions the seeds of sanction for obeisance to a leader.

The wisdom of training children in patriotic impulses by those compulsions which necessarily pervade so much of the educational process is not for our independent judgment.[47]

Though the members of the Court might find "that the deepest patriotism is best engendered by giving unfettered scope to the most crotchety beliefs," it was not for the Court but for the school board to determine that granting the Gobitas children an exemption from the salute "might cast doubts in the minds of other children which would themselves weaken the effect of the exercise," Frankfurter wrote.[48]

Only Justice Stone dissented, choosing religious liberty over political authority. The compulsory salute, Stone said,

does more than suppress freedom of speech and more than prohibit the free exercise of religion, which concededly are forbidden by the First Amendment.... For by this law the state seeks to coerce these children to express a sentiment which, as they interpret it, they do not entertain, and which violates their deepest religious convictions.[49]

Moreover, Stone said the school board could have found ways to instill patriotism in its students without compelling an affirmation some students were unwilling to give:

The very essence of the liberty which they [the First and Fourteenth Amendments] guaranty is the freedom of the individual from compulsion as to what he shall think and what he shall say, at least where the compulsion is to bear false witness to his religion. If these guaranties are to have any meaning they must, I think, be deemed to withhold from the state any authority to compel belief or the expression of it where that expression violates religious convictions, whatever may be the legislative view of the desirability of such compulsion.[50]

The majority's reluctance to review legislative judgment was in this case "no more than the surrender of the constitutional protection of the liberty of small minorities to the popular will," Stone said.[51]

The press and the legal profession responded unfavorably to the decision. One commentator noted that more than 170 leading newspapers condemned the decision, while only a few supported it.[52] Law review articles almost universally opposed it. Two years after *Gobitis*, Justices Douglas, Hugo L. Black, and Frank Murphy announced in a dissent from the majority's holding in an unrelated case that they had changed their minds about compulsory flag salutes. In *Jones v. Opelika* (1942), the majority upheld a statute imposing peddler fees on Jehovah's Witnesses selling religious publications door to door. Dissenting from this decision as an unconstitutional suppression of the free exercise of religion, Black, Douglas, and Murphy described the majority position as a logical extension of the principles in the *Gobitis* ruling:

Since we joined in the opinion in the *Gobitis* case, we think this is an appropriate occasion to state that we now believe that it was ... wrongly decided. Certainly our democratic form of government functioning under the historic Bill of Rights has a high responsibility to accommodate itself to the religious views of minorities however unpopular and unorthodox those views may be. The First Amendment does not put the right freely to exercise religion in a subordinate position. We fear, however, that the opinion in these and in the *Gobitis* case do exactly that.[53]

Flag Salute Cases II

Justice Harlan Fiske Stone, the sole dissenter in *Gobitis*, became chief justice in 1941. The reversal on *Gobitis* by Justices Douglas, Black, and Murphy in 1942 and the appointment in 1943 of Justice Rutledge, a libertarian with well-established views favoring freedom of religion, indicated that *Gobitis* might be overruled if the flag salute issue were reconsidered. That opportunity arose in *West Virginia State Board of Education v. Barnette* (1943). After the *Gobitis* decision, the West Virginia Board of Education required all schools to make flag salutes part of the daily routine, in which all teachers and pupils must participate. Not only would children be expelled if they refused to salute the flag, they would be declared "unlawfully absent" from school and subject to delinquent proceedings. Parents of such children were subject to a fine and imprisonment.

RELIGION AND WAR

Since it instituted compulsory conscription in 1917, Congress has exempted from military service those persons who object to war for religious reasons. In 1917 the exemption was narrow, extending only to adherents of a "well-recognized religious sect or organization ... whose existing creed or principles [forbid] its members to participate in war in any form." Congress expanded the exemption in 1940 to any persons who "by reason of their religious training and belief are conscientiously opposed to participation in war in any form." In 1948 Congress defined "religious training and belief" to mean "an individual's belief in a relation to a Supreme Being involving duties superior to those arising from any human relation but [not including] essentially political, sociological, or philosophical views or a merely personal moral code."

In 1965 this definition was challenged as discriminating against people who hold strong religious convictions but do not believe in a Supreme Being in the orthodox sense. The Supreme Court sidestepped the issue by interpreting Congress's definition very broadly. The "test of belief 'in a relation to a Supreme Being'" is whether a given belief that is sincere and meaningful occupies a place in the life of its possessor parallel to that filled by the orthodox belief in God of one who clearly qualifies for exemption," the Court said in *United States v. Seeger* (1965).[1]

A few years later, the Court construed the exemption to include persons who objected to all war on moral and ethical grounds. To come within the meaning of the law, wrote Justice Hugo L. Black for the Court in *Welsh v. United States* (1970), opposition to the war must "stem from the registrant's moral, ethical, or religious beliefs about what is right and wrong and ... these beliefs [must] be held with the strength of traditional religious convictions."[2]

A year later, however, the Court refused to hold that conscription unconstitutionally infringed on the religious liberty of those opposed to a particular war as unjust. The Court acknowledged that the ruling impinged on those religions that counseled their members to fight only in those wars that were just, but the justices determined that Congress had acted reasonably and neutrally when it decided that the danger of infringing religious liberty did not outweigh the government interest in maintaining a fairly administered draft service. Fairness, the justices ruled, would be threatened by the difficulty of separating sincere conscientious objectors from fraudulent claimants.[3] The Court in another case held that a federal law giving veterans' benefits only to persons who had performed active duty did not unconstitutionally discriminate against conscientious objectors who had performed alternative service.[4]

---

1. *United States v. Seeger*, 380 U.S. 163 at 165–166 (1965).
2. *Welsh v. United States*, 398 U.S. 333 at 340 (1970).
3. *Gillette v. United States*, 401 U.S. 437 (1971).
4. *Johnson v. Robison*, 415 U.S. 361 (1974).

Several families of Jehovah's Witnesses affected by this decree sued for an injunction to stop its enforcement. The federal district court agreed to issue the injunction, and the state school board appealed that decision directly to the Supreme Court.

By a 6-3 vote, the Court upheld the lower federal court, reversing *Gobitis*. In the majority's opinion, which was announced on Flag Day 1943, Justice Jackson rejected the *Gobitis* view that the courts should defer to the legislative judgment in this matter. "The very purpose of a Bill of Rights was to withdraw certain subjects from the vicissitudes of political controversy, to place them beyond the reach of majorities and officials and to establish them as legal principles to be applied by the courts," he said.[54] Jackson then turned to the heart of the issue: "National unity as an end which officials may foster by persuasion and example is not in question," he wrote. "The problem is whether under our Constitution compulsion as here employed is a permissible means for its achievement." Jackson's answer was negative. "Compulsory unification of opinion achieves only the unanimity of the graveyard."[55]

For Jackson, the issues raised by the compulsory flag salute reached beyond questions of religious liberty to broader concerns for the individual's personal liberty. In defense of his view, he wrote one of the most elegant and eloquent passages in Supreme Court history:

The case is made difficult not because the principles of its decision are obscure but because the flag involved is our own. Nevertheless, we apply the limitations of the Constitution with no fear that freedom to be intellectually and spiritually diverse or even contrary will disintegrate the social organization. To believe that patriotism will not flourish if patriotic ceremonies are voluntary and spontaneous instead of a compulsory routine is to make an unflattering estimate of the appeal of our institutions to free minds. We can have intellectual individualism and the rich cultural diversities that we owe to exceptional minds only at the price of occasional eccentricity and abnormal attitudes. When they are so harmless to others or to the State as those we deal with here, the price is not too great. But freedom to differ is not limited to things that do not matter much. That would be a mere shadow of freedom. The test of its substance is the right to differ as to things that touch the heart of the existing order.

If there is any fixed star in our constitutional constellation, it is that no official, high or petty, can prescribe what shall be orthodox in politics, nationalism, religion or other matters of opinion or force citizens to confess by word or act their faith therein. If there are any circumstances which permit an exception, they do not now occur to us.[56]

In dissent, Justices Owen J. Roberts and Stanley F. Reed simply stated that they agreed with the majority opinion in *Gobitis*. Justice Frankfurter's dissent, however, rivaled Jackson's majority opinion in eloquence. Insisting that the majority had failed to exercise proper judicial restraint, Frankfurter maintained that it was within the constitutional authority of the state school board to demand that public school children salute the American flag. Reading the majority a lecture on their duties as interpreters of the Constitution, Frankfurter began with an unusual personal reference to his own heritage:

One who belongs to the most vilified and persecuted minority in history is not likely to be insensible to the freedoms guaranteed by our Constitution. Were my purely personal attitude relevant I should wholeheartedly associate myself with the general libertarian views in the Court's opinion, representing as they do the thought and action of a lifetime. But as judges we are neither Jew nor Gentile, neither Catholic nor agnostic....

As a member of this Court I am not justified in writing my private notions of policy into the Constitution, no matter how deeply I may cherish them or how mischievous I may deem their disregard. The duty of a judge who must decide which of two claims before the Court shall prevail, that of a State to enact and enforce laws within its general competence or that of an individual to refuse obedience because of the demands of his conscience, is not that of an ordinary person. It can never be emphasized too much that one's own opinion about the wisdom or evil of a law should be excluded altogether when one is doing one's duty on the bench. The only opinion of our own even looking in that direction that is material is our opinion whether legislators could in reason have enacted such a law. In the light of all the circumstances, including the history of this question in this Court, it would require more daring than I possess to deny that reasonable legislators could have taken the action which is before us for review.... I cannot bring my mind to believe that the "liberty" secured by the Due Process Clause gives this Court the authority to deny to the State of West Virginia the attainment of that which we all recognize as a legitimate legislative end, namely, the promotion of good citizenship, by employment of the means here chosen.[57]

Religion, Work, and School

In 1961 the Court set out the modern rule for determining when a state may properly compel obedience to a secular law that conflicts with religious beliefs. The case involved an Orthodox Jew who observed the Jewish Sabbath, closing his clothing and furniture store on Saturday. To make up the lost revenue, he opened the store on Sunday. When Pennsylvania enacted a Sunday closing law in 1959, he challenged its constitutionality on the ground that it restricted the free exercise of religion. The Supreme Court found that the law did not violate the First Amendment. Sunday closing of commercial enterprises was an effective means for achieving the valid state purpose of providing citizens with a uniform day of rest. Although it operated indirectly to make observance of certain religious practices more expensive, the law did not make any religious practice illegal, the majority observed in *Braunfeld v.*

Brown (1961). The Court then announced the rule for judging whether a state law unconstitutionally restricts the exercise of religious liberty:

> If the purpose or effect of a law is to impede the observance of one or all religions or is to discriminate invidiously between religions, that law is constitutionally invalid even though the burden may be characterized as being only indirect. But if the State regulates conduct by enacting a general law within its power, the purpose and effect of which is to advance the State's secular goals, the statute is valid despite its indirect burden on religious observance unless the State may accomplish its purpose by means which do not impose such a burden.[58]

Unemployment Compensation

In 1963 the Court significantly modified *Braunfeld* by declaring that only a compelling state interest could justify limitations on religious liberty. *Sherbert v. Verner* (1963) arose after Adell Sherbert was fired from her textile mill job in South Carolina because, as a Seventh-Day Adventist, she refused to work on Saturdays. Because she refused available work, the state denied her unemployment compensation benefits. Overturning the state ruling by a 7-2 vote, the Court, speaking through Justice William J. Brennan Jr., explained that the state's action forced Sherbert either to abandon her religious principles in order to work or to maintain her religious precepts and forfeit unemployment compensation benefits. "Governmental imposition of such a choice puts the same kind of burden upon the free exercise of religion as would a fine imposed against appellant for her Saturday worship," Brennan wrote.[59]

Brennan contended that the state could limit the exercise of an individual's religion only for a compelling state interest. "Only the gravest abuses, endangering paramount interests, give occasion for permissible limitation," he said. Prevention of fraudulent claims was the only reason the state advanced for denying benefits to Sherbert, Brennan noted. To justify that denial, he wrote, the state must show that it cannot prevent such fraud by means less restrictive of religious liberty.[60] In dissent, Justices John Marshall Harlan and Byron R. White held that the Court should have abided

by its *Braunfeld* rule. Unemployment compensation was intended to help people when there was no work available, not to aid those who, for whatever reason, refused available work. Maintenance of such a distinction was a valid goal of the state that affected religion only indirectly, they said.

The Court reaffirmed *Sherbert* twice in the mid-1980s, holding that a state could not deny unemployment benefits to a man in Indiana who quit his job because his religion forbade his participation in weapons production or to a woman in Florida—like Sherbert—fired because she would not work on her Sabbath. On the other hand, the Court has also set limits to state action protecting the right of workers not to work on their Sabbath. The Court in *Thornton v. Caldor Inc.* (1985) ruled unconstitutional a state law giving all employees the right to refuse with impunity to work on their Sabbath. By giving those workers such a right, the state gave religious concerns priority over all others in setting work schedules and thereby advanced religion, the Court held.[61]

Compulsory School Attendance

The *Sherbert* ruling had been reinforced earlier by the Court's decision in *Wisconsin v. Yoder* (1972). Old Order Amish parents refused to send their children to school beyond grade eight, which violated Wisconsin's law compelling all children to attend school until age sixteen. The parents asserted that a high school education would engender values contrary to Amish beliefs, which hold that salvation may be obtained only by living in religious, agrarian communities separate from the world and worldly influences. Expert witnesses testified that compulsory high school education might result not only in psychological harm to Amish children confused by trying to fit into two different worlds, but also in the destruction of the Amish community.

The Wisconsin trial and appeals courts upheld compulsory attendance as a reasonable and constitutional means of promoting a valid state interest. The state supreme court reversed this ruling, holding that the state had not shown that its interest in compelling attendance was sufficient to justify the infringement on the free exercise of religion. The Supreme Court affirmed that decision. Chief Justice Warren E. Burger wrote the Court's opinion. He acknowledged that the provision of public schools was one of the primary functions of the state, but, he added,

> a state's interest in universal education, however highly we rank it, is not totally free from a balancing process when it impinges on fundamental rights and interests, such as those specifically protected by the Free Exercise Clause of the First Amendment, and the traditional interest of parents with respect to the religious upbringing of their children so long as they … "prepare [them] for additional obligations."[62]

The Court accepted that the traditional Amish community life was based on convictions that would be weakened by forcing teenage children into public schools. The Court also noted that the Amish provided their children with alternative modes of vocational education that accommodated all the interests the state advanced in support of its compulsory attendance law.

Religion and Oath Taking

Article VI of the Constitution states that "no religious Test shall ever be required as a Qualification to any Office or public Trust under the United States." The Supreme Court in 1961 ruled that under the First Amendment, states are prohibited from requiring religious test oaths. Ray Torcaso, appointed a notary public in Maryland, was denied his commission when he refused to declare his belief in God, a part of the oath notaries public were required by Maryland law to take. Torcaso sued, challenging the oath as abridging his religious liberty. A unanimous Supreme Court struck down the oath requirement in *Torcaso v. Watkins* (1961). Justice Black wrote,

> We repeat and again affirm that neither a State nor the Federal Government can constitutionally force a person "to profess a belief or disbelief in any religion." Neither can constitutionally pass laws or impose requirements which aid all religions as against non-believers, and neither can aid those religions based on a belief in the existence of God as against those religions founded on different beliefs.[63]

Although the Court unequivocally stated in *Torcaso* that a state may not require a person to swear to a belief he or she does not hold, may government require a person to swear a non-religious oath contrary to religious beliefs? In a series of cases concerning pacifist applicants for U.S. citizenship, the Supreme Court initially said yes but then changed its mind. The naturalization oath requires applicants for citizenship to swear "to support and defend the Constitution and the law of the United States of America against all enemies, foreign and domestic." The naturalization service interpreted the oath to require that prospective citizens be willing to bear arms in defense of the country. It therefore denied citizenship to two pacifist women and to a fifty-four-year-old Yale Divinity School professor who said he would fight only in wars he believed to be morally justified. Although the three were qualified in every other way to be citizens and were extremely unlikely ever to be called into active service, the Court upheld the naturalization service's position as reasonable in *United States v. Schwimmer* (1929) and again in 1931.[64]

Following World War II, the Court reconsidered and reversed these holdings. Again the majority did not reach the constitutional issue but dealt only with the statutory interpretation of the oath. *Girouard v. United States* (1946) concerned a Canadian Seventh-Day Adventist who agreed to serve as a noncombatant in the armed forces but refused to bear arms because killing conflicted with his religious beliefs. The majority noted that the oath did not expressly require naturalized citizens to swear to bear arms and ruled that this interpretation need not be read into the oath. Congress, the majority said, could not have intended to deny citizenship in a country noted for its protection of religious beliefs to persons whose religious beliefs prevented them from bearing arms.[65] In 1945, the year before the Court overruled its earlier decisions in the pacifist naturalization cases, the justices upheld the Illinois bar's decision to deny admission to an attorney because its required oath conflicted with his beliefs. That decision has never been overruled, but its effect has been weakened by subsequent decisions.[66]

Among the more recent of these cases was *McDaniel v. Paty* (1978), in which the Court struck down as unconstitutional a Tennessee law that forbade clergy to hold state offices. Writing the Court's opinion, Chief Justice Burger relied on *Sherbert* as precedent, saying that the state law unconstitutionally restricted the right of free exercise of religion by making it conditional on a willingness to give up the right to seek public office.[67] Justices Potter Stewart, Thurgood Marshall, and Brennan used *Torcaso* as precedent, and Marshall and Brennan held that the law also violated the Establishment Clause.[68] Justice White held that the law denied clergy equal protection of the laws.

ESTABLISHMENT OF RELIGION

The First Amendment forbids laws "respecting an establishment of religion," but it is far from obvious what that means. "In the 50 years since *Everson,* we have consistently struggled to apply these simple words in the context of governmental aid to religious schools," said Justice Clarence Thomas in the opening words of a lengthy opinion in 2000 that upheld the use of federal education aid to buy computers in parochial as well as public schools.[69] Predictably, the decision split the justices. Thomas spoke for a plurality of four, who had no trouble concluding that the aid program was constitutional. The program is "neutral" and offers money "to a broad range of groups or persons without regard to religion."[70] Since all secondary schools can obtain the federal aid to buy computers, "no one would conclude … it results in religious indoctrination by the government," Thomas wrote.[71] Chief Justice William H. Rehnquist and Justices Antonin Scalia and Anthony M. Kennedy agreed.

Justice Sandra Day O'Connor wrote a separate opinion, stating that while she agreed the computer aid program was constitutional, she did so for a quite different reason. Computers cannot be "diverted" and used for religious indoctrination, she said. If it were a cash grant, however, she would have a different view. Justice Stephen G. Breyer said he agreed with O'Connor. In dissent, Justice David H. Souter said the education aid program violates the Establishment Clause because it uses tax money to fund religious teaching. Regardless of how else the government spends its money, it cannot use tax money to teach or promote religion, he said. Justices John Paul Stevens and Ruth Bader Ginsburg agreed with him.

Although this controversy over church and state continues to rage in the twenty-first century, it occupied little of the Court's time during its first century and a half. Its first decision, which came in 1899, sustained a federal construction grant to a Roman Catholic hospital. The Court held that the hospital's purpose was secular and that it did not discriminate among its patients on the basis of religion. The aid therefore only indirectly benefited the church.[72] Most of the Court's Establishment Clause rulings have come since the Court declared the clause applicable to the states in 1947. A few of these cases have concerned taxation, some have concerned public displays of religious symbols, but most have concerned religion and education. The Court has sustained the practice of exempting churches from taxes on the ground that to tax them would be to entangle government excessively with religion. For much the same reason, the Court has also declined to review legal questions involving controversies within churches. *(See box, Internal Church Disputes, p. 143.)*

Three topics in the area of religion and education have particularly drawn the Court's attention: religious readings and prayer in school, state aid to parochial schools, and equal treatment of student religious groups and publications. The Court has barred religious exercises in tax-supported public schools as an unconstitutional government advancement of religion. Prayer recitations, Bible readings, and religious instruction, when denominational, favor one religion over others; when nondenominational, they favor all religion over nonreligious beliefs, the Court has said. The Court, however, has adopted what it describes as a "benevolent neutrality" toward government financial aid to parochial schools. If the aid is secular in its purpose and effect and does not entangle the government excessively in its administration, it is permissible, even if it indirectly benefits church schools. The Court also has held that access to school facilities, and in some cases school support, should be the same for all student groups. The First Amendment protection for free speech requires that religious groups not be treated differently because of the content of their meetings or messages.

Tax Exemptions

The federal government, every state, and the District of Columbia have historically exempted churches from paying property and income taxes. The Supreme Court has sustained such exemptions. *Walz v. Tax Commission* (1970) arose when a property owner in New York challenged the state's property tax exemption for religious institutions as an establishment of religion. He contended that the exemption meant that nonexempt property owners made an involuntary contribution to churches. Writing for the 8-1 majority, Chief Justice Burger observed that churches were only one of several institutions—including hospitals, libraries, and historical and patriotic organizations—exempted from paying property taxes. Such exemptions reflected the state's decision that these groups provided beneficial and stabilizing influences in the community and that their activities might be hampered or destroyed by the need to pay property taxes.

"We cannot read New York's statute as attempting to establish religion," Burger wrote, "it is simply sparing the exercise of religion from the burden of property taxation levied on private profit institutions."[73] The exemption thus met the existing test for determining whether government policy constituted improper establishment of religion; the purpose and the effect of the exemption were primarily secular, having only an indirect benefit to religion. To this test, however, the Court in *Walz* added a new one: whether the exemption resulted in excessive government involvement with religion. To answer this question, Burger said the Court must consider whether taxing the property would result in more or less entanglement than continuing the exemption. Observing that taxation would require government valuation of church property, and possibly tax liens and foreclosures, Burger concluded that the "hazards of churches supporting government are hardly less in their potential than the hazards of government supporting churches." Tax exemption, on the other hand, created "only a

minimal and remote involvement between church and state. It restricts the fiscal relationship between church and state, and tends to complement and reinforce the desired separation insulating each from the other."[74]

As churches have moved into quasi-business areas in recent years, the tax question has returned to the Court in several new ways. In 1981 the Court ruled unanimously that church-run elementary and secondary schools were exempt from paying federal or state unemployment taxes. Four years later, however, the Court made clear that this exemption did not extend so far as to protect commercial enterprises of churches from minimum wage, overtime, and recordkeeping requirements of federal labor law.[75]

Religion and Public Schools

"We are a religious people whose institutions presuppose a Supreme Being," wrote Justice Douglas in 1952.[76] The nation's governmental institutions reflect this belief daily. Each session of the House and Senate opens with a prayer. The Supreme Court begins its sessions with an invocation asking that "God save the United States and this honorable Court." Our currency proclaims, "In God We Trust," and we acknowledge that we are "one nation, under God," each time we recite the pledge of allegiance. These official and public affirmations of religious belief have not escaped legal challenge, but the Supreme Court has dismissed most of them summarily. In 1964 the Court refused to review a lower court decision that held that despite inclusion of the phrase "under God" in the pledge of allegiance, the First Amendment did not bar the New York Education Commission from recommending that the pledge be recited in schools. In 1971 the Court declined to stop astronauts from praying on television for God's blessing for a successful trip to the moon. In the same ruling, the lower court had rejected a challenge to the phrase "So help me God" contained in the oath witnesses are required to take in many courts. In 1979 the Court refused to review a challenge to the words "In God We Trust" on currency.[77]

In 1983 the Court for the first time gave full consideration to a challenge to a state legislature's practice of opening sessions with a prayer. The Court upheld the practice, finding that it dated back to the First

INTERNAL CHURCH DISPUTES

The Supreme Court has been reluctant to involve itself in the internal disputes that occasionally arise within churches. Where judicial intervention is unavoidable, the Court has insisted that courts decline to resolve doctrinal questions. This rule was first developed in *Watson v. Jones* (1872), a dispute over church property between a national church organization and local churches that had withdrawn from the national hierarchy. The case was decided on common law grounds, but it had First Amendment overtones:

> All who unite themselves to [the central church] do so with an implied consent to [its] government, and are bound to submit to it. But it would be a vain consent, and would lead to the total subversion of such religious bodies, if anyone aggrieved by one of their decisions could appeal to the secular courts and have [it] reversed.[1]

In 1952 the Court said that the First Amendment gave religious organizations "power to decide for themselves, free from state interference, matters of church government as well as those of faith and doctrine."[2] In 1969 the Court held that

> First Amendment values are plainly jeopardized when church property litigation is made to turn on the resolution by civil courts of controversies over religious doctrine and practice. If civil courts

undertake to resolve such controversies … the hazards are ever present of inhibiting the free development of religious doctrine and of implicating secular interests in matters of purely ecclesiastical concern…. The Amendment therefore commands civil courts to decide church property disputes without resolving underlying controversies over religious doctrines.[3]

The judicial role is therefore limited to examining the church rules and determining that they have been applied appropriately. Justice Louis D. Brandeis wrote, "In the absence of fraud, collusion, or arbitrariness, the decisions of the proper church tribunals on matters purely ecclesiastical, although affecting civil rights, are accepted in litigation before the secular courts as conclusive."[4]

---

1. *Watson v. Jones*, 13 Wall. (80 U.S.) 679 at 728–29 (1872).

2. *Kedroff v. St. Nicholas Cathedral*, 344 U.S. 94 at 116 (1952); see also *Kreshik v. St. Nicholas Cathedral*, 363 U.S. 190 (1960).

3. *Presbyterian Church in the United States v. Mary Elizabeth Blue Hull Memorial Presbyterian Church*, 393 U.S. 440 at 449 (1969).

4. *Gonzalez v. Archbishop*, 280 U.S. 1 at 16 (1929).

Congress of the United States, the one that also adopted the First Amendment, and had "become part of the fabric of our society."[78] Although the Court has not proscribed government-sponsored public expression of religious belief on the part of adults, it has flatly prohibited states from requiring or permitting religious exercises by children in public elementary and secondary schools.

Released Time

The first two Supreme Court rulings concerning religious exercises in public schools involved "released time" programs. Employed by school districts across the country, these programs released students from regular class work, usually once a week, to receive religious instruction. In some cases the students received the instruction in their regular classrooms; sometimes they met in another schoolroom; at other times they met in churches or synagogues. Students participated

in the programs voluntarily. Students who did not participate had a study period during the time religious instruction was given. The first of the released time cases was *Illinois ex rel. McCollum v. Board of Education* (1948). The Champaign, Illinois, school board operated a released time program in which religion teachers from the private sector came into the public schools once a week to give thirty minutes of religious instruction to voluntary participants. The program was challenged as a violation of the First Amendment's Establishment Clause by the atheist mother of a fifth grader, the only pupil in his class who did not participate in the program.

By an 8-1 vote, the Supreme Court declared the program unconstitutional. "Pupils compelled by law to go to school for secular education are released in part from their legal duty upon the condition that they attend religious classes," wrote Justice Black for the majority. "This is beyond all question a utilization of

Evolution or Creation?

One of the most celebrated trials in U.S history took place in 1925. John Scopes was convicted and fined $100 for teaching the Darwinian theory of evolution in violation of a Tennessee law that made it illegal to teach anything other than a literal biblical theory of human creation. Although the state supreme court reversed Scopes's conviction, the Tennessee statute was left standing and never challenged before the U.S. Supreme Court.[1] Decades later, the Court ruled twice on this issue.

In *Epperson v. Arkansas* (1968), a public school biology teacher challenged a state law that forbade teachers in state-supported schools from teaching or using textbooks that teach "the theory or doctrine that mankind ascended or descended from a lower order of animals." The Supreme Court unanimously held this law in violation of the First Amendment: "Arkansas law selects from the body of knowledge a particular segment which it proscribes for the sole reason that it is deemed to conflict with a particular religious doctrine; that is, with a particular interpretation of the Book of Genesis by a particular religious group," stated the Court.[2]

In the late 1980s, the Court, 7-2, held that Louisiana violated the First Amendment when it required that any public school teacher who taught evolution must also give equal time to teaching "creation science." Writing for the majority in *Edwards v. Aguillard* (1987), Justice William J. Brennan Jr. explained that it was clear that the purpose of the law was "to advance the religious viewpoint that a supernatural being created humankind."[3] Dissenting were Chief Justice William H. Rehnquist and Justice Antonin Scalia, who criticized the Court for presuming the law unconstitutional because "it was supported strongly by organized religions or by adherents of particular faiths.... Political activism by the religiously motivated is part of our heritage," Scalia wrote. "Today's religious activism may give us [this law] ... but yesterday's resulted in the abolition of slavery, and tomorrow's may bring relief for famine victims."[4]

1. *Scopes v. State,* 154 Tenn. 105, 289 S.W. 363 (1927).
2. *Epperson v. Arkansas,* 393 U.S. 97 at 103 (1968).
3. *Edwards v. Aguillard,* 482 U.S. 578 at 592 (1987).
4. Id. at 615.

the tax-established and tax-supported public school system to aid religious groups to spread their faith."[79] Four justices concurred separately. They said the program not only violated the Establishment Clause by tending to advance certain religions over others, but it also threatened to impede the free exercise of religion. Justice Frankfurter explained:

Religious education so conducted on school time and property is patently woven into the working scheme of the school. The Champaign arrangement thus presents powerful elements of inherent pressure by the school system in the interest of religious sects.... That a child is offered an alternative may reduce the constraint; it does not eliminate the operation of influence by the school in matters sacred to conscience and outside the school's domain. The law of imitation operates, and nonconformity is not an outstanding characteristic of children. The result is an obvious pressure upon children to attend. Again, while the Champaign school population represents only a fraction of the more than

two hundred and fifty sects of the nation, not even all the practicing sects in Champaign are willing or able to provide religious instruction.... As a result, the public school system of Champaign actively furthers inculcation in the religious tenets of some faiths, and in the process sharpens the consciousness of religious differences at least among some of the children committed to its care.[80]

Four years later, the Court upheld New York City's released time program in which religious instruction was given during the school day but not in the public schools. In *Zorach v. Clausen* (1952) the Court held, 6-3, that this program did not violate the Establishment Clause. "The First Amendment ... does not say that in every and all respects there shall be a separation of Church and State," wrote Justice Douglas, noting that governments provided churches with general services, such as police and fire protection, and that public officials frequently said prayers before undertaking their official chores.[81] The New York program did not significantly aid religion; it simply required that the public schools "accommodate" a program of outside religious instruction. Government, wrote Douglas,

> may not coerce anyone to attend church, to observe a religious holiday, or to take religious instruction. But it can close its doors or suspend its operations as to those who want to repair to their religious sanctuary for worship or instruction. No more than that is undertaken here.[82]

Justices Black, Frankfurter, and Jackson held that the program was coercive and a direct aid to religion.

School Prayer

A decade after *Zorach*, the Supreme Court set off an intense new round of controversy over such matters of church and state as school prayer and Bible reading as regular devotional exercises in public schools. These exercises, often coupled with recitation of the Pledge of Allegiance, had been common occurrences in classrooms across the country. As early as 1930, the Court had declined to review fully a state court's refusal to order the state school superintendent to require Bible reading in public schools. The question of Bible readings in public schools returned to the Court in 1952, and again the Court dismissed the suit, this time because the parents of the child involved no longer had standing to sue.[83]

Another ten years passed before the Court directly addressed the constitutionality of devotional practices in public schools. When it did, the case involved a recommendation by the New York State Board of Regents that school districts adopt a specified nondenominational prayer to be repeated voluntarily by students at the beginning of each school day. The brief prayer read: "Almighty God, we acknowledge our dependence upon Thee, and we beg Thy blessings upon us, our parents, our teachers, and our country." The prayer was not universally adopted throughout the state. New York City, for example, chose instead to have its students recite the verse of the hymn "America" that asks God's protection for the country.

The school board of New Hyde Park adopted the recommended prayer. Parents of ten pupils in the school district, with the support of the New York Civil Liberties Union, brought suit, claiming that the prayer was contrary to their religious beliefs and practices and that its adoption and use violated the Establishment Clause. The state courts upheld the prayer on the condition that no student be compelled to participate. In *Engel v. Vitale* (1962), the Supreme Court, 6-1, reversed the state courts, holding that this use of the prayer was "wholly inconsistent with the Establishment Clause." In an opinion written by Justice Black, the majority explained its view:

> [T]he constitutional prohibition against laws respecting an establishment of religion must at least mean that in this country it is no part of the business of government to compose official prayers for any group of the American people to recite as a part of a religious program carried on by government.[84]

The fact that the prayer was nondenominational and that students who did not wish to participate could remain silent or leave the room did not free the prayer "from the limitations of the Establishment Clause." Black wrote,

> The Establishment Clause, unlike the Free Exercise Clause, does not depend upon any showing of direct governmental compulsion and is violated by the enactment of laws which establish an official religion whether those laws operate directly to coerce nonobserving individuals or not. This is not to say, of course, that laws officially prescribing a particular form of religious worship do not involve coercion of such individuals. When the power, prestige and financial support of government is placed behind a particular religious belief, the indirect coercive pressure upon religious minorities to conform to the prevailing officially approved religion is plain.[85]

In response to the argument that the prayer—if an establishment of religion at all—was a relatively insignificant and harmless encroachment, Black quoted Madison, the chief author of the First Amendment:

> [I]t is proper to take alarm at the first experiment on our liberties. Who does not see that the same authority which can establish Christianity, in exclusion of all other Religions, may establish with the same ease any particular sect of Christians, in exclusion of all other Sects?[86]

Asserting that "the Court has misapplied a great constitutional principle," Justice Stewart dissented. "I

Deborah Weisman (*right*) and her sister Merith outside the Supreme Court. Deborah's father challenged the practice of a rabbi delivering an invocation and benediction at her public middle school graduation ceremony in Rhode Island. In *Lee v. Weisman* (1992), the Supreme Court ruled in his favor.

cannot see how an 'official religion' is established by letting those who want to say a prayer say it," he said.[87] Stewart compared the regents' prayer to other state-sanctioned religious exercises, such as the reference to God in the pledge to the flag, in the president's oath of office, and in the formal opening of each day's session of the Court itself:

> I do not believe that this Court, or the Congress, or the President has by the actions and practices I have mentioned established an "official religion" in violation of the Constitution. And I do not believe the State of New York has done so in this case. What each has done has been to recognize and to follow the deeply entrenched and highly cherished spiritual traditions of our Nation—traditions which come down to us from those who almost two hundred years ago avowed their "firm Reliance on the Protection of divine Providence" when they proclaimed the freedom and independence of this brave new world.[88]

Bible Readings

A year after *Engel v. Vitale,* the Court affirmed its school prayer decision in two cases concerning the practice of daily Bible readings in public school classrooms: *School District of Abington Township v. Schempp* (1963) and *Murray v. Curlett* (1963). *Schempp* concerned a Pennsylvania statute that required the reading of at least ten verses from the Bible each day, followed by recitation of the Lord's Prayer and the Pledge of Allegiance. Pupils were excused from participating at the request of their parents. The Schempps asserted that certain literal Bible readings were contrary to their Unitarian religious beliefs and brought suit to stop the readings. In *Murray,* the challenged reading from the Bible was required not by state law but by a 1905 city rule. Madalyn Murray and her student son, William, were atheists. They contended that the daily religious exercises placed "a premium on belief as against non-belief and subject[ed] their freedom of conscience to the rule of the majority." They asked that the readings be stopped.

In an 8-1 vote, the Court held that the Bible readings in both cases were unconstitutional. The readings were clearly religious exercises prescribed as part of the school curriculum for students compelled by law to attend school. They were held in state buildings and supervised by teachers paid by the state. By these actions the state abandoned the neutrality toward religion demanded by the Establishment Clause. Justice Tom C. Clark wrote for the majority:

> The place of religion in our society is an exalted one, achieved through a long tradition of reliance on the home, the church and the inviolable citadel of the individual heart and mind. We have come to recognize through bitter experience that it is not within the power of government to invade that citadel, whether its purpose or effect be to aid or oppose, to advance or retard. In the relationship between man and religion, the State is firmly committed to a position of neutrality.[89]

It was no defense that the Bible reading exercises might be "relatively minor" encroachments on the First Amendment. "The breach of neutrality that is today a trickling stream may all too soon become a raging torrent," Clark wrote.[90] The ruling, he contended, did not set up a "religion of secularism" in the schools. Schools could permit the study of the Bible for its literary and historical merits; they were only prohibited from using the Bible as part of a devotional exercise. Concluding, Clark said that the ruling did not deny the majority its right to the free exercise of religion. "While the Free Exercise Clause clearly prohibits the use of state action to deny the rights of free exercise to *anyone,* it has never meant that a majority could use the machinery of the State to practice its beliefs."[91]

Public opposition to the decisions in *Schempp* and *Murray* ran high, encouraging both chambers of Congress to consider constitutional amendments to overrule them. Neither the House nor the Senate, however, was able to produce the two-thirds votes needed to send a proposed amendment to the states for ratification. The Court steered clear of school prayer cases

for well more than twenty years, until *Wallace v. Jaffree* (1985), when it decided to take a long, hard look at the new version of school prayer—a "moment-of-silence." Twenty-three states had passed such laws. They varied in their particulars, but in general they permitted teachers to set aside a moment in each public school classroom each day for students to engage in quiet meditative activity. When Alabama's law was challenged, a federal judge—in blithe disregard of a half-century of Supreme Court decisions—declared that the First Amendment did not preclude Alabama from establishing a state religion. Although an appeals court reversed that ruling, the state—backed by the Reagan administration—asked the Supreme Court to reinstate the law. The Court refused, 6-3, agreeing with the appeals court that the law violated the Establishment Clause.

Some moment-of-silence laws might pass muster, said Justices Lewis F. Powell Jr. and Sandra Day O'Connor, but not one that was so clearly just a subterfuge for returning prescribed prayer to the public schools. Writing for the majority, Justice John Paul Stevens declared that it was "established principle that the government must pursue a course of complete neutrality toward religion." Chief Justice Burger dissented, joined by Justices White and William H. Rehnquist, who said it was time for the Court to reassess its precedents on this issue.[92]

The broadest and most significant dissent in *Wallace v. Jaffree* was by Rehnquist, who challenged the separation of church and state doctrine as wrong-headed and based on a misreading of history. Thomas Jefferson was in France when the Bill of Rights was passed by Congress and adopted by the states, he noted. Yet, Jefferson's 1802 letter to the Danbury Baptists and his comment about "building a wall of separation of church and state" had become the Court's accepted view of the Establishment Clause since 1947. "It is impossible to build a sound constitutional doctrine upon a mistaken understanding of constitutional history, but unfortunately the Establishment Clause has been expressly freighted with Jefferson's misleading metaphor for nearly 40 years," Rehnquist wrote.[93] He also examined Madison's words during the debate over the First Amendment. The

Establishment Clause was "designed to prohibit the establishment of a national religion, and perhaps to prevent discrimination among sects. He [Madison] did not see it as requiring neutrality on the part of government between religion and irreligion," Rehnquist continued.[94] "The 'wall of separation between church and state' is a metaphor based on bad history.... It should be frankly and explicitly abandoned," he concluded.[95]

Rehnquist's dissent signaled the possibility of a significant change in the law. Reagan and the Republican Party platform had called for a return to prayer in the public schools. A year after *Wallace v. Jaffree*, Reagan selected Rehnquist as chief justice. In addition to elevating Rehnquist, Reagan appointed three new justices: Sandra O'Connor, Antonin Scalia, and Anthony M. Kennedy. Reagan's successor, George Bush, added two more: David H. Souter and Clarence Thomas. By 1992 there appeared to be a solid bloc of conservative justices who were ready to cast aside the strict separation of church and state and to allow, at a minimum, religious invocations at school ceremonies. Those hopes were dashed, however.

Principals in Providence, Rhode Island, were given authorization to invite members of the clergy to deliver an invocation and benediction at public school graduation ceremonies. In 1989 a rabbi gave a nondenominational message to the graduates at the Nathan Bishop Middle School: "God of the Free, Hope of the Brave: For the Legacy of America where diversity is celebrated and the rights of minorities are protected, we thank you," he began. He spoke of the importance of liberty and justice and made no overly religious comments, except to repeat the phrase, "We thank You." Fourteen-year-old Deborah Weisman and her father challenged the rabbi's invocation in a lawsuit that named the school principal Robert E. Lee. U.S. solicitor general Kenneth Starr, representing the Bush administration, urged the Court in *Lee v. Weisman* (1992) to rule for the principal and confirm that public schools may acknowledge the nation's religious heritage in their ceremonies. By a 5-4 vote, the Court ruled the school's action unconstitutional because it forced students to participate in "state-sponsored religious activity." Three Reagan-Bush appointees—Justices Kennedy, O'Connor,

and Souter—joined with Justices Blackmun and Stevens—Republican appointees from the 1970s—to form the majority. The move to cast aside the separation of church and state doctrine, inspired by Reagan and pressed by Rehnquist, had fallen one vote short.

"The lessons of the First Amendment are as urgent in the modern world as in the 18th Century when it was written," Kennedy said.[96] "One timeless lesson is that if citizens are subjected to state-sponsored religious exercises, the State disavows its own duty to guard and to respect that sphere of inviolable conscience and belief which is the mark of a free people."[97] The rabbi's invocation may sound beyond objection to many, he said, but consider the view of the "nonbeliever or dissenter." To that person, the religious invocation may look like "an attempt to employ the machinery of the State to enforce a religious orthodoxy.... The Constitution forbids the State to exact religious conformity from a student as the price of attending her own high school graduation. This is the calculus the Constitution commands," wrote Kennedy.[98]

The majority distinguished *Lee v. Weisman* from *Marsh v. Chambers* (1983), in which the Court condoned a prayer at the opening of a state legislature's daily session: "The atmosphere at the opening of a session of a state legislature where adults are free to enter and leave with little comment and for any number of reasons cannot compare with the constraining potential of the one school event most important for the student to attend. The influence and force of a formal exercise in a school graduation are far greater than the prayer exercise we condoned in *Marsh*."[99]

Chief Justice Rehnquist and Justices Scalia, White, and Thomas dissented. Scalia, writing for the group, emphasized the historical and unifying role of prayer in American celebrations: "The history and tradition of our Nation are replete with public ceremonies featuring prayers of thanksgiving and petition.... Most recently, President [George] Bush, continuing the tradition established by President Washington, asked those attending his inauguration to bow their heads, and made a prayer his first official act as president."[100]

The decisions of the 1960s had made clear that teachers and principles cannot lead prayers at a public school. *Lee v. Weisman* extended that prohibition to include clerics who were invited by school officials to speak at school ceremonies. Students, however, have a free speech right to pray on their own at school, the Court said in 1990, and some school officials and religious rights activists took this right a step further and designated students as prayer leaders at school events. This practice was particularly common in Texas. The issue came before the Court in 2000 in a case from Santa Fe, Texas, a city with a population of 8,500, midway between Galveston and Houston. The Santa Fe school board had authorized members of the senior class to elect one student each year to deliver a pregame prayer over the public address system at football games. Two students and their parents challenged this mixing of church and state as unconstitutional, but they did so anonymously because of their fear that they would be harassed and intimidated. Texas governor George W. Bush, campaigning for the presidency, filed an amicus brief supporting the students' right to lead Christian prayers at football games.

In a 6-3 decision in *Santa Fe Independent School District v. Doe (2000)*, the Court struck down the school board's policy, reiterating that "school sponsorship of a religious message is impermissible."[101] Nothing in the law or the Constitution "prohibits any public school student from voluntarily praying at any time before, during or after the school day," said Justice Stevens.[102] He continued, however,

> these invocations are authorized by a government policy and take place on government property at government-sponsored school-related events.... The school allows only one student, the same student for the entire season to give the invocation.... The delivery of such a [religious] message—over the school's public address system, by a speaker representing the student body, under the supervision of the school faculty and pursuant to a school policy that explicitly and implicitly encourages public prayer—is not properly characterized as "private speech."[103]

In dissent, Chief Justice Rehnquist faulted "the tone of the Court's opinion [which] bristles with hostility to all things religious in public life."[104] He was joined by Justices Scalia and Thomas.

Equal Access

Despite the *Santa Fe* setback for advocates of a return to school-sponsored prayer, the Court made clear in a series of rulings that students may meet on their own to pray or read the Bible at a public school. In five decisions between 1981 and 2001, the justices rejected the arguments of school officials that the use of public school facilities to support religious programs would breach the Establishment Clause.

In 1981 the Court ruled that the University of Missouri must allow a student religious group to meet in school buildings on the same terms as other extracurricular groups. Once the campus "has opened its facilities for use by student groups," it cannot now "exclude groups because of the content of their speech," the Court said.[105] In 1984 Congress passed the Equal Access Act, barring high schools from discriminating against clubs or meetings based on the "religious, philosophical [or] political" views of the students involved. The Court upheld the law in 1990, ruling that school officials may not discriminate against student-led Bible clubs or prayer groups. Allowing such groups on campus as part of "the broad spectrum" of student activities counters "any possible message of official endorsement of or preference for religion or a particular religious belief," said Justice O'Connor.[106]

The next test of religious access, in 1993, went beyond student use of public school facilities. The Center Moriches Union Free School District on Long Island, New York, had allowed community groups to use its facilities after hours for social, civic, and recreational purposes, but the district had a formal policy against opening classrooms to groups for religious activities. It rejected a request from an evangelical Christian church that wanted to show a film series addressing various child-rearing issues. This denial of access was unconstitutional, the Court ruled unanimously. Justice Byron R. White, writing for the Court, said "it discriminates on the basis of viewpoint to permit school property to be used for the presentation of all views about family issues and child-rearing except those dealing with the subject matter from a religious standpoint."[107]

Two years later, the Supreme Court examined a University of Virginia policy that denied the use of student activity fees to cover the costs of printing a Christian magazine on campus. Such fees were used to support a broad range of extracurricular activities related to the university's educational purpose, such as the publication of student news, information, and opinion. The Court, 5-4, struck down the policy as a violation of free speech, ruling that a program that distributes funds to religious and nonreligious publications would not violate the Establishment Clause. Justice Kennedy wrote the majority opinion in *Rosenberger v. University of Virginia* (1995):

> There is no difference in logic or principle, and no difference of constitutional significance, between a school using its funds to operate a facility to which students have access, and a school paying a third-party contractor [such as a printer] to operate the facility on its behalf. The latter occurs here.[108]

Kennedy continued:

> It is axiomatic that the government may not regulate speech based on its substantive content or the message it conveys.... Vital First Amendment speech principles are at stake here. The first danger to liberty lies in granting the State the power to examine publications to determine whether or not they are based on some ultimate idea and if so for the State to classify them. The second, and corollary, danger is to speech from the chilling of individual thought and expression. That danger is especially real in the University setting, where the State acts against a background and tradition of thought and experiment that is at the center of our intellectual and philosophic tradition.[109]

Kennedy was joined by Chief Justice Rehnquist and Justices O'Connor, Scalia, and Thomas. Justices Souter, Stevens, Ruth Bader Ginsburg, and Stephen G. Breyer dissented. Justice Souter expressed their concern that

> the Court today, for the first time, approves the direct funding of core religious activities by an arm of the State.... [T]here is no warrant for distinguishing among public funding sources for purposes of applying the First Amendment's prohibition on religious establishment.[110]

Souter concluded with a reference to the 1971 ruling that has defined the modern Court's approach to cases brought under the Establishment Clause:

> [M]y apprehension is whetted by Chief Justice Burger's warning in *Lemon v. Kurtzman*: "in constitutional adjudication some steps, which when taken were thought to approach 'the verge,' have become the platform for yet further steps. A certain momentum develops in constitutional theory and it can be a 'downhill thrust' easily set in motion but difficult to retard or stop."[111]

Sante Fe, Widmar, Lamb's Chapel, and *Rosenberger*—two involving colleges and two involving high schools—stood for the proposition that the Establishment Clause did not require, or even permit, school officials to exclude student activities or groups solely because of their religious beliefs. Although the government cannot sponsor a religious group or single it out for special favor, it also cannot single out a religious group for a special exclusion, the Court said. The justices extended that principle in 2002 to include evangelical groups seeking to meet at public elementary schools after hours.

The Good News Club is a private Christian organization that offers Bible study and Christian teaching to children between the ages of six and twelve. Stephen and Darleen Fournier asked the school superintendent at the Milford Central School in upstate New York to hold the club's weekly meeting in the elementary school cafeteria. The superintendent refused, citing a school board policy that prohibits use of the facilities "for religious purposes." The Court took up the Fournier's appeal and ruled 6-3 in *Good News Club v. Milford Central School District* (2001) that the school's refusal to open its cafeteria to them violated their free speech rights.

Justice Thomas noted that New York law states that school facilities may be open for "social, civil and recreational meetings" as well as educational activities of all sorts. While public facilities need not be open to everyone, a "restriction [on their use] must not discriminate against speech on the basis of viewpoint," he said. He concluded that "Milford's exclusion of the Good News Club [is] based on its religious nature" and thereby violates the freedom of speech guarantee in the First Amendment. He dismissed the Establishment Clause concern raised by school officials as far-fetched. There is "no realistic danger that the community would think that the District was endorsing religion or any particular creed" simply by allowing the Fourniers to meet there, he said.[112]

In dissent, Justice Souter said that the Fourniers wanted to use the school "for an evangelical service of worship" and their victory in the Supreme Court seems to stand "for the remarkable proposition that any public schools opened for civic meetings must be opened for use as a church, synagogue or mosque."[113]

State Aid to Church-Related Schools

While the school prayer and equal access cases concern religious activities in public schools, the Court has struggled just as mightily over whether and when public money can flow to religious schools. Through the mid-twentieth century, the Court took the view that parochial students as well as public students could benefit from state aid, so long as the government did not single out religious schools for special favor. In the 1960s and 1970s, however, the justices took a more stringent view of the Establishment Clause and struck down a series of state laws that subsidized parochial schools by offering their students free textbooks or by giving their parents help with tuition. The justices said these laws had the obvious "effect" of promoting the teaching of religion with tax money, a violation of the clause. Beginning in the 1980s, the Court gradually backed away from this strict ban on aid. Entering the twenty-first century, the Court's majority stressed the principle of neutrality. Under this approach, parochial schools as well as public schools may receive public education aid so long as the religious schools are not singled out for special or favored treatment.

A key decision in the Court's change in approach came in 2002, when the Court upheld the use of state vouchers to pay for children to transfer to religious schools.[114] While this decision marked a clean break from the strict separation between church and state of a few decades earlier, it also could be seen as a return to the Court's original interpretation of the Establishment Clause. The first suit challenging state aid to church-related schools reached the Supreme Court in *Cochran v. Louisiana Board of Education* (1930).[115] Louisiana gave all schoolchildren in the state, including those attending parochial schools, secular textbooks paid for with public funds. Emmett Cochran, a taxpayer, challenged the statute. He contended that this use of public funds violated the Fourteenth Amendment's prohibition against state action depriving persons of their property without due process of law. (In 1930 the Court had not yet specifically stated that the Fourteenth Amendment incorporated the religious guarantees of the First Amendment.) Rejecting Cochran's assertion, the Supreme Court adopted the "child benefit" theory. The provision of free textbooks was designed to further the education of all children in the state and not to benefit church-related schools, the Court maintained.

In *Everson v. Board of Education* (1947), the Court specifically applied the Establishment Clause to the states for the first time.[116] This case was also the first one in which the Court was required to consider whether the clause barred public aid to church-operated schools. *Everson* concerned a New Jersey statute that permitted local boards of education to reimburse parents for the costs of sending their children to school on public transportation. Arch Everson, a local taxpayer, challenged as an impermissible establishment of religion the reimbursement of parents of parochial school students. The Court in *Everson* elaborated on its ruling in *Cochran*, decided seventeen years earlier.

Writing for the five-justice majority, Justice Black offered his famous explanation of the Establishment Clause, including Jefferson's comment about the "wall of separation of church and state." Among its prohibitions, the First Amendment means, Black said, "No tax in any amount, large or small, can be levied to support any religious activities or institutions, whatever they may be called, or whatever form they may adopt to teach or practice religion."[117] Having said that, however, the majority proceeded to uphold the New Jersey statute on the grounds that it did not aid religion but was instead public welfare legislation benefiting children rather than schools:

> It is undoubtedly true that children are helped to get to church schools. There is even a possibility that some of the children might not be sent to the church schools if the parents were compelled to pay their children's bus fares out of their own pockets when transportation to a public school would have

SCHOOL PRAYER AND CONGRESSIONAL BACKLASH

"The Supreme Court has made God unconstitutional," declared Sen. Sam Ervin, D-N.C., in 1962, after the Court's rejection of school prayer in *Engel v. Vitale*.[1] Members of Congress, governors, even a former president all spoke out in opposition to the decision. Although the ruling was greeted favorably by the Jewish community and many Christian leaders, several members of the clergy expressed dismay. "I am shocked and frightened that the Supreme Court has declared unconstitutional a simple and voluntary declaration of belief in God by public school children," said Francis Cardinal Spellman. "The decision strikes at the very heart of the Godly tradition in which America's children have for so long been raised."[2]

Reaction to the Court's Bible reading decision in 1963 was equally adverse and outspoken. "Why should the majority be so severely penalized by the protests of a handful?" asked evangelist Billy Graham.[3] With such proclamations began decades of debate in state legislatures and the halls of Congress over the issue of prayer and Bible reading in school. Despite the opposition of most major religious organizations to a constitutional amendment to overturn the rulings, mail advocating such an amendment began to pour into congressional offices in the days and months after the Supreme Court rulings.

Rep. Frank J. Becker, R-N.Y., proposed an amendment in 1962. It provided that nothing in the Constitution should be interpreted to bar "the offering, reading from, or listening to prayer or biblical scriptures, if participation therein is on a voluntary basis, in any government or public school institution or place." The House Judiciary Committee took no action on the proposal, primarily because of the opposition of its chairman, Emanuel Celler, D-N.Y.

Senate minority leader Everett McKinley Dirksen, R-Ill., proposed in 1966 an amendment stating that the Constitution should not be interpreted to bar any public school authority from providing for or permitting the voluntary participation of students in prayer. His amendment specifically stated that it did not authorize any government official to prescribe the form or content of a prayer. When the Senate voted on this amendment, it fell nine votes short of approval.

In the early 1970s, at the urging of a grassroots organization called the Prayer Campaign Committee, Rep. Chalmers P. Wylie, R-Ohio, supported another proposed amendment to the Constitution. He began to circulate among House members a petition to discharge the amendment, similar to the Dirksen amendment, from a still-opposed House Judiciary Committee. By September 1971, a majority of the House had signed Wylie's petition, and the amendment came to the House floor for debate. On November 8, 1971, the amendment failed by twenty-eight votes to win the approval of the necessary two-thirds majority.

A decade later, the support of President Ronald Reagan for a constitutional amendment on school prayer revived efforts to win congressional approval, but in 1984 the Senate fell eleven votes short of approving the administration's amendment.[4] In October 1994, Congress passed legislation that included a provision withholding federal funds from any public school that willfully violated a court order to allow constitutionally protected voluntary prayer.[5] After the Republicans won majorities in the House and Senate in November 1994, numerous proposals were offered for a constitutional amendment permitting organized school prayer. None has been adopted.

---

1. Quoted in Leo Pfeffer, *Church, State and Freedom*, rev. ed. (Boston: Beacon Press, 1967), 466.

2. Ibid., 467.

3. Quoted in Congressional Quarterly, "Restore Prayers in Schools: The Move That Failed," in *Education for a Nation* (Washington, D.C.: Congressional Quarterly, 1972), 38. The decision was *School District of Abington Township v. Schempp, Murray v. Curlett*, 374 U.S. 203 (1963).

4. *Congress and the Nation* (Washington, D.C.: Congressional Quarterly, 1985), 6:703; *CQ Almanac, 1985* (Washington, D.C.: Congressional Quarterly, 1986), 235.

5. *CQ Almanac, 1994* (Washington, D.C.: Congressional Quarterly, 1995), 389–391.

been paid for by the State.... Similarly, parents might be reluctant to permit their children to attend [church] schools which the state had cut off from such general government services as ordinary police and fire protection, connections for sewage disposal, public highways and sidewalks. Of course, cutting off church schools from these services, so separate and so indisputably marked off from the religious function, would make it far more difficult for the schools to operate. But such is obviously not the purpose of the First Amendment. That Amendment requires the state to be a neutral in its relations with groups of religious believers and nonbelievers; it does not require the state to be their adversary. State power is no more to be used so as to handicap religions, than it is to favor them.[118]

In dissent, Justice Rutledge, joined by Justices Jackson, Frankfurter, and Harold H. Burton, agreed with the majority that the Establishment Clause "forbids state support, financial or other, of religion in any guise, form or degree. It outlaws all use of public funds for religious purposes." To cast this particular case in terms of public welfare, as the majority does, however, is to ignore "the religious factor and its essential connection with the transportation, thereby leaving out the only vital element in the case," said Rutledge.[119] Publicly supported transportation of parochial schoolchildren benefits not only their secular education but also their religious instruction, Rutledge asserted.

> Two great drives are constantly in motion to abridge, in the name of education, the complete division of religion and civil authority which our forefathers made. One is to introduce religious education and observances into the public schools. The other, to obtain public funds for the aid and support of various private religious schools.... In my opinion, both avenues were closed by the Constitution. Neither should be opened by this Court.[120]

Textbooks

It was evident from *Everson* that despite Justice Black's extremely broad interpretation of the Establishment Clause, the line of separation between church and state was, as a later justice would put it, "a blurred, indistinct and variable barrier depending on all the circumstances of a particular relationship."[121] The Court now needed to devise some criteria for assessing whether state aid to religious schools breached that barrier. In the twenty years between *Everson* and the next state aid case—*Board of Education of Central School District No. 1 v. Allen* (1968)—the Supreme Court decided *Vitale, Schempp,* and *Murray,* ruling that the Establishment Clause did not permit public schools to use prayers and Bible reading as part of their daily exercises and that such exercises violated the clause because they were sectarian in purpose and their primary effect was to advance religion. The Court first applied these guidelines to a question of state aid to church-related schools in *Allen.*

The circumstances were similar to those in *Cochran.* New York law required local school boards to lend textbooks purchased with public funds to seventh- through twelfth-grade students, including those attending parochial schools. The requirement was challenged as a violation of the Establishment Clause. The New York Court of Appeals upheld the statute and, by a 6-3 vote, the Supreme Court agreed. Writing for the majority, Justice White explained that the purpose of the requirement was secular—to further the educational opportunities of students at public as well as private schools. Because the subject matter of the books was secular, the loan program neither advanced nor inhibited religion.

To the claim that books were essential for teaching and that the primary goal of parochial schools was to teach religion, White observed that the Court "has long recognized that religious schools pursue two goals, religious instruction and secular education." Without more evidence, White said the majority could not state that "all teaching in a sectarian school is religious or that the processes of secular and religious training are so intertwined that secular textbooks furnished to students by the public are in fact instrumental in the teaching of religion."[122] The majority also held that the loan program conformed to the *Everson* child benefit precedent: "[N]o funds or books are furnished to parochial schools, and the financial benefit is to parents and children, not to schools," White wrote.[123]

In separate dissents, Justices William O. Douglas and Abe Fortas contended that although local public school boards would approve the books for use, in actual practice they would not choose the books to be used in the church schools; sectarian authorities would make that choice. Justice Black also dissented, distinguishing between nonideological aid, such as transportation or school lunch, which was permissible, and books, which were related to substantive religious views and beliefs and thus in his view impermissible.

"Parochiaid"

Allen was decided at a time when rising educational costs compelled more and more parochial school officials to seek direct financial aid from the states. The states, faced with fiscal problems of their own and many

THE *LEMON* DEMON

The Court's modern test for determining whether government policy or action violates the Establishment Clause was first set out in *Lemon v. Kurtzman* (1971) and hence is known as the *Lemon* test.[1] In brief, the test permits government aid to religious entities only if the assistance has a secular purpose, neither advances nor inhibits religion, and does not foster excessive government "entanglement" with the religious entity.

Many of the justices who came to the Court subsequent to *Lemon* believed that it was too strict a test. Because a majority could not agree on an alternative test, the Court used *Lemon* inconsistently during the 1980s and 1990s. In a 1993 opinion, Justice Antonin Scalia mocked the Court's reluctance to rid itself of *Lemon*:

> Like some ghoul in a late-night horror movie that repeatedly sits up in its grave and shuffles abroad, after being repeatedly killed and buried, *Lemon* stalks our Establishment Clause jurisprudence once again, frightening the little children and school attorneys.[2]

Scalia noted that five sitting justices—himself, Anthony M. Kennedy, Sandra Day O'Connor, William H. Rehnquist, and Byron R. White—"have, in their own opinions, personally driven pencils through the creature's heart."[3] He continued:

> The secret of the *Lemon* test's survival, I think, is that it is so easy to kill. It is there to scare us (and our audience) when we wish it to do so, but we can command it to return to the tomb at will. See, *e.g., Lynch v. Donnelly* (1984) (noting instances in which Court has not applied *Lemon* test). When we wish to strike down a practice it forbids, we invoke it, see, *e.g., Aguilar v. Felton* (1985) (striking down state remedial education program administered in part in parochial schools); when we wish to uphold a practice it forbids, we ignore it entirely, *see Marsh v. Chambers* (1983) (upholding state legislative chaplains). Sometimes, we take a middle course, calling its three prongs "no more than helpful signposts," *Hunt v. McNair* (1973). Such a docile and useful monster is worth keeping around, at least in a somnolent state; one never knows when one might need him.[4]

---

1. *Lemon v. Kurtzman,* 403 U.S. 602 (1971).

2. *Lamb's Chapel v. Center Moriches School District,* 508 U.S. 384 (1993).

3. Id.

4. Id.

with large numbers of parochial school students, were willing to comply on the premise that it would be less expensive to give the church schools aid than to absorb their students into the public system if they were forced to close. Several states—notably New York, Pennsylvania, and Ohio—passed statutes authorizing direct aid, such as teacher salary subsidies, tuition reimbursements, and tuition tax credits. The decision in *Allen* and support for such programs from President Richard Nixon and members of Congress encouraged church and state officials to hope that these so-called parochiaid programs might pass constitutional scrutiny.

The first challenges to these direct aid laws reached the Court in the early 1970s. *Lemon v. Kurtzman* (1971) and its companion cases concerned a Rhode Island statute that authorized a salary supplement to certain nonpublic school teachers and a Pennsylvania law that established a program to reimburse nonpublic schools for teachers' salaries, textbooks, and instructional materials. In practice, the Rhode Island law benefited only Roman Catholic schools, while the Pennsylvania law affected more than 20 percent of the students in the state. Both laws stipulated that recipient teachers must teach only secular subjects. The Pennsylvania law stipulated that the textbooks and instructional materials also be secular in nature.

The Court struck down both state laws in unanimous votes. In doing so it added a new requirement to the test for permissible state aid. Writing the Court's opinion, Chief Justice Warren E. Burger said such aid not only must have a secular legislative purpose and a primary effect that neither advanced nor inhibited religion, but it also must not foster "an excessive government entanglement with religion."[124] The latter requirement was drawn from a 1970 ruling upholding property tax exemptions for church property. (*See "Tax Exemptions," p. 142.*) To determine whether state entanglement with religion is excessive, Burger said, the Court "must examine the character and purposes of the institutions that are benefited, the nature of the aid that the State provides, and the resulting relationship between the government and the religious authority."[125]

Applying this new, three-part test to the Rhode Island statute, the majority found that teacher salary supplements did result in excessive state entanglement with religion. Without continual monitoring, the state could not know with certainty whether a parochial school teacher was presenting subject matter to pupils in the required neutral manner, Burger said. Simple assurances were not sufficient:

> We need not and do not assume that teachers in parochial schools will be guilty of bad faith or any conscious design to evade the limitations imposed by the statute and the First Amendment. We simply recognize that a dedicated religious person, teaching in a school affiliated with his or her faith and operated to inculcate its tenets, will inevitably experience great difficulty in remaining religiously neutral.[126]

The only way to ensure that teachers remained neutral, Burger said, is through "comprehensive, discriminating and continuing state surveillance." Such contact between state and church amounted to excessive entanglement.[127] By the same reasoning, the salary reimbursement portion of the Pennsylvania statute was invalid, Burger said. Furthermore, the portion of the Pennsylvania law reimbursing church schools for textbooks and instructional materials constituted direct aid to the school rather than to the pupils and their parents.

School Maintenance, Tuition Grants, Tax Credits

Using the same three-part test, the Court struck down New York statutes that authorized maintenance and repair grants to certain private and parochial schools, reimbursed low-income parents of nonpublic school students for a portion of school tuition, and allowed tax credits to parents of nonpublic school students who did not qualify for the tuition reimbursements. Writing for the majority in *Committee for Public Education and Religious Liberty v. Nyquist* (1973),

Justice Powell said that nothing in the statute stipulated that maintenance grants should be used only for secular purposes. Because the state grant could easily be used to "maintain the school chapel, or [cover] the cost of renovating classrooms in which religion is taught, or the cost of heating and lighting those same facilities," the majority could not deny that the primary effect of the grant was to subsidize directly "the religious activities of sectarian elementary and secondary schools" in violation of the Establishment Clause.[128]

Although the tuition reimbursement law appeared to aid parents, it was ruled to unconstitutionally advance religion, the justices finding its obvious and primary effect to aid church schools. Powell wrote,

> [I]t is precisely the function of New York's law to provide assistance to private schools, the great majority of which are sectarian. By reimbursing parents for a portion of their tuition bill, the State seeks to relieve their financial burdens sufficiently to assure that they continue to have the option to send their children to religion-oriented schools. And while the other purposes for that aid—to perpetuate a pluralistic educational environment and to protect the fiscal integrity of overburdened public schools—are certainly unexceptionable, the effect of the aid is unmistakably to provide desired financial support for nonpublic, sectarian institutions.[129]

It made no difference to the majority that parents might spend the reimbursement money on something other than tuition:

> [I]f the grants are offered as an incentive to parents to send their children to sectarian schools by making unrestricted cash payments to them, the Establishment Clause is violated whether or not the actual dollars given eventually find their way into the sectarian institutions. Whether the grant is labeled a reimbursement, a reward or a subsidy, its substantive impact is still the same.[130]

The majority concluded that the tax credit provisions served to advance religion for the same reasons tuition grants did. Under either the tuition reimbursement or the tax credit, the parent "receives the same form of encouragement and reward for sending his children to nonpublic schools," Powell wrote.[131]

Dissenting from the majority on tuition reimbursement and tax credits, Chief Justice Burger and Justice Rehnquist contended that those two programs aided parents and not schools. Justice White would have upheld both programs as well as the grants for maintenance and repairs. He said that the primary effect of the New York statutes was not to advance religion but to "preserve the secular functions" of parochial schools.

Testing Services

On the same day in 1973 as the *Nyquist* decision, the Court also held invalid a New York law that provided per-pupil payments to nonpublic schools to cover the costs of testing and maintaining state-mandated pupil records. Most of the funds were spent on testing—state-mandated standardized tests and those prepared by teachers to measure the progress of students in regular course work. The Court found that the statute was invalid as it related to this latter sort of testing. "Despite the obviously integral role of testing in the total teaching process," the statute made no attempt to ensure that teacher-prepared tests were "free of religious instruction." Thus the grants used for testing had the primary effect of advancing religion, the Court said, and because the Court could not determine which part of the grants was spent on potentially religious activities and which on permissible secular activities, it invalidated the entire statute.[132]

Several years later the Court found a permissible testing reimbursement arrangement that covered the costs of administering, grading, and reporting the results of standardized tests prepared by the state, as well as the costs of reporting pupil attendance and other basic data required by the state.[133]

Other State Services

In two other cases, *Meek v. Pittinger* (1975) and *Wolman v. Walter* (1977), the Court again used its three-level test to measure the constitutionality of a variety of state services. Under *Lemon*'s three-part test, government aid must have a secular purpose; it can neither advance nor inhibit religion; and it must not foster excessive involvement with religion. The Court in these rulings allowed

states to provide church-affiliated schools with loaned textbooks, standardized testing and scoring services, and speech and hearing diagnostic services. Therapeutic, guidance, and remedial education services could be provided by public school board employees to parochial school students at sites away from the schools, although services by such employees provided at the schools were impermissible.

The Court in *Wolman* ruled unconstitutional an Ohio law that permitted the state to pay the costs of transportation for parochial school field trips. The majority held that because the schools determined the timing and destination of field trips, they and not parents were the true beneficiaries of the statute, and thus could not be reimbursed. "The field trips are an integral part of the educational experience," the majority said, "and where the teacher works within and for a sectarian institution, an unacceptable risk of fostering of religion is an inevitable byproduct."[134]

The Court also held impermissible as a violation of the Establishment Clause the loan of instructional materials and equipment either to sectarian schools themselves or to their pupils. The Court ruled out direct loans to schools in *Meek*. Even though the materials were secular in nature, the loan "has the unconstitutional primary effect of advancing religion because of the predominantly religious character of the schools benefiting from the Act."[135] Later in *Wolman*, the majority would say that it saw no significant difference between lending materials to schools and lending them to pupils; "the state aid inevitably flows in part in support of the religious role of the schools."[136]

The Court's no-aid-to-parochial-schools doctrine reached its high water mark in 1985, when the justices on a 5-4 vote struck down the use of federal tutors in parochial schools. The majority held that Grand Rapids, Michigan, school officials had "established" religion by providing remedial and enrichment classes to students at forty-one nonpublic schools, forty of which were religiously affiliated. Writing for the majority, Justice William J. Brennan Jr. said that these classes—conducted during the school day by public school teachers or after school by parochial school teachers who were paid for this work from public funds—were impermissible. The "symbolic union of church and state inherent in the provision of secular state-provided instruction in the religious school buildings threatens to convey a message of state support for religion," Brennan wrote in *Grand Rapids School District v. Ball*. The vote was 7-2 on the day-hours classes, with Justices Rehnquist and White dissenting; it was 5-4 on the after-school classes, with Chief Justice Burger and Justice O'Connor finding them permissible.[137] That same day the Court, 5-4, also held unconstitutional New York's system for providing remedial and counseling services to disadvantaged children in nonpublic schools.[138]

The pair of rulings set off a backlash in the education community and brought the Court in for sharp criticism. Federal aid to education began in the mid-1960s as part of President Lyndon B. Johnson's War on Poverty, and by law, public school districts were obliged to provide extra tutoring for all of the needy children in their area, regardless of whether they were enrolled in public or parochial schools. Yet, the Court's ruling barred public school officials from sending tutors to the disadvantaged children at their religious schools. Education Secretary William J. Bennett complained that the Court seemed to view religion as "akin to an infectious disease," dangerous to children and teachers alike.

The tide, however, had begun to turn against this strict insistence on separation of church and state. In *Mueller v. Allen* (1983), the Court had upheld a Minnesota state income tax deduction to parents with children in public or parochial schools. Parents could deduct for such expenses as tuition, textbooks, or transportation up to $500 per child in elementary school and up to $700 per child in secondary schools. While the program was open to all, the main beneficiaries were parents who sent their children to private and parochial schools. Speaking for the 5-4 majority, Justice Rehnquist described the tuition deduction as a public program that is "neutral" toward religion and whose benefits are determined by "the private choices of individual parents."[139]

In *Witters v. Washington Department of Services for the Blind* (1986), the Court unanimously ruled that a blind student could use a state tuition grant to enroll in a private Christian college in hopes of becoming a pastor, missionary, or youth director. "The Establishment Clause is not violated every time money previously in the possession of the State is conveyed to a religious institution," wrote Justice Thurgood Marshall. This Washington state program to aid blind students "is in no way skewed toward religion. It creates no financial incentive for students to undertake sectarian education."[140] For some of the justices, this decision was an easy one because it concerned colleges and universities, not elementary schools. In *Tilton v. Richardson* (1971), the Court had upheld federal construction grants to church-affiliated colleges under the Higher Education Act of 1963. There is less need to worry about government support for religious colleges compared to similar support for elementary schools because the students are different, argued Chief Justice Burger. "College students are less impressionable and less susceptible to religious indoctrination," he said.[141] *(See "Aid to Church Colleges," pp. 162–163.)* The *Witters* ruling also contained a seed that would sprout later in aid programs for elementary and secondary children. As Justice Rehnquist and others said in concurring opinions, "state programs that are wholly neutral" in providing education money do not violate the First Amendment just because some of it goes to religious schools. It would take many more cases, however, to establish that principle.

In 1993 the Court upheld the use of a federally funded sign-language interpreter for a deaf student in a Catholic high school. James Zobrest had been deaf since birth and had attended public schools in Tucson, Arizona, with the aid of a sign-language interpreter, thanks to the requirements of the Individuals with Disabilities Education Act. When he was due to enter the ninth grade, his parents enrolled him in Salpointe Catholic High School. They requested that the interpreter go with him, but the school district refused, saying it would be unconstitutional to send the public school teacher on to the premises of a Catholic school.

The Court disagreed in *Zobrest v. Catalina Foothills School District* (1993). "We have consistently held that government programs that neutrally provide benefits to a broad class of citizens defined without reference to

RELIGIOUS SYMBOLS ON DISPLAY

The Supreme Court has frowned upon government-sponsored displays of religious symbols and texts and has provoked frowns and protests from many Americans who do not see any possible harm to others in celebrating Christmas or honoring the Ten Commandments in the public sphere. In 1980 the Court in an unsigned opinion and without hearing arguments on the issue struck down a Kentucky law that required the posting of the Ten Commandments on a wall in each public classroom in the state. Said the Court in *Stone v. Graham,*

> The preeminent purpose for posting the Ten Commandments … is plainly religious in nature. The Ten Commandments are undeniably a sacred text in the Jewish and Christian faiths, and no legislative recitation of a supposed secular purpose can blind us to that fact.[1]

The Ten Commandments can be "integrated into the school curriculum" and used in the "appropriate study of history, civilization, ethics, comparative religion or the like," the Court added, but "the mere posting of the copies under the auspices of the legislature provides the official support of the state government that the Establishment Clause prohibits."[2]

The ruling spoke only for a 5-4 majority. Of the four dissenters, Chief Justice Warren E. Burger and Justices Harry A. Blackmun and Potter Stewart would have heard full arguments on the issue. Justice William H. Rehnquist thought the ruling unequivocally wrong. "The Ten Commandments have had a significant impact on the development of secular legal codes of the Western World" and that alone, according to him, gave state lawmakers ample justification for posting the commandments in the state's classrooms.[3]

In the final months of Rehnquist's life, the Court reconsidered the display of the Ten Commandments on public property and ended with a split decision in June 2005. With Rehnquist speaking for a 5-4 majority, the Court upheld the display of a granite monument displaying the commandments that stood with other monuments and statues on the grounds of the Texas state capitol.[4] The monument had been erected forty years earlier by the Fraternal Order of Eagles, and, as Rehnquist noted, its display recognized the role of religion in American life and history. In a separate 5-4 vote, the Court struck down as unconstitutional the posting of the Ten Commandments inside the courthouses in two counties in Kentucky.[5] Justice David H. Souter acknowledged the commandments as a "sacred text" in the Jewish and Christian faiths, and a "reasonable observer could only think the counties meant to emphasize and celebrate [their] religious message."

Only Justice Stephen G. Breyer was in the majority in both cases. He offered that "no exact formula" can decide these disputes because the First Amendment promotes religious liberty but also limits the government's promotion of religion. Context counts, Breyer noted, and the Texas monument sitting among other historical markers and statues carries a historical and cultural message rather than a solely religious one. At the same time, he agreed with Souter that the Kentucky officials who posted the commandments in their courthouses were publicly endorsing a religious message.

Earlier, the justices had issued two somewhat contradictory rulings on city-sponsored Christmas displays. In a case from Pawtucket, Rhode Island, the Court upheld the display of a crèche in a city park that was surrounded by other traditional holiday symbols, including Santa Claus, a Christmas tree, and colored lights. In *Lynch v. Donnelly* (1984), the Court, by a 5-4 vote, upheld the inclusion of the crèche. Writing for the majority, Chief Justice Burger declared that "the concept of a 'wall' of separation is a useful figure of speech … but … not a wholly accurate description of the practical aspects of the relationship that in fact exists between church and state."[6] Burger rejected a "rigid, absolutist view" of the Establishment Clause.

---

religion are not readily subject to an Establishment Clause challenge just because sectarian institutions may also receive an attenuated financial benefit," wrote Chief Justice Rehnquist for the 5-4 majority.[142] He cited *Mueller* and *Witters* as precedents. "Disabled children, not sectarian schools, are the primary beneficiaries of the IDEA; to the extent sectarian schools benefit at all … they are only incidental beneficiaries," he said. "Not withstanding the Court of Appeals intimations to the contrary, the Establishment Clause lays down no absolute bar to the placing of a public employee in a sectarian school."[143]

What had changed since 1985, when the Court struck down the use of public teachers in parochial schools? A shift of one justice: Justice Thurgood Marshall, a strict separationist, had retired in 1991 and was replaced by Clarence Thomas, who supported nondiscriminatory aid for religious schools. In dissent, Justice Harry A. Blackmun said "government crosses the boundary when it furnishes the medium for communication of

He called this approach "simplistic" because it ignored "an unbroken history of official acknowledgment by all three branches of government of the role of religion in American life from at least 1789."[7] Justices William J. Brennan Jr., Blackmun, Thurgood Marshall, and John Paul Stevens dissented. In their view, the "primary effect of including a nativity scene in the city's display is … to place the government's imprimatur of approval on the particular religious beliefs exemplified by the crèche," which violates the First Amendment.[8]

Five years after *Lynch v. Donnelly,* the Court reverted to the strict separation view when confronted with a scene of Jesus in a manger on display in a county courthouse. Each Christmas season in Pittsburgh, the seat of Allegheny County, the depiction of Christ's birth occupied a prominent place in the courthouse. By the 1980s, officials also erected a menorah outside. Both religious displays were challenged as unconstitutional by the American Civil Liberties Union. The Court upheld the menorah display, but not the crèche. Justice Blackmun explained for the majority that "unlike in *Lynch,* nothing in the context of the display detracts from the crèche's religious message." Rather, it stood alone on the Grand Staircase of the Allegheny County Courthouse. By permitting its prominent display in that particular place, "the county sends an unmistakable message that it supports and promotes … the crèche's message." The Court divided 5-4 on this point. Chief Justice Rehnquist and Justices Anthony M. Kennedy, Byron R. White, and Scalia dissented.[9]

The menorah display was permissible, Blackmun continued, because it was part of an overall display of symbols of the winter holidays, including a Christmas tree outside the City-County Building. Unlike the crèche, he wrote, "the menorah's message is not exclusively religious."[10] The Court divided 6-3 on this point. Blackmun and Justice Sandra Day O'Connor were joined in the majority by the dissenters on the crèche issue. Justices Stevens, Brennan, and Marshall dissented.

Another religion-based case implicating free speech rights arose after Ohio officials denied members of the Ku Klux Klan a permit to erect a large wooden cross in front of the state capitol, where other private groups had been permitted to erect a Christmas tree and a menorah. By a 7-2 vote, the Court held that state officials were wrong to exclude this one privately sponsored religious message from a public forum open to other privately sponsored messages. Justice Scalia, who wrote the opinion, said a reasonable observer would not think the state had endorsed the cross's message. He distinguished the case from the Allegheny County decision, arguing that the Grand Staircase of the courthouse was not open to all on an equal basis, "so the County was *favoring* sectarian religious expression."[11] Most of Scalia's opinion was joined by Chief Justice Rehnquist and Justices O'Connor, Kennedy, Souter, Clarence Thomas, and Breyer. Justices Stevens and Ruth Bader Ginsburg dissented.

---

1. *Stone v. Graham,* 449 U.S. 39 at 41 (1980).
2. Id. at 42.
3. Id. at 45.
4. *Van Orden v. Perry,* 545 U.S. 677 (2005).
5. *McCreary County v. American Civil Liberties Union of Kentucky,* 545 U.S. 844 (2005).
6. *Lynch v. Donnelly,* 465 U.S. 668 at 673 (1984).
7. Id.
8. Id. at 701.
9. *Allegheny County v. American Civil Liberties Union, Chabad v. American Civil Liberties Union, Pittsburgh v. American Civil Liberties Union,* 492 U.S. 573 (1989).
10. Id.
11. *Capitol Square Review and Advisory Board v. Pinette,* 515 U.S. 753 (1995).

a religious message. If [the Zobrests] receive the relief they seek, it is beyond question that a state-employed sign language interpreter would serve as the conduit for James' religious education, thereby assisting Salpointe in its mission of religious indoctrination."[144]

Four years after *Zobrest,* the Rehnquist Court took up a New York City case with the express intent to overrule Justice Brennan's 1985 opinion that had barred public school remedial-reading tutors from parochial schools. Those decisions—*Aguilar v. Felton* and *School District of Grand Rapids v. Ball*—had created a practical problem, because the public schools were required to serve disadvantaged children in parochial schools, but their teachers could not enter the premises to teach them. As a fallback, the New York City school system bought computers and mobile vans, which were parked outside parochial schools. The students came outside and were taught in the vans so as not to cross the imaginary line separating church and state. City school officials told the Court they had

As the Supreme Court heard oral arguments in February 2002 on the constitutionality of school vouchers, supporters and opponents of such plans rallied outside.

spent $100 million over a decade trying to comply with the 1985 rulings.

In *Agostini v. Felton* (1997), Justice O'Connor spoke for the 5-4 majority that overturned the earlier rulings. She candidly described the shift in the Court's thinking:

> We have abandoned the presumption erected in *Meek* and *Ball* that the placement of public employees on parochial school grounds inevitably results in the impermissible effect of state sponsored indoctrination or constitutes a symbolic union between government and religion.... Second, we have departed from the rule relied on [earlier] that all government aid that directly aids the education function of religious schools is invalid.... No Title I funds ever reach the coffers of religious schools.[145]

Reiterating this last point, O'Connor stated, "New York City's Title I program does not run afoul" of the First Amendment by advancing religion: "It does not result in governmental indoctrination; define its recipients by reference to religion; or create an excessive entanglement."[146]

Justice Souter spoke for the four dissenters, contending the ruling "authorize[s] direct state aid to religious institutions on an unparalleled scale, in violation of the Establishment Clause's central prohibition against religious subsidies by the government."[147] He was joined by Justices Stevens, Ginsburg, and Breyer.

The rulings in *Zobrest* and *Agostini* made clear that publicly funded teachers could now work in parochial schools. Could public funds be used to buy computers, textbooks, and other teaching tools for use in religious schools? In the 1970s, the Court had outlawed such subsidies in the cases of *Meek v. Pittinger* and *Wolman v. Walter,* but the Court in 2000 took up a Louisiana case to test these precedents as well. Chapter 2 of the Education Consolidation and Improvement Act of

1981 channels federal money to local school districts to buy instructional and educational materials, including computers, and it obliges the public schools districts to provide roughly equal amounts (per student) for non-profit private schools in their area as well. In Jefferson Parish, Louisiana, about 30 percent of the money went to private institutions, and of these, a solid majority of them were Roman Catholic schools. Mary Helms, a parent, sued the school district on the grounds that it was subsidizing the parochial schools.

Under normal circumstances, taxpayers cannot sue to challenge a government spending program because they have not suffered a direct, personal injury. The Court had established this rule in 1923,[148] but the justices later created an exception for challenges based on the Establishment Clause. It "operates as a specific constitutional limitation upon the exercise by Congress of the taxing and spending power," the Court said in *Flast v. Cohen* (1968).[149] Mrs. Flast had challenged as unconstitutional the new program of federal aid to education because it subsidized parochial as well as public schools. She won the legal "standing" to pursue her challenge in court, but the justices did not resolve the merits of her claim. Decades later, Mary Helms relied on Flast's victory to bring her challenge to the federal subsidies in Jefferson Parish, and she prevailed in the lower courts. Judges in New Orleans said the federal funding violated the rule against subsidies for church schools that the Court had set in the 1970s. Guy Mitchell, the school superintendent, appealed the issue anew to the Supreme Court.

In *Mitchell v. Helms* (2001), the Court upheld the use of tax money to buy computers for parochial schools and declared *Meek* and *Wolman* "no longer good law." Wrote Justice Thomas for a four-member plurality,

> We see no basis for concluding that Jefferson Parish's Chapter 2 program has the effect of advancing religion. Chapter 2 does not result in government indoctrination, because it determines eligibility for aid neutrally, allocates that aid based on the private choices of parents of school children and does not provide aid that has an impermissible content.... A government computer or overhead projector does not itself inculcate a religious message, even when it is conveying one.[150]

Thomas stated that a general aid program should never be struck down as a subsidy for religion simply because a religious school qualifies for the same support as a public school. "If a program offers permissible aid to the religious, the areligious and the irreligious, it is a mystery which view of religion the government has established," he said. He also described as "most bizarre" the dissenters' argument that "reserves special hostility" for what were described as "pervasively sectarian" institutions. "It was an open secret [in the nineteenth and early twentieth centuries] that 'sectarian' was code for 'Catholic,'" he said. "The exclusion of pervasively sectarian schools from otherwise permissible aid programs ... has a shameful pedigree that we do not hesitate to disavow. This doctrine, born of bigotry, should be buried now," he concluded.[151] Chief Justice Rehnquist and Justices Scalia and Kennedy joined his opinion.

Justice Sandra Day O'Connor said she agreed with the outcome, but said Thomas's opinion went too far for her. His "rule of unprecedented breadth" would appear to allow the government to fund church schools on an equal basis with public schools, O'Connor said.[152] Justice Breyer agreed with her. In dissent, again, Justice Souter said the Court should stick with the "principle of no aid to religious teaching" set back in 1947. He called Thomas's opinion

> a sharp break with the Framers' understanding of establishment and this Court's consistent interpretative course.... Together with James Madison, we have consistently understood the Establishment Clause to impose a substantive prohibition against public aid to religion, and hence, to the religious mission of sectarian schools.[153]

The decisions of the 1990s knocked down the old barriers to what the Court called "incidental" aid to parochial schools. They also cleared the way for a far more important ruling to allow the government to pay the full cost of transferring a school child from a public to a religious school. The constitutionality of state vouchers came to the Court in an Ohio case. Earlier, the justices had refused to hear a First Amendment challenge to Wisconsin's vouchers for parents in

Milwaukee. They were obliged to take up the issue when a U.S. court of appeals in Ohio struck down that state's voucher program for parents in Cleveland.

The public schools in Cleveland were among the most troubled in the nation. More than two-thirds of the city's high school students dropped out or failed to graduate. The state legislature enacted a tuition aid program for children from kindergarten through the eighth grade. Parents with low incomes could receive a state voucher for 90 percent of the cost of tuition in a private school, up to $2,250 per year. During the 1999–2000 school year, more than 3,700 children took advantage of the state tuition aid, and 96 percent of them enrolled in a church-related school. A group of taxpayers and parents, led by Doris Simmons-Harris, challenged the program as unconstitutional in a lawsuit backed by the nation's two large teachers unions, the American Federation of Teachers and the National Education Association. A federal judge and the U.S. Court of Appeals in Cincinnati agreed the state aid had the "primary effect" of subsidizing religious instruction, since nearly all of the students transferred to church schools. Ohio appealed on behalf of its school superintendent, Susan Tave Zelman.

The Court upheld the voucher program, arguing that the state was giving parents a choice for their children's education, not subsidizing religion. "We have never found a program of true private choice to offend the Establishment Clause," wrote Chief Justice Rehnquist for the 5-4 majority in *Zelman v. Simmons-Harris* (2002).[154] He continued:

> The Ohio program is neutral in all respects toward religion.... It confers educational assistance directly to a broad class of individuals defined without reference to religion, i.e. any parents of a school-age child who resides in the Cleveland City School District. The program permits the participation of ALL schools within the district, religious or nonreligious.... There are no financial incentives that skew the program toward religious schools.... Any objective observer familiar with the full history and context of the Ohio program would reasonably view it as one aspect of a broader undertaking to assist poor children in failed schools, not as an endorsement of religious school in general.[155]

The ruling marked a special triumph for Chief Justice Rehnquist. Throughout more than three decades on the high court, he had called for upholding public aid to students who attend parochial schools. Rehnquist's opinion was joined in full by Justices O'Connor, Scalia, Kennedy, and Thomas.

In separate dissents, Justice Stevens and Breyer foresaw an increase in "religious strife" if the government insisted on paying for "religious indoctrination." "Whenever we remove a brick from the wall that was designed to separate religion and government, we increase the risk of religious strife and weaken the foundation of our democracy," Stevens wrote.[156] "I hope that a future court will reconsider today's dramatic departure from basic Establishment Clause principle," said Justice Souter in a dissent that was joined by Justice Ginsburg.[157] The dissenters could not claim to be surprised by the outcome. Chief Justice Rehnquist laid the groundwork for a new interpretation of the First Amendment. The government may fund education in a way that allows parents to choose a religious school for their children, so long as church schools are not given special treatment.

Aid to Church Colleges

The Court's decisions concerning government aid to elementary and secondary schools have been made after lengthy deliberations, but the justices' rulings upholding direct government aid to church-affiliated colleges and universities have been arrived at with little difficulty. In three cases decided in the 1970s, the Court approved state and federal programs aiding sectarian institutions of higher education. In *Tilton v. Richardson* (1971), the Court upheld federal construction grants to church-affiliated colleges under the Higher Education Facilities Act of 1963. This federal statute permitted church-related schools to receive grants with the understanding that no federally financed building would be used for sectarian purposes.

Writing the opinion for the majority of five, Chief Justice Burger said that because the grants were available to secular and sectarian schools, the law met the test that government aid be secular in purpose. The majority did not find the involvement between the federal government and church-related schools likely to be excessive. The buildings themselves were religiously neutral in character, and since religious indoctrination was not the primary purpose of the colleges, the necessity for government surveillance to maintain the separation between religious and secular education was minimal. In addition, the federal law did not advance religion. There was no evidence, said Burger, that "religion seeps into the use of any of these facilities."[158]

Underlying the majority's decision was its presumption that there is a significant difference between the religious aspects of church-related colleges and church-related primary and secondary schools and between impressionable youngsters and more skeptical young adults. As Burger explained,

[C]ollege students are less impressionable and less susceptible to religious indoctrination.... The skepticism of the college student is not an inconsiderable barrier to any attempt or tendency to subvert the congressional objectives and limitations. Furthermore, by their very nature, college and postgraduate courses tend to limit the opportunities for sectarian influence by virtue of their own internal disciplines. Many church-related colleges and universities are characterized by a high degree of academic freedom and seek to evoke free and critical responses from their students.[159]

Justice Douglas, speaking for three of the dissenters, objected to the federal law on the grounds that no federal tax revenues should be used to support religious activities of any sort. Justice Brennan also dissented. The majority did declare unconstitutional a section of the law that permitted the schools to use the buildings for sectarian purposes after twenty years.

Using *Tilton* as a precedent, the Court subsequently upheld a South Carolina statute that allowed the state to issue revenue bonds to finance construction of secular facilities at secular and sectarian colleges and universities and a Maryland program of general annual grants to private colleges, including church-related schools.[160]

──────── ★ ────────

NOTES

INTRODUCTION (PP. 22–32)

1. Zechariah Chafee Jr., *Free Speech in the United States* (Cambridge: Harvard University Press, 1941; reprint, New York: Atheneum, 1969), 33.

2. Thomas I. Emerson, *The System of Freedom of Expression* (New York: Random House, Vintage Books, 1970), 7.

3. Thomas M. Cooley, *A Treatise on Constitutional Limitations*, 8th ed., 2 vols. (Boston: Little, Brown, 1927), 2:901.

4. *Whitney v. California*, 274 U.S. 357 at 375–376 (1927).

5. *Reynolds v. United States*, 98 U.S. 145 (1879).

6. *Barron v. Baltimore*, 7 Pet. (32 U.S.) 243 (1833).

7. Alpheus T. Mason and William M. Beaney, *The Supreme Court in a Free Society* (New York: Norton, 1968), 289.

8. *Gilbert v. Minnesota*, 254 U.S. 325 at 343 (1920).

9. *Prudential Insurance Co. v. Cheek*, 259 U.S. 530 at 538 (1922).

10. *Meyer v. Nebraska*, 262 U.S. 390 at 399–400 (1923).

11. *Gitlow v. New York*, 268 U.S. 652 at 666 (1925).

12. *Pierce v. Society of Sisters*, 268 U.S. 510 (1925).

13. *Cantwell v. Connecticut*, 310 U.S. 296 at 303 (1940); *Everson v. Board of Education*, 330 U.S. 1 (1947).

14. *Near v. Minnesota*, 283 U.S. 697 (1931); *DeJonge v. Oregon*, 299 U.S. 353 at 364 (1937).

15. William Blackstone, *Commentaries on the Laws of England*, quoted in Chafee, *Free Speech*, 9.

16. Cooley, *Constitutional Limitations*, 2:885–886.

17. *Cantwell v. Connecticut*, 310 U.S. 296 at 303–304 (1940).

18. *Schenck v. United States*, 249 U.S. 47 (1919).

19. *West Virginia State Board of Education v. Barnette*, 319 U.S. 624 at 642 (1943).

20. *Abrams v. United States*, 250 U.S. 616 at 630 (1919).

21. *Smith v. California*, 361 U.S. 147 at 157 (1959).

22. *Konigsberg v. State Bar of California*, 366 U.S. 36 at 61 (1961).

23. *Palko v. Connecticut*, 302 U.S. 319 at 327, 326 (1937).

24. *United States v. Carolene Products Co.*, 304 U.S. 144 at 152 n. 4 (1938).

25. *Schneider v. Irvington*, 308 U.S. 147 at 161 (1939).

26. *Murdock v. Pennsylvania*, 319 U.S. 105 at 115 (1943).

27. *Thomas v. Collins*, 323 U.S. 516 at 529–530 (1945).

28. *Landmark Communications Inc. v. Virginia*, 435 U.S. 829 at 843–844 (1978).

29. *Kovacs v. Cooper*, 336 U.S. 77 at 90 (1949).

30. *Dennis v. United States*, 341 U.S. 494 at 539–540 (1951).

31. *Schenck v. United States*, 249 U.S. 47 at 52 (1919).

32. See, for example, *Abrams v. United States,* 250 U.S. 616 (1919); *Pierce v. United States,* 252 U.S. 239 (1920); *Gitlow v. New York,* 268 U.S. 652 (1925).

33. *Herndon v. Lowry,* 301 U.S. 242 at 261 (1937).

34. *Thornhill v. Alabama,* 310 U.S. 88 (1940).

35. *Cantwell v. Connecticut,* 310 U.S. 296 at 311 (1940).

36. *Terminiello v. Chicago* 337 U.S. 1 (1949); *Feiner v. New York,* 340 U.S. 315 (1951).

37. *Dennis v. United States,* 341 U.S. 494 at 510 (1951).

38. *Yates v. United States,* 354 U.S. 298 (1957).

39. *American Communications Association v. Douds,* 399 U.S. 382 at 399 (1950).

40. See, for example, *Konigsberg v. State Bar of California,* 366 U.S. 36 (1961).

41. *NAACP v. Alabama ex rel. Patterson,* 357 U.S. 449 (1958); *Edwards v. South Carolina,* 372 U.S. 229 (1963); *Cox v. Louisiana,* 379 U.S. 536 (1965); *Brown v. Louisiana,* 383 U.S. 131 (1966); *Adderly v. Florida,* 385 U.S. 39 (1966); *United States v. Robel,* 389 U.S. 258 (1967).

42. *Brandenburg v. Ohio,* 395 U.S. 444 (1969).

43. *Shelton v. Tucker,* 364 U.S. 479 at 488 (1960).

44. *Virginia v. Black,* 538 U.S. 343 (2003).

FREEDOM OF SPEECH (PP. 33–82)

1. C. Herman Pritchett, *The American Constitution,* 3d ed. (New York: McGraw-Hill, 1977), 314.

2. Ibid., 317.

3. See Rodney A. Smolla, *Free Speech in an Open Society* (New York: Alfred A. Knopf, 1992), 97.

4. *Schenck v. United States,* 249 U.S. 47 at 51 (1919).

5. Id. at 52.

6. Id.

7. *Frohwerk v. United States,* 249 U.S. 204 at 208–209 (1919).

8. *Debs v. United States,* 249 U.S. 211 at 215 (1919).

9. Id.

10. *Abrams v. United States,* 250 U.S. 616 at 623 (1919).

11. Id. at 627, 628.

12. Smolla, *Free Speech,* 101.

13. *Abrams v. United States,* 250 U.S. 616 at 630–631 (1919).

14. *Schaefer v. United States,* 251 U.S. 466 at 481 (1920).

15. Id. at 478.

16. Id. at 479.

17. Id. at 486.

18. Id. at 493–495.

19. *Pierce v. United States,* 252 U.S. 239 at 249 (1920).

20. Id. at 269.

21. Id. at 273. The three minor decisions in this series were *Sugarman v. United States,* 249 U.S. 182 (1919); *Stilson v. United States,* 250 U.S. 583 (1919); *O'Connell v. United States,* 253 U.S. 142 (1920).

22. *Hartzel v. United States,* 322 U.S. 680 (1944).

23. *Gitlow v. New York,* 268 U.S. 652 at 665 (1925).

24. Id. at 667.

25. Id. at 669.

26. Id. at 673.

27. *Whitney v. California,* 274 U.S. 357 at 371–372 (1927).

28. Id. at 373.

29. Id. at 376, 378.

30. *Fiske v. Kansas,* 274 U.S. 380 (1927).

31. *DeJonge v. Oregon,* 299 U.S. 353 at 365 (1937).

32. *Herndon v. Lowry,* 301 U.S. 242 at 258 (1937).

33. Id. at 263–264.

34. Id. at 276.

35. *Brandenburg v. Ohio,* 395 U.S. 444 at 447–448 (1969).

36. *Davis v. Massachusetts,* 167 U.S. 43 at 47 (1897).

37. *Hague v. C.I.O.,* 307 U.S. 496 at 515–516 (1939).

38. *Cox v. New Hampshire,* 312 U.S. 569 (1941).

39. *Cantwell v. Connecticut,* 310 U.S. 296 at 308 (1940).

40. Id. at 310, 311.

41. *Terminiello v. Chicago,* 337 U.S. 1 at 4–5 (1949).

42. Id. at 37.

43. *Feiner v. New York,* 340 U.S. 315 at 320–321 (1951).

44. *Near v. Minnesota,* 283 U.S. 697 (1931).

45. *Cantwell v. Connecticut,* 310 U.S. 296 (1940).

46. *Thomas v. Collins,* 323 U.S. 516 at 534–535 (1945).

47. Id. at 540.

48. *Kunz v. New York,* 340 U.S. 290 at 293 (1951).

49. Id. at 298.

50. *Watts v. United States* 394 U.S. 705 (1969).

51. *Stromberg v. California,* 283 U.S. 359 at 369 (1931).

52. *West Virginia State Board of Education v. Barnette,* 319 U.S. 624 at 632–633 (1943).

53. *Garner v. Louisiana,* 368 U.S. 157 (1961).

54. See, for example, *Peterson v. City of Greenville,* 373 U.S. 244 (1963); *Shuttlesworth v. City of Birmingham,* 373 U.S. 262 (1963); *Lombard v. Louisiana,* 373 U.S. 267 (1963); *Gober v. City of Birmingham,* 373 U.S. 374 (1963); *Avent v. North Carolina,* 373 U.S. 375 (1963).

55. *NAACP v. Claiborne Hardware Co.,* 458 U.S. 886 (1982).

56. *United States v. O'Brien,* 391 U.S. 367 at 376 (1968).

57. *Barnes v. Glen Theatre,* 501 U.S. 560 (1991).

58. *Tinker v. Des Moines School District,* 393 U.S. 503 at 508–509 (1969).

59. *Schacht v. United States,* 398 U.S. 58 at 63 (1970).

60. *Street v. New York,* 394 U.S. 576 (1969).

61. *Smith v. Goguen,* 415 U.S. 566 at 574 (1974).

62. *Spence v. Washington,* 418 U.S. 405 at 410–411 (1974).

63. *Texas v. Johnson,* 491 U.S. 397 at 414 (1989).

64. Id. at 417.

65. Id. at 420.

66. Id. at 420–421.

67. Id. at 426, 428.

68. *United States v. Eichman,* 496 U.S. 310 (1990).

69. *City of Ladue v. Gilleo,* 512 U.S. 687 (1994).

70. *Virginia v. Black,* 538 U.S. 343 (2003).

71. *United States v. Cruikshank,* 92 U.S. 542 at 552 (1876).

72. *DeJonge v. Oregon,* 299 U.S. 353 at 365 (1937).

73. *Hague v. C.I.O.,* 307 U.S. 496 (1939).

74. *Cox v. New Hampshire,* 312 U.S. 569 at 576 (1941).

75. *Forsyth County, Georgia v. Nationalist Movement,* 505 U.S. 123 (1992).

76. *Hurley v. Irish-American Gay, Lesbian and Bisexual Group of Boston,* 515 U.S. 557 (1995).

77. *Edwards v. South Carolina,* 372 U.S. 229 (1963). See also *Fields v. South Carolina,* 375 U.S. 44 (1963); *Cameron v. Johnson,* 390 U.S. 611 (1968).

78. *Edwards v. South Carolina,* 372 U.S. 229 at 235, 237 (1963).

79. Id. at 237; *Terminiello v. Chicago,* 337 U.S. 1 (1949).

80. *Cox v. Louisiana,* 379 U.S. 536 (1965).

81. Id. at 559.

82. *Brown v. Louisiana,* 383 U.S. 131 at 142 (1966).

83. Id. at 166.

84. *Adderly v. Florida,* 385 U.S. 39 at 41, 47–48 (1966).

85. Id. at 49–51.

86. *Gregory v. City of Chicago,* 394 U.S. 111 at 112 (1969).

87. *Frisby v. Schultz,* 487 U.S. 474 (1988).

88. *NAACP v. Claiborne Hardware Co.,* 458 U.S. 886 (1982).

89. *United States v. Grace,* 461 U.S. 171 (1983).

90. *Clark v. Community for Creative Non-Violence,* 468 U.S. 288 (1984).

91. *Madsen v. Women's Health Center,* 512 U.S. 753 at 770 (1994).

92. *Schenck v. Pro-Choice Network of Western New York,* 519 U.S. 357 (1997).

93. *Hill v. Colorado,* 530 U.S. 703 at 716–717 (2000), referring to *Olmstead v. United States,* 277 U.S. 438 at 478 (1928).

94. Id. at 710.

95. Id. at 764–765.

96. *American Steel Foundries v. Tri-City Central Trades Council,* 257 U.S. 184 at 204 (1921).

97. *Senn v. Tile Layers Union,* 301 U.S. 468 at 478 (1937).

98. *Thornhill v. Alabama,* 310 U.S. 88 at 102 (1940).

99. Id. at 104; see also *Carlson v. California,* 310 U.S. 106 (1940).

100. *AFL v. Swing,* 312 U.S. 321 (1941).

101. *Milk Wagon Drivers Union v. Meadowmoor Dairies Inc.,* 312 U.S. 287 at 293, 294 (1941).

102. *Bakery and Pastry Drivers v. Wohl,* 315 U.S. 769 at 775 (1942).

103. *Carpenters and Joiners Union v. Ritter's Cafe,* 315 U.S. 722 at 727 (1942).

104. *Bakery and Pastry Drivers v. Wohl,* 315 U.S. 769 at 776–777 (1942).

105. *Giboney v. Empire Storage & Ice Co.,* 336 U.S. 490 at 502 (1949).

106. *Hughes v. Superior Court of California,* 339 U.S. 460 at 465–466 (1950).

107. *Building Service Employees Union v. Gazzam,* 339 U.S. 532 (1950); *International Brotherhood of Teamsters v. Hanke,* 339 U.S. 470 (1950).

108. *Local Plumbers Union #10 v. Graham,* 345 U.S. 192 (1953).

109. *International Brotherhood of Teamsters, Local 695 v. Vogt,* 354 U.S. 284 at 294–295, 293 (1957).

110. Id. at 296.

111. *Amalgamated Food Employees Union Local 590 v. Logan Valley Plaza,* 391 U.S. 308 (1968), qualified by *Lloyd Corporation Ltd. v. Tanner,* 407 U.S. 551 (1972), and *Hudgens v. National Labor Relations Board,* 424 U.S. 507 (1976).

112. Zechariah Chafee Jr., *Free Speech in the United States* (Cambridge, Mass: Harvard University Press, 1941; reprint, New York: Atheneum, 1969), 405–406.

113. *Cantwell v. Connecticut,* 310 U.S. 296 at 306–307 (1940); see also *Schneider v. Irvington,* 308 U.S. 147 (1939); *Largent v. Texas,* 318 U.S. 418 (1943).

114. *Hynes v. Oradell,* 425 U.S. 610 (1976); *Village of Schaumburg v. Citizens for a Better Environment,* 444 U.S. 620 (1980).

115. *Secretary of State of Maryland v. Joseph H. Munson Co.,* 467 U.S. 947 (1984); *Riley v. National Federation of the Blind of North Carolina,* 487 U.S. 781 (1988).

116. *Thomas v. Collins,* 323 U.S. 516 at 534, 540 (1945). See also *Staub v. City of Baxley,* 355 U.S. 313 (1958).

117. *Martin v. City of Struthers,* 319 U.S. 141 at 145, 146, 154–155 (1943).

118. *Watchtower Bible & Tract Society v. Village of Stratton,* 536 U.S. 205 (2002).

119. *International Society for Krishna Consciousness v. Lee; Lee v. International Society for Krishna Consciousness,* 505 U.S. 672 (1992).

120. *Board of Education of Westside Community School v. Mergens,* 496 U.S. 226 at 250 (1990).

121. Id.

122. *Lamb's Chapel v. Center Moriches Union Free School District,* 508 U.S. 384 at 393 (1993).

123. *Rosenberger v. University of Virginia,* 515 U.S. 819 (1995).

124. Id. at 828.

125. Id. at 863.

126. *Good News Club v. Milford Central School,* 533 U.S. 98 at 120 (2000).

127. *Capitol Square Review Board v. Pinette,* 515 U.S. 753 at 760 (1995).

128. Id. at 771.

129. Alex Kozinski and Stuart Banner, "Who's Afraid of Commercial Speech," *Virginia Law Review* 76 (May 1990): 627.

130. *Schneider v. Irvington,* 308 U.S. 147 (1939).

131. *Valentine v. Chrestensen,* 316 U.S. 52 at 54 (1942).

132. *Breard v. City of Alexandria,* 341 U.S. 622 at 642 (1951).

133. *New York Times Co. v. Sullivan,* 376 U.S. 254 at 266 (1964).

134. *Bigelow v. Virginia,* 421 U.S. 809 (1975).

135. *Virginia State Board of Pharmacy v. Virginia Citizens Consumer Council Inc.,* 425 U.S. 748 at 765 (1976).

136. *Carey v. Population Services International,* 431 U.S. 678 (1977); *Bates v. Arizona State Bar,* 433 U.S. 350 (1977); *Linmark Associates Inc. v. Township of Willingboro,* 431 U.S. 85 (1977); *Bolger v. Youngs Drug Products Corp.,* 463 U.S. 60 (1983).

137. *Bates v. Arizona State Bar,* 433 U.S. 350 (1977); *Ohralik v. Ohio State Bar Association,* 436 U.S. 447 (1978). See also *Friedman v. Rogers,* 440 U.S. 1 (1979); *Zauderer v. Office of Disciplinary Counsel of the Supreme Court of Ohio,* 471 U.S. 626 (1985).

138. *In re R. M. J.,* 455 U.S. 191 (1982); *Shapero v. Kentucky Bar Assn.,* 486 U.S. 466 (1988).

139. *Florida Bar v. Went For It Inc.,* 515 U.S. 618 (1995).

140. *Ibanez v. Florida Department of Business and Professional Regulation, Board of Accountancy,* 512 U.S. 136 (1994); *Edenfield v. Fane,* 507 U.S. 761 (1993).

141. *Central Hudson Gas & Electric Co. v. Public Service Commission of New York,* 447 U.S. 557 (1980).

142. Id. at 566.

143. *Consolidated Edison of New York v. Public Service Commission of New York,* 447 U.S. 530 (1980); *Pacific Gas & Electric Co. v. Public Utilities Commission,* 475 U.S. 1 (1986).

144. *44 Liquormart v. Rhode Island,* 517 U.S. 484 (1996).

145. *Posadas de Puerto Rico Associates v. Tourism Co. of P.R.,* 478 U.S. 328 (1986).

146. *Greater New Orleans Broadcasting Assn. v. United States,* 527 U.S. 173 (1999).

147. *Rubin v. Coors Brewing Co.,* 514 U.S. 476 (1995).

148. *44 Liquormart v. Rhode Island,* 517 U.S. 484 at 504 (1996).

149. *FDA v. Brown & Williamson,* 529 U.S. 120 (2000).

150. *Lorillard Tobacco Co. v. Reilly,* 533 U.S. 525 at 562 (2001).

FREEDOM OF THE PRESS (PP. 83–124)

1. Quoted in Willard Grosvenor Bleyer, *Main Currents in the History of American Journalism* (Boston: Houghton Mifflin, 1927), 103.

2. Dissenting opinion in *Saxbe v. Washington Post,* 417 U.S. 843 at 863 (1974).

3. *New York Times Co. v. United States, United States v. Washington Post,* 403 U.S. 713 (1971).

4. *Nebraska Press Association v. Stuart,* 427 U.S. 539 (1976).

5. *Gannett Co. Inc. v. DePasquale,* 443 U.S. 368 (1979), and *Richmond Newspapers Inc. v. Commonwealth of Virginia,* 448 U.S. 555 (1980).

6. *Branzburg v. Hayes, In re Pappas, United States v. Caldwell,* 408 U.S. 665 at 689–690 (1972).

7. *Zurcher v. The Stanford Daily,* 436 U.S. 547 (1978).

8. Thomas I. Emerson, *The System of Freedom of Expression* (New York: Random House, Vintage Books, 1970), 506.

9. *Near v. Minnesota,* 283 U.S. 697 at 713 (1931).

10. Id. at 716.

11. Id. at 720.

12. Id. at 721.

13. Id. at 722.

14. Id. at 735, 736.

15. Id. at 738.

16. *Simon & Schuster Inc. v. Members of New York State Crime Victims Board,* 502 U.S. 105 (1991).

17. *Grosjean v. American Press Co.,* 297 U.S. 233 at 244–245 (1936).

18. Id. at 250. See also *Minneapolis Star & Tribune Co. v. Minnesota Commissioner of Revenue,* 460 U.S. 575 (1983), and *Arkansas Writers' Project v. Ragland,* 481 U.S. 221 (1987).

19. *Lovell v. Griffin,* 303 U.S. 444 at 452 (1938).

20. Id. at 451.

21. *Schneider v. Irvington,* 308 U.S. 147 (1939); see also *Jamison v. Texas,* 318 U.S. 413 (1943). The other three cases are *Kim Young v. California, Snyder v. Milwaukee, Nichols v. Massachusetts,* 308 U.S. 147 (1939).

22. *Schneider v. Irvington,* 308 U.S. 147 at 160–161 (1939).

23. Id. at 163.

24. *Talley v. California,* 362 U.S. 60 at 64 (1960).

25. *McIntyre v. Ohio Elections Commission,* 514 U.S. 334 (1995).

26. *Organization for a Better Austin v. Keefe,* 402 U.S. 415 at 418, 419, 420 (1971).

27. *Mills v. Alabama,* 384 U.S. 214 at 219 (1966).

28. *New York Times Co. v. United States, United States v. Washington Post,* 403 U.S. 713 at 714 (1971).

29. Id. at 715, 717.

30. Id. at 720.

31. Id. at 725–726.

32. Id. at 730.

33. Id. at 730–731, 732.

34. Id. at 742.

35. Id. at 749.

36. Id. at 751.

37. Id. at 757.

38. Id. at 759.

39. Id. at 761.

40. See Holmes's dissent in *Abrams v. United States,* 250 U.S. 616 at 630 (1919); Black's and Douglas's opinion in *Beauharnais v. Illinois,* 343 U.S. 250 at 272 (1952); majority opinion in *New York Times Co. v. Sullivan,* 376 U.S. 254 (1964).

41. *Coleman v. MacLennan,* 98 P. 281 at 281–282 (1908).

42. *Dun & Bradstreet Inc. v. Greenmoss Builders Inc.*, 472 U.S. 749 (1985).

43. *New York Times Co. v. Sullivan*, 376 U.S. 254 at 257–258 (1964).

44. Id. at 268, 269.

45. Id. at 270–271.

46. Id. at 271–272.

47. Id. at 279.

48. Id. at 279–280.

49. Id. at 288.

50. Id. at 293.

51. Id. at 300.

52. *Garrison v. Louisiana*, 379 U.S. 64 (1964); *Ashton v. Kentucky*, 384 U.S. 195 (1966); *St. Amant v. Thompson*, 390 U.S. 727 at 731 (1968); *Greenbelt Cooperative Publishing Assn. v. Bresler* 398 U.S. 6 (1970); *Time Inc. v. Pape*, 401 U.S. 279 (1971).

53. *Herbert v. Lando*, 441 U.S. 153 (1979).

54. *Rosenblatt v. Baer*, 383 U.S. 75 at 85–86 (1966).

55. Id. at 93.

56. *Monitor Patriot Co. v. Roy*, 401 U.S. 265 (1971); see also *Ocala Star-Banner Co. v. Damron*, 401 U.S. 295 (1971).

57. *Curtis Publishing Co. v. Butts, Associated Press v. Walker*, 388 U.S. 130 (1967).

58. Id.

59. Id. at 155.

60. Id.

61. Id. at 159.

62. *Wolston v. Reader's Digest Association Inc.*, 443 U.S. 157 (1979); *Hutchinson v. Proxmire*, 443 U.S. 111 (1979).

63. *Bose Corp. v. Consumers Union of the United States*, 466 U.S. 485 (1984); *Anderson v. Liberty Lobby*, 477 U.S. 242 (1986); *Hustler Magazine v. Falwell*, 485 U.S. 46 (1988).

64. *Rosenbloom v. Metromedia Inc.*, 403 U.S. 29 at 43 (1971).

65. *Gertz v. Robert Welch Inc.*, 418 U.S. 323 at 345 (1974).

66. Id. at 347.

67. Id. at 352.

68. *Time Inc. v. Firestone*, 424 U.S. 448 at 453 (1976).

69. *Wolston v. Reader's Digest Association Inc.*, 443 U.S. 157 (1979); *Hutchinson v. Proxmire*, 443 U.S. 111 (1979); *Philadelphia Newspapers Inc. v. Hepps*, 475 U.S. 767 (1986).

70. *Hustler Magazine v. Falwell*, 485 U.S. 46 (1988).

71. Id. at 53.

72. Id. at 54.

73. Id. at 54–55.

74. Id. at 55.

75. *Milkovich v. Lorain Journal*, 497 U.S. 1 at 18 (1990).

76. Id. at 18.

77. Id. at 19.

78. Id. at 20.

79. Id. at 21.

80. Id. at 36.

81. *Masson v. New Yorker*, 501 U.S. 496 at 502 (1991).

82. *Cohen v. Cowles Media Co.*, 501 U.S. 663 (1991).

83. Id. at 672.

84. *Sheppard v. Maxwell*, 384 U.S. 333 at 350 (1966).

85. *Toledo Newspaper Co. v. United States*, 247 U.S. 402 (1918).

86. *Nye v. United States*, 313 U.S. 33 (1941).

87. *Patterson v. Colorado*, 205 U.S. 454 at 463 (1907).

88. *Bridges v. California, Times-Mirror Co. v. Superior Court of California*, 314 U.S. 252 at 269 (1941).

89. Id. at 270–271.

90. Id. at 273.

91. Id. at 278.

92. Id. at 284.

93. *Pennekamp v. Florida*, 328 U.S. 331 at 347 (1946).

94. *Craig v. Harney*, 331 U.S. 367 at 378 (1947).

95. *Wood v. Georgia*, 370 U.S. 375 at 389 (1962).

96. *Stroble v. California*, 343 U.S. 181 (1951).

97. *Marshall v. United States*, 360 U.S. 310 (1959).

98. *Irvin v. Dowd*, 366 U.S. 717 at 722–723 (1961).

99. *Beck v. Washington*, 369 U.S. 541 (1962).

100. *Rideau v. Louisiana*, 373 U.S. 723 (1963).

101. *Estes v. Texas*, 381 U.S. 532 at 536 (1965).

102. *Sheppard v. Maxwell*, 384 U.S. 333 at 355, 358 (1966).

103. Id. at 361–362.

104. *Nebraska Press Association v. Stuart*, 427 U.S. 539 (1976).

105. Id. at 559.

106. Id. at 568. See also *Cox Broadcasting Corp. v. Cohn*, 420 U.S. 469 (1975).

107. *Nebraska Press Association v. Stuart*, 427 U.S. 539 at 570 (1976).

108. Id. at 572.

109. *Seattle Times Co. v. Rhinehart*, 467 U.S. 1 (1984).

110. *Gentile v. State Bar of Nevada*, 501 U.S. 1030 (1991).

111. *Gannett Co. Inc. v. DePasquale*, 443 U.S. 368 (1979).

112. *Richmond Newspapers Inc. v. Commonwealth of Virginia*, 448 U.S. 555 (1980). See also *Globe Newspaper Co. v. Superior Court*, 457 U.S. 596 (1982); *Press-Enterprise Co. v. Superior Court of California, Riverside County*, 464 U.S. 501 (1984); *Press-Enterprise Co. v. Superior Court of California*, 464 U.S. 501 (1986).

113. *Chandler v. Florida*, 449 U.S. 560 (1981).

114. *Saxbe v. Washington Post Co.*, 417 U.S. 843 (1974); *Pell v. Procunier*, 417 U.S. 817 (1974).

115. *Pell v. Procunier*, 417 U.S. 817 at 834 (1974).

116. Id. at 835.

117. *Saxbe v. Washington Post Co.*, 417 U.S. 843 at 861 (1974).

118. *Houchins v. KQED Inc.*, 438 U.S. 1 at 15–16 (1978).

119. Id. at 32.

120. *Branzburg v. Hayes, In re Pappas, United States v. Caldwell,* 408 U.S. 665 at 689–690 (1972).

121. Id. at 681–682.

122. Id. at 690–691.

123. Id. at 691, 692.

124. Id. at 725.

125. Id. at 732–733.

126. Id. at 743.

127. *Zurcher v. The Stanford Daily,* 436 U.S. 547 at 565 (1978).

128. Id. at 566.

129. Id. at 571–573.

130. *Red Lion Broadcasting Co. v. Federal Communications Commission,* 395 U.S. 367 at 376 (1969).

131. *National Broadcasting Company v. United States,* 31 U.S. 190 at 226 (1943); see also *Federal Communications Commission v. SNCN Listeners Guild,* 450 U.S. 582 (1981).

132. *Red Lion Broadcasting Co. v. Federal Communications Commission,* 395 U.S. 367 at 388 (1969).

133. *Columbia Broadcasting System Inc. v. Democratic National Committee,* 412 U.S. 94 at 130 (1973).

134. *FCC v. League of Women Voters of California,* 468 U.S. 364 (1984).

135. *Telecommunications Research and Action Center v. Federal Communications Commission,* 801 F. 2d 501, review denied, June 8, 1987.

136. *Arkansas Educational Television Commission v. Forbes,* 523 U.S. 666 at 673 (1998).

137. Id. at 676.

138. *Federal Communications Commission v. Pacifica Foundation,* 438 U.S. 726 at 744 (1978).

139. Id. at 748, 749.

140. *Federal Communications Commission v. National Citizens Committee for Broadcasting,* 436 U.S. 775 (1978).

141. *Turner Broadcasting v. FCC,* 512 U.S. 622 at 639 (1994).

142. Id. at 636.

143. *Denver Area Telecommunications Consortium v. FCC,* 518 U.S. 727 at 741 (1996).

144. *United States v. Playboy Entertainment Group,* 529 U.S. 803 at 814 (2000).

145. Id. at 815.

146. *Turner Broadcasting v. FCC,* 520 U.S. 180 at 191 (1997).

147. *Reno v. ACLU,* 521 U.S. 844 at 852, 853 (1997).

148. Id. at 871.

149. Id. at 868.

150. Id. at 870.

151. Id. at 844.

152. *Ashcroft v. Free Speech Coalition,* 535 U.S. 234 (2002).

153. Id.

154. *United States v. American Library Association,* 539 U.S. 194 (2003).

FREEDOM OF RELIGION (PP. 125–163)

1. Sources on the history of religious freedom in the United States include Loren P. Beth, *The American Theory of Church and State* (Gainesville: University of Florida Press, 1958); and Leo Pfeffer, *Church, State and Freedom,* rev. ed. (Boston: Beacon Press, 1967).

2. Joseph Story, *Commentaries on the Constitution of the United States,* sec. 1879, cited in Charles Evans Hughes, *The Supreme Court of the United States: Its Foundations, Methods, and Achievements. An Interpretation* (New York: Columbia University Press, 1928), 161.

3. *Wallace v. Jaffree,* 472 U.S. 38 (1985). For the letter, see *Writings of Thomas Jefferson,* ed. H. A. Washington (Washington, D.C.: Taylor & Maury, 1853–54), 8:113.

4. *Everson v. Board of Education,* 330 U.S. 1 at 15–16 (1947).

5. "A Bill for Establishing Religious Freedom," in *Papers of Thomas Jefferson,* ed. Julian P. Boyd (Princeton, N.J.: Princeton University Press, 1950), 2:545–546.

6. *Wallace v. Jaffree,* 472 U.S. 38 at 92 (1985).

7. *Mitchell v. Helms,* 530 U.S. 793 at 829 (2000).

8. See id., upholding federal aid to purchase computers in parochial schools, and *Zelman v. Simmons-Harris,* 536 U.S. 639 (2002), upholding Ohio's use of vouchers to send children to religious schools.

9. *Everson v. Board of Education,* 330 U.S. 1 at 15–16 (1947).

10. *Mitchell v. Helms,* 530 U.S. 793 (2000).

11. See *Engel v. Vitale,* 370 U.S. 421 (1962), striking down state-sponsored prayers in the public schools, and *School District of Abington Township v. Schempp,* 374 U.S. 203 (1963), outlawing daily Bible readings in public schools.

12. *Lee v. Weisman,* 505 U.S. 577 (1992).

13. *Santa Fe Independent School District v. Doe,* 530 U.S. 290 (2000).

14. *Agostini v. Felton,* 521 U.S. 203 (1997).

15. *Mitchell v. Helms,* 530 U.S. 793 (2001).

16. *Zelman v. Simmons-Harris,* 536 U.S. 639 (2002).

17. *West Virginia State Board of Education v. Barnette,* 319 U.S. 624 (1943).

18. *Employment Division, Department of Human Resources of Oregon v. Smith,* 494 U.S. 872 at 879 (1990).

19. *City of Boerne v. Flores,* 521 U.S. 507 (1997).

20. *Cantwell v. Connecticut,* 310 U.S. 296 (1940).

21. *Lovell v. Griffin,* 303 U.S. 444 (1938); *Kunz v. New York,* 340 U.S. 290 (1951).

22. *Reynolds v. United States,* 98 U.S. 145 at 165 (1879).

23. *Davis v. Beason,* 133 U.S. 333 at 342–343 (1890).

24. Id. at 345; see also *Cleveland v. United States,* 329 U.S. 14 (1946).

25. *Cantwell v. Connecticut,* 310 U.S. 296 at 306–307 (1940).

26. *Martin v. City of Struthers*, 319 U.S. 141 (1943).

27. *United States v. Ballard*, 322 U.S. 78 at 86, 87 (1944).

28. *Prince v. Massachusetts*, 321 U.S. 158 at 166 (1944).

29. *Sherbert v. Verner*, 374 U.S. 398 (1963).

30. *Employment Division, Department of Human Resources of Oregon v. Smith*, 494 U.S. 872 (1990).

31. *CQ Almanac, 1993* (Washington, D.C.: Congressional Quarterly, 1994), 315.

32. *Church of the Lukumi Babalu Aye v. Hialeah*, 508 U.S. 520 (1993).

33. *Cantwell v. Connecticut*, 310 U.S. 296 at 308, 311 (1940).

34. Id. at 307; see also *Schneider v. Irvington*, 308 U.S. 147 (1939); *Martin v. City of Struthers*, 319 U.S. 141 (1943).

35. *Cox v. New Hampshire*, 312 U.S. 569 (1941).

36. *Kunz v. New York*, 340 U.S. 290 at 293 (1951).

37. *Niemotko v. Maryland*, 340 U.S. 268 (1951).

38. *Fowler v. Rhode Island*, 345 U.S. 67 at 70 (1953).

39. *Jones v. Opelika*, 316 U.S. 584 at 597 (1942).

40. *Murdock v. Pennsylvania*, 319 U.S. 105 at 113, 109 (1943).

41. Id. at 111; see also *Follett v. City of McCormick*, 321 U.S. 573 (1944).

42. *Heffron v. International Society for Krishna Consciousness*, 452 U.S. 640 (1981); *Widmar v. Vincent*, 454 U.S. 263 (1981).

43. *Jacobson v. Massachusetts*, 197 U.S. 11 (1905).

44. *Pierce v. Society of Sisters*, 268 U.S. 510 (1925); *Hamilton v. California Board of Regents*, 293 U.S. 245 (1934).

45. *Leoles v. Landers*, 302 U.S. 656 (1937); *Hering v. State Board of Education*, 303 U.S. 624 (1938); *Gabrielli v. Knickerbocker, Johnson v. Town of Deerfield*, 306 U.S. 621 (1939).

46. *Minersville School District v. Gobitis*, 310 U.S. 586 at 593, 594–595 (1940).

47. Id. at 598.

48. Id. at 598, 600.

49. Id. at 601.

50. Id. at 604.

51. Id. at 606.

52. Irving Dilliard, "The Flag-Salute Cases," in *Quarrels That Have Shaped the Constitution*, ed. John A. Garraty (New York: Harper and Row, 1964), 234.

53. *Jones v. Opelika*, 316 U.S. 584 at 623–624 (1942).

54. *West Virginia State Board of Education v. Barnette*, 319 U.S. 624 at 638 (1943).

55. Id. at 640, 641.

56. Id. at 641–642.

57. Id. at 646–647.

58. *Braunfeld v. Brown*, 366 U.S. 599 at 607 (1961); see also *Gallagher v. Crown Kosher Super Market*, 366 U.S. 617 (1961).

59. *Sherbert v. Verner*, 374 U.S. 398 at 404 (1963).

60. Id. at 406, quoting *Thomas v. Collins*, 323 U.S. 516 at 530 (1945).

61. *Thomas v. Review Board of the Indiana Employment Security Division*, 450 U.S. 707 (1981); *Hobbie v. Unemployment Appeals Commission of Florida*, 480 U.S. 136 (1987); *Estate of Thornton v. Caldor Inc.*, 472 U.S. 703 (1985).

62. *Wisconsin v. Yoder*, 406 U.S. 205 at 214 (1972).

63. *Torcaso v. Watkins*, 367 U.S. 488 at 495 (1961).

64. *United States v. Schwimmer*, 279 U.S. 644 (1929); *United States v. Macintosh*, 283 U.S. 605 (1931); *United States v. Bland*, 283 U.S. 636 (1931).

65. *Girouard v. United States*, 328 U.S. 61 (1946), overturning *United States v. Schwimmer*, 279 U.S. 644 (1929).

66. *In re Summers*, 325 U.S. 561 (1945).

67. *McDaniel v. Paty*, 435 U.S. 618 (1978); *Sherbert v. Verner*, 374 U.S. 398 (1963).

68. *Torcaso v. Watkins*, 367 U.S. 488 (1961).

69. *Mitchell v. Helms*, 530 U.S. 793 at 807 (2000).

70. Id. at 809.

71. Id. at 821.

72. *Bradfield v. Roberts*, 175 U.S. 291 (1899); see also *Quick Bear v. Leupp*, 210 U.S. 50 (1908).

73. *Walz v. Tax Commission*, 397 U.S. 664 at 673 (1970).

74. Id. at 675, 676.

75. *St. Martin Evangelical Lutheran Church and Northwestern Lutheran Academy v. State of South Dakota*, 452 U.S. 640 (1981); *Tony and Susan Alamo Foundation v. Secretary of Labor*, 471 U.S. 290 (1985). See also *Corporation of the Presiding Bishop of the Church of Jesus Christ of the Latter Day Saints v. Amos*, 483 U.S. 327 (1987).

76. *Zorach v. Clausen*, 343 U.S. 306 at 313 (1952).

77. *Lewis v. Allen*, 379 U.S. 923 (1964); *O'Hair v. Paine*, 401 U.S. 955 (1971); *O'Hair v. Blumenthal* 442 U.S. 930 (1979).

78. *Marsh v. Chambers*, 463 U.S. 783 (1983).

79. *Illinois ex rel. McCollum v. Board of Education*, 333 U.S. 203 at 210 (1948).

80. Id. at 227–228.

81. *Zorach v. Clausen*, 343 U.S. 306 at 312 (1952).

82. Id. at 315, 314.

83. *Clithero v. Schowalter*, 284 U.S. 573 (1930); *Doremus v. Board of Education*, 342 U.S. 429 (1952).

84. *Engel v. Vitale*, 370 U.S. 421 at 425 (1962).

85. Id. at 430–431.

86. Id. at 436, quoting James Madison, "Memorial and Remonstrance against Religious Assessments."

87. Id. at 445.

88. Id. at 450.

89. *School District of Abington Township v. Schempp, Murray v. Curlett*, 374 U.S. 203 at 226 (1963).

90. Id. at 225.

91. Id. at 226.

92. *Wallace v. Jaffree*, 472 U.S. 38 (1985).

93. Id. at 92.

94. Id. at 98.

95. Id. at 107–108.

96. *Lee v. Weisman,* 505 U.S. 577 at 592 (1992).

97. Id.

98. Id. at 596.

99. Id. at 597.

100. Id. at 633.

101. *Santa Fe Independent School District v. Doe,* 530 U.S. 290 at 309 (2000).

102. Id. at 313.

103. Id. at 303.

104. Id. at 318.

105. *Widmar v. Vincent,* 454 U.S. 263 at 273 (1981).

106. *Board of Education of the Westside Community Schools (Dist. 66) v. Mergens,* 496 U.S. 226 at 252 (1990).

107. *Lamb's Chapel v. Center Moriches Union Free School District,* 508 U.S. 384 at 393 (1993).

108. *Rosenberger v. Rector and Visitors of University of Virginia,* 515 U.S. 819 at 843 (1995).

109. Id. at 835.

110. Id. at 863–864.

111. Id. at 899.

112. *Good News Club v. Milford Central School District,* 533 U.S 98 at 106, 113 (2001).

113. Id. at 138.

114. *Zelman v. Simmons-Harris,* 536 U.S. 639 (2002).

115. *Cochran v. Louisiana Board of Education,* 281 U.S. 370 (1930).

116. *Everson v. Board of Education,* 330 U.S. 1 (1947).

117. Id. at 15–16.

118. Id. at 17–18.

119. Id. at 33, 50.

120. Id. at 63.

121. *Lemon v. Kurtzman,* 403 U.S. 602 at 614 (1971).

122. *Board of Education of Central School District No. 1 v. Allen,* 392 U.S. 236 at 245, 248 (1968).

123. Id. at 243–244.

124. *Lemon v. Kurtzman,* 403 U.S. 602 at 613 (1971), quoting *Walz v. Tax Commission,* 397 U.S. 664 at 674 (1970).

125. Id. at 615.

126. Id. at 618.

127. Id. at 619.

128. *Committee for Public Education and Religious Liberty v. Nyquist,* 413 U.S. 756 at 774 (1973); *Sloan v. Lemon,* 413 U.S. 825 (1973).

129. Id. at 783.

130. Id. at 786.

131. Id. at 791.

132. *Levitt v. Committee for Public Education and Religious Liberty,* 413 U.S. 472 at 480 (1973).

133. *Committee for Public Education and Religious Liberty v. Regan,* 444 U.S. 646 (1980).

134. *Wolman v. Walter,* 433 U.S. 229 at 254 (1977).

135. *Meek v. Pittinger,* 421 U.S. 349 at 363 (1975).

136. *Wolman v. Walter,* 433 U.S. 229 at 250 (1977).

137. *Grand Rapids School District v. Ball,* 473 U.S. 373 (1985).

138. *Aguilar v. Felton,* 473 U.S. 402 (1985).

139. *Mueller v. Allen,* 463 U.S. 388 at 400 (1983).

140. *Witters v. Washington Department of Services for the Blind,* 474 U.S. 481 at 486, 488 (1986).

141. *Tilton v. Richardson,* 403 U.S. 672 at 681 (1971).

142. *Zobrest v. Catalina Foothills School District,* 509 U.S. 1 at 8 (1993).

143. Id. at 12, 13.

144. Id. at 22.

145. *Agostini v. Felton,* 521 U.S. 203 at 223, 225 (1997).

146. Id. at 234.

147. Id. at 240–241.

148. *Frothingham v. Mellon,* 262 U.S. 447 (1923).

149. *Flast v. Cohen,* 392 U.S. 83 at 104 (1968).

150. *Mitchell v. Helms* 530 U.S. 793 at 823 (2001).

151. Id. at 826–827, 828, 829.

152. Id. 837.

153. Id. at 899.

154. *Zelman v. Simmons-Harris,* 536 U.S. 639 (2002).

155. Id.

156. Id.

157. Id.

158. *Tilton v. Richardson,* 403 U.S. 672 at 681 (1971).

159. Id. at 686.

160. *Hunt v. McNair,* 413 U.S. 734 (1973); *Roemer v. Maryland Board of Public Works,* 426 U.S. 736 (1976).

chapter 3

The Rights of Political Participation

THE POLITICAL HISTORY of the United States is the story of the effort to translate the ideals of equality and freedom into political reality. The elusiveness of these goals is reflected in a long line of Supreme Court decisions that deal with the right to vote, the right to have that vote counted equally with all others, and the freedom to associate with persons of similar political views. Although the right to vote is the cornerstone of the democratic political system, the Constitution until 1868 made almost no mention of that right. For well more than a century, the Supreme Court maintained that state citizenship, not federal citizenship, was the source of the right to vote. Six times the Constitution has been amended to extend and protect this basic political right:

- In 1868 the Fourteenth Amendment appeared to guarantee the right to vote to all citizens—including women and blacks—by forbidding any state to abridge the privileges and immunities of U.S. citizens.

- In 1870 the Fifteenth Amendment explicitly enfranchised former slaves.

- In 1920 the Nineteenth Amendment granted women the right to vote.

- In 1961 the Twenty-third Amendment granted residents of Washington, D.C., the right to vote in presidential elections.

- In 1964 the Twenty-fourth Amendment prohibited use of a poll tax as a reason to deny anyone the right to vote in federal elections.

- In 1971 the Twenty-sixth Amendment lowered the voting age to eighteen.

In the earliest years of the United States, the right to vote was the exclusive prerogative of free white adult males who owned property. Property qualifications were the first restrictions to be rejected, although vestiges of that requirement remained for more than a century in the form of poll taxes. The Civil War and the amendments that marked its close seemed to promise a new era of broadened political participation. The Privileges and Immunities Clause of the Fourteenth Amendment appeared to many to guarantee all citizens—female as well as male, black as well as white—the right to vote: "No state shall make or enforce any law which shall abridge the privileges or immunities of citizens of the United States." Within a decade of its adoption in 1868, however, the Supreme Court made clear that the Fourteenth Amendment had no such practical effect. The Constitution of the United States, declared the Court, still granted no one the right to vote. That was a state prerogative.

The Fifteenth Amendment, ratified in 1870, spoke plainly:

Section 1. The right of citizens of the United States to vote shall not be denied or abridged by the United States or by any State on account of race, color, or previous condition of servitude.

Section 2. The Congress shall have power to enforce this article by appropriate legislation.

Yet Supreme Court decisions continued to perpetuate the view that voter qualifications and election regulations were exclusively state responsibilities. State officials, insulated from federal action by these decisions, successfully employed literacy tests, grandfather clauses, poll taxes, and white primaries to circumvent the amendment's intent for most of another century. Around 1915 the Supreme Court began to edge toward a new view of the amendments and the protection they intended to provide for the right to vote, but it was Congress, spurred by the civil rights movement of the 1960s, that ultimately led the way in fulfilling the promise of the Fifteenth Amendment. The Voting Rights Act of 1965 at last secured for the nation's black citizens the right to vote. To do so, the act asserted federal authority over electoral matters traditionally left in the hands of state officials.

Once Congress acted, the Supreme Court steadily backed its power to ensure the right to vote. The Court listened to the challenges of the states to the new law, but then rejected them resoundingly. A series of rulings in the 1960s were a mirror image of the postwar decisions of the 1870s and 1880s that restricted federal power to protect the citizen's right to vote. The Court of the late twentieth century gave the broadest possible reading to the Fifteenth Amendment, the power of Congress to enforce it, and to the 1965 act, making it the most effective civil rights law ever enacted.

At the same time that the Court's modern voting rights decisions were underwriting the expansion of the right to vote, its plunge into the political morass of redistricting cases revolutionized the balance of political power within Congress and in every state legislature. Electoral districts within state boundaries had been a fact of life since the early nineteenth century, when Congress first directed all states with more than one member in the U.S. House of Representatives to elect House members from separate, compact, and contiguous districts. Later in the century, Congress required that these districts also be as nearly equal in

population as was practicable. Congress, however, omitted those requirements from its revision of the Reapportionment Act of 1929. A few years later, the Supreme Court found the omission purposeful. The lifting of these requirements came just as the nation's population was shifting from primarily rural areas to create an urban majority. From the 1920s until the 1960s, this shift was not reflected in the nation's legislatures. Farm and rural interests continued to dominate in Congress and in state legislatures. Efforts by urban residents to have district lines redrawn to reflect their new strength—and to win equal weight for their votes—failed.

In large part, these attempts were blocked by the insistence of federal courts, led by the Supreme Court, that such challenges were political matters outside judicial power and therefore best dealt with by the malapportioned legislatures that were the heart of the problem. As late as 1946, the Court explicitly reaffirmed this view, describing redistricting challenges as a "political thicket" it would not enter.[1] Within sixteen years, however, the Court had reversed itself. It took the first step in *Baker v. Carr* (1962), ruling that redistricting cases might, after all, present issues suitable for judicial resolution.[2] That ruling opened the doors of the federal courts to a multitude of suits challenging state and congressional districting and apportionment structures.

As the Court dealt with subsequent cases, it translated the Fourteenth Amendment's guarantee of equal protection into the rule of "one person, one vote" as the proper measure for redistricting plans.[3] Within a decade it appeared that the standard was in some ways a dual one, applied to require that a state's congressional districts be almost precisely equal in population, while allowing a state's legislative electoral districts to vary further from the ideal of precise equality. In subsequent rulings, the Court extended the one person, one vote rule to a variety of local electoral districts.

The freedom of political association receives no mention in the Constitution, yet the modern Supreme Court has made clear in decisions concerning communists and civil rights activists, radicals and

Republicans, that it considers the freedom to associate with persons of like political views—without penalty from the government—an essential corollary of the First Amendment freedoms of speech, peaceable assembly, and the right to petition the government for redress of grievances. Like other First Amendment rights—but unlike the right to vote—the freedom of political association may legitimately be restricted by government to further other major interests, thus political association cases present the Court with the task of reconciling individual freedoms and the government's need to preserve public peace and national security.

Nowhere is this more obvious than in the decisions of the 1950s and 1960s concerning the efforts of Congress, the executive branch, and state legislatures to curtail the spread of domestic communism and to protect government against infiltration by disloyal persons. Reconciliation takes place through a process of weighing and balancing, which inevitably reflects the social and political contexts in which the justices live and work. During periods of severe external threat to the United States, the Court has upheld substantial restrictions upon the exercise of this right.

In its early 1950s rulings on these laws and programs, the Court found their restrictive impact on individual freedom justified. As the threat eased, however, the Court found challenges to these laws more and more persuasive. In response, it tightened the standards of proof to ensure that persons were not penalized simply for "guilt by association" or abstract advocacy of revolution, but only for actions that clearly threatened the nation's security. Eventually, this line of rulings vitiated the internal security laws. The right of political association—finally recognized even in internal security cases—found its clearest definition in cases involving homegrown forms of activism and more traditional political activities. In the 1960s, the Court forbade states to interfere with the right of civil rights activists to associate and work for the advancement of blacks and other minorities. Such associations could not be penalized by the state, held the Court. Later rulings recognized the right of national political parties to this freedom—interpreted to shield those parties from the interference of state courts—and the right of persons holding different views from those of an elected officeholder to keep their jobs nonetheless.

Fair Elections and the Right to Vote

The gradually broadening suffrage is one of the most significant characteristics of the continuing U.S. experiment in popular government.[1] In 1792 only propertied white males were granted the privilege of voting. By 1972 all Americans eighteen or older—blacks and whites, women and men—possessed this right. The Constitution barely mentions the right to vote. It provides for the direct election of members of the House of Representatives, permits states to set qualifications for voters, and gives the states the authority to set the times, places, and manner of elections for senators and representatives. Article I, section 4, however, does reserve to Congress the power to override, by law, such state-established election rules.

Early in the history of the republic, popular pressure forced states to drop the restrictive property qualification for voting. The Constitution subsequently has been amended six times to extend the vote to formerly disenfranchised groups. The Fifteenth Amendment, added in 1870, prohibited denial of the right to vote for reasons of race, color, or previous condition of servitude. Women, who had sought to win the right to vote through judicial interpretation of the Privileges and Immunities Clause of the Fourteenth Amendment, were rebuffed in that effort by the Supreme Court.[2] After organizing as a women's suffrage movement, they worked and fought for half a century for the right to vote. Finally, in 1920, the addition of the Nineteenth Amendment forbade restriction of the suffrage on account of sex.

In 1961 the Twenty-third Amendment granted residents of the nation's capital, the District of Columbia, the right to vote in presidential elections. In 1964 the Twenty-fourth Amendment ended all efforts to restrict the right to vote because of lack of wealth or property, outlawing use of a poll tax as a means of abridging the right to vote in federal elections. Next, the age for political participation was formally lowered by the Twenty-sixth Amendment, ratified in 1971 and granting all citizens eighteen and older the right to vote in federal elections. With this amendment—and new civil rights legislation finally implementing the Fifteenth Amendment—virtually every adult citizen possessed the right to vote in the nation's elections by 1972. Among the exceptions today are felons in some states and the residents of the nation's capital, the District of Columbia, the latter of whom cannot vote for senators or representatives.

THE RIGHT AND THE POWER: A NARROW VIEW

No other constitutional promise has gone so long unfulfilled as that of the Fifteenth Amendment. Despite the clear language forbidding abridgment of the right to vote because of race or color, state officials succeeded for almost a full century in denying black citizens the right to vote or to play any significant role in state or national politics. The Supreme Court, by its acquiescence, played a critical role in creating this anomalous situation. The right to vote was viewed by many as doubly guaranteed by the Civil War Amendments—the Fourteenth Amendment, safeguarding the privileges and immunities of citizens against state infringement, and the Fifteenth Amendment, forbidding abridgment of the right to vote because of race, color, or previous condition of servitude. In addition, voting rights for blacks had been made a condition for readmission to the Union for the rebellious states of the Confederacy. Yet, after the presidential election of 1876, the issue of black voting rights was again left to state control. As the southern states returned to white rule under "restored" governments, they passed laws that effectively defeated the purposes of the amendments.

The Supreme Court created the environment for such systematic state obstruction with a set of rulings in which it adopted the narrowest possible view of federal power and responsibility for protecting the individual's right to vote. The Court held that the right to vote was chiefly governed by state laws; that its source was the state, not the U.S. Constitution; and that Congress had only limited power to interfere in state regulation of electoral matters.

No Privilege or Immunity or Federal Voting Right

The first of these restrictive rulings came in 1875, when the Court declared that the U.S. Constitution did not give anyone the right to vote. *Minor v. Happersett* was brought by St. Louis attorney Francis Minor on behalf of his wife, president of the Missouri Woman Suffrage Association. The Minors argued that the right to vote was a privilege of U.S. citizenship, protected by the first section of the Fourteenth Amendment. Therefore, the Minors concluded, states could not deny women the right to vote. Missouri law, however, limited suffrage to males. Happersett, an election registrar, refused to register Mrs. Minor, and the couple filed suit. Just two years earlier, in the *Slaughterhouse Cases,* the Court had described the privileges and immunities of U.S. citizenship: "They may all ... be comprehended under the following general heads: protection by the government, with the right to acquire and possess property of every kind, and to pursue and obtain happiness and safety, subject nevertheless to such restraints as the government may prescribe for the general good of the whole."[3] The right to vote was not mentioned. In line with that decision, the Court rejected the Minors' argument.

Chief Justice Morrison R. Waite wrote for the Court that the right to vote was not a privilege or immunity of federal citizenship. The suffrage, Waite stated, had never been coextensive with citizenship:

> The United States has no voters in the States of its creation....
>
> [T]he Constitution of the United States does not confer the right of suffrage upon anyone.

"EVERY THING POINTS TO A DEMOCRATIC VICTORY THIS FALL."—*Southern Papers.*

Despite adoption of the Fifteenth Amendment, making it illegal to bar citizens from voting because of their color, blacks were turned away from polls by a combination of Ku Klux Klan harassment, intimidation, and various legal gimmicks. The Supreme Court's ruling in *United States v. Reese* (1876) weakened the government's power to impose stiff penalties for interfering with the rights of blacks to vote.

It was still up to the states, Waite said, to define voter qualifications—even for federal elections:

> The [Fourteenth] Amendment did not add to the privileges and immunities of a citizen. It simply furnished an additional guaranty for the protection of such as he already had.
>
> It is clear, therefore, we think, that the Constitution has not added the right of suffrage to the privileges and immunities of citizenship as they existed at the time it was adopted.[4]

In 1876 the Court adopted a similar narrow view of the Fifteenth Amendment. In *United States v. Reese* and *United States v. Cruikshank,* the Court overturned federal convictions of persons charged with violating the Enforcement Act of 1870, the law enforcing the Fifteenth Amendment's guarantee against denial of voting rights because of race. In *Reese,* state election officials were convicted for violating the law by refusing to receive or count a black man's vote. The Court overturned the convictions, finding the section of the law under which they were charged technically defective. The Court, again through Chief Justice Waite, stated that "[t]he Fifteenth Amendment does not confer the right of suffrage upon anyone."[5] The right with which that amendment invests the citizens of the United States, he said, was the right to be free from discrimination (on account of race, color, or previous condition of servitude) in their exercise of the right to vote.

United States v. Cruikshank, decided that same day in 1876, dealt with one of the ninety-six indictments resulting from a massacre of sixty blacks in Colfax, Louisiana, in 1873. Disputes over local elections allegedly led William J. Cruikshank and others to shoot down a posse of blacks who had seized the Colfax Courthouse. Cruikshank and his confederates were indicted under the 1870 Enforcement Act for conspiring to intimidate blacks to prevent their exercise of constitutional rights, including the right to vote. The Supreme Court declared the indictment defective because "it is nowhere alleged in these counts that the wrong contemplated against the rights of these citizens was on account of their race or color."[6] Chief Justice Waite delivered the opinion of the Court. He declared again that the amendment added nothing to the rights a citizen possessed:

> It simply furnishes an additional guaranty as against any encroachment by the States upon the fundamental rights which belong to every citizen as a member of society.... The power of the National Government is limited to the enforcement of this guaranty....
>
> The right to vote in the States comes from the States; but the right of exemption from the prohibited discrimination comes from the United States. The first has not been granted or secured by the Constitution of the United States; but the last has been.
>
> Inasmuch, therefore, as it does not appear in these counts that the intent of the defendants was to prevent these parties from exercising their right to

vote on account of their race ... it does not appear that it was their intent to interfere with any right granted or secured by the Constitution or laws of the United States. We may suspect that race was the cause of the hostility; but it is not so averred.[7]

Exceptions to the View

Despite this limiting interpretation of the new constitutional language concerning the right to vote, the Court upheld federal power to regulate elections under the provisions of Article I. In *Ex parte Siebold* (1880), which did not involve charges of racial discrimination, the Court upheld federal power to ensure that elections of federal officials be fairly conducted. Albert Siebold, a state election official, was convicted of violating federal law by stuffing a ballot box in an election of state and federal officers. The Court upheld his conviction, citing Article I, section 4, to justify federal regulation of the actions of state election officials. The constitutional passage gives Congress broad concurrent powers to regulate elections along with and independent of state power in that area.[8] During the next three decades the Court would reaffirm this position in similar cases.[9]

The Court's narrow view of the Fifteenth Amendment broadened briefly in 1884. *Ex parte Yarbrough* was the only early case in which the Court backed the use of federal power to punish private individuals who obstructed the right to vote in a federal election. In *Yarbrough,* the Court held that once an individual acquired the right to vote for federal officers—by meeting state-established voter qualifications—that right was accorded federal protection. Jasper Yarbrough, a member of the Ku Klux Klan, and some fellow Klansmen attacked a black man named Berry Saunders to prevent his voting in a congressional election. Yarbrough was convicted and sentenced to prison for violating the 1870 Enforcement Act by conspiring to prevent a citizen from voting. He challenged his conviction, arguing that the 1870 law was unconstitutional, because Congress lacked the authority to act to protect the right to vote in federal elections. The Court, however, upheld his conviction, the federal law, and congressional power to protect the right to vote.

Justice Samuel Miller, writing for the majority, made clear that the right to vote for members of

Congress was derived from the federal Constitution—not state laws—and was subject to federal protection:

That a government whose essential character is republican has no power to secure this election from the influence of violence, of corruption, and of fraud, is a proposition so startling as to arrest attention....

If this government is anything more than a mere aggregation of delegated agents of other States and governments, each of which is superior to the General Government, it must have the power to protect the elections on which its existence depends from violence and corruption....

If it has not this power, it is left helpless before the two great natural and historical enemies of all republics, open violence and insidious corruption.

The States in prescribing the qualifications for the most numerous branch of their own Legislatures, do not do this with reference to the election for members of Congress.... They define who are to vote for the popular branch of their own legislature, and the Constitution of the United States says the same persons shall vote for members of Congress in that State. It adopts the qualification thus furnished as the qualification of its own electors for members of Congress.

It is not true, therefore, that electors for members of Congress owe their right to vote to the state law in any sense which makes the exercise of the right to depend exclusively on the law of the State.[10]

The Fifteenth Amendment, said the Court, did operate in some circumstances as the source of a right to vote, and Congress did have the authority "to protect the citizen in the exercise of rights conferred by the Constitution of the United States essential to the healthy organization of the government itself."[11] Thus, the opinion concluded,

If the Government of the United States has within its constitutional domain no authority to provide against these evils [violence and corruption of elections], if the very sources of power may be poisoned by corruption or controlled by violence and outrage, without legal restraint, then, indeed, is the country in danger and its best powers, its highest purposes, the hopes which it inspires ... are at the mercy of the combinations of those who respect no right but brute force, on the one hand, and unprincipled corruptionists on the other.[12]

Despite Justice Miller's strong words, the Court persisted for decades in its narrow view of the right to vote. In the absence of state action, the acts of private individuals to deny the rights of others to vote remained outside the reach of federal power. In 1903 the Court stated that the provisions of the 1870 Enforcement Act, which might be interpreted "to punish purely individual action [to interfere with voting rights,] cannot be sustained as an appropriate exercise of the power conferred by the Fifteenth Amendment upon Congress."[13]

PATTERN OF EXCLUSION

Encouraged by the Court's limiting view of the federal right to vote and of federal power to enforce that right, many southern states during the period from 1890 to 1910 excluded blacks from participating in the political process by rewriting their constitutions or adding new requirements for voters.[14] The Court by and large left major elements of the program of disenfranchisement untouched for decades. The strategy of exclusion employed many methods, among them literacy tests, grandfather clauses, all-white primaries, poll taxes, and the racial gerrymander. Grandfather clauses were held unconstitutional in 1915, and white primaries were finally ruled invalid in 1944, but not until Congress acted did the Court strike down the use of poll taxes and literacy tests.

Ancestry and Literacy

For seventy years, from 1898 until 1965, the Supreme Court upheld the validity of literacy tests for voters. In *Williams v. Mississippi* (1898), Henry Williams, a black man, was indicted for murder by an all-white grand jury. The jurors were selected from the list of registered voters who had, among other qualifications, passed such a literacy test. Williams challenged the use of the test as unconstitutional. Williams's attorneys argued that his conviction was invalid because the laws under which the grand jury was selected allowed discrimination in voter registration, thereby violating the equal protection guarantee of the Fourteenth Amendment. Justice Joseph McKenna, writing for the Court, refused to find the Mississippi statutes in violation of the Equal Protection Clause. The "evil" was not the laws themselves, he wrote, for they did not on their face discriminate against blacks; the only evil resulted from the effect of their discriminatory administration.[15]

Grandfather Clauses

Seventeen years later, however, in *Guinn v. United States* (1915), the Supreme Court held impermissible Oklahoma's combined use of a literacy test and a "grandfather" clause.[16] The state required all voters to pass a literacy test *or* to show that their ancestors had been entitled to vote in 1866. This requirement was challenged as a violation of the Fifteenth Amendment, because in operation it exempted most white males from the literacy test requirement and permitted voter registrars to test primarily blacks, whose ancestors in most cases had not been eligible to vote in 1866. The state defended its system by arguing that the clause did not deny blacks the right to vote outright; it simply required them all to take the literacy tests. The Fifteenth Amendment, the state continued, did not confer the right to vote on all blacks; it merely prevented states from denying them the right to vote on purely racial grounds.

With *Guinn* the Court began moving toward its modern view of the Fifteenth Amendment. The Court unanimously struck down Oklahoma's system as an unconstitutional evasion of the amendment. Chief Justice Edward D. White wrote the Court's opinion. In it, however, the Court continued to affirm state power to require voters to demonstrate some measure of literacy. The establishment of a literacy test requirement was "but the exercise by the state of a lawful power not subject to our supervision."[17] *Guinn* had a limited effect on black voting rights in the South because it dealt only with the grandfather clause. The case, however, was the first in which the Court in a voting rights case looked beyond nondiscriminatory form to discover discriminatory substance.

In a second Oklahoma case decided the same day in 1915, the Court upheld the federal indictments—under the Reconstruction Civil Rights Acts—of county election officials who refused to count certain persons' votes. The Court, in *United States v. Mosely*, declared that "the right to have one's vote counted is as open to protection by Congress as the right to put a ballot in a box."[18] Oklahoma

subsequently adopted a requirement that all voters register within a twelve-day period, exempting from the requirement those who had voted in the 1914 elections, prior to *Guinn*. In 1939 the Court held this, too, was an unconstitutional attempt to disenfranchise blacks in violation of the Fifteenth Amendment. Justice Felix Frankfurter, writing for the majority, said that the Fifteenth Amendment "nullifies sophisticated as well as simpleminded modes of discrimination. It hits onerous procedural requirements which effectively handicap exercise of the franchise by the colored race although the abstract right to vote may remain unrestricted as to race."[19]

Tests of Understanding

In addition to strict literacy tests, some states also required voters to "understand and explain" an article of the Constitution. The vagueness of one such provision was nullified by a federal court as an arbitrary grant of power to election officials who could and did administer the literacy test in a racially discriminatory fashion and thus violated the Fifteenth Amendment. The fact that the provision itself made no mention of race did not save it from being unconstitutional. The Supreme Court affirmed this ruling in 1949.[20] The Court continued, however, to uphold the power of states to require that their voters demonstrate some measure of literacy. For example, in the late 1950s the Court upheld North Carolina's requirement that all voters be able to read and write a section of the state constitution in English. Such a test was not, on its face, a violation of the Fourteenth, Fifteenth, or Seventeenth Amendments, the Court held in *Lassiter v. Northampton County Board of Elections* (1959). Justice William O. Douglas's opinion for the majority stressed that the state had an interest in securing an independent and intelligent electorate. How the state achieved that objective, Douglas said, was a policy question outside the Court's purview:

> Literacy and intelligence are obviously not synonymous. Illiterate people may be intelligent voters. Yet in our society ... a state might conclude that only those who are literate should exercise the franchise.... We do not sit in judgment on the wisdom of that policy. We cannot say, however, that it is not an allowable one measured by constitutional standards.

"NAH, YOU AIN'T GOT ENOUGH EDJICCASHUN TO VOTE"

From 1898 to 1969, the Supreme Court upheld the validity of literacy tests for voters. Election offcials in some states administered these tests in a racially discriminatory fashion. This cartoon observes that many blacks were deemed unqualified to vote by election offcials less educated than they.

Of course a literacy test, fair on its face, may be employed to perpetuate that discrimination which the Fifteenth Amendment was designed to uproot. No such influence is charged here…. The present requirement, applicable to members of all races … seems to us one fair way of determining whether a person is literate. Certainly we cannot condemn it on its face as a device unrelated to the desire of North Carolina to raise the standards for people of all races who cast the ballot.[21]

Six years later, however, the Court held as a violation of the Fifteenth Amendment a Louisiana test requiring voters to display a reasonable knowledge and understanding of any section of the state or federal constitution. The Court's unanimous opinion, written by Justice Hugo L. Black, viewed the requirement in light of the history of voter discrimination in the state:

The applicant facing a registrar in Louisiana thus has been compelled to leave his voting fate to that official's uncontrolled power to determine whether the applicant's understanding of the Federal or State Constitution is satisfactory. As the evidence showed, colored people, even some with the most advanced education and scholarship, were declared by voting registrars with less education to have an unsatisfactory understanding of the Constitution of Louisiana or of the United States. This is not a test but a trap, sufficient to stop even the most brilliant man on his way to the voting booth. The cherished right of people in a country like ours to vote cannot be obliterated by the use of laws like this, which leave the voting fate of a citizen to the passing whim or impulse of an individual registrar.[22]

Suspension of Literacy Tests

As part of the Voting Rights Act of 1965, Congress suspended all literacy tests and similar devices in all areas where less than half the population of voting age had been registered or had voted in the 1964 presidential election. The act was immediately challenged as infringing upon state power to oversee elections. In *South Carolina v. Katzenbach* (1966), the Supreme Court upheld Congress's power to pass the law and backed all its major provisions, including that suspending literacy tests.[23] Chief Justice Earl Warren, who delivered the opinion of the Court, wrote that the provision of the act suspending literacy tests

was clearly a legitimate response to the problem…. Underlying the response was the feeling that States and political subdivisions which had been allowing white illiterates to vote for years could not sincerely complain about "dilution" of their electorates through the registration of Negro illiterates. Congress knew that continuance of the tests and devices in use at the present time, no matter how fairly administered in the future, would freeze the effect of past discrimination in favor of unqualified white registrants. Congress permissibly rejected the alternative of requiring a complete reregistration of all voters, believing that this would be too harsh on many whites who had enjoyed the franchise for their entire adult lives.[24]

That opinion was followed three months later by two decisions that prevented states from disqualifying potential voters simply because they were unable to read or write English.[25] Then, three years later, the Court rejected, 7-1, the effort of a North Carolina county to reinstate a literacy test. The Court declared in *Gaston County v. United States* (1969) that counties and states, by operating separate and unequal schools for blacks and whites, had denied blacks the opportunity to acquire the skills necessary to pass a literacy test. Reinstatement of a literacy test would simply perpetuate the effects of the dual, unequal educational system that had so long operated to disenfranchise blacks, the Court held.[26] Justice John Marshall Harlan wrote for the majority:

> Affording today's Negro youth equal educational opportunity will doubtless prepare them to meet, on equal terms, whatever standards of literacy are required when they reach voting age. It does nothing for their parents, however. From this record, we cannot escape the sad truth that throughout the years, Gaston County systematically deprived its black citizens of the educational opportunities it granted to its white citizens. "Impartial" administration of the literacy test today would serve only to perpetuate those inequities in a different form.[27]

The Voting Rights Act of 1965 was amended in 1970 to suspend literacy tests nationwide and to bring more areas under coverage of its provisions. The Supreme Court upheld the nationwide ban on literacy tests in *Oregon v. Mitchell* (1970).[28] Justice Black explained that such a ban, in light of the long history of discriminatory literacy tests, was well within the power of Congress in enforcement of the Fifteenth Amendment. In 1975 the law was amended to abolish all literacy tests permanently. *(See box, Voter Requirements: Age, Residence, Property, p. 180)*

White Primaries

Southern politics was completely dominated by the Democratic Party during the first half of the twentieth century. In many areas the Democratic primary was the only significant part of the election process. Winning the primary was tantamount to election. Being excluded from voting in the primary was equivalent to being excluded from voting altogether. Not until 1941 was it clear, as the result of a Supreme Court ruling, that Congress had the power to regulate primary elections as well as general elections. In fact, in a decision involving campaign spending—*Newberry v. United States* (1921)—the Court had seemed to say that Congress lacked this very power.[29] This Court-created doubt encouraged the eleven states that had comprised the Confederacy to begin the systematic exclusion of blacks from participation in primaries. The Democratic Party was often organized on a statewide or county basis as a private club or association that could freely exclude blacks. Texas's use of the white primary to shut blacks out of participation in the political process came before the Supreme Court five times.

Nixon v. Herndon (1927)

In 1923 the Texas legislature passed a law forbidding blacks to vote in the state Democratic primary. Dr. L. A. Nixon, a black resident of El Paso, challenged the law, arguing that it clearly violated the Fourteenth and Fifteenth Amendments. In *Nixon v. Herndon* (1927), the Supreme Court agreed with Nixon's Fourteenth Amendment claim. "A more direct and obvious infringement" of the equal protection guarantee would be hard to imagine, wrote Justice Oliver Wendell Holmes Jr. for a unanimous Court.[30]

Nixon v. Condon (1932)

After *Herndon*, the Texas legislature authorized state political parties' executive committees to establish their own qualifications for voting in the primary. Nixon again sued successfully, challenging the law as racially discriminatory. Attorneys for the state argued that the Fourteenth Amendment's Equal Protection Clause did not apply because the party, not state officials, had set up the allegedly discriminatory standards. With Justice Benjamin N. Cardozo writing for the majority of five, the Court held that the executive committee of the Democratic Party acted as a delegate of the state in setting voter qualifications; its action was equivalent to state action and thus within the scope of the equal protection guarantee it violated.[31]

Voter Requirements: Age, Residence, Property

States historically have imposed various nonracial qualifications upon voters. Supreme Court rulings, however, have limited the power to impose voter requirements related to age, to property ownership, and to state residence for any extended period of time. The Court has affirmed the power of states to exclude convicted felons from the exercise of the franchise. In *Green v. New York City Board of Elections* (1968) the Court upheld a New York law that barred convicted, unpardoned felons from voting.[1] In 1974 the Court reaffirmed that position, ruling that denial of the right to vote to convicted felons did not violate the Fourteenth Amendment.[2]

In a 1959 decision the Court declared that states had broad powers to set age and residence rules for voters:

> The states have long been held to have broad powers to determine the conditions under which the right of suffrage may be exercised.... Residence requirements, and age ... are obvious examples indicating factors which a State may take into consideration in determining the qualification of voters.[3]

Eleven years later, in 1970, the Court upheld the power of Congress to lower age and residence requirements for participation in federal, but not state or local, elections.[4] Following that ruling, the Court limited the ability of states to impose a residency requirement for an extended period. In doing so, the justices invalidated a Tennessee law requiring people to be residents of the state for one year before qualifying to vote. The decision in *Dunn v. Blumstein* (1972) held that residency requirements burden fundamental rights to vote and to travel and that the state had shown no compelling interest to justify its one-year demand.[5] This ruling side-stepped but did not overrule a 1904 decision upholding a similar Maryland requirement that voters file a declaration of intent to register one year before their enrollment on the voter lists.[6]

The Court later upheld an Arizona rule cutting off voter registration fifty days before a primary, indicating that the state had shown the fifty-day period necessary to permit preparation of accurate lists of voters.[7] An earlier ruling had held that a state could not prevent military personnel

stationed within its borders from establishing residence for purposes of voting.[8] In 1970 the Court held that a state could not deny the right to vote to persons living in a federal enclave in the state if those persons were otherwise treated as state residents.[9]

By the mid-1970s property requirements for voting in general elections had disappeared from the electoral process. In a set of modern rulings the Court made clear that the equal protection guarantee of the Fourteenth Amendment was infringed by state efforts to restrict the right to vote. In 1969 the justices struck down a Louisiana law that limited to property tax payers the right to vote in elections to approve issuance of utility revenue bonds.[10] The same day the Court held that the equal protection guarantee gave all residents—not only those who owned or leased property or who had children in the public schools—the right to vote in school district elections.[11] In 1970 the same principle was applied to strike down state efforts to exclude people who did not own property from voting in elections held to approve the issue of general obligation bonds.[12] The Court later struck down laws that limited the right to vote in city bond elections only to persons who owned taxable property.[13]

1. *Green v. New York City Board of Elections*, 389 U.S. 1048 (1968).
2. *Richardson v. Ramirez*, 418 U.S. 24 (1974).
3. *Lassiter v. Northampton County Board of Elections*, 360 U.S. 45 at 51 (1959).
4. *Oregon v. Mitchell, Texas v. Mitchell, United States v. Idaho, United States v. Arizona*, 400 U.S. 112 (1970).
5. *Dunn v. Blumstein*, 405 U.S. 330 (1972).
6. *Pope v. Williams*, 193 U.S. 621 (1904).
7. *Marston v. Lewis*, 410 U.S. 679 (1973); *Burns v. Fortson*, 410 U.S. 686 (1973).
8. *Carrington v. Rash*, 380 U.S. 89 (1965).
9. *Evans v. Cornman*, 398 U.S. 419 (1970).
10. *Cipriano v. City of Houma*, 395 U.S. 701 (1969).
11. *Kramer v. Union Free School District No. 15*, 395 U.S. 818 (1969).
12. *Phoenix v. Kolodzieski*, 399 U.S. 204 (1970).
13. *Hill v. Stone*, 421 U.S. 289 (1975); *Quinn v. Millsap*, 491 U.S. 95 (1989).

Grovey v. Townsend (1935)

Undeterred, the Texas Democratic Party, without state direction or authorization, voted to limit party membership to whites. This was permissible, all the justices agreed in *Grovey v. Townsend*. The Supreme Court unanimously held that the political party was not acting as a creature of the state and that its action was thus unreachable under either the Fourteenth or Fifteenth Amendments. The Court in this case viewed the political party as a private club, a voluntary association of private individuals, whose actions—even in controlling access to the vote—were not restricted by the Constitution.[32]

United States v. Classic (1941)

Only six years later, however, the Court began to chip away the foundation on which *Grovey v. Townsend* was based. In *United States v. Classic,* the Court discarded the *Newberry* restriction on federal power to regulate primary elections. *Classic* was not a racial discrimination case at all. Classic, an overzealous opponent of Louisiana governor Huey Long, was convicted of falsifying election returns. His conviction was based on the federal law that made it a crime "to injure, oppress, threaten or intimidate any citizen in the free exercise or enjoyment of any right or privilege secured to him by the Constitution." He challenged his conviction, arguing that the right to vote in a primary election was not a right secured by the Constitution. The prosecution in *Classic* was initiated by the newly formed civil rights section of the Justice Department established by Attorney General Frank Murphy and later directed by Attorney General Robert H. Jackson, both of whom became members of the Supreme Court. The case was argued before the Court by Herbert Wechsler, a former law clerk to Justice Harlan Fiske Stone, and by Jackson.

The Court upheld Classic's conviction and declared that the primary was an integral part of the election process. The authority of Congress under Article I, section 4, to regulate elections included the authority to regulate primary elections, wrote Justice Stone, "when, as in this case, they are a step in the exercise by the people of their choice of representatives in Congress."[33]

Smith v. Allwright (1944)

In 1944 the Court overturned *Grovey* and held the all-white primary unconstitutional. *Smith v. Allwright* arose out of the refusal of S. S. Allwright, a county election official, to permit Lonnie E. Smith, a black man, to vote in the 1940 Texas Democratic primary. Smith sued Allwright for damages. Lower federal courts denied Smith the right to bring suit. *Grovey v. Townsend,* they said, placed this sort of discrimination beyond federal control.

Smith was represented before the Supreme Court by two attorneys for the National Association for the Advancement of Colored People (NAACP):

William H. Hastie and Thurgood Marshall. Both later became distinguished judges, and Marshall went on to become the first African American member of the Court. The Court heard arguments twice in the case. On April 3, 1944, the Court held the white primary unconstitutional as a violation of the Fifteenth Amendment. The seven justices appointed by President Franklin D. Roosevelt since the *Grovey* decision, along with Stone, who had voted with the majority in *Grovey,* found state action evident in the number of state laws regulating primary elections. Writing for the majority, Justice Stanley Reed linked *Classic* and *Smith v. Allwright*: "The fusing by the *Classic* case of the primary and general elections into a single instrumentality for choice of officers has a definite bearing on the permissibility under the Constitution of excluding Negroes from primaries."[34] *Classic* bears upon *Grovey v. Townsend,* Reed explained, because the state had delegated so much responsibility for the primary to the political party that the party became an agent of the state in its actions conducting the primary. Thus, held the Court, Allwright's action was state action abridging Smith's right to vote because of his race, a clear violation of the Fifteenth Amendment.

Only Justice Owen J. Roberts sounded a dissenting voice as the Court overturned *Grovey v. Townsend,* a decision not yet a decade old. Author of the Court's opinion in *Grovey,* Roberts warned that by overruling such a recent decision, the Court "tends to bring adjudications of this tribunal into the same class as a restricted railroad ticket, good for this day and train only."[35]

Terry v. Adams (1953)

In 1953 the relentless effort of Texas Democrats—and politicians in other southern states—to maintain the white primary finally came to an end. Since 1889 the Jaybird Party, an all-white Democratic organization in one Texas county, had declared itself a private club and had submitted political candidates' names in an unofficial county primary for whites only. The successful candidate in the Jaybird primary invariably entered and won the following Democratic primary and general election. The Court struck down this strategem, finding the use of racially exclusive private clubs as a political caucus a violation of the Fifteenth Amendment. Justice Black wrote for the eight-justice majority in *Terry v. Adams*:

> [T]he Jaybird primary has become an integral part, indeed the only effective part, of the elective process that determines who shall rule and govern in the county. The effect of the whole procedure, Jaybird primary plus Democratic primary plus general election, is to do precisely that which the Fifteenth Amendment forbids—strip Negroes of every vestige of influence in selecting the officials who control the local county matters that intimately touch the daily lives of citizens.[36]

Poll Taxes

In the early days of the republic, poll taxes—an annual assessment on each citizen—replaced landholding, property, and other more burdensome requirements for voters, but most poll taxes were eliminated by the time of the Civil War. This type of tax was revived in the early 1890s as one of the devices used to restrict the suffrage to white voters in the South. The ostensible reason for reintroduction of the poll tax was to "cleanse" the state of such election abuses as repeat voting, that is, one person in one election voting more than once.

In *Breedlove v. Suttles* (1937), the Supreme Court upheld the constitutionality of the poll tax against the challenge that it violated the equal protection guarantee of the Fourteenth Amendment. The tax assessed upon voters by Georgia was a legitimate means of raising revenue; it was not a denial of equal protection, held the Court, because on its face it applied to black and white voters alike. The Court, for whom Justice Pierce Butler wrote the opinion, rejected the notion that the Georgia tax was an impermissible levy on a federally guaranteed right.[37]

After the Populist Era, many states had voluntarily dropped use of the poll tax. Proposals to abolish it were introduced in every Congress from 1939 to 1962. By 1960 only four states still required its payment by voters. In August 1962, the House approved a constitutional amendment—already accepted by the Senate—that outlawed poll taxes in federal elections. The poll tax ban was ratified as the Twenty-fourth Amendment January 23, 1964. *Harman v. Forssenius* (1965) became the first Supreme Court decision interpreting the amendment. The Court's decision struck down Virginia's effort (in anticipation of the poll tax ban) to give voters in federal elections the option of paying the levy or filing a certificate of residence before each election. The Court held that the reregistration/residence requirement for persons who chose to exercise their right to vote without paying a poll tax subverted the effect of the Twenty-fourth Amendment.[38]

In 1966 the Court held the poll tax an unconstitutional requirement for voting in state and local elections as well. "Wealth, like race, creed, or color is not germane to one's ability to participate intelligently in the electoral process," wrote Justice Douglas for the Court in *Harper v. Virginia State Board of Elections*.[39] Thus the Court struck down Virginia's $1.50 poll tax as a violation of the Equal Protection Clause, overruling *Breedlove v. Suttles*. Douglas explained the Court's reasoning:

> We conclude that a State violates the Equal Protection Clause of the Fourteenth Amendment whenever it makes the affluence of the voter or payment of any fee an electoral standard. Voter qualifications have no relation to wealth nor to paying or not paying this or any other tax....
>
> To introduce wealth or payment of a fee as a measure of a voter's qualifications is to introduce a capricious or irrelevant factor.... In this context—that is, as a condition of obtaining a ballot—the requirement of fee paying causes an "invidious" discrimination ... that runs afoul of the Equal Protection Clause.[40]

Justices Black and Harlan wrote dissents. Black argued that the majority was merely incorporating its notion of good government policy into the Constitution. Harlan, with whom Justice Potter Stewart concurred, described the majority opinion as "wholly inadequate" to explain why a poll tax was "irrational or invidious."[41]

The Racial Gerrymander

As the white primary, literacy tests, and poll taxes were disappearing from the electoral framework of the South, the Supreme Court struck down still another device used to disenfranchise black voters. Northern and southern states both made some use of the racial gerrymander—the practice of drawing election district boundaries to dilute or eliminate concentrations of black voting strength in a single district. *Gomillion v. Lightfoot* (1960) brought this practice before the Supreme Court, which found it a clear violation of the Fifteenth Amendment. The Court's ruling was notable for two other reasons: it predated by two years the Court's abandonment of its traditional hands-off policy toward redistricting and reapportionment questions, and the majority opinion was written by Justice Frankfurter, who had been the Court's most articulate spokesman for this hands-off policy.

Alabama had redefined the boundaries of the city of Tuskegee to exclude virtually all black voters. The excluded blacks sought a court order halting enforcement of the law, which had changed the shape of the city limits from a square to a twenty-eight-sided figure. The new boundary removed from within the city all but four or five qualified black voters, yet not a single white voter. Professor C. G. Gomillion of Tuskegee Institute and the other affected black citizens argued that the gerrymander denied them due process and equal protection under the Fourteenth Amendment and infringed their right to vote in violation of the Fifteenth Amendment. The Supreme Court unanimously declared the gerrymander unconstitutional. The right of the states to control the boundaries of their political subdivisions is subject to constitutional limitation, it held.

Justice Frankfurter wrote the Court's opinion. Frankfurter had been the author of the Court's opinion in *Colegrove v. Green* (1946), which declared that the Court should not enter the "political thicket" of redistricting questions because they were political matters beyond the competence of the courts to resolve.[42] In *Gomillion*, Frankfurter made the distinction that *Colegrove* involved involuntary nonracial disparities in districts created by population shifts, not state action, while *Gomillion* involved intentional racial discrimination by the state:

> When a legislature thus singles out a readily isolated segment of a racial minority for special discriminatory treatment, it violates the Fifteenth Amendment. In no

In 1812 Elkanah Tinsdale lampooned the political maneuverings of Gov. Elbridge Gerry of Massachusetts, who deftly engineered the construction of constituency boundaries to aid in the election of a member of his own party. Because the district resembled a mythological salamander in the cartoonist's illustration, the term *gerrymander* has come to mean the drawing of political district lines for partisan advantage. Racial gerrymandering was declared unconstitutional by the Supreme Court in *Gomillion v. Lightfoot* (1960).

case involving unequal weight in voting distribution that has come before the Court did the decision sanction a differentiation on racial lines whereby approval was given to unequivocal withdrawal of the vote solely from colored citizens. Apart from all else, these considerations lift this controversy out of the so-called "political" arena and into the conventional sphere of constitutional litigation....

> While in form this is merely an act redefining metes and bounds, if the allegations are established, the inescapable human effect of this essay in geometry and geography is to despoil colored citizens, and only colored citizens, of their theretofore enjoyed voting rights.[43]

Justice Charles E. Whittaker's concurring opinion pointed out that this application of the Fifteenth Amendment extended the meaning of that amendment, guaranteeing not only the right to vote but also the right to vote in a particular district. The Equal Protection Clause of the Fourteenth Amendment would have been a preferable basis for the ruling, Whittaker wrote:

> [I]nasmuch as no one has the right to vote in a political division, or in a local election concerning only an area in which he does not reside, it would seem to follow that one's right to vote in Division A is not abridged by a redistricting that places his residence in Division B if he there enjoys the same voting privileges as all others in that Division.
>
> But it does seem clear to me that accomplishment of a State's purpose ... of "fencing Negro citizens out of" Division A and into Division B is an unlawful segregation of races of citizens in violation of the Equal Protection Clause of the Fourteenth Amendment.[44]

In 1962 Manhattan voters brought suit charging that a New York congressional districting law was irrational, discriminatory, and unequal and segregated voters by race and national origin, concentrating white voters in the Seventeenth—"Silk Stocking"—District, and nonwhite and Puerto Rican voters in the Eighteenth, Nineteenth, and Twentieth Congressional Districts. The Supreme Court in *Wright v. Rockefeller* (1964) found no constitutional violation. Since Manhattan was a mosaic of ethnic and racial groups, it said, almost any combination of arbitrarily drawn congressional district lines would result in some pattern of racial imbalance subject to challenge as unconstitutional.[45] *(See details of Wells v. Rockefeller, p. 201.)*

THE RIGHT AND THE POWER: A BROAD VIEW

Although the Court had struck down the use of grandfather clauses and white primaries before 1950, it was Congress that at last asserted federal power to ensure the right of black citizens to vote. A constitutional amendment ratified in 1964 outlawed the use of poll

THE RIGHT TO RUN FOR PUBLIC OFFICE

In the late 1960s and 1970s, the Supreme Court struck down a number of state-imposed restrictions on the right to run for public office, ruling that such restrictions violated the Fourteenth Amendment's guarantee of equal protection. One state required valid nominating petitions for independent presidential electors to have ten thousand signatures—at least two hundred persons signing from each of fifty counties. In 1969 the Court held that this state law violated the "one person, one vote" rule. By setting this arbitrary quota for each one of so many counties, held the Court, the law discriminated against voters residing in the more heavily populated counties of the state. With this ruling in *Moore v. Ogilvie* (1969), the Court reversed a 1948 decision upholding the same requirement.[1]

In 1972 the justices struck down a state's practice of basing the size of filing fees for candidates on the estimated total cost of an election. This practice, held the Court, discriminated against candidates who could not afford to pay large fees.[2] In 1974 the Court ruled it unconstitutional for a state to set mandatory high filing fees in order to prevent poor people from running for office.[3]

Cases before the Court have also involved state regulations governing new political parties' efforts to win a place on the state ballot. In a 1968 case initiated by the American Independent Party, the Court struck down Ohio's burdensome requirements on the ground that laws that place heavier burdens on parties other than the Republican and Democratic Parties violates the guarantee of equal protection.[4] Six years later, however, the Court held that a state might properly require new and minority parties seeking a spot on the ballot to secure a certain number of voter signatures endorsing its effort and to require that those signatures belong to persons who had not voted in a party primary or otherwise participated in another party's nominating process during that year. This restriction, held the Court, was simply a reasonable means for the state to use in protecting the integrity of its nominating process.[5]

In the context of congressional elections, the Court in 1995 ruled that states may not set a limit on the number of terms their representatives may serve in Congress.[6]

---

1. *Moore v. Ogilvie*, 394 U.S. 814 (1969); *MacDougall v. Green*, 335 U.S. 281 (1948).

2. *Bullock v. Carter*, 405 U.S. 134 (1972).

3. *Lubin v. Panish*, 415 U.S. 709 (1974).

4. *Williams v. Rhodes*, 393 U.S. 23 (1968).

5. *American Party of Texas v. White, Hainsworth v. White*, 415 U.S. 767 (1974); see also *Munro v. Socialist Workers Party*, 479 U.S. 189 (1986).

6. *U.S. Term Limits Inc. v. Thornton*, 514 U.S. 779 (1995).

Electing Judges

The Voting Rights Act as passed by Congress in 1965 clearly applied to the election of state judges as well as to lawmaking representatives. In 1982 Congress amended the act, using the term *representatives* in the amendment. This introduced an ambiguity that led to a pair of Supreme Court rulings on semantics and the scope of the act's protections: *Chisom v. Roemer* (1991) and *Houston Lawyers' Association v. Attorney General of Texas* (1991).[1] The 1982 amendment raised questions over whether judges were still covered by the act. The cases began when voters in Louisiana and Texas challenged those states' system of electing judges through at-large districts. The districts, they said, diluted the power of black and Hispanic votes. State officials countered that judicial elections are not protected by federal voting rights law because judges are not "representatives" under the Voting Rights Act. Lower courts agreed.

The Supreme Court reversed in 1991 by a vote of 6-3 in *Chisom*. The act clearly applied to judicial elections before the 1982 amendments, it said, and those amendments were chiefly aimed at removing a requirement of proof of intentional discrimination for redress under the act. Therefore, no reason existed to believe that Congress intended to eliminate judges from the coverage of the act. The justices noted that the main purpose of Congress's 1982 action was to overturn the Supreme Court's ruling in *City of Mobile, Ala. v. Bolden* (1980), which required challengers to a voting process to show it was intentionally discriminatory.[2] In instituting a test that looked to the actual discriminatory "effects" of an election scheme, Congress happened to use the term *representatives*.

Justice John Paul Stevens, who wrote for the majority, said, "It is difficult to believe that Congress, in an express effort to broaden the protection afforded by the Voting Rights Act, withdrew, without comment, an important category of elections from that protection."[3]

---

1. *Chisom v. Roemer*, 501 U.S. 380 (1991); *Houston Lawyers' Association v. Attorney General of Texas*, 501 U.S. 419 (1991).

2. *City of Mobile, Ala. v. Bolden*, 446 U.S. 55 (1980).

3. *Chisom v. Roemer*, 501 U.S. 380 at 404 (1991).

---

taxes in federal elections, and the Voting Rights Act of 1965 suspended the use of literacy tests and put in place federal machinery to protect the opportunity of blacks to register and vote. Congress had begun reasserting its authority to enforce the Fifteenth Amendment in 1957. The amendment authorizes Congress to pass appropriate legislation to enforce it, but in the years immediately after adoption, efforts to pass enforcing legislation were proscribed by the Court's restrictive view of this power. The Civil Rights Act of 1957 established the Civil Rights Commission, which was charged with, among other tasks, studying the problem of voter discrimination. The act also authorized the attorney general to bring lawsuits to halt public and private interference with the right of blacks to vote, and it expanded federal jurisdiction over such suits. The Court upheld the investigatory procedures of the commission and the authorization of federal voting rights suits.[46]

Responding to reports that progress in securing voting rights for blacks remained slow even under the provisions of the 1957 act, Congress in 1960 passed a measure that permitted the U.S. attorney general to sue a state for deprivation of voting rights if the individuals named initially as defendants—usually voting registrars—should leave office. This provision remedied a situation that had arisen in a suit brought by the United States against Alabama voting officials who had subsequently relinquished their positions.[47] In addition, Title VI of the 1960 law authorized the appointment of special federal "voting referees" to oversee voter registration in selected counties where a federal court found a pattern of voter discrimination.

The Civil Rights Act of 1964, in its first title, mandated state adoption of standard procedures and requirements for all persons seeking to register to vote. The law also required local officials to justify rejecting a potential voter who had completed the sixth grade or had equivalent evidence of intellectual competence. Other provisions of the 1964 law expedited the movement of voting rights cases to the Supreme Court.[48] In two cases brought under the 1964 act, the Supreme Court sanctioned the federal government's efforts to break the pattern of case-by-case litigation of voting rights violations by upholding federal power to challenge a state's entire constitutional legal framework for voter registration and conduct of elections.[49]

Progress was still slow. In Dallas County, Alabama, three new federal laws and four years of litigation had produced the registration of only 383 black voters out of a potential pool of 15,000 blacks of voting age. On March 8, 1965, the Rev. Martin Luther King Jr. led a "Walk for Freedom," from Montgomery to Selma, to dramatize the need for more blacks to register to vote in the South. The violent reaction of local white law enforcement officers and white bystanders to King's peaceful demonstration drew nationwide attention to the problem. A week later, President Lyndon B. Johnson addressed a joint session of Congress to ask passage of a new voting rights measure to close the legal loopholes that had so long allowed local officials to stall black voter registration. Johnson explained that "no law that we now have on the books can ensure the right to vote when local officials are determined to deny it."[50] Later that month, NAACP official Roy Wilkins, appearing on behalf of the Leadership Conference on Civil Rights, testified before a Senate committee on the need for such legislation. He urged Congress to "transform this retail litigation method of registration into a wholesale administration procedure registering all who seek to exercise their democratic birthright."[51]

NAACP official Roy Wilkins and President Lyndon B. Johnson review strategies for securing passage of the Voting Rights Act of 1965.

Voting Rights Act of 1965

In August 1965, Congress approved the sweeping Voting Rights Act. The law suspended literacy tests and provided for the appointment of federal supervisors of voter registration in all states and counties where literacy tests (or similar qualifying devices) were in effect as of November 1, 1964, and where fewer than 50 percent of the voting-age residents were registered to vote or did vote in the 1964 presidential election. The law established criminal penalties for persons found guilty of interfering with the voting rights of others. State or county governments brought under the coverage of the law were required to obtain federal approval of any new voting laws, standards, practices, or procedures. A covered state or county could "escape" from the law's

provisions if it could convince a three-judge federal court in the District of Columbia that no racial discrimination in registration or voting had occurred in the previous five years. The act placed federal registration machinery in six southern states—Alabama, Georgia, Mississippi, South Carolina, Louisiana, and Virginia—Alaska, twenty-eight counties in North Carolina, three counties in Arizona, and one in Idaho. It was the most effective civil rights legislation ever enacted. Within four years almost 1 million blacks had registered to vote under its provisions.[52]

State Challenges

Not surprisingly, the unprecedented assertion of federal power over electoral and voting matters was immediately challenged as exceeding congressional authority and encroaching on states' rights. Times and the Court had, however, changed since the post–Civil War era, and in 1966 the Supreme Court firmly backed the power of Congress to pass such a law. In *South Carolina v. Katzenbach* (1966), the state asked the Court to halt implementation of the Voting Rights Act, charging that Congress had overstepped its bounds in suspending state voting standards, authorizing the use of federal election examiners, and adopting a "triggering" formula that would result in its affecting some states but not others. At the Court's invitation, Alabama, Georgia, Louisiana, Mississippi, and Virginia filed briefs in support of South Carolina's challenge. Twenty other states filed briefs in support of the law.

South Carolina charged that by suspending voter qualification "tests and devices" in some states, Congress violated the principle that all states were equal. It also alleged that the law denied the affected states due process of law by presuming that if the minority population was high and voter participation was low, racially discriminatory voting practices existed. Due process was also denied, argued South Carolina, by the law's failure to allow judicial review of the findings putting the law into effect in a state. Furthermore, the state maintained, the act was an unconstitutional bill of attainder, punishing only certain states, and a violation of the separation of powers because it used legislative means to declare certain states guilty of discrimination.

Taking a far broader view of the right to vote and congressional power to enforce and protect that right than had the Court of the 1870s and 1880s, the Supreme Court in 1966 rejected all challenges to the act. "Congress," wrote Chief Justice Warren for eight members of the Court, "has full remedial powers to effectuate the constitutional prohibition against racial discrimination in voting."[53] He continued:

> The Voting Rights Act was designed by Congress to banish the blight of racial discrimination in voting, which has infected the electoral process in parts of our country for nearly a century.... Congress assumed the power to prescribe these remedies from Section 2 of the Fifteenth Amendment, which authorizes the National Legislature to effectuate by "appropriate" measures the constitutional prohibition against racial discrimination in voting. We hold that the sections of the Act which are properly before us are an appropriate means for carrying out Congress' constitutional responsibilities and are consonant with all other provisions of the Constitution. We therefore deny South Carolina's request that enforcement of these sections of the act be enjoined.[54]

Warren then responded to the challenges to each particular provision. With respect to the triggering formula, he stated that it was "rational in both practice and theory." The suspension of tests and devices "was a legitimate response to the problem for which there is ample precedent in Fifteenth Amendment cases." The

federal approval requirement for new voting rules in the states covered by the act, Warren observed, "may have been an uncommon exercise of congressional power, as South Carolina contends, but the Court has recognized that exceptional conditions can justify legislative measures not otherwise appropriate." The appointment of federal election examiners was "clearly an appropriate response to the problem, closely related to remedies authorized in prior cases."[55]

Justice Black concurred in part and dissented in part. He agreed that Congress had the power under the Fifteenth Amendment to suspend literacy tests and to authorize federal examiners to register qualified voters, but Black objected to the provisions that suspended any changes in state voting laws until the state obtained approval of the change from the attorney general or the federal District Court for the District of Columbia. This provision, Black argued, "so distorts our constitutional structure of government as to render any distinction drawn in the Constitution between state and federal power almost meaningless."[56]

Also in 1966, in *Katzenbach v. Morgan,* the Court upheld the portion of the Voting Rights Act that permitted persons educated in accredited "American-flag" schools to vote even if they were unable to demonstrate literacy in English. The provision was aimed at enfranchising persons educated in schools in Puerto Rico, a commonwealth of the United States, who were unable to read or write English.[57]

Scope and Application

Although the basic constitutionality of the Voting Rights Act was settled, a steady stream of voting rights cases came to the Court well into the mid-1990s that tested the scope and application of the law. The Court steadfastly backed the act through the 1970s and 1980s, but in the 1990s it began to cut back on its scope, concerned that the law was fostering "reverse discrimination." In *Gaston County v. United States* (1969), the Court refused to allow a North Carolina county to reinstate a literacy test. Writing the Court's opinion, Justice Harlan linked the county's earlier maintenance of segregated schools and the literacy level of its blacks and declared that to reinstitute the literacy

Long lines of black voters in Cobb County, Georgia, casting ballots for the 1946 Democratic primary elections showed that when the government removed obstacles to voting, blacks turned up at the polls in large numbers. Nearly twenty years later, the Voting Rights Act of 1965 eliminated the remaining obstacles to voting. Within four years of the act's passage, almost one million blacks had registered to vote.

qualification for voters would simply perpetuate the inequality of the denial of equal educational opportunity.[58] *(See details of the case, p. 180.)*

In a number of other cases, the Court upheld the pre-clearance requirement for a wide variety of laws and practices affecting the right to vote.[59] In 1978 the Court even extended the requirement to apply to a county school board's rule that any employee running for state office take leave from his or her post without pay during the period of active candidacy. The Court held that the rule was a voting standard, practice, or procedure subject to the requirement and that the county school board was a political subdivision subject to the provisions of the Voting Rights Act. Four justices dissented on the first point, three on the second.[60]

Earlier, the Court had held that annexation of contiguous areas by communities covered by the act was prohibited without prior federal approval.[61] In 1975 the Court held in *Richmond v. United States* that a federally approved annexation plan did not violate the Voting Rights Act—even if it reduced the

percentage of black voters in the city's population—so long as there were legitimate objective reasons for the annexation.[62] In two cases decided in 1977—*Briscoe v. Bell* and *Morris v. Gressette*—the Court also sustained the act's limits on judicial review of the formula that put the law into effect in certain areas and on judicial review of the attorney general's decision to approve changes in voting laws or practices.[63]

New Push for Black Representation

In 1980 the Supreme Court for the first time narrowed the reach of the Voting Rights Act, but its decision proved to have a short life. The issue concerned not who could vote, but how those votes were translated into political power. The Court's decision ignited a debate over whether the Voting Rights Act concerned discrimination against individual black voters only or whether it also applied to discrimination against black voters as a group. Mobile, Alabama, was governed by a three-member commission, with each member elected citywide. Although blacks made up 35 percent of the

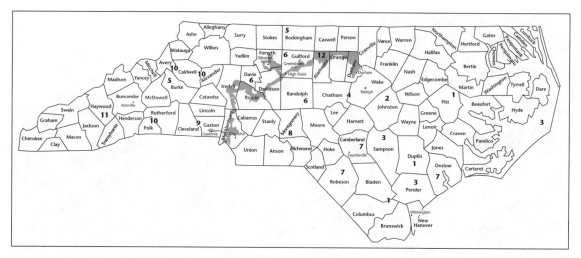

The irregular shape of North Carolina's Twelfth Congressional District was challenged in *Shaw v. Reno* (1993).

city's population, as of 1980 no black had ever been elected to the commission. Nonetheless, in a 6-3 decision in *City of Mobile v. Bolden,* the justices ruled that the Mobile electoral system did not violate the Voting Rights Act or the Constitution because there was no proof that it was created with the intent to discriminate against blacks. The use of at-large elections in a city where two-thirds of the voters were white unquestionably had the effect of preventing blacks from winning representation, but the law forbids only deliberate and intentional discrimination, the Court said.[64] The Voting Rights Act guarantees blacks the right "to register and vote without hindrance," but it does not guarantee them a right to win representation. In dissent, Justice Marshall argued that the majority had watered down the meaning of the Voting Rights Act to the point that the right to vote was "granted in form, but denied in substance."[65]

The *Mobile* decision elicited an immediate response on Capitol Hill, and civil rights activists pressed Congress to reverse the Court's narrow interpretation of the Voting Rights Act. In 1982 the law was amended to overturn the Mobile decision and to state that voting practices that denied blacks and other minorities a chance "to elect representatives of their choice" were illegal, regardless of whether they were created for discriminatory purposes. Four years later,

the Court applied that new test in a North Carolina case. In *Thornburg v. Gingles* (1986), the Court held that the state could not divide large blocs of minority voters among several mostly white districts because it diluted the electoral strength of the minority.[66] This concept of "vote dilution" was not precise or obvious in all circumstances, but the thrust of the law was clear. As the 1990 census began, state officials believed that where it was possible to do so, they should draw electoral districts that would favor the election of black and Hispanic representatives. The pressure to carve out black majority districts in the southern states set off a backlash that would reach the Court a few years later.

Voter Identification

Although states may not deny eligible citizens their right to vote because of their race or economic status, the Supreme Court has ruled that states have broad powers to regulate ballots and the process of voting. The reason for doing so is to make sure elections are fair and honest. In the nineteenth century, city bosses were reputed to control elections by paying for votes or by having supporters and others cast votes in the name of dead persons. By the twentieth century, nearly all the states required voters to register well in advance of an election. This process gave officials time to verify information about those who intended to vote. Of course, a citizen failing to register would mean that he or she could not vote, even if an eligible resident. No one claimed that such a regulation was unconstitutional. Still, the line between a reasonable regulation of the voting process and an unconstitutional burden on the right to vote was none too clear.

The issue came before the Court in 2008, when Indiana Democrats challenged a Republican-sponsored state law that required voters to present photo identification before casting a ballot. A driver's license or a passport would suffice. The Indiana Republicans who had won passage of the photo ID law said it would deter fraud at polling places. The Democrats responded that there was no evidence of persons masquerading as someone else in order to cast an illegal vote. They also said the new requirement could deter tens of thousands of eligible voters—most of them poor, elderly or disabled—who did not drive. Because the law had a partisan motive and would burden the right to vote for many citizens, the Democrats argued that it should be struck down as unconstitutional.

In *Crawford v. Marion County Election Board* (2008), the Court in a 6-3 decision upheld the photo ID law as a reasonable regulation of voting.[67] Justice John Paul Stevens said that the state has a valid interest "in protecting the integrity and reliability of the electoral process," and in particular, in "deterring and detecting voter fraud." He noted that about 99 percent of Indiana voters already had a photo ID card. Further, counties would supply photo identification free of charge to anyone who appeared and requested one. The lawsuit brought by the Democrats was flawed, Stevens argued, while pointing out that it did not cite a single plaintiff who had said that he or she had been deterred from voting because of the photo ID requirement. "In sum, on the basis of the record that has been made in this litigation, we cannot conclude that the statute imposes excessively burdensome requirements on any class of voters," Stevens wrote. Chief Justice John G. Roberts Jr. and Justice Anthony M. Kennedy agreed. Justices Antonin Scalia, Clarence Thomas, and Samuel A. Alito Jr. concurred in the result, but said they would have gone further and closed the door to future claims over voting regulations. The dissenters held that the law would likely deter thousands of voters who were poor or disabled from casting a ballot. "The Indiana Voter ID is thus unconstitutional: the state interests fail to justify the practical limitations placed on the right to vote, and the law imposes an unreasonable and irrelevant burden on voters who are poor and old," wrote Justice David H. Souter.

The Right to an Equal Vote

In the early 1960s, as Congress was moving with judicial backing to fulfill at last the promise of the Fifteenth Amendment, the Supreme Court sparked a second revolution in the nation's electoral system. At issue in this revolution was not every American's right to vote but the right, based on the equal protection guarantee of the Fourteenth Amendment, to an equal vote. In 1962 the Court abandoned its long-standing policy of noninterference in the malapportionment of population among a state's electoral districts. By the end of the decade, the Court's rulings would require that almost all the nation's legislative and congressional districts be redrawn. The equal protection guarantee meant that one person's vote should be counted equally with another's. Thus the standard by which these redistricting efforts were measured was that of "one person, one vote."

CONGRESS, DISTRICTS, AND PEOPLE

Article I, section 4, of the Constitution gives Congress the power to override state-established rules governing the election of senators and representatives:

> The Times, Places and Manner of holding Elections for Senators and Representatives shall be prescribed in each State by the Legislature thereof; but the Congress may at any time by Law make or alter such Regulations, except as to the Places of chusing Senators.

Congress exercised this power in 1842 to require that members of the House be elected from separate districts within each state. In 1872 Congress added the requirement that these congressional districts be of approximately equal population. Subsequent reapportionment statutes, including ones enacted in 1901 and 1911, contained the specification that congressional districts be "contiguous and compact territory and containing as nearly as practicable an equal number of inhabitants."[1] The next such law, passed in 1929, omitted these requirements, however, and the Supreme Court held the omission intentional and the standards thus no longer in effect. In *Wood v. Broom* (1932), the Court upheld a Mississippi redistricting law that failed to provide compact, contiguous, and population-equal districts.[2]

That decision came at a critical time in the nation's demographic history. The 1920 census showed that, for the first time, more Americans lived in cities than in rural settings. The implication was clear: the voice of the farmer in the legislature and in Congress would grow fainter while that of the city dweller would increase in strength. For forty years, however, rural interests delayed the political impact of this shift in population, and the Court steadfastly held that challenges to malapportionment were political questions, outside its purview. In 1946 the Court refused to intervene in Illinois, reaffirming its intention to stay out of the "political thicket" of redistricting and reapportionment. Within two decades, however, in *Baker v. Carr* (1962), the Court would abandon its long-held aversion to ruling on malapportionment. In subsequent cases the Court would move into the thicket to ensure each voter's ballot equal weight in the state electoral process.

The "Political Thicket"

Colegrove v. Green (1946) was brought before the Supreme Court by Kenneth W. Colegrove, a Northwestern University professor of political science who argued that Illinois congressional districts were so unequal in population as to deny voters in the more populous districts the equal protection of the law guaranteed by the Fourteenth Amendment. The numerical disparity between these districts, he pointed out, was as large as 800,000 persons. The Supreme Court, 4-3, threw out his case without addressing the equal protection issue. Justice Robert H. Jackson did not take part in the decision (because he was acting as prosecutor at the Nuremberg trials), and the seat of the chief justice was vacant (as Chief Justice Harlan Fiske Stone had died two months before the decision was announced).[3] Justice Felix Frankfurter wrote the Court's opinion, joined by Justices Stanley F. Reed and Harold H. Burton. Frankfurter noted that the case could be resolved on the same basis as *Wood v. Broom:* Because Congress had omitted the equal population standard from the reapportionment law now in effect, there was no such requirement for states to follow in drawing district lines.

Practical considerations as well as judicial precedent also dictated the Court's decision not to intervene. The issue in the case, Frankfurter noted, was "of a peculiarly political nature" and not fit for judicial determination. He continued:

> Nothing is clearer than that this controversy concerns matters that bring courts into immediate and active relations with party contests. From the determination of such issues this Court has traditionally held aloof. It is hostile to a democratic system to involve the judiciary in the politics of the people....
>
> ... [D]ue regard for the Constitution as a viable system precludes judicial correction [of the evils protested here]. Authority for dealing with such problems resides elsewhere.... The short of it is that the Constitution [Article I, section 4] has conferred upon Congress exclusive authority to secure fair representation by the States in the popular House and left to that House determination whether States have fulfilled their responsibility. If Congress failed in exercising its powers, whereby standards of fairness are offended, the remedy ultimately lies with the people. Whether Congress faithfully discharges its duty or not, the subject has been committed to the exclusive control of Congress....
>
> To sustain this action would cut very deep into the very being of Congress. Courts ought not to enter this political thicket. The remedy for unfairness in districting is to secure State legislatures that will apportion properly, or to invoke the ample powers of Congress.[4]

The critical fourth vote was cast by Justice Wiley B. Rutledge, who wrote a separate opinion. He did not endorse the position set out by Frankfurter that issues of districting were not proper matters for judicial determination, but in this case he thought the Court properly dismissed the matter in order to avoid collision with the political departments of the government.[5]

Justices Hugo L. Black, William O. Douglas, and Frank Murphy dissented, finding Colegrove's complaint well within the power of the federal courts to redress constitutional grievances caused by state action. Black wrote, "What is involved here is the right to vote guaranteed by the Federal Constitution. It has always been the rule that where a federally protected right has been invaded the federal courts will provide the remedy to rectify the wrong done."[6] Population disparities such as those in this case clearly violated the Fourteenth Amendment, the dissenters concluded, and the Court should grant relief. *Colegrove* stood for sixteen years as a firmly planted obstacle to judicial inquiry into the apportionment of state legislatures as well as into the distribution of population among congressional districts.

Race and Redistricting

In 1960—with Justice Frankfurter speaking for the Court—the Supreme Court made an exception to its refusal to intervene in apportionment issues. When civil rights and redistricting converged in the case of *Gomillion v. Lightfoot* (1960), the Supreme Court was persuaded by a claim of racial discrimination to strike down an Alabama law redrawing Tuskegee's voting boundaries to eliminate nearly every black voter from the city's limits.[7] *(See details of this case, pp. 184–185.)* Justice Frankfurter drew a clear line between redistricting challenges based on the Fourteenth Amendment, such as *Colegrove*, and those based on the Fifteenth Amendment, such as *Gomillion:*

> The decisive facts in this case ... are wholly different from the considerations found controlling in *Colegrove.*
>
> That case involved a complaint of discriminatory apportionment of congressional districts. The appellants in *Colegrove* complained only of a dilution of the strength of their votes as a result of legislative inaction over a course of many years. The petitioners here complain that affirmative legislative action deprives them of their vote and the consequent advantages that the ballot affords....
>
> When a state exercises power wholly within the domain of state interest, it is insulated from federal judicial review. But such insulation is not carried over when state power is used as an instrument of circumventing a federally protected right.[8]

POLITICAL QUESTIONS AND JUDICIAL ANSWERS

To avoid addressing the issue of legislative malapportionment, the Supreme Court in *Colegrove v. Green* (1946) invoked the "political question" doctrine. Indeed, it is one of the oldest of the Court's rationales for *not* deciding a case. In the classic discussion of judicial power in *Marbury v. Madison* (1803), Chief Justice John Marshall declared,

> The province of the court is, solely, to decide on the rights of individuals, not to inquire how the executive, or executive officers, perform duties in which they have a discretion. Questions in their nature political, or which are, by the Constitution and laws, submitted to the executive, can never be made in this court.[1]

In the ensuing years the Court used the political question doctrine as a convenient device for avoiding collisions with Congress, the president, or the states on matters ranging from foreign relations to malapportioned congressional districts.

The attributes of the political question doctrine are quite variable. One modern justice has observed that they "in various settings, diverge, combine, appear, and disappear in seeming disorderliness."[2] The Constitution provides that the United States shall guarantee to every state a republican form of government. When the question of enforcing that guarantee came for the first time to the Supreme Court, however, the justices made clear that this was a "political question" beyond the Court's reach. The case *Luther v. Borden* (1849) involved two competing groups, each asserting that it was the lawful government of Rhode Island. Writing for the Court, Chief Justice Roger B. Taney stated firmly that it was up to Congress to decide which government was the legitimate one:

> [W]hen the senators and representatives of a State are admitted into the councils of the Union, the authority of the government under which they are appointed, as well as its republican character, is recognized by the proper constitutional authority.

In addition, Congress's decision is binding on every other department of the government and cannot be questioned in a judicial tribunal.[3]

The Court has consistently applied the political question doctrine to avoid addressing Fourteenth Amendment Guaranty Clause challenges to state action.[4] In another early-nineteenth-century ruling, the Court placed questions of foreign policy and foreign affairs firmly in the political question category. In 1829 the Court refused to settle an international border question, stating that it was not the role of the courts to assert national interests against foreign powers.[5] Throughout its history, the Court has reaffirmed the view that in foreign affairs the nation should speak with a single voice.[6]

In similar fashion, the Court has generally invoked the political question doctrine to refuse to intervene in questions of legislative process or procedure, leaving their resolution to Congress or the states. The exception to that general practice has come in cases raising questions of basic constitutional standards—such as the power of Congress to legislate on

Baker v. Carr (1962)

By 1962 only three members of the *Colegrove* Court remained on the bench: Frankfurter, Black, and Douglas—the latter two, dissenters in the 1946 ruling. By that year as well, the once slight advantage in representation of rural voters in state legislatures had become extremely pronounced. Legislative districts in rural areas held nearly twice as many seats as they would have been entitled to by apportionment on a population basis alone. A similar degree of population imbalance existed with respect to congressional districts. The Supreme Court took its first step into the political thicket of legislative reapportionment with *Baker v. Carr* (1962).[9] The Tennessee legislature had failed to reapportion itself for sixty years, despite the fact that the state constitution required decennial reapportionment, after each census. By 1960 population shifts from rural to urban regions of the state had created dramatic disparities in the pattern of representation for state house and senate seats. As Justice Tom C. Clark would point out in his concurring opinion in *Baker v. Carr,* two-thirds of the members of the state legislature were elected by slightly more than one-third of the state's population.[10]

Appeals to the legislature to reapportion itself were futile. A suit brought in state court was rejected on the grounds that state courts—like federal courts—should stay out of such legislative matters. The city dwellers who brought the state suit then appealed to the federal courts, charging that the "unconstitutional certain matters or the propriety of one chamber's action excluding a member who meets constitutional qualifications[7]—or in matters where Congress and the president are deadlocked over an issue.[8]

For most of the nation's history, the Court also viewed challenges to state decisions allocating population among electoral districts as a political question. It was in this vein that Justice Felix Frankfurter wrote in *Colegrove* that for Courts to involve themselves in malapportionment controversies was "hostile to a democratic system."[9] Sixteen years later, however, the Court in *Baker v. Carr* (1962) found the *Colegrove* ruling to be based on too broad a definition of "political questions." Justice William J. Brennan Jr. explained for the new majority:

> [I]t is the relationship between the judiciary and the coordinate branches of the Federal Government, and not the federal judiciary's relationship to the States, which gives rise to the "political questions."… The nonjusticiability of a political question is primarily a function of the separation of powers.[10]

The basic question of fairness involved in *Baker v. Carr*, wrote Brennan, was constitutional, not political, and was therefore well within the jurisdiction of the Court. Simply "the presence of a matter affecting state government does not [in and of itself] render the case nonjusticiable."[11]

More recently the Court widened what it considered justiciable when it extended federal court jurisdiction to cover the issue of political gerrymanders. In *Davis v. Bandemer* (1986), Justice Byron R. White applied the political questions standard set out in *Baker v. Carr*. Referring to political gerrymanders, he said,

> Disposition of this question does not involve us in a matter more properly decided by a coequal branch of our Government. There is no risk of foreign or domestic disturbance, and … we are not persuaded that there are no judicially discernible and manageable standards by which political gerrymander cases are to be decided.[12]

---

1. *Marbury v. Madison*, 1 Cr. (5 U.S.) 137 at 170 (1803).

2. *Baker v. Carr*, 369 U.S. 186 at 210 (1962).

3. *Luther v. Borden*, 7 How. (48 U.S.) 1 at 42 (1849).

4. *Pacific States Telephone and Telegraph Co. v. Oregon*, 223 U.S. 118 (1912).

5. *Foster v. Neilson*, 2 Pet. (27 U.S.) 253 at 307 (1829).

6. *Oetjen v. Central Leather Co.*, 246 U.S. 297 at 302 (1918); *United States v. Curtiss-Wright Export Corporation*, 299 U.S. 304 (1936).

7. *Hawke v. Smith*, 253 U.S. 221 (1920); *Coleman v. Miller*, 307 U.S. 433 (1939); *Powell v. McCormack*, 395 U.S. 486 (1969).

8. Id. at 457–458.

9. *Colegrove v. Green*, 328 U.S. 549 at 554 (1946).

10. *Baker v. Carr*, 369 U.S. 186 at 210 (1962).

11. Id. at 232.

12. *Davis v. Bandemer*, 478 U.S. 109 at 123 (1986).

and obsolete" apportionment system denied them the equal protection of the laws promised by the Fourteenth Amendment. In *Baker v. Carr*, the Court abandoned the view that such claims were political questions outside the competence of the courts and ruled, 6-2, that constitutional challenges to legislative malapportionment were "justiciable"—that is, suitability for judicial solution—and could thus properly be considered by federal courts. The Court stopped there, choosing not to address the merits of the challenge to malapportionment. Justice Charles E. Whittaker did not participate in the decision.

Justice William J. Brennan Jr. wrote the Court's opinion. The majority resolved the question of federal jurisdiction over the case with surprising ease. The complaint clearly arose under one of the provisions of the U.S. Constitution, Brennan wrote, so it fell within the federal judicial power as defined in Article III: "An unbroken line of our precedents sustains the federal courts' jurisdiction of the subject matter of federal constitutional claims of this nature."[11] Then, turning to the question of the voters' standing to bring the case, Brennan explained that they did have standing because they had been deprived of an interest they sought to defend:

> These appellants seek relief in order to protect or vindicate an interest of their own.… Their constitutional claim is, in substance, that the 1901 statute [setting up the existing districting and apportionment structure] constitutes arbitrary and capricious state action, offensive to the Fourteenth Amendment

in its irrational disregard of the standard of apportionment prescribed by the State's Constitution or of any standard, effecting a gross disproportion of representation to voting population.[12]

This holding did not require the Court to decide the merits of the voters' allegations, Brennan wrote, before going on to consider the critical question of the justiciability of the issue. Did this suit present a "political question" outside the proper scope of the Supreme Court's consideration? Brennan's answer was "no":

> [T]he mere fact that the suit seeks protection of a political right does not mean it presents a political question…. It is argued that apportionment cases, whatever the actual wording of the complaint, can involve no federal constitutional right except one resting on the guaranty of a republican form of government, and that complaints based on that clause have been held to present political questions which are nonjusticiable.
>
> We hold that the claim pleaded here neither rests upon nor implicates the Guaranty Clause and that its justiciability is therefore not foreclosed by our decisions of cases involving that clause. The District Court misinterpreted *Colegrove v. Green* and other decisions of this Court on which it relied.[13]

The Guaranty Clause to which Brennan refers is in Article IV, section 4, of the Constitution: "The United States shall guarantee to every State in this Union a Republican Form of Government." *Luther v. Borden* (1849), which resulted in one of the first major expositions of the "political question" doctrine, involved this guarantee. The Court held the clause's enforcement to be a political question outside judicial competence and one best left to the political branches—Congress and the president.[14] *Baker v. Carr* rendered the Guaranty Clause virtually useless.

Justices Douglas, Clark, and Potter Stewart wrote concurring opinions. Douglas emphasized the Court's frequent role as protector of voting rights. Clark would have gone further and considered the merits of the particular complaint and granted relief: "[No] one, not even the State nor the dissenters, has come up with any rational basis for Tennessee's apportionment statute."[15] Nevertheless, Clark recommended that federal courts

intrude in reapportionment matters only as a last resort. Stewart reiterated that the Court had decided only that such Fourteenth Amendment challenges to malapportionment were justiciable matters and that the persons bringing this case had standing to sue.

Justices Frankfurter and John Marshall Harlan dissented. In what would be his last major opinion, Frankfurter criticized the majority for "[s]uch a massive repudiation of the experience of our whole past in asserting destructively novel judicial power." The Court had, he argued, allowed a "hypothetical claim resting on abstract assumptions" to become "the basis for affording illusory relief for a particular evil even though it foreshadows deeper and more pervasive difficulties in consequence."[16] Frankfurter went on to say that to give judges the task of "accommodating the incommensurable factors of policy" involved in reapportionment plans was "to attribute … omnicompetence to judges." By this decision, he wrote, the Supreme Court gave the nation's courts the power "to devise what should constitute the proper composition of the legislatures of the fifty States." The Court had overlooked the fact, he added, "that there is not under our Constitution a judicial remedy for every political mischief, for every undesirable exercise of legislative power."[17]

Justice Harlan found the Tennessee plan rational. "Nothing in the Equal Protection Clause or elsewhere in the Federal Constitution," he wrote, "expressly or impliedly supports the view that state legislatures must be so structured as to reflect with approximate equality the voice of every voter…. In short, there is nothing in the Federal Constitution to prevent a State, acting not irrationally, from choosing any electoral legislative structure it thinks best suited to the interests, temper, and customs of its people."[18]

Harlan concluded with a strong criticism of the majority's action, saying that "what the Court is doing reflects more an adventure in judicial experimentation than a solid piece of constitutional adjudication."[19]

"One Person, One Vote"

The decision in *Baker v. Carr* opened the doors of federal courtrooms across the country to litigants

Cartoon showing the impact of the Supreme Court's decision in *Gray v. Sanders* on the rural vote in Georgia.

challenging state and congressional apportionment systems, but it provided no standards to guide federal judges in measuring the validity of challenged systems. With its subsequent rulings in 1963 and 1964, the Supreme Court formulated a standard, known far and wide as the "one man, one vote" or "one person, one vote" rule. Two new justices participated in these decisions. After *Baker v. Carr,* Justices Whittaker and Frankfurter retired. President John F. Kennedy appointed Byron R. White to succeed Whittaker and Arthur J. Goldberg to succeed Frankfurter.

Gray v. Sanders (1963): Statewide Equal Weight

The one person, one vote rule was first set out by the Court almost exactly one year after *Baker v. Carr,* but the case in which the announcement came did not involve legislative districts. In *Gray v. Sanders* (1963) the Court found, 8-1, that Georgia's county-unit

primary system for electing state officials—a system that weighted votes to give advantage to rural districts in statewide primary elections—denied voters the equal protection of the laws. Justice Douglas's majority opinion rejected the state's effort to defend this weighted voting system as analogous to the electoral college system. The electoral college system was included in the Constitution because of specific historical concerns, Douglas wrote, but that inclusion "implied nothing about the use of an analogous system by a State in a statewide election."[20] All votes in a statewide election must have equal weight, held the Court:

How then can one person be given twice or 10 times the voting power of another person in a statewide election merely because he lives in a rural area or because he lives in the smallest rural county? Once the geographical unit for which a representative is to be chosen is designated, all who participate in the election are to have an equal vote—whatever their race, whatever their sex, whatever their occupation, whatever their income, and wherever their home may be in that geographical unit. This is required by the Equal Protection Clause of the Fourteenth Amendment. The concept of "we the people" under the Constitution visualizes no preferred class of voters but equality among those who meet the basic qualification. The idea that every voter is equal to every other voter in his State, when he casts his ballot in favor of one of several competing candidates, underlies many of our decisions.... The conception of political equality from the Declaration of Independence to Lincoln's Gettysburg Address, to the Fifteenth, Seventeenth, and Nineteenth Amendments can mean only one thing—one person, one vote.[21]

Justice Harlan again dissented:

The Court's holding surely ... flies in the face of history ... [as] "one person, one vote" has never been the universally accepted political philosophy in England, the American Colonies, or in the United States.... I do not understand how, on the basis of these mere numbers, unilluminated as they are by any of the complex and subtle political factors involved, a court of law can say, except by judicial fiat, that these disparities are in themselves constitutionally invidious.[22]

"ONE PERSON, ONE VOTE" AT CITY HALL

Through several rulings, the Supreme Court has extended the "one person, one vote" rule to some local districts as well as state districts. In 1967 the Court ruled that county school board members (each representing a local board) from districts of disparate population were not subject to this rule because the county board performed administrative, not legislative, functions.[1] In *Avery v. Midland County* (1968), however, the Court ruled that when a state delegates lawmaking power to local government and provides for election by district of the officials exercising that power, those districts must be of substantially equal population.[2] Two years later, the Court ruled that one person, one vote must be applied to *any* election—state or local—of persons performing governmental functions:

> If one person's vote is given less weight through unequal apportionment, his right to equal voting participation is impaired just as much when he votes for a school board member as when he votes for a state legislator.... [T]he crucial consideration is the right of each qualified voter to participate on an equal footing in the election process.[3]

In 1973 the Court held that the constitutional guarantee of equal protection did not, however, demand that one person, one vote be applied to special-purpose electoral districts, such as those devised to regulate water supplies in the West. In such districts, the Court held, states may restrict the franchise to landowners and weigh the votes of each person according to the property he owns.[4]

---

1. *Sailors v. Board of Education,* 387 U.S. 105 (1967); see also *Dusch v. Davis,* 387 U.S. 112 (1967).
2. *Avery v. Midland County,* 390 U.S. 474 (1968).
3. *Hadley v. Junior College District of Metropolitan Kansas City, Mo.,* 397 U.S. 50 at 55 (1970); see also *New York Board of Estimate v. Morris,* 489 U.S. 688 (1989).
4. *Salyer Land Co. v. Tulare Water District; Associated Enterprises Inc. v. Toltec Watershed Improvement District,* 410 U.S. 719 at 743 (1973).

Wesberry v. Sanders (1964): Congressional Districts

The Court's rulings in *Baker* and *Gray* concerned the equal weighting and counting of votes cast in state elections. In deciding *Wesberry v. Sanders* (1964), the Court applied the one person, one vote principle to congressional districts and set equality, not rationality, as the standard for congressional redistricting. Voters in Georgia's Fifth Congressional District—which includes Atlanta—complained that the population of their congressional district was more than twice the ideal state average of 394,312 persons per district and that the state's failure to redistrict denied them equal protection of the laws. They also challenged Georgia's apportionment scheme as a violation of Article I, section 2, of the Constitution that declares that members of the House of Representatives are to be elected "by the people."

A federal district court dismissed the case in 1962, but the Supreme Court, 6-3, reversed that decision in 1964. In the majority opinion Justice Black considered the historical context of the requirement in Article I, section 2, that representatives be chosen "by the People of the several States." This means, he wrote, that as nearly as is practicable, one man's vote in a congressional election is to be worth as much as another's....

To say that a vote is worth more in one district than in another would not only run counter to our fundamental ideas of democratic government, it would cast aside the principle of a House of Representatives elected "by the People."

While it may not be possible to draw congressional districts with mathematical precision, that is no excuse for ignoring our Constitution's plain objective of making equal representation for equal numbers the fundamental goal of the House of Representatives.[23]

Black's view was sharply attacked by Justice Harlan, who dissented:

The upshot of all this is that the language of Art. 1, [sections] 2 and 4, the surrounding text, and the relevant history are all in strong and consistent direct contradiction of the Court's holding. The constitutional scheme vests in the States plenary power to regulate the conduct of elections for Representatives, and, in order to protect the Federal

Government, provides for congressional supervision of the States' exercise of their power. Within this scheme, the appellants do not have the right which they assert, in the absence of provision for equal districts by the Georgia Legislature or the Congress. The constitutional right which the Court creates is manufactured out of whole cloth.[24]

Justice Black did not invoke the Equal Protection Clause in the case. Speculation as to why Black based this ruling on historical grounds rather than on the Fourteenth Amendment suggests that his approach was a compromise among members of the Court.[25] Four months later, eight members would agree on the requirements of the Fourteenth Amendment for state reapportionment.

Reynolds v. Sims (1964): State Legislative Districts

By a vote of 8-1, the Supreme Court ruled in *Reynolds v. Sims* (1964) that the Fourteenth Amendment required equally populated electoral districts for both houses of bicameral state legislatures. The case, which concerned Alabama, was accompanied to the Supreme Court by a number of others involving other state legislatures. Therefore, the Court's decision immediately affected reapportionment not only in Alabama but also in Colorado, Delaware, New York, Maryland, and Virginia. Ultimately, however, every state legislature would feel the impact of *Reynolds v. Sims*. Chief Justice Earl Warren, writing what he would often describe as the most significant opinion of his judicial career, stated that the "controlling criterion" for any reapportionment plan must be equal population.[26]

The Court rejected the suggestion that a state might, by analogy to the federal system, constitute one house of its legislature on the basis of population and the other on an area basis. Chief Justice Warren explained: "The system of representation in the two Houses of Congress is one conceived out of compromise and concession indispensable to the establishment of our federal republic based on the consideration that in establishing our type of federalism a group of formerly independent states bound themselves together under one national government." Political subdivisions of states, like cities and countries, he continued, were never considered "sovereign entities," but rather "subordinate governmental instrumentalities."[27] The Equal Protection Clause required substantially equal representation of all citizens. The Court did not provide any precise formula for defining "substantially equal" and left it to lower courts to work out a useful standard.

Chief Justice Warren set forth the reasoning behind the one person, one vote rule with clarity and firmness:

> The right to vote freely for the candidate of one's choice is of the essence of a democratic society, and any restrictions on that right strike at the heart of representative government. And the right of suffrage can be denied by a debasement of suffrage or dilution of the weight of a citizen's vote just as effectively as by wholly prohibiting the free exercise of the franchise....
>
> Legislators represent people, not trees or acres. Legislators are elected by voters, not farms or cities or economic interests. As long as ours is a representative form of government, and our legislatures are those instruments of government elected directly by and directly representative of the people, the right to elect legislators in a free and unimpaired fashion is a bedrock of our political system....
>
> ... The fact that an individual lives here or there is not a legitimate reason for overweighting or diluting the efficacy of his vote. The complexions of societies and civilizations change, often with amazing rapidity. A nation once primarily rural in character becomes predominantly urban. Representation schemes once fair and equitable become archaic and outdated. But the basic principle of representative government remains, and must remain, unchanged—the weight of a citizen's vote cannot be made to depend on where he lives. Population is, of necessity, the starting point for consideration and the controlling criterion for judgment in legislative apportionment controversies. A citizen, a qualified voter, is no more nor no less so because he lives in the city or on the farm. This is the clear and strong command of our Constitution's Equal Protection Clause. This is an essential part of the concept of a government of laws and not men....
>
> The Equal Protection Clause demands no less than substantially equal state legislative representation for all citizens, of all places as well as of all races.

We hold that as a basic constitutional standard, the Equal Protection Clause requires that the seats in both houses of a bicameral state legislature must be apportioned on a population basis. Simply stated, an individual's right to vote for state legislators is unconstitutionally impaired when its weight is in substantial fashion diluted when compared with votes of citizens living in other parts of the State.[28]

The Court recognized the impossibility of attaining mathematical precision in election district populations:

[T]he Equal Protection Clause requires that a State make an honest and good faith effort to construct districts, in both houses of its legislature, as nearly of equal population as is practicable. We realize that it is a practical impossibility to arrange legislative districts so that each one has an identical number of residents, or citizens, or voters. Mathematical exactness or precision is hardly a workable constitutional requirement.[29]

Warren wrote that in applying the equal population principle, the Court, for the present, considered it

expedient not to attempt to spell out any precise constitutional tests. What is marginally permissible in one State may be unsatisfactory in another, depending on the particular circumstances of the case. Developing a body of doctrine on a case-by-case basis appears to us to provide the most satisfactory means of arriving at detailed constitutional requirements in the area of state legislative apportionment.[30]

Justices Clark and Stewart issued concurring opinions, while Justice Harlan again dissented, arguing that the Court's rule had no constitutional basis and that the drafters of the Fourteenth Amendment had not meant to give the federal government authority to intervene in the internal organization of state legislatures. According to Harlan, judicial intervention in reapportionment questions was "profoundly ill advised and constitutionally impermissible." According to him, this series of decisions—*Baker v. Carr, Gray v. Sanders, Wesberry v. Sanders,* and *Reynolds v. Sims*—would weaken the vitality of the political system and "cut deeply into the fabric of our federalism." The Court's ruling gave

"support to a current mistaken view of the Constitution and the constitutional function of this Court. This view, in a nutshell, is that every major social ill in this country can find its cure in some constitutional 'principle,' and that this Court should 'take the lead' in promoting reform when other branches of government fail to act. The Constitution is not a panacea for every blot upon the public welfare, nor should this Court, ordained as a judicial body, be thought of as a haven for reform movements."[31]

HOUSE DISTRICTS: STRICT EQUALITY

Five years elapsed between the Court's admonition in *Wesberry v. Sanders* (1964), urging states to make a good-faith effort to construct congressional districts as nearly of equal population as is practicable, and the Court's next application of constitutional standards to redistricting. In 1967 the Court hinted at the strict stance it would adopt two years later. With two unsigned opinions, the Court sent back to Indiana and Missouri for revision redistricting plans for congressional districts that allowed variations of as much as 20 percent from the average district population.[32] Two years later, Missouri's revised plan returned to the Court for full review. With its decision in *Kirkpatrick v. Preisler* (1969), the Court, 6-3, rejected the plan. It was unacceptable, held the majority, because it allowed a variation of as much as 3.1 percent from perfectly equal population districts.[33]

The Court thus made clear its strict application of one person, one vote to congressional redistricting. Minor deviations from the strict principle of equal population were permissible only when the state provided substantial evidence that the variation was unavoidable. Writing for the majority, Justice Brennan declared that there was no "fixed numerical or percentage population variance small enough to be considered *de minimis*," and he emphasized the need "to satisfy without question the 'as nearly as practicable' standard."[34] Brennan continued:

The whole thrust of the "as nearly as practicable" approach is inconsistent with adoption of fixed numerical standards which excuse population variances without regard to the circumstances of each particular case....

The extent to which equality may practicably be achieved may differ from State to State and from district to district. Unless population variances among congressional districts are shown to have resulted despite such effort, the State must justify each variance, no matter how small....

... [T]o consider a certain range of variances *de minimis* would encourage legislators to strive for that range rather than for equality "as nearly as practicable."... [T]o accept population variances, large or small, in order to create districts with specific interest orientations is antithetical to the basic premise of the constitutional command to provide equal representation for equal numbers of people.[35]

Justice Abe Fortas concurred with the majority but felt that the Court had set a standard of "near-perfection" difficult to achieve:

Whatever might be the merits of insistence on absolute equality if it could be obtained, the majority's pursuit of precision is a search for a will-o'-the-wisp. The fact is that any solution to the apportionment and districting problem is at best an approximation because it is based upon figures which are always to some degree obsolete. No purpose is served by an insistence on precision which is unattainable because of the inherent imprecisions in the population data on which districting must be based.[36]

Justices Harlan, Stewart, and White dissented. White called the majority's ruling "an unduly rigid and unwarranted application of the Equal Protection Clause which will unnecessarily involve the courts in the abrasive task of drawing district lines."[37] Harlan wrote that the decision transformed "a political slogan into a constitutional absolute. Strait indeed is the path of the righteous legislator. Slide rule in hand, he must avoid all thought of county lines, local traditions, politics, history, and economics, so as to achieve the magic formula: one man, one vote."[38]

In another congressional redistricting case decided the same day, the Court in *Wells v. Rockefeller* (1969) rejected New York's redistricting plan as out of line with equal protection standards. The New York plan resulted in districts of nearly equal size within regions of the state but not of equal population throughout the state. That was unacceptable, held the

Court, because the state could not and did not claim that its legislators had made a good-faith effort to achieve precise mathematical equality among its congressional districts. Brennan wrote again for the Court:

To accept a scheme such as New York's would permit groups of districts with defined interest orientations to be overrepresented at the expense of districts with different interest orientations. Equality of population among districts in a sub-state is not a justification for inequality among all the districts in the State.[39]

The effect of this line of rulings from *Baker* in 1962 through *Kirkpatrick* in 1969 was felt in every state. By the end of the 1960s, thirty-nine of the forty-five states that elect more than one member of the House had redrawn their district lines. Because the new districts were based on 1960 census figures, however, population shifts during the decade left the new districts far from equal in population. The redistricting following the 1970 census resulted in substantial progress toward population equality among each state's congressional districts. Three hundred eighty-five of the four hundred thirty-five members of the House of Representatives elected in 1972 were chosen from districts that varied less than 1 percent from their state's average congressional district population.[40]

In 1973 the Court unanimously reaffirmed the strict standard for congressional districts set out in *Kirkpatrick*. In *White v. Weiser* (1973) the Court invalidated Texas's 1971 redistricting plan, which allowed a difference of almost 5 percent between the most populous and the least populous congressional district.[41] Justice White, writing the opinion in *White v. Weiser*, stated that these differences were avoidable. Chief Justice Warren E. Burger and Justices William H. Rehnquist and Lewis F. Powell Jr. concurred, but they added that had they been members of the Court in 1969, they would have dissented from the rule of strict equality set out in *Kirkpatrick*.

Ten years later, the Court again emphasized the strict standard of one person, one vote, but this time the Court was not unanimous. Divided 5-4 in *Karcher v. Daggett* (1983), the Court struck down a New Jersey congressional redistricting plan that was based on the

1980 census. Although the variation between the most populous district and the least populous district was less than 1 percent, the Court held that the difference must be justified as necessary to achieve some important state goal. New Jersey had not provided that justification, held the Court. Justice Brennan wrote the opinion. Chief Justice Burger and Justices White, Powell, and Rehnquist dissented.[42]

In 1992 the Court rejected a challenge by the state of Montana to the allocation of U.S. House members under a 1941 federal law.[43] After the 1990 census and subsequent reapportionment, Montana lost one of its two seats in the House. If it had kept both seats, each district would have been closer to the nationally ideal size of a congressional district than was the reapportioned single district. State officials argued that the statute violated the principle of one person, one vote. In a unanimous decision, the Court said precise equal representation is impossible to achieve because the Constitution guarantees each state at least one representative and prevents House districts from crossing state lines. Furthermore, the Court said, Congress has broad discretion in apportioning representatives.

STATE DISTRICTS: MORE LEEWAY

In *Baker v. Carr* (1962), the Supreme Court ruled for the first time that federal courts could address the problem of unequal distribution of voters among legislative districts. This decision, which rejected the Court's view in *Colegrove v. Green* (1946) that it should stay out of the "political thicket" of redistricting, began the first phase of changes in state legislatures across the nation. *Reynolds v. Sims* (1964) began the second phase in the process. That decision applied the one person, one vote apportionment rule set forth in *Gray v. Sanders* (1963) to both houses of a state legislature.

The third and longest phase was characterized by the Supreme Court's effort to resolve the tension between the goal of equal population, demanded by the Fourteenth Amendment, and state definitions of democratic representation that often took factors other than population into account. In this effort, which carried on for decades following *Reynolds v.*

Sims, the Court indicated a preference for single-member, not multimember, districts for electing state legislators. It continued to insist that reapportionment is primarily a legislative responsibility. Since 1973 the Court has been willing to tolerate more deviation from absolute population equality for state legislative districts than for congressional districts.

Multimember Districts

In *Fortson v. Dorsey* (1965), the Supreme Court rejected a constitutional challenge to Georgia's use of single-member and multimember districts for electing members of the state senate. That system was challenged as intending to minimize the voting strength of certain minority groups. Although the Court held that that allegation had not been proved, Justice Brennan made clear that the Court was not giving blanket approval to multimember districts:

> It might well be that, designedly or otherwise, a multi-member constituency apportionment scheme, under the circumstances of a particular scheme, would operate to minimize or cancel out the voting strength of racial or political elements of the voting population. When this is demonstrated it will be time enough to consider whether the system still passes constitutional muster.[44]

The following year, the Court refused to disturb a similar electoral system for Hawaii's senate, emphasizing that the task of setting up such systems should be left to legislators, not judges.[45] Again in 1971, in a case from Indiana, the Court refused to hold multimember districts unconstitutional, requiring proof that the challenged districts operated to dilute the votes of certain groups or certain persons.[46] Two years later, the Court did find unconstitutional two multimember districts for electing members of the Texas house; it held them impermissible in light of the history of political discrimination against blacks and Mexican Americans residing in those areas.[47]

Population Equality

Beginning with *Swann v. Adams* (1967), the Court defined the outer limits of population variance for state legislative districts. In that case, the Court held unconstitutional Florida's plan that permitted deviations of as much as 30 percent and 40 percent from population equality. Minor variations from equality would be tolerated if there were special justifications for it, held the Court, but it would be left to the state to prove the justification sufficient. Justice White wrote the opinion:

> *Reynolds v. Sims* ... recognized that mathematical exactness is not required in state apportionment plans. *De minimis* variations are unavoidable, but variations of 30 percent among senate districts and 40 percent among house districts can hardly be deemed *de minimis* and none of our cases suggests that differences of this magnitude will be approved without a satisfactory explanation grounded on acceptable state policy.[48]

White said that the Court in *Reynolds* had limited the permissible deviations to "minor variations" brought about by "legitimate considerations incident to the effectuation of a rational state policy ... such ... as the integrity of political subdivisions, the maintenance of compactness and contiguity in legislative districts or the recognition of natural or historical boundary lines."[49]

Justice Harlan, joined by Justice Stewart, dissented, saying that Florida's plan was a rational state policy. Harlan complained that in striking down the plan because it found the relatively minor variations in population among some districts unjustified, the Court "seems to me to stand on its head the usual rule governing this Court's approach to legislative enactments, state as well as federal, which is that they come to us with a wrong presumption of regularity and constitutionality."[50]

After the Court's insistence in *Kirkpatrick v. Preisler* (1969) that congressional districts be precisely equal in population, states doubted the flexibility left to them in drawing state legislative districts not absolutely equal in the number of inhabitants. The Court in *Mahan v. Howell* (1973) reiterated the more relaxed application to state legislative districts of the one person, one vote standard, declaring that "in the implementation of the basic constitutional principle—equality of population among the districts—more flexibility was constitutionally permissible with respect to state legislative reapportionment than in congressional redistricting."[51]

Virginia's legislative reapportionment statute, enacted after the 1970 census, allowed as much as a 16.4 percent deviation from equal population in the districts from which members of the state house were elected. When this was challenged in federal court as too large a disparity, the lower court agreed, citing *Kirkpatrick v. Preisler* and *Wells v. Rockefeller*, both of which concerned districts from which members of the U.S. House of Representatives were elected. By a 5-3 vote, the Supreme Court reversed the lower court, finding that the population variance was not excessive. Justice Powell did not participate in the decision; Justices Brennan, Douglas, and Thurgood Marshall dissented.

Justice Rehnquist, writing for the majority, cited *Reynolds v. Sims* in support of the majority's view that some deviation from equal population was permissible for state legislative districts so long as it was justified by rational state policy. He explained the reason behind the Court's application of different standards to state and congressional redistricting plans:

> [A]lmost invariably, there is a significantly larger number of seats in state legislative bodies to be distributed within a State than congressional seats and ... therefore it may be feasible for a State to use political subdivision lines to a greater extent in establishing state legislative districts while still affording adequate statewide representation.
>
> By contrast, the court in *Wesberry v. Sanders* ... recognized no excuse for the failure to meet the objective of equal representation for equal numbers of people in congressional districting other than the practical impossibility of drawing equal districts with mathematical precision. Thus, whereas population alone has been the sole criterion of constitutionality in congressional redistricting under Art. I ... broader latitude has been afforded the State under the Equal Protection Clause in state legislative redistricting because of the considerations enumerated in *Reynolds v. Sims*.... The dichotomy between the two lines of cases has consistently been maintained....
>
> Application of the "absolute equality" test of *Kirkpatrick* and *Wells* to state legislative redistricting may impair the normal functioning of state and local governments....

We hold that the legislature's plan for apportionment of the House of Delegates may reasonably be said to advance the rational state policy of respecting the boundaries of political subdivisions. The remaining inquiry is whether the population disparities among the districts which have resulted from the pursuit of this plan exceed constitutional limits. We conclude that they do not.[52]

Rehnquist noted, however, that the 16 percent deviation from equality "may well approach tolerable limits."

In dissent, Justice Brennan, joined by Justices Douglas and Marshall, argued for a stricter application of the one person, one vote principle:

The principal question presented for our decision is whether on the facts of this case an asserted state interest in preserving the integrity of county lines can justify the resulting substantial deviations from population equality....

... The Constitution does not permit a State to relegate considerations of equality to secondary status and reserve as the primary goal of apportionment the service of some other state interest.[53]

Several months later, the Court in *Gaffney v. Cummings* (1973) upheld Connecticut's reapportionment of its legislature, despite a maximum deviation of 7.8 percent from mathematical equality in the population of the districts.[54] Justice White wrote for the majority that state legislative reapportionment plans need not place an "unrealistic emphasis on raw population figures" when to do so might "submerge other considerations and itself furnish a ready tool for ignoring factors that in day-to-day operation are important to an acceptable representation and apportionment arrangement."[55] White also warned that strict adherence to arithmetic could frustrate achievement of the goal of fair and effective representation "by making the standards of reapportionment so difficult to satisfy that the reapportionment task is recurringly removed from legislative hands and performed by federal courts."[56] He continued:

We doubt that the Fourteenth Amendment requires repeated displacement of otherwise appropriate state decision making in the name of essentially minor deviations from perfect census population equality that no one, with confidence, can say will deprive any person of fair and effective representation in his state legislature.

That the Court was not deterred by the hazards of the political thicket when it undertook to adjudicate the reapportionment cases does not mean that it should become bogged down in a vast, intractable apportionment slough, particularly when there is little if anything to be accomplished by doing so.[57]

The same day that it announced its decision upholding Connecticut's reapportionment in *Gaffney*, the Court in *White v. Regester* (1973) upheld a similar plan for the Texas legislature, despite a 9.9 percent variation in the populations of the largest and smallest districts. In the same case, however, the Court required revision of the plan to eliminate two multimember districts in areas with histories of discrimination against racial and ethnic minority-group voters.[58] Ten years later, the Court again affirmed its willingness to give states more leeway in drawing their legislative districts than in drawing their congressional district lines. The same day that it struck down, 5-4, New Jersey's congressional redistricting plan with less than 1 percent variation between districts, it upheld, 5-4, a Wyoming law that gave each county one representative in the state's lower house—even though the population variance among the counties was enormous. The Court said that this arrangement was permissible in light of the state interest in giving each county its own representative.[59]

County governments prevailed in two key voting rights cases in the early 1990s primarily because the Court majority did not view the challenged practices as covered by the Voting Rights Act. In the first case, *Presley v. Etowah County Commission* (1992), the Court said changes in the responsibilities of elected county commissioners are not subject to federal approval under the act, even when the changes adversely affect the political power of black county commissioners.[60] In this Alabama case, the Court ruled, 5-4, that only modifications that directly affect voting itself are covered by the act. In the second case, *Holder v. Hall* (1994), which also was decided 5-4, the Court ruled that the size of a governing body—in this case a single county commissioner with executive and legislative authority in Georgia—is not subject to challenge under the Voting Rights Act.[61]

The decision barred a challenge to the unusual governmental structure used in rural Bleckley County, Georgia. Blacks, who made up about 20 percent of the county's population, claimed the single-member commission violated the Voting Rights Act by "diluting" their opportunity to elect blacks to office. In an opinion joined by Chief Justice Rehnquist and Justice Sandra Day O'Connor, Justice Anthony M. Kennedy wrote that "no objective and workable standard" existed to decide how many members a county commission should have. Justice Clarence Thomas wrote a fifty-nine-page concurring opinion that attacked the use of the Voting Rights Act in any legislative redistricting case. He argued that invoking the law to encourage "racially designated districts" had been a "disastrous adventure in judicial policymaking."[62] Justice Antonin Scalia joined Thomas's opinion.

Court-Ordered Redistricting

Since 1975 the Court has applied stricter standards to state redistricting plans drawn by judges than to those drafted by legislators. In the North Dakota case of *Chapman v. Meier* (1975), the Court disapproved a court-ordered plan for the state legislature that allowed up to a 20 percent population variance among districts.[63] Court-ordered redistricting plans should not include multimember districts or allow more than a minimal variation from the goal of equal population, held the Court, unless unique state features or significant state policy justified those characteristics. Justice Harry A. Blackmun spoke for the unanimous Court, stating that "absent particularly pressing features calling for multimember districts, a United States district court should refrain from imposing them upon a State."[64] A 20 percent population variance, he continued, was not permissible "simply because there is no particular racial or political group whose voting power is minimized or cancelled." Moreover, Blackmun stated, neither sparse population nor the geographic division of the state by

the Missouri River, "warrant[ed] departure from population equality."[65]

Reaffirming this position in *Connor v. Finch* (1977), the Court, by a 7-1 vote, overturned a court-ordered reapportionment plan for the Mississippi state legislature because it allowed population variations of up to 16.5 percent in senate districts and of up to 19.3 percent among house districts. The population variance was defended as necessary to preserve the integrity of county lines within legislative districts.[66] The Court found this insufficient in light of the stricter standards set out in *Chapman v. Meier* for court-ordered plans.

In 1993 the justices ruled unanimously that federal courts generally should defer to state courts if both are hearing legal challenges to a state redistricting plan. The justices also ruled 9-0 that states may create "majority-minority" districts even when such districts are not required to remedy previous Voting Rights Act violations.[67]

Backlash against Majority-Minority Districts

In June 1993, the Supreme Court announced a decision that amounted to a sudden U-turn on the issue of black voting rights and minority representation. Until then, the Court and Congress had pressed the states—particularly those in the South—to elect more black representatives to Congress and their state legislatures. The states had done so by redrawing their electoral districts after the 1990 Census to lump black voters into "majority-minority districts." The effort was successful. In the 1992 election, the number of black representatives elected to Congress nearly doubled, to thirty-nine. Alabama, Florida, Louisiana, North Carolina, South Carolina, and Virginia—all states with large black populations—sent their first black representative to Washington in the twentieth century. The celebratory mood among civil rights activists lasted just months, however.

In *Shaw v. Reno* (1993), the Court condemned "racial gerrymandering" as a threat to the Constitution's guarantee of equal treatment for all because it relied on the use of race as a decision-making factor. Justice O'Connor, speaking for a 5-4 majority, stated that the Equal Protection Clause of the Fourteenth Amendment was intended to eliminate the use of race

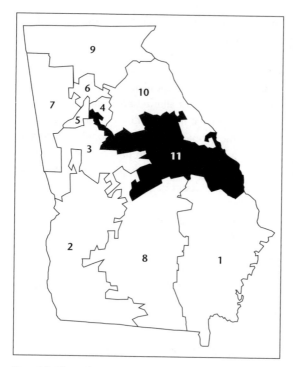

Georgia's Eleventh Congressional District *(above left)* was challenged in *Miller v. Johnson* (1995). Although the district is not generally irregular in shape, note the thin fingerlike extensions in the northwestern, northeastern, and western sections of the district. These were designed to incorporate high concentrations of black voters in Savannah, Augusta, and Atlanta. Pictured *(above right)* are Democratic representatives who protested the Court's decision *(from left to right):* Charles B. Rangel of New York; Cynthia A. McKinney, whose Georgia district was invalidated by the *Miller* decision; and Bobby L. Rush and Luis V. Gutierrez of Illinois.

by the government, not to elevate it as a prime reason for drawing electoral boundaries. At issue in the 1993 case was a district that wound around in a snake-like fashion for 160 miles in central North Carolina, picking up black neighborhoods in four metropolitan areas. The district, about 57 percent black, had been drawn at the urging of the Justice Department, which under the Voting Rights Act's "pre-clearance" procedure was pushing states to maximize the number of black and Hispanic seats created. A group of white voters alleged that North Carolina had set up "a racially discriminatory voting process" and deprived them of the right to vote in "a color-blind" election. A lower court dismissed the complaint. At the time the case came to the justices, the stakes were high: the creation of numerous majority-minority districts had nearly

doubled the number of blacks and Hispanics in Congress in the early 1990s. Critics of such districts, however, contended that the bizarre shapes reflected a racial quota system, violating white voters' rights.

Justice O'Connor acknowledged that racial considerations are legitimately among the myriad of factors that go into redistricting, but she said that in "some exceptional cases" a plan could be "so highly irregular that, on its face, it rationally cannot be understood as anything other than an effort to segregate voters on the basis of race."[68] O'Connor went on to say that "reapportionment is one area in which appearances do matter."

A reapportionment plan that includes in one district individuals who belong to the same race, but who are otherwise widely separated by geographical and political boundaries, and who may have little in common with one another but the color of their skin, bears an uncomfortable resemblance to political apartheid. It reinforces the perception that members of the same racial group—regardless of their education, economic status, or the community in which they live—think alike, share the same political interests, and will prefer the same candidates at the polls. We have rejected such perceptions elsewhere as impermissible racial stereotypes.[69]

O'Connor warned of the "lasting harm to our society" that can be caused by racial classifications.

They reinforce the belief, held by too many for too much of our history, that individuals should be judged by the color of their skin. Racial classifications with respect to voting carry particular dangers. Racial gerrymandering, even for remedial purposes, may balkanize us into competing racial factions; it threatens to carry us further from the goal of a political system in which race no longer matters—a goal that the Fourteenth and Fifteenth Amendments embody, and to which the Nation continues to aspire. It is for these reasons that race-based districting by our state legislatures demands close judicial scrutiny.[70]

Joining O'Connor were Chief Justice Rehnquist and Justices Scalia, Kennedy, and Thomas. Justices White, Blackmun, John Paul Stevens, and David H. Souter dissented. The decision in *Shaw v. Reno* returned the case to a lower court for further hearings to determine whether the reapportionment plan was narrowly tailored to serve a compelling government interest.

In a dissenting opinion, White said the majority never identified the harm that the state's white voters had suffered: "Whites constitute roughly 76 percent of the total population and 79 percent of the voting age population in North Carolina. Yet, under the state's plan, they still constitute a voting majority in ten (or 83 percent) of the 12 congressional districts. Though they might be dissatisfied at the prospect of casting a vote for a losing candidate—a lot shared by many, including a disproportionate number of minority voters—surely they cannot complain of discriminatory treatment."[71]

Blackmun and Stevens joined White's opinion but also wrote biting opinions of their own. Blackmun said it was "ironic" that the Court's ruling came after

North Carolina had elected its first black members of Congress since Reconstruction. Stevens called it "perverse" to permit redistricting plans drawn to provide adequate representation for other groups—mentioning rural voters, union members, Hasidic Jews, Polish Americans, and Republicans—but not for blacks. Souter wrote a separate dissent, contending the majority had no reason for adopting the strict scrutiny test. Instead, he said, the Court should have stuck with previous decisions that required proof of a discriminatory intent and effect to invalidate a district plan because of racial considerations.

The following year the Court returned to the issue of racially drawn districts but ruled narrowly and avoided any reconsideration or enhancement of *Shaw*. In a 7-2 vote, the Court in *Johnson v. DeGrandy* (1994) ruled that the Voting Rights Act does not require legislative districting plans to maximize the number of districts in which minority groups are in the majority. Instead, the Court said that state legislatures usually can satisfy the Voting Rights Act if minority voters form "effective voting majorities in a number of districts roughly proportional to the minority voters' respective shares in the voting-age population." The decision left in place a redistricting plan for the Florida legislature.[72] In *Miller v. Johnson* (1995), the Court revisited *Shaw v. Reno* and expanded its scrutiny for districts drafted on racial lines.[73] The Court said any district in which race was a predominant factor in boundaries deserves strict scrutiny. That meant a larger group of districts would be challenged, not only those that were oddly shaped, as in *Shaw*. The Court said districts in which race is a predominant factor require government to show that its action is narrowly tailored to achieve a compelling interest. The Court ruled, 5-4, that Georgia's creation of a third majority-black congressional district, under pressure from the Justice Department, violated the equal protection rights of white voters in the district. (The boundaries of the central Georgian district were not bizarre or particularly distinctive.) The Justice Department twice had rejected state plans that included only two such majority-minority districts.

When a state follows a Justice Department determination that race-based districting is necessary to comply with the Voting Rights Act, the majority said, federal judges still have an independent obligation to ensure that the state's action is narrowly tailored to achieve a compelling interest. Justice Kennedy, who wrote for the majority, said government should not treat citizens as members of a racial class:

> When the State assigns voters on the basis of race, it engages in the offensive and demeaning assumption that voters of a particular race, because of their race, think alike, share the same political interests, and will prefer the same candidates at the polls. Race-based assignments embody stereotypes that treat individuals as the product of their race, evaluating their thoughts and efforts—their very worth as citizens—according to a criterion barred to the government by history and the Constitution.[74]

Kennedy was joined in *Miller v. Johnson* by the rest of the majority in *Shaw*: Chief Justice Rehnquist and Justices O'Connor, Scalia, and Thomas. Dissenting were Stephen G. Breyer, Ruth Bader Ginsburg, Stevens, and Souter.

By the same 5-4 line-up the following year, the Court invalidated one majority-Hispanic and two majority-black districts in Texas and struck down a majority-black district in North Carolina.[75] Relying on the principles established by earlier rulings and referring to traditional districting practices that until the 1990s had not been invoked in regard to race, Justice O'Connor wrote in the Texas case, "Those practices and our precedents, which acknowledge voters as more than mere racial statistics, play an important role in defining the political identity of the American voter. Our Fourteenth Amendment jurisprudence evinces a commitment to eliminate unnecessary and excessive governmental use and reinforcement of racial stereotypes."[76] In dissent, Justice Stevens countered, "While any racial classification may risk some stereotyping, the risk of true 'discrimination' in this case is extremely tenuous in light of the remedial purpose the classification is intended to achieve and the long history of resistance to giving minorities a full voice in the political process."[77]

The Court's decisions of the 1990s warned state lawmakers that they could not use race as the main factor in redrawing electoral districts after a census, but the justices took some of the edge off that warning

in 2001 by ruling that black voters could be shifted into a reliably Democratic district for partisan political reasons. The Court's decision highlighted a crucial constitutional difference concerning official actions. The Constitution allows the government to make decisions based on politics or partisanship. For example, a Republican president or a Democratic governor would raise no eyebrows if they announced that they would appoint only Republicans or Democrats to their top policymaking posts. The Constitution, however, forbids decision-making based on race, and an elected official would face legal and political trouble if he announced that he would appoint only whites or only blacks to top jobs.

When it comes to drawing electoral districts, politics and race often overlap, the Court noted. If state lawmakers deliberately draw the boundaries to include a precinct that includes mostly black voters who vote reliably for the Democrats, they may do so for political reasons, the justices said. "Race in this case correlates closely with political behavior. The basic question is whether the legislature drew District 12's boundaries because of race rather than because of political behavior," wrote Justice Breyer for the 5-4 majority in *Hunt/Easley v. Cromartie* (2001).[78] Fittingly enough, *Cromartie* involved North Carolina and was the fourth ruling in a decade on the makeup of the Twelfth District, in the central part of the state.

In *Shaw v. Reno* (1993), the Court had cited the district's long, squiggly shape as classic evidence of a racial gerrymandering.[79] After the district was declared unconstitutional in a second ruling, state lawmakers met in a special session in 1997 to redraw the boundaries of their congressional districts, seeking to create one reliably Republican district and one reliably Democratic district in the middle of the state. This type of partisan gerrymandering is permitted under law, despite a 1986 decision that suggested it could be challenged if proof were strong enough.[80] Since blacks registered and voted reliably as Democrats, North Carolina's lawmakers moved mostly black precincts into the Twelfth District. When challenged, they said they did so for political reasons, not racial reasons. After a federal district court struck down this redrawn district, the Court took up the state's appeal and said the matter deserved a full trial. After the trial, the same federal court struck down the district again, prompting the Supreme Court to consider it for the fourth time.

The Twelfth District won the Court's approval on the fourth try. The key vote was cast by Justice O'Connor. She had joined the conservative majority in the series of 5-4 decisions that condemned racial gerrymandering, but a former state legislator herself, she knew the Court had put lawmakers in a difficult spot. Since race closely correlates with voting patterns, lawmakers could be easily accused of making decisions based on race when this correlation was pointed out. Because of O'Connor's switch, state officials again had considerable leeway to draw new districts.

Partisan Gerrymander Withstands Challenge

Although the Supreme Court has rejected legislative districts with lines drawn based on race, it has yet to strike down a redistricting plan because it unduly favored Republicans or Democrats. The Equal Protection Clause forbids the state from making decisions based on race, but it does not forbid public officials from making decisions for political reasons. Nevertheless, "gerrymandering" has been regarded as suspect and unfair for most of the nation's history. The term originated with an 1812 cartoon lampooning Massachusetts governor Elbridge Gerry for drawing a district that resembled a salamander to give his party an advantage in the legislature. With each decade comes a new census, after which political leaders traditionally have redrawn electoral districts to make sure that each district has about the same number of persons. Rare is the party leader in the legislature—Republican or Democrat—who passes up a chance to redraw district boundaries in a way that helps elect more of his or her fellow party members.

In the past, redistricting was considered to be inherently political and beyond the purview of judges. In addition, the Court has been unable to agree on a formula for deciding when a politically inspired redistricting is so unfair as to deprive voters of equal representation in the legislature. In 1986 the Court held for the first time that a political gerrymander could be unconstitutional.[81] Having opened the courtroom door, however, the justices could not decide when a redistricting plan became unconstitutional. In 2004 Democrats challenged a Republican-drawn plan in Pennsylvania. Both parties had received about 50 percent of the statewide vote, but Republicans held twelve of the state's nineteen seats in Congress. The Court rejected the Democrats' claim of partisan gerrymandering. Justices Scalia, Rehnquist, O'Connor, and Thomas said they would overrule *Davis v. Bandemer* and reject all claims of partisan gerrymandering. Since colonial times, politicians have drawn districts to their favor, and there is no legal way to police that, Scalia argued. Justice Kennedy said he would not close the door to such claims, but he agreed that the Pennsylvania plan was constitutional. Justices Stevens, Souter, Ginsburg, and Breyer dissented.[82]

The dispute was revived two years later in a Texas case, but the result was the same. In 2002 elections, the state had relied on a districting plan drawn up a decade earlier by judges that gave Texas Democrats seventeen seats and Republicans fifteen seats in Congress. In statewide voting that year, Republicans won 59 percent of the votes cast to the Democrats' 40 percent. When the GOP took control of both houses of the state legislature, Republicans redrew the districts, and in 2004, they took twenty-one seats in Congress to the Democrats' eleven. The Democrats went to court, arguing that the Republican's mid-decade redistricting was unconstitutional because it was done specifically to give one party an advantage over the other. In *League of Latin American Citizens v. Perry* (2006), the Court disagreed and upheld the Texas districts as constitutional. "There is nothing inherently suspect about a legislature's decision to replace mid-decade a court-ordered plan with one of its own," Kennedy wrote. The justices, however, rejected one south Texas district because it diluted the voting power of Latinos.[83]

BUSH V. GORE: DECIDING WHO BECOMES PRESIDENT

The Supreme Court's willingness to oversee elections and the process of voting grew steadily during the twentieth century. In the 1950s and 1960s, the civil rights

REACTIONS TO *BUSH V. GORE*

"The Court was in a no-win situation. Damage to public respect for the judiciary was inevitable once Gore decided to bring the courts into the process of Presidential selection rather than to accept the machine recount or the decisions of the county canvassing boards. Judges' ire should be directed not at each other, but at him."

> Richard A. Posner, *Breaking the Deadlock: The 2000 Election, the Constitution, and the Courts* (Princeton, N.J.: Princeton University Press, 2001), 176.

"The five justices in the *Bush v. Gore* majority fall uniquely within the category that is most indicative of partisan justice: they made a decision that was consistent with their political preferences but inconsistent with precedent and inconsistent with what would have been predicted given their views in other cases."

> Howard Gillman, *The Votes That Counted: How the Court Decided the 2000 Presidential Election* (Chicago: University of Chicago Press, 2001), 189.

"The majority recognized that their decision would subject them to merciless, politically motivated attacks. But rather than take the easy way out, they courageously accepted their 'unsought responsibility' to require that the Florida court comply with the Constitution.... The blame lies squarely on Florida's supreme court, which violated the Constitution."

> Nelson Lund, "An Act of Courage," *Weekly Standard,* December 25, 2000, 19–20.

"The decision in the Florida election case may be ranked as the single most corrupt decision in Supreme Court history, because it is the only one that I know of where the majority justices decided as they did because of the personal identity and political affiliation of the litigants. That was cheating and a violation of the judicial oath."

> Alan S. Dershowitz, *Supreme Injustice: How the High Court Hijacked Election 2000* (New York: Oxford University Press, 2001), 174.

"The Florida court's decision was so blatantly, one-sidedly pro-Gore that but for the U.S. Supreme Court's intervention, it would have had the foreseeable effect of rigging the recount in the guise of 'counting every vote.' If Gore had pulled ahead of Bush by, say, 300 votes in the further recounts, such phony 'votes' would have provided his entire margin of victory."

> Stuart Taylor Jr., "Why the Florida Recount Was Egregiously One-Sided," *National Journal,* December 23, 2000, 3932–3933.

"The stark reality is that the institution Americans trust the most to protect its freedoms and principles committed one of the biggest and most serious crimes this nation has ever seen—pure and simple, the theft of the presidency.... These five justices are criminals in every true sense of the word."

> Vincent Bugliosi, *The Betrayal of America: How the Supreme Court Undermined the Constitution and Chose Our President* (New York: Thunder's Mouth Press, Nation Books, 2001), 48.

movement in the South highlighted the unfinished business of the Reconstruction era. Despite the Fourteenth Amendment's guarantee of equal protection of the laws and the Fifteenth Amendment's ban on racial discrimination in voting, blacks still were largely excluded from voting in southern states. The Warren Court determined to make these nineteenth-century promises a reality by the second half of the twentieth century. It outlawed the poll taxes and literacy tests used to screen out African American voters, and it struck down local and state gerrymanders driven by racial politics. Further, the newly minted one person, one vote principle had the practical effect of giving voters a

roughly equal voice in the legislature, regardless of whether they lived in the city or the country. The Rehnquist Court in the 1990s invoked the same constitutional principles—equal protection and a prohibition on race discrimination—but did so in a way that limited the chances of blacks to win legislative races. Its justices feared that the new race-driven politics had the potential to divide and "balkanize" the country. The Rehnquist Court declared that states may not configure their electoral districts along racial lines, regardless of whether they seek to aid black or white candidates. The justices handed down seven separate rulings on racial gerrymandering between 1993 and 2001.

Until 2000 the Court had never become involved in a presidential election. The experience of the late twentieth century, however, had laid the groundwork for the belief among lawyers and judges that the U.S. Constitution and the Supreme Court had a role to play in overseeing elections. Regardless, no one could have anticipated that the final and decisive votes in the 2000 election would be cast by the nine justices. Some of what the deadlocked and disputed election revealed came as unpleasant surprises to many. For instance, ordinary voters do not decide who is elected president of the United States. Though Vice President Al Gore received 539,947 more votes than Texas governor George W. Bush, he lost. Gore received 50,996,116 votes, while Bush received 50,456,169. State electors cast the true votes for president, and in all but two states—Maine and Nebraska—the state's electors vote as a bloc for one candidate. The winner of the state's popular vote, even if by a mere handful of votes, receives all of the electors' votes. So, the cliche that "every vote counts" is true, but only in the sense that it can determine who wins a state.

Moreover, the process of counting votes is not as exact as many people might have assumed. Different states and different counties, even neighboring precincts, use varying means of counting votes, and that difference determines the likelihood that a vote will be counted. In Florida, some precincts used paper card ballots that were punched out by the voter and counted by a tabulating machine. Others used more modern computer scanning systems. The older punch card system does not count as high a percentage of ballots as more modern systems, and in a close election such a difference alone can be vital. Justice Stevens pointed out that 3.9 percent of the punch card ballots—that is, nearly 400 out of every 10,000—were not counted as votes. By contrast, Florida's optical scanners failed to count only 1.4 percent of the ballots. Those differences in the ballot-counting systems proved crucial to the outcome in the Florida election, but they did not figure in the Court's rulings.

An even more glaring problem in Florida was the design of the "butterfly" ballot in Palm Beach County. Rather than list all the candidates in a single column,

election officials decided to spread them across two pages that opened to the voter, rather like the wings of a butterfly. The punch holes ran down the middle of the two-page ballot. The result was confusion. Republicans George W. Bush and Richard Cheney were listed first on the left side of the ballot, and underneath them were Democrats Al Gore and Joseph Lieberman. Across the page on the right side was Reform Party candidate Patrick Buchanan, whose punch mark was second in the middle column, between Bush and Gore. Many elderly Democratic voters, seeing Gore and Lieberman listed below Bush, punched the second hole. They had voted unwittingly for the conservative Buchanan. Some tried to correct their mistake by punching a second hole next to Gore's name. Nearly 20,000 ballots in Palm Beach were declared invalid because they displayed a double vote. Buchanan received a surprising 3,407 votes, an outcome that was attributed, even by him, to the confusing ballot. The Palm Beach troubles came to light in the days after the November 7 election, but Gore's lawyers decided against raising the issue in court. Short of rerunning the election in Palm Beach, there was no remedy.

On election night, the television networks first called Gore the winner in Florida but later changed it to Bush. By early the next morning, the networks gave up and said it was too close to call. That is where things stood for more than a month. Elsewhere, Gore had garnered 267 electoral votes, just short of the 271 needed for victory, and Bush had won 246. Florida's twenty-five electoral votes would determine the winner. On election night, Bush had a lead of 1,784 votes in Florida, but his margin decreased to 327 votes after the mandatory machine recount. Gore and his lawyers, convinced a majority of Floridians had voted Democratic, decided to challenge the outcome in court. Bush's advisers said the Texas governor had won narrowly but fairly, and the election was over.

Gore's legal team faced an uphill fight from the start. Florida's election laws were somewhat confused and outmoded. Moreover, they were written to regulate the sixty-seven county election boards, not the state as a whole. Gore could not simply ask for a statewide recount under Florida law. He had to take his fight to the individual counties. One provision of state law held that a losing candidate "shall have the right to protest the returns of the election as being erroneous."[84] "Any candidate whose name appeared on the ballot … may file a written request with the county canvassing board for a manual recount." If a test recount "indicates an error in the vote tabulation which could affect the outcome of the election," county officials should either fix the tabulating machines or manually recount all ballots. This "protest" phase takes place before the county vote totals are sent to the state. Gore's lawyers, relying on these provisions, said the failure of the tabulating machines to count thousands of punch card ballots "could affect the outcome," so they asked for manual recounts in four counties: Miami Dade, Broward, Palm Beach, and Volusia. These were Democratic-leaning counties on the southeast coast. Bush's lawyers went to federal court seeking to block the recounts.

Secretary of State Katherine Harris, an elected Republican, announced two key interpretations of state law that supported Bush's argument that a recount was not called for. First, she said the "inability of voting systems to read an improperly punched punch card ballot is not 'an error in the vote tabulation' and would not trigger the requirement" for a manual recount. Second, she said her office would enforce a one-week deadline for the counties to submit their election tallies. State law says the county's returns must be submitted "on the 7th day following" the election and that "such returns may be ignored" if they are not filed on time.[85] Florida attorney general Robert Butterworth, an elected Democrat, told county officials that he disagreed with Harris's interpretation of the law. If there is evidence of a "discrepancy" between the machine's tabulation of the votes and a hand count of the ballots, a manual recount is required, he said, bolstering Gore's claim.[86]

Fearing that Harris would ignore the recounts, Gore's lawyers appealed to state circuit court judge Terry Lewis, but lost. "I give great deference to the interpretation by the Secretary of the election laws," he said, in addition to concurring that she "may" ignore the manual recounts if they are filed late.[87] Judge

Lewis's ruling did not, however, resolve whether the manual recounts were legal, and several of the counties continued to count their ballots. The Florida Supreme Court stepped in to resolve the legal conflict between the county election boards' duty to manually recount ballots and the secretary of state's refusal to include those votes in the final tally. In the first major ruling of the developing legal dispute, the Florida Supreme Court sided 7-0 with Gore and the county officials, thus rebuking Harris. "[T]he will of the people, not a hyper-technical reliance upon statutory provisions, should be our guiding principle in election cases," the state justices said in *Palm Beach County Canvassing Board v. Harris* (2000).[88] Getting the right result was more important than getting it done on time, they concluded. Their decision, handed down on November 21, extended the time for the counties to recount ballots for five more days, until Sunday, November 26.

The day after the Florida Supreme Court ruled, Washington attorney Theodore B. Olson, representing Bush, asked the U.S. Supreme Court to intervene. Olson had gone to Washington in the early days of the Reagan administration and was well known to the justices on a personal and professional basis. While lawyers for Gore and Bush had been fighting in the Florida state courts, Olson had taken a separate track into the federal courts, believing that the ultimate decision would depend on the Supreme Court. On November 24, to the surprise of most legal analysts, the Court announced that it would hear the Republicans' challenge to the Florida court's decision extending the deadlines. It was not clear what constitutional matters were at issue or whether the extended deadline made much difference. Two days later, on November 26, Harris's office declared Bush the winner of Florida's twenty-five electoral votes. The final tally was 2,912,790 for Bush and 2,912,253 for Gore, a difference of 537 votes.

The second major ruling came on December 4, when the Supreme Court handed down a brief, unanimous, and unsigned opinion that decided very little. The justices "vacated," or set aside, the Florida Supreme Court's ruling, stating that they wished for a clearer explanation of the basis for its decision. State judges are required to interpret laws, but they are not free to change them after the election. The justices could not decide whether the Florida court had interpreted the law or changed it. The Court's ruling on *Bush v. Palm Beach County Canvassing Board* sent the matter back to Florida for clarification.[89]

By then, the fast-moving battle in Florida had entered phase two. Gore's lawyers had challenged the state's decision to certify the winner under a separate provision of state law called a Contest of Election. It states that candidates can contest the result in court if they can point to the "rejection of a number of legal votes sufficient to change or place in doubt the result of the election." A judge who finds merit in the challenge may "provide any relief appropriate under the circumstances."[90] Gore's lawyers noted that more than 9,000 punch card ballots in Miami Dade alone had gone through the tabulating machines, but were not counted as votes. If these ballots contained legal votes, they would certainly "place in doubt" the outcome of the Florida election, they argued. On Friday, December 8, a divided Florida Supreme Court agreed. "This election should be determined by a careful examination of the votes of Florida's citizens," the state court said. "In close elections the necessity for counting all legal votes becomes critical." In a 4-3 vote, it ordered a hand recount of all the remaining untabulated ballots in Florida by December 12, beginning with the 9,000 ballots in Miami Dade. By some estimates, more than 40,000 ballots needed to be tallied by hand.[91]

The December 12 deadline derived from federal law. The disputed presidential election of 1876 between Republican Rutherford B. Hayes and Democrat Samuel Tilden also turned on Florida, which had submitted two slates of electors. In response to this fiasco, Congress passed the Electoral Vote Count Act of 1887 to set rules for resolving such disputes. It says a state's electors "shall meet and give their votes on the first Monday after the second Wednesday in December." In 2000, December 18 was the first Monday after the second Wednesday. Another provision of the law says the state result "shall be conclusive" if all controversy over the selection of the electors is resolved "at least six days before the time fixed for the meeting of electors." In the

fight for Florida, December 12 was therefore the deadline for resolving the controversy.

The Florida Supreme Court, in its concluding sentence, instructed that the recounting teams do their best to determine what the voter intended. "In making the determination of what is a 'legal vote,' the standard to be employed is that established by the Legislature in our Election Code.... [T]he vote shall be counted as a legal vote if there is a clear indication of the intent of the voter." In one sense, the Florida court had ordered a recount that was fairer than the one Gore sought. The Republicans had faulted the use of a "selective" recount in a few Democratic-leaning counties. Taking that criticism into account, the state judges said that all the counties should tabulate their "undervotes," referring to a punch card ballot that did not register as a vote when it went through the tabulating machine. This occurred mostly when the voter had not punched out the paper hole cleanly and instead left a "hanging chad." Sometimes, the voter put only a dent in the card, failing to punch through it. The Florida court's opinion did not establish a standard for whether an indented ballot should be counted as a legal vote. The court also did not order a count of so-called overvotes—ballots with more than one marking—because Gore had not asked for one. For example, if a voter punched out a chad next to Bush-Cheney, and then wrote below "BUSH," the ballot could not be counted because it had two markings, although the voter's intent was entirely clear. Some of the state justices said they would have voted to tally these overvotes as well when the voter's intent was clear. Later analyses showed Gore might have prevailed had all the overvotes been counted.

Time, however, was short. The hurried recount started again on December 9, but at midday it was halted by a surprise order from the U.S. Supreme Court. In a 5-4 vote, the justices had granted an emergency motion filed by Olson to block the Florida court's ruling from taking effect. Under the Court's rules, such emergency stay orders are hard to obtain and rarely granted. Ordinarily, the Supreme Court reviews cases that are finally decided by lower courts. It avoids intervening in pending matters. To obtain an emergency order that stays a lower court decision the appealing party must show he will suffer "an irreparable harm" unless the court intervenes. Beyond that, he must assert convincingly that five justices—a majority—are likely to rule for him and reverse the lower court. For lawyers, showing an "irreparable harm" to their client is quite difficult. One notable exception is a last-minute appeal in a death penalty case.

In Bush's motion, Olson said the Texas governor would suffer an irreparable harm if the Floridians conducted a "standardless" recount. Five members of the Court agreed: Chief Justice Rehnquist, and Justices O'Connor, Scalia, Kennedy, and Thomas. "It suffices to say that … a majority of the Court … believe that the petitioner [Bush] has a substantial probability of success," Scalia said in a statement defending the stay. "The counting of votes that are of questionable legality does in my view threaten irreparable harm to [Bush] and to the country, by casting a cloud upon what he claims to be the legitimacy of his election." Justice Stevens spoke for the four dissenters. "Counting every legally cast vote cannot constitute irreparable harm. On the other hand, there is a danger that a stay may cause irreparable harm to the respondents [Gore and Lieberman]—and, more importantly, the public at large.… Preventing the recount from being completed will inevitably cast a cloud on the legitimacy of the election."[92]

The stay order signaled the end of the fight for Florida and a final victory for George W. Bush. It would have been highly responsible for them to stop the vote recount for several days while they pondered the matter and then allow the counting to continue once the time had expired. Nonetheless, lawyers hastily filed new briefs on Sunday, and on Monday morning, the Court heard an oral argument that was later broadcast nationwide via audiotape. The Florida Supreme Court routinely broadcast its sessions on television and won plaudits for doing so. While their rulings did not persuade the justices in Washington, the Sunshine State judges nudged the Court toward opening its public arguments to a wider audience. During the oral argument, the justices who voted to grant the stay—notably Justices Kennedy and O'Connor—seemed to struggle for the right legal reason for Bush to prevail,

but they left no doubt the Texas governor would prevail.

On December 12, the Court handed out copies of its decision in *Bush v. Gore* (2000). It was an unsigned opinion and labeled a "per curiam," or opinion of the court. This usually refers to a unanimous and uncontroversial ruling, but this decision was anything but. Attached were four separate dissents by Justices Breyer, Ginsburg, Souter, and Stevens. In addition, a concurring opinion written by Chief Rehnquist was joined by Justices Scalia and Thomas. That meant, by a process of deduction, that the authors of the decisive opinion were the two unnamed members of the Court: Justices Kennedy and O'Connor. During the oral argument, Kennedy in particular spoke about the equal protection problem, and he is credited as being the opinion's primary author.

Bush's appeal had raised two questions: whether the Florida courts had violated federal election law by establishing "new standards" for resolving the disputed election and whether the "use of standardless manual recounts violates the Equal Protection and Due Process Clauses" of the Fourteenth Amendment. "[W]e find a violation of the Equal Protection Clause," the Court said.[93] "The individual citizen has no federal constitutional right to vote for electors for the President of the United States," the Court's opinion said, unless and until the state legislature chooses popular election as the means of choosing its electors. Once it has settled on elections, however, the state must give "equal weight … to each vote and equal dignity … to each voter.… The State may not, by later arbitrary and disparate treatment, value one person's vote over that of another."[94] As precedent, the opinion cited the Warren Court rulings that abolished poll taxes and set the "one person, one vote" rule for drawing electoral districts.

Of course, both sides claimed they were protecting the right to vote, as the Court noted. The Democrats said the recounts were needed to assure that every voter's ballot was counted. The Republicans said a flawed recount based on hazy and subjective rules was fundamentally unfair and unreliable. The Court adopted the second argument. "The recount mechanisms … do not satisfy the minimum requirement for non-arbitrary treatment of voters necessary to secure the fundamental right" to vote, the opinion said.[95] Since the case had developed quickly, the justices had only limited information on how the recounts were being conducted. Republican officials complained that some recount teams were counting ballots that were only dented, while others counted them only when the hole was punched through. This difference did not necessarily amount to discrimination against Bush and in favor of Gore, but the Court concluded it did amount to "unequal evaluation of ballots."[96]

The opinion stopped short of setting a clear, constitutional rule. "Our consideration is limited to the present circumstances, for the problem of equal protection in election processes generally presents many complexities," it said.[97] The unsigned opinion also stated, "Seven Justices of the Court agreed that there are constitutional problems with the recount ordered by the Florida Supreme Court that demand a remedy. The only disagreement is as to remedy."[98] This statement fueled a short-lived debate over whether the outcome amounted to a 7-2 decision or a 5-4 ruling. While Justices Souter and Breyer said they believed that the recount raised potential equal protection problems, they dissented in the order that stopped it and dissented again from the final ruling that ended the recount. Both said they favored completing the recount, but with the use of a clear standard for deciding which ballots were legal votes.

Without question, however, the Court's ruling ensured Bush's victory. It said December 12 was indeed the deadline for recounting votes in Florida, and by handing down the opinion at 10 p.m. on December 12, the possibility for any further action in Florida was foreclosed. "That date is upon us, and there is no recount procedure in place ... that comports with minimal constitutional standards," the Court concluded.[99] Chief Justice Rehnquist had drafted a version of the opinion, but it did not attract the votes of Kennedy and O'Connor, so it was issued as a concurring opinion. Rehnquist said he would have reversed the Florida court's ruling on the ground that the state judges "departed" from the state's election law.

"We deal here not with an ordinary election, but with an election for the President of the United States," he began. Normally, the justices defer to a state judge's reading of state law, he said, but presidential elections are different. Article II of the Constitution says that states shall appoint their electors "in such Manner as the Legislature thereof may direct," and Rehnquist said this provision demands that the state's laws be followed precisely. In this case, we "hold that the Florida Supreme Court's interpretation of the Florida election laws impermissibly distorted them beyond what a fair reading required, in violation of Article II."[100] As an example of the Florida court's mistaken interpretations, the chief justice cited its order requiring the recount of "improperly marked" ballots. "No reasonable person would call it an 'error in the vote tabulation' when electronic or electromechanical equipment performs precisely in the manner designed and fails to count the ballots that are not marked in the manner" required, he said.[101] Justices Scalia and Thomas said they agreed with Rehnquist's opinion.

The four dissenters said the Court had no business blocking the state's effort to count all of its votes in a very close election. "The federal questions that ultimately emerged in this case are not substantial," said Justice Stevens, who lives much of the year in Ft. Lauderdale. By intervening, "the majority effectively orders the disenfranchisement of an unknown number of voters whose ballots reveal their intent—and are therefore legal votes under state law—but were for some reason rejected by the ballot-counting machines."[102] He characterized the Court's intervention as unwise and partisan and an affront to the state judges in Florida. "Although we may never know with complete certainty the identity of the winner of this year's Presidential election, the identity of the loser is perfectly clear. It is the Nation's confidence in the judge as an impartial guardian of the rule of law."[103]

Justice Ginsburg faulted the conservative majority for turning its back on its customary stand of deferring to the states. "The extraordinary setting of this case has obscured the ordinary principle that dictates its proper resolution: Federal courts defer to state high courts' interpretations of their state's own law," she said. "Were the other members of this Court as mindful as they generally are of our system of dual sovereignty, they would affirm the judgment of the Florida Supreme Court."[104] Justice Souter, an appointee of the first president Bush, said the Court should not have taken up either of the Republican appeals nor stopped the statewide recount. The "resolution by the majority is another erroneous decision," he wrote. He agreed, however, that it was wrong to continue a recount where the standards are "wholly arbitrary" and differ substantially from county to county. Souter said the case should be sent back to the Florida court to "establish uniform standards" for counting the remaining ballots.[105]

Justice Breyer also left no doubt as to his disagreement. "The Court was wrong to take this case. It was wrong to grant a stay," he began. "By halting the manual recount, and thus ensuring that the uncounted legal votes will not be counted under any standard, this Court … harms the very fairness interests the Court is attempting to protect."[106] Moreover, Breyer pointed out that the Twelfth Amendment and the Electoral Vote Count Act state that state courts and Congress are charged with resolving disputes in presidential elections. The law "nowhere provides for involvement by the United States Supreme Court," he said. If ever there was a case for "judicial restraint," this

was it, he added. "In this highly politicized matter, the appearance of a split decision runs the risk of undermining the public's confidence in the Court itself.... [W]e do risk a self-inflicted wound—a wound that may harm not just the Court, but the Nation," he concluded.[107]

The Court's ruling succeeded in bringing a swift and decisive end to a seemingly endless election battle. Less than twenty-four hours after the decision, Gore conceded defeat. "While I strongly disagree with the Court's decision, I accept it," he said in a televised address. The Court had never previously decided such an intensely political case. Reactions to the ruling divided along ideological lines. Liberals charged the Court with hypocrisy. The conservative justices, who usually tout states' rights and shun those who claim their rights to equal protection have been violated, had reversed a state court's decision based on the Republicans' claims of a novel equal protection violation. Conservatives praised the Court for standing in the way of activist, liberal state judges who were determined to reverse the Florida election result and hand the White House to the Democrats. The public's reaction appeared to be muted. Opinion polls taken after *Bush v. Gore* showed the Court retaining a high level of public confidence.

Freedom of Political Association

The freedom to espouse any political belief and to associate with others sharing that belief is, in the words of the modern Supreme Court, "the core of those activities protected by the First Amendment."[1] Judicial recognition of this freedom is new, exclusively a development of the mid-twentieth century. A corollary of the First Amendment freedoms of speech and belief, the right of political association was first expounded upon by the Court after World War I, when the Court attempted to reconcile the government's need to protect itself against internal subversion with the First Amendment protection for free speech. This freedom is not absolute. The Court has condoned its curtailment, especially during times of perceived or real national peril, when the line between freedom of political association and treasonable conspiracy blurs. The Court labored to strike the proper balance in the cases involving cold war–era anti-subversive programs, which evolved into the longest series of rulings on this freedom. Traced decision by decision, the constitutional freedom is ill defined, but by the end of the 1960s, the Court was firm on one point: guilt by association is impermissible. A person must not be found guilty simply because he or she belongs to a particular group. A government-imposed penalty is proper only after it is shown that the association involves active, knowing participation in efforts to bring about violent revolution.

The nation's first internal security laws were enacted within the same decade as the Bill of Rights. The Alien and Sedition Acts of 1798 set severe penalties for persons found guilty of criticizing the government or government officials. Convictions under these laws—some obtained before Supreme Court justices sitting as circuit judges—aroused public indignation, but the laws expired before they were ever challenged before the Supreme Court. During the Civil War,

military officials imposed restrictions on individual rights and expression, but again, the constitutionality of those actions was never questioned before the Court. The Supreme Court first found itself face to face with the question of permissible government restrictions upon political belief and expression in 1919. During World War I, Congress passed the Espionage Act of 1917 and the Sedition Act of 1918 to penalize persons who spoke or published statements with the intent of interfering with the nation's military success. In addition, persons who brought the flag, the Constitution, the government, or the military uniform into disrepute, or who promoted the cause of the enemy, could be charged under the act. Hundreds of persons were convicted.

In a series of cases decided after the end of the war, the Court upheld these laws but began to formulate tests to gauge when such restriction of speech and expression was permissible and when it was not.[2] Concern about the threat of communism intensified after World War II, sparking the passage of federal laws intended to protect the nation against communist subversion. These laws restricted the exercise—by persons holding certain views—of the freedom of political belief, expression, and association. In cases arising under these laws, the modern Court attempted to reconcile the demands of political freedom with the requirements of internal security.

The famous if often-disregarded "clear and present danger" test for determining when official restriction or punishment may be imposed upon the exercise of the right to speak was set out by the Court in *Schenck v. United States* (1919). Charles Schenck was convicted under the Espionage Act for mailing circulars urging men eligible for the military draft to resist it and describing the draft as unconstitutional despotism. In upholding Schenck's conviction—finding that his

In this 1918 cartoon Uncle Sam rounds up enemies of the United States. During World War I, Congress passed an amendment to the Espionage Act of 1917, imposing severe penalties on speech that interfered with the prosecution of the war. The Court ruled in *Schenck v. United States* (1919) that Schenck's words raised a "clear and present danger" and were not protected by the First Amendment.

actions constituted a clear and present threat that would result in illegal action—the Court set out the new standard. Writing for the unanimous Court, Justice Oliver Wendell Holmes Jr. declared,

> The most stringent protection of free speech would not protect a man in falsely shouting fire in a theatre and causing a panic. It does not even protect a man from an injunction against uttering words that may have all the effect of force.... The question in every case is whether the words used are used in such circumstances and are of such a nature as to create a clear and present danger that they will bring about the substantive evils that Congress has a right to prevent.[3]

Later in 1919—and again in 1920—Holmes dissented with Justice Louis D. Brandeis when the Court upheld three more convictions under the World War I espionage and sedition acts. In these cases, to the dismay of Holmes and Brandeis, the Court relaxed its standard for government curtailment of free expression of political ideas. In *Schaefer v. United States* (1920), the majority espoused the view that the "bad tendency" of an individual's speech or action, rather than the actual threat of danger, was sufficient to justify punishment. The new test, stated the majority, did not require that an utterance's "effect or the persons affected ... be shown.... The tendency of the articles and their efficacy were enough for offense."[4] In dissent, Justice Brandeis opposed this "bad tendency" test because it eliminated consideration of the speaker's intent and because it ignored the relevance of the likelihood that danger would result. The clear and present danger test, he said, "is a rule of reason. Correctly applied, it will preserve the right of free speech both from suppression by tyrannous majorities and from abuse by irresponsible, fanatical minorities."[5]

The 1920s were a period of intolerance in the United States. Many states, following the example of Congress, passed laws penalizing persons for expressing or acting upon views of political truth that were perceived as subversive. In 1925 and again in 1927 the Court upheld convictions of persons holding such views. In both instances, Holmes and Brandeis disagreed with the majority's view that the clear and present danger test had no application at all to laws that punished advocacy of the forcible overthrow of government. In *Gitlow v. New York* (1925), the Court upheld the conviction of Benjamin Gitlow, a leader of the left wing of the Socialist Party, for violating provisions of the New York criminal anarchy statute by publishing thousands of copies of a manifesto setting out his beliefs. In this case the Court for the first time assumed that the First Amendment freedoms of speech and the press—protected from abridgment by Congress—were also among the fundamental personal liberties protected by the Fourteenth Amendment against impairment by the states. The Court made clear, however, that the First Amendment "does not confer an absolute right to speak or publish, without responsibility, whatever one may choose."[6]

Challenges to state laws alleged to restrict the freedom of speech or the press must overcome a strong presumption in favor of the constitutionality of state legislation, the Court said. If the state thought the statute necessary, and the Court agreed, then the only other question was whether the language used or the action punished was prohibited by the state law. In the late 1920s, the Court upheld the conviction of Anita Whitney—who happened to be the niece of former Supreme Court justice Stephen J. Field—for violating the California Syndicalism Act of 1919 by her part in organizing the California Communist Labor Party. Whitney had participated in the convention establishing the state party and was an alternate member of its executive committee. With the decision in *Whitney v. California* (1927), the majority of the Court appeared to allow persons to be punished simply for associating with groups that espoused potentially illegal acts. Justices Holmes and Brandeis agreed in upholding the conviction, because the clear and present danger test had not been used as part of Whitney's defense at trial, but in a concurring opinion that often read like a dissent, Brandeis challenged laws that exalted order over liberty:

> Those who won our independence by revolution were not cowards. They did not fear political change. They did not exalt order at the cost of liberty. To courageous, self-reliant men, with confidence in the power of free and fearless reasoning applied through the processes of popular government, no danger flowing from speech can be deemed clear and present, unless the incidence of the evil apprehended is so imminent that it may befall before there is opportunity for full discussion. If there be time to expose through discussion the falsehood and fallacies, to avert the evil by the processes of education, the remedy to be applied is more speech, not enforced silence. Only an emergency can justify repression. Such must be the rule if authority is to be reconciled with freedom.[7]

During the 1930s, the Supreme Court, now under the leadership of Chief Justice Charles Evans Hughes, extended *Gitlow*'s protection of First Amendment freedoms against state action, while it repudiated the guilt-by-association rule it seemed to adopt in *Whitney*. In 1931 the Court reversed the conviction of Yetta Stromberg, a supervisor in a youth camp operated by the Young Communist League in California, for violating the state law prohibiting display of a red flag as an "emblem of opposition to organized government." Such a flag was raised by Stromberg each morning at the camp for a flag-salute ceremony. The Court ignored Stromberg's Communist Party affiliation in holding the state law invalid under the due process guarantee of the Fourteenth Amendment.[8] Six years later, in 1937, the Court unanimously overturned the conviction of Dirk DeJonge for violating Oregon's criminal syndicalism law after he presided over a public meeting called by the Communist Party to protest police brutality in a longshoremen's strike. That same year, the Court reversed the conviction of a communist organizer in Georgia for attempting to recruit members and distributing literature about the party.[9]

In each of those cases, the Court focused upon the actions of the individual, emphasizing personal guilt rather than guilt by association. In the Court's opinion in *DeJonge v. Oregon*, Chief Justice Hughes wrote that the state could not punish a person making a lawful speech simply because the speech was sponsored by an allegedly "subversive" organization. Hughes's opinion made no reference to the clear and present danger test. He assumed that incitement to violence would not be protected by the First Amendment. The unanimous Court opinion affirmed the political value of the rights of free speech and association:

> The greater the importance of safeguarding the community from incitements to the overthrow of our institutions by force and violence, the more imperative is the need to preserve inviolate the constitutional rights of free speech, free press and free assembly in order to maintain the opportunity for free political discussion, to the end that government may be responsive to the will of the people and that changes, if desired, may be obtained by peaceful means. Therein lies the security of the Republic, the very foundation of constitutional government.... The question, if the rights of free speech and peaceable assembly are to be preserved, is not as to the auspices under which the meeting is held but as to its purpose; not as to the relations of the speakers, but whether their utterances transcend the bounds of the freedom of speech.[10]

COMMUNISM AND COLD WAR

World communism posed a double-edged threat to the survival of the U.S. system. Militarily, the spread of communist-dominated regimes across the globe was thought to pose the most serious external challenge the West had ever faced. The appeal of communist ideology to some people in the United States resulted in enactment of laws intended to curtail the advocacy of those ideas and penalize those who espoused them. Some observers of this reaction wondered if legislators at home would strangle the very freedoms that military and diplomatic personnel abroad were working to preserve. Justice William O. Douglas expressed this concern in 1951:

> In days of great tension when feelings run high, it is a temptation to take shortcuts by borrowing from the totalitarian techniques of our opponents. But when we do, we set in motion a subversive influence of our own design that destroys us from within.[11]

The three major federal laws enacted to discourage the growth of communist-affiliated organizations in the United States were the Smith Act of 1940, the McCarran Act of 1950, and the Communist Control Act of 1954. The Smith Act made it a crime to advocate the violent overthrow of the government or to organize or to belong to any group advocating such revolutionary action. The McCarran Act required all communist-action groups or communist-front groups to register with the Justice Department and disclose their membership lists. The act further penalized members of such groups by prohibiting them from holding government or defense-related jobs or using U.S. passports. The Communist Control Act declared that the Communist Party was an instrument of treasonable conspiracy against the U.S. government and thus deprived of all the rights and privileges of political parties and legal entities in the United States.

Debate over the constitutionality of these laws—and the loyalty-security programs and oath requirements that accompanied them—resounded frequently in the nation's courtrooms, including that of the Supreme Court. Views of communism differed. Was it

a valid political movement, espousal of which and association with which was protected by the First Amendment or was it a treasonable conspiracy, which the Constitution viewed as punishable?[12] During the first decade of the cold war, 1947 to 1957, the Supreme Court—reflecting the mood of the nation—generally upheld the provisions and application of the anticommunism laws. In so doing, the majority avoided ruling directly on the challenge that they impermissibly abridged the First Amendment guarantee of freedom of political association. Beginning in 1957, as the cold war thawed, the Court began to restrict their application, finding them often used in too sweeping a fashion. The Constitution specifies that no one shall be found guilty of treason without evidence of overt treasonous acts. The Court began to insist that these internal security laws be used only to penalize persons who knowingly and actively sought to promote communist revolution in the United States, not simply to punish persons who had at some time found other social and economic or philosophical tenets of the movement attractive.

In the decade from 1957 through 1967, a libertarian majority coalesced on the Court under Chief Justice Earl Warren and forced the government to cease prosecuting persons under the Smith Act, to abandon its effort to force registration of the Communist Party and other communist-affiliated groups, and to cease denying passports and defense industry jobs to members of such groups. Although the Court had earlier condoned the use of loyalty oaths for state and local employees, it now struck down many of them as improper restrictions upon the freedom to believe and to speak freely and to associate with others of like belief. Article VI of the Constitution requires state and federal officeholders to swear to uphold the Constitution of the United States. Congress and state legislatures during the cold war era in particular imposed additional oaths deemed appropriate as a condition of public office.

The Smith Act

The Alien Registration Act of 1940—also known as the Smith Act, after its sponsor, Rep. Howard Smith,

ALIENS AND COMMUNIST PARTY MEMBERSHIP

Congress, by virtue of its control over immigration and naturalization, has virtually unlimited power to regulate the activities of aliens in the United States and to deport those it finds undesirable. In several decisions, the modern Supreme Court has, however, curtailed this power when it was used to penalize aliens for membership in the Communist Party. Party membership alone—without evidence of the member's advocacy of forcible or violent overthrow of the government—was insufficient reason to revoke an individual's naturalization, the Court ruled in *Schneiderman v. United States* (1943). By a 6-3 vote, the Court reversed the government's decision to revoke naturalization papers granted to William Schneiderman in 1927 when he was a member of the Communist Party.[1]

The Alien Registration Act of 1940 had provided for deportation of aliens who were members of the party. In 1952 the Court upheld the application of this provision even to aliens whose membership had terminated before the 1940 law took effect.[2] Congress included similar provisions in the Internal Security Act of 1950 and the Immigration and Nationality Act of 1952.

In 1954 the Court upheld deportation of a resident alien because of his Communist Party membership, even though it was not clear that he was aware of the party's advocacy of the violent overthrow of the government. Congress, said the Court, had virtually unrestricted power to deport aliens.[3] In the 1950s and 1960s, however, the Warren Court applied stricter standards to similar deportation decisions. In *Rowoldt v. Perfetto* (1957) and *Gastelum-Quinones v. Kennedy* (1963), the Court required the government to prove not only that the alien was a member of the party but also that he understood the political implications of that membership before it might permissibly order him to leave the country.[4] Writing for the Court in *Gastelum-Quinones*, Justice Arthur J. Goldberg explained:

> [T]here is a great practical and legal difference between those who firmly attach themselves to the Communist Party being aware of all of the aims and purposes attributed to it, and those who temporarily join the Party, knowing nothing of its international relationships and believing it to be a group solely trying to remedy unsatisfactory social or economic conditions, carry out trade-union objectives, eliminate racial discrimination, combat unemployment, or alleviate distress and poverty.[5]

1. *Schneiderman v. United States*, 320 U.S. 118 (1943).

2. *Harisiades v. Shaughnessy*, 342 U.S. 580 (1952).

3. *Galvan v. Press*, 347 U.S. 522 (1954).

4. *Rowoldt v. Perfetto*, 355 U.S. 115 (1957); *Gastelum-Quinones v. Kennedy*, 374 U.S. 469 (1963).

5. *Gastelum-Quinones v. Kennedy*, 374 U.S. 469 at 473 (1963).

D-Va.—required all aliens living in the United States to register with the government; any alien found to have past ties to "subversive organizations" could be deported. *(See box, Aliens and Communist Party Membership)* Title I of the act affected citizens as well as aliens. Intended to thwart communist activity in the United States, the measure was the nation's first peacetime sedition law since the infamous Sedition Act of 1798. Yet the Smith Act attracted little attention at the time of its passage in 1940. Thomas I. Emerson observes that "enactment of the bill reflected not so much a deliberate national determination that the measure was necessary to protect internal security as an unwillingness of members of Congress to vote against legislation directed at the Communist Party."[13]

The Smith Act made it a crime "to knowingly or willfully advocate, abet, advise, or teach the duty, necessity, desirability, or propriety of overthrowing or destroying any government in the United States by force or violence." It forbade the publication or display of printed matter teaching or advocating forcible overthrow of the government, and in language directly curtailing the freedom of association, made it a crime to organize any group teaching, advocating, or encouraging the overthrow or destruction of government by force. It also was a crime to become a "knowing" member of any organization or group dedicated to the violent overthrow of any government in the United States.

Dennis v. United States (1951)

In 1948 the government indicted eleven leaders of the Communist Party in the United States, charging them with violating the Smith Act by conspiring to form groups teaching the overthrow of the government. The

Politics and the Right to a Passport

Cold war legislation forbade any member of the Communist Party to apply for a U.S. passport, but that was not the first time this privilege had been denied to people who seemed ideologically out of sync with prevailing U.S. beliefs or politics. The Passport Act of 1926, the basis for modern passport administration, authorized the State Department to deny travel documents to applicants with criminal records and to noncitizens.

From 1917 until 1931, passports generally were refused to members of the American Communist Party. During the cold war, the State Department resumed the practice. The 1950 McCarran Act forbade members of any registered communist political action or front organization to apply for or use a U.S. passport. Although the registration provisions were resisted, the State Department nevertheless denied passports to a number of individuals thought to be communists, acting under its own rules and the discretion granted it by the Immigration and Nationality Act of 1952.

FREEDOM TO TRAVEL

In *Kent v. Dulles* (1958), the Supreme Court held that Congress had not authorized the secretary of state to deny passports to persons because of their beliefs or associations. Furthermore, held the Court, the right to travel is an aspect of a citizen's protected personal liberty of which he cannot be deprived without due process. The Court, 5-4, thus reversed the State Department's denial of a passport to artist Rockwell Kent, who refused to submit an affidavit disclaiming any affiliation with communist groups. Justice William O. Douglas wrote,

> [W]e are dealing here with citizens who have neither been accused of crimes or found guilty. They are being denied their freedom of movement solely because of their refusal to be subjected to inquiry into their beliefs and associations. They do not seek to escape the law nor to violate it. They may or may not be Communists. But assuming they are, the only law which Congress has passed expressly curtailing the movement of Communists across our borders has not yet become effective. It would therefore be strange to infer that pending the effectiveness of that law, the Secretary has been silently granted by Congress the larger, the more pervasive power to curtail in his discretion the free movement of citizens in order to satisfy himself about their beliefs or associations.[1]

The dissenting justices—Harold H. Burton, John Marshall Harlan, Charles E. Whittaker, and Tom C. Clark—found the denial proper.

In the wake of *Kent,* the Eisenhower administration asked Congress to authorize the State Department to deny passports to persons with Communist Party affiliations. Congress did not do so.[2] The Court's decision in *Communist Party v. Subversive Activities Control Board* (1961) upheld the order to the party to register under the McCarran Act and made operative the provisions of the act denying passports to party members. *(See details of this case, pp. 230–232.)*

The State Department revoked the passports of several leading communists, including Herbert Aptheker, one of the party's leading intellectuals. In *Aptheker v. Secretary of State* (1964), the Court in a 6-3 vote declared the passport denial provisions of the McCarran Act as unconstitutional infringements of the freedom to travel. Writing for the majority, Justice Arthur J. Goldberg explained that the law violated the guarantee of due process by failing to distinguish between knowing and unknowing party membership and by arbitrarily excluding any consideration of the purpose of the proposed travel.[3] Justices Harlan, Clark, and Byron R. White dissented.

The following year, the Court in *Zemel v. Rusk* upheld the power of the State Department to impose geographic area limitations on the use of U.S. passports,[4] but subsequent decisions made clear that such limitations, forbidding Americans to travel to certain countries, although valid were unenforceable.[5]

FREEDOM TO TRAVEL DENIED

The Court in *Haig v. Agee* (1981) upheld the power of the secretary of state to revoke a citizen's passport. Philip Agee was not a communist but a former Central Intelligence Agency official who had become disillusioned with the agency. He had worked as an undercover agent, and upon leaving the agency, undertook to expose CIA agents abroad in order to drive them out of the countries where they were working. Secretary of State Alexander Haig revoked Agee's passport, stating that his activities caused serious damage to national security. Agee challenged the revocation as a violation of his First Amendment right to criticize the government, but the Court decided against him, 7-2.[6]

---

1. *Kent v. Dulles,* 357 U.S. 117 at 130 (1958).

2. *Congress and the Nation* (Washington, D.C.: Congressional Quarterly, 1965), 1:1650.

3. *Aptheker v. Secretary of State,* 378 U.S. 500 (1964).

4. *Zemel v. Rusk,* 381 U.S. 1 (1965).

5. *United States v. Laub,* 385 U.S. 475 (1967); *Travis v. United States,* 385 U.S. 491 (1967).

6. *Haig v. Agee,* 453 U.S. 280 (1981).

Eugene Dennis, general secretary of the Communist Party, boards the bus at the New York City Federal House of Detention. Eleven leaders of the party were arrested and jailed in 1951 after Congress passed the Smith Act, which made it illegal to belong to an organization designated as subversive. In *Dennis v. United States* (1951), the Court upheld the act, asserting that the threat of communism justified a restriction on the rights of free expression.

eleven were convicted after a long and sensational trial. In upholding the convictions, Judge Learned Hand spoke for the federal court of appeals and used a "sliding scale" rule for applying the clear and present danger test in sedition cases: "In each case [courts] must ask whether the gravity of the 'evil,' discounted by its improbability, justifies such invasion of free speech as is necessary to avoid the danger."[14] In 1951 the Supreme Court by a vote of 6–2 upheld the convictions and the constitutionality of the Smith Act. Justice Tom C. Clark did not take part in the Court's decision in *Dennis v. United States*. The eight voting members disagreed

widely about the proper way to measure the validity of sedition laws against the restraints they placed on First Amendment freedoms of expression and association.[15]

Chief Justice Fred M. Vinson, speaking for Justices Stanley F. Reed, Harold H. Burton, and Sherman Minton, gave lip service to *Schenck*'s clear and present danger test but seemed in fact to apply the "sliding scale" rule. The Smith Act, wrote Vinson, did not allow persons to be punished simply for peaceful study and discussion of revolutionary concepts: "Congress did not intend to eradicate the free discussion of political theories, to destroy the traditional rights of Americans to discuss and evaluate ideas without fear of governmental sanction."[16] He went on to write, however,

Overthrow of the Government by force and violence is certainly a substantial enough interest for the Government to limit speech. Indeed, this is the ultimate value of any society, for if a society cannot protect its very structure from armed internal attack, it must follow that no subordinate value can be protected. If, then, this interest may be protected, the literal problem which is presented is what has been meant by the use of the phrase "clear and present danger" of the utterances bringing about the evil within the power of Congress to punish.

Obviously, the words cannot mean that before the Government may act, it must wait until the putsch is about to be executed, the plans have been laid and the signal is awaited. If Government is aware that a group aiming at its overthrow is attempting to indoctrinate its members and to commit them to a course whereby they will strike when the leaders feel the circumstances permit, action by the Government is required.... Certainly an attempt to overthrow the Government by force, even though doomed from the outset because of inadequate numbers or power of the revolutionists is a sufficient evil for Congress to prevent....

The damage which such attempts create both physically and politically to a nation makes it impossible to measure the validity in terms of the probability of success....

The formation ... of such a highly organized conspiracy, with rigidly disciplined members subject to call when the leaders ... felt that the time had come for action, coupled with the inflammable nature of world conditions ... convince us that their convictions were justified.... And this analysis disposes of the contention that a conspiracy to advocate, as distinguished from the advocacy itself, cannot be constitutionally restrained, because it comprises only the preparation. It is the existence of the conspiracy which creates the danger. If the ingredients of the reaction are present we cannot bind the Government to wait until the catalyst is added....

... Petitioners intended to overthrow the Government of the United States as speedily as the circumstances would permit. Their conspiracy to organize the Communist Party and to teach and advocate the overthrow of the Government of the United States by force and violence created a "clear and present danger" of an attempt to overthrow the Government by force and violence. They were properly and constitutionally convicted for violation of the Smith Act.[17]

Concurring in judgment, Justice Felix Frankfurter observed,

Suppressing advocates of overthrow inevitably will also silence critics who do not advocate overthrow but fear that their criticism may be so construed. No matter how clear we may be that the defendants now before us are preparing to overthrow our Government at the propitious moment, it is self-delusion to think that we can punish them for their advocacy without adding to the risks run by loyal citizens who honestly believe in some of the reforms these defendants advance. It is a sobering fact that in sustaining the convictions before us we can hardly escape restriction on the interchange of ideas.[18]

First Amendment guarantees must be balanced against the nation's need to protect itself, Frankfurter stated:

The appellants maintain that they have a right to advocate a political theory, so long, at least, as their advocacy does not create an immediate danger of obvious magnitude to the very existence of our present scheme of society. On the other hand, the Government asserts the right to safeguard the security of the Nation by such a measure as the Smith Act. Our judgment is thus solicited on a conflict of interests of the utmost concern to the well-being of the country.[19]

The responsibility for reconciling this conflict of values lay primarily with Congress, not the Court, wrote Frankfurter. The Court should set aside the laws reflecting the judgment of Congress in such matters only if it found no reasonable basis for the judgment, or if it found the law too indefinite to meet the demands of due process or breaching the separation of powers. The Court was responsible for ensuring fair procedures in the enforcement of the law and for requiring substantial proof to justify conviction, but "[b]eyond these powers we must not go; we must scrupulously observe the narrow limits of judicial authority even though self-restraint is alone set over us."[20]

Justice Robert H. Jackson, in his concurring opinion, declared that the clear and present danger test was inadequate when applied to laws intended to curtail the spread of the communist conspiracy:

The authors of the clear and present danger test never applied it to a case like this, nor would I. If applied as it is proposed here, it means that the Communist plotting is protected during its period of incubation; its preliminary stages of organization and preparation are immune from the law; the Government can move only after imminent action is manifest, when it would, of course, be too late.[21]

The law of conspiracy was "an awkward and inept remedy" when applied to the threat of subversion presented by the Communist Party, which Jackson described as "a state within a state, an authoritarian dictatorship within a republic." Despite the awkwardness of the instrument, however, Jackson found no constitutional reason for denying the government its use: "There is no constitutional right to gang up on the Government."[22]

Justices Hugo L. Black and William O. Douglas dissented. Black argued that the conspiracy section of the Smith Act should be held void as a prior restraint on the exercise of First Amendment freedoms of speech and the press. Black noted that the eleven communist leaders had not been charged with an actual attempt to overthrow the government but only with agreeing "to assemble and to talk and publish certain ideas at a later date. The indictment is that they conspired to organize the Communist Party and to use speech or newspapers ... to teach and advocate the forcible overthrow of the Government. No matter how it is worded, this is a virulent form of prior censorship of speech and press, which I believe the First Amendment forbids."[23]

Douglas also reminded his colleagues that the defendants were not on trial for conspiring to overthrow the government but only for organizing groups advocating its overthrow. He warned of the "vice of treating speech as the equivalent of overt acts of a treasonable or seditious character," noting that the Constitution allowed punishment for treason only upon evidence of overt treasonable acts:

[N]ever until today has anyone seriously thought that the ancient law of conspiracy could constitutionally be used to turn speech into seditious conduct. Yet that is precisely what is suggested.... We deal here with speech alone, not with speech plus acts of sabotage or unlawful conduct. Not a single seditious act is charged in the indictment....

Free speech has occupied an exalted position because of the high service it has given our society. Its protection is essential to the very existence of a democracy.... We have founded our political system on it. It has been the safeguard of every religious, political, philosophical, economic, and racial group amongst us. We have counted on it to keep us from embracing what is cheap and false; we have trusted the common sense of our people to choose the doctrine true to our genius and to reject the rest.... We have above all else feared the political censor....

There comes a time when even speech loses its constitutional immunity. Speech innocuous one year may at another time fan such destructive flames that it must be halted in the interests of the safety of the Republic. That is the meaning of the clear and present danger test. When conditions are so critical that there will be no time to avoid the evil that the speech threatens, it is time to call a halt. Otherwise, free speech which is the strength of the Nation will be the cause of its destruction.

Yet free speech is the rule, not the exception. The restraint to be constitutional must be based on more than fear, on more than passionate opposition ... on more than a revolted dislike for its contents....

Free—speech the glory of our system of government—should not be sacrificed on anything less

than plain and objective proof of danger that the evil advocated is imminent. On this record no one can say that petitioners and their converts are in such a strategic position as to have even the slightest chance of achieving their aims.[24]

In the wake of the *Dennis* decision, conspiracy prosecutions under the Smith Act were brought involving 121 defendants—all second-rank officials in the U.S. Communist Party. Other prosecutions were brought against individuals for party membership. Convictions were secured in every case brought to trial between 1951 and 1956. The courts of appeal affirmed the convictions, and the Supreme Court denied petitions for review.

Yates v. United States (1957)

Late in 1955 the Court agreed to review the convictions of fourteen persons charged with Smith Act violations. The decision of the Court in these cases is generally known by the name of one of them, *Yates v. United States* (1957). By imposing strict standards of proof upon the government in such prosecutions, the Court effectively curtailed further use of the Smith Act to prosecute members of the Communist Party. The decision marked a major shift in the Court's attitude toward the Smith Act, although it left untouched its earlier declaration in *Dennis* that the act was constitutional. The defendants who brought before the Court the cases of *Yates v. United States, Schneiderman v. United States*, and *Richmond v. United States* were charged with organizing and participating in a conspiracy, namely the Communist Party U.S.A, to advocate the overthrow of the government by force.

By a 6-1 vote, the Supreme Court in *Yates* found that the government had waited too long to indict these persons for their involvement in the organization of the party in the United States, that the trial judge had erred in his instructions to the jury concerning what they must find to convict the defendants on the advocacy charges, and that the evidence in several cases was insufficient to prove the charges. The Court reversed all the convictions, acquitting those of the defendants against whom the evidence was insufficient and ordering new trials for the others. Justices William J. Brennan

This 1948 cartoon suggests that the United States uproot the "tree of communism" with enlightened policies rather than cutting away at free speech. That same year twelve leaders of the Communist Party were indicted for advocating the overthrow of the government. In *Dennis v. United States* (1951), the Supreme Court upheld the constitutionality of a federal law criminalizing such advocacy, even if the threat is not imminent.

Jr. and Charles E. Whittaker did not participate in the rulings.[25] The majority took a narrow view of the scope of the Smith Act provision making it unlawful to organize a group advocating violent overthrow of the government. The majority, explained Justice John Marshall Harlan in the Court's opinion, defined "organize" with respect to the formation of the Communist Party as an activity that took place in 1945 with the party's founding in this country, rejecting the government's definition of "organize" as an ongoing process. Because the defendants were not indicted on this charge until 1951, the three-year statute of limitations on such charges rendered that part of the indictment invalid, held the Court:

> Stated most simply, the problem is to choose between two possible answers to the question: when was

the Communist Party "organized"? Petitioners contend that the only natural answer to the question is the formation—date in this case, 1945. The Government would have us answer the question by saying that the Party today is still not completely "organized"; that "organizing" is a continuing process that does not end until the entity is dissolved....

> We conclude ... that since the Communist Party came into being in 1945, and the indictment was not returned until 1951, the three-year statute of limitations had run on the "organizing" charge, and required the withdrawal of that part of the indictment from the jury's consideration.[26]

Furthermore, held the Court, the trial judge had misinterpreted the Court's meaning in *Dennis* when he instructed the jury. He failed to distinguish properly between advocacy of an abstract doctrine, a protected activity, and advocacy intended to promote unlawful action, a punishable activity under the Smith Act. In restating Vinson's ruling in *Dennis,* Justice Harlan discarded the clear and present danger test altogether. In *Dennis,* he wrote, the punishable advocacy did not create any danger of immediate revolution but "was aimed at building up a seditious group and maintaining it in readiness for action at a propitious time."[27] Harlan continued:

> In failing to distinguish between advocacy of forcible overthrow as an abstract doctrine and advocacy of action to that end, the District Court appears to have been led astray by the holding in *Dennis* that advocacy of violent action to be taken at some future time was enough.... The District Court apparently thought that *Dennis* obliterated the traditional dividing line between advocacy of abstract doctrine and advocacy of action....

> The essence of the *Dennis* holding was that indoctrination of a group in preparation for future violent action, as well as exhortation to immediate action, by advocacy found to be directed to "action for the accomplishment" of forcible overthrow, to violence as "a rule or principle of action," and employing "language of incitement,"... is not constitutionally protected when the group is of sufficient size and cohesiveness, is sufficiently oriented towards action, and other circumstances are such as reasonable to justify apprehension that action will occur.

> This is quite a different thing from the view of the District Court here that mere doctrinal

justification of forcible overthrow, if engaged in with the intent to accomplish overthrow, is punishable per se under the Smith Act. That sort of advocacy, even though uttered with the hope that it may ultimately lead to violent revolution, is too remote from concrete action to be regarded as the kind of indoctrination preparatory to action which was condemned in *Dennis*....

The essential distinction is that those to whom the advocacy is addressed must be urged to do something, now or in the future, rather than merely to believe in something....

We recognize that distinctions between advocacy and teaching of abstract doctrines, with evil intent, and that which is directed to stirring people to action, are often subtle and difficult to grasp, for in a broad sense, as Mr. Justice Holmes said.... "Every idea is an incitement." But the very subtlety of these distinctions required the most clear and explicit instructions with reference to them.[28]

The Court, wrote Harlan, also found the evidence of advocacy geared to action deficient in a number of the cases: "however much one may abhor even the abstract preaching of forcible overthrow or believe that forcible overthrow is the ultimate purpose to which the Communist Party is dedicated, it is upon the evidence in the record that the petitioners must be judged in this case."[29]

Justices Black and Douglas concurred in part and dissented in part. Both felt that all the prosecutions of these defendants should be dropped because the Smith Act provisions upon which the charges were based "abridge freedom of speech, press and assembly in violation of the First Amendment."[30] "I believe that the First Amendment forbids Congress to punish people for talking about public affairs, whether or not such discussion incites to action, legal or illegal," Black wrote.[31] In a separate dissenting opinion, Justice Clark said that all of the convictions should be upheld, in line with *Dennis*. Clark noted that although the communists in *Yates* were lower in the hierarchy than the defendants in *Dennis*, they served "in the same army and were engaged in the same mission."[32]

The *Yates* requirement that the government show a connection between advocacy and action, between participation in the Communist Party and forcible overthrow of the government, ended most Smith Act prosecutions. The government decided to drop charges against those of the *Yates* defendants who, in light of the Court's ruling, could have been retried.

Membership Prosecutions

Despite the Court's narrow view of the Smith Act's "organizing" and "advocating" provisions, prosecutions remained possible under the clause that forbade "knowing" membership in any group advocating forcible overthrow of the government. When coupled with the registration provisions of the 1950 McCarran Act, this provision seemed to constitute compulsory self-incrimination in violation of the Fifth Amendment guarantee against such coercion. (*See "The McCarran Act,"* pp. 229–233.) In 1961 the Supreme Court for the first time reviewed convictions of persons under the membership clause of the Smith Act. In those rulings, the Court upheld the constitutionality of the provision but measured the government's proof in such cases against the strict *Yates* standard of evidence.

In the case of *Scales v. United States* (1961), the Court in a vote of 5-4 affirmed the conviction of Junius Scales, director of a communist training school, and upheld the constitutionality of the membership clause. Chief Justice Warren and Justices Black, Douglas, and Brennan dissented. Justice Harlan, the spokesman for the majority as he had been in *Yates,* distinguished between active, "knowing" membership and passive, merely nominal membership in a subversive organization. The membership clause, properly applied, did not violate the First Amendment guarantees of free political expression and association, he explained. In *Dennis* the Court had established two points in that regard:

the advocacy with which we are here concerned is not constitutionally protected speech, and ... that a combination to promote such advocacy, albeit under the aegis of what purports to be a political party, is not such association as is protected by the First Amendment.

We can discern no reason why membership, when it constitutes a purposeful form of complicity in a group engaging in this same forbidden advocacy, should receive any greater degree of protection from the guarantees of that amendment.[33]

No Bills of Attainder or Ex Post Facto Laws

One of the few provisions of the original Constitution affecting individual rights is this terse command in Article I, section 9: "No Bill of Attainder or ex post facto Law shall be passed." Only three acts of Congress have been held to be bills of attainder, and one of those is the only instance in which the Court has found that Congress passed an ex post facto law. A bill of attainder, stated the Court in 1867, is "a legislative act which inflicts punishment without a judicial trial."[1] An ex post facto law makes an action a crime after it has already been committed or otherwise penalizes some past action.

Ex parte Garland

In *Ex parte Garland* (1867), the Court struck down a law enacted in 1865 that barred attorneys from practicing before federal courts unless they swore an oath that they had remained loyal to the Union throughout the Civil War. Persons who swore falsely could be charged with and convicted of perjury. A. H. Garland of Arkansas had been admitted to practice law before the federal courts during the 1860 Supreme Court term. When Arkansas seceded from the Union, Garland went with his state, becoming first a representative and later a senator in the Confederate Congress.

He received a full pardon in 1865 from President Andrew Johnson for his service to the Confederacy. In *Ex parte Garland,* he argued that he should be allowed to resume his federal practice without taking the required oath.[2] The Supreme Court agreed with him, 5–4, finding the test oath requirement invalid as a bill of attainder. Justice Stephen J. Field explained that lawyers who had served the Confederacy could not take the oath without perjuring themselves. Therefore,

> the act, as against them, operates as a legislative decree of perpetual exclusion. And exclusion from any of the professions or any of the ordinary avocations of life for past conduct can be regarded in no other light than as punishment for such conduct.[3]

In addition, the Court held the test oath invalid as an ex post facto law, prohibiting attorneys from practicing before a federal court if they did not take the oath, thus punishing them for past acts not defined as illegal at the time they were committed.

United States v. Lovett

Almost eighty years passed before the Court again applied the Bill of Attainder Clause to hold a law invalid. *United States v. Lovett* (1946) arose after Rep. Martin Dies, D-Texas, chairman of the House Committee on Un-American Activities, listed thirty-nine federal employees as "irresponsible, unrepresentative, crackpot, radical bureaucrats" who were affiliated with "communist front organizations." Dies urged that Congress refuse to appropriate the funds necessary to pay these employees' salaries.

After a special subcommittee of the House Appropriations Committee heard testimony in secret session, it pronounced three of the thirty-nine federal employees—individuals named Lovett, Watson, and Dodd—guilty of subversive activities and unfit to hold their government jobs. Congress then added specific language to an appropriations bill forbidding the use of any of the funds it contained to pay the salaries of the three. President Franklin D. Roosevelt signed the bill but made clear that he viewed that particular provision as an unconstitutional bill of attainder. A majority of the Court agreed with Roosevelt.

Justice Hugo L. Black wrote that "legislative acts, no matter what their form, that apply either to named individuals or to easily ascertainable members of a group in such a way as to inflict punishment on them without a judicial trial are bills of attainder prohibited by the Constitution."[4]

United States v. Brown

United States v. Brown (1965) concerned a provision of the Labor-Management Reporting and Disclosure Act of 1959 making it a crime for anyone to serve as an officer or employee of a labor union if he or she were a member of the Communist Party or had been a member at any time in the previous five years.[5] Designed to prevent politically motivated strikes, the provision replaced a section of the Taft-Hartley Act of 1947 that had required unions seeking access to the National Labor Relations Board to file affidavits swearing that none of the union's officers was a member of or affiliated with the Communist Party. In 1950 the Court had upheld that requirement.[6] *(See "American Communications Association v. Douds," pp. 236–237.)*

The Court, however, found the successor provision unconstitutional as a bill of attainder. "The statute," wrote Chief Justice Earl Warren, "designates in no uncertain terms the persons who possess the feared characteristics and therefore cannot hold union office without incurring criminal liability—members of the Communist Party."[7] *Brown* differed from the 1950 case, Warren said, because the Taft-Hartley provision could be escaped by persons who resigned from the Communist Party. The newer provision applied to persons who had been members of the party before its enactment.[8]

---

1. *Cummings v. Missouri,* 4 Wall. (71 U.S.) 277 (1867).

2. *Ex parte Garland,* 4 Wall. (71 U.S.) 333 (1867).

3. Id. at 377.

4. *United States v. Lovett,* 328 U.S. 303 at 315 (1946).

5. *United States v. Brown,* 381 U.S. 437 (1965).

6. *American Communications Association v. Douds,* 339 U.S. 382 (1950).

7. *United States v. Brown,* 381 U.S. 437 at 450 (1965).

8. Id. at 457–458.

Harlan continued:

> The clause does not make criminal all association with an organization which has been shown to engage in illegal advocacy. There must be clear proof that a defendant "specifically intend[s] to accomplish [the aims of the organization] by resort to violence."... Thus the member for whom the organization is a vehicle for the advancement of legitimate aims and policies does not fall within the ban of the statute: he lacks the requisite specific intent "to bring about the overthrow of the government as speedily as circumstances would permit." Such a person may be foolish, deluded, or perhaps merely optimistic, but he is not by this statute made a criminal.[34]

Justices Douglas and Brennan and Chief Justice Warren based their dissent primarily on the view that the 1950 Internal Security Act specifically immunized persons from prosecution under the Smith Act membership clause. In a separate opinion, Justice Douglas charged that the Court was legalizing guilt by association, an action with which he strongly disagreed. In another separate opinion, Justice Black reiterated his view that the First Amendment "absolutely forbids Congress to outlaw membership in a political party or similar association merely because one of the philosophical tenets of that group is that the existing government should be overthrown by force at some distant time in the future when circumstances may permit."[35]

In a companion case, *Noto v. United States* (1961), the Court reversed the membership clause conviction of John Francis Noto, holding the evidence insufficient under the *Yates* rule to justify the conviction. Justice Harlan wrote for the unanimous Court:

> [T]he mere abstract teaching of Communist theory, including the teaching of the moral propriety or even moral necessity for a resort to force and violence, is not the same as preparing a group for violent action and steeling it to such action. There must be some substantial direct or circumstantial evidence of a call to violence now or in the future which is both sufficiently strong and sufficiently pervasive to lend color to the otherwise ambiguous theoretical material regarding Communist Party teaching, and to justify the inference that such a call to violence may fairly be imputed to the Party as a whole, and not merely to some narrow segment of it.[36]

The McCarran Act

Deeming the Smith Act insufficient protection against the domestic communist movement, Congress in 1950 approved the Internal Security Act over the veto of President Harry S. Truman, who felt its vague language endangered First Amendment freedoms of speech, press, and assembly. The act, also known as the McCarran Act, after its sponsor, Sen. Pat McCarran, D-Nev., was to expose Communist Party leaders and members of communist-front organizations by requiring that all communist-front and communist-action organizations register with the attorney general. Public exposure, it was thought, would curtail the activities of such groups.

The Subversive Activities Control Act of 1950 was Title I of the McCarran Act. It established a five-member Subversive Activities Control Board (SACB), appointed by the president, to determine, subject to judicial review, whether a particular organization was a communist-action or communist-front group and whether certain individuals were among the members. Once the SACB decided that an organization was indeed a communist group, the organization was required to register with the Justice Department and provide to the government lists of its officers and members. Once registered, these members would be barred from federal jobs, jobs in defense-related industries, and from applying for or using U.S. passports.[37] Failure to register would lead to heavy fines and long prison terms. Compliance with the law, however, made the subject a likely candidate for investigation by a legislative committee or prosecution under the Smith Act. The act did state, however, that holding offices in, or being a member of, a communist organization should not in itself be a crime and that registration should not be used as evidence against a person being prosecuted for violating any criminal law.

In November 1950, the attorney general filed a petition with the SACB to compel the Communist Party of the United States to register as a communist-action organization. That action began an unsuccessful fifteen-year battle to force registration on the party. The SACB twice ordered the party to register, but the party appealed both orders to the courts. The judicial

THE COURT AND STATE SEDITION LAWS

Loyalty oath requirements and loyalty dismissal programs were not the only state response to concern about communist subversion. Many states during the 1940s and 1950s passed their own sedition laws to punish persons for plotting to overthrow the U.S. government. In *Pennsylvania v. Nelson* (1956), however, the Supreme Court held that Congress had preempted such state laws, occupying the field of federal sedition prosecutions with passage of the Smith Act of 1940, the McCarran Act of 1950, and the Communist Control Act of 1954. This decision limited state sedition statutes to punishing sedition against state or local government but not the federal government.

Steve Nelson, an avowed communist, had been convicted for violating Pennsylvania's sedition law by his words and actions concerning the federal government. He was sentenced to serve twenty years in prison and to pay a $10,000 fine and prosecution costs of $13,000. The state supreme court held that the state law had been superseded by the Smith Act, a ruling the Supreme Court upheld and extended. Chief Justice Earl Warren surveyed the relevant provisions of the Smith, McCarran, and Communist Control Acts and declared,

> the conclusion is inescapable that Congress has intended to occupy the field of sedition. Taken as a whole they evince a congressional plan which makes it reasonable to determine that no room has been left for the States to supplement it.

Therefore, a state sedition statute is superseded regardless of whether it purports to supplement the federal law.[1]

"Since 1939," he noted, "in order to avoid a hampering of uniform enforcement of its program by sporadic local prosecutions, the Federal Government has urged local authorities not to intervene in such matters, but to turn over to the federal authorities immediately and unevaluated all information concerning subversive activities."[2] Justices Stanley F. Reed, Harold H. Burton, and Sherman Minton dissented. Following the decision, all pending proceedings under state sedition laws were dismissed or abandoned. Congress considered a measure reversing the Court's decision but did not complete action on such a bill.

In 1965 the Court further curtailed state subversion laws, holding Louisiana's Subversive Activities Criminal Control Act unconstitutionally vague.[3] In *Brandenburg v. Ohio* (1969) the Court struck down Ohio's Criminal Syndicalism Act, declaring illegal the use of advocacy of violence, crime, sabotage, and terrorism to accomplish industrial or political reform. This ruling overturned the Court's decision in *Whitney v. California* (1927), upholding an almost identical California law.[4] *(See details of this case, p. 48.)*

---

1. *Pennsylvania v. Nelson,* 350 U.S. 497 at 504 (1956).
2. Id. at 505–506.
3. *Dombrowski v. Pfister,* 380 U.S. 479 (1965).
4. *Brandenburg v. Ohio,* 395 U.S. 444 (1969), overturning *Whitney v. California,* 274 U.S. 357 (1927).

record involved three decisions by the court of appeals and two reviews by the Supreme Court. The case record includes 15,000 pages of testimony and 507 documentary exhibits.[38]

Communist Party v. Subversive Activities Control Board (1961)

In 1961 the Supreme Court upheld by a 5-4 vote the second order for the Communist Party to register with the attorney general, an apparent victory for the government. The majority rejected the party's arguments that the registration provisions were unconstitutional as a bill of attainder and as violations of the First Amendment's guarantees of freedom.[39] Joined by Justices Clark, Harlan, Whittaker, and Potter Stewart,

Justice Frankfurter wrote one of the longest opinions in the Court's history. The evidence, he concluded, confirmed the SACB ruling that the party was a communist-action group within the scope of the McCarran Act registration provisions. The provisions of that law, Frankfurter declared, did not constitute a bill of attainder—a legislative act pronouncing a particular individual guilty of a crime without trial or conviction and imposing a sentence upon him. The McCarran Act

> attaches not to specified organizations but to described activities in which an organization may or may not engage. The singling out of an individual for legislatively prescribed punishment constitutes an attainder whether the individual is called by name or described in terms of conduct

The House Un-American Activities Committee, which reported the bill that became the McCarran Act, holds a press conference December 3, 1948, after a closed session. Standing are two committee investigators. Seated are several reporters and (*left to right*) Richard Nixon, R-Calif., John Rankin, D-Miss., and John McDowell, R-Pa.

which, because it is past conduct, operates only as a designation of particular persons.... The Subversive Activities Control Act is not of that kind. It requires the registration only of organizations which, after the date of the Act, are found to be under the direction, domination, or control of certain foreign powers and to operate primarily to advance certain objectives.[40]

The majority also held that the law did not violate First Amendment guarantees. In requiring registration, Congress balanced private rights of free speech and association against the public interest in disclosure.

Where the mask of anonymity which an organization's members wear serves the double purpose of protecting them from popular prejudice and of enabling them to cover over a foreign-directed conspiracy, infiltrate into other groups, and enlist the support of persons who would not, if the truth were revealed, lend their support ... it would be a

distortion of the First Amendment to hold that it prohibits Congress from removing the mask.[41]

Frankfurter emphasized the foreign-dominated character of the Communist Party in the United States:

There is no attempt here to impose stifling obligations upon the proponents of a particular political creed as such, or even to check the importation of particular political ideas from abroad for propagation here. The Act compels the registration of organized groups which have been made the instruments of a long-continued, systematic, disciplined activity directed by a foreign power and purposing to overthrow existing government in this country.[42]

The majority found it premature to consider the challenge that the registration provisions violated the Fifth Amendment privilege against compelled self-incrimination: "No person ... shall be compelled in any criminal case to be a witness against himself." This privilege, it pointed out, must be claimed by an individual, and it was not evident that the party officers would make such a claim. In similar fashion, the majority refused to rule on the constitutionality of any other sanctions that might be imposed upon members of the party, once it was registered.

Chief Justice Warren and Justices Brennan, Black, and Douglas dissented in separate opinions, citing a wide variety of reasons for their disagreement with the majority. Warren would have remanded the case to the SACB for reconsideration of credibility of the testimony of two key government witnesses. Justice Black protested that the Subversive Activities Control Act effectively outlawed the Communist Party, a direct violation of the First Amendment:

The first banning of an association because it advocates hated ideas—whether that association be called a political party or not—marks a fateful moment in the history of a free country. That moment seems to have arrived for this country.... This whole Act, with its pains and penalties, embarks this country, for the first time, on the dangerous adventure of outlawing groups that preach doctrines nearly all Americans detest. When the practice of outlawing parties and various public groups begins, no one can say where it will end. In most countries such a practice once begun ends with a one-party government.[43]

Justices Douglas and Brennan found the registration provisions in violation of the Fifth Amendment. Douglas wrote,

Signing as an officer or director of the Communist Party—an ingredient of an offense that results in punishment—must be done under the mandate of law. That is compulsory incrimination of those individuals and, in my view, a plain violation of the Fifth Amendment.[44]

Albertson v. Subversive Activities Control Board (1965)

As subsequent rulings made clear, the Court had upheld only the power of Congress under the McCarran Act to require registration of communist-front and communist-action groups; it would not give similar sanction to the implementing provisions of the act. In 1964 the Court held invalid the passport restrictions imposed by the act on members of registered organizations. (See box, Politics and the Right to a Passport, p. 222.) In Albertson v. Subversive Activities Control Board (1965), the Court held that the registration requirements, when applied to individuals, violated the Fifth Amendment privilege against compelled self-incrimination. In 1967 the Court declared unconstitutional the provision that barred members of registered organizations from jobs in defense-related facilities. Congress responded, first by rewriting the registration provisions and eventually by allowing the SACB to die.[45]

The most severe of these Court-inflicted blows to the McCarran Act was its 1965 ruling in Albertson v. Subversive Activities Control Board, a sequel to the 1961 decision upholding the SACB registration order to the Communist Party. Party officers refused to comply with a final notice from the Justice Department that set November 19, 1961, as the deadline for registration. The government subsequently obtained criminal indictments against the party for its failure to register, and an SACB order directed party officers to register personally. The officers refused and appealed to the federal courts, citing their Fifth Amendment privilege against self-incrimination. With the Court's decision in Albertson, the officers of the party won a clear-cut victory. The Court held unanimously that the information sought in the registration forms included material that was self-incriminating. Thus compulsion to register did violate the officers' Fifth Amendment privilege. Justice Brennan wrote the Court's opinion.

The Court rejected the government's argument that the information sought through the registration forms was no more incriminating than that on a tax return. While questions on tax returns were "neutral on their face and directed at the public at large," wrote Brennan, the registration questions were aimed at "a highly selective group inherently suspect of criminal activities." In this case, he explained, the Fifth Amendment privilege was asserted "not ... in an essentially non-criminal and regulatory area of inquiry, but against an inquiry in an area permeated with criminal statutes where response to any of the form's questions in context might involve the petitioners in the admission of a crucial element of a crime."[46] This ruling effectively ended the long effort by the government to force registration of the party.[47]

United States v. Robel (1967)

Two years after *Albertson,* in *United States v. Robel,* the Court declared that the McCarran Act also abridged the right of political association insofar as it denied all members of communist-action or communist-front organizations the right to hold jobs in defense-related industries. The Court held 6-2 that the ban was too broad, taking in all types of members, not simply active and knowing advocates of violent revolution. Eugene Frank Robel, a member of the Communist Party, worked as a machinist in a Seattle shipyard determined by the secretary of defense to be a defense facility. Robel stayed on the job after the final registration deadline for the party and so was charged with violation of the act. Chief Justice Warren's opinion for the majority viewed this portion of the law as establishing guilt purely by association:

> When Congress' exercise of one of its enumerated powers clashes with those individual liberties protected by the Bill of Rights, it is our "delicate and difficult" task to determine whether the resulting restriction on freedom can be tolerated.... The Government emphasizes that the purpose of ... [the contested ban] is to reduce the threat of sabotage and espionage in the nation's defense plants. The Government's interest in such a prophylactic measure is not insubstantial. But it cannot be doubted that the means chosen to implement that governmental purpose in this instance cut deeply into the right of association. [It] ... put appellee to the choice of surrendering his organizational affiliation, regardless of whether his membership threatened the security of a defense facility or giving up his job.... The statute quite literally establishes guilt by association alone, without any need to establish that an individual's association poses the threat feared by the Government in proscribing it. The inhibiting effect on the exercise of First Amendment rights is clear.

Warren added, however, that "nothing we hold today should be read to deny Congress the power under narrowly drawn legislation to keep from sensitive positions in defense facilities those who would use their positions to disrupt the Nation's production facilities."[48]

Brennan did not join the majority, but issued his own concurring opinion. Justices Byron R. White and Harlan dissented. White wrote that in Robel's case

> the interest in anticipating and preventing espionage or sabotage would outweigh the deterrent impact of job disqualification.... In the case before us the Court simply disagrees with the Congress and the Defense Department, ruling that Robel does not present a sufficient danger to the national security to require him to choose between membership in the Communist Party and his employment in a defense facility.... I much prefer the judgment of Congress and the Executive Branch that the interest of respondent in remaining a member of the Communist Party ... is less substantial than the public interest in excluding him from employment in critical defense industries.[49]

In the fall of 1967, Congress revised the definition of communist-front organization in the McCarran Act. Another amendment to the act eliminated the registration requirement and authorized the SACB to place on a public register the names of individuals and organizations it found to be communist. In 1968 Attorney General Ramsey Clark asked the board to conduct hearings on seven individuals thought to be members of the Communist Party. The SACB issued orders against three of them, declaring they were members of a communist-action organization. The board's order was set aside by the District of Columbia Court of Appeals in 1969, holding that membership in the Communist Party was protected by the First Amendment.[50]

Federal Loyalty Programs

To ensure that only "loyal" persons held federal jobs, Presidents Harry S. Truman and Dwight D. Eisenhower instituted federal loyalty programs that provoked considerable controversy. Critics of the programs argued that through them the government penalized persons for a state of mind rather than for overt acts of disloyalty, and it dismissed persons from jobs purely on the grounds of guilt by association. Defenders of the programs pointed out that there was no constitutional right to hold a government job and that the government had a right to protect itself from internal subversion. Moreover, dismissal from a government job did not imply guilt but only that some question existed as to one's fitness for government employment.

In 1947 President Truman by executive order established a loyalty program for all civilian employees of the executive branch. Executive Order 9835 established a Loyalty Review Board within the Civil Service Commission to coordinate agency loyalty policies and to serve as the final board of appeal in loyalty dismissal cases. Loyalty investigations were required for all persons employed by the government and for all applicants for government jobs. Dismissal of individuals from government posts or denial of a job was permitted when "on all the evidence, reasonable grounds exist for belief that the person involved is disloyal to the Government of the United States." (In 1951 this standard was modified to allow dismissal when "there is a reasonable doubt as to the loyalty of the person involved.") In the 1940s, Congress authorized summary dismissal of employees of the Departments of State, Defense, Army, Navy, and Air Force and the Atomic Energy Commission when dismissal was considered necessary or advisable in the interest of national security. In 1950 Congress extended this authority to the Departments of the Treasury, Commerce, and Justice.

In 1953 President Eisenhower extended this summary dismissal power to all executive branch agencies and replaced the Truman loyalty program with a more stringent loyalty-security program established by Executive Order 10450. Under the Eisenhower program, a suspected employee bore the burden of proving his employment "clearly consistent" with national security. The order also sanctioned dismissal for reasons other than disloyalty: for example, personal behavior, sexual misconduct, excessive use of drugs or alcohol, and physical or mental disorders.[51]

The Supreme Court never squarely addressed the substantial constitutional questions raised by the federal loyalty and security programs, although it did rule in a number of cases during the 1950s concerning individual dismissals. Three constitutional provisions were implicated in the programs: the First Amendment guarantees of freedom of expression and political association; the Fifth Amendment guarantee that government not deprive one of liberty or property without due process of law; and the Article I ban on the passage of bills of attainder. Only the due process issue received any extended consideration by the Court in these cases.

The first ruling was a 5-3 decision in *Joint Anti-Fascist Refugee Committee v. McGrath* (1951), in which the Court upheld the authority of the attorney general, under the Truman loyalty program, to maintain and furnish to the Loyalty Review Board a list of allegedly subversive organizations. The Court held, however, that the attorney general had exceeded that authority and had acted arbitrarily in placing the names of three particular organizations—including the Anti-Fascist Refugee Committee—on that list.

Justice Clark, attorney general when the case was filed, did not participate in the decision. Justice Burton—joined only by Justice Douglas—wrote the opinion announcing the judgment of the Court. That opinion carefully avoided the First Amendment issues of political association raised by use of this list. In concurring opinions, Justices Black, Douglas, Frankfurter, and Jackson questioned the constitutionality of the list in light of the guarantee of due process and the prohibition on a bill of attainder. Justice Frankfurter wrote that although the designation as "communist" actually imposed no legal sanction on the listed organizations,

> in the conditions of our time such designation drastically restricts the organizations, if it does not proscribe them…. Yet, designation has been made without notice, without disclosure of any reasons justifying it, without opportunity to meet the undisclosed evidence or suspicion on which designation may have been based, and without opportunity to establish affirmatively that the aims and acts of the organization are innocent.

Frankfurter continued, stating that such action

> to maim or decapitate, on the mere say-so of the Attorney General, an organization to all outward-seeming engaged in lawful objectives is so devoid of fundamental fairness as to offend the Due Process Clause of the Fifth Amendment.[52]

Justices Reed and Minton and Chief Justice Vinson dissented, finding the due process guarantee inapplicable and rejecting any First Amendment challenge to use of the list. Justice Reed explained:

> So long as petitioners are permitted to voice their political ideas … it is hard to understand how any advocate of freedom of expression can assert that their right has been unconstitutionally abridged. As nothing in the orders or regulations concerning this list limits the teachings or support of these organizations, we do not believe that any right of theirs under the First Amendment is abridged by publication of the list.[53]

The same day a Court vote of 4-4 left standing an appeals court ruling upholding the decision of the loyalty board to dismiss Dorothy Bailey, a training officer in the United States Employment Service. Justice Clark again did not participate in the decision. There was no opinion from the Supreme Court, as is the practice in cases in which the justices are evenly divided.[54] Because there was no constitutional right to federal employment, Bailey's dismissal did not violate due process, and, the majority of the lower court continued, the First Amendment did not bar removal of persons from office for political reasons.

In 1955 the Court ruled that the Loyalty Review Board had exceeded its authority in discharging a public health officer as a security risk, after the officer had twice been cleared of any suspicion of disloyalty by agency loyalty boards.[55] In 1956 the Court held unjustified the summary dismissal of an inspector with the Food and Drug Administration on loyalty grounds. The Court ruled that dismissal from a nonsensitive position could not be justified as necessary in the interest of national security.[56]

In 1959 the Court weakened the federal government's effort to carry out its loyalty program by casting doubt on the propriety of the procedures used in revoking security clearances and dismissing employees on the basis of information from anonymous sources. With its ruling in *Greene v. McElroy,* the Court forced the president to revise those procedures.[57] William L. Greene had lost his job as vice president of an engineering firm engaged in defense contract work after his security clearance was revoked. The review board revoking the clearance relied on confidential reports, never made available to Greene, even though he appeared at the hearings of the board to respond to the charges against him.

When Greene lost his clearance, he was unable to find another job in the field of aeronautical engineering. He challenged the revocation of his clearance as depriving him of his livelihood and thus of liberty and property without due process of law guaranteed by the Fifth Amendment. The Court, 8-1, agreed that the denial of access to the evidence against Greene had been improper, depriving him of the opportunity to respond and rebut the charges. Neither Congress nor the president had authorized the Defense Department thus to classify the employees of a contractor as security risks without giving them the opportunity to confront and examine the evidence against them, held the Court. Chief Justice Warren, writing for five members of the majority, carefully narrowed the reach of the ruling:

> [P]etitioner's work opportunities have been severely limited on the basis of a fact determination rendered after a hearing which failed to comport with our traditional ideas of fair procedure. The type of hearing was the product of administrative decision not explicitly authorized by either Congress or the President. Whether those procedures under the circumstances comport with the Constitution we do not decide. Nor do we decide whether the President has inherent authority to create such a program, whether congressional action is necessary, or what the limits on executive or legislative authority may be. We decide only that in the absence of explicit authorization from the President or Congress the respondents were not empowered to deprive petitioner of his job in a proceeding in which he was not afforded the safeguards of confrontation and cross-examination.[58]

Justices Frankfurter, Harlan, and Whittaker concurred with the Court's judgment. Justice Clark dissented, arguing that no one has "a constitutional right to have access to the Government's military secrets.... What for anyone else would be considered a privilege at best has for Greene been enshrouded in constitutional protection. This sleight of hand is too much for me." Clark warned that the majority was casting a cloud over the entire federal loyalty-security program, which could result in "a rout of our internal security."[59]

Early in 1960 President Eisenhower issued an executive order restricting the use of informants whose identities must be protected. The order also granted to persons accused of being security risks the right to confront and cross-examine their accusers.[60] In 1961, however, the Court upheld the national security dismissal of a short-order cook in a cafeteria on the premises of the Naval Gun Factory in Washington, D.C. The Court, 5-4, held this action well within the authority granted by Congress to the executive to control security on military bases.[61]

Loyalty Oaths and the Labor Movement

Along with the institution of the federal loyalty-security program came the proliferation of requirements that persons holding certain posts take loyalty oaths or sign affidavits to demonstrate their loyalty to the U.S. government. In a long line of rulings, the Supreme Court first upheld and then circumscribed the use and the usefulness of such requirements.

American Communications Association v. Douds (1950)

Concern over communist infiltration of the labor movement and "political strikes" spurred passage of the Labor Management Relations Act of 1947, sponsored by Sen. Robert Taft, R-Ohio, and Rep. Fred Hartley Jr., R-N.Y. A provision in the Taft-Hartley Act required officers of all labor organizations wishing to benefit from the protections and guarantees of federal labor law to sign affidavits that they were not members of, or affiliated with, the Communist Party, and that they did not believe in or hold membership in any organization teaching or believing in the forcible, illegal, or unconstitutional overthrow of the federal government. Unions whose officers did not sign such affidavits were denied all protection of and services from the National Labor Relations Board. In *American Communications Association v. Douds* (1950), the Supreme Court, 5-1, upheld the affidavit requirement as within the power of Congress. Chief Justice Vinson wrote the opinion. Justices Douglas, Clark, and Minton did not take part.

"There can be no doubt that Congress may, under its constitutional power to regulate commerce among the several States, attempt to prevent political strikes and other kinds of direct action designed to burden and interrupt the free flow of commerce," Vinson said.[62] The affidavit requirement, Vinson explained, was a reasonable means of attaining that end. Vinson continued:

> Congress could rationally find that the Communist Party is not like other political parties in its utilization of positions of union leadership as means by which to bring about strikes and other obstructions of commerce for purposes of political advantage.[63]

The affidavit requirement, "by exerting pressures on unions to deny office to communists and others identified therein,"

> undoubtedly lessens the threat to interstate commerce, but it has the further necessary effect of discouraging the exercise of political rights protected by the First Amendment. Men who hold union offices often have little choice but to renounce Communism or give up their offices.[64]

Vinson rejected the challenge that the affidavit requirement was an unconstitutional curtailment of individual freedom. The requirement, Vinson wrote,

> does not interfere with speech because Congress fears the consequences of speech; it regulates harmful conduct which Congress has determined is carried on by persons who may be identified by their political affiliations and beliefs. The [National Labor Relations] Board does not contend that political strikes, the substantive evil at which [the requirement] is aimed, are the present or impending products of advocacy of the doctrines of Communism or the expression of belief in overthrow of the Government by force.... Speech may be fought with speech.

Falsehoods and fallacies must be exposed, not suppressed, unless there is not sufficient time to avert the evil consequences of noxious doctrine by argument and education. That is the command of the First Amendment. But force may and must be met with force.... [The affidavit requirement] is designed to protect the public not against what Communists and others identified therein advocate or believe, but against what Congress has concluded they have done and are likely to do again.[65]

Justice Frankfurter concurred in upholding the membership portion of the affidavit but dissented from the majority opinion upholding the portion involving belief alone. Justice Jackson also concurred in part and dissented in part, making a similar distinction between the membership and the belief portions of the affidavit:

[A]ll parts of this oath which require disclosure of overt acts of affiliation or membership in the Communist Party are within the competence of Congress to enact ... any parts of it that call for a disclosure of belief unconnected with any overt act are beyond its power.[66]

Earlier in Jackson's opinion, he had phrased his view in less abstract terms:

I think that under our system, it is time enough for the law to lay hold of the citizen when he acts illegally, or in some rare circumstances when his thoughts are given illegal utterance. I think we must let his mind alone.[67]

In a vigorous dissenting opinion, Justice Black criticized his colleagues for allowing the government to restrict the right to think:

Freedom to think is inevitably abridged when beliefs are penalized by imposition of civil disabilities.... Like anyone else, individual Communists who commit overt acts in violation of valid laws can and should be punished. But the postulate of the First Amendment is that our free institutions can be maintained without proscribing or penalizing political belief, speech, press, assembly, or party affiliation. This is a far bolder philosophy than despotic rulers can afford to follow. It is the heart of the system on which our freedom depends.[68]

United States v. Brown (1965)

In 1959 Congress replaced the affidavit requirement—which proved ineffective since some communists were willing to take the oath and risk prosecution for perjury—with a flat prohibition against members of the Communist Party holding any union office. The new section of the federal labor law, part of the Labor-Management Reporting and Disclosure Act of 1959, also disqualified anyone who had been a member of the party during the last five years.[69] In 1965 the Supreme Court held this ban unconstitutional as a violation of the provision forbidding Congress to pass bills of attainder. Archie Brown, a member of the Communist Party, challenged the operation of the law that forbade him to serve on the executive board of a local of the International Longshoremen's and Warehousemen's Union. He based his challenge on First and Fifth Amendment grounds, but the Court found it unnecessary to consider those. (See box, Politics and Loyalty at the Bar, p. 240.) By a 5-4 vote in United States v. Brown, the Supreme Court ruled in his favor. Chief Justice Earl Warren wrote,

Congress undoubtedly possesses power under the Commerce Clause to enact legislation designed to keep from positions affecting interstate commerce persons who may use such positions to bring about political strikes. In ... [this prohibition,] however, Congress has exceeded the authority granted it by the Constitution. The statute does not set forth a generally applicable rule decreeing that any person who commits certain acts or possesses certain characteristics (acts and characteristics which, in Congress' view, make them likely to initiate political strikes) shall not hold union office, and leave to courts and juries the job of deciding what persons have committed the specified acts or possess the specified characteristics. Instead, it designates in no uncertain terms the persons who possess the feared characteristics and therefore cannot hold union office without incurring criminal liability—members of the Communist Party....

We do not hold today that Congress cannot weed dangerous persons out of the labor movement.... Rather, we make again the point ... that Congress must accomplish such results by rules of general applicability. It cannot specify the people upon whom the sanction it prescribes is to be levied. Under our Constitution, Congress possesses full legislative authority, but the task of adjudication must be left to other tribunals.[70]

In dissent, Justice White, joined by Justices Clark, Harlan, and Stewart, criticized the majority's distinction between the legislative function of making rules and the judicial function in applying those rules to particular individuals or groups. White wrote that the Court took "too narrow [a] view of the legislative process."[71]

In the 1960s, the Court ruled on two other cases related to the Taft-Hartley Act requirement that officers of labor organizations sign affidavits that they were not Communist Party members. The decisions reversed convictions of union members who had sworn falsely that they were not communists. The Court decided both cases without dealing with the First Amendment claim of freedom of political association or the Fifth Amendment privilege protecting individuals against compelled self-incrimination.[72]

Oaths and State and Local Employees

The most frequent state reaction to the threat of communist subversion was passage of a law requiring public employees—particularly teachers—to take a loyalty oath affirming that they had not been and were not members of the Communist Party. During the 1950s, the Court upheld the constitutionality of such oaths, but by 1967 it had reversed itself, finding that most oaths came too close to guilt by association, demanding little evidence of actual subversive activity. In the 1970s, the Court upheld several laws requiring state employees to take affirmative oaths promising to uphold the Constitution and to oppose the violent overthrow of the government.

Gerende and Garner

The Court handed down its first loyalty oath rulings in 1951. In *Gerende v. Board of Supervisors of Elections*, it upheld a Maryland law requiring every candidate for public office to file an affidavit disavowing involvement in any attempt to overthrow the government by force or violence.[73] Two months later, on the same day

that it upheld the constitutionality of the Smith Act in *Dennis*, the Court in *Garner v. Board of Public Works of the City of Los Angeles* (1951) upheld a Los Angeles ordinance requiring city employees to affirm their loyalty through oath and affidavit. Public employees had to state whether they ever had been members of the Communist Party and to swear that they had not advocated the overthrow of state or federal government in the previous five years, that they had not and would not be affiliated with any group advocating such overthrow during the period they held a city job. Seventeen employees refused to comply and were dismissed. They sued for reinstatement, challenging the oath and affidavit requirement as unconstitutional as a bill of attainder, an ex post facto law, and a violation of their freedom of speech, assembly, and right to petition the government for redress of grievances.[74]

In *Garner,* the Court upheld the affidavit requirement 7-2, but the oath by only 5-4. Justice Clark, writing for the majority, explained that they did not view the Los Angeles ordinance as a bill of attainder because it did not punish anyone, but simply set standards of qualification and eligibility for city jobs. It was not an ex post facto law, he continued, because it involved activity that for the seven previous years had been proscribed for city employees. The majority did not address the First Amendment issues directly. Justices Frankfurter and Burton concurred in the decision to uphold the affidavit requirement, but they dissented from the majority's ruling upholding the oath. Frankfurter wrote,

> The Constitution does not guarantee public employment. City, State and Nation are not confined to making provisions appropriate for securing competent professional discharge of the functions pertaining to diverse governmental jobs. They may also assure themselves of fidelity to the very presuppositions of our scheme of government on the part of those who seek to serve it.[75]

Frankfurter explained that he would have overturned the oath requirement because it was "not limited to affiliation with organizations known at the time to have advocated overthrow of government.... How can anyone be sure that an organization with which he affiliates will not at some time in the future be found … to advocate overthrow of government by 'unlawful means'?"[76] Burton found the retroactive nature of the oath invalid under the Court's decisions concerning bills of attainder and ex post facto laws. Justices Black and Douglas found all aspects of the ordinance objectionable, holding both the oath and the affidavit requirements invalid as bills of attainder.

Loyalty Dismissals

Loyalty oath requirements for state or city employees were often linked with programs for the removal of public employees whose loyalty was suspect. In *Adler v. Board of Education, City of New York* (1952), the Supreme Court in a 6-3 vote upheld a New York law setting up a state list of subversive organizations—those advocating the violent overthrow of the government—and providing that membership in any listed organization would constitute prima facie evidence justifying dismissal from a public post.[77] The law was intended to ensure the doctrinal orthodoxy of teachers and other officials in the New York public school system. Before dismissal, persons who were members of such an organization were entitled to a full hearing and judicial review of the decision to dismiss them. For the majority, Justice Minton wrote,

> That the school authorities have the right and the duty to screen the officials, teachers and employees as to their fitness to maintain the integrity of the schools as a part of ordered society, cannot be doubted. One's associates, past and present, as well as one's conduct, may properly be considered in determining fitness and loyalty. From time immemorial, one's reputation has been determined in part by the company he keeps.[78]

Disqualification from a job under the law, wrote Minton, did not deny one the right of free speech and assembly: "His freedom of choice between membership in the organization and employment in the school system might be limited, but not his freedom of speech or assembly."[79]

Justices Frankfurter, Black, and Douglas dissented. Frankfurter argued that the Court should have dismissed the case without ruling on the law. Douglas

and Black found the law a violation of the First Amendment. It "proceeds on a principle repugnant to our society—guilt by association," wrote Douglas.[80] He elaborated:

> Youthful indiscretions, mistaken causes, misguided enthusiasms—all long forgotten—become the ghosts of a harrowing present. Any organization committed to a liberal cause, any group organized to revolt against a hysterical trend, any committee launched to sponsor an unpopular program becomes suspect. These are the organizations into which Communists often infiltrate. Their presence infects the whole, even though the project was not conceived in sin. A teacher caught in that mesh is almost certain to stand condemned. Fearing condemnation, she will tend to shrink from any association that stirs controversy. In that manner freedom of expression will be stifled.…
>
> What happens under this law is typical of what happens in a police state. Teachers are under constant surveillance; their pasts are combed for signs of disloyalty; their utterances are watched for cues to dangerous thoughts. A pall is cast over the classrooms. There can be no real academic freedom in that environment. Where suspicion fills the air and holds scholars in line for fear of their jobs, there can be no exercise of the free intellect.…
>
> Of course the school systems … need not become cells for Communist activities; and the classrooms need not become forums for propagandizing the Marxist creed. But the guilt of the teacher should turn on overt acts. So long as she is a law-abiding citizen, so long as her performance within the public school system meets professional standards, her private life, her political philosophy, her social creed should not be the cause of reprisals against her.[81]

Late in 1952, however, the Court unanimously struck down an Oklahoma loyalty program that penalized knowing *and* unknowing members of certain proscribed organizations. (The Smith Act of 1940 had made it a crime to become a knowing member of any organization or group dedicated to the violent overthrow of any government in the United States.) The law challenged in *Wieman v. Updegraff* (1952) required all state officers and employees to take a loyalty oath and excluded from public jobs those persons who had

POLITICS AND LOYALTY AT THE BAR

Concerned about communist infiltration of the legal profession, several states in the 1950s began inquiring into the political affiliation and associations of individuals seeking admission to the practice of law. This line of inquiry—and resulting state decisions to deny certain persons admission—produced a series of Supreme Court rulings over some twenty years. The first case was that of George Anastaplo. When Illinois bar examiners questioned him about his political beliefs, he refused on principle to respond, asserting that the questions invaded areas protected by the First and Fourteenth Amendments from state infringement. He was denied admission to the bar. The Supreme Court upheld the denial by refusing to review his appeal.[1]

Two years after *In re Anastaplo* (1955), however, the Court ruled in two cases that questionable political affiliations alone or the simple refusal to answer questions about one's political associations did not give a state a basis for concluding that an applicant lacked the proper moral character for admission to the practice of law. In *Schware v. New Mexico Board of Bar Examiners* (1957), the board had concluded that Rudolph Schware lacked the requisite "good moral character" because he had used aliases during the 1930s to obtain jobs in businesses that discriminated against Jews, because he had been arrested several times, and because he had been a member of the Communist Party from 1932 to 1940. The Supreme Court unanimously reversed the board's decision. Justice Hugo L. Black wrote the opinion, refuting the board's inference that because Schware had belonged to the Communist Party he was of bad moral character.[2]

Raphael Konigsberg was denied admission to the California bar because he, like Anastaplo, refused to answer questions about his political affiliations. The Court overturned the state's action the same day it reversed the lower court decision in *Schware*. Konigsberg's record of public and military service testified sufficiently to his loyalty, the Supreme Court held, reversing the state board's rulings as contrary to the evidence.[3]

ADMISSION NOT GUARANTEED

Supreme Court reversal of the state's initial refusal to admit Anastaplo and Konigsberg to the practice of law did not guarantee their admission. On the basis of *Schware* and *Konigsberg*, Anastaplo asked the Illinois bar to reconsider his application. After lengthy proceedings, the state again rejected it. In 1961 the Supreme Court, 5-4, upheld the state's action. The majority said that the state had a legitimate interest in examining the qualifications of persons seeking to practice law in the state and that questions about Anastaplo's political background were a proper element in that examination. The Court held that by continuing to refuse to answer the questions

posed, Anastaplo obstructed the state's inquiry; therefore, denial of admission was a legitimate response.[4]

A second ruling in Konigsberg's case was announced the same day. Also 5-4, the Court upheld California bar officials' refusal to admit Konigsberg, not because of concern about his character but simply because he too persisted in his refusal to answer questions germane to its inquiry, thereby obstructing the state's examining process.[5]

EVIDENCE OF CHARACTER

In two decisions announced on the same day in 1971, the Supreme Court marked the boundary for questioning about political affiliation. By a 5-4 vote, the Court made it harder for a state to exclude an applicant from admission to the bar. Without any other evidence of the applicant's disloyalty or unfitness, a state may not refuse the applicant solely on the basis of his refusal to state whether he had ever belonged to an organization advocating the violent overthrow of the government. Justice Black wrote the opinion. Justices John Marshall Harlan, Byron R. White, and Harry A. Blackmun and Chief Justice Warren Burger dissented.[6]

In the other case, with Justice Potter Stewart joining those dissenters, the Court, 5-4, held that states could require applicants for admission to the bar to be of good moral character and loyal to the Constitution. It made no difference that the "loyalty" requirement included taking an oath in support of the state and federal constitutions and responding to two questions concerning membership in any organization advocating overthrow of the government by force or violence, with the specific intent of furthering that goal.[7]

The majority was careful to point out that there was no indication that any applicant had been denied admission to the bar because of his or her answers to these questions or the refusal to answer them. "It is well settled," wrote Justice Stewart, "that Bar Examiners may ask about Communist affiliation as a preliminary to further inquiry into the nature of the association and may exclude an applicant for refusal to answer."[8]

---

1. *In re Anastaplo,* 348 U.S. 946 (1955).

2. *Schware v. New Mexico Board of Bar Examiners,* 353 U.S. 232 (1957).

3. *Konigsberg v. State Bar of California,* 353 U.S. 252 (1957).

4. *In re Anastaplo,* 366 U.S. 82 (1961).

5. *Konigsberg v. State Bar of California,* 366 U.S. 36 (1961).

6. *In re Stolar, Baird v. State Bar of Arizona,* 401 U.S. 23 (1971).

7. *Law Students Civil Rights Research Council v. Wadmond,* 401 U.S. 154 (1971).

8. Id. at 165–166.

POLITICS AND PUBLIC EMPLOYEES

Despite the First Amendment's guarantee of freedom for political associa-tion, the Supreme Court has consistently upheld the power of Congress and state legislatures to limit the political activity of public employees. The Court first made this point in 1947: the limited burden such laws place upon the right of political association is justified by the government's inter-est in having its employees chosen on the basis of merit, not political loyalty. The end of the spoils system for filling federal posts brought with it laws limiting the political activities of government workers.

In 1876 Congress prohibited government employees from requesting, giving, or receiving money for political purposes from any federal official. The Civil Service Act of 1883 forbade federal officials to use their positions to influence the political action of their subordi-nates. The Hatch Act of 1939 prohibited federal employees from taking active part in political campaigns or the management of political party activities. Office of Personnel Management (formerly the Civil Service Commission) regulations subsequently have denied govern-ment workers the right to participate in the following political activi-ties: running for office, distributing campaign literature, taking an active role in political campaigns, circulating nominating petitions, attending political conventions as anything other than a spectator, and publishing or signing a letter soliciting votes for a candidate. The Supreme Court in *United Public Workers v. Mitchell* (1947) upheld, 4-3, these restrictions.

Justices Frank Murphy and Robert H. Jackson did not take part in the decision. Justices Wiley Rutledge, Hugo L. Black, and William O. Douglas dissented. Justice Stanley F. Reed, speaking for the Court, declared that there was no constitutional objection to the finding of Congress that an efficient public service was best obtained by prohibit-ing active participation by public employees in political campaigns. The conclusion was a reasonable one, well within the power of Congress. Reed continued:

For regulation of employees it is not necessary that the act regulated be anything more than an act reasonably deemed by Congress to interfere with the efficiency of the public service....

We have said that Congress may regulate the political conduct of Government employees "within reasonable limits," even though the regulation trenches to some extent upon unfettered political action. The determination of the extent to which political activities of governmental employees shall be regulated lies pri-marily in Congress. Courts will interfere only when such regulation passes beyond the generally existing conception of governmental power.[1]

Reed warned, however, that the concept of government power might change. Some future Court might find these restrictions impermissible.

Twenty-six years later, in *Civil Service Commission v. Letter Carriers* (1973), the Court again rebuffed First Amendment challenges to federal and state prohibitions on partisan political activity by public employees. By 6-3, the Court reaffirmed the validity of the Hatch Act. Justice Byron R. White wrote for the majority:

[I]t is in the best interest of the country, indeed essential, that federal service should depend upon meritorious performance rather than political service, and that the political influence of federal employees on others and on the electoral process should be limited.[2]

Justices Douglas, William J. Brennan Jr., and Thurgood Marshall dissented.

In a companion case, *Broadrick v. Oklahoma State Personnel Board* (1973), the Court 5-4 sustained a state law prohibiting employees from partisan political activity.[3] Justice Potter Stewart, who voted with the majority in the Hatch Act case, joined the dissenters in this case.

---

1. *United Public Workers v. Mitchell,* 330 U.S. 75 at 101, 102 (1947).

2. *Civil Service Commission v. Letter Carriers,* 413 U.S. 548 at 557 (1973).

3. *Broadrick v. Oklahoma State Personnel Board,* 413 U.S. 601 (1973).

been members of certain organizations, regardless of their knowledge of the organization's purposes. With this ruling the Court began to impose limits upon state loyalty oaths. Membership in an organization could not be used as a basis for a state-imposed penalty, the Court said, unless the member consciously endorsed the organization's aims and doctrines.

Justice Jackson, who had not heard the case argued, did not participate in the decision. Justice Clark, writing for the unanimous Court, made clear that in *Garner* and *Adler* only "knowing" membership resulted in disquali-fication for or dismissal from a public job. Under Okla-homa law, "membership alone disqualifies."[82] This was a critical difference. Under the challenged law the fact of association alone determines disloyalty and disqualification; it matters not whether association existed innocently or knowingly. To thus inhibit individual freedom of movement is to stifle the flow of democratic expression and controversy at one of its chief sources.... Indiscriminate classification of innocent with knowing activity must fall as an assertion of arbitrary power. The oath offends due process.[83]

Four years later, the Court held it unconstitutional for a state or city automatically to dismiss employees if they invoked their constitutional privilege against self-incrimination to avoid answering questions about their political associations. At issue in *Slochower v. Board of Higher Education of New York City* (1956) was the city's summary dismissal of a Brooklyn College professor because, in testimony before the Senate internal security subcommittee, he had refused to answer questions about his political associations before 1941, invoking the Fifth Amendment. Slochower was suspended without notice, hearing, or an opportunity to explain or discuss the reasons for the termination of his tenure. This action came under a provision of the city charter that automatically terminated the tenure of any public official who invoked the Fifth Amendment to avoid answering questions related to official conduct. Slochower sued, challenging his dismissal as improper and the city charter provision as unconstitutional because it penalized the exercise of a federally guaranteed constitutional right. The Court ruled in Slochower's favor but on different grounds.

Summary dismissal, the Court held 5-4, violated Slochower's right to due process of law. The city board of education, wrote Justice Clark for the majority, had erred in treating his assertion of his Fifth Amendment privilege as a "conclusive presumption of guilt." Such interpretation of the assertion of a constitutional right was impermissible. Clark continued: "The privilege against self-incrimination would be reduced to a hollow mockery if its exercise could be taken as equivalent to a confession of guilt."[84] Because no valid inference of guilt could be made, the Court sustained Slochower's claim of privilege before the Senate subcommittee and ruled that there was no basis for his dismissal.

Justice Reed, speaking also for Justices Burton and Minton, dissented. He argued that "the city does have reasonable ground to require its employees either to give evidence regarding facts of official conduct within their knowledge or to give up the positions they hold."[85] Justice Harlan, in a separate dissenting opinion, wrote that the majority had "misconceived" the nature of the city charter provision in question and had "unduly circumscribed the power of the State to ensure the qualifications of its teachers."[86]

Two years later, the Court again upheld the right of states to question employees about their associations when examining their overall qualifications for state employment. In *Lerner v. Casey* (1958), a subway conductor refused to tell his superiors whether he was a member of the Communist Party, after which he was dismissed as a person of doubtful loyalty and reliability.[87] In *Beilan v. Board of Public Education, School District of Philadelphia* (1958), a schoolteacher who refused to tell his superintendent whether he had earlier held a position in the Communist Party was dismissed as incompetent.[88] The five-man majority in both cases—Harlan, Burton, Frankfurter, Clark, and Whittaker—stressed that the subway conductor and the school teacher were dismissed because they refused to answer questions put by their employers—action that constituted evidence of incompetency and unreliability.

In a concurring opinion, Justice Frankfurter said the two employees were "terminated because of their refusals to answer questions relevant ... to an inquiry by their supervisors into their dependability. When these two employees were discharged, they were not labeled 'disloyal.' They were discharged because governmental authorities, like other employers, sought to satisfy themselves of the dependability of employees in relation to their duties."[89] In dissent, Chief Justice Warren and Justices Brennan, Black, and Douglas argued that the two employees had been branded disloyal by the inquiry into their political associations and activities. In his dissenting opinion, Brennan wrote that "more is at stake here than the loss of positions of public employment for unreliability or incompetence. Rather, it is the simultaneous public labeling of the employees as disloyal that gives rise to our concern."[90]

The Shift of the Sixties

With a series of decisions beginning in 1958—initially involving civil rights, not communist, groups—the Supreme Court gave formal recognition to a First Amendment freedom of political association. *(See box, The Right and Freedom of Association, pp. 42–43.)* In line with this development came a clear shift in the Court's willingness to back government inquiry into the affiliations of its employees. The Court also was less willing to uphold government-imposed penalties for persons whose affiliations seemed suspect. The *Aptheker* and *Robel* rulings of 1964 and 1967, respectively, reflected the change. *(See details on these two cases, pp. 222, 233.)*

In a set of rulings in the mid-1960s, the Court effectively reversed most of its key decisions upholding state government loyalty oath and loyalty program requirements, finding that they were too broad to comport with the freedom guaranteed by the First Amendment. The first of these freedom-of-association rulings was *National Association for the Advancement of Colored People v. Alabama* (1958).[91] Two years later, the Court struck down a state law that required public school teachers to file affidavits listing all their organizational memberships. In its opinion in *Shelton v. Tucker* (1960), the Court found this requirement to go "far beyond what might be justified in the exercise of the State's legitimate inquiry into the fitness and competency of its teachers."[92]

In 1961 the Court first applied its new view of loyalty oaths, striking down a Florida law that required state employees to swear that they had never lent "aid, support, advice, counsel or influence to the Communist Party." Employees who did not sign the oath were fired. In *Cramp v. Board of Public Instruction, Orange County, Fla.*, the Court held this oath far too vague, "completely lacking in ... terms susceptible of objective measurement."[93] A law describing prohibited acts "in terms so vague that men of common intelligence must necessarily guess at its meaning and differ as to its application violates the first essential of due process of law," wrote Justice Stewart for the unanimous Court.[94] In 1964 Washington State's loyalty oath for teachers was struck down on the basis of similar reasoning.[95]

Elfbrandt and Garner

In 1966 and 1967 the Court's shift in thinking culminated in decisions effectively nullifying *Gerende, Garner,* and *Adler.* The first of these rulings came in the case of *Elfbrandt v. Russell* (1966). Barbara Elfbrandt, a Quaker teacher in Arizona, challenged the constitutionality of the state laws that required state employees to take a loyalty oath. The oath itself simply affirmed support for the constitutions and laws of the state and the United States, but the state legislature had by law provided that the oath would be considered violated by knowing membership in the Communist Party. The law made clear that any employee who took the oath and at the time or later became a willing, knowing member of the Communist Party could be prosecuted for perjury. In a 5-4 vote, the Supreme Court held this combination of oath and interpretive statute too broad to meet constitutional standards. Justice Douglas explained that the major flaw was the failure of the state to acknowledge that many people might join organizations such as the Communist Party without actually sharing the organization's unlawful purposes. The challenged law, he continued, was predicated on the doctrine of guilt by association:

> Those who join an organization but do not share its unlawful purposes and who do not participate in its unlawful activities surely pose no threat, either as citizens or as public employees.... This Act threatens the cherished freedom of association protected by the First Amendment, made applicable to the States through the Fourteenth Amendment.... A law which applies to membership without the "specific intent" to further the illegal aims of the organization infringes unnecessarily on protected freedoms. It rests on the doctrine of "guilt by association" which has no place here.[96]

With this ruling, the Court effectively, if implicitly, overturned *Garner,* which had upheld that sort of oath. The four dissenting justices—White, Clark, Harlan, and Stewart—said that the oath should be upheld in light of the Court's earlier decisions acknowledging the right of states to condition public employment upon the requirement that employees abstain from knowing membership in subversive organizations.

Keyishian and Adler

The following year the Court struck down the New York law it had upheld in *Adler*. The vote in *Keyishian v. Board of Regents of the University of the State of New York* (1967) was again 5-4. Justice Brennan wrote the majority opinion. The law authorized the board of regents to prepare a list of subversive organizations and to deny jobs to teachers belonging to those organizations. The law made membership in the Communist Party prima facie evidence for disqualification from employment. Four university faculty members subject to dismissal under the law challenged its constitutionality. The Court found the law too vague and too sweeping, penalizing "[m]ere knowing membership without a specific intent to further the unlawful aims" of the Communist Party.[97] The question of vagueness, noted Brennan, had not been placed before the Court in *Adler*. The majority described New York's complex of criminal anarchy and loyalty laws as "a highly efficient *in terrorem* mechanism" that operated to curtail First Amendment freedom:

> It would be a bold teacher who would not stay as far as possible from utterances or acts which might jeopardize his living by enmeshing him in this intricate machinery....
>
> Our Nation is deeply committed to safeguarding academic freedom, which is of transcendent value to all of us and not merely to the teachers concerned. That freedom is therefore a special concern of the First Amendment, which does not tolerate laws that cast a pall of orthodoxy over the classroom.[98]

Four justices—Clark, Harlan, Stewart, and White—dissented. Justice Clark declared: "[T]he majority has by its broadside swept away one of our most precious rights, namely, the right of self preservation."[99]

A few months later the Court, 6-3, struck down the Maryland loyalty oath law it had upheld in *Gerende*. Justice Douglas explained that the oath was so vague that it violated the due process guarantee of the Fourteenth Amendment. Its capricious application could "deter the flowering of academic freedom as much as successive suits for perjury," he wrote.[100] Justices Harlan, Stewart, and White dissented.

POLITICAL ASSOCIATION: A CONTEMPORARY VIEW

As the threat of domestic subversion faded, and questions of domestic politics came again to the foreground of national attention, the Supreme Court through the 1990s continued to define various aspects of the freedom of political association.

Loyalty Oaths

The Court continued to support state requirements that employees take loyalty oaths that are worded affirmatively, that is, when employees declare their support for the existing system of constitutional government rather than disavow any affiliation with groups intending to overthrow that system. In 1971 the Court upheld a state requirement that teachers take such an oath, making clear in its opinion that persons could be properly dismissed for refusing to take such an oath only after they were given a hearing.[101] The following year the Court, 4-3, upheld a state requirement that all employees swear to "oppose the overthrow of the government by force, violence or by any illegal or unconstitutional method."[102] Also in 1971 and 1972 the Court upheld state requirements that applicants for admission to the state bar take affirmative oaths of loyalty to the state and federal constitutions, but the Court at the same time limited strictly the power of state officials to penalize those who would not take such oaths.[103] *(See box, Politics and Loyalty at the Bar, p. 240.)* In 1974 the Court held unanimously that a state infringed the freedom of political association when it required political parties seeking a place on the ballot to swear that they did not advocate the violent overthrow of local, state, or federal government. In *Communist Party of Indiana v. Whitcomb* (1974), Justice Brennan reaffirmed the Court's view that "the constitutional guarantees of free speech and free press do not permit a State to forbid or proscribe advocacy of the use of force or of law violation except where such advocacy is directed to inciting or producing imminent lawless action and is likely to incite or produce such action."[104]

Political Parties

Political parties—and in one case a radical student organization—have won Court rulings making clear their right of association and the point at which state officials could limit its exercise. The case of *Healy v. James* (1972) concerned a local chapter of Students for a Democratic Society. The Court held that without evidence that the chapter would have adverse effects on campus life, university officials could not constitutionally refuse to recognize it.[105]

Several decisions in the early 1970s set out the Court's view of the permissible restrictions a state might place on voters or candidates wishing to change political parties. In 1973 the Court upheld a state requirement that voters who wish to vote in a party's primary enroll in that party at least thirty days before the last general election.[106] Later in the year, the Court held that the First Amendment limited the scope of such a state requirement, striking down as abridging the right of political association a state rule forbidding persons to vote in the primary of one party if they had voted in that of another party within the preceding twenty-three months.[107] Early in 1974, however, the Court upheld a state requirement that independent candidates disaffiliate themselves from a party one year before the primary election of the year in which they wish to run as independents.[108]

In the mid-1970s, the Court held that national political parties, as well as individuals, have a constitutional right of political association. In *Cousins v. Wigoda* (1975), the Court ruled that Illinois law infringed the Democratic Party's First Amendment right by penalizing one set of party delegates recognized and seated, instead of an alternative delegation, by the Democratic National Convention. The case arose from the 1972 convention, to which two opposing sets of Democratic delegates went from Illinois—one committed to the presidential candidacy of Sen. George S. McGovern of South Dakota and the other chosen and led by Mayor Richard J. Daley of Chicago.[109] The right of association of political parties was further defined in 1981, when the Court, 6-3, upheld Wisconsin's right to hold an open primary in which voters participate without declaring their allegiance to a particular party. The Court also held, however, that the state could not compel the national party to recognize the primary results if to do so would violate the party's rules and infringe on its right of association.[110] A year later, the Court struck down Ohio's law requiring candidates for office to disclose the names and addresses of campaign contributors. By a 6-3 vote, the Court held that such disclosure, particularly of contributors to minor parties, might subject the persons whose names were disclosed to harassment, violating their freedom of association.[111]

In June 2000, the Court struck down California's open primary law in a 7-2 ruling, a ringing endorsement to the right of political parties and their faithful members to choose their own candidates and to exclude independents from the process. "Representative democracy … is unimaginable without the ability of citizens to band together in promoting among the electorate candidates who espouse their political views," said Justice Antonin Scalia. "[A] corollary of [this] right to associate is the right not to associate," he added in *California Democratic Party v. Jones.*[112]

In 1996 California voters had approved a measure that called for opening primary elections to all voters, regardless of whether they belonged to a party. It adopted the most expansive version of the open primary, so on the day of the primary voters could freely choose from the full menu of candidates. For example, a single voter could select a Republican for governor, a Democrat for the U.S. Senate, and a Libertarian to run for the House. The winners, and thus the parties' nominees, would be the Republican and the Democrat who received the most votes. Proponents said this system would increase participation in the elections, since more voters, particularly independents, could cast a primary ballot, and the process would likely promote more centrist candidates because they could draw support across party lines, state lawyers said. As Justice Scalia countered, however, the "Republican" nominee may not represent the views of true Republicans, since he or she could win thanks to an outpouring of votes from Democrats and independents. Lawyers for both major parties in California challenged the measure as unconstitutional, and they prevailed.

In dissent, Justice Stevens said he agreed with Californians who believed that open primaries would "foster democratic government by increasing the representativeness of elected officials, giving voters greater choice and increasing voter turnout."[113] The large number of independent or disaffected voters could participate in these primaries. "In my view, the First Amendment does not inhibit the State from acting to broaden voter access to state-run, state-financed elections," Stevens said.[114] Only Justice Ruth Bader Ginsburg agreed with him. Scalia, however, said the states were not free to "weaken" political parties by depriving them of the full right to decide who will be their candidate. Selecting a candidate is "the basic function of a political party." "We can think of no heavier burden on a political party's associational freedom" than by forcibly "opening it up to persons wholly unaffiliated with the party."[115]

Patronage Hiring and Firing

Twice the Court has upheld laws restricting the partisan political activity of federal and state workers. Curtailment of their First Amendment rights may be justified, the Court has ruled, by the interest in having government jobs filled on the basis of merit, not political loyalty. *(See box, Politics and Public Employees, p. 241.)* The Court has also dealt with the other side of the patronage hiring issue—patronage firing—and in those decisions has held that the freedom of political association was violated by that practice.

Elrod v. Burns (1976), like *Cousins,* arose in Illinois. At the time, all employees of the Cook County sheriff's office who were not covered by civil service regulations or who were not of the same party as the newly elected sheriff were fired by the incoming sheriff, with the intent of replacing them with persons of political affiliation similar to his. This practice, held the Court 5-3, violated the First Amendment. Justice Brennan, writing for the majority, first quoted the Court's earlier declaration in *Buckley v. Valeo* (1976) that the "First Amendment protects political association as well as political expression." He then continued, "There can no longer be doubt that freedom to associate with others for the common advancement of political beliefs and ideas is a form of 'orderly group activity' protected by the First and Fourteenth Amendments."[116]

Brennan cited as precedent the decision in *Keyishian* nine years earlier, noting that in that case the Court "squarely held that political association alone could not, consistently with the First Amendment, constitute adequate ground for denying public employment."[117] *(See details of Keyishian v. Board of Regents of the University of the State of New York, p. 244.)* Then, moving to weigh the state's justification for patronage firing against its curtailment of individual freedom, Brennan cited the cases in which the Court had upheld the Hatch Act limitations on partisan political activity by government employees—*United Public Workers v. Mitchell* (1947) and *Civil Service Commission v. Letter Carriers* (1973).[118] Those limitations were upheld, he explained, as a justifiable way of eliminating patronage, the very practice that Illinois now argued to preserve. By forbidding the firing of persons simply because of their political affiliation, Brennan continued, the Court was not outlawing political parties:

> Parties are free to exist and their concomitant activities are free to continue. We require only that the rights of every citizen to believe as he will and to act and associate according to his beliefs be free to continue as well.
>
> In summary, patronage dismissals severely restrict political belief and association. Though there is a vital need for government efficiency and effectiveness, such dismissals are on balance not the least restrictive means for fostering that end.... [P]atronage dismissals cannot be justified by their contribution to the proper functioning of our democratic process through their assistance to partisan politics since political parties are nurtured by other, less intrusive and equally effective methods. More fundamentally, however, any contribution of patronage dismissals to the democratic process does not suffice to override their severe encroachment on First Amendment freedoms.[119]

Justices Lewis F. Powell Jr. and William H. Rehnquist dissented, as did Chief Justice Warren E. Burger. They held that the patronage system contributed to the democratization of politics and to sustaining grassroots interest in government—considerations that outweighed the limited intrusion of patronage firing on First Amendment freedoms. Powell wrote, "Before patronage practices developed fully, an 'aristocratic' class dominated political affairs, a tendency that persisted in areas where patronage did not become prevalent. Patronage practices broadened the base of political participation by providing incentives to take part in the process, thereby increasing the volume of political discourse in society."[120]

Four years later, in *Branti v. Finkel* (1980), the Court expanded the First Amendment's protections for non–civil service workers.[121] Then, in 1990, the Court went beyond the context of dismissals and held that it was unconstitutional for states, cities, or counties to hire, promote, or transfer most public employees based on party affiliation.[122] The Court, 5-4, ruled that patronage violates the right of free association when government workers who are not in policy or confidential positions are denied advancement because of their party membership. Justice Brennan, writing for the majority in *Rutan v. Republican Party of Illinois* (1990), opened his opinion with this quip: "To the victor belong only those spoils that may be constitutionally obtained."[123] Brennan was joined by Justices Byron R. White, Thurgood Marshall, Harry A. Blackmun, and John Paul Stevens.

Justice Scalia's strongly worded dissent was joined by Chief Justice Rehnquist, Justice Anthony M. Kennedy, and in part by Justice Sandra Day O'Connor. Wrote Scalia, "There is little doubt that our decisions in *Elrod* and *Branti*, by contributing to the decline of party strength, have also contributed to the growth of interest-group politics in the last decade. Our decision today will greatly accelerate the trend."[124] Casting the discussion as a conflict between patronage and the merit principle, Scalia explained, "As the merit principle has been extended and its effects increasingly felt; as the Boss Tweeds, the Tammany Halls, the Pendergast machines, the Byrd machines and the Daley machines have faded into history; we find that political leaders at all levels increasingly complain of the helplessness of elected government before the demands of small and cohesive interest-groups."[125]

Despite Justice Scalia's plea that city leaders be left free to run their cities, the Court in 1996 extended free speech protections to the vast number of independent government contractors. You can fight City Hall, even if you work for it as a contractor, the 7-2 majority said. In one case, *Board of County Commissioners, Wabaunsee County v. Umbehr*, a trash hauler from Kansas had his contract terminated by the county board after he wrote several letters to the local newspaper criticizing the board for allegedly misusing tax dollars. In a second case, *O'Hare Truck Service v. City of Northlake*, a tow truck driver lost his privilege to tow autos in the city of Northlake, Illinois, a Chicago suburb, after he refused to donate money to the mayor's reelection campaign. Instead, he had supported his opponent, who lost. Both men sued, alleging that they had lost their contracts in retaliation for their political statements or political associations.[126]

The government is entitled to terminate contractors, as it can its employees, for many reasons, including poor performance, the Court said. The First Amendment does not, however, allow the government to terminate contractors, or employees, solely because of their statements "on matters of public concern" or their "exercise of rights of political association," the justices said.[127] The Court did not say that the two fired contractors were entitled to win their lawsuit, because the outcome depended on whether the government had a good reason for terminating their contracts. If the reason was retaliation for their political actions, they deserved to win. Justices Scalia and Thomas dissented, saying they feared a wave of lawsuits against local officials for favoring their friends over their political enemies.

NOTES

INTRODUCTION (PP. 171–173)

1. *Colegrove v. Green*, 328 U.S. 549 (1946).
2. *Baker v. Carr*, 369 U.S. 186 (1962).
3. For example, see *Gray v. Sanders*, 372 U.S. 368 (1963).

FAIR ELECTIONS AND THE RIGHT TO VOTE (PP. 174–191)

1. See generally, Alexander Keyssar, *The Right to Vote: The Contested History of Democracy in the United States* (New York: Basic Books, 2000).

2. *Minor v. Happersett*, 21 Wall. (88 U.S.) 162 (1875). See also, Sandra F. VanBurkleo, *"Belonging to the World": Women's Rights and American Constitutional Culture* (New York: Oxford University Press, 2001).

3. *Slaughterhouse Cases (Butchers' Benevolent Association of New Orleans v. The Crescent City Livestock Landing and Slaughterhouse Company, Esteben v. Louisiana)*, 16 Wall (83 U.S.) 36 at 75 (1873).

4. *Minor v. Happersett*, 21 Wall. (88 U.S.) 162 (1875).

5. *United States v. Reese*, 92 U.S. 214 at 564 (1876).

6. *United States v. Cruikshank*, 92 U.S. 542 at 555 (1876).

7. Id. at 554–556.

8. *Ex parte Siebold*, 100 U.S. 371 (1880).

9. *Ex parte Clarke*, 100 U.S. 399 (1880); *United States v. Gale*, 109 U.S. 65 (1883); *In re Coy*, 127 U.S. 731 (1888); *United States v. Mosely*, 238 U.S. 383 (1915).

10. *Ex parte Yarbrough*, 110 U.S. 651 at 657–658, 663–664 (1884).

11. Id. at 666.

12. Id. at 667.

13. *James v. Bowman*, 190 U.S. 127 at 139 (1903).

14. C. Vann Woodward, *The Strange Career of Jim Crow*, 2d rev. ed. (New York: Oxford University Press, 1966), 82–93.

15. *Williams v. Mississippi*, 170 U.S. 213 at 225 (1898).

16. *Guinn v. United States*, 238 U.S. 347 (1915).

17. Id. at 366.

18. *United States v. Mosley*, 238 U.S. 383 at 386 (1915).

19. *Lane v. Wilson*, 307 U.S. 268 at 275 (1939).

20. *Davis v. Schnell*, 336 U.S. 933 (1949).

21. *Lassiter v. Northampton County Board of Elections*, 360 U.S. 45 at 51–54 (1959).

22. *Louisiana v. United States*, 380 U.S. 145 at 152–153 (1965).

23. *South Carolina v. Katzenbach*, 383 U.S. 301 (1966). See also Steven F. Lawson, *Black Ballots: Voting Rights in the South, 1944–1969* (New York: Columbia University Press, 1976).

24. *South Carolina v. Katzenbach*, 383 U.S. 301 at 328, 334 (1966).

25. *Katzenbach v. Morgan*, 384 U.S. 641 (1966); *Cardona v. Power*, 384 U.S. 672 (1966).

26. *Gaston County v. United States*, 395 U.S. 285 (1969).

27. Id. at 296–297.

28. *Oregon v. Mitchell*, 400 U.S. 112 (1970).

29. *Newberry v. United States*, 256 U.S. 232 (1921).

30. *Nixon v. Herndon*, 273 U.S. 536 at 541 (1927).

31. *Nixon v. Condon*, 286 U.S. 73 (1932). See also Conrey Bryson, *Dr. Lawrence A. Nixon and the White Primary* (El Paso: Texas Western Press, 1974).

32. *Grovey v. Townsend*, 295 U.S. 45 (1935).

33. *United States v. Classic*, 313 U.S. 299 at 317 (1941).

34. *Smith v. Allwright*, 321 U.S. 649 at 660 (1944).

35. Id. at 669.

36. *Terry v. Adams*, 345 U.S. 461 at 469–470 (1953).

37. *Breedlove v. Suttles*, 302 U.S. 277 (1937).

38. *Harman v. Forssenius*, 380 U.S. 528 (1965).

39. *Harper v. Virginia State Board of Elections*, 383 U.S. 663 at 668 (1966).

40. Id. at 666, 668.

41. Id. at 683, 686.

42. *Colegrove v. Green*, 328 U.S. 549 (1946).

43. *Gomillion v. Lightfoot*, 364 U.S. 339 at 346–347 (1960). See also Richard C. Cortner, *The Apportionment Cases* (Knoxville: University of Tennessee Press, 1970).

44. *Gomillion v. Lightfoot*, 364 U.S. 339 at 349 (1960).

45. *Wright v. Rockefeller*, 376 U.S. 52 (1964).

46. *United States v. Raines*, 362 U.S. 17 (1960); *Hannah v. Larch*, 363 U.S. 420 (1960).

47. *Congress and the Nation* (Washington, D.C.: Congressional Quarterly, 1965), 1:1628; *United States v. Alabama*, 362 U.S. 602 (1960).

48. *Congress and the Nation*, 1:1638.

49. *United States v. Louisiana*, 380 U.S. 145 (1965); *United States v. Mississippi*, 380 U.S. 128 (1965).

50. Speech of March 15, 1965, in *Public Papers of the Presidents of the United States, Lyndon B. Johnson, 1965* (Washington, D.C.: U.S. Government Printing Office, 1966), 1:282.

51. Senate Judiciary Committee, *Voting Rights*, 89th Cong., 1st sess., 1965, pt. 2: 1005.

52. *Congress and the Nation* (Washington, D.C.: Congressional Quarterly, 1969), 2:354, 356–365.

53. *South Carolina v. Katzenbach*, 383 U.S. 301 at 326 (1966).

54. Id. at 308.

55. Id. at 330, 334, 336.

56. Id. at 358.

57. *Katzenbach v. Morgan*, 384 U.S. 641 (1966).

58. *Gaston County v. United States*, 395 U.S. 285 (1969).

59. *Allen v. Virginia Board of Elections*, 393 U.S. 544 (1969); *Hadnott v. Amos*, 394 U.S. 358 (1969); *McDaniel v. Sanchez*, 452 U.S. 130 (1981); *Hathorn v. Lovorn*, 457 U.S. 255 (1982); *City of Port Arthur, Texas v. United States*, 459 U.S. 159 (1982); *NAACP v. Hampton County Election Commission*, 470 U.S. 166 (1985); *Morse v. Republican Party of Virginia*, 517 U.S. 186 (1996).

60. *Dougherty County Board of Education v. White*, 435 U.S. 921 (1978).

61. *Perkins v. Mathews*, 400 U.S. 379 (1971); see also *City of Pleasant Grove v. United States*, 479 U.S. 462 (1987).

62. *Richmond v. United States*, 422 U.S. 358 (1975).

63. *Briscoe v. Bell*, 432 U.S. 404 (1977); *Morris v. Gressette*, 432 U.S. 491 (1977).

64. *City of Mobile v. Bolden*, 446 U.S. 55 (1980).

65. Id. at 141.

66. *Thornburg v. Gingles*, 478 U.S. 30 (1986).

67. *Crawford v. Marion County Election Board*, 553 U.S. __ (2008).

THE RIGHT TO AN EQUAL VOTE (PP. 192–216)

1. For general background see *Congressional Quarterly's Guide to U.S. Elections*, 4th ed. (Washington, D.C.: CQ Press, 2001), 2:807–826.

2. *Wood v. Broom*, 287 U.S. 1 (1932).

3. *Colegrove v. Green*, 328 U.S. 549 (1946).

4. Id. at 552, 553–554, 556.

5. Id. at 564.

6. Id. at 574.

7. *Gomillion v. Lightfoot*, 364 U.S. 339 (1960).

8. Id. at 346, 347.

9. *Baker v. Carr*, 369 U.S. 186 (1962). See also Richard C. Cortner, *The Apportionment Cases* (Knoxville: University of Tennessee Press, 1970).

10. *Baker v. Carr*, 369 U.S. 186 at 253 (1962).

11. Id. at 201.

12. Id. at 207.

13. Id. at 209.

14. *Luther v. Borden*, 7 How. (48 U.S.) 1 (1849).

15. *Baker v. Carr*, 369 U.S. 186 at 258 (1962).

16. Id. at 267.

17. Id. at 268–270.

18. Id. at 332, 334.

19. Id. at 339.

20. *Gray v. Sanders*, 372 U.S. 368 at 378 (1963).

21. Id. at 379–381.

22. Id. at 384, 388.

23. *Wesberry v. Sanders*, 376 U.S. 1 at 7–8 (1964).

24. Id. at 42.

25. Richard O. Claude, *The Supreme Court and the Electoral Process* (Baltimore: John Hopkins University Press, 1970), 213n–214n.

26. *Reynolds v. Sims*, 377 U.S. 533 at 567 (1964).

27. Id. at 573–574.

28. Id. at 555, 562, 567–568.

29. Id. at 577.

30. Id. at 578.

31. Id. at 624–625.

32. *Duddleston v. Grills*, 385 U.S. 155 (1967); *Kirkpatrick v. Preisler*, 385 U.S. 450 (1967).

33. *Kirkpatrick v. Preisler*, 394 U.S. 526 (1969).

34. Id. at 530.

35. Id. at 530–531, 533.

36. Id. at 538–539.

37. Id. at 553.

38. Id. at 549–550.

39. *Wells v. Rockefeller*, 394 U.S. 542 at 546 (1969).

40. *Guide to U.S. Elections*, 2:823.

41. *White v. Weiser*, 412 U.S. 783 (1973).

42. *Karcher v. Daggett*, 462 U.S. 725 (1983).

43. *United States Department of Commerce v. Montana*, 503 U.S. 442 (1992).

44. *Fortson v. Dorsey*, 379 U.S. 433 at 439 (1965).

45. *Burns v. Richardson*, 384 U.S. 73 (1966).

46. *Whitcomb v. Chavis*, 403 U.S. 124 (1971).

47. *White v. Regester*, 412 U.S. 755 (1973).

48. *Swann v. Adams*, 385 U.S. 440 at 444 (1967).

49. Id.

50. Id. at 447.

51. *Mahan v. Howell*, 410 U.S. 315 at 321 (1973).

52. Id. at 321–323, 328.

53. Id. at 339–340.

54. *Gaffney v. Cummings*, 412 U.S. 736 (1973).

55. Id. at 749.

56. Id.

57. Id. at 749–750.

58. *White v. Regester*, 412 U.S. 755 (1973).

59. *Brown v. Thomson*, 462 U.S. 835 (1983).

60. *Presley v. Etowah County Commission*, 502 U.S. 491 (1992).

61. *Holder v. Hall*, 512 U.S. 874 (1994).

62. Id.

63. *Chapman v. Meier*, 420 U.S. 1 (1975).

64. Id. at 19.

65. Id. at 24–25.

66. *Connor v. Finch*, 431 U.S. 407 (1977).

67. *Growe v. Emison*, 507 U.S. 25 (1993); *Voinovich v. Quilter*, 507 U.S. 146 (1993).

68. *Shaw v. Reno*, 509 U.S. 630 at 658 (1993).

69. Id. at 647.

70. Id. at 657.

71. Id. at 666–667.

72. *Johnson v. DeGrandy*, 512 U.S. 997 (1994).

73. *Miller v. Johnson*, 515 U.S. 900 (1995).

74. Id. at 912.

75. *Bush v. Vera*, 517 U.S. 952 (1996); *Shaw v. Hunt*, 517 U.S. 899 (1996).

76. *Bush v. Vera*, 517 U.S. 952 at 985 (1996).

77. Id. at 1011.

78. *Hunt/Easley v. Cromartie*, 532 U.S. 234 at 257 (2001).

79. *Shaw v. Reno*, 509 U.S. 630 (1993).

80. *Davis v. Bandemer*, 478 U.S. 109 (1986).

81. *Davis v. Bandemer*, 478 U.S. 109 (1986).

82. *Vieth v. Jubelier*, 541 U.S. 267 (2004).

83. *League of Latin American Citizens v. Perry*, 548 U.S. __ (2006).

84. Florida Election Code, sec. 102.166.

85. Florida Election Code, sec. 102.112; Florida Department of State, advisory opinion DE00-10, November 13, 2000.

86. Advisory Legal Opinion 2000-65, November 14, 2000.

87. *Canvassing Board of Volusia County v. Secretary of State, State of Florida*, CV00-2700.

88. *Palm Beach County Canvassing Board v. Harris*, SC00-2346.

89. *Bush v. Palm Beach County Canvassing Board,* 531 U.S. 70 (2000).

90. Florida Election Code, sec. 102.168.

91. *Gore v. Harris,* SC00-2431.

92. Scalia and Stevens' remarks were issued in response to the order staying the recount: application for stay granted, 00A504, and petition for certiorari, 00-949 granted, December 9, 2000, 513 U.S. at 1046, 1047.

93. *Bush v. Gore,* 531 U.S. 98 at 103 (2000).

94. Id. at 104.

95. Id. at 105.

96. Id.

97. Id. at 109.

98. Id. at 111.

99. Id. at 110.

100. Id. at 112.

101. Id. at 119.

102. Id. at 123.

103. Id. at 128–129.

104. Id. at 142–143.

105. Id. at 129, 134.

106. Id. at 144.

107. Id. at 153, 157–158.

FREEDOM OF POLITICAL ASSOCIATION (PP. 217–247)

1. *Elrod v. Burns,* 427 U.S. 347 at 356 (1976).

2. *Schenck v. United States,* 249 U.S. 47 (1919); *Frohwerk v. United States,* 249 U.S. 204 (1919); *Debs v. United States,* 249 U.S. 211 (1919).

3. *Schenck v. United States,* 249 U.S. 47 at 52 (1919).

4. *Schaefer v. United States,* 251 U.S. 466 at 482 (1920).

5. Id. at 479.

6. *Gitlow v. New York,* 268 U.S. 652 at 666 (1925).

7. *Whitney v. California,* 274 U.S. 357 at 377 (1927).

8. *Stromberg v. California,* 283 U.S. 359 (1931).

9. *DeJonge v. Oregon,* 299 U.S. 353 (1937); *Herndon v. Lowry,* 301 U.S. 242 (1937).

10. *DeJonge v. Oregon,* 299 U.S. 353 at 365 (1937).

11. *Joint Anti-Fascist Refugee Committee v. McGrath,* 341 U.S. 123 at 174 (1951).

12. *Congress and the Nation* (Washington, D.C.: Congressional Quarterly, 1965), 1:1645–1670.

13. Thomas I. Emerson, *The System of Freedom of Expression* (New York: Random House, 1970), 110.

14. *United States v. Dennis,* 183 F. 2d. 201, 212 (2d Cir. 1950).

15. *Dennis v. United States,* 341 U.S. 494 (1951). See also Michal R. Belknap, *Cold War Political Justice: The Smith Act, the Communist Party, and American Civil Liberties* (Westport, Conn.: Greenwood Press, 1977).

16. *Dennis v. United States,* 341 U.S. 494 at 502 (1951).

17. Id. at 509, 510–511, 516–517.

18. Id. at 549.

19. Id. at 518–520.

20. Id. at 525–526.

21. Id. at 570.

22. Id. at 577.

23. Id. at 579.

24. Id. at 584–585, 590.

25. *Yates v. United States,* 354 U.S. 298 (1957); see also the Court's review of Yates's conviction for contempt: *Yates v. United States,* 355 U.S. 66 (1957); 356 U.S. 363 (1958).

26. *Yates v. United States,* 354 U.S. 298 at 306–307, 312 (1957).

27. Id. at 321.

28. Id. at 320–322, 324–325, 326–327.

29. Id. at 329–330.

30. Id. at 339.

31. Id. at 340.

32. Id. at 345.

33. *Scales v. United States,* 367 U.S. 203 at 228–229 (1961).

34. Id. at 229–230.

35. Id. at 260.

36. *Noto v. United States,* 367 U.S. 290 at 297–298 (1961).

37. *Congress and the Nation,* 1:1650–1651.

38. Ibid., 1:1653.

39. *Communist Party v. Subversive Activities Control Board,* 367 U.S. 1 (1961).

40. Id. at 86.

41. Id. at 102–103.

42. Id. at 105.

43. Id. at 137, 145.

44. Id. at 181.

45. *Congress and the Nation* (Washington, D.C.: Congressional Quarterly, 1969), 2:413–415; (1973), 3:489; and (1977), 4:570.

46. *Albertson v. Subversive Activities Control Board,* 382 U.S. 70 at 79 (1965).

47. *Congress and the Nation,* 2:418.

48. *United States v. Robel,* 389 U.S. 258 at 265, 266–267 (1967).

49. Id. at 285.

50. *Boorda v. Subversive Activities Control Board,* 421 F. 2d 1142 (D.C. Cir. 1969).

51. For general background on loyalty programs, see *Congress and the Nation,* 1:1663–1668.

52. *Joint Anti-Fascist Refugee Committee v. McGrath,* 341 U.S. 123 at 161 (1951).

53. Id. at 200.

54. *Bailey v. Richardson,* 341 U.S. 918 (1951).

55. *Peters v. Hobby,* 349 U.S. 331 (1955).

56. *Cole v. Young,* 351 U.S. 536 (1956); see also *Service v. Dulles,* 354 U.S. 363 (1957).

57. *Greene v. McElroy*, 360 U.S. 474 (1959).

58. Id. at 508.

59. Id. at 511, 524.

60. *Congress and the Nation*, 1:1667–1668.

61. *Cafeteria and Restaurant Workers Union v. McElroy*, 367 U.S. 886 (1961).

62. *American Communications Association v. Douds*, 339 U.S. 382 at 390 (1950).

63. Id. at 391.

64. Id. at 393.

65. Id. at 396.

66. Id. at 445.

67. Id. at 444.

68. Id. at 446, 452–453.

69. *Congress and the Nation*, 1:568, 611.

70. *United States v. Brown*, 381 U.S. 437 at 449–450, 461 (1965).

71. Id. at 474.

72. *Killian v. United States*, 368 U.S. 231 (1961); *Raymond Dennis et al. v. United States*, 384 U.S. 855 (1966).

73. *Gerende v. Board of Supervisors of Elections*, 341 U.S. 56 (1951).

74. *Garner v. Board of Public Works of the City of Los Angeles*, 341 U.S. 716 (1951).

75. Id. at 724–725.

76. Id. at 726, 728.

77. *Adler v. Board of Education, City of New York*, 342 U.S. 485 (1952).

78. Id. at 493.

79. Id.

80. Id. at 508.

81. Id. at 509, 510, 511.

82. *Wieman v. Updegraff*, 344 U.S. 183 at 190 (1952).

83. Id. at 191.

84. *Slochower v. Board of Higher Education of New York City*, 350 U.S. 551 at 557 (1956).

85. Id. at 561.

86. Id. at 565.

87. *Lerner v. Casey*, 357 U.S. 468 (1958).

88. *Beilan v. Board of Public Education, School District of Philadelphia*, 357 U.S. 399 (1958).

89. Id. at 410.

90. Id. at 418; see also *Speiser v. Randall*, 357 U.S. 513 (1958).

91. *National Association for the Advancement of Colored People v. Alabama*, 357 U.S. 449 (1958).

92. *Shelton v. Tucker*, 364 U.S. 479 at 490 (1960).

93. *Cramp v. Board of Public Instruction, Orange County, Fla.*, 368 U.S. 278 at 286 (1961).

94. Id. at 287.

95. *Baggett v. Bullitt*, 377 U.S. 360 at 367 (1964).

96. *Elfbrandt v. Russell*, 384 U.S. 11 at 17–19 (1966).

97. *Keyishian v. Board of Regents of the University of the State of New York*, 385 U.S. 589 at 606 (1967).

98. Id. at 601, 603.

99. Id. at 628.

100. *Whitehill v. Elkins*, 389 U.S. 54 at 62 (1967).

101. *Connell v. Higginbotham*, 403 U.S. 207 (1971).

102. *Cole v. Richardson*, 405 U.S. 676 (1972).

103. *In re Stolar, Baird v. State Bar of Arizona*, 401 U.S. 23, 1 (1971); *Law Students Civil Rights Research Council v. Wadmond*, 401 U.S. 154 (1971).

104. *Communist Party of Indiana v. Whitcomb*, 414 U.S. 441 at 448 (1974).

105. *Healy v. James*, 408 U.S. 169 (1972).

106. *Rosario v. Rockefeller*, 410 U.S. 752 (1973).

107. *Kusper v. Pontikes*, 414 U.S. 51 (1973).

108. *Storer v. Brown, Frommhagen v. Brown*, 415 U.S. 724 (1974).

109. *Cousins v. Wigoda*, 419 U.S. 477 (1975).

110. *Democratic Party of the United States v. La Follette*, 450 U.S. 107 (1981).

111. *Brown v. Socialist Workers '74 Campaign Committee*, 459 U.S. 81 (1982).

112. *California Democratic Party v. Jones*, 530 U.S. 567 at 574 (2000).

113. Id. at 590.

114. Id. 600–601.

115. Id. at 588–589.

116. *Elrod v. Burns*, 427 U.S. 347 at 357 (1976). See also *Buckley v. Valeo*, 424 U.S. 1 at 11 (1976). The reference to "orderly group activity" is from *National Association for the Advancement of Colored People v. Button*, 371 U.S. 415 at 430 (1963).

117. *Elrod v. Burns*, 427 U.S. 347 at 358 (1976).

118. *United Public Workers v. Mitchell*, 330 U.S. 75 (1947); *Civil Service Commission v. Letter Carriers*, 413 U.S. 548 (1973).

119. *Elrod v. Burns*, 427 U.S. 347 at 372–373 (1976).

120. Id. at 379.

121. *Branti v. Finkel*, 445 U.S. 507 (1980).

122. *Rutan v. Republican Party of Illinois*, 497 U.S. 62 (1990).

123. Id. at 64.

124. Id. at 93.

125. Id. at 93–94.

126. *Board of County Commissioners, Wabaunsee County v. Umbehr*, 518 U.S. 668 (1996); *O'Hare Truck Service v. City of Northlake*, 518 U.S 712 (1996).

127. *Board of County Commissioners, Wabaunsee County v. Umbehr*, 518 U.S. 668 at 685 (1996).

chapter 4

The Second Amendment and the Right to Bear Arms

For much of the Supreme Court's history, the Second Amendment was treated as the forgotten amendment. Although drafted by James Madison and added to the Constitution as one of the first ten amendments in 1791, its impact was initially minimal. It reads, "A well-regulated Militia, being necessary to the security of a free State, the right of the people to keep and bear Arms, shall not be infringed." Madison's first draft had included a third clause, which was later dropped. It stated, "But no person religiously scrupulous of bearing arms, shall be compelled to render military service in person."

The Second Amendment made clear that Congress could not abolish a state's militia. The so-called Anti-Federalists of the time feared an all-powerful central government as well as professional standing armies. In the South, the prospect of a slave revolt haunted many. To win support for the Constitution, Madison promised that he would protect the states' right to have a militia of well-armed citizens. The Second Amendment and the Third Amendment succeeded in their initial aims and then withered. No one proposed to do away with state militias in violation of the Second Amendment, and no one in government proposed having soldiers "quartered in any house" in violation of the Third Amendment.

In the view of many, however, the Second Amendment and right "to keep and bear arms" went beyond militias. They understood it to protect an individual's right to possess a gun for self-defense. They also could point to a strong historical tradition. In England as well as in colonial America, the right to self-defense was considered to be a basic right. The 1689 English Bill of Rights states, "Protestants may have arms for their defense," and Blackstone describes "the right of having arms and using arms for self-preservation and defence" as among the fundamental rights of liberty. Some of the early state constitutions that preceded the U.S. Constitution contained similar declarations. Pennsylvania, for example, declared that "the people have a right to bear arms for the defence of themselves and the state."[1]

ONLY FEDERAL GUN LAWS LIMITED

The Supreme Court gave the Second Amendment short shrift for two centuries. Until the Civil War, it was understood that the Bill of Rights restricted only the federal government, not states or local governments. The Reconstruction Congress intended to change that in order to protect the rights of citizens. In particular, northern lawmakers intended to give the newly freed slaves the protections of the Constitution and federal civil rights law so they could do business, arm themselves to protect their freedom, and vote (in the case of men). In 1875, however, the Court dismantled these protections in a ruling that dismissed a series of criminal charges against several white men who had led a

RESOURCES ON THE SECOND AMENDMENT IN HISTORY AND IN LAW

Cornell, Saul. *A Well-Regulated Militia: The Founding Fathers and the Origins of Gun Control in America.* Oxford and New York: Oxford University Press, 2006.

   Tells the history of the gun rights in colonial America and describes how this right evolved in the nineteenth and twentieth centuries.

Doherty, Brian. *Gun Control on Trial: Inside the Supreme Court Battle over the Second Amendment.* Washington, D.C.: Cato Institute, 2008.

   Tells the story of the lawyers who fashioned and won the *Heller* case.

Halbrook, Stephen P. *The Founders' Second Amendment: Origins of the Right to Bear Arms.* Chicago: Independent Institute, 2008.

   Focuses on the framers of the U.S. Constitution and their support for the right to bear arms.

Malcolm, Joyce Lee. *To Keep and Bear Arms: The Origins of an Anglo-American Right.* Cambridge, Mass.: Harvard University Press, 1996.

   Focuses on the English origins of the right that became the Second Amendment.

massacre of blacks in Colfax, Louisiana. One count charged that the black men had been deprived of their right to "bear arms for a lawful purpose," but the Court stated in *United States v. Cruikshank,* "This is not a right granted by the Constitution.... The Second Amendment declares that it shall not be infringed; but this, as has been seen, means no more than it shall not be infringed by Congress. This is one of the amendments that has no other effect than to restrict the powers of the national government."[2] In *Presser v. Illinois* (1886), the Court reasserted this view when it upheld an Illinois man's conviction for organizing a private military unit outside the control of the state national guard in violation of state law. "We think it clear that the sections [of the Illinois law] under consideration ... do not infringe the right of the people to keep and bear arms. But a conclusive answer to the contention that this [second] amendment prohibits the legislation in question lies in the fact that the amendment is a limitation only upon the power of Congress and the National government, and not upon that of the States."[3]

The *Miller* Decision and the Effectiveness of the Militia

The Second Amendment fared no better throughout the twentieth century, even when federal gun laws were at issue. In 1939 the Court rejected a Second

As these bumper stickers displayed at a 2003 National Rifle Association meeting bear witness, the NRA is a powerful opponent of gun control legislation.

Amendment challenge to the National Firearms Act, which made it a crime to transport machine guns and sawed-off shotguns across state lines. Jack Miller and Frank Layton had been indicted for carrying a double-barreled shotgun from Oklahoma into Arkansas. They contended that the firearms act infringed their right to keep and bear arms. The Court disagreed unanimously in *United States v. Miller*. Its opinion examined the colonial history of the Second Amendment and determined that it was intended to protect state militias. Wrote Justice James C. McReynolds, "The sentiment of the time strongly disfavored standing armies; the common view was that adequate defense of country and laws could be secured through the Militia—civilians primarily, soldiers on occasion.... With the obvious purpose to assure the continuation and render possible the effectiveness of such forces, the declaration and guarantee of the Second Amendment were made. It must be interpreted and applied with that end in view."[4]

With that understanding, the Court rejected Miller's appeal. "In the absence of any evidence tending to show that possession or use of a shotgun having a barrel of less than eighteen inches in length at this time has some reasonable relationship to the preservation or efficiency of a well-regulated militia, we cannot say that the Second Amendment guarantees the right to keep and bear such an instrument. Certainly it is not within judicial notice that this weapon is any part of the ordinary military equipment or that its use could contribute to the common defense."[5] There, the law stood for decades. The Second Amendment was about militias and militia service. It did not protect someone's right to have a gun for his personal use.

By the latter decades of the twentieth century, this view of the Second Amendment struck many as peculiar. The Bill of Rights had come to be understood as a set of legal protections for individual rights. The First Amendment protected the free speech rights of individuals, and it shielded persons whose "free exercise of religion" did not comport with the majority's view. The Fourth Amendment referred to the "right to the people" to be shielded from "unreasonable searches and seizures"; this too was understood to protect individuals. What then to make of the Second Amendment

and its reference to the "right of the people to keep and bear arms"? The National Rifle Association (NRA) incorporated these words into a powerful advertising campaign against gun control. The phrase was repeated so often that the right to "keep and bear arms" became one of the best-known phrases in the Constitution, even as the Second Amendment itself had virtually vanished from the law. Repeatedly, the Court turned down appeals that cited the Second Amendment to challenge convictions on gun possession charges.

SECOND AMENDMENT REVIVAL: A LOSS FOR THE DISTRICT OF COLUMBIA'S HANDGUN BAN

Lawyers at the libertarian Cato Institute in Washington, D.C., believed that the Constitution strongly protects the rights of individuals and limits the powers of the government, and they had often championed rights that were out of favor, including property rights. A senior Cato lawyer, Robert A. Levy, sought to mount a legal challenge to the *Miller* decision and to revive the Second Amendment as a protection for individual gun rights. He found a suitable target close to home—the District of Columbia's gun control law, the strictest such statute in the nation. Enacted in 1976, the law prohibited residents from possessing a handgun, even if kept at home. Residents could apply for a permit to have a rifle or shotgun, but only if those weapons were kept disassembled or under lock. A successful entrepreneur before joining Cato, Levy decided in 2002 to finance a lawsuit challenging the D.C. ordinance and therefore enlisted six plaintiffs who lived in the city. One of them, Dick Heller, worked as a guard at the Federal Judicial Center and carried a handgun. He applied for a permit to keep his handgun at home, but he was denied. Another plaintiff, Shelly Parker, said she lived in a high-crime neighborhood and wanted a handgun for self-defense. A federal judge rejected their Second Amendment claim, citing the decision in *Miller*, but the U.S. Court of Appeals for the District of Columbia sided with the plaintiffs in 2007, ruling that the D.C. ordinance violated the Second Amendment.

REACTIONS TO THE *HELLER* DECISION

The following are press statements issued on June 26, 2008, following the Supreme Court's announcement of its decision in *District of Columbia v. Heller* (2008).

"As a longstanding advocate of the rights of gun owners in America, I applaud the Supreme Court's historic decision today confirming what has always been clear in the Constitution: the Second Amendment protects an individual right to keep and bear firearms."

—President George W. Bush

"I have always believed that the Second Amendment protects the rights of individuals to bear arms, but I also identify with the need for crime-ravaged communities to save their children from violence that plagues our streets through common-sense, effective safety measures. I know what works in Chicago may not work in Cheyenne. We can work together to enact common-sense laws, like closing the gun-show loophole and improving our

background-check system, so that guns do not fall into the hands of terrorists or criminals."

—Sen. Barack Obama, Democratic nominee for U.S. president

"It looks to be a phenomenal day for gun owners and District of Columbia residents. The next step is to ensure that every American has access to this right."

—Wayne LaPierre, chief executive of the National Rifle Association

"While we disagree with the Supreme Court's ruling, which strips citizens of the District of Columbia of a law they strongly support, the decision clearly suggests that other gun laws are entirely consistent with the Constitution."

—Paul Helmke, president of the Brady Campaign to Prevent Handgun Violence

---

The city appealed, and the Supreme Court agreed to decide the case of *District of Columbia v. Heller* (2008).[6]

Scalia and Originalism

Justice Antonin Scalia had long been the Court's foremost proponent of deciding cases based on the original meaning and text of the Constitution. Scalia's approach may seem unremarkable, but justices often look to the Court's precedents as the starting point for making decisions in cases before them. In one famous example, Justice Harry A. Blackmun in *Roe v. Wade* cited prior cases that referred to a right to "privacy," but he did not quote wording in the Constitution that could serve as the source of this right. Scalia, however, has insisted on focusing on the words of the Constitution and what they originally meant, an approach that legal scholars call originalism. Scalia was also the Court's most avid hunter. He regularly went hunting.[7] Because of the dearth of Second Amendment cases over the years, the D.C. handgun case allowed the

Court to write on a nearly blank slate. When the Court voted 5-4 to strike down the law, Chief Justice John G. Roberts Jr. chose Scalia, the hunter and originalist, to write the opinion. The Court announced the decision on June 26, 2008.

Scalia's sixty-four-page opinion analyzed the text and history of the Second Amendment and past cases involving it. At the outset, he acknowledged that there are two quite different ways to read the Second Amendment. One view, held by the city and the dissenters, believes "it protects only the right to possess and carry a firearm in connection with military service." The other view, endorsed by the Court's majority, holds that "it protects an individual right to possess a firearm unconnected with service in a militia, and to use that arm for traditionally lawful purposes, such as self-defense within the home." Scalia concluded that "because the inherent right of self-defense has been central to the Second Amendment right," the D.C. ban was unconstitutional. It "amounts to a prohibition on

Gun rights supporters cheer the Supreme Court's 2008 decision in *District of Columbia v. Heller* that struck down the District of Columbia's strictest-in-the-nation handgun ban. In *Heller*, the Court heard detailed arguments on the Second Amendment's right "to keep and bear arms" for the first time in nearly 70 years.

an entire class of arms that is overwhelmingly chosen by American society for that lawful purpose."

Scalia asserted that the words and history of the Second Amendment show that it protects the "right of the people" as individuals to defend themselves and, when necessary, defend their community. "Nowhere else in the Constitution does a 'right' attributed to 'the people' refer to anything other than an individual right," he wrote. Some argued that the phrase "keep and bear arms" refers to military service only, but Scalia said the phrase was used more broadly in the seventeenth and eighteenth centuries. "'Keep arms' was simply a common way of referring to possessing arms, for militiamen and everyone else," he said.

Looking to history, Scalia said the Second Amendment wrote into the Constitution a "preexisting right." The American colonists, as well as the

English, believed that they had a right to have firearms to protect themselves "against both public and private violence." As for the prefatory clause—a "well-regulated militia, being necessary to the security of a free State"—Scalia said,

> It fits perfectly, once one knows the history.... That history showed that the way tyrants had eliminated a militia consisting of all able-bodied men was not by banning the militia but simply by taking away the people's arms.... The prefatory clause does not suggest that preserving the militia was the only reason Americans valued the ancient right; most undoubtedly thought it even more important for self-defense and hunting. But the threat that the new Federal Government would destroy the citizens' militia by taking away their arms was the reason that right—unlike some other English rights—was codified in the written Constitution.

Scalia dismissed the Court's earlier gun cases as having little significance. The *Miller* decision held only that the sawed-off shotgun had no military value, he said. "We conclude that nothing in our precedents forecloses our adoption of the original understanding of the Second Amendment." No sooner had Scalia stated that Americans have an individual right to a gun, however, he followed with a lengthy passage to limit the significance of this ruling:

> Like most rights, the right secured by the Second Amendment is not unlimited. From Blackstone through the 19th-century cases, commentators and courts routinely explained that the right was not a right to keep and carry any weapon whatsoever in any manner whatsoever and for whatever purpose. For example, the majority of the 19th-century courts to consider the question held that prohibitions on carrying concealed weapons were lawful under the Second Amendment or state analogues. Although we do not undertake an exhaustive historical analysis today of the full scope of the Second Amendment, nothing in our opinion should be taken to cast doubt on longstanding prohibitions on the possession of firearms by felons and the mentally ill, or laws forbidding the carrying of firearms in sensitive places such as schools and government buildings, or law imposing conditions and qualifications on the commercial sale of arms.

Nonetheless, the D.C. ordinance could not stand, Scalia said, because it is a total ban on a weapon that is most useful to self-defense. "In sum, we hold that the District's ban on handgun possession in the home violates the Second Amendment, as does its prohibition against rendering any lawful firearm in the home operable for the purpose of immediate self-defense," he said. Chief Justice Roberts and Justices Anthony M. Kennedy, Clarence Thomas, and Samuel A. Alito Jr. agreed entirely with Scalia's opinion in *Heller*.

Scalia did not seek to answer two important questions: First, how is this right to be judged? For example, is the Second Amendment right like the First Amendment right to freedom of speech? If so, any infringement on this right would be subjected to strict scrutiny by judges and would be unconstitutional unless the government had a compelling need for it. Scalia's comment above suggests that many, if not most, gun control restrictions would survive despite a reinvigorated Second Amendment. Second, does the right to a gun extend to state laws and local ordinances? The logic of Scalia's opinion suggests that it does because it is a constitutional right; he states, however, in footnote 23 that the question of state or local law is "not presented by this case," because the District of Columbia is a federal district—not a state. The Court would leave it to another day to decide the reach of the Second Amendment.

Justices John Paul Stevens, David H. Souter, Ruth Bader Ginsburg, and Stephen G. Breyer dissented. In his forty-six-page dissent, Stevens asserted that Scalia was wrong on virtually every point. He argued that the text and original history show that the Second Amendment was about protecting militias, not hunters. "The Second Amendment was adopted to protect the right of the people of each of the several states to maintain a well-regulated militia," he wrote. It had nothing to do with the "use or possession of firearms for purely civilian purposes." James Madison's original draft confirms the "distinctly military" character of the Second Amendment in its statement that no "religiously scrupulous" person—what we call today a conscientious objector—"shall be compelled to render military service."

Stevens said a proper reading of the words "keep and bear arms" confirms that the amendment concerns military service. He quotes a state judge in 1840 who wrote, "A man in the pursuit of deer, elk and buffaloes might carry his rifle every day, for forty years, and yet, it would never be said of him that he had borne arms" (footnote 10). Stevens accused Scalia and the majority of ignoring two centuries of settled law and adopting a new definition of the Second Amendment that could undercut popular gun control measures. "The right the Court announces was not 'enshrined' in the Second Amendment by the Framers; it is a product of today's law-changing decision.... Until today, it has been understood that legislatures may regulate the civilian use and misuse of firearms so long as they do not interfere with the preservation of a well-regulated militia," he wrote. "I fear that the District's policy choice may well be just the first of an unknown number of dominoes to be knocked off the table."

In a separate dissent, Breyer said that cities with rampant gun violence need more authority to restrict guns and that nothing in the Second Amendment forecloses that choice. He noted that Boston, Philadelphia, and New York City, the three largest cities in colonial America, restricted the firing of a gun within city limits. If those ordinances were seen as reasonable regulations in the late eighteenth century, why should the Second Amendment of 1791 be read now to forbid city gun regulations, he asked. He too said he worried about the future implications of the *Heller* decision. It "threatens to throw into doubt the constitutionality of gun laws throughout the United States," Breyer said. "In my view, there simply is no untouchable constitutional right guaranteed by the Second Amendment to keep loaded handguns in the house in crime-ridden urban areas."

NOTES

1. 1 Blackstone, *Commentaries*, 139–140 (1765).
2. *United States v. Cruikshank,* 92 U.S. 542 at 553 (1875).
3. *Presser v. Illinois,* 116 U.S. 252 at 264 (1886).
4. *United States v. Miller,* 307 U.S. 174 at 178–179 (1939).
5. Id. at 178.
6. *District of Columbia v. Heller,* 554 U.S. __ (2008).
7. In 2004 Scalia had accompanied Vice President Dick Cheney on a hunting trip shortly after the Court had agreed to decide a case challenging the secrecy surrounding the vice president's energy policy task force.

chapter 5

Crime and Punishment

More of the Bill of Rights is devoted to crime and punishment than to any other topic. This should come as little surprise given that the government's power to arrest, punish, and imprison people can make for a police state if this authority is not strictly limited by law. The framers of the Constitution had a healthy fear of unchecked government power because they had experienced it themselves during the colonial era.

The king of England and his agents in the colonies depended for revenue on taxes and duties on all sorts of goods and imports, not just taxes on tea, but on soap, salt, paper, glass, and alcohol, among others. Despite the well-known English maxim that "A man's house is his castle," British officers relied on general warrants to search and seize property at will for untaxed items. In Parliament in 1763, William Pitt had given voice to the home as castle: "The poorest man may, in his cottage, bid defiance to all the forces of the Crown. It may be frail; its roof may shake. The wind may blow through it. The storm may enter. The rain may enter, but the King of England may not enter. All his force dare not cross the threshold of the ruined tenement." Yet the colonists across the Atlantic were experiencing something quite different.

British colonial forces relied on indiscriminate searches of homes, stables, and warehouses as "the ordinary means of collecting royal revenues," wrote constitutional historian Leonard W. Levy.[1] The Fourth Amendment of the Constitution was intended to prohibit unrestricted searches by the government: "The right of the people to be secure in their persons, papers and effects, against unreasonable searches and seizures, shall not be violated, and no Warrants shall issue, but upon probable cause, supported by Oath and affirmation, and particularly describing the place to be searched, and the persons or things to be seized." The principle of limited searches continues to resonate every day. It forbids police from forcibly entering homes and apartments without a warrant from a magistrate. It limits what officers can search for in cars stopped along the highway or on pedestrians on the sidewalk. Its limits extend even to school lockers and to drug tests required by the government.

The Fifth and Sixth Amendments established rules for trials by jury. The framers knew the history of sixteenth- and seventeenth-century political trials in England, when the king's men met in secret and served as inquisitors and judges. In the Star Chamber, they could force men to confess to treasonous acts and these confessions used in turn to convict others. Sir Walter Raleigh, a hero of Queen Elizabeth's reign, was tried and convicted of treason after her death in 1603. The evidence against him consisted mostly of a statement that Lord Cobham, his supposed co-conspirator, had given to inquisitors. Raleigh demanded that Cobham testify at his trial and state his accusation. "Let Cobham be here. Let him speak it. Call my accuser before my face," he said.[2] His request was denied, but the injustice of Raleigh's conviction led to the so-called confrontation right in the Sixth Amendment: "In all criminal prosecutions, the accused shall enjoy the right ... to be confronted with the witnesses against him."

In Roman times and during the Spanish inquisition, accused persons were forced to take an oath to tell the truth and to confess their crimes and sins. In 1637 John Lilburne, a Puritan agitator, was brought before the Star Chamber, where he refused to take the oath or answer questions. His example is cited often in English law and became the basis for the right against self-incrimination in the Fifth Amendment: "No person shall ... be compelled in any criminal case to be a witness against himself." In the landmark decision in *Miranda v. Arizona* (1966) establishing the "right to remain silent," Chief Justice Earl Warren cited Lilburne's trial, calling it "the critical historical event" leading to Anglo-American rule against compelled self-incrimination.

According to some scholars, the most important right in the Constitution may be the right to a jury trial. Yale law professor Akhil Amar asserts that the framers acted on the assumption that judges could be agents of the state, but that ordinary jurors would act as "populist protectors." In adopting the Bill of Rights, "The dominant strategy to keep agents of the central government under control was to use the populist and local institution of the jury," he wrote.[3] The Fifth Amendment says no person may be prosecuted for a "capital or otherwise infamous crime, unless on presentment or indictment of a Grand Jury." Once indicted for a crime, "the accused shall enjoy the right to a speedy and public trial, by an impartial jury of the state," the Sixth Amendment states.

Beyond these specific rights, the Fifth Amendment includes a catch-all procedural right that has come to have broad importance: "No person shall ... be deprived of life, liberty or property, without due process of law." This phrase appears again in the Fourteenth Amendment. Over time, the notion of "due process of law" in a criminal proceeding came to stand for the principle of fundamental fairness. "It is procedure that spells much of the difference between rule by law and rule by whim or caprice," wrote Justice William O. Douglas.[4]

People convicted of crimes perhaps deserve to be punished, but there too, the Constitution set limits. The framers knew of ghastly stories from English history involving beheadings and burnings at the stake. They also knew of prisoners who had had their eyes gouged and their ears severed; some had been tortured on the rack. The Eighth Amendment did not exclude particular punishments, but instead adopted the principle that "cruel and unusual punishments [shall not be] inflicted."

Despite the hard-won victories that led to the Constitution and the Bill of Rights, these enumerated rights had little impact on the law or the lives of ordinary Americans and residents through much of the nation's history. Because the Bill of Rights begins with the phrase, "Congress shall make no law ...," the Supreme Court determined that its limits applied only to Congress, and by extension, the federal government. Crime and punishment has always been, and remains today, largely a matter for state law and local police. Moreover, rights are meaningless unless they can be enforced. What, for example, would be the significance if the police, acting on no more than a hunch, could break into a house or a car and seize evidence? The rule against "unreasonable searches and seizures" had teeth only after the courts said that illegally seized evidence would be thrown out. It was not until the 1960s that the Supreme Court decided that the rights set out in the Fourth, Fifth, Sixth, and Eighth Amendments apply to the states and that violations of those rights would result in suppressing the evidence or a confession.

THE LONG MARCH TOWARD TODAY'S BILL OF RIGHTS

In the 1800s during the tenure of Chief Justice John Marshall, the Supreme Court held that the Bill of Rights limited only the federal government, not the states. The Court set out this conclusion in *Barron v. Baltimore* (1833), which was decided without dissent.[5] With Marshall writing, the Court rejected the argument of a Baltimore wharf owner that the Fifth Amendment guarantee of just compensation to persons whose private property was taken for public use applied against all governments, not just the federal government. This was not the intent of the Bill of Rights, according to Marshall:

> The Constitution was ordained and established by the people of the United States for themselves, for their own government, and not for the government of the individual States…. The powers they conferred on this government were to be exercised by itself; and the limitations on power, if expressed in general terms, are naturally, and, we think, necessarily applicable to the government created by the instrument.
>
> … the provision in the fifth amendment to the Constitution, declaring that private property shall not be taken for public use without just compensation, is intended solely as a limitation on the exercise of power by the government of the United States, and is not applicable to the legislation of the States.[6]

Although the justices refused to extend the Fifth Amendment's guarantee of due process against *state* action, the Court in the 1850s applied that guarantee to legislative action by Congress, making clear that all branches of the *federal* government were bound by it. In *Murray's Lessee v. Hoboken Land and Improvement Company* (1856), the Court upheld an act of Congress authorizing the Treasury Department to issue warrants against the property of federal revenue collectors who were indebted to the federal government.[7] The law had been challenged as allowing the taking of property without due process. In the majority opinion by Justice Benjamin R. Curtis, the Court began its effort to define due process as any process that did not conflict with specific constitutional provisions or established judicial practices.

> That the warrant now in question is legal process, is not denied. It was issued in conformity with an act of Congress. But is it "due process of law?" The Constitution contains no description of those processes which it was intended to allow or forbid. It does not even declare what principles are to be applied to ascertain whether it be due process. It is manifest that it was not left to the legislative power to enact any process which might be devised. The article is a restraint on the legislative as well as on

the executive and judicial powers of the government, and cannot be so construed as to leave Congress free to make any process "due process of law," by its mere will. To what principles, then, are we to resort to ascertain whether this process enacted by Congress, is due process? To this the answer must be twofold. We must examine the Constitution itself, to see whether this process be in conflict with any of its provisions. If not found to be so, we must look to those settled usages and modes of proceeding existing in the common and statute law of England, before the emigration of our ancestors and which are shown not to have been unsuited to their civil and political condition by having been acted on by them after the settlement of this country.[8]

In 1868, twelve years after *Hoboken*, the Fourteenth Amendment became part of the Constitution. Its framers intended it to forbid the states to deprive any person of life, liberty, or property without due process of law. The due process guarantee was, however, initially used with a great deal more effect to protect property than to protect life or liberty. This was the result of the development of the doctrine of substantive due process, that is, the view that the substance, as well as the procedures, of a law must comply with due process. *(See box, The Protection of Substantive Due Process, pp. 478–479.)* In the mid-twentieth century, Justice Robert H. Jackson compared the two types of due process:

> Procedural due process is more elemental and less flexible than substantive due process. It yields less to the times, varies less with conditions, and defers much less to legislative judgment. Insofar as it is technical law, it must be a specialized responsibility within the competence of the judiciary on which they do not bend before political branches of the Government, as they should on matters of policy which comprise substantive law.[9]

For sixty-five years after the Fourteenth Amendment was ratified, its Due Process Clause provided little protection to persons tried in state and local courts. In 1884 the Court held that due process did not require states to use indictments to charge persons with capital crimes, despite the Fifth Amendment provision requiring indictments in similar federal cases. In 1900 the

STUDENTS AND CRIME AND PUNISHMENT

In the 1970s, the Court recognized the constitutional rights of students in the area of discipline and punishment, but more recently it has moved toward giving school officials greater authority over students. Before a student is suspended from school, he is entitled to a hearing and "an opportunity to present his side of the story," the Court had held in *Goss v. Lopez* (1975).[1] The Fourteenth Amendment says that a state may not deprive a person of "liberty (or) property without due process of law," and the right to public education is a type of property, the justices said. "At the very minimum, therefore, students facing suspension ... must be given some kind of notice and afforded some kind of hearing," the Court held.[2] While the school need not adopt "trial-type procedures" with a lawyer, witnesses, and cross-examination, it must tell the student why he is being suspended, explain the evidence against him, and allow him "to give his version of events." The ruling in *Goss v. Lopez* stemmed from a period of racial unrest in Columbus, Ohio, where nine African American students were suspended for at least ten days without a hearing.

The Court later refused to require school officials to hold a hearing before administering a paddling or otherwise to limit the paddling of students. The Eighth Amendment prohibits "cruel and unusual punishment," and on that ground in 1970 sixteen students from a junior high in Miami sued after they had been paddled severely; one student received fifty licks for making an obscene phone call. While the Court agreed that the punishment was "exceptionally harsh," the 5-4 majority ruled in *Ingraham v. Wright* (1977) that the Eighth Amendment was "designed to protect those convicted of crimes," not to regulate the schools.[3] Since then, however, half of the states have banned corporal punishment, and some lower courts have upheld awards of monetary damages for students who were injured in beatings administered by teachers or principals.

In 1985 the Court declared "reasonableness" the rule governing searches of students, including their purses and lockers. This legal standard generally did not allow a school principal to inspect all of the lockers or all of the bags of students, but instead could trigger a search when there was reason to believe an individual student had violated the rules. The case involved a fourteen-year-old freshman known by her initials, T.L.O., who had done just that. A teacher at Piscataway High School found her and a girlfriend smoking in the lavatory in 1980. The two were taken to the principal's office, where one girl admitted to smoking. T.L.O. denied it. The assistant principal took her in his office and examined her purse. He not only found cigarettes, but also a small amount of marijuana, a wad of money, and a list of students. T.L.O. later confessed to selling marijuana at school and was put on probation for a year. She contended that the search of her purse was illegal, and the evidence should therefore have been suppressed. The New Jersey state courts agreed with her, but the Supreme Court did not.

On the one hand, the justices held that the Fourth Amendment's ban on "unreasonable searches and seizures applies to searches by public school officials," but on the other, however, school authorities do not need "probable cause" or a search warrant before they look into a student's purse or locker, they added. "Under ordinary circumstances, a search of a student by a teacher or other school officials will be justified ... when there are reasonable grounds for suspecting that the search will turn up evidence that the student has violated or is violating either the law or the rules of the school," wrote Justice Byron R. White in *New Jersey v. T.L.O.* (1985).[4] The search of her purse was reasonable, the justices said, because T.L.O. had been seen smoking, yet denied having cigarettes. Because this initial search was reasonable, the other evidence found in her purse may be used against her, the Court concluded.

Court held that the due process guarantee did not require states to use twelve-person juries. In 1908 the Court held that the Fifth Amendment privilege against compelled self-incrimination did not protect state defendants.

In *Hurtado v. California* (1884), the Court upheld the murder conviction and death sentence of Joseph Hurtado, who was charged without an indictment.[10] He

challenged his conviction, arguing that under Justice Curtis's definition of due process in *Hoboken*, he had been denied due process. The Court's ruling, relaxing the earlier standard for the demands of due process upon state criminal procedures, blurred the *Hoboken* definition. Writing for the seven-man majority, Justice Stanley Matthews redefined due process as "any legal proceeding enforced by public authority, whether sanctioned by age

By the 1990s, the reasonableness standard had faded and was replaced by rules allowing routine searches of all students whenever there was a "special need" cited. One such special need was to keep guns and knives out of schools. When metal detectors were put at the doors of some high schools, no one seriously contended that such searches were unconstitutional. Some schools adopted policies of drug testing students who participated in sports or other extracurricular activities, and these were challenged as unconstitutional because they were not triggered by evidence that an individual had used drugs. In the mid-1990s, the Court rejected such a challenge and upheld an Oregon school district's policy of testing the urine of athletes, once before the season and randomly during the season.

The Court cited at least five reasons for its conclusion in *Vernonia School District v. Acton* (1995). Drug abuse was a national problem, and it had become a local problem in the small logging community of Vernonia, Oregon, in the late 1980s, school officials said. Students are not adults, but are in the "temporary custody" of the schools. Beyond that, sports can be dangerous if athletes are impaired by drugs. Further, because athletes are "role models" for other students, it is important that they be drug free. Finally, giving a urine sample is not a severe invasion of privacy, particularly in the context of a school locker room. "School sports are not for the bashful," Justice Antonin Scalia commented.[5] In passing, Scalia also noted that a positive drug test did not trigger a criminal charge, but instead a meeting with the student's parents and, at worse, a suspension from playing sports. "Taking account all of the factors we have considered above,… we conclude Vernonia's policy is reasonable and hence constitutional," Scalia said.[6] Justices Sandra Day O'Connor, John Paul Stevens, and David H. Souter dissented, saying that an individual student should be tested only when there is reason to believe he has used drugs.

In 2002 the Court went a step further and upheld a drug-testing program that covered all students participating in extracurricular activities. Lindsay Earls, a member of the choir and the marching band, challenged these searches as unconstitutional and won before the U.S. Court of Appeals, which noted the absence of an "identifiable drug abuse problem" in her rural Oklahoma high school. The Court, however, in a 5-4 ruling, upheld the school's policy in *Board of Education v. Earls* (2002). "Given a nationwide epidemic of drug use,… it was entirely reasonable for the school district to enact this particular drug testing policy," said Justice Clarence Thomas. "The invasion of students' privacy is not significant."[7]

In a concurring opinion, Justice Stephen G. Breyer said the testing policy seeks to "change the school's environment in order to combat the single most important factor leading children to take drugs, namely, peer pressure.… I cannot know whether the school's drug testing program will work. But, in my view, the Constitution does not prohibit the effort."[8] The dissenters, led by Justice Ruth Bader Ginsburg, said the "particular testing program upheld today is not reasonable. It is capricious, even perverse: [It] targets for testing a student population least likely to be at risk from illicit drugs and their damaging effects."[9]

---

1. *Goss v. Lopez,* 419 U.S. 565 (1975).

2. Id at 579.

3. *Ingraham v. Wright,* 430 U.S. 651 (1977).

4. *New Jersey v. T.L.O.,* 469 U.S. 325 at 341–342 (1985).

5. *Vernonia School District v. Acton,* 515 U.S. 646 at 657 (1995).

6. Id. at 665.

7. *Board of Education v. Earls,* 536 U.S. 822 (2002).

8. Id.

9. Id.

---

and custom, or newly devised in the discretion of the legislative power, in furtherance of the general public good, which regards, and preserves these principles of liberty and justice."[11] Matthews further explained, however, that "not every Act, legislative in form,… is law":

Law is something more than mere will exerted as an act of power. It must be not a special rule for a particular person or a particular case,… thus excluding, as not due process of law, Acts of attainder, Bills of pains and penalties, Acts of confiscation, Acts reversing judgments, and Acts directly transferring one man's estate to another, legislative judgments and decrees, and other similar, special, partial and arbitrary exertions of power under the forms of legislation. Arbitrary power, enforcing its edicts to the injury of the persons and property of its subjects, is not law, whether manifested as the decree of a personal monarch or of an impersonal multitude.[12]

Adopting reasoning diametrically opposed to that of Justice Curtis in *Hoboken,* the majority ruled that because the Fifth Amendment expressly included *both* the indictment requirement *and* the due process guarantee, the indictment requirement was obviously not included as an element of due process.

In lone dissent, Justice John Marshall Harlan set out the "incorporation" approach. In his view, the Fourteenth Amendment guarantee of due process incorporated many of the specific guarantees of the Bill of Rights, effectively nullifying *Barron v. Baltimore* by applying those guarantees against state action. Harlan argued that the Court's reasoning in *Hurtado* could open the door for states to deny defendants many other rights:

> If the presence in the Fifth Amendment of a specific provision for grand juries in capital cases, alongside the provision for due process of law in proceedings involving life, liberty or property, is held to prove that "due process of law" did not, in the judgment of the framers of the Constitution, necessarily require a grand jury in capital cases, inexorable logic would require it to be, likewise, held that the right not to be put twice in jeopardy of life and limb for the same offense, nor compelled in a criminal case to testify against one's self—rights and immunities also specifically recognized in the Fifth Amendment—were not protected by that due process of law required by the settled usages and proceedings existing under the common and statute law of England at the settlement of this country. More than that, other Amendments of the Constitution proposed at the same time, expressly recognize the right of persons to just compensation for private property taken for public use; their right, when accused of crime, to be informed of the nature and cause of the accusation against them, and to a speedy and public trial, by an impartial jury of the State and district wherein the crime was committed; to be confronted by the witnesses against them; and to have compulsory process for obtaining witnesses in their favor. Will it be claimed that these rights were not secured by the "law of the land" or by "due process of law," as declared and established at the foundation of our government?[13]

Eventually the Court would adopt an approach of "selective incorporation" of the guarantees of the Bill of Rights into the Due Process Clause of the Fourteenth Amendment. Justice Samuel F. Miller wrote:

> If … it were possible to define what it is for a State to deprive a person of life, liberty or property without due process of law, in terms which would cover every exercise of power thus forbidden to the State, and exclude those which are not, no more useful construction could be furnished by this or any other court to any part of the fundamental law.
>
> But, apart from the imminent risk of failure to give any definition which would be at once perspicuous, comprehensive and satisfactory, there is wisdom, we think, in the ascertaining of the intent and application of such an important phrase in the Federal Constitution, by the gradual process of judicial inclusion and exclusion, as the cases presented for decision shall require, with the reasoning on which such decisions may be founded. This court is, after … nearly a century, still engaged in defining … other powers conferred on the Federal Government, or limitations imposed upon the States.[14]

The Court ruled in *Maxwell v. Dow* (1900) that the Fourteenth Amendment did not require state juries to be composed of twelve persons. Justice Harlan again dissented, protesting the contrast between the Court's vigorous use of substantive due process and its reluctance to enforce procedural due process:

> If then the "due process of law" required by the Fourteenth Amendment does not allow a State to take private property without just compensation, but does allow the life or liberty of the citizen to be taken in a mode that is repugnant to the settled usages and the modes of proceeding authorized at the time the Constitution was adopted and which was expressly forbidden in the National Bill of Rights, it would seem that the protection of private property is of more consequence than the protection of the life and liberty of the citizen.[15]

Eight years later, the Court in *Twining v. New Jersey* (1908) permitted a judge to call attention to defendants' failure to testify in their own defense. Despite the trial judge's implication that the silence was an admission of guilt, the Court ruled that due process was not denied the defendants. The defendants had claimed that the judge's comments violated their Fifth Amendment right to remain silent rather than incriminate themselves. They argued that this right was a fundamental "privilege or immunity" of federal citizenship protected against state action by the Fourteenth Amendment. The Court rejected the claim and upheld the decision of the state court, sustaining conviction. Justice William H. Moody's opinion also denied that the Fourteenth Amendment guarantee of due process extended the protection of the first eight amendments against state action:

> The essential elements of due process of law, already established ... are singularly few, though of wide application and deep significance.... Due process requires that the court which assumes to determine the rights of parties shall have jurisdiction ... and that there shall be notice and opportunity for hearing given the parties.[16]

Moody, however, left open the possibility that additional due process requirements could be imposed upon the states.

> It is possible that some of the personal rights safeguarded by the first eight Amendments against national action may also be safeguarded against state action, because a denial of them would be a denial of due process of law.... If this is so, it is not because those rights are enumerated in the first eight Amendments, but because they are of such a nature that they are included in the conception of due process of law.[17]

In the 1920s and 1930s, the Court began to rule that some rights were so fundamental to fair treatment that the due process guarantee required states to observe them. In *Palko v. Connecticut* (1937), the Court explained that some rights were "implicit in the concept of ordered liberty" and thus protected by due process against state infringement. Frank Palko had been tried twice by Connecticut for the same murder. He challenged his conviction, arguing that the second trial violated the Fifth Amendment guarantee against double jeopardy. The Court refused to reverse his conviction, declaring that the protection against double jeopardy was not one of those rights that due process required the states to observe. For the Court, divided 8-1, Justice Benjamin N. Cardozo gave a "status report" on due process and state action:

> The right to trial by jury and the immunity from prosecution except as the result of an indictment may have value and importance. Even so, they are not of the very essence of a scheme of ordered liberty. To abolish them is not to violate a "principle of justice so rooted in the traditions and conscience of our people as to be ranked as fundamental." ... What is true of jury trials and indictments is true also, as the cases show, of the immunity from compulsory self-incrimination.... This too might be lost, and justice still be done.... The exclusion of these immunities and privileges from the privileges and immunities protected against the action of the states has not been arbitrary or casual. It has been dictated by a study and appreciation of the meaning, the essential implications, of liberty itself.
>
> We reach a different plane of social and moral values when we pass to the privileges and immunities that have been taken over from the earlier articles of the federal bill of rights and brought within the Fourteenth Amendment by a process of absorption.... [T]he process of absorption has had its source in the belief that neither liberty nor justice would exist if they were sacrificed.... This is true ... of freedom of thought and speech.... Fundamental too in the concept of due process, and so in that of liberty, is the thought that condemnation shall be rendered only after trial.... The hearing, moreover, must be a real one, not a sham or a pretense, *Moore v. Dempsey*.... For that reason, ignorant defendants in a capital case were held to have been condemned unlawfully when in truth, though not in form, they were refused the aid of counsel, *Powell v. Alabama*.[18]

In *Palko*, the Court again rejected the incorporation theory, first expressed in Harlan's dissent from *Hurtado*. A decade after *Palko*, the Court in *Adamson v. California* (1947) reaffirmed that the self-incrimination guarantee did not operate against state action—its holding in *Twining*—and its general view that the Fourteenth Amendment did not incorporate the Bill of Rights.[19]

Justices Hugo L. Black, Frank Murphy, William O. Douglas, and Wiley B. Rutledge dissented in *Adamson,* arguing in favor of incorporation. They asserted that the Fourteenth Amendment was originally intended "to extend to all the people of the nation the complete protection of the Bill of Rights."[20] In the late 1960s, the battle for incorporation was finally won. Black and Douglas, who served on the Court through the 1960s, had their views at last espoused by a majority of the Court as it extended virtually all of the Bill of Rights' protections to all persons. The debate is now largely forgotten. The Bill of Rights and its protection for criminal defendants extend to every police station, every county courthouse, and every state trial. The rights it establishes extend to all Americans. Under Chief Justice John G. Roberts Jr., the Court has expressed misgivings about the exclusionary rule and whether a minor mistake by a police officer should result in excluding valid evidence against a crime suspect, but the Court is united in the view that the rights set out in the Constitution protect all Americans and bind the government at every level.

A Fair Trial by Jury

Trial by jury is a distinctive feature of the Anglo-American system of justice, dating back to the fourteenth century. The framers of the Constitution included in Article III the requirement that "the Trial of all Crimes, except in Cases of Impeachment, shall be by Jury." Not content with this single provision, those who drafted the Bill of Rights included additional guarantees of that right. The Fifth Amendment begins: "No person shall be held to answer for a capital, or otherwise infamous crime, unless on a presentment or indictment of a Grand Jury," except in matters of the military and war. The Sixth Amendment begins, "In all criminal prosecutions, the accused shall enjoy the right to a speedy and public trial, by an impartial jury of the State and district wherein the crime shall have been committed." The Seventh Amendment extends the right to a jury to civil cases. This right to a jury has been the subject of many Supreme Court rulings, which have involved the size, selection, and unanimity of juries, as well as a defendant's decision to waive the right to a jury trial, usually as a result of plea bargaining.

THE RIGHT TO A JURY TRIAL

In federal cases, the Supreme Court has been unwavering in insisting that a jury in a criminal case must consist of twelve people and must reach a unanimous verdict. (In federal civil cases, however, juries may be as small as six members.)[1] The Court in *Patton v. United States* (1930) explained that a jury trial "includes all the essential elements as they were recognized in this country and England when the Constitution was adopted":

> Those elements were: 1) That the jury should consist of twelve men, neither more nor less; 2) that the trial should be in the presence and under the superintendence of a judge having power to instruct them as to the law and advise them in respect of the facts; and 3) that the verdict should be unanimous.[2]

Not until 1968, a full century after ratification of the Fourteenth Amendment and its Due Process Clause, did the Court apply the right to trial by jury to the states. In *Walker v. Sauvinet* (1876), the Court held that the Seventh Amendment right to trial by jury in civil cases was not a privilege or immunity of federal citizenship protected against state action.[3] Later, in *Maxwell v. Dow* (1900), the Court ruled that neither the Privileges and Immunities Clause of the Fourteenth Amendment nor the Due Process Clause required that state juries consist of twelve persons. "Trial by jury has never been affirmed to be a necessary requisite of due process of law," declared the Court.[4]

With a line of decisions beginning in the 1930s, however, the Court made clear that *if* a state provided a trial by jury to a defendant, it was required to use fair procedures in selecting a jury that would represent a cross section of the community and would be relatively unbiased. In *Duncan v. Louisiana*, decided in 1968, the centennial of the adoption of the Fourteenth Amendment, the Court finally held that the right to trial by jury for persons charged with serious crimes applied to the states. According to the Court, the Sixth Amendment right to a jury trial is a necessary ingredient of due process.[5] The Sixth Amendment's guarantee reads,

> In all criminal prosecutions, the accused shall enjoy the right to a speedy and public trial, by an impartial jury of the State and district wherein the crime shall have been committed, which district shall have been previously ascertained by law, and to be informed of the nature and cause of the accusation; to be confronted with the witnesses against him; to have compulsory process for obtaining witnesses in his favor, and to have the Assistance of Counsel for his defence.

Gary Duncan, charged with battery in Louisiana courts, had been denied a jury trial; he was convicted and sentenced to a fine and two years in prison. Duncan appealed to the Supreme Court, arguing that this

DUE PROCESS FOR DELINQUENTS

Juveniles, the Supreme Court has ruled, possess some but not all of the due process rights assured to adults by the Fifth Amendment's Due Process Clause and the Sixth Amendment. Juvenile court proceedings are considered civil, not criminal, hearings. They are designed to shelter young offenders from the exposure of a public trial, giving them the opportunity to begin anew without the handicap of publicity or a criminal record. Until 1967 only general elements of due process and fair treatment were applied to these proceedings, but in *In re Gault* (1967) the Court held that juveniles charged with violating the law did have the right to confront and cross-examine persons presenting the evidence against them. Furthermore, the Court declared that juveniles had the same rights as adults to notice, aid of counsel, and protection against self-incrimination.[1]

Juveniles must be found delinquent by proof beyond a reasonable doubt rather than by any lesser standard, the Court held in *In re Winship* (1970). In this case, the justices held that Samuel Winship, a twelve-year-old found guilty by a preponderance of the evidence of stealing money from a woman's pocketbook, had been denied his due process rights. The stricter standard of proof of guilt, beyond a reasonable doubt, was an essential element of due process and fair treatment applicable to juvenile as well as adult proceedings, said the Court.[2] The following year, however, in *McKeiver v. Pennsylvania* and *In re Burrus* (1971), the Court refused to extend the right to trial by jury to juvenile court proceedings.[3] Justice Harry A. Blackmun explained:

> If the jury trial were to be injected into the juvenile court system as a matter of right, it would bring with it into that system the traditional delay, the formality and the clamor of the adversary system and, possibly, the public trial....

> If the formalities of the criminal adjudicative process are to be superimposed upon the juvenile court system, there is little need for its separate existence. Perhaps that ultimate disillusionment will come one day, but for the moment we are disinclined to give impetus to it.[4]

Four years later, the Court extended the Fifth Amendment protection against double jeopardy to minors, ruling that a defendant found in juvenile court to have violated the law could not subsequently be tried for the same act as an adult.[5]

---

1. *In re Gault*, 387 U.S. 1 (1967).

2. *In re Winship*, 397 U.S. 358 (1970).

3. *McKeiver v. Pennsylvania, In re Burrus*, 403 U.S. 528 (1971).

4. Id. at 550–551.

5. *Breed v. Jones*, 421 U.S. 519 at 529 (1975).

---

denial of a jury trial violated his right to due process. The Court agreed. Wrote Justice Byron R. White,

> Because we believe that trial by jury is fundamental to the American scheme of justice, we hold that the Fourteenth Amendment guarantees a right of jury trial in all criminal cases which—were they to be tried in a federal court—would come within the Sixth Amendment's guarantee.[6]

State Trials: Juror Numbers and Unanimity

Having ruled that trial by a jury is a fundamental right in state as well as federal prosecutions, the Court created two new questions: Are states now required to use only twelve-person juries? Must all state jury verdicts be unanimous? The answer to both questions is "no," the Court said, although nearly all the states required unanimous verdicts from twelve-member juries in criminal cases. In *Williams v. Florida* (1970), the Court held it proper for states to use juries composed of as few as six persons in noncapital cases.[7] Johnny Williams was tried for robbery by a six-man jury, which Florida law allowed in all noncapital cases. Writing for the Court, Justice White acknowledged the following:

> We do not pretend to be able to divine precisely what the word "jury" imported to the Framers, the First Congress, or the States in 1789. It may well be that the usual expectation was that the jury would consist of 12, and that hence, the most likely conclusion to be drawn is simply that little thought was actually given to the specific question we face today. But there is absolutely no indication in "the intent

of the Framers" of an explicit decision to equate the constitutional and common law characteristics of the jury. Nothing in this history suggests, then, that we do violence to the letter of the Constitution by turning to other than purely historical considerations to determine which features of the jury system, as it existed at common law, were preserved in the Constitution. The relevant inquiry, as we see it, must be the function which the particular feature performs and its relation to the purposes of the jury trial. Measured by this standard, the 12-man requirement cannot be regarded as an indispensable component of the Sixth Amendment....

... [T]he essential feature of a jury obviously lies in the interposition between the accused and his accuser of the common-sense judgment of a group of laymen, and in the community participation and shared responsibility which results from the group's determination of guilt or innocence. The performance of this role is not a function of the particular number of the body which makes up the jury. To be sure the number should probably be large enough to promote group deliberation, free from outside attempts at intimidation, and to provide a fair possibility for obtaining a representative cross section of the community. But we find little reason to think that these goals are in any meaningful sense less likely to be achieved when the jury numbers six, than when it numbers 12— particularly if the requirement of unanimity is retained. And, certainly the reliability of the jury as a factfinder hardly seems likely to be a function of its size.[8]

In 1978 the Supreme Court made plain that juries must consist of at least six persons, rejecting Georgia's use of a five-person jury.[9] The same day the Court in *Williams* resolved the question of jury size, it answered another question: What crimes were serious enough to require states to provide a jury trial? In *Baldwin v. New York* (1970), the Court held that states must provide trial by jury for all persons charged with offenses that could be punished by more than six months in prison.[10]

In the early 1970s, the Court held that state juries need not reach their verdicts unanimously. This ruling came in *Johnson v. Louisiana* (1972) and *Apodaca v. Oregon* (1972).[11] In the Louisiana case, the

Court upheld a state jury's 9-3 verdict convicting a man of robbery. Writing for the majority, Justice White declared that "want of jury unanimity is not to be equated with the existence of a reasonable doubt" concerning a defendant's guilt. The Court rejected the defendant's argument "that in order to give substance to the reasonable doubt standard which the State, by virtue of the Due Process Clause of the Fourteenth Amendment, must satisfy in criminal cases ... that clause must be construed to require a unanimous jury verdict in all criminal cases."[12] White responded,

[T]his Court has never held jury unanimity to be a requisite of due process of law.... Appellant offers no evidence that majority jurors simply ignore the reasonable doubts of their colleagues or otherwise act irresponsibly in casting their votes in favor of conviction, and before we alter our own longstanding perceptions about jury behavior and overturn a considered legislative judgment that unanimity is not essential to reasoned jury verdicts, we must have some basis for doing so other than unsupported assumptions....

Of course, the State's proof could perhaps be regarded as more certain if it had convinced all 12 jurors instead of only nine.... But the fact remains that nine jurors—a substantial majority of the jury—were convinced by the evidence. In our view disagreement of three jurors does not alone establish reasonable doubt.... That rational men disagree is not in itself equivalent to a failure of proof by the State, nor does it indicate infidelity to the reasonable-doubt standard.[13]

In the Oregon case, Robert Apodaca and two other men had been convicted (of burglary, larceny, and assault with a deadly weapon) by twelve-member juries voting 11-1 and 10-2. Oregon law required that juries reach their verdicts by no less a majority than 10-2. The Supreme Court affirmed these convictions, using reasoning similar to that in the Louisiana case.

In *Burch v. Louisiana* (1979), the Court addressed a question posed by the "intersection" of its decisions allowing states to use juries of fewer than twelve persons and those allowing state juries to reach their verdicts by less than unanimous votes. The Court held that a jury as small as six persons must reach its verdict unanimously. The Court held that a defendant charged with a nonpetty crime was denied his Sixth Amendment right to trial by jury if the state allowed him to be convicted by a less than unanimous vote of a six-member jury.[14]

An Impartial Jury

The Constitution does not state that defendants have a right to a "jury of their peers." It does, however, say that they have a right to "an impartial jury." The Court has interpreted this phrase to mean that the jury should broadly represent the community. The defendant is protected against prejudice based on race, sex, employment, or class by the "cross section" principle espoused in *Williams,* which forbids systematic exclusion from juries of identifiable segments of the community.

Long before 1968, when *Duncan v. Louisiana* required states to provide jury trials, the Court had demanded that state juries, if provided, be fairly selected. "It is part of the established tradition in the use of juries as instruments of public justice," declared the Court in 1940, "that the jury be a body truly representative of the community. For racial discrimination to result in the exclusion from jury service of otherwise qualified groups not only violates our Constitution and the laws enacted under it but is at war with our basic concepts of a democratic society and a representative government."[15] Three decades later the Court reiterated this point, holding that state laws were unconstitutional if they resulted in the exclusion of women from juries. In these rulings the Court reaffirmed the fair cross-section requirement as fundamental to the right to a jury trial.[16] Congress incorporated this principle into the Federal Jury Selection and Service Act of 1968, which—a century after adoption of the Fourteenth Amendment—forbade discrimination in the selection of jury panels based on race, color, religion, sex, national origin, or economic status.[17]

Racial Bias

Racial discrimination in jury selection has been the subject of Supreme Court rulings for more than one hundred years. The due process and equal protection guarantees of the Fourteenth Amendment furnish a basis for federal courts to review state jury selection practices alleged to be discriminatory. Most often the Equal Protection Clause has served as the more effective of the two provisions in this area.

In 1880 the Court struck down Virginia and West Virginia laws that excluded blacks from jury service,[18] but the Court made clear in another decision the same year that it would not require state officials to ensure that blacks actually did serve on juries.[19] In other words, the mere absence of black jurors from any particular panel would not serve as a constitutional basis for challenging the jury's decision. For the next half-century, this superficial approach prevailed, and blacks continued to be excluded from local juries. Then in *Norris v. Alabama* (1935), the *Second Scottsboro Case*—named for the town in which the trial was held—the Court looked behind the language of the state law to its effect, finding it unconstitutional.[20]

One of the so-called Scottsboro Boys, Clarence Norris, a black convicted of raping a white woman, challenged his conviction as a violation of equal protection. Norris pointed out that blacks were systematically eliminated from the pools of potential state jurors, including those who indicted and tried him. The Supreme Court reversed his conviction. Chief Justice Charles Evans Hughes said the Court's responsibility was to decide whether the equal protection guarantee was denied "not merely … in express terms but also whether it was denied in substance and effect."[21] He noted that no black had served on a jury in that county within the memory of any person living. Hughes found that sufficient basis for reversing Norris's conviction.

Twelve years later, in *Patton v. Mississippi* (1947), the Court found similar justification for reversing the murder conviction of a black man indicted and convicted by all-white juries. The Supreme Court held the long exclusion of blacks from juries a denial of equal protection. Justice Hugo L. Black delivered the opinion of a unanimous Court:

When a jury selection plan, whatever it is, operates in such way as always to result in the complete and

DUE PROCESS: THE RIGHT TO NOTICE

Formal notice of charges—or of legal proceedings affecting one's rights—is one of the essential elements of due process of law. All parties who are to become involved in legal proceedings must be informed in advance of trial of the specific charges against them to give them time to prepare their defense or, in the case of modern class action cases, to withdraw from the affected class. In civil and criminal proceedings alike, notice must be given promptly and with sufficient specificity to permit preparation of an adequate defense. In addition, the Court has extended the due process requirement of notice to protect consumers from a unilateral seizure of property by creditors and to shield individuals from some administrative actions.

The concept of notice is included in the Fifth and Sixth Amendments. The Fifth Amendment provides that no one "shall be held to answer for a capital, or otherwise infamous crime, unless on a presentment or indictment of a Grand Jury, except in cases arising in the land or naval forces, or in the militia." The Court in *Hurtado v. California* (1884) held that this requirement of an indictment applied only to persons charged with federal crimes. That decision has never been reversed.[1] The Sixth Amendment states that in *all* criminal prosecutions the defendant has the right "to be informed of the nature and cause of the accusation." This more general rule has been accepted as basic to a fair trial. Both the Sixth Amendment and due process require that laws describing certain actions as criminal be sufficiently specific to place persons on notice as to what acts are proscribed. As the Court wrote in 1926, "a statute which either forbids or requires the doing of an act in terms so vague that men of common intelligence must necessarily guess at its meaning and differ as to its application, violates the first essential of due process of law."[2]

For that reason, the Court has held some laws "void for vagueness." These laws do not define with reasonable specificity the nature of forbidden conduct. For the same reason, the Court has set aside indictments that are insufficiently precise in stating the charges against an individual. In testing laws challenged as unconstitutionally vague, the Court balances the right to notice against the imprecise language and political considerations inherent in the process of writing laws. Justice Tom C. Clark in 1952 set out the Court's view of these factors:

> A criminal statute must be sufficiently definite to give notice of the required conduct to one who would avoid its penalties, and to guide the judge in its application and the lawyer in defending one

charged with its violation. But few words possess the precision of mathematical symbols, most statutes must deal with untold and unforeseen variations in factual situations, and the practical necessities of discharging the business of government inevitably limit the specificity with which legislators can spell out prohibitions.[3]

In later rulings, the Supreme Court extended the concept of notice, holding that it is required in a variety of situations outside of those occurring in the enforcement of the criminal law. In 1969 and 1972, the Court held that due process requires that consumers be notified before their wages are garnished or property repossessed for nonpayment of debts.[4] The Court in 1970 applied the notice requirement to termination of welfare benefits.[5] Two years later it held that a teacher fired after ten years of service was entitled to notice and a hearing.[6] In 1975 the justices ruled that students were entitled to notice of charges before being suspended from public schools for misbehavior.[7]

Chief Justice John G. Roberts Jr., in his first term on the Court, invoked the right-to-notice to return an Arkansas man's home that had been seized for unpaid taxes. Gary Jones had paid the mortgage and taxes on a house in Little Rock, even after he had separated from his wife and moved into an apartment. When the mortgage was paid off, however, he did not receive a bill for the taxes, and his wife did not pay them either. The state sent a certified letter to the home, but when it was return as undelivered, the house was sold. Jones sued, but lost in the Arkansas courts. Chief Justice Roberts said that the state's bureaucratic response violated Jones's right to due process of law before losing his property. "Due process requires the government to provide adequate notice of the impending taking," Roberts said in the opinion for the 5-3 majority in *Jones v. Flowers* (2006).[8] Officials could have posted a notice on the house or sent a notice to Jones's apartment, as he was listed in the state tax records.

---

1. *Hurtado v. California,* 110 U.S. 516 (1884).

2. *Connally v. General Construction Co.,* 269 U.S. 385 at 391 (1926).

3. *Boyce Motor Lines Inc. v. United States,* 342 U.S. 337 at 340 (1952).

4. *Sniadach v. Family Finance Corp. et al.,* 395 U.S. 337 (1969); *Fuentes v. Shevin,* 407 U.S. 67 (1972).

5. *Goldberg v. Kelly,* 397 U.S. 254 (1970).

6. *Perry v. Sinderman,* 408 U.S. 593 (1972).

7. *Goss v. Lopez,* 419 U.S. 565 (1975).

8. *Jones v. Flowers,* 547 U.S. 220 (2006).

WITNESSES FOR THE DEFENSE

The right to present a defense includes the power to use subpoenas and similar legal means to compel witnesses to appear on one's behalf at trial. In the 1960s, the Supreme Court ruled that this right applied in state as well as federal trials. In *Washington v. Texas* (1967), Chief Justice Earl Warren explained for the unanimous Court:

> The right to offer the testimony of witnesses, and to compel their attendance if necessary, is in plain terms the right to present a

defense, the right to present the defendant's version of the facts as well as the prosecution's to the jury so it may decide where the truth lies. Just as an accused has a right to confront the prosecution's witnesses for the purpose of challenging their testimony, he has the right to present his own witnesses to establish a defense. This right is a fundamental element of due process of law.[1]

---

1. *Washington v. Texas*, 388 U.S. 14 at 19 (1967).

---

long-continued exclusion of any representative at all from a large group of negroes, or any other racial group, indictments and verdicts returned against them by juries thus selected cannot stand.... [O]ur holding does not mean that a guilty defendant must go free. For indictments can be returned and convictions can be obtained by juries selected as the Constitution commands.[22]

In subsequent cases, the Court upheld good-faith efforts by state officials to secure competent juries representative of the community. In 1953 the Court approved the use of taxpayers' rolls as the basis from which names were selected for jury service.[23] The Court then began to rule against the token selection of blacks for jury duty, or systems of jury selection that made it easy to exclude blacks. In *Avery v. Georgia* (1952), the Court struck down a system in which different colored pieces of paper were used to indicate whether a potential juror was black or white. The juries in this case were selected by a judge drawing pieces of paper from a box. In *Whitus v. Georgia* (1967), the justices invalidated the selection of jurors from racially separated tax records.[24]

In *Hernandez v. Texas* (1954), the Court held that the Fourteenth Amendment forbids the systematic or arbitrary exclusion of any substantial racial group from jury service. A unanimous Court ruled that in a county where 14 percent of the population was of Mexican or Latin American descent, it violated equal protection to exclude all such persons from juries.[25] In the mid-1980s, the Court reaffirmed the importance of eliminating racial bias from the jury room. In *Vasquez v. Hillery* (1986), the Court ruled that anyone indicted by a grand jury selected in a racially discriminatory fashion had the right to a new trial, regardless of the length of time since the discriminatory indictment. Such discrimination is a "grave constitutional trespass," wrote Justice Marshall. It "undermines the structural integrity of the criminal tribunal itself."[26]

Limiting Peremptory Challenges

Despite the Court's many pronouncements against excluding blacks from juries, many black defendants have been tried before all-white or nearly all-white juries. This was the result often of so-called peremptory challenges by prosecutors. The juries that decide cases are formed in a three-step process. First, citizens are called to appear for jury duty. Second, from the pool of eligible jurors, some are eliminated "for cause." This occurs when the judge, a prosecutor, or a defense lawyer excludes a particular juror because he or she has a connection to the defendant, the prosecutor, the victim, or the crime. Third, the two sides are permitted to remove a fixed number of potential jurors for any reason, including a hunch that they might not rule

THE DISRUPTIVE DEFENDANT

Inherent in the defendant's right to confront and cross-examine witnesses is the right to attend the trial.[1] The Supreme Court has held, however, that this right is not absolute and that a defendant who persistently disrupts trial proceedings by noisy and disorderly conduct is not denied his constitutional rights if the judge has him removed from the courtroom.

In *Illinois v. Allen* (1970), the defendant had repeatedly interrupted the trial proceedings with noisy outbursts and insulting language. The judge finally ordered him removed from the courtroom until he agreed to behave. At the conclusion of the trial, which resulted in a conviction, the defendant filed a petition for habeas corpus relief, claiming that he had been denied his right to a fair trial because of his enforced absence from the courtroom during the presentation of most of the state's case against him. A unanimous Supreme Court rejected that argument. Wrote Justice Hugo L. Black,

It is essential to the proper administration of criminal justice that dignity, order, and decorum be the hallmarks of all court proceedings in our country. The flagrant disregard in the courtroom of elementary standards of proper conduct should not and cannot be tolerated. We believe trial judges confronted with disruptive, contumacious, stubbornly defiant defendants must be given sufficient discretion to meet the circumstances of each case. No one formula for maintaining the appropriate courtroom atmosphere will be best in all situations. We think there are at least three constitutionally permissible ways for a trial judge to handle an obstreperous defendant like Allen: 1) bind and gag him, thereby keeping him present; 2) cite him for contempt; 3) take him out of the courtroom until he promises to conduct himself properly.[2]

---

1. *Lewis v. United States*, 146 U.S. 370 (1892).

2. *Illinois v. Allen*, 397 U.S. 337 at 343–344 (1970); see also *Mayberry v. Pennsylvania*, 400 U.S. 455 (1971).

---

favorably for their side. For example, in many states, the prosecution and the defense can each "strike" twelve potential jurors. The theory behind peremptory challenges is that by giving both sides an equal opportunity to eliminate some possibly biased jurors, the resulting twelve-member jury is more likely to be impartial. However, this system also allowed prosecutors to eliminate all or nearly all of the black jurors from a trial involving a black defendant.

The Court adopted a major change in the law in *Batson v. Kentucky* (1986).[27] Speaking for a 7-2 majority, Justice Lewis F. Powell Jr. said that prosecutors can be forced to justify why they had "struck" blacks from serving on a particular jury. If a defense lawyer sees a "pattern" of excluding blacks or other minorities, he or she can challenge the prosecutor's actions before the judge who is supervising the jury selection process. At that point, the burden shifts to the prosecutor, Powell said. "Once the defendant makes a *prima facie* showing, the burden shifts to the State to come forward with a neutral explanation for challenging black jurors," he

wrote. The trial judge has a duty to weigh the explanation. If the reason for excluding a juror has nothing to do with race, the prosecutor's decision should be upheld. If not, the judge must recall the excluded person and add him or her to the jury.[28]

In the case before the Court, James Batson, an African American, had been prosecuted and convicted of burglary before an all-white jury in Louisville. The prosecutor had used peremptory challenges to remove the blacks in the jury pool. Batson's lawyer objected to the all-white jury, but the trial proceeded, and the Kentucky Supreme Court upheld the conviction. In the U.S. Supreme Court's reversal of the conviction, Powell said such discrimination against black jurors and a black defendant violates the Equal Protection Clause of the Fourteenth Amendment. "The core guarantee of equal protection … would be meaningless," he wrote, if prosecutors can exclude blacks from juries for secretly held racial reasons. "The harm from discriminatory jury selection [can] touch the entire community … [and] undermine public confidence in the fairness of our system of justice," Powell wrote. In a concurring opinion, Justice Thurgood Marshall said that the Court should have gone further and outlawed peremptory challenges entirely. Chief Justice Warren Burger and soon-to-be chief justice William H. Rehnquist dissented, questioning whether eliminating jurors through peremptory challenges violated the guarantee of equal protection of the laws.

Thereafter, the phrase "*Batson* challenge" came to be heard often in courtrooms and in legal opinions discussing jury selection. The underlying premise of *Batson*—that racial bias in jury selection corrupts the integrity of the judicial system—was subsequently extended to apply in other trial contexts. For example, in *Edmonson v. Leesville Concrete Co.* (1991), the Court ruled that jurors in civil cases cannot be excluded because of their race;[29] in another case that year, it ruled that a defendant may object to race-based exclusions even if he or she is not the same race as the excluded jurors;[30] and in 1992 the Court in a 7-2 vote completed the prohibition on race bias in jury selection, ruling that defense attorneys, as well as prosecutors, cannot eliminate prospective jurors because of race. The majority held that any racially motivated approach to choosing a jury violates the constitutional guarantee of equal protection of the laws.[31]

The Court also continued to review cases in which *Batson* challenges had been rejected. In 2005 the justices in a 6-3 decision overturned the murder conviction and death sentence of a black Texas defendant who had been tried nearly twenty years earlier by a nearly all-white jury. Dallas prosecutors during the 1960s had an explicit policy of excluding blacks and Jews from juries, the Court noted in *Miller-El v. Dretke* (2005).[32] When Thomas Miller-El was on trial for shooting two hotel employees, prosecutors used ten peremptory challenges to exclude blacks from his jury. In 2008 in *Snyder v. Louisiana,* the Roberts Court in a 7-2 decision reversed the murder conviction and death sentence of a black man who had been tried by an all-white jury. Prosecutors had used peremptory challenges to exclude all five blacks from the jury. Justice Samuel A. Alito Jr. faulted the trial judge, whom he said had "committed a clear error" by allowing the

prosecutor to exclude qualified black jurors.[33] Justices Clarence Thomas and Antonin Scalia dissented in both the *Miller-El* and *Snyder* cases.

Women on Juries

Although the Court as early as 1946 disapproved of the exclusion of women from federal jury panels, it took thirty more years before that disapproval extended to state juries. In *Hoyt v. Florida* (1961), the Court upheld a Florida statute that made jury service by women voluntary. Women interested in being included on jury lists had to record with the county their willingness to serve.[34] Gwendolyn Hoyt, accused of murdering her husband with a baseball bat, challenged the constitutionality of the voluntary jury service statute. Failure to include women on the jury, she claimed, denied women defendants the equal protection of the law. The Court rejected this argument, saying that Florida law did not exclude all women from jury service but simply permitted them to avail themselves of a broad exemption from that duty. At the time, the Court noted, seventeen states made jury service by women voluntary. For the unanimous Court, Justice John Marshall Harlan wrote that "woman is still regarded as the center of home and family life." In light of that, he continued, "We cannot say that it is constitutionally impermissible for a State … to conclude that a woman should be relieved from the civic duty of jury service unless she herself determines that such service is consistent with her own special responsibilities."[35]

Fourteen years later, the Court overturned *Hoyt*. In *Taylor v. Louisiana* (1975), the Court found no rational, let alone compelling, reason for exempting women from jury duty. The Court found the law unconstitutional, in conflict with the Sixth Amendment right of a defendant to be tried by an impartial jury drawn from a fair cross section of the community.[36] The justices reaffirmed this position in 1979, striking down a Missouri law that exempted women from jury duty upon their request. Leaving room for states to exempt from jury duty persons responsible for the care of children and other dependents, the Court held that the broader, sex-based exemption denied defendants their right to a jury that fairly represented their community.[37] The

1986 *Batson* prohibition of race discrimination in jury selection was extended to sex discrimination in *J.E.B. v. Alabama ex rel. T.B.* (1994). By 6-3, the justices ruled that the use of gender-based peremptory challenges to eliminate female jurors "serves to ratify and perpetuate invidious, archaic, and overbroad stereotypes about the relative abilities of men and women."[38]

Blue Ribbon Juries

The Supreme Court has upheld the use of specially qualified panels of jurors for difficult cases. In *Fay v. New York* (1947), the Court considered a New York law that forbade selection of jury panels on the basis of race, creed, color, or occupation but provided for the use of such "blue ribbon" juries. Two union officials convicted of conspiracy and extortion by a blue ribbon jury claimed that these panels excluded laborers, craftsmen, and service employees, discriminating against certain economic classes and thus violating the due process and equal protection guarantees. The Court, 5-4, upheld the system and the convictions. Justice Robert H. Jackson explained:

> We fail to perceive on its face any constitutional offense in the statutory standards prescribed for the special panel. The Act does not exclude, or authorize the clerk to exclude, any person or class because of race, creed, color or occupation. It imposes no qualification of an economic nature beyond that imposed by the concededly valid general panel statute. Each of the grounds of elimination is reasonably and closely related to the juror's suitability for the kind of service the special panel requires or to his fitness to judge the kind of cases for which it is most frequently utilized. Not all of the grounds of elimination would appear relevant to the issues of the present case. But we know of no right of defendants to have a specially constituted panel which would include all persons who might be fitted to hear their particular and unique case.[39]

In dissent Justices Frank Murphy, Hugo L. Black, Wiley B. Rutledge, and William O. Douglas protested that use of blue ribbon juries conflicted with the fair cross-section requirement. Wrote Murphy,

> There is no constitutional right to a jury drawn from a group of uneducated and unintelligent persons.

Nor is there any right to a jury chosen solely from those at the lower end of the economic and social scale. But there is a constitutional right to a jury drawn from a group which represents a cross-section of the community. And a cross-section of the community includes persons with varying degrees of training and intelligence and with varying economic and social positions. Under our Constitution, the jury is not to be made the representative of the most intelligent, the most wealthy or the most successful, nor of the least intelligent, the least wealthy or the least successful. It is a democratic institution, representative of all qualified classes of people.[40]

Decision Makers: Juries v. Judges

The Court strengthened the right to a jury trial in 2000. The 5-4 ruling in *Apprendi v. New Jersey* (2000) called a halt to the practice of allowing judges to tack on extra prison time based on certain "sentencing factors."[41] For example, if the judge found that the convicted defendant was carrying a gun during the commission of a drug crime, the magistrate could increase the prison term. The Court held such judge-imposed punishments unconstitutional if they go beyond the maximum sentence for the crime on which the jury voted. "The founders of the American Republic were not prepared to leave it to the state" to decide who is guilty and what punishment is deserved, wrote Justice Antonin Scalia in a concurring opinion. "Judges, it is sometimes necessary to remind ourselves, are part of the State," he added.[42]

Though Scalia is often described as a conservative, this label does not describe well his approach to constitutional questions. Many conservatives favor law enforcement and oppose rulings that favor the rights of criminal defendants. Scalia's conservatism, by contrast, looks to the original understanding of the Constitution, and sometimes, as in the area of jury trials, his view of what the Constitution originally required favors criminal defendants. The right to a jury trial "has never been efficient, but it has always been free," he wrote. It means "the criminal will never get more punishment than he bargained for when he did the crime, and his guilt of the crime (and hence the length

THE RIGHT TO A PUBLIC TRIAL

The Sixth Amendment guarantees persons charged with crimes a public trial. The First Amendment guarantees the press and public the right to attend criminal trials. In the late 1970s, the Supreme Court held that the Sixth Amendment guarantee is solely for the benefit of the defendant, not for the public in general or the press. *(See "Access and Confidentiality," pp. 116–124; see also "Introduction to Freedom of the Press," pp. 83–84.)*

In *Gannett Co. v. DePasquale* (1979), the Court held that a trial judge could close to the press and the public a pretrial hearing on evidence in a murder case, if closure was needed to protect the defendant's right to a fair trial.[1] "To safeguard the due process rights of the accused, a trial judge has an affirmative constitutional duty to minimize the effects of prejudicial pretrial publicity," wrote Justice Potter Stewart, noting that one of the most effective means of minimizing publicity is to close pretrial proceedings to the public and to the press.[2] The Sixth Amendment, Stewart continued,

> surrounds a criminal trial with guarantees … that have as their overriding purpose the protection of the accused from prosecutorial and judicial abuses. Among the guarantees that the Amendment provides to a person charged with the commission of a criminal offense, and to him alone, is the "right to a speedy and public trial, by an impartial jury." The Constitution nowhere mentions any right of access to a criminal trial on the part of the public; its guarantee, like the others enumerated, is personal to the accused.[3]

Gannett has not been overruled, but a series of subsequent decisions have established a growing presumption of openness. That series began the year after *Gannett*, when the Supreme Court found in the First Amendment the very guarantee of access that it had found absent in the Sixth Amendment. In *Richmond Newspapers v. Virginia* (1980), the Court agreed with a First Amendment challenge brought by the press and overturned the decision of a trial judge to close a murder trial to the press

and public.[4] "We hold that the right to attend criminal trials is implicit in the guarantees of the First Amendment," wrote Chief Justice Warren E. Burger. "[W]ithout the freedom to attend such trials, which people have exercised for centuries, important aspects of freedom of speech and 'of the press could be eviscerated.'"[5] Burger acknowledged that in some situations the only way to preserve the right to a fair trial is to limit the access of press and public to the courtroom. If such limitations are necessary, however, they must be outlined clearly and backed by written findings on the part of the judge that closure is essential to preserve an overriding state interest.

In *Waller v. Georgia* (1984), the Court held that a defendant's right to a public trial means that a judge may close pretrial hearings to the public over a defendant's objection only if there is some overriding interest that will be prejudiced by an open hearing.[6] Two years later, in still another case on these points, Chief Justice Burger declared that the defendant's right to a fair trial need not be in conflict with the public's right to access. In *Press-Enterprise Co. v. Superior Court* (1986), the justices ruled that a newspaper could have access to the transcript of a preliminary hearing in a criminal case. Burger wrote to emphasize that one important way to assure the defendant's right to a fair trial is to keep the process open to neutral observers.[7]

---

1. *Gannett Co. v. DePasquale,* 443 U.S. 368 (1979).

2. Id. at 378.

3. Id. at 379.

4. *Richmond Newspapers v. Virginia,* 448 U.S. 555 (1980).

5. Id. at 580.

6. *Waller v. Georgia,* 467 U.S. 39 (1984).

7. *Press-Enterprise Co. v. Superior Court,* 478 U.S. 1 (1986).

of the sentence to which he is exposed) will be determined beyond a reasonable doubt by the unanimous vote of 12 of his fellow citizens."[43]

Apprendi involved a neighborhood shooting and allegations of racism. In the early morning hours of December 22, 1994, Charles Apprendi Jr. fired several bullets at the home of an African American family that

had recently moved into a previously all-white neighborhood in Vineland, New Jersey. He was arrested within an hour, admitted to the shooting, and commented that he had fired the shots at his neighbor's home "because they are black." He was indicted on a series of weapons charges and agreed to plead guilty to two counts that could result in his serving ten years in prison. At the sentencing hearing, prosecutors asked the judge to extend his sentence because his action was a hate crime under New Jersey law. Apprendi denied that he was racially biased and said he was drunk on the night of the shootings. The judge, disagreeing, said the evidence suggested the crime "was motivated by racial bias." He sentenced Apprendi to twelve years in prison.

The Court overturned the additional two years added to Apprendi's prison term and called the judge's sentencing "an unacceptable departure from the jury tradition that is an indispensable party of our criminal justice system."[44] Justice Stevens, speaking for the Court, set out a clear rule: "Other than the fact of a prior conviction, any fact that increases the penalty for a crime beyond the prescribed statutory maximum must be submitted to a jury, and proved beyond a reasonable doubt."[45] He was joined by Justices Scalia, David H. Souter, Clarence Thomas, and Ruth Bader Ginsburg. In dissent, Justice Sandra Day O'Connor called the ruling "a watershed change in constitutional law."[46] It threatens to reverse thousands of sentences imposed by judges, including the death sentences in her home state of Arizona, she said. Her warning did not change any votes, but her prophecy proved accurate.

Two years after *Apprendi,* the Court struck down Arizona's death sentencing system, because it put the crucial decision in the hands of a judge, not the jury. Timothy Ring, a one-time police officer, was convicted by a jury for his role in the robbery of $562,000 from a Wells Fargo armored van and the murder of the driver. The jury heard evidence that Ring had $271,000 hidden in his garage and that he had spoken with two accomplices about the heist. For this crime, he could be sentenced to life in prison or death. Under Arizona law, the judge decided which it would be. In a hearing before the judge alone, an accomplice testified that Ring planned the crime and shot the driver. Afterward, the judge concluded that Ring indeed was the murderer and sentenced him to die.

By a 7-2 vote, the Court reversed the sentence in *Ring v. Arizona* (2002), because the jury had not decided, beyond a reasonable doubt, that Ring had committed the murder. "Capital defendants, no less than non-capital defendants, are entitled to a jury determination of any fact on which the legislature conditions an increase in their maximum punishment," said Justice Ruth Bader Ginsburg.[47] The decision gave hundreds of death row inmates in Arizona and seven other states a chance for new sentencing hearings before a jury. Only Chief Justice Rehnquist and Justice O'Connor dissented.

In 2004 the Court dealt a blow to the sentencing rules that had been adopted by the federal government and many states. Twenty years earlier, Congress had passed the Sentencing Reform Act in hopes of bringing about more consistent and uniform prison terms for federal crimes. Lawmakers on the left and right believed that judges had too much leeway when imposing sentences. As a result of such discretion, prison terms for a particular crime—bank robbery or fraud, for example—varied widely, depending on the judge. The federal sentencing guidelines came with a detailed manual to determine whether the criminal deserved more or less time in prison. Did the bank robber carry a gun? Was the weapon discharged? Was the money recovered? And so on. Although these rules were referred to as "guidelines," they were binding on judges.

The guidelines, however, ran afoul of the constitutional principle established in the *Apprendi* decision. In jurisdictions across the country, the sentencing judge, not the jury, normally took into consideration the facts—such as whether a bank robber fired his gun or whether the robber was contrite after being caught—that determined the length of a prison term. In *Blakely v. Washington* (2004), the Court struck down the sentencing guidelines used in Washington state because they required judges to increase a prison term if certain aggravating factors were found to be involved. Ralph Blakeley had pleaded guilty to kidnapping his estranged wife, which called for a prison term of up to fifty-three months. The judge then determined that Blakely had acted with deliberate cruelty and therefore increased his sentence to ninety months. This extra prison time violated Blakely's right to a jury trial, Scalia asserted for a 5-4 majority. The same unusual line-up as in *Apprendi* decided the case, with Justices Stevens, Souter, Thomas, and Ginsberg joining him.[48]

The *Blakely* ruling jeopardized the sentencing guidelines because they operated in the manner prohibited by the Court in that case. A year after *Blakely*, in *Booker v. United States* (2005), the Court decided, as expected, that the sentencing rules were unconstitutional because they permitted judges to increase prison terms based on aggravating facts that were not determined by the jury.[49] Freddie Booker had been caught in Wisconsin with 92 grams of crack cocaine, and a jury found him guilty of possessing cocaine with the intent to sell it. Possession of more than 50 grams of crack called for a mandatory ten-year prison term, but the judge in the case held a hearing and agreed with prosecutors that Booker possessed at least 566 grams of crack and had obstructed justice. Based on these facts, the judge imposed a thirty-year prison term. Once again, Justices Stevens, Scalia, Souter, Thomas, and Ginsburg agreed that the extra prison time violated the Sixth Amendment because it allowed the judge, not jurors, to decide on key facts that determined the sentence.

In a surprise announcement, and an effort to save the U.S. sentencing system, a separate five-member majority ruled that judges should approach the sentencing guidelines as advisory, not as mandatory. Justice Stephen G. Breyer, an architect of the guidelines during the 1980s, wrote the 5-4 decision that preserved them. Justice Ginsburg cast the key vote, but wrote nothing to explain her view. Because of Ginsburg's vote, the Court ruled simultaneously that binding sentencing rules were unconstitutional, but advisory guidelines were acceptable.

With this new authority, some judges gave drug defendants shorter prison terms than called for by the federal guidelines, and in 2007 the Court upheld these decisions in two cases. In *Kimbrough v. United States* (2007), the Court ruled that a judge had acted reasonably when he gave a fifteen-year prison term, rather than the twenty-two years called for in the guidelines, to an army veteran who had been arrested in Norfolk, Virginia, with crack cocaine and a gun in his car.[50] In *Gall v. United States* (2007), the Court affirmed a judge's decision not to impose prison time on an Arizona construction worker who had sold the drug

ecstasy several years before when he was a college student in Iowa. When the drug ring was exposed, Brian Gall was contacted by federal agents, and he pleaded guilty to being involved. The federal guidelines called for him to serve about three years in prison, but the Court agreed that the sentencing judge had good reason for ignoring the guideline—Gall had rehabilitated himself and should not go to prison for past drug use.[51]

THE RIGHT TO A SPEEDY TRIAL

In 1905 the Supreme Court made clear that the right to a speedy trial is a relative matter, "consistent with delays and depend[ent] upon circumstances."[52] The Court has adopted a balancing approach in cases alleging that a defendant has been denied this right. The justices weigh the particular facts to determine the reasons for the delay as well as the effect of the delay on the defendant. In *United States v. Provoo* (1955), the Court upheld the dismissal of an indictment of a defendant who—although ready for trial since 1951 and protesting governmental requests for delay—had not been tried. The Court explained that the lapse of time, the death or disappearance of witnesses, and the protracted confinement of the defendant had seriously jeopardized his opportunity to defend himself.[53] In *Strunk v. United States* (1973), dismissal of the charges, the unanimous Court held firmly, is the only appropriate remedy for denial of this right. The justices found sentence reduction an insufficient remedy for delay of trial.[54]

The right to a speedy trial does not apply to delays before a person is accused of a crime but only to the interval between arrest and trial. In a 1971 case Justice White explained:

> [T]he Sixth Amendment speedy trial provision has no application until the putative defendant becomes an "accused."...
>
> ... On its face, the protection of the amendment is activated only when a criminal prosecution has begun and extends only to those persons who have been "accused" in the course of that prosecution. These provisions would seem to afford no protection to those not yet accused, nor would they

HABEAS CORPUS: A RETURN TO THE GREAT WRIT

In modern U.S. law, "habeas corpus" usually refers to a second-chance appeal for criminals who are convicted and imprisoned. These defendants are due all the protections of the Constitution when they are arrested and put on trial. If they are convicted and their appeals are rejected by the state courts, these defendants can try again by appealing to the federal courts. They do so by filing a writ of habeas corpus and asking a U.S. judge to decide whether their constitutional rights have been violated.

The Supreme Court was called upon to revisit the writ of habeas corpus after President George W. Bush's administration launched a "war on terror" following the al-Qaida attacks of September 11, 2001. Bush authorized the Defense Department to create a prison at the U.S. naval base at Guantánamo Bay, Cuba, to detain and question hundreds of men who had been captured in Afghanistan, Pakistan, and elsewhere; they were suspected of being Islamic extremist allies of al-Qaida. The military referred to these men as "unlawful enemy combatants" and said that they were not entitled to legal rights, including the protections of the Geneva Conventions concerning the humane treatment of prisoners.

Human rights lawyers took up the prisoners' cause, arguing that they were entitled to the protections of U.S. law. The legal dispute became a battle over habeas corpus. At issue was whether the Guantánamo prisoners could file a writ of habeas corpus and plead for their freedom before a federal judge.

In old English law, a writ of habeas corpus was sent to the king's jailer, calling upon him to bring an imprisoned man before the judge. "Habeus corpus" translates from the Latin as "you should have the body." This right to question one's detention before a judge was written into the Constitution: "The Privilege of the Writ of Habeas Corpus shall not be suspended, unless when in Cases of Rebellion or Invasion the public Safety may require it," states Article I, section 9. Congress in the Judiciary Act of 1789 also authorized federal judges to issue writs of habeas corpus for prisoners "in custody" of the United States. Prior to the events that transpired after September 11, the Court had rarely ruled on the reach of this right. In three decisions arising from the Guantánamo prison, the Court ruled that these long-detained prisoners had rights to habeas corpus.

In *Rasul v. Bush* (2004), the Court in a 6-3 vote determined that the "habeas statute confers a right to judicial review of the legality of Executive detention of aliens in a territory over which the United States exercises plenary and exclusive jurisdiction." Justice John Paul Stevens noted that these prisoners had not been tried or convicted on any charges. Moreover, they were held in a territory over which the United States "exercises complete jurisdiction and control."[1]

Two years later, in *Hamdan v. Rumsfeld* (2006), the Court struck down the use of "military commissions" to prosecute these men because the trial system, set up by the Bush administration, had not been authorized by Congress. A threshold question in that case had been whether the men had a right to appear before a court or whether military reviews of their detention status were sufficient. Congress in the Detainee Treatment Act of 2005 had denied habeas rights for foreigners held as enemy combatants. Stevens, speaking for the Court again, said that the law did not apply to the pending cases.[2]

A few months later, Congress passed, and Bush signed into law, the Military Commission Act to resolve the matter. This time, Congress made clear that the limits on habeas corpus applied to the pending cases from Guantánamo. Besides authorizing military trials, it specifically stripped the habeas rights from the prisoners. "No court, justice or judge shall have the jurisdiction to hear or consider an application for a writ of habeas corpus filed by or on behalf of an alien detained by the United States" for engaging in hostile acts or for aiding terrorists, the MCA said.

In its third decision on this issue, the Court ruled that the Constitution gave the prisoners a right to habeas corpus. The 5-4 decision in *Boumediene v. Bush* (2008) struck down the key habeas provision in the Military Commissions Act. "The Framers considered the writ a vital instrument for the protection of liberty," Justice Anthony M. Kennedy wrote. The Constitution states that habeas corpus may not be suspended except in times of "rebellion or invasion," Kennedy noted, and because Congress had not declared such a state of emergency, the "MCA thus effects an unconstitutional suspension of the writ." The ruling cleared the way for the prisoners at Guantánamo to appeal to federal judges and seek their freedom, but it did not ensure that any of them would go free.[3]

---

1. *Rasul v. Bush*, 542 U.S. 466 (2004).

2. *Hamdan v. Rumsfeld*, 548 U.S. 557 (2006).

3. *Boumediene v. Bush*, 553 U.S. ___ (2008).

JAIL BEFORE TRIAL

Twice during the 1980s, the Supreme Court approved of preventive detention, the practice of holding certain defendants in jail before their trial. The first case involved the pretrial detention of dangerous juveniles, the second the pretrial detention of organized crime figures. In *Schall v. Martin, Abrams v. Martin* (1984), the Court voted 6-3 to uphold a New York law permitting pretrial detention of juveniles when there is a serious risk that the juvenile may commit a serious crime before trial. Detention fell well within the bounds of due process, wrote Justice William H. Rehnquist for the Court. In such a case, he continued, detention protects the juvenile as well as society. Justices William J. Brennan Jr., Thurgood Marshall, and John Paul Stevens dissented.[1]

Three years later, the Court reaffirmed and broadened its approval for pretrial detention, upholding the relevant provisions of a 1984 federal law. The case of *United States v. Salerno* (1987) arose from the pretrial detention of Anthony Salerno and Vincent Cafaro, who were indicted in New York on racketeering charges. The Court ruled—again 6-3—that neither due process nor the ban on excessive bail was violated when a judge decided that freeing the suspect on bail pending trial would pose a danger to the community.[2]

---

1. *Schall v. Martin, Abrams v. Martin,* 467 U.S. 253 (1984).
2. *United States v. Salerno,* 481 U.S. 739 (1987).

---

seem to require the Government to discover, investigate, and accuse any person within any particular period of time.[55]

The Court reaffirmed this point in its decision in *United States v. Lovasco* (1977), rejecting the argument that a defendant was denied due process by a good-faith investigative delay between the commission of an offense and the time of his indictment.[56] Justice Marshall wrote,

[P]rosecutors do not deviate from "fundamental conceptions of justice" when they defer seeking indictments until they have probable cause to believe an accused is guilty; indeed it is unprofessional conduct for a prosecutor to recommend an indictment on less than probable cause.... From the perspective of potential defendants, requiring prosecutions to commence when probable cause is established is undesirable because it would increase the likelihood of unwarranted charges being filed, and would add to the time during which defendants stand accused but untried....

Penalizing prosecutors who defer action ... would subordinate the goal of "orderly expedition" to that of "mere speed." This the Due Process Clause does not require. We therefore hold that to prosecute a defendant following investigative delay does not deprive him of due process, even if his defense might have been somewhat prejudiced by the lapse of time.[57]

In *Klopfer v. North Carolina* (1976), the Court held that the Due Process Clause requires protection of the right to speedy trial against abridgment by the states.[58] The Court unanimously struck down a North Carolina law that allowed indefinite postponement of a criminal prosecution without dismissal of the indictment. The defendant would remain at liberty, but the prosecutor could restore the case to the docket any time a judge agreed such action to be appropriate. Speaking for the Court, Chief Justice Earl Warren explained that this procedure "clearly denies the petitioner the right to a speedy trial which we hold is guaranteed to him by the Sixth Amendment.... We hold here that the right to a speedy trial is as fundamental as any of the rights secured by the Sixth Amendment."[59]

Federal and state officials operated until the 1970s on the assumption that an accused's failure to demand a speedy trial meant that he acquiesced in delay of proceedings. In *Barker v. Wingo* (1972), the

Court rejected the view "that a defendant who fails to demand a speedy trial forever waives his right."[60] Justice Lewis F. Powell Jr. reaffirmed the Court's "balancing approach" to speedy trial claims:

> The approach we accept is a balancing test, in which the conduct of both the prosecution and the defendant are weighed.
>
> A balancing test necessarily compels courts to approach speedy-trial cases on an ad-hoc basis. We can do little more than identify some of the factors which courts should assess in determining whether a particular defendant has been deprived of his right. Though some might express them in different ways, we identify four such factors: Length of delay, the reason for the delay, the defendant's assertion of his right, and prejudice to the defendant....
>
> We regard none of the four factors identified above as either a necessary or sufficient condition to the finding of a deprivation of the right of speedy trial. Rather they are related factors and must be considered together with such other circumstances as may be relevant. In sum, these factors have no talismanic qualities; courts must still engage in a difficult and sensitive balancing process. But, because we are dealing with a fundamental right of the accused, this process must be carried out with full recognition that the accused's interest in a speedy trial is specifically affirmed in the Constitution.[61]

Barker v. Wingo prompted Congress—against the advice of the Justice Department and federal judges—to pass the Speedy Trial Act of 1974 to reduce delays in federal trials. The act established a deadline of one hundred days between arrest or indictment and trial. Failure to meet the deadline would result in dismissal of the charges.[62]

In *United States v. MacDonald* (1982), the Court further defined the right to a speedy trial, ruling that this guarantee applied to the period between arrest and indictment, and in this specific case not to a period after military charges have been dropped and before a civilian indictment has been obtained. The right was not intended to prevent prejudice to the defense as a result of the passage of time but to limit the impairment of liberty of an accused before trial and to

shorten the disruption of life caused by pending criminal charges.[63]

In 1990 the Court said an eight-year delay between indictment and arrest violated the Sixth Amendment right to a speedy trial. The defendant in this case was indicted on federal drug charges in 1980 but left the country, apparently unaware of his indictment, before he could be arrested. After several years, he returned to the United States, married, earned a college degree, found steady employment, and lived under his own name. He was arrested after a routine credit check. By 5-4, the Court ruled that he could not be tried after such a long delay. The justices said U.S. officials were negligent in tracking the defendant.[64]

THE RIGHT TO CONFRONT WITNESSES

The Sixth Amendment guarantees that "in all criminal prosecutions, the accused shall enjoy the right ... to be confronted with the witnesses against them." This right had ancient roots in the notion that accusers must come forward and face those they are accusing. In seventeenth-century England, the importance of this right became clear when prominent figures of the day, including Sir Walter Raleigh, were tried for treason and convicted based on statements supposedly given by witnesses to the king's men. Raleigh had no chance to confront his accuser or to question his account. In *Mattox v. United States* (1895), the Supreme Court defined the purpose of this rule:

> The primary object ... was to prevent depositions or ex parte affidavits ... being used against the prisoner in lieu of a personal examination and cross-examination of the witness in which the accused has an opportunity, not only of testing the recollection and sifting the conscience of the witness, but of compelling him to stand face to face with the jury in order that they may look at him, and judge by his demeanor upon the stand and manner in which he gives his testimony whether he is worthy of belief.[65]

The Court subsequently struck down an act of Congress for violating this right. The act allowed the court record of a person convicted of stealing

Televising Trials

Although Chief Justice Warren E. Burger steadfastly opposed the introduction of cameras into the Supreme Court chamber, he nonetheless wrote the Court's 1981 opinion permitting states to televise trials.[1] For almost half a century, cameras had been unwelcome in the nation's courtrooms in reaction to sensational news coverage during some trials of the 1920s and 1930s. The American Bar Association (ABA) had in fact declared, as one of the canons of judicial ethics, that all photographic and broadcast coverage of trials should be prohibited. During the 1970s, however, attitudes started to change. In 1978 the ABA began considering relaxation of this ban, and the Conference of State Chief Justices voted to allow each state to develop guidelines for the use of cameras in the courtroom.

Florida began to experiment with televised trials in 1977. One of the trials covered by television was that of Noel Chandler and Robert Granger, former Miami Beach police officers charged with burglary. They challenged their convictions, arguing that the television coverage had denied them a fair trial. In their defense, Chandler and Granger cited the Court's ruling in *Estes v. Texas* (1964).[2] This decision, they said, had declared that all photographic or broadcast coverage of a criminal trial was a denial of due process. No, it did not, responded Chief Justice Burger for the Court in *Chandler v. Florida* (1981). *Estes* "does not stand as an absolute ban on state experimentation with an evolving technology, which, in terms of modes of mass communication, was in its relative infancy in 1964, and is, even now, in a state of continuing change."[3] Burger continued:

Any criminal case that generates a great deal of publicity presents some risks that the publicity may compromise the right of the defendant to a fair trial. The risk of juror prejudice in some cases does not justify an absolute ban on news coverage of trials by the printed media [or of] ... all broadcast coverage.[4]

"Dangers lurk in this, as in most experiments, but unless we were to conclude that television coverage under all conditions is prohibited by the Constitution, the states must be free to experiment," Burger concluded.[5] Most states allowed trials to be televised, typically at the judge's discretion, but the federal courts continued to oppose cameras in the courtroom in criminal cases. In a small step toward greater public access, the Judicial Conference of the United States, which oversees the lower federal courts, voted in March 1996 to give appellate judges the option of allowing television coverage of appellate arguments. This action did not apply to the U.S. Supreme Court, and the justices showed no signs of budging from their firm policy against cameras in the high court.

---

1. *Chandler v. Florida*, 449 U.S. 560 (1981).

2. *Estes v. Texas*, 381 U.S. 532 (1964).

3. *Chandler v. Florida*, 449 U.S. 560 at 574 (1981).

4. Id.

5. Id. at 582.

government property to be used against the person charged with receiving that property. The act said that the record from the first case could be used as evidence that the property was stolen. In the opinion the Court further explained the purpose of this Confrontation Clause:

> [A] fact which can be primarily established only by witnesses cannot be proved against an accused ... except by witnesses who confront him at the trial, upon whom he can look while being tried, whom he is entitled to cross-examine, and whose testimony he may impeach.... The presumption of the innocence of an accused attends him throughout the trial, and has relation to every fact that must be

established to prove his guilt beyond a reasonable doubt.[66]

This presumption was denied the defendant in this case because "he was put upon the defensive almost from the outset of the trial by reason alone of what appeared to have been *said* in another criminal prosecution with which he was not connected and at which he was not entitled to be represented."[67]

Many of the Court's pronouncements on the Confrontation Clause have focused on efforts by prosecutors to use at trial hearsay evidence—prior, out-of-court statements of persons unavailable to testify and be cross-examined. In general, the Court allows use of such evidence only when there is sufficient reason to consider it credible. In *Pointer v. Texas* (1965), the Court held this right of confrontation to be "a fundamental right essential to a fair trial in a criminal prosecution" and therefore applicable to defendants in state trials through the Due Process Clause.[68] *Pointer* involved a trial in which a state prosecutor attempted to use the transcript of a witness's testimony taken at a preliminary hearing, where he was not subject to cross-examination. The prosecutor had made no effort to secure the personal appearance of the witness at the trial. The Court threw out that evidence.

Although in recent years the Court seems to have relaxed some of its earlier restrictions on the use of hearsay evidence or out-of-court statements, it has reaffirmed the high priority it places upon this right in ensuring a fair trial.[69] In 1973 the Court, 8-1, held that a defendant on trial for murder had been denied a fair trial and due process by the state judge's strict application of the hearsay rule. That application wrongly prevented the introduction of testimony by three men to whom a fourth had confessed the crime with which the defendant was charged.[70] In 1974, with Chief Justice Burger writing the opinion, the Court held that a defendant was denied his right of confrontation when the trial judge forbade cross-examination of a key witness, a juvenile, about his delinquency record and probationary status, matters that could have impeached the credibility of his testimony.[71]

To protect the victims in child abuse cases from possible additional trauma caused by testifying at the trial of his or her alleged attacker, a number of states in the 1980s passed laws that permitted the victims to testify shielded from the view of the defendant. In *Coy v. Iowa* (1988), the Supreme Court held unconstitutional Iowa's law that permitted child victims to testify behind a screen because the law denied the defendant his right to meet face-to-face with his accusers in front of a judge and a jury. This guarantee of confrontation, wrote Justice Antonin Scalia, "serves ends related both to appearances and to reality.... The perception that confrontation is essential to fairness has persisted over the centuries because there is much truth to it.... That face-to-face presence may, unfortunately, upset the

truthful rape victim or abused child; but by the same token it may confound and undo the false accuser, or reveal the child coached by a malevolent adult.... Constitutional protections have costs."[72]

Two years later, Scalia was in dissent when the Court ruled 5-4 that states may shield victims of child abuse by allowing them to testify on closed-circuit television rather than face the person accused of abusing them. Writing for the majority in *Maryland v. Craig* (1990), Justice Sandra Day O'Connor said the state interest in protecting child witnesses from the trauma of testifying may justify permitting them to answer questions without a confrontation with the defendant.[73] In another 1990 decision the Court, again 5-4, ruled that hearsay statements from a child who is unable to testify in an abuse case can be admitted at trial if the child's story is tested for trustworthiness, including how well the child knew the accused and whether the child would make up the story.[74]

In another sensitive area, the Court ruled that while the Confrontation Clause does guarantee an alleged rapist the right to face his accuser, it does not assure him the opportunity to counter the charge by introducing evidence of their prior romantic relationship. The defendant in a 1991 case from Michigan was barred from introducing such evidence because he failed to notify prosecutors within ten days after arraignment that he wished to introduce such testimony. The Court said the state's "notice" requirement and ten-day rule served legitimate interests of protecting rape victims against surprise, harassment, and unnecessary invasions of privacy.[75]

Justice Scalia breathed new life into the confrontation right in the case of *Crawford v. Washington* (2004).[76] He had long argued that the Court should interpret this right in light of its original meaning, and he had strenuously objected when exceptions were permitted. Since 1980 the Court had said that some out-of-court statements could be used as evidence if they were viewed as reliable and trustworthy. For example, a person may have given the police a recorded statement or testified before a grand jury. If that person were later unavailable to testify at trial, the Court had ruled in *Ohio v. Roberts* (1980), the witness's statement could be introduced as evidence.[77] In *Crawford,* Scalia spoke for a 7-2 majority in overruling *Roberts* and insisting that the accused had a right to block the use of statements by persons unavailable for cross examination.

Michael Crawford had objected when a tape-recorded statement from his wife Sylvia was used at his trial. He had been accused of stabbing Kenneth Lee at the man's apartment, but he argued that he had acted in self-defense. When Sylvia was questioned by the police, she had suggested that her husband had approached Lee with a knife, not fought back from an attack by Lee. Because a husband can prevent a wife from testifying against him, Sylvia was not called to the witness stand. Instead, her tape-recorded statement was used, over his objection. Scalia said her statement may have been reliable, but it nonetheless violated Michael Crawford's right to confront his accuser.

"Where testimonial evidence is at issue, the Sixth Amendment demands what the common law required: unavailability and a prior opportunity for cross examination," Scalia wrote. "We leave for another day any effort to spell out a comprehensive definition of 'testimonial.' Whatever else the term covers, it applies at a minimum to prior testimony at a preliminary hearing, before a grand jury, or at a former trial, and to police interrogations." Scalia said the defendant retains his right to confront his accusers in court, even if enforcing it means that crucial and reliable evidence will be lost. Chief Justice William H. Rehnquist and Justice Sandra Day O'Connor dissented.

The *Crawford* decision had a wide impact, particularly in cases of domestic violence and child abuse. Victims of such abuse oftentimes give statements to police investigators, nurses, or counselors, and these statements have been used in court as a substitute for testimony. Scalia's opinion allowed no such exceptions, although, as he noted, it is not entirely clear what a "testimonial" is. In 2006 the Court tried to answer this question and drew a fine line: Statements given in response to a police officer's questions are "testimonial," the Court ruled, and therefore, these words cannot be used in court against a defendant unless the

witness testifies. On the other hand, a caller's frantic words when speaking to a 911 operator can be used because they involve reporting an event in progress, not building a case against a defendant. The Court reached these conclusions in the combined case known as *Davis v. Washington* (2006).[78]

In the first of the cases, a woman called 911 and said, "He's here ... And jumping on me again." She was referring to her boyfriend, Adrian Davis. She gave the operator his name and was told that the police were on the way. Davis was arrested and charged with violating a restraining order. His girlfriend disappeared and did not testify at Davis's trial, at which the 911 recording was played. The jury convicted Davis, and the Court upheld the verdict in a 9-0 decision. Scalia wrote that the girlfriend was reporting "an ongoing emergency. She simply was not acting as a witness. She was not testifying."

The second case involved a police visit to the home of Amy and Herschel Hammon in Peru, Indiana. The officers, responding to a domestic disturbance call, found Amy on the front porch looking scared. An officer took her into the living room and asked her what had happened. She said that she and her husband had had an argument, and that he had broken a lamp and thrown her to the ground. She signed a statement describing what happened. Amy did not testify at her husband's trial, but the police officer reported what she had said. The judge and the Indiana courts upheld the use of her signed statement and affirmed his conviction on the grounds that hers was an "excited utterance" at a crime scene.

Scalia spoke for an 8-1 majority in overturning the husband's conviction in *Hammon v. Indiana* (2006). "There was no emergency in progress," he said. The wife had recounted what had happened in response to the officer's questions. Scalia characterized her statement as "inherently testimonial" because it served as an accusation in court. Justice Thomas dissented on the ground that persons who speak to the police are not "witnesses" unless they testify at trial.

In 2008 the Court issued a ruling in *Giles v. California* allowing a killer to block the jury from hearing from his victim.[79] On September 29, 2002, Dwayne Giles had shot his unarmed ex-girlfriend Brenda Avie six times near the garage of his home in south Los Angeles. She had come to see him, and they had quarreled. Giles fled, but when arrested, he admitted to the shooting, claiming that he had acted in self-defense. At trial, however, a police officer testified that he had spoken to Avie three weeks earlier, when he had responded to a domestic disturbance call from her home. She said that she and Giles had had a fight, and he had pulled out a knife and threatened to kill her. The jury convicted Giles of first-degree murder, and the California Supreme Court upheld his conviction, ruling that the defendant had forfeited his confrontation right when he killed the witness.

Scalia spoke for a 6-3 majority in reversing Giles's conviction because the use of Avie's words violated his confrontation right. Scalia agreed that "deliberate witness tampering" would void the defendant's right, but there was no evidence that Giles had shot Avie with the intent of preventing her from testifying against him. He cited several cases from seventeenth-century England and said that they had established the rule "that unconfronted testimony would not be admitted without a showing that the defendant intended to prevent the witness from testifying." Giles had caused Avie to be absent, but he did not kill her to prevent her testimony, Scalia asserted. "We decline to approve an exception to the Confrontation Clause unheard of at the time of the founding or for 200 years thereafter," Scalia wrote. Chief Justice Roberts and Justices Thomas and Alito agreed. Justices Souter and Ginsburg concurred in the outcome. Justices Breyer, Stevens, and Kennedy dissented. Breyer said that Scalia's approach threatens to create "great practical difficulties" in domestic violence cases, like this one. The defendant gains a "windfall," he said, by killing the main witness to the crime.

Search and Seizure

The Fourth Amendment's protection against "unreasonable searches and seizures" by the government is one of the best known and most vital "rights of the people" in U.S. law. Its origins echo in the old English maxim "A man's house is his castle," off-limits to intrusions by the king's men. No wonder then that the Fourth Amendment stands strongest as a legal barrier to police searches of homes. This right against "unreasonable searches" is not, however, limited to a residence. "The Fourth Amendment protects people, not places," the Court said famously in *Katz v. United States* (1967), when it extended this privacy protection to a phone booth that had been wiretapped by the FBI.[1]

Like the First Amendment's protection for the freedom of speech and of religion, the Fourth Amendment protects something many people hold dear: their privacy. It adds to the law the principle that within the private sphere, the right to be let alone stands as a barrier to spying and prying by agents of the government. Of note, the Court has repeatedly said that the most important word in the Fourth Amendment is "unreasonable." The Constitution does not forbid *all* searches; it does not even require judicial warrants for all searches. Rather, it forbids those searches that are deemed unreasonable. The 1967 wiretapping decision set out a formula the Court has since followed. Its opinion in *Katz* rejected two extreme views: One side contended that the Fourth Amendment applied narrowly—only to "protected areas," such as a home. The other side held that it created a broad "general right to privacy." The right answer is somewhere in the middle, the Court said. The Constitution protects persons and their belongings when and where they have a "reasonable expectation of privacy." This privacy right may vanish with exposure. "What a person knowingly exposes to the public, even in his home or office, is not a subject of Fourth Amendment protection," wrote Justice Potter Stewart. "But what he seeks to preserve, as private, even in an area accessible to the public, may be constitutionally protected.[2]

This formula is not easy to apply, but apply it the Court has. For example, it ruled that a list of phone calls made by a homeowner is not private and protected by the Fourth Amendment, even if the contents of the calls are protected.[3] This permits police or the FBI to obtain phone records without a search warrant, but if they want to listen to the calls, however, they need a warrant from a magistrate. The Court held similarly that persons have no reasonable expectation of privacy in their bank or tax records. "Checks are not confidential communications, but negotiable instruments to be used in commercial transactions," the Court said in 1976. These papers "contain only information voluntarily conveyed to the banks and … exposed to their employees in the ordinary course of business."[4]

When motorists get in a car and drive it on a public road, they relinquish much of their "expectation of privacy." They can be stopped by a police officer if they are speeding or weaving across lanes. If they appear to be inebriated, an officer can order them out of the car. If an officer sees signs of drugs or a gun, he or she can search the inside of the automobile. The Court has deemed all these actions as reasonable searches. If a person enters an airport or a government building where security is crucial, he or she can be stopped and searched. In these high-security areas, a person has no "reasonable expectation of privacy."

The Fourth Amendment states a general proposition and a means for enforcing it. "The right of the people to be secure in their persons, houses, papers, and effects, against unreasonable searches and seizures, shall not be violated," it says. The second clause reads, "and no Warrants shall issue, but upon probable cause, supported by Oath or affirmation, and particularly describing the place to be searched, and the persons or things to be seized." If these two clauses were interpreted as one, the Fourth Amendment could require that government agents need a warrant whenever they conduct a search. A valid warrant—one issued by a neutral and detached magistrate based upon probable cause—offers significant protection for privacy. Government agents must show they have good evidence that a crime is being committed and that they need to search for certain evidence to confirm this crime. The Court has refused to require warrants for all searches, but instead has focused on those that would violate a person's reasonable expectation of privacy.

The Court has recognized two primary exceptions to search warrant requirements: a search related to a lawful arrest or a search of a moving vehicle that has been halted by police. Although the Court generally has resisted arguments for new exceptions to the warrant requirement, it has held that neither aerial surveillance nor police searches of privately owned open fields need to be authorized by warrant. It has steadily lengthened the list of situations in which police are permitted to search cars without first obtaining warrants.[5]

The justices continue to struggle over when a warrant is required. Two recent rulings illustrate their difficulties. One involved the use of a "thermal imager" that shows sources of heat in a home. Federal agents in Oregon had suspected Danny Kyllo of growing marijuana plants. Standing on the street, they focused the thermal imager at his house and found an unusual level of heat radiating from the roof. They used this image to obtain a search warrant; once inside, they discovered 100 marijuana plants. In its 5-4 decision in *Kyllo v. United States* (2001), the Court ruled that the use of the thermal imager was an unconstitutional search because it allowed agents "to explore details of the home," said Justice Antonin Scalia for the majority. The more liberal justice John Paul Stevens spoke for the dissenters. He said the thermal imager did not look into the house, but instead detected heat waves radiating from it.[6]

A search is legal when police are given consent to enter, but in 2006 the Court split over whether a wife may give consent to search her home if the husband disagrees. Scott Randolph's estranged wife had told police that he used cocaine and she gave them permission to search the house to find the evidence. Her husband stood at the door and refused to consent to the search, but an officer entered without a warrant and found the evidence in an upstairs bedroom. In *Georgia v. Randolph* (2006), the Court ruled in a 5-3 decision that the search was unconstitutional.[7] The ruling prompted Chief Justice John G. Roberts Jr. to write his first dissent.

How to enforce the Fourth Amendment's privacy protection has always been the subject of great controversy and continuing dispute. The rule would be meaningless if the police could violate it without penalty. Suing police officers or FBI agents was seen as impractical and ineffective. Over time, the Court adopted the "exclusionary rule" as a method of enforcing the Fourth Amendment guarantee. In effect in federal courts since 1914, this rule provides that evidence obtained in violation of the Fourth Amendment rights of a defendant may not be used as evidence against the defendant at trial. *(See box, The Exclusionary Rule, pp. 296–297.)* Not until 1949 did the Supreme Court consider applying the Fourth Amendment guarantee and the exclusionary rule to state defendants. In *Wolf v. Colorado* (1949), the Court seemed to say that the rights protected by the Fourth Amendment were so basic to "the concept of ordered liberty" that they were protected against state action through the Due Process Clause of the Fourteenth Amendment. Nevertheless, the Court in *Wolf* expressly declined to apply the exclusionary rule against state officials.[8] Twelve years later, however, the Court reversed *Wolf* and in *Mapp v. Ohio* (1961) extended to state defendants the full protection of the guarantee.[9] *Mapp* was one of the momentous decisions of the Warren Court because it brought the full power of the Fourth Amendment to bear on everyday encounters between residents and local law enforcement. In *Ker v. California* (1963), the Court stated that the Fourth Amendment guarantee as applied to state action was in all respects the same as that applied to federal action.[10]

THE NEUTRAL MAGISTRATE

The Court has interpreted the Constitution to require that search and arrest warrants be issued by a neutral

PRIVATE SEARCH

The Fourth Amendment protects individuals only against searches and seizures by government agents, not by private individuals. The Supreme Court set out this rule in *Burdeau v. McDowell* (1921).[1] After J.C. McDowell was dismissed from his corporate job, his former employers blew open the lock on his private office safe, broke the lock on his desk drawer, and delivered the contents of the desk and safe to the Justice Department, which was investigating McDowell's role in a mail fraud scheme. McDowell challenged the seizure of the evidence as a violation of his right to be secure in his "papers and effects" against unreasonable search and seizure.

The Supreme Court rebuffed McDowell's challenge, holding that the Fourth Amendment reached only government action; acts committed by private individuals, as in McDowell's case, were outside the protection of that guarantee. McDowell could, however, the Court noted, institute a private suit against those individuals who took his papers and turned them over to the government.

1. *Burdeau v. McDowell*, 256 U.S. 465 (1921).

---

and detached magistrate. In 1948 Justice Robert H. Jackson explained why:

> The point of the Fourth Amendment, which often is not grasped by zealous officers, is not that it denies law enforcement the support of the usual inferences which reasonable men draw from evidence. Its protection consists in requiring that those inferences be drawn by a neutral and detached magistrate instead of being judged by the officer engaged in the often competitive enterprise of ferreting out crime. Any assumption that evidence sufficient to support a magistrate's disinterested determination to issue a search warrant will justify the officers in making a search without a warrant would reduce the Amendment to a nullity and leave the people's homes secure only in the discretion of police officers.... When the right of privacy must reasonably yield to the right of search is, as a rule, to be decided by a judicial officer, not by a policeman or Government enforcement agent.[11]

The Court emphasized the importance of this requirement again in the 1970s. In *Coolidge v. New Hampshire* (1971), the Court forbade the use of evidence obtained in a police search based on a warrant issued by the state official who was the chief investigator and prosecutor in the case. "Since he was not the neutral and detached magistrate required by the Constitution," stated the Court, "the search stands on no firmer ground than if there had been no warrant at all."[12] The following year, however, the Court

ruled that municipal court clerks may issue search warrants in cases involving the breach of municipal laws. There was no Fourth Amendment "commandment that all warrant authority must reside exclusively in a lawyer or judge." Justice Lewis F. Powell Jr. wrote the Court's opinion:

> The substance of the Constitution's warrant requirements does not turn on the labeling of the issuing party. The warrant traditionally has represented an independent assurance that a search and arrest will not proceed without probable cause to believe that a crime has been committed and that the person or place named in the warrant is involved in the crime. Thus an issuing magistrate must meet two tests. He must be neutral and detached, and he must be capable of determining whether probable cause exists for the requested arrest or search.... If ... detachment and capacity do conjoin, the magistrate has satisfied the Fourth Amendment's purpose.[13]

PROBABLE CAUSE

A magistrate must find "probable cause" to issue a warrant. Probable cause has been variously defined. Although the term "means less than evidence which would justify condemnation,"[14] probable cause does require "belief that the law was being violated on the premises to be searched; and ... the facts ... are such that a reasonably discreet and prudent man would be led to believe that there was a commission of the offense charged."[15] A warrant is not valid, the Court has held, if it is based only upon a sworn allegation without adequate support in fact. In *Nathanson v. United States* (1933), the Court set out this rule:

> Under the Fourth Amendment, an officer may not properly issue a warrant to search a private dwelling unless he can find probable cause therefore from facts or circumstances presented to him under oath or affirmation. Mere affirmance of belief or suspicion is not enough.[16]

The Court has held valid, however, warrants based on hearsay, and it has not required direct personal observation of the facts or circumstances justifying the warrant by the individual who seeks it.[17] The magistrate, however, must be satisfied that the informant, whose identity need not be disclosed, is credible or his information reliable.[18]

In the late 1970s, the Court granted the right to a trial court hearing to a defendant who claimed that police had obtained evidence against him by using lies to convince a magistrate of probable cause. Justice Harry A. Blackmun, writing for the Court in *Franks v. Delaware* (1978), made clear the majority's view that "a warrant ... would be reduced to a nullity if a police officer was able to use deliberately falsified allegations to demonstrate probable cause."[19]

Only if an individual cannot or does not consent to a search are police required to obtain a warrant. Voluntary consent of the individual who owns or occupies the place to be searched validates the search, but the Court has held that the individual who is asked to consent to a search need not be informed that he or she may refuse. In *Schneckloth v. Bustamonte* (1973), the Court discussed the elements of voluntary consent. Justice Potter Stewart wrote for the majority:

> We hold only that when the subject of a search is not in custody and the State attempts to justify the search on the basis of his consent, the Fourth and Fourteenth Amendments require that it demonstrate that the consent was in fact voluntarily given, and not the result of duress or coercion, express or implied. Voluntariness is a question of fact to be

determined from all the circumstances, and while the subject's knowledge of a right to refuse is a factor to be taken into account, the prosecution is not required to demonstrate such knowledge as a prerequisite to establishing a voluntary consent.[20]

Justices William J. Brennan Jr., William O. Douglas, and Thurgood Marshall dissented, arguing that they failed to see "how our citizens can meaningfully be said to have waived something as precious as a constitutional guarantee without ever being aware of its existence."[21]

The following year in *United States v. Matlock* (1974), the Court held that when one occupant of a house consents to search of the premises, the search is proper, and evidence uncovered in it may be used against another occupant.[22] In 1990 in another case involving multiple occupants of a residence, the Court ruled that an overnight houseguest has a legitimate expectation of privacy and is entitled to Fourth Amendment protection against police intrusion at the house. By 7-2, the justices said the guest has sufficient interest in the home to challenge the legality of his warrantless arrest there.[23] A homeowner has a right, however, to refuse entrance to the police, even if his spouse consents to a search, the Court said in 2006. Unlike in the *Matlock* case, Scott Randolph was at home in Americus, Georgia, when an officer came to the door and sought permission to enter. He was there because Randolph's estranged wife Janet had called the police and reported that her husband was a drug user. In *Georgia v. Randolph*, the Court said that the officer's entrance into the house and his search of the premises were unconstitutional. Justice David H. Souter, speaking for the 5-3 majority, said that the homeowner retains the right to keep out a police officer who does not have a search warrant. Chief Justice John G. Roberts Jr. dissented, along with Justices Antonin Scalia and Clarence Thomas. "A warrantless search is reasonable if the police obtain the voluntary consent of a person authorized to give it," he wrote, and this was a "search of what is, after all, her home, too."[24]

PROPERTY, PAPERS, AND EFFECTS

Most of the individual rights in the Constitution were given a narrow reach in the Supreme Court's first century. Their true significance came much later, after the mid-twentieth century when the Court breathed new life into the Bill of Rights. The Fourth Amendment's privacy protection for "papers and effects" is the exception. The Court gave this provision a robust reading in its first major decision, but it scaled back the privacy protection for private papers in the 1970s.

The Supreme Court's first major ruling on the scope of the Fourth Amendment's protection for individual privacy and security came in *Boyd v. United States* (1886).[25] In *Boyd*, the Court established that the Fourth Amendment protected individuals against subpoenas, as well as searches, for private business papers, and it forbade such subpoenas as unreasonable if they forced the person to whom they were directed to produce self-incriminating evidence, contrary to their Fifth Amendment right. E. A. Boyd and Sons had contracted with the federal government to furnish plate glass for a post office and courthouse building in Philadelphia. They agreed to discount the price of the glass in return for permission to import it duty free. The government subsequently charged that the Boyds had taken advantage of the agreement by importing more glass than the contract permitted and therefore sought forfeiture of the contract. At trial, the judge ordered the Boyds to produce the invoice showing the amount of imported glass they had received. Under protest, the Boyds complied with the order. They were convicted.

The Supreme Court reversed their conviction and ordered a new trial, declaring that the subpoena had violated the Boyds' Fourth Amendment and Fifth Amendment rights. For the majority, Justice Joseph P. Bradley explained that compulsory production of a man's private papers was an unreasonable search and seizure under the Fourth Amendment. He also explained how the Boyds' Fifth Amendment rights were infringed:

> The principles laid down in this opinion affect the very essence of constitutional liberty and security … they apply to all invasions, on the part of the Government and its employees, of the sanctity of a man's home and the privacies of life. It is not the breaking of his doors and the rummaging of his drawers that constitutes the essence of the offence: but it is the invasion of his indefeasible right of personal security, personal liberty and private property, where

that right has never been forfeited by his conviction of some public offense.… Breaking into a house and opening boxes and drawers are circumstances of aggravation; but any forcible and compulsory extortion of a man's own testimony or of his private papers to be used as evidence to convict him of crime or to forfeit his goods is within the condemnation of that judgment. In this regard the Fourth and Fifth Amendments run almost into each other.…

> We have already noticed the intimate relation between the two Amendments. They throw great light on each other. For the "unreasonable searches and seizures" condemned in the Fourth Amendment are almost always made for the purpose of compelling a man to give evidence against himself, which in criminal cases is condemned in the Fifth Amendment; and compelling a man "in a criminal case to be a witness against himself," which is condemned in the Fifth Amendment, throws light on the question as to what is an "unreasonable search and seizure" within the meaning of the Fourth Amendment. And we have been unable to perceive that the seizure of a man's private books and papers to be used in evidence against him is substantially different from compelling him to be a witness against himself.[26]

The Exclusionary Rule

To avoid the cumbersome and expensive remedy of retrial for persons convicted on the basis of evidence seized in violation of their Fourth Amendment rights, the Court in the early twentieth century adopted the exclusionary rule. Set out first by the Court in *Weeks v. United States* (1914), the rule allows a defendant who feels that evidence obtained in violation of his rights will be used against him to require the trial court to exclude it from use.[27] Fremont Weeks was arrested without a warrant. Federal agents searched his home, also without a warrant, and took from it documents and letters used as evidence against him at trial. After his conviction, he challenged the conviction as obtained in violation of his rights. The Supreme Court agreed. In its unanimous opinion, Justice William R. Day explained that exclusion of such evidence was necessary to discourage unlawful practices by law enforcement agents:

The tendency of those who execute the criminal laws of the country to obtain conviction by means of unlawful seizures and enforced confessions ... should find no sanction in the judgments of the courts, which are charged ... with the support of the Constitution.

... If letters and private documents can thus be seized and held and used in evidence against a citizen accused of an offense, the protection of the 4th Amendment, declaring his right to be secure against such searches and seizures, is of no value, and, so far as those thus placed are concerned, might as well be stricken from the Constitution.[28]

The Court concluded that the seizure of the letters by a federal agent and the refusal of the judge to honor Weeks's request for their return before they were used as evidence were violations of his constitutional rights. (*See box, The Exclusionary Rule, pp. 296–297.*)

Business, Tax, and Phone Records

Three decisions in 1976 curtailed Fourth Amendment protection for private papers that had been established in *Boyd* nearly a century before. In *United States v. Miller* (1976), the Court ruled that bank records of a depositor's transactions were not private papers protected by the amendment,[29] and in *Andresen v. Maryland* (1976), it undercut *Boyd* to allow the use of an attorney's business records as evidence against him.[30] Because police had a warrant for the search in which they seized these papers, there was no valid Fourth Amendment challenge to their use, the Court held, in the case of *Andresen* rejecting the attorney's argument that as in *Boyd*, the use of his papers against Andresen violated his Fifth Amendment privilege against compelled self-incrimination. In *Fisher v. United States* (1976), the Court said that tax records, even those held by an attorney, are not shielded from being turned over to the government by either the Fourth Amendment's privacy protection or the Fifth Amendment's protection against self-incrimination. "Several of *Boyd's* express or implicit declarations have not stood the test of the time," Justice Byron White said in the *Fisher* case.[31]

The Court explained that bank, business, and tax records are not inherently private papers, but rather flow in the public stream of commerce. Check and deposit slips "are not confidential communications," Justice Lewis F. Powell Jr. wrote in the *Miller* decision.

They "contain only information voluntarily conveyed to the banks and exposed to their employees in the ordinary course of business," he said. Therefore, neither a bank customer, a taxpayer, nor a business owner has a reasonable expectation of privacy in these records and papers, the Court said.

In 1979 the Court said that phone records are not private and may be obtained by the government without a warrant. "We doubt that people in general entertain any actual expectation of privacy in the numbers they dial," wrote Justice Harry A. Blackmun. The dialing records are kept at the office of the telephone company, and most phone users see a list of their long-distance calls on their monthly bill.[32]

The Court also expanded the reach of authorized searches to include "third parties" who are not suspected of a crime. In *Zurcher v. The Stanford Daily* (1978), the Court rejected the argument of a campus newspaper that a search of its offices by police with a warrant violated the First and the Fourth Amendments. The *Stanford Daily* offices were searched by police looking for photographs or notes revealing the identity of individual demonstrators responsible for injuries to police during a protest. Such documents were clearly mere evidence, and there was no allegation that the newspaper or any of its employees had engaged in any wrongdoing. The newspaper contended that police should have subpoenaed the information, rather than searching its offices. The Court ruled that the Fourth Amendment did not restrict permissible searches to only those places occupied by persons suspected of crimes. "Under existing law," wrote Justice Byron R. White for the five-justice majority, "valid warrants may be issued to search *any* property, whether or not occupied by a third party, at which there is probable cause to believe that the fruits, instrumentalities, or evidence of a crime will be found."[33] Justice John Paul Stevens, one of the dissenters from the *Zurcher* decision, took this opportunity to express his concern about the Court's departure from the so-called mere evidence rule in *Warden v. Hayden* (1967):

Countless law abiding citizens ... may have documents in their possession that relate to an ongoing criminal investigation. The consequences of subjecting this large category of persons to unannounced police searches are extremely serious.[34]

"STOP AND FRISK" SEARCHES HELD REASONABLE

The Supreme Court has held that the police practice of stopping suspicious persons and "frisking" them for weapons is a reasonable "search" within the boundaries of the Fourth Amendment. According to the justices, such searches are permissible even without a search warrant or enough information to constitute probable cause for arrest. In *Terry v. Ohio* (1968), Chief Justice Earl Warren announced,

> there must be a narrowly drawn authority to permit a reasonable search for weapons for the protection of the police officer....Where a police officer observes unusual conduct which leads him reasonably to conclude in the light of his experience that criminal activity may be afoot and that the person with whom he is dealing may be armed and presently dangerous,... he is entitled for the protection of himself and others in the area to conduct a carefully limited search of the outer clothing of such persons in an attempt to discover weapons which might be used to assault him.[1]

Warren, however, emphasized the limited nature of this authority. It is not a general or unlimited power to stop every pedestrian. Rather, it is triggered whenever the officer has some specific reason to suspect wrongdoing by a pedestrian, the Court said. The brief search itself consists "solely of a limited patting of the outer clothing of the suspect for concealed weapons," Warren stated.[2] It is not to be used as a pretext to search the suspect for drugs or other illegal items. Nonetheless, the Court has been reluctant to restrain officers further by second-guessing their reason for stopping a suspect or by rejecting evidence that was found after an initial frisk.

In 1989 the Court upheld the use of "drug courier" profiles by federal agents operating at airports and train stations. Persons who fit the profiles sometimes are stopped for questioning, even if agents have no other reason to suspect them of a crime. Andrew Sokolow triggered suspicion when he went to the airport in Honolulu in 1984 dressed in a black jumpsuit and wearing a gold chain. He used a large roll of $20 bills to purchase two round-trip tickets to Miami. He and his female companion planned to stay in Florida less than two days before they returned to Hawaii on the long cross-country flight. Upon his return, Sokolow looked "very nervous," the agents said. In addition, they had learned that he had used a false name on his ticket. The agents pulled him aside before he could leave the airport and found 1,063 grams of cocaine in one of his carry-on bags. A federal appeals court threw out the evidence on the ground that the agents did not have reasonable suspicion to stop Sokolow because none of his actions—paying cash for his tickets, flying to Miami for a short stay, and looking nervous—amounted to criminal behavior.

Disagreeing with the lower court, Chief Justice William H. Rehnquist said reasonable suspicion must be judged "by the totality of the circumstances—the whole picture."[3] He cited the series of facts relied upon by the agents, including the cash purchases and the unusual itinerary. "Any one of these factors is not by itself proof of any illegal conduct and is quite consistent with innocent travel. But we think that taken together they amount to reasonable suspicion," he said for a 7-2 majority. Justices Thurgood Marshall and William J. Brennan Jr. dissented.

Just as "nervous, evasive behavior" at an airport counter may give agents reason to detain a traveler, "unprovoked flight upon noticing the police" gives officers good reason to pursue and stop an individual, Chief Justice Rehnquist said in *Illinois v. Wardlow* (2002).[4] This case of the fleeing suspect began at midday on September 9, 1995, when four squad cars from the Chicago Police Department turned on to the 4000 block of West Van Buren Street, an area known for drug dealing. An officer saw one man, later identified as Sam Wardlow, turn and run down an alley when the police cars approached. The officers turned another corner and stopped him. When an officer patted down Wardlow, he found a bag with a hard object inside. It proved to be a .38 caliber handgun with five loaded bullets. Wardlow was convicted of the unlawful use of a concealed weapon by a felon, but he appealed, contending that he had been subjected to an

ARRESTS AND SEARCHES

The Supreme Court has never applied the warrant requirement of the Fourth Amendment as strictly to arrests—the seizure of one's person—as to searches. The Court has applied the common law rule to arrests, approving warrantless arrests by law enforcement officers for crimes committed in their presence and for other crimes where there are reasonable grounds for their action.[35] In 1925 the Court stated that "[t]he usual rule is that a police officer may arrest without warrant one believed by the officer upon reasonable cause to have been guilty of a felony."[36] Half a century later, the Court noted that it had never unreasonable search. The Illinois courts agreed and said every person has a right to "go on one's way." In a 5-4 decision, however, the Court reinstated the conviction. Fleeing from the police, wrote Chief Justice Rehnquist, "is not necessarily indicative of wrongdoing, but it is certainly suggestive of such....Reasonable suspicion must be based on common-sense judgments and inferences about human behavior," he added.[5]

The Court has, however, refused to give officers broader authority to search presumably innocent pedestrians and seize evidence from them. In 1993 Justice Byron R. White, the last surviving member of the Warren Court, stressed that a "stop and frisk" was a "strictly circumscribed search for weapons," not a "general warrant to rummage and search at will."[6] White spoke for a 6-3 majority in *Minnesota v. Dickerson* (1993) that said police cannot feel around in a detained person's pockets and clothing in hopes of finding drugs. In this case, a Minneapolis police officer had stopped Timothy Dickerson after observing him leaving a notorious crack house. In patting down the man, he found no weapons, but instead he "felt a small lump in the front pocket." Inside, he found a plastic bag containing one-fifth of one gram of crack cocaine. The Court held that the stop of Dickerson was legal, but the seizure of the drug evidence was not. Feeling around for the drug evidence "amounted to the sort of evidentiary search that *Terry* expressly refused to authorize," White said in his final month on the Court.[7]

The justices have also insisted that police have "reliable" evidence of wrongdoing before they stop someone. An anonymous caller reporting that a man at a bus stop is carrying a hidden gun is not reliable enough, the Court said in *Florida v. J.L.* (2000). In October 1995, the Miami-Dade police had received a call from an unidentified person who said that a young black male standing on a corner and wearing a plaid shirt had a gun. A patrol car was dispatched, and at the bus stop an officer saw three young men, one of whom was wearing a plaid shirt. Nothing else appeared suspicious. When the youth, identified only as "J.L.," was patted down, the officer

felt a gun in his pocket. In a unanimous decision, the Court said this stop-and-frisk based entirely on an "anonymous tip" was unreasonable because police had no way to judge the reliability of the tipster. The information proved to be accurate, but it came from "an unknown, unaccountable informant who neither explained how he knew about the gun nor supplied any basis for believing he had inside information about J.L.," said Justice Ruth Bader Ginsburg.[8]

When police stop a suspicious person, they may require him to give his name, the Court said in 2004. "It is well established that an officer may ask a suspect to identify himself in the course of a Terry stop," wrote Justice Anthony M. Kennedy for a 5-4 majority in *Hiibel v. Sixth Judicial District Court of Nevada* (2004).[9] A deputy had responded to a call reporting a woman being beaten in a pickup truck when he came upon a man standing beside a parked pickup. A woman sat inside. The officer asked him repeatedly—11 times in all—to identify himself. The man refused and was arrested. In court, Larry Hiibel insisted that he had a right to remain silent and that his arrest violated the Fourth Amendment's ban on unreasonable searches and the Fifth Amendment's protection against self-incrimination. The Court disagreed. Because the officer had reason to stop Hiibel, he could require Hiibel to disclose his name, Kennedy said. This does not make for an unreasonable search, nor did his name alone incriminate him.

---

1. *Terry v. Ohio*, 392 U.S. 1 at 27, 30 (1968).

2. Id. at 30, 31.

3. *United States v. Sokolow*, 490 U.S. 1 at 8 (1989).

4. *Illinois v. Wardlow*, 528 U.S. 119 at 124 (2002).

5. Id. at 124–125.

6. *Minnesota v. Dickerson*, 508 U.S. 366 at 378 (1993).

7. Id.

8. *Florida v. J.L.*, 529 U.S. 266 at 271 (2000).

9. *Hiibel v. Sixth Judicial District Court of Nevada*, 542 U.S. 177 (2004).

---

invalidated an arrest supported by probable cause just because the arresting officer did not have an arrest warrant. To impose a warrant requirement on all arrests, the Court said, would "constitute an intolerable handicap for legitimate law enforcement." [37]

Probable cause, however, is essential to justify a warrantless arrest.[38] The Court has declared unconstitutional

the warrantless detention of suspects apprehended in a police dragnet, declaring that such "investigatory arrests" must be authorized by warrants if the evidence they uncover is to be used in court.[39] In *United States v. Watson* (1976), the Court upheld the warrantless arrest of a suspect in a public place based upon probable cause.[40] Justice White elaborated on

Searches at the Border and Beyond

Since the earliest days of the nation's history, Congress has authorized warrantless searches of persons entering the country at its borders. The Court has upheld checkpoints near the border where cars and trucks are required to stop for a brief inspection. In a series of rulings in the mid-1970s, however, the Court held that the Fourth Amendment did apply to searches that were part of the U.S. Border Patrol's effort to control illegal immigration.

In *Almeida-Sanchez v. United States* (1973), the Court held that roving patrols violated the Fourth Amendment guarantee when they searched vehicles as far as one hundred miles from the border without a search warrant or probable cause to suspect that the car contained illegal aliens.[1] Two years later, a unanimous Court extended *Almeida-Sanchez* to hold that roving patrols could not even stop a car for questioning of its occupants unless there was more cause than the fact that the occupants appeared to be Mexican.[2] The same day, the Court held that border patrol officers at fixed checkpoints away from the border itself must have probable cause or a warrant before they searched cars at the checkpoint without the driver's consent.[3] In 1976 the Court held that border patrol officers need not have probable cause or a warrant before they stopped cars for brief questioning at fixed checkpoints. Justice Lewis F. Powell Jr. made clear the Court's distinction between searches and stops for questioning:

> While the need to make routine checkpoint stops is great, the consequent intrusion on Fourth Amendment interests is quite limited....
>
> Neither the vehicle nor its occupants is searched, and visual inspection of the vehicle is limited to what can be seen without a search. This objective intrusion—the stop itself, the questioning, and the visual inspection—also existed in roving-patrol stops. But we view checkpoint stops in a different light because the subjective intrusion—the generating of concern or

even fright on the part of lawful travelers—is appreciably less in the case of a checkpoint stop....

> ... [T]he reasonableness of the procedures followed in making these checkpoint stops makes the resulting intrusion on the interests of the motorists minimal. On the other hand, the purpose of the stops is legitimate and in the public interest.... Accordingly, we hold that the stops and questioning at issue may be made in the absence of any individualized suspicion at reasonably located checkpoints.[4]

In 1990 the Supreme Court addressed the question of whether the Fourth Amendment limited searches outside the borders of the United States. In an opinion by Chief Justice William H. Rehnquist, the Court ruled 5-4 that U.S. law enforcement agents operating without warrants may search a foreigner's property in a foreign country without violating the constitutional prohibition against unreasonable searches and seizures. The Court's ruling in *United States v. Verdugo-Urquidez* (1990) overturned a federal appeals court decision that had excluded from trial evidence seized in a warrantless search in Mexico of a man who was arrested there and brought back to the United States on drug charges. The Fourth Amendment's protection of the rights of "the people" was limited "to a class of persons who are part of a national community or who have otherwise developed sufficient connection with this country to be considered part of that community," wrote Rehnquist. The foreigner in this case did not fall within that group.[5] Justices William J. Brennan Jr., Thurgood Marshall, Harry A. Blackmun, and John Paul Stevens dissented.

---

1. *Almeida-Sanchez v. United States,* 413 U.S. 266 (1973).

2. *United States v. Brignoni-Ponce,* 422 U.S. 873 (1975).

3. *United States v. Ortiz,* 422 U.S. 891 (1975).

4. *United States v. Martinez, Sifuentes v. United States,* 428 U.S. 543 at 557–558, 561–562 (1976).

5. *United States v. Verdugo-Urquidez,* 494 U.S. 258 at 265 (1990).

---

the Court's view of the warrant requirement for arrests:

> Law enforcement officers may find it wise to seek arrest warrants where practicable to do so, and their judgments about probable cause may be more readily accepted where backed by a warrant issued

by a magistrate.... But we decline to transform this judicial preference into a constitutional rule when the judgment of the Nation and Congress has for so long been to authorize warrantless public arrests on probable cause rather than to encumber criminal prosecutions with endless litigation with respect to the existence of exigent circumstances, whether it was practicable to get a warrant, whether the suspect was about to flee, and the like.[41]

The Court drew a line at the entrance of a home, ruling that police may not enter a residence to make a routine arrest without a warrant. "The physical entry of the home is the chief evil against which the wording of the Fourth Amendment is directed," Justice John Paul Stevens wrote for the 6-3 majority in *Payton v. New York* (1980). "At the very core of this (amendment) stands the right of a man to retreat into his own home and there be free from unreasonable governmental intrusion."[42] In this instance, New York police had probable cause to believe that Theodore Payton had shot a gas station attendant two days earlier. At dawn they used a crow bar to break into his Bronx apartment without bothering to obtain an arrest warrant. The Court ruled that this forced entry without a warrant violated the Fourth Amendment. Police may not "make a warrantless and nonconsensual entry into a suspect's home in order to make a routine felony arrest," the justices held.[43]

Knock First, Then Enter

In the mid-1990s, police were told that they usually must knock on the door and announce their presence before entering a home, even if they have a warrant. Police in Arkansas had made an unannounced entry into the home of Sharlene Wilson and arrested her on drug charges. The Court unanimously reversed her conviction, tracing some basis of its decision back centuries. According to the statement of an English judge in 1604, "[T]he house of every one is to him as his castle and fortress." William Blackstone repeated this famous observation in *Commentaries on the Laws of England*. Justice Clarence Thomas, who frequently cites old English law, noted in *Wilson v. Arkansas* (1995) that the king's men were required to announce themselves before entering a home, and "the common law knock-and-announce principle was woven quickly into the fabric of early American law."[44] He further concluded that the knock-and-announce principle was incorporated into the Fourth Amendment's ban on unreasonable searches. Thomas did not, however, endorse an absolute rule requiring police to announce their presence. While police normally must knock on the door,

officers may enter unannounced if they face a serious threat or if evidence is likely to be destroyed.

In carrying out drug raids, police must move quickly and need not wait for a resident to answer the door, the justices ruled in 2003, upholding as reasonable a decision by police in Las Vegas to break down the door of a man's apartment less than twenty seconds after knocking on it. LaShawn Banks, the target of the search warrant, emerged from his shower to find police and FBI agents in his apartment. They found guns, cocaine, and $6,000 in cash. Since "15 or 20 seconds does not seem an unrealistic guess about the time someone would need to get in a position to rid his quarters of cocaine," fifteen or twenty seconds is a reasonable wait before forcibly entering, wrote Justice Souter in *United States v. Banks* (2003). The required wait may be longer, he added, if police had been searching for a stolen piano.[45]

If the police violate the knock-and-announce rule by entering too quickly, the evidence they find need not be thrown out, the Court said in 2006. "Suppression of evidence has always been our last resort, not our first impulse," wrote Justice Antonin Scalia in *Hudson v. Michigan* (2006).[46] Police in Detroit had obtained a warrant to search for drugs at the home of Booker Hudson. They announced their presence, and after three to five seconds they turned the door knob and burst into the house. They found Hudson sitting in a chair with a gun and a large quantity of drugs. He was convicted on drug charges, but appealed, arguing that the evidence should have been suppressed because the police had violated the knock-and-announce rule. The Court rejected his claim in a 5-4 ruling. "Suppression of all evidence, amounting in many cases to a get-out-of-jail free card" is too high a price to pay for entering too quickly, Scalia wrote, particularly since the police had a valid warrant to enter and search Hudson's home. Chief Justice John G. Roberts Jr. and Justices Clarence Thomas and Samuel A. Alito Jr. agreed entirely. Justice Anthony M. Kennedy joined him to form the majority, but added a caution: Despite some of Scalia's comments, "The continued operation of the exclusionary rule, as settled and defined by our precedents, is not in doubt," Kennedy said.

THE EXCLUSIONARY RULE: HOW RIGHTS ARE ENFORCED

The Constitution protects the rights of individuals against agents of the government, but it does not say how those rights are to be enforced. What should be done, for example, if police officers break into a home without a search warrant and find evidence of a crime? To deter just such violations, the Court adopted the controversial exclusionary rule, which requires that illegally obtained evidence be excluded from use as evidence, that is, thrown out. The reach of the exclusionary rule remains in dispute.

"The benefits of deterrence must outweigh the costs," Chief Justice John G. Roberts Jr. said in 2009. "The principal cost of applying the rule is, of course, letting the guilty and possibly dangerous defendants go free—something that offends basic concepts of the criminal justice system."[1] In this instance, he was speaking for a 5-4 majority in upholding gun and drug charges against Bennie D. Herring, an Alabama man who had been stopped on the highway and searched based on a supposedly outstanding arrest warrant. It turned out that the warrant had been revoked five months earlier, but the Dale County police department had failed to update this fact in its computer. The arresting officer learned of the mistake fifteen minutes after he had stopped Herring and found him in possession of methamphetamine and a pistol.

In *Herring v. United States* (2009), the Court ruled that honest mistakes by the police do not require that evidence be thrown out. "To trigger the exclusionary rule, police conduct must be sufficiently deliberate that exclusion can meaningfully deter it, and sufficiently culpable that such deterrence is worth the price paid by the justice system," Roberts wrote. "The exclusionary rule serves to deter deliberate, reckless, or grossly negligent conduct, or in some circumstances recurring or systematic negligence. The error in this case does not rise to that level." Justices Antonin Scalia, Anthony M. Kennedy, Clarence Thomas, and Samuel A. Alito Jr. agreed.

LONG HISTORY, RECURRING CONTROVERSY

The Court first put forward the exclusionary rule in *Weeks v. United States* (1914). Its decision in this case prohibited the use in federal courts of evidence seized by federal agents in violation of the Fourth Amendment ban against unreasonable search and seizure.[2] The Court applied the rule subsequently to forbid the use of evidence taken in violation of other constitutional rights as well, in particular the Fifth Amendment privilege against self-incrimination and the Sixth Amendment right to counsel. Not until *Mapp v. Ohio* (1961), however, did the Court extend the exclusionary rule to state trials.[3]

By denying prosecutors the use of certain evidence, the rule can cause the collapse of the government's case and allow a guilty person to go free. As Benjamin Cardozo wrote before he sat on the Court, "The criminal is to go free because the constable has blundered."[4] Chief Justices Warren E. Burger and William H. Rehnquist, like Chief Justice Roberts, also questioned whether such an outcome is too high a price for society to pay for inadvertent violations of constitutional guarantees.

In *Silverthorne Lumber Co. v. United States* (1920), the Court made clear that the exclusionary rule announced in *Weeks* forbade *all* use of illegally obtained evidence in federal courts. The ruling ordered the government to return to the owner physical evidence illegally seized by federal officials.[5] Justice Oliver Wendell Holmes Jr., speaking for the majority, stated that the decision also ruled photocopied evidence inadmissible: "The essence of a provision forbidding the acquisition of evidence in a certain way is that not merely evidence so acquired shall not be used before the court, but that it shall not be used at all."[6]

In 1954, however, the Court held that narcotics illegally seized by federal officials, while not admissible as evidence at trial, could be used to impeach a defendant's credibility after he has testified that he had never used them.[7] In other decisions, the Court made clear that only the person whose rights are violated by the search and seizure can invoke the exclusionary rule.[8]

WOLF v. COLORADO

The Court in *Wolf v. Colorado* (1949) took a half step toward extending the exclusionary rule to all courts and all law enforcement when it held that the Fourth Amendment guarantee protects individuals against state as well as federal action. The Court declined, however, to apply the exclusionary rule to enforce this guarantee against state officials.[9] Dr. Julius Wolf challenged the use of such evidence, arguing that it had been illegally seized and should be excluded. The Supreme Court, however, sustained his conviction. In this case, a deputy sheriff had seized Wolf's appointment book without a warrant, interrogated patients whose names he found in the book, and thereby obtained evidence to charge Wolf with performing illegal abortions. Justice Felix Frankfurter wrote for the majority. "The immediate question," he said,

> is whether the basic right to protect against arbitrary intrusion by the police demands the exclusion of logically relevant evidence obtained by an unreasonable search and seizure because, in a federal prosecution for a federal crime, it would be excluded.... When we find that in fact most of the English-speaking world does not regard as vital to such protection the exclusion of evidence thus obtained, we must hesitate to treat this remedy as an essential ingredient of the right.[10]

Shocking conduct by police, however, did cause the Court to reverse state convictions obtained by an unreasonable search and seizure, even before it applied the exclusionary rule to states. One such case was *Rochin v. California* (1952). In *Rochin*, state police officers had "seized" evidence from a suspect by pumping his stomach to recover two capsules of drugs he had swallowed at the time of his arrest. The Court held the resulting conviction invalid. Justice Frankfurter wrote the opinion for the unanimous Court, decrying such methods as "conduct that shocks the conscience,... methods too close to the rack and the screw to permit of constitutional differentiation."[11] The Court's earlier refusal in *Wolf* to exclude *all* illegally obtained evidence, however, was subsequently reaffirmed in cases involving eavesdropping, illegal entry, and the taking of a blood sample from an unconscious, injured suspect.[12]

The Supreme Court announced a major change in the law in *Mapp v. Ohio* (1961) when it extended the exclusionary rule to the states. In this case, the Court finally declared that "the exclusionary rule is an essential part of both the Fourth and Fourteenth Amendments."[13] Cleveland police, suspecting that a criminal was hiding in a house, broke in the door, manhandled the woman resident, a Miss Mapp, and searched the entire premises without a warrant. The police found a trunk containing obscene materials in the house. Mapp was tried and convicted for possession of obscene materials. The Supreme Court overturned Mapp's conviction because the evidence used against her had been unconstitutionally seized. The majority opinion by Justice Tom C. Clark reversed *Wolf* insofar as it dealt with the exclusionary rule:

> Nothing can destroy a government more quickly than its failure to observe its own laws, or worse, its disregard of the charter of its own existence....
>
> The ignoble shortcut to conviction left open to the State [by allowing use of illegally obtained evidence] tends to destroy the entire system of constitutional restraints on which the liberties of the people rest. Having once recognized that the right to privacy embodied in the Fourth Amendment is enforceable against the States, and that the right to be secure against rude invasions of privacy by state officers is, therefore, constitutional in origin, we can no longer permit that right to remain an empty promise.[14]

The *Mapp* decision was one of the far-reaching rulings of the Warren Court because it applied the full force of the Constitution to everyday encounters between local police and the public. In the 1970s, however, the Court limited the use of the exclusionary rule to overturn convictions, reflecting the lack of enthusiasm of some members of the Court for the rule. Chief Justice Burger said in *Bivens v. Six Unknown Named Agents* (1971) that he preferred an alternative remedy, perhaps a damage suit against the offending officials.[15]

The Court subsequently said that prosecutors may use illegally obtained evidence when questioning witnesses before grand juries. It also refused to extend the exclusionary rule to habeas corpus hearings before a federal judge. So long as the state has provided an opportunity for a full, fair hearing of the defendant's challenge to the use of illegally obtained evidence, there is no constitutional duty for federal courts to use the writ of habeas corpus to enforce the exclusionary rule, the Court held.[16]

In the 1980s, the Court approved several exceptions to the exclusionary rule. A "good faith" exception permits the use of illegally obtained evidence at trial if the police who seized it had a search warrant and thought they were acting legally only to find that because of some "technical" flaw, their search was in fact illegal. In such a case where the police were acting in good faith, wrote Justice Byron R. White in *United States v. Leon* (1984), the exclusion of valid evidence has no deterrent effect and exacts too high a price from society.[17] The same year the Court also approved an "inevitable discovery" exception to the exclusionary rule, permitting evidence taken in violation of a defendant's rights to be used at trial if the prosecutor can show that the evidence ultimately would have been discovered by lawful means.[18]

In 1995 the Court extended the good faith exception to mistakes made by judicial personnel. The case of *Arizona v. Evans* (1995) involved a courthouse computer mistake, which led a police officer to believe that a warrant that actually had been quashed remained valid. After the officer arrested the individual involved, he discovered a bag of marijuana in the man's car. The Supreme Court ruled 7-2 that errors made by clerical employees resulting in an unconstitutional arrest do not invoke the exclusionary rule and that the drug evidence need not be suppressed.[19] The *Herring* decision in 2009 went a step further in ruling that illegal searches caused by an error in a police department's computer do not trigger the exclusionary rule. In between these cases, the Court in *Hudson v. Michigan* (2006) had said that the evidence need not be excluded if police with a search warrant fail to "knock and announce" before entering. "Suppression of evidence has always been our last resort, not our first impulse," wrote Justice Scalia.[20]

1. *Herring v. United States* 555 U.S. ___ (2009).

2. *Weeks v. United States,* 232 U.S. 383 (1914).

3. *Mapp v. Ohio,* 367 U.S. 643 (1961).

4. *People v. Defore,* 242 N.Y. 13 at 21, 150 N.B. 585 (1926).

5. *Silverthorne Lumber Co. v. United States,* 251 U.S. 385 (1921).

6. *Id.* at 392.

7. *Walder v. United States,* 347 U.S. 62 (1954); see also *Stefanelli v. Minard,* 342 U.S. 117 (1951).

8. *Goldstein v. United States,* 316 U.S. 114 (1942).

9. *Wolf v. Colorado,* 338 U.S. 25 (1949).

10. *Id.* at 28–29, 31, 33.

11. *Rochin v. California,* 342 U.S. 165 (1952).

12. *Irvine v. California,* 347 U.S. 128 (1954); *Breithaupt v. Abrams,* 352 U.S. 432 (1957).

13. *Mapp v. Ohio,* 367 U.S. 643 at 657 (1961).

14. *Id.* at 659, 660.

15. *Bivens v. Six Unknown Named Agents,* 403 U.S. 388 (1971); see also *Monroe v. Pape,* 365 U.S. 176 (1961).

16. *United States v. Calandra,* 414 U.S. 338 (1974); *Stone v. Powell, Wolff v. Rice,* 428 U.S. 465 (1976); see also *United States v. Janis,* 428 U.S. 433 (1976).

17. *United States v. Leon,* 468 U.S. 897 (1984); *Massachusetts v. Sheppard,* 468 U.S. 981 (1984); see also *Maryland v. Garrison,* 480 U.S. 79 (1987); *Illinois v. Krull,* 480 U.S. 340 (1987).

18. *Nix v. Williams,* 467 U.S. 431 (1984).

19. *Arizona v. Evans,* 514 U.S. 1 (1995).

20. *Hudson v. Michigan,* 547 U.S. 586 (2006).

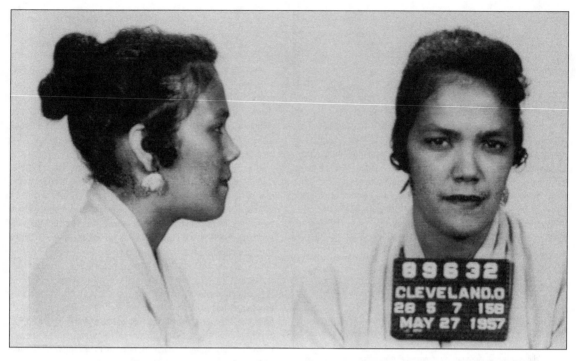

In 1957 Dollree Mapp was arrested for possession of obscene materials, which the police seized during an unconstitutional search. In *Mapp v. Ohio* (1961), the Supreme Court reversed her conviction holding that evidence obtained through an illegal search was inadmissible in court.

Media Ride-Alongs

Obtaining a warrant and knocking on the door are not the only Fourth Amendment requirements for entering a home, the Court has said. Keeping the media out is another. In 1999 the justices ruled that "media ride-alongs"—when the police allow reporters and camera operators to enter a residence as officers make an arrest—are unconstitutional. The decision came in the case of an elderly Maryland couple who were awakened at dawn when U.S. marshals, accompanied by a reporter and a photographer for the *Washington Post*, charged into their living room. The startled homeowner, Charles Wilson, was wrestled to the floor while his wife watched in horror. The marshals later realized that they had made a mistake; they possessed a warrant to arrest the couple's son, but he was not there. While the *Post* did not publish photographs from the raid, the Wilsons sued for invasion of privacy and won a symbolic victory at the Supreme Court. In the unanimous decision in *Wilson v. Layne* (1999), the Court said the media has no right to enter a private home, and police violate the Fourth Amendment if they bring such non–law enforcement personnel with them. "Surely the possibility of good public relations for the police is simply not enough, standing alone, to justify the ride-along intrusion into a private home," said Chief Justice Rehnquist.[47] Because the law had not been clear, however, the Wilsons could not be awarded damages from the U.S. Marshal's Service. In a partial dissent, Justice Stevens said the officers in this case should have been hit with damages. "The Court today authorizes one free violation of the well-established rule it reaffirms," Stevens said.[48]

Arrests for Misdemeanors

Although homeowners are entitled to privacy, the Court has continued to stress that police officers retain broad power to make arrests on the streets if they observe

A RIGHT TO LOITER?

Laws against loitering and vagrancy had been on the books since colonial times, but they came under challenge during the civil rights movement. In 1965 the Court ruled that while the police have the power to keep the peace, they may not use this power to harass or arrest those peacefully going about their business. Fred Shuttlesworth, a black minister in Birmingham, Alabama, was arrested for standing outside a downtown department store. He was not accused of obstructing others, but of failing to "move on" when told to do so by a police officer.

The city code said it was "unlawful for any person to stand or loiter upon any street or sidewalk of the city after having been requested by any police officer to move on." Shuttlesworth was sentenced to 180 days hard labor, but in a unanimous decision reversing the conviction in *Shuttlesworth v. Birmingham* (1965), Justice Potter Stewart said the Constitution does not give a city the total power to permit persons "to stand on a public sidewalk ... only at the whim of any police officer." To act otherwise "bears the hallmark of a police state."[1]

A few years later, the Court intervened again, after Birmingham authorities arrested, convicted, and sentenced Shuttlesworth to ninety days in prison for walking at the head of a group of marchers on Good Friday. Once again, he was not charged with blocking the sidewalk or obstructing traffic. Instead, he was charged under a city ordinance that made it a crime to "participate in any parade or procession" without a permit. Although the Alabama Supreme Court upheld Shuttlesworth's conviction, the Supreme Court unanimously reversed it. Police cannot be given "unbridled and absolute power to prohibit any parade or procession on the city's streets and public ways," said Justice Stewart.[2] "[T]he peaceful enjoyment of freedoms which the Constitution guarantees [is not] contingent upon the uncontrolled will of an official."[3]

In 1972 the Court swept aside the remnants of antiquated laws against vagrancy and loitering. Justice William O. Douglas waxed poetically on the virtues of loafing and wandering and cited as authorities the poets Walt Whitman and Vachel Lindsay and author Henry David Thoreau. The case before the Court arose when several white women, including Margaret Papachristou, and several black men were arrested in Jacksonville, Florida, for riding together in a car. They were charged with "vagrancy," being "vagabonds" or "loitering." None was accused of a specific crime, such as speeding or theft. According to a Jacksonville ordinance, "Rogues and vagabonds or dissolute persons" as well as "common drunkards, common nightwalkers, lewd, wanton and lascivious persons,... habitual loafers [and] disorderly persons ... shall be deemed vagrants" and arrested.

This ordinance "makes criminal activities which by modern standards are normally innocent," said Justice Douglas in *Papachristou v. City of Jacksonville* (1972).[4] Moreover, it "fails to give a person of ordinary intelligence a fair notice" of just what is forbidden by law. It also "encourages arbitrary and erratic arrests and convictions," he said.[5] "Of course, vagrancy statutes are useful to the police. They are nets making easy the round-up of the so-called undesirables," Douglas said for a 7-0 majority.[6] Because these laws are so vague, however, they "cannot be squared with our constitutional standards." Justices William H. Rehnquist and Lewis F. Powell Jr. had arrived a month after the case was argued, so they took no part in the decision.

In the late 1990s, the Rehnquist Court revisited the issue of loitering when Chicago officials employed a new anti-loitering law against gangs. The so-called Gang Congregation Ordinance allowed Chicago police officers to arrest anyone who is "reasonably believe[d] to be a criminal street gang member loitering in any public place" and who fails to disperse when warned. Police made more than 42,000 arrests under the ordinance until it was struck down by the Illinois courts. They cited the 1965 *Shuttlesworth* decision and *Papachristou* as precedents, but the Court took up Chicago's appeal.

The justices in a 6-3 decision declared the Chicago ordinance unconstitutional because it failed to spell out the "forbidden conduct" and because it gave police too much power to interfere with the innocent. "The freedom to loiter for innocent purposes is part of the 'liberty' protected by the Due Process Clause of the 14th Amendment," said Justice John Paul Stevens, joined by Justice David H. Souter and Ruth Bader Ginsburg.[7] Separately, Justices Sandra Day O'Connor, Stephen G. Breyer, and Anthony M. Kennedy agreed that police cannot be given an open-ended authority to arrest persons on a "whim." O'Connor stressed that police can by law, however, arrest persons who are loitering for an illegal purpose, such as for prostitution or to intimidate others.

---

1. *Shuttlesworth v. Birmingham*, 382 U.S. 87 at 90, 91 (1965).

2. *Shuttlesworth v. Birmingham*, 394 U.S. 147 at 150 (1969).

3. Id at 151.

4. *Papachristou v. City of Jacksonville*, 405 U.S. 156 at 161 (1972).

5. Id. at 156.

6. Id. at 171.

7. *Chicago v. Morales*, 527 U.S. 41 at 53 (1999).

persons breaking the law, including committing the most minor of offenses. In March 1997, Gail Atwater was driving her two children home from a soccer practice when she was stopped by Officer Bart Turek of the Lago Vista, Texas, police department. The two had exchanged words before, and when he saw that neither she nor the children were wearing their seat belts, he said, "You're going to jail." The offense, a misdemeanor, was punishable by a fine of $25 to $50 under Texas law. Atwater was arrested, handcuffed, and jailed. After paying a $50 fine, Atwater sued, alleging that her arrest amounted to an unreasonable seizure under the Fourth Amendment. She argued that her offense did not amount to a "breach of peace," nor was her crime punishable by jail time. Therefore, it was unreasonable to take her to jail for violating a fine-only ordinance.

In a 5-4 decision, the Court refused to limit the authority of officers to make arrests. "If an officer has probable cause to believe that an individual has committed even a very minor criminal offense in his presence, he may, without violating the Fourth Amendment, arrest the offender," said Justice David H. Souter in *Atwater v. Lago Vista* (2001).[49] His opinion examined the history of medieval England and the American colonies. In England, the so-called nightwalker statutes had given constables and night watchmen the power to arrest and hold until morning "any suspicious nightwalker ... till he give [*sic*] good account of himself."[50] From this history, Souter concluded that the framers of the Constitution were not "at all concerned about warrantless arrests by local constables."[51] He was joined by Chief Justice Rehnquist and Justices Antonin Scalia, Anthony M. Kennedy, and Thomas. In dissent, Justice Sandra Day O'Connor said that Souter and the majority had focused on the wrong question: It was not whether all such arrests are unreasonable, but instead whether this one was, she argued. The arrest of Atwater and the "pointless indignity" she suffered were unjustified and unreasonable and thereby violated the Fourth Amendment. O'Connor also feared that the "unbounded discretion" given to police officers carries with it "grave potential for abuse."[52]

48 Hours: From Arrest to Seeing a Judge

How long can the police hold an arrested person before giving him a hearing before a magistrate? No longer than forty-eight hours, the Court ruled in *County of Riverside v. McLaughlin* (1991). While an officer may arrest a person based on his belief that a suspect has violated the law, the detained individual has a right to a "prompt" hearing to challenge this decision, the justices said. Although "warrantless arrests are permitted,... persons arrested without a warrant must promptly be brought before a neutral magistrate for a judicial determination of probable cause," Justice Sandra Day O'Connor explained for the 5-4 majority.[53] It would be best if such hearings were held immediately after the suspect was booked, the Court held, but sometimes, such as late at night or on weekends, a magistrate is not available. In light of these "practical realities," individuals can be detained for a short time without a hearing, but "in no event later than 48 hours after arrest."[54] Justice Scalia, speaking for the four dissenters, would have set a stricter rule, requiring a hearing within twenty-four hours:

> Hereafter a law-abiding citizen wrongfully arrested may be compelled to await the grace of a Dickensian bureaucratic machine, as it churns its cycles for up to two days, never once given the opportunity to show a judge that there is absolutely no reason to hold him, that a mistake has been made.[55]

Searches Incident to Arrest

When police arrest a suspect, the Court has held it reasonable for them to search—even without a search warrant—the person arrested and, to some limited extent, the suspect's immediate surroundings. The justices have viewed such searches as necessary to protect the lives of the arresting officers, to prevent the fugitive's escape, and to prohibit the destruction of evidence. The Court acknowledged such exceptions to the warrant requirement in *Agnello v. United States* (1925):

> The right without a search warrant contemporaneously to search persons lawfully arrested while committing crime, and to search the place where the arrest is made in order to find and seize things connected with the crime as its fruits, or as the means by which it was committed, as well as weapons and other things to effect an escape from custody is not to be doubted.[56]

Twenty-two years later, in *Harris v. United States* (1947), the Court interpreted this exception broadly.[57] Harris was arrested in his apartment by FBI agents and charged with mail fraud and forgery. Without a search warrant, the agents searched his entire apartment for five hours. They found no evidence of mail fraud or forgery, but they did discover several stolen Selective Service draft cards. Harris was subsequently convicted for illegal possession of those cards. He challenged the validity of the search and the seizure of the cards, but the Court upheld the search as valid, incident to his arrest. Harris was in control of the entire four-room apartment, it reasoned, and thus the search could extend beyond the room in which he was arrested.

Chief Justice Fred M. Vinson declared that "[s]earch and seizure incident to lawful arrest is a practice of ancient origin and has long been an integral part of the law-enforcement procedures of the United States."[58] Justices Felix Frankfurter, Robert H. Jackson, Wiley B. Rutledge, and Frank Murphy dissented. Wrote Murphy,

> The Court today has resurrected and approved, in effect, the use of the odious general warrant or writ of assistance, presumably outlawed forever from our society by the Fourth Amendment. A warrant of arrest, without more, is now sufficient to justify an unlimited search of a man's home from cellar to garret for evidence of any crime, provided only that he is arrested in his home. Probable cause for the search need not be shown; an oath or affirmation is unnecessary; no description of the place to be searched or the things to be seized need be given; and the magistrate's judgment that these requirements have been satisfied is now dispensed with. In short, all the restrictions put upon the issuance and execution of search warrants by the Fourth Amendment are now dead letters as to those who are arrested in their homes.[59]

The following year, however, the Court seemed to narrow the definition of a permissible search, without a warrant, pursuant to a valid arrest. *Trupiano v. United States* (1948) involved the arrest of several persons on a farm in New Jersey for operating an illegal still and the seizure, without a warrant, of the still, which the arresting agents had observed in operation during the arrest.[60] The Supreme Court held the warrantless arrest valid but not the seizure of the still. For the majority, Justice Murphy wrote that no reason was offered why the federal agents

could not have obtained a search warrant before moving in to make the arrest "except [their] indifference to the legal process for search and seizure which the Constitution contemplated."[61] Murphy continued:

> A search or seizure without a warrant as an incident to a lawful arrest has always been considered to be a strictly limited right. It grows out of the inherent necessities of the situation at the time of the arrest. But there must be something more in the way of necessity than merely a lawful arrest.... Otherwise the exception swallows the general principle, making a search warrant completely unnecessary wherever there is a lawful arrest, and so there must be some other factor in the situation that would make it unreasonable or impracticable to require the arresting officer to equip himself with a search warrant.[62]

The Court reiterated this last point in its ruling in *McDonald v. United States* (1948):

> Where ... officers are not responding to an emergency, there must be compelling reasons to justify the absence of a search warrant. A search without a warrant demands exceptional circumstances.... We cannot ... excuse the absence of a search warrant without a showing by those who seek exemption from the constitutional mandate that the exigencies of the situation made that course imperative.[63]

Although the "exigent circumstances" requirement of *McDonald* for warrantless searches generally has survived, the *Trupiano* ruling that a warrant be required whenever obtaining one was practicable was short-lived. The Court in *United States v. Rabinowitz* (1950) declared that "[t]o the extent that *Trupiano* ... requires a search warrant solely upon the basis of the practicability of procuring it rather than upon the reasonableness of the search after a lawful arrest, that case is overruled."[64] In *Rabinowitz*, the Court separated the question of the reasonableness of a search from the warrant requirement. Justice Sherman Minton explained:

> What is a reasonable search is not to be determined by any fixed formula. The Constitution does not define what are "unreasonable" searches and, regrettable, in our discipline we have no ready litmus-paper test. The recurring questions of the reasonableness of searches must find resolution in the facts and circumstances of each case....

THE FOURTH AMENDMENT AND ADMINISTRATIVE SEARCHES

The Fourth Amendment requires building, health, and fire inspectors to obtain warrants for administrative searches of private premises, the Court has ruled, but the justices have also held that warrants for such searches do not need to meet the same strict "probable cause" standards mandated for warrants in criminal investigations. Further, the Court has held that warrants are not required when welfare workers enter the homes of clients for interviews, nor when inspectors visit regulated business establishments, such as gun and liquor stores and junkyards. The Court in *Frank v. Maryland* (1959) upheld the warrantless inspection of a private dwelling by a city health official seeking the source of a rat infestation. The protection of the Fourth Amendment did not apply in this case:

> No evidence for criminal prosecution is sought.... Appellant is simply directed to do what he could have been ordered to do without any inspection, and what he cannot properly resist, namely, act in a manner consistent with the maintenance of minimum community standards of health.[1]

Eight years later, the Court overturned *Frank*. In *Camara v. Municipal Court* (1967), it declared that administrative searches were indeed "significant intrusions upon the interests protected by the Fourth Amendment."[2] Roland Camara had refused to permit a housing inspector of the San Francisco Health Department to make an inspection of his apartment without a search warrant. The Court upheld Camara's position:

> We may agree that a routine inspection of the physical condition of private property is a less hostile intrusion than the typical

policeman's search for the fruits and instrumentalities of crime. For this reason alone, *Frank* differed from the great bulk of Fourth Amendment cases.... But we cannot agree that the Fourth Amendment interests at stake in these inspection cases are merely "peripheral." It is surely anomalous to say that the individual and his private property are fully protected by the Fourth Amendment only when the individual is suspected of criminal behavior.[3]

In a second ruling announced the same day, the Court declared that government agents must obtain a warrant for administrative entries into the nonpublic portions of commercial establishments. In *See v. City of Seattle* (1967), the Court established broad guidelines for such searches.[4] The Court in *Marshall v. Barlow's Inc.* (1978) denied government inspectors from the Occupational Safety and Health Administration the right to make warrantless random safety inspections of nonpublic working areas on business premises over the owner's objection. If consent is not given to the search, a warrant must be obtained, the Court determined. Relying on *Camara*, the justices held that the

> Warrant Clause of the Fourth Amendment protects commercial buildings as well as private homes.... That an employee is free to report, and the Government is free to use, any evidence of noncompliance with OSHA that the employee observes furnishes no justification for federal agents to enter a place of business from which the public is restricted and to conduct their own warrantless search.[5]

The Court has made exceptions to the warrant requirement for administrative searches of premises occupied by gun dealers and liquor

The relevant test is not whether it is reasonable to procure a search warrant, but whether the search was reasonable. That criterion in turn depends on the facts and circumstances—the total atmosphere of the case.[65]

The attempted separation of the reasonableness standard from the warrant requirement and the use of the "total atmosphere" test resulted in considerable confusion over what warrantless searches were permissible incident to a valid arrest.[66] In *Chimel v. California* (1969), the Court overruled *Rabinowitz* and *Harris*,

and returned to the view that the warrant and reasonableness requirements were indeed linked.[67] The decision in *Chimel* overturned a burglary conviction because it was based on evidence seized without a warrant incident to arrest, but the search was too extensive to be justified by the arrest alone. Searches incident to arrest were only reasonable insofar as they involved the person arrested and the area immediately under his control, from which he could obtain a weapon or within which he could destroy evidence, declared the Court. Justice Stewart wrote for the majority:

establishments, both of which are regulated by federal law. The premises of such business establishments may be inspected during regular business hours by government agents without a warrant. In *Colonnade Catering Corp. v. United States* (1970), the Court held that in certain industries subject to particular government oversight there can be no expectation of privacy for the proprietor or the premises. A federal agent of the alcohol and tobacco tax division of the Internal Revenue Service had made a warrantless inspection of a locked storeroom and forcibly seized illegal liquor. Justice William O. Douglas declared that "Congress has broad power to design such powers of inspection under the liquor laws as it deems necessary to meet the evils at hand."[6]

In *United States v. Biswell* (1972), the Court upheld the warrantless search of a pawnbroker's storeroom by a federal agent who discovered two illegal weapons there. Relying on *Colonnade Catering,* the Court declared that in this case "regulatory inspections further urgent federal interest, and the possibilities of abuse and the threat to privacy are not of impressive dimensions." Therefore, "the inspection may proceed without a warrant where specifically authorized by statute."[7] In *New York v. Burger* (1987), the Court brought auto junkyards, which are regulated by the state, within this exception to the warrant requirement.[8]

The Court has twice insisted that fire officials inspecting the premises on which a suspicious fire has occurred must have a warrant, unless the inspection occurs during or immediately after the fire. In *Michigan v. Tyler* (1978), the Court held that

an entry to fight a fire requires no warrant, and ... once in the building, officials may remain there for a reasonable time to investigate the cause of the fire. Thereafter, additional entries to investigate ... must be made pursuant to the warrant procedures governing administrative searches.[9]

The Court underscored this point in *Michigan v. Clifford* (1984), declaring that the warrantless entry and search of a burned residence five hours after the fire was extinguished, without notice to the absent residents, was a violation of the Fourth Amendment.[10] In contrast, the Court has held since *Wyman v. James* (1971) that home visits by a welfare worker to a prospective client raised no valid Fourth Amendment issues. The visit, agreed the Court, might be "rehabilitative and investigative," but it nevertheless was not "a search in the traditional criminal law context" to which the warrant requirement applies.[11]

---

1. *Frank v. Maryland,* 359 U.S. 360 at 366 (1959).
2. *Camara v. Municipal Court,* 387 U.S. 523 at 530 (1967).
3. Id.
4. *See v. City of Seattle,* 387 U.S. 541 (1967).
5. *Marshall v. Barlow's Inc.,* 436 U.S. 307 at 311, 315 (1978).
6. *Colonnade Catering Corp. v. United States,* 397 U.S. 72 at 76 (1970).
7. *United States v. Biswell,* 406 U.S. 311 at 317 (1972).
8. *New York v. Burger,* 482 U.S. 691 (1987).
9. *Michigan v. Tyler,* 436 U.S. 499 at 511 (1978).
10. *Michigan v. Clifford,* 464 U.S. 287 (1984).
11. *Wyman v. James,* 400 U.S. 309 at 317–318 (1971).

No consideration relevant to the Fourth Amendment suggests any point of rational limitation, once the search is allowed to go beyond the area from which the person arrested might obtain weapons or evidentiary items. The only reasoned distinction is one between a search of the person arrested and the area within his reach on the one hand, and more extensive searches on the other....

The search here went far beyond the petitioner's person and the area from within which he might have obtained either a weapon or something that could have been used as evidence against him. There was no constitutional justification, in the absence of a search warrant, for extending the search beyond that area. The scope of the search was, therefore, "unreasonable" under the Fourth and Fourteenth Amendments, and the petitioner's conviction cannot stand.[68]

Justice White, joined by Justice Hugo L. Black, dissented:

[W]here as here the existence of probable cause is independently established and would justify a warrant for a broader search for evidence, I would follow past cases and permit such a search to be carried out without a warrant, since the fact of arrest supplies an exigent circumstance justifying police action before the evidence can be removed, and also alerts the suspect to the fact of the search so that he can immediately seek judicial determination of probable cause in an adversary proceeding and appropriate redress.[69]

The following year, in *Vale v. Louisiana* (1970), the Court held that a street arrest of a narcotics suspect did not constitute an "exigent circumstance" to justify a warrantless search of his house.[70] Then, in *Coolidge v. New Hampshire* (1971), it ruled that the arrest of a suspect inside his house did not justify a search of his automobile parked in the driveway.[71] The Court, however, has never retreated from its view that a suspect under lawful arrest may properly be subjected to the full search of his person without a warrant, that such a search is reasonable under the Fourth Amendment, and that evidence found in such a search is admissible. The Court reaffirmed these points in *United States v. Robinson* (1973) and *Gustafson v. Florida* (1973), cases involving motorists stopped for violations of auto or traffic laws and found to possess illegal drugs. The subsequent narcotics convictions of both motorists were upheld.[72]

Automobile Searches

The Fourth Amendment's rule on unreasonable searches and seizures extends to automobiles, including to their drivers and passengers, but it is considerably less strict when compared to the rule governing searches of homes and other private spaces. Police officers generally do not need warrants to stop cars and to search the vehicle or its passengers and luggage. If an officer has "reasonable suspicion" that a driver is intoxicated or otherwise violating the law, he may pull the vehicle to the side of the road and investigate further. He may look inside for a weapon, and if he sees evidence of illegal drugs or alcohol, he can search the car. Because the Fourth Amendment forbids "unreasonable searches"—not *all* searches—the justices hold that the privacy interests of individuals must be balanced against the government's interest in enforcing the law. When a driver gets behind the wheel and takes his car on the public roadways, the balance tips in favor of the government.

The landmark case in this area is *Carroll v. United States* (1925).[73] George Carroll was convicted of transporting liquor for sale in violation of the federal prohibition law and the Eighteenth Amendment. The contraband liquor used as evidence against him had been taken from his car by federal agents acting without a search warrant. The Supreme Court sustained Carroll's conviction against his contention that this seizure violated his Fourth Amendment rights. Writing for the Court, Chief Justice William Howard Taft explained:

> [T]he guaranty of freedom from unreasonable searches and seizures by the Fourth Amendment has been construed, practically since the beginning of the government, as recognizing a necessary difference between a search of a store, dwelling house, or other structure in respect of which a proper official warrant readily may be obtained and a search of a ship, motor boat, wagon, or automobile for contraband goods, where it is not practicable to secure a warrant, because the vehicle can be quickly moved out of the locality or jurisdiction in which the warrant must be sought.[74]

Subsequent rulings involving police searches of automobiles, without warrants, for contraband, have made clear the breadth of this exception to the warrant requirements. In 1931 the Court upheld the search of a parked car as reasonable because police could not know when the suspect might move it.[75] The Court in 1948 appeared to limit this exception to situations in which Congress had authorized warrantless searches of moving vehicles suspected of involvement in violating federal laws.[76] Then the justices in *Brinegar v. United States* (1949) upheld, as reasonable, warrantless searches of automobiles whenever police had probable cause to believe the cars were involved in illegal activity.[77] This remains the rule, as the Court has repeatedly emphasized in cases in which it has refused to declare evidence to be admissible when it was discovered in a search for which there was no probable cause.[78] After the Court in *Mapp v. Ohio* (1961) applied the exclusionary rule to state proceedings—and in *Ker v. California* (1963) adopted a uniform standard for state and federal action under the Fourth Amendment—it applied the same rules for warrantless auto searches to state police and federal agents.

The Court gives police leeway in warrantless searches of cars. It has upheld the search of a car without a warrant as long as a week after the arrest of its owner,

Since 1925 the Court has made numerous decisions dealing with searches of automobiles, their occupants, and even closed packages found in a car. In general, the Court has decided that people and their paraphernalia are entitled to less privacy in cars than in their homes or places of business.

when the government had a proprietary interest in the car because it was subject to forfeiture under state law.[79] It has allowed police to make such searches of autos after they have been towed to the police garage from the site of an arrest.[80] The justices have refused to exclude evidence obtained in the routine warrantless search of an impounded vehicle as inadmissible[81] or to require that a warrant be obtained before police take paint samples from the exterior of a car parked in a public parking lot.[82] In *Rakas v. Illinois* (1978), the Court held that passengers did not have the right to challenge the warrantless search of the vehicle in which they were riding or the use of evidence seized in that search against them. That decision tied the Fourth Amendment rights of persons in cars more closely to ownership concepts than in earlier cases.

For the five-man majority, Justice Rehnquist emphasized that Fourth Amendment rights could be asserted only by the person whose privacy was invaded: "A person who is aggrieved by an illegal search and seizure only through the introduction of damaging evidence secured by a search of a third person's premises or property has not had any of his Fourth Amendment rights infringed."[83] The warrantless search in *Rakas* was proper because it was based on probable cause: the car fit the description of a getaway car used in a nearby robbery. In addition, because the passengers did not claim that they owned either the car or the items seized, they could not challenge the search, the seizure, or the use of discovered evidence against them as a violation of the Fourth Amendment guarantee.

DRUG TESTING: A LIMITED EXCEPTION TO THE FOURTH AMENDMENT

Before individuals are subjected to searches by the government, officials need some reason to suspect that the person is violating the law. In 1989, however, the Court ruled that mandatory drug testing of some employees—and later, high school students—was an exception to this rule. After a series of deadly accidents and train derailments, the Federal Railroad Administration required blood and urine testing of all train crews after accidents. The Court had no trouble upholding those regulations.

When there are "special needs, beyond the normal need for law enforcement," the government does not always need a warrant or individualized suspicion to conduct searches, the Court said in its 7-2 decision in *Skinner v. Railway Labor Executives Association* (1989).[1] In this instance, the justices held, the need for safety on the railroads outweighs the privacy rights of the workers. The same day, the Court by a 5-4 vote upheld a drug-testing program for U.S. Customs Agents. Justice Anthony M. Kennedy, who wrote both opinions, said the government needs to have a high level of trust in agents who carry guns and serve on the front line in the war on drugs.[2]

The Court continued to hold, however, that mass drug testing could be used only in "certain limited circumstances." In an 8-1 decision, the Court struck down a novel Georgia law that required candidates for high state offices to submit urine samples. Walker Chandler, a Libertarian candidate for lieutenant governor, lost his bid for office, but won a legal battle when he took his own case to the Supreme Court. The Georgia law sacrifices "personal privacy for a symbol's sake," said Justice Ruth Bader Ginsburg in *Chandler v. Miller* (1997).[3]

Four years later, the Court struck down another unique and, by then, discontinued, drug-testing policy at a public hospital in Charleston, South Carolina, where nurses tested the blood of pregnant patients, and the hospital turned over the results to the police. Some women who tested positive were taken away in handcuffs and charged with drug offenses. Although this program began with a medical purpose, it crossed the line and violated the Fourth Amendment when the "the searches generate[d] evidence for law enforcement purposes," the Court said in a 6-3 ruling that upheld a lawsuit brought on behalf of ten patients in *Ferguson v. City of Charleston* (2001).[4] Justice Antonin Scalia, Chief Justice William H. Rehnquist, and Justice Clarence Thomas dissented, contending that officials had a "special need" in this instance to prevent these women from using drugs and harming their unborn children.

High school students have lesser rights than adults, the Court said in upholding drug testing for student athletes and other students who participate in such extracurricular activities as band. Athletes risk injury if they use drugs, Justice Scalia noted in a ruling upholding an Oregon school's policy of drug testing its sports teams.[5] Justices Sandra Day O'Connor, John Paul Stevens, and David H. Souter dissented. In 2002 the Court went a step further and upheld drug testing of students who volunteer for extracurricular activities. "Given the nationwide epidemic of drug use, it was entirely reasonable for the [Tecumseh, Oklahoma] school district to enact this particular drug testing policy," said Justice Thomas for a 5-4 majority.[6] *(See box, Students and Crime and Punishment, pp. 262–263.)*

---

1. *Skinner v. Railway Labor Executives Association,* 489 U.S. 602 (1989).

2. *National Treasury Employees Union v. Von Rabb,* 489 U.S. 656 (1989).

3. *Chandler v. Miller,* 520 U.S. 305 at 322 (1997).

4. *Ferguson v. City of Charleston,* 532 U.S. 67 (2001).

5. *Vernonia School District v. Acton,* 515 U.S. 646 (1995).

6. *Board of Education v. Earls,* 536 U.S 822 (2002).

The decision in *United States v. Ross* (1982) cleared the way for full searches of cars. Justice Stevens wrote that police officers who have probable cause to suspect that drugs or other contraband are in a car they have stopped may search the entire vehicle as thoroughly as if they had a warrant, including all containers and packages in the car that might contain the object of the search. Justices White, Brennan, and Marshall dissented.[84] Nine years later the Court, 6-3, allowed police even more leeway. The justices ruled in *California v. Acevedo* (1991) that police do not need a warrant to search a car and all closed containers inside if they have probable cause to believe that one of the containers holds contraband, even if they lack probable cause for the entire vehicle.[85]

On a few occasions, the Court has ruled that the police went too far in stopping or searching a car for no specific reason. In *Delaware v. Prouse* (1979), the Court

THE ULTIMATE ARREST

The Supreme Court invoked the Fourth Amendment guarantee against unreasonable seizure in the mid-1980s to declare that police may not use deadly force to stop a fleeing felon unless they have reason to believe that the felon threatens the life of people nearby.

In *Tennessee v. Garner* (1985), the father of an unarmed fifteen-year-old boy, who was shot and killed by police as he fled a burglarized house, won a 6-3 decision declaring that "a police officer may not seize an

unarmed non-dangerous suspect by shooting him dead." Over the dissenting votes of Chief Justice Warren E. Burger and Justices Sandra Day O'Connor and William H. Rehnquist, Justice Byron R. White wrote for the Court that "the use of deadly force to prevent the escape of all felony suspects, whatever the circumstances, is constitutionally unreasonable."[1]

---

1. *Tennessee v. Garner*, 471 U.S. 1 (1985).

---

rejected a police officer's decision to randomly stop motorists, without any probable cause, to check for their license and registration. These "spot checks" amount to "unreasonable seizures," the Court held. To permit officers "standardless and unconstrained discretion" to stop motorists on a mere whim would violate the essence of the Fourth Amendment, wrote Justice White for the 8-1 majority.[86] The Court also has rejected a police policy of using routine traffic stops as a reason to search cars for drugs. In this case, Patrick Knowles was pulled over in Newton, Iowa, for driving forty-three miles per hour in a twenty-five-mile-per-hour zone. The officer gave him a speeding ticket and then searched the entire car. He found a bag of marijuana under the seat, and Knowles was charged with a drug violation. In *Knowles v. Iowa* (1998), the Court reversed the drug conviction and ruled unanimously that the Iowa police violated the Fourth Amendment by relying on a traffic stop as the basis to "conduct a full-blown search of an automobile and driver."[87] Chief Justice Rehnquist said officers need a specific reason to search further, and a simple speeding violation does not supply it.

Stopping Cars to Search for Drugs

Rarely has the Court rejected searches and seizures on highways so long as the police could furnish a specific reason for their actions. Moreover, the reason cited by an officer for stopping a car need not be the true reason, the

Court ruled unanimously in *United States v. Whren* (1996). Rather, officers may stop cars for minor traffic violations as a "pretext" to search for drugs. In this case, plainclothes officers patrolling a "high drug area" in the District of Columbia noticed a car with several young black men inside that first stopped at a corner and then sped away—failing to give a turn signal—when another police car approached. When the drug patrol officers stopped the vehicle, they noticed what turned out to be a bag of crack cocaine being held by passenger Michael Whren. In court, Whren argued that the search and seizure violated the Fourth Amendment because this was not a normal traffic stop, but instead a pretext to search for drugs.

Justice Antonin Scalia dismissed Whren's assertion on the ground that the "actual motivations" of the officers were irrelevant. So long as the police observed a traffic violation, they were entitled to stop the car. Scalia wrote, "We think these [past] cases foreclose any argument that the constitutional reasonableness of traffic stops depends on the actual motivations of the individual officers involved. We of course agree with petitioners that the Constitution prohibits selective enforcement of the law based on considerations such as race. But the constitutional basis for objecting to intentionally discriminatory application of laws is the Equal Protection Clause, not the Fourth Amendment. Subjective intentions play no role in ordinary, probable cause Fourth Amendment analysis."[88]

High-Speed Chases

The Court also has shielded the police from being sued over high-speed chases. Some lower court judges had ruled that the police can be sued for a constitutional violation if their reckless speeding causes death or injuries. In *County of Sacramento v. Lewis* (1998), however, the justices held that a police officer violates the Constitution only if his "purpose is to cause harm."[89] The Sacramento, California, police were sued by the parents of a sixteen-year-old boy who died when he fell off the back of a speeding motorcycle and was struck by a pursuing police car. The two young men on the cycle had sped away after an officer had warned them to stop. The officer reached a speed of 100 miles per hour during the pursuit. Although a high-speed chase on city streets may have been reckless, said Justice Souter for a 9-0 Court, "the officer's instinct was to do his job as a law enforcement officer, not ... to terrorize, cause harm or kill."[90]

In 2007 the Court extended this shield of liability to include cases where a police officer rams a speeding car and drives it off the road. In rural Georgia, Victor Harris sped away when a patrol car flashed its blue lights; he reached 85 miles per hour on a two-lane road. Deputy Timothy Scott gave chase, and after nearly ten miles, he decided to force Harris's Cadillac off the road. He bumped hard against the back of the speeding car, and Harris lost control, sending the car over an embankment. The crash rendered Harris a quadriplegic. He sued Scott, alleging that his actions amounted to an "unreasonable seizure" and the unjustified use of deadly force. In *Scott v. Harris* (2007), the Court ruled Deputy Scott's actions were reasonable because the speeding car posed a danger to other motorists and pedestrians.[91]

This case is notable also because the Court said that it had studied a videotape of the chase submitted with the legal briefs. "What we see on the video more closely resembles a Hollywood-style car chase of the most frightening sort, placing police officers and innocent bystanders alike at great risk of serious injury," wrote Justice Scalia. He rejected a legal rule that would allow motorists to escape "whenever they drive so recklessly that they put other people's lives in danger.... Instead, we lay down a more sensible rule: A police officer's attempt to terminate a dangerous high-speed car chase that threatens the lives of innocent bystanders does not violate the Fourth Amendment, even when it places the fleeing motorist at risk of serious injury or death." Justice Stevens dissented alone. He said that the jury should have been permitted to view the videotape and hear the evidence to decide whether ramming Harris's car and forcing it off the road had been reasonable under the circumstances.

The Court also has given traffic police more authority over passengers as well as motorists than over pedestrians or residents in homes. In the late 1990s, the justices ruled that an officer who pulls over a vehicle may order the passengers as well as the driver to get out of the car. There is a "weighty interest in officer safety," which outweighs the privacy rights of the car's occupants, Chief Justice Rehnquist wrote in *Maryland v. Wilson* (1997).[92] In this case, a Maryland trooper had stopped a car for speeding on Interstate 95 near Baltimore. As the officer spoke to the driver outside the car, he noticed that the two passengers inside appeared nervous, so he ordered them to get out. When one, Jerry Wilson, did so, he dropped a vial of crack cocaine. In court, Wilson argued that the search was unreasonable. He won in the Maryland courts, but lost in the Supreme Court. Twenty years earlier, the justices had rule that a driver may be ordered from his or her car.[93] The same rule applies to passengers, the chief justice said, because they might have a gun or other weapon that could be used to attack the officer. The 7-2 ruling reinstated the drug evidence against Wilson.

In 1999 the Court said officers who have probable cause to search a car may inspect the purses and luggage of the passengers. When a Wyoming highway patrol officer stopped a motorist for speeding, he noticed a hypodermic syringe in the driver's pocket. A second officer ordered two women out of the car and searched it. In a purse on the back seat, he found methamphetamine. The purse belonged to Sandra Houghton, who was arrested and charged with a drug crime. While the Wyoming courts said the officers had no authority to search "the personal effects of a passenger," the Court disagreed and upheld her conviction on a 6-3 vote. "The sensible rule (and the one supported by history and case law) is that such a package may be searched, whether or not its owner is present as a passenger or otherwise, because it may contain the contraband that the officer has reason to believe is in the car," Justice Scalia said in *Wyoming v. Houghton* (1997).[94] Justices Stevens, Souter, and Ginsburg dissented.

Sniffing Dogs: Buses and Trains

The government's "war on drugs" has affected searches and seizures in a number of areas. In 2005 the Court said that the police may use drug-sniffing dogs during a routine traffic stop. When Roy Caballes was stopped for speeding on an interstate highway in Illinois, a second officer overheard the radio report and brought a drug-sniffing dog to the scene. The dog alerted officers to the trunk, where inside they found a large quantity of marijuana. In *Illinois v. Caballes* (2005), the Court ruled that use of the sniffing dog had not violated any privacy rights. "In our view, conducting a dog sniff would not change the character of a traffic stop that is lawful at its inception," said Justice Stevens for a 6-2 majority. "The use of a well-trained narcotics detection dog ... during a lawful traffic stop generally does not implicate legitimate privacy interests."[95]

Passengers on buses and trains also have limited privacy rights. In airplanes, the overriding concern for safety allows officials to search passengers and their belongings to check for weapons. By contrast, bus searches usually target illegal drugs. In *Florida v. Bostick* (1991), the Court upheld the police policy of boarding Greyhound buses at station stops and asking all the passengers to consent to a search of their bags. Technically, a passenger can refuse and leave the bus, so these searches were described as "consensual."[96] In February 1999, Christopher Drayton was traveling on a Greyhound that stopped in Tallahassee, Florida. When the driver stepped off the bus, three armed officers entered to conduct a drug search. One officer asked Drayton if he could check his bags in the overhead rack. He consented, and the officer found nothing. "Mind if I check you?" the officer asked Drayton. The passenger lifted his hands a few inches, and the officer patted down his baggy pant leg. He felt a hard plastic object that turned

out to be a tightly wrapped bundle of cocaine. A year later, the U.S. Court of Appeals in Atlanta threw out the drug evidence against Drayton because he and his fellow passengers felt trapped and compelled to permit the search. Disagreeing in *United States v. Drayton* (2002), the Court described the search as "voluntary.... There was nothing coercive or confrontational about the encounter."[97] Justice Kennedy also rejected the notion that "police officers must always inform citizens of their right to refuse when seeking permission to conduct a warrantless consent search."[98] In dissent, Justice Souter noted that "there is an air of unreality about the Court's explanation," since "no reasonable passenger" would have thought he was free to ignore the police and leave.[99] Justices Stevens and Ginsburg agreed.

ELECTRONIC EAVESDROPPING

Not until 1967 did the Supreme Court bring electronic eavesdropping and surveillance techniques within the scope of the Fourth Amendment guarantee of security against unreasonable search and seizure. From 1928 until 1967, the Court held firmly that the Fourth Amendment applied only when there was physical entry and seizure of tangible items; it did not apply to overheard conversations. This rule was set out in *Olmstead v. United States* (1928). Through the use of wiretaps, police had gathered evidence against a bootlegging operation. The defendants challenged this method of obtaining evidence, arguing that it violated their Fourth Amendment rights. The Court, with Chief Justice Taft writing its opinion, rejected that claim:

> The well-known historical purpose of the 4th Amendment, directed against general warrants and writs of assistance, was to prevent the use of governmental force to search a man's house, his person, his papers, and his effects, and to prevent their seizure against his will....
>
> The Amendment itself shows that the search is to be of material things—the person, the house, his papers or his effects. The description of the warrant necessary to make the proceeding lawful is that it must specify the place to be searched and the person or things to be seized....

The Amendment does not forbid what was done here. There was no searching. There was no seizure. The evidence was secured by the use of the sense of hearing and that only. There was no entry of the houses or offices of the defendants....

The language of the Amendment can not be extended and expanded to include telephone wires reaching to the whole world from the defendant's house or office....

Congress may, of course, protect the secrecy of telephone messages by making them, when intercepted, inadmissible in evidence in Federal criminal trials.... But the courts may not adopt such a policy by attributing an enlarged and unusual meaning to the 4th Amendment.[100]

In dissent Justice Oliver Wendell Holmes Jr. wrote, "[A]part from the Constitution, the government ought not to use evidence obtained, and only obtainable, by a criminal act.... I think it a less evil that some criminals should escape than that the government should play an ignoble part."[101] Justice Louis D. Brandeis also dissented, arguing that wiretapping was clearly a search within the meaning of the Fourth Amendment, which he described as intended to protect "the sanctities of a man's home and the privacies of life." He added that the Fourth Amendment guarantee must, to retain its validity, be read with an awareness of new threats to the security it was intended to protect:

Subtler and more far-reaching means of invading privacy have become available to the government. Discovery and invention have made it possible for the government, by means far more effective than stretching upon the rack, to obtain disclosure in court of what is whispered in the closet.

Furthermore, Brandeis argued, wiretapping was itself a crime under federal law, and government agents should not be allowed to commit crimes to catch criminals:

Decency, security, and liberty alike demand that government officials shall be subjected to the same rules of conduct that are commands to the citizen. In a government of laws, existence of the government will be imperiled if it fails to observe the law scrupulously. Our government is the potent, the omnipresent, teacher. For good or ill, it teaches the whole people by its example. Crime is contagious. If the government becomes a law-breaker, it breeds contempt for law; it invites every man to become a law unto himself; it invites anarchy. To declare that in the administration of the criminal law the end justifies the means—to declare that the government may commit crimes in order to secure the conviction of a private criminal—would bring terrible retribution. Against that pernicious doctrine this court should resolutely set its face.[102]

In 1934 Congress included in the Federal Communications Act the statement that "no person not being authorized by the sender shall intercept any communication and divulge or publish the existence, contents, substance, purport, effect or meaning of such intercepted communication to any person." Three years later, in *Nardone v. United States* (1937), the Court read this provision as forbidding federal agents, as well as all other persons, to intercept and disclose telephone messages by the use of wiretaps. In that and a similar case in 1939, the Court excluded from use in federal courts any evidence obtained, directly or indirectly, from wiretaps.[103] Two wartime rulings, however, allowed some use of evidence obtained by electronic surveillance. In *Goldstein v. United States* (1942), the Court held that wiretap evidence could be used against persons other than those whose conversations had been overheard, and in *Goldman v. United States* (1942), the Court held that the use of a "bug"—an electronic listening device, not a wiretap on telephone lines—was not in violation of the communications act provision, which applied only to actual interference with communication wires and telephone lines.[104]

In the 1960s, the Court began to take a tougher view of electronic surveillance as an impermissible intrusion into personal privacy. In *Silverman v. United States* (1961), the Court held that the Fourth Amendment was violated by the use of a "spike-mike" driven into a building wall to allow police to overhear conversations within the building. The fact that the device, although tiny, actually penetrated the building wall was sufficient to constitute physical intrusion in violation of the search-and-seizure provision.[105] Six years later, the Court finally abandoned *Olmstead* and brought electronic surveillance of all types within the proscription of the Fourth Amendment.

Katz v. United States (1967) involved evidence obtained by government agents who had placed a listening device on the outside of a public telephone booth. The information from the telephone conversations led to the prosecution of individuals involved in illegal bookmaking activities.[106] Justice Stewart explained, "The fact that the electronic device employed ... did not happen to penetrate the wall of the booth can have no constitutional significance."[107] He continued:

> [T]he Fourth Amendment protects people, not places. What a person knowingly exposes to the public, even in his own home or office, is not a subject of Fourth Amendment protection.... But what he seeks to preserve as private, even in an area accessible to the public, may be constitutionally protected....
>
> ... [W]hat he [Katz] sought to exclude when he entered the booth was not the intruding eye—it was the uninvited ear. He did not shed his right to do so simply because he made his calls from a place where he might be seen.[108]

Two years after *Katz*, the Court made clear its intention of penalizing government agents for engaging in improper electronic surveillance. In *Alderman v. United States, Butenko v. United States,* and *Ivanov v. United States* (1969), the Court held that the government must turn over all material obtained by illegal surveillance to the defendant whose Fourth Amendment rights had been violated by its collection and against whom such evidence might be used. The defendant could then examine the information to ascertain what parts of it the government might plan to use against him and to challenge its use. The government, dismayed by this ruling, chose to drop a number of prosecutions rather than disclose the method and the content of some particular instances of surveillance.[109]

Congress in the Crime Control and Safe Streets Act of 1968 provided statutory authorization for federal use of judicially approved electronic surveillance. The law set out procedures to be followed by federal agents in obtaining approval for such surveillance, first from Justice Department officials and then from a federal judge who would issue a warrant for this type of search and seizure. The law provided that applications for warrants must be approved either by the attorney general or by a specially designated assistant attorney general.[110] Twice in the 1970s the Court signaled its determination to apply the warrant requirement to wiretaps at least as strictly as it applied it to other types of searches. In 1972 the Court unanimously rejected the contention of the Nixon administration that the 1968 law did not require judicial approval of warrants for wiretaps or surveillance in national security cases.[111] Two years later, the Court effectively nullified hundreds of criminal prosecutions based on evidence obtained by electronic surveillance because Attorney General John N. Mitchell had not himself signed the applications for the warrants authorizing the surveillance and had allowed an aide other than the designated assistant attorney general to approve the applications.[112] In 1979 the Court held that because Congress must have recognized that most electronic bugs can be installed only by agents who secretly enter the premises, warrants authorizing such surveillance need not explicitly authorize covert entry.[113]

In the so-called war on drugs, police have used new high-tech methods to search for narcotics, and most of them have won the Court's approval. In 1986 the justices upheld the use of low-flying aircraft to search fields and backyards. Flying at a thousand feet, police in Santa Clara, California, saw tall marijuana plants growing in a backyard. They photographed the area and used the images as evidence to obtain a warrant to search the house and arrest the owner. In a 5-4 decision, the Court rejected the claim that the aerial search violated the privacy rights of the homeowner. "The Fourth Amendment simply does not require the police traveling in the public airways at this altitude to obtain a warrant in order to observe what is visible to the naked eye," said Chief Justice Warren E. Burger.[114] In 1989 the Court also upheld backyard drug searches by helicopters hovering at four hundred feet. In both instances, police used their own eyes from a public vantage point to look for drugs. "What a person knowingly exposes to the public, even in his home or office, is not a subject of Fourth Amendment protection," the Court ruled.[115]

The justices, however, drew a line at sensing devices that can look into a house. Federal agents had used a "thermal imager" on the street outside the home of Danny Kyllo in Florence, Oregon, to detect heat emissions. In doing so, they identified hot spots indicating that high-intensity lamps were being used to cultivate marijuana. With that evidence, agents obtained a search warrant to raid Kyllo's house. Their suspicions proved correct, but in *Kyllo v. United States* (2001) the Court declared the search an unconstitutional invasion of privacy. Obtaining by "sense-enhancing technology any information regarding the interior of the home" crosses the line protected by the Fourth Amendment, said Justice Scalia for a 5-4 majority.[116] "In the home, all details are intimate details, because the entire area is held safe from prying government eyes," he added.[117] In dissent, Justice Stevens said he would have upheld this use of the heat imager because "heat waves, like aromas that are generated in the kitchen," waft outside and can be lawfully detected there. Chief Justice Rehnquist along with Justices O'Connor and Kennedy joined his dissent.

Self-Incrimination

The Fifth Amendment privilege against self-incrimination is stated clearly: no one "shall be compelled in any criminal case to be a witness against himself." A person may not be forced to confess, required to testify, or provide evidence that could convict him. When charged with a crime, an individual defendant is free to plead not guilty, and no inference of guilt may be drawn either from his decision not to testify at his own trial or to remain silent when interrogated by police.[1] The privilege is not, however, an absolute right to silence. The right must be claimed; it is waived unless invoked, and when it is claimed, a judge decides whether its assertion is justified.[2] The accused waives that right when he agrees to testify in his own defense, and thus becomes subject to cross-examination.

A witness called to testify before a grand jury, a congressional committee, or an administrative hearing risks a contempt citation if he refuses to appear. Once on the stand, however, he may refuse to answer particular questions on the grounds that the answers will tend to incriminate him.[3] He may not assert the privilege just because he fears other adverse consequences of his testimony, such as public ridicule or general disrepute.[4] Once incriminating facts have been revealed voluntarily, a witness cannot then assert a Fifth Amendment privilege to avoid disclosure of further details.[5] The privilege is a personal one and may not be invoked to protect anyone else. It is to be asserted only by "natural" persons, not by corporations, labor unions, or other organizations.[6] Individuals in possession of public records or those of an organization cannot claim the Fifth Amendment privilege to protect those records, even if they contain information incriminating to the witness. Only purely personal and private documents and papers in the possession of the owner are protected by the privilege.[7] The Court has affirmed repeatedly that innocent persons as well as guilty ones may invoke this privilege. In doing so, it rejected the assumption that anyone who "takes the Fifth" must be guilty.

The Court has declared it unconstitutional for a state to punish employees who refuse to testify about employment-related activities after being ordered to waive their privilege against self-incrimination. It has reversed convictions of public employees based on testimony obtained through such coercion and held that states may not fire persons just because they invoke this privilege.[8] Congress, in the course of regulating certain forms of business and political activity found highly susceptible to illegal diversion or influence, has passed a number of federal laws requiring detailed records, reports, registration, and tax payments related to membership in some groups, to drug and firearms transactions, and to gambling. Until the 1960s, the Court generally upheld such registration and tax provisions,[9] but beginning with its decision in *Albertson v. Subversive Activities Control Board* (1965), involving Communist Party registration, the Court held that such requirements violated the Fifth Amendment.[10] *(See details of the case, pp. 232–233.)* In the late 1960s and early 1970s, the Court struck down many of these registration provisions on Fifth Amendment grounds. Congress subsequently rewrote some of the offending laws and omitted the self-incriminatory provisions.[11]

The Court has cautioned that the Fifth Amendment does not provide a general right against self-incrimination, but rather a right of the accused not to be required to be a "witness" whose words are used against him. The Fifth Amendment does not, for example, shield from the government his or her fingerprints, blood, or hair samples, DNA, or handwriting, any of which could be incriminating. "We adhere to the view that the Fifth Amendment protects against compelled self-incrimination, not the disclosure of private information," the Court stated in *Fisher v. United States* (1976).[12] In that case, a taxpayer had tried to shield from the Internal Revenue Service some documents that could prove incriminating and which he had given to his lawyer. The Court said that the tax records were not truly private papers, and even if they were, they were not shielded by the Constitution. "The Fifth Amendment does not independently proscribe the compelled production of every sort of incriminating evidence, but applies only when the accused is compelled to make a testimonial communication that is incriminating," wrote Justice Byron R. White.

In 1990 the Court cited *Fisher* when it rejected a self-incrimination claim from a mother suspected of having killed her child. Jacqueline Bouknight had abused her infant Maurice, and the Baltimore City Department of Social Services had taken the child into custody for a time. When the child was returned to Bouknight, she promised to comply with its conditions. She did not, however, and when the child disappeared, Bouknight was ordered to produce Maurice; the court held her in contempt for refusing to do so. In *Baltimore v. Bouknight* (1990), the Court ruled that the Fifth Amendment did not shield the mother from an order compelling her to produce her child. Bouknight served seven years in jail without revealing the whereabouts of her missing son.[13]

PRIVILEGE AND IMMUNITY

Immunity statutes, in use throughout U.S. history, represent the government's effort to reconcile its need for information with the Fifth Amendment privilege against compelled self-incrimination. These laws protect individuals who furnish information to the government from prosecutions based on their own coerced testimony. Most immunity laws contain an exception for perjury: if immunized witnesses provide false information, they are subject to prosecution for perjury using their own words. Justice Lewis F. Powell Jr. noted once that immunity laws "seek a rational accommodation between the imperatives of the privilege and the legitimate demands of government to compel citizens to testify."[14]

The modern Court has condoned as constitutional a narrower form of immunity than that approved during the nineteenth century. Early statutes allowed immunization of witnesses from prosecution for any crime revealed in their testimony, a so-called "immunity bath." Later statutes, however, allowed some indirect use of immunized testimony to obtain other evidence of wrongdoing by the witness. In the late 1890s, in one of its earliest rulings concerning the Fifth Amendment privilege, the Supreme Court had held this more limited immunity insufficient protection for the witness. In *Counselman v. Hitchcock* (1892), the Court unanimously ordered the release from custody of Charles Counselman, a railroad official held in contempt of court. Asserting his constitutional privilege against compelled self-incrimination, he had declined to answer certain questions from a grand jury. Counselman challenged his detention as a violation of his Fifth Amendment rights and sought release through a writ of habeas corpus. The Supreme Court agreed with his challenge.

The Court's opinion, written by Justice Samuel Blatchford, held that grand jury witnesses, as well as persons already charged with crimes, could assert this privilege. In addition, the Court found this limited immunity, which left the witness still subject to indirect use of his testimony against him, insufficient because it "does not supply a complete protection from all the perils against which the constitutional prohibition was designed to guard, and is not a full substitute for that prohibition."[15] "In view of the constitutional provision," concluded Blatchford, "a statutory enactment, to be valid, must afford absolute immunity against future prosecution for the offense to which the question relates."[16] This decision was interpreted as a requirement that immunity must protect a witness from all prosecution for the criminal "transactions" revealed in immunized testimony, not just against the "use" of the testimony itself as evidence.

Concerned that the Fifth Amendment privilege could be used to block inquiry into alleged violations of the Interstate Commerce Act, Congress in 1892 provided that witnesses appearing in Interstate Commerce Commission investigations could be granted this type of "transactional" immunity. The Court, 5-4, upheld the new law in *Brown v. Walker* (1896). In so doing, the Court made clear that the privilege was to be claimed only to protect the witness alone, not any third party, and only to protect the witness from prosecution, not simply from "personal odium and disgrace." The Court upheld the contempt sentence of Brown, a railway company auditor who had refused to answer certain questions from a grand jury, claiming his Fifth Amendment privilege. The Court held that this assertion was not appropriate, since the privilege was being claimed to shield others from prosecution. Justice Henry B. Brown, who viewed the privilege as meaning only that the witness was secure from criminal prosecution, held that this interpretation established an appropriate equilibrium between the private right and the public welfare:

> The clause of the Constitution in question is obviously susceptible of two interpretations. If it be construed literally, as authorizing the witness to refuse to disclose any fact that might tend to incriminate, disgrace, or expose him to unfavorable comments, then, as he must necessarily to a large extent determine upon his own conscience and responsibility whether his answer to the proposed question will have that tendency ... the practical result would be, that no one could be compelled to testify to a material fact in a criminal case.... If, upon the other hand, the object of the provision be to secure the witness against a criminal prosecution, which might be aided directly or indirectly by his disclosure, then, if no such prosecution be possible,—in other words, if his testimony operate as a complete pardon for the offense to which it relates,—a statute absolutely securing to him such immunity from prosecution would satisfy the demands of the clause in question....
>
> It can only be said in general that the clause should be construed, as it was doubtless designed, to effect a practical and beneficent purpose—not necessarily to protect witnesses against every possible detriment which might happen to them from their testimony, nor to unduly impede, hinder, or obstruct the administration of criminal justice....
>
> The design of the constitutional privilege is not to aid the witness in vindicating his character but to protect him against being compelled to furnish evidence to convict him of a criminal charge.... While the constitutional provision in question is justly regarded as one of the most valuable prerogatives of the citizen, its object is fully accomplished by the statutory immunity, and we are therefore of opinion that the witness was compellable to answer.[17]

The issue of what constitutes true immunity was again raised during the 1950s, when the Eisenhower administration proposed, and Congress approved, the Immunity Act of 1954. Its purpose was to prevent witnesses called to testify in government subversion inquiries from refusing to answer questions on grounds of self-incrimination. The act granted immunity from prosecution for criminal activity revealed during compelled testimony, but in congressional testimony, Communist Party members challenged the law. They alleged that the act did not provide true immunity in light of the many disabilities—including loss of employment and public criticism—imposed on party members. The Court upheld the act in *Ullmann v. United States* (1956). Justice Felix Frankfurter described the 1893 immunity statute upheld in *Brown* as now "part of our constitutional fabric."[18] He continued:

> We are not dealing here with one of the vague, undefinable, admonitory provisions of the Constitution whose scope is inevitably addressed to changing circumstances.... [T]he history of the privilege establishes not only that it is not to be interpreted literally, but also that its sole concern is ... with the danger to a witness forced to give testimony leading to the infliction of "penalties affixed to the criminal acts."... Immunity displaces the danger. Once the reason for the privilege ceases, the privilege ceases.[19]

Justices William O. Douglas and Hugo L. Black dissented, urging the Court to overrule *Brown v. Walker* and adopt the literal view "that the right of silence created by the Fifth Amendment is beyond the reach of Congress."[20] Wrote Douglas,

> [T]he Fifth Amendment was written in part to prevent any Congress, any court, and any prosecutor from prying open the lips of an accused to make incriminating statements against his will. The Fifth Amendment protects the conscience and the dignity of the individual, as well as his safety and security, against the compulsion of the government....
>
> The critical point is that the Constitution places the right of silence beyond the reach of government. The Fifth Amendment stands between the citizen and his government. When public opinion casts a person into the outer darkness, as happens today when a person is exposed as a Communist, the government

brings infamy on the head of the witness when it compels disclosure. That is precisely what the Fifth Amendment prohibits.[21]

In the Organized Crime Control Act of 1970, Congress approved a more limited grant of "use" immunity to witnesses in organized crime cases. Rather than providing immunity from prosecution for any offense in which the witness was implicated through his testimony, the law simply forbade the use of any of his compelled testimony or derivative evidence against him. Under the 1970 act, however, a witness could be prosecuted for crimes mentioned in his testimony if the evidence used in the prosecution was developed independently of his testimony.[22] In *Kastigar v. United States* (1972), the Court found this narrower "use" immunity constitutional:

> The privilege has never been construed to mean that one who invokes it cannot subsequently be prosecuted. Its sole concern is to afford protection against being forced to give testimony leading to the infliction of "penalties affixed to … criminal acts." Immunity from the use of compelled testimony, as well as evidence derived directly and indirectly therefrom, affords this protection.[23]

The Court found this use immunity sufficient, because the law required the state—in prosecuting an immunized witness—to show that its evidence had not been derived from his immunized testimony. Justice Powell wrote,

> A person accorded this immunity…, and subsequently prosecuted, is not dependent for the preservation of his rights upon the integrity and good faith of the prosecuting authorities…. This burden of proof which we reaffirm as appropriate … imposes on the prosecution the affirmative duty to prove that the evidence it proposes to use is derived from a legitimate source wholly independent of the compelled testimony.[24]

Justices Douglas and Thurgood Marshall dissented. Wrote Douglas,

> When we allow the prosecution to offer only "use" immunity we allow it to grant far less than it has taken away. For while the precise testimony that is compelled may not be used, leads from that testimony may be pursued and used to convict the witness. My view is that the Framers put it beyond

the power of Congress to compel anyone to confess his crimes…. Government acts in an ignoble way when it stoops to the end which we authorize today.[25]

EXPANDING PROTECTION

Twice—in 1908 and in 1947—the Supreme Court rejected arguments that the due process guarantee of the Fourteenth Amendment extended the privilege against self-incrimination to state defendants. In both cases, the Court permitted state officials to draw unfavorable inferences from a defendant's failure to testify in his own behalf. In *Twining v. New Jersey* (1908), the Court stated that the privilege was not inherent in due process, but "separate from and independent of" it.[26] The decision in *Adamson v. California* (1947) reaffirmed this stance in refusing to find the privilege essential to a system of "ordered liberty."[27] Furthermore, in several cases the justices held that the Fifth Amendment did not protect an individual from a state's use of testimony compelled by federal authority or from federal use of testimony compelled by state authority.[28] In *Malloy v. Hogan* (1964), however, the Court reconsidered *Twining* and *Adamson* and declared that the Fifth Amendment guarantee against self-incrimination did indeed extend to state proceedings.

William Malloy, convicted of illegal gambling activities, refused to testify before a state investigation of gambling operations in Hartford County, Connecticut. Malloy claimed that to testify would compel him to incriminate himself. He was held in contempt and sentenced to prison. Malloy appealed, but the Connecticut Supreme Court held that the Fifth Amendment's privilege against self-incrimination was not available to a witness in a state proceeding. The Supreme Court, 5-4, reversed the state court and upheld Malloy's claim, holding that the Fourteenth Amendment guaranteed him the protection of the Fifth Amendment's privilege against self-incrimination. Justice William J. Brennan Jr. wrote the majority opinion:

> The Fourteenth Amendment secures against state invasion the same privilege that the Fifth Amendment guarantees against federal infringement—the

right of a person to remain silent unless he chooses to speak in the unfettered exercise of his own will, and to suffer no penalty … for such silence.…

It would be incongruous to have different standards determine the validity of a claim of privilege based on the same feared prosecution, depending on whether the claim was asserted in a state or federal court. Therefore, the same standards must determine whether an accused's silence in either a federal or state proceeding is justified.… It must be considered irrelevant that the petitioner was a witness in a statutory inquiry and not a defendant in a criminal prosecution, for it has long been settled that the privilege protects witnesses in similar federal inquiries.[29]

Justices Byron R. White, Potter Stewart, John Marshall Harlan, and Tom C. Clark dissented from what they viewed as the step-by-step incorporation of the first eight amendments under the Due Process Clause of the Fourteenth Amendment. According to Harlan,

The consequence of such an approach … is inevitable disregard of all relevant differences which may exist between state and federal criminal law and its enforcement.…

The Court's approach in the present case is in fact nothing more or less than "incorporation" in snatches. If, however, the Due Process Clause is something more than a reference to the Bill of Rights and protects only those rights which derive from fundamental principles … it is just as contrary to precedent and just as illogical to incorporate the provisions of the Bill of Rights one at a time as it is to incorporate them all at once.[30]

On the same day the Court announced its decision in *Malloy v. Hogan*, it decided *Murphy v. The Waterfront Commission of New York Harbor* (1964). The Court said the Fifth Amendment protects a state witness against incrimination under federal as well as state law and a federal witness against incrimination under state as well as federal law. Immunity granted under federal law protects against state prosecution and vice versa. In that case, William Murphy, a labor union official subpoenaed to testify about a work stoppage at New Jersey piers, refused to answer questions on the grounds that his answers would tend to incriminate him. Granted immunity

under New York and New Jersey laws, Murphy still refused to testify because the immunity failed to protect him from federal prosecution. The court held Murphy in contempt, but the Supreme Court vacated the judgment. Justice Arthur J. Goldberg's opinion for a unanimous Court set out the constitutional rule:

[A] state witness may not be compelled to give testimony which may be incriminating under federal law unless the compelled testimony and its fruits cannot be used in any manner by federal officials in connection with a criminal prosecution against him. We conclude, moreover, that in order to implement this constitutional rule and accommodate the interests of the State and Federal Governments in investigating and prosecuting crime, the Federal Government must be prohibited from making any such use of compelled testimony and its fruits.[31]

The Court reinforced the *Malloy* ruling in *Griffin v. California* (1965). Effectively reversing *Twining* and *Adamson* in holdings concerning judicial or prosecutorial comment on the silence of defendants, the Court held that the Fifth Amendment "forbids either comment by the prosecution on the accused's silence or instructions by the Court that such silence is evidence of guilt."[32] Writing for the Court in *Griffin*, Justice Douglas explained:

[C]omment on the refusal to testify is a remnant of the "inquisitorial system of criminal justice,"… which the Fifth Amendment outlaws. It is a penalty imposed by courts for exercising a constitutional privilege. It cuts down on the privilege by making its assertion costly.[33]

COERCED CONFESSIONS

Confessions, the Court stated in 1884, are "among the most effectual proofs in the law," but they are admissible as evidence only when given voluntarily.[34] This requirement has long been the rule in federal courts, where the Fifth Amendment clearly applies.[35] Since 1936 the same rule has governed the use of confessions in state courts. The inevitable question is how to determine when a confession is voluntary. The Court ruled on the use of confessions for the first time in 1884. An involuntary confession, it said, is one that "appears to have been made, either in

THE QUESTION OF QUESTIONING

Critical to the meaning of *Miranda v. Arizona* (1966), the case that forbade police to continue questioning a suspect after he invoked his right to remain silent or to have his lawyer present, was the meaning of the term *interrogation.*[1] Fourteen years after *Miranda,* the Court adopted a broad definition of the word. *Interrogation,* the Court declared unanimously in *Rhode Island v. Innis* (1980), means more than just the direct questioning of a suspect by police. It includes other "techniques of persuasion," such as staged lineups, intended to evoke statements from a suspect. Indeed, said the Court, interrogation occurs any time police use words or actions "that they *should have known* were reasonably likely to elicit an incriminating response" from a suspect.[2]

This broad definition of interrogation did not, however, encompass events that transpired in *Rhode Island,* the Court held 6-3. Thomas Innis, arrested for murder, led police to the murder weapon after he overheard policemen conversing among themselves about the possibility of children finding and being harmed by the weapon they were seeking. Because this evocative conversation occurred in a police car without Innis's attorney present, he challenged his eventually incriminating statements as obtained in violation of *Miranda.* The Supreme Court rejected this argument, holding that the conversation he overheard did not qualify as interrogation.[3]

In 1981 the Court reaffirmed its broad view of interrogation, ruling that a defendant should be warned, prior to an interview with a state-appointed psychiatrist, that he had the right to refuse to answer the psychiatrist's questions and to have his attorney present during the interview.[4] The whole area of police conversation with a suspect raises difficult points of distinction. In *Edwards v. Arizona* (1981), the Court was unanimous in insisting that once a defendant has said he wants his attor-

ney present, all interrogation must cease and may not resume until the attorney is present or the defendant starts a new conversation with police.[5] Two years later, the Court emphasized the latter point, ruling 5-4 that a suspect who invokes his right to counsel but later, before counsel arrives, asks police, "Well, what is going to happen to me now?" is not denied his rights when police remind him of his request for counsel but then continue to talk with him.[6]

Police use of a well-placed informer can also constitute interrogation, the Court has held. In *United States v. Henry* (1980), the Court held that a suspect was denied the right to counsel when the government obtained and used incriminating statements by planting an informer in his cell prior to trial.[7] The Court reaffirmed this ruling in *Maine v. Moulton* (1985), but a year later it drew the line between solicited and unsolicited incriminating statements, permitting police to use *unsolicited* remarks made by a suspect to a police informer in his cell.[8] *(See "Miranda v. Arizona" for other rulings on invocation of privilege, pp. 322–325.)*

---

1. *Miranda v. Arizona,* 384 U.S. 436 (1966), reaffirmed in *Michigan v. Jackson, Michigan v. Bladel,* 475 U.S. 625 (1986).

2. *Rhode Island v. Innis,* 446 U.S. 291 (1980).

3. Id.

4. *Estelle v. Smith,* 451 U.S. 454 (1981); *Satterwhite v. Texas,* 486 U.S. 249 (1988).

5. *Edwards v. Arizona,* 451 U.S. 477 (1981), applied retroactively to cases pending on appeal; *Shea v. Louisiana,* 470 U.S. 51 (1985). See also *Arizona v. Roberson,* 486 U.S. 675 (1988), *Patterson v. Illinois,* 487 U.S. 285 (1988).

6. *Oregon v. Bradshaw,* 462 U.S. 1039 (1983).

7. *United States v. Henry,* 447 U.S. 264 (1980).

8. *Maine v. Moulton,* 474 U.S. 159 (1985); *Kuhlmann v. Wilson,* 477 U.S. 436 (1986).

---

consequence of inducements of a temporal nature ... or because of a threat or promise ... which, operating upon the fears or hopes of the accused ... deprive him of that freedom of will or self-control essential to make his confession voluntary within the meaning of the law."[36]

A dozen years later, in 1896, the Court restated the standard for determining when a confession was admissible: "The true test of admissibility is that the confession is made freely, voluntarily, and without compulsion or inducement of any sort."[37] This test, as the Court reaffirmed in 1897, had to be applied every time the use of a confession was challenged. The judge should consider "the circumstances surrounding, and the facts established to exist, in reference to the confession, in order to determine whether it was shown to have been voluntarily made." In all federal trials, the resolution of this issue was controlled by the Fifth Amendment command that no person be compelled to incriminate himself.[38]

Delay in charging a suspect with a crime is a significant factor in determining if a confession is admissible. Several federal laws made clear that when persons are arrested, they should be taken promptly before a magistrate and charged. In the 1940s, the Supreme Court gave compelling force to this requirement by holding that confessions obtained after "unnecessary delay" in a suspect's arraignment could not be used as evidence in federal court. In *McNabb v. United States* (1943), the justices overturned the convictions of several men for murdering a federal revenue agent. The most important elements in the prosecution's case were incriminating statements made by the defendants after three days of questioning by federal officers in the absence of any defense counsel and before they were formally charged with any crime.

The Court based its decision on the statutory requirements of prompt arraignment, and on the Court's general power to supervise the functioning of the federal judicial system, rather than on the Fifth Amendment. Justice Frankfurter explained that the Court's supervisory role obligated it to establish and maintain "civilized standards of procedure and evidence" for federal courts.[39] The purpose of the ban on unnecessary delay between arrest and arraignment, he continued, was plain:

A democratic society, in which respect for the dignity of all men is central, naturally guards against the misuse of the law enforcement process. Zeal in tracking down crime is not in itself an assurance of soberness of judgment. Disinterestedness in law enforcement does not alone prevent disregard of cherished liberties. Experience has therefore counseled that safeguards must be provided against the dangers of the overzealous as well as the despotic. The awful instruments of the criminal law cannot be entrusted to a single functionary. The complicated process of criminal justice is therefore divided into different parts, responsibility for which is separately vested in the various participants upon whom the criminal law relies for its vindication. Legislation ... requiring that the police must with reasonable promptness show legal cause for detaining arrested persons, constitutes an important safeguard—not only in assuring protection for the innocent but also in securing conviction of the guilty by methods that commend themselves to a progressive and self-confident society. For this procedural requirement checks resort to those reprehensible practices known as the "third degree" which, though universally rejected as indefensible, still find their way into use. It aims to avoid all the evil implications of secret interrogation of persons accused of crime. It reflects not a sentimental but a sturdy view of law enforcement. It outlaws easy but self-defeating ways in which brutality is substituted for brains as an instrument of crime detection.[40]

The Federal Rules of Criminal Procedure subsequently incorporated this rule, and the Court in *Mallory v. United States* (1957) reaffirmed its importance. In *Mallory*, the justices nullified a death sentence imposed upon a rapist who "confessed" to the crime during a delay of more than eighteen hours between his arrest and his arraignment. They warned that such "unwarranted detention" could lead "to tempting utilization of intensive interrogation, easily gliding into the evils of 'the third degree'"—precisely what the rule was intended to avoid.[41] *Mallory* generated fierce criticism and prompted Congress to revise the statutory rule to allow some use of evidence obtained during such delays. In 1968 the national legislature included in the Crime Control and Safe Streets Act a provision stating that delay in arraignment was not an absolute bar to federal use of a confession obtained during a period of delay.

Decades before the Supreme Court applied the Fifth Amendment to state action, it unanimously forbade states to use coerced confessions to convict persons of crimes. The concept of basic fairness implicit in the Fourteenth Amendment guarantee of due process served as the basis for the Court's declaration of this prohibition in *Brown v. Mississippi* (1936). With that decision the Court for the first time overturned a state conviction because it was obtained by using a confession extracted by torture. Mississippi defended its use of this confession by citing *Twining v. New Jersey* (1908), a ruling that state defendants did not enjoy the protection of the Fifth Amendment privilege against compelled self-incrimination. The Court rejected that defense, stating flatly that "the question of the right of the state to withdraw the privilege against self-incrimination is not here involved."[42] Chief Justice Charles Evans Hughes saw a distinction between compulsion forbidden by the Fifth Amendment and compulsion forbidden by the Fourteenth Amendment's Due Process Clause.

> The compulsion to which the ... [Fifth Amendment] refer[s] is that of the processes of justice by which the accused may be called as a witness and required to testify. Compulsion by torture to extort a confession is a different matter....
>
> Because a state may dispense with a jury trial, it does not follow that it may substitute trial by ordeal. The rack and torture chamber may not be substituted for the witness stand.... It would be difficult to conceive of methods more revolting to the sense of justice than those taken to procure the confessions of these petitioners, and the use of the confessions thus obtained as the basis for conviction and sentence was a clear denial of due process.[43]

Over the next three decades, the Court judged each case in which state use of a confession was challenged by looking at the "totality of the circumstances" surrounding the arrest and interrogation. In these cases, Chief Justice Hughes's neat distinction between physical coercion and other forms of compulsion soon blurred.

The Court affirmed *Brown* in *Chambers v. Florida* (1940). In that case, four black men had been convicted of murder on the basis of confessions obtained after days of being held incommunicado and interrogated by law enforcement officials. The unanimous Court overturned their convictions, acknowledging that psychological coercion, as well as physical torture, could produce involuntary confessions whose use violated due process. Justice Black wrote the Court's opinion:

> The determination to preserve an accused's right to procedural due process sprang in large part from knowledge of the historical truth that the rights and liberties of people accused of crime could not be safely entrusted to secret inquisitorial processes....
>
> For five days petitioners were subjected to interrogations culminating in ... [an] all night examination. Over a period of five days they steadily refused to confess and disclaimed any guilt. The very circumstances surrounding their confinement and their questioning without any formal charges having been brought, were such as to fill petitioners with terror and frightful misgivings. Some were practically strangers in the community.... The haunting fear of mob violence was around them in an atmosphere charged with excitement and public indignation.... To permit human lives to be forfeited upon confessions thus obtained would make of the constitutional requirement of due process of law a meaningless symbol....
>
> Due process of law, preserved for all by our Constitution, commands that no such practice as that disclosed by this record shall send any accused to his death.[44]

The Court in subsequent decisions acknowledged that some situations were so inherently coercive that evidence produced from them was inadmissible, but not until the mid-1960s did it develop any hard-and-fast rules concerning the admissibility of the products of prolonged interrogation of suspects in police custody.[45] Voluntariness, not veracity, was the key to whether a confession was admissible. As Justice Frankfurter explained in the Court's decision in *Rogers v. Richmond* (1961),

> Our decisions ... have made clear that convictions following the admission into evidence of confessions which are involuntary ... cannot stand. This is so not because such confessions are unlikely to be true but because the methods used to extract them offend an underlying principle in the enforcement of our criminal law: that ours is an accusatorial and not an inquisitorial system—a system in which the State must establish guilt by evidence independently and freely secured and may not by coercion prove its own charge against an accused out of his own mouth.[46]

CONFESSIONS AND COUNSEL

The Fifth Amendment privilege against compelled self-incrimination was inextricably linked with the Sixth Amendment right to counsel by the Court's rulings in *Escobedo v. Illinois* (1964) and *Miranda v. Arizona* (1966). The Court had ruled in 1958 that confessions could be voluntary and admissible even when obtained from a suspect who was denied the opportunity to consult with legal counsel during interrogation by police.[47] A few years later, however, it reversed that view. In *Massiah v. United States* (1964), the justices declared that an indicted person could not properly be questioned or otherwise persuaded to make incriminating remarks in the absence of his lawyer.[48] Coupled with the Court's ruling later that term in *Malloy v. Hogan* extending the Fifth Amendment privilege to state defendants, *Massiah* laid the groundwork for *Escobedo*.

Escobedo v. Illinois

A week after *Malloy*, the Court announced its decision in the case of Danny Escobedo, who was convicted of murder in Illinois on the basis of his own words. In *Escobedo v. Illinois* (1964), the Court discarded the voluntarism standard for determining the admissibility of confessions, moving away from the "totality of the circumstances" approach to concentrate on the procedures followed by police in obtaining a confession.[49] Escobedo repeatedly asked for and was denied the opportunity to see his attorney during his interrogation by police. Incriminating statements he made during this time were used as evidence against him. He challenged his conviction as a denial of his right to counsel. The Court agreed, ruling that a defendant has a right to remain silent rather than be forced to incriminate himself. If police do not warn a suspect of his "absolute constitutional right to remain silent," said the Court, he has been denied "the assistance of counsel" in violation of the Sixth Amendment. Justice Goldberg wrote the majority opinion. Justices Harlan, White, Clark, and Stewart dissented.

The year before, the Court had declared in *Gideon v. Wainwright* (1963) that the Sixth Amendment required that every person accused of a serious crime be provided the aid of an attorney.[50] Justice Goldberg reasoned in *Escobedo* that the right guaranteed in *Gideon* would be a hollow one if it did not apply until after police obtained a confession:

> We have ... learned ... that no system of criminal justice can, or should, survive if it comes to depend for its continued effectiveness on the citizens' abdication through unawareness of their constitutional rights. No system worth preserving should have to fear that if an accused is permitted to consult with a lawyer, he will become aware of, and exercise, these rights. If the exercise of constitutional rights

Danny Escobedo's arrest and conviction for the murder of his brother-in-law led to a Supreme Court decision that expanded constitutional protections for criminal defendants during police interrogations. This photograph of Escobedo was taken as he awaited processing on charges of burglarizing a hot dog stand not long after the Supreme Court issued its landmark ruling in *Escobedo v. Illinois*.

> will thwart the effectiveness of a system of law enforcement, then there is something very wrong with that system.
>
> We hold, therefore, that where, as here, the investigation is no longer a general inquiry into an unsolved crime but has begun to focus on a particular suspect, the suspect has been taken into police custody, the police carry out a process of interrogations that lends itself to eliciting incriminating statements, the suspect has requested and been denied an opportunity to consult with his lawyer, and the police have not effectively warned him of his absolute constitutional right to remain silent, the accused has been denied "the Assistance of Counsel" in violation of the Sixth Amendment ... and that no statement elicited by police during the interrogation may be used against him at a criminal trial.[51]

Justice White's dissenting opinion, joined by Justices Clark and Stewart, criticized the majority's holding that any incriminating statement made by an arrested suspect who was denied the opportunity to see his lawyer was inadmissible:

> By abandoning the voluntary-involuntary test ... the Court seems driven by the notion that it is uncivilized law enforcement to use an accused's own admissions against him at his trial. It attempts to find a home for this new and nebulous rule of due process by attaching it to the right of counsel guaranteed in the federal system by the Sixth Amendment and binding upon the States by virtue of the due process guarantee of the Fourteenth Amendment.... The right to counsel now not only entitles the accused to counsel's advice and aid in preparing for trial but stands as an impenetrable barrier to any interrogation once the accused has become a suspect.[52]

Miranda v. Arizona

Two years after *Escobedo*, the Supreme Court in *Miranda v. Arizona* (1966) set out "concrete constitutional guidelines" for the custodial interrogation practices of state and local police.[53] Ernesto Miranda was convicted of kidnapping and rape in Arizona. The prosecution used as evidence against him statements Miranda had made to police during his interrogation. He was not advised of his rights to remain silent and to consult an attorney. Miranda challenged his conviction as obtained in violation of the Fifth Amendment privilege. By the same 5-4 vote as in *Escobedo*, the Court upheld his challenge. It ruled that prosecutors were constitutionally forbidden to use incriminating statements obtained from suspects during interrogation unless strict procedural safeguards had been followed to guarantee that the suspect was aware of his constitutional rights to remain silent and to have the aid of an attorney. "The presence of counsel," stated Chief Justice Earl Warren for the majority, was "the adequate protective device" to "insure that statements made in the government-established atmosphere are not the product of compulsion."[54] Warren, summarizing the Court's holding, wrote that

> the prosecution may not use statements, whether exculpatory or inculpatory, stemming from custodial interrogation of the defendant unless it demonstrates the use of procedural safeguards effective to secure the privilege against self-incrimination. By custodial

interrogation, we mean questioning initiated by law enforcement officers after a person has been taken into custody or otherwise deprived of his freedom of action in any significant way. As for the procedural safeguards to be employed, unless other fully effective means are devised to inform accused persons of their right of silence and to assure a continuous opportunity to exercise it, the following measures are required. Prior to any questioning, the person must be warned that he has a right to remain silent, that any statement he does make may be used as evidence against him, and that he has a right to the presence of an attorney, either retained or appointed. The defendant may waive effectuation of these rights, provided the waiver is made voluntarily, knowingly and intelligently. If, however, he indicates in any manner and at any stage of the process, that he wishes to consult with an attorney before speaking there can be no questioning. Likewise, if the individual is alone and indicates in any manner that he does not wish to be interrogated, the police may not question him. The mere fact that he may have answered some questions or have volunteered some statements on his own does not deprive him of the right to refrain from answering any further inquiries until he has consulted with an attorney and thereafter consents to be questioned.[55]

The Fifth Amendment, explained Warren, required that whenever a suspect indicated, before or during interrogation, that he wished to remain silent, all interrogation must cease. "At this point he has shown that he intends to exercise his Fifth Amendment privilege," wrote the chief justice. Therefore "any statement taken after the person invokes his privilege cannot be other than the product of compulsion, subtle or otherwise."[56]

Justices Clark, Harlan, White, and Stewart dissented, arguing that they felt the Court should continue to use the "totality of the circumstances" approach to determining the admissibility of confessions. Justice Harlan criticized the ruling as "poor constitutional law":

> I think it must be frankly recognized at the outset that police questioning allowable under due process precedents may inherently entail some pressure on the suspect and may seek advantage in his ignorance or weaknesses.... Until today, the role of the Constitution has been only to sift out undue pressure, not to assure spontaneous confessions. The Court's new rules aim to offset these minor pressures and disadvantages

```
DEFENDANT                              LOCATION

     SPECIFIC WARNING REGARDING INTERROGATIONS

 1. YOU HAVE THE RIGHT TO REMAIN SILENT.

 2. ANYTHING YOU SAY CAN AND WILL BE USED AGAINST YOU IN A COURT
    OF LAW.

 3. YOU HAVE THE RIGHT TO TALK TO A LAWYER AND HAVE HIM PRESENT
    WITH YOU WHILE YOU ARE BEING QUESTIONED.

 4. IF YOU CANNOT AFFORD TO HIRE A LAWYER ONE WILL BE APPOINTED
    TO REPRESENT YOU BEFORE ANY QUESTIONING, IF YOU WISH ONE.

 SIGNATURE OF DEFENDANT                           DATE

 WITNESS                                          TIME

 REFUSED SIGNATURE     SAN FRANCISCO POLICE DEPARTMENT      PR.9.1.4
```

As a result of the ruling in *Miranda v. Arizona* (1966) a police officer must advise a person placed under arrest of his or her right to remain silent and to be represented by an attorney.

intrinsic to any kind of police interrogation. The rules do not serve due process interests in preventing blatant coercion since ... they do nothing to contain the policeman who is prepared to lie from the start.[57]

White argued that the majority had misread the Fifth Amendment prohibition against compelled self-incrimination:

Confessions and incriminating admissions, as such, are not forbidden evidence; only those which are compelled are banned. I doubt that the Court observes these distinctions today....

The obvious underpinning of the Court's decision is a deep-seated distrust of all confessions....

The rule announced today ... is a deliberate calculus to prevent interrogations, to reduce the incidence of confessions and pleas of guilty and to increase the number of trials. Criminal trials, no matter how efficient the police are, are not sure bets for the prosecution, nor should they be if the

evidence is not forthcoming.... There is, in my view, every reason to believe that a good many criminal defendants, who otherwise would have been convicted on what this Court has previously thought to be the most satisfactory kind of evidence, will now, under this new version of the Fifth Amendment, either not be tried at all or will be acquitted if the State's evidence, minus the confession, is put to the test of litigation.[58]

A week after *Miranda*, the Court held that it would not apply the decision retroactively to invalidate convictions obtained in trials begun before its announcement on June 13, 1966. A similar rule applied in cases to which *Escobedo* might apply, held the Court.[59]

Mallory v. United States, Escobedo v. Illinois, and *Miranda v. Arizona*, together with rulings extending the specific protections of the Bill of Rights to state defendants, brought criticism of the Warren Court to a crescendo in the late 1960s. One of the major themes of the 1968 presidential campaign was "law and order"—a phrase that Richard Nixon, the successful candidate, used as a basis for his criticism of the Court's rulings. Many members of Congress were persuaded that the Court was, in fact, encouraging crime by impeding law enforcement officers in their duties. In the Crime Control and Safe Streets Act of 1968, Congress included provisions intended to blunt or overrule the effect of *Mallory* and *Miranda*. By stating that confessions could be used in federal courts whenever the judge found them voluntary, Congress attempted to abandon the procedural guidelines set out in *Miranda* and return to the old voluntary-involuntary test for prosecutorial use of incriminating statements. The 1968 law, however, affected only federal trials, not state trials. The states remained bound by the *Miranda* requirements.

Despite opposition to *Miranda*, the Supreme Court stood by that decision. Early in 1969, the Court held that *Miranda* required that police, before questioning an individual in his own home, warn him of his constitutional rights as soon as he was effectively in custody.[60] President-elect Nixon promised during his 1968 campaign to appoint justices to the Supreme Court who would be less receptive to the arguments of criminal defendants and more responsive to the reasoning of law enforcement officers. In spring 1969, Nixon named—and the Senate confirmed—Warren E. Burger, a conservative appeals court judge, as the successor to Chief Justice Warren, who had announced his plans to retire even before the election. In 1970 Burger was joined on the bench by another Nixon appointee, Harry A. Blackmun. In 1971 Nixon filled two more seats on the Court with Justices Powell and William H. Rehnquist.

Although the Court with its new chief justice and new members did not overturn *Miranda*, it did, over the next twenty-five years, decline to extend *Miranda*, and it allowed a number of indirect uses of statements and other evidence obtained from persons not warned of their rights. The first of these rulings came in *Harris v. New York* (1971). By a 5-4 vote, the Court held that although statements made by a defendant before he was advised of his rights could not be used as evidence against him, they could be used to impeach his credibility if he took the stand in his own defense and contradicted what he had said before trial. Chief Justice Burger observed:

> Some comments in the *Miranda* opinion can indeed be read as indicating a bar to use of an uncounseled statement for any purpose, but discussion of that issue was not at all necessary to the Court's holding, and cannot be regarded as controlling. *Miranda* barred the prosecution from making its case with statements of an accused while in custody prior to having or effectively waiving counsel. It does not follow from *Miranda* that evidence inadmissible against an accused in the prosecution's case in chief is barred for all purposes, provided of course that the trustworthiness of the evidence satisfies legal standards....
>
> The shield provided by *Miranda* cannot be perverted into a license to use perjury by way of a defense, free from the risk of confrontation with prior inconsistent utterances.[61]

Justices Black, Brennan, Douglas, and Marshall dissented, warning that this ruling "goes far toward undoing much of the progress made in conforming police methods to the Constitution."[62]

Three years later, the Court in *Michigan v. Tucker* (1974) upheld the prosecution's use of a statement made by a suspect not fully warned of his rights as a "lead" for locating a prosecution witness. Writing the opinion, Justice Rehnquist emphasized that the procedures *Miranda* required were safeguards for constitutional rights but were not themselves constitutionally guaranteed.[63] In *United States v. Mandujano* (1976), the Court refused to require that *Miranda* warnings be given to grand jury witnesses before they testify—even though they may be potential defendants.[64] In the early 1980s, the Court for the first time approved an exception to the strict requirement of *Miranda* that police advise a suspect in custody of his rights to remain silent and to have the aid of an attorney before the suspect can be questioned. That exception was called the "public safety" exception and was recognized in *New York v. Quarles* (1984). In that case, police were arresting a suspect in a grocery store and did not see the gun they expected him to be carrying. Instead of first warning him of his rights under *Miranda*, police asked, "Where's the gun?" and only then advised him of his rights. The Court by votes of 5-4 and 6-3 held that the police acted appropriately to protect the public safety and that the suspect's answer to the question of the gun's whereabouts, and any evidence that answer produced, could be used against him.[65] Rehnquist wrote the Court's opinion.

Justice Sandra Day O'Connor, then a junior member of the Court, wrote a dissenting opinion that attracted considerable attention. Demonstrating the degree to which *Miranda* had become an established part of U.S. law, O'Connor refused to agree with the majority that this public safety exception should be permitted. "Were the Court writing from a clean slate, I could agree," she wrote. "But *Miranda* is now the law ... and the Court has not provided sufficient justification for blurring its now clear strictures."[66] Also in 1984, the Court ruled that an initial unwarned admission of guilt—given voluntarily in a non-coercive environment—does not so taint any subsequent confession as to bar its use in a trial.[67] In 1990 the Court ruled 8-1 that videotaped sobriety tests can be used as evidence against a suspect even if he has not been warned of his rights before the test is administered. The Court said police may videotape people answering routine "booking" questions, including name, address, and date of birth, without first telling them they have a right to remain silent. The majority said their replies were physical evidence, comparable to blood or a handwriting sample, not evidence that is "testimonial."[68]

The Court has been asked on numerous occasions to define what action by a suspect constitutes assertion of his rights to counsel and to silence and what limits such action places on police. In 1975 the Court ruled that, although a suspect's assertion of his right to silence must terminate police interrogation of him about one crime, it does not foreclose subsequent police efforts, after an interval and a second warning of his rights, to question him about another crime.[69] Fifteen years later, in 1990, the Court said again that once a suspect has invoked his right to counsel, police may not resume questioning about the crime of which he is suspected until his lawyer is present,

even if the suspect has consulted with counsel in the meantime. The Court affirmed and extended the rule, established in *Edwards v. Arizona* (1981), requiring the police to stop interrogation after the accused asks for a lawyer.[70] In 1994, however, the Court held 5-4 that police need not stop questioning unless a suspect makes "an unambiguous or unequivocal request for counsel."[71] If the suspect makes an ambiguous statement, one that is not clearly a request for counsel, the police are not required to ask the suspect for clarification, the majority said.

The Court had held earlier that a juvenile suspect's request to see his probation officer is not an assertion of his Fifth Amendment privilege against self-incrimination, requiring police to cease questioning him, and that a probationer does not need *Miranda* warnings before being asked about crimes by his probation officer.[72] Mental illness, the Court has held, 7-2, does not necessarily disable someone from voluntarily and intelligently waiving his constitutional rights to silence and the aid of an attorney.[73]

Miranda Upheld

William H. Rehnquist had been a critic of the *Miranda* ruling and its required warnings throughout his career on the Supreme Court. He believed that while the Fifth Amendment prohibited the use of "compelled" testimony from a defendant, it did not forbid the police from seeking to obtain a voluntary confession from a crime suspect. In spring 2002, when the Court had an opportunity to overrule *Miranda*, Chief Justice Rehnquist, in dramatic fashion, announced the ruling affirming *Miranda* and its requiring warnings. He said that over the previous decades—and thanks to countless TV police dramas—most Americans had come to accept these warnings as a fundamental part of the law. "*Miranda* has become embedded in routine police practice to the point where the warnings have become part of our national culture," the chief justice said in *Dickerson v. United States* (2000). "We decline to overrule *Miranda*."[74] Rehnquist had a second reason for his seeming about-face: He did not believe that Congress could overturn a constitutional ruling of the Supreme Court, and that was the issue posed by the case of Charles Dickerson.

An alleged accomplice in a bank robbery, Dickerson had discussed the robbery with an FBI agent who had come to his house but did not warn him of his rights as required by *Miranda*. Because of the agent's lapse, a federal judge said that Dickerson's statements could not be used against him in court. The Justice Department appealed the issue to the U.S. Court of Appeals in Richmond, Virginia, citing a 1968 law passed by Congress stating that in any federal criminal case, a "confession … shall be admissible in evidence if it is voluntarily given." This law had been enacted shortly after the *Miranda* ruling and was intended to overturn it for federal cases, but it had gone essentially unused by the Justice Department until Dickerson's case. By the standard of the 1968 law, Dickerson's admissions could be used against him, because he had spoken voluntarily to the agent. In a 2-1 vote, the appeals court agreed with the Justice Department and held that the 1968 law essentially overruled the Court's *Miranda* decision.

In *Dickerson*, Rehnquist spoke for a 7-2 majority voiding the 1968 law and upholding what he called *Miranda*'s "core ruling that unwarned statements may not be used as evidence in the prosecution's case in brief.… Congress may not legislatively supersede decisions interpreting and applying the Constitution," he added.[75] In dissent, Justice Scalia accused his colleagues of glossing over the main issue: Does police questioning without *Miranda* warnings "violate the Constitution of the United States?" Rehnquist and his colleagues "cannot say that [it does], because a majority of the Court does not believe it," Scalia wrote.[76] Further, he stated, the *Dickerson* decision stands for the proposition "that this Court has the power, not merely to apply the Constitution, but to expand it, imposing what it regards as useful 'prophylactic' restrictions upon Congress and the States. That is an immense and frightening antidemocratic power, and it does not exist."[77] Justice Thomas joined Scalia's dissent.

Despite the dramatic decision in *Dickerson*, the dispute over *Miranda* continued. Scalia and Thomas insisted that the "right to remain silent" was not a true constitutional right; their view won a majority in a civil case involving a California man who was shot by the police and then pressed by a patrol supervisor to admit that he had prompted the shooting. Oliverio Martinez, a farm worker, had been riding a creaky bike at night in Oxnard, California, when two officers on patrol stopped him while looking for drug dealers. A fight ensued, and Martinez was shot six times, leaving him blind and paralyzed. Ben Chavez, a patrol supervisor, arrived and climbed into the ambulance with Martinez. While the badly injured man awaited treatment, Chavez can be heard on a tape recording pressing Martinez to admit that he had grabbed the officer's gun. "I'm dying!" Martinez is heard to scream. The questioning continued for forty-five minutes.

Martinez later sued Chavez and the Oxnard Police Department, alleging that they had violated his rights through coercive interrogation and tortuous treatment. In *Chavez v. Martinez* (2003), a fractured Court ruled that the officer's persistent questioning in the ambulance and at the hospital did not violate the Fifth Amendment because the paralyzed man was not charged with a crime.[78] "We conclude that Chavez did not deprive Martinez of a constitutional right," Thomas said, joined by Chief Justice Rehnquist and Justices O'Connor and Scalia. Souter concurred. Kennedy disagreed with this analysis. "In my view the Self-Incrimination Clause is applicable at the time and place police use compulsion to extract a statement from a subject," he wrote. He also joined Justices Stevens, Ginsburg, Breyer, and Souter to rule that Martinez could sue Chavez under the Fourteenth Amendment for engaging in official action that "shocks the conscience."

In 2004 the Court ruled that the police cannot evade the *Miranda* ruling by questioning suspects first and giving them their warnings after they have confessed. On the same day, however, the Court ruled that officers may use physical evidence they discover through questioning a suspect without giving him the required warnings. Both decisions came on a 5-4 votes, with Kennedy alone in both majorities. He stressed that the Fifth Amendment protects against "admitting into trial an accused's coerced incriminating statements," not physical evidence that he voluntarily reveals.

In the 1990s, some police departments instructed officers to question suspects about a crime. If they obtained a confession, the officers could then warn the suspect of his rights and have him sign a waiver. The Court called a halt to this practice in *Missouri v. Seibert* (2004).[79] Justice Souter said the "*Miranda* warnings" were ineffective and meaningless if they were given after a police interrogation. "We hold that a statement repeated after a warning in such circumstances is inadmissible," he wrote. Justices Stevens, Ginsburg, Breyer, and Kennedy agreed.

Patrice Seibert had been suspected of allowing her disabled son and a mentally ill boy to die in a house fire. An officer awakened her at 3:00 a.m. and took her to a police station in Rolla, Missouri, for questioning. The officer was told not to give her *Miranda* warnings. After Seibert admitted that she knew that other teenagers had set the fire, an officer took a short break. He then gave her the *Miranda* warnings and asked her to repeat what she had said. The Court ruled that her subsequent statement could not be used against her.

In *United States v. Patane* (2004), the Court said that police and prosecutors could use as evidence a Glock pistol that they had found by questioning a suspect.[80] Samuel Patane had been arrested for harassing a girlfriend. He was released on bond, but later violated a restraining order by calling her. Officers in Colorado Springs, Colorado, joined by an agent of the federal Bureau of Alcohol, Tobacco, and Firearms, went to Patane's residence, knowing that he had a pistol. At the door, as the officer was giving him *Miranda* warnings, Patane stopped him. "Where's the Glock?" the officer asked. Patane said that it was in the bedroom. He was later convicted of gun possession by a felon, but he appealed, alleging that the use of the gun as evidence violated the *Miranda* rule. The Court disagreed. "The *Miranda* rule protects against violations of the Self-Incrimination Clause, which, in turn, is not implicated by the introduction at trial of physical evidence resulting from voluntary statements," Thomas said.

The Aid of Legal Counsel

"In all criminal prosecutions," the Sixth Amendment stipulates, "the accused shall enjoy the right ... to have the assistance of counsel for his defense." Despite this unambiguous language, only persons charged with federal crimes punishable by death have been guaranteed this right throughout American history.[1] The right of all other defendants, federal and state, to the aid of an attorney traditionally depended upon their ability to hire and pay their own lawyer. Beginning in the 1930s, however, the Supreme Court vastly enlarged the class of persons who have the right to legal counsel—appointed and paid by the state if necessary—in preparing and presenting a defense. In 1932 the Court declared this right so fundamental that the Fourteenth Amendment's Due Process Clause required states to provide the effective aid of counsel to all defendants charged with capital crimes.[2] Six years later, the Court held that the Sixth Amendment required that all federal defendants be provided an attorney.[3] This expansion of the Sixth Amendment right to counsel continued during the 1960s and 1970s, when the Court ruled that the amendment guaranteed the aid of an attorney to all state defendants charged with crimes that could be considered serious. In the 1980s, the Court further expanded the right to include a guarantee that indigents defending themselves with a claim of insanity are entitled to the aid of a court-appointed and publicly paid psychiatrist.[4]

A FUNDAMENTAL RIGHT

The Court's first modern ruling on the right to counsel came in the first Scottsboro Boys case—*Powell v. Alabama* (1932). Nine young illiterate black teenagers were charged with the rape of two white girls on a freight train passing through Tennessee and Alabama. Their trial was held in Scottsboro, Alabama, where community hostility toward the defendants was intense. The trial judge appointed all the members of the local bar to serve as defense counsel, but when the trial began no attorney appeared to represent the defendants. The judge, on the morning of the

trial, appointed a local lawyer who undertook the task with reluctance. The defendants were convicted. They challenged their convictions, arguing that they were effectively denied aid of counsel because they did not have the opportunity to consult with their lawyer and prepare a defense. The Supreme Court agreed, 7-2. Writing for the Court, Justice George Sutherland explained:

> It is hardly necessary to say that the right to counsel being conceded, a defendant should be afforded a fair opportunity to secure counsel of his own choice. Not only was that not done here, but such designation of counsel as was attempted was either so indefinite or so close upon the trial as to amount to a denial of effective and substantial aid.[5]

The action of the judge in appointing all members of the local bar as defense counsel was "little more than an expansive gesture" that resulted in no aid to the defendants in the critical pretrial period, the Court said.[6] In *Twining v. New Jersey* (1908), the Court had acknowledged that some of the rights guaranteed in the Bill of Rights might be so fundamental that a denial of them by a state would be a denial of due process. Citing *Twining*, the Court declared that "the right to the aid of counsel is of this fundamental character."[7] *(See details of Twining v. New Jersey, pp. 264–265.)*

In *Powell v. Alabama*, the Court leaned heavily upon the circumstances of the case and the characteristics of the defendants in finding the denial of effective aid of counsel a denial of due process. Wrote Sutherland,

> In the light of the facts ... the ignorance and illiteracy of the defendants, their youth, the circumstances of public hostility, the imprisonment and the close surveillance of the defendants by the military forces, the fact that their friends and families were all in other states and communication with them necessarily difficult, and above all that they stood in deadly peril of their lives—we think the failure of the trial court to give them reasonable time and opportunity to secure counsel was a clear denial of due process.

But ... assuming their inability, even if opportunity had been given, to employ counsel, as the trial court evidently did assume, we are of opinion that, under the circumstances just stated, the necessity of counsel was so vital and imperative that the failure of the trial court to make an effective appointment of counsel was likewise a denial of due process within the meaning of the Fourteenth Amendment. Whether this would be so in other criminal prosecutions, or under other circumstances, we need not determine. All that it is necessary now to decide, as we do decide, is that in a capital case, where the defendant is unable to employ counsel, and is incapable adequately of making his own defense because of ignorance, feeblemindedness, illiteracy or the like, it is the duty of the court, whether requested or not, to assign counsel for him as a necessary requisite of due process of law; and that duty is not discharged by an assignment at such a time or under such circumstances as to preclude the giving of effective aid in the preparation and trial of the case.[8]

Since 1790 federal law implementing the Sixth Amendment guarantee has required that persons charged with capital crimes in federal courts be provided an attorney.[9] Close to a century and a half later, the Court held that the Sixth Amendment required this assurance for *all* federal defendants in *Johnson v. Zerbst* (1938).[10] In this case, John Johnson, a marine, was charged with passing counterfeit money. He was tried and convicted in civil court without the aid of an attorney to act in his defense. He challenged his conviction as obtained in violation of his constitutional rights. The Supreme Court found his argument persuasive and upheld his claim. Justice Hugo L. Black spoke for a majority of the Court:

The Sixth Amendment ... embodies a realistic recognition of the obvious truth that the average defendant does not have the professional legal skill to protect himself when brought before a tribunal with power to take his life or liberty, wherein the prosecution is presented by experienced and learned counsel. That which is simple, orderly and necessary to the lawyer—to the untrained laymen ... may appear intricate, complex, and mysterious....

... The Sixth Amendment withholds from federal courts, in all criminal proceedings, the power

and authority to deprive an accused of his life or liberty unless he has or waives the assistance of counsel....

... While an accused may waive the right to counsel, whether there is a proper waiver should be clearly determined by the trial court....

Since the Sixth Amendment constitutionally entitles one charged with crime to the assistance of counsel, compliance with this constitutional mandate is an essential jurisdictional prerequisite to a federal court's authority to deprive an accused of his life or liberty [unless the right has been properly waived].... If the accused, however, is not represented by counsel and has not competently and intelligently waived his constitutional right, the Sixth Amendment stands as a jurisdictional bar to a valid conviction and sentence depriving him of his life or his liberty.[11]

THE APPOINTMENT OF COUNSEL

Johnson v. Zerbst, with its emphatic declaration of the right of federal defendants to have an attorney, provided no aid to state defendants, and for thirty years after *Powell v. Alabama*, the Court refused to rule that the Sixth Amendment, in addition to the general due process guarantee of the Fourteenth Amendment, extended the right to legal counsel to state defendants. The primary effect of this judicial posture was to withhold the aid of counsel from indigent state defendants charged with noncapital crimes. The Court first declared in *Betts v. Brady* (1942) that "appointment of counsel is not a fundamental right" for such state defendants.[12] The due process guarantee of the Fourteenth Amendment, held the Court, did not require states to appoint counsel in every criminal case where it was requested by the defendant. A state legislature, however, might choose to write such a requirement into state law, the Court added. The vote was 6-3. Justice Owen J. Roberts declared for the majority,

The Sixth Amendment of the national Constitution applies only to trials in federal courts. The due process clause of the Fourteenth Amendment does not incorporate, as such, the specific guarantees found in the Sixth Amendment although a denial by a state of rights or privileges specifically embodied in that and

"GUIDING HAND"

A classic description of the "guiding hand" of an attorney at trial came in the landmark decision in *Powell v. Alabama* (1932), the first of the Scottsboro Boys cases. Writing for the Court, Justice George Sutherland discussed the basic requirements of due process and the importance, to the defendant, of the aid of counsel:

> It has never been doubted by this court, or any other so far as we know, that notice and hearing are preliminary steps essential to the passing of an enforceable judgment, and that they, together with a legally competent tribunal having jurisdiction of the case, constitute basic elements of the constitutional requirement of due process....
>
> What, then, does a hearing include? Historically and in practice, in our own country at least, it has always included the right to the aid of counsel when desired and provided by the party asserting the right. The right to be heard would be, in many cases, of little avail if it did not comprehend the right to be heard by counsel. Even the intelligent and educated layman has small and sometimes no skill in the science of law. If charged with crime, he is incapable, generally, of determining for himself whether the indictment is good or bad. He is unfamiliar with the rules of evidence. Left without the aid of counsel he may be put on trial without a proper charge, and convicted upon incompetent evidence, or evidence irrelevant to the issue or otherwise inadmissible. He lacks both the skill and knowledge adequately to prepare his defense, even though he have a perfect one. He requires the guiding hand of counsel at every step in the proceedings against him. Without it, though he be not guilty, he faces the danger of conviction because he does not know how to establish his innocence. If that be true of men of intelligence, how much more true is it of the ignorant and illiterate, or those of feeble intellect. If in any case, civil or criminal, a state or federal court were arbitrarily to refuse to hear a party by counsel, employed by and appearing for him, it reasonably may not be doubted that such a refusal would be a denial of a hearing, and, therefore, of due process in the constitutional sense.[1]

---

1. *Powell v. Alabama*, 287 U.S. 45 at 68–69 (1932).

---

others of the first eight amendments may, in certain circumstances, or in connection with other elements, operate, in a given case, to deprive a litigant of due process of law in violation of the Fourteenth. Due process of law is secured against invasion by the federal Government by the Fifth Amendment and is safeguarded against state action in identical words by the Fourteenth. The phrase formulates a concept less rigid and more fluid than those envisaged in other specific and particular provisions of the Bill of Rights. Its application is less a matter of rule. Asserted denial is to be tested by an appraisal of the totality of facts in a given case. That which may, in one setting, constitute a denial of fundamental fairness, shocking to the universal sense of justice, may, in other circumstances, and in the light of other considerations, fall short of such denial.[13]

Justice Roberts acknowledged that *Johnson v. Zerbst* raised the issue of "whether the constraint laid by the [Sixth] amendment upon the national courts expresses a rule so fundamental and essential to a fair trial, and so, to due process of law, that it is made obligatory upon the States by the Fourteenth Amendment."[14] The Court thought not. Roberts wrote that Smith Betts—unlike Ozie Powell of the Scottsboro case—was a man of forty-three years and "of ordinary intelligence and ability." He was not so handicapped by lack of counsel that he was denied the fundamental fairness promised by the Due Process Clause. Thus, concluded the Court, while "the Fourteenth Amendment prohibits the conviction and incarceration of one whose trial is offensive to the common and fundamental ideas of fairness and right, and while want of counsel in a particular case may result in a conviction lacking in such fundamental fairness, we cannot say that the amendment embodies an inexorable command that no trial for any offense, or in any court, can be fairly conducted and justice accorded a defendant who is not represented by counsel."[15]

Justice Black, joined by Justices Frank Murphy and William O. Douglas in dissent, urged that the same rule apply in state as in federal courts:

The plight of the nine "Scottsboro boys," arrested in rural Alabama in 1931 for allegedly raping two white females, spawned numerous legal actions including *Powell v. Alabama* (1932), which expanded the rights of indigents to legal representation. Samuel Leibowitz, a prominent attorney and later a judge, handled the defendants' cases after their original conviction. He is shown here conferring with his clients.

A practice cannot be reconciled with "common and fundamental ideas of fairness and right," which subjects innocent men to increased dangers of conviction merely because of their poverty....

Denial to the poor of the request for counsel in proceedings based on charges of serious crime has long been regarded as shocking to the "universal sense of justice" throughout this country.[16]

Under *Betts* then, the Court considered the special circumstances of each case to determine if denial of counsel denied the defendant fair treatment. The Court upheld some state convictions that challenged due to lack of counsel, but in most cases it found circumstances that warranted reversal. Among those were the conduct of the trial judge or the youth, ignorance, or lack of legal sophistication of the defendants.[17] In the landmark *Gideon v. Wainwright* (1963), the Supreme Court would unanimously discard this case-by-case approach, overruling *Betts v. Brady* to hold that the right to the assistance of counsel was so fundamental that the Fourteenth Amendment's Due Process Clause extended the Sixth Amendment guarantee to state defendants.[18] States would thereafter be required to provide counsel for all defendants charged with felonies and unable to pay a lawyer.

Clarence Earl Gideon, an indigent, was tried and convicted in a Florida state court of a felony—breaking and entering a poolroom to commit a misdemeanor. He requested but was denied a court-appointed attorney. The judge based his refusal on the fact that Gideon's offense—unlike that in *Powell*—was not a capital crime. Gideon conducted his own defense. Convicted and sentenced to spend five years in prison, Gideon prepared his own petitions asking a federal court to declare his conviction invalid, because it was obtained in violation of his constitutional right to counsel, and to order his release. The Supreme Court agreed to hear Gideon's case and appointed a well-known Washington attorney, Abe Fortas, to argue on his behalf. The Court also requested that both sides in the case argue an additional question: Should *Betts v. Brady* be reconsidered?

The Court's opinion in *Gideon*, reconsidering and reversing *Betts v. Brady*, was written by Justice Black, who had dissented from *Betts*. Looking back to *Powell*, in which the Court had described the right to counsel as fundamental to a fair trial, Black wrote,

The fact is that the Court in *Betts v. Brady* made an abrupt break with its own well-considered precedents. In returning to these old precedents, sounder we believe than the new, we but restore constitutional principles established to achieve a fair system of justice. Not only these precedents but also reason and reflection require us to recognize that in our adversary system of criminal justice, any person haled into court, who is too poor to hire a lawyer, cannot be assured a fair trial unless counsel is provided for him. This seems to us to be an obvious truth.... Lawyers to prosecute are everywhere deemed essential to protect the public's interest in an orderly society....

That government hires lawyers to prosecute and defendants who have the money hire lawyers to

Clarence Earl Gideon *(right),* a penniless convict who had not been able to afford a defense attorney, sent a handwritten petition *(left)* from prison to the Supreme Court to hear his case. The Supreme Court granted his petition, heard his case, and ruled unanimously in 1963 that every state must provide counsel to an indigent charged with a felony.

defend are the strongest indications of the widespread belief that lawyers in criminal courts are necessities, not luxuries.[19]

"Adequate Protective Device"

A year after *Gideon,* the Supreme Court further tightened the requirement that states observe the right to counsel. With the controversial ruling in *Escobedo v. Illinois* (1964), the justices linked that right to the Fifth Amendment privilege against self-incrimination. In *Escobedo,* a divided Court held that a suspect in custody had an absolute right to the aid of an attorney during police interrogation.[20] *(See details of Escobedo v. Illinois, pp. 321–322.)* With its decision in *Miranda v. Arizona*

(1966), the Court declared the presence of counsel "the adequate protective device necessary to make the process of police interrogation conform to the dictates of the [Fifth Amendment] privilege."[21] "Accordingly," wrote Chief Justice Earl Warren, "we hold that an individual held for interrogation must be clearly informed that he has the right to consult with a lawyer and to have the lawyer with him during interrogation."[22] Six years later, the Court held that the right to counsel applied not only to state defendants charged with felonies but in all trials of persons for offenses serious enough to warrant a jail sentence. Speaking for the unanimous Court in *Argersinger v. Hamlin* (1972), Justice Douglas looked back to *Powell* and *Gideon:*

THE RIGHT TO REFUSE COUNSEL

Defendants have a right to a lawyer to assist them, but they do not have to accept the offer. In a case that seemed to turn inside-out the series of rulings expanding the right to an attorney, the Supreme Court in the mid-1970s held that defendants also have the right to *refuse* legal assistance. In *Faretta v. California* (1975), the Court ruled that individuals have the right to conduct their own defense and to reject counsel who have been appointed to represent them.

Justice Potter Stewart said that the right to self-representation had been recognized by the federal government and many states. He acknowledged that declaring it a constitutional right seemed "to cut against the grain of this court's decisions holding that the Constitution requires that no accused can be convicted and imprisoned unless he has been accorded the right to the assistance of counsel." Stewart noted, however, that "it is one thing to hold that every defendant, rich or poor, has the right to the assistance of counsel, and quite another to say that a state may compel a defendant to accept a lawyer he does not *want*."[1] The dissenters foresaw problems ahead. Justice Harry A. Blackmun, in one dissent, commented, "If there is any truth to the old proverb 'One who is his own lawyer has a fool for a client', the Court by its opinion today now bestows a constitutional right on one to make a fool of himself."[2]

This right to "go it alone" does not extend to appeals. A trial poses a factual question: Did the defendant commit the crime? By contrast, an appeal is purely a dispute over the law, and it can be handled only by a trained lawyer, the Court ruled in *Martinez v. Court of Appeals of California* (2000).[3] The right to self-representation has other limits as well. In 2008 the Court ruled that defendants who are not "mentally competent" may be denied the right to represent themselves. Ahmad Edwards, who suffers from schizophrenia, tried to steal a pair of shoes and shot at a store guard who had tried to stop him. After several years of treatment, he was judged competent to stand trial. He insisted on representing himself, but the judge refused. The Court affirmed that decision in *Indiana v. Edwards* (2008). "The Constitution permits judges to take realistic account of the particular defendant's mental capacities by asking whether a defendant who seeks to conduct his own defense at trial is mentally competent to do so," said Justice Stephen J. Breyer. (Ftn. 3) Justices Antonin Scalia and Clarence Thomas dissented, saying "the defendant's right to make his own case before the jury" cannot be taken away.[4]

---

1. *Faretta v. California*, 422 U.S. 806 at 832–833 (1975).

2. Id. at 853.

3. *Martinez v. Court of Appeals of California*, 528 U.S. 152 (2000).

4. *Indiana v. Edwards*, 544 U.S. ___ (2008).

Both *Powell* and *Gideon* involved felonies. But their rationale has relevance to any criminal trial, where an accused is deprived of liberty. *Powell* and *Gideon* suggest that there are certain fundamental rights applicable to all such criminal prosecutions....

The requirement of counsel may well be necessary for a fair trial even in a petty offense prosecution. We are by no means convinced that legal and constitutional questions involved in a case that actually leads to imprisonment even for a brief period are any less complex than when a person can be sent off for six months or more....

Under the rule we announce today, every judge will know when the trial of a misdemeanor starts that no imprisonment may be imposed, even though local law permits it, unless the accused is represented by counsel.[23]

Thirty years later, the Court went a step further and ruled that states must provide lawyers for indigent defendants who may only receive a suspended sentence or probation. Although convicted of a minor offense, such persons could later be sent to jail if they violate the terms of probation. Whenever a defendant "may" face jail time for a conviction, he "is entitled to appointed counsel at the critical stage when his guilt or innocence of the charged crimes is decided and his vulnerability to imprisonment is determined," said Justice Ruth Bader Ginsburg for a 5-4 majority in *Alabama v. Shelton* (2002).[24] In dissent, Justice Antonin Scalia faulted the majority for imposing a costly new burden on states to provide lawyers for untold numbers of petty cases. Chief Justice Rehnquist along with Justices Anthony M. Kennedy and Clarence Thomas joined in dissent.

"Critical Stage"

In *Powell v. Alabama* (1932), the Court indicated the importance of timing in the provision of legal assistance to a defendant, describing the period between arrest and trial as a critical one in the preparation of a defense.[25] Many subsequent rulings on the right to counsel have contributed to defining the "critical stage" at which the right applies—the time counsel must be made available if requested by the suspect or defendant. In *Hamilton v. Alabama* (1961), the Court held that arraignment was such a critical stage, at least in some states.[26] Later, *Escobedo* and *Miranda* emphatically held that the right applied once a suspect was in custody and subject to interrogation.[27] In *United States v. Wade* (1967)—and its state counterpart, *Gilbert v. California*—the Court held that police lineups also were such a critical stage.[28] In this case, the Court declared inadmissible any in-court identification of defendants based on pretrial lineups conducted in the absence of the defendant's attorney. Justice William J. Brennan Jr., writing for a unanimous Court in *Wade*, observed,

> [T]he principle of *Powell v. Alabama* and succeeding cases requires that we scrutinize any pretrial confrontation of the accused to determine whether the presence of his counsel is necessary to preserve the defendant's basic right to a fair trial as affected by his right meaningfully to cross-examine the witnesses against him and to have effective assistance of counsel at the trial itself.[29]

In *Gilbert*, the Court applied the same rule to state proceedings.

Wade was undercut by Congress in the Crime Control and Safe Streets Act of 1968, which included a provision allowing the use of such lineup identification evidence at trial in federal courts, even if obtained in the absence of counsel. A few years later, the Court further limited the effect of *Wade* and *Gilbert*. The defendants in those cases had already been indicted when they were placed in the lineup. In *Kirby v. Illinois* (1972), the Court ruled that the right to counsel did not apply to persons in such lineups who had not yet been indicted. The right did not take effect, the Court held, until "formal prosecutorial proceedings" were under way.[30] Justice Potter Stewart explained:

> The initiation of judicial criminal proceedings is far from a mere formalism. It is the starting point of our whole system of adversary criminal justice. For it is only then that the Government has committed itself to prosecute and only then that the adverse positions of Government and defendant have solidified. It is then that a defendant finds himself faced with the prosecutorial forces of organized society, and immersed in the intricacies of substantive and procedural criminal law. It is this point, therefore, that marks the commencement of the "criminal prosecutions" to which alone the explicit guarantees of the Sixth Amendment are applicable.[31]

The principle of *Wade* and *Gilbert* was further eroded in 1973 when the Court held that it was not necessary for a defendant's attorney to be present at a postindictment photographic identification session with potential witnesses.[32]

At the other end of the criminal justice process—appeal of conviction—the Court in the 1970s called a halt to the gradual extension of the right to appointed counsel. In *Ross v. Moffit* (1974), the justices held that the state's constitutional obligation to provide appointed counsel for indigents appealing their convictions did not extend past the point where their right to appeal had been effectively exhausted.[33] The Court in 2001 gave police additional leeway to question a criminal defendant without a lawyer present when the interrogation concerns charges different from those already being prosecuted.[34]

"Effective" Aid

As the Court made clear in *Powell v. Alabama*, the effective aid of counsel means more than the mere physical presence of an attorney at trial. In *Powell* the Court held that the judge's gesture of appointing the entire local bar as defense counsel—and the failure of any particular individuals to assume that role before trial—had deprived the defendants of the *effective* aid of counsel. Other factors can deprive defendants of the sort of legal representation to which the Sixth Amendment or due process generally entitles them. Conflict of interest is one.

In *Glasser v. United States* (1942), the Court found that a judge had denied two defendants the effective aid of counsel by requiring a single attorney to represent them both.[35] The majority declared,

> Upon the trial judge rests the duty of seeing that the trial is conducted with solicitude for the essential rights of the accused.... Of equal importance with the duty of the court to see that an accused has the assistance of counsel is its duty to refrain from embarrassing counsel in the defense of an accused by insisting, or indeed, even suggesting, that counsel undertake to concurrently represent interests which might diverge from those of his first client, when the possibility of that divergence is brought home to the court.[36]

The Court elaborated on this point, stating in *Holloway v. Arkansas* (1978),

> Joint representation of conflicting interests is suspect because of what it tends to prevent the attorney from doing.... Generally speaking, a conflict may ... prevent an attorney from challenging the admission of evidence prejudicial to one client but perhaps favorable to another, or from arguing at the sentencing hearing the relative involvement and culpability of his clients in order to minimize the culpability of one by emphasizing that of another.... The mere physical presence of an attorney does not fulfill the Sixth Amendment guarantee when the advocate's conflicting obligations has [*sic*] effectively sealed his lips on crucial matters.[37]

Competence of counsel, however, is more difficult to challenge. The Court in the 1970s rejected the argument of several persons that their convictions, based on guilty pleas, were the result of advice from incompetent counsel. The Court declared that defendants must assume a certain degree of risk that their attorneys might make some "ordinary error" in assessing the facts of their case and the law that applies, and that such error was not a basis for reversing a conviction.[38]

Ineffective Assistance by Counsel

In the 1980s, the Supreme Court for the first time set out a standard for use in reviewing a defendant's claim that he had been denied the effective aid of an attorney.

Justice Sandra Day O'Connor, who had been a trial judge in Arizona prior to her appointment to the Court, wrote the opinion in *Strickland v. Washington* (1984). "The benchmark for judging any claim of ineffectiveness," wrote O'Connor, "must be whether counsel's conduct so undermined the proper functioning of the adversarial process that the trial cannot be relied on as having produced a just result." She explained that to win reversal of a conviction or invalidation of a sentence, a defendant must show that his attorney made errors so serious at trial that they resulted in his being denied a fair trial. The proper standard, O'Connor continued, is "reasonably effective assistance." The lawyer, she said, deserves the benefit of the doubt. "Judicial scrutiny of counsel's performance must be highly deferential.... Because of the difficulties inherent in making the evaluation, a court must indulge a strong presumption that counsel's conduct falls within the wide range of reasonable professional assistance."[39]

The Court applied that standard to another case decided the same day. In *United States v. Cronic* (1984), it unanimously held that an appeals court was wrong to infer that a defendant was denied the right to counsel because the appointed counsel lacked criminal law experience and was given only a brief time to prepare for trial. Such a conclusion, wrote Justice John Paul Stevens, must be supported by evidence of serious errors by the lawyer so prejudicial that the defendant was denied a fair trial.[40] The following year, the Court for the first time found a case in which this standard worked to prove the defendant's claim. In *Evitts v. Lucey* (1985), the Court held that an attorney's failure to file a statement of appeal by the legal deadline constituted evidence that he was not providing his client the effective aid of counsel.[41]

In *Roe, Warden v. Flores-Ortega* (2000), the Court adopted a case-by-case approach to evaluate whether a court-appointed lawyer's failure to file an appeal for an indigent defendant violated the defendant's right to effective assistance of counsel. By a 6-3 vote, the Court said the per se rule was "inconsistent" with its ruling in *Strickland v. Washington* (1984), requiring a case-by-case evaluation of ineffective assistance of counsel claims. "We cannot say, as a *constitutional* matter, that in every case counsel's failure to consult with the defendant about an appeal is necessarily unreasonable, and therefore deficient," Justice O'Connor wrote.[42] Nonetheless, O'Connor said that lawyers would have such a duty "in the vast majority of cases." She added that a defendant would be entitled to a new chance to file an appeal if he showed that "but for counsel's deficient conduct, he would have appealed."[43]

In 2002 the Court held that a defendant's right to fair representation is not violated simply because his lawyer was shown to have a conflict of interest. In the case of Walter Mickens, a Virginia inmate facing execution, it was revealed that his trial lawyer had been assigned briefly to represent the young man that Mickens was convicted of murdering. In a 5-4 decision, the Court ruled that there was no evidence that this potential conflict affected the attorney's performance and therefore a reversal of the conviction was not required. Shortly after the ruling, Mickens was executed.[44]

Death Row Inmates and Incompetent Lawyers

The issue of incompetent lawyering often arises in the cases of state inmates on death row. Their appeals sometimes assert that they would not have been convicted had their lawyer fully investigated the crime or that the jury would not have sentenced them to death had their lawyer presented all the evidence that called for leniency. Both Congress and the Court have, however, made it harder for inmates to win a belated hearing on such claims before a federal judge.

The Antiterrorism and Effective Death Penalty Act of 1996 set new and stricter standards for filing a writ of habeas corpus, which is the means by which state prisoners appeal to a federal court. Inmates who lost a final state appeal were given one year to file a writ of habeas corpus in federal court. This limit was intended to prevent inmates from delaying for years as their execution date approached. In addition, the law said that a habeas appeal "shall not be granted" except when the state court's decision has "resulted in a decision that was contrary to, or involved an unreasonable application of, clearly established Federal law, as determined by the Supreme Court of the United States." Sponsors of the law said they wanted to prevent state inmates from having a second chance to litigate the same claims in a federal court. The law also carried a message for federal judges: Do not second-guess rulings of the state courts unless they are clearly wrong.

The Supreme Court enforced the hands-off message by reversing federal judges who were too quick to intervene. For example, the Ninth Circuit Court of Appeals reversed the California death sentence meted out to John Visciotti, who had robbed and shot two co-workers on payday in a scheme to steal their money. One survived and testified against the shooter. Nearly fifteen years after the crime, the federal appellate judges ruled that his trial lawyer had acted unreasonably because he had not told the sentencing jury about Visciotti's "dysfunctional family" and possible brain damage.

In *Woodford v. Visciotti* (2002), the Court reversed that ruling in a short, unsigned opinion, stating that the writ of habeas corpus should not have been granted. The California court rulings that had upheld the death sentence were not "contrary to" or "an unreasonable application" of the standard set in *Strickland v. Washington* (1984), because there was no reason to believe the jury would have changed its verdict if it had known about Visciotti's troubled family.[45] "The federal habeas scheme leaves primary responsibility with state courts for these judgments, and authorizes federal-court intervention only when a state-court decision is objectively unreasonable. It is not that here," the justices said.[46]

The Court, however, continued to insist that trial lawyers in death penalty cases have a duty to investigate their client's background, and a total failure to present a true picture of the defendant's difficult upbringing might be grounds for overturning a death sentence. Kevin Wiggins, a yard worker at a Baltimore area apartment building who had no criminal record, was convicted of drowning a seventy-seven-year-old woman in her bathtub. Police found no evidence that Wiggins had entered the apartment, but he and his girlfriend were found in possession of the victim's car and some of her belongings. His two public defenders devoted their efforts to proving their client's innocence, but neither looked into his background, which included an alcoholic mother, sexual abuse, and borderline mental retardation.

Wiggins was convicted and sentenced to death, but the Court reversed his death sentence in *Wiggins v. Maryland* (2003).[47] "Counsel did not conduct a reasonable investigation" in this case, said Justice Sandra Day O'Connor, the author of the *Strickland* standard. "Any reasonably competent attorney" would know that the abuse Wiggins had suffered, coupled with his otherwise clean record, probably would have persuaded the jury to sentence him to prison, not to death, she said for a 7-2 majority. Therefore, the Maryland courts made an "unreasonable application" of the *Strickland* standard, and the federal courts were justified in granting his writ of habeas corpus and overturning his death sentence.

Double Jeopardy

To restrain the government from repeated prosecutions of an individual for one particular offense, the prohibition against double jeopardy was included in the Fifth Amendment: "nor shall any person be subject for the same offense to be twice put in jeopardy of life or limb." The Supreme Court has held that this guarantee protects an individual against multiple prosecutions for the same offense as well as against multiple punishments for the same crime. Until the late 1960s, the Double Jeopardy Clause applied only to federal prosecutions. In that year, the Court in *Benton v. Maryland* (1969) held that the due process guarantee of the Fourteenth Amendment extended this protection to persons tried by states as well.[1]

A defendant is placed in jeopardy at the time his jury is sworn in,[2] although if a mistrial is declared under certain circumstances[3] or if the jury fails to agree on a verdict,[4] the Double Jeopardy Clause does not forbid his retrial. If he is convicted, he may waive his immunity against double jeopardy and seek a new trial, or he may appeal the verdict to a higher court. If the conviction is set aside for a reason other than insufficient evidence, he may be tried again for the same offense.[5] If he is acquitted, the Double Jeopardy Clause absolutely bars any further prosecution of him for that crime, even if the acquittal results from error.[6]

ONE TRIAL PER SOVEREIGN

The double jeopardy guarantee protects only against repeated prosecutions by a single sovereign government. Thus, it is not violated when a person is tried on state as well as federal charges arising from a single offense. Many offenses are crimes under both federal and state laws. The Court established this rule in *United States v. Lanza* (1922). In this case, Vito Lanza was convicted for violating Washington State's prohibition law. He was then indicted on the same grounds for violating the

federal prohibition law. The federal district judge dismissed his indictment as a violation of the double jeopardy guarantee. The government appealed the dismissal, and the Supreme Court reversed it, 6-3. Chief Justice William Howard Taft explained:

> We have here two sovereignties, deriving power from different sources, capable of dealing with the same subject-matter within the same territory. Each may, without interference by the other, enact laws to secure prohibition.... Each government, in determining what shall be an offense against its peace and dignity, is exercising its own sovereignty, not that of the other.
>
> It follows that an act denounced as a crime by both national and state sovereignties is an offense against the peace and dignity of both, and may be punished by each. The 5th Amendment, like all the other guaranties in the first eight amendments, applies only to proceedings by the Federal government ... and the double jeopardy therein forbidden is a second prosecution under authority of the Federal government after a first trial for the same offense under the same authority. Here the same act was an offense against the state of Washington, because a violation of its law, and also an offense against the United States under the National Prohibition Act. The defendants thus committed two different offenses by the same act, and a conviction by a court of Washington of the offense against that state is not a conviction of the different offense against the United States, and so is not double jeopardy.[7]

The *Lanza* rule survives. The Court repeatedly has reaffirmed that multiple prosecutions by different sovereigns—including two states—for the same offense does not violate the Double Jeopardy Clause.[8] Because a state and a city are not separate sovereigns, however, the double jeopardy guarantee does protect an individual against prosecution by both for one offense.[9]

The separate sovereignties doctrine was applied by the Court in *United States v. Wheeler* (1978), in which it ruled that the Double Jeopardy Clause did not protect an American Indian defendant convicted in tribal court from being tried by federal authorities for the same offense.[10] Seven years later, the Court allowed a defendant to be tried in two different states for two parts of the same crime—the murder of his wife. One state—where the murder was committed—charged him for the murder; the second—where he dumped the body—charged him for that crime. The Supreme Court, with Justice Sandra Day O'Connor writing the opinion in *Heath v. Alabama* (1985), found nothing to violate the double jeopardy guarantee.[11]

The Double Jeopardy Clause also protects an individual who successfully appeals his conviction on a lesser charge from being retried on the original charge. In *Green v. United States* (1957), the Court ruled that Everett Green—tried for first-degree murder but convicted of murder in the second degree, a verdict that he successfully appealed—could not be tried again for first-degree murder after he had won a new trial for second-degree murder on appeal. The Court said that Green had been once in jeopardy for first-degree murder and that appeal of his conviction for a different crime did not constitute a waiver of his protection against double jeopardy. The Court explained:

> The underlying idea, one that is deeply ingrained in at least the Anglo-American system of jurisprudence, is that the State with all its resources and power should not be allowed to make repeated attempts to convict an individual for an alleged offense, thereby subjecting him to embarrassment, expense and ordeal and compelling him to live in a continuing state of anxiety and insecurity, as well as enhancing the possibility that even though innocent he may be found guilty.[12]

STATE ACTION

In the often-cited decision in *Palko v. Connecticut* (1937), the Court rejected the idea that the Fourteenth Amendment Due Process Clause applies the double jeopardy guarantee to state action. Frank Palko was convicted of second-degree murder and sentenced to life imprisonment. The state sought and won a new trial claiming that legal errors had occurred at trial. At a second trial, Palko was found guilty of first-degree murder and sentenced to die. He challenged his second conviction as a violation of the double jeopardy guarantee and of due process. The Court rejected this argument, excluding the double jeopardy guarantee from the list of guarantees that had been "absorbed" into due process. That protection, Justice Benjamin N. Cardozo wrote for the majority, was not "of the very essence of a scheme of ordered liberty":[13]

> Is that kind of double jeopardy to which the statute has subjected him a hardship so acute and shocking that our polity will not endure it? Does it violate those "fundamental principles of liberty and justice which lie at the base of all our civil and political institutions?"… The answer surely must be "no."… The state is not attempting to wear the accused out by a multitude of cases with accumulated trials. It asks no more than this, that the case against him shall go on until there shall be a trial free from the corrosion of substantial legal error.… This is not cruelty at all, nor even vexation in any immoderate degree. If the trial had been infected with error adverse to the accused, there might have been review at his instance, and as often as necessary to purge the vicious taint. A reciprocal privilege, subject at all times to the discretion of the presiding judge …, has now been granted to the state. There is here no seismic innovation. The edifice of justice stands, its symmetry, to many, greater than before.[14]

Thirty-two years later, the Court overruled *Palko* by a vote of 6-2. In its last announced decision under Chief Justice Earl Warren, the Court in *Benton v. Maryland* (1969) declared that the Double Jeopardy Clause indeed applies to the states through the due process guarantee of the Fourteenth Amendment. Justice Thurgood Marshall delivered the majority opinion:

> Our recent cases have thoroughly rejected the *Palko* notion that basic constitutional rights can be denied by the States so long as the totality of the circumstances does not disclose a denial of "fundamental fairness." Once it is decided that a particular Bill of Rights guarantee is "fundamental to the American scheme of justice,"… the same constitutional standards apply against both the State and Federal Governments. *Palko*'s roots had thus been cut away years ago. We today only recognize the inevitable.[15]

Justices John Marshall Harlan and Potter Stewart dissented from this "march toward 'incorporating' much, if not all, of the Federal Bill of Rights into the Due Process Clause."[16]

RESENTENCING RESTRICTIONS

Bullington v. Missouri (1981), a case similar to *Palko*, arose after Robert Bullington was convicted of murder, for which he could have been sentenced to death. Instead, the jury sentenced him to life in prison without eligibility for parole for fifty years. Bullington won a new trial, and the state declared that it would again seek a death sentence. Bullington objected, arguing that the Double Jeopardy Clause precluded his being once again placed in jeopardy of a death sentence after a jury had already decided that he should not be executed. The Supreme Court, 5-4, agreed with him. The state should not have a second chance to try to convince a jury to sentence Bullington to death, wrote Justice Harry A. Blackmun. Once a jury had decided that he should not die for his crime, Bullington's right to be secure against double jeopardy forbade the state, even at a new trial, to seek the death penalty. Dissenting were Chief Justice Warren E. Burger and Justices Byron R. White, Lewis F. Powell Jr., and William H. Rehnquist.[17]

The same day that the Court announced its decision in *Benton*, it held in *North Carolina v. Pearce* (1969) that the double jeopardy guarantee limited the authority of a judge to impose a harsher sentence than the original upon a defendant whose first conviction had been set aside for a new trial.[18] Clifton Pearce was convicted of assault with intent to rape and sentenced to twelve to fifteen years in prison. After serving several years, he won reversal of his conviction and a new trial. Convicted in the second trial, Pearce was sentenced to eight years in prison. When this new sentence was added to the time he had already served, it amounted to a longer sentence than the original one.

Justice Stewart wrote the Court's opinion, holding that unless there were objective reasons related to the conduct of the defendant after the imposition of the first sentence, and unless those reasons were set out

in the record of the case, a judge could not impose a harsher sentence after retrial. In addition, the new sentence would be a violation of the double jeopardy guarantee unless the time already served was credited against it:

> The Court has held today, in *Benton v. Maryland* ... that the Fifth Amendment guarantee against double jeopardy is enforceable against the States through the Fourteenth Amendment. That guarantee has been said to consist of three separate constitutional protections. It protects against a second prosecution for the same offense after acquittal. It protects against a second prosecution for the same offense after conviction. And it protects against multiple punishments for the same offense. This last protection is what is necessarily implicated in any consideration of the question whether, in the imposition of sentence for the same offense after retrial, the Constitution requires that credit must be given for punishment already endured....
>
> We hold that the constitutional guarantee against multiple punishments for the same offense absolutely requires that punishment already exacted must be fully "credited" in imposing sentence upon a new conviction for the same offense. If upon a new trial, the defendant is acquitted, there is no way the years he spent in prison can be returned to him. But if he is reconvicted, those years can and must be returned—by subtracting them from whatever new sentence is imposed.[19]

In 1973, however, the Court refused to apply these limitations to resentencing by a *jury* after retrial.[20]

APPEALING DISMISSALS

In the mid-1970s, the Supreme Court began to expand the government's right to appeal a judge's decision to dismiss charges against a defendant after the trial was under way. Such appeals had been thought impermissible under the general rule that the prosecution may not appeal a verdict of acquittal. In *United States v. Wilson* (1975), the Court held that the double jeopardy guarantee did not foreclose a government appeal of a trial judge's decision to dismiss charges against a defendant who had already been found guilty.[21] The

CONFINING SEXUAL PREDATORS AFTER PRISON

The 1990s saw a wave of new laws that locked up "sexual predators" after they had served their prison sentences. These men had a record of sex crimes and were seen as strong bets to repeat their offenses if presented with the opportunity. The Court upheld these tough new laws, even though they seemed to skirt the normal rules for double punishment and after-the-fact penalties.

A 5-4 ruling in 1997 upheld a Kansas law that allowed state authorities to confine in locked treatment centers sex criminals who had completed their prison terms. Leroy Hendricks, a pedophile who had served a ten-year prison term for taking "indecent liberties" with two boys, was due to be released in 1994. The new law, however, allowed prosecutors to seek the continued confinement of persons who, due to a "mental abnormality," were likely to commit future sex crimes. A jury agreed that Hendricks posed such a danger, and he was confined in a separate prison-like treatment facility on the grounds of the state prison. He sued, contending that the extra prison time for a past crime was unconstitutional. The Court upheld the law in *Kansas v. Hendricks* (1997).[1]

"Involuntary confinement pursuant to the [Kansas Sexually Violent Predator] Act is not punitive," and therefore, does not violate the Constitution's ban on double jeopardy or ex-post-facto laws, said Justice Clarence Thomas. The forced confinement of a "narrow class of particularly dangerous individuals" can be seen as a "civil commitment scheme designed to protect the public from harm," not a means of imposing extra punishment, he wrote in an opinion joined by Chief Justice William H. Rehnquist and Justices Sandra Day O'Connor, Antonin Scalia, and Anthony M. Kennedy. The ruling affirmed similar laws in five other states.[2]

Five years later, the Court by the same 5-4 margin upheld a Kansas prison rule that required sex criminals to reveal details about their past sex crimes. Those who refused lost prison privileges and would delay their possible release. Officials also reserved the right to prosecute the men for the crimes they revealed. Nonetheless, the Court rejected one inmate's claim that these forced admissions would violate his right against self-incrimination. Justice Anthony Kennedy, speaking for the Court, called the treatment program "a sensible approach to reducing the serious danger that repeat sex offenders pose to many innocent persons."[3]

A year later, the Court upheld the so-called Megan's Laws, which require released sex offenders to register with authorities and have their names, addresses, and photos put on the Internet. In a Connecticut case, the Court said these convicted criminals do not have a right to a hearing to contest whether they remain dangerous. A "John Doe" had sued, contending that posting his name and face on the Internet as a registered sex offender tells the public he is a danger, which he asserted was false and defamatory and thus a violation of what he contended was a due process right not to be defamed by the government. The Court unanimously rejected this claim and said the state may post accurate information about past criminal convictions. Whether he is "currently dangerous is of no consequence," declared Chief Justice Rehnquist.[4] "Connecticut has decided that the registry information of all sex offenders—currently dangerous or not—must be publicly disclosed," he wrote.[5] In an Alaska case, the Court said these laws may be applied retroactively to persons whose crimes predate the law. In a 6-3 decision, the justices again characterized the sex registry as a "civil regulatory scheme" designed to protect the public, not an extra punishment for past crimes.[6]

---

1. *Kansas v. Hendricks,* 521 U.S. 346 (1997).

2. Id. at 369, 364.

3. *McKune v. Lile,* 536 U.S 24 (2002).

4. *Connecticut v. Doe,* 538 U.S. 1 (2003).

5. Id.

6. *Smith v. Doe,* 538 U.S. 84 (2003).

Court reasoned that the Double Jeopardy Clause did not foreclose an appeal of such a postverdict dismissal of charges inasmuch as the success of the appeal would only result in reinstatement of the verdict, not in a new trial.

In another case decided that same day, the Court seemed to make the possibility of further proceedings against the defendant a crucial element in determining the permissibility of such appeals. In *United States v. Jenkins* (1975), the Court held that the Double Jeopardy Clause forbids the government from appealing a ruling dismissing an indictment when a successful appeal might result in further proceedings.[22] Three years later, however, the Court overruled *Jenkins* with its decision in *United States v. Scott* (1978).[23] By a 5-4 vote, the Court held that the government could appeal a trial judge's decision to grant a defendant's motion to dismiss charges in midtrial. The Court held that the double jeopardy guarantee did not forbid an appeal of that ruling—or retrial of the defendant—because a defendant, in seeking dismissal of the charges based on grounds unrelated to his guilt or innocence, had made a voluntary choice to risk retrial for the same offense. The Double Jeopardy Clause, held the majority, protected an individual against government oppression through multiple prosecutions but not against the consequences of his own voluntary choice.

ONE OFFENSE, TWO TRIALS?

For a brief few years in the early 1990s, the Court broadened the double jeopardy provision to bar multiple prosecutions whenever the two offenses charged involved the same conduct. In this case, the Court ruled, 5-4, that the test for double jeopardy was whether a second prosecution was based on conduct that had already been prosecuted. In *Grady v. Corbin* (1990), a driver was ticketed and fined for the misdemeanors of driving while intoxicated and failing to keep right of the median. Later, prosecutors who were unaware of the earlier court action sought to try the driver for the death of a motorist he allegedly hit in the oncoming lane.[24] Writing for the Court, Justice William J. Brennan Jr. said a defendant should be protected from repeated government attempts to convict him for a single action. Joining Brennan in the majority were Justices White, Marshall, Blackmun, and John Paul Stevens. Chief Justice William H. Rehnquist and Justices Sandra Day O'Connor and Anthony M. Kennedy dissented, as did Antonin Scalia. Scalia argued that the Double Jeopardy Clause protects an individual against a second prosecution for the same offense, not the same conduct.

Three years later, Scalia and the three other *Grady* dissenters, joined by a new justice, Clarence Thomas, reversed the 1990 ruling, holding that multiple prosecutions are permitted if the two offenses contain different elements. Dissenting were Justices White, Blackmun, Stevens, and David H. Souter, who had succeeded Brennan in the interim.[25]

FINES AND FORFEITURES

The Court in the mid-1990s upheld government's use of fines and forfeitures, even in cases in which the prosecutor's target had already served a prison term. The lawyers for the convicted had maintained that the government cannot impose a double punishment for the same crime. Justice Scalia said the focus on "double punishment" was misleading, since the word *jeopardy* referred to being in jeopardy of going to prison and losing your liberty. "In my view, the Double Jeopardy Clause prohibits successive prosecution, not successive punishment," he said in *United States v. Ursery* (1996).[26] Guy Ursery, a Michigan farmer, had been found to be growing marijuana plants in a field near his home. Prosecutors moved to seize his home and his land on the theory that they were being used as instruments of crime. Ursery was later indicted for growing marijuana, convicted, and sentenced to sixty-three months in prison. His case raised the question of whether the forfeiture of his house, followed by criminal prosecution, amounted to a double punishment for the same crime.

The Court held that "civil forfeitures do not constitute 'punishment' for the purposes of the Double Jeopardy Clause."[27] Justice Thomas agreed with Scalia, and although Chief Justice Rehnquist did not adopt this view, he spoke for the Court in limiting the scope of the Double Jeopardy Clause in cases involving illegal drugs, bank fraud, and sex crimes. The Court said that losing your house, your money, or your liberty are not always punishment and therefore, these government actions do not trigger the ban on double jeopardy.

Chief Justice Rehnquist noted that since the days of pirate ships, the government had had the authority to seize vehicles or other property used in the commission of a crime. In a concurring opinion, Justice Kennedy noted that these actions rely on "the legal fiction" that the piece of property, not the owner, is guilty of the offense. "Civil in rem forfeiture (focusing on the thing) has long been understood as independent of criminal punishments," Kennedy agreed.[28] The Court's opinion in *Ursery* cleared away most constitutional doubts about the government's seizure of boats, cars, airplanes, and other property as part of the so-called war on drugs. *(See box, Forfeiting the Goods, p. 352.)* In a solo dissent, Justice Stevens said he could not agree with the "surprising conclusion that the owner is not punished by the loss of his residence."[29] He faulted his colleagues for undercutting "a guarantee deemed fundamental by the Founders" and "dramatically expanding the sovereign's power to forfeit private property."[30]

The following year, the Court ruled that a civil penalty imposed by the government is not punishment either. In 1989 John Hudson, the chairman of the First National Bank of Tipton, Oklahoma, was hit with a $16,500 fine by federal bank regulators and barred from the banking business for his part in a scheme that allowed him to benefit from loans to others. In 1992 he was indicted for bank fraud based upon the same scheme. In *Hudson v. United States* (1997), the Court ruled that the Double Jeopardy Clause does not stop the government from bringing the second set of punishments against the former bank president. The "money penalties and occupational debarment" were "civil, not criminal" measures, Rehnquist said, and therefore, do not amount to a double punishment for the same crime.[31]

Cruel and Unusual Punishment

The Eighth Amendment prohibits "cruel and unusual punishments" as well as "excessive fines (or) bail," but it does not define the key words. Like the Fourth Amendment's ban on "unreasonable" searches, the Eighth Amendment virtually requires the justices to decide for themselves what is meant by the terms "cruel and unusual" or "excessive." Whether the Court is bound by the original understanding of these words when they were drafted or by contemporary and evolving standards, or some other means of balancing the rights of the accused with the legitimate police power of government is not clear. Justices Antonin Scalia and Clarence Thomas look to history to find the answer. They say cruel and unusual punishment should be defined today by the standards of 1791, when the Bill of Rights was added to the Constitution. For example, they have said that a long prison term for a minor crime is never cruel and unusual punishment, since confinement in prison was not seen as a cruel punishment in 1791. A solid majority of the Court, however, has looked instead to contemporary views, or what Chief Justice Earl Warren in 1958 called the "evolving standards of decency that mark the progress of a maturing society."[1]

The Court has invoked the Eighth Amendment to outlaw torture and to demand humane conditions for prisoners. In 2002 the justices in a 6-3 decision ruled that Alabama prison guards violated the Eighth Amendment when they chained an inmate to a "hitching post" and left him for seven hours in the hot sun without water or his shirt. No doubt prisoners suffered worse treatment during the eighteenth and nineteenth centuries, and chain gangs were common during most of the twentieth century. Justice John Paul Stevens noted, however, that it violates current notions of "human dignity" to permit guards to inflict "wanton and unnecessary pain" on an inmate.[2] Still, the Eighth Amendment is triggered only in extreme circumstances, as the Court has been careful to defer to the judgment of legislators and the general public on what is the proper punishment for crime. In *Lockyer v Andrade* (2003), the Court upheld California's "three strikes and you're out" law, which resulted in a fifty-year prison term for a petty thief who had stolen videotapes from a K-Mart.[3] Despite fervent pleas, the Court also has rejected the claim that the death penalty itself is cruel and unusual punishment. Most states and the general public, as measured by opinion surveys, strongly support capital punishment for murderers. Therefore, it would be difficult for the justices to conclude that the death penalty is either cruel or unusual when measured by contemporary standards in the United States.

THE EIGHTH AMENDMENT AND THE STATES

Like other provisions of the Bill of Rights, the Eighth Amendment had little practical effect until the Court decided it applied to state and local governments. Initially, it extended only to Congress and the federal government, and relatively few crimes were federal in nature prior to the twentieth century. In 1892 the Court turned away an early challenge raising the issue of cruel and unusual punishment by ruling that the amendment did not extend to state action.[4] The first victory for an Eighth Amendment claim came in 1910, when the Court rescued a Coast Guard officer in the new territory of the Philippines who had been sentenced to fifteen years at hard labor for falsifying documents. Finding this punishment excessive and cruel, the Court said "it is a precept of justice that the punishment for crime should be graduated and proportioned to the offense."[5] This notion that the punishment should fit the crime would be cited often in later Eighth Amendment cases, including as a challenge to California's three-strikes law.

In the mid-twentieth century, the Court quietly began applying the ban to states, but not until 1962 did it strike down a state-imposed punishment as a violation of the Eighth Amendment. One of the most bizarre of the Court's early Eighth Amendment cases was *Louisiana ex rel. Francis v. Resweber* (1947), in which the Court assumed for the first time that the Eighth Amendment ban on cruel and unusual punishment could be enforced against the states. Willie Francis had been sentenced by a Louisiana court to be electrocuted. On the appointed day, Francis was put in the electric chair, the switch was thrown, but nothing happened. A failure in the operating mechanism prevented the electricity from reaching Francis. Francis appealed to the Supreme Court, asking it to forbid the state a second attempt at execution because it would constitute cruel and unusual punishment. The Court denied Francis's appeal, by a vote of 5-4.[6] Justice Stanley F. Reed, who wrote for the majority, clearly saw the Eighth Amendment ban as applicable to state action, but he did not find that action in Francis's case to be cruel and unusual:

> [T]he fact that petitioner has already been subjected to a current of electricity does not make his subsequent execution any more cruel in the constitutional sense than any other execution. The cruelty against which the Constitution protects a convicted man is cruelty inherent in the method of punishment, not the necessary suffering involved in any method employed to extinguish life humanely. The fact that an unforeseeable accident prevented the prompt consummation of the sentence cannot, it seems to us, add an element of cruelty to a subsequent execution. There is no purpose to inflict unnecessary pain nor any unnecessary pain involved in the proposed execution.... We cannot agree that the hardship imposed upon the petitioner rises to that level of hardship denounced as denial of due process because of cruelty.[7]

Justice Harold H. Burton, joined by Justices William O. Douglas, Frank Murphy, and Wiley B. Rutledge, dissented.

Fifteen years after *Louisiana ex rel. Francis v. Resweber*, the Court for the first time used the Eighth Amendment to invalidate a state law. In *Robinson v. California* (1962), the justices held it impermissibly cruel and unusual punishment for a state to impose prison sentences upon persons found to be drug addicts. Justice Potter Stewart wrote the majority opinion for six members of the Court:

> This statute ... is not one which punishes a person for the use of narcotics, for their purchase, sale or possession, or for antisocial or disorderly behavior resulting from their administration. It is not a law which even purports to provide or require medical treatment. Rather, we deal with a statute which makes the "status" of narcotic addiction a criminal offense....
>
> It is unlikely that any State ... would attempt to make it a criminal offense for a person to be mentally ill, or a leper, or to be afflicted with a venereal disease ... in the light of contemporary human knowledge, a law which made a criminal offense of such a disease would doubtless be universally thought to be an infliction of cruel and unusual punishment in violation of the Eighth and Fourteenth Amendments....
>
> ... We hold that a state law which imprisons a person thus afflicted as a criminal ... inflicts a cruel and unusual punishment in violation of the Fourteenth Amendment.[8]

Justices Byron R. White and Tom C. Clark dissented.

In the late 1960s, the Court refused to apply *Robinson* to forbid states to punish public drunkenness. In a case from Texas, Leroy Powell had been convicted of being intoxicated in a public place. He attacked the law as cruel and unusual punishment, because it punished him for being a chronic alcoholic. By a 5-4 vote in *Powell v. Texas* (1968), the Court rejected that challenge. Justice Thurgood Marshall delivered the majority opinion, distinguishing the law in *Powell* from that in *Robinson*:

> [A]ppellant was convicted, not for being a chronic alcoholic, but for being in public while drunk on a particular occasion. The State of Texas thus has not sought to punish a mere status, as California did in *Robinson*; nor has it attempted to regulate appellant's behavior in the privacy of his home. Rather, it has imposed upon appellant a criminal sanction for public behavior which may create substantial health and safety hazards, both for appellant and for members of the general public, and which offends the moral and esthetic sensibilities of a large segment of the community.[9]

Justice Abe Fortas, in a dissent joined by Justices Douglas, Stewart, and William J. Brennan Jr., said the appellant was powerless to avoid drinking and, once intoxicated, could not prevent himself from appearing in public places.

PRISON CONDITIONS

Since 1976 the Court has held that the Eighth Amendment forbids the "unnecessary and wanton infliction of pain" on prisoners. Amid the fierce contemporary debate over the legitimacy of the death penalty, it had been almost forgotten that the main concern for the framers of the Eighth Amendment was prohibiting torture and other "barbarous" methods of punishment, the justices noted. Because prisoners are under the control of the government, officials must take responsibility for their basic care. Not providing them with food, water, and shelter is not physical torture in the usual sense of the term, but it would inflict pointless and "unnecessary suffering" and violate "contemporary standards of decency," the Court said in *Estelle v. Gamble* (1976).[10]

The case that elicited this response concerned medical treatment for prisoners. J.W. Gamble, a Texas inmate, injured his back while working in prison. He claimed that he was in severe pain, but the prison's doctors, after giving him pain pills, sent him back to work in a few days. He sued on his own, contending that the doctors' action amounted to mistreatment that violated his constitutional rights. Gamble lost before the Supreme Court, but his case established an important precedent. Gamble had been seen seventeen times over a three-month period by doctors and nurses at the prison, so the Court determined that he had no basis to argue that his condition was callously and deliberately ignored. For the first time, however, the Court made clear that the deliberate mistreatment of prisoners violated the Eighth Amendment: "We conclude that deliberate indifference to serious medical needs of prisoners constitutes the unnecessary and wanton infliction of pain proscribed by the Eighth Amendment," said Justice Marshall for an 8-1 majority.[11]

In subsequent rulings, the Court defined more clearly what it meant by "unnecessary and wanton

infliction of pain." In the 1980s, the justices ruled that an Oregon inmate who had been shot during a prison disturbance did not have a claim for cruel and unusual punishment. "It is obduracy and wantonness, not inadvertence or error" by prison guards that rises to the level of an Eighth Amendment violation, said Justice Sandra O'Connor for the 5-4 majority in *Whitley v. Albers* (1986).[12] Prison guards need to have the power to maintain security and quell disturbances, she said, and they cannot be sued simply because they may have erred and used too much force.

O'Connor also spoke for the Court in 1992 in upholding a lawsuit by a Louisiana inmate who was handcuffed and then punched in the mouth by a guard. Kevin Hudson, the inmate, was shackled and held by one guard while the other, Jack McMillian, punched and kicked him repeatedly. The blows bruised Hudson's face, loosened his teeth, and cracked his dental plate. When he sued, a magistrate awarded him $800 in damages. The state appealed, contending "minor injuries" suffered by prisoners cannot be considered cruel and unusual punishment. In a 7-2 decision, the Court sided with the inmate. "When prison officials maliciously and sadistically use force to cause harm, contemporary standards of decency are always violated. This is true whether or not significant injury is evident," O'Connor wrote in *Hudson v. McMillian* (1992).[13]

This latter decision is noteworthy as well for the dissent by Justice Clarence Thomas. The case came before the Court in November 1991 during Thomas's first weeks on the bench and prompted his first written dissent. In it, he boldly accused his new colleagues of ignoring "all bounds of history and precedent" to turn the Eighth Amendment into "a National Code of Prison Regulation." "Abusive behavior by prison guards is deplorable conduct that properly evokes outrage and contempt. But that does not mean that it is invariably unconstitutional," Thomas wrote. Looking back to English history, he said, the word "punishments" in the Eighth Amendment refers to penalties imposed by the courts. It does not therefore "protect inmates from harsh treatment" in prison, he said. Because Hudson's injuries were "minor" and left no permanent damage, his suit should have been dismissed, according to Thomas.[14] Justice Scalia agreed. In a concurring statement in *Hudson*, Justice Harry Blackmun took Thomas to task and said his view, if adopted in law, would allow "various kinds of state-sponsored torture and abuse" by prison authorities, including the use of electric shocks and beatings with rubber hoses.[15]

In later dissents, Thomas called for overruling *Estelle v. Gamble*, Justice Marshall's path-breaking decision. In *Helling v. McKinney* (1993), he wrote, "Judges or juries—but not jailers—impose punishment," and therefore, prison guards cannot violate the Eighth Amendment.[16] The rest of his colleagues, including Chief Justice Rehnquist, distanced themselves from his view. In *Helling v. McKinney*, the Court had ruled that a prisoner who was put into a cell with another who smoked five packs of cigarettes a day might win a claim of cruel and unusual punishment. The 7-2 majority saw such an action as "deliberate indifference" to the inmate's health and safety. The justices' decision was moot, however, as the inmate had been transferred soon after he filed his complaint. Thomas and Scalia in their dissent faulted the Court for treating "a prisoner's mere risk of injury" as potentially cruel and unusual punishment.[17]

A year later, the Court ruled that prison officials can be sued if they knowingly expose an inmate to being raped. "The Constitution does not mandate comfortable prisons, but neither does it permit inhumane ones," wrote Justice David H. Souter in *Farmer v. Brennan* (1994).[18] Dee Farmer, a transsexual who "projects feminine characteristics," sued federal prison authorities because he said he was raped shortly after being transferred to a penitentiary in Indiana. The Court stressed that prison officials are not liable for all prison rapes. Rather, an official can be sued "only if he knows inmates face a substantial risk of serious harm and disregards that risk by failing to take reasonable measures to abate it," Souter stated.[19]

In the Alabama "hitching post" case, *Hope v. Pelzer* (2002), the Court said prisoners cannot be subjected to a slow form of torture simply because they get into a squabble with a guard. Larry Hope, the inmate, fell asleep on a bus on the way to a work site and then got into a vulgar shouting match with the guards. According to Hope's complaint, they handcuffed him to a railing with his hands above his head and left him there for seven hours without water or his shirt. "The obvious cruelty inherent in this practice" should have been evident, said Justice Stevens. "Handcuffing Hope to a hitching post for an extended period apparently to inflict gratuitous pain or discomfort" is cruel and unusual punishment, and the guards can be held liable for violating the Eighth Amendment, he concluded.[20] Thomas dissented, joined by Chief Justice Rehnquist and Justice Scalia.

CAPITAL PUNISHMENT

The Constitution was written with the idea that death was the proper punishment for some crimes. There are, however, limits to this practice. The Fifth Amendment states, "No person shall be held to answer for a capital or otherwise infamous crime," unless he has been indicted by a grand jury. The Fourteenth Amendment holds that a State shall not "deprive any person of life … without due process of law." In the late 1960s, however, civil rights lawyers broadly challenged the death penalty as violating basic notions of due process of law and equal protection as well as the ban on cruel and unusual punishment. The problem of continued resistance to equal rights for African Americans in the South and the nexus between race and criminal justice administration played a central role in the rising tide of opposition to capital punishment, although the justices shied from explicitly discussing either.

During the nineteenth century, the death penalty had been abolished in parts of the Midwest and Northeast, including in Iowa, Michigan, Wisconsin, Rhode Island, and Maine. Southern states not only retained capital punishment, but also used it for crimes such as rape and robbery. As of 1954, rape was still punishable by death in sixteen of these states, and robbery could result in a death sentence in eight of them: Alabama, Georgia, Kentucky, Mississippi, Missouri, Oklahoma,

"THREE-TIME LOSERS" LOSE AGAIN

It is commonly said that the punishment should fit the crime, and the Court has voiced the view that a prison sentence that is "grossly disproportionate" to the crime would violate the ban on cruel and unusual punishment. The justices, however, have upheld exceedingly stiff sentences for rather minor crimes. In 2003, the Court upheld a fifty-year prison term for a petty criminal who shoplifted videotapes from two K-Marts in Southern California. Leandro Andrade, an army veteran and a heroin addict, had been convicted years earlier of two burglaries. He ran afoul of a new law adopted by California and half the states in the mid-1990s that borrowed a rule from baseball: "Three strikes and you're out." Under this law, a third conviction could trigger a prison term of twenty-five years to life. California passed it in the wake of the murder of twelve-year-old Polly Klass by Richard Allen Davis, a career criminal who had been released on parole after two earlier kidnapping convictions. Despite its origin in a kidnapping and murder case, the three strikes law snared petty criminals as well.

In a second case before the Court, Gary Ewing, another repeat criminal, had been given a twenty-five-year prison term for stealing three golf clubs from a pro shop. In a pair of 5-4 rulings, the Court upheld the three strikes law and rejected the claims that these punishments went too far. Career criminals pose "a serious public safety concern," and states are entitled to decide these persons "must be incapacitated," said Justice Sandra Day O'Connor. Moreover, these two criminals are not being sent away for their most recent thefts but for their "long history of crime," she added.[1]

The dissenters—Justice Stephen G. Breyer, John Paul Stevens, Ruth Bader Ginsburg, and David H. Souter—said such sentences for nonviolent thieves were far beyond any imposed in other states, and therefore, should be seen as both cruel and unusual.

In 1991 the Court had handed down a similar 5-4 ruling that upheld a life prison term for a first-time drug offender. Ronald Harmelin was arrested with a block of cocaine in his car, an offense that triggered a life prison term.[2] The 1980s had seen two conflicting decisions. One upheld a life term for a Texas man whose crimes consisted of misusing credit cards and writing bad checks.[3] A second ruling struck down a life term for a man whose seventh nonviolent offense was writing a bad check for $100.[4] Both cases were decided by a 5-4 vote, and until 2003 the Court had been divided on which to follow. The decision in the three strikes case from California suggests that only a truly extraordinary prison sentence will be struck down under the Eighth Amendment. "We do not sit as a 'Super Legislature' to second-guess these policy choices," said Justice O'Connor, herself a former Arizona legislator.[5]

---

1. *Ewing v. California, Lockyer v. Andrade,* 538 U.S. 63 (2003).

2. *Harmelin v. Michigan,* 501 U.S. 957 (1991).

3. *Rummel v. Estelle,* 445 U.S. 263 (1980).

4. *Solem v. Helm,* 463 U.S. 277 (1983).

5. *Ewing v. California, Lockyer v. Andrade,* 538 U.S. 63 (2003).

Texas, and Virginia.[21] This system gave white prosecutors and jurors wide discretion to impose the ultimate punishment, and blacks were on the receiving end of a disproportionate percentage of death sentences. During the years of the Warren Court, the justices repeatedly tangled with southern courts and became acutely aware of the possibility of racial bias in the justice system. Of 771 persons who were executed for rape between 1870 and 1950, 701 of them were black.[22] These did not include men killed in the mob lynchings that had continued throughout the South in the early decades of the twentieth century. Even Justices Byron R. White and Potter Stewart, neither of whom would

be considered liberal in criminal cases, were troubled by what they encountered: A rape or robbery in a small southern town, particularly when committed by a black person, might result in a death sentence although a conviction for the same crime elsewhere in the nation would yield only a few years in prison.

Lawyers for the NAACP Legal Defense Fund were riding a wave of success in civil rights cases when they launched their effort to abolish capital punishment in the mid-1960s. The justices, or at least several of them, had signaled that they had doubts about the death sentencing system across the states, but neither the defense lawyers nor the justices anticipated that lightening would strike in 1972. When the justices voted to take up the case of *Furman v. Georgia*, only Justices Brennan and perhaps Marshall were absolutely opposed to capital punishment. Marshall's years as an NAACP lawyer in the South had convinced him that racial bias plagued the system. When the justices gathered in conference to vote on the outcome, it turned out that Brennan and Marshall were not alone. A majority of them agreed, albeit for different reasons, that the system as it existed could not stand.

Death penalty laws, held the majority, left too much discretion to juries in imposing this ultimate penalty. The result was a "wanton and freakish" pattern of its use that violated the Eighth Amendment ban on cruel and unusual punishment. The majority was composed of the five justices who had served under Chief Justice Warren: Douglas, Brennan, Stewart, White, and Marshall. Each wrote a separate opinion. Dissenting were the four members named to the Court by President Richard Nixon: Chief Justice Warren E. Burger and Justices Harry A. Blackmun, Lewis F. Powell Jr., and William H. Rehnquist. Concerning the death penalty laws existing in Georgia and Texas, Justice Douglas wrote,

no standards govern the selection of the penalty. People live or die, dependent on the whim of one man or of 12....
... [T]hese discretionary statutes are unconstitutional in their operation. They are pregnant with discrimination and discrimination is an ingredient not compatible with the idea of equal protection of the laws that is implicit in the ban on "cruel and unusual" punishments.[23]

Justice Brennan found the death penalty "uniquely degrading to human dignity" no matter how the decision is reached:[24]

Death is an unusually severe and degrading punishment; there is a strong probability that it is inflicted arbitrarily; its rejection by contemporary society is virtually total; and there is no reason to believe that it serves any penal purpose more effectively than the less severe punishment of imprisonment. The function of these principles is to enable a court to determine whether a punishment comports with human dignity. Death, quite simply, does not.[25]

Justice Stewart found critical how this penalty was applied under existing law:

These death sentences are cruel and unusual in the same way that being struck by lightning is cruel and unusual. For, of all the people convicted of rapes and murders in 1967 and 1968, many just as reprehensible as these, the petitioners are among a capriciously selected random handful upon whom the sentence of death has in fact been imposed.... [T]he Eighth and Fourteenth Amendments cannot tolerate the infliction of a sentence of death under legal systems that permit this unique penalty to be so wantonly and so freakishly imposed.[26]

Justice White took a similar view:

The imposition and execution of the death penalty are obviously cruel in the dictionary sense. But the penalty has not been considered cruel and unusual punishment in the constitutional sense because it was thought justified by the social ends it was deemed to serve. At the moment that it ceases realistically to further these purposes, however, the emerging question is whether its imposition ... would violate the Eighth Amendment. It is my view that it would, for its imposition would then be the pointless and needless extinction of life with only marginal contributions to any discernible social or public purposes....
It is ... my judgment that this point has been reached with respect to capital punishment as it is presently administered under the statutes involved in these cases.[27]

Justice Marshall found the death penalty both "excessive" and "morally unacceptable." He wrote that "the average citizen would, in my opinion, find it shocking to his conscience and sense of justice. For this reason alone capital punishment cannot stand."[28] Justice Burger, writing for the dissenting justices, based their position in large part on their view of the respective roles of judges and legislators:

If legislatures come to doubt the efficacy of capital punishment, they can abolish it, either completely or on a selective basis. If new evidence persuades them that they have acted unwisely, they can reverse their field and reinstate the penalty to the extent it is thought warranted. An Eighth Amendment ruling by judges cannot be made with such flexibility or discriminating precision.[29]

BAIL: NEITHER ABSOLUTE NOR EXCESSIVE

The Eighth Amendment states that "[e]xcessive bail shall not be required." Throughout U.S. history, federal law has provided that persons arrested for noncapital offenses shall be granted the right to post bail and win release to participate in preparing their defense. Bail is money or property pledged by an accused person to guarantee his or her appearance at trial. Failure to appear at trial—"jumping bail"—carries criminal penalties, plus forfeiture of the pledged bond. The Supreme Court has held that a presumption in favor of granting bail exists in the Bill of Rights. Wrote Justice Horace Gray in 1895,

> The statutes of the United States have been framed upon the theory that a person accused of crime shall not, until he has been finally adjudged guilty in the court of last resort, be absolutely compelled to undergo imprisonment or punishment, but may be admitted to bail, not only after arrest and before trial, but after conviction and pending a writ of error.[1]

In *McKane v. Durston* (1894), the Court affirmed that the Eighth Amendment's bail provisions limit federal courts but not state courts.[2]

The Federal Rules of Criminal Procedure provide that the amount of bail shall be determined by the nature and circumstances of the offense, the weight of the evidence, the defendant's ability to pay, and his or her general character.[3] Under the 1966 Bail Reform Act, almost all persons charged with noncapital federal offenses are able to obtain release on personal recognizance or unsecured bond.[4] The leading Supreme Court decision on the question of excessive bail is *Stack v. Boyle* (1951). In this case, twelve communist leaders in California were indicted for conspiracy under the Alien Registration Act of 1940. Bail was fixed at $50,000 for each defendant. The defendants moved to reduce the amount of bail on the grounds that it was excessive in violation of the Eighth Amendment. The Supreme Court agreed. Chief Justice Fred M. Vinson delivered the opinion of the unanimous Court:

> This traditional right to freedom before conviction permits the unhampered preparation of a defense, and serves to prevent the infliction of punishment prior to conviction.... Unless this right to bail before trial is preserved, the presumption of innocence, secured only after centuries of struggle, would lose its meaning.
>
> The right to release before trial is conditioned upon the accused's giving adequate assurance that he will stand trial and submit to sentence if found guilty.... Bail set at a figure higher than an amount reasonably calculated to fulfill this purpose is "excessive" under the Eighth Amendment....
>
> If bail in an amount greater than that usually fixed for serious charges of crimes is required in the case of any of the petitioners, that is a matter to which evidence should be directed in a hearing....
>
> In the absence of such a showing, we are of the opinion that the fixing of bail before trial in these cases cannot be squared with the statutory and constitutional standards for admission to bail.[5]

The following spring, however, the Court held that the Eighth Amendment does not guarantee an absolute right to bail. Certain alien

---

The *Furman* decision effectively struck down all existing death penalty laws, but it did not close the door to enacting new measures to replace them. The Court's decision also seemed to trigger a shift in public opinion in favor of capital punishment. During the 1960s, opposition to the death penalty had grown steadily. In March 1972, shortly before the *Furman* decision was announced, a Gallup Poll found that supporters edged opponents by 50 percent to 42 percent. After the Court's ruling, Gallup's pollsters found a dramatic shift in favor of capital punishment. By 1976 the margin had grown to more than two to one, 65 percent for capital punishment and 28 percent against.[30] Although Justices Brennan and Marshall, the Court's two abolitionists, maintained that the "evolving standards of decency" called for ending the death penalty, public opinion surveys suggested that American standards were evolving in the other direction.

A close reading of the various opinions in the *Furman* case suggested the states had two options for restoring capital punishment. They could remove almost all jury discretion from the decision by making death the mandatory punishment for certain crimes, or they could provide a two-stage procedure in capital cases—a trial at which the issue of guilt or innocence is determined and then, for those persons found guilty, a second proceeding at which evidence might be presented before the decision is reached communists had been detained prior to a final determination on their deportation. Their application for bail was denied by the attorney general acting under provisions of the Internal Security Act of 1950. The Court divided 5–4 in rejecting their argument that bail should be granted. Justice Stanley F. Reed, writing for the majority in *Carlson v. Landon* (1952), stated that the Eighth Amendment does not guarantee everyone detained by federal authority the right to be released on bail:

> The bail clause was lifted … from the English Bill of Rights Act. In England that clause has never been thought to accord a right to bail in all cases, but merely to provide that bail shall not be excessive in those cases where it is proper to grant bail. When this clause was carried over into our Bill of Rights, nothing was said that indicated any different concept. The Eighth Amendment has not prevented Congress from defining the classes of cases in which bail shall be allowed in this country. Thus, in criminal cases, bail is not compulsory where the punishment may be death.…We think, clearly, here that the Eighth Amendment does not require that bail be allowed.[6]

Justices Hugo L. Black, Felix Frankfurter, William O. Douglas, and Harold H. Burton dissented. Black wrote, "The plain purpose of our bail Amendment was to make it impossible for any agency of Government, even the Congress, to authorize keeping people imprisoned a moment longer than was necessary."[7] Twice in the 1980s the Supreme Court approved the denial of bail to certain suspects. In 1984 it upheld the denial to dangerous juveniles, and in 1987 to

organized crime figures.[8] In *United States v. Salerno* (1987), Chief Justice William H. Rehnquist discussed the Eighth Amendment guarantee, pointing out that it "says nothing about whether bail shall be available at all."[9] The primary function of bail, he acknowledged, "is to safeguard the courts' role in adjudicating the guilt or innocence of the defendants [by preventing flight]." The Eighth Amendment does not, however, deny the government the opportunity to regulate pretrial release for other reasons. "We believe," Rehnquist concluded, "that when Congress has mandated detention on the basis of a compelling interest other than prevention of flight, as it has here, the Eighth Amendment does not require release on bail."[10]

---

1. *Hudson v. Parker,* 156 U.S. 277 at 285 (1895).

2. *McKane v. Durston,* 153 U.S. 684 (1894).

3. Federal Rules of Criminal Procedure, Rule 46(c).

4. *Congress and the Nation* (Washington, D.C.: Congressional Quarterly, 1969), 2:315–316.

5. *Stack v. Boyle,* 342 U.S. 1 at 4–5, 6, 7 (1951).

6. *Carlson v. Landon,* 342 U.S. 524 at 545–546 (1952).

7. Id. at 557–558.

8. *Schall v. Martin, Abrams v. Martin,* 467 U.S. 253 (1984); *United States v. Salerno,* 481 U.S. 739 (1987).

9. *United States v. Salerno,* 481 U.S. 739 at 752 (1987).

10. Id. at 753, 755.

on whether to impose a sentence of death. Thirty-five states passed new death penalty statutes. Ten chose the mandatory route, while the other twenty-five preferred the two-stage procedure. By 1976 both types of laws were back before the bench for the Court to again determine whether death in and of itself was a cruel and unusual—and hence unconstitutional—punishment for any crime in the United States.

In *Gregg v. Georgia* (1976) and two companion cases, *Proffitt v. Florida* and *Jurek v. Texas*, the Court refused to declare the death penalty unconstitutional in all circumstances. Justice Stewart set out the majority position:

> [W]e are concerned here only with the imposition of capital punishment for the crime of murder, and when a life has been taken deliberately by the offender, we cannot say that the punishment is invariably disproportionate to the crime. It is an extreme sanction, suitable to the most extreme of crimes.[31]

In short the Court would not overrule the judgment of state legislatures and declare capital punishment per se as unconstitutional. Justice Stewart continued:

> Considerations of federalism, as well as respect for the ability of a legislature to evaluate, in terms of its particular State, the moral consensus concerning the death penalty and its social utility as a sanction,

FORFEITING THE GOODS

As part of the so-called war on drugs, Congress and many states gave prosecutors and the police new powers to seize money, boats, cars, and other property from suspected drug dealers. In theory, these "forfeitures" were supposed to be limited to a criminal's ill-gotten gains or to items that were used to further the crime. For example, a drug dealer who used a speedboat or an airplane to ship narcotics was in danger of having his boat or plane seized by the government. Sometimes, however, these seizures went well beyond money or goods that were linked to the crime, and on a few occasions, the Court said the forfeitures were so excessive as to violate the Eighth Amendment clause against excessive fines.

Richard Austin, who repaired cars, was convicted of selling two grams of cocaine to an undercover policeman in Sioux Falls, South Dakota. The government then moved to seize his auto body shop and his mobile home. In *Austin v. United States* (1993), the Court unanimously agreed that this seizure could be challenged as unconstitutionally excessive. "The purpose of the Eighth Amendment ... was to limit the government's power to punish," wrote Justice Harry A. Blackmun. He left it to the lower courts to determine when a forfeiture becomes "excessive."[1]

In a separate case, the Court said that the government cannot seize property bought with drug money by someone who did not know the source of the funds.[2] The Court also said that a property owner ordinarily is entitled to notice and a hearing before his property is forfeited to the government.[3] In 1998 the Court for the first time overturned a forfeiture as unconstitutionally excessive under the Eighth Amendment. In this case, Hosep Bajakajian, a Syrian immigrant to Los Angeles, was trying to return to his homeland when customs inspectors found $357,144 in his family's luggage. The law requires filing a currency transaction form whenever $10,000 in cash is moved across the border. Bajakajian pled guilty to that offense, and he was fined $20,000. Authorities then moved to seize the entire $357,000, even though a judge had concluded that Bajakajian had lawfully earned the money. "We hold that ... full forfeiture of [his] currency would be grossly disproportional to the gravity of his offense [and] would violate the Excessive Fines Clause of the Eighth Amendment," said Justice Clarence Thomas for the 5-4 majority.[4] Chief

Justice William H. Rehnquist and Justices Sandra Day O'Connor, Antonin Scalia, and Anthony M. Kennedy dissented.

The Court has refused to block forfeitures as a second punishment for the same crime.[5] *(See "Fines and Forfeitures," p. 342–343.)* The justices also refused to shield an "innocent owner" from losing her property in a forfeiture. Tina Bennis had the double misfortune of having a husband who was arrested with a prostitute and in a family car that she owned, at least in part. After John Bennis was convicted of gross indecency, Detroit prosecutors seized the eleven-year-old Pontiac sedan under the state's public nuisance law. In her appeal, she argued that since she owned half of the car, she was entitled to half of its value. By a 5-4 vote, the Court disagreed.[6] Chief Justice Rehnquist said that since the days of pirate ships, the government has had the power to seize vehicles that are used for illicit purposes. In a key concurring opinion, Justice Ruth Bader Ginsburg applauded the authorities for seeking "to deter Johns from using the cars they own (or co-own) to contribute to neighborhood blight."[7] Besides, the old Pontiac was practically worthless, she said. In dissent, Justice John Paul Stevens noted that for centuries, prostitutes have been "plying their trade on other people's property," including in luxury hotels and cruise ships.[8] Surely, the Court does not mean to say those too are subject to forfeitures, he wondered. Justices Kennedy, David H. Souter, and Stephen G. Breyer joined him in dissent.

---

1. *Austin v. United States,* 509 U.S. 602 at 609 (1993). See also *Alexander v. United States,* 509 U.S. 544 (1993).

2. *United States v. A Parcel of Land, Buildings, Appurtenances and Improvements, known as 92 Buena Vista Ave.,* 507 U.S. 111 (1993).

3. *United States v. James Daniel Good Real Property,* 510 U.S. 43 (1993).

4. *Bajakajian v. United States,* 524 U.S. 321 at 324 (1998).

5. *United States v. Ursery,* 518 U.S. 267 (1996). See also *Libretti v. United States,* 516 U.S. 29 (1996).

6. *Bennis v. Michigan,* 516 U.S. 442 (1996).

7. Id. at 458.

8. Id.

require us to conclude, in the absence of more convincing evidence, that the infliction of death as a punishment for murder is not without justification and thus is not unconstitutionally severe....

... We hold that the death penalty is not a form of punishment that may never be imposed, regardless of the circumstances of the offense, regardless

of the character of the offender, and regardless of the procedure followed in reaching the decision to impose it.[32]

Justices Brennan and Marshall dissented. Brennan argued that death was now an uncivilized and unconstitutional punishment. The Court "inescapably

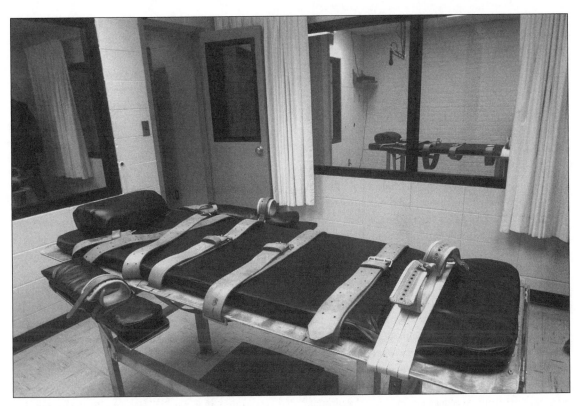

The Rehnquist Court has rejected most broad challenges to death penalty procedures and tightened standards for reviewing individual challenges. In *Atkins v. Virginia* (2002), however, the Court barred the execution of mentally retarded offenders, and in *Ring v. Arizona* (2002) it said that jurors, not judges, decide who deserves the death penalty. Pictured here is the lethal injection room at the Mississippi State Penitentiary in Parchman.

has the duty, as the ultimate arbiter of the meaning of our Constitution, to say whether ... 'moral concepts' require us to hold that the law has progressed to the point where we should declare that the punishment of death, like punishments on the rack, the screw and the wheel, is no longer morally tolerable in our civilized society."[33] Justice Marshall found death an excessive, shocking, and unjust punishment in all cases and would declare it invariably cruel and unusual punishment, forbidden by the Eighth Amendment.

Of equal or greater practical significance, the Court in *Gregg, Jurek,* and *Proffitt* approved as constitutional the new two-stage procedure adopted by Georgia, Florida, Texas, and twenty-two other states for imposing the death sentence. This procedure, wrote

Justice Stewart, met the objections that had caused the Court in *Furman* to invalidate the existing state laws:

The basic concern of *Furman* centered on those defendants who were being condemned to death capriciously and arbitrarily. Under the procedures before the Court in that case, sentencing authorities were not directed to give attention to the nature of circumstances of the crime committed or to the character or record of the defendant. Left unguided, juries imposed the death sentence in a way that could only be called freakish. The new ... sentencing procedures, by contrast, focus the jury's attention on the particularized nature of the crime and the particularized characteristics of the individual defendant. While the jury is permitted to consider any aggravating or mitigating circumstances, it must find and identify at least one statutory aggravating factor before it may impose a penalty of death. In this way the jury's discretion is channeled. No longer can a jury wantonly and freakishly impose the death sentence; it is always circumscribed by the legislative guidelines.[34]

On the same day, the Court struck down state laws that made death the mandatory penalty for first-degree murder. This ruling came in *Woodson v. North Carolina* (1976) and *Roberts v. Louisiana* (1976).[35] The Court divided 5-4; Justices Brennan and Marshall became part of the majority with Justices Stewart, Powell, and Stevens. Chief Justice Burger and Justices Blackmun, White, and Rehnquist dissented.

The Court held that mandatory death penalty statutes "simply papered over the problem of unguided and unchecked jury discretion" and were constitutionally unsatisfactory because they failed to allow room for consideration of the individual defendant and the particular crime.[36] The majority refused to approve "[a] process that accords no significance to relevant facets of the character and record of the individual offender or the circumstances of the particular offense." Such a process "excludes from consideration in fixing the ultimate punishment of death the possibility of compassionate or mitigating factors stemming from the diverse frailties of humankind."[37]

In capital cases, the majority opinion concluded, "the fundamental respect for humanity underlying the Eighth Amendment ... requires consideration of the character and record of the individual offender and the circumstances of the particular offense as a constitutionally indispensable part of the process of inflicting the penalty of death."[38] Subsequently, the Court used similar reasoning in striking down a state law that made death the mandatory sentence for anyone convicted of the first-degree murder of a police officer or for a prison inmate serving a life sentence without possibility of parole and yet convicted of murdering a fellow inmate.[39]

Last Hope for Ending the Death Penalty?

For opponents of capital punishment, the last best hope for ending the death penalty came before the Court in 1987. Anti–death penalty activists had maintained that

racism permeated the prosecution of crime in much of the nation, and this helped explain which accused murderers ended up on death row. A statistical analysis of all the homicides in Georgia between 1974 and 1979 showed a clear pattern of racial bias. Surprisingly, the apparent bias did not turn on the race of the defendant. Instead, it turned on the race of the victim. Local prosecutors sought the death penalty often when the victims were white but only rarely when they were black. David Baldus, a University of Iowa professor, analyzed 2,484 homicides in Georgia and found that 11 percent of those involving white victims resulted in a death sentence compared to 1 percent when blacks were the victims. At first glance, perhaps this might be so because whites were more likely than blacks to be storeowners or police officers. An additional bias might be that murders of strangers are often prosecuted more severely than crimes involving family members, friends, or neighbors. Baldus, however, controlled statistically for 230 variables and concluded in the end that murders of whites were 4.3 times more likely to result in a death sentence than similar crimes against blacks.

Georgia had had a long history of racial discrimination. The Equal Protection Clause was added to the Constitution after the Civil War specifically to stop discrimination against blacks in the South. Justice Brennan commented that at the time of amendment, Georgia had "a dual system of crime and punishment" that turned on the race of the victim and the race of the perpetrator.[40] NAACP Legal Defense Fund lawyers brought the Baldus study before the Court in the case of Warren McCleskey, a black man who was sentenced to death for shooting a white police officer during the robbery of a furniture store. His lawyers urged the Court to overturn Georgia's system of capital punishment as unconstitutional because it was infected with a racial bias. With success, the death penalty in other states would be vulnerable to the same challenge and possibly swept aside. Their legal attack in *McCleskey v. Kemp* (1987) fell short by one vote in the Supreme Court.

"At most, the Baldus study indicates a discrepancy that appears to correlate with race," said Justice Lewis F. Powell Jr. for the 5-4 majority.[41] The statistics do not, however, prove that prosecutors deliberately discriminate based on race when they bring their cases, he said.

Warren McCleskey based the appeal of his death sentence on a study showing that someone convicted of killing a white person was four times more likely to receive the death penalty than someone convicted of killing a black person. His appeal was rejected in *McCleskey v. Kemp* (1987), and he was executed in 1991.

"There can be no perfect procedure for deciding which cases" merit a death sentence.[42] "We hold that the Baldus study does not demonstrate a constitutionally significant risk of racial bias affecting the Georgia capital sentencing system," he concluded.[43] Chief Justice Rehnquist and Justices White, O'Connor, and Scalia agreed.

The four dissenters—Brennan, Marshall, Blackmun, and Stevens—said that the state, at minimum, should be compelled to explain the basis for what appeared to be a systematic racial bias. "Suffusing the Court's opinion in *McCleskey* was a weariness, a pessimism about the possible," wrote legal historian Stuart Banner.[44] "Fifteen years after *Furman*, the Court had given up hope of eliminating the racism and the arbitrariness that had once been the motors of constitutional change. Racism and irrationality were facts of life, and that was that."[45]

Limiting the Use of the Death Penalty

By the 1980s, the fight over capital punishment had reached a standoff at the Supreme Court, and the justices, like the nation, agreed to disagree over the value and virtue of death penalty. In 2008, fourteen states—mostly in New England and the upper Midwest—did not authorize capital punishment. Although thirty-six allowed convicted killers to be sentenced to death, only a handful of them—mostly in the South—carried out executions. Between 1976 and 2008, there were 1,132 executions in the United States, according to the Death Penalty Information Center, and of those, more than a third (422) took place in Texas. Next in line were Virginia (102), Oklahoma (88), Missouri (66), and Florida (66). Large states, such as California, Pennsylvania, Illinois, and Arizona, had hundreds of inmates on death row, but they rarely carried out executions. California had by far the largest death row—with 667 inmates in 2008—yet it had carried out only thirteen executions in the thirty-two years since the Court restored capital punishment.

Each year, the justices continued to closely examine death sentences. In rulings that stretched from 1977 to 2008, the Court imposed two kinds of restrictions: It insisted that jurors be provided a full picture of the defendant before deciding whether he or she should be sentenced to death, and it placed categorical limits on the death penalty, prohibiting the execution of rapists, the mentally retarded, and juveniles under age 18 at the time they committed the crime in question. The Court in 1986 also ruled that an inmate who becomes insane behind bars may not executed.

Repeatedly, the Court focused on the jury and its crucial role in deciding whether a convicted murderer deserved to die. In 1978 the Court held that after a defendant is convicted of murder, the sentencing jury must be allowed to consider any "mitigating factor" that would call for sparing the killer's life.[46] This might include testimony about the defendant's abusive childhood or statements from family members speaking well of his character and so on. In *Simmons v. South Carolina* (1994), the Court said jurors, for the purposes of sentencing, must be told that the defendant will never leave prison if they decide on a life term rather than death.[47] Many jurors believed, and correctly so, that the phrase "life in prison" did not always mean that a criminal sentenced to life would stay in prison for the rest of his life. They had heard of too many instances in which such a defendant was released on parole and committed additional crimes. In response, many states amended their death penalty laws to include a sentence of "life without the possibility of parole." Nonetheless, many jurors continued to suspect that a murderer given a life sentence might leave prison someday. Thus judges must explain to jurors that if they choose a life sentence, the defendant will stay behind bars until he dies. This decision in *Simmons*, though it drew little attention, was credited by death penalty experts with reducing the number of death sentences handed down in the decade afterward.

The Court also ruled that jurors, not judges, must decide whether a defendant is factually guilty of murder before he is sentenced to die. The 7-2 decision in *Ring v. Arizona* (2002) overturned Arizona's death-sentencing system, which called for judges to decide whether a murder defendant deserved to die.[48] *(See discussion of Apprendi v. New Jersey, pp. 275–278.)*

Exclusion for Rapists, the Mentally Retarded, and Youths

The Court has handed down four significant limitations on who can be executed. The first came just a year after the *Gregg* decision, with the justices in *Coker v. Georgia* (1977) outlawing capital punishment for rape. "We have the abiding conviction that the death penalty, which is unique in its severity and irrevocability, is an excessive penalty for the rapist who does not take human life," said Justice White in a 7-2 decision.[49] In subsequent rulings, the Court made clear that the death penalty is reserved for murderers and those who play key roles in a murder plot. In *Enmund v. Florida* (1982), a 5-4 decision overturned the death sentence imposed on the driver of the getaway car in an armed robbery of a house.[50] Earl Enmund's accomplices shot and killed the elderly couple who resisted. Because the driver neither killed the victims nor intended they be killed, the death penalty was disproportionate to Enmund's guilt, the Court said.

Five years after *Enmund*, however, the Court narrowed that decision and ruled that a "major" participant in a crime that leads to murder may be sentenced to die, even if that person did not intend that the victims be killed. In 1978 brothers Ricky and Raymond Tison went to an Arizona prison with an ice chest full

of guns and helped their father Gary and another prisoner escape. When their getaway car broke down on a remote highway, Raymond flagged down another vehicle, which stopped to help. After the gang moved their belongings into the captured car, the father took the four occupants aside and shot them. Gary Tison later died in the desert, but Ricky and Raymond were convicted and sentenced to death.

In a 5-4 decision in *Tison v. Arizona* (1987), the Court upheld the death sentences, even though neither brother had fired a shot or intended the victims to be killed.[51] The Court said the two brothers played a key role in springing their father from prison, and they knew or had reason to believe that he would kill again, because he had earlier killed a prison guard. "We hold that major participation in the felony committed, combined with reckless indifference to human life, is sufficient" to warrant the ultimate punishment, Justice O'Connor wrote.[52] When combined, the *Coker*, *Enmund*, and *Tison* decisions have been interpreted to hold that the death penalty is reserved for murder but is not limited to actual killers.

In the 1980s, the Court announced a second categorical limitation involving the death penalty: inmates who are insane may not be put to death. "The execution of an insane person simply offends humanity [and] contributes nothing to whatever deterrence value is intended to be served by capital punishment," said Justice Marshall for the 7-2 majority in *Ford v. Wainwright* (1986).[53] Chief Justice Burger and soon-to-be chief justice Rehnquist dissented.

In the late 1980s, the Court found itself badly split over whether to set an age limit for capital punishment. In a pair of divided rulings, the Court overturned as unconstitutional a death sentence given to a fifteen-year-old in Oklahoma, but upheld the death sentence for a seventeen-year-old defendant in Kentucky. The outcome meant that no one under age sixteen at the time of his crime could be sentenced to death. "Such a young person is not capable of acting with the degree of culpability that can justify the ultimate punishment," said Justice John Paul Stevens for the splintered court in *Thompson v. Oklahoma* (1988).[54] The key vote was cast by Justice O'Connor. The four liberal justices favored abolishing the death penalty for everyone under eighteen, while O'Connor's conservative colleagues would have left the matter to the states. Although O'Connor agreed with the liberal faction to void the death sentence for a fifteen-year-old in *Thompson*, a year later she joined the four conservatives to reject a challenge to a death sentence for a murderer who had been seventeen at the time of his crime.[55]

The third categorical bar on capital punishment came in 2002 when the Court eliminated the death penalty for defendants who are mentally retarded. In *Atkins v. Virginia* (2002), the Court declared that the mentally retarded "should be categorically excluded from execution."[56] These offenders deserve to be punished, but their "subaverage intellectual functioning" and difficulty in adapting "diminishes their personal culpability," noted Justice Stevens. They are less likely to foresee the consequences of their actions and more likely to "act on impulse," he said. While his opinion did not define mental retardation, he referred to the American Psychiatric Association's definition of "mild mental retardation," which refers to persons who, when tested as youths, have I.Q. scores between 50 and 70. In the case before the Court, Daryl R. Atkins had been convicted of murder and sentenced to death for robbing and killing an airman stationed at the Langley Air Force Base. Virginia authorities disputed that Atkins was retarded, but a defense psychologist testified that he had an I.Q. of 59. The Court's 6-3 majority held that it was influenced by a shift in opinion by state legislators.

In 1989, when the justices had last considered the issue, only two states specifically exempted mentally retarded defendants from capital punishment. Since that time, however, sixteen more states and the federal government had moved to exempt mentally retarded persons from the death penalty. In the 1990s, only five states—Alabama, Louisiana, South Carolina, Texas, and Virginia—allowed execution of the mentally retarded, Stevens pointed out. "The practice, therefore, has become truly unusual, and it is fair to say that a national consensus has developed against it," he wrote in *Atkins v. Virginia*.[57]

In dissent, Chief Justice Rehnquist disputed whether there was a "national consensus" on the issue. In all, twenty states would permit capital punishment for a retarded murderer, and according to Rehnquist, it should be left to prosecutors, judges, and juries to decide the proper punishment for particular crimes and criminals.[58] In a much harsher dissent, Justice Scalia accused his colleagues of fabricating constitutional rules based on their "personal views" and "turning the process of capital trial into a game.... Society's moral outrage sometimes demands execution of retarded offenders."[59] He dismissed the "empty talk of a national consensus" on the issue, stating that the Court's view of the Constitution is "that really good lawyers have moral sentiments superior to those of the common herd, whether in 1791 or today. The arrogance of this assumption of power takes one's breath away."[60] Justice Thomas joined both dissents.

In 2005 the Court took the next step and abolished capital punishment for people under age eighteen at the time of their crimes. In *Roper v. Simmons*, Justice Kennedy noted that most states had limited the death penalty to adult murderers. Only three states—Oklahoma, Texas, and Virginia—had carried out executions of juvenile killers in the ten years prior to the ruling, he noted. If the death penalty is the ultimate punishment reserved for the "worst offenders," juveniles do not qualify, Kennedy said. "As any parent knows and as the scientific and sociological studies ... tend to confirm, 'a lack of maturity and an underdeveloped sense of responsibility are found in youth more often than in adults.'" This reckless and immature behavior does not excuse brutal crimes by the young, but a young murderer is "not as morally reprehensible" as an adult killer, he said.[61]

The ruling freed Christopher Simmons from Missouri's death row. His crime was certainly heinous. At seventeen, Simmons enlisted two other teenage boys to break into the home of a woman in their neighborhood. They tied her up and dropped her from a bridge into the Meramec River. Simmons confessed shortly after being arrested. Justices Stevens, Souter, Ginsburg, and Breyer joined Kennedy's opinion. Justices Rehnquist, O'Connor, Scalia, and Thomas dissented.

The most controversial passages in the Court's opinion referred to international law and world opinion. "Our determination that the death penalty is disproportionate punishment for offenders under 18 finds confirmation in the stark reality that the United States is the only country in the world that continues to give official sanction to the juvenile death penalty. This reality does not become controlling, for the task of interpreting the Eighth Amendment remains our responsibility," Kennedy wrote. He noted that the United Nations Convention on the Rights of the Child has been ratified by every country in the world, except the United States and Somalia, and it "contains an express prohibition on capital punishment for crimes committed by juveniles under age 18.... In sum, it is fair to say that the United States now stands alone in a world that has turned its face against the juvenile death penalty."

"It does not lessen our fidelity to the Constitution or our pride in its origins," Kennedy concluded, "to acknowledge that the express affirmation of certain fundamental rights by other nations and peoples simply underscores the centrality of those same rights without our own heritage of freedom."

In 2008 the Court reaffirmed its holding that the death penalty must be reserved for murderers. In another 5-4 decision, it struck down a Louisiana law that in 1995 authorized capital punishment for the rape of a child under age twelve. The first man sentenced to die under this law was Patrick Kennedy, who had been convicted of raping his twelve-year-old stepdaughter. By the time his case reached the Court, four other states had adopted similar laws. In *Kennedy v. Louisiana* (2008), however, the Court held to its view that "the death penalty should not be expanded to instances where the victim's life was not taken."[62] Between 1930 and 1964, 455 persons were executed for the crime of rape, the Court noted, and none since then. While the rape of a child is a heinous crime deserving of severe punishment, it is not the same as murder, said Justice Kennedy. His opinion left open the possibility that "offenses against the state," such as treason, espionage, or terrorism, could result in a death penalty, even when no life was taken. The majority consisted of Justices Kennedy, Stevens, Souter,

Ginsburg, and Breyer. In dissent, Justice Alito said there was no "national consensus" against executing child rapists, since the number of states enacting such laws had been increasing. Chief Justice Roberts and Justices Scalia and Thomas joined him in dissent.

The Court in 2008 also rejected a challenge to the use of lethal injections to carry out the death penalty. By the middle of the nineteenth century, hanging had become the "nearly universal form of execution" in the United States. In 1888, however, New York looked to modern science for the "most humane and practical method" of carrying out executions and so became the first to adopt electrocution. Throughout much of the twentieth century, the electric chair was the most common method of execution, although a few states used lethal gas or a firing squad. State officials were in search of a more humane method when in 1977, Oklahoma became the first to switch to lethal injections. Within two decades, all the states had followed suit. They also followed the same protocol whereby three drugs are administered: the first drug, sodium thiopental, induces unconsciousness; the second drug, pancuronium bromide, causes paralysis; and a third, potassium chloride, stops the heart from beating.

Those challenging this method conceded that if these drugs were administered properly, the condemned inmate would be rendered unconscious and would die peacefully. They also maintained, however, that if the first drug were administered improperly, the inmate would be paralyzed and could be subjected to searing pain by the heart-stopping drug. In *Baze v. Rees*, the Court upheld Kentucky's use of lethal injections and concluded there was no evidence that prison officials would botch the procedure.[63]

Chief Justice Roberts noted that when the framers of the Constitution adopted the ban on "cruel and unusual punishments," they did so against a backdrop of history when executioners deliberately inflicted pain. English history was replete with tortuous executions involving disemboweling, quartering, dissecting, and burning alive, he said. No one today contends the states are seeking to inflict great pain when they carry out an execution; they are understood to be seeking the most humane method of execution, he asserted.

"To constitute cruel and unusual punishment, an execution method must present a substantial or objectively intolerable risk of serious harm," Roberts wrote. He added that there was no evidence that the warden in Kentucky would not or could not follow the recommended protocol and administer the death penalty humanely. The chief justice left the door open to a future challenge involving lethal injections, but to win, the condemned prisoner would need evidence that the state's execution procedure "creates a demonstrated risk of severe pain," Roberts said. This is a high standard, and one not likely to be met. Justices Kennedy and Alito joined with Roberts, and Justices Stevens, Scalia, Thomas, and Breyer concurred in the outcome.

In a separate opinion, Justice Stevens said that he had concluded that "state-sanctioned killing" should be abolished. He said he had become convinced that capital punishment cannot be administered fairly and that its costs outweigh its benefits. "I have relied on my own experience in reaching the conclusion that the imposition of the death penalty represents the pointless and needless extinction of life with only marginal contributions to any discernible social or public purposes," Stevens wrote. "A penalty with such negligible returns to the States is patently excessive and cruel and unusual punishment violative of the Eighth Amendment." Over his many years on the Court, Stevens had succeeded in limiting the use of the death penalty, but he lacked the votes to end it.

NOTES

INTRODUCTION (PP. 259–266)

1. Leonard W. Levy, *Original Intent and the Framers Constitution* (Chicago: Ivan R. Dee, 2000), 224.

2. See *Crawford v. Washington*, 541 U.S. 36 (2004).

3. Akhil Amar, *The Bill of Rights: Creation and Reconstruction* (New Haven, Conn.: Yale University Press, 1998), 83.

4. *Joint Anti-Fascist Refugee Committee v. McGrath*, 341 U.S. 123 at 179 (1951).

5. *Barron v. Baltimore*, 7 Pet. (32 U.S.) 243 (1833).

6. Id. at 247, 250–251.

7. *Murray's Lessee v. Hoboken Land and Improvement Co.*, 18 How. (59 U.S.) 272 (1856).

8. Id. at 276–277.

9. *Shaughnessy v. United States ex rel. Mezei*, 345 U.S. 206 at 224 (1953).

10. *Hurtado v. California*, 110 U.S. 516 (1884); see also *Pennoyer v. Neff*, 95 U.S. 714 (1878).

11. *Hurtado v. California*, 110 U.S. 516 at 537 (1884).

12. Id. at 535–536.

13. Id. at 547–548.

14. *Davidson v. New Orleans*, 95 U.S. 97 at 104 (1878).

15. *Maxwell v. Dow*, 1976 U.S. 581 at 614 (1900).

16. *Twining v. New Jersey*, 211 U.S. 78 at 110–111 (1908).

17. Id. at 99.

18. *Palko v. Connecticut*, 302 U.S. 319 at 325 (1937).

19. *Adamson v. California*, 332 U.S. 46 at 53 (1947).

20. Id. at 89.

A FAIR TRIAL BY JURY (PP. 267–285)

1. *Colgrove v. Battin*, 413 U.S. 149 (1973).

2. *Patton v. United States*, 281 U.S. 276 at 288 (1930); see also *Singer v. United States*, 380 U.S. 24 (1965).

3. *Walker v. Sauvinet*, 92 U.S. 90 (1876).

4. *Maxwell v. Dow*, 176 U.S. 581 at 603 (1900).

5. *Duncan v. Louisiana*, 391 U.S. 145 (1968); but see *Blanton v. City of North Las Vegas*, 489 U.S. 538 (1989).

6. *Duncan v. Louisiana*, 391 U.S. 145 at 149 (1968).

7. *Williams v. Florida*, 399 U.S. 78 (1970).

8. Id. at 98–101.

9. *Ballew v. Georgia*, 435 U.S. 223 (1978).

10. *Baldwin v. New York*, 399 U.S. 66 (1970).

11. *Johnson v. Louisiana*, 406 U.S. 356 (1972); *Apodaca v. Oregon*, 406 U.S. 404 *(1972)*.

12. *Johnson v. Louisiana*, 406 U.S. 356 at 359 (1972).

13. Id. at 359, 362.

14. *Burch v. Louisiana*, 441 U.S. 130 (1979); *Brown v. Louisiana*, 447 U.S. 323 (1980).

15. *Smith v. Texas*, 311 U.S. 128 at 130 (1940).

16. *Taylor v. Louisiana*, 419 U.S. 522 (1975); *Duren v. Missouri*, 439 U.S. 357 (1979).

17. *Congress and the Nation* (Washington, D.C.: Congressional Quarterly, 1969), 2:385.

18. *Ex parte Virginia*, 100 U.S. 339 (1880); *Strauder v. West Virginia*, 100 U.S. 303 (1880); see also *Rose v. Mitchell*, 443 U.S. 545 (1979).

19. *Virginia v. Rives*, 100 U.S. 313 (1880).

20. *Norris v. Alabama*, 294 U.S. 587 (1935).

21. Id. at 590.

22. *Patton v. Mississippi*, 332 U.S. 463 at 469 (1947).

23. *Brown v. Allen*, 344 U.S. 443 (1953).

24. *Cassell v. Texas*, 339 U.S. 282 (1950); *Whitus v. Georgia*, 385 U.S. 545 (1967); *Avery v. Georgia*, 345 U.S. 559 (1952).

25. *Hernandez v. Texas*, 347 U.S. 475 (1954).

26. *Vasquez v. Hillery*, 474 U.S. 254 (1986).

27. *Batson v. Kentucky*, 476 U.S. 79 (1986).

28. *Id.*; see also *Griffith v. Kentucky, Brown v. United States*, 479 U.S. 314 (1987).

29. *Edmonson v. Leesville Concrete Co.*, 500 U.S. 614 (1991).

30. *Powers v. Ohio*, 499 U.S. 400 (1991).

31. *Georgia v. McCollum*, 505 U.S. 42 (1992).

32. *Miller-El v. Dretke*, 545 U.S. 231 (2005).

33. *Snyder v. Louisiana*, 552 U.S. __ (2008).

34. *Ballard v. United States*, 329 U.S. 187 (1946); *Hoyt v. Florida*, 368 U.S. 57 (1961).

35. Id. at 62.

36. *Taylor v. Louisiana*, 419 U.S. 522 (1975).

37. *Duren v. Missouri*, 439 U.S. 357 (1979).

38. *J.E.B. v. Alabama ex rel. T.B.*, 511 U.S. 127 (1994).

39. *Fay v. New York*, 332 U.S. 261 at 270–272 (1947); see also *Moore v. New York*, 333 U.S. 565 (1948).

40. Id. at 299–300.

41. *Apprendi v. New Jersey*, 530 U.S. 466 (2000).

42. Id. at 498.

43. Id.

44. Id. at 497.

45. Id. at 490.

46. Id. at 524.

47. *Ring v. Arizona*, 536 U.S. __ (2002).

48. *Blakely v. Washington*, 542 U.S. 296 (2004).

49. *Booker v. United States*, 543 U.S. 220 (2005).

50. *Kimbrough v. United States*, 552 U.S. __ (2007).

51. *Gall v. United States*, 552 U.S. __ (2007).

52. *Beavers v. Haubert*, 198 U.S. 77 at 87 (1905).

53. *United States v. Provoo*, 350 U.S. 857 (1955); see also *Pollard v. United States*, 352 U.S. 354 (1957); *United States v. Ewell*, 383 U.S. 116 (1966).

54. *Strunk v. United States*, 412 U.S. 434 (1973).

55. *United States v. Marion*, 404 U.S. 307 at 313 (1971).

56. *United States v. Lovasco*, 431 U.S. 783 (1977).

57. Id. at 790–791, 795–796.

58. *Klopfer v. North Carolina*, 386 U.S. 213 (1967).

59. Id. at 222–223.

60. *Barker v. Wingo*, 407 U.S. 514 (1972).

61. Id. at 530, 533.

62. *Congress and the Nation* (Washington, D.C.: Congressional Quarterly, 1977), 4:576; see also *United States v. Taylor*, 485 U.S. 902 (1988).

63. *United States v. MacDonald*, 435 U.S. 850 (1982); see also *United States v. Loud Hawk*, 474 U.S. 302 (1986).

64. *Doggett v. United States*, 505 U.S. 647 (1990).

65. *Mattox v. United States*, 156 U.S. 237 at 242–243 (1895).

66. *Kirby v. United States*, 174 U.S. 47 at 55 (1899).

67. Id. at 56.

68. *Pointer v. Texas*, 380 U.S. 400 (1965); see also *Douglas v. Alabama*, 380 U.S. 415 (1965).

69. *California v. Green*, 399 U.S. 149 (1970); *Dutton v. Evans*, 400 U.S. 74 (1970). See also *Harrington v. California*, 395 U.S. 250 (1969); *Nelson v. O'Neil*, 402 U.S. 622 (1971); *Schneble v. Florida*, 405 U.S. 427 (1972); *United States v. Inadi*, 475 U.S. 387 (1986); *Delaware v. Van Arsdall*, 475 U.S. 673 (1986); *Richardson v. Marsh*, 481 U.S. 200 (1987); *Cruz v. New York*, 482 U.S. 186 (1987).

70. *Chambers v. Mississippi*, 410 U.S. 284 (1973).

71. *Davis v. Alaska*, 415 U.S. 308 (1974).

72. *Coy v. Iowa*, 487 U.S. 1012 (1988).

73. *Maryland v. Craig*, 497 U.S. 836 (1990).

74. *Idaho v. Wright*, 497 U.S. 805 (1990); see also *White v. Illinois*, 502 U.S. 346 (1992).

75. *Michigan v. Lucas*, 500 U.S. 145 (1991).

76. *Crawford v. Washington*, 541 U.S. 36 (2004).

77. *Ohio v. Roberts*, 448 U.S. 56 (1980).

78. *Davis v. Washington*, 547 U.S. 813 (2006).

79. *Giles v. California*, 554 U.S. __ (2008).

SEARCH AND SEIZURE (PP. 286–312)

1. *Katz v. United States*, 389 U.S. 347 (1967).

2. Id. at 352.

3. *Smith v. Maryland*, 442 U.S. 735 (1979).

4. *United States v. Miller*, 425 U.S. 435 (1976).

5. *GM Leasing Corporation v. United States*, 429 U.S. 338 (1977); *Michigan v. Tyler*, 436 U.S. 499 (1978); *Mincey v. Arizona*, 437 U.S. 385 (1978); cf. *Oliver v. United States, Maine v. Thornton*, 466 U.S. 170 (1984); *California v. Ciraolo*, 476 U.S. 207 (1986); *Dow Chemical v. United States*, 476 U.S. 227 (1986); *California v. Acevedo*, 500 U.S. 565 (1991).

6. *Kyllo v. United States*, 533 U.S. 27 (2001).

7. *Georgia v. Randolph*, 547 U.S. 103 (2006).

8. *Wolf v. Colorado*, 338 U.S. 25 (1949).

9. *Mapp v. Ohio*, 367 U.S. 643 (1961).

10. *Ker v. California*, 374 U.S. 23 (1963).

11. *Johnson v. United States*, 333 U.S. 10 at 13–14 (1948).

12. *Coolidge v. New Hampshire*, 403 U.S. 443 at 453 (1971); see also *Lo-Ji Sales v. New York*, 442 U.S. 319 (1979).

13. *Shadwick v. City of Tampa, Fla.*, 407 U.S. 345 at 350 (1972).

14. *Locke v. United States*, 7 Cr. (11 U.S.) 339 at 348 (1813); see *Arizona v. Hicks*, 480 U.S. 321 (1987).

15. *Dumbra v. United States*, 268 U.S. 435 at 441 (1925); see also *Byars v. United States*, 273 U.S. 28 (1927); *Draper v. United States*, 358 U.S. 307 (1959).

16. *Nathanson v. United States*, 290 U.S. 41 at 47 (1933); see also *Giordanello v. United States*, 357 U.S. 480 (1958); *Aguilar v. Texas*, 378 U.S. 108 (1964); *Spinelli v. United*

States, 393 U.S. 410 (1969); *United States v. Ventresca,* 380 U.S. 102 at 108–109 (1965).

17. *Jones v. United States,* 362 U.S. 257 (1960).

18. *Rugendorf v. United States,* 367 U.S. 528 (1964); *McCray v. Illinois,* 386 U.S. 300 (1967); see also *Whitely v. Warden,* 401 U.S. 560 (1971); *United States v. Harris,* 403 U.S. 573 (1971); *Adams v. Williams,* 407 U.S. 143 (1972); *Alabama v. White,* 496 U.S. 325 (1990).

19. *Franks v. Delaware,* 438 U.S. 154 at 168 (1978).

20. *Schneckloth v. Bustamonte,* 412 U.S. 218 at 248–249 (1973).

21. Id. at 277.

22. *United States v. Matlock,* 415 U.S. 164 (1974).

23. *Minnesota v. Olson,* 495 U.S. 91 (1990); see also *United States v. Padilla,* 508 U.S. 77 (1993).

24. *Georgia v. Randolph,* 547 U.S. 103 (2006).

25. *Boyd v. United States,* 116 U.S. 616 (1886).

26. Id. at 630, 633.

27. *Weeks v. United States,* 232 U.S. 383 (1914).

28. Id. at 392–393.

29. *United States v. Miller,* 425 U.S. 435 (1976).

30. *Andresen v. Maryland,* 427 U.S. 463 (1976).

31. *Fisher v. United States,* 425 U.S. 391 (1976).

32. *Smith v. Maryland,* 442 U.S. 735 (1979).

33. *Zurcher v. The Stanford Daily,* 436 U.S. 547 at 554 (1978).

34. Id. at 579.

35. *Ex parte Burford,* 3 Cr. (7. U.S.) 448 (1805); *Kurtz v. Moffitt,* 115 U.S. 487 (1885).

36. *Carroll v. United States,* 267 U.S. 132 at 156 (1925).

37. *Gerstein v. Pugh,* 420 U.S. 103 at 113 (1975).

38. *Ker v. California,* 374 U.S. 23 (1963).

39. *Davis v. Mississippi,* 394 U.S. 721 at 727 (1969); *Dunaway v. New York,* 442 U.S. 200 (1979).

40. *United States v. Watson,* 423 U.S. 411 (1976).

41. Id. at 423–424.

42. *Payton v. New York,* 445 U.S. 573 at 590 (1980).

43. Id. at 591.

44. *Wilson v. Arkansas,* 514 U.S. 927 at 933 (1995).

45. *United States v. Banks,* 540 U.S. 31 (2003).

46. *Hudson v. Michigan,* 547 U.S. 586 (2006).

47. *Wilson v. Layne,* 526 U.S. 603 at 613 (1999).

48. Id. at 625.

49. *Atwater v. Lago Vista,* 532 U.S. 318 at 354 (2001).

50. Id. at 333.

51. Id. at 339–340.

52. Id. at 360, 372.

53. *County of Riverside v. McLaughlin,* 500 U.S. 44 at 53 (1991).

54. Id. at 55, 56.

55. Id. at 71.

56. *Agnello v. United States,* 269 U.S. 20 at 30 (1925); *Marron v. United States,* 275 U.S. 192 (1927).

57. *Harris v. United States,* 331 U.S. 145 (1947).

58. Id. at 150–151.

59. Id. at 183.

60. *Trupiano v. United States,* 334 U.S. 699 at 706 (1948).

61. Id. at 708.

62. Id.

63. *McDonald v. United States,* 335 U.S. 451 at 454, 456 (1948).

64. *United States v. Rabinowitz,* 339 U.S. 56 at 66 (1950).

65. Id. at 63, 66.

66. *Kremen v. United States,* 353 U.S. 346 (1957); *Abel v. United States,* 362 U.S. 217 at 238 (1960); *Chapman v. United States,* 365 U.S. 610 (1961); *Ker v. California,* 374 U.S. 23 (1963).

67. *Chimel v. California,* 395 U.S. 752 (1969).

68. Id. at 766, 768.

69. Id. at 780.

70. *Vale v. Louisiana,* 399 U.S. 30 (1970).

71. *Coolidge v. New Hampshire,* 403 U.S. 443 (1971); see also *United States v. Edwards,* 415 U.S. 800 (1974).

72. *United States v. Robinson,* 414 U.S. 218 (1973); *Gustafson v. Florida,* 414 U.S. 260 (1973).

73. *Carroll v. United States,* 267 U.S. 132 (1925).

74. Id. at 153.

75. *Husty v. United States,* 282 U.S. 694 (1931); see also *Scher v. United States,* 305 U.S. 251 (1938).

76. *United States v. Di Re,* 332 U.S. 581 (1948).

77. *Brinegar v. United States,* 338 U.S. 160 (1949); see also *California v. Carney,* 471 U.S. 386 (1985).

78. *Henry v. United States,* 361 U.S. 98 (1959); *Rios v. United States,* 364 U.S. 253 (1960).

79. *Cooper v. California,* 386 U.S. 58 (1967).

80. *Chambers v. Maroney,* 399 U.S. 42 (1970); *Preston v. United States,* 376 U.S. 364 (1964).

81. *Cady v. Dombrowski,* 413 U.S. 433 (1973); *South Dakota v. Opperman,* 428 U.S. 364 (1976).

82. *Cardwell v. Lewis,* 417 U.S. 583 (1974).

83. *Rakas v. Illinois,* 439 U.S. 128 (1978).

84. *United States v. Ross,* 456 U.S. 798 (1982).

85. *California v. Acevedo,* 500 U.S. 565 (1991).

86. *Delaware v. Prouse,* 440 U.S. 648 at 661 (1979).

87. *Knowles v. Iowa,* 525 U.S. 113 at 115 (1998).

88. *United States v. Whren,* 517 U.S. 806 at 813 (1996).

89. *County of Sacramento v. Lewis,* 523 U.S. 833 at 836 (1998).

90. Id. at 855.

91. *Scott v. Harris* 550 U.S. __ (2007).

92. *Maryland v. Wilson,* 519 U.S. 408 at 413 (1997).

93. *Pennsylvania v. Mimms,* 434 U.S. 106 (1977).

94. *Wyoming v. Houghton,* 526 U.S. 295 at 307 (1997).

95. *Illinois v. Caballes,* 543 U.S. 405 (2005).

96. *Florida v. Bostick,* 501 U.S. 429 (1991).

97. *United States v. Drayton*, 536 U.S. 194 (2002).

98. Id.

99. Id.

100. *Olmstead v. United States*, 277 U.S. 438 at 463–466 (1928).

101. Id. at 469–470.

102. Id. at 473, 485.

103. *Nardone v. United States*, 302 U.S. 379 (1937); *Weiss v. United States*, 308 U.S. 321 (1939); *Nardone v. United States*, 308 U.S. 338 (1939); see also *Rathbun v. United States*, 355 U.S. 107 (1957); *Benanti v. United States*, 355 U.S. 96 (1957).

104. *Goldstein v. United States*, 316 U.S. 114 (1942); *Goldman v. United States*, 316 U.S. 129 (1942); see also *On Lee v. United States*, 343 U.S. 747 (1952).

105. *Silverman v. United States*, 365 U.S. 505 (1961); see also *Wong Sun v. United States*, 371 U.S. 471 (1963); *Berger v. New York*, 388 U.S. 41 (1967); *Osborn v. United States*, 385 U.S. 323 (1966).

106. *Katz v. United States*, 389 U.S. 247 (1967).

107. Id. at 353.

108. Id. at 351.

109. *Alderman v. United States, Butenko v. United States, Ivanov v. United States*, 394 U.S. 165 (1969).

110. *Congress and the Nation* (Washington, D.C.: Congressional Quarterly, 1969), 2:326–327.

111. *United States v. U.S. District Court, Eastern Michigan*, 407 U.S. 297 (1972).

112. *United States v. Giordano*, 416 U.S. 505 (1974).

113. *Dalia v. United States*, 441 U.S. 238 (1979).

114. *California v. Ciraolo*, 476 U.S. 207 at 215 (1986).

115. *Florida v. Riley*, 488 U.S. 445 at 449 (1989).

116. *Kyllo v. United States*, 533 U.S. 27 at 34 (2001).

117. Id. at 37.

SELF-INCRIMINATION (PP. 313–327)

1. *Bruno v. United States*, 308 U.S. 287 (1939); *Griffin v. California*, 380 U.S. 609 (1965); *United States v. Hale*, 422 U.S. 171 (1975); *Doyle v. Ohio, Wood v. Ohio*, 427 U.S. 610 (1976).

2. *Hoffman v. United States*, 341 U.S. 479 (1951); *Mason v. United States*, 244 U.S. 362 (1917); *Rogers v. United States*, 340 U.S. 367 (1951); *United States v. Monia*, 317 U.S. 424 (1943).

3. *Emspak v. United States*, 349 U.S. 190 (1955).

4. *Heike v. United States*, 227 U.S. 131 (1913); *Brown v. Walker*, 161 U.S. 591 (1896).

5. *Rogers v. United States*, 340 U.S. 367 at 372–374 (1951); see also *Blau v. United States*, 340 U.S. 159 (1950).

6. *Hale v. Henkel*, 201 U.S. 43 (1906); *United States v. White*, 322 U.S. 694 (1944); *Bellis v. United States*, 417 U.S. 85 (1974).

7. *Wilson v. United States*, 221 U.S. 361 (1911); *Shapiro v. United States*, 335 U.S. 1 (1948); see also *Mancusi v. DeForte*, 392 U.S. 364 (1968); *Couch v. United States*, 409 U.S. 322 (1973); *United States v. Kasmir, Fisher v. United States*, 425 U.S. 391 (1976).

8. *Garrity v. New Jersey*, 385 U.S. 493 (1967); *Spevack v. Klein*, 385 U.S. 511 (1967); *Slochower v. Board of Higher Education of New York City*, 350 U.S. 551 (1956); *Garner v. Broderick*, 392 U.S. 273 (1968); *Lefkowitz v. Cunningham*, 431 U.S. 801 (1977).

9. *United States v. Doremus*, 249 U.S. 86 (1919); *United States v. Sanchez*, 340 U.S. 42 (1950); *Sonzinsky v. United States*, 300 U.S. 506 (1937); *United States v. Kahriger*, 345 U.S. 22 (1953).

10. *Albertson v. Subversive Activities Control Board*, 382 U.S. 70 (1965).

11. *Grosso v. United States*, 390 U.S. 62 (1968); *Marchetti v. United States*, 390 U.S. 39 (1968); *Haynes v. United States*, 390 U.S. 85 (1968); *Leary v. United States*, 395 U.S. 6 (1969); see also *Minor v. United States, Buie v. United States*, 396 U.S. 87 (1969); *United States v. Freed*, 41 U.S. 601 (1971).

12. *Fisher v. United States*, 425 U.S. 391 (1976).

13. *Baltimore v. Bouknight*, 493 U.S. 549 (1990).

14. *Kastigar v. United States*, 406 U.S. 441 at 446 (1972).

15. *Counselman v. Hitchcock*, 142 U.S. 547 at 585–586 (1892).

16. Id.

17. *Brown v. Walker*, 161 U.S. 591 at 595, 596, 605–606, 610 (1896).

18. *Ullmann v. United States*, 350 U.S. 422 at 438 (1956).

19. Id. at 438–439.

20. Id. at 440.

21. Id. at 449, 454.

22. *Congress and the Nation* (Washington, D.C.: Congressional Quarterly, 1973), 3:273.

23. *Kastigar v. United States*, 406 U.S. 441 at 453 (1972).

24. Id. at 460.

25. Id. at 466–467.

26. *Twining v. New Jersey*, 211 U.S. 78 at 106 (1908).

27. *Adamson v. California*, 332 U.S. 46 at 54 (1947).

28. *United States v. Murdock*, 284 U.S. 141 (1931); *Feldman v. United States*, 322 U.S. 487 (1944); *Knapp v. Schweitzer*, 357 U.S. 371 (1958).

29. *Malloy v. Hogan*, 378 U.S. 1 at 8, 11 (1964).

30. Id at 16, 27.

31. *Murphy v. The Waterfront Commission of New York Harbor*, 378 U.S. 52 at 79 (1964).

32. *Griffin v. California*, 380 U.S. 609 at 615 (1965).

33. Id. at 614; see also *Lakeside v. Oregon*, 435 U.S. 333 (1978).

34. *Hopt v. Utah*, 110 U.S. 574 at 585 (1884).

35. *Bram v. United States*, 168 U.S. 532 (1897).

36. *Hopt v. Utah,* 110 U.S. 574 at 584–585 (1884).

37. *Wilson v. United States,* 162 U.S. 613 at 623 (1896).

38. *Bram v. United States,* 168 U.S. 532 at 561, 542 (1897).

39. *McNabb v. United States,* 318 U.S. 332 at 340 (1943).

40. Id. at 343–344.

41. *Mallory v. United States,* 354 U.S. 449 at 453 (1957).

42. *Brown v. Mississippi,* 297 U.S. 278 at 285 (1935).

43. Id. at 285–286.

44. *Chambers v. Florida,* 309 U.S. 227 at 237, 239–240, 241 (1940).

45. *Lisenba v. California,* 314 U.S. 219 (1941); *Ashcraft v. Tennessee,* 322 U.S. 143 (1944); *Fikes v. Alabama,* 352 U.S. 191 (1957); *Spano v. New York,* 360 U.S. 315 (1959); *Lynumn v. Illinois,* 372 U.S. 528 (1963); *Townsend v. Sain,* 372 U.S. 293 (1963); *Haynes v. Washington,* 373 U.S. 503 (1963).

46. *Rogers v. Richmond,* 365 U.S. 534 at 540–541 (1961); see also *Stein v. New York,* 346 U.S. 156 (1953); *Jackson v. Denno,* 378 U.S. 368 (1964).

47. *Crooker v. California,* 357 U.S. 433 (1958); *Cicencia v. LaGay,* 357 U.S. 504 (1958), overruled by *Miranda v. Arizona,* 384 U.S. 436 (1966).

48. *Massiah v. United States,* 377 U.S. 201 (1964).

49. *Escobedo v. Illinois,* 378 U.S. 478 (1964).

50. *Gideon v. Wainwright,* 372 U.S. 335 (1963).

51. *Escobedo v. Illinois,* 378 U.S. 478 at 490–491 (1964).

52. Id. at 496.

53. *Miranda v. Arizona,* 384 U.S. 436 at 441–442 (1966). *Miranda* was one of four cases reviewed by the Court and resolved together. The others were *Vignera v. New York, Westover v. United States,* and *California v. Stewart.*

54. *Miranda v. Arizona,* 384 U.S. 436 at 466 (1966).

55. Id. at 444–445.

56. Id. at 474.

57. Id. at 515–516.

58. Id. at 536, 537, 541–542.

59. *Johnson v. New Jersey,* 384 U.S. 719 (1966).

60. *Orozco v. Texas,* 394 U.S. 324 (1969).

61. *Harris v. New York,* 401 U.S. 222 at 224, 226 (1971).

62. Id. at 232.

63. *Michigan v. Tucker,* 417 U.S. 433 (1974); see also *Oregon v. Hass,* 420 U.S. 714 (1975).

64. *United States v. Mandujano,* 425 U.S. 564 (1976).

65. *New York v. Quarles,* 467 U.S. 649 (1984).

66. Id. at 660.

67. *Minnesota v. Murphy,* 465 U.S. 420 (1984); see also *Oregon v. Elstad,* 470 U.S. 298 (1985).

68. *Pennsylvania v. Muniz,* 496 U.S. 582 (1990).

69. *Michigan v. Mosley,* 423 U.S. 96 (1975).

70. *Minnick v. Mississippi,* 498 U.S. 146 (1990); *Edwards v. Arizona,* 451 U.S. 477 (1981).

71. *Davis v. United States,* 512 U.S. 452 (1994).

72. *Fare v. Michael C.,* 442 U.S. 707 (1979).

73. *Colorado v. Connelly,* 479 U.S. 157 (1986).

74. *Dickerson v. United States,* 530 U.S. 428 (2000).

75. Id. at 437.

76. Id. at 446.

77. Id.

78. *Chavez v. Martinez,* 538 U.S. 760 (2003).

79. *Missouri v. Seibert,* 542 U.S. 600 (2004).

80. *United States v. Patane,* 542 U.S. 630 (2004).

THE AID OF LEGAL COUNSEL (PP. 328–337)

1. 1 Stat. 73, 92 (1789); 1 Stat. 112, 118 (1790); now U.S. Code 18, sec. 563.

2. *Powell v. Alabama,* 287 U.S. 45 (1932).

3. *Johnson v. Zerbst,* 304 U.S. 458 (1938).

4. *Gideon v. Wainwright,* 372 U.S. 335 (1963); *Argersinger v. Hamlin,* 407 U.S. 25 (1972); *Ake v. Oklahoma,* 470 U.S. 68 (1985).

5. *Powell v. Alabama,* 287 U.S. 45 at 53 (1932).

6. Id. at 56–57.

7. Id. at 68.

8. Id. at 71.

9. 1 Stat. 73, 92 (1789); 1 Stat. 112, 118 (1790); now U.S. Code 18, sec. 563.

10. *Johnson v. Zerbst,* 304 U.S. 458 (1938).

11. Id. at 462–463, 465, 467–468.

12. *Betts v. Brady,* 316 U.S. 455 (1942).

13. Id. at 461–462.

14. Id. at 465.

15. Id. at 473.

16. Id. at 476.

17. *Canizio v. New York,* 327 U.S. 82 (1946); *Bute v. Illinois,* 333 U.S. 640 (1948); *Tomkins v. Missouri,* 323 U.S. 485 (1945); *Townsend v. Burk,* 334 U.S. 736 (1948); *White v. Ragen,* 324 U.S. 760 (1945); *DeMeerleer v. Michigan,* 329 U.S. 663 (1947); *Marino v. Ragen,* 332 U.S. 561 (1947); *Rice v. Olsen,* 324 U.S. 786 (1945).

18. *Gideon v. Wainwright,* 372 U.S. 335 (1963).

19. Id. at 343–344.

20. *Escobedo v. Illinois,* 378 U.S. 478 (1964).

21. *Miranda v. Arizona,* 384 U.S. 436 at 466 (1966).

22. Id. at 471; see also *Duckworth v. Eagan,* 492 U.S. 195 (1989).

23. *Argersinger v. Hamlin,* 407 U.S. 25 at 32–33, 40 (1972).

24. *Alabama v. Shelton,* 536 U.S. 654 (2002).

25. *Powell v. Alabama,* 287 U.S. 45 (1932).

26. *Hamilton v. Alabama,* 368 U.S. 52 (1961).

27. *Escobedo v. Illinois,* 378 U.S. 478 (1964); *Miranda v. Arizona,* 384 U.S. 436 (1966).

28. *United States v. Wade,* 388 U.S. 218 (1967); *Gilbert v. California,* 388 U.S. 263 (1967).

29. *United States v. Wade,* 388 U.S. 218 at 227 (1967).

30. *Kirby v. Illinois,* 406 U.S. 682 (1972); but see also *Coleman v. Alabama,* 399 U.S. 1 (1970).

31. *Kirby v. Illinois,* 406 U.S. 682 at 689–690 (1972).

32. *United States v. Ash,* 413 U.S. 300 (1973).

33. *Ross v. Moffit,* 417 U.S. 600 (1974).

34. *Texas v. Cobb,* 532 U.S. 162 (2001).

35. *Glasser v. United States,* 315 U.S. 60 (1942).

36. Id. at 71, 76.

37. *Holloway v. Arkansas,* 435 U.S. 475 at 489–490 (1978).

38. *Mann v. Richardson,* 397 U.S. 759 (1970); *Tollett v. Henderson,* 411 U.S. 258 (1973).

39. *Strickland v. Washington,* 466 U.S. 668 at 689 (1984).

40. *United States v. Cronic,* 466 U.S. 648 (1984).

41. *Evitts v. Lucey,* 469 U.S. 387 (1985).

42. *Roe, Warden v. Flores-Ortega,* 528 U.S. 470 at 479 (2000).

43. Id. at 480.

44. *Mickens v. Taylor,* 535 U.S. 162 (2002).

45. See *Strickland v. Washington,* 466 U.S. 668 (1984).

46. *Woodford v. Visciotti,* 537 U.S. 19 (2002).

47. *Wiggins v. Maryland,* 539 U.S. 510 (2003).

DOUBLE JEOPARDY (PP. 338–343)

1. *Benton v. Maryland,* 395 U.S. 784 (1969).

2. *Downum v. United States,* 372 U.S. 734 (1963); *Crist v. Bretz,* 437 U.S. 28 (1978).

3. *Wade v. Hunter,* 336 U.S. 684 (1949); *United States v. Dinitz,* 424 U.S. 600 (1976); *Lee v. United States,* 432 U.S. 23 (1977); *Oregon v. Kennedy,* 456 U.S. 667 (1982).

4. *United States v. Perez,* 9 Wheat. (22 U.S.) 579 (1824); *Richardson v. United States,* 468 U.S. 317 (1984).

5. *United States v. Ball,* 163 U.S. 662 (1896); *Hudson v. Louisiana,* 450 U.S. 40 (1981); *Smalis v. Pennsylvania,* 476 U.S. 140 (1986); but see *Tibbs v. Florida,* 457 U.S. 31 (1982).

6. *United States v. Sanges,* 144 U.S. 310 (1892); *United States v. Ball,* 163 U.S. 662 (1896); *Fong Foo v. United States,* 369 U.S. 141 (1962); *Sanabria v. United States,* 437 U.S. 54 (1978).

7. *United States v. Lanza,* 260 U.S. 377 at 382 (1922).

8. *Abbate v. United States,* 359 U.S. 187 (1959); *Bartkus v. Illinois,* 359 U.S. 121 (1959); see also *Petite v. United States,* 361 U.S. 529 (1960); *Heath v. Alabama,* 474 U.S. 82 (1985).

9. *Waller v. Florida,* 397 U.S. 387 (1970).

10. *United States v. Wheeler,* 435 U.S. 313 (1978).

11. *Heath v. Alabama,* 474 U.S. 82 (1985); see also *Grady v. Corbin,* 495 U.S. 508 (1990); *United States v. Dixon,* 509 U.S. 688 (1993).

12. *Green v. United States,* 355 U.S. 184 at 187–188 (1957); see also *Price v. Georgia,* 398 U.S. 323 (1970).

13. *Palko v. Connecticut,* 302 U.S. 319 at 325 (1937).

14. Id. at 328.

15. *Benton v. Maryland,* 395 U.S. 784 at 795 (1969).

16. Id. at 808.

17. *Bullington v. Missouri,* 451 U.S. 430 (1981); see also *Arizona v. Rumsey,* 467 U.S. 203 (1984); *Poland v. Arizona,* 476 U.S. 147 (1986).

18. *North Carolina v. Pearce,* 395 U.S. 711 (1969); but see *Texas v. McCullough,* 475 U.S. 134 (1986); *Alabama v. Smith,* 490 U.S. 794 (1989).

19. *North Carolina v. Pearce,* 395 U.S. 711 at 717 (1969).

20. *Chaffin v. Stynchcombe,* 412 U.S. 17 (1973).

21. *United States v. Wilson,* 420 U.S. 332 (1975).

22. *United States v. Jenkins,* 420 U.S. 358 (1975).

23. *United States v. Scott,* 437 U.S. 82 (1978).

24. *Grady v. Corbin,* 495 U.S. 508 (1990).

25. *United States v. Dixon,* 509 U.S. 688 (1993).

26. *United States v. Ursery,* 518 U.S. 267 at 297 (1996).

27. Id. at 288.

28. Id. at 295.

29. Id. at 301.

30. Id. at 320.

31. *Hudson v. United States,* 522 U.S. 93 at 95–96 (1997).

CRUEL AND UNUSUAL PUNISHMENT (PP. 344–359)

1. *Trop v. Dulles,* 356 U.S. 86 at 101 (1958).

2. *Hope v. Pelzer,* 536 U.S 730 (2002).

3. *Lockyer v Andrade,* 538 U.S. 63 (2003).

4. *O'Neil v. Vermont,* 144 U.S. 323 (1892).

5. *Weems v. United States,* 217 U.S. 349 at 367 (1910).

6. *Louisiana ex rel. Francis v. Resweber,* 329 U.S. 459 (1947).

7. Id. at 464.

8. *Robinson v. California,* 370 U.S. 660 at 666, 667 (1962).

9. *Powell v. Texas,* 392 U.S. 514 at 532 (1968).

10. *Estelle v. Gamble,* 429 U.S. 97 (1976).

11. Id. at 104.

12. *Whitley v. Albers,* 475 U.S. 312 at 319 (1986).

13. *Hudson v. McMillian,* 503 U.S. 1 at 9 (1992).

14. Id. at 28.

15. Id. at 13–14.

16. *Helling v. McKinney,* 509 U.S. 25 at 40 (1993).

17. Id. at 37.

18. *Farmer v. Brennan,* 511 U.S. 825 at 832 (1994).

19. Id. at 847.

20. *Hope v. Pelzer,* 536 U.S 730 (2002).

21. See Stuart Banner, *The Death Penalty: An American History* (Cambridge, Mass.: Harvard University Press, 2002), 228.

22. Ibid., 230.

23. *Furman v. Georgia*, 408 U.S. 238 at 253, 256–257 (1972).

24. Id. at 291.

25. Id. at 305.

26. Id. at 309–310.

27. Id. at 312–313.

28. Id. at 369.

29. Id. at 404.

30. Banner, *Death Penalty*, 268.

31. *Gregg v. Georgia*, 428 U.S. 153 at 187 (1976); *Proffitt v. Florida*, 428 U.S. 242 (1976); *Jurek v. Texas*, 428 U.S. 262 (1976).

32. *Gregg v. Georgia*, 428 U.S. 153 at 186–187 (1976).

33. Id. at 229.

34. Id. at 206–207.

35. *Woodson v. North Carolina*, 428 U.S. 280 (1976); *Roberts v. Louisiana*, 428 U.S. 325 (1976).

36. *Woodson v. North Carolina*, 428 U.S. 280 at 302 (1976).

37. Id. at 304.

38. Id.

39. *Roberts v. Louisiana*, 431 U.S. 633 (1977); *Sumner v. Shuman*, 483 U.S. 66 (1987).

40. *McCleskey v. Kemp*, 481 U.S. 279 at 329 (1987).

41. Id. at 312.

42. Id.

43. Id.

44. Banner, *Death Penalty*, 290.

45. Ibid.

46. *Lockett v. Ohio*, 438 U.S. 586 (1978).

47. *Simmons v. South Carolina*, 512 U.S. 154 (1994).

48. *Ring v. Arizona*, 536 U.S. 584 (2002).

49. *Coker v. Georgia*, 433 U.S. 584 at 598 (1977).

50. *Enmund v. Florida*, 458 U.S. 782 (1982).

51. *Tison v. Arizona*, 481 U.S. 137 (1987).

52. Id. at 158.

53. *Ford v. Wainwright*, 477 U.S. 399 at 407 (1986).

54. *Thompson v. Oklahoma*, 487 U.S. 815 at 823 (1988).

55. *Stanford v. Kentucky*, 492 U.S. 361 (1989).

56. *Atkins v. Virginia*, 536 U.S. 304 (2002).

57. Id.

58. Id.

59. Id.

60. Id.

61. *Roper v. Simmons*, 543 U.S. 551 (2005).

62. *Kennedy v. Louisiana*, 554 U.S. __ (2008).

63. *Baze v. Rees*, 553 U.S. __ (2008).

chapter 6

Equal Rights and Equal Protection of the Laws

EQUAL RIGHTS AND EQUAL PROTECTION of the laws are two of the great promises of American democracy. They are also great embarrassments to the U.S. Constitution as practiced for centuries in U.S. history. The Declaration of Independence in 1776 had proclaimed what its authors saw as the "self-evident" truth that "all men are created equal." This was a call to revolution, one that inspired its generation and generations to follow. The Constitution of 1787 was more practically minded. It set out a structure and plan for a stronger federal government, but it made no mention of equality or equal rights for all. Many of its framers owned slaves in the South, and their rights were protected. Article I of the Constitution extended the slave trade for another generation. Congress was prohibited from forbidding the importation of slaves before 1808; future lawmakers were told they could impose a tax "not exceeding ten dollars for each Person." As for African Americans, they had no prospect of equal rights, or any rights, under this Constitution. Women of the day had no right to own property, to vote, or to hold public office. By this reckoning, "We the People" referred to in the Constitution's preamble did not include the majority of Americans.

When the United States celebrated the two hundredth anniversary of the Constitution in 1987, Justice Thurgood Marshall, the Court's first African American justice, gave a speech that read like a dissenting opinion. He rebuked those who focus on the original meaning of the Constitution: "I do not believe that the meaning of the Constitution was forever 'fixed' at the Philadelphia Convention. Nor do I find the wisdom, foresight and sense of justice exhibited by the framers particularly profound. To the contrary, the government they devised was defective from the start, requiring several amendments, a Civil War, and momentous social transformation to attain the system of constitutional government, and its respect for the individual freedoms and human rights, we hold as fundamental today," Marshall said. Stating that he did not plan to join "the celebration of the 'Miracle of Philadelphia,'" the justice concluded "the true miracle was not the birth of the Constitution but its life, a life nurtured through two turbulent centuries of our own making."[1]

As Marshall remarked, equal rights under law evolved over two centuries, and the Supreme Court played little role for much of that time. The Civil War ended slavery, and the Fourteenth Amendment that followed in 1868 sought to give equal rights to the freed slaves. It states, "No state shall ... deny to any person within its jurisdiction the equal protection of the laws." The amendment gave Congress the authority to enforce this provision. Two years before, the Reconstruction Congress had adopted the Civil Rights Act of 1866, the nation's first civil rights measure. It reads, in part, "citizens of every race and color ... shall have the same right ... to make and enforce contracts ... and to full and equal benefit of all laws and proceedings for the security of person and property, as is enjoyed by white citizens." In 1875 Congress extended the reach of federal civil rights protections to give all persons the right to "the full and equal enjoyment" of public transportation, inns, and theaters. The Supreme Court, however, struck down this law in 1883, ruling that the Congress that had written the Fourteenth Amendment had misunderstood its reach. Another eight decades would pass before Congress negated this court decision.

Relying on its power over interstate commerce, Congress adopted the Civil Rights Act of 1964 and prohibited discrimination against blacks in hotels, restaurants, schools, colleges, and workplaces. By that time, the Supreme Court had changed its course and had become an ally of the civil rights movement. The key moment had transpired in 1954, when a new chief justice, Earl Warren, spoke for a unanimous Court in holding that racial segregation of public schools was "inherently unequal" and unconstitutional. No longer would the Court look the other way and rationalize laws and official practices that excluded blacks as "separate but equal." The Court's decision in *Brown v. Board of Education* (1954) did not transform the schools immediately. Southern states resisted compliance for more than a decade, but the institution that had done so much to weaken the civil rights advances of the Reconstruction era helped launch a second civil rights movement that reshaped the nation in the 1960s.

The women's rights movement gained strength throughout the 1960s, and its impact was eventually felt by a nine-man Supreme Court. During the 1970s, the Court moved, step by step, toward outlawing nearly all gender discrimination in the law. One of the leading voices pressing for gender equality was Ruth Bader Ginsburg, a lawyer for the Women's Rights Project of the American Civil Liberties Union. In 1993 Ginsburg would become the second woman appointed to the Supreme Court. In the 1990s, the

Court confronted the growing gay rights movement. In its first major ruling on gay rights, a 6-3 majority would strike down as unconstitutional a voter initiative in Colorado that deprived gays and lesbians of all protections of antidiscrimination law. Led by Justice Anthony M. Kennedy, the Court conceded that it had not settled on a neat formula for deciding cases involving discrimination against gays. Nonetheless, a discriminatory law "born of animosity toward the class of persons affected" cannot stand, he said.[2]

WHAT IS EQUAL PROTECTION?

The guarantee of "equal protection of the laws" has never been interpreted to require that all persons and all groups are treated in exactly the same way. Laws by their very nature distinguish between categories of people, classes of property, and kinds of action. For the most part, such distinctions are desirable and necessary in an organized society. For example, most states will license a sixteen-year-old to drive a car but will not do the same for a fifteen-year-old. Similarly, persons with a degree from an accredited medical school can be licensed to practice medicine, while those without such a credential are denied the same privilege. These distinctions and classifications treat persons differently, but they are not seen as denying individuals the equal protection of the law. Other distinctions, however, are seen as unfair, irrational, and even malicious. The question the Court must answer is whether legal classifications are permissible or result from a distinction that is unacceptable.

The first standard developed by the Supreme Court for measuring a particular classification against the equal protection guarantee grew largely out of its review of state tax and economic regulation. Here the Court deferred more often than not to the judgment of the states; its standard for review of such alleged violations was thus, not surprisingly, minimal. The Court was satisfied that a classification was valid if a state could show that it had a reasonable basis. This traditional standard for testing the validity of

FEDERAL EQUAL PROTECTION

Nowhere does the Constitution explicitly require the federal government to ensure equal protection of its laws against arbitrary discrimination. The Supreme Court, however, has found this requirement implicit in the Fifth Amendment's guarantee of due process of law. The Court explained this finding in *Bolling v. Sharpe* (1954), in which it struck down the federal government's requirement that black and white pupils in the District of Columbia attend separate schools:

> The Fifth Amendment ... does not contain an equal protection clause as does the Fourteenth Amendment which applies only to the states. But the concepts of equal protection and due process, both stemming from our American ideal of fairness, are not mutually exclusive. The "equal protection of the law" is a more explicit safeguard of prohibited unfairness than "due process of law," and, therefore, we do not imply that the two are always interchangeable phrases. But, as this Court has recognized, discrimination may be so unjustifiable as to be violative of due process.[1]

The Court reaffirmed this finding in several later cases.[2]

---

1. *Bolling v. Sharpe,* 347 U.S. 483 at 499 (1954).

2. *Weinberger v. Wiesenfeld,* 420 U.S. 636 at 638, note 2 (1975); *Buckley v. Valeo,* 424 U.S. 1 at 93 (1976); *Hampton v. Mow Sun Wong,* 426 U.S. 88 at 100 (1976); and *Davis v. Passman,* 442 U.S. 228 (1979).

classifications—still pertinent to certain cases today—was summarized by the Court in 1911:

> The equal protection clause of the Fourteenth Amendment does not take from the State the power to classify in the adoption of police laws, but admits of the exercise of a wide scope of discretion in that regard, and avoids what is done only when it is without any reasonable basis and is therefore purely arbitrary....
>
> A classification having some reasonable basis does not offend against the clause merely because it is not made with mathematical nicety or because in practice it results in some inequality....
>
> When the classification in such a law is called in question, if any state of facts reasonably can be conceived that would sustain it, the existence of that state of facts at the time the law was enacted must be assumed....
>
> One who assails the classification in such a law must carry the burden of showing that it does not rest upon any reasonable basis, but is essentially arbitrary.[3]

Invoking only this permissive standard, the Court upheld few challenges to laws on equal protection grounds. The Court noted in 1927 that the clause had become no more than "the usual last resort of constitutional arguments."[4]

MODERN STANDARD

The Court's shift in focus from property rights to individual rights in the late 1930s led it to develop a more probing standard for examining charges of denial of equal protection. Under this so-called active standard, classifications that are "inherently suspect" or that affect what the Court considers to be fundamental rights or interests require a greater degree of justification for their existence than simple rationality. A state must prove not only that it has a compelling governmental interest for making the challenged classification, but also that the classification is narrowly tailored to achieve that interest. The development of this modern standard came in distinct stages. In 1944 the Court declared race to be a suspect category requiring heightened judicial scrutiny, and later applied this standard of equal protection in *Brown v. Board of Education* (1954), its most important decision on racial discrimination. Classifications by alienage came in for heightened review as early as 1948, but not until 1971 did the Court explicitly describe alienage as a suspect category.

As early as 1942, the Court had indicated that the Equal Protection Clause protected all individuals from state deprivation of certain fundamental rights, but

STANDARDS OF REVIEW: EQUAL PROTECTION CLAIMS

The Equal Protection Clause of the Fourteenth Amendment forbids a state to "deny to any person within its jurisdiction the equal protection of the laws." The clause has been applied by the Supreme Court to prevent states from enforcing laws that discriminate on the basis of race, creed, gender, and national or ethnic origin. The Court applies a multitiered system of review to cases involving equal protection claims. The standard it applies depends on how the victim is classified and whether the government has a reasonable basis or a compelling state interest to act. The Court's standards follow, arranged from the most permissive government classification to the strictest.

Standard of Review	Definition	Classification	Key Cases
Rational basis (also referred to as the traditional standard or minimum scrutiny)	The government need only show that the challenged classification is rationally related to serving a legitimate government interest	Economic interests and non-suspect classifications	*Lindsley v. Natural Carbonic Gas Co.*, 220 U.S. 61 (1911) *Kotch v. Board of River Port Pilot Commissioners*, 330 U.S. 552 (1947) *Williamson v. Lee Optical of Oklahoma*, 348 U.S. 483 (1955) *McGowan v. Maryland*, 336 U.S. 420 (1961) *Plyler v. Doe*, 457 U.S. 202 (1982)
Intermediate scrutiny (also referred to as middle-tier scrutiny or heightened scrutiny)	The government must show that the challenged classification serves an important government interest and that the classification is at least substantially related to serving that interest	Quasi-suspect classifications including gender and illegitimacy	*Craig v. Boren*, 429 U.S. 190 (1976) *Central Hudson Gas & Electric Co. v. Public Service Commission of New York*, 447 U.S. 557 (1980)
Exceedingly persuasive justification (also referred to as skeptical scrutiny)	The government must show an "exceedingly persuasive justification" for the challenged classification	Quasi-suspect classifications including gender	*Mississippi University for Wmen v. Hogan*, 458 U.S. 718 (1982) *United States v. Virgnia et al.*, 518 U.S. 515 (1996)
Strict scrutiny (also referred to as the active standard, the modern standard, or rigid scrutiny)	The government must show that the challenged classification serves a compelling government interest and that the classification is necessary to serve that interest	Suspect classifications, based on race, national origin, alienage, and classifications affecting fundamental rights	*United States v. Carolene Products Co.*, 304 U.S. 144 (1938) *Skinner v. Oklahoma*, 316 U.S. 535 (1942) *Korematsu v. United States*, 323 U.S. 214 (1944) *Loving v. Virginia*, 388 U.S. 1(1967) *Wygant v. Jackson Board of Education*, 476 U.S. 267 (1986)

SOURCES: Lee Epstein and Thomas G. Walker, *Constitutional Law for a Changing America: Rights, Liberties, and Justice,* 5th ed. (Washington, D.C.: CQ Press, 2004); Douglas O. Linder, "Levels of Scrutiny under the Equal Protection Clause," *Exploring Constitutional Conflicts,* www.law.umkc.edu/faculty/projects/ftrials/conlaw/epcscrutiny.htm, 2003.

twenty years passed before it began to elaborate on this premise. Much of the development of this modern equal protection standard began after Congress passed the Civil Rights Act of 1964, which prohibited discrimination on the grounds of race, color, national origin, or religion in most privately owned public accommodations. It also prohibited job discrimination on these grounds and on the basis of sex. Passage of the Voting Rights Act of 1965 authorized federal action to enforce the rights of blacks to vote, and in 1968 Congress barred discrimination in the sale and rental of housing. As a result of these federal laws, minorities and other groups traditionally victimized by discrimination brought increasing numbers of lawsuits charging a denial of equal protection. In reviewing these cases, the Court moved away from the traditional "reasonable basis" standard. Race and alienage are the only two categories to which the Supreme Court has accorded suspect status.

RACIAL CLASSIFICATIONS

There is more than a little irony in the case of *Korematsu v. United States* (1944). It is considered by most scholars to be one of the worst rulings in Supreme Court history. The justices upheld as constitutional the rounding up and detention of more than 120,000 innocent persons on the West Coast solely because they were of Japanese descent. At the same time, the Court for the first time declared that the government's categorizing of persons based on their race was highly suspect under the Fourteenth Amendment.

Under a World War II military order, Japanese Americans in the West were detained shortly after the Japanese navy and air force attacked Pearl Harbor, in Hawaii. The U.S. military had feared a possible invasion of the West Coast. The Supreme Court ruled against Toyosaburo Korematsu, who had defied the detention order, holding that the wartime emergency necessitated the mass imprisonment. In so deciding, it also announced that it would give classifications by race increased attention:

> It should be noted ... that all legal restrictions which curtail the civil rights of a single racial group are immediately suspect. That is not to say that all such restrictions are unconstitutional. It is to say that courts must subject them to the most rigid scrutiny. Pressing public necessity may sometimes justify the existence of such restrictions; racial antagonism never can.[5]

The Court's 1954 school desegregation decisions made abundantly clear the meaning of "rigid scrutiny," but it would take another thirteen years for the Court to expressly declare all racial classifications "inherently suspect." This rather anticlimactic declaration came in *Loving v. Virginia* (1967), a case in which the Court struck down a Virginia statute making it a crime for residents to enter into interracial marriages. *(See details of Brown v. Board of Education, pp. 384–390; Loving v. Virginia, p. 477.)*

DISCRIMINATION AGAINST ALIENS

As early as 1886, the Court had held that the Fourteenth Amendment protected aliens as well as citizens, but during the next sixty years, the justices, applying the traditional standard of review, found that most statutes challenged as discriminating against aliens were in fact based on some reasonable—and therefore permissible—objective. In 1948 the Court began to require more than simple rationality to justify such laws, but not until 1971 did the Court explicitly acknowledge that such classifications were inherently suspect, requiring a compelling interest as justification. "Aliens as a class are a prime example of a 'discrete and insular' minority ... for whom ... heightened judicial solicitude is appropriate," said the Court.[6] Because the Constitution gives Congress exclusive authority over naturalization and, by extension, immigration, however, the Court has been reluctant to judge federal alienage classification laws as strictly as similar state laws. *(See "Aliens and the Law," pp. 440–441.)*

SEX DISCRIMINATION

All the modern cases challenging discrimination on the basis of sex have occurred since 1969. In the earliest of those cases, the Court applied the traditional standard of review and more often than not found that the state had a rational basis to justify treating women differently from men. In a line of cases involving the defense of administrative efficiency, however, the Court held that classification by sex was impermissible.

The statutes struck down in these cases presumed that all men behaved in one way and all women in another, failing to allow for any variation from their unproved assumption. The Court found such presumptions arbitrary, too broad, and unjustified by mere administrative convenience.

In *Craig v. Boren* (1976), a slim majority of the Court adopted a test that fell between the reasonable basis standard and the compelling governmental interest test. This standard requires the state to show that its sex-based classification is necessary to achieve some "important governmental objective."[7] Ever since, the Court has used such intermediate scrutiny for classifications based on gender. Regulations that discriminate against women are usually held invalid if they serve no important interest of government. The Court stressed in 1996 that governments defending gender-based action must demonstrate an "exceedingly persuasive justification."[8]

The Court upheld the 1964 Civil Rights Act ban on job discrimination on the grounds of sex and the 1963 Equal Pay Act requiring that men and women be paid the same for the same work, but it has steadily refused to describe differential treatment of pregnant women as sex discrimination. Such a classification is based not on gender but on physical condition, a majority of the Court has held, ruling that classification by physical condition did not violate either the Equal Protection Clause or the 1964 Civil Rights Act. (See "Romantic" Paternalism, pp. 453–454.)

The Court has refused to apply the compelling interest standard to test laws that discriminate against illegitimate children and the poor. Nonetheless, it has treated most cases involving classification by legitimacy with more than minimal scrutiny, striking down several laws distinguishing illegitimate children from their legitimate siblings on the grounds that such classifications are arbitrary and archaic. The Court has found discrimination against the poor unconstitutional when it deprives the indigent of a fundamental right or interest, but it has not applied the Equal Protection Clause to protect the poverty-stricken from deprivation of rights not considered "fundamental."

FUNDAMENTAL INTERESTS

The Court first articulated its fundamental interest standard in *Skinner v. Oklahoma* (1942). The decision not only advanced the concept of equal protection but also contributed to the contemporary interpretation of an implicit constitutional right of privacy. *Skinner* marked the first time that the Court declared a fundamental right to marriage and procreation. The justices were unanimous in striking down an Oklahoma statute that authorized sterilization of criminals who had committed two felonies "involving moral turpitude":

> We are dealing here with legislation which involves one of the basic civil rights of man. Marriage and procreation are fundamental to the very existence and survival of the race. The power to sterilize, if exercised, may have subtle, far-reaching and devastating effects. In evil or reckless hands it can cause races or types which are inimical to the dominant group to wither and disappear. There is no redemption for the individual whom the law touches.... He is forever deprived of a basic liberty. We mention these matters ... merely in emphasis of our view that strict scrutiny of the classification which a State makes in a sterilization law is essential, lest unwittingly or otherwise invidious discriminations are made against groups or types of individuals in violation of the constitutional guaranty of just and equal laws.[9]

The expansive ruling in *Skinner*, merging due process values and equal protection, would lead two decades later to significant decisions in the areas of personal liberty and electoral equality.

Substantive Due Process and the Right to Privacy

The Court had applied a theory of substantive due process in the early 1900s to protect economic and property rights—in effect "a liberty to contract"—but the era of economic rights ended in the 1930s. When the Court revived substantive due process in the 1960s, personal liberties, rather than economic ones, were at stake. Substantive due process extends judicial scrutiny beyond the procedures, or methods, of government to the substance, or fundamental value, at the heart of the law. In the Court's first modern invocation of substantive due process, it struck down a ban on the use of contraceptives. That law, it said, infringed on "the zone of privacy" protected by fundamental constitutional guarantees. Justice William O. Douglas wrote in *Griswold v. Connecticut* (1965):

> Would we allow the police to search the sacred precincts of marital bedrooms for telltale signs of the use of contraceptives? The very idea is repulsive to the notions of privacy surrounding the marriage relationship. We deal with a right of privacy older than the Bill of Rights—older than our political parties, older than our school system. Marriage is a coming together for better or for worse, hopefully enduring, and intimate to the degree of being sacred. The association promotes a way of life, not causes; a harmony in living, not political faiths; a bilateral loyalty, not commercial or social projects. Yet it is an association for as noble a purpose as any involved in our prior decisions.[10]

Eight years later, that generous view of the right of privacy exploded into public consciousness when the Court made abortion legal nationwide in *Roe v. Wade* (1973), the most controversial ruling of the modern era. Justice Harry A. Blackmun wrote that the right of privacy implicit in the Fourteenth Amendment guarantee of liberty is "broad enough to encompass a woman's decision whether or not to terminate her pregnancy."[11] Despite intense political pressure to repudiate that ruling and that position, the belief in the right of privacy has endured through the ensuing decades. In *Planned Parenthood of Southeastern Pennsylvania v. Casey* (1992), almost twenty years after *Roe*, the Court reaffirmed this position:

> Our law affords constitutional protection to personal decisions relating to marriage, procreation, contraception, family relationships, child rearing, and education.... These matters, involving the most intimate and personal choices a person may make in a lifetime, choices central to personal dignity and autonomy, are central to the liberty protected by the Fourteenth Amendment. At the heart of liberty is the right to define one's own concept of existence, of meaning, of the universe, and of the mystery of human life. Beliefs about these matters could not define the attributes of personhood were they formed under compulsion of the state.[12]

Electoral Equality

The fundamental interest doctrine, set forth in *Skinner v. Oklahoma* (1942), next emerged in the area of equal protection twenty years later, when the Court held that state electoral districts must each contain substantially the same number of voters. In *Reynolds v. Sims* (1964), the Court wrote,

> Undoubtedly, the right of suffrage is a fundamental matter in a free and democratic society. Especially since the right to exercise the franchise in a free and unimpaired manner is preservative of other basic civil and political rights, any alleged infringement of the right of citizens to vote must be carefully and meticulously scrutinized.[13]

In 1969 the Court elaborated:

> [I]f a challenged state statute grants the right to vote to some bona fide residents of requisite age and citizenship and denies the franchise to others, the Court must determine whether the exclusions are necessary to promote a compelling state interest.
>
> ... [T]he deference usually given to the judgment of legislators does not extend to decisions concerning which resident citizens may participate in the election of legislators and other public officials.... [W]hen we are reviewing statutes which deny some residents the right to vote, the general presumption of constitutionality afforded state statutes and the traditional approval given state classifications if the Court can conceive of a "rational basis" for the distinctions made are not applicable.[14]

Applying this stricter standard, the Court struck down a number of statutes because they restricted the right to vote. States have no compelling reason to deny the right to vote to persons simply because they have not resided in the state for a certain period of time, or because they are too poor to pay a poll tax. Filing fees that prevent poor candidates from seeking office also are unconstitutional, as are statutes that keep off the ballot all candidates except those belonging to the two major political parties. (*See voting participation cases, pp. 177–183.*)

The Right to Travel

Durational residency requirements also violate another fundamental interest guarded by the Equal Protection Clause—the right to travel unrestricted from state to state. The Court has debated for several decades the source of this right, sometimes finding it in the Interstate Commerce Clause of Article I of the Constitution, at other times in the Privileges and Immunities Clause of the Fourteenth Amendment. In 1966 the Court abandoned the debate:

> The constitutional right to travel from one State to another … occupies a position fundamental to the concept of our Federal Union. It is a right that has been firmly established and repeatedly recognized.… Although there have been recurring differences in emphasis within the Court as to the source of the constitutional right of interstate travel, there is no need here to canvass those differences further. All have agreed that the right exists.[15]

Using this reasoning, the Court in 1969 declared requirements that persons live in a state for a certain period of time before becoming eligible for welfare benefits to be a violation of equal protection and thus unconstitutional. The Court said such requirements unconstitutionally restricted the poor in the exercise of their right to travel interstate.

Access to Justice for the Poor

The Supreme Court has designated access to justice a fundamental right. It had been foreclosed at times to poor people who could not afford the fees required either to file suit or hire an attorney or pay for a transcript to prepare an appeal. In many of these instances, the Court held that requiring a fee impermissibly violates the indigent's guarantee of due process as well as equal protection of the laws. *(See "Access to Justice," pp. 446–448.)*

The fundamental interest doctrine has been criticized from the bench, first by Justice John Marshall Harlan and then by Justice William H. Rehnquist, who replaced him on the Court. Both contended that the Court exceeds its power when it singles out certain rights and interests for special protection. Wrote Harlan in 1969,

> [W]hen a statute affects only matters not mentioned in the Federal Constitution and is not arbitrary or irrational, I must reiterate that I know of nothing which entitles this Court to pick out particular human activities, characterize them as "fundamental," and give them added protection under an unusually stringent equal protection test.[16]

In 1972 Rehnquist added that "[t]his body of doctrine created by the Court can only be described as a judicial superstructure, awkwardly engrafted upon the Constitution itself."[17]

Since 1969 the Court has refused to classify any other right or interest as fundamental. Although it hinted in 1969 that it might place "food, shelter and other necessities of life" in the fundamental right category, in 1972 the justices held that the assurance of adequate housing was not a fundamental interest.[18] In 1973 a majority of the Court held that the right to an education was neither explicitly nor implicitly guaranteed by the Constitution. The majority added that it was "not the province of this Court to create substantive constitutional rights in the name of guaranteeing equal protection of the laws."[19]

Racial Equality

The Fourteenth Amendment, said the Supreme Court in 1880,

> was designed to assure to the colored race the enjoyment of all the civil rights that under the law are enjoyed by white persons, and to give to that race the protection of the general government, in that enjoyment, whenever it should be denied by the States. It not only gave citizenship and the privileges of citizenship to persons of color, but it denied to any State the power to withhold from them the equal protection of the laws, and authorized Congress to enforce its provisions.[1]

Another seventy-five years would pass before black people would receive any substantial benefit from the Fourteenth Amendment's protections. Even as the Court spoke in 1880, southern states had begun to separate white from black in what would result in almost complete social, legal, and political segregation of the two races. Although the Court's first actions regarding blacks after the Civil War were favorable to them—admitting a black attorney to the Supreme Court bar and ruling that a black woman could sue a railroad company for damages after it had forcibly removed her from a train after she refused to sit in the "colored" car—the Court nonetheless played a role in creating the climate that allowed segregation to flourish.[2]

In the *Slaughterhouse Cases* (1873), the justices divided 5-4 in ruling that citizens held two distinct types of citizenship—one federal and one state. The Fourteenth Amendment, the majority held, protected a person only from state infringement on such privileges and immunities of national citizenship as the right to petition the federal government and the right to vote in federal elections. The privileges and immunities conferred by citizenship in a state were outside federal protection. This decision, intact today, divested the Privileges and Immunities Clause of any substantive protection it might have afforded citizens of either race.[3] In the *Slaughterhouse* opinion, the majority characterized the Fourteenth Amendment's Equal Protection Clause as primarily of use to protect blacks from unjust discrimination. In deciding *Strauder v. West Virginia* (1880), the Court utilized the clause to strike down a state law that barred blacks from jury service.

Three years later, however, the Court significantly narrowed the protection of the clause for blacks. In the *Civil Rights Cases* (1883) the Court nullified an 1875 federal law that gave all persons, regardless of color, "the full and equal enjoyment" of public transportation, inns, theaters, and "other places of public amusement."[4] The Court held that the Fourteenth Amendment prohibited only state-imposed discrimination and not that imposed by individuals acting privately. Congress therefore had overstepped its authority when it sought to stop private businesspersons from discriminating against blacks. Furthermore, the Court said, the amendment only empowered Congress to remedy acts of state discrimination. Congress could not enact a general law in anticipation of discriminatory state actions.

By 1883 the fervor of Reconstruction had worn thin. As one historian wrote, "Other than Negroes and their faithful friends, the people were tired of giving special protection to the former slaves. It was felt to be time for the return to power of the dominant factions in the several communities."[5] Against this background, the decision in the *Civil Rights Cases* had particular significance. Political scientist Alan F. Westin attributed two primary effects to it:

> [F]irst, it destroyed the delicate balance of federal guarantee, Negro protest and private enlightenment which was producing a steadily widening area of peacefully integrated public facilities in the North and South during the 1870s and early 1880s. Second, it had an immediate and profound effect on national and state politics as they related to the Negro. By denying Congress power to protect the Negro's rights to equal treatment, the Supreme Court wiped the issue of civil rights from the Republican party's agenda of national responsibility. At the same time, those Southern political leaders who saw anti-Negro politics as the most promising avenue to power could now rally the "poor whites" to the banner of segregation.[6]

THE *AMISTAD*: SLAVES OR FREE MEN

In 1841 abolitionists won a victory, but not necessarily an important legal precedent, when they persuaded the Supreme Court to free fifty-three Africans who had been held as slaves aboard the schooner *Amistad*.[1] After leaving port in Havana, Cuba, the Africans broke their shackles and killed most of the crew. Don Jose Ruiz and Don Pedro Montez, the two Spaniards who held them as slaves, steered the ship on a zigzag course until it ran aground near Montauk Point on Long Island. U.S. officials took custody of the ship into New London, Connecticut.

The federal courts had jurisdiction over maritime and salvage disputes and therefore the authority to decide the fate of these Africans: Were they slaves and murderers or free men who had been kidnapped? Abolitionist lawyers proved the men were not native-born Cuban slaves, as the two Spaniards had said, but rather Africans who had been captured and held as slaves, in violation of Spanish law. They hired former president John Quincy Adams to argue the case on behalf of the Africans. The U.S.

government intervened to argue that the slaves and the ship should be returned to Spanish custody.

The Court rejected the government's argument in *United States v. Claimants of the Schooner Amistad* (1841).[2] "These Negroes never were the lawful slaves of Ruiz or Montez or of any other Spanish subjects. They are natives of Africa, and were kidnapped there, and were unlawfully transported to Cuba," wrote Justice Joseph Story. He ordered that "said Negroes be declared free and be dismissed from the custody of the court and go without day."[3] The *Amistad* case was the subject of the 1998 film by Steven Spielberg named for the schooner.

---

1. See Howard Jones, *Mutiny on the Amistad: The Saga of a Slave Revolt and Its Impact on American Abolition, Law, and Diplomacy* (New York: Oxford University Press, 1987).

2. *United States v. Claimants of the Schooner Amistad*, 40 U.S. 518 (1841).

3. Id. at 593, 597.

Thirteen years later, the Supreme Court sanctioned the "separate but equal" doctrine developed to justify state-imposed racial segregation. In *Plessy v. Ferguson* (1896), a majority of the Court held that so long as the facilities provided blacks were equal to those provided whites, state laws requiring segregation did not violate the Equal Protection or Due Process Clauses of the Fourteenth Amendment. The justices did not view separation of the races as pinning on blacks a badge of slavery in violation of the Thirteenth Amendment.[7]

In the wake of *Plessy*, state-ordered segregation invaded almost every aspect of daily life in the former Confederate states. Blacks throughout the South were required to use separate streetcars, waiting rooms, toilets, and water fountains. They attended different schools and were segregated in parks and theaters, mental hospitals, and prisons. At the same time, blacks were almost completely disenfranchised in those states by such devices as the poll tax, property and literacy tests, and the white primary. (*See "The Pattern of Exclusion," pp. 177–183.*)

Although there was comparatively little official segregation in northern and western states, whites there generally regarded blacks as inferiors, and there was little intermingling of the two races. When the United States entered its brief but intense period of imperialism at the end of the nineteenth century, bringing some 8 million nonwhites under its domination, northern attitudes grew steadily more sympathetic to the racist views of southern whites. As the U.S. Commission on Civil Rights wrote in understatement: at the end of the nineteenth century, the "very concept of civil rights seemed to have passed out of existence, and the prospects for the future were not encouraging."[8]

SEGREGATION UNDER ATTACK

During the first third of the twentieth century, segregation by law appeared firmly entrenched, but the events that would lead to its demise were taking shape. The National Association for the Advancement of Colored People

(NAACP), which would lead the legal fight to end racial discrimination, was founded in 1909, and the National Urban League began operating in 1911. World War I contributed markedly to the rising aspirations of blacks. Many of the 360,000 blacks who fought to make the world safe for democracy began to wonder when they might begin to enjoy democracy's benefits. The Great War also spurred a black migration to the North, where blacks found work in the defense industry. Racial tension escalated during this period. In the first year after the war's end, more than seventy blacks were lynched. The Ku Klux Klan enjoyed revived popularity in the North as well as in the South. In 1919 bloody race riots broke out in twenty-five cities across the nation. Historian John Hope Franklin described this time as "the greatest period of interracial strife the nation had ever witnessed."[9]

In three school segregation cases, the Supreme Court refused to review the separate but equal doctrine, although in 1914 it did strike down a state law because it did not provide blacks with exactly the same train accommodations it provided whites. In 1917 the Court struck down a municipal ordinance that prohibited blacks from living on the same streets as whites. This decision did not end residential segregation, however, because private restrictive covenants quickly replaced the illegal ordinances. These covenants, attached to the deed or title to property, forbade the white owner to sell to blacks. The Supreme Court upheld the covenants in 1926, reiterating its view that the Fourteenth Amendment did not reach private discrimination.

Blacks as a group were among the most severely burdened by the Great Depression of the 1930s. Many blacks had left the Republican Party to vote for Woodrow Wilson in 1912, only to be disillusioned when he did little to advance their civil rights, and many thousands more swung their support to Franklin D. Roosevelt in the 1936 and 1940 elections. The Democratic administration did try to improve the economic condition of both races, but segregation continued unabated. Blacks nonetheless had won recognition as a political power, and by the 1940s militant individuals and organized groups demanding an end to segregation were beginning to make themselves heard. These demands steadily gained adherents as the ironies of World War II became increasingly apparent. The inconsistency of sending black and white soldiers to fight against Germany's racial policies while continuing to practice racial segregation at home became too obvious to ignore.

The cold war further intensified this paradox. Communist countries pointed to U.S. racial policies and problems in an effort to undermine the appeal of the democratic system. No reasonable person could deny the irony, as C. Vann Woodward observed, of the United States competing with the Soviet Union for the friendship of the people of Asia and Africa while continuing to treat Asians and blacks in the United States as second-class citizens.

Supreme Court Shifts Focus

Against this backdrop, the Supreme Court began to take a closer look at the laws that discriminated on the basis of race. From the end of the Civil War until 1937, the Supreme Court's primary concern was the protection of business from what it considered excessive regulation by the federal government. When these laissez-faire views jeopardized Roosevelt's New Deal programs, the president threatened in 1937 to "pack" the Court with additional justices, who would construe the Constitution to support his economic policies. The Court responded by relaxing its vigilant attitude toward economic regulation and shifting its focus to individual rights and liberties. A harbinger of this shift came in 1938 in what became famously known as "Footnote Four," an eventful note to an otherwise routine decision. In it, Justice Harlan Fiske Stone implied that the Court might soon be required to decide whether

> statutes directed at particular religious ... or national ... or racial minorities ... [or] whether prejudice against discrete and insular minorities may be a special condition which tends seriously to curtail the operation of those political processes ordinarily to be relied upon to protect minorities, and which may call for a correspondingly more searching judicial inquiry.[10]

SLAVE OR FREE: THE DRED SCOTT CASE

Dred Scott, a slave seeking his freedom, brought about the first major individual rights ruling from the U.S. Supreme Court. Scott lost his case, but the Court's decision inflamed public opinion and contributed to the outbreak of the Civil War, which finally settled the question of slavery in the United States. *Scott v. Sandford* (1857) was brought with the financial support of Scott's owners to test whether a slave who lived for a time on free soil would become free as a result. Scott had lived in Illinois and Wisconsin, where slavery was not permitted, but later returned to the slave state of Missouri, contending that he was free.

The Missouri Supreme Court held that under state law, Scott remained a slave. The case moved into the federal courts. The first federal court dismissed the case, finding that Scott, as a slave, was not a citizen of Missouri and so could not invoke the jurisdiction of the federal courts over suits between citizens of different states. By this time Scott had been sold outside of Missouri. Scott appealed his case to the U.S. Supreme Court, which heard it argued twice in 1856. The nine justices voted 7-2 against him.

The majority would have resolved the case simply by declaring that Scott's status was a matter for Missouri, not federal officials, to decide, but the two dissenters, both fiercely antislavery, announced that their dissents would address broader issues: whether a slave could ever become a citizen, whether a stay on free soil made a slave free, and whether Congress had the power to ban slavery in the territories. In response, each of the seven-majority justices wrote his own opinion, setting out his views on these matters. The result was confusion. The opinion by Chief Justice Roger B. Taney is generally considered the official majority view.

Dred Scott could not be a citizen, declared Taney, nor could any slave or his descendant. Thus, the chief justice continued, blacks could "claim none of the rights and privileges which ... [the Constitution] provides for and secures to citizens of the United States."[1] When the Constitution used the word "citizens," it did not include slaves, Taney explained, reasoning from the fact that slaves "had for more than a century before [ratification of the Constitution] been regarded as being of an inferior order, and altogether unfit to associate with the white race, either in social or political relations; and so far inferior, that they had no rights which the white man was bound to respect."[2]

This last statement, taken out of its context as Taney's observation upon the historical view of slaves, was quoted time and again in the incendiary debates of the years before the war. Northern abolitionists were particularly incensed by it, viewing it as a statement of Taney's own belief in the inferiority of blacks. Furthermore, wrote Taney, slaves were not included in the statement in the Declaration of Independence that "all men are created equal."[3] Indeed, slaves were viewed as property, and the Constitution reflects this view. "The only two provisions which point to them and include them, treat them as property, and make it the duty of the government to protect it; no other power, in relation to this race, is to be found in the Constitution."[4]

Taney could have stopped there. He had given ample reason for dismissing Scott's case on the grounds that he was not a citizen, but Taney continued. Congress lacked the power to declare certain territory "free" of slavery, he wrote, and so the "free territory" in which Scott had lived could not actually be so designated. For Congress to do so, Taney reasoned, deprived slave-owning citizens of their property when they came into that territory and thus denied slave owners due process of law, in violation of the Fifth Amendment.[5] Congress was officially declared powerless to stop the spread of slavery through the expanding nation.

The Civil War rendered moot the question of congressional power over slavery, and in 1868 ratification of the Fourteenth Amendment reversed the Court's declaration that blacks were not and could not be citizens under the Constitution. The first section of the amendment declares that all persons born or naturalized in the United States and subject to its jurisdiction are citizens of the United States and the state in which they live. That same section prohibits states from making any law abridging the privileges and immunities of citizens, depriving any person of life, liberty, or property without due process of law, or denying to anyone equal protection of the law. This set of guarantees, indirectly the legacy of Dred Scott, a slave who sought to be free, provided the basis for the modern revolution in civil rights.

---

1. *Scott v. Sandford,* 19 How. (60 U.S.) 393 at 404 (1857).

2. Id. at 407.

3. Id. at 410.

4. Id. at 425.

5. Id. at 450.

Also in 1938, the Court determined that the separate but equal rule required a state to provide law schools for blacks if it provided them for whites, even though there might be only a single black law student. The Court also upheld the right of blacks to picket an employer to persuade the employer to hire more black workers. In 1944, six years after Stone's Footnote Four, the Court announced that it would give closer scrutiny to laws that treated one race differently from another, upholding such distinctions only if they were justified by a pressing governmental need. In that same year the Court held it unconstitutional for states to exclude black voters from primary elections, and in the first modern decision on job discrimination, the Court ruled in favor of black railroad workers.

In 1948 the Court took another look at restrictive covenants, ruling that although the Fourteenth Amendment did not prohibit them, it did prohibit states from enforcing them. With this decision, the Court began to expand its definition of state action covered by the Fourteenth Amendment to include private discrimination promoted in any way by official state action, even if the state action itself was not discriminatory. The decisions that portended the most for the future of black civil rights, however, dealt with the question of whether separate facilities could be equal.

In June 1950, the Court held that Texas violated the Equal Protection Clause because its black state law school was not the equivalent of the white school either in tangible aspects (such as the number of books in the library) or in intangible aspects (such as the prestige of its faculty and alumni). In a second case decided the same day, the Court ruled that Oklahoma violated the equal protection guarantee when it separated a black from his white colleagues in classes, the library, and the cafeteria. Four years later in the public school desegregation cases familiarly known as *Brown v. Board of Education* (1954), the unanimous Court declared that separation of the races in public schools was "inherently unequal."[11] After sixty years, the *Plessy* doctrine—and a way of life for an entire section of the nation—was officially renounced. The *Brown* decisions, wrote G. Theodore Mitau,

acknowledged judicially what many people had known or felt for a long time: Segregation was morally indefensible, socially irrational and politically undemocratic. It perpetuated a racial myth which imprisoned American values at home and weakened America's leadership abroad. Equally important to many, it defiled this country's claim to stand as a world model of freedom and human dignity in defense of which whites and Negroes fought side by side in all of this nation's major wars.[12]

In 1955 the Court issued guidelines directing school officials to desegregate schools with "all deliberate speed." Although many states complied with the Court order, many others embarked on programs of "massive resistance" in defiance of the Supreme Court order. The governor of Arkansas in 1958 called out the National Guard to prevent black students from entering a formerly all-white high school in Little Rock. In an extraordinary session, the Supreme Court demanded unanimously that the state cease its resistance and that the students be admitted to the school. For ten years after *Brown,* the Court left it to lower courts to implement school desegregation. The pace was slow: by 1964 less than 2 percent of black pupils in the former Confederate states were in desegregated schools.[13]

Civil Rights Revolution

During this period, the Court frequently cited *Brown* as precedent for rulings striking down other forms of segregation throughout the South in parks and beaches, traffic courts and theaters, railroad cars and bus terminals. These decisions spurred a revolution in civil rights. Blacks were no longer willing to let whites deny them their rights. Beginning in 1957 with a Montgomery, Alabama, bus boycott led by Dr. Martin Luther King Jr., blacks organized to protest racial segregation and discrimination in jobs, housing, and public accommodations. The student sit-ins and "freedom rides" of the early 1960s sensitized the rest of the nation to the black dilemma. The violence with which whites frequently countered black demonstrations grabbed the nation's sympathy.

The year that marked the one hundredth anniversary of the Emancipation Proclamation was particularly

In the early 1960s Freedom Riders, like these having breakfast at a lunch counter in Montgomery, Alabama, in 1961, traveled throughout the South to test the effectiveness of the Supreme Court's decision in *Boynton v. Virginia* (1960), which outlawed segregation in privately owned facilities on public property. Many southern towns refused, however, to comply with the Court's ruling, so the Freedom Riders often encountered arrests and resistance from local whites.

turbulent. In May 1963, police loosed dogs and turned high-pressure fire hoses on demonstrators in Birmingham, Alabama. Sympathizers soon held demonstrations in several other cities. In August, some 200,000 blacks and whites marched peacefully in Washington, D.C., to protest the status of blacks. March leaders presented blacks' demands for equal treatment to Congress, the president, and a closely watching country. One month later, a bomb thrown into a black church in Birmingham killed four little girls. On November 22, an assassin

shot and killed President John F. Kennedy, an advocate of civil rights.

Hope, frustration, and outrage impelled Congress in 1964 to approve the most comprehensive civil rights act since Reconstruction. It barred discrimination in most public accommodations, prohibited job discrimination on the basis of race, and established a procedure for withholding federal funds from any program or institution, including schools, that continued to discriminate against blacks. The year 1964 also marked the end of the Court's silence on continuing questions of school desegregation. There has been "too much deliberation and not enough speed" in desegregating public schools, the Court declared in 1964, holding that a county could not close its schools to avoid desegregating them. Later in the year, the Court upheld that section of the 1964 Civil Rights Act barring racial discrimination in most public accommodations. In 1966 the Court upheld the Voting Rights Act of 1965.

In 1968 the Court reinterpreted part of the 1866 Civil Rights Act as barring private individuals from refusing to sell their homes to persons of a different race. The Court also declared that state and school officials must do more than simply end segregation; they had a duty to take affirmative action to ensure effective school desegregation. The Court also gave lower courts new guidelines for determining whether desegregation efforts were sincere.

The Court's Remedies

Chief Justice Earl Warren's replacement in 1969 by Warren E. Burger coincided with a new phase in the civil rights movement and the Court's role in it. It was clear that racial discrimination was illegal; the Court's task was now to define the scope of remedies available to its victims. The Burger Court approved a wide variety of measures to remedy school segregation, including busing, gerrymandered attendance zones, limited use of mathematical ratios, and compensatory education programs. The Court also extended the obligation to desegregate to non-southern school districts where existing segregation had not been required by law but rather imposed as a matter of school board policy.

The Court insisted that the remedies selected be tailored to fit the extent of the proven discrimination. Thus a multidistrict busing plan was found too sweeping a remedy when deliberate discrimination had been found in only one of the affected districts. In another instance, a district-wide plan was held to be too broad because the proven discrimination had not been shown to affect the entire school district. The Court also held that once a school district was desegregated, school officials were not required to remedy its resegregation so long as it did not result from official state action.

In addition to reinterpreting the 1866 Civil Rights Act as barring housing discrimination by private individuals, the Court also read the act to prohibit private schools from refusing to admit black pupils and to invalidate neighborhood recreational association policies excluding black homeowners and renters from membership. In a major case in which federal and city housing officials admitted they had been guilty of intentional racial segregation, the Court backed a lower court's remedy that covered a metropolitan area. In a second case, however, the justices held there to be no constitutional violation by a community charged with exercising its zoning power to exclude blacks by omitting low-income housing. The Court held that there was no evidence that the charges were true or that the zoning decision was motivated by racial considerations.

When charges of racial discrimination in employment have been brought under Title VII of the Civil Rights Act of 1964, the Court has placed the burden of proving nondiscrimination on the employer. Few employers have met this test. When charges of job discrimination have been brought under the Fourteenth Amendment, the Court has shifted the burden to the employees, requiring them to prove that the employer intended to discriminate; the discriminatory effect of an employment policy is not sufficient proof of intent. Few employees have met this test. Where job discrimination has been proved, however, the Court has sanctioned far-reaching remedies, including awards of back pay and retroactive seniority.

The success of the civil rights movement encouraged other victims of discrimination, particularly women, to assert their right to equal treatment. It also prompted some members of the majority to complain of "reverse discrimination," that is, that affirmative action programs to remedy past discrimination against minorities in turn discriminate against whites. The Court has held that the Civil Rights Act of 1964 provides remedies to whites as well as to blacks who have been discriminated against in employment because of their race and that it bars universities receiving federal funds from setting aside a specific number of seats in each class for minority applicants. The Court has, however, endorsed as within the bounds of the Constitution and

Under the rule of law established in *Plessy v. Ferguson* (1896), states could require racial separation if facilities for blacks and whites were of equal quality. In public education black schools were not always equal to those reserved for whites.

the law the use of affirmative action, a program that deliberately takes into account the personal characteristics of an individual (such as race, color, or sex) to remedy society's past discrimination against racial minorities and women.

EQUAL OPPORTUNITY FOR EDUCATION

When the Supreme Court in 1896 ruled that separate public facilities for blacks and whites did not violate the Equal Protection Clause of the Fourteenth Amendment, it pointed to the nation's schools as "the most common instance" of segregation. "Establishment of separate schools for white and colored children has been held to be a valid exercise of the legislative power," the Court said in *Plessy v. Ferguson*, "even by courts of States where the political rights of the colored race have been longest and most earnestly enforced."[14] The Court was referring to Massachusetts, and it used a case from Boston to support its decision in *Plessy*.

Roberts v. City of Boston

The city of Boston had maintained separate schools for blacks and whites since 1820. Sarah Roberts, a five-year-old black child, was forced, as a result of this segregation, to walk past five white primary schools on her way to the black school. When repeated attempts to place her in one of the closer white schools failed, Sarah's father hired Charles Sumner, the future senator and abolitionist, and went to court. Appearing before Chief Justice Lemuel Shaw of the Massachusetts Supreme Judicial Court, Sumner made one of his most eloquent pleas, contending that the segregated schools violated state law, which held all persons, "without distinction of age or sex, birth or color, origin or condition," to be equal before the law. Noting the general soundness of Sumner's contention, the state supreme court nonetheless rejected Roberts's challenge. Shaw wrote that

> when this great principle [of equality before the law] comes to be applied to the actual and various conditions of persons in society, it will not warrant the assertion, that men and women are legally clothed with the

same civil and political powers, and that children and adults are legally to have the same functions and be subject to the same treatment; but only that the rights of all, as they are settled and regulated by law, are equally entitled to the paternal consideration and protection of the law, for their maintenance and security. What those rights are, to which individuals, in the infinite variety of circumstances by which they are surrounded in society, are entitled, must depend on laws adapted to their respective relations and conditions.[15]

To Sumner's contention that segregation "brand[s] a whole race with the stigma of inferiority and degradation," Shaw responded,

> It is urged, that this maintenance of separate schools tends to deepen and perpetuate the odious distinction of caste, founded in a deep-rooted prejudice in public opinion. This prejudice, if it exists, is not created by law, and probably cannot be changed by laws.[16]

Massachusetts abolished the dual school system six years after *Roberts*. In citing this case to support *Plessy,* the Court overlooked the fact that the state case was decided almost twenty years before ratification of the Fourteenth Amendment made blacks citizens and required the states to give all citizens equal protection of the laws.

Plessy and the Schools

While the *Plessy* decision did not deal directly with school segregation, the Supreme Court in that opinion clearly condoned the practice. The Court confirmed this position in three subsequent cases challenging the "separate" half of the "separate but equal" doctrine as states applied it to schools. In all three instances, the Court bowed to the right of the state to run its own schools, refusing to consider the constitutional question of whether state-required segregation denied black children equal protection of the laws. The first of these cases was *Cumming v. Richmond (Ga.) County Board of Education* (1899). The school board had discontinued operating the black high school in order to use the building as an additional facility for black primary school pupils. The board continued to operate a high school for white girls and one for white boys. Blacks in

the county sought an injunction to prevent taxes from being used to operate the white schools until a black high school was reestablished. Refusing to grant the injunction, the Court said it would not address the issue of equal protection because it was not raised in the case. The Court then stated,

> [W]hile all admit that the benefits and burdens of public taxation must be shared by citizens without discrimination against any class on account of their race, the education of the people in schools maintained by state taxation is a matter belonging to the respective States, and any interference on the part of the federal authority with the management of such schools cannot be justified except in the case of a clear and unmistakable disregard of rights secured by the supreme law of the land.[17]

Ironically, this opinion was written by Justice John Marshall Harlan, who had so vigorously dissented from *Plessy. (See "Plessy v. Ferguson," pp. 407–408.)*

In 1908 Berea College, a private Christian school incorporated in Kentucky, challenged in the Supreme Court a state law requiring that any institution that taught both blacks and whites conduct separate classes for the two races. The school said the state had illegally impaired the school's charter by denying it the right to teach students of both races together. The Court rejected the challenge, holding that since the college could still teach members of both races, the law had not significantly injured the school's charter.[18] Twenty years later, a girl of Chinese descent challenged her assignment to an all-black school in Mississippi as a denial of equal protection. In *Gong Lum v. Rice* (1927), the Court upheld her assignment to the black school, saying that the question raised "has been many times decided to be within the constitutional power of the state legislature to settle without intervention of the federal courts under the Federal Constitution."[19]

Separate and Unequal

In none of these early cases did the Court consider whether the segregated facilities were in fact equal, nor was school segregation challenged on that basis. During the 1930s, the NAACP determined that the separate but equal doctrine was most vulnerable on this point. Studies of dual school systems, particularly in the South, showed disproportionate amounts of money spent on white and black school facilities, materials, salaries, and transportation. The NAACP decided first to attack the lack of equality in institutions of higher education. Inequality of facilities and instruction was even more apparent at the university level than at the primary and secondary school levels. Many states provided no school at all to blacks seeking certain advanced degrees, and NAACP officials reasoned that integration of a college or university by a few black students represented less of a threat to the segregated southern lifestyle than did wholesale integration of entire school districts.[20]

Missouri ex rel. Gaines v. Canada (1938) became the first of these cases decided by the Court. Because there were no black law schools in Missouri, Lloyd Gaines, a qualified black undergraduate, applied to the all-white University of Missouri Law School, which refused him admission solely because of his race. The school said it would pay Gaines's tuition at any law school in an adjacent state that would accept him. At the time, law schools in Illinois, Iowa, Kansas, and Nebraska accepted black out-of-state students. This solution was unacceptable to Gaines, who sued to compel the University of Missouri to admit him. The Supreme Court ruled, 6-2, that Gaines had been denied equal protection and that he was entitled to be admitted to the state's all-white law school. Dismissing the state's contention that it intended to establish a black law school when it became practical, Chief Justice Charles Evans Hughes wrote,

> The question here is not of a duty of the State to supply legal training, or of the quality of the training which it does supply, but of its duty when it provides such training to furnish it to the residents of the State upon the basis of an equality of right. By the operation of the laws of Missouri, a privilege has been created for white law students which is denied to Negroes by reason of their race.[21]

The majority also rejected as inadequate the state's promise to pay tuition at an out-of-state school:

> We find it impossible to conclude that what otherwise would be an unconstitutional discrimination, with respect to the legal right to the enjoyment of opportunities within the State, can be justified by requiring resort to opportunities elsewhere. That resort may mitigate the inconvenience of the discrimination but cannot serve to validate it.[22]

Ten years later, the Court reaffirmed this ruling in *Sipuel v. Board of Regents of the University of Oklahoma* (1948). A law school applicant had been refused admission to the University of Oklahoma because she was black. In a per curiam opinion, the Court held that the state must provide Ada Lois Sipuel with legal training "in conformity with the equal protection clause."[23] The next case, *Sweatt v. Painter* (1950), focused on the inequality of two state institutions at which legal training was provided. Refused admission to the all-white University of Texas law school, Heman Marion Sweatt sued in state court. The court agreed that Sweatt had been denied equal protection but gave the state time to create a black law school. Sweatt refused to apply to the new school on the ground that its instruction would be inferior to the education he would receive at the University of Texas. After state courts held the new school "equal" to the long-established university law school, Sweatt appealed to the Supreme Court. The Court unanimously ordered that Sweatt be admitted to the University of Texas. The Court "cannot find substantial equality in the educational opportunities offered white and Negro law students by the state," wrote Chief Justice Fred M. Vinson. He elaborated:

> In terms of number of the faculty, variety of courses and opportunity for specialization, size of the student body, scope of the library, availability of law review and similar activities, the University of Texas Law School is superior. What is more important, the University of Texas Law School possesses to a far greater degree those qualities which are incapable of objective measurement but which make for greatness in a law school. Such qualities, to name but a few, include reputation of the faculty, experience of the administration, position and influence of the alumni, standing in the community, traditions and prestige. It is difficult to believe that one who had a free choice between these law schools would consider the question close.[24]

For the first time the Court had ordered a state to admit a black to an all-white school because the education provided by a black school was inferior. Vinson, however, added that the Court saw no necessity to go on—as Sweatt's attorney, Thurgood Marshall, had asked it to do—to reexamine the separate but equal doctrine "in the light of contemporary knowledge respecting the purposes of the Fourteenth Amendment and the effects of racial segregation."[25]

A second case decided on the same day cast even more doubt upon the premise that separate could be equal. A black student named G. W. McLaurin was admitted to the all-white University of Oklahoma as a candidate for a doctorate in education and assigned to a special seat in the classroom and to special tables in the library and cafeteria. The Supreme Court held that such state-imposed requirements produced inequities that could not be tolerated. The restrictions, the Court wrote, "impair and inhibit [McLaurin's] ability to study, to engage in discussion and exchange views with other students, and, in general, to learn his profession."[26] It was only McLaurin's segregation from the rest of the students that made his treatment unequal, the Court recognized. He heard the same lectures, had access to the same books, and ate the same food.

Brown v. Board of Education

Even as the Court announced its decisions in *Sweatt* and *McLaurin,* the five cases in which the Court would make the implicit explicit were taking shape. In each of the five cases, parents of black schoolchildren had asked lower courts to order school boards to stop enforcing laws requiring or permitting segregated schools.

The Cases

The challenge that gave the landmark school desegregation decision its name, *Brown v. Board of Education of Topeka* (1954), was brought in 1951 by Oliver Brown in behalf of his daughter Linda.[27] Under Kansas law permitting cities with populations over 15,000 to operate dual school systems, Topeka had opted to segregate its primary schools. As a result, Linda Brown was

forced to walk twenty blocks to an all-black grade school rather than attend an all-white school in her neighborhood. Several other black families joined the challenge. In 1951 a federal district court found Topeka's segregation detrimental to black children but found no constitutional violation because the black and white primary schools were substantially equal with respect to buildings, curricula, transportation, and teachers.

The case of *Briggs v. Elliott* was actually the first to reach the Supreme Court. Federal proceedings began in 1950, when parents of black elementary and secondary school-aged children in Clarendon County, South Carolina, asked a federal district court to enjoin enforcement of state constitutional and statutory provisions requiring segregation in public schools. The court denied the request, but it found the black schools inferior to the white and ordered the school board to equalize them immediately. The court refused, however, to order the school board to admit black children to the white school while the equalization took place. The children's parents then appealed to the Supreme Court, which in 1952 returned the case to the lower court to consider a report on the progress of the equalization program. The lower court found that the school board had either achieved substantial equality in all areas or soon would, and it again upheld the separate but equal doctrine. The case then returned to the Court.

Davis v. County School Board of Prince Edward County, Va. was almost identical to *Briggs v. Elliott.* Parents of black high school students sued to stop enforcement of the state's constitutional provisions requiring separate schools. Although the district court found the black high school to be inferior and ordered its equalization, it upheld the validity of the segregation provisions. It also refused to admit the black students to white high schools while the black schools were being brought up to par with the white schools. The fourth case, *Gebhart v. Belton,* involved the schools of New Castle County, Delaware. As in the other cases, parents of black children sued to stop enforcement of the constitutional provisions

Famous Footnote: *PLESSY* REFUTED

One of the more controversial footnotes in Supreme Court history is footnote eleven in *Brown v. Board of Education* (1954). That footnote cites seven sociological and psychological studies of the effects of racial segregation that support the unanimous Court's contention that segregation on the basis of race generates a feeling of inferiority among blacks that might never be erased:

> 11. K. B. Clark, *Effect of Prejudice and Discrimination on Personality Development* (Midcentury White House Conference on Children and Youth, 1950); Witner and Kotinsky, *Personality in the Making* (152), c. VI; Deutscher and Chein, *The Psychological Effects of Enforced Segregation; A Survey of Social Science Opinion*, 26 J. Psychol. 259 (1948); Chein, *What are the Psychological Effects of Segregation Under Conditions of Equal Facilities?*, 3 Int. J. Opinion and Attitude Res. 229 (1949); Brameld, Educational Costs, in *Discrimination and National Welfare* (McIver, ed., 1949), 44–48; Frazier, *The Negro in the United States* (1949), 674–681. And see generally Myrdal, *An American Dilemma* (1944).[1]

In *Simple Justice*, Richard Kluger quotes Chief Justice Earl Warren as saying of the footnote, "We included it because I thought the point it made was the antithesis of what was said in *Plessy*. They had said there that if there was any harm intended, it was solely in the mind of the Negro. I thought these things—these cited sources—were sufficient to note as being in contradistinction to that statement in *Plessy*."[2] In *Brown*, Warren restated that point with poignant clarity:

> We then come to the question presented: Does segregation of children in public schools solely on the basis of race, even though the physical facilities and other "tangible" factors may be equal, deprive the children of the minority group of equal educational opportunities? We believe that it does.... To separate them from others of similar age and qualifications solely because of their race generates a feeling of inferiority as to their status in the community that may affect their hearts and minds in a way unlikely ever to be undone.[3]

Kluger's research indicates that at least two of the justices questioned inclusion of the footnote in the school desegregation opinion, but their objections were minor compared to those that came from critics of the decision. Democratic senator James O. Eastland of Mississippi, in a May 27, 1954, speech in the Senate, said,

> The Supreme Court could not find the authority for its decisions in the wording of the 14th Amendment, in the history of the amendment or in the decision of any court. Instead, the Court was forced to resort to the unprecedented authority of a group of recent

partisan books on sociology and psychology. If this is the judicial calibre of the Court, what can the Nation expect from it in the future? What is to prevent the Court from citing as an authority in some future decision the works of Karl Marx?[4]

Even some who favored desegregation were displeased with the footnote. "It is one thing to use the current scientific findings, however ephemeral they may be, in order to ascertain whether the legislature has acted reasonably, in adopting some scheme of social or economic regulation.... It is quite another thing to have our fundamental rights rise, fall or change along with the latest fashions of psychological literature," wrote Professor Edmond Cahn.[5] Another respected law professor, Alexander Bickel, concluded:

> It was a mistake to do it this way. If you're going to invoke sociology and psychology, do it right.... No matter how it had been done, no doubt, the enemies of the opinion were certain to seize upon it and proclaim the ruling unjudicial and illegal. The opinion therefore should have said straight-forwardly that *Plessy* was based on a self-invented philosophy, no less psychologically oriented than the Court was being now in citing these sources that justify the holding that segregation inflicted damage. It was clear, though, that Warren wanted to present as small a target as possible, and that was wise. He did not want to go out to the country wearing a Hussar's uniform.[6]

Thurgood Marshall biographer Mark V. Tushnet later reexamined the footnote and its importance:

> Warren later denied that the material was crucial to the Court's decision, and in some sense it clearly was not. The footnote references were asides. And yet, [the] strategy of introducing the evidence [at trial] paid off. Something had to bridge the gap between the intangibles of [a college's] reputation and the [opportunities for] networking in the university cases and the intangibles in lower schools. Warren's statement about damage to hearts and minds shows that psychological intuitions, if not necessarily the trial court testimony, provided the bridge.[7]

1. *Brown v. Board of Education*, 347 U.S. 483 at 495 (1954).

2. Richard Kluger, *Simple Justice: The History of* Brown v. Board of Education *and Black America's Struggle for Equality* (New York: Knopf, 1976), 706.

3. *Brown v. Board of Education*, 347 U.S. 483 at 493 (1954).

4. *Congressional Record*, May 27, 1954, 100:7252.

5. Edmond Cahn, "Jurisprudence," *New York University Law Review* 30 (1955): 150, 159.

6. Kluger, *Simple Justice*, 707.

7. Mark V. Tushnet, *Making Civil Rights Law: Thurgood Marshall and the Supreme Court, 1946–1961* (New York: Oxford University Press, 1994), 214.

mandating a dual school system, but unlike the other cases, the state court granted the request. Finding the black schools inferior on a number of points, the court ordered white schools to admit black children. The state supreme court affirmed the decree, which the school board then appealed to the U.S. Supreme Court.

The fifth case, although argued with the other four, was decided separately.[28] *Bolling v. Sharpe* concerned public schools in the District of Columbia. Because the Fourteenth Amendment's guarantee of equal protection of the laws applies only to states, parents of black pupils based their challenge to school segregation in the District on the Fifth Amendment's guarantee of due process. A district court dismissed the suit, and the Supreme Court granted review of the dismissal. *(See box, Federal Equal Protection, p. 368.)* Together, the five cases brought to the Court grade school pupils and high school students, mandatory segregation laws and more permissive laws, the Equal Protection Clause of the Fourteenth Amendment and the Due Process Clause of the Fifth Amendment. Geographically, the five cases came from two southern states, one border state, a Plains state, and the nation's capital. As one commentator noted, the "wide geographical range gave the anticipated decision a national flavor and would blunt any claim that the South was being made a whipping boy."[29] In all five cases, the lower courts found that the education offered black students was substantially equal, or soon would be, to that given in the white schools. Thus the question presented to the Court was whether public school segregation per se was unconstitutional.

The Arguments

The school cases were argued in December 1952. In June 1953, the Court requested reargument, asking the attorneys to address three main questions:

- What historical evidence was there that the framers of the Fourteenth Amendment intended it to apply to segregation in public schools?

- If the answer to the first question was inconclusive, was it within the power of the Court to abolish segregation?

- If school segregation was found unconstitutional, what approach should the Court take to end it?

The cases were reargued in December 1953. Two months earlier, former California governor Earl Warren had become chief justice, replacing Vinson, who had died in September. Because Congress had already adjourned when he was named, Warren presided over the Court by virtue of a recess appointment until his unanimous confirmation on March 1, 1954.

Although there were several lawyers on both sides, the two leading adversaries were Marshall, director of the NAACP Legal Defense Fund, which had been instrumental in guiding the challenge to school segregation through the courts, and John W. Davis, a former U.S. representative, D-W.Va., solicitor general, and ambassador to Great Britain. In addition to being the 1924 Democratic presidential nominee, Davis had argued more cases before the Supreme Court than any other lawyer of his era. Marshall, then forty-five, would become in 1967 the first African American to sit *on* the Supreme Court. Davis, at age eighty, was making his final appearance before the Court, arguing in behalf of South Carolina in *Briggs* for the continuation of school segregation. It is one of the ironies of these cases that in 1915 Davis as solicitor general had successfully persuaded the Court to strike down Oklahoma's grandfather clause that prohibited blacks from voting. In that case, the fledgling NAACP supported Davis's position in its first friend-of-the-court brief.[30] *(See details of Guinn v. United States, p. 178.)*

Davis was first to present an answer to the Court's three questions. He contended that the Fourteenth Amendment was never intended to bar segregation in the nation's public schools. In addition to an intensive examination of the legislative history surrounding enactment of the amendment, Davis also recited the names of the states, both North and South, that instituted or continued to conduct segregated

The landmark decision in *Brown v. Board of Education of Topeka* (1954) overturned the "separate but equal" doctrine of *Plessy v. Ferguson* (1896). Linda Brown Smith, Ethel Louise Belton Brown, Harry Briggs Jr., and Spottswood Bolling Jr. were the plaintiffs.

schools after the amendment was ratified. Several of these same states had voted to ratify. To the question whether the Court had the authority on its own to overturn the separate but equal doctrine, Davis reminded the Court that the doctrine had been upheld not only by the lower courts but also by the Supreme Court and had therefore become part of the law of the land. "[S]omewhere, sometime to every principle comes a moment of repose when it has been so often announced, so confidently relied upon, so long continued, that it passes the limits of judicial discretion and disturbance," he said.[31] Making clear what he thought of earlier expert testimony concerning the detrimental effects of segregation on black children, Davis rhetorically asked what impact a desegregation order might have on a

predominantly black school district such as Clarendon County:

> If it is done on the mathematical basis, with 30 children as a maximum … you would have 27 Negro children and three whites in one school room. Would that make the children any happier? Would they learn any more quickly? Would their lives be more serene?
>
> Children of that age are not the most considerate animals in the world, as we all know. Would the terrible psychological disaster being wrought, according to some … to the colored child be removed if he had three white children sitting somewhere in the same school room?
>
> Would white children be prevented from getting a distorted idea of racial relations if they sat with 27 Negro children? I have posed that question because it is the very one that cannot be denied.[32]

Davis also said he did not believe the courts had the power to tell the states how to desegregate their schools. "Your Honors do not sit, and cannot sit as a glorified Board of Education for the State of South Carolina or any other state. Neither can the District Court," he declared. Davis then concluded:

> Let me say this for the State of South Carolina…. It believes that its legislation is not offensive to the Constitution of the United States.
>
> It is confident of its good faith and intention to produce equality for all of its children of whatever race or color. It is convinced that the happiness, the progress and the welfare of these children is best promoted in segregated schools, and it thinks it a thousand pities that by this controversy there should be urged the return to an experiment which gives no more promise of success today than when it was written into their Constitution during what I call the tragic era.
>
> I am reminded—and I hope it won't be treated as a reflection on anybody—of Aesop's fable of the dog and the meat: The dog, with a fine piece of meat in his mouth, crossed a bridge and saw the shadow in the stream and plunged for it and lost both substance and shadow.
>
> Here is equal education, not promised, not prophesied, but present. Shall it be thrown away on some fancied question of racial prestige?[33]

Marshall's response to Davis the following day illustrated the difference between the two men's styles and philosophies:

> I got the feeling on hearing the discussion yesterday that when you put a white child in a school with a whole lot of colored children, the child would fall apart or something. Everybody knows that is not true.
>
> Those same kids in Virginia and South Carolina—and I have seen them do it—they play in the streets together, they play on their farms together, they go down the road together, they separate to go to school, they come out of school and play ball together. They have to be separated in school.
>
> There is some magic to it. You can have them voting together, you can have them not restricted because of law in the houses they live in. You can have them going to the same state university and the same college, but if they go to elementary and high school, the world will fall apart.... They can't take race out of this case. From the day this case was filed until this moment, nobody has in any form or fashion ... done anything to distinguish this [segregation] statute from the Black Codes, which they must admit, because nobody can dispute ... the Fourteenth Amendment was intended to deprive the states of power to enforce Black Codes or anything else like it.
>
> ... [T]he only way that this Court can decide this case in opposition to our position, is that there must be some reason which gives the state the right to make a classification that they can make in regard to nothing else in regard to Negroes, and we submit the only way to arrive at this decision is to find that for some reason Negroes are inferior to all other human beings....
>
> It can't be because of slavery in the past, because there are very few groups in this country that haven't had slavery some place back in the history of their groups. It can't be color because there are Negroes as white as the drifted snow, with blue eyes, and they are just as segregated as the colored man.
>
> The only thing [it] can be is an inherent determination that the people who were formerly in slavery, regardless of anything else, shall be kept as near that stage as possible, and now is the time, we submit, that this Court should make it clear that that is not what our Constitution stands for.[34]

The Decision

All nine justices—including Robert H. Jackson, who had left a hospital bed—were present on May 17, 1954, when Chief Justice Warren read the unanimous decision in *Brown v. Board of Education*. The opinion, described by many as the most socially and ideologically significant decision in the Court's history, was just thirteen paragraphs long. Warren quickly disposed of the Court's first question—whether the framers of the Fourteenth Amendment intended it to bar school segregation. The evidence was inconclusive. The chief justice then turned to the separate but equal doctrine. Children attending the segregated public schools in these cases (unlike in *Sweatt*) were—or soon would be—receiving substantially equal treatment so far as "tangible" factors were concerned. Therefore, said Warren, the Court must look at the "effect of segregation itself on public education."[35] That assessment could not be made by turning the clock back to 1868, when the amendment was adopted, or to 1896 when the *Plessy* decision was written. "We must consider public education in the light of its full development and its present place in American life throughout the Nation," wrote Warren. "Only in this way can it be determined if segregation in public schools deprives these plaintiffs of the equal protection of the laws."[36]

The Court found that education was "perhaps the most important function" of state and local government, as evidenced by their compulsory attendance laws and considerable expenditures. Education, wrote Warren, was the foundation of good citizenship and the basis for professional training and adjustment to society. "In these days, it is doubtful that any child may reasonably be expected to succeed in life if he is denied the opportunity of an education," said Warren, adding that where the state had undertaken to make education available it must be available to all on equal terms.[37] Warren then posed this question: "Does segregation of children in public schools solely on the basis of race, even though the physical facilities and other 'tangible' factors may be equal, deprive the children of the minority group of equal educational opportunities?" The Court's answer: "We believe that it does."[38] Observing that intangible factors were considered in finding the

Pictured on the steps of the U.S. Supreme Court are the NAACP Legal Defense and Educational Fund lawyers who argued the school segregation cases resulting in the May 17, 1954, *Brown v. Board of Education* decision. *Left to right*: Howard Jenkins, James M. Nabrit, Spottswood W. Robinson III, Frank Reeves, Jack Greenberg, Special Counsel Thurgood Marshall, Louis Redding, U. Simpson Tate, and George E.C. Hayes. Missing from the photograph is Robert L. Carter, who argued the Topeka, Kansas, case.

treatment accorded *Sweatt* and *McLaurin* unequal, Warren said,

> Such considerations apply with added force to children in grade and high schools. To separate them from others of similar age and qualifications solely because of their race generates a feeling of inferiority as to their status in the community that may affect their hearts and minds in a way unlikely ever to be undone.[39]

This belief "was amply supported by modern authority," Warren asserted. In a footnote he cited seven sociological studies on the detrimental effects of enforced racial segregation. *(See box, Famous Footnote, p. 385.)* Warren continued:

> We conclude that in the field of public education the doctrine of "separate but equal" has no place. Separate educational facilities are inherently unequal. Therefore, we hold that the plaintiffs and others similarly situated for whom the actions have been brought are, by reason of the segregation complained of, deprived of the equal protection of the laws guaranteed by the Fourteenth Amendment.[40]

In the District of Columbia case, considered separately from the other four because it involved a question of due process under the Fifth Amendment, Warren wrote:

> Liberty under law extends to the full range of conduct which the individual is free to pursue, and it cannot be restricted except for a proper governmental objective. Segregation in public education is not reasonably related to any proper governmental objective, and thus it imposes on Negro children of the District of Columbia a burden that constitutes an arbitrary deprivation of their liberty in violation of the Due Process Clause.
>
> In view of our decision that the Constitution prohibits the states from maintaining racially segregated public schools, it would be unthinkable that the same Constitution would impose a lesser duty on the Federal Government.[41]

In the four state cases and in the District of Columbia suit, the Court postponed its decision on a remedy for school segregation until after the parties presented their views on that question.

DE FACTO SEGREGATION: FROM DENVER TO DAYTON

The Fourteenth Amendment prohibits state action denying anyone the equal protection of the law. It clearly applies to de jure segregation, that is, segregation imposed by law, like that the Court declared unconstitutional in *Brown v. Board of Education* (1954). De jure segregation existed throughout most southern and border states. School segregation also existed in the North and West, particularly in major cities, but most of the northern and western communities had repealed their segregation laws decades before *Brown* or had never required segregation by law. Their so-called de facto segregation resulted from economic status, residential patterns, and other factors outside the usual scope of the Equal Protection Clause.

DENVER 1973

Almost twenty years after *Brown,* the Court decided the first school segregation case from a state that had not imposed separation by law. In *Keyes v. School District #1, Denver* (1973), the Court, 7-1, ruled that under certain circumstances segregation in such school systems was unconstitutional. The case concerned two sets of schools in the Denver school system that were governed by one school board. The first were schools segregated by deliberate actions of the school board, and core city schools that were segregated but not—a lower court had held—as a result of school board action.

The Supreme Court directed the lower court to determine whether the school board's deliberate action in regard to the first set of schools so affected the other schools that it made the entire district a dual (that is, segregated) system. If not, the lower court was to consider proof that the core city schools were not intentionally segregated. If this proof produced by the school board was not persuasive, the court should order desegregation.

With this decision the Court expanded the definition of de jure segregation to include that fostered by intentional school board policies, even in the absence of state law. Without a showing of intent to segregate, however, no constitutional wrong existed. "We emphasize that the differentiating factor between *de jure* segregation and so-called *de facto* segregation ... is *purpose or intent to* segregate," Justice William J. Brennan Jr. wrote.[1] The majority indicated that the deliberate segregation of some of a system's schools could make the entire system a segregated one:

> [C]ommon sense dictates the conclusion that racially inspired school board actions have an impact beyond the particular schools that are the subjects of those actions.... Plainly a finding of intentional segregation as to a portion of a school system is not devoid of probative value in assessing the school authorities' intent with respect to other parts of the same school system.[2]

"All Deliberate Speed"

Among the issues the Court asked the parties to address in argument on appropriate remedies were the following:

- Should the Supreme Court formulate a detailed decree in each of the five cases, and if so, what specific issues should be addressed?

- Should the Court appoint a special master to take evidence and then make specific recommendations to the Court on the contents of the decrees?

- Should the Court remand the cases to the lower courts to fashion the decrees, and if so,

what directions and procedural guidelines should the Supreme Court give the lower courts?

- Should black pupils be admitted to schools of their choice "forthwith" or might desegregation be brought about gradually?

In addition to hearing from the parties involved in the five cases, the Court invited the Eisenhower administration and every state that required or permitted segregated public schools to submit their answers to these questions. The administration, Arkansas, Florida, Maryland, North Carolina, Oklahoma, and Texas accepted the invitation and participated in the oral argument in April 1955. Several states declined the

Justice Lewis F. Powell Jr. agreed with the decision but not with retention of the de jure–de facto distinction. He contended that the Court should adopt instead the rule that

> where segregated public schools exist within a school district to a substantial degree, there is a prima facie case that the duly constituted public authorities ... are sufficiently responsible [for the segregation] to warrant imposing upon them a nationally applicable burden to demonstrate they nevertheless are operating a genuinely integrated school system.[3]

DISCRIMINATORY INTENT

Disregarding Powell's suggestion, the Court continued to maintain the distinction between de jure and de facto segregation. In *Austin Independent School District v. United States* (1976), the justices told lower federal court judges to reconsider the school case of Austin, Texas, in light of *Washington v. Davis* (1976). In the latter case, the Court ruled that discriminatory intent, as well as discriminatory effect, must be shown for a denial of equal protection to be proved.[4]

DAYTON 1979

The Court's decision in *Dayton (Ohio) Board of Education v. Brinkman* (1977) held that a lower court had erred in asserting that the simple existence of racial imbalance in a city's schools constituted proof of deliberate segregation.[5] When the Dayton case, along with a case from Columbus, returned to the Court two years later, however, the Court abandoned the effort to distinguish between de jure and de facto segregation. It upheld massive court-ordered busing for both school systems, backing the finding of lower courts that both systems were unconstitutionally segregated.[6]

The majority stated that because the Dayton and Columbus systems had been largely segregated by race in 1954—at the time of *Brown*—the school boards in those cities had an affirmative constitutional responsibility to end that segregation. Because they had not, the busing orders were justified, declared the majority: the board's actions after 1954 "having foreseeable and anticipated disparate [racial] impact" were relevant evidence "to prove ... forbidden purpose."[7]

---

1. *Keyes v. School District #1, Denver,* 413 U.S. 189 at 208 (1973); see also *Columbus (Ohio) Board of Education v. Penick,* 443 U.S. 449 (1979).

2. Id. at 203, 207 passim.

3. Id. at 224.

4. *Austin Independent School District v. United States,* 429 U.S. 990 (1976); *Washington v. Davis,* 426 U.S. 229 (1976).

5. *Dayton (Ohio) Board of Education v. Brinkman,* 433 U.S. 406 (1977).

6. *Dayton Board of Education v. Brinkman, Columbus Board of Education v. Penick,* 443 U.S. 526 (1979).

7. Id.

invitation. On May 31, 1955, Chief Justice Warren announced the Court's final decision in an opinion commonly known as *Brown II,* to distinguish it from the 1954 decision. Warren first noted that the District of Columbia and the school districts in Kansas and Delaware had made substantial progress toward desegregation in the year since the first *Brown* decision. Virginia and South Carolina, he said, were awaiting the Court's final decision before acting. Warren then moved to the heart of the matter:

> Full implementation of these constitutional principles may require solution of varied local school problems. School authorities have the primary responsibility for elucidating, assessing, and solving these problems; courts will have to consider whether the action of school authorities constitutes good faith implementation of the governing constitutional principles. Because of their proximity to local conditions and the possible need for further hearings, the courts which originally heard these cases can best perform this judicial appraisal. Accordingly, we believe it appropriate to remand the cases to those courts.
>
> In fashioning and effectuating the decrees, the courts will be guided by equitable principles.... At stake is the personal interest of the plaintiffs in admission to public schools as soon as practicable on a nondiscriminatory basis. To effectuate this interest may call for elimination of a variety of obstacles in making the transition to school systems operated in accordance with the constitutional principles set forth in our May 17, 1954,

decision. Courts of equity may properly take into account the public interest in the elimination of such obstacles in a systematic and effective manner. But it should go without saying that the vitality of these constitutional principles cannot be allowed to yield simply because of disagreement with them.

While giving weight to these public and private considerations, the courts will require that the defendants make a prompt and reasonable start toward full compliance with our May 17, 1954, ruling. Once such a start has been made, the courts may find that additional time is necessary to carry out the ruling in an effective manner. The burden rests upon the defendants to establish that such time is necessary in the public interest and is consistent with good faith compliance at the earliest practicable date. To that end, the courts may consider problems related to administration, arising from the physical condition of the school plant, the school transportation system, personnel, revision of school districts and attendance areas into compact units to achieve a system of determining admission to the public schools on a nonracial basis, and revision of local laws and regulations which may be necessary in solving the foregoing problems. They will also consider the adequacy of any plans the defendants may propose to meet these problems and to effectuate a transition to a racially nondiscriminatory school system. During this period of transition, the courts will retain jurisdiction of these cases.[42]

Desegregation of public schools, Warren concluded, was to proceed "with all deliberate speed."[43]

Reaction and Resistance

Reaction to the two *Brown* decisions was immediate. At one extreme were those committed to segregation as a way of life. They castigated the Court, called its decisions a usurpation of state prerogatives, and urged defiance. The height of the rhetoric opposing the *Brown* decisions may have been the March 1956 "Declaration of Constitutional Principles," a tract signed by 101 of 128 members of Congress from eleven southern and border states. The signers called the *Brown* decisions "a clear abuse of judicial power" and commended those states that intended to "resist enforced integration by any means."[44] At the other end of the spectrum were those

who hailed the demise of the separate but equal doctrine as long overdue but felt that the Court seriously erred in *Brown II* by not ordering immediate desegregation. Many found themselves somewhere in the middle, unhappy with the command to desegregate but unwilling to defy it.

"Massive resistance"—a phrase coined by Democratic senator Harry F. Byrd of Virginia—did not begin in earnest until late 1955 and early 1956. Relieved that the Court had not ordered immediate desegregation, many southern leaders opposed to desegregation apparently presumed that lower courts would ignore or otherwise delay implementation of the *Brown* decisions. By January 1956, however, nineteen lower courts had used the *Brown* precedents to invalidate school segregation and, as historian C. Vann Woodward characterized it, "[s]omething very much like panic seized many parts of the South … a panic bred of insecurity and fear."[45] White citizens councils, created to preserve segregation, spread throughout the South. The NAACP was barred from operating in some states, and many state and local officials sought ways to delay desegregation in the schools.

Official resistance took three main paths. Several states enacted "interposition" statutes declaring the *Brown* decisions of no effect. Mississippi and Louisiana also passed laws requiring school segregation in order to promote public health and morals and preserve the public peace. Several states also adopted superficially neutral laws that resulted in separation of pupils by race. Among these types of statutes were laws that assigned pupils to specific schools and classes on the basis of their scholastic aptitude and achievement. Since black children had rarely received adequate educations, they were thus easily isolated. Another tactic was to allow pupils to attend any public school (of the correct grade level) they chose. Few blacks had the courage to attend hostile white schools, and even fewer whites chose to attend black schools. Some states barred public funds to any school district that integrated, while others permitted public schools to close rather than to accept black children. In some instances, compulsory attendance laws were repealed, and in still other cases states and localities allocated public funds

White students at Arkansas' North Little Rock High School block the school doors in September 1957, denying access to six enrolled black students in defiance of Supreme Court rulings ordering desegregation of the nation's public schools. Moments later the black students were shoved down a flight of stairs and onto the sidewalk.

to private segregated schools. Many states employed more than one of these methods to perpetuate segregation in their public schools.

Brown as Precedent

Adverse reaction to the desegregation decision did not deter the Court from applying it to other areas of life. In 1955 the Court ordered the University of Alabama to admit two blacks to its undergraduate program.[46] The Court in a per curiam opinion declared in *Florida ex rel. Hawkins v. Board of Control* (1956) that it would not permit institutes of higher education to delay desegregation.[47] Beginning with *Muir v. Louisville Park Theatrical Assn.* (1954) the justices, in brief orders that cited *Brown* as authority, struck down the separate but equal doctrine as it applied to state-imposed segregation of

public places, such as parks, and vehicles of interstate transportation.[48] *(See "Travel and Public Accommodations," pp. 406–414.)*

Resistance Rebuked

The Court first addressed the problem of massive resistance in *Cooper v. Aaron* (1958), which resulted when Arkansas officials openly defied the Court's order to abandon segregation. Less than a week after the Supreme Court struck down the separate but equal doctrine, the Little Rock school board announced its intention to develop a desegregation plan for the city schools. One year later—a week before the Court announced its decision in *Brown II*—the school board approved a plan that called for gradual desegregation beginning with Central High School in fall 1957.

Meanwhile, the state adopted a constitutional amendment commanding the legislature to oppose the *Brown* decisions. In response, the state legislature enacted a law permitting children in racially mixed schools to ignore compulsory attendance laws.

On September 2, 1957, Governor Orval Faubus sent units of the Arkansas National Guard to Central High to prevent nine black students scheduled to attend the school from entering. Obeying a federal district court order, the school board proceeded with its integration plan, and on September 4 the nine students tried to enter the school, but found their way blocked by guardsmen standing shoulder to shoulder, along with a mob of hostile onlookers. This situation prevailed until September 20, when Faubus decided to obey a court order and withdraw the troops. On September 23, the black students entered the high school but were quickly removed by police when a mob outside grew unruly. Two days later, President Dwight D. Eisenhower sent federal troops to protect the blacks as they entered and left the school. Federal troops remained there until November 27, when they were replaced by federalized national guardsmen who remained for the duration of the school year.

In the face of such official and public hostility, the Little Rock school board in February 1958 asked the district court for permission to withdraw the black students from Central High and to postpone any further desegregation for two and a half years. Finding the situation at Central intolerable, the court agreed to the request. An appeals court reversed the decision, and the school board appealed to the Supreme Court.

A Special Term

The Court convened a special summer term on August 28, 1958, to render its opinion before the school year began. Arguments were heard September 11. The next day the Court issued an unsigned per curiam opinion affirming the appeals court's denial of the postponement. On September 29, the Court issued its formal opinion in *Cooper v. Aaron*, which sharply rebuked Faubus and the Arkansas legislature for their obstructive actions.[49] The Court indicated its sympathy for the Little Rock school board, which it said had acted in

good faith, but the Court added that the "constitutional rights of [black] respondents are not to be sacrificed or yielded to the violence and disorder which have followed upon the actions of the Governor and Legislature."[50] The Court then reminded those officials that the Fourteenth Amendment prohibited state officials from denying anyone equal protection of the laws and said that it would not tolerate any state action perpetuating segregation in schools:

> State support of segregated schools through any arrangement, management, funds or property cannot be squared with the [Fourteenth] Amendment's command that no State shall deny to any person within its jurisdiction the equal protection of the laws.... The basic decision in *Brown* was unanimously reached by this Court only after the case had been briefed and twice argued and the issues had been given the most serious consideration.
>
> Since the first *Brown* opinion three new Justices have come to the Court. They are at one with the Justices still on the Court who participated in that basic decision as to its correctness, and that decision is now unanimously reaffirmed. The principles announced in that decision and the obedience of the States to them, according to the command of the Constitution, are indispensable for the protection of the freedoms guaranteed by our fundamental charter for all of us. Our constitutional ideal of equal justice under law is thus made a living truth.[51]

To emphasize the gravity with which the Court viewed the defiance of the Arkansas officials, each of the nine justices personally signed the opinion.

Governor Faubus and the Arkansas legislature chose to ignore this warning. With the approval of the legislature, Faubus shut down all four Little Rock high schools, which remained closed for the entire 1958–1959 school year. In June 1959, a federal district court declared the statute authorizing the closures a violation of due process and equal protection, and the Supreme Court affirmed that opinion.[52] Little Rock high schools opened to black and white students in fall 1959.

Other Decisions

Despite the Court's protestation in the Arkansas case that it would not tolerate schemes to evade segregation, in November 1958 it affirmed without opinion an appeals court decision upholding Alabama's pupil placement law as constitutional on its face. (The lower court had made clear, however, that the law might be found unconstitutional if its application resulted in racial discrimination.)[53] In two 1959 cases the Supreme Court refused to review lower court rulings requiring that all state remedies for segregation be exhausted before a case could move into federal court.[54] Over the next three years, the Court affirmed lower court decisions striking down Louisiana laws clearly designed to continue school segregation.[55]

In June 1963, the Court began to express its impatience with dilatory school boards. In the first signed opinion on school desegregation since *Cooper v. Aaron,* the Court struck down a transfer scheme that worked to preserve segregated schools. Its decision in *Goss v. Board of Education of Knoxville* (1963) reversed the lower courts' approval of transfer plans in two Tennessee cities that allowed students assigned to schools where they were in the minority to transfer to schools where their race was in the majority. The unanimous Court declared that because it was "readily apparent" that the plan would continue segregation, it was unconstitutional.[56] In a second case, *McNeese v. Board of Education* (1963), the Court ruled that where federal rights were at stake, all state remedies need not be exhausted before relief was sought in federal court.[57]

Too Much Deliberation

A full ten years after *Brown I,* the Court announced that there had been too much deliberation and not enough speed in the effort to desegregate the nation's public schools. The case of *Griffin v. County School Board of Prince Edward County* (1964) originated in the same Virginia county involved in *Brown.* Despite that decision in 1954, the county's schools remained segregated. In 1959 the county closed its schools rather than obey a lower court order to desegregate. The county then replaced the public schools for whites with private schools, partially financed by public funds. The county offered to set up similar schools for blacks, but blacks refused the offer and pursued the legal battle for integrated public schools. Consequently, black children in Prince Edward County could not attend public school there from 1959 until 1963. Federal, state, and local officials eventually cooperated to open some desegregated public schools in the county.

In 1961 a federal district court ordered a halt in the flow of public funds to the all-white private schools. In 1962 it ordered the county to reopen the public schools, ruling that it could not constitutionally close the schools to avoid segregating them while all the other public schools in the state remained open. The county appealed the ruling to the Supreme Court. "Whatever nonracial grounds might support a State's allowing a county to abandon public schools, the object must be a constitutional one, and grounds of race and opposition to desegregation do not qualify as constitutional," the Court said in 1964 affirming the lower court order.[58] Dismissing the county's contention that the state courts should have been given an opportunity to determine whether the schools should be opened before the federal district court acted, the Court declared,

[W]e hold that the issues here imperatively call for decision now. The case has been delayed since 1951 by resistance at the state and county level, by legislation, and by lawsuits. The original plaintiffs have doubtless all passed high school age. There has been entirely too much deliberation and not enough speed in enforcing the constitutional rights which we held in *Brown* ... had been denied Prince Edward County Negro children.[59]

The Court spoke even more sharply a year later. "Delays in desegregating public school systems are no longer tolerable," the justices declared in a per curiam opinion in *Bradley v. School Board of City of Richmond* (1965).[60] Three weeks later, in *Rogers v. Paul* (1965), the Court in another per curiam opinion ordered an Arkansas school district to permit a black student "immediate transfer" to an all-white high school, adding that "those similarly situated" might transfer as well.[61] In December 1967, the Court affirmed without opinion lower court rulings requiring Alabama to desegregate its schools. It was the first time that a state was ordered to take such action. All previous desegregation orders had been directed only to local school systems.[62]

"Affirmative Duty"

In May 1968, the Supreme Court put its foot down. The unanimous Court ordered all remaining segregated school systems to devise desegregation plans that promised to be effective. In *Green v. County School Board of New Kent County, Va.* (1968), the Court held that the county's freedom of choice plan did not accomplish the goals set out in *Brown I* and *Brown II*. Freedom of choice plans allowed students to choose which school within the district they wanted to attend. Details varied from district to district, but in most instances custom and residential patterns served to keep the schools under such plans racially segregated.

Rural New Kent County, with a population divided almost evenly between whites and blacks, was originally segregated by Virginia law. In 1965 the school board adopted a freedom of choice plan, but, as the Court noted, in three years of operation no white pupil chose to attend the black school and only 15 percent of the black children were enrolled in the formerly all-white school. In an opinion written by Justice William J. Brennan Jr., the Court said the school board's adoption of a freedom of choice plan did not fulfill its obligation to desegregate the county schools:

> In the context of the state-imposed segregated pattern of long standing, the fact that in 1965 the Board opened the doors of the former "white" school to Negro children and of the "Negro" school to white children merely begins, not ends, our inquiry whether the Board has taken steps adequate to abolish its dual, segregated system. *Brown II* was a call for the dismantling of well-entrenched dual systems tempered by an awareness that complex and multifaceted problems would arise which would require time and flexibility for a successful resolution. School boards such as the respondent then operating state-compelled dual systems were nevertheless clearly charged with the affirmative duty to take whatever steps might be necessary to convert to a unitary system in which racial discrimination would be eliminated root and branch.[63]

Observing that it had taken eleven years after *Brown I* for the district to begin desegregating, Brennan continued:

> This deliberate perpetuation of the unconstitutional dual system can only have compounded the harm of such a system.... Moreover, a plan that at this late date fails to provide meaningful assurance of prompt and effective disestablishment of a dual system is also intolerable.... The burden on a school board today is to come forward with a plan that promises realistically to work, and promises realistically to work now.[64]

Effective Remedy

The Court refused to say that any one type of desegregation plan promised to be more effective than another—leaving it up to each individual school district to fashion a remedy best suited to its situation and needs—but it did give the district courts some guidance in assessing the effectiveness of desegregation plans. Wrote Brennan:

> It is incumbent upon the district court to weigh that claim [of plan effectiveness] in light of the facts at hand and ... any alternatives which may be shown as feasible and more promising in their effectiveness. Where the court finds the board to be acting in good faith and the proposed plan to have real prospects for dismantling the state-imposed dual system "at the earliest practicable date," then the plan may be said to provide effective relief. Of course, the availability to the board of other, more promising courses of action may indicate a lack of good faith; and at the least it places a heavy burden upon the board to explain its preference for an apparently less effective method.[65]

Although the Court did not rule out freedom of choice plans entirely, it stated that experience indicated they were usually ineffective. Certainly, the Court said, New Kent County's plan was ineffective. There "the plan has operated simply to burden children and their parents with a responsibility which *Brown II* places squarely on the School Board." The Court ordered the board to formulate a new plan that promised to convert the county schools "to a system, without a 'white' school and a 'Negro' school, but just schools."[66]

In two other cases decided on the same day, the Court applied *Green* to find a freedom of choice plan in an Arkansas school district and a free transfer plan

TWO RACES, TWO DISTRICTS?

One way some towns and cities avoided desegregation was to divide a school district so that most black children would attend the schools of one district and most white children the schools in another. The Supreme Court did not view this ploy sympathetically. *Wright v. Emporia City Council* (1972) concerned a Virginia city whose schools were part of the surrounding county school system. When the county was ordered to desegregate its schools, the city petitioned to operate its own school system. Although the city and county school systems both would have had a majority of black students, the county schools would have been more heavily black if the city school district were created than if the city's students were part of a countywide plan. By a 5-4 vote the Court ruled the city's proposal impermissible because it would hinder desegregation:

> Certainly desegregation is not achieved by splitting a single school system operating "white schools" and "Negro schools" into two new systems, each operating unitary schools within its borders, where one of the two new systems is, in fact, "white" and the other is, in fact, "Negro."[1]

The four dissenters denied that creation of the second school system would interfere with the desegregation process. A second system should not be rejected if its only effect was a slightly greater racial imbalance in both school systems, they said.

In a second case, the Court was unanimous in its opinion that the creation of a new school district was impermissible. *United States v. Scotland Neck City Board of Education* (1972) involved the North Carolina legislature's creation of a school district for the city of Scotland Neck, which had been part of a county school system that was in the process of implementing a desegregation plan. The Court said there was no question that the statute was motivated by a desire to create a predominantly white school system in the city, and so it must be struck down.[2]

---

1. *Wright v. Emporia City Council*, 407 U.S. 451 at 463 (1972).
2. *United States v. Scotland Neck Board of Education*, 407 U.S. 484 (1972).

---

in Jackson, Tennessee, unlikely to achieve desegregation.[67] *Green* was the last major school desegregation case in which Chief Justice Warren participated; he would retire in June 1969. In the first case heard by Chief Justice Burger, the Court reversed an appeals court order that allowed indefinite postponement of desegregation in thirty-three Mississippi school districts so long as they took "significant steps" in the forthcoming school year to dismantle their dual school systems. The Court's brief decision in *Alexander v. Holmes Board of Education* (1969) took on added significance because the administration of President Richard Nixon had argued for allowing delay. In an unsigned opinion, the Court said that the standard of "all deliberate speed" was "no longer constitutionally permissible," and it ordered the school districts to begin immediate operation of unitary school systems. The Court defined these as "systems within which no person is to be effectively excluded from any school because of race or color."[68]

The Scope of the Remedy

Chief Justice Burger's appointment to the Court coincided with a shift in the focus of school desegregation cases. It became clear with *Green* that schools could no longer avoid the duty to desegregate; the issue thus shifted to the methods used to accomplish that end. A major question was whether schools were required to reflect the racial balance that existed in the community. Would neighborhood schools, whatever their racial balance, satisfy the desegregation requirement so long as they were open to students of all races or must pupils be transported beyond their normal geographic school zones to achieve some sort of racial balance?

The Swann Decision

School officials, the Court held, could choose from a broad range of desegregation tools those that would most effectively eliminate segregation in their district. In a unanimous decision, the Court ruled in *Swann v. Charlotte-Mecklenburg County Board of Education*

(1971) that busing, racial balance quotas, and gerrymandered school districts were all appropriate interim methods of eliminating the vestiges of school segregation. The case arose from controversy over the desegregation of the Charlotte-Mecklenburg County, North Carolina, school system. That system in the 1969–1970 school year had 84,000 students, 71 percent white and 29 percent black. In that year, almost 29,000 of those students were bused to school in an effort to desegregate the school system.

Of the 24,000 black students, 21,000 lived within the city of Charlotte. Because of the smaller number and dispersed residences of black pupils in the rural part of the county, there were no all-black schools in that part of the system. In the city, however, most schools remained racially identifiable, and two of every three of the city's black students attended one of twenty-five schools that were 98 percent to 100 percent black. Three of every four of the area's white students attended schools that were primarily white. In February 1970, a federal district judge ordered 13,000 additional students bused. More than 9,000 of these pupils were elementary school children. Under the order, no school remained all black, and the effort was made to reach a 71:29 white-black ratio in each school, reflecting the overall white-black ratio in the system.

The Fourth Circuit Court of Appeals first delayed, then reversed the elementary school part of the plan as imposing an unreasonable burden upon the school board. The NAACP Legal Defense Fund, representing the black parents concerned, appealed to the Supreme Court, arguing that the order should have been left intact. The school board also appealed, arguing that more of the order should have been modified. Chief Justice Burger wrote the Court's opinion. He pointed out that federal courts became involved in the desegregation process only when local school authorities failed to fulfill their obligation to eliminate a dual school system. If school authorities defaulted—as the lower federal court found that the Charlotte school board had in *Swann*—then the federal judge had wide discretion to select the means of desegregating the school system. Burger then discussed the four main issues

Swann presented: racial balance, one-race schools, attendance zones, and busing.

Racial Balance. The Court held that the federal district court had properly used mathematical ratios of whites and blacks as "a starting point in the process of shaping a remedy." Burger asserted, however, that a court could not require "as a matter of substantive constitutional right" any specific degree of racial mixing. "The constitutional command to desegregate schools does not mean that every school in every community must always reflect the racial composition of the school system as a whole."[69]

One-Race Schools. The Court acknowledged that residential patterns often result in schools that are attended only by children of one race. The presence of such schools does not necessarily indicate a system that is still segregated, but, wrote Burger, school authorities or the district court

> should make every effort to achieve the greatest possible degree of actual desegregation and will thus necessarily be concerned with the elimination of one-race schools. No per se rule can adequately embrace all the difficulties of reconciling the competing interests involved; but in a system with a history of segregation, the need for remedial criteria of sufficient specificity to assure a school authority's compliance with its constitutional duty warrants a presumption against schools that are substantially disproportionate in their racial composition.... [T]he burden upon the school authorities will be to satisfy the court that their racial composition is not the result of present or past discriminatory action on their part.[70]

The Court endorsed plans that allowed a child attending a school where his or her race was a majority to transfer to a school where the child's race was a minority, but to be successful, the justices added, such plans must ensure the transferring pupil available space in the school and free transportation.

Attendance Zones. To overcome the effects of segregated residential patterns, the Court endorsed drastic gerrymandering of school districts and pairing, clustering, and grouping of schools that were not necessarily contiguous. "As an interim corrective measure, this cannot be said to be beyond the broad remedial powers of a court," the chief justice wrote.[71]

Busing. Bus transportation of students had been an "integral part of the public education system for years," Burger wrote, and was a permissible remedial technique to help achieve desegregation. The Court conceded that objections to busing might be valid "when the time or distance of travel is so great as to either risk the health of the children or significantly impinge on the educational process." The limits to busing would vary with many factors, "but probably with none more than the age" of the children, the Court said.[72] The Court acknowledged that some of these remedies might be "administratively awkward, inconvenient and even bizarre in some situations and may impose burdens on some; but all awkwardness and inconvenience cannot be avoided in the interim period when the remedial adjustments are being made to eliminate the dual school systems."[73]

The Court was careful to say that its decision did not deal with de facto segregation, that is, discrimination resulting from factors other than state law, nor did it reach the question of what action might be taken against schools that were segregated as a result of "other types of state action, without any discriminatory action by the school authorities."[74] In reference to the potential problem of resegregation, which might occur after achievement of a unitary school system, the Court concluded,

> Neither school authorities nor district courts are constitutionally required to make year-by-year adjustments of the racial composition of student bodies once the affirmative duty to desegregate has been accomplished and racial discrimination through official action is eliminated from the system. This does not mean that federal courts are without power to deal with future problems; but in the absence of a showing that either the school authorities or some other agency of the state has deliberately attempted to fix or alter demographic patterns to affect the racial composition of the schools, further intervention by a district court should not be necessary.[75]

Related Rulings

The Court handed down three related school desegregation decisions the same day as the Charlotte-Mecklenburg ruling. In *North Carolina State Board of Education v. Swann* (1971), the Court struck down a state law that forbade school systems to bus or assign students to schools on the basis of race. The Court said the law was invalid because it prevented implementation of desegregation plans:

> [I]f a state-imposed limitation on a school authority's discretion operates to inhibit or obstruct the operation of a unitary school system or impede the disestablishing of a dual school system, it must fall; state policy must give way when it operates to hinder vindication of federal constitutional guarantees.... [T]he statute exploits an apparently neutral form to control school assignment plans by directing that they be "color-blind"; that requirement, against the background of segregation, would render illusory the promise of *Brown*.... Just as the race of students must be considered in determining whether a constitutional violation has occurred, so also must race be considered in formulating a remedy. To forbid, at this stage, all assignments made on the basis of race would deprive school authorities of the one tool absolutely essential to fulfillment of their constitutional obligation to eliminate existing dual school systems.[76]

In *Davis v. Board of School Commissioners of Mobile County, Ala.* (1971), the Court ordered an appeals court to reexamine its desegregation order for Mobile in light of the guidelines set down in *Swann*. The Court said the appeals court had not considered all the available techniques for desegregation. The plan included no busing for black children attending predominantly black high schools, and its insistence on geographically unified school zones tended to preserve single-race schools.[77] In the third case, *McDaniel v. Barresi* (1971), the Court upheld a Georgia county desegregation plan that assigned black pupils living in heavily black areas to schools in other attendance zones. The state supreme court had declared the plan invalid on the grounds that busing only black pupils denied equal protection of the laws, but the Supreme

Court said the school board had acted properly in considering race as a factor in a desegregation plan.[78]

"Tailoring" the Remedy

In the early 1970s, opposition to court-ordered desegregation focused on the school bus. The nearly universal antipathy to busing did not cause the Supreme Court to retract its opinion that busing was an appropriate remedy for segregation, but in 1974 the Court began to insist that the scope of the remedy not exceed the extent of the violation causing the segregation.

Busing across Boundaries: Richmond and Detroit

The first time the Court considered whether federal courts could require busing between school districts as part of a desegregation plan, it did not reach a conclusion. The case of *Richmond School Board v. Virginia State Board of Education* (1973) came to the Court after a federal district judge ordered school officials to consolidate the predominantly black Richmond school district with the two neighboring, mostly white, county systems in order to desegregate the city schools.[79] The court of appeals overturned the order as too drastic. The Supreme Court divided 4-4, automatically upholding the court of appeals. Justice Lewis F. Powell Jr. did not participate in the case; he had formerly served on both the Richmond and Virginia school boards. There was no Court opinion, and because of the even vote, the case carried no weight as precedent.

Slightly more than a year later, the Court, 5-4, struck down a district court plan to desegregate Detroit, Michigan, schools by busing students among fifty-four school districts in three counties. The majority held that a multidistrict remedy was not appropriate unless all of the districts were responsible for the segregation. *Milliken v. Bradley* (1974) originated when a federal district judge concluded that both the Detroit school board and state officials had taken actions that fostered school segregation in the city. Because the city school system was predominantly black, the judge declared that a plan limited to its boundaries would fail to provide meaningful desegregation of the schools. He therefore ordered the multidistrict remedy. "[S]chool district lines are simply matters of political convenience and

may not be used to deny constitutional rights," the judge ruled.[80] A court of appeals affirmed the order, but a Supreme Court majority overturned the order.

Chief Justice Burger explained that both lower courts erred when they assumed that desegregation could not be achieved unless the Detroit schools reflected the racial balance of the surrounding metropolitan area. Although "boundary lines may be bridged where there has been a constitutional violation calling for interdistrict relief," wrote Burger, "... the notion that school district lines may be casually ignored or treated as a mere administrative convenience is contrary to the history of public education in our country."[81] In any school desegregation case, said Burger, the scope of the remedy should not exceed the extent of the violation:

> Before the boundaries of separate and autonomous school districts may be set aside by consolidating the separate units for remedial purposes or by imposing a cross-district remedy, it must first be shown that there has been a constitutional violation within one district that produces a significant segregative effect in another district. Specifically, it must be shown that racially discriminatory acts of the state or local school districts, or of a single school district, have been a substantial cause of interdistrict segregation. Thus an interdistrict remedy might be in order where the racially discriminatory acts of one or more school districts caused racial segregation in an adjacent district or where district lines have been deliberately drawn on the basis of race. In such circumstances, an interdistrict remedy would be appropriate to eliminate the interdistrict segregation directly caused by the constitutional violation. Conversely, without an interdistrict violation and interdistrict effect, there is no constitutional wrong calling for an interdistrict remedy.[82]

Since none of the other fifty-three school districts had been shown to practice segregation or to have been affected by Detroit's segregation, the proposed remedy was "wholly impermissible," the majority concluded. That state officials had contributed to the segregation did not empower the federal court to order the multidistrict remedy. "Disparate treatment of white and Negro students occurred within the

Detroit school system, and not elsewhere, and on this record the remedy must be limited to that system," Burger wrote.[83]

Without an interdistrict remedy, wrote Justice Marshall in a dissenting opinion, "Negro children in Detroit will receive the same separate and inherently unequal education in the future as they have been unconstitutionally afforded in the past."[84] Marshall insisted that the segregative actions of state officials justified the multidistrict remedy:

> The essential foundation of interdistrict relief in this case was not to correct conditions within outlying districts.... Instead, interdistrict relief was seen as a necessary part of any meaningful effort by the State of Michigan to remedy the state-caused segregation within the city of Detroit.[85]

Remedying the System: Detroit and Dayton

The Supreme Court remanded *Milliken* to the district court to fashion a new remedy that affected only the Detroit city schools. In an opinion affirmed by the appeals court, the district court ordered the school board as part of the new remedy to institute comprehensive remedial education, testing, training, counseling, and guidance programs in the city schools. It also directed the state to pay half the costs of implementing these programs. These two parts of the remedy were appealed to the Supreme Court, which upheld them in 1977 by a 9-0 vote.

The Court found the comprehensive remedial programs appropriate to remedy the educational conditions caused by the segregation. "Pupil assignment alone does not automatically remedy the impact of previous unlawful educational isolation; the consequences linger and can be dealt with only by independent measures," the Court said.[86] The justices also held that the order to the state to pay half the costs was not equivalent, as the state claimed, to an award for damages. In a non-school-related case, the Court in 1974 had ruled that the Eleventh Amendment protected states against such payments of damages,[87] but the school payments

were permissible, held the Court, because they amounted to prospective relief "designed to wipe out continuing conditions of inequality" caused by the state.[88]

Reflecting the 1974 *Milliken* holding that where segregation affects only one school district, a multidistrict remedy is excessive, the Court also held that where segregation does not affect an entire school district, a system-wide desegregation plan is excessive. A federal district court found in *Dayton (Ohio) Board of Education v. Brinkman* (1977) that the city school board had discriminated against minority students in three specific instances. After a court of appeals rejected more limited remedies, the district court proposed a desegregation plan that involved the entire school district. The appeals court affirmed this plan, but the Supreme Court struck it down, 8-0. In an opinion written by Justice William H. Rehnquist, the Court questioned the validity of the district court's finding of discrimination in two of the instances and observed that the discrimination in the third affected only high school students. Under these circumstances, the Court said, the appeals court overstepped its proper role when it ordered the district court to develop a system-wide plan without disputing the district court's findings of fact or legal opinion:

> The duty of both the district Court and of the Court of Appeals in a case such as this, where mandatory segregation by law of the races in the schools has long since ceased, is to first determine whether there was any action in the conduct of the business of the school board which was intended to, and did in fact, discriminate against minority pupils, teachers or staff.... If such violations are found, the District Court in the first instance, subject to review by the Court of Appeals, must determine how much incremental segregative effect these violations had on the racial distribution of the Dayton school population as presently constituted, when that distribution is compared to what it would have been in the absence of such constitutional violations. The remedy must be designed to redress that difference, and only if there has been a systemwide impact may there be a systemwide remedy.[89]

Discrimination and Private Schools: Textbooks to Taxes

Private schools proliferated in most areas under pressure to desegregate public schools. Many private schools were created specifically as havens for whites fleeing desegregation. In the 1920s, the Supreme Court acknowledged the right of parents to send their children to private schools. In *Pierce v. Society of Sisters* (1925), the Court ruled that an Oregon statute requiring all children to attend public schools "unreasonably interferes with the liberty of parents and guardians to direct the upbringing and education of children under their control."[1]

This holding, coupled with the Court's view that the Fourteenth Amendment does not prohibit acts of private discrimination, appeared to immunize private schools with racially discriminatory admissions policies from desegregation efforts. Two Supreme Court rulings in the 1970s, however, curtailed the forms of support that state and local governments can provide to racially discriminatory private schools. In a third case, the Court significantly narrowed the freedom of such schools to discriminate, and in 1983 it held that racial discrimination by a private university was grounds for denial, or withdrawal, of that university's tax-exempt status.

TEXTBOOKS

In *Norwood v. Harrison* (1973), a unanimous Court held that it was not permissible for Mississippi to lend textbooks to private schools that discriminated on the basis of race. Lending textbooks was direct state aid in violation of the Fourteenth Amendment.[2] Noting that the Court had affirmed lower court rulings barring state tuition grants to students attending racially discriminatory private schools, Chief Justice Warren E. Burger wrote,

> Free textbooks, like tuition grants directed to private school students, are a form of financial assistance inuring to the benefit of the private schools themselves. An inescapable educational cost for students in both public and private schools is the expense of providing all necessary learning materials. When, as here, that necessary expense is borne by the State, the economic consequence is to give aid to the enterprise; if the school engages in discriminatory practices the State by tangible aid in the form of textbooks thereby supports such discrimination.

Racial discrimination in state-operated schools is barred by the Constitution and "[i]t is also axiomatic that a State may not induce, encourage or promote private persons to accomplish what it is constitutionally forbidden to accomplish."[3]

The Court rejected Mississippi's contention that to deny such private schools state aid would deny them equal protection of the laws. "It is one thing to say that a State may not prohibit the maintenance of private schools and quite another to say that such schools must, as a matter of equal protection, receive state aid," declared the Court.[4]

ATHLETIC FACILITIES

In the early 1970s, the Court affirmed a lower court order forbidding Montgomery, Alabama, to permit racially discriminatory private schools to have exclusive use of its park and recreational facilities. Such permission "created, in effect, 'enclaves of segregation'" that deprived black children and their families of equal access to the parks.[5] Furthermore, the city's action ran counter to the intent of a court order directing it to desegregate its public schools. Justice Harry A. Blackmun explained that the city, by permitting these schools to have exclusive use of public recreational facilities, enhanced the attractiveness of segregated private schools—formed in reaction to the desegregation order—by enabling them to offer athletic programs to their students at public expense.

Because the city provided the schools with stadiums and other recreational facilities, the schools were able to spend money they would have spent on athletic programs or other educational projects. At the same time, the schools realized revenue from the concessions operated at the stadiums and other facilities. "We are persuaded," concluded Blackmun in *Gilmore v. City of Montgomery* (1974), "... that this assistance significantly tended to undermine the federal court order mandating the establishment and maintenance of a unitary school system in Montgomery."[6] The Court was, however, unable to decide whether it was unconstitutional for the state to allow the segregated private schools to use the facilities in common with other schoolchildren and private nonschool organizations.

In 1979 the Court held that the board's discrimination had a system-wide impact and thus necessitated a system-wide remedy. *(See box, De Facto Segregation, pp. 390–391.)*

Balance, Not Rebalance: Pasadena

The Court in *Swann* said that once a school system was desegregated, school authorities would not be required to make annual adjustments in order to maintain a

ADMISSIONS POLICIES

Racially discriminatory admissions policies of private schools were directly challenged in *Runyon v. McCrary, Fairfax-Brewster School v. Gonzales* (1976). Two private schools in northern Virginia, Bobbe's Private School and Fairfax-Brewster School, refused to admit Michael McCrary and Colin Gonzales solely because they were black. Their parents filed suit on behalf of the boys, charging that discriminatory admissions policies violated the Civil Rights Act of 1866 that gives "all persons within the jurisdiction of the United States the same right … to make and enforce contracts … as is enjoyed by white citizens." A federal district court and court of appeals agreed with the parents, and the Supreme Court affirmed the lower courts by a 7-2 vote.[7]

The majority, with Justice Potter Stewart as its spokesman, rejected the argument that the 1866 law did not reach private contracts. That claim was inconsistent with the Court's earlier rulings, said Stewart, in particular the decision in *Jones v. Alfred H. Mayer Co.* (1968). In that case, the Court held that a companion provision of the 1866 act forbade private racial discrimination in the sale or rental of property.[8] *(See details of this case, p. 418.)* The Court also rejected the arguments that application of the 1866 law to admissions policies violated the constitutional right of parents to have their children associate only with certain persons and to send their children to schools that promote racial segregation. "[P]arents have a First Amendment right to send their children to educational institutions that promote the belief that racial segregation is desirable, and … the children have an equal right to attend such institutions," Stewart wrote. "But it does not follow that the *practice* of excluding racial minorities from such institutions is also protected" by the right of association.[9]

In dissent, Justice Byron R. White, joined by Justice William H. Rehnquist, took issue with the extension of the contract provision of the 1866 law to private action. No person, black or white, has a right to enter into a contract with an unwilling party, White said.[10] In 1989 the Court unanimously reaffirmed its decision in *Runyon*. This time Rehnquist, now chief justice, and White agreed with the majority. Justice Anthony M. Kennedy's opinion stressed adherence to precedent, *stare decisis*, asserting that

the Civil Rights Act of 1866 did indeed continue to prohibit racial discrimination in the making and enforcing of private contracts.[11]

TAX-EXEMPT STATUS

Citing the national interest in ending race discrimination, the Court had ruled in the 1980s that the federal government could deny tax-exempt status to private schools, including universities, that discriminate against blacks. By an 8-1 vote in *Bob Jones University v. United States* (1983), the justices upheld the decision of the Internal Revenue Service in 1970 to stop granting tax-exempt status to discriminatory private schools. The school in this case argued that its policy of discriminating against black students was based upon sincerely held religious beliefs. Writing for the Court, Chief Justice Burger countered that the national interest in eradicating racial discrimination in education "substantially outweighs whatever burden denial of tax benefits places" on the exercise of the freedom of religion.[12] Only Justice Rehnquist dissented.

---

1. *Pierce v. Society of Sisters*, 268 U.S. 510 at 534–535 (1925).

2. In other cases the Court has held that the First Amendment's clause prohibiting government establishment of religion bars states from lending textbooks to parochial schools but not from lending them to children who attend those schools. *(See "State Aid to Church-Related Schools," pp. 151–162.)*

3. *Norwood v. Harrison*, 413 U.S. 455 at 463–465 (1973); for state tuition grants cases, see *Brown v. South Carolina Board of Education*, 296 F. Supp. 199 (S.C. 1968), affirmed per curiam 393 U.S. 222 (1968); *Poindexter v. Louisiana Finance Commission*, 275 F. Supp. 833 (E D La. 1967), affirmed per curiam 389 U.S. 571 (1968).

4. *Norwood v. Harrison*, 413 U.S. 455 at 462 (1973).

5. *Gilmore v. City of Montgomery*, 417 U.S. 556 at 566 (1974).

6. Id. at 569.

7. *Runyon v. McCrary, Fairfax-Brewster School v. Gonzales*, 427 U.S. 160 (1976).

8. *Jones v. Alfred H. Mayer Co.*, 392 U.S. 409 (1968).

9. *Runyon v. McCrary*, 427 U.S. 160 at 176 (1976).

10. Id. at 195.

11. *Patterson v. McLean Credit Union*, 491 U.S. 1644 (1989).

12. *Bob Jones University v. United States*, 461 US 574 (1983).

---

specific racial balance in each school. In *Pasadena City Board of Education v. Spangler* (1976), the Court elaborated on that point. The Pasadena, California, school board adopted a desegregation plan stipulating that as

of the 1970–1971 school year, no school in the district could have a majority of students of a minority race. In 1974 the school board asked the district court to lift or modify the "no-majority" requirement. Observing that

BILINGUAL EDUCATION

A unanimous Supreme Court in *Lau v. Nichols* (1974) ruled that a public school system must make some effort to ensure that students who do not speak English are equipped with language skills necessary to profit from their required attendance at school.[1] Non-English-speaking Chinese students in San Francisco charged that the city school board's failure to provide them with bilingual lessons or remedial English resulted in unequal educational opportunities and therefore violated the Fourteenth Amendment.

The Court found it unnecessary to address the equal protection issue, ruling that the school board had violated the Civil Rights Act of 1964, which forbids discrimination based on national origin, race, or color in any program receiving federal aid, and a Department of Health, Education, and Welfare regulation requiring such school districts "to rectify ... language deficiency" to ensure that instruction is meaningful to non-English-speaking pupils.

---

1. *Lau v. Nichols*, 414 U.S. 563 (1974).

---

the board had complied with that requirement only in the initial year of the plan's implementation, the district court refused the request. It held that the requirement was applicable every year, even though residential patterns and other factors outside the school board's control resulted in a changing racial composition of the schools. The Supreme Court, 6-2, reversed the district court, holding that its literal interpretation required the board to maintain a specific racial balance, something that the Court in *Swann* said it would disapprove:

> No one disputes that the initial implementation of the plan accomplished [its] objective. That being the case, the District Court was not entitled to require the [school district] to rearrange its attendance zones each year so as to ensure that the racial mix desired by the court was maintained in perpetuity. For having once implemented a racially neutral attendance pattern in order to remedy the perceived constitutional violations on the part of the defendants [the school board], the District Court has fully performed its function of providing the appropriate remedy for previous racially discriminatory attendance patterns.[90]

Joined in dissent by Justice Brennan, Justice Marshall noted that the desegregation plan fulfilled the no-majority requirement only for one year and that

without its continued maintenance immediate resegregation of the school system was likely. Because a lasting unitary school system had apparently not been achieved, Marshall said the majority's application of *Swann* was improper. *Swann*, wrote Marshall,

> recognizes on the one hand that a fully desegregated school system may not be compelled to adjust its attendance zones to conform to changing demographic patterns. But on the other hand, it also appears to recognize that until such a unitary system is established, a district court may act with broad discretion—discretion which includes the adjustment of attendance zones—so that the goal of a wholly unitary system might be sooner achieved.[91]

Judicial Withdrawal: Kansas City

For the next twenty years, the Court continued down the path of *Milliken* and *Pasadena,* easing judges out of the business of desegregating schools. In a 1991 Oklahoma City case, the Court emphasized that desegregation decrees were meant to be temporary.[92] In that decision, the justices, 5-3, said formerly segregated school districts may free themselves of court orders directing school busing if they can prove that elements of past discrimination have been removed to all "practicable" extent.

Federal judges' role in local school desegregation was further diminished as a result of the Court's ruling in *Missouri v. Jenkins* (1995).[93] Five years earlier, when the Kansas City, Missouri, case appeared first before the Court, the justices had endorsed broad judicial authority to move school systems toward desegregation. By 5-4, the Court allowed a judge to order a local government to levy taxes in excess of state statutory limits to correct school segregation.[94] In 1995, however, when the Court again reviewed the situation in Kansas City, the conservative majority prevailed. Writing for the Court, Chief Justice William H. Rehnquist said that the federal judge overseeing the Kansas City schools had exceeded his authority by ordering salary increases and the creation of magnet schools to attract white students from neighboring districts to remedy the "vestiges" of previous legal segregation. Rehnquist was joined by Justices Sandra Day O'Connor, Antonin Scalia, Anthony M. Kennedy, and Clarence Thomas. Justices David H. Souter, John Paul Stevens, Ruth Bader Ginsburg, and Stephen G. Breyer dissented.

The decision required lower courts to reconsider parts of a showcase plan aimed at increasing the attractiveness of a predominantly black school district. The state of Missouri, which had challenged the judge's remedial plan, specifically attacked two orders requiring salary increases for most of the school district's employees and converting all high schools and middle schools and half of the district's elementary schools into magnet schools. Rehnquist said the effort to attract white students from adjoining suburban districts amounted to an impermissible "interdistrict remedy," and he criticized the judge's use of below-normal achievement scores to justify his continued supervision over the school system. "Insistence upon academic goals unrelated to the effects of legal segregation unwarrantably postpones the day when the [Kansas City district] will be able to operate on its own," the chief justice wrote.[95]

Justice Souter, writing for the four dissenters, asserted that the majority had not followed proper procedure in reviewing the judge's remedy. On the merits, he contended that the lower courts had properly concluded that past segregation had contributed to white flight and that the desegregation decree could include steps to draw them back to the Kansas City system.

End to Voluntary Desegregation

In 2007 Chief Justice John G. Roberts Jr., in just his second term, led the Court in calling a halt to school integration policies that assign some students based on their race. He described such policies as "racial balancing" and invoked the 1954 decision in *Brown v. Board of Education* to explain why they were unconstitutional: "Before *Brown*, school children were told where they could and could not go to school based on the color of their skin. The school districts in these cases have not carried the heavy burden of demonstrating that we should allow this again—even for very different reasons," Roberts wrote. "For schools that never segregated on the basis of race, such as Seattle, or that have removed the vestiges of past segregation, such as Jefferson County [Ky.], the way to achieve a system of determining admission to the public schools on a nonracial basis is to stop assigning students on a racial basis. The way to stop discrimination on the basis of race is to stop discriminating on the basis of race."[96]

In one case, parents in Seattle had challenged as unconstitutional a policy that allotted some spots in high schools to students who would add to the racial diversity of the school. The second case, from Jefferson County, Kentucky, which includes Louisville, arose when a white parent sued after her son, Joshua McDonald, could not enroll in the elementary school nearest their home. Louisville once had segregated schools and was forced in the 1970s to bus students to bring about desegregation. After court-ordered busing ended, the school board in 2001 adopted the racial balancing guidelines to maintain integration.

The Roberts Court ruled for the parents in both cases in 5-4 votes. The chief justice was joined by Justices Scalia, Kennedy, Thomas, and Alito. In a concurring opinion, Kennedy said that school officials may "adopt general policies to encourage a diverse student body," so long as they do not assign students based just on their race. For example, school boards may locate new schools between mostly white and mostly black neighborhoods with the goal of achieving integrated classes, he said.

The dissenters—Stevens, Souter, Ginsburg, and Breyer—described the ruling as a sad retreat from the goal of achieving racial integration. Stevens, the eighty-seven-year-old senior justice, added a personal note despairing of how far the Court had moved during his tenure. "It is my firm conviction," he wrote, "that no member of the Court that I joined in 1975 would have agreed with today's decision."

TRAVEL AND PUBLIC ACCOMMODATIONS

During the first few years after the Civil War, blacks in many localities were treated substantially the same as whites. In the 1870s, there was little state-imposed segregation of the races in transportation or public accommodations. In fact, three states—Massachusetts, New York, and Kansas—specifically prohibited separation of the races in public places. Whether to accept the patronage of blacks was left largely to individual choice, and the majority of operators of public transport systems, hotels, restaurants, theaters, and other amusements admitted blacks, if not always to first class accommodations, then at least to second class.[97] Nonetheless, many proprietors, especially in the rural South, refused to serve blacks. Enactment of the 1866 Civil Rights Act—granting blacks the same rights as whites to bring lawsuits—encouraged blacks to challenge such exclusion. Although many of these suits brought by blacks were successful, some courts upheld the right of individual proprietors to deny service to whomever they chose. In an attempt to reverse such rulings, the Republican Congress enacted the Civil Rights Act of 1875, declaring that "all persons within the jurisdiction of the United States shall be entitled to the full and equal enjoyment of the accommodations ... of inns, public conveyances on land or water, theaters, and other places of public amusement; subject only to the conditions and limitations established by law, and applicable alike to citizens of every race or color." Persons violating the act were subject to fine or imprisonment.

Civil Rights Cases

This law became the basis for several dozen suits protesting denial of equal treatment to blacks. Federal courts in some states upheld the constitutionality of the act, while others found it invalid. Five of these cases—known collectively as the *Civil Rights Cases* (1883)—reached the Supreme Court: *United States v. Singleton, United States v. Ryan, United States v. Nichols, United States v. Stanley,* and *Robinson & Wife v. Memphis and Charleston Railroad Company.* They involved theaters in New York and California that would not seat blacks, a hotel in Missouri and a restaurant in Kansas that would not serve blacks, and a train in Tennessee that prohibited a black woman from riding in the "ladies'" car.

By an 8-1 vote, the Court declared that Congress had exceeded its authority to enforce the Thirteenth and Fourteenth Amendments in passing the 1875 act, and so it was invalid. Justice John Marshall Harlan was the lone dissenter. According to the majority, the Fourteenth Amendment applied only to discriminatory *state* actions. "Individual invasion of individual rights is not the subject-matter of the amendment," the Court asserted.[98] Furthermore, said the majority, private discrimination against blacks did not violate the Thirteenth Amendment abolishing slavery:

> [S]uch an act of refusal has nothing to do with slavery or involuntary servitude.... It would be running the slavery argument into the ground to make it apply to every act of discrimination which a person may see fit to make as to the guests he will entertain, or as to the people he will take into his coach or cab or car, or admit to his concert or theater.[99]

Although public opinion generally supported the Court's decision in the *Civil Rights Cases,* four states in 1884 barred discrimination in public places. By 1897 eleven more states, all in the North and West, had enacted similar laws. Those that were challenged were sustained as a proper exercise of state police power.[100]

Segregation and Commerce

The decision in the *Civil Rights Cases* left open the possibility that Congress, through its constitutional authority over interstate commerce, might bar private discrimination against blacks on public carriers. By the close of the Civil War, the Court had interpreted that authority to deny the states power to regulate anything other than local commerce with no significant impact on other states. In 1878 a unanimous Supreme Court had declared unconstitutional a Louisiana law *forbidding* segregation on public carriers. So far as the state law required desegregation on carriers that traveled interstate, it was a burden on interstate commerce, the Court said in *Hall v. DeCuir* (1878). Prohibition of segregation in interstate transportation was a matter on which there should be national uniformity, and thus only Congress could adopt that policy. "If each state was at liberty to regulate the conduct of carriers while within its jurisdiction, the confusion likely to follow could not but be productive of great inconvenience and unnecessary hardship," the Court concluded.[101]

Hoping that the Court would apply this same reasoning to strike down state segregation laws, opponents of segregation challenged a Mississippi law *requiring* segregation on public transportation. Their hopes went unfulfilled. Distinguishing *Louisville, New Orleans and Texas Railway v. Mississippi* (1890) from *DeCuir*, the Court ruled that the Mississippi law applied only to intrastate traffic and was therefore within a state's power to regulate local commerce.[102]

Plessy v. Ferguson

Six years later, the Supreme Court gave its blessing to segregation in the case of *Plessy v. Ferguson* (1896). The case was a deliberate test of the constitutionality of a Louisiana statute requiring separate but equal railroad accommodations for the races. Louisiana was one of six states that by 1896 had enacted such Jim Crow laws segregating blacks from whites on public carriers. The suit was brought by Homer Plessy, a citizen of the United States and a Louisiana resident who was one-eighth black and appeared white. Plessy bought a first-class ticket to travel from New Orleans to Covington, Louisiana, and took a seat in the coach reserved for whites. When he refused to move to the black coach, he was arrested. The state courts upheld the constitutionality of the state law. Plessy then appealed to the Supreme Court, which affirmed the holdings of the state courts.

A Reasonable Rule

Writing for the majority, Justice Henry B. Brown said the state law did not infringe on congressional authority over commerce. "In the present case," said Brown, "no question of interference with interstate commerce can possibly arise, since the East Louisiana Railway appears to have been purely a local line, with both its termini within the State."[103] The state statute also did not violate the Thirteenth Amendment:

> A statute which implies merely a legal distinction between the white and colored races—a distinction which is founded in the color of the two races, and which must always exist so long as white men are distinguished from the other race by color—has no tendency to destroy the legal equality of the two races, or reestablish a state of involuntary servitude.[104]

Plessy's challenge to the law as a violation of the Fourteenth Amendment also failed, the majority said, because that amendment guaranteed only political equality and did not encompass what the Court considered social distinctions:

> The object of the [Fourteenth] Amendment was undoubtedly to enforce the absolute equality of the two races before the law, but in the nature of things it could not have been intended to abolish distinctions based upon color, or to enforce social, as distinguished from political equality, or a commingling of the two races upon terms unsatisfactory to either. Laws permitting, and even requiring, their separation in places where they are liable to be brought into contact do not necessarily imply the inferiority of either race to the other, and have been generally recognized as within the competency of the state legislatures in the exercise of their police powers.[105]

The question then, Brown continued, was whether the law was an unreasonable use of the state's police power. Noting that the Court thought it reasonable for a state to consider the traditions and customs of its people and to want to protect their comfort and peace, Brown wrote,

> [W]e cannot say that a law which authorizes or even requires the separation of the two races in public conveyances is unreasonable, or more obnoxious to the Fourteenth Amendment than the

act of Congress requiring separate schools for colored children in the District of Columbia, the constitutionality of which does not seem to have been questioned, or the corresponding acts of state legislatures.

We consider the underlying fallacy of [Plessy's] argument to consist in the assumption that the enforced separation of the two races stamps the colored race with a badge of inferiority. If this be so, it is not by reason of anything found in the act, but solely because the colored race chooses to put this construction upon it.... Legislation is powerless to eradicate racial instincts or to abolish distinctions based upon physical differences, and the attempt to do so can only result in accentuating the difficulties of the present situation. If the civil and political rights of both races be equal one cannot be inferior to the other civilly, or politically. If one race be inferior to the other socially, the Constitution of the United States cannot put them upon the same plane.[106]

A Colorblind Constitution

In lone dissent, as in the *Civil Rights Cases,* Justice John Marshall Harlan predicted that the decision would prove "quite as pernicious" as had the Court's ruling in *Scott v. Sandford* (1857). The Kentucky-born Harlan, himself a former slaveholder, acknowledged that whites were the dominant race in prestige, education, wealth, and power, "[b]ut in view of the Constitution," he declared, "in the eye of the law, there is in this country no superior, dominant, ruling class of citizens. There is no caste here. Our Constitution is colorblind and neither knows nor tolerates classes among citizens."[107] *(See box, Slave or Free: The Dred Scott Case, p. 377.)* Charging that the majority had glossed over the fact that the Louisiana law segregated blacks because whites considered them inferior, Harlan wrote,

The arbitrary separation of citizens, on the basis of race, while they are on a public highway, is a badge of servitude wholly inconsistent with the civil freedom and the equality before the law established by the Constitution. It cannot be justified upon any legal grounds.... We boast of the freedom enjoyed by our people above all other peoples. But it is

difficult to reconcile that boast with a state of the law, which, practically, puts the brand of servitude and degradation upon a large class of our fellow-citizens, our equals before the law. The thin disguise of "equal" accommodations for passengers in railroad coaches will not mislead any one, nor atone for the wrong this day done.[108]

Equal Treatment

For sixty years the Court's stance in regard to segregation on public carriers was similar to the stance it maintained on school segregation. The Court upheld the right of the states to separate the races while requiring that their treatment be equal. This insistence on equal treatment in transportation was first apparent in *McCabe v. Atchison, Topeka and Santa Fe Railroad* (1914). Oklahoma law required companies operating trains within the state to provide separate coaches for whites and blacks. McCabe sued the railroad because it provided sleeping cars for whites but none for blacks. The railroad argued that there was not sufficient demand by blacks for sleeping-car accommodations. The Court rejected this defense. In an opinion written by Justice Charles Evans Hughes, the Court said the railway's contention

makes the constitutional right depend upon the number of persons who may be discriminated against, whereas the essence of the constitutional right is that it is a personal one. Whether or not particular facilities shall be provided may doubtless be conditioned upon there being a reasonable demand therefore, but, if facilities are provided, substantial equality of treatment of persons traveling under like conditions cannot be refused. It is the individual who is entitled to the equal protection of the laws, and if he is denied by a common carrier, acting in the matter under the authority of a state law, a facility or convenience in the course of his journey which under substantially the same circumstances is furnished to another traveler, he may properly complain that his constitutional privilege has been invaded.[109]

In 1941 the Court extended this principle to the case of an interstate traveler. A black member of the U.S. House of Representatives, Arthur W. Mitchell, D-Ill., held a first-class ticket for a trip from Chicago to Hot Springs,

DISCRIMINATORY WILLS

In two sets of cases, the Supreme Court has held that the Fourteenth Amendment forbids a state agency, but not a private one, from acting as trustee for wills that discriminate against blacks. *Pennsylvania v. Board of Directors of City Trusts of Philadelphia* (1957) concerned a will that left money in trust for the establishment and maintenance of a school for poor white orphan boys. The trust was administered by a state agency. The case arose when the agency refused admittance to two black orphan boys. In a per curiam opinion, the Court said the agency's refusal to admit the two boys amounted to state discrimination in violation of the Fourteenth Amendment. Administration of the school was then turned over to private trustees who continued to follow the discriminatory terms of the will. This policy was again challenged, but the Court in 1958 refused to review it.[1]

Close to a decade later, in 1966, the Court decided a case concerning a park in Macon, Georgia, that, under the terms of the will bequeathing the land, could serve only whites. In this case the Court held that even though the city, refusing to operate the park on a segregated basis, had turned over its management to private trustees, the park retained a public character that made it subject to the prohibitions of the Fourteenth Amendment.[2] As a result, the park reverted to the original heirs and was closed. A group of blacks sued, claiming the closing violated their right to equal protection of the laws, but the Court in 1970 found no constitutional violation. Closing the park to the public did not treat one race differently from the other but deprived both blacks and whites equally of the facility, the majority said.[3]

---

1. *Pennsylvania v. Board of Directors of City Trusts of Philadelphia*, 353 U.S. 230 (1957); 357 U.S. 570 (1958).

2. *Evans v. Newton*, 382 U.S. 296 (1966).

3. *Evans v. Abney*, 396 U.S. 435 (1970); see also *Palmer v. Thompson*, 403 U.S. 217 (1971).

Arkansas. When the train reached the Arkansas border, Mitchell was required by state law to move to a car reserved for blacks where there were no first-class accommodations. Mitchell challenged the state law as a violation of the Interstate Commerce Act of 1887, which prohibited public carriers from subjecting "any person ... to any undue or unreasonable prejudice or disadvantage in any respect whatsoever." The Interstate Commerce Commission (ICC) dismissed the complaint, but Mitchell appealed to the Supreme Court, which held that he was entitled to first-class accommodations just as any white would be. The Court, however, did not question Arkansas's right to require the segregated coaches.[110]

Five years later, the Court took a significant step toward overturning segregation in public interstate transportation. The case of *Morgan v. Virginia* (1946) concerned a black woman traveling on a bus from Virginia to Maryland. Upon entering Virginia, she defied that state's law when she refused to move to the back of the bus to make her seat available to whites. Noting that ten states specifically required segregation in interstate bus travel and that eighteen specifically prohibited it, the Court said

that a "burden [on interstate commerce] might arise from a state statute which requires interstate passengers to order their movements on the vehicle in accordance with local rather than national requirements."[111] The Court thus held that "seating arrangements for the different races in interstate motor travel require a single, uniform rule to promote and protect national travel."[112] The state law violated the Commerce Clause.

In 1948 the Court upheld a Michigan law prohibiting segregation in public transportation. The law did not interfere with Congress's power to regulate interstate and foreign commerce, it said. In 1950 the Court struck down segregated but unequal dining facilities on trains. In 1953 the justices applied two seldom-used laws to prohibit restaurants in the District of Columbia from discriminating against blacks.[113]

Plessy Overturned

Beginning with *Muir v. Louisville Park Theatrical Association* (1954), the Court summarily declared that state-imposed segregation in public accommodations and transportation was unconstitutional. Relying on the precedent of *Brown v. Board of Education of Topeka* (1954), the Court ordered an end to state-imposed segregation on public beaches, municipal golf courses, vehicles of interstate transportation, in public parks, municipal auditoriums and athletic contests, seating in traffic court, and in prisons and jails.[114] Most of these decisions were issued without opinion. The Court did, however, issue a full opinion in one case to emphasize its expectation that the states would proceed expeditiously to eliminate state-imposed segregation in public areas. The question in *Watson v. City of Memphis* (1963) was whether the Tennessee city should be granted more time to desegregate its public parks and other municipal facilities. Warning that it would not countenance indefinite delays, the Court said,

> The rights here asserted are, like all such rights, present rights; they are not merely hopes to some future enjoyment of some formalistic constitutional promise. The basic guarantees of our Constitution are warrants for the here and now and, unless there is an overwhelmingly compelling reason, they are to be promptly fulfilled.[115]

In contrast to its continued insistence on school desegregation, a sharply divided Court held in the 1970s that a city under a court order to desegregate its public facilities could close its public swimming pools rather than operate them on an integrated basis. For the five-man majority in *Palmer v. Thompson* (1971), Justice Hugo L. Black maintained that the Fourteenth Amendment did not impose an affirmative obligation on a local government to maintain public swimming pools. According to Black, so long as the city government denied the same facility to both races, it was not denying either equal protection. For the dissenters, Justice Byron R. White said that "a state may not have an official stance against desegregating public facilities in response to a desegregation order. The fact is that closing the pools is an expression of public policy that Negroes are unfit to associate with whites."[116]

Semipublic Business

In a pair of cases in the 1960s, the Court prohibited racial discrimination by privately owned businesses operated on public property. *Boynton v. Virginia* (1960) concerned a privately owned restaurant in an interstate bus terminal that refused to serve a black interstate traveler. The question presented to the Court was whether the refusal violated the Interstate Commerce Act. The Court decided that it did:

> [I]f the bus carrier has volunteered to make terminal and restaurant facilities and service available to its interstate passengers as a regular part of their transportation, and the terminal and restaurant have acquiesced and cooperated in this undertaking, the terminal and restaurant must perform these services without discriminations prohibited by the Act. In performance of these services under such conditions, the terminal and the restaurant stand in the place of the bus company.[117]

The second case involved an intrastate situation and a constitutional question rather than a question of statutory law. *Burton v. Wilmington Parking Authority* (1961) concerned the Eagle restaurant, which leased space in a city-owned parking building. The parking authority rented out the space in order to procure additional revenue to redeem its bonds. When the restaurant refused to serve a black, the question was whether the restaurant was so closely associated with the municipal parking authority as to make its discriminatory action state action in violation of the Equal Protection Clause.

"Only by sifting facts and weighing circumstances can the nonobvious involvement of the State in private conduct be attributed its true significance," the Court said in answering the question.[118] It then pointed out that the land on which the parking garage and restaurant sat was publicly owned and that the restaurant was there for the purpose of maintaining the public garage as a self-sustaining entity. Thus, the Court concluded,

> The State has so far insinuated itself into a position of interdependence with [the] Eagle [restaurant] that it must be recognized as a joint participant in the challenged activity, which, on that account, cannot be considered to have been so "purely private" as to fall without the scope of the Fourteenth Amendment.[119]

As the civil rights movement gained strength, demonstrators demanding service at whites-only lunch counters were not only arrested and convicted but also were ill-treated by private citizens. In this 1963 incident in Jackson, Mississippi, demonstrators were sprayed with condiments and were physically abused by spectators.

Sit-In Cases

Boynton and *Burton* served as precedent for a series of five cases commonly known as the *Sit-In Cases* (1962). Four of these concerned young blacks who had been convicted of criminal trespass after they had protested racially discriminatory policies of privately owned stores and restaurants by seeking service at "whites only" lunch counters and tables. The fifth case involved two ministers convicted of aiding and abetting persons to commit criminal trespass by encouraging them to sit in. The Supreme Court earlier had decided such cases involving civil rights activists on First Amendment grounds. The *Sit-In Cases* were the only major cases decided on equal protection grounds. In each, a majority of the Court found sufficient state involvement with the private act of discrimination to warrant coverage by the Fourteenth Amendment's Equal Protection Clause.

In the first case, *Peterson v. City of Greenville* (1963), an eight-justice majority overturned the convictions of ten youthful protesters who attempted to

desegregate a department store lunch counter in Greenville, South Carolina. A city ordinance required racial segregation of public eating places. By having the protesters arrested, the store's managers did what the ordinance required, and therefore, held the Court, the subsequent convictions amounted to state enforcement of the city ordinance denying equal protection. It was no defense that the store managers would have brought criminal trespass charges in the absence of the ordinance, the majority said:

> When a state agency passes a law compelling persons to discriminate against other persons because of race, and the State's criminal processes are employed in a way which enforces the discrimination mandated by that law, such a palpable violation of the Fourteenth Amendment cannot be saved by attempting to separate the mental urges of the discriminators.[120]

Peterson became the rule for overturning similar criminal trespass convictions in *Gober v. City of*

Birmingham (1963) and *Avent v. North Carolina* (1963).[121] In both cases, city ordinances required separation of the races in eating places. Having overturned trespass convictions in *Gober,* the Court also overturned aiding and abetting convictions of the two ministers who had urged participation in that sit-in. "It is generally recognized that there can be no conviction for aiding and abetting someone to do an innocent act," the majority wrote in *Shuttlesworth v. Birmingham* (1963).[122] In *Lombard v. Louisiana* (1963), there was no law requiring segregated eating places in New Orleans. Nonetheless, the Court found that public statements of the city mayor and police chief effectively "required" that public eating facilities be segregated. If it is constitutionally impermissible for a state to enact a law segregating the races, "the State cannot achieve the same result by an official command which has at least as much coercive effect as an ordinance," the justices said.[123]

Individual Discrimination

Despite the Court's rulings in the *Sit-In Cases,* most private owners of hotels, stores, restaurants, theaters, and other public accommodations remained "without the scope of the Fourteenth Amendment" until passage in 1964 of the most comprehensive civil rights act since 1875. The act barred discrimination in employment, provided new guarantees to ensure blacks the right to vote, and authorized the federal government to seek court orders for the desegregation of public schools. Title II of the act was aimed at discrimination in public accommodations. It prohibited discrimination on grounds of race, color, religion, or national origin in public accommodations if the discrimination was supported by state law or other official action, if lodgings or other service were provided to interstate travelers, or if a substantial portion of the goods sold or entertainment provided moved in interstate commerce.

There was no question that the Fourteenth Amendment barred state officials from requiring or supporting segregation in public places, but the power of Congress to use the Commerce Clause as authority for barring private discrimination was uncertain. A case challenging that exercise of the commerce power reached the Supreme Court just six months after the Civil Rights Act of 1964 was enacted.

Heart of Atlanta Motel

The case of *Heart of Atlanta Motel v. United States* (1964) involved a motel in downtown Atlanta that refused to serve blacks in defiance of the new federal law. The motel owner charged that Congress had exceeded its authority under the Commerce Clause when it enacted Title II, and that the property owner's Fifth Amendment rights were denied when Congress deprived him of the freedom to choose his customers. A unanimous Supreme Court upheld Title II.

Writing for the Court, Justice Tom C. Clark first outlined the interstate aspect of the motel's business, noting that it was accessible to interstate travelers, that it sought out-of-state patrons by advertising in nationally circulated publications, and that 75 percent of its guests were interstate travelers. Clark then cited the testimony at the congressional hearings on the act that showed that blacks were frequently discouraged from traveling because of the difficulty encountered in obtaining accommodations. Congress had reasonably concluded that discrimination was an impediment to interstate travel, the Court said. Clark next turned to the commerce power of Congress, finding that it had the authority not only to regulate interstate commerce but also to regulate intrastate matters that affected interstate commerce:

> [T]he power of Congress to promote interstate commerce includes the power to regulate the local incidents thereof, including local activities in both the States of origin and destination, which might have a substantial and harmful effect upon that commerce. One need only examine the evidence ... to see that Congress may—as it has—prohibit racial discrimination by motels serving travelers, however "local" their operations may appear.[124]

The Court also said that it made no difference that Congress had used its power under the Commerce Clause to achieve a moral goal. That fact, wrote Clark,

PRIVATE CLUBS

The freedom to associate with persons of one's own choosing is protected by the First Amendment, at least up to a point. Consequently, private clubs with racially discriminatory admissions policies are generally considered beyond the reach of the Fourteenth Amendment. In the 1970s, the Supreme Court held, 6-3, that the issuance of a liquor license by the state to a private club that discriminates against blacks is not discriminatory state action in violation of the Fourteenth Amendment. In *Moose Lodge 107 v. Irvis* (1972), the majority said the Court had never forbidden a state to provide services to a private individual or group that practiced discrimination.[1] Such a ruling would mean that the state could not provide vital essentials, such as fire and police protection, electricity, and water, to private individuals who discriminate.

The degree of state involvement necessary to constitute state action varies from case to case, the majority continued. In this situation the liquor regulations, with one exception, in no way promoted discrimination and therefore did not involve the state in the private discriminatory policy,

it concluded. The exception was the liquor board's requirement that all club bylaws be obeyed. The majority found that in cases where the bylaws restricted membership by race, the state regulation amounted to enforcement of a discriminatory practice and the requirement should not be applied to the private club.

In a second case, the Court rejected the claim of a community recreation association that it was a private club exempt from the Civil Rights Act of 1964. The association limited membership in its swimming pool to white residents of the community and their white guests. In *Tillman v. Wheaton-Haven Recreation Association* (1973), the Court ruled that the association was not entitled to the exemption because it had no selection criteria for membership other than race and residence in the community.[2]

---

1. *Moose Lodge 107 v. Irvis*, 407 U.S. 163 (1972).

2. *Tillman v. Wheaton-Haven Recreation Association*, 410 U.S. 431 (1973).

does not detract from the overwhelming evidence of the disruptive effect that racial discrimination has had on commercial intercourse. It was this burden which empowered Congress to enact appropriate legislation, and, given this basis for the exercise of its power, Congress was not restricted by the fact that the particular obstruction to interstate commerce with which it was dealing was also deemed a moral and social wrong.[125]

The Court also rejected the claim that Title II violated the motel owner's Fifth Amendment rights. Congress acted reasonably to prohibit racial discrimination, the Court said, noting that thirty-two states had civil rights laws that were similar to the 1964 federal law. Furthermore, "in a long line of cases this Court has rejected the claim that the prohibition of racial discrimination in public accommodations interferes with personal liberty."[126]

The Court's decision upholding the constitutionality of the use of the commerce power to bar private discrimination seemed to conflict with its decision in the *Civil Rights Cases* (1883) that Congress lacked the power to enforce the Thirteenth and Fourteenth Amendments by barring private acts of discrimination in public accommodations. The Court said in its 1964 ruling that it found the 1883 decision "without precedential value" since Congress in 1875 had not limited prohibition of discrimination to those businesses that impinged on interstate commerce. Wrote Clark of that case,

> Since the commerce power was not relied on by the Government and was without support in the [trial] record it is understandable that the Court narrowed its inquiry and excluded the Commerce Clause as a possible source of power. In any event, it is clear that such a limitation renders the opinion devoid of authority for the proposition that the Commerce Clause gives no power to Congress to regulate discriminatory practices now found substantially to affect interstate commerce.[127]

Ollie's Barbecue

In the companion case *Katzenbach v. McClung* (1964), the Court upheld the section of Title II barring discrimination by private proprietors who served to their clientele goods that moved in interstate commerce. Ollie's Barbecue, a Birmingham, Alabama, restaurant that discriminated against blacks, did not seek to serve customers from out of state, but 46 percent of the food it served was supplied through interstate commerce. The restaurant claimed that the amount of food it purchased in interstate commerce was insignificant compared to the total amount of food in interstate commerce. The Court rejected this argument. The restaurant's purchase might be insignificant, the Court said, but added to all other purchases of food through interstate commerce by persons who discriminate against blacks, the impact on interstate commerce was far from insignificant.[128]

Commerce and Recreation

In *Daniel v. Paul* (1969), the Court, 7-1, upheld Title II as applied to a small recreational area near Little Rock, Arkansas. The area admitted only whites, but claimed that it did not fall under Title II because it did not seek interstate travelers and sold little food purchased through interstate commerce. The Court disagreed, pointing out that the food sold was composed of ingredients produced in other states. Moreover, the facility advertised in Little Rock and at a military base, and it was unreasonable to think that the ads would not attract some interstate travelers.[129] Justice Hugo L. Black, the sole dissenter, objected to connecting the recreational area to interstate commerce, saying he would have supported a decision based on the Fourteenth Amendment.

THE RIGHT TO FAIR HOUSING

Even as the Supreme Court in the *Civil Rights Cases* (1883) held that Congress lacked authority to protect blacks against persons who refused them public accommodations, it acknowledged in those cases the power of Congress to erase "the necessary incidents of slavery" and "to secure to all citizens of every race and color, without regard to previous servitude, those fundamental rights which are

the essence of civil freedom." Among these, the Court said, was the right "to inherit, purchase, lease, sell and convey property."[130] With this statement the Court by indirection upheld the Civil Rights Act of 1866, enacted by Congress to enforce the Thirteenth Amendment, which abolished slavery. The act gave blacks the same rights as whites to buy, lease, hold, and sell property. *(See box, Civil Rights Act of 1866, p. 417.)*

State Discrimination

As states and cities adopted more laws segregating blacks and whites, the fundamental rights of blacks concerning property fell victim to Jim Crow laws. In the early twentieth century, the Supreme Court struck down one such housing law. *Buchanan v. Warley* (1917) began in Louisville, Kentucky, where a city ordinance forbade members of one race to buy, reside on, or sell property on streets where a majority of the residents were of the other race. Charles Buchanan, a white property owner, entered into a contract for the sale of his property to a black man named William Warley. When Warley found the Louisville law prevented him from living on the property, he exercised a contract proviso allowing him to break his agreement to purchase. Buchanan then sued for performance of the contract and charged that the Louisville ordinance violated the Fourteenth Amendment.

Defenders of the ordinance claimed that it was a valid exercise of the city's police power to prevent racial conflict, maintain racial purity, and prevent deterioration in property values. The Supreme Court acknowledged a broad police power but also recalled the Court's 1883 opinion that acquisition, use, and disposal of property were fundamental rights available to all citizens without regard to race or color. The Court then unanimously struck down the ordinance. Justice William R. Day wrote for the Court.

> That there exists a serious and difficult problem arising from a feeling of race hostility which the law is powerless to control, and to which it must give a measure of consideration, may be freely admitted. But its solution cannot be promoted by depriving citizens of their constitutional rights and privileges.... The right which the ordinance annulled was the civil right of a white man to dispose of his property if he saw fit to do so to

a person of color, and of a colored person to make such disposition to a white person.... We think this attempt to prevent the alienation of the property in question ... was not a legitimate exercise of the police power of the state, and is in direct violation of the fundamental law enacted in the Fourteenth Amendment of the Constitution preventing state interference with property rights except by due process of law.[131]

Citing *Buchanan,* the Court subsequently upheld several lower court decisions invalidating similar laws.[132]

Restrictive Covenants

Officially imposed housing segregation was quickly replaced in many localities by private restrictive covenants. Under such covenants, the white residents of a particular block or neighborhood agreed to refuse to sell or lease their homes to blacks. A challenge to the constitutional validity of such private covenants came before the Supreme Court in the 1920s. Adhering to earlier rulings that Congress had no authority to protect individuals from private discrimination, the Court dismissed *Corrigan v. Buckley* (1926), effectively upholding as valid private restrictive covenants. The arguments that the covenant violated the Fifth, Thirteenth, and Fourteenth Amendments, the Court said, were

> entirely lacking in substance or color of merit. The Fifth Amendment "is a limitation only upon the powers of the General Government,"... and is not directed against the action of individuals. The Thirteenth Amendment denouncing slavery ... does not in other matters protect the individual rights of persons of the Negro race.... And the prohibitions of the Fourteenth Amendment "have reference to state action exclusively, and not to any action of private individuals."[133]

No State Enforcement

The Court eventually nullified restrictive covenants by forbidding states to enforce them. *Shelley v. Kraemer* (1948) arose when a black couple bought property to which a restrictive covenant applied. A white couple who owned restricted property in the same neighborhood sued to stop the Shelleys from taking possession of the property. The trial court denied that request, holding

that the covenant was not effective because it had not been signed by all the property owners in the affected area. The supreme court of Missouri reversed the decision, ruling the covenant effective and not a violation of the Shelleys' rights under the Fourteenth Amendment. The Shelleys appealed to the Supreme Court, where their case was combined with a similar one, *McGhee v. Sipes* (1948).[134]

Writing for a unanimous Court (although three members did not participate), Chief Justice Fred M. Vinson repeated the Court's earlier opinion that the Fourteenth Amendment does not reach "private conduct, however discriminatory or wrongful." Therefore, Vinson wrote, private restrictive covenants "effectuated by voluntary adherence to their terms" are not in violation of the amendment.[135] Official actions by state courts and judicial officers, however, have never been considered to be outside the scope of the Fourteenth Amendment, the chief justice continued. In the two cases before the Court, Vinson said,

> the States have made available to [private] individuals the full coercive power of government to deny to petitioners, on the grounds of race or color, the enjoyment of property rights in premises which petitioners are willing and financially able to acquire and which the grantors are willing to sell. The difference between judicial enforcement and nonenforcement of the restrictive covenants is the difference to petitioners between being denied rights of property available to other members of the community and being accorded full enjoyment of these rights on an equal footing....
>
> We hold that in granting judicial enforcement of the restrictive agreements in these cases, the States have denied petitioners the equal protection of the laws and that, therefore, the action of the state courts cannot stand.[136]

Two companion cases, *Hurd v. Hodge* and *Urciola v. Hodge* (1948), challenged restrictive covenants in the District of Columbia. Because the Fourteenth Amendment applied only to states, the District covenants could not be challenged on that basis. Instead, the covenants were alleged to violate the Due Process Clause of the Fifth Amendment. The Court, however, found it unnecessary to address the constitutional issue,

In 1948 the Supreme Court held that the state of Missouri had engaged in unconstitutional discrimination when it enforced a restrictive covenant that prevented J.D. and Ethel Lee Shelley and their six children from retaining ownership of their newly purchased St. Louis home.

holding that the district courts were barred from enforcing the covenants by the Civil Rights Act of 1866.[137]

No Penalty

The Court expanded *Shelley v. Kraemer* five years later in *Barrows v. Jackson* (1953), in which it ruled that state courts could not require a person who had violated a restrictive covenant to pay damages to other covenantors who claimed that her action had reduced the value of their property. Court enforcement of such a damage claim constitutes state action that violates the Fourteenth Amendment if it denies any class the equal protection of the laws, the Court said. "If a state court awards damages for breach of a restrictive covenant," the Court reasoned, "a prospective seller of restricted

land will either refuse to sell to non-Caucasians or else will require non-Caucasians to pay a higher price to meet the damage which the seller may incur."[138] In either event, the Court concluded, non-Caucasians would be denied equal protection.

Housing Referenda

In *Reitman v. Mulkey* (1967), the Court applied *Shelley v. Kraemer* to nullify a 1964 California constitutional amendment barring the state from interfering with the right of any person to sell or refuse to sell his property to anyone for any reason. The amendment effectively had nullified several state fair housing laws. When the Mulkeys sued Neil Reitman on the grounds that he had declined to rent them an apartment solely because they were black, Reitman moved for dismissal of the

CIVIL RIGHTS ACT OF 1866

Congress enacted the Civil Rights Act of 1866 to enforce the newly ratified Thirteenth Amendment prohibiting slavery. Following is the text of the portion of the act that the Supreme Court ruled in 1968 bars individuals from discriminating against racial minorities in the sale or rental of housing:

Section 1. Be it enacted by the Senate and House of Representatives of the United States of America in Congress assembled, That all persons in the United States and not subject to any foreign power,... are hereby declared to be citizens of the United States; and such citizens, of every race and color, without regard to any previous condition of servitude ... shall have the same right, in every State and Territory in the United States, to make and enforce contracts, to sue, be parties, and give evidence, to inherit, purchase, lease, sell, hold, and convey real and personal property, and to full and equal benefit of all laws and proceedings for the security of person and property, as is enjoyed by white citizens, and shall be subject to like punishment, pains, and penalties, and to none other, any law, statute, ordinance, regulation, or custom, to the contrary notwithstanding.

Section 2. That any person who, under color of any law, statute, ordinance, regulation, or custom, shall subject, or cause to be subjected, any inhabitant of any State or Territory to the deprivation of any right secured or protected by this act, or to different punishment, pains, or penalties on account of such person having at any time been held in a condition of slavery or involuntary servitude,... or by reason of his color or race, than is prescribed for the punishment of white persons, shall be deemed guilty of a misdemeanor, and, on conviction, shall be punished by fine not exceeding one thousand dollars, or imprisonment not exceeding one year, or both, in the discretion of the court.

complaint, citing the newly enacted constitutional amendment. The California Supreme Court, however, held that by the amendment the state had acted "to make private discriminations legally possible" and thus had violated the Equal Protection Clause. By a 5-4 vote, the Supreme Court affirmed that ruling. For the majority, Justice Byron R. White wrote that adoption of the amendment meant that

> [t]he right to discriminate, including the right to discriminate on racial grounds, was now embodied in the State's basic charter, immune from legislative, executive or judicial regulation at any level of the state government. Those practicing racial discriminations need no longer rely solely on their personal choice. They could now invoke express constitutional authority, free from censure or interference of any kind from official sources.[139]

Justice Harlan, writing for the dissenters, said the amendment was neutral on its face and did not violate the Equal Protection Clause. By maintaining that the amendment actually encourages private discrimination, Harlan said, the majority "is forging a slippery and unfortunate criterion by which to measure the constitutionality of a statute simply permissive in purpose and effect, and inoffensive on its face."[140]

Two years later, the Court struck down a newly added provision of the Akron, Ohio, city charter that required a majority of voters to approve any ordinance dealing with racial, religious, or ancestral discrimination in housing. Noting that the charter did not require similar referenda for other housing matters, such as rent control, public housing, and building codes, the majority in *Hunter v. Erickson* (1969) held that the charter singled out a special class of people for special treatment in violation of the Equal Protection Clause. "[T]he State may no more disadvantage any particular group by making it more difficult to enact legislation in its behalf than it may dilute any person's vote or give any group a smaller representation than another of comparable size," the majority wrote.[141] Justice Black dissented, protesting "against use of the Equal Protection Clause to bar States from repealing laws that the Court wants the States to retain."[142]

In *James v. Valtierra* (1971), however, the Court upheld a California constitutional amendment providing that no local government agency could construct low-income housing projects without first receiving the approval of a majority of those voting in a local referendum. Distinguishing this case from *Hunter,* the majority said the city charter at issue in *Hunter* created a classification based solely upon race, while the constitutional amendment involved in *James* "requires referendum approval for any low-rent public housing project, not only for projects ... occupied by a racial minority."[143] In dissent, Justice Thurgood Marshall contended that the California amendment created a classification based on poverty that violated the Equal Protection Clause just as much as classifications based on race. "It is far too late in the day to contend that the Fourteenth Amendment prohibits only racial discrimination," Marshall wrote, "and, to me, singling out the poor to bear a burden not placed on any other class of citizens tramples the values that the Fourteenth Amendment was designed to protect."[144] *(See "Poverty and Equal Protection," pp. 446–452.)*

Individual Discrimination

Despite the Court's rulings on state enforcement of restrictive covenants and housing referenda, blacks and other minorities still had little protection from housing discrimination by individual home and apartment owners until the late 1960s.

Old Law, New Life

In 1968, just weeks after Congress enacted the first federal fair housing law, the Supreme Court, 7-2, held that the 1866 Civil Rights Act barred individual as well as state-backed discrimination in the sale and rental of housing. The case was brought by Joseph Lee Jones, who contended that the Alfred H. Mayer Company violated the 1866 act by refusing to sell him a home in the Paddock Woods section of St. Louis County, Missouri, because he was black. A federal district court dismissed the case; the court of appeals affirmed the dismissal on the grounds that the 1866 act (in modern form Section 1982 of Title 42 of the U.S. Code) applied only to state discrimination and not to the segregative actions of private individuals.

The Supreme Court reversed the court of appeals. Writing in *Jones v. Alfred H. Mayer Co.* (1968), Justice Potter Stewart said that the legislative history of the 1866 act persuaded the Court that Congress intended to ban private as well as state-backed discrimination:

> In light of the concerns that led Congress to adopt it and the contents of the debates that preceded its passage, it is clear that the Act was designed to do just what its terms suggest: to prohibit all racial discrimination, whether or not under color of law, with respect to the rights enumerated therein— including the right to purchase or lease property.[145]

The question then became whether Congress had the power to enact the 1866 act. For the answer, Stewart looked to the Thirteenth Amendment rather than to the Equal Protection Clause of the Fourteenth Amendment. The Thirteenth Amendment was adopted to remove the "badges of slavery" from the nation's blacks, Stewart observed, and it gave Congress the power to enforce that removal:

> If Congress has power under the Thirteenth Amendment to eradicate conditions that prevent Negroes from buying and renting property because of their race or color, then no federal statute calculated to achieve that objective can be thought to exceed the constitutional power of Congress simply because it reaches beyond state action to regulate the conduct of private individuals.... Surely Congress has the power under the Thirteenth Amendment rationally to determine what are the badges and the incidents of slavery, and the authority to translate that determination into effective legislation. Nor can we say that the determination Congress has made is an irrational one.... [W]hen racial discrimination herds men into ghettoes and makes their ability to buy property turn on the color of their skin, then it too is a relic of slavery....
>
> At the very least, the freedom that Congress is empowered to secure under the Thirteenth Amendment includes the freedom to buy whatever a white man can buy, the right to live wherever a white man can live. If Congress cannot say that being a free man means at least this much, then the Thirteenth

THE RIGHT TO CHALLENGE

The Supreme Court ordinarily does not allow a person to come before it to defend someone else's rights, but it has sometimes bent this rule in housing discrimination cases. *Barrows v. Jackson* (1953) concerned a woman who violated a restrictive covenant by selling her property to blacks. Other covenantors in the neighborhood sued her for damages, claiming that her action reduced their property values.

The restrictive covenant did not affect the constitutional rights of the white seller who had breached its terms, but in defense of her action, she argued that the covenant infringed on the rights of racial minorities by forbidding them to buy homes in the neighborhood. The Court allowed her to make this defense in behalf of minority group members. The reasons for ordinarily prohibiting such a third-party defense were "outweighed [in this case] by the need to protect the fundamental rights which would be denied by permitting the damages action to be maintained," the Court said.[1]

In 1972 the Court again took a broad view of the right to bring housing discrimination cases. Two white tenants in an apartment building claimed that their landlord's discriminatory policy against nonwhites harmed them by denying them social, business, and professional advantages gained from association with minorities. The tenants filed a complaint with the U.S. Department of Housing and Urban Development (HUD) under Section 810 of the Civil Rights Act of 1968. When the complaint came to trial, a federal judge held that the tenants were not within the class of persons entitled to sue under the 1968 act. The Supreme Court reversed the lower court decision. "We can give vitality to [Section] 810 ...," wrote Justice William O. Douglas, "only by a generous construction which gives standing to sue to all in the same housing unit who are injured by racial discrimination in the management of those facilities within the coverage of the statute."[2]

The Court has not, however, been consistently generous in construing standing to challenge alleged housing discrimination. In *Warth v. Seldin* (1975), a five-justice majority deflected an effort to attack a town's zoning ordinance that effectively excluded low-income and moderate-income persons from living in the town. The majority held that none of the groups or individuals seeking to bring the suit had the legal standing because none could show that a decision in their favor would have a direct ameliorative effect on the injury they claimed to suffer as a result of the zoning ordinance.[3]

---

1. *Barrows v. Jackson*, 346 U.S. 249 at 257 (1953).

2. *Trafficante v. Metropolitan Life Insurance Company*, 409 U.S. 205 at 212 (1972); see also *Gladstone Realtors v. Village of Bellwood*, 441 U.S. 91 (1979).

3. *Warth v. Seldin*, 422 U.S. 490 (1975).

Amendment made a promise the Nation cannot keep.[146]

Justice Harlan, in a dissent joined by Justice White, said that the 1866 act was meant only to protect people from state-imposed discrimination.

Community Clubs, Pools

In 1969 the Court held that the 1866 act also prohibited a community recreational club from refusing membership to a black man who received membership as part of his lease of a home in the neighborhood.[147] The justices also ruled that a community recreation area violated the 1866 Civil Rights Act when it limited membership in its swimming pools to white residents of the community and their white guests. In *Tillman v. Wheaton-Haven Recreation Association* (1973), a unanimous Court wrote,

When an organization links membership benefits to residence in a narrow geographical area, that decision infuses those benefits into the bundle of rights for which an individual pays when buying or leasing within the area. The mandate of [the 1866 Civil Rights Act] then operates to guarantee a non-white resident, who purchases, leases or holds this property, the same rights as are enjoyed by a white resident.[148]

Remedies for Discrimination

Although the Court has struck down several varieties of housing discrimination, it has had little occasion to consider remedies for that discrimination. In the one case the Court has heard on the remedy issue, however, it unanimously upheld the power of a federal judge to order a metropolitan area-wide remedy for segregated public housing in Chicago. The question in *Hills v. Gautreaux* (1976) was whether the remedy for racial discrimination in public housing caused by state and federal officials must be confined to the city in which the discrimination occurred or whether it could include the surrounding metropolitan area.[149] In holding that the remedy need not be restricted to the city alone, the Court made an important distinction between the facts in that case and those in *Milliken v. Bradley* (1974), which overturned a metropolitan area-wide plan of school desegregation.[150] *(See details of Milliken v. Bradley, pp. 400–401.)*

In *Hills*, the Chicago Housing Authority (CHA) was found guilty of discrimination in placing most of the city's public housing in black ghettos, and the Department of Housing and Urban Development (HUD) was found guilty of sanctioning and aiding this discriminatory public housing program. A court of appeals ordered a metropolitan area-wide plan to eliminate the segregated public housing system, but HUD asked the Supreme Court to reverse it, citing *Milliken v. Bradley*. Distinguishing between the two cases, Justice Stewart said the Court struck down the school desegregation plan because "there was no finding of unconstitutional action on the part of the suburban school officials and no demonstration that the violations committed in the operation of the Detroit school system had any significant segregative effects in the suburbs."[151]

The situation in the Chicago housing case was different, Stewart said. HUD did not contest the finding that it had violated the Constitution and the Civil Rights Act of 1964, nor did it dispute the appropriateness of its being ordered to help develop public housing:

> The critical distinction between HUD and the suburban school districts in *Milliken* is that HUD has been found to have violated the Constitution.... Nothing in the *Milliken* decision suggests a *per se* rule that federal courts lack authority to order parties found to have violated the Constitution to undertake remedial efforts beyond the municipal boundaries of the city where the violation occurred.[152]

The Court continued:

> [I]t is entirely appropriate and consistent with *Milliken* to order CHA and HUD to attempt to create housing alternatives for the respondents [the black plaintiffs] in the Chicago suburbs. Here the wrong committed by HUD confined the respondents to segregated public housing. The relevant geographic area for purposes of the respondents' housing option is the Chicago housing market, not the Chicago city limits.... To foreclose such relief solely because HUD's constitutional violation took place within the city limits of Chicago would transform *Milliken*'s principled limitation on the exercise of federal judicial authority into an arbitrary ... shield for those found to have engaged in unconstitutional conduct.[153]

A metropolitan remedy need not impermissibly interfere with local governments that had not been involved in the unconstitutional segregation, Stewart continued:

> The remedial decree would neither force suburban governments to submit public housing proposals to HUD nor displace the rights and powers accorded local government entities under federal or state housing statutes or existing land-use laws. The order would have the same effect on the suburban governments as a discretionary decision by HUD to use its statutory powers to provide the respondents with alternatives to the racially segregated Chicago public housing system created by CHA and HUD.[154]

The following year the Court seemed to limit the potential impact of *Gautreaux*. In *Village of Arlington Heights v. Metropolitan Housing Development Corporation* (1977), the Court said that, without a showing of discriminatory motive, the village's refusal to rezone property to permit building of a housing development for low- and moderate-income persons of both races did not violate the Fourteenth Amendment.[155] The Court's decision left open the possibility that the zoning decision might, however, have violated the 1968 Fair Housing Act. *(See box, The Zoning Power and Fair Housing, p. 421.)*

THE ZONING POWER AND FAIR HOUSING

Since 1926, when the Supreme Court first upheld a comprehensive local zoning law, it has seldom interfered with state power over land use, even when those laws were challenged as violating the Equal Protection Clause of the Fourteenth Amendment. Such a challenge was raised in 1974 against a New York village's zoning ordinance that prohibited more than two unrelated persons from sharing a single-family home. The ordinance placed no limit on the number of family members that could share a house. Rejecting an equal protection challenge to the ordinance, the Court wrote that the law was a reasonable means of attaining a permissible objective—the preservation of the family character of the village.[1]

DISCRIMINATORY INTENT

In *Village of Arlington Heights v. Metropolitan Housing Development Corporation* (1977), the Court again turned back an equal protection challenge to a local zoning decision. This case arose when a housing developer requested the predominantly white Chicago suburb of Arlington Heights to rezone certain land so that he could build housing for low- and moderate-income persons of both races there. When zoning officials refused the request, the developer went to court, charging the denial was motivated by a desire to keep black families from moving into the suburb.

By a 5-3 vote, the Supreme Court upheld the village's refusal to rezone, finding no evidence that it was racially motivated. Instead the evidence showed that the zoning decision was the result of the legitimate desire to protect property values.[2] Without discriminatory intent, wrote Justice Lewis F. Powell Jr., the fact that the refusal to rezone had a racially discriminatory effect was "without independent constitutional significance." The Court referred to its job discrimination ruling in *Washington v. Davis* (1976).[3] There, said Powell, the Court made clear "that official action will not be held unconstitutional solely because it results in a racially disproportionate impact.... Proof of racially discriminatory intent or purpose is required to show a violation of the Equal Protection Clause."[4] *(See box, The Question of Intent, p. 424.)*

Powell said that the factors that might be examined to determine whether a decision had been motivated by racial discrimination included its potential impact, the historical background, the sequence of events leading up to the decision, departures from normal procedures, and the legislative or administrative history. For example, Powell proffered, the Arlington Heights decision to refuse to rezone would appear in a different light if the village had not consistently applied its zoning policy, if unusual procedures had been followed in handling this particular request, or if the zoning for the particular parcel had been recently changed from multi-family to single-family use. Justice Byron R. White, author of the Court's opinion in *Washington v. Davis*, dissented, arguing that the majority should not have applied that ruling to this case.

DISCRIMINATORY EFFECT

The Court sent the case back to the court of appeals to consider whether the zoning decision violated the Fair Housing Act of 1968. In July 1977, that court held that the village's refusal to rezone would violate the act if it had a discriminatory effect even though there was no intent to discriminate. "Conduct that has the necessary and foreseeable consequences of perpetuating segregation can be as deleterious as purposefully discriminating conduct in frustrating" the national goal of integrated housing, the appeals court wrote.[5]

---

1. *Village of Belle Terre v. Boraas*, 416 U.S. 1 (1974).

2. *Village of Arlington Heights v. Metropolitan Housing Development Corporation*, 429 U.S. 252 (1977).

3. *Washington v. Davis*, 426 U.S. 229 (1976).

4. *Village of Arlington Heights v. Metropolitan Housing Development Corporation*, 429 U.S. 252 at 264–265 (1977).

5. *Metropolitan Housing Development Corporation v. Village of Arlington Heights*, 558 F. 2d 1283 at 1289 (1977).

EQUAL EMPLOYMENT OPPORTUNITY

Civil war and emancipation did little to free blacks from job discrimination. Most of the southern states enacted Black Codes restricting the kinds of jobs blacks could hold, thereby limiting competition with white workers and forcing blacks to continue as farm and plantation workers. South Carolina enacted one of the harshest of these codes. It prohibited a black from working as an artisan or mechanic unless he obtained a license that cost ten dollars and from becoming a shopkeeper unless he had a license costing one hundred dollars. Licenses were issued by judges who decided whether the black applicants were skilled and morally fit for the work.

The only jobs that blacks could obtain without a license were as farm workers or servants, and in both cases they were required to sign labor contracts with their employers. In South Carolina, as in many other southern states, failure to fulfill the labor contract was a crime, and a black worker could avoid a jail term only by agreeing to work off the original contract, his or her fine for defaulting, and court costs. The Supreme Court struck down such peonage laws as unconstitutional in the early 1900s.[156]

Despite industrialization, blacks remained relegated to low-paying, unskilled jobs that promised little, if any, advancement. Even if blacks qualified for a better job, they were often passed over in favor of white employees. Until the enactment of state fair employment laws in the mid-1940s, few blacks who had been refused jobs because of their race had any legal recourse. The employer-employee relationship was considered private, outside the protection of the Fourteenth Amendment. Private employers and labor unions could discriminate against blacks with impunity and many of them did.[157]

Early Rulings

Because there were so few legal protections available for minorities, only a handful of employment discrimination cases reached the Court before 1964, the year that Congress prohibited such job bias. In almost all of these early cases, however, the Supreme Court interpreted available law to protect blacks. The first of these cases came in 1938. Blacks organized a picket line outside a District of Columbia grocery to force the proprietor to hire blacks. A federal court ordered the picketing stopped; the blacks charged that the order violated the Norris-LaGuardia Act, which prohibited federal courts from issuing injunctions in legal labor disputes. The issue was whether picketing to force someone to hire blacks was a legal labor objective within the meaning of the law. By 7-2, the Court held that

[r]ace discrimination by an employer may be reasonably deemed more unfair and less excusable than discrimination against workers on the ground of union affiliation. There is no justification … for limiting [the act's] definition of labor disputes and cases arising therefrom by excluding those which arise with respect to discrimination in terms and condition of employment based upon differences of race or color.[158]

The Court modified this position in 1950 when it held that picketing to demand that a store owner increase the number of blacks he employed constituted discrimination against already-hired white clerks.[159]

The first case involving union discrimination came in 1944, when the Court was asked to decide whether a union acting under federal law as the exclusive bargaining agent for a class of workers was obligated by that law to represent all workers without regard to race. *Steele v. Louisville and Nashville Railroad Co.* (1944) involved the Brotherhood of Locomotive Firemen, the exclusive bargaining representative for train firemen of twenty-one railroad companies. The union, which excluded blacks from membership, agreed with the railroad companies to amend the work contract to end all employment of blacks as firemen. As a result, Steele, a black fireman, was reassigned to more difficult, less remunerative work, and his job was given to a white man with less seniority and no more qualifications.

In an opinion that carefully avoided any constitutional issues, the Court ruled that the Railway Labor Act of 1930 compelled the exclusive bargaining agent for an entire class of employees to represent all those employees fairly "without hostile discrimination" against any of them.[160] The Court reached a similar conclusion in *Brotherhood of Railroad Trainmen v. Howard* (1952). A white brakemen's union threatened to strike unless the railroad company fired all its black "train porters," who performed the same functions as brakemen, and replaced them with white union members. Unlike the blacks in the *Steele* case, however, the black train porters had long been represented by their own union. Nonetheless, a majority of the Supreme Court saw no significant difference in the two cases.

The black "train porters are threatened with loss of their jobs because they are not white and for no other reason," wrote Justice Black. "The Federal [Railway Labor] Act ... prohibits bargaining agents it authorizes from using their position and power to destroy colored workers' jobs in order to bestow them on white workers."[161]

State Antidiscrimination Laws

Black workers won another measure of job protection in 1945, when the Court upheld the validity of state fair-employment laws. The New York Civil Rights Act contained a provision—one of the first of its kind enacted—prohibiting a union from denying membership on the basis of race, creed, or color. The Railway Mail Association, which represented postal clerks in New York and other states and which limited its membership to whites and Indians, appealed the state's judgment that this law applied to its policy of excluding blacks. The association claimed the state law violated the organization's right to due process and equal protection and encroached on Congress's power to regulate the mails. The Supreme Court denied all three claims:

> We see no constitutional basis for the contention that a state cannot protect workers from exclusion solely on the basis of race, color or creed by an organization functioning under the protection of the state, which holds itself out to represent the general business needs of employees.[162]

The question of whether a state fair-employment practices act placed an impermissible burden on interstate commerce came to the Court in *Colorado Anti-Discrimination Commission v. Continental Airlines* (1963).[163] A black man named Marion Green applied for a job as a pilot with the interstate airline, which had its headquarters in Denver. He was rejected solely because of his race. The Colorado Anti-Discrimination Commission found the company had discriminated in violation of state law and ordered it to give Green the first opening in its next training course. A state court overruled the order because the law unduly burdened interstate commerce. The Supreme Court reversed the trial court and upheld the commission's order.

The state antidiscrimination law did not conflict with or frustrate any federal law that might also regulate employment discrimination by airlines, said the Court, nor did it deny the airlines any rights granted by Congress. Unlike several cases in which the Court has found that state-required racial separation of passengers in public transportation unduly burdened interstate commerce, the Court found hiring within a state, even for an interstate job, a "much more localized matter." Furthermore, the potential for diverse and conflicting hiring regulations among the states, which might hamper interstate commerce, was "virtually nonexistent." (*See details of Plessy v. Ferguson and McCabe v. Atchison, Topeka and Santa Fe Railroad, pp. 407–408.*)

Civil Rights Act of 1964

In 1964 Congress enacted the first federal law prohibiting job discrimination. Title VII of the Civil Rights Act of that year prohibited unions representing more than twenty-five workers as well as employers with that same number of employees, union hiring halls, and employment agencies from discriminating on the grounds of race, color, religion, sex, or national origin in the hiring, classification, training, or promotion of anyone. The act also created the Equal Employment Opportunities Commission (EEOC) to hear complaints and seek compliance with the law. In 1972 Congress extended coverage to employers and unions with fifteen or more employees or members, state and local governments, and educational institutions. The only major group left uncovered were federal government employees. The 1972 act also authorized the EEOC to go into federal courts to enforce the law. Federal courts were authorized to order employers to remedy proven discrimination by reinstating or hiring the employees concerned, with or without back pay, and by any other remedial measures the courts found appropriate.

Job Qualifications

The Supreme Court first fully discussed the scope of Title VII in *Griggs v. Duke Power Co.* (1971). Black employees charged that the North Carolina power

THE QUESTION OF INTENT

In distinguishing between cases based on the Constitution's guarantee of equal protection and those based on civil rights laws, the Supreme Court has made clear that it is sometimes more difficult to prove actions unconstitutional than to prove them illegal. The seminal case is *Washington v. Davis* (1976). In order to prove an employer guilty of unconstitutional discrimination, his action must be shown to be discriminatory in effect and intent, the Court held.

The case arose when two blacks challenged as unconstitutionally discriminatory the District of Columbia police department's requirement that recruits pass a verbal ability test. The two men argued that the number of black police officers did not reflect the city's large black population, that more blacks than whites failed the test, and that the test was not significantly related to job performance. Their challenge was based not on the Civil Rights Act of 1964, but on the Due Process Clause of the Fifth Amendment, which implicitly includes the equal protection guarantee. *(See box, Federal Equal Protection, p. 368.)*

A federal district court rejected the challenge because there was no evidence of intent to discriminate. The appeals court reversed, citing *Griggs v. Duke Power* (1971). *(See details of this case, pp. 423–425.)* The Supreme Court, however, reversed again, agreeing with the district court, 7-2, that there was no constitutional violation without proof of discriminatory intent. Justice Byron R. White wrote that the Court had "not held that a law, neutral on its face and serving ends otherwise within the power of the government to pursue, is invalid under the Equal Protection Clause simply because it may affect a greater proportion of one race than another."[1]

The Court subsequently applied this principle—that a law or other official action must reflect some racially discriminatory intent to violate the equal protection guarantee—in other areas of discrimination, including schools and housing.[2] *(See Austin Independent School District v. United States, p. 391; Village of Arlington Heights v. Metropolitan Housing Development Corporation, p. 421.)* For example, it extended this intent requirement to challenged voting practices in *Mobile v. Bolden* (1980), ruling 6-3 that before it would strike down an at-large system for electing city officials as a violation of the equal protection guarantee or of the law barring racial discrimination in voting, the system must be found intentionally discriminatory as well as discriminatory in effect.

Congress quickly overrode this latter ruling with amendments in 1982 to the Voting Rights Act, which made plain that there was no need for this finding of intent to justify holding a voting practice impermissible under that law.[3] Two years later, the Court again applied the intent requirement in the employment arena, ruling 5-4 that workers challenging a seniority system as discriminatory under the 1964 act must prove both a discriminatory intent and effect.[4]

---

1. *Washington v. Davis*, 426 U.S. 229 at 242 (1976).
2. *Austin Independent School District v. United States*, 429 U.S. 990 (1976); *Village of Arlington Heights v. Metropolitan Housing Development Corporation*, 429 U.S. 252 (1977).
3. *City of Mobile, Ala. v. Bolden*, 446 U.S. 55 (1980); *Congress and the Nation* (Washington, D.C.: Congressional Quarterly, 1985), 6:680.
4. *American Tobacco Co. v. Patterson*, 456 U.S. 63 (1982); see also *U.S. Postal Service Board of Governors v. Aikens*, 460 U.S. 711 (1983).

---

company had unfairly discriminated when it required them to have a high school diploma or pass a generalized intelligence test as a condition for employment or promotion. The black workers claimed that neither requirement was related to successful job performance, that the requirements disqualified a substantially higher number of blacks than whites, and that the jobs in question had been filled by whites under the company's former longstanding policy of giving whites first preference. The Court ruled 8-0 that under those circumstances the job qualification requirements were discriminatory. Chief Justice Burger set out the Court's interpretation of Title VII:

> [T]he Act does not command that any person be hired simply because he was formerly the subject of discrimination, or because he is a member of a minority group. Discriminatory preference for any group, minority or majority, is precisely and only what Congress has proscribed. What is required by Congress is the removal of artificial, arbitrary, and unnecessary barriers to employment when the barriers operate invidiously to discriminate on the basis of racial or other impermissible classification.[164]

Black *and* White

Title VII of the Civil Rights Act of 1964 prohibits racial discrimination against whites as well as against blacks in the workplace, the Court has ruled. In *McDonald v. Santa Fe Trail Transportation Co.* (1976), a freight company fired two white men who had stolen sixty cans of antifreeze, but the company did not dismiss a black man who had also participated in the theft. The Court held this differential treatment a clear violation of Title VII.

The law in its language and its legislative history makes plain that whites are to be protected as well as members of racial minorities, said Justice Thurgood Marshall. "While Santa Fe may decide that participation in a theft of cargo may render an employee unqualified for employment, this criterion must be 'applied alike to members of all races,' and Title VII is violated if … it was not."[1] The Court held, 7-2, that the two white men were also protected from such treatment by a provision of the 1866 Civil Rights Act, embodied in existing law as Section 1981 of Title 42 of the U.S. Code. The section declares that "all persons within the jurisdiction of the United States shall have the same right … to make and enforce contracts … as is enjoyed by white citizens." *(See box, Civil Rights Act of 1866, p. 417.)*

---

1. *McDonald v. Santa Fe Trail Transportation Co.,* 427 U.S. 273 at 283 (1976).

Any test that operates to exclude blacks, even one that is neutral on its face, must be shown to have a significant relation to job performance, Burger continued. Neither the requirement for a high school diploma nor the intelligence test had this relation. The Court agreed that there was no evidence that the company had intended to discriminate against its black employees, but, wrote Burger, "Congress directed the thrust of the Act to the consequences of employment practices, not simply the motivation."[165]

The Supreme Court in 1975 reaffirmed its view that tests that excluded more blacks than whites and were not proven to be job-related were discriminatory.[166] More than a decade later, the Court backed away from *Griggs*. In *Wards Cove Packing Co. v. Atonio* (1989), the Court, 5-4, held that workers charging an employer with discrimination had to do more to prove the charge than simply show that there was a high proportion of nonwhite workers in low-status jobs and a high proportion of white workers in high-status jobs. To hold otherwise, wrote Justice White for the Court, would be to encourage employers to adopt racial quotas to make certain that no portion of the workforce deviated in racial composition from the other parts of the workforce. Congress and the Court had rejected that idea, he said. The dissenting justices criticized the majority for "tipping the scales in favor of employers."[167] Two years later, Congress reversed some of the effects of the *Wards Cove* decision by easing the burden of proof for aggrieved workers in the Civil Rights Act of 1991.[168]

Proving Bias

A unanimous Court held in 1973 that the Civil Rights Act of 1964 did not require a company to rehire a black employee who had engaged in deliberate unlawful protests against it, but neither was the company permitted to use the protests as a pretext for refusing to rehire the employee because of his race. The former employee should have an opportunity to prove that the employer was using the illegal protest as an excuse to carry out a discriminatory hiring policy, the Court said in *McDonnell Douglas Corp. v. Green* (1973). If he could not show this, the refusal to rehire him could stand.[169] Twenty years later, the Court held that a worker is not automatically entitled to a judgment when a judge or jury rejects his employer's explanations for an adverse employment action. Instead, the Court held, the worker must prove a discriminatory motive for the action taken against him or her.[170]

In *Furnco Construction Corp. v. Waters* (1978), the Supreme Court held that an appeals court erred in ordering a construction company to adopt nondiscriminatory hiring practices before the company had been found guilty of job discrimination. The Court also said that an employer may point to the fact that he has hired a substantial number of black workers as part of his proof that he is not guilty of discrimination, but wrote the Court, "a racially balanced work force cannot immunize an employer from liability for specific acts of discrimination."[171]

Remedies

The Supreme Court has upheld the broad authority of lower federal courts under Title VII of the Civil Rights Act of 1964 to award back wages and retirement benefits to persons who have suffered illegal job discrimination.

Back Pay. The first compensation case was *Albemarle Paper Co. v. Moody* (1975). A federal district court found that the North Carolina paper mill had discriminated against blacks prior to enactment of Title VII and that the effects of that discrimination were apparent for several years afterward. Because the company no longer discriminated, however, the lower court decided against a back pay award. A court of appeals reversed the decision, and the paper mill appealed. In a 7-1 vote, the Court ruled that back pay was a proper remedy for past job discrimination. Wrote Justice Stewart,

> If employers faced only the prospect of an injunctive order, they would have little incentive to shun practices of dubious legality. It is the reasonably certain prospect of a backpay award that "provide[s] the spur or catalyst which causes employers and unions to self-examine and to self-evaluate their employment practices and to endeavor to eliminate, so far as possible, the last vestiges of an unfortunate and ignominious page in this country's history."… It is also the purpose of Title VII to make persons whole for the injuries suffered on account of unlawful employment discrimination.[172]

Back pay should be awarded in most cases where job discrimination in violation of Title VII has been proved, the majority held, even in cases such as this one, where the employer had acted in good faith to end discrimination. If back pay were awarded only for acts of bad faith, the majority said, "the remedy would become a punishment for moral turpitude, rather than

a compensation for workers' injuries…. [A] worker's injury is no less real simply because his employer did not inflict it in 'bad faith.'"[173] In *Fitzpatrick v. Bitzer* (1976), the Court upheld the award of retroactive retirement benefits to male employees of the state of Connecticut who had been required to work longer than women employees before they could retire.[174]

One of the first Supreme Court opinions by Justice Sandra Day O'Connor concerned back pay awards. In *Ford Motor Co. v. Equal Employment Opportunity Commission* (1982), she explained the Court's view that an employer charged with job bias can terminate the period for which he may be held liable for back pay by unconditionally offering the person charging bias the job he had previously refused to offer. "The victims of job discrimination want jobs, not lawsuits," she wrote, expressing the hope that this ruling would encourage employers to make such offers.[175]

Seniority Rights. The Court also has upheld the authority of federal courts to award retroactive seniority rights to persons denied employment or promotion by biased policies. In *Franks v. Bowman Transportation Co. Inc.* (1976), the Court, 5-3, approved seniority awards by lower courts dating back to rejection of the job application. Retroactive seniority was an appropriate remedy, and such awards should be made in most cases where a seniority system exists and discrimination is proved, the Court said. Such awards fulfill the "make-whole" purposes of Title VII. Without them, Justice Brennan wrote, the victim of job discrimination "will never obtain his rightful place in the hierarchy of seniority according to which these various employment benefits are distributed. He will perpetually remain subordinate to persons who, but for the illegal discrimination, would have been in respect to entitlement to these benefits his inferiors."[176]

The Court did not distinguish between benefit seniority, which determines matters such as length of vacation and pension benefits, and competitive seniority, which determines issues such as the order in which employees are laid off and rehired, promoted, and transferred. In dissent, Justice Powell opposed the award of retroactive competitive seniority because it did not affect the employer but rather "the rights and expectations of perfectly innocent employees. The economic benefits awarded discrimination victims would be derived not at the expense of the employer but at the expense of other workers."[177]

Retroactive Seniority Limited. Little more than a year later, the Court qualified its holding in *Franks.* Its decision in *Teamsters v. United States* and *T.I.M.E.-D.C. v. United States* (1977) barred the award of retroactive seniority benefits dating before July 2, 1965, the effective date of the Civil Rights Act of 1964. In Title VII, Congress specifically included language that immunized existing bona fide seniority systems from attack as discriminatory. The Court held, 7-2, that this immunity precluded any award of retroactive seniority benefits that would have been accumulated prior to July 2, 1965, absent racial discrimination.

This case concerned a nationwide trucking firm and the truckers' union.[178] Lower courts found that the firm systematically denied intercity-line driver jobs to blacks and Spanish-surnamed employees and applicants. Seniority became an issue in determining the remedy for this discrimination. Under the company's collective bargaining agreement with the Teamsters, competitive seniority for a line driver was counted from the time he took the post, not from the time he joined the company. Thus a black employee transferring to the line driver job would be required to give up any competitive seniority he had accumulated.

Citing *Franks,* the unanimous Court held that persons discriminated against after the effective date of the 1964 act were entitled to retroactive seniority as far back as that date. With Justices Brennan and Marshall dissenting, however, the Court refused to order seniority awards stretching back further than July 2, 1965, for victims of discrimination. Were it not for the specific immunity granted by the act to bona fide seniority systems, wrote Stewart for the majority, the seniority system challenged in this case would probably have been found invalid. The language of the immunization provision and the legislative history, however, demonstrated that an

otherwise neutral, legitimate seniority system does not become unlawful under Title VII simply because it may perpetuate pre-Act discrimination. Congress did not intend to make it illegal for employees with vested seniority rights to continue to exercise those rights, even at the expense of pre-Act discriminatees.[179]

Marshall and Brennan based their dissent on their view that a seniority system that perpetuated the effect of pre-1965 discrimination was not a bona fide system protected by Title VII.

In 1983 the Court, by a splintered majority, held that without proof of intent to discriminate, private persons suing their employer, a recipient of federal funds, for discrimination in violation of Title VI of the 1964 Civil Rights Act, may not win back pay or retroactive seniority, but only an injunction against the continuation of such conduct.[180]

AFFIRMATIVE ACTION

After 1954 the Court insisted that the Fourteenth Amendment's equal protection guarantee prohibited racial discrimination by state governments, and the Fifth Amendment's Due Process Clause prohibited racial discrimination by the federal government.[181] In the 1960s, Congress outlawed racial discrimination in employment, education, and housing, but by the 1970s the clarity of these civil rights era measures was tested by a long and divisive struggle over whether extra steps could be taken to benefit blacks and other minorities in order to achieve greater equality. These extra steps became known as "affirmative action." Critics described these measures as "reverse discrimination" or "racial preferences."

The phrase "affirmative action" originated with an executive order issued by President John F. Kennedy in 1961. Setting the goal of achieving "equal opportunity" in federally funded projects, Kennedy said contractors should "take affirmative action" to make sure the hiring of workers was free of racial bias. The concept's origin, however, is credited to President Lyndon B. Johnson. The year after winning passage of the Civil

Rights Act of 1964, Johnson told the graduating class at Howard University that ending discrimination was not enough. "You do not wipe away the scars of centuries by saying: 'Now, you are free to go where you want, do as you desire, and choose the leaders you please.' You do not take a man who for years has been hobbled by chains, liberate him, bring him to the starting line of a race, saying, 'You are free to compete with all the others,' and still justly believe you have been completely fair," he said. "This is the next and more profound stage of the battle for civil rights. We seek not just freedom but opportunity, not just legal equity but human ability, not just equality as a right and a theory, but equality as a fact and as a result."[182]

Johnson's speech accurately foresaw the "next and more profound stage of the battle for civil rights." Advocates for minority rights took up his call for "equality as a fact and as a result." They would not accept as sufficient the use of strict standards of "legal equity" if the result was that only a tiny percentage of blacks obtained jobs, housing, or college opportunities. They insisted on "goals and timetables" that would measure racial progress in numbers, but this insistence on measurable progress triggered a backlash, particularly among white conservatives, who argued the law demanded equal treatment for individuals, not equal results for groups. In a series of lawsuits that reached the Court, the justices grappled with the practical meaning of equality in the law and in society. In a nation whose history includes black slavery and blatant racial bias, may employers and colleges give qualified black applicants an edge in order to achieve overall equality, or does that system of advantages for some violate the rights of whites who lose out?

The Court found itself as divided and uncertain as the nation. The justices were unable to agree on clear, decisive rulings that either allowed the "affirmative" use of race, or rejected it entirely. In the most significant opinions, however, the Court left the door open for employers and colleges to make a limited use of affirmative action. Two early cases established rules that have survived through the decades. A divided Court in *Regents of the University of California v. Bakke* (1978)

held that colleges and universities may use a black applicant's race as a "plus factor" in admissions.[183] A year later, the Court ruled that a company may give blacks an advantage over whites in seeking promotions. The Civil Rights Act of 1964, despite its strict nondiscrimination clause, did not outlaw "all voluntary, private race-conscious efforts" to achieve greater equality, the Court said in *United Steelworkers of America v. Weber* (1979).[184] So long as these decisions stood, college officials and employers were free to use affirmative action.

Since affirmative action's inception, its underlying rationale has shifted considerably. At first, its proponents said "goals and timetables" were needed to stop discrimination. In the construction trades, for example, federal regulators feared union leaders and work foremen would likely exclude blacks unless they were pressured to hire them. The regulators said their goal was equal opportunity for all. Later cases tested whether seniority rules or promotion tests could be eased for blacks and Hispanics. Advocates stressed then that these "affirmative" steps were needed to make up for past discrimination. Like President Johnson, they said it was unfair and illogical to ignore centuries of oppression of blacks by whites. By the late 1980s, however, the Court had rejected past "societal discrimination" as a rationale for continuing affirmative action. Rather, advocates switched the focus to "diversity," a notion that Justice Lewis F. Powell Jr. launched in his separate opinion in *Bakke*. Colleges seek a diverse student body because of its educational benefit. Education officials argued that having students from rural as well as urban backgrounds, from small towns and big cities, from blue-collar homes as well as from those of highly paid professionals, makes for a richer experience for all. Agreeing, Powell said that in such a context it makes sense that a minority student's race could be a "plus factor" to an admission officer seeking to achieve a diverse student body.

Once born in *Bakke*, arguments for diversity grew through the 1980s and 1990s to become the predominant rationale for affirmative action. In 2003 the Court finally endorsed diversity as a "compelling" justification for affirmative action in colleges and universities. "Today we endorse Justice Powell's view that student body diversity is a compelling state interest that can justify the use of race in university admissions," wrote Justice Sandra Day O'Connor for a five-member majority in upholding the admissions policy at the University of Michigan Law School. "Access to legal education (and thus the legal profession) must be inclusive of talented and qualified individuals of every race and ethnicity," she said. If admissions officers must give extra consideration to minority applicants to achieve this goal, so be it. "The Equal Protection Clause does not prohibit the Law School's narrowly tailored used of race in admissions decisions to further a compelling interest in obtaining the educational benefits that flow from a diverse student body," she concluded.[185]

In one sense, the Court had gone back to where it started. The justices remained divided and skeptical of "race-conscious" policies. O'Connor's opinion stressed that she was not endorsing "racial balancing, which is patently unconstitutional." On the same day as the ruling in the law school case, a 6-3 majority struck down an admissions policy for undergraduates at the University of Michigan that awarded points for being a minority. Still, skepticism aside, the Court was not willing to require colleges or employers to close the door to aspiring minority applicants.

Beginning with *Bakke*

The first time the issue of affirmative action came to the Court, in *DeFunis v. Odegaard* (1974), a five-justice majority sidestepped the issue, ruling on the reverse discrimination issue by finding the case moot, that is, no longer presenting a live controversy. The white plaintiff, who charged that he was denied admission to a state law school so that the school might accept a less-qualified minority student, had been admitted under court order. He was scheduled to graduate from law school in the spring of 1974, only months after the Court heard arguments in his case.

The majority held that the case was moot because their decision on the equal protection issue would have

no effect on the plaintiff. The dissenting justices would, however, have preferred to resolve the substantive question.[186] When the Court finally dealt with a live case of reverse discrimination—*University of California Regents v. Bakke* (1978)—it found itself just as divided as the rest of the country over the issue. On one point, the Court, 5-4, told state universities that they may not set aside a fixed quota of seats in each class for minority group members, denying white applicants the opportunity to compete for those places. On a second point, a different five-justice majority held that admissions officers do not violate the equal protection guarantee when they consider race as one of many factors that determine which applicant is accepted and which rejected.

Allan Bakke, a thirty-eight-year-old white engineer, was twice denied admission to the medical school at the University of California at Davis. To ensure minority representation in the student body, the university had set aside sixteen seats for minority applicants in each medical school class of one hundred students. Challenging the set-aside as a violation of his constitutional right to equal protection of the laws, Bakke contended that he would have been admitted had it not been for this rigid preference system. In each year his application was rejected, the school had accepted some minority applicants with qualifications inferior to his.

Justice Powell was the key to the *Bakke* decision: He was the only justice who was in both majorities. On the first point—the decision to strike down the Davis quota system—Powell voted with Chief Justice Warren E. Burger and Justices William H. Rehnquist, Potter Stewart, and John Paul Stevens, who saw *Bakke* as a controversy between litigants that could be settled by applying the Civil Rights Act of 1964 without involving constitutional issues. Title VI of the act, they pointed out, barred any discrimination on the grounds of race, color, or national origin in any program receiving federal financial assistance. When that ban was placed alongside the facts of the case, it was clear to them that the university had violated the statute. Stevens explained:

The University, through its special admissions policy, excluded Bakke from participation in its program of medical education because of his race. The University also acknowledges that it was, and still is, receiving federal financial assistance.... The meaning of the Title VI ban on exclusion is crystal clear: Race cannot be the basis of excluding anyone from participation in a federally funded program.[187]

Powell's reasoning on this point differed from the view of the four dissenters. Where they found no constitutional involvement, he found the scope of the Title VI ban and the Equal Protection Clause of the Fourteenth Amendment identical: What violated one therefore violated the other, so he based his vote against the university's preference system on both the law and the Constitution.

The Davis admissions program used an explicit racial classification, Powell noted. Such classifications were not always unconstitutional, he continued, "[b]ut when a state's distribution of benefits or imposition of burdens hinges on ... the color of a person's skin or ancestry, that individual is entitled to a demonstration that the challenged classification is necessary to promote a substantial state interest." Powell could find no substantial interest that justified establishment of the university's specific quota system. Not even the desire to remedy past discrimination was a sufficient justification, he said; such a desire was based on "an amorphous concept of injury that may be ageless in its reach into the past."[188]

Powell did not believe, however, that all racial classifications were unconstitutional. He voted with Justices William J. Brennan Jr., Thurgood Marshall, Byron R. White, and Harry A. Blackmun to approve the use of some race-conscious affirmative action programs. These four contended that the university's wish to remedy past societal discrimination was sufficient justification. For the four, Brennan wrote,

> Government may take race into account when it acts not to demean or insult any racial group, but to remedy disadvantages cast on minorities by past racial prejudice, at least when appropriate findings have been made by judicial, legislative, or administrative bodies with competence to act in this area.[189]

The four endorsed the broad remedial use of race-conscious programs, even in situations where no specific constitutional violation had been found.

Voluntary Affirmative Action

The Court's next affirmative action case, *United Steelworkers of America v. Weber* (1979), did not raise the constitutional issue of equal protection. Rather, it posed only the question whether the Civil Rights Act of 1964 barred an employer from voluntarily establishing an affirmative action training program that preferred blacks over whites. By a 5-2 vote, the Court held that Title VII did not bar such a program. Justice Stewart, who had voted against racial quotas in the *Bakke* case, joined the four justices who had endorsed use of race-conscious programs in that case to form the majority in *Weber*. Chief Justice Burger and Justice Rehnquist dissented; Justices Powell and Stevens did not participate in the case.

In 1974 Kaiser Aluminum and the United Steelworkers of America agreed upon an affirmative action plan that reserved 50 percent of all in-plant craft training slots for minorities. The agreement was a voluntary effort to increase the number of minority participants holding skilled jobs in the aluminum industry. Brian Weber, a white, applied for a training program at the Kaiser plant where he worked in Gramercy, Louisiana. He was rejected. Weber, who had more seniority than the most junior black accepted for the program, charged that he had been a victim of "reverse discrimination." He won at the federal district court and the court of appeals levels. The union, the company, and the Justice Department then asked the Supreme Court to review the appeals court decision.[190] Reversing the lower courts, the majority said that in passing Title VII Congress could not have intended to prohibit private employers from voluntarily instituting affirmative action plans to open opportunities for blacks in job areas traditionally closed to them:

> It would be ironic indeed if a law triggered by a Nation's concern over centuries of racial injustice and intended to improve the lot of those who had "been excluded from the American dream for so

long" … constituted the first legislative prohibition of all voluntary, private, race-conscious efforts to abolish traditional patterns of racial segregation and hierarchy.[191]

The majority carefully distinguished between the language of Title VII, prohibiting racial discrimination in employment, and Title VI, the section of the act reviewed in *Bakke* and held to mean that programs receiving federal aid could not discriminate on the basis of race. In Title VI, Brennan said for the majority, "Congress was legislating to assure federal funds would not be used in an improper manner. Title VII, by contrast, was enacted pursuant to the Commerce power to regulate purely private decisionmaking and was not intended to incorporate and particularize the commands of the Fifth and Fourteenth Amendments" that guarantee equal protection of the laws against federal and state infringement.[192]

In separate dissents, Chief Justice Burger and Justice Rehnquist objected to the majority's interpretation of Title VII and its legislative history. The Court's judgment, Burger wrote,

> is contrary to the explicit language of the statute and arrived at by means wholly incompatible with long-established principles of separation of powers. Under the guise of statutory "construction," the Court effectively rewrites Title VII to achieve what it regards as a desirable result. It "amends" the statute to do precisely what both its sponsors and its opponents agreed the statute was not intended to do.[193]

Rehnquist charged that the majority had contorted the language of Title VII. Its opinion, he said, is "reminiscent not of jurists such as Hale, Holmes and Hughes, but of escape artists such as Houdini." The Court, he continued, "eludes clear statutory language, 'uncontradicted' legislative history, and uniform precedent in concluding that employers are, after all, permitted to consider race in making employment decisions."[194]

Federal Affirmative Action

The following year, in *Fullilove v. Klutznick* (1980), the Court faced a constitutional challenge to affirmative action that was not voluntary but mandated by federal law. In the Public Works Employment Act of 1977, Congress set aside a certain percentage of federal funds for contracts with minority-owned businesses. The Court, 6-3, held the set-aside permissible. This program, explained Chief Justice Burger, "was designed to ensure that, to the extent federal funds were granted under … [this law], grantees who elect to participate would not employ procurement practices that Congress had decided might result in perpetuation of the effects of prior discrimination which had impaired or foreclosed access by minority businesses to public contracting opportunities."[195]

"In the continuing effort to achieve the goal of equality of economic opportunity," wrote Burger, "Congress has necessary latitude to try new techniques such as the limited use of racial and ethnic criteria to accomplish remedial objectives; this is especially so in programs where voluntary cooperation with remedial measures is induced by placing conditions on federal expenditures."[196] The justices in the majority were Burger, Brennan, Powell, Marshall, White, and Blackmun. Justices Rehnquist, Stewart, and Stevens dissented.

Layoff Cases

Affirmative action was anathema to Ronald Reagan's administration, which saw it as impermissible reverse discrimination, penalizing innocent whites—usually white men—for past discrimination by others against blacks and women. The first two affirmative action cases heard by the Court during the Reagan years brought results the administration found quite congenial. Twice, the Court ruled that affirmative action was not appropriately used in layoff situations to protect the jobs of more recently hired blacks at the cost of the jobs of more senior white employees.

In December 1983, the Court heard arguments in *Firefighters Local Union No. 1784 v. Stotts, Memphis Fire Department v. Stotts*. After the Memphis fire department, operating under a consent decree settling charges of racial discrimination against the department, hired a number of black firefighters, budget cutbacks required some firemen to be laid off. The black fire captain, Carl

Stotts, who had won the consent decree, persuaded a federal judge to order that whites with more seniority be laid off in order to preserve the jobs of more recently hired blacks. With the backing of the Reagan administration, the city and the firefighters' union came to the Court seeking reversal of this order. They argued that layoffs should proceed along the general rule of "last hired, first fired." The administration's friend-of-the-court argument contended that the firefighters' seniority system was immunized by the Civil Rights Act of 1964 against such judicial tampering unless the system was shown to have been designed to discriminate against minority employees, a finding not made in the Memphis case.

Stotts Ruling

In June 1984, the Court agreed with the challenge, holding that the federal judge had overstepped his powers when he overrode the usual seniority rule to preserve the jobs of the junior firefighters who were black. The administration hailed the decision as a victory, reading into it a broad disavowal of affirmative action. In fact, Justice White tied the Court's opinion closely to the particular facts of this case, namely, the court order directing the city to ignore its usual rules for layoffs in order to preserve gains achieved under a consent decree.[197] White and the four other justices in the majority—Burger, Powell, Rehnquist, and O'Connor—did, however, declare that Congress, in the 1964 Civil Rights Act, had intended to provide remedies of this affirmative sort only to persons who had themselves been the victims of illegal discrimination. Because there was no finding in this case that any of the newly hired black firefighters had suffered such personal rejection, the judge's order was unwarranted, they said. Justice Stevens joined the majority but not White's opinion. Justices Brennan, Blackmun, and Marshall dissented.

Wygant Decision

Two years later, the Court underscored its doubts about the use of affirmative action in layoff situations, ruling 5-4 that it was unconstitutional for a school board to lay off white teachers to preserve the jobs of blacks with less seniority. That, the Court held in *Wygant v. Jackson Board of Education* (1986), denied the whites equal protection.[198] The voluntary adoption of an agreement protecting blacks' jobs in time of layoffs was not based on any showing by the board of actual past discrimination, nor was it narrowly tailored enough to be permitted, the majority held. It was one thing to use affirmative action in hiring, when "the burden to be borne by innocent individuals is diffused ... generally," wrote Powell, but quite another to use it to deprive people of their existing jobs.[199]

The decision was notable, in light of the Reagan administration's position, that the Court went out of its way to point out that although the school board's use of affirmative action in this case was not permissible, some affirmative action was appropriate. "We have recognized ... that in order to remedy the effects of prior discrimination, it may be necessary to take race into account," wrote Justice Powell. "As part of this nation's dedication to eradicating racial discrimination, innocent persons may be called upon to bear some burden of the remedy."[200]

Justice O'Connor also wrote to emphasize the Court's agreement on "core principles" concerning affirmative action. "The Court is in agreement," she wrote, that "remedying past or present racial discrimination by a state actor is a sufficiently weighty state interest to warrant the remedial use of a carefully constructed affirmative action program."[201] O'Connor's opinion rejected the administration's position, which *Stotts* had seemed to endorse, that affirmative action was constitutional only when used to benefit specific identified victims of bias. This opinion, O'Connor's first substantive writing on the issue, moved her into the decisive "swing" position between the four justices who usually favored affirmative action—Brennan, Marshall, Blackmun, and Stevens—and the four who generally disapproved it—Burger, Rehnquist, White, and Powell.

Affirmative Action Upheld

Wygant marked a turning point. Within the next ten months, the Court removed all doubt that affirmative action, properly used in the proper circumstance, was a constitutionally permissible remedy for past discrimination. Six weeks after *Wygant,* the Court ruled in two more affirmative action cases. In both of them, the Court rebuffed the administration's argument against affirmative action. Only Chief Justice Burger and Justice Rehnquist accepted the administration's view. Justice Brennan, the Court's most staunchly liberal member, spoke for the majority in both cases, holding that neither court-ordered minority quotas for union admission nor race-based job promotions violated the Civil Rights Act of 1964.

In *Local #28 of the Sheet Metal Workers' International v. Equal Employment Opportunity Commission* (1986), the Court, 5-4, upheld an order requiring the union, which had persistently refused to admit blacks, to increase its nonwhite membership to 29.23 percent by August 1987.[202] In *Local #93, International Association of Firefighters v. City of Cleveland and Cleveland Vanguards* (1986), the Court, 6-3, held that the Civil Rights Act did not prevent the city from resolving a bias complaint by agreeing to promote one black firefighter for every white promoted.[203] O'Connor, who had dissented in the sheet metal workers' case, joined the majority in the Cleveland case, leaving Burger, Rehnquist, and White in dissent.

Paradise: Promotion Quota

For the third time in less than a year, the Supreme Court upheld a challenged affirmative action plan. Against a challenge that a one-black-for-one-white promotion quota denied white troopers the equal protection of the law, the Court, 5-4, sustained the plan imposed on Alabama's state troopers by a federal judge.[204] Justice Brennan spoke for the Court in *United States v. Paradise* (1987): "Strong measures were required in light of the ... long and shameful record of delay and resistance." The Alabama Department of Public Safety had hired no blacks before it was sued for discrimination in 1972.

Eleven years later, a federal judge found racial discrimination still pervasive and conspicuous in the department and therefore imposed the promotion quota. This quota "was amply justified and narrowly tailored to serve the legitimate and laudable purposes" of eradicating this history of discrimination, wrote Brennan.[205] Justice Powell, but not O'Connor, joined the majority in this case. Dissenting with O'Connor were Chief Justice William H. Rehnquist and Justices White and Antonin Scalia, the latter the Court's newest member.

Johnson: A Boost for Women

In *Johnson v. Transportation Agency, Santa Clara County, Calif.* (1987), the Court laid to rest any remaining doubts about its endorsement of the careful use of affirmative action. This case was the first before the Court concerning the use of affirmative action to benefit women. The vote was 6-3. Justices O'Connor and Powell joined the usual foursome of affirmative action advocates—Justices Brennan, Marshall, Blackmun, and Stevens. Their decision upheld a voluntary affirmative action plan adopted by the Santa Clara County Transportation Department to move women into higher ranking positions than they had previously held. The plan resulted in the promotion of Diane Joyce to road dispatcher. Competing with Joyce for the job was Paul Johnson, who scored two points higher on a qualifying interview, but because of the affirmative action plan, lost out on the promotion.

It was appropriate, under the circumstances, to take Joyce's sex into account as a plus, wrote Justice Brennan for the majority:

> The decision to do so was made pursuant to an affirmative action plan that represents a moderate, flexible, case-by-case approach to effecting a gradual improvement in the representation of minorities and women in the agency's work force.... Such a plan is fully consistent with Title VII [of the Civil Rights Act of 1964], for it embodies the contribution that voluntary employer action can make in eliminating the vestiges of discrimination in the workplace.[206]

Brennan looked back to the 1979 *Weber* ruling in writing this opinion, extending its approval of voluntary affirmative action to include public as well as private employers. As in *Weber,* the plan in *Johnson* was permissible because it did not require white men to be fired and replaced by blacks or women nor impose an absolute bar to advancement by white males, and it was only a temporary remedy.

In dissent, Scalia said the Court had all but repealed the federal antidiscrimination law for ordinary white workers, like Paul Johnson. He quoted the Civil Rights Act of 1964 that makes it an "unlawful employment practice for an employer ... to discriminate against any individual ... because of such individual's race, color, religion, sex or national origin." Although Johnson had lost a promotion to a woman with lesser credentials, the Court had upheld the employer's action, he noted. "A statute designed to establish a color-blind and gender-blind workplace has thus been converted into a powerful engine of racism and sexism," Scalia wrote. "In fact, the only losers in this process are the Johnsons of the country, for whom Title VII had been not merely repealed but actually inverted. The irony is that these individuals—predominantly unknown, unaffluent, unorganized—suffer this injustice at the hands of a Court fond of thinking of itself the champion of the politically impotent."[207] Chief Justice Rehnquist and Justice White joined Scalia's dissent.

A Tightening Standard

After the Court's 1980 ruling in *Fullilove,* dozens of state and local governments set aside a certain portion of their public works dollars for minority-owned businesses. Those programs boosted the economic prospects of racial minorities and women but sometimes at the expense of more established contractors, a number of whom went to court to protest.

Richmond: Rigid Set-Aside

The week that President George H.W. Bush succeeded Ronald Reagan as president, the Supreme Court announced a strict new approach to government-sponsored preferences for minorities. For the first time, a majority ruled that racial discrimination of any sort is subject to "strict scrutiny," regardless of whether blacks are the victims or the beneficiaries. When examining a city or state's use of race, "the standard of review under the Equal Protection Clause is not dependent on the race of those burdened or benefited by a particular classification," wrote Justice O'Connor in *City of Richmond v. J.A. Croson Co.* (1989).[208] The 6-3 decision struck down a southern city's rigid set-aside plan. Richmond, Virginia, the former capital of the Confederacy, had adopted the measure after the city council learned that less than 1 percent of the city's contract dollars went to minority entrepreneurs. The Court's decision cast doubt on all programs that included special benefits or set asides that were based on race.

Richmond's program required that the prime contractor on every city construction project subcontract at least 30 percent of the dollar amount of the contract to minority-owned businesses. *City of Richmond v. J.A. Croson Co.* was a challenge to that plan by a company that had lost a contract for installing plumbing fixtures at the city jail because it could not find a qualified minority subcontractor. The states do not share Congress's broad power to enforce the Fourteenth Amendment, which operates as a direct restriction on the power of the states to use racial classifications, said the Court. Therefore, *Fullilove* does not govern city and state minority set-aside plans, it declared. Richmond's plan violated the Fourteenth Amendment promise that "no state shall ... deny to any person within its jurisdiction the equal protection of the laws," wrote Justice O'Connor, joined by Chief Justice Rehnquist and Justices White, Stevens, and Anthony M. Kennedy. Justice Scalia concurred; Justices Marshall, Brennan, and Blackmun dissented.

The plan's primary defect, O'Connor explained, was its lack of justification by specific evidence of racial discrimination within the city's construction industry. Echoing her opinion in *Wygant,* she wrote, "a generalized assertion that there has been past discrimination in an entire industry provides no guidance for a legislative body to determine the precise scope of the injury it seeks to remedy."[209] O'Connor continued:

Two editorial cartoonists respond to the Supreme Court's recent rulings on affirmative action. In *Adarand Constructors Inc. v. Peña* (1995), the Court decided that federal affirmative action policies are subject to strict scrutiny.

While there is no doubt that the sorry history of both private and public discrimination in this country has contributed to a lack of opportunities for black entrepreneurs, this observation, standing alone, cannot justify a rigid racial quota in the awarding of public contracts in Richmond, Virginia. An amorphous claim that there has been past discrimination in a particular industry cannot justify the use of an unyielding racial quota. The 30 percent quota cannot in any realistic sense be tied to any injury suffered by anyone.[210]

States and cities "may take remedial action when they possess evidence that their own spending practices are exacerbating a pattern of prior discrimination," said O'Connor, but "they must identify that discrimination, public or private, with some specificity before they use race-conscious relief."[211] Further, she stated,

To accept Richmond's claim that past societal discrimination alone can serve as the basis for rigid racial preferences would be to open the door to competing claims for "remedial relief" for every disadvantaged group. The dream of a Nation of equal citizens in a society where race is irrelevant to personal opportunity and achievement would be lost in a mosaic of shifting preferences based on inherently immeasurable claims of past wrongs."...

Proper findings in this regard are necessary to define both the scope of the injury and the extent of the remedy necessary to cure its effects. Such findings also serve to assure all citizens that the deviation from the norm of equal treatment for all racial and ethnic groups is a temporary matter, a measure taken in the service of the goal of equality itself. Absent such findings, there is a danger that a racial classification is merely the product of unthinking stereotypes or a form of racial politics.[212]

Later in 1989, the Court seemed to encourage the testing of affirmative action plans when it ruled that such settlements could be challenged, after their adoption, by white workers who felt themselves adversely affected by the terms. Until the Court's ruling in *Martin v. Wilks* (1989), a suit between black firefighters and the city of Birmingham, such "third-party" challenges generally were not permitted.[213] Writing for the Court, divided 5-4, Chief Justice Rehnquist declared that the Court felt it must permit such challenges in order to honor the principle that a person could not be deprived of his legal rights in a proceeding to which he was not a party.

Federal Preferences

In 1990 Justice William J. Brennan Jr., the long-time leader of the Court's liberal faction, surprised many observers when in his final month on the Court, the eighty-four-year-old mustered a 5-4 majority to uphold "benign race-conscious measures" by the federal government. Just a year earlier, Justice White had joined Justice O'Connor's opinion for a conservative majority that said all racial classifications by state and local officials were suspect and subject to "strict scrutiny." White maintained, however, that Congress deserved greater deference than city and state officials, so he joined

Brennan's opinion. The decision in *Metro Broadcasting Inc. v. Federal Communications Commission* (1990) upheld a congressional plan to foster diversity on the airwaves by encouraging the sale of radio and television licenses to blacks and Hispanics.[214] Justice Stevens who was skeptical of the set-asides in the construction industry also joined Brennan's opinion upholding the FCC.

Strict Scrutiny

Five years after *Metro Broadcasting*, the Court overruled that decision and brought all governmental action based on race under the most searching judicial inquiry. By 5-4, with Justice O'Connor writing for the majority, the Court held that affirmative action policies, including federal minority contracting provisions, are subject to strict scrutiny by the courts. That means that such policies will survive judicial scrutiny only if they serve a compelling governmental interest and are narrowly tailored to achieve that goal.[215] With that decision in *Adarand Constructors Inc. v. Peña* (1995), the justices returned to lower courts the case begun by a white contractor in Colorado.

Adarand's guardrail construction company had challenged a U.S. Transportation Department program that gave contractors a financial incentive to award subcontracts to minority-owned businesses. The company sued after it lost a bid on a federal highway project to a Hispanic-owned company. Not surprisingly, the lower federal courts hearing the case rejected the challenge and upheld the program, applying the intermediate standard of review used by the Court in *Metro Broadcasting*. The Supreme Court overruled them.

Justice O'Connor said in her opinion that the Court was generally skeptical of racial classifications and had imposed identical standards under the Equal Protection Clause on federal, state, or local governments. *Metro Broadcasting*, she said, had departed from those precedents. "[W]henever the government treats any person unequally because of his or her race, that person has suffered an injury that falls squarely within the language and spirit of the Constitution's guarantee of equal protection," she wrote.[216] O'Connor stopped short of saying that strict scrutiny would prevent the government from ever using racial classifications. "[W]e wish to dispel the notion that strict scrutiny is 'strict in theory, but fatal in fact,'" she said, quoting a passage by Justice Marshall in *Fullilove*. "The unhappy persistence of both the practice and lingering effects of racial discrimination against minority groups in this country is an unfortunate reality, and government is not disqualified from acting in response to it."[217]

Chief Justice Rehnquist and Justices Scalia, Kennedy, and Clarence Thomas joined most of O'Connor's opinion. (Thomas, who succeeded Thurgood Marshall, one of the five justices in the *Metro Broadcasting* majority, effectively made the difference in shifting the Court toward strict judicial scrutiny for federal affirmative action programs.) Dissenting in *Adarand* were Justices Stevens, David H. Souter, Ruth Bader Ginsburg, and Stephen G. Breyer. Stevens, the most senior of the group, criticized the majority's "inability to differentiate between 'invidious' and 'benign' discrimination." The ruling, Stevens said, "would disregard the difference between a 'No Trespassing' sign and a welcome mat. It would treat a Dixiecrat Senator's decision to vote against Thurgood Marshall's confirmation in order to keep African Americans off the Supreme Court as on a par with President Johnson's evaluation of his nominee's race as a positive factor."[218]

College Affirmative Action Survives

The *Croson* and *Adarand* opinions appeared to doom affirmative action. If a race-conscious government plan that favors blacks was subjected to the same strict scrutiny used against racial bias against blacks, it would almost certainly be struck down, legal experts said. In the lower courts, the *Croson* and *Adarand* decisions prompted judges in the 1990s to strike down affirmative action programs at the University of Texas and the University of Georgia, but the Court had yet to decide whether the *Bakke* decision set an entirely different rule for colleges and universities.

That issue came before the Court in 2003 in two cases from the University of Michigan. In *Bakke*, Justice Powell, speaking only for himself, had said college admission officers had a "compelling interest" in having

Barbara Grutter (*left*) and Jennifer Gratz (*right*) brought cases against the University of Michigan alleging reverse discrimination in the school's affirmative action admissions policies. In *Grutter v. Bollinger* (2003), the Court upheld the law school's policy, asserting that the university could take into consideration an individual's race as part of a holistic approach to achieve the compelling interest of diversity. It ruled against the undergraduate admissions policy in *Gratz v. Bollinger* (2003) because it made race a decisive factor.

a diverse student body. For that reason, they may consider a minority applicant's race as a "plus factor." At the same time, they may not use rigid quotas that make race the only factor, Powell said. Although colleges and universities relied on Powell's opinion, critics of affirmative action contended his solo opinion had been implicitly overruled by the *Croson* and *Adarand* decisions.

In the late 1990s, the Center for Individual Rights, a Washington-based law firm that opposed affirmative action, sued on behalf of two white women who had been rejected by the University of Michigan. Barbara Grutter applied to the law school in 1996 with a 3.8 grade average and a 161 score on the Law School Admissions Test (LSAT). Each year, the school enrolled

about 350 new students, and it said it sought a "critical mass" of minority students. These "underrepresented" minorities—African Americans, Hispanics, and Native Americans—made up roughly 15 percent of the class. Grutter was rejected, although her grades and test scores were better than most of the minority students who were accepted. In 1997 she sued Lee Bollinger, who was then dean of the law school, alleging she was denied the equal protection of the laws. During the trial, an expert for the law school testified that if a "race-blind admissions system" had been used, the percentage of minority students would have fallen from 14.5 percent to 4 percent in the entering law class of 2000.

Jennifer Gratz had a 3.8 high school grade point average and an American College Test (ACT) score of 25 when she applied in 1995 to the University of Michigan campus in Ann Arbor. Her qualifications would have won her automatic admission if she were a minority applicant. The admissions office ranked applicants based on a 150-point index, and all minority applicants were awarded 20 bonus points. After Gratz was rejected, she too sued, and Bollinger, who had become the university president, was named as the defendant.

Justice O'Connor, like her friend and mentor Justice Lewis Powell Jr., held the crucial middle position between the Court's conservative and liberal factions. She affirmed Powell's approach in *Bakke*. Colleges and universities may consider an individual minority applicant's race as a plus in order to achieve diversity, but they may not use a "mechanized selection" system, she said. O'Connor spoke for a 5-4 majority that upheld the law school's admissions policy in *Grutter v. Bollinger* (2003).[219] She also joined the 6-3 majority in *Gratz v. Bollinger* (2003) that struck down Michigan's undergraduate admissions policy because of its point system.[220]

Though O'Connor had been skeptical of the government's use of race-based criteria for awarding construction contracts or broadcast licenses, she said higher education was different. College officials had a duty to educate the next generation of leaders, and the nation needs leaders who reflect the diversity of the United States, she said. She pointed to friend-of-the-court briefs that influenced her thinking. One from former military leaders stressed the importance of an officer corps that included blacks and Hispanics. To achieve an officer corps that is "both highly qualified and racially diverse" requires a "limited use of race-conscious recruiting and admissions policies" at the U.S. service academies, she said. Similarly, corporate executives stressed that they too need a diverse group to serve a global market.

"We agree that ... our country's most selective institutions must remain both diverse and selective," O'Connor wrote in *Grutter v. Bollinger*. "In order to cultivate a set of leaders with legitimacy in the eyes of the citizenry, it is necessary that the path to leadership be visibly open to talented and qualified individuals of every race and ethnicity.... Just as growing up in a particular region or having particular professional experiences is likely to affect an individual's views, so too is one's own, unique experience of being a racial minority in a society, like our own, in which race unfortunately still matters." The law school's leaders said they need affirmative action to achieve diversity, and, she added, "Our holding today is in keeping with our tradition of giving a degree of deference to a university's academic decisions, within constitutionally prescribed limits."[221]

Besides fulfilling a "compelling" goal, the law school's admissions policy also passes the Court's "narrow-tailoring" test, she said. "When using race as a 'plus' factor in university admissions, a university admissions program must remain flexible enough to ensure that each applicant is evaluated as an individual and not in a way that makes an applicant's race or ethnicity the defining feature of his or her application." The law school "engages in a highly individualized, holistic review of each applicant's file," she said, and "awards no mechanical, predetermined diversity 'bonuses' based on race or ethnicity."[222]

In a concluding comment, O'Connor repeated her earlier view that affirmative action should be a "temporary matter," not a "permanent justification for racial preferences.... We expect that 25 years from now, the use of racial preferences will no longer be necessary to further the interest approved today."[223] Justices Stevens, Souter, Ginsburg, and Breyer joined O'Connor's opinion in the law school case. In a concurring opinion, Ginsburg and Breyer cast doubt on O'Connor's twenty-five-year limit for affirmative action. "It remains the current reality that many minority students encounter markedly inadequate and unequal educational opportunities," Ginsburg wrote. "From today's vantage point, one may hope, but not firmly forecast, that over the next generation's span, progress toward nondiscrimination and genuinely equal opportunity will make it safe to sunset affirmative action."[224]

Two dissenters, Justices Scalia and Thomas, said they saw nothing to like in O'Connor's opinion, except her comment that affirmative action should end in twenty-five years. Scalia called the law school's admissions policy "a sham to cover a scheme of racially proportionate admissions."[225] In the longest dissent, Justice Clarence Thomas quoted abolitionist Frederick Douglass and his speech to a Boston audience in 1865: "What I ask for the Negro is not benevolence, not pity, not sympathy, but simple justice.... Do nothing with us. If the Negro cannot stand on his own legs, let him fall also. All I ask, give him a chance to stand on his own legs! Let him alone."[226] "Like Douglass, I believe blacks can achieve in every avenue of American life without the meddling of university administrators. Because I wish to see all students succeed whatever their color, I share, in some respect, the sympathies of those who sponsor the type of discrimination advanced by the University of Michigan Law School. The Constitution does not, however, tolerate institutional devotion to the status quo in admissions policies when such devotion ripens into racial discrimination," Thomas wrote. "The Constitution abhors classifications based on race, not only because those classifications can harm favored races or are based on illegitimate motives, but also because every time the government places citizens on racial registers and makes race relevant to the provision of burdens or benefits, it demeans us all."[227]

Chief Justice Rehnquist and Justice Kennedy also dissented.

In *Gratz v. Bollinger*, Rehnquist said Michigan's undergraduate admissions policy put too much emphasis on race. The system of bonus points "makes race a decisive factor for virtually every minimally qualified underrepresented minority student," he wrote.[228] Justices O'Connor, Scalia, Kennedy, and Thomas joined his opinion, while Justice Breyer concurred in the result. Two of the dissenters, Justices Ginsburg and Souter, questioned striking down the undergraduate admissions policy if its goal—achieving racial diversity—is deemed as legitimate. If colleges may consider a minority applicant's race in order to enroll more minorities, they asked, why not use numbers? "If honesty is the best policy, surely Michigan's accurately described, fully disclosed college affirmative action program is preferable to achieving similar numbers through winks, nods and disguises," Ginsburg said.[229]

Despite the split decisions in the two cases, university officials and civil rights advocates hailed the Court for preserving affirmative action in higher education. While colleges are not required to consider the race of applicants, they may do so in a limited way if they focus on individuals, the Court concluded.

Equal Protection: The Alien and the Poor

The Supreme Court's protection of aliens—persons born in another country who have not become U.S. citizens—expanded gradually, as it did for blacks and other racial minorities. In time, laws discriminating against aliens would receive the greatest scrutiny under the Fourteenth Amendment's guarantee of equality. Other cases would test whether strict scrutiny applied to discrimination based on sex, relative wealth, or education. By the mid-1990s, the Court still reserved the greatest protection and strictest judicial scrutiny for race and alienage alone. *(See "Compromise Standard," pp. 459–462.)*

ALIENS AND THE LAW

Congress has exclusive authority to determine who may enter the United States, and once an alien is admitted, he or she is entitled to the equal protection of its laws. In *Yick Wo v. Hopkins* (1886), the Court declared that the Fourteenth Amendment protected persons, not just citizens. The Civil War amendment applies "to all *persons* within the territorial jurisdiction, without regard to any differences of race, of color, or of nationality; and the equal protection of the laws is a pledge of the protection of equal laws."[1] In eighty-five more years the Supreme Court would declare alienage, like race, a "suspect" category justifiable only by a compelling government interest. Before then, however, the justices, beginning with *Yick Wo* and with one period of exception, had required states to show more than a merely rational basis for a legal distinction between aliens and citizens. As a result, aliens initially fared better under the Court's application of the Fourteenth Amendment's Equal Protection Clause than did the blacks who were expected by the authors of the clause to be its primary beneficiaries.

In *Yick Wo v. Hopkins* (1886), involving a Chinese laundry owner whose license to operate in San Francisco had not been renewed by city officials, the Supreme Court ruled that the Fourteenth Amendment protects all persons, not just citizens of the United States.

Yick Wo involved a San Francisco ordinance that, to minimize fire hazards, required operators of wooden laundries to obtain a license from the city. Although Yick Wo's laundry had been declared safe by city fire and health officials, municipal authorities declined to renew his license. When he discovered that most Chinese owners of wooden laundries had been denied permits, while most white laundry owners were granted them, he sued, charging that he had been denied equal protection of the laws. Sustaining the charge, a unanimous Supreme Court wrote,

> Though the law itself be fair on its face and impartial in appearance, yet, if it is applied and administered

by public authority with an evil eye and an unequal hand, so as practically to make unjust and illegal discriminations between persons in similar circumstances, material to their rights, the denial of equal justice is still within the prohibition of the Constitution.[2]

Because the city offered no explanation for its discrimination, "the conclusion cannot be resisted, that no reason for it exists except hostility to the race and nationality to which the petitioners belong, and which in the eye of the law is not justified," the Court wrote.[3] Yick Wo's case involved his right to earn a living, a right the Court said that was "essential to the enjoyment of life." The Court amplified this holding in *Truax v. Raich* (1915). Arizona law required that 80 percent of the workers in establishments with more than five employees be U.S. citizens. When a restaurant owner fired Mike Raich, an Austrian native, in order to comply with the statute, Raich charged that he had been denied equal protection. Agreeing, the Supreme Court declared the state law unconstitutional. Justice Charles Evans Hughes wrote the opinion:

It requires no argument to show that the right to work for a living in the common occupations of the community is of the very essence of the personal freedom and opportunity that it was the purpose of the [Fourteenth] Amendment to secure.... If this could be refused solely upon the ground of race or nationality, the prohibition of the denial to any person of the equal protection of the laws would be a barren form of words."[4]

Within twelve years *Raich* would prove rather barren. In 1915 the country was already growing suspicious of and antagonistic toward immigrants from certain countries. Historians Alfred H. Kelly and Winfred A. Harbison describe that prejudice, which would peak in the 1920s:

The average middle class "old American" of the twenties believed firmly that both the Communist and anarchist menaces and the contemporary alarming increase in urban crime were due to the presence of undesirable aliens in the country. Much contemporary xenophobic sentiment also was laden with religious and racial prejudice. Conservative Protestants feared and resented the recent heavy influx of Catholic immigrants from Italy and Poland, while the swarthy new-comers from southern and eastern Europe as well as those from Japan and Asia were looked upon as "unassimilable" and a threat to American racial purity.[5]

Congress passed laws requiring the deportation of aliens convicted of crimes and subversive activity. It also established immigration quotas, based on national origin, that heavily favored the immigrants of northwestern Europe. In 1924 the legislature passed a second law that effectively barred most immigration from Asia.

State Government

Like Congress, the Supreme Court was not immune to public prejudice against aliens. Beginning in 1914, it condoned state laws excluding aliens from certain activities and jobs cloaked with a special public interest. The Court had ruled in *McCready v. Virginia* (1877) that the state could prohibit residents of other states from planting oysters in its tidal streams. The right to use such streams was a property right, and the Privilege and Immunity Clause did not invest "the citizens of one state ... with any interest in the common property of the citizens of another state."[6] The Court extended this special public interest rule to aliens in 1914, when it upheld a Pennsylvania statute forbidding aliens to shoot wild game and, to that end, to possess shotguns and rifles.

Wild game, like a tidal stream, was a natural resource that a state may preserve for its own citizens "if it pleases," the Court said in *Patsone v. Pennsylvania* (1914). To that purpose, the state may make classifications, and if the class "discriminated against is or reasonably might be considered to define those from whom the evil mainly is to be feared," the classification is permissible, wrote Justice Oliver Wendell Holmes Jr.[7] No evidence was presented to support a contention that aliens shot more game than any other class, but the majority would not say the state was wrong in identifying aliens "as the peculiar source of the evil that it desired to prevent."[8] In 1915 the Court used the special public interest test to uphold the right of a state to confine hiring on state public works projects to U.S. citizens.[9]

In the early 1920s, several western states seeking to discourage Japanese immigration passed laws barring aliens ineligible for citizenship from owning or leasing agricultural lands. The Court in 1922 interpreted the federal laws restricting citizenship as allowing only whites and blacks of African descent to become citizens.[10] As a result, the alien land laws applied primarily to Japanese aliens. In 1923 the Court upheld these laws. Because the federal government recognized only two classes of aliens—those who were eligible for citizenship and those who were not—the states were not required to justify similar laws passed by their legislatures. "The rule established by Congress on this subject, in and of itself, furnishes a reasonable basis for classification in a state law," the Court said in *Terrace v. Thompson* (1923).[11]

In 1927 the Court appeared to abandon its 1915 decision that states may not deny aliens opportunities to hold "the common occupations of the community" solely because they are aliens. At the same time the Court adopted a more relaxed standard of review for state classifications based on alienage. *Clarke v. Deckebach* (1927) concerned a Cincinnati ordinance that barred aliens from operating pool and billiards halls. The city justified this classification by arguing that pool halls were evil places frequented by lawbreakers and were the scenes of many crimes. Because aliens were less familiar with the laws and customs of the country, their operation of these pool halls constituted a menace to the public, the city claimed. Upholding the ordinance, the unanimous Court said that while the Fourteenth Amendment prohibits "plainly irrational discrimination against aliens … it does not follow that alien race and allegiance may not bear in some instances such a relation to a legitimate object of legislation as to be made the basis of a permissible classification."[12] Enunciating its new standard of scrutiny, the Court wrote,

> It is enough for present purposes that the ordinance, in the light of facts admitted or generally assumed, does not preclude the possibility of a rational basis for the legislative judgment and that we have no such knowledge of local conditions as would enable us to say that it is clearly wrong.

It was competent for the city to make such a choice, not shown to be irrational, by excluding from the conduct of a dubious business an entire class rather than its objectionable members selected by more empirical means.[13]

Thus the Fourteenth Amendment no longer protected aliens seeking to work at ordinary jobs. The Court now allowed a city or state to deny rights to all aliens on the presumption that some aliens would act in an unacceptable manner. It was left to the alien class to prove the presumption irrational. Fortunately for aliens, this standard was relatively short-lived.

A Closer Scrutiny

The Court first indicated a changed attitude toward questions of alienage and national origin in two World War II cases that concerned U.S. citizens of Asian descent. Both involved Japanese Americans who had failed to comply with military orders first restricting the movements of Japanese Americans living on the West Coast and then confining them to detention camps for eventual relocation away from the coast. In both cases, the Court held that such extreme discrimination against these citizens was justified by the necessities of war and the need to protect the country from the possibility that some disloyal Japanese Americans might collaborate with the Japanese enemy. In both cases, however, the Court said distinctions based on race and ancestry merited close scrutiny and could be justified only by such "pressing public necessity" as war.[14]

In the late 1940s, the Court effectively reversed its position on alien land laws. *Oyama v. California* (1948) involved a Japanese alien, Kajiro Oyama, who had purchased some agricultural property as a gift to his minor son, Fred Oyama, a U.S. citizen by birth. Kajiro Oyama was then appointed his son's guardian, which allowed him to work the land for the benefit of his son. The state charged Oyama with attempting to evade the alien land law, and Oyama in turn charged that both he and his son were denied equal protection of the laws by that law. The Supreme Court ruled, 6-3, that the state law indeed deprived the citizen son of equal protection:

There remains the question of whether discrimination between citizens on the basis of their racial descent, as revealed in this case, is justifiable. Here we start with the proposition that only the most exceptional circumstances can excuse discrimination on that basis in the face of the equal protection clause and a federal statute giving all citizens the right to own land.... The only justification urged upon us by the State is that the discrimination is necessary to prevent evasion of the Alien Land Law.... In the light most favorable to the State, this case presents a conflict between the State's right to formulate a policy of landholding within its bounds and the right of American citizens to own land anywhere in the United States. When these two rights clash, the rights of a citizen may not be subordinated merely because of his father's country of origin.[15]

The majority did not decide whether the alien father had been denied equal protection of the laws, but the decision stripped the law of much of its effectiveness.

Six months later, the Court, 7-2, rejected its reasoning in *Deckebach* and returned to its earlier position that the right to earn a living was a liberty that could not be denied an alien solely on the basis of race or national origin. *Takahashi v. Fish and Game Commission* (1948) involved a 1943 California law that prohibited alien Japanese from fishing in the state's coastal waters. In 1945 the state amended the law to extend the ban to all aliens ineligible for citizenship. In effect, this meant Japanese aliens, because a 1946 federal law made Filipinos and persons of races indigenous to India eligible for citizenship. Torao Takahashi, a fisherman denied a license, charged that he had been denied equal protection by the 1945 state law.

Sustaining the charge, the Court reversed its previous position that a state could make the same alienage classifications as the federal government. "It does not follow," wrote Justice Hugo L. Black for the majority, "that because the United States regulates immigration and naturalization in part on the basis of race and color classifications, a state can adopt one or more of the same classifications."[16] The Constitution gives Congress complete authority over admission and naturalization of aliens. "State laws which impose discriminatory burdens

upon the entrance or residence of aliens lawfully within the United States conflict with this constitutionally derived federal power to regulate immigration," Black wrote.[17] Furthermore, the majority rejected California's claim that the fish in its offshore waters were a natural resource that the state could reserve for its own citizens under the special public interest rule:

> To whatever extent the fish in the three-mile belt off California may be "capable of ownership" by California, we think that the "ownership" is inadequate to justify California in excluding any or all aliens who are lawful residents of the State from making a living by fishing in the ocean off its shores while permitting all others to do so.[18]

The Modern Standard

Questions of discrimination against aliens did not come before the Court again until the 1970s. In its first important alien case of this period, *Graham v. Richardson* (1971), a unanimous Court asserted that

> classifications based on alienage, like those based on nationality or race, are inherently suspect and subject to close judicial scrutiny. Aliens as a class are a prime example of a "discrete and insular" minority ... for whom such heightened judicial solicitude is appropriate.[19]

Graham concerned an Arizona statute that restricted certain welfare benefits to citizens and aliens who had resided in the United States for at least fifteen years. A second case, consolidated with *Graham,* tested a Pennsylvania statute that denied certain welfare benefits to all aliens. By its declaration that classification by alienage was inherently suspect, the Court required states to show a compelling governmental interest to justify making that distinction. The claim that the special public interest rule allows a state to "preserve limited welfare benefits for its own citizens is inadequate" to justify the classification, the Court said.[20] Aliens as well as residents pay state and federal taxes. "There can be no 'special public interest' in tax revenues to which aliens have contributed on an equal basis with the residents of the State," the Court said.[21]

Over the next few years, the Court applied close judicial scrutiny and found no compelling interest in several state laws denying aliens certain benefits or the opportunity to work in certain professions. The Court struck down a Connecticut law that barred aliens from being licensed as lawyers, a Puerto Rico law that barred them from becoming engineers, a New York law that excluded aliens from the state's competitive civil service, and a Texas law barring resident aliens from the job of notary public. It also struck down a New York law that excluded resident aliens who did not intend to become citizens from eligibility for state financial aid for higher education.[22]

In *Sugarman v. Dougall* (1973), the New York case concerning civil service employment, the state contended that it should be allowed to exclude aliens from governmental policymaking positions because aliens might not be "free of competing obligations to another power."[23] The Court observed that not all members of the competitive civil service held policy-formulating positions. At the same time, the state allowed aliens to serve in other branches of the state civil service in both policymaking and non-policymaking jobs. Applying strict scrutiny, the Court held that the statute must fall because it "is neither narrowly confined nor precise in its application."[24] In *dicta* at the end of that unanimous opinion, however, the Court said states might require a person to be a citizen in order to exercise certain rights, such as voting, or to hold certain positions essential to the maintenance of representative government. Among these positions were "state elective or important non-elective executive, legislative, and judicial positions, for officers who participate directly in the formulation, execution, or review of broad public policy perform functions that go to the heart of representative government."[25]

The Court further stated that its scrutiny would "not be so demanding where we deal with matters resting firmly within the State's constitutional prerogatives."[26] In 1978 this statement provided the basis for a decision in which the Supreme Court, 6-3, upheld a New York statute requiring all its state police to be U.S. citizens. Writing for the majority, Chief Justice Warren E. Burger found police among the category of those who participated in making or carrying out governmental policy. Therefore, the state could require them to be citizens. Burger explained: "The essence of our holdings to date is that although we extend to aliens the right to education and public welfare, along with the ability to earn a livelihood and engage in licensed professions, the right to govern is reserved to citizens."[27] Because the right to govern fell within the state's constitutional prerogatives, the state needed only to prove that it had a rational basis for excluding aliens from police positions. Because police generally execute public policy and exercise a wide variety of discretionary powers that have a significant impact on citizens, the majority felt it was rational for the state to restrict such jobs to citizens. "Clearly the exercise of police authority calls for a very high degree of judgment and discretion, the abuse or misuse of which can have serious impact on individuals," Burger said. "In short, it would be as anomalous to conclude that citizens may be subjected to the broad discretionary powers of noncitizen police officers as it would be to say that judicial officers and jurors with power to judge citizens may be aliens."[28]

In 1979 the Court, 5-4, sustained a New York law prohibiting aliens who refuse to apply for U.S. citizenship the opportunity to work as public school teachers. Because teachers play a critical role in developing the attitudes of their students toward government, society, and the political process, they fall into the category of occupations "so bound up with the operation of the State as a governmental entity" as to permit the restriction of those jobs to citizens, the majority wrote.[29] Subsequently, the Court, 5-4, upheld a California requirement that all peace officers—that is, persons with law enforcement responsibilities—be U.S. citizens. These officers, explained Justice Byron R. White in *Cabell v. Chavez-Salido* (1982), exercise and symbolize the power of the political community, and it is reasonable to require that they be citizens.[30]

The Court did not, however, see the education of children the same way. By refusing to educate illegal alien children in the public schools, Texas sought to curtail the costs those residents imposed on the state budget. This policy was challenged, and the Court, 5-4, ruled it unconstitutional in *Plyler v. Doe, Texas v. Certain Named and Unnamed Undocumented Alien Children* (1982). Illegal aliens present in the United States are accorded the full protection of the Equal Protection Clause, wrote Justice William J. Brennan Jr. for the majority. Regardless of their illegal status, they are clearly persons and may not be denied the right to a free public education. There is no national policy nor state interest sufficient to justify denying them this right, held the Court:[31]

> It is difficult to understand precisely what the State hopes to achieve by promoting the creation and perpetuation of a subclass of illiterates within our boundaries, surely adding to the problems and costs of unemployment, welfare, and crime. It is thus clear that whatever savings might be achieved by denying these children an education, they are wholly insubstantial in light of the costs involved to these children, the State, and the Nation.... If the State is to deny a discrete group of innocent children the free public education that it offers to other children residing within its borders, that denial must be justified by a showing that it furthers some substantial state interest.[32]

Federal Government

The Court has traditionally allowed the federal government to treat citizens and aliens differently. Because the Constitution gives Congress absolute authority over immigrants' admission to the United States and their naturalization, the Supreme Court requires Congress only to present some rational basis for making a distinction between citizen and alien or between some aliens and other aliens. A unanimous Court in *Mathews v. Diaz* (1976) upheld a Medicare regulation that made aliens who were not permanent residents of the country for at least five years ineligible for supplementary medical benefits:

> [T]he fact that Congress has provided some welfare benefits for citizens does not require it to provide like benefits for all aliens. Neither the overnight visitor, the unfriendly agent of a hostile foreign power, the resident diplomat, nor the illegal entrant, can advance even a colorable constitutional claim to a

share in the bounty that a conscientious sovereign makes available to its own citizens and some of its guests. The decision to share that bounty with our guests may take into account the character of the relationship between the alien and this country: Congress may decide that as the alien's tie grows stronger, so does the strength of his claim to an equal share of the munificence....

> ... In short, it is unquestionably reasonable for Congress to make an alien's eligibility depend on both the character and the duration of his residence. Since neither requirement is wholly irrational, this case essentially involves nothing more than a claim that it would have been more reasonable for Congress to select somewhat different requirements of the same kind.[33]

In addition, because the benefit issue raised was a question of degree rather than kind, the Court said it was "especially reluctant to question the exercise of congressional judgment."[34]

In a second case decided the same day, the Court, 5-4, ruled that the Civil Service Commission violated the Fifth Amendment due process guarantee by excluding all aliens from the federal competitive civil service and therefore denying them the opportunity for employment in a major sector of the economy. The denial affected an aspect of liberty protected by the Fifth Amendment, the majority said in *Hampton v. Mow Sun Wong* (1976):

> Since these resident ... [aliens] were admitted as a result of decisions made by the Congress and the President ... due process requires that the decision to impose that deprivation of an important liberty be made either at a comparable level of government or, if it is permitted to be made by the Civil Service Commission, that it be justified by reasons which are properly the concern of that agency.[35]

The only reason offered that properly concerned the agency was administrative efficiency, noted the majority. Although it was reasonable for the agency to make a single rule applicable to all aliens, such an arbitrary rule did not outweigh "the public interest in avoiding the wholesale deprivation of employment opportunities caused" by the rule, which therefore must fall.[36] Three months later, President Gerald R.

Ford issued an executive order authorizing the Civil Service Commission to continue to exclude noncitizens from the federal competitive civil service.

POVERTY AND EQUAL PROTECTION

Discrimination against poor people because of their poverty has not been declared inherently unconstitutional by the Supreme Court, but individual justices have endorsed that belief. The Court, however, has found wealth-based classifications in violation of the equal protection guarantee when they deprive poor people of fundamental rights and interests with no compelling state interest to justify the discrimination. On this basis, the Court has invalidated classifications by wealth that impede access to justice, the right to travel freely between states, and the right to vote and run for public office.

Efforts to persuade the Court to classify all distinctions based on wealth as inherently suspect and to raise vital interests, such as education, to the status of fundamental rights have been unsuccessful. Where the Court has found that a classification by wealth does not involve a fundamental interest, it has applied the traditional equal protection test in which the state must only show a rational basis to justify the distinction between rich and poor.

Access to Justice

Griffin v. Illinois (1956) was the first case in which the Court held a wealth-based classification to violate the equal protection guarantee. Judson Griffin and James Crenshaw were convicted of armed robbery. Because they were indigent, the two asked for a free transcript of their trial for use in preparing an appeal. After their request was refused, the two charged that the refusal denied them due process and equal protection. The Supreme Court agreed, 5-4. Justice Hugo L. Black wrote the opinion, joined by only three other justices. Justice Felix Frankfurter concurred in the judgment with a separate opinion. Wrote Black,

> Both equal protection and due process emphasize the central aim of our entire judicial system—all

people charged with crime must, so far as the law is concerned, "stand on an equality before the bar of justice in every American court."... [*Chambers v. Florida*, 309 U.S. 227 at 241 (1940)] Surely no one would contend that either a State or the Federal Government could constitutionally provide that defendants unable to pay court costs in advance should be denied the right to plead not guilty or to defend themselves in court. Such a law would make the constitutional promise of a fair trial a worthless thing. Notice, the right to be heard, and the right to counsel would under such circumstances be meaningless promises to the poor. In criminal trials a State can no more discriminate on account of poverty than on account of religion, race, or color. Plainly the ability to pay costs in advance bears no rational relationship to a defendant's guilt or innocence and could not be used as an excuse to deprive a defendant of a fair trial.[37]

A state is not required by the Constitution to provide an appeals procedure, but if it chooses to do so it may not limit access to it on the basis of wealth, Black continued. "There can be no equal justice where the kind of a trial a man gets depends on the amount of money he has."[38] The four dissenters held that so long as Illinois followed its established procedure for appellate review, due process had not been denied. In addition, so long as the state opened its appeals procedure to all defendants convicted of the same crime, it did not violate equal protection even though

> some may not be able to avail themselves of the full appeal because of their poverty.... The Constitution requires the equal protection of the law, but it does not require the States to provide equal financial means for all defendants to avail themselves of such laws.[39]

An Equal Right to Appeal

By the 1970s, however, the entire Court agreed that poverty alone should not bar an indigent from appealing his or her conviction. In *Mayer v. Chicago* (1971), a unanimous Court expanded *Griffin* to hold that a state's refusal to provide a free transcript to a man so that he might appeal his misdemeanor

CLEARING THE "SLUMS" AND SEIZING HOMES

The government has the broad power of eminent domain to seize private property for public use, so long as it pays the owner "just compensation." Critics point out, however, that when eminent domain is applied, the poor and powerless often lose out to well-connected developers working with city officials. In such instances, they fault the Court for failing to protect the rights of the property owners. The case of *Kelo v. City of New London* (2005) put a national spotlight on this issue.

The state of Connecticut declared New London to be "economically distressed" after the U.S. Navy closed its Undersea Warfare Center there. To revitalize the downtown and waterfront, a city agency planned to buy up ninety acres of land in hopes of attracting hotels, restaurants, and stores and building urban townhouses. The pharmaceutical company Pfizer announced plans to build a research center there. City planners said the new development would bring jobs and more tax revenue to New London.

Susette Kelo and a few of her neighbors refused to sell their homes, even though the city would pay them at far more than their fair market value. Kelo's small, pink Victorian-style home offered a view of Long Island Sound. Neither her home nor her neighborhood could be described as "blighted." She and her neighbors sued to block the seizure of their homes. The libertarian Institute for Justice took up their case and argued that it was unconstitutional for the government to seize private property to make way for private development. They relied on the Fifth Amendment, which states that "private property [shall not] be taken for public use, without just compensation."

In *Kelo v. New London* (2005), the Supreme Court in a 5-4 decision upheld the city's authority to seize the land and the homes.[1] Justice John Paul Stevens cited a long series of rulings "reflecting our longstanding policy of deference to legislative judgment in this field." He noted how in the nineteenth century the government had seized land to build railroads and to flood fields with water that drove grist mills and factories. He also cited *Berman v. Parker* (1954), in which the Court upheld the razing of a neighborhood in Washington, D.C., including a department store, for the "public purpose" of revitalizing the area. Justice William O. Douglas, writing then for the same unanimous Court that had handed down the decision in *Brown v. Board of Education* (1954), described a mostly black neighborhood in Washington as a "slum area" that could "spread disease and crime and immorality." Douglas lauded the work of city planners; the Court's opinion in *Berman* gave the stamp of approval to urban renewal projects in the decades that followed.

In the *Kelo* decision, Stevens did not lavish praise on city planners, but said that judges were not well suited to decide the public value of development projects. "Promoting economic development is a traditional and long accepted function of government," he wrote. "Just as we decline to second-guess the city's considered judgments about the efficacy of its development plan, we also decline to second-guess the city's determinations as to what lands it needs to acquire in order to effectuate the project." Justices Anthony M. Kennedy, David H. Souter, Ruth Bader Ginsburg, and Stephen G. Breyer agreed.

In dissent, Justice Sandra Day O'Connor faulted the Court for abandoning a "long-held basic limitation on government power. Under the banner of economic development, all private property is now vulnerable to being taken and transferred to another private owner, so long as it might be upgraded," she wrote. "The specter of condemnation hangs over all property. Nothing is to prevent the State from replacing any Motel 6 with a Ritz-Carlton, any home with a shopping mall, or any farm with a factory." Chief Justice William H. Rehnquist and Justices Antonin Scalia and Clarence Thomas agreed. In a separate dissent, Thomas said the Court had gone wrong by ignoring the language of the Constitution and relying on its own "misguided" precedents. "Something has gone seriously awry with this Court's interpretation of the Constitution. Though citizens are safe from the government in their homes, the homes themselves are not," Thomas wrote. He and O'Connor said the victims of these redevelopment projects are most likely to be low-income, powerless persons. "Urban renewal projects have long been associated with the displacement of blacks," Thomas wrote. "In cities across the country, urban renewal came to be known as 'Negro removal,'" he said, quoting a critic of urban renewal.[2]

Justices Rehnquist, O'Connor, and Scalia also joined his dissent.

Stevens stressed that states could revise their laws to limit such seizures. "Nothing in our opinion precludes any state from placing further restrictions on its exercise of the takings power," he wrote. In the wake of the ruling, many states adopted new measures to forbid or limit the use of the eminent domain power to take homes or for the purpose of private development.

---

1. *Kelo v. New London*, 545 U.S. 469 (2005).

2. Wendall E. Pritchett, "The 'Public Menace' of Blight: Urban Renewal and the Private Uses of Eminent Domain," *Yale Law and Policy Review* 21 (2003).

conviction was a violation of equal protection. "The size of the defendant's pocketbook bears no more relationship to his guilt or innocence in a nonfelony than in a felony case," the Court declared.[40] Five years later, however, the Court limited the circumstances under which the federal government must provide transcripts at public expense. In *United States v. Mac-Collum* (1976), the justices declared that indigent convicts did not have an unlimited constitutional right to a free transcript of their trial. Congress did not violate the equal protection guarantee implicit in the Fifth Amendment when it made provision of such a transcript conditional upon a finding that the challenge to the conviction was not frivolous and that the transcript was necessary to resolve the issues presented. These conditions, the five-justice majority conceded,

> place an indigent in somewhat less advantageous position than a person of means. But neither the Equal Protection Clause of the Fourteenth Amendment nor … the Fifth Amendment … guarantees "absolute equality or precisely equal advantages."… [*San Antonio School District v. Rodriguez*, 411 U.S. 1 at 24 (1973)] In the context of a criminal proceeding, they require only an "adequate opportunity to present [one's] claims fairly." [*Ross v. Moffitt*, 417 U.S. 600 at 616 (1974)][41]

The Right to Legal Counsel

The Supreme Court held in *Gideon v. Wainwright* (1963) that a state violated due process when it refused to provide court-appointed attorneys to indigents charged with felonies. On the same day, the Court also held that a state violated equal protection if it provided attorneys to indigents appealing convictions only when the appellate court decided legal counsel would be advantageous to the success of the appeal. For the majority in *Douglas v. California*, Justice William O. Douglas wrote,

> There is lacking that equality demanded by the Fourteenth Amendment where the rich man, who appeals as of right, enjoys the benefit of counsel's examination into the record, research of the law,

and marshaling of arguments on his behalf, while the indigent, already burdened by a preliminary determination that his case is without merit, is forced to shift for himself.[42]

Justice John Marshall Harlan, who dissented in *Griffin*, also dissented in *Douglas*. He argued that the Court should have relied on the Due Process Clause rather than the equal protection guarantee to invalidate the state law:

> The States, of course, are prohibited by the Equal Protection Clause from discriminating between "rich" and "poor" as such in the formulation and application of their laws. But it is a far different thing to suggest that this provision prevents the State from adopting a law of general applicability that may affect the poor more harshly than it does the rich, or, on the other hand, from making some effort to redress economic imbalances while not eliminating them entirely.[43]

In subsequent cases the Court held that neither due process nor equal protection required a state to provide a convicted defendant with counsel so that he could seek discretionary review of his case in the state's higher courts or in the Supreme Court, rather than in an appeal to which he had a right. The state also does not deny equal protection when it requires a convicted indigent who subsequently becomes capable of repayment to reimburse the state for the costs of his court-appointed attorney.[44]

Court Costs

Justice Harlan eventually persuaded a majority of the Court that due process was the proper constitutional basis for striking down state laws discriminating against the poor. People who could not afford the sixty dollars in court costs associated with divorce proceedings were barred by Connecticut from filing for separation. Ruling against the state in *Boddie v. Connecticut* (1971), Justice Harlan for the majority pointed out that the only way to obtain a divorce was in court. By denying access to court to persons too poor to pay the fees, the state—in the absence of a "sufficient countervailing" justification—denied them due process. Harlan acknowledged that the state had an interest in curbing frivolous suits and in using court fees to offset court costs, but these reasons were not sufficient, he said, "to override the interest of these [indigents] in having access to the only avenue open for dissolving their ... marriages."[45]

Justices Douglas and William J. Brennan Jr. concurred in the result but argued that the case presented a classic denial of equal protection. "Affluence does not pass muster under the Equal Protection Clause for determining who must remain married and who shall be allowed to separate," wrote Douglas.[46]

Bankruptcy

By a 5-4 vote the Court sustained a federal law that required indigents to pay a fee to declare bankruptcy. "There is no constitutional right to obtain a discharge of one's debts in bankruptcy," the majority wrote in *United States v. Kras* (1973).[47] Because the right to file for bankruptcy was not a fundamental one, the majority ruled that the federal government need only meet the rationality test. Because it was reasonable that the bankruptcy system be self-sufficient, the government met the test. In dissent, Justice Potter Stewart said he could not agree with a decision that made "some of the poor too poor even to go bankrupt."[48]

Fines and Terms

In two unanimous decisions the Court has held that states may not substitute imprisonment for a fine that an indigent is unable to pay. In *Williams v. Illinois* (1970), the Court ruled that states could not hold poor people in prison beyond the length of the maximum sentence merely to work off a fine they were unable to pay. Forty-seven of the fifty states allowed such imprisonment. For the Court, Chief Justice Warren E. Burger wrote,

> On its face the statute extends to all defendants an apparently equal opportunity for limiting confinement to the statutory maximum simply by satisfying a money judgment. In fact, this is an illusory choice for Williams or any indigent who ... is with-

out funds. By making the maximum confinement contingent upon one's ability to pay, the State has visited different consequences on two categories of people.[49]

In 1971 the Court ruled that a "$30 or 30 days" sentence was also an unconstitutional denial of equal protection. That provision of the Fourteenth Amendment, held the Court, barred any state or municipality from limiting punishment for an offense to a fine for those who could pay, but expanding punishment for the same offense to imprisonment for those who could not.[50]

The Poor, the Right to Travel, and Political Rights

The Supreme Court has ruled that states may not discriminate against visitors and new residents. "Citizens of the United States, whether rich or poor, have the right to choose to be citizens of the state where they reside. The states, however, do not have any right to select their citizens," the Court said in *Saenz v. Roe* (1999), striking down a California law that allotted lower welfare payments to new residents.[51] The justices have not settled on which clause of the Constitution protects an individual's right to travel from state to state, but they have agreed that it is a fundamental, protected right.[52]

In 1941 the Court had unanimously struck down a depression-era law in California that made it a crime to bring "an indigent person" into the state. Fred Edwards had been convicted of having brought his wife's nearly penniless brother to California from Texas. Some of the justices had felt that the state law placed an unconstitutional burden on interstate commerce, but others considered the right to travel a "right of national citizenship" that cannot be infringed by a state.[53]

In the late 1960s, the Court struck down two state laws and a District of Columbia statute setting residence requirements for welfare recipients. In *Shapiro v. Thompson* (1969), the Court ruled, 6-3, that the residency requirements infringed on the right of poor people to move from state to state and thereby denied them due process and equal protection of the laws. "[A]ny classification which serves to penalize the exercise of that right [to travel], unless shown to be necessary to promote a *compelling* governmental interest is unconstitutional," the Court held.[54] The majority recognized the state's valid interest in maintaining the fiscal integrity of its welfare plan but did not find this interest a compelling justification for making "invidious distinctions between classes of its citizens."[55] The Court reiterated its *Shapiro* decision in 1974 when it ruled that Arizona had violated the Equal Protection Clause by requiring indigent persons to live in a county for a year before becoming eligible for free non-emergency medical care.[56]

In the 1990s, California did not deny welfare benefits to new residents, but instead sought to pay them the lower amount that they would have received in the state they had left. Justice Stevens spoke for a 7-2 majority in ruling this approach unconstitutional. The "right to travel embraces the citizen's right to be treated equally in her new state of residence," he said in *Saenz v. Roe*. Stevens described this right as one of the "privileges and immunities" protected by the Fourteenth Amendment.

The Court has ruled consistently that states may not place financial impediments in the way of a person's right to vote or otherwise participate in the political process. Rights associated with political participation are of fundamental interest to citizens, and classifications that prevent a group of people from participating may be justified only by a compelling governmental interest. *(See "Fundamental Interests," pp. 371–373.)* The poll tax was the major financial barrier to voting for many people for years. Originally conceived of as an additional source of revenue, the poll tax became in the early 1900s a discriminatory tool to bar blacks from voting. In *Breedlove v. Suttles* (1937), the Court had turned aside a charge that the poll tax denied equal protection of the laws, upholding it as a valid source of revenue.[57] In *Harper v. Virginia State Board of Elections* (1966), however, the Court overruled its 1937 decision on the ground that the poll tax denied equal protection to the poor by depriving them of the freedom to exercise their right to vote. "Wealth, like race, creed, or color, is not germane to one's ability to participate intelligently in the electoral process," the majority declared.[58] *(See "Poll Taxes," p. 183.)*

Twice the Court has held that states may not use filing fee requirements to keep poor candidates off the ballot for public office. Such restrictions violate the guarantee of equal protection not only to candidates but also to voters by limiting the choice of candidates, the Court reasoned. *Bullock v. Carter* (1972) concerned a Texas statute that based the size of primary election filing fees on the costs of conducting those elections. The fees ran as high as $8,900 for some races. Although keeping spurious candidates off the ballot was a legitimate state objective, the method selected to achieve that objective was arbitrary, the Court held, since some serious candidates were unable to pay the high filing fees while some frivolous candidates could afford them. The test applied to the challenged law was not as demanding as the compelling interest test generally used for classifications affecting fundamental interests, but it was more rigorous than the traditional equal protection test that simply required the state to show that the challenged classification had a rational basis.[59]

Bullock was expanded when the Court held that California could not deny an indigent candidate a spot on the ballot simply because he was too poor to pay the filing fee, no matter how reasonable that fee was considered to be. In *Lubin v. Panish* (1974), the Court said the state must provide alternative means for indigents to qualify for a ballot position.[60]

Education and Wealth

In 1973 the Court refused to make classifications by wealth inherently suspect or to give education the status of a "fundamental interest." This meant that the Court would not closely scrutinize a state's decision to continue financing public schools from local property taxes although that resulted in wide disparities in the amount spent per pupil in different districts. It also meant that the state would not have to prove that its financing system served a compelling state interest. In *San Antonio School District v. Rodriguez* (1973), the Court, 5-4, upheld this system of financing public education, challenged as a denial of equal protection of the laws.

FAMILY MATTERS

Because some matters of family and marital relations are of fundamental interest, classifications that restrict these relationships can be justified only by a compelling reason. The Supreme Court ruled, however, that a state statute that appeared to discriminate against large families was constitutional because it had a rational basis.

Dandridge v. Williams (1970) concerned a Maryland law that limited the maximum amount of welfare a family could receive.[1] This meant that large families received less per child in benefits than families with fewer children. Large poor families consequently charged that the state had impermissibly denied them equal protection. The Court held that the statute did not deliberately discriminate against large families but was simply a reasonable means for a state to use to allocate scarce welfare funds.

---

1. *Dandridge v. Williams*, 397 U.S. 471 (1970).

In the early 1970s, school districts in every state but Hawaii operated primarily with money raised from taxing the real property within the district. Variations in districts—the amount of taxable property, the value of the property, and the tax rate—resulted in widely differing amounts that school districts in the same state could spend for the education of their children. In Texas, where the case arose, the wealthiest district spent $594 for each schoolchild, while the poorest spent only $356. A bombshell shook the foundations of public school financing in August 1971, when the California Supreme Court declared the traditional fee structure unconstitutional because it resulted in less being spent to educate a child in one school district than in another.[61] Similar rulings followed from other state and federal courts. In Texas, the parents of Mexican American pupils in San Antonio brought a similar suit, and in December 1971 a federal court found the Texas system unconstitutional. The state appealed to the Supreme Court.

Critical to the holding of the five-justice majority, for whom Justice Lewis F. Powell Jr. wrote, were its findings that the Texas system did not disadvantage an identifiable group of poor persons and that the Constitution makes no mention of a right to education. In previous cases classifications by wealth were found unconstitutionally discriminatory, wrote Powell, because the groups or individuals affected "were completely unable to pay for some desired benefit, and as a consequence, they sustained an absolute deprivation of a meaningful opportunity to enjoy that benefit." In *Rodriguez*, however, there was no showing that the financing system disadvantaged any definable indigent group or that the poorest people were concentrated in the poorest school districts. Justice Powell explained:

> The argument here is not that the children in districts having relatively low assessable property values are receiving no public education; rather, it is that they are receiving a poorer quality education than that available to children in districts having more assessable wealth. Apart from the unsettled and disputed question whether the quality of education may be determined by the amount of money expended for it, a sufficient answer … is that at least where wealth is involved, the Equal Protection Clause does not require absolute equality or precisely equal advantages.[62]

"It is not the province of this Court to create substantive constitutional rights in the name of guaranteeing equal protection of the laws," Powell said. "[T]he undisputed importance of education will not alone cause this Court to depart from the usual standard for reviewing a State's societal and economic legislation."[63] The question remaining was whether it was reasonable for the state to use the property tax to finance public schools. The majority concluded that it was rational:

> [T]o the extent that the Texas system of school finance results in unequal expenditures between children who happen to reside in different districts, we cannot say that such disparities are the product of a system that is so irrational as to be invidiously discriminatory.... The Texas plan is not the result of hurried, ill-conceived legislation. It certainly is not the product of purposeful discrimination against any group or class. On the contrary, it is rooted in decades of experience in Texas and elsewhere, and in major part is the product of responsible studies by qualified people.... One must also remember that the system here challenged is not peculiar to Texas.... In its essential characteristics, the Texas plan for financing public education reflects what many educators for a half century have thought was an enlightened approach to a problem for which there is no perfect solution. We are unwilling to assume for ourselves a level of wisdom superior to that of legislators, scholars, and educational authorities in 50 States, especially where the alternatives proposed are only recently conceived and nowhere yet tested. The constitutional standard under the Equal Protection Clause is whether the challenged state action rationally furthers a legitimate state purpose or interest.... We hold that the Texas plan abundantly satisfies this standard.[64]

The four dissenters wanted to overturn the Texas system. Justices Douglas and Thurgood Marshall contended that classification by wealth demanded strict scrutiny and that education was a fundamental interest. Children in property-poor districts were unconstitutionally discriminated against, wrote Marshall, and the Court should not judge the instrument of their discrimination against the "lenient standard of rationality which we have traditionally applied ... in the context of economic and commercial matters."[65] Marshall rejected "the majority's labored efforts to demonstrate that fundamental interests ... encompass only established rights which we are somehow bound to recognize from the text of the Constitution itself."[66] The right to an education was fundamental, he said, because it was so intimately related to such rights as the right of expressing and receiving information and ideas as guaranteed by the First Amendment. Justices Douglas, Brennan, and Byron R. White said that the school financing system was not rational.

Following the *Rodriguez* decision, Texas school finance reform advocates, along with advocates for reform in other states, turned to litigating this issue in state courts on independent state constitutional grounds during the 1980s. With the rise of the new judicial federalism, many state judges have interpreted state constitutional provisions more broadly than their federal counterparts. In the case of public education, a number of state constitutions include provisions dealing directly with public provision of education, something about which the federal constitution is silent. In Texas, and in several other states, the state supreme court has overturned grossly inequitable financing schemes.

Sex Discrimination

It took the Supreme Court almost a century to extend the guarantee of equal protection to blacks, and it took even longer for it to extend the same guarantee to women. Only in the 1970s did the Court begin to apply the equal protection guarantee to gender-based discrimination. This form of discrimination is still measured against a lower standard than is racial discrimination. The Court has taken important steps toward placing men and women on an equal footing before the law, but it continues to uphold some laws—most notably those excluding women from the military draft—based on traditional beliefs about the respective roles of men and women.

"ROMANTIC PATERNALISM"

The Supreme Court's attitude toward women and their role in the political and economic life of the nation has tended to reflect the prevailing societal attitudes of the time. Early on, the Court adopted a protectionist philosophy, described as "romantic paternalism," to justify discrimination against women. In *Bradwell v. Illinois* (1873), a Chicago woman appealed to the Supreme Court to overturn a state law barring women from practicing law. Relying on the view of woman as wife, mother, and homemaker, the Court upheld the statute. In the Court's opinion, Justice Samuel F. Miller did not discuss the gender issue but simply held that the Fourteenth Amendment did not affect state authority to regulate admission of members to its bar. In a concurring opinion, Justice Joseph P. Bradley gave judicial cognizance to the then-common belief that women were unfit by nature to hold certain occupations:

> [T]he civil law, as well as nature herself, has always recognized a wide difference in the respective spheres and destinies of man and woman. Man is, or should be, woman's protector and defender. The natural

and proper timidity and delicacy which belongs to the female sex evidently unfits it for many of the occupations of civil life. The constitution of the family organization, which is founded in divine ordinance, as well as in the nature of things, indicates the domestic sphere as that which properly belongs to the domain and functions of womanhood.[1]

The Fourteenth Amendment did not compel the states to admit women to the bar or to allow women to vote or serve on juries. In *Minor v. Happersett* (1875), the Court held that although women were citizens, the right to vote was not a privilege or immunity of national citizenship before adoption of the Fourteenth Amendment nor did the amendment add suffrage to the privileges and immunities of national citizenship. Therefore, the national government could not require states to permit women to vote.[2] In this respect, women fared worse than blacks, whose right to vote was specifically protected by the Fifteenth Amendment. Not until ratification in 1920 of the Nineteenth Amendment were women assured of the right to vote. *(See "No Privilege or Immunity or Federal Voting Right," pp. 175–176.)* The Court in 1880 ruled that the Fourteenth Amendment did not prohibit the states from excluding women from jury duty. This position, reaffirmed as recently as 1961, was overturned by the Court's decision in *Taylor v. Louisiana* (1975).[3] *(See box, Women on Jury Duty, p. 458.)*

Romantic paternalism again came into play when the Court upheld laws intended to protect women's morals. In 1904 it affirmed the validity of a Denver ordinance prohibiting the sale of liquor to women and barring women from working in bars or stores where liquor was sold.[4] Four decades later, in *Goesaert v. Cleary* (1948), the Court sustained a Michigan law that forbade a woman to serve as a bartender unless she was the wife or daughter of the bar's owner. The majority thought it was reasonable for Michigan to believe "that the oversight assured through ownership of a bar by a barmaid's husband or father minimizes hardships that may confront a barmaid without such protecting oversight."[5] Three justices, however, disagreed, contending that the statute made an unjustifiable and therefore unconstitutional distinction between male and female bar owners. "A male bar owner, although he himself is always absent from his bar, may employ his wife and daughter as barmaids," they wrote, while a "female [bar] owner may neither work as a barmaid herself nor employ her daughter in that position."[6] The real purpose of the statute, implied the dissenters, was not to protect women's morals but men's jobs.

Paternalism was also evident in the Court's response to other cases involving working women. In the early 1900s, the Court upheld state laws setting maximum hours and minimum wages for women while holding similar regulations for men a violation of the right to contract their labor. The typical justification of this distinction was provided by the Court's unanimous decision in *Muller v. Oregon* (1908) upholding a state law that set maximum hours for women laundry workers:

> The two sexes differ in structure of body, in the functions to be performed by each, in the amount of physical strength, in the capacity for long-continued labor, particularly when done standing, the influence of vigorous health upon the future well-being of the race, the self-reliance which enables one to assert full rights, and in the capacity to maintain the struggle for subsistence. This difference justifies a difference in legislation and upholds that which is designed to compensate for some of the burdens which rest upon [women].[7]

The civil rights movement of the 1950s and 1960s aroused a new national sensitivity to all forms of discrimination, including that based on sex. Even a cursory examination of the record showed that the traditional protectionist view of women as wives and mothers had contributed substantially to the discrimination they suffered in a modern era in which more and more women worked to support themselves and their families. Because women had been expected to remain at home, they were generally less well educated

than men. As a result, women seeking jobs outside the home usually qualified only for low-paying, low-skill jobs where opportunities for advancement were limited. Frequently women were paid less than men who performed the same job, often on the theory that women's earnings were less vital to the support of their families than were men's. Certain legal rights and benefits accrued to women only through their presumed dependency on their husbands and not to them as individuals. As a lower court wrote in 1971, "The pedestal upon which women have been placed has,... upon closer inspection, been revealed as a cage."[8]

Congress began to act to remedy some of the more obvious inequities in 1963 when it adopted the Equal Pay Act. Title VII of the Civil Rights Act of 1964 prohibited employment discrimination on the basis of sex. In 1972 Congress barred gender-based discrimination in all education programs that received federal support. It also passed the proposed Equal Rights Amendment to the Constitution, which would guarantee women and men equal rights under the law if ratified by three-fourths of the states. In 1973 it approved a bill prohibiting lenders from denying credit on the basis of sex or marital status.

Challenges to laws and practices that discriminated against women, and occasionally against men, began to reach the Court in the 1970s. Although the Court consistently held that classifications based on sex could be challenged as violating the equal protection guarantee, the justices were unable for several years to agree on the standard to use in deciding whether such classifications were justified and constitutional. An intermediate scrutiny test, used first in a 1976 case and adopted by majorities in the 1980s, eventually became the rule. Some individual justices, however, continued to press for measuring sex discrimination against the same tough standard of strict scrutiny that is applied to charges of racial bias.

THE SEARCH FOR A STANDARD

Rationality was the standard applied in *Reed v. Reed* (1971). The case arose after a minor child in Idaho died intestate, without a will. His adoptive parents, Sally and

Cecil Reed, were separated; both filed competing petitions to serve as administrator of the child's estate. The Court awarded the appointment to the father because the Idaho statute designating those eligible to administer intestate estates gave preference to males. Sally Reed challenged the statute as a violation of the Equal Protection Clause of the Fourteenth Amendment. In an opinion written by Chief Justice Warren E. Burger, a unanimous Court struck down the Idaho statute. It was the first time that the Supreme Court had held a state law invalid because it discriminated against women.

Quoting from a 1920 decision, Burger said that to be constitutionally permissible, a gender-based classification "must be reasonable, not arbitrary, and must rest upon some ground of difference having a fair and substantial relation to the object of the legislation so that all persons similarly circumstanced shall be treated alike."[9] Applying that standard, the Court could find no rational basis for giving men preference over women. The statute's purpose was to reduce the work of probate courts by eliminating one source of controversy in probate cases, the Court said. But "[t]o give a mandatory preference to members of either sex over members of the other, merely to accomplish the elimination of hearings on the merits, is to make the very kind of arbitrary legislative choice forbidden by the Equal Protection Clause," the Court concluded.[10] Using the rationality standard, the Court in several cases upheld gender-based classifications, sustaining the following:

- *Kahn v. Shevin* (1974), a Florida property tax exemption for widows but not for widowers. The majority found the exemption "reasonably designed to further the state policy of cushioning the financial impact of spousal loss upon the sex for whom that loss imposes a disproportionately heavy burden."[11]

- *Schlesinger v. Ballard* (1975), a federal law that allows certain female naval officers to serve longer than male officers before mandatory discharge upon failure to win promotion. Observing that female officers could not compete with male officers to win promotion through combat or sea duty, the majority thought it reasonable for Congress to give them a longer period in which to earn advancement.[12]

- *Weinberger v. Salfi* (1975), a Social Security regulation that denies survivors' benefits to widows married less than three months before their husband's death. The majority said such denials were a rational means of preventing sham marriages solely for the purpose of obtaining Social Security benefits.[13]

- *Mathews v. De Castro* (1976), a Social Security regulation providing benefits to married women under age sixty-two with a minor dependent whose husbands were retired or disabled but not to divorced women in the same circumstances.[14]

In the 1970s, the Court used the rationality standard to strike down a Utah law that required divorced fathers to support their sons to age twenty-one but their daughters only to age eighteen. The Court in *Stanton v. Stanton* (1975) rejected arguments that boys needed the longer period of parental support to obtain education and training and that girls needed a shorter period of support because they tended to mature and marry earlier than males. Present realities make education for girls as important as for boys, the majority said. "And if any weight remains in this day in the claim of earlier maturity of the female, with a concomitant inference of absence of need for support beyond 18, we fail to perceive its unquestioned truth or its significance," the Court added.[15]

Stricter Standard Advocated

In the early 1970s, four members of the Court argued for adoption of a stricter standard for gender-based laws. *Frontiero v. Richardson* (1973) involved a female air force officer who sought increased benefits for her husband as a dependent. Her request was denied because the law stipulated that while wives of members of the uniformed services were assumed to be dependents eligible for additional benefits, husbands were not and must prove actual dependence in order to be eligible. Because a federal law was involved, the officer could not challenge it under the Fourteenth Amendment's guarantee of equal protection of the laws against state action. Instead, she challenged the law as a violation of the Due Process Clause of the Fifth

THE EXTENDED FAMILY: RIGHTS OF "ILLEGITIMATE" CHILDREN, UNWED FATHERS, AND GRANDPARENTS

With the exception of designating as a "fundamental liberty" the right of fit parents to raise their children without undue state interference, the Supreme Court has been cautious about using the Constitution to decide matters of family law. On occasion, it has struck down state laws that unfairly punished children who were born out of wedlock or that denied unwed fathers all chance to raise their children. Beginning with cases in the late 1960s and early 1970s, the Court allowed "illegitimate" children the same basic rights under the Equal Protection Clause as legitimate children. For example, in 1972 it struck down a state law that denied illegitimate children any share in workers' compensation survivors' benefits paid automatically to legitimate children. "The status of illegitimacy has expressed through the ages society's condemnation of irresponsible liaisons beyond the bonds of marriage," the Court said.

> But visiting this condemnation on the head of an infant is illogical and unjust. Moreover, imposing disabilities on the illegitimate child is contrary to the basic concept of our system that legal burdens should bear some relationship to individual responsibility or wrongdoing. Obviously, no child is responsible for his birth and penalizing the illegitimate child is an ineffectual—as well as an unjust—way of deterring the parent.[1]

Using similar reasoning, the Court rejected state laws forbidding illegitimate children to recover damages in the wrongful death of their mother and, conversely, a mother from recovering damages for the wrongful death of her illegitimate child.[2] It also voided a state law giving legitimate, but not illegitimate, children an enforceable right to support from their natural fathers.[3]

RIGHTS OF UNWED FATHERS

In the early 1970s, the Court for the first time said unwed fathers had constitutional rights in regard to their children. Until then, many state laws failed to take them into consideration. Joan Stanley lived intermittently with Peter Stanley for eighteen years, during which time they had three children. When she died, Illinois law declared their children wards of the state, but in *Stanley v. Illinois* (1972), the Court said the state violated the Due Process and Equal Protection Clauses by excluding the father from the proceedings on the fate of his children. "[Peter] Stanley was entitled to a hearing on his fitness as a parent before his children were taken from him," the Court said.[4] In later rulings, however, the Court held that unwed fathers are not entitled to a veto over the adoption of their children, especially when they have not established a parental relationship with their offspring.[5]

In 1989 the Court further restricted the rights of unwed fathers, ruling that a state can deny child visitation rights to a biological father. The child at issue had a mother and father by marriage, but her biological father was Michael H. A blood test showed by a 98 percent probability that he was her natural father. He petitioned a court for visitation rights, while Gerald D., the married father, opposed his claim. In a 5-4 decision, the Court upheld the California law that gave parental rights to the married father and excluded the biological father.[6] Justice Antonin Scalia drew a distinction between the

Amendment, which applies to federal action. Although the Fifth Amendment does not specifically guarantee equal protection, the Court has long held that some discriminations are so unjustifiable as to be violations of the amendment's promise of due process. (*See box, Federal Equal Protection, p. 368.*)

The Court struck down the law in an 8-1 vote. In a plurality opinion announcing the decision, Justice William J. Brennan Jr. contended that gender-based classifications, like distinctions based on race and alienage, were inherently suspect. Brennan observed that a person's sex was a noncontrollable and immutable characteristic, and added

what differentiates sex from such nonsuspect statuses as intelligence or physical disability, and aligns it with the recognized suspect criteria, is that the sex characteristic frequently bears no relation to ability to perform or contribute to society. As a result, statutory distinctions between the sexes often have the effect of invidiously relegating the entire class of females to inferior legal status without regard to the actual capabilities of its individual members.[16]

Such inherently suspect classifications may be justified only by a compelling governmental interest, argued Brennan, but the government's only purpose for the gender-based distinction in this case appeared unwed father who had established a family, as had Peter Stanley, and an unwed father, like Michael H., whose claim rested on a blood test.

GRANDPARENT RIGHTS

In 2000 the Court dealt a setback to grandparents by ruling that parents are entitled to decide what's best for their children, which might in some cases involve denying grandparents visitation with their grandchildren. States began enacting visitation laws in the 1970s to help maintain extended families. Children were increasingly being cared for by persons other than their parents as they grew, and these laws were intended to resolve disputes among these caregivers. In practice, such laws also gave judges the power to take children away from mothers (and fathers) for a time so the grandchildren could be with their grandparents. In a 6-3 decision, the Court overturned a Washington state judge's order granting visitation rights to grandparents Jenifer and Gary Troxel and held that states must honor the parent's wishes.[7]

"The liberty interest at issue in this case—the interest of parents in the care, custody and control of their children—is perhaps the oldest of the fundamental liberty interests recognized by this Court," said Justice Sandra Day O'Connor.[8] The case before the Court illustrates the difficulty of the issue. The mother, Tommie Granville, had two children with Brad Troxel, but after they separated, he committed suicide. His parents sought to maintain regular contact with their granddaughters. Though the mother favored an occasional one-day visit, the Troxels went to a Washington court and sought an order that would allow them to have the granddaughters for two weekends a month and two weeks during the summer. The judge agreed, saying it would be in the best interest of the girls.

Disagreeing, the Supreme Court ruled that the state had overstepped its bounds. The Constitution "does not permit a state to infringe on the fundamental right of parents to make childbearing decisions simply because a state judge believes a 'better' decision could be made," O'Connor said.[9] Chief Justice William H. Rehnquist and Justices Ruth Bader Ginsburg and Stephen G. Breyer agreed. Justice David H. Souter concurred on the ground that Washington's law was too broad. Justice Clarence Thomas concurred as well, contending that the state had no business "secondguessing a fit parent's decision regarding visitation with third parties."[10]

---

1. *Weber v. Aetna Casualty and Surety Co.,* 406 U.S. 164 at 175 (1972).

2. *Levy v. Louisiana,* 391 U.S. 68 (1968); *Glona v. American Guarantee and Liability Insurance Co.,* 391 U.S. 73 (1968); see also *Parham v. Hughes,* 441 U.S. 347 (1979).

3. *Gomez v. Perez,* 409 U.S. 535 (1973).

4. *Stanley v. Illinois,* 405 U.S. 645 (1972).

5. *Quilloin v. Walcott,* 434 U.S. 246 (1978); *Lehr v. Robertson,* 463 U.S. 248 (1983).

6. *Michael H. v. Gerald D.,* 491 U.S. 110 (1989).

7. *Troxel v. Granville,* 530 U.S. 57 (2000).

8. Id. at 65.

9. Id. at 72–73.

10. Id. at 80.

---

to be administrative convenience, he said. Even under the less exacting standard of rationality, gender-based classifications made solely to suit administrative convenience were constitutionally impermissible.

Only three other justices agreed with Brennan's reasoning, so his view that gender-based classifications were inherently suspect remained simply an opinion without the force of law. Justice Lewis F. Powell Jr., joined by Chief Justice Burger and Justice Harry A. Blackmun, said he agreed that the classification under consideration violated the Due Process Clause. He objected, however, to placing sex-based classifications among those considered inherently suspect and

justifiable only by a compelling government interest. He maintained that application of the rationality standard to this case would have resulted in the same outcome. Justice Potter Stewart concurred in the result without subscribing to either opinion.

Arbitrary Presumptions

In *Frontiero,* the law fell because the legislators had made the unproven assumption that wives depended on their husbands for support while men did not so depend on their wives. Because this assumption did not take into account those situations in which wives are financially independent of their husbands and

Women on Jury Duty

For nearly one hundred years, the Supreme Court held that because a woman's place was in the home, she did not have to perform jury duty unless she expressed a wish to do so. Further, the exclusion of women from state court jury panels did not violate the Fourteenth Amendment, the Court ruled in *Strauder v. West Virginia* (1880).[1]

In *Hoyt v. Florida* (1961), Gwendolyn Hoyt sought to overturn her murder conviction, arguing that Florida's jury selection procedures were unconstitutional because only women who had registered for jury duty could be called, which excluded most women from service. The Court majority found the statute valid. "[W]oman is still regarded as the center of home and family life," wrote Justice John Marshall Harlan. "We cannot say that it is constitutionally impermissible for a State ... to conclude that a woman should be relieved from the civic duty of jury service unless she herself determines that such service is consistent with her own special responsibilities."[2]

Fourteen years later, the Court reversed itself. In *Taylor v. Louisiana* (1975), it ruled unconstitutional the automatic exemption of women. Billy Taylor, convicted of a crime by an all-male jury, challenged the Louisiana law that exempted women from jury service unless they volunteered. He said the law denied him his right to a fair trial. The Court agreed, reasoning that a jury comprised of a fair cross-section of the community was fundamental to the right to jury trial guaranteed by the Sixth Amendment. That guarantee was denied "if the jury pool is made up of only special segments of the populace or if large, distinctive groups are excluded from the pool," the majority said. Because 53 percent of the community was female—a large, distinctive group—the question then became whether women served "such a distinctive role" that their exclusion from jury service was justifiable.

The majority answered that it was "no longer tenable to hold that women as a class may be excluded or given automatic exemptions based solely on sex if the consequence is that criminal jury venires are almost totally male.... If it was ever the case that women were unqualified to sit on juries or were so situated that none of them could be required to perform jury service, that time has long since passed."[3]

The Court later ruled that lawyers may not exclude people from serving on juries solely because of their sex. The decision in *J.E.B. v. Alabama ex rel. T.B.* (1994) extended the reasoning of a line of cases beginning in 1986 that barred lawyers from excluding potential jurors on account of race. Referring to the guarantee of the Equal Protection Clause, the Court said, "Discrimination in jury selection, whether based on race or on gender, causes harm to the litigants, the community, and the individual jurors who are wrongfully excluded from participation in the judicial process."[4]

---

1. *Strauder v. West Virginia*, 100 U.S. 303 (1880).

2. *Hoyt v. Florida*, 368 U.S. 57 at 62 (1961).

3. *Taylor v. Louisiana*, 419 U.S. 522 at 537 (1975).

4. *J.E.B. v. Alabama ex rel. T.B.*, 511 U.S. 127 (1994).

---

where husbands are in fact dependent on their wives, the Court held that the law was too broad and therefore a violation of the equal protection guarantee. In three subsequent cases, the Court found similar presumptions invalid.

In 1975 the Court struck down that portion of the Social Security Act that provided survivors' benefits to widows with small children but not to widowers with small children. Finding this distinction the same as the invalid classification in *Frontiero*, the Court ruled that it violated the Due Process Clause by providing working women fewer benefits for their Social Security contributions than working men received. The distinction challenged here was based on an "archaic and overbroad" generalization, said the Court in *Weinberger v. Wiesenfeld* (1975). The idea that men more frequently than women are the primary supporters of their families is "not without empirical support," Justice Brennan wrote. "But such a gender-based generalization cannot suffice to justify the denigration of the efforts of women who do work and whose earnings contribute significantly to their families' support."[17] Pointing out that the intended purpose of the benefit was to allow a mother to stay home to care for her young children, Brennan said the distinction between surviving mothers and surviving fathers was "entirely irrational.... It is no less important for a child to be cared for by its sole surviving parent when that parent is male rather than female."[18]

Two years later, a five-justice majority invalidated a Social Security Act provision that provided survivors' benefits to widows regardless of their financial dependence on their husbands, but to widowers only if they proved they had received more than half their income from their wives. In *Califano v. Goldfarb* (1977), four members of the majority found that this impermissibly discriminated against female wage earners by diminishing the protection, relative to male wage earners, that they provided for their families. Wrote Justice Brennan,

> The only conceivable justification for writing the presumption of wives' dependency into the statute is the assumption, not verified by the Government ... but based simply on "archaic and overbroad" generalizations ... that it would save the Government time, money and effort simply to pay benefits to all widows, rather than to require proof of dependency of both sexes. We held in *Frontiero,* and again in *Wiesenfeld,* and therefore hold again here, that such assumptions do not suffice to justify a gender-based discrimination in the distribution of employment-related benefits.[19]

The fifth member of the majority, Justice John Paul Stevens, found that the provision impermissibly discriminated against the dependent widowers. For the minority, Justice William H. Rehnquist argued that the classification was a rational one substantially related to the intended goal, which Rehnquist defined as a wish to aid "the characteristically [economically] depressed condition of aged widows."[20]

In 1980 the Court struck down another such law, this time a state statute making widows automatically eligible for death benefits after the work-related death of their husband, but requiring widowers—in order to be eligible for such benefits—to prove that they were physically or mentally unable to earn a living or that they were dependent upon their wives' earnings.[21]

Compromise Standard

Although Justice Brennan had been unable to convince a majority of the Court that gender-based discrimination was so invidious as to require a compelling government interest to justify it, he in 1976 won majority support for a standard that was midway between the standards of rationality and a compelling governmental interest. *Craig v. Boren* (1976) involved a challenge to an Oklahoma law that permitted the sale of 3.2 percent beer to women at age eighteen but not to men until age twenty-one. Four justices agreed with Brennan that to "withstand constitutional challenge ... classifications by gender must serve important governmental objectives and must be substantially related to achievement of those objectives."[22] It was not enough that the classification was rational, Brennan said; the distinction must serve some "important governmental objective." Applying this standard, the majority found that Oklahoma's desire to promote traffic safety was an important goal but that the gender-based distinction prohibiting the sale, but not the possession, of a low-alcohol beverage to males under age twenty-one was not substantially related to the attainment of that objective. The classification was therefore invalid.

Five years later, the Court upheld a sex-based distinction in criminal law, finding it justified as an appropriate means of accomplishing an important state end. California's statutory rape law permitted a man to be prosecuted for having sexual relations with a woman younger than eighteen to whom he is not married. The woman was exempted from criminal liability. Challenged as discriminating against the man, the state law was upheld by the Court, 5-4, as an appropriate means of preventing illegitimate teenage pregnancies.[23] The Court also gave at least lip service to this standard when it decided, 6-3, that Congress was well within its authority when it decided to exclude women from the military draft. Writing for the majority in *Rostker v. Goldberg* (1981), Justice Rehnquist declared this distinction justified because women were barred from combat and thus were not "similarly situated" with men for the purposes of maintaining a ready military force.[24]

Women demonstrated outside the Supreme Court during arguments in *United States v. Virginia* (1996), in which the justices ordered the historically all-male Virginia Military Institute to admit women or forgo state funding.

Brennan's position gained strength when Justice Sandra Day O'Connor joined the Court in 1981. In one of her first Court opinions, *Mississippi University for Women v. Hogan* (1982), O'Connor described the test for determining the validity of a classification based on sex as "straightforward." She then went on to invoke the "important governmental objectives" test. The case involved a Mississippi state statute that barred men from enrolling in a state-supported nursing school:[25]

> Our decisions ... establish that the party seeking to uphold a statute that classifies individuals on the basis of their gender must carry the burden of showing an "exceedingly persuasive justification" for the classification. The burden is met only by showing at least that the classification serves "important governmental objectives and that the discriminatory means employed" are "substantially related to the achievement of those objectives."[26]

The Court struck down the admissions policy and said excluding males from nursing training "tends to perpetuate the stereotyped view of nursing as an exclusively women's job."[27] That same year, 1982, however, saw the deadline pass for ratification by the states of the Equal Rights Amendment, which stated "Equality of rights under the law shall not be denied or abridged by the United States or by any State on account of sex." The proposed amendment had been approved by Congress and submitted to the states a decade earlier. It failed when three-fourths of the states failed to ratify it.

The standard of intermediate scrutiny as articulated in *Mississippi University for Women v. Hogan* would prevail through 1996. That year the Court declined to raise the judicial standard to strict scrutiny for classifications based on sex, but in striking down the Virginia Military Institute's (VMI) traditional policy excluding women students, it broadly interpreted the standards for protecting victims of sex discrimination. The decision stressed that government must demonstrate an "exceedingly persuasive justification" for gender-based action.[28] The opinion in *United States v. Virginia* (1996) was written by Justice Ruth Bader Ginsburg, a well-known advocate for women's rights before her appointment to the Court in 1993. The case may well turn out to be a milestone in sex discrimination decisions to come. According to legal scholar Cass Sunstein, *United States v. Virginia*'s "exceedingly persuasive justification" legal standard "now seems to have become the basic test for sex discrimination."[29]

VMI, Virginia's publicly funded military-style academy, had admitted only men since its founding in 1839. It had become one of the state's most prestigious colleges, boasting the largest per-student endowment of any undergraduate institution in the nation. VMI attracted the interest of some women, and in 1990 the Justice Department sued Virginia, alleging that VMI's exclusively male admission policy violated the Fourteenth Amendment's guarantee of equal protection. VMI countered that its distinctive approach, marked by a mentally and physically grueling regimen and an absence of student privacy, would be compromised by the admission of women. Midway through the litigation, in response to an initial federal appeals court ruling, Virginia developed a parallel program for women, the Virginia Women's Institute for Leadership (VWIL), at the nearby Mary Baldwin College, a private liberal arts school for women. Although the women's program lacked VMI's distinctive "adversative" training, its well-credentialed faculty, and high admissions standards, the U.S. Court of Appeals for the Fourth Circuit said the dual programs met the test of whether students at the respective institutions could obtain "substantially comparable benefits."

In reversing that decision and ordering VMI to choose between admitting women and retaining its state support or going private and continuing as a male-only institution, the Supreme Court said that although the state's educational options may be serving "the state's sons, it makes no provision whatever for her daughters. That is not *equal* protection."[30] The vote against VMI's position was 7-1. Ginsburg was joined by Justices John Paul Stevens, Sandra Day O'Connor, Anthony M. Kennedy, David H. Souter, and Stephen G. Breyer. Chief Justice William H. Rehnquist wrote a statement concurring in the judgment but disagreeing with the "exceedingly persuasive justification" legal standard used by the majority. Justice Antonin Scalia dissented, and Justice Clarence Thomas, whose son Jamal was attending VMI at the time, took no part in the case. In explaining the standard used for judging sex discrimination, the Ginsburg majority adopted language from precedent but cast the constitutional protection broadly:

> [T]he reviewing court must determine whether the proffered justification is exceedingly persuasive. The burden of justification is demanding and it rests entirely on the State. The State must show at least that the challenged classification serves important governmental objectives and that the discriminatory means employed are substantially related to the achievement of those objectives. The justification must be genuine, not hypothesized or invented *post hoc* in response to litigation. And it must not rely on overbroad generalizations about the different talents, capacities, or preferences of males and females.[31]

Rejecting VMI's defense that women were not suited to the arduous program, Ginsburg noted that similar concerns were voiced when women first sought admission to law schools and the bar. She wrote, "There is no reason to believe that the admission of women capable of all the activities required of VMI cadets would destroy the Institute rather than enhance its capacity to serve the 'more perfect Union.'"[32]

Rehnquist referred to the state's asserted justification of educational diversity: "The difficulty with its position is that the diversity benefitted only one sex; there was single-sex public education available for men at VMI, but no corresponding single-sex public education available for women."[33] He added, however, that the majority's broad rendering of the constitutional protection for sex discrimination left the intermediate scrutiny traditionally used for sex discrimination muddled. Scalia's dissent targeted the majority's legal analysis and its rejection of the values underlying the venerable military institute: "In an odd sort of way, it is precisely VMI's attachment to such old-fashioned concepts as manly 'honor' that has made it, and the system it represents, the target of those who today succeed in abolishing public single-sex education."[34] He said Virginia was appropriately providing different programs to meet the different developmental needs of men and women students.

DISCRIMINATION IN EMPLOYMENT

Because women traditionally have had the primary responsibility for raising children, employers have used potential pregnancy as an argument against hiring, training, and promoting women. Employers' policies on pregnancy have been a major target of women's rights advocates who see this issue as the heart of sex discrimination. The Supreme Court has found it difficult to deal with cases involving pregnancy-related discrimination. For a time the Court declared that pregnancy classifications did not discriminate between men and women but rather between pregnant persons and nonpregnant persons. After Justice John Paul Stevens took issue with that view, lecturing his brethren in 1976 that "it is the capacity to become pregnant which primarily differentiates the female from the male," it was rarely invoked again.[35]

Hiring Standards

Title VII of the Civil Rights Act of 1964 forbids discrimination on the basis of sex as well as race in employment. It took seven years for the first Title VII sex discrimination case—*Phillips v. Martin Marietta Corp.* (1971)—to come to the Court. Martin Marietta refused to hire women with preschool children, although it hired men regardless of the age of their children. The Court said that Title VII did not permit such a distinction unless it was "a bona fide occupational qualification reasonably necessary to the normal operation of that particular business or enterprise."[36]

Six years later, in *Dothard v. Rawlinson* (1977), the Court struck down as discrimination on the basis of sex a state law that set minimum height and weight requirements for certain jobs, in this case that of a prison guard. Dianne Rawlinson was rejected for a job as a prison guard in Alabama because she did not meet the requirement that guards be at least five feet, two inches tall and weigh at least 120 pounds. She challenged the law on the grounds that it would disqualify more than 40 percent of the women in the country but less than 1 percent of the men. The Court ruled this prima facie evidence of sex discrimination because the apparently neutral physical requirements "select applicants for hire in a significantly discriminatory pattern." The state was then required to show that the height and weight requirements had a "manifest relationship" to the job in question. This the state failed to do, the Court said.[37]

The Court did uphold, however, a provision of the Alabama statute that prohibited women from filling positions that brought them into close proximity with inmates. In this case, the majority said an employee's "very womanhood" would make her vulnerable to sexual and other attacks by inmates and thus "undermine her capacity to provide the security that is the essence of a correctional counselor's responsibility."[38] Justices Brennan and Thurgood Marshall dissented. The majority decision "perpetuates one of the most insidious of the old myths about women—that women, wittingly or not, are seductive sexual objects," wrote Marshall. The majority, he said, makes women "pay the price in lost job opportunities for the threat of depraved conduct by prison inmates.... The proper response to inevitable attacks on both female and male guards is ... to take swift and sure punitive actions against the inmate offenders."[39]

Maternity Leave

The Court's first major modern constitutional decisions on sex discrimination in the workplace came in the early 1970s and required employers to be more flexible in administering maternity leave. The Court, 7-2, held that it violated the due process guarantee to require all pregnant women to leave their jobs at the same point in pregnancy. *Cleveland Board of Education v. LaFleur* and *Cohen v. Chesterfield County School Board* (1974), decided together, involved school board policies that forced teachers to stop teaching midway through pregnancy. "[F]reedom of personal choice in matters of marriage and family life is one of the liberties protected by the due process clause," the majority wrote. Due process requires that maternity leave regulations "not needlessly, arbitrarily, or capriciously impinge upon this vital area of a teacher's constitutional liberty."[40]

The Court rejected the school boards' arguments that mandatory leave policies ensured continuity of instruction by giving the school time to find qualified substitute teachers. Such an absolute requirement violated the test of rationality, the Court said, because in many instances it would interrupt continuity by requiring a teacher to leave her classroom in the middle of a term. "As long as the teachers are required to give substantial advance notice of their condition, the choice of firm dates later in pregnancy would serve the boards' objectives just as well, while imposing a far lesser burden on the women's exercise of constitutionally protected freedom," the majority wrote.[41]

The Court also held that the regulations were too broad because they presumed that all women reaching the fifth or sixth month of pregnancy were physically incapable of continuing in their jobs. Such a presumption, which denies a pregnant woman the opportunity to prove she is fit to continue working, is contrary to the due process guarantees of the Fifth and Fourteenth Amendments. "If legislative bodies are to be permitted to draw a general line anywhere short of the delivery room, I can find no judicial standard of measurement which says the lines drawn here are invalid," said Justice Rehnquist, dissenting for himself and Chief Justice Burger.[42]

Pregnancy and Disability

In examining an employer's obligation to provide disability payments to women unable to work because of pregnancy and childbirth, the Court has been distinctly less sympathetic to the needs of working women. After the Court twice ruled against women workers in this context, Congress stepped in to correct the trend by amending Title VII to prohibit discrimination against pregnant women in all areas of employment. Six months after the maternity leave decision in *Cleveland Board of Education v. LaFleur,* the Court in *Geduldig v. Aiello* (1974) upheld a state disability insurance program excluding coverage of disabilities related to normal pregnancy and childbirth. The six-justice majority said the exclusion was based on physical condition, not sex:

> The California insurance program does not exclude anyone from benefit eligibility because of gender but merely removes one physical condition—pregnancy—from the list of compensable disabilities. While it is true that only women can become pregnant, it does not follow that every legislative classification concerning pregnancy is a sex-based classification.... Normal pregnancy is an objectively identifiable physical condition with unique characteristics. Absent a showing that distinctions involving pregnancy are mere pretexts designed to effect an invidious discrimination against the members of one sex or the other, lawmakers are constitutionally free to include or exclude pregnancy from the coverage of legislation such as this on any reasonable basis, just as with respect to any other physical condition.[43]

The question then became simply whether the exclusion was reasonable. Justice Stewart observed that disability coverage for pregnancy would increase costs that would have to be offset by increased contributions by employees, changes in other coverage, or lower benefit levels. He continued:

> The state has a legitimate interest in maintaining the self-supporting nature of its insurance program. Similarly, it has an interest in distributing the available resources in such a way as to keep benefit payments at an adequate level for disabilities that are covered, rather than to cover all disabilities inadequately. Finally, California has a legitimate concern in maintaining the contribution rate at a level that will not unduly burden participating employees, particularly low-income employees who may be most in need of the disability insurance.

These policies provide an objective and wholly non-invidious basis for the State's decision not to create a more comprehensive insurance program than it has. There is no evidence in the record that the selection of the risks insured by the program worked to discriminate against any definable group or class in terms of the aggregate risk protection derived by that group or class from the program. There is no risk from which men are protected and women are not. Likewise, there is no risk from which women are protected and men are not.

The appellee simply contends ... she has suffered discrimination because she encountered a risk that was outside the program's protection.... [W]e hold that this contention is not a valid one under the Equal Protection Clause of the Fourteenth Amendment.[44]

In dissent Justice Brennan argued as he had in previous sex discrimination cases that the Court should regard gender-based classifications as inherently suspect, justifiable only to achieve a compelling government interest that could not otherwise be met. He also asserted that the Court misapplied the more lenient standard it did use:

[T]he economic effects caused by pregnancy-related disabilities are functionally indistinguishable from the effects caused by any other disability: wages are lost due to a physical inability to work, and medical expenses are incurred for the delivery of the child and for post-partum care. In my view, by singling out for less favorable treatment a gender-linked disability peculiar to women, the State has created a double standard for disability compensation: a limitation is imposed upon the disabilities for which women workers may recover, while men receive full compensation for all disabilities suffered, including those that affect only or primarily their sex.... Such dissimilar treatment of men and women, on the basis of physical characteristics inextricably linked to one sex, inevitably constitutes sex discrimination.[45]

Two years later, the Court upheld a similar exclusion from a disability plan maintained by a private employer, General Electric. "[E]xclusion of pregnancy from a disability benefits plan providing general coverage is not a gender-based discrimination at all," wrote

Justice Rehnquist for the six-justice majority in *General Electric Co. v. Gilbert* (1976).[46] The plan covered some risks, but not others; there was no risk from which men were protected, but not women, or vice versa. Wrote Rehnquist:

[I]t is impossible to find any gender-based discriminatory effect in this scheme simply because women disabled as a result of pregnancy do not receive benefits; that is to say, gender-based discrimination does not result simply because an employer's disability benefits plan is less than all-inclusive. To hold otherwise would endanger the common-sense notion that an employer who has no disability benefits program at all does not violate Title VII [of the 1964 Act].[47]

"Surely it offends common sense to suggest ... that a classification revolving around pregnancy is not, at the minimum, strongly 'sex related,'" wrote Justice Brennan in dissent. "Pregnancy exclusions ... both financially burden women workers and act to break down the continuity of the employment relationship, thereby exacerbating women's comparatively transient role in the labor force."[48]

Sick Pay and Seniority

Almost exactly one year after *General Electric*, the Court ruled that employers can refuse sick pay to women employees absent from work due to pregnancy and childbirth, but they cannot divest those women of their accumulated seniority for taking maternity leave. All the justices concurred in the ruling in *Nashville Gas Co. v. Satty* (1977). For the Court, Justice Rehnquist wrote that the divestiture of seniority clearly violated the 1964 Civil Rights Act's Title VII, which prohibits employment discrimination on the basis of sex. Although the policy appeared neutral—divesting of seniority all persons who took leaves of absence from work for any reason other than illness, a category from which childbirth-related absences were excluded—its effect was clearly discriminatory, depriving far more women than men of job opportunities and adversely affecting their status as employees.

The denial of sick pay was permissible, wrote Rehnquist, under the *General Electric* reasoning, which permitted disabilities arising from pregnancy to be treated differently from similar disabilities caused by other medical conditions. Attempting to distinguish the seniority policy from the sick pay and disability benefits policies, Rehnquist emphasized that the gas company

has not merely refused to extend to women a benefit [sick pay, disability insurance] that men cannot and do not receive, but has imposed on women a substantial burden that men need not suffer. The distinction between benefits and burdens is more than one of semantics. We held in *Gilbert* that ... [Title VII] did not require that greater economic benefits be paid to one sex or the other "because of their differing roles in the scheme of human existence." ... But that holding does not allow us to read ... [Title VII] to permit an employer to burden female employees in such a way as to deprive them of employment opportunities because of their different role.[49]

Finding Rehnquist's distinction between General Electric's seniority policy and its sick pay and disability benefits policy somewhat confusing, Justice Stevens said he saw the difference between the two policies as one of short-term versus long-term effect. Denial of sick pay did not affect the woman worker beyond the period of her leave; loss of seniority resulted in permanent disadvantage. In a concurring opinion, Justices Brennan, Powell, and Marshall suggested that the combination of the seniority and sick pay policies violated Title VII by resulting in less net compensation for women than for men employees.

Frustrated by the Court's complicated position, women's rights activists turned to Congress for relief. It responded in 1978 by amending Title VII to prohibit discrimination against pregnant women in any area of employment, including hiring, promotion, seniority rights, and job security. The Pregnancy Discrimination Act of 1978 also required employers who offered health insurance and temporary disability plans to provide coverage to women for pregnancy, childbirth, and related medical conditions.[50] That meant, the Court held later, that employers must provide health insurance pregnancy coverage for the wives of male employees that was as comprehensive as that provided for the female employees. On the other hand, the Court held in 1987, the new law did not preclude states from requiring more benefits for workers disabled by pregnancy than for other temporarily disabled workers.[51]

Four years later, in the Court's first "fetal protection" case, the justices ruled unanimously that companies may not exclude women from jobs that might harm a developing fetus. The justices, however, divided over whether an employer could restrict working conditions for pregnant women, but not for other workers, and still satisfy the standards of Title VII. Five members of the Court, led by Justice Blackmun, said Congress had intended to forbid any discrimination based on a worker's ability to have children. He wrote that "Congress has left this choice to the woman as hers to make," and he was joined by Justices Marshall, Stevens, O'Connor, and Souter.[52] Justices Byron R. White, Rehnquist, Anthony M. Kennedy, and Scalia said that situations could arise in which a company, because of personal injury liability and workplace costs, could exclude women based on hazards to the unborn.

Pension Rights, Sexual Harassment

Women, as a group, live longer than men as a group. That disparity has been reflected traditionally in differing treatment of men and women by life insurance plans, but the Supreme Court has made clear that the Civil Rights Act of 1964 bars the use of this collective difference to discriminate, in premiums or annuities, against women by charging them more than the generally shorter lived men. In the 1970s, the Court ruled, 5–3, that a municipal employer could not require female employees to make higher contributions to a pension fund than male employees earning the same salary. In *Los Angeles v. Manhart* (1978), the city contended that the differential contributions were not based on sex but on longevity. Justice Stevens for the majority acknowledged that women usually lived longer than men and that without the differential, men would, in effect, subsidize the pension benefits eventually paid to women. Stevens said, however, that such subsidies are the essence of group insurance:

> Treating different classes of risk as though they were the same for purposes of group insurance is a common practice which has never been considered inherently unfair. To insure the flabby and the fit as though they were equivalent risks may be more common than treating men and women alike; but nothing more than habit makes one "subsidy" seem less fair than the other.[53]

It is the individual that the 1964 Civil Rights Act protects from discrimination: "Even a true generalization about the class is an insufficient reason for disqualifying an individual to whom the generalization does not apply."[54] Even though most women live longer than most men, many women workers who paid the larger contribution would not, in fact, live longer than some of their male colleagues, Stevens pointed out. In dissent, Chief Justice Burger said if employers

> are to operate economically workable group pension programs, it is only rational to permit them to rely on statistically sound and proven disparities in longevity between men and women. Indeed, it seems to me irrational to assume Congress intended to outlaw use of the fact that, for whatever reasons or combination of reasons, women as a class outlive men....
>
> An effect upon pension plans so revolutionary and discriminatory—this time favorable to women at the expense of men—should not be read into the statute without either a clear statement of that intent in the statute, or some reliable indication in the legislative history that this was Congress' purpose.[55]

The majority may have been influenced by Burger's warning of the decision's revolutionary effect on pension plans. By a 7-1 vote, the Court reversed the lower court order awarding retroactive relief to the women contributors. In this instance, the majority felt that retroactive relief was inappropriate because it "could be devastating for a pension fund."[56] Payment of the award from the pension fund would diminish the fund's assets; that might then prove inadequate to meet obligations, which in turn might decrease benefits to all employees or increase the contribution rates for current employees, the Court said. In lone dissent on this point, Justice Marshall said the majority had been shown no proof of the predicted "devastating" effect. Repayment to women of their earlier excessive contributions was the only way to make them whole for the discrimination they had suffered, he said.

In an earlier case involving remedies for proven sex discrimination, the Court had held that the Eleventh Amendment, which prohibits private suits in federal courts against unwilling states, did not protect a state from an order to pay retroactive benefits to employees who were discriminated against by the state. In *Fitzpatrick v. Bitzer* (1976), the Court upheld a federal court order to Connecticut to pay retroactive benefits to men who had been forced by state law to work longer than women employees before they could retire.[57] The Court said Congress had the power to enforce the guarantees of the Fourteenth Amendment by authorizing orders requiring expenditures of states' funds. States, by ratifying that amendment, surrendered some of their sovereign immunity to federal orders, it said.

The proper allocation of retirement rights and costs is still a matter that closely divides the Court. In the early 1980s, the Court divided, 5-4, in resolving a challenge to an employer's retirement plan under which women workers upon retirement received smaller monthly payments than did men who had contributed the same amounts during their working years. In *Arizona Governing Committee for Tax Deferred Annuity and Deferred Compensation Plans v. Norris* (1983), the Court held—with reasoning similar to that set out by Justice Stevens in *Manhart*—that the greater longevity of women than men was not a permissible basis for paying them different monthly benefits.[58] Voting together on that point were Justices Marshall, Brennan, Stevens, O'Connor, and White. On a point of considerable practical importance to women who had already retired under this plan, however, the Court held that this decision would apply only to retirement benefits derived from contributions made after the ruling. O'Connor joined the dissenters from the other point—Burger, Blackmun, Powell, and Rehnquist—to form this majority.

In June 1986, during the week Rehnquist was promoted to chief justice, the Court unanimously applied Title VII to ban sexual harassment in the workplace as a form of sexual discrimination, and the usually conservative Rehnquist wrote the majority's opinion. Such harassment is illegal not only when it results in the loss of a job or promotion, but also when it creates an offensive or hostile working environment:

> The language of Title VII is not limited to "economic" or "tangible" discrimination. The phrase "terms, conditions, or privileges of employment" evinces a congressional intent "to strike at the entire spectrum of disparate treatment of men and women" in employment.[59]

An employee claiming sexual harassment must prove the existence of a hostile or abusive work environment, said the unanimous Court in the early 1990s, but there is no need for a showing that he or she suffered serious psychological injury as a result. The prohibition on sex discrimination contained in Title VII of the Civil Rights Act of 1964 "comes into play before the harassing conduct leads to a nervous breakdown," explained Justice O'Connor in *Harris v. Forklift Systems Inc.* (1993). She added, "So long as the environment would reasonably be perceived, and is perceived, as hostile or abusive, there is no need for it also to be psychologically injurious."[60]

In 1998 the Court put employers on notice that they can be held liable for sexual harassment of an employee by a mid-level supervisor, even if top officials are unaware of the situation. In a pair of 7-2 decisions handed down on June 26, 1998, the Court ruled that companies and agencies are generally responsible if their male supervisors harass female employees, unless they have taken strong steps to prevent such harassment. In one case, Beth Faragher, a lifeguard, sued the city of Boca Raton, Florida, after two men in charge of the lifeguards had subjected her and other women to lewd comments and unwanted touching. In the second case, Kimberly Ellerth quit her sales job for Burlington Industries and sued the company after she had been repeatedly subjected to sexual advances by a supervisor. In neither case did the women show that they had suffered a specific job loss (such as a demotion) because they had rebuffed the

unwanted advances, but they had experienced a hostile and abusive work environment, for which the Court said federal law allowed the employers to be held liable. The justices also ruled, however, that employers can fend off such claims with an "affirmative defense" if they maintain a strong and clear policy against sexual harassment and a confidential reporting system for complaints. If an employee then fails to voice a complaint, she may have her suit thrown out, the Court determined.[61]

Pay Discrimination

In 2007 the Roberts Court was sharply criticized by women's rights advocates when it threw out a jury's verdict in favor of a female manager who had been paid far less than her male counterparts. The 5-4 decision relied on a strict and literal reading of the statute of limitations in the Civil Rights Act of 1964.

After retiring in 1998 from the Goodyear Tire & Rubber Company, Lilly Ledbetter sued for sex discrimination under Title VII of the Civil Rights Act as well as for unequal pay under the Equal Pay Act (EPA). A judge ruled that she could not prevail under EPA, but he allowed a jury to decide the discrimination issue. Ledbetter showed that she had been paid 15 percent to 40 percent less than men who had held the same jobs, and she blamed a male manager for discriminating against her years earlier because she had rejected his advances. The jury ruled that Ledbetter had been a victim of illegal sex discrimination, but on appeal, the company pointed out that none of the discriminatory pay decisions cited by Ledbetter under her Title VII claim had taken place in the 180 days before her suit was filed, as required by the Civil Rights Act. The appeals court agreed with Goodyear.

In *Ledbetter v. Goodyear Tire & Rubber Co.* (2007), the Supreme Court ruled against Ledbetter, finding her claim untimely. The justices pointed to the strict statute of limitations in the Civil Rights Act, which states that claims must be filed within 180 days "after the alleged unlawful employment practice occurred." Citing this timeframe, the Court found that Ledbetter had waited too long to sue her employer for paying her less than men during her nearly twenty-year career as a manager with Goodyear. In short, women who believe that they have been paid less than men for the same work would find it difficult to sue under Title VII for sex discrimination involving past claims. Suing under the EPA remained an option, however, because it does not have a 180-day time limitation.

"We apply the statute as written," Justice Alito said in rejecting Ledbetter's claim of discrimination under Title VII. Chief Justice Roberts and Justices Scalia, Kennedy, and Thomas agreed with him. Justice Ginsburg, the only female on the Court, dissented and stated that the ruling ignores "the realities of the workplace" and the "problem of concealed pay discrimination." Ledbetter had no way of knowing that she was being paid far less than the men, Ginsburg argued, and by the time she realized this, it was too late to sue. Ginsburg urged Congress to revise the laws.[62] In January 2009, the 111th Congress did so, and President Barack Obama signed the Lilly Ledbetter Fair Pay Act into law as the first major piece of legislation enacted during his administration. Under the revised law, each new paycheck can be considered an act of discrimination if an employee was paid less because of her gender.

NOTES

INTRODUCTION (PP. 366–373)

1. Thurgood Marshall, "Reflections on the Bicentennial of the United States Constitution," remarks delivered before the San Francisco Patent and Trademark Law Association, Maui, Hawaii, May 6, 1987.

2. *Romer v. Evans,* 517 U.S. 620 at 634 (1996).

3. *Lindsley v. Natural Carbonic Gas Co.,* 220 U.S. 61 at 78–79 (1911); see also *McGowan v. Maryland,* 366 U.S. 420 (1951); *Williamson v. Lee Optical of Oklahoma,* 348 U.S. 483 (1955); *Kotch v. Board of River Pilot Commissioners,* 330 U.S. 552 (1947); *Royster Guano Co. v. Virginia,* 253 U.S. 412 (1920).

4. *Buck v. Bell,* 274 U.S. 200 at 208 (1927).

5. *Korematsu v. United States,* 323 U.S. 214 at 216 (1944).

6. *Graham v. Richardson,* 403 U.S. 365 at 372 (1971).

7. *Craig v. Boren,* 429 U.S. 190 at 197 (1976).

8. *United States v. Virginia,* 518 U.S. 515 (1996).

9. *Skinner v. Oklahoma,* 316 U.S. 535 at 541 (1942).

10. *Griswold v. Connecticut,* 381 U.S. 479 (1965).

11. *Roe v. Wade,* 410 U.S. 113 (1973).

12. *Planned Parenthood of Southeastern Pennsylvania v. Casey,* 505 U.S. 833 (1992).

13. *Reynolds v. Sims,* 377 U.S. 533 at 561–562 (1964).

14. *Kramer v. Union Free School District,* 395 U.S. 621 at 627–628 (1969).

15. *United States v. Guest,* 383 U.S. 745 at 757, 759 (1966).

16. *Shapiro v. Thompson,* 394 U.S. 618 at 662 (1969).

17. *Weber v. Aetna Casualty & Surety Co.,* 406 U.S. 164 at 179 (1972).

18. *Shapiro v. Thompson,* 394 U.S. 618 at 627 (1969); *Lindsey v. Normet,* 405 U.S. 56 (1972).

19. *San Antonio Independent School District v. Rodriguez,* 411 U.S. 1 at 33 (1973).

RACIAL EQUALITY (PP. 374–439)

1. *Strauder v. West Virginia,* 100 U.S. 303 at 306–307 (1880).

2. John P. Frank, *Marble Palace: The Supreme Court in American Life* (New York: Knopf, 1961), 204. Other sources include John Hope Franklin, *From Slavery to Freedom: A History of Negro Americans,* 3d ed. (New York: Random House, Vintage Books, 1969); John A. Garraty, ed., *Quarrels That Have Shaped the Constitution* (New York: Harper and Row, 1964); U.S. Commission on Civil Rights, *Freedom to the Free: Century of Emancipation, 1863–1963* (Washington, D.C.: U.S. Government Printing Office, 1963); C. Vann Woodward, *The Strange Career of Jim Crow,* 2d rev. ed. (New York: Oxford University Press, 1966).

3. *Slaughterhouse Cases,* 16 Wall. (83 U.S.) 36 (1873).

4. *Civil Rights Cases,* 109 U.S. 3 (1883).

5. Carl B. Swisher, "Dred Scott One Hundred Years After," *Journal of Politics* 19 (May 1957): 167–174, quoted in Frank, *Marble Palace,* 205.

6. Alan P. Westin, "The Case of the Prejudiced Doorkeeper," in Garraty, *Quarrels That Have Shaped the Constitution,* 143.

7. *Plessy v. Ferguson,* 163 U.S. 537 (1896).

8. U.S. Commission on Civil Rights, *Freedom to the Free,* 71.

9. Franklin, *From Slavery to Freedom,* 480.

10. *United States v. Carolene Products Co.,* 304 U.S. 144 at 152–153, footnote 4 (1938).

11. *Brown v. Board of Education of Topeka,* 347 U.S. 483 (1954).

12. G. Theodore Mitau, *Decade of Decision: The Supreme Court and the Constitutional Revolution, 1954–1964* (New York: Scribner's, 1967), 62–63.

13. Franklin, *From Slavery to Freedom,* 644.

14. *Plessy v. Ferguson,* 163 U.S. 537 at 544 (1896).

15. *Roberts v. City of Boston,* 59 Mass. 198 at 206 (1849).

16. Id. at 209.

17. *Cumming v. Richmond County Board of Education,* 175 U.S. 528 at 545 (1899).

18. *Berea College v. Kentucky,* 211 U.S. 45 (1908).

19. *Gong Lum v. Rice,* 275 U.S. 78 at 86 (1927).

20. For general background, see Alfred H. Kelly and Winfred A. Harbison, *The American Constitution: Its Origins and Development,* 5th ed. (New York: Norton, 1976), 860; Richard Kluger, *Simple Justice* (New York: Knopf, 1976), 126–137.

21. *Missouri ex rel. Gaines v. Canada,* 305 U.S. 337 at 349 (1938).

22. Id. at 350.

23. *Sipuel v. Board of Regents of the University of Oklahoma,* 332 U.S. 631 at 633 (1948).

24. *Sweatt v. Painter,* 339 U.S. 629 at 633–634 (1950).

25. Id. at 636.

26. *McLaurin v. Oklahoma State Regents for Higher Education,* 339 U.S. 637 at 641 (1950).

27. *Brown v. Board of Education of Topeka, Briggs v. Elliott, Davis v. County School Board of Prince Edward County, Va., Gebhart v. Belton,* 347 U.S. 483 (1954).

28. *Bolling v. Sharpe,* 347 U.S. 497 (1954).

29. Loren Miller, *The Petitioners: The Story of the Supreme Court of the United States and the Negro* (New York: Random House, Pantheon Books, 1966), 345.

30. *Guinn v. United States,* 238 U.S. 347 (1915); see also Kluger, *Simple Justice,* 527.

31. Quoted in Leon Friedman, ed., *Argument: The Oral Argument before the Supreme Court in Brown v. Board of Education of Topeka, 1952–55* (New York: Chelsea House, 1969), 215.

32. Ibid.

33. Ibid., 216.

34. Ibid., 239–240.

35. *Brown v. Board of Education of Topeka,* 347 U.S. 483 at 492 (1954).

36. Id. at 492–493.

37. Id. at 493.

38. Id.

39. Id. at 494.

40. Id. at 495.

41. *Bolling v. Sharpe,* 347 U.S. 497 at 499–500 (1954).

42. *Brown v. Board of Education of Topeka,* 349 U.S. 294 at 299–301 (1955).

43. Id. at 301.

44. U.S. Senate, "Declaration of Constitutional Principles," *Congressional Record,* 84th Cong., 2d sess., March 12, 1956, 102:4460.

45. Woodward, *Strange Career of Jim Crow,* 154.

46. *Lucy v. Adams,* 350 U.S. 1 (1955).

47. *Florida ex rel. Hawkins v. Board of Control,* 350 U.S. 413 (1956).

48. *Muir v. Louisville Park Theatrical Assn.,* 347 U.S. 971 (1954); see also *Mayor and City Council of Baltimore v. Dawson,* 350 U.S. 877 (1955); *Holmes v. City of Atlanta,* 350 U.S. 879 (1955); *New Orleans City Park Improvement Assn. v. Detiege,*

358 U.S. 54 (1959); *Gayle v. Browder,* 352 U.S. 903 (1956); *Wright v. Georgia,* 373 U.S. 284 (1963).

49. *Cooper v. Aaron,* 358 U.S. 1 (1958).

50. Id. at 16.

51. Id. at 19–20.

52. *Faubus v. Aaron,* 361 U.S. 197 (1959).

53. *Shuttlesworth v. Birmingham Board of Education,* 162 F. Supp. 372, affirmed 358 U.S. 101 (1958).

54. *Holt v. Raleigh,* 265 F. 2d 95, cert. denied, 361 U.S. 818 (1959); *Covington v. Edwards,* 264 F. 2d 780, cert. denied, 361 U.S. 840 (1959).

55. *Bush v. Orleans Parish School Board,* 364 U.S. 500 (1960); *Orleans Parish School Board v. Bush,* 365 U.S. 569 (1961); *St. Helena Parish School Board v. Hall,* 368 U.S. 515 (1962).

56. *Goss v. Board of Education of Knoxville,* 373 U.S. 683 (1963).

57. *McNeese v. Board of Education for Community School District 187, Cahokia, Ill.,* 373 U.S. 668 (1963).

58. *Griffin v. County School Board of Prince Edward County,* 377 U.S. 218 at 231 (1964).

59. Id. at 229.

60. *Bradley v. School Board, City of Richmond,* 382 U.S. 103 (1965).

61. *Rogers v. Paul,* 382 U.S. 198 (1965).

62. *Wallace v. United States, Bibb County Board of Education v. United States,* 386 U.S. 976 (1967).

63. *Green v. County School Board of New Kent County, Va.,* 391 U.S. 430 at 437–438 (1968).

64. Id. at 438–439.

65. Id. at 439.

66. Id. at 441, 442.

67. *Raney v. Board of Education of Gould School District,* 391 U.S. 443 (1968); *Monroe v. Board of Commissioners, City of Jackson,* 391 U.S. 450 (1968).

68. *Alexander v. Holmes Board of Education,* 396 U.S. 19 (1969); see also *Carter v. West Feliciana Parish School Board,* 396 U.S. 290 (1970); *Northcross v. Board of Education, City of Memphis,* 397 U.S. 232 (1970).

69. *Swann v. Charlotte-Mecklenburg County Board of Education,* 402 U.S. 1 at 25, 24 (1971).

70. Id. at 26.

71. Id. at 27.

72. Id. at 30–31.

73. Id. at 28.

74. Id. at 23.

75. Id. at 31–32.

76. *North Carolina State Board of Education v. Swann,* 402 U.S. 43 at 45–46 (1971).

77. *Davis v. Board of School Commissioners of Mobile County, Ala.,* 402 U.S. 33 (1971).

78. *McDaniel v. Barresi,* 402 U.S. 39 (1971).

79. *Richmond School Board v. Virginia State Board of Education*, 412 U.S. 92 (1973).

80. Quoted by Chief Justice Warren E. Burger in *Milliken v. Bradley*, 418 U.S. 717 at 733 (1974).

81. Id. at 741.

82. Id. at 744–745.

83. Id. at 746.

84. Id. at 752.

85. Id. at 789.

86. *Milliken v. Bradley*, 433 U.S. 267 at 287–288 (1977).

87. *Edelman v. Jordan*, 415 U.S. 651 (1974).

88. *Milliken v. Bradley*, 433 U.S. 267 at 290 (1977).

89. *Dayton (Ohio) Board of Education v. Brinkman*, 433 U.S. 406 at 420 (1977); *Dayton Board of Education v. Brinkman*, 443 U.S. 526 (1979).

90. *Pasadena City Board of Education v. Spangler*, 427 U.S. 424 at 437 (1976).

91. Id. at 443.

92. *Board of Education of Oklahoma City Public Schools v. Dowell*, 498 U.S. 237 (1991).

93. *Missouri v. Jenkins*, 515 U.S. 70 (1995).

94. *Missouri v. Jenkins*, 495 U.S. 33 (1990).

95. *Missouri v. Jenkins*, 515 U.S. 70 (1995).

96. *Parents Involved in Community Schools v. Seattle School District #1*, 551 U.S. __ (2007).

97. For general historical background in this area, see U.S. Commission on Civil Rights, *Freedom to the Free*, 60–71; Woodward, "The Case of the Louisiana Traveler," in Garraty, *Quarrels That Have Shaped the Constitution*, 145; Woodward, *Strange Career of Jim Crow*.

98. *Civil Rights Cases*, 109 U.S. 3 at 11 (1883).

99. Id. at 24.

100. Milton Konvitz and Theodore Leskes, *A Century of Civil Rights, with a Study of State Law against Discrimination* (New York: Columbia University Press, 1961), 157. The states that passed antidiscrimination laws were Connecticut, Iowa, New Jersey, and Ohio in 1884; Colorado, Illinois, Indiana, Michigan, Minnesota, Nebraska, and Rhode Island in 1885; Pennsylvania in 1887; Washington in 1890; Wisconsin in 1895; and California in 1897.

101. *Hall v. DeCuir*, 95 U.S. 485 at 489 (1878).

102. *Louisville, New Orleans and Texas Railway v. Mississippi*, 133 U.S. 587 (1890).

103. *Plessy v. Ferguson*, 163 U.S. 537 at 548 (1896).

104. Id. at 543.

105. Id. at 544.

106. Id. at 550–551.

107. Id. at 559.

108. Id. at 560–561.

109. *McCabe v. Atchison, Topeka and Santa Fe Railroad*, 235 U.S. 151 at 161–162 (1914).

110. *Mitchell v. United States*, 313 U.S. 80 (1941).

111. *Morgan v. Virginia*, 328 U.S. 373 at 380–381 (1946).

112. Id. at 386.

113. *Bob-Lo Excursion Co. v. Michigan*, 333 U.S. 28 (1948); *Henderson v. United States*, 339 U.S. 816 (1950); *District of Columbia v. Thompson Co.*, 346 U.S. 100 (1953).

114. *Mayor and City Council of Baltimore v. Dawson*, 350 U.S. 877 (1955); *Holmes v. City of Atlanta*, 350 U.S. 879 (1955); *New Orleans City Park Improvement Assn. v. Detiege*, 358 U.S. 54 (1959); *Gayle v. Browder*, 352 U.S. 903 (1956); *Muir v. Louisville Park Theatrical Assn.*, 347 U.S. 971 (1954); *Wright v. Georgia*, 373 U.S. 284 (1963); *Schiro v. Bynum*, 375 U.S. 395 (1964); *State Athletic Commission v. Dorsey*, 359 U.S. 533 (1959); *Johnson v. Virginia*, 373 U.S. 61 (1963); *Lee v. Washington*, 390 U.S. 333 (1968).

115. *Watson v. City of Memphis*, 373 U.S. 526 at 533 (1963).

116. *Palmer v. Thompson*, 403 U.S. 217 (1971).

117. *Boynton v. Virginia*, 364 U.S. 454 at 460–461 (1960).

118. *Burton v. Wilmington Parking Authority*, 365 U.S. 715 at 722 (1961).

119. Id. at 725.

120. *Peterson v. City of Greenville*, 373 U.S. 244 at 248 (1963).

121. *Gober v. City of Birmingham*, 373 U.S. 374 (1963); *Avent v. North Carolina*, 373 U.S. 375 (1963).

122. *Shuttlesworth v. Birmingham*, 373 U.S. 262 at 265 (1963).

123. *Lombard v. Louisiana*, 373 U.S. 267 at 273 (1963).

124. *Heart of Atlanta Motel v. United States*, 379 U.S. 241 at 258 (1964).

125. Id. at 257.

126. Id. at 260.

127. Id. at 252.

128. *Katzenbach v. McClung*, 379 U.S. 294 (1964).

129. *Daniel v. Paul*, 395 U.S. 298 (1969).

130. *Civil Rights Cases*, 109 U.S. 3 at 22 (1883).

131. *Buchanan v. Warley*, 245 U.S. 60 at 80–82 (1917).

132. See, for example, *Harmon v. Tyler*, 273 U.S. 668 (1927); *City of Richmond v. Deans*, 281 U.S. 704 (1930).

133. *Corrigan v. Buckley*, 271 U.S. 323 at 330 (1926).

134. *Shelley v. Kraemer, McGhee v. Sipes*, 334 U.S. 1 (1948).

135. Id. at 13.

136. Id. at 19–20.

137. *Hurd v. Hodge, Urciola v. Hodge*, 334 U.S. 24 (1948).

138. *Barrows v. Jackson*, 346 U.S. 254 (1953).

139. *Reitman v. Mulkey*, 387 U.S. 369 at 377 (1967).

140. Id. at 393.

141. *Hunter v. Erickson*, 393 U.S. 385 at 393 (1969).

142. Id. at 396–397.

143. *James v. Valtierra*, 402 U.S. 137 at 141 (1971).

144. Id. at 145.

145. *Jones v. Alfred H. Mayer Co.*, 392 U.S. 409 at 436 (1968).

146. Id. at 438–443, passim.

147. *Sullivan v. Little Hunting Park Inc.*, 396 U.S. 229 (1969).

148. *Tillman v. Wheaton-Haven Recreation Association*, 410 U.S. 431 at 437 (1973).

149. *Hills v. Gautreaux*, 425 U.S. 284 (1976).

150. *Milliken v. Bradley*, 418 U.S. 717 (1974).

151. *Hills v. Gautreaux*, 425 U.S. 284 at 294 (1976).

152. Id. at 297.

153. Id. at 298–300.

154. Id. at 306.

155. *Village of Arlington Heights v. Metropolitan Housing Development Corporation*, 429 U.S. 252 (1977).

156. *Bailey v. Alabama*, 219 U.S. 219 (1911); *United States v. Reynolds*, 235 U.S. 133 (1914); see also *Taylor v. Georgia*, 315 U.S. 25 (1942); *Pollock v. Williams*, 322 U.S. 4 (1944).

157. For general historical accounts of job discrimination against blacks, see Miller, *Petitioners*; Woodward, *Strange Career of Jim Crow*.

158. *New Negro Alliance v. Sanitary Grocery Co.*, 303 U.S. 552 at 561 (1938).

159. *Hughes v. Superior Court*, 339 U.S. 460 (1950).

160. *Steele v. Louisville and Nashville Railroad Co.*, 323 U.S. 192 (1944); see also *Tunstall v. Brotherhood*, 323 U.S. 210 (1944); *Graham v. Brotherhood*, 338 U.S. 232 (1949); *Conley v. Gibson*, 355 U.S. 41 (1957).

161. *Brotherhood of Railroad Trainmen v. Howard*, 343 U.S. 768 at 774 (1952); see also *Syres v. Oil Workers International Union*, 350 U.S. 892 (1955).

162. *Railway Mail Association v. Corsi*, 326 U.S. 88 (1945).

163. *Colorado Anti-Discrimination Commission v. Continental Airlines*, 372 U.S. 714 (1963).

164. *Griggs v. Duke Power Co.*, 401 U.S. 424 at 430–431 (1971).

165. Id. at 432.

166. *Albemarle Paper Company v. Moody*, 422 U.S. 405 (1975).

167. *Wards Cove Packing Co. v. Atonio*, 490 U.S. 642 (1989); see also *Lorance v. AT&T Technologies Inc.*, 490 U.S. 900 (1989).

168. *CQ Almanac, 1991* (Washington, D.C.: Congressional Quarterly, 1992), 251–261.

169. *McDonnell Douglas Corporation v. Green*, 411 U.S. 807 (1973).

170. *St. Mary's Honor Center v. Hicks*, 509 U.S. 502 (1993).

171. *Furnco Construction Corporation v. Waters*, 438 U.S. 567 at 579 (1978).

172. *Albemarle Paper Company v. Moody*, 422 U.S. 405 at 417–418 (1975).

173. Id. at 422.

174. *Fitzpatrick v. Bitzer*, 427 U.S. 445 (1976).

175. *Ford Motor Co. v. Equal Employment Opportunity Commission*, 458 U.S. 219 (1982).

176. *Franks v. Bowman Transportation Co. Inc.*, 424 U.S. 747 at 768 (1976).

177. Id. at 788–789.

178. *Teamsters v. United States, T.I.M.E.-D.C. v. United States*, 431 U.S. 324 (1977).

179. Id. at 354.

180. *Guardians Association v. Civil Service Commission of City of New York*, 463 U.S. 482 (1983).

181. *Brown v. Board of Education of Topeka*, 347 U.S. 483 (1954); *Bolling v. Sharpe*, 347 U.S. 483 (1954).

182. "To Fulfill These Rights," *Public Papers of the Presidents of the United States: Lyndon B. Johnson* (Washington, D.C., U.S. Government Printing Office, 1966), 2:635–640.

183. *University of California Regents v. Bakke*, 438 U.S. 265 (1978).

184. *United Steelworkers of America v. Weber, Kaiser Aluminum & Chemical Corp. v. Weber, United States v. Weber*, 443 U.S. 193 (1979).

185. *Grutter v. Bollinger*, 539 U.S. 306 (2003).

186. *DeFunis v. Odegaard*, 416 U.S. 312 (1974).

187. *University of California Regents v. Bakke*, 438 U.S. 265 at 412, 418 (1978).

188. Id. at 320, 307.

189. Id. at 325.

190. *United Steelworkers of America v. Weber, Kaiser Aluminum & Chemical Corp. v. Weber, United States v. Weber*, 443 U.S. 193 (1979).

191. Id. at 204.

192. Id. at 206, footnote 6.

193. Id. at 216.

194. Id. at 222.

195. *Fullilove v. Klutznick*, 448 U.S. 448 at 473 (1980).

196. Id. at 490.

197. *Firefighters Local No. 1784 v. Stotts, Memphis Fire Department v. Stotts*, 467 U.S. 561 (1984).

198. *Wygant v. Jackson Board of Education*, 476 U.S. 267 (1986).

199. Id. at 282.

200. Id. at 280–281.

201. Id. at 286.

202. *Local #28 of the Sheet Metal Workers' International v. Equal Employment Opportunity Commission*, 478 U.S. 421 (1986).

203. *Local #93, International Association of Firefighters v. City of Cleveland and Cleveland Vanguards*, 478 U.S. 501 (1986).

204. *United States v. Paradise*, 480 U.S. 149 (1987).

205. Id.

206. *Johnson v. Transportation Agency of Santa Clara County, Calif.*, 480 U.S. 616 (1987).

207. Id. at 677.

208. *City of Richmond v. J. A. Croson Co.*, 488 U.S. 469 at 491–492 (1989).

209. Id. at 498.

210. Id. at 499.

211. Id. at 504.

212. Id. at 505–506, 510.

213. *Martin v. Wilks*, 490 U.S. 755 (1989).

214. *Metro Broadcasting Inc. v. Federal Communications Commission*, 497 U.S. 547 (1990).

215. *Adarand Constructors Inc. v. Peña*, 515 U.S. 200 (1995).

216. Id. at 229–230.

217. Id.

218. Id. at 245.

219. *Grutter v. Bollinger*, 539 U.S. 306 (2003).

220. *Gratz v. Bollinger*, 539 U.S. 244 (2003).

221. *Grutter v. Bollinger*, 539 U.S. 306 (2003).

222. Id.

223. Id.

224. Id.

225. Id.

226. Id.

227. Id.

228. *Gratz v. Bollinger*, 539 U.S. 244 (2003).

229. Id.

EQUAL PROTECTION: THE ALIEN AND THE POOR (PP. 440–452)

1. *Yick Wo v. Hopkins*, 118 U.S. 356 at 369 (1886).

2. Id. at 373–374.

3. Id. at 374.

4. *Truax v. Raich*, 239 U.S. 33 at 41 (1915).

5. Alfred H. Kelly and Winfred A. Harbison, *The American Constitution: Its Origins and Development*, 5th ed. (New York: Norton, 1976), 666.

6. *McCready v. Virginia*, 94 U.S. 391 at 395 (1877).

7. *Patsone v. Pennsylvania*, 232 U.S. 138 at 144 (1914).

8. Id.

9. *Heim v. McCall*, 239 U.S. 175 (1915); *Crane v. New York*, 239 U.S. 195 (1915).

10. *Ozawa v. United States*, 260 U.S. 178 (1922).

11. *Terrace v. Thompson*, 263 U.S. 197 at 220 (1923); see also *Porterfield v. Webb*, 263 U.S. 225 (1923); *Webb v. O'Brien*, 263 U.S. 313 (1923); *Frick v. Webb*, 263 U.S. 326 (1923); *Cockrill v. California*, 268 U.S. 258 (1925).

12. *Clarke v. Deckebach*, 274 U.S. 392 at 396 (1927).

13. Id. at 397.

14. *Hirabayashi v. United States*, 320 U.S. 81 (1943); *Korematsu v. United States*, 323 U.S. 214 (1944).

15. *Oyama v. California*, 332 U.S. 633 at 646 (1948).

16. *Takahashi v. Fish and Game Commission*, 334 U.S. 410 at 418 (1948).

17. Id. at 419.

18. Id. at 421.

19. *Graham v. Richardson*, 403 U.S. 365 at 372 (1971).

20. Id. at 374.

21. Id. at 376.

22. *In re Griffiths*, 413 U.S. 717 (1973); *Examining Board of Engineers, Architects and Surveyors v. de Otero*, 426 U.S. 572 (1976); *Sugarman v. Dougall*, 413 U.S. 634 (1973); *Nyquist v. Mauclet*, 432 U.S. 1 (1977); *Bernal v. Fainter*, 467 U.S. 216 (1984).

23. *Sugarman v. Dougall*, 413 U.S. 634 at 641 (1973).

24. Id. at 643.

25. Id. at 647.

26. Id. at 648.

27. *Foley v. Connelie*, 435 U.S. 291 at 297 (1978).

28. Id. at 298–299.

29. *Ambach v. Norwick*, 441 U.S. 68 (1979).

30. *Cabell v. Chavez-Salido*, 454 U.S. 432 (1982).

31. *Plyler v. Doe, Texas v. Certain Named and Unnamed Undocumented Alien Children*, 457 U.S. 202 (1982).

32. Id. at 230.

33. *Mathews v. Diaz*, 426 U.S. 67 at 80–83, passim (1976).

34. Id. at 84.

35. *Hampton v. Mow Sun Wong*, 426 U.S. 88 at 1 (1976).

36. Id. at 115.

37. *Griffin v. Illinois*, 351 U.S. 12 at 12–13 (1956).

38. Id. at 19.

39. Id. at 28–29.

40. *Mayer v. Chicago*, 404 U.S. 189 at 196 (1971).

41. *United States v. MacCollum*, 426 U.S. 317 at 324 (1976).

42. *Douglas v. California*, 372 U.S. 353 at 357–358 (1963).

43. Id. at 361.

44. *Ross v. Moffitt*, 417 U.S. 600 (1974); *Fuller v. Oregon*, 417 U.S. 40 (1974).

45. *Boddie v. Connecticut*, 401 U.S. 371 at 381 (1971).

46. Id. at 386.

47. *United States v. Kras*, 409 U.S. 434 at 446 (1973).

48. Id. at 457.

49. *Williams v. Illinois*, 399 U.S. 235 (1970).

50. *Tate v. Short*, 401 U.S. 395 (1971).

51. *Saenz v. Roe*, 526 U.S. 489 (1999).

52. *United States v. Guest*, 383 U.S. 745 (1966).

53. *Edwards v. California*, 314 U.S. 160 (1941).

54. *Shapiro v. Thompson*, 394 U.S. 618 at 634 (1969).

55. Id. at 633.

56. *Memorial Hospital v. Maricopa County*, 415 U.S. 250 (1974).

57. *Breedlove v. Suttles*, 302 U.S. 277 (1937).

58. *Harper v. Virginia State Board of Elections*, 383 U.S. 663 at 668 (1966).

59. *Bullock v. Carter*, 405 U.S. 134 (1972).

60. *Lubin v. Panish*, 415 U.S. 709 (1974).

61. *Serrano v. Priest*, 96 Cal. Rptr. 601, 487 P. 2d 1241; 5 Cal. 3d 584 (1971).

62. *San Antonio Independent School District v. Rodriguez*, 411 U.S. 1 at 23–24 (1973); see also *Kadrmas v. Dickinson Public Schools*, 487 U.S. 450 (1988).

63. Id. at 33, 35.

64. Id. at 54–55.

65. Id. at 98.

66. Id. at 99.

SEX DISCRIMINATION (PP. 453–468)

1. *Bradwell v. Illinois*, 16 Wall. (83 U.S.) 130 at 141 (1873).

2. *Minor v. Happersett*, 21 Wall. (88 U.S.) 162 (1875).

3. *Strauder v. West Virginia*, 100 U.S. 303 (1880); *Hoyt v. Florida*, 368 U.S. 57 (1961), overruled by *Taylor v. Louisiana*, 419 U.S. 522 (1975).

4. *Cronin v. Adams*, 192 U.S. 108 (1904).

5. *Goesaert v. Cleary*, 335 U.S. 464 at 466 (1948).

6. Id. at 468.

7. *Muller v. Oregon*, 208 U.S. 412 at 422–423 (1908); see also *Riley v. Massachusetts*, 232 U.S. 671 (1914); *Miller v. Wilson*, 236 U.S. 373 (1915); *Bosley v. McLaughlin*, 236 U.S. 385 (1915); *West Coast Hotel v. Parrish*, 300 U.S. 379 (1937).

8. *Sail'er Inn Inc. v. Kirby*, 5 Cal. 3d 1.20, 485 P. 2d 529 (1971).

9. *Reed v. Reed*, 404 U.S. 71 at 76 (1971), quoting *Royster Guano Co. v. Virginia*, 253 U.S. 412 at 415 (1920).

10. *Reed v. Reed*, 404 U.S. 71 at 76 (1971).

11. *Kahn v. Shevin*, 416 U.S. 351 (1974).

12. *Schlesinger v. Ballard*, 419 U.S. 498 (1975).

13. *Weinberger v. Salfi*, 422 U.S. 749 (1975).

14. *Mathews v. De Castro*, 429 U.S. 181 (1976).

15. *Stanton v. Stanton*, 421 U.S. 7 at 15 (1975).

16. *Frontiero v. Richardson*, 411 U.S. 677 at 686–687 (1973).

17. *Weinberger v. Wiesenfeld*, 420 U.S. 636 at 645 (1975).

18. Id. at 651–652.

19. *Califano v. Goldfarb*, 430 U.S. 199 at 217 (1977).

20. Id. at 242.

21. *Wengler v. Druggists Mutual Insurance Co.*, 446 U.S. 142 (1980).

22. *Craig v. Boren*, 429 U.S. 190 at 197 (1976); see also *Orr v. Orr*, 440 U.S. 268 (1979).

23. *Michael M. v. Superior Court of Sonoma County*, 450 U.S. 464 (1981).

24. *Rostker v. Goldberg*, 453 U.S. 57 (1981).

25. *Mississippi University for Women v. Hogan*, 458 U.S. 718 (1982).

26. Id. at 724.

27. Id. at 729.

28. *United States v. Virginia*, 518 U.S. 515 at (1996).

29. Cass Sunstein, *One Case at a Time* (Cambridge, Mass.: Harvard University Press, 1999).

30. *United States v. Virginia*, 518 U.S. 515 at 540 (1996).

31. Id. at 533.

32. Id. at 558.

33. Id. at 562.

34. Id. at 601.

35. *General Electric Co. v. Gilbert*, 429 U.S. 125 at 162 (1976).

36. *Phillips v. Martin Marietta Corp.*, 400 U.S. 542 (1971).

37. *Dothard v. Rawlinson*, 433 U.S. 321 at 329 (1977).

38. Id. at 336.

39. Id. at 345–346.

40. *Cleveland Board of Education v. LaFleur, Cohen v. Chesterfield County School Board*, 414 U.S. 632 at 639–640 (1974).

41. Id. at 643.

42. Id. at 660.

43. *Geduldig v. Aiello*, 417 U.S. 484 at 496–497, note 20 (1974).

44. Id. at 496–497.

45. Id. at 500–501.

46. *General Electric Co. v. Gilbert*, 429 U.S. 125 at 136 (1976).

47. Id. at 138–139.

48. Id. at 149, 158.

49. *Nashville Gas Co. v. Satty*, 434 U.S. 136 at 142 (1977).

50. *Congress and the Nation* (Washington, D.C.: Congressional Quarterly, 1981), 5:796.

51. *Newport News Shipbuilding & Dry Dock Co. v. Equal Employment Opportunity Commission*, 462 U.S. 669 (1983); *California Federal Savings & Loan v. Guerra*, 479 U.S. 272 (1987).

52. *UAW v. Johnson Controls*, 499 U.S. 187 (1991).

53. *Los Angeles v. Manhart*, 435 U.S. 702 at 710 (1978).

54. Id. at 708.

55. Id. at 726.

56. Id. at 722.

57. *Fitzpatrick v. Bitzer*, 427 U.S. 445 (1976).

58. *Arizona Governing Committee for Tax Deferred Annuity and Deferred Compensation Plans v. Norris*, 463 U.S. 1073 (1983); see also *Florida v. Long*, 487 U.S. 223 (1988).

59. *Meritor Savings Bank v. Vinson*, 477 U.S. 57 (1986).

60. *Harris v. Forklift Systems Inc.*, 510 U.S. 17 (1993).

61. *Faragher v. City of Boca Raton*, 524 U.S. 775 (1998), and *Burlington Industries v. Ellerth*, 524 U.S.742 (1998).

62. *Ledbetter v. Goodyear Tire & Rubber Co.*, 550 U.S. __ (2007).

chapter 7

Liberty and Privacy

EW WOULD DISAGREE that freedom and individual liberty are among the most cherished values of American democracy. The Declaration of Independence set out a truth its authors saw as "self-evident" that all persons had rights to "Life, Liberty and the Pursuit of Happiness" and that government was instituted "to secure these rights." The Constitution professes to "secure the Blessings of Liberty to ourselves and our Posterity." Defining the reach of this protected liberty has prompted fierce disputes, even war. Whose liberty is to be protected? Should the Court decide or leave it to the will of the majority?

The greatest conflict of the nineteenth century concerned slavery. Southern plantation owners said they had the right and the freedom to own slaves. Northern abolitionists said the African slaves had a right to live in freedom. While the Supreme Court sided with the slave owners in the *Dred Scott* decision of 1857, the Union's victory in the Civil War gave the slaves their freedom. Early in the twentieth century, laws were passed to protect workers from long hours and low pay. The Supreme Court struck down some of these laws on the grounds that they interfered with the worker's "liberty" to work even longer and for less. In 1905, when the Court voided a New York law that limited bakers to working no more than sixty hours per week, Justice Rufus Peckham argued that bakers' liberty was at issue. "The right to purchase or sell labor is part of the liberty protected by this [Fourteenth] Amendment," he said. "There is no reasonable ground for interfering with the liberty of person or right of free contract by determining the hours of labor," he concluded.[1] These pro-business decisions were denounced at the time as flawed in their reasoning and perverse in their result. The Fourteenth Amendment said no state shall "deprive any person of life, liberty or property without due process of law." Because the New York law had been duly enacted, it was not obvious how its limit on work hours for bakers deprived anyone of liberty "without due process of law." These decisions were repudiated during the New Deal era as overreaching by the judiciary. In 1937, after President Franklin D. Roosevelt's landslide reelection, the Court backed away from reviewing workplace laws on constitutional grounds. Commercial arrangements are the province of the elected branches of government, the Court decided.

On occasion, the Court ruled against peculiar state laws on the grounds that they violated the liberty protected by the Fourteenth Amendment. In 1923 a Nebraska law that forbade the teaching of foreign languages was struck down on the ground that it violated the liberty rights of parents and teachers.[2] A Connecticut law that prohibited the selling or using of birth control pills was struck down in 1965. This law may have been "uncommonly silly," said dissenting Justice Potter Stewart, but he doubted it violated a particular provision in the Constitution. Speaking for the majority in *Griswold v. Connecticut,* Justice William O. Douglas conceded the point, but said the "specific guarantees in the Bill of Rights have penumbras, formed by emanations from those guarantees that help give them life and substance.... Various guarantees create zones of privacy," Douglas said. "Would we allow the police to search the sacred precincts of marital bedrooms for telltale signs of the use of contraceptives?"[3]

Critics of the Court mocked Douglas's vaporizing about "emanations" and "penumbras," but his opinion laid the basis for a far-reaching and far more controversial decision less than ten years later. Then, forty-six of the fifty states made nearly all abortions a crime, and they had done so for more than a century. The Court's ruling in *Roe v. Wade* (1973) struck down all these laws as unconstitutional and declared that abortion may not be prohibited until after six months of a pregnancy. Public opinion polls suggested then, as now, that the nation was deeply split over the legality and morality of abortion. Many believed that because an unwanted pregnancy profoundly affected the life and liberty of a woman, she should have the right and the freedom to decide whether to end it. Others maintained that the life and liberty of an unborn child was at stake; by this light, an abortion was akin to murder.

The women's rights movement was surging in strength in the early 1970s, and many saw the strict laws against abortion as archaic, a remnant of the Victorian era. It was commonly said that if men could become pregnant, the law would not punish abortion as a crime. The Court did not decide, however, to invalidate the abortion laws as a type of sex discrimination against women. Instead, Justice Harry A. Blackmun said the newly minted right to abortion grew from the liberty and privacy protected by the Constitution. "This right to privacy, whether it is founded in the Fourteenth Amendment's concept of personal liberty and restrictions upon state action, as we feel it is, or, as the District Court determined, in the Ninth Amendment's reservations of rights to the people, is broad enough to encompass a woman's decision whether or not to terminate her pregnancy," Blackmun wrote for a 7-2 majority. The ruling set off a public firestorm that has roared steadily to the present. The furor is fueled by the strong emotions that surround the intensely personal nature of abortion, the related issues of life and

death, the continuing struggle of women for sexual equality, and the unique political and social character of the United States.

Far from resolving the issue through a legal ruling, the Court's decision in *Roe* launched a powerful "right to life" movement that has reshaped American politics and affected the confirmation of presidential nominees to the Court. "The war over abortion seems fiercer and more violent in America than anywhere else," notes Ronald Dworkin, a liberal scholar. He attributes this reaction to a combination of America's contradictory public and private attitudes toward religion and the nature of the women's movement. While the country demands strict separation of church and state, Dworkin observes, religious faith is nonetheless a powerful force in American life. Meanwhile, the women's movement has sought to free women from traditional notions of sexuality and duty.[4] Critics of the *Roe* ruling, including Justice Antonin Scalia, blame the Court for the continuing controversy. By removing abortion from the political arena, the justices prevented elected state lawmakers from making compromises that reflect the will of the people, he has said.

In 1980 Ronald Reagan ran for the presidency and vowed to try to overturn *Roe v. Wade.* His victory put the Republican Party on a course to represent "pro-life" voters. The Democratic Party spoke for "pro-choice" voters, and its platform had vowed to defend *Roe* and a woman's right to abortion. Reagan appointed three new justices to the Court and elevated William H. Rehnquist, one of the two dissenters to the *Roe* decision, to be chief justice. Reagan's vice president and successor, President George H. W. Bush, appointed two more justices. Nonetheless, the Court in *Planned Parenthood of Southeastern Pennsylvania v. Casey* (1992) affirmed the right to an abortion. "Some of us as individuals find abortion offensive to our most basic principles of morality, but that cannot control our decision. Our obligation is to define the liberty of all, not to mandate our own moral code," wrote Justices Sandra Day O'Connor, Anthony M. Kennedy, and David H. Souter in an unusual joint opinion.[5] O'Connor and Kennedy were Reagan appointees, and Souter had been appointed by Bush.

Although the Court held the line on abortion, it retreated from the frontiers of liberty and privacy. In 1986 the justices heard a challenge to a Georgia law that made it a crime for gays to have sex, even at home. If the Constitution indeed protected a "right to privacy," this law would appear to be more suspect than a ban on abortion. This medical procedure takes place in a doctor's office or in a hospital or clinic, not in the privacy of a home. The Court, however, upheld antisodomy laws in *Bowers v. Hardwick* (1986). The right-to-die issue came before the Court in the 1990s, posing the question of whether a dying person has a right to end his or her life at home with a dose of lethal medication. Unanimously, in *Washington v. Glucksberg* (1997), the Court in 1997 upheld a state law prohibiting assisted suicide and refused to extend the right to liberty and privacy to a patient's dying days.[6]

The gay rights movement could not be denied, however. Hundreds of cities and states had enacted laws protecting gays and lesbians from discrimination, but Texas had kept on the books a law that made sex between gays a crime. In 2003 in *Lawrence v. Texas,* the Court overturned *Bowers v. Hardwick* and struck down the Texas law. Justice Kennedy sounded a tone that had not been heard for some time and said that the Court has a duty to protect liberty and privacy. The "intimate, consensual conduct" of two adults at home is surely within the realm of liberty protected by the Constitution, he said, and off-limits to the government.[7]

ORIGINS OF PERSONAL PRIVACY

Judicial recognition of a protected category of personal rights dates back to the early 1920s, during the era when the Court interpreted the liberty guarantee as "the liberty to contract." In *Meyer v. Nebraska* (1923), the Court extended the liberty guarantee to cover rights that were personal as well as economic. That case involved a Nebraska law that forbade any school from teaching a modern foreign language other than English to children in the first eight grades. The Court held that the statute violated the Fourteenth Amendment's due process guarantee by depriving the teacher who had been convicted and the affected parents and children of a measure of personal liberty—the right to choose this area of instruction:

> Without doubt, it [liberty] denotes not merely freedom from bodily restraint but also the right of the individual to contract, to engage in any of the common occupations of life, to acquire useful knowledge, to marry, establish a home and bring up children, to worship God according to the dictates of his own conscience, and generally to enjoy those privileges long recognized at common law as essential to the orderly pursuit of happiness by free men.[8]

Two years later the Court struck down an Oregon law that required all children to attend public schools. The challenge was brought by the Society of the Sisters of the Holy Names of Jesus and Mary, which ran orphanages and parochial schools. The Court in *Pierce v. Society of Sisters* declared that the statute "unreasonably interferes with the liberty of parents ... to direct the upbringing and education of [their] children." The Court said parents may educate children as they choose: "The child is not the mere creature of the State; those who nurture him and direct his destiny have the right, coupled with the high duty, to recognize and prepare him for additional obligations."[9]

Marriage and Procreation

In the 1940s the Court recognized another fundamental right of liberty that had no clear constitutional roots: the freedom to marry and procreate. Oklahoma law provided that persons convicted three times of crimes of "moral turpitude" were to be sterilized. The Supreme Court in *Skinner v. Oklahoma* (1942) invalidated the law because it did not treat all persons convicted of similar crimes in a similar way:

> We are dealing here with legislation which involves one of the basic civil rights of man. Marriage and procreation are fundamental to the very existence and survival of the race. The power to sterilize, if exercised, may have subtle, far-reaching and devastating effects. In evil or reckless hands it can cause races or types which are inimical to the dominant group to wither and disappear.... [T]he individual whom the law touches ... is forever deprived of a basic liberty.[10]

Estelle Griswold *(left)* and Mrs. Ernest Jahncke, president of Parenthood League of Connecticut, Inc., celebrate the Supreme Court's ruling in *Griswold v. Connecticut* (1965). Griswold had opened a birth control clinic in New Haven in violation of an 1879 Connecticut law prohibiting the use of contraceptives. The Court struck down the law and established a constitutionally protected right to privacy.

As a result of this decision, laws that affected such fundamental rights as marriage and procreation were now subject to close scrutiny and could be justified only by a pressing governmental objective. Such protection for the right of personal privacy was reinforced by the Court's evolving fundamental interest standard for equal protection cases. Twenty-five years after *Skinner,* the Court affirmed the Constitution's protection for choice in marriage. In the case of *Loving v. Virginia* (1967), the Court struck down a Virginia law that punished persons for marrying someone of a different race. This law, the unanimous Court held, violated the Equal Protection Clause and denied those it affected due process:

The freedom to marry has long been recognized as one of the vital personal rights essential to the orderly pursuit of happiness by free men.... To deny this fundamental freedom on so unsupportable a basis as the racial classification embodied in these statutes ... is surely to deprive all the State's citizens of liberty without due process of law. The Fourteenth Amendment requires that the freedom of choice to marry not be restricted by invidious racial discriminations. Under our Constitution, the freedom to marry or not marry a person of another race resides with the individual and cannot be infringed by the State.[11]

Contraceptives

Two years before *Loving,* in *Griswold v. Connecticut* (1965), the Court had held that the Constitution

THE PROTECTION OF SUBSTANTIVE DUE PROCESS: FROM PROPERTY TO PRIVACY

Within the awkward phrase "substantive due process" lies a fierce debate spanning more than 130 years over the Supreme Court's role in protecting liberty as a fundamental right. The Fifth and Fourteenth Amendments do not unequivocally guarantee a right to liberty. Rather, they state that a person may not be "deprived of life, liberty or property, without due process of law." Constitutional literalists, such as Justice Antonin Scalia, say that this provision does not give the Court the authority to determine the substance of liberty. Instead, they contend it may rule only on the fairness of the procedures used by the government.

For more than a century, however, the Court has adopted a broader view of its authority to protect liberty itself as a fundamental right, including by defining the substance of liberty. Early in the twentieth century, the Court struck down labor laws, including limits on working hours, on the theory that this restriction infringed the "liberty" of individuals to work as long as they chose. In 1923 the Court struck down a Nebraska law that prohibited the teaching of German and other foreign languages in the schools. The law had been challenged by a German teacher. Two years later, the Court struck down an Oregon law that required all children to attend public schools and not religious or parochial schools. In both cases, the justices said that the Constitution and the Fourteenth Amendment protect the right to live freely in a democratic society. This includes the right "to engage in any of the common occupations of life, to acquire useful knowledge, to marry, establish a home and bring up children."[1] Decades later, these opinions giving the "liberty" clause a broad reading were relied upon as precedents to strike down state laws forbidding contraceptives, abortion, and sodomy. Critics of these decisions faulted the Court for overstepping its authority and writing into the Constitution its view of liberty. They referred to this overreaching as "substantive due process."

A DEVELOPING CONCEPT

The first hint of the doctrine of substantive due process is found in a dissenting opinion in the *Slaughterhouse Cases* (1873). New Orleans butchers challenged a state-granted slaughterhouse monopoly as denying them due process—the opportunity to practice their trade. The Court rejected this Fourteenth Amendment challenge. In dissent, Justice Joseph P. Bradley agreed that "a law which prohibits a large class of citizens from adopting ... or from following a lawful employment ... does deprive them of liberty as well as property, without due process of law."[2]

Four years later, in *Munn v. Illinois* (1877), the Court edged closer to Bradley's view. Although the justices upheld a state law that regulated grain elevator rates, they did so only after considering the substance of the business regulated. The Court found that grain storage was one of a class of businesses "affected with a public interest" and therefore subject to state regulation.[3] In this decision, the first in a line of rulings stretching over half a century, the Court looked to the character of the activity regulated to determine whether it was properly within the state's domain. In *Mugler v. Kansas* (1887), concerning a state prohibition law, Justice John Marshall Harlan explained the Court's view:

> The courts are not bound by mere forms, nor are they to be misled by mere pretenses. They are at liberty—indeed, are under a solemn

duty—to look at the substance of things, whenever they enter upon the inquiry whether the legislature has transcended the limits of its authority. If, therefore, a statute purporting to have been enacted to protect the public health, the public morals, or the public safety, has no real or substantial relation to those objects, or is a palpable invasion of rights secured by the fundamental law, it is the duty of the courts to so adjudge, and thereby give effect to the Constitution.[4]

In *Chicago, Milwaukee and St. Paul R. R. Co. v. Minnesota* (1890), the Court first used substantive due process to strike down a state law regulating economic matters, ruling that the courts should have the final word on the reasonableness of railroad rates.[5] In 1898 the Court declared that courts should review public utility rates for reasonableness and to see that they allowed a fair return to the utility.[6]

FREEDOM OF CONTRACT: ECONOMIC SUBSTANTIVE DUE PROCESS

Although many laws in which states exercised their police power were challenged as a denial of due process in the nineteenth and early twentieth centuries, the Supreme Court generally found these laws valid.[7] In the areas of rate setting, price regulation, and wage-and-hour laws, however, the Court was far less disposed to defer to the judgment of state legislators.[8] Two key doctrines emerged: business in which there is a public interest can be regulated by the state, and government should not interfere with the freedom of contract. With these doctrines, the Supreme Court plunged into a new role as judge of the substance of state economic regulation.

Under the public interest rubric, the Court upheld state regulation of such varied matters as insurance and stockyards,[9] but beginning in the 1920s it found fewer and fewer areas of economic life to be properly included in this category.[10] To protect the freedom of contract, the Court struck down a number of the first wage-and-hour laws passed by the states. In *Holden v. Hardy* (1898), the Court upheld a law setting the eight-hour day as the maximum that miners might work,[11] but seven years later, in *Lochner v. New York* (1905), the justices struck down a law setting the ten-hour day and the sixty-hour week as the maximum for bakers.[12] The Court saw a critical difference between the working conditions of mines and bakeries. Miners worked in palpably unhealthy conditions, to which their exposure should be limited, while bakers were subject to less risk of injury or illness in their working environment. The Court subsequently dropped its opposition to maximum-hour laws.[13] It was not, however, so tolerant when it considered the first minimum-wage statutes. In *Adkins v. Children's Hospital* (1923), the Court struck down the District of Columbia's minimum-wage law for women. Justice George Sutherland, for the five-man majority, described the law as "simply and exclusively a price-fixing law" in violation of the freedom of contract.[14]

DEMISE OF ECONOMIC SUBSTANTIVE DUE PROCESS

The Great Depression and the New Deal created pressures that inexorably forced the Supreme Court to drop its use of substantive due process to monitor economic regulation. Beginning with *Nebbia v. New York* (1934), the Court abdicated its role as "super-legislature," leaving decisions on the wisdom and appropriateness of economic legislation to legislators. In *Nebbia*, the Court upheld a state law regulating milk prices, although the milk industry was not one "affected with a public interest."[15] The Court thus ceased to distinguish between some lines of business and others for the purpose of finding some subject to state regulation and others exempt. Nevertheless, the Court used the freedom of contract doctrine to nullify a state minimum-wage law for women. In *Morehead v. New York ex rel. Tipaldo* (1936), a five-justice majority declared, "The right to make contracts about one's affairs is a part of the liberty protected by the due process clause. Within this liberty are provisions of contracts between employer and employee fixing the wages to be paid."[16] The tide of public opinion had, however, turned against this sort of judicial second-guessing. In 1936 both major parties repudiated the *Morehead* decision. Then in *West Coast Hotel v. Parrish* (1937), the Court upheld a Washington state minimum-wage law for women, overruling *Adkins* and *Morehead*.[17]

FROM PROPERTY TO PRIVACY

Yet even as the Court wrote the epitaph for the use of substantive due process to justify its supervision of economic regulation, it was developing a line of rulings under the equal protection guarantee that led it again to consider the substance of state legislation. In *Skinner v. Oklahoma* (1942), the Court struck down a state law that allowed habitual criminals to be sterilized. This law was a denial of equal protection, held the justices, because of its substance—because it allowed the state to deprive an individual of "one of the basic civil rights of man."[18] Matters of personal choice in family life have been the primary beneficiary of the "new substantive due process" approach foreshadowed in *Skinner*.

One landmark in this area was the Court's declaration in *Griswold v. Connecticut* (1965) that privacy was a value protected by the Constitution.[19] In that case, the Court struck down a state law forbidding all use of birth control devices. Although Justice William O. Douglas, writing the majority opinion, was careful not to rest the conclusion upon the Due Process Clause, Justice Hugo L. Black—in dissent—found the ruling a direct descendant of *Lochner v. New York*. This too was substantive due process, he warned, and it was "no less dangerous when used to enforce this Court's views about personal rights than those about economic rights."[20]

Eight years later Justice William H. Rehnquist sounded the same complaint, dissenting from the Court's decision in *Roe v. Wade* (1973), which struck down state laws banning abortion. "As in *Lochner* and similar cases applying substantive due process standards," Rehnquist wrote, the standard adopted in *Roe v. Wade* "will inevitably require this Court to examine the legislative policies and pass on the wisdom of these policies."[21] In the 1990s the Court narrowly affirmed the essential holding of *Roe*, voting 5-4 in *Planned Parenthood of Southeastern Pennsylvania v. Casey* (1992). The three justices whose votes effectively preserved the right to abortion wrote in their plurality opinion

> Neither the Bill of Rights nor the specific practices of the States at the time of the adoption of the Fourteenth Amendment marks the outer limits of the substantive sphere which the Fourteenth Amendment protects....It is settled now, as it was when the Court heard arguments in *Roe v. Wade*,

that the Constitution places limits on a State's right to interfere with a person's most basic decisions about family and parenthood.[22]

The Court again invoked the Liberty and Due Process Clauses to strike down homosexual sodomy laws. The Fourteenth Amendment's Liberty Clause "gives substantial protection to adult persons in deciding how to conduct their private lives in matters pertaining to sex," the Court said in *Lawrence v. Texas* (2003).[23]

1. *Meyer v. Nebraska*, 262 U.S. 390 (1923), and *Pierce v. Society of Sisters*, 268 U.S. 510 (1925).

2. *Slaughterhouse Cases*, 16 Wall. (83 U.S.) 36 at 122 (1873).

3. *Munn v. Illinois*, 94 U.S. 113 (1877).

4. *Mugler v. Kansas*, 123 U.S. 623 at 661 (1887).

5. *Chicago, Milwaukee and St. Paul R. R. Co. v. Minnesota*, 134 U.S. 418 (1890).

6. *Smyth v. Ames*, 169 U.S. 466 (1898).

7. *Powell v. Pennsylvania*, 127 U.S. 678 (1888); *Jacobson v. Massachusetts*, 197 U.S. 11 (1905); *Austin v. Tennessee*, 179 U.S. 343 (1900); *Packer Corp. v. Utah*, 285 U.S. 105 (1932); *Euclid v. Ambler Realty Co.*, 272 U.S. 365 (1926).

8. *Allgeyer v. Louisiana*, 165 U.S. 578 at 589 (1897).

9. *German Alliance Insurance Co. v. Lewis*, 233 U.S. 389 (1914); *Cotting v. Godard*, 183 U.S. 79 (1901).

10. *Tyson & Brother v. Banton*, 273 U.S. 418 (1927); *Ribnik v. McBride*, 277 U.S. 350 (1928); *Wolff Packing Co. v. Court of Industrial Relations*, 262 U.S. 522 (1923); *Burns Baking Co. v. Bryan*, 264 U.S. 504 (1924).

11. *Holden v. Hardy*, 169 U.S. 366 (1898).

12. *Lochner v. New York*, 198 U.S. 45 (1905).

13. *Muller v. Oregon*, 208 U.S. 412 (1908); *Bunting v. Oregon*, 243 U.S. 426 (1917). For examples of substantive due process and labor matters, see *Adair v. United States*, 208 U.S. 161 (1908); *Coppage v. Kansas*, 236 U.S. 1 (1915); *Lincoln Federal Labor Union v. Northwestern Iron & Metal Co.*, 335 U.S. 525 (1949).

14. *Adkins v. Children's Hospital*, 261 U.S. 525 at 554 (1923).

15. *Nebbia v. New York*, 291 U.S. 502 (1934); see also *Petersen Baking Co. v. Burns*, 290 U.S. 570 (1934).

16. *Morehead v. New York ex rel. Tipaldo*, 298 U.S. 587 at 610 (1936).

17. *West Coast Hotel v. Parrish*, 300 U.S. 379 (1937); see also *United States v. Darby Lumber Co.*, 312 U.S. 100 (1941); *Olsen v. Nebraska*, 313 U.S. 236 (1941); *Federal Power Commission v. Hope Natural Gas*, 320 U.S. 551 (1944); *Day-Brite Lighting Inc. v. Missouri*, 342 U.S. 421 at 423 (1952); *Williamson v. Lee Optical of Oklahoma*, 348 U.S. 483 (1955).

18. *Skinner v. Oklahoma*, 316 U.S. 535 (1942).

19. *Griswold v. Connecticut*, 381 U.S. 479 (1965); see also *Eisenstadt v. Baird*, 405 U.S. 438 (1972); *Roe v. Wade*, 410 U.S. 113 (1973); *Doe v. Bolton*, 410 U.S. 179 (1973).

20. *Griswold v. Connecticut*, 381 U.S. 479 at 522 (1965).

21. *Roe v. Wade*, 410 U.S. 113 at 174 (1973).

22. *Planned Parenthood of Southeastern Pennsylvania v. Casey*, 505 U.S. 833 (1992).

23. *Lawrence v. Texas*, 539 U.S. 558 (2003).

forbade a state to prohibit married couples from using contraceptives. Estelle Griswold, the executive director of the Planned Parenthood League of Connecticut, gave medical advice to married persons who wished to prevent conception, and she challenged the Connecticut law.

The progeny of this case would greatly expand the scope of constitutional liberties. The individual votes in the seven-justice majority rested on a variety of reasons. Justice William O. Douglas, for the Court, found the basis for his vote in a right of personal privacy, an independent right implicit in the First, Third, Fourth, Fifth, and Ninth Amendments. "[S]pecific guarantees in the Bill of Rights have penumbras, formed by emanations from those guarantees that help give them life and substance," he wrote. "Various guarantees create zones of privacy."[12] Marriage was within a protected zone of privacy, Douglas continued, and the state impermissibly invaded that zone by prohibiting married couples from using contraceptives. "Would we allow the police to search the sacred precincts of marital bedrooms for telltale signs of the use of contraceptives? The very idea is repulsive to the notions of privacy surrounding the marriage relationship," he concluded.[13]

In an opinion by Justice Arthur J. Goldberg, joined by Chief Justice Earl Warren and Justice William J. Brennan Jr., the right to personal privacy was declared to be one of those rights "retained by the people" under the Ninth Amendment, which states that the "enumeration in the Constitution of certain rights shall not be construed to deny or disparage others retained by the people."[14] Justice John Marshall Harlan, it was cited, had seen marriage as one of the basic values that the Court had found "implicit in the concept of ordered liberty" protected by the Fourteenth Amendment.[15] Justice Byron R. White held that because marriage was a fundamental interest, the Connecticut law deprived married couples of "liberty" without due process of law.[16] The dissenting justices, Potter Stewart and Hugo L. Black, found no right of personal privacy expressed or implied in the Constitution. In 1972 the Court struck down a state law that permitted the distribution of contraceptives to single persons to prevent the spread of disease but not to prevent conception, finding it a violation of the equal protection guarantee.[17]

ABORTION, *ROE V. WADE,* AND THE CONTROVERSY THAT NEVER ENDS

In June 1971, the Court agreed for the first time to hear a constitutional challenge to the long-standing laws against abortion. Texas had made it a crime since 1854 to "procure" an abortion, unless it was done to save the life of the mother. Thirty-one states besides Texas had similar laws on the books in 1971. Georgia and thirteen other states had adopted somewhat more lenient measures. Abortions were permitted for certain reasons, such as if the mother's health were endangered, if the fetus had a severe defect, or if the pregnancy were the result of rape. In Georgia, such abortions had to be performed in a hospital and required the approval of three physicians.

The Court voted to hear a challenge to the Texas law in *Roe v. Wade* and to the Georgia law in *Doe v. Bolton.* It took two rounds of arguments and about nineteen months for the Court to decide the cases. During that time, Justices Hugo L. Black and John Marshall Harlan retired and died and were replaced by President Richard Nixon's third and fourth appointees: Justices Lewis F. Powell Jr. and William H. Rehnquist. Justice Harry A. Blackmun was in just his second year on the Court when Chief Justice Warren Burger assigned him to write the opinions in the two abortion cases. A former legal counsel for the Mayo Clinic in Minnesota, Blackmun had a deep respect for doctors, and his opinion in *Roe* described abortion as "inherently, and primarily, a medical decision, and basic responsibility for it must rest with the physician." It seems that Blackmun perhaps did not understand, or perhaps did not foresee, that doctors would routinely perform abortions upon request if the practice were legal.

Blackmun's opinion evolved over the nineteen months. In the Court's first conference, in December 1971, he described the Georgia law as a "fine statute" and "perfectly workable." It "strikes a balance that is fair," according to notes taken by Justices Douglas and Brennan. By contrast, he and the other six justices—Powell and Rehnquist had yet to arrive–agreed that the Texas law was too strict. It would prohibit abortions even if the doctor believed the mother's health was in danger. All the justices—except for perhaps Byron White—voted to strike down the Texas law. They were more closely divided on the Georgia law. Two major questions were before Blackmun and the Court: Is there a constitutional right to abortion? If so, how far does it extend?

After six months had elapsed, Blackmun sent around a seventeen-page opinion that he called "a first and tentative draft" for *Roe v. Wade*. "I come out on the theory that the Texas statute, despite its narrowness, is unconstitutionally vague." It does not clearly tell doctors whether they can perform an abortion if, for example, a pregnancy might threaten a woman's life. "I think that this would be all that is necessary for the disposition of the case, and that we need not get into the more complex Ninth Amendment issue. This may or may not appeal to you. In any event, I am still flexible as to results."[18] Blackmun's draft did not appeal to liberal justices William O. Douglas, William J. Brennan Jr., and Thurgood Marshall. They wanted a strong statement declaring a right to abortion. Had Blackmun's draft been issued as the Court's opinion, it would have struck down nearly all the abortion laws on the books and forced states to rewrite the measures. This would have likely led to years of more litigation over the contours of the abortion right. Chief Justice Burger proposed to issue no decision and instead to have the cases reargued in the fall with the new justices, Powell and Rehnquist, on the bench. Blackmun reluctantly agreed.

By the fall, Blackmun had drafted a much longer opinion that delved into the history of abortion in ancient Greece and Rome. On November 22, 1972, he sent this draft to his colleagues and noted that his opinion would permit abortion for the first three months of a pregnancy. "You will observe that I have concluded that the end of the first trimester is critical.

That is arbitrary, but perhaps any other selected point, such as quickening or viability, is equally arbitrary," he wrote in a memo now on file at the Library of Congress. His draft said that states may restrict abortion after the first trimester to "reasonable therapeutic categories." This would follow the model of the Georgia law.

Several justices, led by Marshall and Lewis F. Powell Jr., objected. They argued that abortion should be legal to the point of "viability," which occurs around month six, when the baby may be able to live on its own. Blackmun agreed and revised his opinion so that it could be released in January 1973. To the end, however, he was convinced that his opinion was measured and did not authorize "abortion on demand." In an unusual move, he wrote, an explanatory memo that would be released to the press. "Abortion is essentially a medical decision," he wrote, "I fear what the headlines may be, but it should be stressed that the Court does not today hold that the Constitution compels abortion on demand." Brennan persuaded Blackmun not to release the memo and instead let the opinion speak for itself.[19]

On January 22, the Court released the opinions in the two abortion cases. The *Roe v. Wade* opinion was long on medical history and short on constitutional analysis. "The Constitution does not explicitly mention any right of privacy," wrote Justice Blackmun. "[H]owever,… the Court has recognized that a right of personal privacy, or a guarantee of certain areas or zones of privacy does exist under the Constitution."[20] Whatever its source, Blackmun declared, "[t]his right of privacy … is broad enough to encompass a woman's decision whether or not to terminate her pregnancy."[21] Blackmun cautioned, however, that a woman's right to have an abortion is qualified:

> [A] state may properly assert important interests in safeguarding health, in maintaining medical standards, and in protecting potential life. At some point in pregnancy, these respective interests become sufficiently compelling to sustain regulation of the factors that govern the abortion decision.[22]

Blackmun summarized the key points:

- "For the stage prior to approximately the end of the first trimester, the abortion decision and its effectuation must be left to the medical judgment of the pregnant woman's attending physician," he wrote. Though this was later referred to as a woman's right to abortion, Blackmun focused on the doctor, not the patient.

- "For the stage prior to approximately the end of the first trimester, the State, in promoting its interest in the health of the mother, may, if it chooses, regulate the abortion procedure in ways that are reasonably related to maternal health." At first, this was seen as giving states some regulatory authority over abortion, but it soon became clear that no regulations could stand if they interfered significantly with abortions. The only measures upheld were those that required abortions to be performed by physicians.

- "For the stage subsequent to viability, the State in promoting its interest in the potentiality of human life may, if it chooses, regulate, and even proscribe, abortion except where it is necessary, in appropriate medical judgment, for the preservation of the life or health of the mother." This too was seen as giving states the power to prohibit late abortions. In the separate *Doe v. Bolton* decision, however, Blackmun defined the word *health* very broadly, so doctors could justify performing an abortion in nearly any circumstance. Abortion rests with the "medical judgment" of the physician, and the doctor may decide "in light of all factors—physical, emotional, psychological, familial and the woman's age—relevant to the wellbeing of the patient. All these factors may relate to health," he wrote. This sentence was the focus of much future controversy. Supporters of abortion rights argued that the laws must permit abortions to protect the "health" of the mother, but critics contended that this exception permits all abortions if "health" is defined so broadly. The companion ruling in *Doe v. Bolton* also struck

down the parts of the Georgia law that required abortions to be performed in hospitals and with the approval of three doctors.[23]

Justices White and Rehnquist dissented. Both said the Court had overstepped its authority. "The Court apparently values the convenience of the pregnant mother more than the continued existence and development of the life or potential life she carries. Whether or not I might agree with the marshaling of values, I can in no event join the Court's judgment because I find no constitutional warrant for imposing such an order of priorities on the people and the legislatures of the States," White wrote in *Doe v. Bolton*.[24] "In a sensitive area such as this, involving as it does issues on which reasonable men can easily and heatedly differ, I cannot accept the Court's exercise of its clear power of choice by interposing a constitutional barrier to state efforts to protect human life and by investing mothers and doctors with the constitutionally protected right to exterminate it. This issue, for the most part, should be left with the people and to the political processes the people have devised to govern their affairs."[25]

Rehnquist noted that Texas law and most of the state restrictions on abortion had been adopted in the mid-nineteenth century, roughly during the time when the Fourteenth Amendment was written and ratified. He said it was hard to understand as a matter of history or logic that this same amendment invalidated the anti-abortion laws.

Chief Justice Burger issued a short concurring opinion that suggests that he, like Blackmun, did not understand the reach of the decision. "I do not read the Court's holdings today as having the sweeping consequences attributed to them by the dissenting Justices; the dissenting views discount the reality that the vast majority of physicians observe the standards of the profession, and act only on the basis of carefully deliberated medical judgments relating to life and health. Plainly, the Court today rejects any claim that the Constitution requires abortions on demand."[26]

State Restrictions Increase, Right to Abortion Affirmed

In a 1976 case, the Court ruled that a mature woman has a right to have an abortion, even in the face of strong family opposition. The justices held that states cannot require the consent of the husband or, if the woman is an unmarried minor, the consent of her parents as an essential condition for a first-trimester abortion.[27] The Court declined, however, in 1980 to require that public funds, state or federal, be used for abortions for poor women.[28] In the 1980s, dissenting *Roe* justices White and Rehnquist were joined by three other justices, all new to the Court since 1973, whose votes created a majority willing to give states more authority to regulate abortions. As chief justice, Rehnquist wrote the Court's opinion in *Webster v. Reproductive Health Services* (1989), pointedly omitting any discussion—indeed, any mention—of the right of privacy. The Court, in a 5-4 decision, upheld the state's right to prohibit the use of public facilities and of public employees to perform abortions. It also upheld the state's right to require physicians to test for fetal viability before permitting an abortion on a woman believed to be as much as twenty weeks pregnant.

In an impassioned dissent, Justice Blackmun criticized the majority for refusing to debate whether the Constitution includes a general right to privacy. "A chill wind blows," he warned, as the majority "casts into darkness the hopes and visions of every woman in this country who had come to believe that the Constitution guaranteed her the right to exercise some control over her unique ability to bear children." They did so, he continued, "either oblivious or insensitive to the fact that millions of women and their families have ordered their lives around this right to reproductive choice, and that this right has become vital to the full participation of women in the economic and political walks of American life."[29] In the term immediately after the *Webster* decision, the Court upheld state laws requiring teenage girls to notify their parents of abortion decisions.[30] A more fundamental battle would come two years later, in 1992.

As *Roe v. Wade* neared its twentieth anniversary, the abortion controversy continued to be a driving force in U.S. politics and in the courts. In the early 1990s, President George H. W. Bush asked the Supreme Court, as Ronald Reagan had before him, to overturn *Roe*. The opportunity came in the case of *Planned Parenthood of Southeastern Pennsylvania v. Casey* (1992),

but the conservative-dominated bench defied all predictions. The Court, 5-4, affirmed a right to abortion while upholding Pennsylvania's abortion regulations that had earlier been found to conflict with the standard adopted in *Roe*. In short, in *Casey* the Court held that states may not prohibit abortions performed early in a pregnancy, when the fetus has no reasonable chance of survival outside the womb. The ruling, however, adopted a new, more lenient standard for determining whether particular state restrictions infringe too far on the right to abortion.[31] The decision upheld a list of requirements that Pennsylvania placed on a woman seeking an abortion, including a twenty-four-hour waiting period between being given certain information and having the abortion and parental or judicial approval for minors seeking abortions. The Court struck down a requirement that a woman seeking an abortion notify her husband.

There was no majority opinion. The plurality opinion, written jointly by Justices Sandra Day O'Connor, Anthony M. Kennedy, and David H. Souter, constitutes the ruling in *Casey*. The decision to uphold *Roe* was the result of these three justices' unexpected votes. Until 1992 O'Connor's position on abortion had been unclear. She had described the legal framework of *Roe v. Wade* as "problematic" but had stopped short of saying it should be overturned. Souter, appointed to the Court in 1990, had never voted in an abortion rights case. Kennedy's vote was perhaps the most surprising. He had signed the plurality opinion in *Webster*, which would have overturned *Roe* had a fifth justice joined it. Justices Blackmun and John Paul Stevens joined Justices O'Connor, Souter, and Kennedy to declare that *Roe v. Wade* created a "rule of law and a component of liberty we cannot renounce."[32] Blackmun, the author of *Roe*, praised the three-justice opinion as an "act of personal courage and Constitutional principle,"[33] but he dissented from all the portions upholding the state regulations. In that position he was joined by Justice Stevens on all but one point.

Chief Justice Rehnquist and Justices White, Antonin Scalia, and Clarence Thomas dissented from the affirmation of *Roe* and agreed with the sections of the opinion upholding the Pennsylvania regulations. In the first paragraph of the plurality opinion that spoke for the Court, the justices noted that five times in the past decade presidents had asked the Court to overturn *Roe*. The justices added, "Liberty finds no refuge in the jurisprudence of doubt."[34] The three-justice opinion affirmed what it called the "essential holding" of *Roe v. Wade*: recognition of a woman's right to obtain an abortion without undue interference from the state before a fetus becomes viable; confirmation of the state's power to restrict abortions after viability, if the law contains exceptions for abortions necessary to save the mother's life or health; and affirmation of legitimate state interests in protecting the health of the woman and the life of the fetus.

"Some of us as individuals find abortion offensive to our most basic principles or morality," wrote O'Connor, Kennedy, and Souter, "but that cannot control our decision. Our obligation is to define the liberty of all, not to mandate our own moral code."[35] They upheld *Roe v. Wade* because of their regard for individual liberty and adherence to precedent. To overturn *Roe* would have serious social repercussions, they acknowledged. For twenty years, people have lived with the idea that abortion is available if contraception fails. By making it more possible for women to control their reproductive lives, *Roe* has helped women achieve economic and social equality, they noted.

Altering the legal test for determining whether a state is interfering with an abortion choice, the justices abandoned the *Roe* standard allowing interference only when the state has a "compelling interest." Under that strict standard, virtually all restrictions on abortion through the first two trimesters—six months—of a pregnancy were invalid. The plurality in *Casey* said that the standard should be whether the regulation puts an "undue burden" on a woman seeking an abortion. An undue burden exists if the law places substantial obstacles in the path of a woman before the fetus is viable. The Court said a state may put regulations in place to further the health or safety of a woman, but it may not impose unnecessary health regulations.

The plurality rejected *Roe*'s trimester framework but said a state may not prohibit any woman from deciding to end her pregnancy before viability. The Court effectively overruled two earlier decisions that struck down "informed consent" provisions—*City of Akron v. Akron Center for Reproductive Health Inc.* (1983) and *Thornburgh v. American College of Obstetricians and Gynecologists* (1986).[36] Informed consent refers to written consent from a woman who is about to have an abortion, indicating she understands the abortion procedure, its risks, and the alternatives.

Among the dissenters, Rehnquist wrote, "Because abortion involves the purposeful termination of potential life, the abortion decision must be recognized as *sui generis,* different in kind from the rights protected in earlier cases under the rubric of personal or family privacy and autonomy."[37] In a separate dissent, Scalia said the abortion issue should be returned to state legislatures: "[B]y foreclosing all democratic outlet for the deep passions this issue arouses, by banishing the issue from the political forum that gives all participants, even the losers, the satisfaction of a fair hearing and an honest fight, by continuing the imposition of a rigid national rule instead of allowing for regional differences, the Court merely prolongs and intensifies the anguish."[38] While abortion remains contentious socially and politically, as a constitutional matter, *Roe v. Wade* endures.

"Partial Birth" Abortion

After narrowly affirming the basic right to abortion in 1992, the Court refused to revisit the issue for eight years. It turned away a series of appeals that dealt with regulatory questions on abortion. Within the Court, pro–abortion rights justices were strengthened by two appointees of President Bill Clinton. Justice White had dissented from the original *Roe v. Wade* ruling and voted to overturn it in 1992. A life-long Democrat, he announced his retirement in 1993, shortly after Clinton became president. Judge Ruth Bader Ginsburg, a pioneering women's rights advocate, was chosen to replace White. A year later, Justice Blackmun, the author of the *Roe* ruling, retired, and Clinton chose Judge Stephen G. Breyer, a moderate liberal jurist, to take his place. Throughout Clinton's term, it appeared

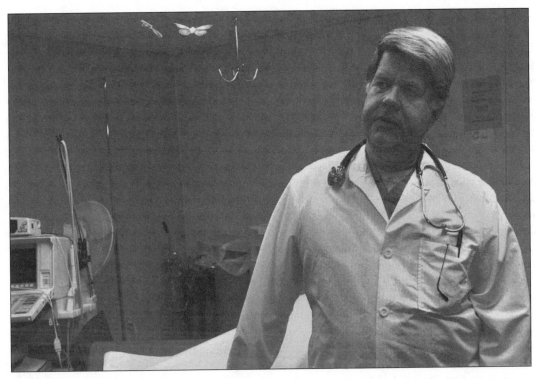

Dr. Leroy Carhart, at one time the only doctor in Nebraska who performed abortions during the second trimester of a pregnancy, challenged the state's ban on so-called partial-birth abortions. In *Stenberg v. Carhart* (2000), the Supreme Court struck down the law, declaring that it was so broad that it could apply to other, more common abortion procedures. The ruling also noted that the law excluded a constitutionally protected exception allowing the procedure when pregnancy threatens the health of the woman.

that six of the nine justices supported the constitutional right to abortion announced in *Roe v. Wade.*

The Court, however, was badly and bitterly split when the issue of "partial birth" abortion came before it. The phrase had been coined by Florida representative Charles Canaday in 1995 and popularized by the National Right to Life Committee through a series of line drawings depicting a baby about to be born only to have its skull pierced by scissors. The gruesome image spurred thirty-one states, including Nebraska, to outlaw this procedure. Doctors who performed abortions objected, arguing that this description of the procedure presented by abortion opponents was inflammatory and misleading. Nebraska passed a law

making it a crime punishable by up to twenty years in prison to "partially deliver vaginally a living unborn child before killing the unborn child and completing the delivery." Leroy Carhart, the only doctor in Nebraska who performed abortions during the second trimester of a pregnancy, challenged the law as unconstitutional. He sued the state's attorney general, Don Stenberg, to stop its enforcement.

In *Stenberg v. Carhart* (2000), the Court engaged in a detailed discussion of abortion procedures, which Justice Breyer conceded may seem "clinically cold or callous" to some, but unavoidable in this case.[39] He began by restating the principles that the Court had adopted earlier in *Roe* and *Casey.* First, pregnant women may choose abortion before viability, the time when a baby can live on its own; this occurs around the twenty-fourth week of a pregnancy. Second, states may not regulate abortion in a way that places "a substantial obstacle in the path of a woman seeking an abortion of a nonviable fetus." States may prohibit abortions after viability, "except where it is necessary, in appropriate medical judgment, for the preservation of the life or health of the mother."

Carhart had testified in Nebraska that for patients between the sixteenth and twentieth week of a pregnancy, he would attempt to remove the fetus intact. At this stage, the fetus would be about six inches in length, and its lungs not developed enough to breathe. After the woman's cervix is dilated, forceps are used to remove the fetus. Sometimes it comes out in pieces, but in other instances the fetus is intact, and the umbilical cord is cut. Because the head is the largest bone at this stage, doctors often have to crush the tiny skull to remove the fetus. Medical experts refer to this procedure as an "intact D&E," or "intact dilation and evacuation." The medical experts testified, most significantly, and the trial judge concluded, that compared to other types of surgical procedures, "intact" removal is safer for some patients because there is less bleeding, less chance of injuring the woman's uterus, and a lower chance of infection because all the fetal material is removed.

In a 5-4 ruling, the Court in June 2000 struck down the Nebraska "partial birth abortion" law because it would force some women to undergo riskier surgery. A state "may not endanger a woman's health when it regulates the methods of abortions," Justice Breyer wrote in *Stenberg v. Carhart*.[40] He also said that the law's wording could also apply to "the most commonly used method" of performing mid-term abortions, the "D&E," or dilation and evacuation procedure. If put into effect, any doctor who performed second-term abortions could be threatened with arrest and prosecution, Breyer said. Justices Stevens, O'Connor, Souter, and Ginsburg joined his opinion. O'Connor, widely seen as the deciding vote, said in a concurring opinion that she would have viewed the state's ban differently

had it included an exception to allow the banned procedure when it is "necessary to preserve the health of the mother."

In another concurring statement, Justices Stevens and Ginsburg objected to the dissenters' insistence that the Court had condoned a gruesome and abhorrent procedure. Since the two procedures—D&E and intact D&E—are similar and "equally gruesome," it is "simply irrational" to say one must be banned while the other remains legal, Stevens wrote. He also pointed out that in the twenty-seven years since *Roe* had been decided, its "central holding has been endorsed by all but 4 of the 17 justices who have addressed the issue."[41] Three of these dissenters—Chief Justice William H. Rehnquist and Justices Antonin Scalia and Clarence Thomas—reiterated their view that the decision in *Roe v. Wade* was "grievously wrong," as Thomas put it. "Today's decision is extraordinary. Today, the Court inexplicably holds that States cannot constitutionally prohibit a method of abortion that millions find hard to distinguish from infanticide," Thomas wrote.[42] Justice Kennedy, who cast a key vote in 1992 to uphold the right to abortion, dissented in the Nebraska case. There are "critical moral differences" between the two abortion procedures, and the state was entitled to demand that doctors "refrain from using the natural delivery process to kill the fetus," Kennedy wrote.[43]

Seven years later, after a change in its membership, the Court changed course on abortion and upheld the federal Partial-Birth Abortion Ban Act of 2003. Congress had directly challenged the Court's decision in *Stenberg v. Carhart* and passed a measure that described "partial birth abortion [as] a gruesome and inhumane procedure that is never medically necessary and should be prohibited." Though signed into law by President George W. Bush, the ban could not go into effect unless the Supreme Court cleared the way. While the measure was being contested in the lower courts, Justice Sandra Day O'Connor announced her retirement. She was replaced early in 2006 by Justice Samuel A. Alito Jr., Bush's second appointee. The switch proved decisive. Justices Kennedy, Scalia, and Thomas, the dissenters in the Nebraska case, were joined by Alito and Chief Justice John G. Roberts Jr. to form a majority to uphold the federal ban.

"The government has a legitimate and substantial interest in preserving and promoting fetal life," Kennedy said in *Gonzales v. Carhart* (2007).[44] The ban on the use of this second-term procedure "does not ... impose a substantial obstacle" to women seeking an abortion, he said, because other safe methods are available. Moreover, "abortions that involve partial delivery of a living fetus ... devalue human life," Kennedy said, agreeing with Congress that the banned procedure "had a disturbing similarity to the killing of a newborn infant." Kennedy also foresaw that the law might affect women, not just their doctors. "Some women come to regret their choice to abort the infant life they once created and sustained," he wrote. "It is a reasonable inference" that the law and the harsh public attention on partial birth abortions "will encourage some women to carry the infant to full term, thus reducing the absolute number of late-term abortions."

In dissent, Ginsburg called the decision "alarming. It tolerates, indeed applauds, federal intervention to ban nationwide a procedure found necessary and proper in certain cases by the American College of Obstetricians and Gynecologists.... And for the first time since *Roe*, the Court blesses a prohibition with no exception safeguarding a woman's health." Speaking as the only woman on the Court, she also attacked Kennedy's prediction on how the law would affect pregnant women: "The law saves not a single fetus from destruction, for it targets only a method of performing abortion," she said. "The notion that the [ban] furthers any legitimate governmental interest is, quite simply, irrational." Instead, she foresaw the ruling as a first step toward overturning *Roe v. Wade*. "In candor, the Act, and the Court's defense of it, cannot be understood as anything other than an effort to chip away at a right declared again and again by this Court—and with increasing comprehension of its centrality to women's lives."

The Court's opinion, and the 5-4 split, indicated that strict regulation of abortion would be upheld by the Roberts Court, but a prohibition on abortion would be struck down if Kennedy adhered to his view in the *Casey* decision.

A LIMITED "RIGHT TO DIE"

In the 1990s the Court grappled with the rights of persons at the end of their lives. While dying was anything but new, advances in medicine presented new, agonizing questions since the "human body [can be kept] alive for longer than any reasonable person would want to inhabit it," as Justice Scalia put it in *Cruzan v. Missouri* (1990).[45] Many people dread the prospect of being hooked to life-support machines more than they fear death. Others dread the pain and utter helplessness of a slow death from a terminal disease. As a result, a growing movement formed around the concept of "death with dignity." Its proponents argued that dying persons—not their doctors, their family members, or the government—had the right to decide to hasten their death. This was referred to generally as the "right to die."

In sharp contrast to the Court's action toward the right to abortion in the 1970s, the Rehnquist Court took a cautious approach to this newly asserted right. In the former case, as support for legalized abortion was growing in many states, the Court stepped forward and announced a new constitutional right to abortion. The *Roe v. Wade* ruling failed to quell the dispute over abortion, and indeed, it was credited with inspiring a national "right to life" movement. When the right to die emerged, the justices, liberal and conservative, thought it wise to move slowly and await a public consensus, rather than attempt to create one with a declaration of constitutional law.

A Right to Refuse Treatment

In 1990 the Court had taken up the case of Nancy Beth Cruzan, the victim of an auto accident who had suffered irreversible brain damage. For seven years, she had been in what doctors called a "persistent vegetative state," with some motor reflexes but no other brain activity. Her condition was hopeless. Her parents, Lester and Joyce Cruzan, said their daughter would not want to exist this way, so they asked state hospital officials to remove the water and feeding tube that kept her alive. They refused, citing Missouri's strong "right to life" policy. The Cruzans went to court to obtain an order to remove the life-sustaining tubes. A trial judge ruled for the parents, citing statements that Nancy had made before her accident indicating that she would not want to be kept alive in such a fashion. The Missouri Supreme Court reversed that decision, holding that the state must have clear and convincing proof of a hospitalized person's wishes before it could act to end his or her life.

The U.S. Supreme Court took up the Cruzan's appeal and in a 5-4 decision upheld Missouri authorities. The ruling was not, however, a total loss for advocates of the right to die. "We assume the United States Constitution would grant a competent person a constitutionally protected right to refuse lifesaving hydration and nutrition," said Chief Justice William H. Rehnquist in *Cruzan v. Missouri Department of Health* (1990).[46] If so, a dying or disabled person may choose to die by starvation and dehydration. All nine justices agreed that there was a basic right to refuse unwanted medical treatment. The Court split, however, on whether one person or persons—in this case, Nancy's parents—could decide for another to end his or her life. "We do not think the Due Process Clause [of the Fourteenth Amendment] requires the State to repose judgment on these matters with anyone but the patient herself," the chief justice wrote. Therefore, Missouri may "require clear and convincing evidence of the patient's wishes … [and] choose to defer only to those wishes, rather than confide the decision to close family members."[47] Justices Byron R. White, Sandra Day O'Connor, Antonin Scalia, and Anthony M. Kennedy agreed.

In a concurring opinion, Justice O'Connor said patients and others who are in good health should consider drawing up a "living will" so that their views on such end-of-life matters would be known. She also said that states had the freedom to rethink their laws in this area: "No national consensus has yet emerged on the best solution for this difficult and sensitive problem. Today, we decide only that one state's practice does not violate the Constitution; the more challenging task for crafting appropriate procedures for safeguarding incompetents' liberty interest is entrusted to the laboratories of the states," she said. In another concurring opinion, Justice Scalia expressed his wish that

the Court would have closed the door to further legal disputes. "I would have preferred that we announce, clearly and promptly, that the federal courts have no business in this field," he wrote. The answers to these end-of-life questions "are neither set forth in the Constitution nor known to the nine justices of this Court any better than they are known to nine people picked at random from the Kansas City telephone book."[48]

The four dissenters—Justices William J. Brennan Jr., Thurgood Marshall, Harry A. Blackmum, and John Paul Stevens—said the Cruzans' request should have been honored. "Nancy Cruzan has dwelt in [a] twilight zone for six years," Brennan noted, even though she had told friends she would wish to forgo medical treatment in such a situation. Rather than honor her rights and her wishes, Missouri officials have "determined that an irreversibly vegetative patient will remain a passive prisoner of medical technology—for Nancy, perhaps for the next 30 years," said Brennan in his last days as a justice.[49] A month later, he would suffer a stroke and be forced to retire. Nancy Cruzan remained a "passive prisoner of medical technology" for only a few more months. After the Court's ruling, her parents went back to the trial judge and presented more evidence of Nancy's wishes. He granted the order to remove her feeding tube, and in December 1990, Nancy died.

State Laws against Suicide Upheld

Seven years after the *Cruzan* decision, the Court squarely faced the broader question of whether the Constitution gave a mentally competent and terminally ill person a right to die. If so, could these dying persons seek the aid of a doctor to end their lives? Two separate cases resulted in lower court rulings that a state's absolute ban on assisted suicide violated the "liberty" and "equal protection" rights of a dying person. In Seattle, Washington, the group Compassion in Dying had formed to support the terminally ill and persons near death. Their patients included people suffering from AIDS and elderly persons. In 1994 four physicians, including Dr. Harold Glucksberg, joined a lawsuit with three dying patients to elicit a ruling that would void in part the state's law against suicide and instead allow "a mentally competent, terminally ill adult" to make the "personal choice" to die through an assisted suicide. If given legal permission, the doctors said they could give these patients medications to permit them to quietly and peacefully end their lives at home. A federal judge in Seattle and the U.S. Court of Appeals in San Francisco agreed with the plaintiffs and ruled Washington's total ban on assisted suicide "places an undue burden" on the dying person's "constitutionally protected liberty."

Meanwhile on the East Coast, Dr. Timothy Quill was pushing a similar lawsuit in New York. In 1992 he had startled the medical community by describing in a journal article how he had used heavy doses of pain-killing medication to help cancer patients die. Two years later, he joined a lawsuit with several doctors that asserted that prescribing lethal medication for a "mentally competent, terminally ill patient" who is in great pain should be seen as an act of compassion, not a crime. The U.S. Court of Appeals in Manhattan agreed, ruling that the system in place provided unequal treatment to dying persons. For example, those persons on a respirator or other life-sustaining equipment have the right to end their lives, while those who are not are left with no such choice, the appeals court noted. The nation's attention had been focused on Dr. Jack Kevorkian, a retired Michigan pathologist who had helped more than fifty dying persons end their lives. Kevorkian had found no success in the lower courts, so the justices took up the cases of Drs. Glucksberg and Quill to decide the issue.

In a pair of 9-0 decisions announced on the same day, the Court ruled for the states, rejecting the claim that the assisted suicide laws were unconstitutional. Chief Justice Rehnquist stressed that the legal bans on suicide were time-honored and traditional. "For over 700 years, the Anglo American common law tradition has punished or otherwise disapproved of both suicide and assisting suicide," he wrote in *Washington v. Glucksberg* (1997).[50] It is thus far-fetched, he said, to say that the Constitution incorporates an exception that allowed doctor-assisted suicide. He spoke for a conservative method of interpreting the Constitution and the right to "liberty" in the Fourteenth Amendment. Although the clause in question "protects the traditional right to refuse unwanted lifesaving medical treatment,... we have always been reluctant to expand the concept of (a substantive liberty right) in this uncharted area.... We must therefore exercise the utmost care whenever we are asked to break new ground in this field, lest the liberty protected by the Due Process Clause be subtly transformed into the policy preferences of the members of this Court," Rehnquist wrote. "Throughout the Nation, Americans are engaged in an earnest and profound debate about the morality, legality and practicality of physician assisted suicide. Our holding permits this debate to continue, as it should in a democratic society," he concluded.[51]

In the New York case, *Vacco v. Quill* (1997), the Court also rejected the claim that it is unfair and unequal for a state to deny some patients a right to assisted suicide, asserting that a clear difference exists between a doctor's withdrawing a breathing tube and giving medication that causes death: "When a patient refuses life sustaining medical treatment, he dies from an underlying fatal disease or pathology, but if a patient ingests lethal medication prescribed by a physician, he is killed by that medication," Rehnquist wrote. "The two acts are different, and New York may therefore, consistent with the Constitution, treat them differently," he concluded.[52]

While the outcomes were unanimous, the justices were more divided than their 9-0 votes suggests. Only four justices—O'Connor, Scalia, Kennedy, and Thomas—signed Rehnquist's opinion. In concurring opinions, O'Connor and the four others left open a future ruling that would allow a dying person in pain to seek medication that would have the foreseeable effect of ending life. In her opinion, O'Connor noted that there are "no legal barriers" to a patient obtaining pain medication "to alleviate suffering, even to the point of causing unconsciousness and hastening death." For that reason, "there is no need to address the question" now of whether the dying patient has a right to take medication that ends his life. Expressing her faith in state legislators, O'Connor also said, "There is no reason to think the democratic process will not strike the proper balance between the interests of terminally ill, mentally competent individuals who would seek to end their suffering, and the State's interests in protecting those who might seek to end life mistakenly or under pressure," she wrote.[53]

In another concurring opinion, Justice Stevens said that while he supported the general state ban on suicide, there may be future cases where "preserving a dying patient's dignity and alleviating her intolerable suffering" will outweigh the state's interest.[54] Justice David H. Souter said he agreed that the Court is wise to "stay its hand to allow reasonable legislative consideration" of the rights of the terminally ill.[55] Justices Ruth Bader Ginsburg and Stephen G. Breyer said they largely agreed with O'Connor's view. The key issue is the suffering of a dying person. Breyer said that he might in a future case support a "right to die with dignity," which he said would include "the avoidance of severe physical pain connected with death." If the world of medicine and the law do not protect the dying from serious pain, Breyer said, the Court "might have to revisit its conclusions in these cases."[56]

Oregon's Death with Dignity Act

When the Court refused to recognize a constitutional right to die in *Washington v. Glucksberg,* Chief Justice Rehnquist said this difficult issue should be left to the states, their legislators, and their voters. In 1994 Oregon's voters approved the first measure to legally permit dying persons to receive a dose of lethal medication from a doctor. Known as the Death with Dignity Act, the law was limited to those who, in the opinion of doctors, had an irreversible condition or an incurable disease that would cause death within six months. Though hundreds of dying persons consulted doctors under the law, only thirty-seven patients had ended their lives by ingesting lethal medication by 2004.

The George W. Bush administration decided to challenge the state law as a violation of the federal Controlled Substances Act of 1970. This drug-control measure classified certain narcotics as illegal, and it authorized the U.S. attorney general to revoke a physician's license to prescribe drugs if he or she illegally dispensed "controlled substances." In 2001 Attorney General John Ashcroft announced that "assisting suicide is not a legitimate medical purpose." Further, physicians in Oregon who prescribe lethal medication would violate the federal law and therefore lose their privilege to dispense drugs, he said.

Several doctors, patients, and the state of Oregon sued to block Ashcroft's order from taking effect, and the Court struck it down in a 6-3 decision in *Gonzales v. Oregon* (2006). Justice Kennedy said the states had the long-standing power to regulate the practice of medicine, including the licensing of physicians, and there was no evidence that Congress intended to give this authority to the U.S. Justice Department and the attorney general. Ashcroft's order, if upheld, would "delegate to a single executive officer the power to effect a radical shift of authority from the states to the federal government to define general standards of medical practice in every locality," Kennedy wrote.[57] Justices Stevens, O'Connor, Souter, Ginsburg, and Breyer agreed. The case had been argued in the first week in October, which was also the first week on the job for new chief justice John G. Roberts Jr., a Bush appointee. Roberts joined Justices Scalia and Clarence Thomas in dissent. Scalia said the Court should have deferred to Ashcroft's interpretation of the federal drug-control law.

GAY RIGHTS

For most of the Court's history, the justices have wanted nothing to do with claims brought by homosexuals. It has rejected without comment numerous appeals from persons who were fired from government jobs, slated for deportation, or dismissed from the military because of their homosexuality.[58] The civil rights movement of the 1960s inspired various groups to stand up for their rights, including advocates for gay rights taking to the political arena and the courts to demand full equality for homosexuals. By the 1980s, the Supreme Court could no longer ignore this growing movement. Nonetheless, its first decision on the issue resulted in a stunning setback for the gay rights cause.

Sodomy Laws Upheld

In August 1982, Michael Hardwick, an Atlanta bartender, was arrested in the bedroom of his apartment when a police officer discovered him having sex with another man. He was charged with violating Georgia's sodomy law, which made it a crime punishable by up to twenty years in prison to "perform or submit to any sexual act involving the sex organs of one person and the mouth or anus of another." The Georgia statute had gone unenforced for decades, and prosecutors decided against bringing an indictment in the bartender's case. Hardwick said forthrightly, however, that he was a homosexual, and he challenged the sodomy law as unconstitutional. The U.S. Court of Appeals in Atlanta agreed with him, citing the Court's decisions on contraception and abortion as establishing the principle that certain private, intimate conduct is off-limits to state regulation. Michael Bowers, Georgia's attorney general, appealed.

In *Bowers v. Hardwick* (1986), the Court upheld criminal laws against sodomy, ruling that the Constitution does not "confer a fundamental right upon homosexuals to engage in sodomy."[59] Although Georgia's law prohibited sodomy by all persons, heterosexuals as well as homosexuals, Justice White referred to it as only applying to homosexuals. He also took the opportunity to distance himself from the "privacy cases"—*Griswold v. Connecticut* and *Roe v. Wade*—that "discover new fundamental rights imbedded in the Due Process Clause. The Court is most vulnerable and comes nearest to illegitimacy when it deals with judge-made constitutional law having little or no cognizable roots in the language or design of the Constitution," White wrote.[60] The proper interpretation of the "Liberty" Clause should be limited to freedoms that "are deeply rooted in this Nation's history and standard." By that standard, the right to marry is a fundamental right, but to claim that a right to homosexual sodomy is rooted in the nation's history and tradition "is, at best, facetious," according to White.[61] Until 1961 all fifty states outlawed sodomy, he noted. In 1986 twenty-four states and the District of Columbia continued to do so. In a concurring opinion, Chief Justice Warren E. Burger said the laws against sodomy have "very ancient roots" and are "firmly rooted in Judeo-Christian moral and ethical standards.... To hold that the act of homosexual sodomy is somehow protected as a fundamental right would be to cast aside millennia of moral teaching."[62]

The crucial vote was cast by a wavering justice, Lewis F. Powell Jr. At first, Powell voted with the liberals to strike down the Georgia law, but a week later changed his mind and supplied the fifth vote to uphold it. Powell thought it would be cruel and unusual punishment to imprison a gay person for sex, but he did not think that acts that had been deemed crimes for centuries could be deemed suddenly as "fundamental rights" protected by the Constitution. Twice during the weeks as the Court deliberated, Powell commented that he had never met a homosexual. (Of note, Powell was apparently unaware that the clerk to whom he had made these comments was gay.) Undecided until the end, he joined White's opinion, noting that Hardwick had not been prosecuted.[63] "The history of non-enforcement suggests the moribund character today of laws criminalizing this type of private, consensual conduct," Powell wrote.[64] In 1990, after Powell had retired from the Court, a law student at New York University asked him to reconcile his vote in favor of privacy in the abortion cases with his vote in *Bowers*. Powell replied, "I think I probably made a mistake in [*Bowers*]. When I had the opportunity to reread the opinions a few months later, I thought the dissent had the better of the arguments."[65] In the lead dissent, Justice Blackmum faulted White for focusing narrowly on the supposed "right to engage in homosexual sodomy." To the contrary, "this case is about 'the most comprehensive of rights and the right most valued by civilized men,' namely the 'right to be let alone,'" Blackmum wrote, quoting Justice Louis D. Brandeis.[66] Justices Brennan, Marshall, and Stevens had joined Blackmun in dissent.

Despite Powell's comment that antisodomy laws were "moribund," they had a significant impact on gays and lesbians, especially after the Court officially upheld them. These laws branded homosexuals as criminals in their private lives, and in state cases involving child custody, adoptions, and visitations, judges cited *Bowers* as a basis for turning away gays and lesbians who sought to care for children. In several states, gays and lesbians were rejected for jobs as police officers or government lawyers on the ground that their private lives made them criminals.

First Victory for Gay Rights

Despite the *Bowers* decision, gay rights advocates subsequently won protections from discrimination in hundreds of cities and several states. In Colorado, the cities of Aspen, Boulder, and Denver enacted ordinances that barred employers, landlords, and businesses from discriminating against persons because of their sexual orientation. These victories for gay rights were met, however, with a backlash. In 1992 Colorado voters narrowly approved a state constitutional amendment designed to override local antibias ordinances. Amendment 2 stated that there is "no protected status based on homosexual, lesbian or bisexual orientation." It voided any ordinance or regulation that protected gays from discrimination. Gay rights lawyers sued on behalf of Richard G. Evans, a gay man who worked for the city of Denver, and they succeeded in persuading a judge to block the measure from taking effect. The Colorado Supreme Court ruled the measure unconstitutional on the grounds that it blocked homosexuals from participating in the political process and lobbying for antidiscrimination ordinances. The U.S. Supreme Court voted to take up an appeal filed on behalf of Gov. Roy Romer.

In a 6-3 decision in *Romer v. Evans* (1996), gays and lesbians won their first major victory before the Supreme Court, as the justices ruled that laws "born of animosity" toward homosexuals as a group violate the Constitution's guarantee of equal protection.[67] "One century ago, the first Justice Harlan admonished this Court that the Constitution 'neither knows nor tolerates

classes among citizens,'" began Justice Kennedy, referring to Harlan's famous dissent in *Plessy v. Ferguson* (1896) arguing that racial segregation was unconstitutional.[68] Although Harlan's words went unheeded at the time, Kennedy noted that it is now established that the Constitution prohibits "laws singling out a certain class of citizens for disfavored legal status or general hardships."[69] In this case, Colorado's amendment "has the peculiar property of imposing a broad and undifferentiated disability on a single named group," he said. It "seems inexplicable by anything but animus toward the class it affects; it lacks a rational relationship to legitimate state interests."[70]

The amendment was so broadly written that it appeared to strip gays and lesbians of all legal protections, the majority said. Gays could be excluded from housing, jobs, insurance coverage, and education. During oral arguments, Justice O'Connor said that if a public library refused to loan books to a homosexual, the amendment would prevent the victim of this discrimination from making an official complaint. Justice Kennedy would later write, "We must conclude that Amendment 2 classifies homosexuals not to further a proper legislative end but to make them unequal to everyone else. This Colorado cannot do. A state cannot so deem a class of persons a stranger to its laws."[71] Justices O'Connor, Stevens, Souter, Ginsburg, and Breyer joined him. Although the Court did not hold that all legal discrimination based on sexual orientation demanded a "heightened scrutiny" from the courts, Kennedy's opinion suggested that the majority viewed this sort of bias as intolerable.

In dissent, Justice Scalia wrote, "The Court has mistaken a Kulturkampf [culture war] for a fit of spite."[72] He characterized Colorado's voter initiative as "a modest attempt by seemingly tolerant Coloradans to preserve traditional sexual mores against the efforts of a politically powerful minority to revise those mores through use of the laws."[73] Whether right or wrong, the matter should be resolved through the political process, not the courts, Scalia argued. He continued:

Since the Constitution of the United States says nothing about this subject, it is left to be resolved by normal democratic means, including the democratic adoption of provisions in state constitutions. This Court has no business imposing upon all Americans the resolution favored by the elite class from which the Members of this institution are selected, pronouncing that "animosity" toward homosexuality is evil. I vigorously dissent.... Striking down [Amendment 2] is an act, not of judicial judgment, but of political will.[74]

Chief Justice Rehnquist and Justice Thomas joined Scalia in dissent.

Exclusion of Gays from Parades and Boy Scouts

Although the Court's ruling in *Romer v. Evans* held that homosexuals could not be singled out for exclusion, advocates for gays were later rebuffed twice when they sought a right to inclusion. In 1995 the Court unanimously upheld the free speech rights of a veterans' group in Boston to exclude a gay contingent from marching in its annual St. Patrick's Day parade. Massachusetts courts had sided with the gays, who wanted to march in the parade and had argued that their exclusion violated a state civil rights law banning discrimination in places of "public accommodation." The Supreme Court, however, ruled that a parade is not like a hotel or restaurant, but is instead "a form of expression." The veterans council "clearly decided to exclude a message it did not like," and the First Amendment gives it the right to do so, wrote Justice Souter in *Hurley v. Irish-American Gay, Lesbian and Bisexual Group of Boston* (1995).[75]

A sharply divided Court came to a similar conclusion in 2000, when it ruled that the Boy Scouts of America had a free speech right to exclude a gay scoutmaster. James Dale, an Eagle Scout and adult scoutmaster in Monmouth, New Jersey, was kicked out of the organization after he had revealed his homosexuality in a newspaper article. He sued and won a ruling in the New Jersey courts determining that his exclusion violated the state's antidiscrimination law. The First Amendment does not mention a "freedom of association," but the Court had ruled previously that political activists and civil rights organizers have a First Amendment right to associate

without interference by the government. This right to associate also includes a right not to associate, and in a 5-4 decision the Court applied that principle in *Boy Scouts v. Dale* (2000).[76] Chief Justice Rehnquist stressed that the Boy Scouts are a private, nonprofit organization with the right to define its mission and beliefs. "The forced inclusion of an unwanted person in a group infringes the group's freedom of expressive association," he wrote.[77] The Boy Scouts organization maintained that "homosexual conduct is not morally straight" and conflicts with the Scout code. While not endorsing that view, Rehnquist said the Court had to defer to the group's definition of its own membership code. Justices O'Connor, Scalia, Kennedy, and Thomas agreed.

In dissent, Justice Stevens questioned whether the Scouts' mission statement expressed an antigay policy. The issue had not arisen until lawsuits arose, he said. He also faulted the Court for its adherence to the opinion in *Bowers v. Hardwick* and its statement that condemnation of homosexuality has "ancient roots." "Like equally atavistic opinions about certain racial groups, those roots have been nourished by sectarian doctrine," he wrote.[78] "Over the years, however, interaction with real people, rather than mere adherence to traditional ways of thinking about members of unfamiliar classes, has modified those opinions."[79] It is time for the Court to rethink its view of homosexuality, Stevens said. "If we would guide by the light of reason, we must let our minds be bold," he concluded.[80]

Anti-Sodomy Laws Voided

In 2003 the Supreme Court agreed to hear a direct challenge to the *Bowers v. Hardwick* decision when it decided to review a Texas prosecution of two gay men. Justice Kennedy's earlier gay rights opinion in the Colorado case did not mention *Bowers*, an unusual omission for a relatively recent precedent. The reason soon became clear.

The Texas case had begun with the arrest of two gay men at home. In 1997 police officers were sent to an apartment in Houston on a false report that a gun had been discharged. They discovered John Geddes Lawrence and Tyron Garner having sex. They were

Tyron Garner (*left*) and John Lawrence (*right*) celebrate the landmark decision in *Lawrence v. Texas* (2003) striking down a Texas sodomy law and along with it similar laws in thirteen other states.

taken into custody and charged with engaging in "deviate sexual intercourse," a violation of the Texas Homosexual Conduct Law. They challenged the law as unconstitutional under the Equal Protection and Due Process Clauses of the Constitution, but were convicted and fined $200 each. The Texas courts upheld the conviction, relying on the *Bowers* decision. Texas was one of only four states that maintained a sodomy law directed only at same-sex behavior. The other states were Kansas, Missouri, and Oklahoma. Nine others still had general antisodomy laws on the books.

In *Lawrence v. Texas* (2003), the Court struck down all laws against private, consensual sex, ruling that they violate the "liberty" right in the Fourteenth Amendment. "Our obligation is to define the liberty of all, not to mandate our own moral code," said Justice Kennedy.[81] In the past half century, it has become accepted that "liberty gives substantial protection to adult persons in deciding how to conduct their private lives in matters pertaining to sex."[82]

Kennedy's opinion is notable for at least three reasons. First, it sharply criticizes the *Bowers* Court for its "demeaning" references to homosexuals and its reliance on a questionable history. In the Georgia case, Justice White had described the issue as whether there is a "fundamental right to engage in homosexual sodomy." This narrow focus "discloses the Court's own failure to appreciate the extent of the liberty at stake," Kennedy said. Just as no one would call marriage the "right to have sexual intercourse," it demeans homosexual persons to focus just on a "particular sex act," he said. Further,

When sexuality finds overt expression in intimate conduct with another person, the conduct can be but one element in a personal bond that is more enduring. The liberty protected by the Constitution allows homosexual persons the right to make this choice.[83]

The *Bowers* opinion also put forth a false history of anti-homosexual laws having "ancient roots." According to Kennedy, legal historians had contended that laws concerning "crimes against nature" had been applied to women and men, not just same-sex conduct, and that virtually all prosecutions had arisen from "predatory acts" against minors or public misconduct, not private consensual sex between adults. "Far from possessing 'ancient roots,' American laws targeting same-sex couples did not develop until the last third of the 20th Century," he stated.[84]

Second, Kennedy's opinion relies on—and bolsters—the much-disputed "privacy" decisions involving contraceptives and abortion. Conservative critics and some legal scholars had faulted *Griswold v. Connecticut* (1965), *Roe v. Wade* (1973), and *Planned Parenthood of Pennsylvania v. Casey* (1992) for having relied on an invented right to privacy that is not spelled out in the Fourteenth Amendment's assertion that the state may not "deprive any person of life (or) liberty ... without due process of law." Justice Scalia, among others, thinks that "due process" means the procedures of law, not the substance of what is "liberty." Kennedy, however, voiced the much broader view of the Liberty Clause:

> *Roe* recognized the right of a woman to make certain fundamental decisions affecting her destiny and confirmed once more that the protection of liberty under the Due Process Clause has a substantive dimension of fundamental significance in defining the rights of the person.[85]

The *Casey* decision, in which Kennedy played a key role, confirmed that "personal decisions relating to marriage, procreation, contraception, family relationships, child rearing and education" are within this realm of protected liberty. "These matters, involving the most intimate and personal choices a person may make in a lifetime, choices central to personal dignity and autonomy, are central to the liberty protected by the 14th Amendment," Kennedy wrote, restating a passage from the *Casey* opinion.[86]

Third, Kennedy's opinion cites a ruling of the European Court of Human Rights as a precedent for striking down homosexual sodomy laws. An adult homosexual from Northern Ireland had challenged its laws against private homosexual conduct, and in *Dudgeon v. United Kingdom* (1981), the European Court ruled that these laws were invalid under the European Convention on Human Rights. In *Bowers*, Chief Justice Burger had claimed that criminal laws against sodomy were an accepted tradition "in our Western civilization." Kennedy commented that other centers of Western civilization did not agree with him, noting "the protected right of homosexual adults to engage in intimate, consensual conduct ... has been accepted as an integral part of human freedom in many countries."[87] While the European Court's decision in the *Dudgeon* case was not a true precedent, Kennedy's reference marked the first time that the Court had cited guidance in part from a decision of an international court.

"*Bowers* was not correct when it was decided, and it is not correct today. It ought not to remain binding precedent. *Bowers v. Hardwick* should be and now is overruled," Kennedy stated.[88] He stressed that the case before the Court did not involve minors or any claim of coercion. He continued:

> It does not involve public conduct or prostitution. It does not involve whether the government must give formal recognition to any relationship that homosexual persons seek to enter. The case does involve two adults who, with full and mutual consent from each other, engaged in sexual practices common to a homosexual lifestyle. The petitioners [Lawrence and Garner] are entitled to respect for their private lives. The State cannot demean their existence or control their destiny by making their private sexual conduct a crime. Their right to liberty under the Due Process Clause gives them the full right to engage in their conduct without the intervention of the government.[89]

Justice Stevens, the lone remaining dissenter from *Bowers*, joined Kennedy's opinion, as did Justices Souter, Ginsburg, and Breyer. Justice O'Connor had voted in the majority in the *Bowers* case and did not join Kennedy's opinion overruling it. She did, however, vote to strike down the Texas law on equal protection grounds. "The Texas statute makes homosexuals unequal in the eyes of the law," she said in a concurring opinion. "A law branding one class of persons as criminal solely based on the State's moral disapproval of that class and the conduct associated with that class runs contrary to the values of the Constitution and the Equal Protection Clause," she said.[90]

Gay rights advocates hailed the ruling as a true landmark in their struggle for acceptance and equality. "Today the U.S. Supreme Court closed the door on an era of intolerance and ushered in a new era of respect and equal treatment for gay Americans," said Ruth Harlow, legal director of the Lambda Legal Defense Fund, which represented Lawrence and Garner.[91] She and other advocates predicted that the Court's opinion would have a broad impact and prevent discrimination against gays and lesbians in child custody and adoption disputes. They also felt that the logic of the opinion—if not the Court's holding—would lead to official recognition of same-sex marriages in the future. They received an unexpected confirmation of this view from Justice Scalia, who, in dissent, said the opinion "effectively decrees the end of all morals legislation.... If moral disapproval of homosexual conduct is 'no legitimate state interest' for purposes of proscribing that conduct,... what justification could there possibly be for denying the benefits of marriage to homosexual couples exercising the 'liberty protected by the Constitution'?"[92] Scalia denounced the ruling and the Court's method of deciding the case. He said the majority was mistaken in believing that the Constitution protects "liberty" in general. It was also mistaken in striking down the laws based on commonly held moral views. "There is no right to 'liberty' under the Due Process Clause, though today's opinion repeatedly makes that claim," Scalia observed. He continued:

> Today's opinion is the product of a Court, which is the product of a law-profession culture, that has largely signed on to the so-called homosexual agenda, by which I mean the agenda promoted by some homosexual activists directed at eliminating the moral opprobrium that has traditionally attached to homosexual conduct.... The Court has taken sides in the culture war, departing from its role of assuring, as neutral observers, that the democratic rules of engagement are observed. Many Americans do not want persons who engage in homosexual conduct as partners in

their business, as scoutmasters for their children, as teachers in their children's schools, or as boarders in their home. They view this as protecting themselves and their families from a lifestyle that they believe to be immoral and destructive.... Let me be clear that I have nothing against homosexuals, or any other group, promoting their agenda through normal democratic means. Social perceptions of sexual and other morality change over time, and every group has the right to persuade its fellow citizens that its view of such matters is the best.... What Texas has chosen to do is well within the range of traditional democratic action, and its hand should not be stayed through the invention of a brand-new 'constitutional right' by a Court that is impatient of democratic change.[93]

Chief Justice Rehnquist and Justice Thomas joined Scalia's dissent. In a separate statement, Thomas compared the Texas anti-sodomy law to Connecticut's ban on contraceptives, which Justice Potter Stewart had called "uncommonly silly" in 1965 in *Griswold*. "If I were a member of the Texas legislature, I would vote to repeal it. Punishing someone for expressing his sexual preference … does not appear to be a worthy way to expend valuable law enforcement resources," Thomas stated. Nonetheless, he continued, he did not believe the law was unconstitutional. "Just like Justice Stewart, I can find [neither in the Bill of Rights nor any other part of the Constitution a] general right to privacy," Thomas wrote. The strong dissents aside, this gay rights ruling demonstrated that a solid majority of the Court had come to believe that the Constitution promises liberty and equality to all, and the Court has a special duty to make that promise a reality.

NOTES

1. *Lochner v. New York*, 198 U.S. 45 (1905).
2. *Meyer v. Nebraska*, 262 U.S. 390 (1923).
3. *Griswold v. Connecticut*, 381 U.S. 479 at 484 and 485–486 (1965).
4. Ronald Dworkin, *Life's Dominion: An Argument about Abortion, Euthanasia, and Individual Freedom* (New York: Knopf, 1993), 6.
5. *Planned Parenthood of Southeastern Pennsylvania v. Casey*, 505 U.S. 833 (1992).
6. *Washington v. Glucksberg*, 521 U.S. 702 (1997).
7. *Lawrence v. Texas*, 539 U.S. 558 (2003).
8. *Meyer v. Nebraska*, 262 U.S. 390 at 399 (1923).

9. *Pierce v. Society of Sisters,* 268 U.S. 510 at 534–535 (1925).

10. *Skinner v. Oklahoma,* 316 U.S. 535 at 541 (1942).

11. *Loving v. Virginia,* 388 U.S. 1 at 12 (1967).

12. *Griswold v. Connecticut,* 381 U.S. 479 at 484 (1965).

13. Id. at 485–486.

14. Id. at 499.

15. Id. at 500, quoting from *Palko v. Connecticut,* 302 U.S. 319 at 325 (1937).

16. Id. at 502.

17. *Eisenstadt v. Baird,* 405 U.S. 438 (1972).

18. See David J. Garrow, *Liberty and Sexuality: The Right to Privacy and the Making of Roe v. Wade* (Berkeley: University of California Press, 1998), 547.

19. Ibid., 587.

20. *Roe v. Wade,* 410 U.S. 113 at 152 (1973).

21. Id. at 153.

22. Id. at 154.

23. Id. at 163–165.

24. *Doe v. Bolton,* 410 U.S. 179 at 222 (1973).

25. Id.

26. Id. at 208.

27. *Planned Parenthood of Central Missouri v. Danforth,* 428 U.S. 52 (1976); *Bellotti v. Baird,* 443 U.S. 622 (1979); *H.L. v. Matheson,* 450 U.S. 398 (1981); *City of Akron v. Akron Center for Reproductive Health Inc.,* 462 U.S. 416 (1983); *Planned Parenthood Association of Kansas City, Mo. v. Ashcroft,* 462 U.S. 476 (1983).

28. *Harris v. McRae,* 448 U.S. 297 (1980); *Williams v. Zbaraz,* 448 U.S. 358 (1980).

29. *Webster v. Reproductive Health Services,* 492 U.S. 490 (1989).

30. *Hodgson v. Minnesota,* 497 U.S. 417 (1990); *Ohio v. Akron Center for Reproductive Health Inc.,* 497 U.S. 502 (1990).

31. *Planned Parenthood of Southeastern Pennsylvania v. Casey,* 505 U.S. 833 at 871 (1992).

32. Id. at 923.

33. Id. at 844.

34. Id. at 850.

35. Id. at 875.

36. *City of Akron v. Akron Center for Reproductive Health Inc.,* 462 U.S. 416 (1983); *Thornburgh v. American College of Obstetricians and Gynecologists,* 476 U.S. 747 (1986).

37. *Planned Parenthood of Southeastern Pennsylvania v. Casey,* 505 U.S. 833 (1992).

38. Id.

39. *Stenberg v. Carhart,* 530 U.S. 914 (2000).

40. Id. at 931.

41. Id. at 946.

42. Id. at 982.

43. Id. at 964.

44. *Gonzales v. Carhart,* 550 U.S. __ (2007).

45. *Cruzan v. Missouri Department of Health,* 497 U.S. 261 at 292 (1990).

46. Id. at 279.

47. Id. at 286.

48. Id. at 293.

49. Id. at 301–302.

50. *Washington v. Glucksberg,* 521 U.S. 702 at 711 (1997).

51. Id. at 720, 735.

52. *Vacco v. Quill,* 521 U.S. 793 at 801, 808 (1997).

53. Id. at 737.

54. Id. at 752.

55. Id. at 789.

56. Id. at 791, 792.

57. *Gonzales v. Oregon,* 546 U.S. 243 (2006).

58. See Joyce Murdoch and Deb Price, *Courting Justice: Gay Men and Lesbians v. the Supreme Court* (New York: Basic Books, 2001).

59. *Bowers v. Hardwick,* 478 U.S. 186 at 190 (1986).

60. Id. at 194.

61. Id.

62. Id. at 197.

63. See John C. Jeffries Jr., *Justice Lewis F. Powell Jr.: A Biography* (New York: Scribners, 1994), 511–530.

64. *Bowers v. Hardwick,* 478 U.S. 186 at 198 (1986).

65. Jeffries, *Justice Lewis F. Powell Jr.,* 511.

66. *Bowers v. Hardwick,* 478 U.S. 186 at 199 (1986). Brandeis is quoted from *Olmstead v. United States,* 277 U.S. 478 (1928).

67. *Romer v. Evans,* 517 U.S. 620 (1996).

68. Id. at 623.

69. Id. at 633.

70. Id. at 632.

71. Id. at 635.

72. Id. at 636.

73. Id.

74. Id. at 636.

75. *Hurley v. Irish-American Gay, Lesbian and Bisexual Group of Boston,* 515 U.S. 557 (1995).

76. *Boy Scouts v. Dale,* 530 U.S. 640 (2000).

77. Id. at 648.

78. Id. at 699.

79. Id.

80. Id. at 700.

81. *Lawrence v. Texas,* 539 U.S. 558 (2003).

82. Id.

83. Id.

84. Id.

85. Id.

86. Id.

87. Id.

88. Id.

89. Id.

90. Id.

91. Lambda Legal Defense Fund, press statement, June 26, 2003.

92. *Lawrence v. Texas,* 539 U.S. 558 (2003).

93. Id.

CONTENTS

Reference Materials

GLOSSARY OF LEGAL TERMS

Accessory. A person not present at the commission of a criminal offense who commands, advises, instigates, or conceals the offense.

Acquittal. Discharge of a person from a charge of guilt. A person is acquitted when a jury returns a verdict of not guilty; a person may also be acquitted when a judge determines that there is insufficient evidence to convict him or that a violation of due process precludes a fair trial.

Adjudicate. To decide by the exercise of judicial authority.

Affidavit. A voluntary, written statement of facts or charges affirmed under oath.

A fortiori. With stronger force or more reason (in drawing a conclusion).

Amicus curiae. A friend of the court; a person not a party to litigation who volunteers or is invited by the court to give his or her views on a case.

Appeal. To take a case to a higher court for review. In general, the losing party in a trial court may appeal once to an appellate court as a matter of right. If he loses in the appellate court, appeal to a higher court is within the discretion of the higher court. Most appeals to the U.S. Supreme Court are at the Court's discretion.

Appellant. The party that appeals a lower court decision to a higher court.

Appellee. One who has an interest in upholding the decision of a lower court and is compelled to respond when the case is appealed to a higher court by the appellant.

Arraignment. The formal process of charging a person with a crime, reading him the charge, asking whether he pleads guilty or not guilty, and entering his plea.

Attainder, Bill of. A legislative act pronouncing a particular individual guilty of a crime without trial or conviction and imposing a sentence upon him or her.

Bail. The security, usually money, given as assurance of a prisoner's due appearance at a designated time and place (as in court) in order to procure in the interim his or her release from jail.

Bailiff. A minor officer of a court usually serving as an usher or a messenger.

Brief. A document prepared by counsel to serve as the basis for an argument in court and setting out the facts of and the legal arguments in support of the case at hand.

Burden of proof. The need or duty of affirmatively proving a fact or facts in dispute.

Case law. The law as defined by previously decided cases, distinct from statutes and other sources of law.

Cause. A civil or criminal case, suit, litigation, or action.

Certiorari, Writ of. An order issued by the Supreme Court, at its discretion, to order a lower court to prepare the record of a case and send it to the Court for review.

Civil law. Body of law dealing with the private rights of individuals, as distinguished from criminal law.

Class action. A lawsuit brought by one person or group on behalf of all persons similarly situated.

Code. A collection of laws arranged systematically.

Comity. Courtesy, respect; usually used in the legal sense to refer to the proper relationship between state and federal courts.

Common law. Collection of principles and rules of action, particularly from unwritten English law, that derive their authority from long-standing usage and custom or from courts recognizing and enforcing these customs; sometimes used synonymously with case law.

Consent decree. A court-sanctioned agreement settling a legal dispute and entered into by the consent of the parties.

Contempt. Civil contempt—the failure to comply with an order by the court to do something for the benefit of another party; criminal contempt—when a person willfully exhibits disrespect for the court or obstructs the administration of justice.

Conviction. Final judgment or sentence that the defendant is guilty as charged.

Criminal law. Branch of law that deals with the enforcement of laws and the punishment of persons who, by breaking laws, commit crimes.

Declaratory judgment. A court pronouncement declaring a legal right or interpretation but not ordering a specific action.

De facto. "In fact"; in reality.

Defendant. The party denying or defending itself in a civil action against charges brought by a plaintiff; the person indicted in a criminal action for commission of an offense.

De jure. "As a result of law"; as a result of official action.

Deposition. Oral testimony by a witness in preparation of a case. It is taken outside of court in response to written or oral questions and committed to in writing.

Dicta. See *Obiter dictum*.

Dismissal. Order disposing of a case without a trial.

Docket. See *Trial docket*.

Due process. Fair and regular procedure. The Fifth and Fourteenth Amendments guarantee persons that they will not be deprived of life, liberty, or property by the government until fair and usual procedures have been followed.

Error, Writ of. An order issued by an appeals court to a lower court requiring it to send to the appeals court the record of a case in which it has entered a final judgment and which the appeals court will now review for error.

Ex parte. "Only from one side" or "only on one side"; type of application to a court for some ruling or action on behalf of only one party.

Ex post facto. "After the fact." An ex post facto law makes an action a crime after it has already been committed or otherwise changes the legal consequences of some past action.

Ex rel. "Upon information from"; usually used to describe legal proceedings begun by an official in the name of the state, but at the instigation of and with information from a private individual interested in the matter.

Grand jury. Group of twelve to twenty-three persons impaneled to hear in closed sessions evidence presented by the state against persons accused of crime and to issue indictments when a majority of the jurors find probable cause to believe that the accused has committed a crime; called a "grand" jury because it comprises a greater number of persons than a "petit" jury.

Grand jury report. A public report released by a grand jury after an investigation into activities of public officials that fall short of criminal actions; often called "presentments."

Guilty. The word used by a defendant in entering a plea for having committed crime or other wrongdoing and by a jury in returning a verdict indicating that the defendant is legally responsible as charged.

Habeas corpus. "You have the body"; a writ issued to inquire whether a person is lawfully imprisoned or detained, demanding that the persons holding the prisoner justify his detention or release him. In current law, a habeas corpus appeal in a federal court allows a state prisoner to challenge his conviction or sentence as unconstitutional under federal law.

Immunity. A grant of exemption from prosecution in return for evidence or testimony.

In camera. "In chambers"; refers to court hearings in private, without spectators or jurors present.

Indictment. A formal, written statement based on evidence presented by the prosecutor from a grand jury that has decided by a majority vote that sufficient evidence exists to charge one or more persons with specified offenses.

In forma pauperis. "In the manner of a pauper"; without liability for court costs.

Information. A written set of accusations, similar to an indictment, but filed directly by a prosecutor (without the involvement of a grand jury).

Injunction. A court order prohibiting the person to whom it is directed from performing a particular act.

In personam. "Against the person"; done or directed against a particular person.

In re. "In the affair of" or "concerning"; title of judicial proceedings in which there are no adversaries, but the matter itself—for example, a bankrupt's estate—requires judicial action.

In rem. "Against a thing"; done or directed against the thing, not the person.

Interlocutory decree. A provisional decision of the court that temporarily settles an intervening matter before completion of a legal action.

Judgment. Official decision of a court based on the rights and claims of the parties to a case that was submitted for determination.

Jurisdiction. The power of a court to hear the case in question; exists when the proper parties are present and when the issue to be decided is among those authorized to be handled by the particular court.

Juries. See *Grand jury* and *Petit jury*.

Magistrate. A judicial officer having jurisdiction to try minor criminal cases and conduct preliminary examinations of persons charged with serious crimes.

Mandamus. "We command"; an order issued by a superior court directing a lower court or other authority to perform a particular act.

Moot. Unsettled, undecided. For example, a moot question is one that is no longer material; a moot case is one that has become hypothetical.

Motion. Written or oral application to a court or a judge to obtain a rule or an order.

Nolo contendere. "I will not contest it"; plea entered by a defendant, at the discretion of the judge, that has the same legal effect as a plea of guilty but may not be cited in other proceedings as an admission of guilt.

Obiter dictum. Statement by a judge or justice expressing an opinion and included with (but not essential to) an opinion resolving a case before the court. Dicta are not necessarily binding in future cases.

Parole. A conditional release from imprisonment by which a person who abides by the law and other restrictions that may be placed upon him is not required to serve the remainder of his sentence; failure to abide by the specified rules will result in being returned to prison.

Per curiam. "By the court"; an unsigned opinion of the court or an opinion written by the whole court.

Petitioner. One who files a petition with a court seeking action or relief, including a plaintiff or an appellant; also a person who files for other court action where charges are not necessarily made, for example, requesting an order requiring another person or party to produce documents. (The opposing party is called the respondent.) When a writ of certiorari is granted by the Supreme Court, the parties to the case are called petitioner and respondent, in contrast to the appellant and appellee terms used in an appeal.

Petit jury. A trial jury; originally a panel of twelve persons who tried to reach a unanimous verdict on questions of fact in criminal and civil proceedings. Since 1970 the Supreme Court has upheld the legality of state juries with fewer than twelve persons; called a "petit" jury because it comprises fewer persons than a "grand" jury.

Plaintiff. A party who brings a civil action or sues to obtain a remedy for injury to his rights. The party against whom action is brought is called the defendant.

Plea bargaining. Negotiations between prosecutor and defendant aimed at exchanging a plea of guilty from the defendant for concessions by the prosecutor, such as a reduction of charges or a request for leniency.

Pleas. See *Guilty* and *Nolo contendere.*

Presentment. See *Grand jury report.*

Prima facie. "At first sight"; referring to a fact or other evidence presumably sufficient to establish a defense or a claim unless otherwise contradicted.

Probation. Process under which a person convicted of an offense, usually a first offense, receives a suspended sentence and is given his or her freedom, usually under the guardianship of an appointed officer.

Quash. To overthrow, annul, or vacate; used in relation to actions taken involving subpoenas, indictments, and so on.

Recognizance. An obligation entered into before a court or magistrate requiring the performance of a specified act—usually to appear in court at a later date; is used as an alternative to bail for pretrial release.

Remand. To send back; act by which a higher court returns for further action a decision to the court from which it came.

Respondent. One who is compelled to answer the claims or questions posed in court by a petitioner. A defendant and an appellee may be called respondents, but the term also includes those parties who answer in court during actions where charges are not necessarily brought or where the Supreme Court has granted a writ of certiorari.

Seriatim. Separately; individually; one by one.

Stare Decisis. "Let the decision stand"; principle of adherence to settled cases; the doctrine that principles of law established in earlier judicial decisions should be accepted as authoritative in similar subsequent cases.

Statute. A written law enacted by a legislature. A collection of statutes for a particular governmental division is called a code.

Stay. To halt or suspend further judicial proceedings.

Subpoena. An order to present one's self before a grand jury, court, or legislative hearing.

Subpoena duces tecum. An order to produce specified documents or papers.

Tort. An injury or wrong to the person or property of another.

Transactional immunity. Status that protects a witness from prosecution for any offense mentioned in or related to his testimony, regardless of independent evidence against him or her.

Trial docket. A calendar prepared by the clerks of the court listing the cases set to be tried.

Use immunity. Status that protects a witness against the use of his own testimony against him for prosecution.

Vacate. To make void, annul, or rescind.

Writ. A written court order commanding the designated recipient to perform or not perform acts specified in the order.

SOURCES OF SUPREME COURT DECISIONS

PAPER SOURCES

The primary print source for Supreme Court decisions is *United States Reports,* the official record of Supreme Court decisions and opinions, published by the U.S. Government Printing Office. This source can be supplemented by *United States Law Week,* published by the Bureau of National Affairs; *Supreme Court Reporter,* published by West; and *United States Supreme Court Reports, Lawyers' Edition,* published by Lawyers Cooperative Publishing Company.

ONLINE SOURCES

The full text of recent Supreme Court opinions as well as decisions from the past are available on the Internet. The following four Web sites offer decisions and other Court information at no cost:

U.S. Supreme Court

www.supremecourtus.gov

The Supreme Court's Web site offers easy access to the Court's recent decisions as well as links to other sites that post opinions issued prior to 1990. It also has information on the Court's rules and procedures, current cases, transcripts of oral arguments, and a description and history of the building in which the Court sits.

Findlaw

www.findlaw.com/casecode/supreme.html

Findlaw features Court opinions dating back to 1893. These cases can be retrieved by name, by year, or by volume and page citations from *United States Reports.* The site also contains information on the Court's calendar and current cases, including key briefs of the opposing sides.

Cornell University Law School / Legal Information Institute

http://supct.law.cornell.edu

Cornell's easy-to-use cite offers Supreme Court opinions from 1990 to the present. The opinions can be accessed by topic, as well as by the name of a party, the date, or the official citation. The site features fifty historic Supreme Court decisions since World War II, including *Brown v. Board of Education* (1954), *Gideon v. Wainwright* (1963), *New York Times v. Sullivan* (1964), and *Roe v. Wade* (1973). Links provide access to other Court opinions dating back to the 1890s.

Oyez: U.S. Supreme Court Media

www.oyez.org

Oyez, sponsored by Northwestern University, provides access to Supreme Court decisions in addition to multimedia presentations, including audio versions of past arguments before the Court, and previews of upcoming cases written for lay readers.

HOW TO READ A COURT CITATION

The official versions of Supreme Court decisions and opinions appear in *United States Reports*. Although there are several unofficial compilations of Court opinions—*United States Law Week, Supreme Court Reporter,* and *United States Supreme Court Reports, Lawyers' Edition*—the official record is the one generally cited. An unofficial version or the official slip opinion might be cited if a decision has not yet been officially reported.

A citation to a case includes, in order, the names of the parties to the case, the volume of *United States Reports* in which the decision appears, the page in the volume that the opinion begins on, the page from which any quoted material is taken, and the year the decision was made. For example, the citation *Colegrove v. Green,* 328 U.S. 549 at 553 (1946), indicates that the Supreme Court decision and opinion in the case that Colegrove brought against Green can be found in volume 328 of *United States Reports* beginning on page 549. The specific quotation in question appears on page 553. The Court announced the decision in 1946.

Until 1875 the official reports of the Court were published under the names of the Court reporters. In these cases, the reporters' names, or abbreviated versions of them, appear in the citations. For example, the citation *Marbury v. Madison,* 1 Cranch 137 (1803), means that the opinion in the case that Marbury brought against Madison is found in the first volume of the reporter Cranch beginning on page 137. Of note, between 1875 and 1883, a Court reporter named William T. Otto compiled the decisions and opinions. His name appears on the volumes for those years along with the *United States Reports* volume number, but Otto is seldom cited. Some citations reference reporter and *United States Reports* volumes, as in the case of *Barron v. Baltimore,* 7 Pet. (32 U.S.) 243 (1833).

The titles of the volumes to 1875, the full names of the reporters, and the corresponding *United States Reports* volumes are as follows:

Reporter Volumes	Court Reporter	*United States Reports*
1–4 Dall.	Dallas	1–4 U.S.
1–9 Cranch or Cr.	Cranch	5–13 U.S.
1–12 Wheat.	Wheaton	14–25 U.S.
1–16 Pet.	Peters	26–41 U.S.
1–24 How.	Howard	42–65 U.S.
1–2 Black	Black	66–67 U.S.
1–23 Wall.	Wallace	68–90 U.S.

SUPREME COURT JUSTICES

The justices of the Supreme Court are listed below in alphabetical order, with years of birth and death; the state from which they were appointed; political party affiliation at the time of appointment; educational institutions attended; significant pre-appointment offices and positions; appointing president; confirmation status, year, and vote; and date of service termination.

Alito, Samuel Anthony, Jr. (1950–). New Jersey. Republican. Princeton, Yale. Assistant U.S. attorney general, federal appeals court judge. Nominated associate justice by George W. Bush; confirmed 2006, 58–42 vote.

Baldwin, Henry (1780–1844). Pennsylvania. Democrat. Yale. U.S. representative. Nominated associate justice by Andrew Jackson; confirmed 1830, 41–2 vote; died in office 1844.

Barbour, Philip Pendleton (1783–1841). Virginia. Democrat. College of William and Mary. Virginia state legislator, U.S. representative, U.S. Speaker of the House, state court judge, federal district court judge. Nominated associate justice by Andrew Jackson; confirmed 1836, 30–11 vote; died in office 1841.

Black, Hugo Lafayette (1886–1971). Alabama. Democrat. Birmingham Medical College, University of Alabama. Alabama police court judge, county solicitor, U.S. senator. Nominated associate justice by Franklin D. Roosevelt; confirmed 1937, 63–16 vote; retired 1971.

Blackmun, Harry Andrew (1908–1999). Minnesota. Republican. Harvard. Federal appeals court judge. Nominated associate justice by Richard Nixon; confirmed 1970, 94–0 vote; retired 1994.

Blair, John, Jr. (1732–1800). Virginia. Federalist. College of William and Mary, Middle Temple (England). Virginia legislator, state court judge, delegate to Constitutional Convention. Nominated associate justice by George Washington; confirmed 1789, voice vote; resigned 1796.

Blatchford, Samuel (1820–1893). New York. Republican. Columbia. Federal district court judge, federal circuit court judge. Nominated associate justice by Chester A. Arthur; confirmed 1882, voice vote; died in office 1893.

Bradley, Joseph P. (1813–1892). New Jersey. Republican. Rutgers. Private practice. Nominated associate justice by Ulysses S. Grant; confirmed 1870, 46–9 vote; died in office 1892.

Brandeis, Louis Dembitz (1856–1941). Massachusetts. Republican. Harvard. Private practice. Nominated associate justice by Woodrow Wilson; confirmed 1916, 47–22 vote; retired 1939.

Brennan, William Joseph, Jr. (1906–1997). New Jersey. Democrat. University of Pennsylvania, Harvard. New Jersey Supreme Court judge. Recess appointment by Dwight D. Eisenhower to be associate justice, 1956; confirmed 1957, voice vote; retired 1990.

Brewer, David Josiah (1837–1910). Kansas. Republican. Wesleyan, Yale, Albany Law School. Kansas state court judge, federal circuit court judge. Nominated associate justice by Benjamin Harrison; confirmed 1889, 53–11 vote; died in office 1910.

Breyer, Stephen G. (1938–). Massachusetts. Democrat. Stanford, Oxford, Harvard. Law professor, chief counsel of the Senate Judiciary Committee, federal appeals court judge. Nominated associate justice by Bill Clinton; confirmed 1994, 87–9 vote.

Brown, Henry B. (1836–1913). Michigan. Republican. Yale, Harvard. Michigan state court judge, federal district court judge. Nominated associate justice by Benjamin Harrison; confirmed 1890, voice vote; retired 1906.

Burger, Warren Earl (1907–1995). Minnesota. Republican. University of Minnesota, St. Paul College of Law. Assistant U.S. attorney general, federal appeals court judge. Nominated chief justice by Richard Nixon; confirmed 1969, 74–3 vote; retired 1986.

Burton, Harold Hitz (1888–1964). Ohio. Republican. Bowdoin College, Harvard. Ohio state legislator, mayor of Cleveland, U.S. senator. Nominated associate justice by Harry S. Truman; confirmed 1945, voice vote; retired 1958.

Butler, Pierce (1866–1939). Minnesota. Republican. Carleton College. Minnesota county attorney, private practice. Nominated associate justice by Warren G. Harding; confirmed 1922, 61–8 vote; died in office 1939.

Byrnes, James Francis (1879–1972). South Carolina. Democrat. Privately educated. South Carolina local solicitor, U.S. representative, U.S. senator. Nominated associate justice by Franklin D. Roosevelt; confirmed 1941, voice vote; resigned 1942.

Campbell, John Archibald (1811–1889). Alabama. Democrat. Franklin College (University of Georgia), U.S. Military Academy. Alabama state legislator. Nominated associate justice by Franklin Pierce; confirmed 1853, voice vote; resigned 1861.

Cardozo, Benjamin Nathan (1870–1938). New York. Democrat. Columbia. State court judge. Nominated associate justice by Herbert Hoover; confirmed 1932, voice vote; died in office 1938.

Catron, John (1786–1865). Tennessee. Democrat. Self-educated. Tennessee state court judge, state chief justice. Nominated associate justice by Andrew Jackson; confirmed 1837, 28–15 vote; died in office 1865.

Chase, Salmon Portland (1808–1873). Ohio. Republican. Dartmouth. U.S. senator, Ohio governor, U.S. secretary of the Treasury. Nominated chief justice by Abraham Lincoln; confirmed 1864, voice vote; died in office 1873.

Chase, Samuel (1741–1811). Maryland. Federalist. Privately educated. Maryland state legislator, delegate to Continental Congress, state court judge. Nominated associate justice by George Washington; confirmed 1796, voice vote; died in office 1811.

Clark, Tom Campbell (1899–1977). Texas. Democrat. University of Texas. Texas local district attorney, U.S. attorney general. Nominated associate justice by Harry S. Truman; confirmed 1949, 73–8 vote; retired 1967.

Clarke, John Hessin (1857–1945). Ohio. Democrat. Western Reserve University. Federal district judge. Nominated associate justice by Woodrow Wilson; confirmed 1916, voice vote; resigned 1922.

Clifford, Nathan (1803–1881). Maine. Democrat. Privately educated. Maine state legislator, state attorney general, U.S. representative, U.S. attorney general, minister to Mexico. Nominated associate justice by James Buchanan; confirmed 1858, 26–23 vote; died in office 1881.

Curtis, Benjamin Robbins (1809–1874). Massachusetts. Whig. Harvard. Massachusetts state legislator. Nominated associate justice by Millard Fillmore; confirmed 1851, voice vote; resigned 1857.

Cushing, William (1732–1810). Massachusetts. Federalist. Harvard. Massachusetts state court judge, electoral college delegate. Nominated associate justice by George Washington; confirmed 1789, voice vote; died in office 1810.

Daniel, Peter Vivian (1784–1860). Virginia. Democrat. Princeton. Virginia state legislator, state Privy Council, federal district court judge. Nominated associate justice by Martin Van Buren; confirmed 1841, 22–5 vote; died in office 1860.

Davis, David (1815–1886). Illinois. Republican. Kenyon College, Yale. Illinois state legislator, state court judge. Nominated associate justice by Abraham Lincoln; confirmed 1862, voice vote; resigned 1877.

Day, William Rufus (1849–1923). Ohio. Republican. University of Michigan. Ohio state court judge, U.S. secretary of state, federal appeals court judge. Nominated associate justice by Theodore Roosevelt; confirmed 1903, voice vote; resigned 1922.

Douglas, William Orville (1898–1980). Connecticut. Democrat. Whitman College, Columbia. Law professor, Securities and Exchange Commission. Nominated associate justice by Franklin D. Roosevelt; confirmed 1939, 62–4 vote; retired 1975.

Duvall, Gabriel (1752–1844). Maryland. Democratic/Republican. Privately educated. Maryland state legislator, U.S. representative, state court judge, presidential elector, comptroller of the U.S. Treasury. Nominated associate justice by James Madison; confirmed 1811, voice vote; resigned 1835.

Ellsworth, Oliver (1745–1807). Connecticut. Federalist. Princeton. Connecticut state legislator, delegate to the Continental Congress and Constitutional Convention, state court judge, U.S. senator. Nominated chief justice by George Washington; confirmed 1796, 21–1 vote; resigned 1800.

Field, Stephen J. (1816–1899). California. Democrat. Williams College. California state legislator, California Supreme Court judge. Nominated associate justice by Abraham Lincoln; confirmed 1863, voice vote; retired 1897.

Fortas, Abe (1910–1982). Tennessee. Democrat. Southwestern College, Yale. Counsel for numerous federal agencies, private practice. Nominated associate justice by Lyndon B. Johnson; confirmed 1965, voice vote; resigned 1969.

Frankfurter, Felix (1882–1965). Massachusetts. Independent. College of the City of New York, Harvard. Law professor, law officer at the War Department, assistant to the secretary of war, assistant to the secretary of labor, chairman of the War Labor Policies Board. Nominated associate justice by Franklin D. Roosevelt; confirmed 1939, voice vote; retired 1962.

Fuller, Melville Weston (1833–1910). Illinois. Democrat. Bowdoin College, Harvard. Illinois state legislator. Nominated chief justice by Grover Cleveland; confirmed 1888, 41–20 vote; died in office 1910.

Ginsburg, Ruth Bader (1933–). New York. Democrat. Columbia. Professor, federal appeals court judge. Nominated associate justice by Bill Clinton; confirmed 1993, 96–3 vote.

Goldberg, Arthur J. (1908–1990). Illinois. Democrat. Northwestern. Secretary of labor. Nominated associate justice by John F. Kennedy; confirmed 1962, voice vote; resigned 1965.

Gray, Horace (1828–1902). Massachusetts. Republican. Harvard. Massachusetts Supreme Court judge. Nominated associate justice by Chester A. Arthur; confirmed 1881, 51–5 vote; died in office 1902.

Grier, Robert Cooper (1794–1870). Pennsylvania. Democrat. Dickinson College. Pennsylvania state court judge. Nominated associate justice by James Polk; confirmed 1846, voice vote; retired 1870.

Harlan, John Marshall (1833–1911). Kentucky. Republican. Centre College, Transylvania University. Kentucky attorney general. Nominated associate justice by Rutherford B. Hayes; confirmed 1877, voice vote; died in office 1911.

Harlan, John Marshall, II (1899–1971). New York. Republican. Princeton, Oxford, New York Law School. Chief counsel for the New York State Crime Commission, federal appeals court judge. Nominated associate justice by Dwight D. Eisenhower; confirmed 1955, 71–11 vote; retired 1971.

Holmes, Oliver Wendell, Jr. (1841–1935). Massachusetts. Republican. Harvard. Law professor, Supreme Judicial Court of Massachusetts justice and chief justice. Nominated associate justice by Theodore Roosevelt; confirmed 1902, voice vote; retired 1932.

Hughes, Charles Evans (1862–1948). New York. Republican. Colgate, Brown, Columbia. New York governor, U.S. secretary of state, Court of International Justice judge. Nominated associate justice by William Howard Taft; confirmed 1910, voice vote; resigned 1916; nominated chief justice by Herbert Hoover; confirmed 1930, 52–26 vote; retired 1941.

Hunt, Ward (1810–1886). New York. Republican. Union College. New York state legislator, mayor of Utica, state court judge. Nominated associate justice by Ulysses S. Grant; confirmed 1872, voice vote; retired 1882.

Iredell, James (1751–1799). North Carolina. Federalist. English schools. Customs official, state court judge, state attorney general. Nominated associate justice by George Washington; confirmed 1790, voice vote; died in office 1799.

Jackson, Howell Edmunds (1832–1895). Tennessee. Democrat. West Tennessee College, University of Virginia, Cumberland University. Tennessee state legislator, U.S. senator, federal circuit court judge, federal appeals court judge. Nominated associate justice by Benjamin Harrison; confirmed 1893, voice vote; died in office 1895.

Jackson, Robert Houghwout (1892–1954). New York. Democrat. Albany Law School. Counsel for the Internal Revenue Bureau and Securities and Exchange Commission, U.S. solicitor general, U.S. attorney general. Nominated associate justice by Franklin D. Roosevelt; confirmed 1941, voice vote; died in office 1954.

Jay, John (1745–1829). New York. Federalist. King's College (Columbia University). Delegate to the Continental Congress, chief justice of New York, minister to Spain and Great Britain, secretary of foreign affairs. Nominated chief justice by George Washington; confirmed 1789, voice vote; resigned 1795.

Johnson, Thomas (1732–1819). Maryland. Federalist. Privately educated. Delegate to the Annapolis Convention and the Continental Congress, governor, state legislator, state court judge. Nominated associate justice by George Washington; confirmed 1791, voice vote; resigned 1793.

Johnson, William (1771–1834). South Carolina. Democratic/Republican. Princeton. South Carolina state legislator, state court judge. Nominated associate justice by Thomas Jefferson; confirmed 1804, voice vote; died in office 1834.

Kennedy, Anthony McLeod (1936–). California. Republican. Stanford, London School of Economics, Harvard. Federal appeals court judge. Nominated associate justice by Ronald Reagan; confirmed 1988, 97–0 vote.

Lamar, Joseph Rucker (1857–1916). Georgia. Democrat. University of Georgia, Bethany College, Washington and Lee. Georgia state legislator, Georgia Supreme Court judge. Nominated associate justice by William Howard Taft; confirmed 1910, voice vote; died in office 1916.

Lamar, Lucius Quintus Cincinnatus (1825–1893). Mississippi. Democrat. Emory College. Georgia state legislator, U.S. representative, U.S. senator, U.S. secretary of the interior. Nominated associate justice by Grover Cleveland; confirmed 1888, 32–28 vote; died in office 1893.

Livingston, Henry Brockholst (1757–1823). New York. Democratic/Republican. Princeton. New York state legislator, state court judge. Nominated associate justice by Thomas Jefferson; confirmed 1806, voice vote; died in office 1823.

Lurton, Horace Harmon (1844–1914). Tennessee. Democrat. University of Chicago, Cumberland. Tennessee Supreme Court judge, federal appeals court judge. Nominated associate justice by William Howard Taft; confirmed 1909, voice vote; died in office 1914.

Marshall, John (1755–1835). Virginia. Federalist. Privately educated, College of William and Mary. Virginia state legislator, minister to France, U.S. representative, U.S. secretary of state. Nominated chief justice by John Adams; confirmed 1801, voice vote; died in office 1835.

Marshall, Thurgood (1908–1993). New York. Democrat. Lincoln University, Howard University. NAACP Legal Defense Fund attorney, federal appeals court judge, U.S. solicitor general. Nominated associate justice by Lyndon B. Johnson; confirmed 1967, 69–11 vote; retired 1991.

Matthews, Stanley (1824–1889). Ohio. Republican. Kenyon College. Ohio state legislator, state court judge, U.S. attorney for southern Ohio, U.S. senator. Nominated associate justice by Rutherford B. Hayes; no Senate action on nomination; renominated associate justice by James A. Garfield; confirmed 1881, 24–23 vote; died in office 1889.

McKenna, Joseph (1843–1926). California. Republican. Benicia Collegiate Institute. California state legislator, U.S. representative, federal appeals court judge, U.S. attorney general. Nominated associate justice by William McKinley; confirmed 1898, voice vote; retired 1925.

McKinley, John (1780–1852). Alabama. Democrat. Self-educated. Alabama state legislator, U.S. senator, U.S. representative. Nominated associate justice by Martin Van Buren; confirmed 1837, voice vote; died in office 1852.

McLean, John (1785–1861). Ohio. Democrat. Privately educated. U.S. representative, Ohio Supreme Court judge, commissioner of the U.S. General Land Office, U.S. postmaster general. Nominated associate justice by Andrew Jackson; confirmed 1829, voice vote; died in office 1861.

McReynolds, James Clark (1862–1946). Tennessee. Democrat. Vanderbilt, University of Virginia. U.S. attorney general. Nominated associate justice by Woodrow Wilson; confirmed 1914, 44–6 vote; retired 1941.

Miller, Samuel Freeman (1816–1890). Iowa. Republican. Transylvania University. Medical doctor, private law practice, justice of the peace. Nominated associate justice by Abraham Lincoln; confirmed 1862, voice vote; died in office 1890.

Minton, Sherman (1890–1965). Indiana. Democrat. Indiana University, Yale. U.S. senator, federal appeals court judge. Nominated associate justice by Harry S. Truman; confirmed 1949, 48–16 vote; retired 1956.

Moody, William Henry (1853–1917). Massachusetts. Republican. Harvard. Massachusetts local district attorney, U.S. representative, secretary of the navy, U.S. attorney general. Nominated associate justice by Theodore Roosevelt; confirmed 1906, voice vote; retired 1910.

Moore, Alfred (1755–1810). North Carolina. Federalist. Privately educated. North Carolina legislator, state attorney general, state court judge. Nominated associate justice by John Adams; confirmed 1799, voice vote; resigned 1804.

Murphy, Francis William (1880–1949). Michigan. Democrat. University of Michigan, London's Inn (England), Trinity College (Ireland). Michigan state court judge, mayor of Detroit, governor of the Philippines, governor of Michigan, U.S. attorney general. Nominated associate justice by Franklin D. Roosevelt; confirmed 1940, voice vote; died in office 1949.

Nelson, Samuel (1792–1873). New York. Democrat. Middlebury College. Presidential elector, state court judge, New York Supreme Court chief justice. Nominated associate justice by John Tyler; confirmed 1845, voice vote; retired 1872.

O'Connor, Sandra Day (1930–). Arizona. Republican. Stanford. Arizona state legislator, state court judge. Nominated associate justice by Ronald Reagan; confirmed 1981, 99–0 vote; retired 2006.

Paterson, William (1745–1806). New Jersey. Federalist. Princeton. New Jersey attorney general, delegate to the Constitutional Convention, U.S. senator, governor. Nominated associate justice by George Washington; confirmed 1793, voice vote; died in office 1806.

Peckham, Rufus Wheeler (1838–1909). New York. Democrat. Albany Boys' Academy. New York local district attorney, city attorney, state court judge. Nominated associate justice by Grover Cleveland; confirmed 1895, voice vote; died in office 1909.

Pitney, Mahlon (1858–1924). New Jersey. Republican. Princeton. U.S. representative, New Jersey state legislator, New Jersey Supreme Court judge, chancellor of New Jersey.

Nominated associate justice by William Howard Taft; confirmed 1912, 50–26 vote; retired 1922.

Powell, Lewis Franklin, Jr. (1907–1998). Virginia. Democrat. Washington and Lee, Harvard. Private practice, member of the Virginia State Board of Education, president of the American Bar Association, president of the American College of Trial Lawyers. Nominated associate justice by Richard Nixon; confirmed 1971, 89–1 vote; retired 1987.

Reed, Stanley Forman (1884–1980). Kentucky. Democrat. Kentucky Wesleyan, Yale, Virginia, Columbia, University of Paris. Federal Farm Board general counsel, Reconstruction Finance Corporation general counsel, U.S. solicitor general. Nominated associate justice by Franklin D. Roosevelt; confirmed 1938, voice vote; retired 1957.

Rehnquist, William Hubbs (1924–2005). Arizona. Republican. Stanford, Harvard. Private practice, assistant U.S. attorney general. Nominated associate justice by Richard Nixon; confirmed 1971, 68–26 vote; nominated chief justice by Ronald Reagan; confirmed 1986, 65–33 vote; died in office 2005.

Roberts, John Glover, Jr. (1955–). Maryland. Republican. Harvard. Deputy solicitor general, federal appeals court judge. Nominated associate justice by George W. Bush July 2005; nomination elevated to chief justice in September 2005 by George W. Bush; confirmed 2005, 78–22 vote.

Roberts, Owen Josephus (1875–1955). Pennsylvania. Republican. University of Pennsylvania. Private practice, Pennsylvania local prosecutor, special U.S. attorney. Nominated associate justice by Herbert Hoover; confirmed 1930, voice vote; resigned 1945.

Rutledge, John (1739–1800). South Carolina. Federalist. Middle Temple (England). Nominated associate justice by George Washington; confirmed 1789, voice vote; resigned 1791. South Carolina legislator, state attorney general, governor, chief justice of South Carolina, delegate to the Continental Congress and Constitutional Convention. Nominated chief justice by George Washington August 1795 and served as recess appointment; confirmation denied and service terminated December 1795.

Rutledge, Wiley Blount (1894–1949). Iowa. Democrat. Maryville College, University of Wisconsin, University of Colorado. Law professor, federal appeals court judge. Nominated associate justice by Franklin D. Roosevelt; confirmed 1943, voice vote; died in office 1949.

Sanford, Edward Terry (1865–1930). Tennessee. Republican. University of Tennessee, Harvard. Assistant U.S. attorney general, federal district court judge. Nominated associate justice by Warren G. Harding; confirmed 1923, voice vote; died in office 1930.

Scalia, Antonin (1936–). District of Columbia. Republican. Georgetown, Harvard. Assistant U.S. attorney general, federal appeals court judge. Nominated associate justice by Ronald Reagan; confirmed 1986, 98–0 vote.

Shiras, George, Jr. (1832–1924). Pennsylvania. Republican. Ohio University, Yale. Private practice. Nominated associate justice by Benjamin Harrison; confirmed 1892, voice vote; retired 1903.

Souter, David Hackett (1939–). New Hampshire. Republican. Harvard, Oxford. New Hampshire attorney general, state court judge, federal appeals court judge. Nominated associate justice by George H.W. Bush; confirmed 1990, 90–9 vote; retired 2009.

Stevens, John Paul (1920–). Illinois. Republican. Chicago, Northwestern. Federal appeals court judge. Nominated associate justice by Gerald R. Ford; confirmed 1975, 98–0 vote.

Stewart, Potter (1915–1985). Ohio. Republican. Yale, Cambridge. Cincinnati city council, federal appeals court judge. Recess appointment by Dwight D. Eisenhower to be associate justice in 1958; confirmed 1959, 70–17 vote; retired 1981.

Stone, Harlan Fiske (1872–1946). New York. Republican. Amherst College, Columbia. Law professor, U.S. attorney general. Nominated associate justice by Calvin Coolidge; confirmed 1925, 71–6 vote; nominated chief justice by Franklin D. Roosevelt; confirmed 1941, voice vote; died in office 1946.

Story, Joseph (1779–1845). Massachusetts. Democratic/Republican. Harvard. Massachusetts state legislator, U.S. representative. Nominated associate justice by James Madison; confirmed 1811, voice vote; died in office 1845.

Strong, William (1808–1895). Pennsylvania. Republican. Yale. U.S. representative, Pennsylvania Supreme Court judge. Nominated associate justice by Ulysses S. Grant; confirmed 1870, voice vote; retired 1880.

Sutherland, George (1862–1942). Utah. Republican. Brigham Young, University of Michigan. Utah state legislator, U.S. representative, U.S. senator. Nominated associate justice by Warren G. Harding; confirmed 1922, voice vote; retired 1938.

Swayne, Noah Haynes (1804–1884). Ohio. Republican. Privately educated. Ohio state legislator, local prosecutor, U.S. attorney for Ohio, Columbus city council.

Nominated associate justice by Abraham Lincoln; confirmed 1862, 38–1 vote; retired 1881.

Taft, William Howard (1857–1930). Ohio. Republican. Yale, Cincinnati. Ohio local prosecutor, state court judge, U.S. solicitor general, federal appeals court judge, governor of the Philippines, secretary of war, U.S. president. Nominated chief justice by Warren G. Harding; confirmed 1921, voice vote; retired 1930.

Taney, Roger Brooke (1777–1864). Maryland. Democrat. Dickinson College. Maryland state legislator, state attorney general, acting secretary of war, secretary of the Treasury (nomination later rejected by the Senate). Nominated associate justice by Andrew Jackson; nomination not confirmed 1835; nominated chief justice by Andrew Jackson; confirmed 1836, 29–15 vote; died in office 1864.

Thomas, Clarence (1948–). Georgia. Republican. Holy Cross, Yale. Assistant secretary for civil rights in the Department of Education, chairman of the Equal Employment Opportunity Commission, federal appeals court judge. Nominated associate justice by George H.W. Bush; confirmed 1991, 52–48 vote.

Thompson, Smith (1768–1843). New York. Democratic/ Republican. Princeton. New York state legislator, state court judge, secretary of the navy. Nominated associate justice by James Monroe; confirmed 1823, voice vote; died in office 1843.

Todd, Thomas (1765–1826). Kentucky. Democratic/ Republican. Liberty Hall (Washington and Lee). Kentucky state court judge, state chief justice. Nominated associate justice by Thomas Jefferson; confirmed 1807, voice vote; died in office 1826.

Trimble, Robert (1776–1828). Kentucky. Democratic/ Republican. Kentucky Academy. Kentucky state legislator, state court judge, U.S. attorney, federal district court judge. Nominated associate justice by John Quincy Adams; confirmed 1826, 27–5 vote; died in office 1828.

Van Devanter, Willis (1859–1941). Wyoming. Republican. Indiana Asbury University, University of Cincinnati. Cheyenne city attorney, Wyoming territorial legislature, Wyoming Supreme Court judge, assistant U.S. attorney general, federal appeals court judge. Nominated associate justice by William Howard Taft; confirmed 1910, voice vote; retired 1937.

Vinson, Frederick Moore (1890–1953). Kentucky. Democrat. Centre College. U.S. representative, federal appeals court judge, director of the Office of Economic Stabilization, secretary of the Treasury. Nominated chief justice by Harry S. Truman; confirmed 1946, voice vote; died in office 1953.

Waite, Morrison Remick (1816–1888). Ohio. Republican. Yale. Private practice, Ohio state legislator. Nominated chief justice by Ulysses S. Grant; confirmed 1874, 63–0 vote; died in office 1888.

Warren, Earl (1891–1974). California. Republican. University of California. California local district attorney, state attorney general, governor. Recess appointment as chief justice by Dwight D. Eisenhower 1953; confirmed 1954, voice vote; retired 1969.

Washington, Bushrod (1762–1829). Virginia. Federalist. College of William and Mary. Virginia state legislator. Nominated associate justice by John Adams; confirmed 1798, voice vote; died in office 1829.

Wayne, James Moore (1790–1867). Georgia. Democrat. Princeton. Georgia state legislator, mayor of Savannah, state court judge, U.S. representative. Nominated associate justice by Andrew Jackson; confirmed 1835, voice vote; died in office 1867

White, Byron Raymond (1917–2002). Colorado. Democrat. University of Colorado, Oxford, Yale. Deputy U.S. attorney general. Nominated associate justice by John F. Kennedy; confirmed 1962, voice vote; retired 1993.

White, Edward Douglass (1845–1921). Louisiana. Democrat. Mount St. Mary's College, Georgetown. Louisiana state legislator, Louisiana Supreme Court judge, U.S. senator. Nominated associate justice by Grover Cleveland; confirmed 1894, voice vote; nominated chief justice by William Howard Taft; confirmed 1910, voice vote; died in office 1921.

Whittaker, Charles Evans (1901–1973). Missouri. Republican. University of Kansas City. Federal district court judge, federal appeals court judge. Nominated associate justice by Dwight D. Eisenhower; confirmed 1957, voice vote; retired 1962.

Wilson, James (1742–1798). Pennsylvania. Federalist. University of St. Andrews (Scotland). Delegate to the Continental Congress and Constitutional Convention. Nominated associate justice by George Washington; confirmed 1789, voice vote; died in office 1798.

Woodbury, Levi (1789–1851). New Hampshire. Democrat. Dartmouth, Tapping Reeve Law School. New Hampshire state legislator, state court judge, governor, U.S. senator, secretary of the navy, secretary of the Treasury. Nominated associate justice by James K. Polk; confirmed 1846, voice vote; died in office 1851.

Woods, William B. (1824–1887). Georgia. Republican. Western Reserve College, Yale. Ohio state legislator, Alabama chancellor, federal circuit court judge. Nominated associate justice by Rutherford B. Hayes; confirmed 1880, 39–8 vote; died in office 1887.

Constitution of the United States

The United States Constitution was written at a convention that Congress called on February 21, 1787, for the purpose of recommending amendments to the Articles of Confederation. Every state but Rhode Island sent delegates to Philadelphia, where the convention met that summer. The delegates decided to write an entirely new constitution, completing their labors on September 17. Nine states (the number the Constitution itself stipulated as sufficient) ratified by June 21, 1788.

The framers of the Constitution included only six paragraphs on the Supreme Court. Article III, section 1, created the Supreme Court and the federal system of courts. It provided that "[t]he judicial power of the United States, shall be vested in one supreme Court," and whatever inferior courts Congress "from time to time" saw fit to establish. Article III, section 2, delineated the types of cases and controversies that should be considered by a federal—rather than a state—court. But beyond this, the Constitution left many of the particulars of the Supreme Court and the federal court system for Congress to decide in later years in judiciary acts.

We the People of the United States, in Order to form a more perfect Union, establish Justice, insure domestic Tranquility, provide for the common defence, promote the general Welfare, and secure the Blessings of Liberty to ourselves and our Posterity, do ordain and establish this Constitution for the United States of America.

ARTICLE I

Section 1. All legislative Powers herein granted shall be vested in a Congress of the United States, which shall consist of a Senate and House of Representatives.

Section 2. The House of Representatives shall be composed of Members chosen every second Year by the People of the several States, and the Electors in each State shall have the Qualifications requisite for Electors of the most numerous Branch of the State Legislature.

No Person shall be a Representative who shall not have attained to the age of twenty five Years, and been seven Years a Citizen of the United States, and who shall not, when elected, be an Inhabitant of that State in which he shall be chosen.

[Representatives and direct Taxes shall be apportioned among the several States which may be included within this Union, according to their respective Numbers, which shall be determined by adding to the whole Number of free Persons, including those bound to Service for a Term of Years, and excluding Indians not taxed, three fifths of all other Persons.][1] The actual Enumeration shall be made within three Years after the first Meeting of the Congress of the United States, and within every subsequent Term of ten Years, in such Manner as they shall by Law direct. The Number of Representatives shall not exceed one for every thirty Thousand, but each State shall have at Least one Representative; and until such enumeration shall be made, the State of New Hampshire shall be entitled to chuse three, Massachusetts eight, Rhode-Island and Providence Plantations one, Connecticut five, New-York six, New Jersey four, Pennsylvania eight, Delaware one, Maryland six, Virginia ten, North Carolina five, South Carolina five, and Georgia three.

When vacancies happen in the Representation from any State, the Executive Authority thereof shall issue Writs of Election to fill such Vacancies.

The House of Representatives shall chuse their Speaker and other Officers; and shall have the sole Power of Impeachment.

Section 3. The Senate of the United States shall be composed of two Senators from each State, [chosen by the Legislature thereof,][2] for six Years; and each Senator shall have one Vote.

Immediately after they shall be assembled in Consequence of the first Election, they shall be divided as equally as may be into three Classes. The Seats of the Senators of the first Class shall be vacated at the Expiration of the second Year, of the second Class at the Expiration of the fourth Year, and of the third Class at the Expiration of the sixth Year, so that one third may be chosen every second Year; [and if Vacancies happen by Resignation, or otherwise, during the Recess of the Legislature of any State, the Executive thereof may make temporary Appointments until the next Meeting of the Legislature, which shall then fill such Vacancies.][3]

No Person shall be a Senator who shall not have attained to the Age of thirty Years, and been nine Years a Citizen of the United States, and who shall not, when elected, be an Inhabitant of that State for which he shall be chosen.

The Vice President of the United States shall be President of the Senate, but shall have no Vote, unless they be equally divided.

The Senate shall chuse their other Officers, and also a President pro tempore, in the Absence of the Vice President, or when he shall exercise the Office of President of the United States.

The Senate shall have the sole Power to try all Impeachments. When sitting for that Purpose, they shall be on Oath or Affirmation. When the President of the United States is tried, the Chief Justice shall preside: And no Person shall be convicted without the Concurrence of two thirds of the Members present.

Judgment in Cases of Impeachment shall not extend further than to removal from Office, and disqualification to hold and enjoy any Office of honor, Trust or Profit under the United States: but the Party convicted shall nevertheless be liable and subject to Indictment, Trial, Judgment and Punishment, according to Law.

Section 4. The Times, Places and Manner of holding Elections for Senators and Representatives, shall be prescribed in each State by the Legislature thereof; but the Congress may at any time by Law make or alter such Regulations, except as to the Places of chusing Senators.

The Congress shall assemble at least once in every Year, and such Meeting shall [be on the first Monday in December],[4] unless they shall by Law appoint a different Day.

Section 5. Each House shall be the Judge of the Elections, Returns and Qualifications of its own Members, and a Majority of each shall constitute a Quorum to do Business; but a smaller Number may adjourn from day to day, and may be authorized to compel the Attendance of absent Members, in such Manner, and under such Penalties as each House may provide.

Each House may determine the Rules of its Proceedings, punish its Members for disorderly Behaviour, and, with the Concurrence of two thirds, expel a Member.

Each House shall keep a Journal of its Proceedings, and from time to time publish the same, excepting such Parts as may in their Judgment require Secrecy; and the Yeas and Nays of the Members of either House on any question shall, at the Desire of one fifth of those Present, be entered on the Journal.

Neither House, during the Session of Congress, shall, without the Consent of the other, adjourn for more than three days, nor to any other Place than that in which the two Houses shall be sitting.

Section 6. The Senators and Representatives shall receive a Compensation for their Services, to be ascertained by Law, and paid out of the Treasury of the United States. They shall in all Cases, except Treason, Felony and Breach of the Peace, be privileged from Arrest during their Attendance at the Session of their respective Houses, and in going to and returning from the same; and for any Speech or Debate in either House, they shall not be questioned in any other Place.

No Senator or Representative shall, during the Time for which he was elected, be appointed to any civil Office under the Authority of the United States, which shall have been created, or the Emoluments whereof shall have been encreased during such time; and no Person holding any Office under the United States, shall be a Member of either House during his Continuance in Office.

Section 7. All Bills for raising Revenue shall originate in the House of Representatives; but the Senate may propose or concur with Amendments as on other Bills.

Every Bill which shall have passed the House of Representatives and the Senate, shall, before it become a Law, be presented to the President of the United States; If he approve he shall sign it, but if not he shall return it, with his Objections to that House in which it shall have originated, who shall enter the Objections at large on their Journal, and proceed to reconsider it. If after such Reconsideration two thirds of that House shall agree to pass the Bill, it shall be sent, together with the Objections, to the other House, by which it shall likewise be reconsidered, and if approved by two thirds of that House, it shall become a Law. But in all such Cases the Votes of both Houses shall be determined by yeas and Nays, and the Names of the Persons voting for and against the Bill shall be entered on the Journal of each House respectively. If any Bill shall not be returned by the President within ten Days (Sundays excepted) after it shall have been presented to him, the Same shall be a Law, in like Manner as if he had signed it, unless the Congress by their Adjournment prevent its Return, in which Case it shall not be a Law.

Every Order, Resolution, or Vote to which the Concurrence of the Senate and House of Representatives may be necessary (except on a question of Adjournment) shall be presented to the President of the United States; and before the Same shall take Effect, shall be approved by him, or being disapproved by him, shall be repassed by two thirds of the Senate and House of Representatives, according to the Rules and Limitations prescribed in the Case of a Bill.

Section 8. The Congress shall have Power To lay and collect Taxes, Duties, Imposts and Excises, to pay the Debts and provide for the common Defence and general Welfare of the United States; but all Duties, Imposts and Excises shall be uniform throughout the United States;

To borrow Money on the credit of the United States;

To regulate Commerce with foreign Nations, and among the several States, and with the Indian Tribes;

To establish an uniform Rule of Naturalization, and uniform Laws on the subject of Bankruptcies throughout the United States;

To coin Money, regulate the Value thereof, and of foreign Coin, and fix the Standard of Weights and Measures;

To provide for the Punishment of counterfeiting the Securities and current Coin of the United States;

To establish Post Offices and post Roads;

To promote the Progress of Science and useful Arts, by securing for limited Times to Authors and Inventors the exclusive Right to their respective Writings and Discoveries;

To constitute Tribunals inferior to the supreme Court;

To define and punish Piracies and Felonies committed on the high Seas, and Offences against the Law of Nations;

To declare War, grant Letters of Marque and Reprisal, and make Rules concerning Captures on Land and Water;

To raise and support Armies, but no Appropriation of Money to that Use shall be for a longer Term than two Years;

To provide and maintain a Navy;

To make Rules for the Government and Regulation of the land and naval Forces;

To provide for calling forth the Militia to execute the Laws of the Union, suppress Insurrections and repel Invasions;

To provide for organizing, arming, and disciplining, the Militia, and for governing such Part of them as may be employed in the Service of the United States, reserving to the States respectively, the Appointment of the Officers, and the Authority of training the Militia according to the discipline prescribed by Congress;

To exercise exclusive Legislation in all Cases whatsoever, over such District (not exceeding ten Miles square) as may, by Cession of particular States, and the Acceptance of Congress, become the Seat of the Government of the United States, and to exercise like Authority over all Places purchased by the Consent of the Legislature of the State in which the Same shall be, for the Erection of Forts, Magazines, Arsenals, dock-Yards, and other needful Buildings;—And

To make all Laws which shall be necessary and proper for carrying into Execution the foregoing Powers, and all other Powers vested by this Constitution in the Government of the United States, or in any Department or Officer thereof.

Section 9. The Migration or Importation of such Persons as any of the States now existing shall think proper to admit, shall not be prohibited by the Congress prior to the Year one thousand eight hundred and eight, but a Tax or duty may be imposed on such Importation, not exceeding ten dollars for each Person.

The Privilege of the Writ of Habeas Corpus shall not be suspended, unless when in Cases of Rebellion or Invasion the public Safety may require it.

No Bill of Attainder or ex post facto Law shall be passed.

No Capitation, or other direct, Tax shall be laid, unless in Proportion to the Census or Enumeration herein before directed to be taken.[5]

No Tax or Duty shall be laid on Articles exported from any State.

No Preference shall be given by any Regulation of Commerce or Revenue to the Ports of one State over those of another; nor shall Vessels bound to, or from, one State, be obliged to enter, clear, or pay Duties in another.

No Money shall be drawn from the Treasury, but in Consequence of Appropriations made by Law; and a regular Statement and Account of the Receipts and Expenditures of all public Money shall be published from time to time.

No Title of Nobility shall be granted by the United States: And no Person holding any Office of Profit or Trust under them, shall, without the Consent of the Congress, accept of any present, Emolument, Office, or Title, of any kind whatever, from any King, Prince, or foreign State.

Section 10. No State shall enter into any Treaty, Alliance, or Confederation; grant Letters of Marque and Reprisal; coin Money; emit Bills of Credit; make any

Thing but gold and silver Coin a Tender in Payment of Debts; pass any Bill of Attainder, ex post facto Law, or Law impairing the Obligation of Contracts, or grant any Title of Nobility.

No State shall, without the Consent of the Congress, lay any Imposts or Duties on Imports or Exports, except what may be absolutely necessary for executing its inspection Laws: and the net Produce of all Duties and Imposts, laid by any State on Imports or Exports, shall be for the Use of the Treasury of the United States; and all such Laws shall be subject to the Revision and Controul of the Congress.

No State shall, without the Consent of Congress, lay any Duty of Tonnage, keep Troops, or Ships of War in time of Peace, enter into any Agreement or Compact with another State, or with a foreign Power, or engage in War, unless actually invaded, or in such imminent Danger as will not admit of delay.

ARTICLE II

Section 1. The executive Power shall be vested in a President of the United States of America. He shall hold his Office during the Term of four Years, and, together with the Vice President, chosen for the same Term, be elected, as follows

Each State shall appoint, in such Manner as the Legislature thereof may direct, a Number of Electors, equal to the whole Number of Senators and Representatives to which the State may be entitled in the Congress: but no Senator or Representative, or Person holding an Office of Trust or Profit under the United States, shall be appointed an Elector.

[The Electors shall meet in their respective States, and vote by Ballot for two Persons, of whom one at least shall not be an Inhabitant of the same State with themselves. And they shall make a List of all the Persons voted for, and of the Number of Votes for each; which List they shall sign and certify, and transmit sealed to the Seat of the Government of the United States, directed to the President of the Senate. The President of the Senate shall, in the Presence of the Senate and House of Representatives, open all the Certificates, and the Votes shall then be counted. The Person having the greatest Number of Votes shall be the President, if such Number be a Majority of the whole Number of Electors appointed; and if there be more than one who have such Majority, and have an equal Number of Votes, then the House of Representatives shall immediately chuse by Ballot one of them for President; and if no Person have a Majority, then from the five highest on the list the said House shall in like Manner chuse the President. But in chusing the President, the Votes shall be taken by States,

the Representation from each State having one Vote; A quorum for this Purpose shall consist of a Member or Members from two thirds of the States, and a Majority of all the States shall be necessary to a Choice. In every Case, after the Choice of the President, the Person having the greatest Number of Votes of the Electors shall be the Vice President. But if there should remain two or more who have equal Votes, the Senate shall chuse from them by Ballot the Vice President.][6]

The Congress may determine the Time of chusing the Electors, and the Day on which they shall give their Votes; which Day shall be the same throughout the United States.

No Person except a natural born Citizen, or a Citizen of the United States, at the time of the Adoption of this Constitution, shall be eligible to the Office of President; neither shall any Person be eligible to that Office who shall not have attained to the Age of thirty five Years, and been fourteen Years a Resident within the United States.

In Case of the Removal of the President from Office, or of his Death, Resignation, or Inability to discharge the Powers and Duties of the said Office,[7] the Same shall devolve on the Vice President, and the Congress may by Law provide for the Case of Removal, Death, Resignation or Inability, both of the President and Vice President, declaring what Officer shall then act as President, and such Officer shall act accordingly, until the Disability be removed, or a President shall be elected.

The President shall, at stated Times, receive for his Services, a Compensation, which shall neither be encreased nor diminished during the Period for which he shall have been elected, and he shall not receive within that Period any other Emolument from the United States, or any of them.

Before he enter on the Execution of his Office, he shall take the following Oath or Affirmation:—"I do solemnly swear (or affirm) that I will faithfully execute the Office of President of the United States, and will to the best of my Ability, preserve, protect and defend the Constitution of the United States."

Section 2. The President shall be Commander in Chief of the Army and Navy of the United States, and of the Militia of the several States, when called into the actual Service of the United States; he may require the Opinion, in writing, of the principal Officer in each of the executive Departments, upon any Subject relating to the Duties of their respective Offices, and he shall have Power to grant Reprieves and Pardons for Offences against the United States, except in Cases of Impeachment.

He shall have Power, by and with the Advice and Consent of the Senate, to make Treaties, provided two thirds of the Senators present concur; and he shall nominate, and by and with the Advice and Consent of the Senate, shall appoint Ambassadors, other public Ministers and Consuls, Judges of the supreme Court, and all other Officers of the United States, whose Appointments are not herein otherwise provided for, and which shall be established by Law: but the Congress may by Law vest the Appointment of such inferior Officers, as they think proper, in the President alone, in the Courts of Law, or in the Heads of Departments.

The President shall have Power to fill up all Vacancies that may happen during the Recess of the Senate, by granting Commissions which shall expire at the End of their next Session.

Section 3. He shall from time to time give to the Congress Information of the State of the Union, and recommend to their Consideration such Measures as he shall judge necessary and expedient; he may, on extraordinary Occasions, convene both Houses, or either of them, and in Case of Disagreement between them, with Respect to the Time of Adjournment, he may adjourn them to such Time as he shall think proper; he shall receive Ambassadors and other public Ministers; he shall take Care that the Laws be faithfully executed, and shall Commission all the Officers of the United States.

Section 4. The President, Vice President and all civil Officers of the United States, shall be removed from Office on Impeachment for, and Conviction of, Treason, Bribery, or other high Crimes and Misdemeanors.

ARTICLE III

Section 1. The judicial Power of the United States, shall be vested in one supreme Court, and in such inferior Courts as the Congress may from time to time ordain and establish. The Judges, both of the supreme and inferior Courts, shall hold their Offices during good Behaviour, and shall, at stated Times, receive for their Services, a Compensation, which shall not be diminished during their Continuance in Office.

Section 2. The judicial Power shall extend to all Cases, in Law and Equity, arising under this Constitution, the Laws of the United States, and Treaties made, or which shall be made, under their Authority; — to all Cases affecting Ambassadors, other public Ministers and Consuls; —to all Cases of admiralty and maritime Jurisdiction; —to Controversies to which the United States shall be a Party; —to Controversies between two or more States; —between a State and Citizens of another State;[8] —between Citizens of different States; —between Citizens of the same State claiming Lands under Grants of different States, and between a State, or the Citizens thereof, and foreign States, Citizens or Subjects.[8]

In all Cases affecting Ambassadors, other public Ministers and Consuls, and those in which a State shall be Party, the supreme Court shall have original Jurisdiction. In all the other Cases before mentioned, the supreme Court shall have appellate Jurisdiction, both as to Law and Fact, with such Exceptions, and under such Regulations as the Congress shall make.

The Trial of all Crimes, except in Cases of Impeachment, shall be by Jury; and such Trial shall be held in the State where the said Crimes shall have been committed; but when not committed within any State, the Trial shall be at such Place or Places as the Congress may by Law have directed.

Section 3. Treason against the United States, shall consist only in levying War against them, or in adhering to their Enemies, giving them Aid and Comfort. No Person shall be convicted of Treason unless on the Testimony of two Witnesses to the same overt Act, or on Confession in open Court.

The Congress shall have Power to declare the Punishment of Treason, but no Attainder of Treason shall work Corruption of Blood, or Forfeiture except during the Life of the Person attainted.

ARTICLE IV

Section 1. Full Faith and Credit shall be given in each State to the public Acts, Records, and judicial Proceedings of every other State. And the Congress may by general Laws prescribe the Manner in which such Acts, Records and Proceedings shall be proved, and the Effect thereof.

Section 2. The Citizens of each State shall be entitled to all Privileges and Immunities of Citizens in the several States.

A Person charged in any State with Treason, Felony, or other Crime, who shall flee from Justice, and be found in another State, shall on Demand of the executive Authority of the State from which he fled, be delivered up, to be removed to the State having Jurisdiction of the Crime.

[No Person held to Service or Labour in one State, under the Laws thereof, escaping into another, shall, in Consequence of any Law or Regulation therein, be discharged from such Service or Labour, but shall be delivered up on Claim of the Party to whom such Service or Labour may be due.][9]

Section 3. New States may be admitted by the Congress into this Union; but no new State shall be formed or erected within the Jurisdiction of any other State; nor any State be formed by the Junction of two or more States, or Parts of States, without the Consent of the Legislatures of the States concerned as well as of the Congress.

The Congress shall have Power to dispose of and make all needful Rules and Regulations respecting the Territory or other Property belonging to the United States; and nothing in this Constitution shall be so construed as to Prejudice any Claims of the United States, or of any particular State.

Section 4. The United States shall guarantee to every State in this Union a Republican Form of Government, and shall protect each of them against Invasion; and on Application of the Legislature, or of the Executive (when the Legislature cannot be convened) against domestic Violence.

ARTICLE V

The Congress, whenever two thirds of both Houses shall deem it necessary, shall propose Amendments to this Constitution, or, on the Application of the Legislatures of two thirds of the several States, shall call a Convention for proposing Amendments, which, in either Case, shall be valid to all Intents and Purposes, as Part of this Constitution, when ratified by the Legislatures of three fourths of the several States, or by Conventions in three fourths thereof, as the one or the other Mode of Ratification may be proposed by the Congress; Provided [that no Amendment which may be made prior to the Year One thousand eight hundred and eight shall in any Manner affect the first and fourth Clauses in the Ninth Section of the first Article; and][10] that no State, without its Consent, shall be deprived of its equal Suffrage in the Senate.

ARTICLE VI

All Debts contracted and Engagements entered into, before the Adoption of this Constitution, shall be as valid against the United States under this Constitution, as under the Confederation.

This Constitution, and the Laws of the United States which shall be made in Pursuance thereof; and all Treaties made, or which shall be made, under the Authority of the United States, shall be the supreme Law of the Land; and the Judges in every State shall be bound thereby, any Thing in the Constitution or Laws of any State to the Contrary notwithstanding.

The Senators and Representatives before mentioned, and the Members of the several State Legislatures, and all executive and judicial Officers, both of the United States and of the several States, shall be bound by Oath or Affirmation, to support this Constitution; but no religious Test shall ever be required as a Qualification to any Office or public Trust under the United States.

ARTICLE VII

The Ratification of the Conventions of nine States, shall be sufficient for the Establishment of this Constitution between the States so ratifying the Same.

Done in Convention by the Unanimous Consent of the States present the Seventeenth Day of September in the Year of our Lord one thousand seven hundred and Eighty seven and of the Independence of the United States of America the Twelfth. IN WITNESS where of We have hereunto subscribed our Names,

George Washington,
President and deputy from Virginia.

New Hampshire:
John Langdon,
Nicholas Gilman.

Massachusetts:
Nathaniel Gorham,
Rufus King.

Connecticut:
William Samuel Johnson,
Roger Sherman.

New York:
Alexander Hamilton.

New Jersey:
William Livingston,
David Brearley,
William Paterson,
Jonathan Dayton.

Pennsylvania:
Benjamin Franklin,
Thomas Mifflin,
Robert Morris,
George Clymer,
Thomas FitzSimons,
Jared Ingersoll,
James Wilson,
Gouverneur Morris.

Delaware:
George Read,
Gunning Bedford Jr.,
John Dickinson,
Richard Bassett,
Jacob Broom.

Maryland:
James McHenry,
Daniel of St. Thomas Jenifer,
Daniel Carroll.

Virginia:
John Blair,
James Madison Jr.

North Carolina:.
William Blount,
Richard Dobbs Spaight,
Hugh Williamson.

South Carolina:
John Rutledge,
Charles Cotesworth
    Pinckney,
Charles Pinckney,
Pierce Butler.

Georgia:
William Few,
Abraham Baldwin.

[The language of the original Constitution, not including the Amendments, was adopted by a convention of the states on September 17, 1787, and was subsequently ratified by the states on the following dates: Delaware, December 7, 1787; Pennsylvania, December 12, 1787; New Jersey, December 18, 1787; Georgia, January 2, 1788; Connecticut, January 9, 1788; Massachusetts, February 6,

1788; Maryland, April 28, 1788; South Carolina, May 23, 1788; New Hampshire, June 21, 1788.

Ratification was completed on June 21, 1788.

The Constitution subsequently was ratified by Virginia, June 25, 1788; New York, July 26, 1788; North Carolina, November 21, 1789; Rhode Island, May 29, 1790; and Vermont, January 10, 1791.]

AMENDMENTS

Amendment I

(First ten amendments ratified December 15, 1791.)

Congress shall make no law respecting an establishment of religion, or prohibiting the free exercise thereof; or abridging the freedom of speech, or of the press; or the right of the people peaceably to assemble, and to petition the Government for a redress of grievances.

Amendment II

A well regulated Militia, being necessary to the security of a free State, the right of the people to keep and bear Arms, shall not be infringed.

Amendment III

No Soldier shall, in time of peace be quartered in any house, without the consent of the Owner, nor in time of war, but in a manner to be prescribed by law.

Amendment IV

The right of the people to be secure in their persons, houses, papers, and effects, against unreasonable searches and seizures, shall not be violated, and no Warrants shall issue, but upon probable cause, supported by Oath or affirmation, and particularly describing the place to be searched, and the persons or things to be seized.

Amendment V

No person shall be held to answer for a capital, or otherwise infamous crime, unless on a presentment or indictment of a Grand Jury, except in cases arising in the land or naval forces, or in the Militia, when in actual service in time of War or public danger; nor shall any person be subject for the same offence to be twice put in jeopardy of life or limb; nor shall be compelled in any criminal case to be a witness against himself, nor be deprived of life, liberty, or property, without due process of law; nor shall private property be taken for public use, without just compensation.

Amendment VI

In all criminal prosecutions, the accused shall enjoy the right to a speedy and public trial, by an impartial jury of the State and district wherein the crime shall have been committed, which district shall have been previously ascertained by law, and to be informed of the nature and cause of the accusation; to be confronted with the witnesses against him; to have compulsory process for obtaining witnesses in his favor, and to have the Assistance of Counsel for his defence.

Amendment VII

In Suits at common law, where the value in controversy shall exceed twenty dollars, the right of trial by jury shall be preserved, and no fact tried by a jury, shall be otherwise re-examined in any Court of the United States, than according to the rules of the common law.

Amendment VIII

Excessive bail shall not be required, nor excessive fines imposed, nor cruel and unusual punishments inflicted.

Amendment IX

The enumeration in the Constitution, of certain rights, shall not be construed to deny or disparage others retained by the people.

Amendment X

The powers not delegated to the United States by the Constitution, nor prohibited by it to the States, are reserved to the States respectively, or to the people.

Amendment XI (Ratified February 7, 1795)

The Judicial power of the United States shall not be construed to extend to any suit in law or equity, commenced or prosecuted against one of the United States by Citizens of another State, or by Citizens or Subjects of any Foreign State.

Amendment XII (Ratified June 15, 1804)

The Electors shall meet in their respective states and vote by ballot for President and Vice-President, one of whom, at least, shall not be an inhabitant of the same state with themselves; they shall name in their ballots the person voted for as President, and in distinct ballots the person voted for as Vice-President, and they shall make distinct lists of all persons voted for as President, and of all persons voted for as Vice-President, and of the number of votes for each, which lists they shall sign and certify, and transmit sealed to the seat of the government of the

United States, directed to the President of the Senate; — The President of the Senate shall, in the presence of the Senate and House of Representatives, open all the certificates and the votes shall then be counted; — The person having the greatest number of votes for President, shall be the President, if such number be a majority of the whole number of Electors appointed; and if no person have such majority, then from the persons having the highest numbers not exceeding three on the list of those voted for as President, the House of Representatives shall choose immediately, by ballot, the President. But in choosing the President, the votes shall be taken by states, the representation from each state having one vote; a quorum for this purpose shall consist of a member or members from two-thirds of the states, and a majority of all the states shall be necessary to a choice. [And if the House of Representatives shall not choose a President whenever the right of choice shall devolve upon them, before the fourth day of March next following, then the Vice-President shall act as President, as in the case of the death or other constitutional disability of the President. —][11] The person having the greatest number of votes as Vice-President, shall be the Vice-President, if such number be a majority of the whole number of Electors appointed, and if no person have a majority, then from the two highest numbers on the list, the Senate shall choose the Vice-President; a quorum for the purpose shall consist of two-thirds of the whole number of Senators, and a majority of the whole number shall be necessary to a choice. But no person constitutionally ineligible to the office of President shall be eligible to that of Vice-President of the United States.

Amendment XIII (Ratified December 6, 1865)

Section 1. Neither slavery nor involuntary servitude, except as a punishment for crime whereof the party shall have been duly convicted, shall exist within the United States, or any place subject to their jurisdiction.

Section 2. Congress shall have power to enforce this article by appropriate legislation.

Amendment XIV (Ratified July 9, 1868)

Section 1. All persons born or naturalized in the United States, and subject to the jurisdiction thereof, are citizens of the United States and of the State wherein they reside. No State shall make or enforce any law which shall abridge the privileges or immunities of citizens of the United States; nor shall any State deprive any person of life, liberty, or property, without due process of law; nor deny to any person within its jurisdiction the equal protection of the laws.

Section 2. Representatives shall be apportioned among the several States according to their respective numbers, counting the whole number of persons in each State, excluding Indians not taxed. But when the right to vote at any election for the choice of electors for President and Vice President of the United States, Representatives in Congress, the Executive and Judicial officers of a State, or the members of the Legislature thereof, is denied to any of the male inhabitants of such State, being twenty-one years of age,[12] and citizens of the United States, or in any way abridged, except for participation in rebellion, or other crime, the basis of representation therein shall be reduced in the proportion which the number of such male citizens shall bear to the whole number of male citizens twenty-one years of age in such State.

Section 3. No person shall be a Senator or Representative in Congress, or elector of President and Vice President, or hold any office, civil or military, under the United States, or under any State, who, having previously taken an oath, as a member of Congress, or as an officer of the United States, or as a member of any State legislature, or as an executive or judicial officer of any State, to support the Constitution of the United States, shall have engaged in insurrection or rebellion against the same, or given aid or comfort to the enemies thereof. But Congress may by a vote of two-thirds of each House, remove such disability.

Section 4. The validity of the public debt of the United States, authorized by law, including debts incurred for payment of pensions and bounties for services in suppressing insurrection or rebellion, shall not be questioned. But neither the United States nor any State shall assume or pay any debt or obligation incurred in aid of insurrection or rebellion against the United States, or any claim for the loss or emancipation of any slave; but all such debts, obligations and claims shall be held illegal and void.

Section 5. The Congress shall have power to enforce, by appropriate legislation, the provisions of this article.

Amendment XV (Ratified February 3, 1870)

Section 1. The right of citizens of the United States to vote shall not be denied or abridged by the United States or by any State on account of race, color, or previous condition of servitude.

Section 2. The Congress shall have power to enforce this article by appropriate legislation.

Amendment XVI (Ratified February 3, 1913)

The Congress shall have power to lay and collect taxes on incomes, from whatever source derived, without apportionment among the several States, and without regard to any census or enumeration.

Amendment XVII (Ratified April 8, 1913)

The Senate of the United States shall be composed of two Senators from each State, elected by the people thereof, for six years; and each Senator shall have one vote. The electors in each State shall have the qualifications requisite for electors of the most numerous branch of the State legislatures.

When vacancies happen in the representation of any State in the Senate, the executive authority of such State shall issue writs of election to fill such vacancies: Provided, That the legislature of any State may empower the executive thereof to make temporary appointments until the people fill the vacancies by election as the legislature may direct.

This amendment shall not be so construed as to affect the election or term of any Senator chosen before it becomes valid as part of the Constitution.

Amendment XVIII (Ratified January 16, 1919)

[**Section** 1. After one year from the ratification of this article the manufacture, sale, or transportation of intoxicating liquors within, the importation thereof into, or the exportation thereof from the United States and all territory subject to the jurisdiction thereof for beverage purposes is hereby prohibited.

Section 2. The Congress and the several States shall have concurrent power to enforce this article by appropriate legislation.

Section 3. This article shall be inoperative unless it shall have been ratified as an amendment to the Constitution by the legislatures of the several States, as provided in the Constitution, within seven years from the date of the submission hereof to the States by the Congress.][13]

Amendment XIX (Ratified August 18, 1920)

The right of citizens of the United States to vote shall not be denied or abridged by the United States or by any State on account of sex.

Congress shall have power to enforce this article by appropriate legislation.

Amendment XX (Ratified January 23, 1933)

Section 1. The terms of the President and Vice President shall end at noon on the 20th day of January, and the terms of Senators and Representatives at noon on the 3d day of January, of the years in which such terms would have ended if this article had not been ratified; and the terms of their successors shall then begin.

Section 2. The Congress shall assemble at least once in every year, and such meeting shall begin at noon on the 3d day of January, unless they shall by law appoint a different day.

Section 3.[14] If, at the time fixed for the beginning of the term of the President, the President elect shall have died, the Vice President elect shall become President. If a President shall not have been chosen before the time fixed for the beginning of his term, or if the President elect shall have failed to qualify, then the Vice President elect shall act as President until a President shall have qualified; and the Congress may by law provide for the case wherein neither a President elect nor a Vice President elect shall have qualified, declaring who shall then act as President, or the manner in which one who is to act shall be selected, and such person shall act accordingly until a President or Vice President shall have qualified.

Section 4. The Congress may by law provide for the case of the death of any of the persons from whom the House of Representatives may choose a President whenever the right of choice shall have devolved upon them, and for the case of the death of any of the persons from whom the Senate may choose a Vice President whenever the right of choice shall have devolved upon them.

Section 5. Sections 1 and 2 shall take effect on the 15th day of October following the ratification of this article.

Section 6. This article shall be inoperative unless it shall have been ratified as an amendment to the Constitution by the legislatures of three-fourths of the several States within seven years from the date of its submission.

Amendment XXI (Ratified December 5, 1933)

Section 1. The eighteenth article of amendment to the Constitution of the United States is hereby repealed.

Section 2. The transportation or importation into any State, Territory, or possession of the United States for delivery or use therein of intoxicating liquors, in violation of the laws thereof, is hereby prohibited.

Section 3. This article shall be inoperative unless it shall have been ratified as an amendment to the Constitution by conventions in the several States, as provided in the Constitution, within seven years from the date of the submission hereof to the States by the Congress.

Amendment XXII (Ratified February 27, 1951)

Section 1. No person shall be elected to the office of the President more than twice, and no person who has held the office of President, or acted as President, for more than two years of a term to which some other person was elected President shall be elected to the office of the President more than once. But this Article shall not apply to any person holding the office of President when this Article was proposed by the Congress, and shall not prevent any person who may be holding the office of President, or acting as President, during the term within which this Article becomes operative from holding the office of President or acting as President during the remainder of such term.

Section 2. This article shall be inoperative unless it shall have been ratified as an amendment to the Constitution by the legislatures of three-fourths of the several States within seven years from the date of its submission to the States by the Congress.

Amendment XXIII (Ratified March 29, 1961)

Section 1. The District constituting the seat of Government of the United States shall appoint in such manner as the Congress may direct:

A number of electors of President and Vice President equal to the whole number of Senators and Representatives in Congress to which the District would be entitled if it were a State, but in no event more than the least populous State; they shall be in addition to those appointed by the States, but they shall be considered, for the purposes of the election of President and Vice President, to be electors appointed by a State; and they shall meet in the District and perform such duties as provided by the twelfth article of amendment.

Section 2. The Congress shall have power to enforce this article by appropriate legislation.

Amendment XXIV (Ratified January 23, 1964)

Section 1. The right of citizens of the United States to vote in any primary or other election for President or Vice President, for electors for President or Vice President, or for Senator or Representative in Congress, shall not be denied or abridged by the United States or any State by reason of failure to pay any poll tax or other tax.

Section 2. The Congress shall have power to enforce this article by appropriate legislation.

Amendment XXV (Ratified February 10, 1967)

Section 1. In case of the removal of the President from office or of his death or resignation, the Vice President shall become President.

Section 2. Whenever there is a vacancy in the office of the Vice President, the President shall nominate a Vice President who shall take office upon confirmation by a majority vote of both Houses of Congress.

Section 3. Whenever the President transmits to the President pro tempore of the Senate and the Speaker of the House of Representatives his written declaration that he is unable to discharge the powers and duties of his office, and until he transmits to them a written declaration to the contrary, such powers and duties shall be discharged by the Vice President as Acting President.

Section 4. Whenever the Vice President and a majority of either the principal officers of the executive departments or of such other body as Congress may by law provide, transmit to the President pro tempore of the Senate and the Speaker of the House of Representatives their written declaration that the President is unable to discharge the powers and duties of his office, the Vice President shall immediately assume the powers and duties of the office as Acting President.

Thereafter, when the President transmits to the President pro tempore of the Senate and the Speaker of the House of Representatives his written declaration that no inability exists, he shall resume the powers and duties of his office unless the Vice President and a majority of either the principal officers of the executive departments or of such other body as Congress may by law provide, transmit within four days to the President pro tempore of the Senate and the Speaker of the House of Representatives their written declaration that the President is unable to discharge the powers and duties of his office. Thereupon Congress shall decide the issue, assembling within forty-eight hours for that purpose if not in session. If the Congress, within twenty-one days after receipt of the latter written declaration, or, if Congress is not in session, within twenty-one days after Congress is required to assemble, determines by two-thirds vote of both Houses that the President is unable to discharge the powers and duties of his office, the Vice President shall continue to discharge the same as Acting President; otherwise, the President shall resume the powers and duties of his office.

Amendment XXVI (Ratified July 1, 1971)

Section 1. The right of citizens of the United States, who are eighteen years of age or older, to vote shall not be denied or abridged by the United States or by any State on account of age.

Section 2. The Congress shall have power to enforce this article by appropriate legislation.

Amendment XXVII (Ratified May 7, 1992)

No law varying the compensation for the services of the Senators and Representatives shall take effect, until an election of Representatives shall have intervened.

Source: U.S. Congress, House, Committee on the Judiciary, The Constitution of the United States of America, as Amended, 100th Cong., 1st sess., 1987, H Doc 100–94.

Notes: 1. The part in brackets was changed by section 2 of the Fourteenth Amendment.

2. The part in brackets was changed by the first paragraph of the Seventeenth Amendment.

3. The part in brackets was changed by the second paragraph of the Seventeenth Amendment.

4. The part in brackets was changed by section 2 of the Twentieth Amendment.

5. The Sixteenth Amendment gave Congress the power to tax incomes.

6. The material in brackets was superseded by the Twelfth Amendment.

7. This provision was affected by the Twenty-fifth Amendment.

8. These clauses were affected by the Eleventh Amendment.

9. This paragraph was superseded by the Thirteenth Amendment.

10. Obsolete.

11. The part in brackets was superseded by section 3 of the Twentieth Amendment.

12. See the Nineteenth and Twenty-sixth Amendments.

13. This amendment was repealed by section 1 of the Twenty-first Amendment.

14. See the Twenty-fifth Amendment.

SELECTED BIBLIOGRAPHY

INDIVIDUAL RIGHTS AND JUDICIAL REVIEW: GENERAL SOURCES

Baum, Lawrence. *The Supreme Court.* 8th ed. Washington, D.C.: CQ Press, 2003.

Bickel, Alexander M. *The Least Dangerous Branch.* Indianapolis: Bobbs-Merrill, 1962.

—— *Politics and the Warren Court.* 1965. Reprint, Jersey City, N.J.: Da Capo, 1973.

Black, Charles L., Jr. *The People and the Court.* New York: Macmillan, 1960.

——. *Perspectives in Constitutional Law.* Englewood Cliffs, N.J.: Prentice-Hall, 1963.

Carp, Robert A., and Ronald Stidham. *The Federal Courts.* 4th ed. Washington, D.C.: CQ Press, 2001.

Carp, Robert A., Ronald Stidham, and Kenneth L. Manning. *Judicial Process in America.* 7th ed. Washington, D.C.: CQ Press, 2007.

Dunne, Gerald T. *Hugo Black and the Judicial Revolution.* New York: Simon and Schuster, 1977.

Epstein, Lee, et al. *The Supreme Court Compendium: Data, Decisions and Development.* 4th ed. Washington, D.C.: CQ Press, 2007.

Finkelman, Paul, and Melvin I. Urofsky. *Landmark Decisions of the United States Supreme Court.* 2d ed. Washington, D.C.: CQ Press, 2002.

Fleming, James E. *Securing Constitutional Democracy: The Case of Autonomy.* Chicago: University of Chicago Press, 2006.

Frank, John P. *Marble Palace: The Supreme Court in American Life.* New York: Knopf, 1961.

Freund, Paul A., and Stanley N. Katz, gen. eds. *History of the Supreme Court of the United States.* Vol. 1, *Antecedents and Beginnings to 1801,* by Julius Goebel Jr., 1971; Vol. 2, *Foundations of Power: John Marshall, 1801–1815,* by George L. Haskins and Herbert A. Johnson, 1981; Vols. 3–4, *The Marshall Court and Cultural Change, 1815–1835,* by G. Edward White, 1988; Vol. 5, *The Taney Period, 1836–1864,* by Carl B. Swisher, 1974; Vol. 6, *Reconstruction and Reunion, 1864–1888,* Part One, by Charles Fairman, 1971; Vol. 7, *Reconstruction and Reunion, 1864–1888,* Part Two, by Charles Fairman, 1987; Supplement to Vol. 7, *Five Justices and the Electoral Commission of 1877,* by Charles Fairman, 1988; Vol. 8, *Troubled Beginnings of the Modern State, 1888–1910,* by Owen M. Fiss, 1993; Vol. 9, *The Judiciary and Responsible Government, 1910–1921,* by Alexander M. Bickel and Benno C. Schmidt Jr., 1984. New York: Macmillan.

Friedman, Lawrence M. *American Law in the 20th Century.* New Haven, Conn.: Yale University Press, 2002.

Garraty, John A., ed. *Quarrels That Have Shaped the Constitution.* Rev. ed. New York: Perennial Library, 1987.

Graber, Mark A., and Michael Perhac, eds. *Marbury versus Madison: Documents and Commentary.* Washington, D.C.: CQ Press, 2002.

Hand, Learned. *The Bill of Rights.* New York: Atheneum, 1964.

Harrell, Mary Ann. *Equal Justice under Law: The Supreme Court in American Life.* 5th ed. Washington, D.C.: The Foundation of the Federal Bar Association, with the cooperation of the National Geographic Society, 1988.

Hirschfield, Robert S. *The Constitution and the Court.* New York: Random House, 1962.

Jackson, Robert H. *The Struggle for Judicial Supremacy.* New York: Knopf, 1941.

——. *The Supreme Court in the American System of Government.* Cambridge, Mass.: Harvard University Press, 1955.

James, Leonard F. *The Supreme Court in American Life.* 2d ed. Glenview, Ill.: Scott, Foresman, 1971.

Kurland, Philip B. *Politics, the Constitution and the Warren Court.* Chicago: University of Chicago Press, 1970.

Kutler, Stanley I., ed. *The Supreme Court and the Constitution: Readings in American Constitutional History.* 3d ed. New York: Norton, 1984.

Lasser, William. *The Limits of Judicial Power: The Supreme Court in American Politics.* Chapel Hill: University of North Carolina Press, 1988.

Levy, Leonard W. *Original Intent and the Framers' Constitution.* Chicago: Ivan R. Dee, 2000.

Lively, Donald E. *Foreshadows of the Law: Supreme Court Dissents and Constitutional Development.* Westport, Conn.: Praeger, 1993.

Madison, James, Alexander Hamilton, and John Jay. *The Federalist Papers.* Edited by Clinton Rossiter. New York: New American Library, 1961.

Mason, Alpheus T. *The Supreme Court from Taft to Burger.* 3d ed. Baton Rouge: Louisiana State University Press, 1979.

——. *The Supreme Court in a Free Society.* New York: Norton, 1968.

Mason, Alpheus T., and Donald Grier Stephenson Jr. *American Constitutional Law: Introductory Essays and Selected Cases.* 15th ed. Upper Saddle River, N.J.: Pearson Prentice Hall, 2009.

McCloskey, Robert G., and Sanford Levinson. *The Modern Supreme Court.* 2d ed. Chicago: University of Chicago Press, 1994.

O'Brien, David M. *Storm Center: The Supreme Court in American Politics.* New York: Norton, 1986.

Pacelle, Richard L., Jr. *The Transformation of the Supreme Court's Agenda: From the New Deal to the Reagan Administration.* Boulder: Westview Press, 1991.

Schwartz, Bernard. *A History of the Supreme Court.* New York: Oxford University Press, 1993.

Swindler, William F. *Court and Constitution in the 20th Century: The New Legality, 1932–1968.* Indianapolis: Bobbs-Merrill, 1970.

Swisher, Carl B. *American Constitutional Development.* Reprint, Westport, Conn.: Greenwood Press, 1978.

Tomlins, Christopher, ed. *The United States Supreme Court: The Pursuit of Justice.* Boston: Houghton Mifflin, 2005.

Tribe, Laurence H. *God Save This Honorable Court.* New York: Random House, 1985.

Warren, Charles. *Congress, the Constitution and the Supreme Court.* Boston: Little, Brown, 1925.

——. *The Supreme Court in United States History.* Rev. ed., 2 vols. Boston: Little, Brown, 1926.

THE COURT AND THE INDIVIDUAL: FREEDOM OF EXPRESSION

Barker, Lucius J., and Twiley W. Barker Jr. *Civil Liberties and the Constitution: Cases and Commentaries.* 7th ed. Englewood Cliffs, N.J.: Prentice-Hall, 1994.

Bearinger, David, ed. *The Bill of Rights, the Courts, and the Law: Landmark Cases That Have Shaped American History.* 3d ed. Charlottesville: Virginia Foundation for the Humanities, 1999.

Berman, Harold J. "Religion and Law: The First Amendment in Historical Perspective." *Emory Law Journal* 35 (1986): 777–793.

Beth, Loren P. *The American Theory of Church and State.* Gainesville: University of Florida Press, 1958.

Bodenhamer, David J., and James W. Ely Jr. *The Bill of Rights in Modern America After 200 Years.* Bloomington: Indiana University Press, 1993.

Bogen, David S. *Bulwark of Liberty: The Court and the First Amendment.* Port Washington, N.Y.: Associated Faculty Press, 1984.

Bollinger, Lee C. *Images of a Free Press.* Chicago: University of Chicago Press, 1991.

——. *The Tolerant Society: Freedom of Speech and Extremist Speech in America.* New York: Oxford University Press, 1986.

Branit, James R. "Reconciling Free Speech and Equality: What Justifies Censorship?" *Harvard Journal of Law and Public Policy* 9 (1986): 429–460.

Choper, Jess H. *Securing Religious Liberty.* Chicago: University of Chicago Press, 1995.

CQ Press. *Guide to Congress.* 6th ed. Washington, D.C.: CQ Press, 2007.

Cushman, Robert F. *Cases in Civil Liberties.* 6th ed. Englewood Cliffs, N.J.: Prentice-Hall, 1994.

Dowling, Noel T. *Cases on Constitutional Law.* 7th ed. Brooklyn, N.Y.: The Foundation Press, 1965.

Emerson, Thomas I. *The System of Freedom of Expression.* New York: Random House, Vintage, 1970.

Epstein, Lee, and Thomas G. Walker. *Constitutional Law for a Changing America.* 5th ed. Washington, D.C.: CQ Press, 2004.

Esbeck, Carl H. "1985 Survey of Trends and Developments on Religious Liberty in the Courts." *Journal of Law and Religion* 4 (1986): 211–240.

Forer, Lois G. *A Chilling Effect: The Mounting Threat of Libel and Invasion of Privacy Actions to the First Amendment.* New York: Norton, 1987.

Hamilton, Marci A. *God vs. the Gavel: Religion and the Rule of Law.* New York: Cambridge University Press, 2005.

Hemmer, Joseph J. *The Supreme Court and the First Amendment.* New York: Praeger, 1986.

Kalven, Harry, Jr. *The Negro and the First Amendment.* Chicago: University of Chicago Press, Phoenix Books, 1966.

Kelly, Alfred H., and Winfred A. Harbison. *The American Constitution: Its Origin and Development.* 7th ed. New York: Norton, 1991.

Konvitz, Milton R. *Fundamental Liberties of a Free People: Religion, Speech, Press, Assembly.* 1957. Reprint, Ithaca, N.Y.: Cornell University Press, 1978.

Lewis, Anthony. *Make No Law: The Sullivan Case and the First Amendment.* New York: Random House, 1991.

Madison, James. *The Federalist Papers.* Edited by Isaac Kramnick. New York: Penguin Books, 1987.

Marshall, William P. "Discrimination and the Right of Association." *Northwestern Law Review* 81 (1986): 68–105.

Mason, Alpheus T., and William M. Beaney. *The Supreme Court in a Free Society.* New York: Norton, 1968.

Miller, William Lee. *The First Liberty: Religion and the American Republic.* New York: Knopf, 1985.

Miller, William, and Charles Cureton. *Supreme Court Decisions on Church and State.* Charlottesville, Va.: Ibis Publications, 1986.

Murphy, Paul L. *The Constitution in Crisis Times, 1918–1969.* New York: Harper and Row, 1972.

Peters, Shawn Francis. *The Yoder Case: Religious Freedom, Education, and Parental Rights.* Landmark Law Cases and American Society. Lawrence: University Press of Kansas, 2003.

Pfeffer, Leo. *Church, State and Freedom.* Rev. ed. 2 vols. Boston: Beacon Press, 1967.

Ravitch, Frank S. *Masters of Illusion: The Supreme Court and the Religion Clauses.* New York: New York University Press, 2007.

Redish, Martin H. *Freedom of Expression: A Critical Analysis.* Charlottesville, Va.: Michie, 1984.

Scherer, Mark R. *Rights in the Balance: Free Press, Fair Trial, and Nebraska Press Association v. Stuart.* Lubbock: Texas Tech University Press, 2008.

Spitzer, Matthew Laurence. *Seven Dirty Words and Six Other Stories: Controlling the Content of Print and Broadcast.* New Haven, Conn.: Yale University Press, 1986.

Sunstein, Cass R. *Democracy and the Problem of Free Speech.* New York: Free Press, 1993.

Tedford, Thomas L. *Freedom of Speech in the United States.* New York: Random House, 1985.

Van Alstyne, William W. *Interpretations of the First Amendment.* Durham, N.C.: Duke University Press, 1984.

Wittern-Keller, Laura, and Raymond Haberski Jr. *The Miracle Case: Film Censorship and the Supreme Court.* Lawrence: University Press of Kansas, 2008.

THE SECOND AMENDMENT AND THE RIGHT TO BEAR ARMS

Cornell, Saul. A *Well-Regulated Militia: The Founding Fathers and the Origins of Gun Control in America.* Oxford and New York: Oxford University Press, 2006.

Doherty, Brian. *Gun Control on Trial: Inside the Supreme Court Battle over the Second Amendment.* Washington, D.C.: Cato Institute, 2008.

Halbrook, Stephen P. *The Founders' Second Amendment: Origins of the Right to Bear Arms.* Chicago: Independent Institute, 2008.

Malcolm, Joyce Lee. *To Keep and Bear Arms: The Origins of an Anglo-American Right.* Cambridge, Mass.: Harvard University Press, 1996.

POLITICAL PARTICIPATION

Anzalone, Christopher A., ed. *Supreme Court Cases on Political Representation, 1787–2001.* Armonk, N.Y.: M. E. Sharpe, 2002.

Atleson, James B. "The Aftermath of *Baker v. Carr:* An Adventure in Judicial Experimentation." *California Law Review* 51 (1963): 535–572.

Auerbach, Carl E. "The Reapportionment Cases: One Person, One Vote--One Vote, One Value." In *Supreme Court Review 1964,* ed. Philip B. Kurland. Chicago: University of Chicago Press, 1964.

Banzhaf, John F., III. "Multi-Member Electoral Districts—Do They Violate the 'One Man, One Vote' Principle?" *Yale Law Journal* 75 (1966): 1309–1338.

Bickel, Alexander M. "The Voting Rights Cases." In *Supreme Court Review 1966,* ed. Philip B. Kurland. Chicago: University of Chicago Press, 1966.

Bontecou, Eleanor. *The Federal Loyalty-Security Program.* 1953. Reprint, Westport, Conn.: Greenwood Press, 1974.

Brown, Ralph S., Jr. *Loyalty and Security: Employment Tests in the United States.* 1958. Reprint, Jersey City, N.J.: Da Capo, 1972.

Cushman, Robert E. *Civil Liberties in the United States.* 1956. Reprint, Ithaca, N.Y.: Cornell University Press, 1969.

Davidson, Chandler, and Bernard Grofman, eds. *Quiet Revolution in the South: The Impact of the Voting Rights Act, 1965–1990.* Princeton, N.J.: Princeton University Press, 1994.

DeGrazia, Alfred. *Essay on Apportionment and Representative Government.* 1963. Reprint, Westport, Conn.: Greenwood Press, 1983.

Elliott, Ward E. Y. *The Rise of Guardian Democracy: The Supreme Court's Role in Voting Rights Disputes, 1845–1969.* Cambridge, Mass.: Harvard University Press, 1974.

Irwin, William P. "Representation and Election: The Reapportionment Cases in Retrospect." *Michigan Law Review* 67 (1969): 73–82.

Konvitz, Milton R. *Fundamental Liberties of a Free People.* 1957. Reprint, Westport, Conn.: Greenwood Press, 1978.

Lahava, Prina. *Press Law in Modern Democracies: A Comparative Study.* New York: Longman, 1985.

Latham, Earl. *The Communist Controversy in Washington.* Ann Arbor, Mich.: UMI, Books on Demand, 1966.

McKay, Robert. *Reapportionment: The Law and Politics of Equal Representation.* New York: Twentieth Century Fund, 1965.

Meiklejohn, Alexander. *Political Freedom: The Constitutional Powers of the People.* 1960. Reprint, Westport, Conn.: Greenwood Press, 1979.

Mendelson, Wallace E. "Clear and Present Danger—From *Schenck* to *Dennis.*" *Columbia Law Review* 52 (1952): 313–333.

Murray, Robert K. *Red Scare: A Study in National Hysteria, 1919–1920.* Minneapolis: University of Minnesota Press, 1955.

Nathanson, Nathaniel L. "The Communist Trial and the Clear and Present Danger Test." *Harvard Law Review* 63 (1950): 1167–1175.

Polsby, Nelson W., ed. *Reapportionment in the 1970s.* Berkeley: University of California Press, 1971.

Pritchett, C. Herman. *Congress versus the Supreme Court, 1957–1960.* Reprint, New York: Da Capo Press, 1973.

Thompson, Kenneth. *The Voting Rights Act and Black Electoral Participation.* Washington, D.C.: Joint Center for Political Studies, 1984.

Woodward, C. Vann. *Origins of the New South, 1877–1913.* Baton Rouge: Louisiana State University Press, 1971.

——. *The Strange Career of Jim Crow.* 3d rev. ed. New York: Oxford University Press, 1974.

DUE PROCESS

Alexander, Frederick, and John L. Amsden. "Scope of the Fourth Amendment." *Georgetown Law Journal* 75 (1987): 713–727.

Allen, Francis A. "Federalism and the Fourth Amendment: A Requiem for Wolf." In *Supreme Court Review 1961,* ed. Philip B. Kurland. Chicago: University of Chicago Press, 1961.

Amsterdam, Anthony. "Perspectives on the Fourth Amendment." *Minnesota Law Review* 58 (1974): 349.

Angotti, Donna Louise, and Michael D. Warden. "Warrantless Searches and Seizures." *Georgetown Law Journal* 75 (1987): 742–790.

Barnett, Edward L., Jr. "Personal Rights, Property Rights and the Fourth Amendment." In *Supreme Court Review 1960,* ed. Philip B. Kurland. Chicago: University of Chicago Press, 1960.

Beaney, William M. "The Constitutional Right to Privacy in the Supreme Court." In *Supreme Court Review 1962,* ed. Philip B. Kurland. Chicago: University of Chicago Press, 1962.

——. *The Right to Counsel in American Courts.* Westport, Conn.: Greenwood Press, 1972.

Black, Charles L. *Capital Punishment: The Inevitability of Caprice and Mistake.* Rev. ed. New York: Norton, 1982.

Epstein, Lee, and Joseph F. Kobylka. *The Supreme Court and Legal Change: Abortion and the Death Penalty.* Chapel Hill: University of North Carolina Press, 1992.

Essaye, Anne. "Cruel and Unusual Punishment." *Georgetown Law Journal* 75 (1987): 1168–1195.

Fellman, David. *The Defendant's Rights Today.* Madison: University of Wisconsin Press, 1976.

Fingarette, Herbert. "Addiction and Criminal Responsibility." *Yale Law Journal* 84 (1975): 413.

Fisher, George. *Plea Bargaining's Triumph: A History of Plea Bargaining in America.* Stanford, Calif.: Stanford University Press, 2003.

Fisher, Louis. "Congress and the Fourth Amendment." *Georgia Law Review* 21 (1986): 107–170.

Goldberger, Peter. "A Guide to Identifying Fourth Amendment Issues." *Search and Seizure Law Report* 13 (1986): 33–40.

Green, John Raeburn. "The Bill of Rights, the Fourteenth Amendment, and the Supreme Court." *Michigan Law Review* 46 (1948): 869.

Griswold, Erwin N. *Search and Seizure: A Dilemma of the Supreme Court.* Lincoln: University of Nebraska Press, 1975.

Hall, Livingston, et al. *Modern Criminal Procedure.* 6th ed. St. Paul, Minn.: West, 1986.

Herman, Michele G. *Search and Seizure Checklists.* 4th ed. New York: Boardman, 1985.

Israel, Jerrold H. "*Gideon v. Wainwright:* The Art of Overruling." *Supreme Court Review 1963,* ed. Philip B. Kurland. Chicago: University of Chicago Press, 1963.

James, Joseph B. *The Ratification of the Fourteenth Amendment.* Macon, Ga.: Mercer University Press, 1984.

Kalven, Harry A., Jr., and Hans Zeisel. *The American Jury.* Chicago: University of Chicago Press, 1986.

Kroll, Robert. "Can the Fourth Amendment Go High Tech?" *American Bar Association* 73 (1987): 70–74.

LaFave, Wayne R. "'Case-by-Case Adjudication' versus 'Standardized Procedures': The *Robinson* Dilemma." *Supreme Court Review 1974,* ed. Philip B. Kurland. Chicago: University of Chicago Press, 1974.

——. *Search and Seizure: A Treatise on the Fourth Amendment.* 2d ed. St. Paul, Minn.: West, 1986.

Landynski, Jacob W. *Searches and Seizures and the Supreme Court: A Study in Constitutional Interpretation.* Baltimore, Md.: Johns Hopkins Press, 1966.

Leo, Richard A., and George C. Thomas III, eds. *The Miranda Debate: Law, Justice, and Policing.* Boston: Northeastern University Press, 2000.

Levy, Leonard W. *Origins of the Fifth Amendment: The Right against Self-Incrimination.* New York: Macmillan, 1986.

Lewis, Anthony. *Gideon's Trumpet.* New York: Random House, 1964.

Long, Carolyn N. *Mapp v. Ohio: Guarding against Unreasonable Searches and Seizures.* Lawrence: University Press of Kansas, 2006.

Marshaw, Jerry L. *Due Process in the Administrative State.* New Haven, Conn.: Yale University Press, 1985.

Mason, Alpheus T., and Donald G. Stephenson, Jr. *American Constitutional Law.* 11th ed. Englewood Cliffs, N.J.: Prentice-Hall, 1995.

Moore, Tim. "Constitutional Law: The Fourth Amendment and Drug Testing in the Workplace." *Harvard Journal of Law and Public Policy* 10 (1987): 762–768.

Oaks, Dallin. "Studying the Exclusionary Rule in Searches and Seizures." *University of Chicago Law Review* 37 (1970): 665.

Oldham, James. *Trial by Jury: The Seventh Amendment and Anglo-American Special Juries.* New York: New York University Press, 2006.

Port, Joseph Clinton, Jr., and James D. Mathias. "Right to Counsel." *Georgetown Law Journal* 75 (1987): 1029–1052.

Rossum, Ralph A. "New Rights and Old Wrongs: The Supreme Court and the Problem of Retroactivity." *Emory Law Journal* 23 (1974).

Sit, Po Yin. "Double Jeopardy, Due Process, and the Breach of Plea Agreements." *Columbia Law Review* 87 (1987): 142–160.

Strong, Frank R. *Substantive Due Process of Law: A Dichotomy of Sense and Nonsense.* Durham, N.C.: Carolina Academic Press, 1986.

White, James B. "The Fourth Amendment as a Way of Talking About People: A Study of *Robinson* and *Matlock.*" In *Supreme Court Review 1974,* ed. Philip B. Kurland. Chicago: University of Chicago Press, 1974.

White, Welsh S. *The Death Penalty in the Eighties: An Examination of the Modern System of Capital Punishment.* Ann Arbor: University of Michigan Press, 1987.

EQUAL RIGHTS

Abernathy, M. Glenn. *Civil Liberties under the Constitution.* 4th ed. Columbia: University of South Carolina Press, 1985.

Amar, Akhil Reed. *The Bill of Rights: Creation and Reconstruction.* New Haven, Conn.: Yale University Press, 1998.

Anzalone, Christopher A., ed. *Supreme Court Cases on Gender and Sexual Equality, 1787–2001.* Armonk, N.Y.: M.E. Sharpe, 2002.

Berger, Morroe. *Equality by Statute: The Revolution in Civil Rights.* 1967. Reprint, New York: Hippocrene Books, 1978.

Bickel, Alexander M. *Politics and the Warren Court.* 1965. Reprint, Jersey City, N.J.: Da Capo, 1973.

Blaustein, Albert P., and Clarence Clyde Ferguson Jr. *Desegregation and the Law: The Meaning and Effect of the School Segregation Cases.* 1957. Reprint, Littleton, Colo.: Rothman, 1985.

Carter, Stephen L. *Reflections of an Affirmative Action Baby.* New York: Basic Books, 1991.

Craig, Barbara Hinkson, and David M. O'Brien. *Abortion and American Politics.* Chatham, N.J.: Chatham House, 1993.

Cushman, Clare, ed. *Supreme Court Decisions and Women's Rights: Milestones to Equality.* Washington, D.C.: CQ Press, 2001.

"Developments in the Law: Equal Protection." *Harvard Law Review* 82 (March 1969): 1065.

Dunn, Joshua M. *Complex Justice: The Case of Missouri v. Jenkins.* Chapel Hill: University of North Carolina Press, 2008.

Dworkin, Ronald. *Life's Dominion: An Argument about Abortion, Euthanasia and Individual Freedom.* New York: Knopf, 1993.

Esdall, Thomas Byrne. *The New Politics of Inequality.* New York: Norton, 1984.

Fisher, Louis. *American Constitutional Law: Civil Rights and Civil Liberties.* 4th ed. Durham, NC: Carolina Academic Press, 2001.

Franklin, John Hope. *From Slavery to Freedom: A History of African Americans.* 7th ed. New York: McGraw-Hill, 1994.

Galloway, Russell W. *Justice for All? The Rich and Poor in Supreme Court History, 1790–1990.* Durham, N.C.: Carolina Academic Press, 1991.

Garraty, John A., ed. *Quarrels That Have Shaped the Constitution.* Rev. ed. New York: Harper and Row, 1987.

Garrow, David J. *Liberty and Sexuality: The Right to Privacy and the Making of* Roe v. Wade. New York: Macmillan, 1994.

Glick, Henry R. "The Impact of Permissive Judicial Policies: The U.S. Supreme Court and the Right to Die." *Political Research Quarterly* 47 (1994): 207–222.

Graber, Mark A. Dred Scott *and the Problem of Constitutional Evil.* New York: Cambridge University Press, 2006.

Gunther, Gerald. "In Search of Evolving Doctrine on a Changing Court: A Model for a Newer Equal Protection." *Harvard Law Review* 86 (November 1972): 1.

Hartmann, Heidi I. *Comparable Worth: New Direction for Research.* Washington, D.C.: National Academy Press, 1985.

Hull, Elizabeth. *Without Justice for All: The Constitutional Rights of Aliens.* Westport, Conn.: Greenwood Press, 1985.

Ivers, Gregg. *American Constitutional Law: Power and Politics.* Vol. 2, *Civil Rights and Liberties.* Boston: Houghton Mifflin, 2002.

Johnson, John W. Griswold v. Connecticut: *Birth Control and the Constitutional Right of Privacy.* Lawrence: University Press of Kansas, 2005.

Karst, Kenneth L. "Equal Citizenship under the Fourteenth Amendment." *Harvard Law Review* 91 (November 1977): 1.

Kelly, Alfred H., and Winfred A. Harbison. *The American Constitution: Its Origins and Development.* 7th ed. New York: Norton, 1991.

Kirp, David L., Mark G. Yudof, and Marlene Strong Franks. *Gender Justice.* Chicago: University of Chicago Press, 1985.

Kluger, Richard. *Simple Justice: The History of* Brown v. Board of Education *and Black America's Struggle for Equality.* New York: Knopf, 1976.

Konvitz, Milton R., and Theodore Leskes. *A Century of Civil Rights, with a Study of State Law against Discrimination.* 1961. Reprint, Westport, Conn.: Greenwood Press, 1983.

Lawson, Steven F. *In Pursuit of Power: Southern Blacks and Electoral Politics, 1965–1982.* New York: Columbia University Press, 1985.

Levin-Epstein, Michael D., and Howard J. Anderson. *Primer of Equal Employment Opportunity.* 3d ed. Washington, D.C.: Bureau of National Affairs, 1984.

Morris, Frank C. *Judicial Wage Determination: A Volatile Spectre: Perspectives on Comparable Worth.* Washington, D.C.: National Legal Center for the Public Interest, 1984.

Murdoch, Joyce, and Deb Price. *Courting Justice: Gay Men and Lesbians v. the Supreme Court.* New York: Basic Books, 2001.

Phelps, Glenn A., and Robert A. Poirer. *Contemporary Debates on Civil Liberties: Enduring Constitutional Questions.* Lexington, Mass.: Lexington Books, 1985.

Remick, Helen. *Comparable Worth and Wage Discrimination: Technical Possibilities and Political Realities.* Philadelphia: Temple University Press, 1984.

Reskin, Barbara F., and Heidi I. Hartmann. *Women's Work, Men's Work: Sex Segregation on the Job.* Washington, D.C.: National Academy Press, 1985.

Schiller, Bradley R. *The Economics of Poverty and Discrimination.* 4th ed. Englewood Cliffs, N.J.: Prentice-Hall, 1984.

Schmid, Gunther, and Renata Weitzel. *Sex Discrimination and Equal Opportunity: The Labor Market and Employment Policy.* New York: St. Martin's Press, 1984.

Schuman, Howard, Charlotte Steeh, and Lawrence Bobo. *Racial Attitudes in America: Trends and Interpretations.* Cambridge, Mass.: Harvard University Press, 1985.

Solove, Daniel J. *Understanding Privacy.* Cambridge, Mass.: Harvard University Press, 2008.

Sunstein, Cass. *One Case at a Time.* Cambridge, Mass.: Harvard University Press, 1999.

Tushnet, Mark V. *Making Civil Rights Law: Thurgood Marshall and the Supreme Court, 1936–1961.* New York: Oxford University Press, 1994.

Tussman, Joseph, and Jacobus tenBroek. "The Equal Protection of the Laws." *California Law Review* 37 (1949): 341.

U.S. Commission on Civil Rights. *Comparable Worth: Issue for the 80's--A Consultation of the U.S. Commission on Civil Rights, June 6–7, 1984.* Washington, D.C.: Commission on Civil Rights, 1984.

Wechsler, Herbert. "Toward Neutral Principles of Constitutional Law." *Harvard Law Review* 73 (November 1959): 31.

Woodward, C. Vann. *The Strange Career of Jim Crow.* 3d rev. ed. New York: Oxford University Press, 1974.

★ ILLUSTRATION CREDITS AND ACKNOWLEDGMENTS

1. THE COURT AND THE INDIVIDUAL

8 Library of Congress; 14 Library of Congress

2. FREEDOM FOR IDEAS: THE FIRST AMENDMENT AND THE RIGHT TO BELIEVE, TO SPEAK, TO ASSEMBLE, TO PETITION, AND TO PUBLISH

23 CQ Photo/R. Michael Jenkins; 37 (left) Library of Congress, (right) from the Collection of Paul Avrich; 45 © Bettmann/CORBIS; 49 Library of Congress; 58 © Bettmann/CORBIS; 61 Bill Pierce; 65 Library of Congress; 69 CQ Photo/Scott J. Ferrell; 85 Minnesota Historical Society; 95 AP Images; 114 AP Images; 131 © The Miami Herald; 146 Daniel Weisman; 160 AP Images/Rick Bowmer

3. THE RIGHTS OF POLITICAL PARTICIPATION

175 Collections of the New York Public Library, Astor, Lenox and Tilden Foundations; 179 A 1958 Herblock Cartoon, copyright by The Herb Block Foundation; 184 The Granger Collection, New York; 187 LBJ Library photo by Yoichi R. Okamoto; 189 © Bettmann/CORBIS; 190 CQ Press; 197 Gene Basset; 206 (left) CQ Press, (right) CQ Photo/Scott J. Ferrell; 218 Library of Congress; 223 AP Images; 226 Paul Carmack / © 1948 The Christian Science Monitor (www.csmonitor.com) Reproduced with permission; 231 © Bettmann/CORBIS

4. THE SECOND AMENDMENT AND THE RIGHT TO BEAR ARMS

253 © Shannon Stapleton/Reuters/Corbis; 256 Newscom/AFP Photo/Tim Sloan

5. CRIME AND PUNISHMENT

298 AP Images; 305 Reuters; 321 © Bettmann/CORBIS; 323 © Bettmann/ CORBIS; 331 Brown Brothers; 332 (left) National Archives and Records Administration, (right) AP Images; 353 AP Images/Rogelio Solis; 355 AP Images/ Atlanta Journal Constitution/Marlene Karas

6. EQUAL RIGHTS AND EQUAL PROTECTION OF THE LAWS

379 AP Images; 381 Library of Congress; 387 Library of Congress; 389 NAACP; 393 AP Images/William P. Straeter; 411 © Bettmann/CORBIS; 416 George Harris; 435 (top) Mike Peters, (bottom) © 1995 John Trever, Albuquerque Journal. Reprinted by permission; 437 AP Images/Paul Sancya; 440 Library of Congress; 460 AP Images/Denis Paquin

7. LIBERTY AND PRIVACY

477 © Bettmann/CORBIS; 485 AP Images/Nati Harnik; 494 Reuters

★ SUBJECT INDEX

Page numbers in italics indicate illustrations and photos.

531

★ CASE INDEX